READINGS IN
AGENTS

READINGS IN
AGENTS

Edited by

Michael N. Huhns
University of South Carolina

Munindar P. Singh
North Carolina State University

MORGAN KAUFMANN PUBLISHERS, INC.
SAN FRANCISCO, CALIFORNIA

Sponsoring Editor Michael B. Morgan
Production Manager Yonie Overton
Production Editor Cheri Palmer
Production Assistant Pamela Sullivan
Editorial Coordinator Marilyn Alan
Editorial Assistant Meghan Keeffe
Cover Design Jamison Chandler/MacTemps
Cover Photograph © John Lund/Tony Stone Images
Text Design, Composition, and Pasteup Susan M. Sheldrake
Copyeditor Jennifer McClain
Proofreader Pamela Sullivan
Printer Edwards Brothers, Inc.

Morgan Kaufmann Publishers, Inc.
Editorial and Sales Office
340 Pine Street, Sixth Floor
San Francisco, CA 94104-3205
USA
Telephone 415 / 392-2665
Facsimile 415 / 982-2665
Email mkp@mkp.com
WWW http://www.mkp.com
Order toll free 800 / 745-7323

02 01 00 5 4 3

Library of Congress Cataloging-in-Publication Data

Readings in agents / edited by Michael N. Huhns, Munindar P. Singh.
p. cm.
Includes bibliographical references and indexes.
ISBN 1-55860-495-2
1. Intelligent agents (Computer software) I. Huhns, Michael N.
II. Singh, Munindar P. (Munindar Paul), date.
QA76.76.I58R43 1997 97-37818
006.3--dc21 CIP

Foreword

by Les Gasser
University of Southern California

It's hardly news these days that rapid proliferation of computing power, connectivity, and on-line content is transforming many of the ways that people work and play. New visions of interactivity suggest that all manner of scientific, educational, commercial, and industrial enterprises will be internally and externally linked, and human spheres previously untouched by computing and digital content—community and family life, for example—are being swept up with the tide. Indeed, along with the family itself, the family toaster and the family pet are soon expected to have their own attachments to the on-line fabric emerging around us.

Along with this new infrastructure, content, and participation come new opportunities for inventing the technologies that will help carry out intricate tasks and assist in managing the complexity of interactions within such a diffuse and open electronic weave. One of the most provocative and promising of these is intelligent agent technologies. The modern concept of intelligent agents has roots that extend back to the foundations of artificial intelligence (AI), object-oriented computing, and distributed systems, as well as into areas of philosophy, the social sciences, and economics. AI has long been concerned with constructing active, integrated models of intelligent behavior as well as with building autonomous computational entities that can actually perform serious and realistic tasks outside the research laboratory. As advances in software architectures, representation methods, and problem-solving technologies have met the massively increased capabilities of modern computing platforms and the broad spectrum of new content, the vision and possibility of integrated intelligent agents have flowered. Similarly, developments in object-based concurrent and distributed computation, mobile computing techniques, and increased standardization through efforts such as CORBA and KQML are beginning to make it possible to reliably program sophisticated applications that have the integrated, encapsulated, and dynamic properties of intelligent agents. Growing practice and experience with agents such as "softbots" and actual robots are contributing to the increased sense of possibility and promise. Finally, some of the long-standing, basic, and high-impact questions of fields such as philosophy, sociology, and economics—issues such as how knowledge is grounded in experience or physicality, the nature of interaction through symbols, the emergence and maintenance of order in collectives, the mechanics and algorithmics of markets, and the economic properties of information—are finding both clear expression and increased salience as people grapple with how to build and sustain the behavior of intelligent agents in realistic, open environments. All in all, this convergence is driving both increased need and increased opportunity for research and practice that integrate approaches to these and other related issues.

The contemporary community of agents researchers and practitioners has pooled itself from many streams and groups, and chief among these is the 25-year-old family of researchers in Distributed AI and Multiagent Systems (DAI/MAS). In the mid to late 1970s DAI/MAS researchers began formulating some of the basic theories, architectures, and experiments that showed, computationally, how interaction and division of labor could be effective in problem solving, how inherent uncertainties introduced by knowledge and action distribution could be managed, and how formal theories of knowledge and action could be extended into localized, distributed, and multiagent contexts.

Michael Huhns and Munindar Singh have long been participants in the DAI/MAS arena and are widely known as two of the area's most dedicated, productive, and insightful researchers. Together in this volume they have crafted a singular and informative collection of some of the best technical material to date in the research area of intelligent agents. Huhns has held a long-standing interest in cooperative information systems—the merging of databases, distributed systems, artificial intelligence, and human-centered approaches. Singh is one of the principal contemporary theorists of agency, with a special focus on theories and models of commitment and knowledge. Together, their expertise is complementary, and it informs the perspective of this book in unique ways. Huhns and Singh have chosen to orient the book around several of the critical issues in research on agents: (1) key characteristics that differentiate agents-oriented thinking from other conceptual and software approaches, (2) emerging applications of agents technologies, (3) architectures and infrastructures for actually building agents, and (4) theoretical models of agency. While there have been several conference and workshop overview papers on the subject, this book presents the best synthesis of current thinking on the unique properties of the agent-oriented perspective. It considers the nature and type of agent autonomy as a critical dimension of agenthood and treats rational, social, interactive, and adaptive agency as four different viewpoints on the agents puzzle. Breaking the agents picture down into these several components makes it easy to identify critical problems and insights posed in the research presented here. The book's primary strengths are its breadth of coverage and its strong theoretical component.

I'm personally excited at the emergence and evident strength of this area of computing and at the intellectual and experimental challenges it presents. This book lays a firm foundation for those interested in quickly and thoroughly apprehending the state of the art in agents, and it will surely lead to a significant synthesis and greater cohesion of research and practice in the field.

Contents

Preface

Agents are garnering an enormous amount of interest from the academic and industrial research communities, software developers, and even the lay press. Work on various aspects of agents has progressed over a number of years, but references to the work are scattered over many publications. We attempt to remedy this situation by collecting and organizing some of the most important papers on agents. We also take the opportunity to provide an overview of agents and a commentary on the collection.

The papers we have collected discuss the major applications of agents, the classical techniques of constructing agents, and theories to model and understand agents, as well as areas on the intellectual boundaries of the science of agents. There are several papers in each category, not only describing different topics but also offering different perspectives on each subject. We believe the different perspectives offer a strength for a new area such as agents.

READERSHIP

The included papers provide the essential background and perspective needed to understand and appreciate any other paper on agents. The book is written for a broad audience of computer scientists including

- Software practitioners who have heard of the wonderful things agents can do, but who want to take a closer look at the many shapes of agent technology and to understand the key concepts behind it
- Graduate students who wish to complete their knowledge of agents before setting out to perform research in the area or to develop advanced applications of them
- Senior researchers who are specialists in some of the aspects of agents, but who wish to understand other applications and research areas and explore possible connections and synergies
- Professors and their students who wish to attain any of the above goals in their courses

Like most *Readings* volumes, this book can be used as a supplementary text in graduate and advanced undergraduate courses. We ourselves have used several of the papers in courses on cooperative information systems, advanced database management, and multiagent systems, as well as for introducing graduate students to the area in self-study courses.

FEATURES

Application Focus

Our intention in this book is to present agents in as broad a sense as possible. By showing several interesting and successful applications of agents first, we hope to draw the readers into the subject and demonstrate for them that the theories that interest researchers are also of value in practice. The book is application oriented and not designed exclusively for the consumption of academic researchers. However, we believe that academic researchers will also benefit from its application focus and its inclusion of areas beyond their specialization.

We first present papers that deal with various applications and follow with architectures and theories. Inevitably, the application papers refer to theories and vice versa. This is beneficial because the reader is drawn into theories by the application papers and kept in touch with applications by the theory papers.

Multiple Viewpoints

We present agents from different viewpoints. A wide variety of viewpoints gives readers a truer flavor of agents than a narrow, ideologically loaded analysis. Consequently, we consider agents from the perspectives of artificial intelligence, databases, distributed computing, and programming languages. Of course, we do take a stance as to how agents ought to be studied and developed—this is inevitable in any book on a lively subject—but we attempt to base it on major conceptual points rather than on narrow distinctions.

To make the coverage as broad as possible, we include contributions by many of the active researchers, while avoiding presentation of several papers by any single author. Consequently, this book has contributions by almost 100 authors from more than 40 sources in its 51 papers.

Timeliness of Contributions

Agents have been studied in one form or another for thousands of years. Talk of computational agents goes back to the early days of computing. However, in light of the rapid advances being made in agent science and technology, we are restricting ourselves to papers that were written in the 1990s. These newer papers have assimilated and extended the key points of the earlier papers.

ACKNOWLEDGMENTS

We would like to thank the authors of the included articles for permission to present their work. Literally, this book could not exist without their efforts! We also thank Diane Cerra and Mike Morgan for assisting us in the conception of this book and Marilyn Uffner Alan, Cheri Palmer, and Meghan Keeffe for managing its publication.

Over the years, we have benefited from discussions with a number of people who have helped shape our view of agents, though not always as they would have preferred! In particular, we would like to thank the following for their time and patience: Manny Aparicio, Nicholas Asher, Ronald Bonnell, Cristiano Castelfranchi, Allen Emerson, Les Gasser, Mike Georgeff, Carl Hewitt, Anuj Jain, Nick Jennings, Tomasz Ksiezyk, Yannis Labrou, Greg Lavender, Vic Lesser, James Lester, Kuha Mahalingam, Abe Mamdani, Jürgen Müller, Anand Rao, David Sadek, Sandip Sen, Robert St. Amant, Larry Stephens, Katia Sycara, Chris Tomlinson, Mladen Vouk, Mike Wooldridge, and Wlodek Zadrozny.

Over the course of this project, Michael Huhns was supported by NIST, DARPA, and EPA. Munindar Singh was supported by the NSF under grants IRI-9529179 and IRI-9624425, by IBM Corporation, and by the NCSU College of Engineering. To all of these agencies we extend our thanks.

Last, but definitely not least, we would like to thank our families for their support and tolerance during this project. We would like to dedicate this book to Mary Huhns and Mona Singh, model spousal agents!

Acknowledgments

Chaib-draa, B. (1995) Industrial applications of distributed AI. *Communications of the ACM* 38(11):49–53. © Association of Computing Machinery, Inc. Reprinted by permission.

Huhns, Michael, N.; Singh, Munindar P.; and Ksiezyk, Tomasz (1994) Global information management via local autonomous agents. In *Proceedings of the ICOT International Symposium on Fifth Generation Computer Systems: Workshop on Heterogeneous Cooperative Knowledge Bases.* 1–15.

Cutkosky, Mark R.; Engelmore, Robert S.; Fikes, Richard E.; Genesereth, Michael R.; Gruber, Thomas R.; Mark, William S.; Tenenbaum, Jay M.; and Weber, Jay C. (1993) PACT: An experiment in integrating concurrent engineering systems. ©1993 IEEE. Reprinted with permission from IEEE Computer 26(1):28–37.

Petrie, Charles (1993) The *Redux'* server. ©1991 IEEE. Reprinted with permission from *International Conference on Intelligent and Cooperative Information Systems* (CoopIS). 134–143.

Sandholm, Tuomas and Lesser, Victor (1995) Issues in automated negotiation and electronic commerce: Extending the contract net framework. In *Proceedings of the International Conference on Multiagent Systems.* 328–335. ©1995 American Association for Artificial Intelligence.

Etzioni, Oren and Weld, Daniel (1994) A softbot-based interface to the Internet. *Communications of the ACM* 37(7):72–76. © Association of Computing Machinery, Inc. Reprinted by permission.

Arens, Yigal; Hsu, Chun-Nan; and Knoblock, Craig A. (1996) Query processing in the SIMS information mediator. In *Proceedings of the ARPA/Rome Laboratory Knowledge-Based Planning and Scheduling Initiative Workshop,* 1996.

Kuokka, Daniel and Harada, Larry (1995) Matchmaking for information agents. In *Proceedings of the 14th International Joint Conference on Artificial Intelligence,* 1995. 672–678. © International Joint Conferences on Artificial Intelligence, Inc.

Durfee, E. H.; Kiskis, D. L.; and Birmingham, W. P. (1997) The agent architecture of the University of Michigan Digital Library. *IEE Proceedings-Software Engineering,* Vol. 144, No. 1, Feb. 1997, pp 61–71. Reprinted with permission.

Lashkari, Yezdi; Metral, Max; and Maes, Pattie (1994) Collaborative interface agents. In *Proceedings of the National Conference on Artificial Intelligence.* 444–449. ©1994 American Association for Artificial Intelligence.

Rich, Charles and Sidner, Candace L. (1997) Collagen: When agents collaborate with people. In *Proceedings of the First International Conference on Autonomous Agents.* ©1997 American Association for Artificial Intelligence.

Kautz, Henry; Selman, Bart; Coen, Michael; Ketchpel, Steven; and Ramming, Chris (1994) An experiment in the design of software agents. In *Proceedings of the National Conference on Artificial Intelligence.* 438–443. ©1994 American Association for Artificial Intelligence.

St. Amant, Robert and Cohen, Paul R. (1996) A planner for exploratory data analysis. In *Proceedings of the Third Annual Conference on AI Planning Systems.* 205–212. ©1996 American Association for Artificial Intelligence.

Hayes-Roth, Barbara; Brownston, Lee; and van Gent, Robert (1995) Multiagent collaboration in directed improvisation. In *Proceedings of the First International Conference on Multiagent Systems.* 148–154. ©1995 American Association for Artificial Intelligence.

Cassell, Justine; Pelachaud, Catherine; Badler, Norman; Steedman, Mark; Achorn, Brett; Becket, Tripp; Douville, Brett; Prevost, Scott; and Stone, Matthew (1994) Animated conversation: Rule-based generation of facial expression, gesture and spoken intonation for multiple conversational agents. In *Proceedings of the ACM SIGGRAPH Conference.* 413–420. © Association of Computing Machinery, Inc. Reprinted by permission.

Stone, Brian A. and Lester, James C. (1996) Dynamically sequencing an animated pedagogical agent. In *Proceedings of the National Conference on Artificial Intelligence.* 424–431. ©1996 American Association for Artificial Intelligence.

Liu, Jyi-Shane and Sycara, Katia P. (1996) Multiagent coordination in tightly coupled task scheduling. In *Proceedings of the First International Conference on Multiagent Systems.* 181–188. ©1996 American Association for Artificial Intelligence.

Ishizaki, Suguru (1996) Multiagent model of dynamic design: Visualization as an emergent behavior of active design agents. In *Proceedings of the ACM Conference on Computer Human Interaction.* 347–354. © Association of Computing Machinery, Inc. Reprinted by permission.

Wiederhold, Gio (1992) Mediators in the architecture of future information systems. ©1992 IEEE. Reprinted with permission from *IEEE Computer* 25(3):38–49.

Cohen, Philip R.; Cheyer, Adam; Wang, Michelle; and Baeg, Soon Cheol (1994) An open agent architecture. In *Proceedings of the AAAI Spring Symposium on Software Agents.* 1–8. ©1994 American Association for Artificial Intelligence.

Bayardo, R. J., Jr.; Bohrer, W.; Brice, R.; Cichocki, A.; Fowler, J.; Helal, A.; Kashyap, V.; Ksiezyk, T.; Martin, G.; Nodine, M.; Rashid, M.; Rusinkiewicz, M.; Shea, R.; Unnikrishnan, C.; Unruh, A.; and Woelk, D. (1997) InfoSleuth: Agent-based semantic integration of information in open and dynamic environments. *ACM SIGMOD.* 195–206. ©1997 Association of Computing Machinery, Inc. Reprinted by permission.

Fischer, Klaus; Müller, Jörg P.; and Pischel, Markus (1996) A pragmatic BDI architecture. In *Intelligent Agents II: Agent Theories, Architectures, and Languages.* 203–218. ©1996 Springer-Verlag.

Bates, Joseph; Loyall, A. Bryan; and Reilly, W. Scott (1994) An architecture for action, emotion, and social behavior. *Artificial Social Systems: Fourth European Workshop on Modeling Autonomous Agents in a Multi-Agent World.* Cristiano Castelfranchi and Eric Werner (eds.). 55–68. ©1994 Springer-Verlag.

Labrou, Yannis and Finin, Tim (1997) Semantics and conversations for an agent communication language. In *Proceedings of the Fifteenth International Conference on Artificial Intelligence.* 584–591. © International Joint Conferences on Artificial Intelligence, Inc.

Patil, Ramesh S.; Fikes, Richard E.; Patel-Schneider, Peter F.; McKay, Don; Finin, Tim; Gruber, Thomas; and Neches, Robert (1992) The DARPA knowledge sharing effort: Progress report. In *Proceedings of the Third International Conference on Principles of Knowledge Representation and Reasoning.* 777–787.

Dowell, Michael L.; Stephens, Larry M.; and Bonnell, Ronald D. (1995) Using a domain-knowledge ontology as a semantic gateway among information resources. In *Proceedings of the IJCAI Workshop on Basic Ontological Issues in Knowledge Sharing.* Chapter 4, 1–9.

Johansen, Dag; van Renesse, Robbert; and Schneider, Fred B. (1995) Operating system support for mobile agents. ©1995 IEEE. Reprinted with permission from *Proceedings of the 5th IEEE Workshop on Hot Topics in Operating Systems.* 42–45.

Chess, David; Grosof, Benjamin; Harrison, Colin; Levine, David; Parris, Colin; and Tsudik, Gene (1995) Itinerant agents for mobile computing. ©1995 IEEE. Reprinted with permission from *IEEE Personal Communications* 2(5):34–49.

Rus, Daniela; Gray, Robert; and Kotz, David (1997) Transportable information agents. In *Proceedings of the International Conference on Autonomous Agents.* 228–236. © Association of Computing Machinery, Inc. Reprinted by permission.

Borenstein, Nathaniel (1994) Email with a mind of its own: The Safe-Tcl language for enabled mail. In *Proceedings of the IFIP International Working Conference on Upper Layer Protocols and Architectures* (ULPAA). 389–402.

Sirbu, Marvin A. (1997) Credits and debits on the Internet. ©1997 IEEE. Reprinted with permission from *IEEE Spectrum* 34(2):23–29.

Reiter, Michael K. (1996) Distributing trust with the Rampart toolkit. *Communications of the ACM* 39(4):71–74. © Association of Computing Machinery, Inc. Reprinted by permission.

Rao, Anand S. and Georgeff, Michael P. (1991) Modeling rational agents within a BDI-architecture. In *Proceedings of the International Conference on Principles of Knowledge Representation and Reasoning.* 473–484.

Shoham, Yoav (1993) Agent-oriented programming. Reprinted from *Artificial Intelligence* 60(1):51–92 with permission from Elsevier Science - NL, Sara Burgerhartstraat 25, 1055 KV Amsterdam, The Netherlands.

Rosenschein, Jeffrey and Zlotkin, Gilad (1994) Designing conventions for automated negotiation. *AI Magazine* 15(3). 29–46. ©1994 American Association for Artificial Intelligence.

Wellman, Michael P. (1995) A computational market model for distributed configuration design. *AI EDAM* 9:125–133. Reprinted with the permission of Cambridge University Press.

Fenster, Maier; Kraus, Sarit; and Rosenschein, Jeffrey S. (1995) Coordination without communication: Experimental validation of focal point techniques. In *Proceedings of the International Conference on Multiagent Systems.* 102–108. ©1995 American Association for Artificial Intelligence.

Gasser, Les (1991) Social conceptions of knowledge and action: DAI foundations and open systems semantics. Reprinted from *Artificial Intelligence* 47:107–138 with permission from Elsevier Science - NL, Sara Burgerhartstraat 25, 1055 KV Amsterdam, The Netherlands.

Hewitt, Carl and Inman, Jeff (1991) DAI betwixt and between: From "intelligent agents" to open systems science. ©1991 IEEE. Reprinted with permission from *IEEE Transactions on Systems, Man, and Cybernetics* 21(6):1409–1419.

Sichman, Jaime Simão; Conte, Rosaria; Demazeau, Yves; and Castelfranchi, Cristiano (1994) A social reasoning mechanism based on dependence networks. In *Proceedings of the 11th European Conference on Artificial Intelligence.* 188–192. ©1994 American Association for Artificial Intelligence.

Tokoro, Mario (1993) The society of objects. In Addendum to the *Proceedings of the International Conference on Object-Oriented Programming Systems, Languages, and Applications* (OOPSLA). 3–11. © Association of Computing Machinery, Inc. Reprinted by permission.

Wooldridge, Michael and Jennings, Nicholas R. (1994) Formalizing the cooperative problem solving process. In *Proceedings of the 13th International Workshop on Distributed Artificial Intelligence.* 403–417.

Haddadi, Afsaneh (1995) Towards a pragmatic theory of interactions. In *Proceedings of the International Conference on Multiagent Systems.* 133–139. ©1995 American Association for Artificial Intelligence.

Decker, Keith S. and Lesser, Victor R. (1995) Designing a family of coordination algorithms. In *Proceedings of the International Conference on Multiagent Systems.* 73–80. © 1995 American Association for Artificial Intelligence.

Singh, Munindar P. (1993) A semantics for speech acts. *Annals of Mathematics and Artificial Intelligence* 8(I–II):47–71. By permission of Baltzer Science Publishers, Amsterdam.

Lux, Andreas and Steiner, Donald (1995) Understanding cooperation: An agent's perspective. In *Proceedings of the International Conference on Multiagent Systems.* 261–268. © 1995 American Association for Artificial Intelligence.

Weiss, Gerhard (1993) Learning to coordinate actions in multiagent systems. In *Proceedings of the Thirteenth International Conference on Artificial Intelligence.* 311–316. © International Joint Conferences on Artificial Intelligence, Inc.

Tan, Ming (1993) Multi-agent reinforcement learning: Independent vs. cooperative agents. In *Proceedings of the 10th International Conference on Machine Learning.* 330–337.

Littman, Michael L.; Cassandra, Anthony R.; and Kaelbling, Leslie Pack (1995) Learning policies for partially observable environments: Scaling up. In *Proceedings of the 12th International Conference on Machine Learning.* 362–370.

Tambe, Milind; Johnson, Lewis; and Shen, Wei-Min (1996) Adaptive agent tracking in real-world multi-agent domains: A preliminary report. In *Proceedings of the AAAI Spring Symposium on Adaptation, Coevolution, and Learning in Multiagent Systems.* © 1996 American Association for Artificial Intelligence.

Sen, Sandip; Sekaran, Mahendra; and Hale, John (1994) Learning to coordinate without sharing information. In *Proceedings of the National Conference on Artificial Intelligence.* AAAI Press. 426–431. © 1994 American Association for Artificial Intelligence.

Chapter 1

Agents and Multiagent Systems: Themes, Approaches, and Challenges

We present some of the key themes in agent research, approaches for building agent systems and tools, and the challenges that remain.

1 INTRODUCTION

Due to the proliferation of computing and networking, the desires of almost everyone to be interconnected, and the needs to make data accessible at any time and any place, modern information environments have become large, open, and heterogeneous. They are composed of distributed, largely autonomous, often legacy components. Recent approaches introduce software agents into such environments to deal with these characteristics. The agents represent the components in interactions, where they mediate differences and provide a syntactically uniform and semantically consistent middleware. Their greatest difficulty in achieving uniformity and consistency is the dynamism that open environments introduce. At the same time, the complexity and dynamism of the information environments has led to a pressing need for user interfaces that are active and adaptive personal assistants—in other words, agents.

Applications such as information access, information filtering, electronic commerce, workflow management, intelligent manufacturing, education, and entertainment are becoming ever more prevalent. What these applications have in common is a need for mechanisms for advertising, finding, fusing, using, presenting, managing, and updating information. Since the underlying environment is open—in that the sources of information are autonomous and heterogeneous and may be added or removed dynamically—the associated mechanisms must be extensible and flexible. Increasingly, people are coming to the conclusion that agents are an integral part of such mechanisms. The charm of agents is that they provide a natural means for performing the above tasks over uncontrollable environments. Further, agents are inherently modular and can be constructed locally for each resource, provided they satisfy some high-level protocol of interaction.

1.1 Agents

So, what exactly is an agent? Must it be intelligent? Adaptive? Itinerant? There are almost as many opinions on this as there are agents themselves, leading to frequent debates flaring up on several Internet forums. There is a common core of concepts among these opinions, however, which we have synthesized into our own definition: *Agents are active, persistent (software) components that perceive, reason, act, and communicate.*

Some researchers add further properties, such as being autonomous, goal directed, reactive, or declaratively programmed. Others limit agents to the role of representing a user or database.

There are two extreme views of agents. One long-standing tradition takes agents as essentially conscious, cognitive entities that have feelings, perceptions, and emotions just like humans. Under this view, all of the computational work on agents is inherently inadequate. An alternative view is that agents are merely automata and behave exactly as they are designed or programmed. This view admits a large variety of computations, including computational agents. A concern is that it might be too permissive.

Which of these views is correct? The truth lies somewhere in between. Here, we shall desist from attempting a precise definition and will instead discuss the kinds of applications, architectures, and models that are typically associated with agents. A key issue is that of complexity. The pure automaton view of agents fails to involve the kinds of abstractions that are often essential in describing, analyzing, understanding, or explaining the behavior of agents. The traditional view has many of the abstractions, which work well for people but does not allow their usage for artificial systems. However, in the study of agents, it is often helpful to use the folk abstractions that were meant for people but give them specific technical meanings that are applicable for computational agents. We discuss some of these in Section 4.

In any case, as a practical matter we should always ask the question, What is special about an entity that it may be called an agent? or What does calling it an agent buy us? The answer would not be the same in each case, but it should be nonempty for the notion of agency to be nonvacuously applied.

1.2 Multiagent Systems

All too often, agents are best developed not in isolation but as parts of a multiagent system. The motivation for this claim is entirely practical. Consider the case of the web. The computational architecture that seems to be evolving out of an informationally chaotic web consists of numerous agents representing users, services, and data resources. A typical paradigm of usage is as follows. The resource agents advertise to the services; the user agents use the services to find the resource agents and then query them for the information they need.

A web agent can do its job well only if it can take advantage not only of all the information resources in the web but also of all the other agents that might be operating there. Agents representing different users might collaborate in finding and fusing information, but they might compete for goods and resources. Similarly, the service agents may collaborate or compete with user, resource, and other service agents.

Whether they are collaborators or competitors, the agents will be interacting with each other. They will be interacting not unwittingly, but purposefully. Most purposeful interactions—whether to inform, query, or deceive—require that the agents talk to one another, be aware of each other, and reason about each other. In other words, the agents would be developed to perform as members of a multiagent system.

1.3 Key Characteristics

A taxonomy of agents requires identifying the key characteristics of agent systems, including the characteristics of the agents, the multiagent systems they participate in, the frameworks they are developed in, the roles they play, and the environments they inhabit. We discuss these next. In the interest of brevity, we do not elaborate many of the characteristics, which can be understood from their short definitions or admissible ranges of values. However, some of the characteristics, especially autonomy, rationality, construction, sociability, and mobility, are discussed in greater detail.

1.3.1 Agents

The characteristics of agents are fundamentally tied to not only their intrinsic properties, which are defined for an agent by itself, but also their extrinsic properties, which are defined for an agent in the context of other agents. Tables 1 and 2 enumerate the intrinsic and extrinsic characteristics of agents, respectively.

Property	Range of Values
Lifespan	Transient to Long-Lived
Level of cognition	Reactive to Deliberative
Construction	Declarative to Procedural
Mobility	Stationary to Itinerant
Adaptability	Fixed to Teachable to Autodidactic
Modeling	Of environment, themselves, or other agents

Table 1: Agent Characteristics: Intrinsic

Property	Range of Values
Locality	Local to Remote
Social autonomy	Independent to Controlled
Sociability	Autistic, Aware, Responsible, Team Player
Friendliness	Cooperative to Competitive to Antagonistic
Interactions	Logistics: direct or via facilitators, mediators, or nonagents Style/Quality/Nature: with agents/world/both Semantic Level: declarative or procedural communications

Table 2: Agent Characteristics: Extrinsic

1.3.2 System

Table 3 enumerates the key attributes of multiagent systems, independent of the agents that constitute them.

1.3.3 Frameworks

An agent execution environment or framework includes a number of concerns, which are enumerated as possible characteristics in Table 4.

1.3.4 Environments

Table 5 lists some key properties of an environment with respect to a specific agent that inhabits it. These generalize the presentation in [Russell & Norvig 1995].

1.3.5 Autonomy

Autonomy is often cited as an important property of agents (and other systems), yet it is difficult to define. We find it useful to distinguish different varieties of autonomy, which serve different purposes in the study and design of agents.

Property	Range of Values
Uniqueness	Homogeneous to Heterogeneous
Granularity	Fine-Grained to Coarse-Grained
Control structure	Hierarchy to Democracy
Interface autonomy	Communication: specify vocabulary, language, protocol Intellect: specify goals, beliefs, ontologies Skills: specify procedures, behaviors
Execution autonomy	Independent to Controlled

Table 3: System Characteristics

Property	Range of Values
Design autonomy	Platform/language/internal architecture/interaction protocol
Communication infrastructure	Shared memory (blackboard) or message-based Connected or connectionless (email) Point-to-point, multicast, or broadcast Push or pull Synchronous or asynchronous
Directory service	White pages, yellow pages
Message protocol	KQML HTTP and HTML OLE, CORBA, DSOM
Mediation services	Ontology-based? Transactional (updates)?
Security services	Timestamps/authentication
Remittance services	Billing/currency
Operations support	Archiving/redundancy/restoration/accounting

Table 4: Framework Characteristics

Property	Definition
Knowable	To what extent is the environment known to the agent?
Predictable	To what extent can it be predicted by the agent?
Controllable	To what extent can the agent modify the environment?
Historical	Do future states depend on the entire history, or only the current state?
Teleological	Are parts of it purposeful (i.e., are there other agents)?
Real time	Can the environment change while the agent is deliberating?

Table 5: Environment-Agent Characteristics

It is important to identify the intended unit of autonomy. This could be the computational agent plus its human owner, or an agent plus some associated information resource. An agent that appears autonomous to other agents may in fact be a slave for the human or information resource to which it is attached.

Absolute Autonomy. Autonomy is intuitively related to predictability—the less predictable an agent is the more autonomous it appears. This view is autonomy as arbitrariness; thus, an absolutely autonomous agent may do anything it pleases. An *autistic* agent—one that is simply unaware of the other agents inhabiting its environment or indeed of the environment itself—may be observed to be performing actions absolutely autonomously. It wouldn't heed to requests of others because it would not even recognize them.

Absolute autonomy is rarely useful in the design of an agent system because agents typically must serve some purpose, which constrains them. However, a multiagent system may be able to tolerate some absolutely autonomous agents: we discuss that feature under "Execution Autonomy."

Social Autonomy. A more interesting case is social autonomy, where an agent is aware of its colleagues and is sociable, but nevertheless exercises its autonomy in certain circumstances. Autonomy is in natural tension with coordination or with higher-level notions such as commitments (Section 4.3). To be coordinated with other agents or to keep its commitments, an agent must lose some of its autonomy. However, an agent that is sociable and responsible can still be autonomous. It would attempt to coordinate with others where appropriate and to keep its commitments as much as possible. However, it would exercise its autonomy in entering into those commitments in the first place.

Consequently, social autonomy is not an intrinsic property, but an extrinsic property, and is included in Table 2.

Interface Autonomy. In most practical systems, where absolute autonomy is not feasible, the most autonomy we can hope for is autonomy with respect to the internal design, provided some application programming interface (API) is maintained. The API defines what is exposed by the agent but doesn't guarantee that the agent will always do as requested—that is a matter of execution autonomy. The interface requirements are imposed by a system on the agents that might join it. For this reason, this property appears as a system characteristic in Table 3.

Execution Autonomy. Execution autonomy corresponds to the freedom an agent has while executing in an environment. For example, personal assistants can be constrained to behave in a helpful manner—they must always speak the truth and believe and help the user. However, since agents can represent different interests, some execution autonomy is generally required even when interface autonomy is constrained. Execution autonomy is crucial to the openness of a system. Restrictions on execution autonomy can be imposed by specific systems, for specific roles. Thus, this is a system characteristic in Table 3.

Design Autonomy. Design autonomy deals with how the agents are constructed—it is the autonomy of the designers. Design autonomy is crucial if we want a system to be truly open, in that people should be able to contribute their agents to the system while having to satisfy as few requirements as possible. Thus, design autonomy corresponds to heterogeneity of the agents. It is orthogonal to execution autonomy because agents of a fixed design might choose their own actions, while agents of different designs might be controlled externally.

Different agent frameworks come with different requirements that impinge upon design autonomy. Some require that all agents be built using a specific language. Some approaches (e.g., for agent communication) require that the agents must necessarily represent beliefs, must be able to perform logical inferences and plan, and must be rational. Design autonomy is listed as a property of frameworks in Table 4.

1.3.6 Intelligence and Rationality

Intelligence is notoriously difficult to define precisely. However, we know intuitively when a system is behaving intelligently. One simplistic, but sometimes useful, definition of an intelligent system is one that performs a task that, if performed by a human, would earn the human the attribute "intelligent." However, many tasks that are performed routinely by humans are difficult to realize in a computational system. By contrast, some tasks that are difficult for a human, such as various forms of arithmetic, are easy for a machine.

The concept of rationality is intimately related to intelligence but can be formalized more easily. Most formalizations require that the agent have preferences about states of the world and choose actions that maximize the preferences. Thus, rationality depends on the following attributes [Russell & Norvig 1995]:

- The performance measure for success
- What the agent has perceived so far
- What the agent knows about the environment
- The actions the agent can perform

An ideal rational agent is defined as follows: for each possible percept sequence, it acts to maximize its expected utility, on the basis of its knowledge and the evidence from the percept sequence.

Logical rationality considers qualitative notions such as the consistency of beliefs or the consistency of beliefs, intentions, and desires with chosen actions (these terms are revisited in Section 4). Economic rationality assumes that the agent has utility functions to guide its choice of actions.

Although rationality is a compelling notion for several purposes, it imposes certain artificial constraints on how we understand the world and the agents that inhabit it. Agents—artificial and human—are limited in their computational powers and their knowledge of their environment and may not be quite as rational as we might like. The study of *bounded rationality* remains an important, yet difficult, subject [Simon 1996].

1.3.7 Procedural vs. Declarative Construction

Procedural approaches to programming specify exactly how a computation should proceed; declarative approaches specify what it should do without giving too much detail of how. There is a long-standing debate in computer science about the relative merits of procedural and declarative approaches. For example, the seventies saw the famous procedural-declarative controversy [Winograd 1975].

Given the way computing systems develop, procedural approaches are the first ones to come about before the necessary generalizations have been made to yield declarative approaches. Also, in a narrow sense, procedural approaches can be more efficient. However, when the flexibility of solutions and the productivity of programmers are taken into consideration, declarative approaches usually pay off. Declarative approaches offer advantages in

- Modularity: requirements can be captured independently from each other.
- Incremental change: it is much easier to add or remove components from a declarative specification than to rewrite procedural programs.
- Semantics: declarative notations can be given a formal semantics directly, whereas procedural languages must first be mapped to declarative structures. Formal semantics is crucial for validating tools for building agents and their interaction protocols. It assures predictable behavior and enables efficiencies in implementation without jeopardizing soundness.
- User interfaces: declarative specifications are easier to generate than procedural code, leading to greater productivity for interface developers and, coupled with clean semantics, greater predictability for users.
- Inspectability: being explicit, declarative specifications can be examined to determine (a) the current constraints on an agent and its interactions, (b) how far the constraints have been satisfied, and (c) the rationales for different actions.
- Learnability: declarative specifications are easier to learn, enabling an agent to discover how other agents behave and how to participate in an ongoing "discussion" among agents.

For these reasons, time and again throughout the history of computing, higher-level declarative techniques have won out. Examples include high-level programming languages versus assembly languages, SQL versus navigational queries, conceptual versus physical data models, and formal grammars and compiler generators versus hard-coded compilers. However, declarative approaches can be significantly inefficient for some problems and can require a heavy infrastructure to interpret declarative specifications.

1.4 Historical Remarks

Agents and agency have been the object of study for centuries. They were first considered in the philosophy of action and ethics. In this century, with the rise of psychology as a discipline, human agency has been studied intensively.

During the five decades of artificial intelligence (AI), computational agents have been an active topic of exploration. The AI work in its earliest stages investigated agents explicitly, albeit with simple models. However, the optimism of building truly intelligent systems with the theories and technologies of the fifties and sixties faded. In the seventies and eighties, the trend of AI research turned toward narrower studies of specific techniques. To some extent this was justifiable, because researchers had come to realize that there were a number of technical problems to be solved before any progress could be made on a general notion of intelligent agency. There was much work in knowledge representation, search techniques, game playing, expert systems, machine learning, and natural language. However, the specialization had the unfortunate effect of fragmenting the field while reducing the payoffs from pursuing further research.

From the late seventies onward, while mainstream AI was turning toward specific capabilities, a research community was forming under the rubric of *distributed AI* (DAI) [Bond & Gasser 1988; Gasser & Huhns 1989; Huhns 1987]. The DAI community concerned itself with agents as computational entities that interacted with each other to solve various kinds of distributed problems. Although there are specific techniques in DAI, just as in the rest of AI, large systems were more important to this community. To this end, whereas AI at large borrowed abstractions such as beliefs and intentions from psychology, the DAI community borrowed abstractions and insights from sociology, organizational theory, economics, and the philosophies of language and linguistics. These abstractions complement rather than oppose the psychological abstractions but, being about groups of agents, are fundamentally better suited to large distributed systems.

The term *agent* also came to be used in the eighties and nineties by the traditional computing communities of database, operating systems, and networking. An agent was essentially a proxy for a computation or a site—a transaction, a process, or a network router—that could be used to poll the state of the underlying entity. Agents were thus a formal interface to an arbitrary system. For example, the Simple Network Management Protocol (SNMP) defines certain kinds of agents upon which a network management application can be designed. This application can in principle execute in a multivendor environment, as long as the agents implemented by the different vendors yield the same functionality while hiding the internal details of the proprietary components, such as network routers.

With the expansion of the Internet and the web in the nineties, we witnessed the emergence of software agents geared to open information environments. These agents perform tasks on behalf of a user or serve as nodes—brokers or information sources—in the global information system. Although software agents of this variety do not involve especially innovative techniques, it is their synthesis of existing techniques and their suitability to their application that makes them powerful and popular. Thus, much of the attention they have received is well deserved. However, we believe that their fundamental shortcoming, which will require significant changes in their design, is their centralization. The enhancement of conventional software agents through distribution will be one of the major areas of expansion in agent technology.

The past few years have also seen the development of user interface agents or personal assistants. These agents help a human user deal with a complex environment. Increasingly, they are called upon to be natural interlocutors with personalities and emotions of their own. This is another promising direction in agent technology.

1.5 Organization

The literature on agents poses some special challenges to classification. Since agent technology is a new area, applications and architectures are usually developed hand in hand. Similarly, architectures and theories or models are also intimately related because the models inherently make architectural assumptions, and architectures often assume a model of agency.

However, in keeping with our present goals, we categorize the literature into applications, architectures and infrastructure, and models, which we discuss in the following sections, followed by some speculations on future trends and challenges.

2 APPLICATIONS

There are numerous applications for agents. Many involve varieties of personal assistants, and others are specialized for information-rich environments. Still others involve topics such as art, drama, and design—well beyond the traditional applications of computing, but increasingly important.

2.1 Information-Rich Environments

Information-rich or open environments are broadly defined as environments consisting of a large number and variety of distributed and heterogeneous information sources. The associated applications are varied. They involve the purely informational ones, such as database access, information malls, workflow management, electronic commerce, and virtual enterprises. They also include the information component of physical ones, such as sensor arrays, manufacturing, transportation, energy distribution, and telecommunications. By way of distinction, open environments

- Span enterprise boundaries
- Have components that are heterogeneous in the underlying database management systems used or the semantics associated with the information stored or manipulated
- Comprise information resources that can be added or removed in a loosely structured manner
- Lack global control of the content of those resources or how that content may be updated
- Incorporate intricate interdependencies among their components

Thus, open information environments are partially knowable, predictable, and controllable. They are often teleological but mostly not historical or real time.

Cooperative Information Systems (CISs) are multiagent systems with organizational and database abstractions geared to open environments. Each component of the environment, as well as the human user(s), is modeled as associated with an agent. The agents capture and enforce the requirements of their associated parties. They interact with one another appropriately and help achieve the necessary robustness and flexibility.

2.1.1 Enterprises

The enterprise applications of interest always involve heterogeneity and often the updating of information. Updates are qualitatively more complex than retrievals because they can potentially introduce inconsistencies. This is especially the case when several databases are involved and there are subtle interdependencies among them. This is the province of a *workflow*, a composite activity to solve some business need that accesses different resources and may involve human interaction.

Traditional database transactions satisfy the so-called ACID properties [Gray & Reuter 1993]. A transaction happens entirely or not at all, does not violate consistency, does not expose any partial results, and, if successful, has permanent results. Transactions are effective in homogeneous and centralized databases but cannot model workflows, as shown in Table 6. For example, atomicity requires the component databases to expose their internal control states and operations, violating their execution autonomy and often their interface autonomy as well. Isolation requires locking data items even when it is essential to let a collaborator access them.

In many cases, multiple workflows can arise and interact with each other. For example, in a telecommunications setting, a channel assignment workflow must wait until enough channels have been created by another workflow. Some of

Property	Meaning	Undesirable When
Atomicity	All or nothing	Legacy systems or nonterminating processes are involved
Consistency	Integrity preserving	Integrity conditions cannot be defined or data values expire
Isolation	Hidden partial results	Collaboration is desired
Durability	Permanent committed results	Backing out is necessary

Table 6: The ACID Properties

these interactions can be pernicious in that one workflow may cause the failure of another workflow. Some of the interactions, however, are useful. The challenge is to identify the (potential) interactions and to control them appropriately.

Agents can manage individual workflows, especially through potential exception conditions. They can also model and manage their interactions with one another.

2.1.2 Network Information Access

Network information access involves accessing information from intranets or the Internet. It involves the tasks of

- Resource discovery—finding the proper source to query or search
- Information retrieval—querying unstructured or semi-structured data
- Database querying—querying structured data of different formats
- Information filtering—obtaining information from a source that is producing a stream of data
- Information fusion—merging results in a meaningful manner

The size of the information space, and the variety of the sources in it, make network information access a daunting task. Unstructured data prove especially challenging because the absence of a clear semantics makes it difficult to reliably relate results from a query to the original information needs of the user [Croft 1993]. Thus, the user must actively participate in the querying process, making information access a prime candidate for personal assistants (Section 2.2).

As a specific example of the use of agents in these applications, consider Warren, which is a system of intelligent agents for helping someone manage a financial portfolio [Sycara & Zeng 1996]. It coalesces market data, financial report data, technical models, analysts' reports, and breaking news with current prices from a stock ticker. For example, while one agent finds and plots the current price of a company's stock, another monitors the newswire for anything that mentions the company. Later, it might be seen that a sharp drop in the price occurred shortly after a news release from a brokerage that downgraded the stock. All of the information is already available in some form on the web—Warren simply integrates it by having a specialized agent responsible for each resource and then presenting it to, or alerting, a user. The agents operate on behalf of users for months, whether they are logged on or not.

Several other applications include aspects of personal assistance:

- Decision support from Firefly, AgentSoft, Verity, and Amulet—information agents that learn and adapt to users' information needs and then proactively retrieve and organize targeted information; Firefly uses collaborative filtering
- Information filtering from Intel—a Smart News Reader sorts and ranks newsgroup articles based on learned user preferences

2.2 Personal Assistants

User interfaces are now widely recognized as one of the booming areas of computing. Interface technologies such as graphics, animation, virtual reality, and wearable or mobile interfaces are becoming ever more common.

Whereas traditional user interfaces were rigid and not helpful, the decreasing cost of computers and physical interface devices, coupled with the spread of computing to the lay population, has supported an increasing trend toward intelligent, cooperative interfaces. Also, whereas traditional user interfaces were for applications such as database access, modern applications involve the control of software and hardware tools in general. These can be as varied as tools for scheduling meetings, finding people with similar interests carrying out statistical reasoning, designing artificial environments, animating entities in virtual worlds, and educating.

Traditional AI sought to develop automated tools for solving problems that required some intelligence—not necessarily using human mechanisms of intelligence, which are not well understood, but at least addressing problems of sufficient complexity that a human solving them would be considered intelligent. Recent successes of computing, AI included, have taken a radically different approach. Rather than attempting to automate the reasoning process fully, the current trend is to develop tools that assist humans in carrying out the reasoning. There are a number of good motivations for the trend:

- Many interesting problems are too complex to have tractable solutions that are fully automated.
- In many settings, for issues of ethics and responsibility, computers cannot be trusted to perform critical actions unilaterally. In such settings, it is crucial to keep a human in the decision loop.
- Some applications inherently require the active participation of a human because the problem cannot be specified in a form that will admit to automatic solution. An important case is information retrieval, where users typically do not have a precise query that can be processed automatically. Instead, users need to ask some leading queries to understand the information space they are searching and to formulate a precise query only gradually (Section 2.1.2). Another example is education: it would be inappropriate with current technology to eliminate the human user from an educational system!

As a consequence of the above trend, modern user interfaces are playing an increasing role in complex systems. The trend has shifted from passive interfaces to active interfaces, those that have a life of their own—that is agents! Such interfaces are *dialogue based* to some extent—not because they must carry out spoken or textual dialogues, but because they are aware of users and interact with them dynamically. In this respect, they typically support *mixed-initiative* interactions in which neither the computer nor the human is master or slave, but equal partners—either party can take initiative in the dialogue as appropriate.

In many applications, it is important to have interfaces that not only get the job done but also exude a *persona*. In such interfaces, the agent has an explicit presence, for example, as an on-screen animated figure. Such agents are called *believable agents* and are suited for applications involving instruction through the means of an animated tutor figure or role in a game or dramatic play.

Thus, personal assistants can be characterized as

- Multimodal: support interactions in different input and output modalities, such as voice or typing
- Dialogue based: carry out a conversation, not necessarily spoken, with the user
- Mixed-initiative: if dialogue based, let the user control the dialogue dynamically or make unexpected requests
- Anthropoid: endowed with a personality; typically emotional
- Cooperative: assist the user in defining the user's real needs—this typically requires some ability to model the user and the task the user is engaged in
- Adaptive: learn from past interactions with the user

A major challenge for agent-based interfaces is the development of toolkits and methodologies through which they can be engineered to have as many of the above characteristics as desired in an application.

The environment of a personal assistant has two main components: the human user and the back-end information system. These have different properties, which place interesting requirements on the designs of the assistants. Table 7 lists the key properties of users and back-end systems using the terms introduced in Table 5. We assume that an assistant can find all that is relevant about the user and system. It can partially predict the user's behavior, which motivates having adaptive user modeling. Since the user is historical and teleological, a dialogue functionality is required along with some task modeling. Since the assistant cannot control the user and users can change their minds in real time, it must allow interrupts, that is, be mixed-initiative.

3 ARCHITECTURES AND INFRASTRUCTURE

Table 8 reviews the development of software architectures leading to agent-based ones. In traditional terms, an agent might be a client and do everything itself or might tell a server how to do something. Correspondingly, an agent may be a server and do nothing or do exactly as told. In peer-to-peer settings with smarter agents, the client need only tell a server what it would like to have done, and the server may satisfy high-level requests. The client and server autonomously preserve their own interests. The traditional case has a mobile variant in which the messages are procedural scripts rather than declarative invocations of services.

Property	User	Backend System
Knowable	Yes	Yes
Predictable	Partially	No
Controllable	No	Partially
Historical	Yes	No
Teleological	Yes	Maybe
Real time	Yes	Possibly

Table 7: A Personal Assistant's Environment

Role Architecture	Entity1	Entity2	Communication
Client-server	Master: Full control	Slave: No control	RPC
	Tells how	Does as told	
Distributed	Peer: Assigns tasks	Peer: Satisfies requests	Asynchronous declarative messages
	Self-interested	Autonomous	
Agent based	Peer: Creates or invokes commitments	Peer: Keeps commitments	Speech act
	Self-interested	Autonomous	

Table 8: Roles of Computations

3.1 Agent Architectures

Agents are constructed and operate in environments whose characteristics we described in Section 1. The environments impose constraints on the behavior of the agents and provide services and facilities that can be used by the agents. A number of agent architectures have been proposed. These are typically layered in some way with components for perception and action at the bottom and reasoning at the top. The perception feeds the reasoning subsystem, which governs the actions, including deciding what to perceive next.

A challenge that agent architectures must surmount is arranging for the reasoning and perception to be both engaged and disengaged as appropriate. For example, it is undesirable for the agent to keep reasoning about some future event while there is a crisis in its immediate environment; conversely, if its perceptions continually interrupt the reasoning, it would not be able to perform any complex chains of reasoning. Agents in which perception or reasoning dominates are called reactive or deliberative, respectively. There are no general, domain-independent approaches that will do the right thing in all circumstances. Some useful papers are [Bonasso et al. 1996; Fischer et al. 1996; Norman & Long 1996]. We revisit related issues in Section 4.

3.2 Agent System Architectures

Agent architectures look at agents in the small. It is often more important to consider agents in the large. This is where agent system architectures come in. These are meant to facilitate agents' actions in obeying the constraints of their environments while taking advantage of available services and facilities. Additionally, the system architectures provide for different types of specialized agents to operate and interact with the environments and each other.

One type of agent manages protocols on behalf of applications and resources. In this capacity, the agents produce a layer of homogeneity among the heterogeneous components of an environment. The layer might be at a low communication level, such as produced by Aides [Singh & Huhns 1994], heads [Lux & Steiner 1995], and front-end processors [Zhang & Bell 1991]; at a semantic level, such as produced by knowledge handlers [Wong 1993], ontology agents [Bayardo et al. 1997], type brokers, and wrappers [Gray 1991]; or at an information management level, such as produced by mediators [Wiederhold 1992], routers [Sayre & Gray 1993], intelligent information agents [Papazoglou et al. 1992], and facilitators [Neches et al. 1991].

Type brokers provide a means to manage the structure and semantics of information and query languages. They define standard types by which computations can communicate. Most of this work pertains to lower-level issues, which typically involve a set of such type brokers and a way to distribute type information. An application uses the broker to find a service and then communicates directly with the desired service. Type brokers give slightly more semantics than directories by including the type signature of methods, not just their names. With more sophisticated notions of service semantics, these could be more useful.

Other types of agents access information from heterogeneous sources on behalf of users or other agents. One of the best examples of these is a mediator [Wiederhold 1992]. A *mediator* is a simplified agent that acts on behalf of a set of information resources or applications. Mediators come in a wide range of capabilities, from database and protocol converters to intelligent modules that capture the semantics of the domain and learn from the data. The basic idea is that a mediator is responsible for mapping the resources or applications to the rest of the world. Mediators thus shield the different components of a system from each other. To construct mediators effectively requires some common representation of the meanings of the resources and applications they connect, which are discussed in Section 3.4.1.

3.3 Agent Frameworks

A number of research groups have made tools available for constructing agents of the types described above:

- Agent Building Environment (ABE) from IBM is written in C++ and Java; agents in ABE have rule-based reasoning and interfaces to the web (HTTP), newsgroups (NNTP), and email (SMTP).
- The Java Agent Template (JAT) and JAT-Lite from Stanford enable simple Java agents to communicate over a LAN via KQML.
- Java Expert System Shell (JESS) is basically CLIPS in Java; it enables solitary reasoning agents to be constructed.
- Voyager from ObjectSpace Inc. provides an Object Request Broker for Java agents.
- Open Agent Architecture (OAA) from SRI enables the construction of agents that are based on a logic-based declarative InterAgent Communication Language and run on top of CORBA. One of the agents, a facilitator, distributes tasks to other agents, with results sent to user agents.

Table 9 shows how these tools can be categorized according to the features described in Table 4. One can see that the feature space has not nearly been explored by these tools.

3.4 Agent Infrastructures

The above tools and architectures presume or provide an infrastructure within which the agents operate and interact. The infrastructure might supply the means for an agent to communicate, to be understood, and to move. A key aspect of the infrastructure is the facilities for communications and knowledge sharing it offers.

3.4.1 Common Ontologies

A major challenge to agents' understanding each other is that they may have different systems of belief; that is, different terms for the same concept, the same term for different concepts, different class systems or schemas, or differences in depth and breadth of coverage. Intuitively, a shared representation is essential to successful communication and coordination. For humans, this is provided by the physical, biological, and social world. For computational agents, this is provided by a *common ontology*—a representation of knowledge, typically taxonomic, of some

Property	ABE	JAT	JESS	Voyager	OAA
Design autonomy	Platform Language Internal architecture	Platform Language Internal architecture	Platform Language Internal architecture	Platform Language Internal architecture	Platform Language Internal architecture
Communication infrastructure	Message based Connectionless Multicast Push Asynchronous	Message based Connected Point-to-point Push Synchronous	None	Message based Connectionless Point-to-point Push Asynchronous	Message based Connected Point-to-point Push Synchronous
Directory service	None	Name server	None	ORB	ORB
Message protocol	HTTP, NNTP, SMTP	KQML	None	IIOP	IIOP
Mediation services	None	None	None	None	Facilitator
Security services	None	None	None	None	None
Remittance services	None	None	None	None	None
Operations support	None	None	None	None	None

Table 9: Characteristics of Agent-Building Tools

domain of discourse that is made available to all the agents and other components in an information system [Neches et al. 1991].

For the present purpose, it is convenient to think of the agents—or, more properly, the information sources that underlie the agents—as databases, although they may in fact be files or sensors without all of the database functionalities [Elmasri & Navathe 1994]. In heterogeneous environments, it is possible and indeed common that, when different databases store information on related topics, each provides a unique model of it. The databases might use different terms (e.g., **`employee`** or **`staff`**) to refer to the same concept. Worse still, they might use the same term to have different meanings. For example, one database may use **`employee`** to mean anyone currently on the payroll, whereas another may use **`employee`** to mean anyone currently receiving benefits. The former will include assigned contractors; the latter will include retirees. Consequently, merging information meaningfully is nontrivial. The problem is exacerbated by competitive pressures to use advances in communications infrastructure: different companies or divisions of a large company, which previously proceeded independently of one another, are now expected to have some linkage with each other.

The linkages can be thought of as semantic mappings between the application (which consumes or produces information) and the various databases. If the application somehow knows that **`employee`** from a database has one meaning, it can insert appropriate tests to eliminate spurious records. Clearly, this approach would be a nightmare to maintain. The slightest changes in a database would require modifying all the applications that access its contents! This would be a fundamental step backward from the very idea of the database architecture [Elmasri & Navathe 1994 (ch.1)], which sought to separate and shield applications from the storage of data.

As we hinted above, common ontologies can be used to mediate among the semantic representations of different databases or agents. They thus promise to simplify the creation and maintenance of semantic mappings. There are two big challenges in using ontologies for this purpose: (1) to build them and (2) to link to them. There are several large-scale efforts underway to build ontologies. These include Cyc [Lenat & Guha 1989], DARPA ontology sharing project [Patil et al. 1992], Ontology Base (ISI) [Knight & Luk 1994], and WordNet (Princeton) [Miller 1995]. Tools for creating semantic mappings are also being built (e.g., [Woelk et al. 1996]), but greater sophistication would be welcome. We revisit this point in Section 5.3.

3.4.2 Communication Protocols

For interoperability, agents should be able to communicate with agents supplied by different implementors or vendors. The obvious solution is a lingua franca, whereby all the agents who implement the (same) lingua franca can communicate. To approach this ideal, an agent communication language (ACL) must be standardized so that different parties can build their agents to interoperate. Further, it must have a formal semantics so that different implementations preserve the essential features of the language. By specifying an ACL, we effectively codify the atoms of the interactions that can take place among autonomously developed agents. This is what makes ACLs and their standards and semantics worth studying.

KQML. The Knowledge Query and Manipulation Language (KQML) [Finin et al. 1994] was defined under the DARPA-sponsored Knowledge Sharing Effort. KQML assumes a layered architecture. It assumes, at the bottom, functionality for message transport or communication. It leaves, at the top, the content to be specified by the applications, typically in some formal language such as Knowledge Interchange Format (KIF) [Genesereth 1991] or Structured Query Language (SQL) [Elmasri & Navathe 1994]. It provides, in the middle, the primitives with which agents can exchange meaningful messages. In other words, KQML provides a way to structure the messages, but lets the agent designers decide what is in them.

KQML provides a large set of primitives through which agents may **`tell`** facts to other agents, evaluate expressions for other agents or **`subscribe`** to services. The primitives are based on speech acts (Section 4.4.1). The KQML primitives fall into a few major classes. One class, which includes **`tell`**, **`evaluate`**, and **`subscribe`**, is geared toward the communication of content. Another class includes primitives to control the flow of information by, for example, using the performative **`next`** to request answers one at a time. Yet another class of primitives allows for **`recruiting`** agents and performing other brokering and facilitator functions.

KQML assumes the message transport is reliable and preserves the order of messages but may not guarantee delivery times. For this reason, the underlying paradigm of communication is asynchronous; at the application level, the effect of synchronous communication is achieved for primitives such as query and reply. KQML allows tagging messages to relate messages (e.g., responses to corresponding queries). In this way, KQML supports some elementary protocols, although more sophisticated protocols must be defined externally.

The KQML semantics is given informally. KQML agents are assumed to have a virtual knowledge base (VKB) containing beliefs and goals. They can communicate about the virtual knowledge base of themselves and others. Thus a **`tell`** directs the recipient to change its VKB; an **`evaluate`** directs the recipient to produce a response based on its VKB.

Arcol and FIPA. Arcol is another ACL based on speech acts [Breiter & Sadek 1996; Sadek 1991]. Arcol was the basis for the first version of the proposed standard of the Foundation for Intelligent Physical Agents (FIPA) standard, and many of its components survive in the second version as well. Agents conforming to the FIPA specification can deal explicitly with actions. They make requests, and they can nest the speech acts. The FIPA specification has a formal semantics.

Comparison. KQML suffers from as yet poorly defined semantics. As a result, of the many implementations of KQML, each seems unique. This makes communication difficult, and a KQML agent might not be understood. Security has not been a major issue in the KQML work. The FIPA specification, by contrast, attempts to formalize the semantics and a security model. However, in view of its recency, it has not been widely tested or adopted. We evaluate these approaches conceptually in Section 4.4.

3.4.3 Interaction with the Infrastructure

An agent communication language (ACL) must inevitably interact with the infrastructure on which the agents are created and managed and over which the communications are effected. Although a number of the transport issues can be separated from the ACL—and have been traditionally—certain issues merit further attention. These include provisions in the infrastructure for multicasting, making the identity of message receivers known, and covering important locutions and conversational structures.

Coverage of Locutions and Conversational Structures. An ACL should include locutions for dealing appropriately with the underlying information system, for example, in terms of initiating and maintaining sessions, authorizing actions, committing to actions, and rolling back to a previous state in the dialogue in case of corruption or error. Additional locutions are required for human-computer dialogue, where the dialogue is mixed-initiative and prolonged and the participants have limited memory or attention spans. A classification of conversational locutions along these lines is being developed [Singh et al. 1997]; the sessional, commissive, and authorizational locutions, in particular, are applicable to ACLs.

Identity of Receivers. At some point in the course of sending a message, the identity of the receiver must be determined so the message can be delivered. How late in the flow of control can this binding be established? In some applications (e.g., workflow management), the receiver is only known by its role until a specific message needs to be sent. The management of roles is an intrinsic part of designing and implementing multiagent systems. We believe there should be functionality for role management in the agent infrastructure with corresponding primitives in the ACL component.

Knowing the identity of the receivers bears on the ACL semantics. When a message is to be sent to a potential receiver whose identity is unknown, the sender can make no assumptions about the receiver's beliefs or intentions because the lower (transport) layer cannot validate them. Consequently, a semantics that requires the sender to reason about the receiver leads to an ACL in which known agents are preferred.

Cardinality of Receivers. Although early approaches generally considered exactly one receiver for each message, many applications require multicasting. Multicasting is typically worked in through some additional mechanism, for example, a special forwarding or broadcast agent, which is not a part of the ACL. However, distributed systems are emerging that support multicast, and an ACL should exploit these distributed systems where available. The challenge as before is to ensure that the reasoning required about the beliefs and intentions of the potential receivers is minimized.

3.4.4 Interaction Protocols

Several interaction protocols have been devised for systems of agents. In cases where the agents have conflicting goals or are simply self-interested, the objective of the protocols is to maximize the payoffs (utilities) of the agents [Rosenschein & Zlotkin 1994]. In cases where the agents have similar goals or common problems, as in distributed problem solving (DPS), the objective of the protocols is to maintain globally coherent performance of the agents without violating autonomy, that is, without explicit global control [Durfee 1988]. For the latter cases, important aspects include how to determine shared goals, determine common tasks, avoid unnecessary conflicts, and pool knowledge and evidence.

A basic strategy shared by many of the protocols for DPS is to decompose and then distribute tasks. Such a divide-and-conquer approach can reduce the complexity of a task: smaller subtasks require less capable agents and fewer resources. However, the system must decide among alternative decompositions, if available, and the decomposition process must consider the resources and capabilities of the agents. Also, there might be interactions among the subtasks and conflicts among the agents.

Task decomposition can be done by the system designer, whereby decomposition is programmed during implementation, or by the agents using hierarchical planning, or it might be inherent in the representation of the problem, as in an AND-OR graph. Task decomposition might be done spatially, based on the layout of information sources or decision points, or functionally, according to the expertise of available agents.

Once tasks are decomposed, they can be distributed according to the following criteria [Durfee et al. 1987]:

- Avoid overloading critical resources
- Assign tasks to agents with matching capabilities
- Make an agent with a wide view assign tasks to other agents
- Assign overlapping responsibilities to agents to achieve coherence
- Assign highly interdependent tasks to agents in spatial or semantic proximity to minimize communication and synchronization costs
- Reassign tasks if necessary for completing urgent tasks

Mechanisms that are commonly used to distribute tasks include

- Market mechanisms: tasks are matched to agents by generalized agreement or mutual selection (analogous to pricing commodities)
- Contract net: announce, bid, and award cycles
- Multiagent planning: planning agents have the responsibility for task assignment
- Organizational structure: agents have fixed responsibilities for particular tasks

Of these, the best known and most widely applied is the contract net protocol [Davis & Smith 1983]. This generic protocol repeats the following steps:

1. A manager announces the existence of tasks via a (possibly selective) multicast. The task announcement describes the tasks and the criteria and format for bidding.

2. Agents evaluate the announcement, and some of these agents submit bids. A bid specifies the agent's relevant capabilities for performing the task.
3. The manager evaluates the bids and awards a contract to the most appropriate agent. The award consists of a complete specification of the task.
4. The manager and contractor then communicate privately as necessary.

The contract net is best used when the application has a well-defined hierarchy of tasks, the problem has a coarse-grained decomposition, and the subtasks minimally interact with each other but cooperate when they do. The result is not only a high-level communication protocol for distributing tasks but also a means of self-organization for a group of agents.

3.4.5 Mobility

While most agents are static in that they exist as a single process or thread on one host computer, others can pick up and move their code and data to a new host in the web, where they then resume executing.

Are such agents mobile, itinerant, dynamic, wandering, roaming, or migrant? Are they sent, beamed, teleported, transported, moved, relocated, or RPC'd? These are some of the questions swirling around web discussion groups these days. However, since anything that can be done with mobile agents can be done with conventional software techniques, the key questions are really

- Are mobile agents a useful part of a distributed computing system?
- Are there applications that are easier to develop using mobile agents?
- Under what circumstances is it useful for an agent to be mobile?

We find that there are very few such circumstances, in spite of all the effort being spent on developing techniques for mobility. And there is a fundamental reason—the dichotomy between procedural and declarative constructions (Section 1.3.7)—why this is so. Nevertheless, there are several interesting uses for mobile agents.

- Distributed software updates: In general, the best applications for mobility might be those that involve the dynamic installation of code to update software or extend the functionality of an existing system. This would address a potential limitation of current static systems, which are not easily enhanced. However, new functionality can be installed without requiring a full-blown mobile agent, by using the standard message type **`install(function_name, version, argument_types, code)`**. The receiving agent can autonomously decide—based among other things on its level of trust in the sender—whether to install the corresponding code; if it does, new functionality becomes available. And state information never needs to be shipped around.
- Disconnected operation: A major consideration for personal digital assistants (PDAs) is battery capacity and therefore connect time. Because of this, PDAs are forced to spend most of their existence off-line. Now, suppose you have constructed an agent that knows your preferences and interests and can filter information sent to you from multiple sources. Further, suppose your agent can provide real-time feedback to the sources that would enable them to improve the precision of their information. This agent can run on your PDA, where you can interact with it and instruct it. However, you do not want your agent to stop functioning when you turn off your PDA; when this happens, your agent should move to a host that is on-line.
- Multihop applications: Mobile agents appear suited to testing distributed network hardware. For example, a distributed telecommunication switch is built out of thousands of different cards, with different test rules. The code for thorough testing can be quite large and can improve over time. A traditional approach is to load the board-level testing code directly into the boards and have these boards self-test periodically, sending their results to a main testing controller. The system-level tests do not fit into the boards and consume too much network bandwidth, so they are loaded remotely when the system is inactive.

  A mobile agent approach is to launch testing agents into the active network. These agents can roam between boards, performing tests stochastically. This allows boards to accommodate many testing strategies with a small amount of memory since the agents can come and go over time. Testing agents carry with them both their previous testing history and the means to perform the test. Testing agents can make local decisions, repeating tests or testing neighboring boards without having to report back to a central controller.
- Information commerce: There are times when an information consumer would like to apply proprietary algorithms from one company to proprietary data from another company. A solution would be to find a trusted third party to which both the data and the algorithms, encoded in a mobile agent, could be sent.
- Customized searches on servers: A frequently proposed use for mobile agents is to send them to execute on servers, particularly when the servers have more information than can reasonably be communicated back to a client for processing there and lack the necessary procedures to perform the desired processing themselves.

Procedural vs. Declarative. We view the mobility of agents as primarily an issue of infrastructure—a matter of how agent functionality might be realized. A client seeking information from a server can either send a procedure to execute on the server and find the desired information or send a message requesting the server to find the information using its own procedure. Our criticism of mobile agents is that they are a low-level procedural means to achieve what communication techniques can support at a higher declarative level.

For example, to customize searches on a server, a declarative approach would implement a protocol of search primitives that could be invoked via messages. This approach would mitigate the security worries that the mobile agent would run amok, intentionally or otherwise. It would also offer efficiency advantages. When a mobile agent runs remotely, the server gives up control of disk, memory, and processor resources to the agent. Instead, if the server accepted a sequence of declarative search primitives, it could schedule and carry them out in a way that is optimized to its current state. For example, a modern DBMS could use its own optimized techniques to compute a join much more efficiently than a remote user could program an agent.

Mobility includes procedural encodings in two distinct respects. One, the behavior of a mobile agent is procedurally coded. This might be reasonable for some static agents as well. Two, the interactions of a mobile agent are implicit in the code that constitutes it. This is unnecessary when the agent is static. A static agent's interactions can be explicitly specified in terms of protocols involving its communications. Static agents can then be supplied by different vendors and programmed in different languages as long as they communicate properly with each other.

Ultimately, there is no difference between a complex request language and a simple programming language. There is in fact a continuum of approaches.

Mobile Agent Frameworks. There are a number of active efforts under way to develop systems, protocols, and frameworks for both the construction and use of mobile agents. Most of the following frameworks allow agents to be started, stopped, and moved, and a few allow them to be monitored.

There is an effort by the Object Management Group (OMG) to establish industry standards for mobile agent technology and interoperability among agent systems, such as Odyssey, Aglets, and MOA. The OMG intends to define a mobile agent facility (MAF) for CORBA.

Security Concerns. There are two main aspects to security involving mobile agents. The first and most commonly considered is protection of the server against intentionally or accidentally malicious agents. The second is protection of a mobile agent against malicious servers. The former aspect has been dealt with extensively in the context of operating systems, which establish and maintain protection levels for process execution. Security in the latter aspect cannot be guaranteed because, in order for the mobile agent's code to be executed, the agent has to expose both its code and data to the server. A detection, but not prevention, mechanism is to have the agent return itself with its data to verify that it has not been altered.

A prevention mechanism might hinge on a determination of legal responsibility: are you liable or not for your agent's deeds? And who pays if, for example, a malicious server causes you to buy something on another server?

Authentication, integrity, confidentiality, and nonrepudiation are other important aspects of security. Authentication validates the identity of the person or agent with which you are interacting. Integrity ensures that what you see has not been tampered with, confidentiality ensures that what you intend to be private remains so, and nonrepudiation means you are liable and cannot change your mind.

Challenges for Mobile Agents. We believe that mobility has a useful, albeit limited, role to play in agent computing. For it to be successful in that role, agent languages are needed that can express useful remote computations, that do not violate the security of the sender or receiver, and that are portable and extensible.

Mobility can improve the survivability of an agent—it can move if its execution on a host is threatened—but it can also result in the agent continuing to exist long after its usefulness has ended. Once mobile agents are launched, it is nontrivial to monitor and manage them. The problem is compounded when agents are given the ability to replicate. Consequently, techniques for managing distributed computations are needed that can

- Disseminate extensions to the programming language interpreter
- Ensure security
- Control agent lifetimes
- Prevent the flooding of communication or storage resources

4 MODELS OF AGENCY

The study of agents inevitably includes some model of agency. There is an immense body of literature on philosophies and theories of agents, which we could not hope to review here. The interested reader may consult [Barwise & Perry 1983; Brand 1984; Bratman 1987; Davidson 1980; Dennett 1987; Goldman 1970; Miller et al. 1960; Pylyshyn 1984; Ryle 1949; Simon 1996; Stalnaker 1984].

Simply put, there are three major classes of models or philosophies of agents and their environments.

- *Behaviorism* or *positivism* is the doctrine that considers only the direct behaviors of agents and their environments. In its most rigid form, this doctrine takes the view that the universe involves plain sequences of events; any patterns are in the eye of the beholder. Therefore, even causality might not be a first-class concept. The agents do not have any mental states such as intentions or beliefs; multiagent systems have no social states such as commitments.
- *Subjectivism*, by contrast, takes the view that there are intentions and commitments, but they are as represented in an agent. Similarly, the universe can have causation but only as represented in an agent.
- *Realism* takes the middle ground. The universe has causes; the agents have intentions and beliefs; multiagent systems exist and involve the agents' commitments. These abstract notions are somehow grounded in the universe.

Of the above, behaviorism essentially throws away the abstractions that are crucial for modeling a complex world and for designing agents to operate in it. Subjectivism admits the abstractions but puts few bounds on them, thus leaving it susceptible to charges of being ad hoc. Realism takes a pragmatic position in admitting the necessary abstractions but asking that they be related to the model of the world independent of the views of a specific agent. This position is attractive in many respects but is technically more challenging, because it is often nontrivial to relate high-level abstractions to the "real" world.

The models are related to the perspective a given theory of agency might take. These perspectives can be the agents', the designers', or the evaluators'. Table 10 shows how the model and the perspective interact. Under subjectivism, the external evaluators' perspective is impossible, but the agents' perspective is natural, as in traditional AI. Similarly, in behaviorism, the agents' perspective is meaningless, but the evaluators' perspective is natural, as in traditional distributed computing (DC). The designers' perspective, which relates the agents' and the evaluators' perspectives, is unnatural and can be carried out only with additional assumptions. Under realism, the agents' perspective guides their action (as in subjectivism), the evaluators' perspective enables testing compliance (as in behaviorism), and the designers' perspective enables relating the two. However, as remarked above, it is nontrivial to carry this out.

4.1 Rational Agency: Logical

Logical rationality includes logical, typically qualitative concepts, such as consistency of beliefs or the suitability of actions given beliefs and intentions.

4.1.1 Consistency Maintenance

A somewhat limited, but widely employed, class of logical models involves the single abstraction of belief. The models capture relationships among the beliefs of an agent, which enables maintaining consistency of the beliefs. There are two main views of the consistency. One is *well-foundedness*, which states that all beliefs, except premises, should be justified by other beliefs and these justifications should be acyclic. The other view is *coherence*, which states that the beliefs should hold together as a coherent body even if they lack external justification. Under well-foundedness an agent cannot hold unsupported beliefs, but under coherence it can. It is recognized that human behavior is often closer to coherence than well-foundedness, although traditional logic favors the latter. Both approaches are used successfully for agents through tools called truth maintenance systems (TMSs).

The well-founded view is implemented as justification-based TMSs (JTMSs) [Doyle 1979] and the coherent view as assumption-based TMSs (ATMSs) [de Kleer 1979]. In general, a TMS performs some form of propositional reasoning to update beliefs incrementally when data are added or removed. Using a TMS imposes a special architecture on an agent, in which the problem-solving or reasoning component is separated from the TMS. The former represents domain knowledge (e.g., as rules or procedures) and chooses what to focus on next. The TMS keeps track of the current state of the actions of the problem solver. It uses constraint satisfaction to maintain consistency in the inferences made by the problem solver. Table 11 shows how the integrity of knowledge should be maintained by an agent.

Single-agent TMSs meet all the requirements of Table 11. However, additional problems arise when knowledge is distributed and different agents must achieve consistency. The kinds of inconsistency include

- Both a fact and its negation are believed
- A fact is both believed and disbelieved
- An object is believed to be of two incompatible types (i.e., two terms are used for the same object)
- Two different objects are believed to be the same
- A single-valued fact is given multiple values

In light of this information, different degrees of logical consistency in a multiagent system may be defined as shown in Table 12 [Huhns & Bridgeland 1991]. Local consistency leaves open the possibility that the different agents may be in serious disagreement. However, global consistency is typically not tractable or even essential. In many cases, it is enough that the agents are in agreement about the data that they share. For this reason, the distributed JTMS (DTMS) maintains local-and-shared consistency and well-foundedness [Huhns & Bridgeland 1991]. In this approach, each agent has a justification-based TMS, but the justifications can be external, that is, based on what another agent said. Agents keep track of what they told to which agent so they can suggest updates when their original assertions are no longer supported.

The Distributed ATMS was introduced in [Mason & Johnson 1989]. In this approach, the agents are locally but not globally consistent, based on a local ATMS. The agents believe only results they can substantiate locally and communicate by explicitly contradicting their previous assertions that have been invalidated.

4.1.2 Mental Agency

The consistency maintenance view is useful and attractive. However, it fails to tell the whole story of agency. What goes

Perspective Dimension	Agents'	Designers'	Evaluators'
Subjectivism	Traditional AI	With caveats	Impossible
Realism	Guide action	Implement	Test compliance
Behaviorism	Impossible	With caveats	Traditional DC

Table 10: Dimensions of Models Related to Perspective

Property	Meaning
Stability	Believe everything justified validly; disbelieve everything justified invalidly
Well-foundedness	Beliefs are not circular
Consistency	No contradictions
Completeness	Find a consistent state, if any

Table 11: Knowledge Integrity

Degree	Meaning
Inconsistency	One or more agents are inconsistent
Local consistency	Agents are locally consistent
Local-and-shared consistency	Agents are locally consistent and all agents are consistent about shared data
Global consistency	Agents are globally consistent

Table 12: Degrees of Logical Consistency

in the reasoner component of an agent? How might it affect the so-called beliefs of that agent? What other abstractions would we need to characterize the agent's actions and purposeful behavior?

Some powerful abstractions are based on the mental concepts of folk psychology. Roughly, *beliefs* characterize what an agent imagines the state of the world to be, that is, the state of the world as "represented" by the agent; *know-how* characterizes what the agent can really control in its environment; *goals* describe what states the agent would prefer; *desires* describe the agent's preferences and may sometimes have a motivational aspect; and *intentions* characterize the goals or desires that the agent has selected to work on. Table 13 puts these concepts in broad categories, which resemble the characteristics of environments of Table 5 but with respect to the agent. The above concepts have been extensively studied (e.g., see [Belnap & Perloff 1988; McDermott 1982; Singh 1992] and the citations below).

There are a large number of variations on the formalizations of beliefs and intentions, but they fall into two main categories. One class of definitions includes what we term the "implicit" versions of these concepts (e.g., [Cohen & Levesque 1990; Moore 1984; Rao & Georgeff 1991; Singh 1994]). These approaches are technically more tractable. However, they support the inference that if an agent believes or intends a proposition, it believes or intends all propositions that are logically equivalent. This is, of course, patently false when applied to the actual beliefs or intentions of limited agents. However, it can be justified for modeling agents from a designer's or evaluator's perspective, in which only the relevant beliefs and intentions need to be explicitly considered. The second class of definition takes a "representationalist" stance toward beliefs and intentions [Fagin & Halpern 1988; Konolige 1986; Konolige & Pollack 1989; Singh & Asher 1993]. These are more accurate from the agents' perspective because they do not support the above inference. However, they tend to support few inferences in general, which makes them less tractable technically.

The philosophical positions of the *intentional stance* [Dennett 1987; McCarthy 1979] or the *knowledge level* [Newell 1982] are that any system can in principle be described using "intentional" terms, such as beliefs and intentions. This is indeed a compelling view for the purposes of understanding or designing intelligent systems. However, this view does not guarantee that there is a unique representation of a complex system in terms of beliefs and intentions. In other words, it does not solve the practical problem of how the beliefs and intentions are mapped from the design of an arbitrary agent. For example, how can we just look at the source code in Figure 1 and say whether agent Al believes that it is raining or not (to decice, in this case, if Al was being sincere)? A narrow definition is that the agent should have the string **raining** in a data structure labeled **beliefs**. But this violates design autonomy. Moreover, two agents with the same **beliefs** data structure could act differently enough that it wouldn't be clear whether they *really* had the same beliefs.

The mental states of agents are important only because they are related to the agents' actions, through which the agents attempt to control their environment and satisfy their ends. There is a long tradition in AI for reasoning about actions and planning, which we could not hope to summarize here [Allen et al. 1990]. This work, which considers models of actions and reasons about their preconditions and effects, is intimately related to studies of know-how and intentions [Lespérance et al. 1996; Singh 1994].

In addition to defining the above concepts, we must also characterize their evolution: how do the beliefs and intentions of an agent change in response to fresh evidence or in response to additional reasoning? This remains an unsolved problem in general, although good progress has been made in some areas, especially belief revision [Gärdenfors 1988; Haddawy 1996]. There has also been some preliminary work on intention adoption, maintenance, and revision [Georgeff & Rao 1995; Singh 1997b; Wobcke 1995].

Many current theories include the notion of *commitments*, which are understood as being internal, that is, applying only to the given agent's "attachment" to their beliefs or intentions. An agent that is committed to its beliefs may keep holding them even when the justification is lost [Gärdenfors 1988; Harman 1986]; this is closely related to the coherence view of TMSs discussed above. Similarly, an agent may be committed to its intentions and will not give them up easily [Brand 1984; Bratman 1987]. These might appear to be patently irrational behaviors, but they usually are not because the agents are computationally limited. Reconsidering beliefs and intentions presupposes a computationally expensive process of deliberation. There is a tradeoff between (a) doggedly holding beliefs and intentions longer than warranted and (b) paying the price of reasoning about them. Option (a) can be seen as a form of *satisficing*, in which an agent merely seeks a "good enough" or acceptable solution, not the optimal solution [Simon 1996]. [Singh 1997b] suggests a way to reconcile commitments with rationality, but the problem is still wide open.

Abstraction	**Rough Meaning**
Belief, knowledge	Information about environment
Ability, know-how, Seeing-to-it-that	Control of environment
Goals, desires, intentions	Purposeful behavior

Table 13: Mental Abstractions for Agents

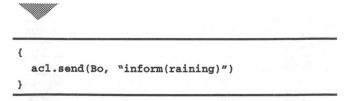

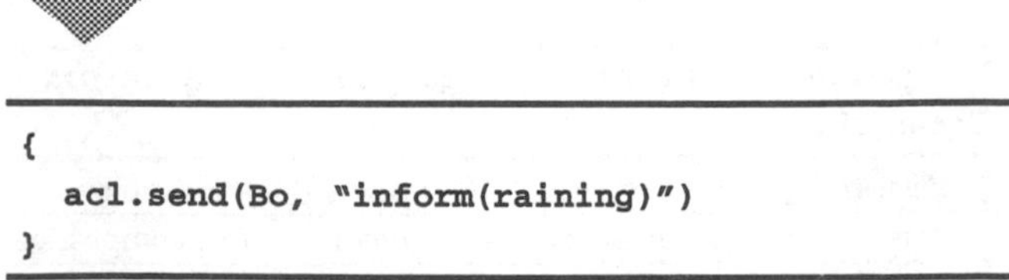
```
{
  acl.send(Bo, "inform(raining)")
}
```

Figure 1: Al, a Very Simple Agent: Does It Comply?

4.2 Rational Agency: Economic

Economic approaches assume that the agent's preferences are given along with knowledge of the effects of the agent's actions. From these, the rational action is the one that maximizes preferences.

Economic rationality has the charm of being a simple, least-common-denominator approach—if you can reduce everything to money, you can talk about maximizing it. But to apply it well requires a careful selection of the target problem.

One of the oldest applications of economic rationality is in decision-theoretic planning, which models the costs and effects of actions quantitatively and probabilistically. For many applications, where the probabilities can be estimated reliably, this leads to highly effective plans of actions [Haddawy 1996; Horvitz & Rutledge 1991].

The need to maximize preferences essentially requires that there be a scalar representation for all the true preferences of an agent. In other words, all of the preferences must be reduced to a single scalar that can be compared effectively with other scalars. This is often difficult unless we can carefully circumscribe the application domain. Otherwise, we end up essentially re-creating all of the other concepts under a veneer of rationality. For example, if we would like an agent to be governed by its past commitments, not just the most attractive choice at the present time, then we can develop a utility function that gives additional weight to past commitments. This approach may work in principle, but in practice it only serves to hide the structure of commitments in the utility function that we choose.

4.2.1 Principles of Negotiation

One of the important applications of economic rationality is in certain kinds of negotiation. These involve a small set of agents with a common language, problem abstraction, and solution. In the unified negotiation protocol of [Rosenschein & Zlotkin 1994], a *deal* is a joint plan between two agents that would satisfy both of their goals. The utility of a deal for an agent is the amount it is willing to pay minus the cost of the deal. The negotiation set is the set of all deals that have a positive utility for every agent. There are three possible situations:

1. Conflict—the negotiation set is empty
2. Compromise—agents prefer to be alone but will agree to a negotiated deal
3. Cooperative—all deals in the negotiation set are preferred by both agents over achieving their goals alone

Since the agents have some execution autonomy, they can in principle deceive or mislead each other. Therefore, an interesting research problem is to develop protocols or societies in which the effects of deception and misinformation can be contained and under which it is rational for agents to be honest with each other.

The connections of the economic approaches with human-oriented negotiation and argumentation have not been fully worked out.

4.2.2 Market-Oriented Programming

Computational markets are an approach to distributed computation based on market mechanisms [Wellman 1995]. These are effective for coordinating the activities of many agents with minimal direct communication among the agents. The research challenge is to build computational economies to solve problems of distributed resource allocation.

Everything of interest to an agent is described by current prices—the preferences or abilities of others are irrelevant except insofar as they (automatically) affect the prices. Agents offer to exchange goods at various prices. There are two types of agents: *consumers*, who exchange goods, and *producers*, who transform some goods into other goods. All agents bid so as to maximize profits or utility.

The important property is that an equilibrium corresponds—in a sense, optimally—to an allocation of resources and dictates the activities and consumptions of the agents. In general, equilibria need not exist or be unique, but under certain conditions, such as when the effect of an individual on the market is assumed negligible, they can be guaranteed to exist uniquely.

4.3 Social Agency

Social agency involves abstractions from sociology and organizational theory to model societies of agents. Since agents are often best studied as members of multiagent systems, this view of agency is important and gaining recognition. Sociability is essential to cooperation, which itself is essential for moving beyond the somewhat rigid client-server paradigm of today to a true peer-to-peer distributed and flexible paradigm that modern applications call for and where agent technology finds its greatest payoffs.

Although the mental primitives are appropriate for a number of applications and situations, they are not suitable in themselves for understanding all aspects of social interactions. Further, economic models of agency, although quite general in principle, are typically limited in practice. This is because the value functions that are tractable essentially reduce an agent to a selfish agent. [Conte & Castelfranchi 1995] argue that a self-interested agent need not be selfish because it may have other interests than its immediate personal gain. This is certainly true in many cases when describing humans and is likely to be a richer assumption for modeling artificial agents in settings that are appropriately complex.

Social commitments are the commitments of an agent to another agent. These must be carefully distinguished from internal commitments, as discussed in Section 4.1. Social commitments have been studied by a number of researchers, including [Gasser 1991; Jennings 1993]. There are a number of definitions in the literature, which add components such as witnesses [Castelfranchi 1995] or contexts [Singh 1997a]. Social commitments are a flexible means through which the behavior of autonomous agents is constrained. This can be voluntary when the agents adopt the roles that bind them to certain commitments.

Coordination is a property of a system of agents performing some activity in a shared environment. The degree of coordination is the extent to which they avoid extraneous activity by reducing resource contention, avoiding livelock and deadlock, and maintaining applicable safety conditions. Cooperation is coordination among nonantagonistic agents.

Typically, to cooperate successfully, each agent must maintain a model of the other agents and also develop a model of future interactions. This presupposes sociability.

Coherence is how well a system behaves as a unit. It requires some form of organization. Social commitments are a means to achieve coherence. [Simon 1996] argues eloquently that, although markets are excellent for *clearing* all goods (i.e., finding a price at which everything is sold), they are less effective in computing optimal allocations of resources. Organizational structures are essential for that purpose. We believe that coherence and optimality are intimately related.

4.4 Interactive Agency

Interactions occur when agents exist and act in close proximity. Interactions can be of various kinds but can be classified into two main categories: intended or otherwise. The best example of unintended interactions is resource contention; for example, when an agent accidentally bumps into another or inadvertently deletes files another needs to access. Intended interactions are primarily communications; these may occur through shared resources, which can then be viewed as a kind of shared memory. For example, an agent may delete a file to indicate that the other agent is prohibited from proceeding. Typically, for such communication to take place, some shared conventions must be in place—just as for communications based on language.

Communication is generally more expensive and less reliable than computation:

- Recomputing is often faster than requesting information over a communication channel.
- Communication can lead to prolonged negotiation.
- Chains of belief and goal updates caused by communication might not terminate.

However, communication is qualitatively superior because information cannot always be reconstructed locally, and communication can be avoided only when the agents are set up to share all necessary knowledge a priori. This is a highly limiting assumption, of course.

4.4.1 Speech Acts

Speech acts are used to motivate message types in agent systems, although speech act theory was invented in the fifties and sixties to help understand human language. The idea is that language is not only for making statements but also for *performing actions* [Austin 1962]. For example, when you request something, you do not just report on a request, but you actually cause the request; when a justice of the peace declares a couple husband and wife, she is not reporting on their marital status but changing it. The stylized syntactic form for speech acts that begins "I hereby request . . ." or "I hereby declare . . ." is called a performative. With a performative, literally, saying it makes it so [Austin 1962 (p. 7)]. Interestingly, verbs that cannot be put in this form are not speech acts. For example, "solve" is not a performative because "I hereby solve this problem" just doesn't work out—or students would be a much happier lot!

In natural language, it is not always obvious what speech act is being performed. For example, if Mike says, "It's cold here," he might be telling you about the temperature, or he may be requesting that you turn up the heat. Artificial languages can avoid this problem.

Several hundred verbs in English have performative forms. This obviously calls for classifications, and many have been given. For most computing purposes, speech acts are classified into assertives (informing), directives (requesting or querying), commissives (promising), prohibitives, declaratives (causing events in themselves; e.g., what the justice of the peace does in a marriage ceremony), and expressives (expressing emotions).

The speech acts have a social component, which relies upon commitments. For example, a commissive creates a commitment from the sender to the receiver to do as promised. An assertion might create a commitment from the sender about the veracity of the asserted proposition. A directive might presuppose some commitment on the part of the receiver to do as told.

4.4.2 Compliance

When different vendors build their products to a standard, there must be a normative means to verify that the products are indeed compliant. If an interaction breaks down, the different developers should be able to determine which of the components were not complying with the standard so they can be fixed. In our view, a "standard" is meaningless if it does not yield some tests of compliance.

One can be sure that agents who are communicating are interacting with other agents and are therefore—by that fact alone—social. To preserve design autonomy, we cannot require that they are mentalistic. For example, consider the agent Al as given in Figure 1. Does Al comply? In fact, in one approach, if Al's designer simply wanted it to comply, it does! This is obviously not practical.

4.4.3 Dimensions of Meaning

We use the terms *meaning* and *understanding* informally and the terms *semantics* and *pragmatics* technically. Any agent communication language (ACL) must—explicitly or implicitly—take specific positions along the *dimensions of meaning*. We describe these next.

One design issue is whether the given ACL semantics is designed to mirror human languages or not. Traditional theories of computational linguistics and discourse build upon work in linguistics and philosophy. However, the needs of human communication are potentially very different from the needs of communication for artificial agents. This makes traditional discourse approaches unsuitable for ACLs in general, although they apply well to personal assistants [Breiter & Sadek 1996].

Personal vs. Conventional Meaning. Personal meaning is based on the "intent" or interpretation assigned by one of the participants. It is a generalization over Grice's notion of utterer's meaning [Grice 1969]. The personal meaning doctrine bases the meaning of the speech acts on the intentions of the agent that performs the given act or even the intentions of the agent(s) toward which the act is directed.

Conventional meaning is based on the conventions of usage. The very idea of an agent lingua franca is founded on there being a well-defined conventional meaning. Indeed, having different explicit acts is a way of streamlining the conventional meaning. Inherently, no formal specification can avoid the conventions of having different labels for the different speech acts.

However, traditional approaches indicate a bias toward personal (utterer's) meaning (e.g., [Sadek 1991]). If an agent says `inform` but lacks the corresponding beliefs and intentions, then under traditional theories an `inform` does not occur. Conversely, if an agent says `request` but has beliefs and intentions corresponding to an `inform` then an `inform` does occur.

There is effectively no conventional meaning, just idiolects of different agents—and idiolects cannot be standardized!

Perspective. There are potentially three different perspectives on each communicative act: those of the sender, the receiver, or the society or other observers. Whereas the personal versus conventional dichotomy discussed above has to do with the meaning of specific communicative acts, the perspective has to do with whose viewpoint that meaning is expressed in. Traditional approaches are concerned only with the sender. This is not a popular view even in the recent discourse literature, where the sender and receiver are treated as equal participants in the discourse. However, a recent proposal looks at the postconditions of communications, which also take the receiver's perspective [Labrou & Finin 1997]. The social perspective should not be ignored in specifying the meaning of an ACL because testing compliance presupposes a public perspective.

Semantics vs. Pragmatics. There are classically three aspects to the formal study of language: syntax, semantics, and pragmatics [Morris 1938]. *Syntax* deals with how the symbols are structured, *semantics* with what they denote, and *pragmatics* with how they are interpreted (or used). Intuitively, the meaning of a communication is a combination of its semantics and pragmatics. Pragmatics inherently includes considerations, such as the environment and mental states of the communicating agents, that are external to the language proper. The Gricean maxims of communication are a prime example of pragmatics [Grice 1975].

- *Quantity:* make your contribution (to the conversation) as informative as necessary, but no more informative (to reduce confusion)
- *Quality:* try to make only true contributions—don't say what you believe is false or what you lack adequate evidence to state
- *Relation:* be relevant
- *Manner:* avoid obscurity and ambiguity; be brief and orderly

The Gricean maxims are a cornerstone of discourse processing. They are used as requirements for cooperation and as bases for performing additional inference (implicature) when they are (apparently) violated. Interestingly, the performance conditions of Arcol essentially follow the discourse literature but embody primarily the maxim of quality. Although the Gricean maxims are important, their suitability for artificial languages is not established. In any case the maxims are pragmatic, and it is not conceptually clean to include them in the semantics of an ACL.

Contextuality. In general, it is impossible to understand communications on purely conventional terms without regard to context. There are a number of components to context, several of which involve the particular physical (or simulated) environment in which the agents are situated. For example, in understanding definite descriptions, such as "the user," we need to know who the given (user interface) agent is dealing with. This form of context is crucial in human-computer applications and where artificial agents collaborate in a shared environment. By and large, this form of context applies to the content language, although it could apply in the ACL itself in terms of identifying the appropriate agent.

Another component of context that we must deal with is social context. It suffices to state that social context determines the agents' expectations of one another—in terms of expected ranges of responses, sincerity, and so on.

Importantly, context can play a role in the meaning of a language only if the semantics is not overspecified. For example, consider the simple communicative act of informing. Arcol requires that the informing agent believe that the proposition being asserted is true, that the informed agent does not already believe it, and that the informer intends that the informed agent come to believe it. This is an instance of overspecification because some agents (e.g., politicians) may say only what they believe their interlocutors agree with [Huhns & Singh 1997]. The ACL cannot prevent that behavior without violating execution autonomy.

Summary of Meaning Dimensions. By addressing the dimensions of meaning, we can talk of compliance more reasonably. In a fundamental sense, whether Al from Figure 1 complies or not depends on Al's actions viewed from the public perspective, contextualized by the protocol or society in which Al participates. Table 14 summarizes our views of what an appropriate ACL should be like and contrasts them with Arcol and KQML. This table considers only the dominant position of each view on each axis.

4.5 Adaptive Agency

One of the important properties of agents, and one that lay users expect, is that agents are adaptive. This typically presupposes that the agents are persistent and can learn. Much of the learning that we encounter in connection with agents has to do with learning values for some parameters, for example, to personalize a user interface by modeling the user. This and some other work essentially applies ideas from traditional

Dimension	Desired	Arcol	KQML
Conventional?	Yes	No	No
Pragmatic?	No	Yes	Yes
Perspective:	Social	Sender's	Sender's
Contextual?	Yes	No	No

Table 14: Dimensions of Meaning

machine learning to agents, which is indeed valuable. The challenge is to cast agent learning in terms of existing approaches. For example, learning from an environment is appropriate for agents that behave autonomously to some extent. A good introduction to this literature is [Shen 1993].

5 FUTURE DIRECTIONS AND CHALLENGES

The successes that agent technology has enjoyed in distributed sensing, information retrieval, and collaborative filtering has led to many other efforts to address new application areas and to research additional capabilities. Three of the most important directions are (1) using agents as a basis for software and its development, (2) formulating principles for the design and description of agent-based systems, and (3) adding a learning capability to agents.

5.1 Agent-Based Software Engineering

The field of software engineering has exhibited almost glacial progress over the last 20 years. Programmers still produce approximately the same number of lines of tested and debugged code per day as they did in 1975, in spite of such "silver bullets" as structured programming, declarative specifications, object-oriented programming, formal methods, and visual languages. This should not be surprising, for three reasons:

1. Software systems are the most complicated artifacts people have ever attempted to construct.
2. Software systems are (supposedly) guaranteed to work correctly only when all errors have been detected and removed, which is infeasible in light of the above complexity.
3. The effect of an error is unrelated to its size; that is, a single misplaced character out of millions can render a system useless or, worse, harmful.

Software engineering attempts to deal with these problems by considering both the process of producing software and the software that is produced. The major goal for the software is that it be correct, and the major goal for the process is that it be conducted efficiently. One fundamental approach to meeting these goals is to exploit modularity and reuse of code. The expectations are that small modules are easier to test, debug, and verify and are therefore more likely to be correct; that small modules will be more likely to be reused; and that reusing debugged modules is more efficient than coding them afresh. This is the major result of the series of programming paradigms that have evolved from the machine language of the 1950s:

- Imperative: procedure-oriented programming
- Declarative: functional and logic programming
- Interactive: object-based and distributed programming

However, software has not kept pace with the increased rate of performance for processors, communication infrastructure, and the computing industry in general [Lewis 1996]. Whereas processor performance has been increasing at a 48% annual rate and network capacity at a 78% annual rate, software productivity has been growing at a 4.6% annual rate and the power of programming languages and tools has been growing at an 11% annual rate. CASE tools, meant to formalize and promote reuse, have not been widely adopted [Iivari 1996]. In addition to these sluggish rates for software, there is a legacy of approximately 50 billion (10^9) lines of Cobol, representing roughly 80% of all software written since 1960. It is unlikely that we can replace it anytime soon, even though maintaining it is a $3 billion annual expense.

The current "hot" computing paradigm is based on Java and the ability it provides for users to download the specific functionality they want when they request it. This is leading to the rise of a software component industry, which will produce and then distribute on demand the components that have the user's unique desired functionality [Yourdon 1995]. However, because of this uniqueness, how can component providers be confident that their components will behave properly? This is a problem that can be solved by agent-based components that actively cooperate with other components to realize the user's goals.

5.1.1 Requirements for New Applications

Evolving applications have characteristics that lead naturally to an agent-based approach to their development [Woelk et al. 1995]:

- They solve a specific business problem by providing a user with seamless interaction with remote information, application, and human resources.
- The identities of the resources to be used are mostly unknown at the time the application is developed.
- The pattern of interaction (workflow) among the resources is a critical part of the application, but the pattern might be unknown at the time the application is developed and might vary over time.

The development of these new applications requires improved programming languages and improved system services. These are not alternatives to such capabilities as OMG CORBA and Microsoft DCOM but, rather, advanced features implemented at a higher level of abstraction and useful across multiple heterogeneous distributed computing environments.

Because each application executes as a set of geographically distributed parts, a distributed active-object architecture is required. It is likely that the objects taking part in the application were developed in various languages and execute on various hardware platforms. A simple, powerful paradigm is needed for communications among these heterogeneous objects. Due to the distributed nature of the application, an object might not always be available when it is needed. For example, an object executing on a PDA might be out of physical communication with the rest of the application.

Because the identities of the resources are not known when the application is developed, there must be an infrastructure to enable the discovery of pertinent objects. Once an object has been discovered, the infrastructure must facilitate the establishment of constructive communication between the new object and existing objects in the application.

Fundamentally, most business software modules are intended to be models of some real object within the business. A problem is that these modules are passive, unlike most of the objects they represent.

5.1.2 Multiagent-Based Development

Therefore, it is appropriate to consider a completely different approach to software systems. We propose one based on the (intentionally provocative) recognition of the following:

- Errors will always be a part of complex systems.
- Error-free code can at times be a disadvantage.
- Where systems interact with the complexities of the physical world, there is a concomitant power that can be exploited.

We suggest an open architecture consisting of multiple, redundant, agent-based modules interacting via a verified kernel. The appropriate analogy is that of a large, robust, natural system.

Multiagent-based interoperation is a new paradigm distinguished by such features as requests that are specified in terms of *what* and not *how*; agents that can take an active role, monitoring conditions in their environment and reacting accordingly; and agents that may be seen as holding beliefs about the world.

5.2 Interaction-Oriented Programming

Although multiagent systems are inherently superior to single-agent systems, they are difficult to construct. The designer of a multiagent system must handle not only the application-specific aspects of the various agents but also their interactions with one another. However, constructing multiagent systems manually can lead to unnecessarily rigid or suboptimal designs, wasted development effort, and violations to the autonomy of the agents.

We propose *interaction-oriented programming* (IOP) as a class of languages, techniques, and tools to develop multiagent systems. Briefly, IOP focuses on what is between, rather than within, agents. Interactions may conveniently be classified into three layers (lower to upper):

1. *Coordination*, which enables the agents to operate in a shared environment [Hewitt 1977]
2. *Commitment*, which adds coherence to the agents' actions [Castelfranchi 1995; Singh 1997a]
3. *Collaboration*, which includes knowledge-level protocols on commitments and communications [Grosz & Kraus 1996; Singh 1994]

Informal interaction concepts, such as competition, may be classified into different layers: auctions require only coordination, whereas commerce involves commitments and negotiation involves sophisticated protocols.

The key tenets of IOP (which we describe and defend in some of our other work) are as follows:

1. Correctness or data integrity may be difficult to characterize, but coherence is still crucial.
2. Complex interactions greatly exacerbate the difficulties in developing robust multiagent systems.
3. Customizable approaches can yield productivity gains that far outweigh any performance penalties.

Interaction has been studied, albeit fragmentarily, in distributed computing (DC) [Agha et al. 1993; Milner 1993], databases (DB) [Gray & Reuter 1993], and DAI. The DB and DC work focuses on narrower problems and eschews high-level concepts. Thus, it is less flexible but more robust than the DAI work. The challenge is in achieving both rigor and flexibility in the abstractions for building multiagent systems.

5.2.1 Commitments and Societies

Social commitment is a key abstraction for supporting coherent interactions while preserving autonomy. In order to formalize commitments, we observe that

- Agents can be structured and are recursively composed of heterogeneous individuals or groups of agents [Singh 1991].
- Agents are autonomous but constrained by commitments—or we would have chaos!
- Social commitments cannot be reduced to internal commitments, which apply within an agent.
- Commitments are, in general, revocable; the clauses for revoking them are no less important than the conditions for satisfying them.
- Commitments arise, exist, and are satisfied or revoked all in a social context; commitments not only rely on the social structure of the groups in which they exist but also help create that structure.

The observations above motivate a view of commitments as relating a *debtor*, a *creditor*, and a *context*. A number of natural operations can be defined on commitments, along with social policies that agents acquire when they (autonomously, in some cases) adopt a role.

A group of agents can form a small society in which they play different roles. The group defines the roles, and the roles define the commitments associated with them. When an agent joins a group, it joins in one or more roles and acquires the commitments of that role. Agents join a group autonomously but are then constrained by the commitments for the roles they adopt. The group defines the *social context* in which the agents interact.

5.2.2 Protocols

Different protocols are suited for different applications and usage scenarios. For example, there would be protocols for electronic commerce, travel applications, student registration, and so on. Different vendors can supply agents to play different roles in these protocols. Each vendor's agent must comply with the protocols in which it participates. The designers who agree on standard protocols can assume a lot more about each other's agents, but not in general. However, the implementation of the agent is known only to the vendor.

Protocols are defined and publicly known. By adopting them, agents are committed to playing specific roles, and guaranteeing properties such as sincerity and producing appropriate responses. The commitments associated with each role are metacommitments because the base-level commitments are created during execution from these metacommitments. For example, an agent may inform another agent of a value but become committed to proactively notifying the other of any changes. This is a metacommitment; when the value changes, the metacommitment leads to a base-level commitment to actually send the specific notification.

The protocols can be specified using some formal notation, such as temporal logic, finite state machines, Petri Nets, or constraint languages. These have all been used in specifying protocols in distributed systems. For the more rigidly defined protocols, the first three approaches are practically equivalent; for more flexible protocols, a rule-based notation is likely to be the most effective.

The framework above presupposes a richer infrastructure for agent management that we term *society management*. This infrastructure has support for defining commitments, roles, and groups. It supports operations for agents to join a society in some roles, to change roles, and to exit the society. These operations must, of course, respect the definitions of the given groups.

The challenge is to develop formal semantics, methodologies, and tools to sustain this vision.

5.3 Adaptive Agents

We restrict our attention to adaptivity applied in open, information-rich environments. To build systems that work effectively within such environments requires balancing ease of construction and robustness with flexibility. This presents a number of technical difficulties. Foremost among these is the need to handle the unpredictability in the environment as new components appear and old ones disappear or change. Since the information components in the environment cannot easily be altered, the agents that represent them must be able to learn and adapt. Table 15 summarizes the associated challenges for machine learning.

5.3.1 Learning about Passive Components

Agents need to learn about the databases and knowledge bases within their environment and be able to form relationships among what they learn.

Relationship Formation. The major problem with ontology-based approaches is the effort required to build an ontology and to relate different resources and applications to it. As agents extend their world model, they need to be able to acquire and integrate ontologies autonomously. They also should learn the ontologies of other agents. In other cases, tools that assist a human designer are needed. These tools must have a strong machine learning component, to be able to not only relate concepts across databases but also help identify relationships within an ontology. Such relationships (e.g., generalization or containment) are necessary for CIS query processing approaches [Arens et al. 1996; Huhns et al. 1994]. For example, `port` is a generalization of `airport` and can be used to answer queries about airports only if additional restrictions are added.

Further, different domains often have a rich variety of relationships that compose elegantly with each other [Huhns & Stephens 1989]. To give a simple, albeit somewhat contrived, example, if a person owns a car and the car contains a wheel, then the person also owns the wheel. These relationships form part of the commonsense knowledge that is essential in relating information from different databases: the two tables `car-ownership` and `car-parts` in one database may correspond to a single table `auto-part-ownership` in another database.

Concept Acquisition. How may we identify the concepts in a remote knowledge base? This is potentially useful but extremely difficult when dealing with a previously unknown source. It remains useful and becomes more tractable when the structure of the database is known, but the structure does not faithfully reflect the meaning of the content. In other words, the concepts are hidden inside the data values. A challenge is to discover the rules for partitioning the mixed-up concepts into the correct categories. Some progress is already being made, mostly under the rubric of *data mining* (e.g., [Fayyad 1996]). An issue that has not drawn much attention is collaborative and context-dependent learning of the concepts. This can be important because different uses of the data might treat the implicit concepts differently.

5.3.2 Learning about Active Components

The active components of an environment are workflows and agents and their interactions. The challenge is to learn the potential coordination constraints of the workflows, to infer the activities or plans of other agents, and to learn from repeated interactions with them. Related problems arise when the information environment is truly open and new agents are added dynamically or when the agents involved do not repeat interactions. In such cases, an agent still needs to learn how to collaborate with classes of agents and to categorize them appropriately. For example, an agent may infer that agents who request a price quote for valves will often also want a price quote on matching hoses.

The foregoing can be generalized still further to learning about the agents' dispositions to one another. For example, it is important to learn to what extent other agents will cooperate with the given agent. Indeed, if the agents form a team or coalition, they will be able to assist each other and prevent mishaps [Shehory & Kraus 1996]. It is also useful to have models of the learning abilities of the other agents.

5.3.3 Themes

Many applications of agents have the unifying themes that (a) the effect of logical homogeneity and centralization must be

Source of Uncertainty	Traditional	Agent-Based
Environment	Agent learns about a predictable, but not teleological, environment	Agent learns about an unpredictable, teleological environment
Environment and Agent's Sensors/Inputs	Agent might have imprecise sensors that yield inaccurate data	Agent might be misled deliberately

Table 15: Challenges for Machine Learning in Agent Systems

attained despite physical distribution and heterogeneity and (b) logical openness must be supported. Openness translates into a number of interesting systemic challenges relating to how a system may initialize and stabilize when some agents meet, are added, or leave. These lead to the following challenges:

- Learning about each other
- Learning about society and the environment
- Learning from repeated interactions with changing agent instances
- Learning biased by social structure
- Forgetting by a group about its former members

The further development of agents that learn will undoubtedly lead to significant new applications for agents.

REFERENCES

[Agha et al. 1993] Agha, Gul; Frølund, Svend; Kim, WooYoung; Panwar, Rajendra; Patterson, Anna; and Sturman, Daniel; 1993. Abstraction and modularity mechanisms for concurrent computing. *IEEE Parallel and Distributed Technology*. 3–14.

[Allen et al. 1990] Allen, James; Hendler, James; and Tate, Austin, editors; 1990. *Readings in Planning*. Morgan Kaufmann, San Francisco.

[Arens et al. 1996] Arens, Yigal; Hsu, Chun-Nan; and Knoblock, Craig A.; 1996. Query processing in the SIMS information mediator. In *Proceedings of the ARPA/Rome Laboratory Knowledge-Based Planning and Scheduling Initiative Workshop*. AAAI Press, Menlo Park, CA.

[Austin 1962] Austin, John L.; 1962. *How to Do Things with Words*. Clarendon Press, Oxford.

[Barwise & Perry 1983] Barwise, Jon and Perry, John; 1983. *Situations and Attitudes*. MIT Press, Cambridge, MA.

[Bayardo et al. 1997] Bayardo, R.; Bohrer, W.; Brice, R.; Chichocki, A.; Fowler, G.; Helal, A.; Kashyap, V.; Ksiezyk, T.; Martin, G.; Nodine, M.; Rashid, M.; Rusinkiewicz, M.; Shea, R.; Unnikrishnan, C.; Unruh, A.; and Woelk, D.; 1997. InfoSleuth: Agent-based semantic integration of information in open and dynamic environments. In *Proceedings of the ACM SIGMOD Conference*. 195–206.

[Belnap & Perloff 1988] Belnap, Nuel and Perloff, Michael; 1988. Seeing to it that: A canonical form for agentives. *Theoria* 54(3):175–199.

[Bonasso et al. 1996] Bonasso, R. Peter; Kortenkamp, David; Miller, David P.; and Slack, Marc; 1996. Experiences with an architecture for intelligent, reactive agents. In *Intelligent Agents II: Agent Theories, Architectures, and Languages*. 187–202.

[Bond & Gasser 1988] Bond, Alan and Gasser, Les, editors; 1988. *Readings in Artificial Intelligence*. Morgan Kaufmann, San Francisco.

[Brachman & Levesque 1985] Brachman, Ronald and Levesque, Hector, editors; 1985. *Readings in Knowledge Representation*. Morgan Kaufmann, San Francisco.

[Brand 1984] Brand, Myles; 1984. *Intending and Acting*. MIT Press, Cambridge, MA.

[Bratman 1987] Bratman, Michael E.; 1987. *Intention, Plans, and Practical Reason*. Harvard University Press, Cambridge, MA.

[Breiter & Sadek 1996] Breiter, P. and Sadek, M. D.; 1996. A rational agent as a kernel of a cooperative dialogue system: Implementing a logical theory of interaction. In *ECAI-96 Workshop on Agent Theories, Architectures, and Languages*. Springer-Verlag, Heidelberg, Germany. 261–276.

[Bukhres & Elmagarmid 1996] Bukhres, Omran A. and Elmagarmid, Ahmed K., editors; 1996. *Object-Oriented Multidatabase Systems: A Solution for Advanced Applications*. Prentice Hall, Englewood Cliffs, NJ.

[Castelfranchi 1995] Castelfranchi, Cristiano; 1995. Commitments: From individual intentions to groups and organizations. In *Proceedings of the International Conference on Multiagent Systems*. 41–48.

[Cohen & Levesque 1990] Cohen, Philip R. and Levesque, Hector J.; 1990. Intention is choice with commitment. *Artificial Intelligence* 42:213–261.

[Conte & Castelfranchi 1995] Conte, Rosaria and Castelfranchi, Cristiano; 1995. *Cognitive and Social Action*. UCL Press, London.

[Croft 1993] Croft, W. Bruce; 1993. Knowledge-based and statistical approaches to text retrieval. *IEEE Expert* 8(2):8–12.

[Davidson 1980] Davidson, Donald; 1980. *Essays on Actions and Events*. Oxford University Press, Oxford.

[Davis & Smith 1983] Davis, Randall and Smith, Reid G.; 1983. Negotiation as a metaphor for distributed problem solving. *Artificial Intelligence* 20:63–109. Reprinted in [Bond & Gasser 1988].

[de Kleer 1979] de Kleer, Johan; 1979. An assumption-based truth maintenance system. *Artificial Intelligence* 28(2):127–162.

[Dennett 1987] Dennett, Daniel C.; 1987. *The Intentional Stance*. MIT Press, Cambridge, MA.

[Doyle 1979] Doyle, Jon; 1979. A truth maintenance system. *Artificial Intelligence* 12(3):231–272.

[Durfee 1988] Durfee, Edmund H.; 1988. *Coordination of Distributed Problem Solvers*. Kluwer, Norwell, MA.

[Durfee et al. 1987] Durfee, Edmund H.; Lesser, Victor R.; and Corkill, Daniel D.; 1987. Coherent cooperation among communicating problem solvers. *IEEE Transactions on Computers* C-36(11):1275–1291.

[Elmasri & Navathe 1994] Elmasri, Ramez and Navathe, Shamkant; 1994. *Fundamentals of Database Systems*, second edition. Benjamin/Cummings, Redwood City, CA.

[Fagin & Halpern 1988] Fagin, Ronald and Halpern, Joseph Y.; 1988. Belief, awareness, and limited reasoning. *Artificial Intelligence* 34:39–76.

[Fayyad 1996] Fayyad, Usama, editor; 1996. Special issue on data mining, *Communications of the ACM* 39 (11). ACM Press, New York.

[Finin et al. 1994] Finin, Tim; Fritzson, Richard; McKay, Don; and McEntire, Robin; 1994. KQML as an agent communication language. In *Proceedings of the International Conference on Information and Knowledge Management*. ACM Press, New York.

[Fischer et al. 1996] Fischer, Klaus; Müller, Jörg; and Pischel, Markus; 1996. A pragmatic BDI architecture. In *Intelligent Agents II: Agent Theories, Architectures, and Languages*. 203–218.

[Gärdenfors 1988] Gärdenfors, Peter; 1988. *Knowledge in Flux: Modeling the Dynamics of Epistemic States*. MIT Press, Cambridge, MA.

[Gasser 1991] Gasser, Les; 1991. Social conceptions of knowledge and action: DAI foundations and open systems semantics. *Artificial Intelligence* 47:107–138.

[Gasser & Huhns 1989] Gasser, Les and Huhns, Michael N., editors; 1989. *Distributed Artificial Intelligence, Volume II*. Pitman, London; available in the Western Hemisphere by Morgan

Kaufmann, San Francisco.

[Genesereth 1991] Genesereth, Michael R.; 1991. Knowledge interchange format. In *Proceedings of the 2nd International Conference on Principles of Knowledge Representation and Reasoning*. 599–600.

[Georgeff & Rao 1995] Georgeff, Michael P. and Rao, Anand S.; 1995. The semantics of intention maintenance for rational agents. In *Proceedings of the International Joint Conference on Artificial Intelligence (IJCAI)*. 704–710.

[Goldman 1970] Goldman, Alvin I.; 1970. *A Theory of Human Action*. Prentice Hall, Englewood Cliffs, NJ.

[Gray 1991] Gray, Michael A.; 1991. On integrating expert system programs into cooperative systems. In *Proceedings of the IEEE/ACM International Conference on Developing and Managing Expert System Programs*. 90–97.

[Gray & Reuter 1993] Gray, Jim and Reuter, Andreas; 1993. *Transaction Processing: Concepts and Techniques*. Morgan Kaufmann, San Francisco.

[Grice 1969] Grice, Paul; 1969. Utterer's meaning and intentions. *Philosophical Review*. Reprinted in [Martinich 1985].

[Grice 1975] Grice, H. P.; 1975. Logic and conversation. In Cole, P. and Morgan, J. L., editors, *Syntax and Semantics, Volume 3*. Academic Press, New York. Reprinted in [Martinich 1985].

[Grosz & Kraus 1996] Grosz, Barbara J. and Kraus, Sarit; 1996. Collaborative plans for complex group action. *Artificial Intelligence* 86(2):269–357.

[Haddawy 1996] Haddawy, Peter; 1996. Believing change and changing belief. *IEEE Transactions on Systems, Man, and Cybernetics Special Issue on Higher-Order Uncertainty* 26(5).

[Harman 1986] Harman, Gilbert; 1986. *Change in View*. MIT Press, Cambridge, MA.

[Hewitt 1977] Hewitt, Carl; 1977. Viewing control structures as patterns of passing messages. *Artificial Intelligence* 8(3):323–364.

[Horvitz & Rutledge 1991] Horvitz, Eric and Rutledge, Geoffrey; 1991. Time-dependent utility and action under uncertainty. In *Proceedings of the 7th Conference on Uncertainty in Artificial Intelligence*. 151–158.

[Huhns 1987] Huhns, Michael N., editor; 1987. *Distributed Artificial Intelligence*. Pitman, London; available in the Western Hemisphere by Morgan Kaufmann, San Francisco.

[Huhns & Bridgeland 1991] Huhns, Michael N. and Bridgeland, David M.; 1991. Multiagent truth maintenance. *IEEE Transactions on Systems, Man, and Cybernetics* 21(6):1437–1445.

[Huhns & Singh 1997] Huhns, Michael N. and Singh, Munindar P.; 1997. Conversational agents. *IEEE Internet Computing* 1(2):73–75. In the column "Agents on the Web."

[Huhns & Stephens 1989] Huhns, Michael N. and Stephens, Larry M.; 1989. Plausible inferencing using extended composition. In *Proceedings of the International Joint Conference on Artificial Intelligence*. 1420–1425.

[Huhns et al. 1994] Huhns, Michael N.; Singh, Munindar P.; and Ksiezyk, Tomasz; 1994. Global information management via local autonomous agents. In *Proceedings of the ICOT International Symposium on Fifth Generation Computer Systems: Workshop on Heterogeneous Cooperative Knowledge Bases*. 1–15.

[Iivari 1996] Iivari, Juhani; 1996. Why are CASE tools not used? *Communications of the ACM* 39(10):94–103.

[Jennings 1993] Jennings, N. R.; 1993. Commitments and conventions: The foundation of coordination in multi-agent systems. *The Knowledge Engineering Review* 2(3):223–250.

[Knight & Luk 1994] Knight, Kevin and Luk, Steve K.; 1994. Building a large knowledge base for machine translation. In *Proceedings of the National Conference on Artificial Intelligence*. 773–778.

[Konolige 1986] Konolige, Kurt; 1986. *A Deduction Model of Belief*. Morgan Kaufmann, San Francisco.

[Konolige & Pollack 1989] Konolige, Kurt G. and Pollack, Martha E.; 1989. A representationalist theory of intentions. In *Proceedings of the International Joint Conference on Artificial Intelligence (IJCAI)*. 924–930.

[Labrou & Finin 1997] Labrou, Yannis and Finin, Tim; 1997. Semantics and conversations for an agent communication language. In *Proceedings of the International Joint Conference on Artificial Intelligence*. (IJCAI). 584–591.

[Lenat & Guha 1989] Lenat, Douglas B. and Guha, R. V.; 1989. *Building Large Knowledge Base Systems*. Addison-Wesley, Reading, MA.

[Lespérance et al. 1996] Lespérance, Yves; Levesque, Hector J.; Lin, Fangzhen; Marcu, Daniel; Reiter, Raymond; and Scherl, Richard B.; 1996. Foundations of a logical approach to agent programming. In *Intelligent Agents II: Agent Theories, Architectures, and Languages*. 331–346.

[Lewis 1996] Lewis, Ted; 1996. The next $10{,}000_2$ years: Part II. *IEEE Computer* 30(5):78–86.

[Lux & Steiner 1995] Lux, Andreas and Steiner, Donald; 1995. Understanding cooperation: An agent's perspective. In *Proceedings of the International Conference on Multiagent Systems*. 261–268.

[Martinich 1985] Martinich, Aloysius P., editor; 1985. *The Philosophy of Language*. Oxford University Press, New York.

[Mason & Johnson 1989] Mason, Cindy L. and Johnson, Rowland R.; 1989. DATMS: A framework for distributed assumption-based reasoning. In [Gasser & Huhns 1989]. 293–318.

[McCarthy 1979] McCarthy, John; 1979. Ascribing mental qualities to machines. In Ringle, Martin, editor, *Philosophical Perspectives in Artificial Intelligence*. Harvester Press, Brighton, England.

[McDermott 1982] McDermott, Drew; 1982. A temporal logic for reasoning about processes and plans. *Cognitive Science* 6(2):101–155.

[Miller 1995] Miller, George A.; 1995. WordNet: A lexical database for English. *Communications of the ACM* 38(11):39–41.

[Miller et al. 1960] Miller, George A.; Galanter, Eugene; and Pribram, Karl; 1960. *Plans and the Structure of Behavior*. Henry Holt, New York.

[Milner 1993] Milner, Robin; 1993. Elements of interaction. *Communications of the ACM* 36(1):78–89. Turing Award Lecture.

[Moore 1984] Moore, Robert C.; 1984. A formal theory of knowledge and action. In Hobbs, Jerry R. and Moore, Robert C., editors, *Formal Theories of the Commonsense World*. 319–358. Ablex, Norwood, NJ.

[Morris 1938] Morris, Charles, editor; 1938. *Foundations of the Theory of Signs*. University of Chicago Press, Chicago and London.

[Neches et al. 1991] Neches, Robert; Fikes, Richard; Finin, Tim; Gruber, Tom; Patil, Ramesh; Senator, Ted; and Swartout, William R.; 1991. Enabling technology for knowledge sharing. *AI Magazine* 12(3):36–56.

[Newell 1982] Newell, Allen; 1982. The knowledge level. *Artificial Intelligence* 18(1):87–127.

[Norman & Long 1996] Norman, Timothy J. and Long, Derek; 1996.

Alarms: An implementation of motivated agency. In *Intelligent Agents II: Agent Theories, Architectures, and Languages*. 219–234.

[Papazoglou et al. 1992] Papazoglou, Mike P.; Laufmann, Steven C.; and Sellis, Timothy K.; 1992. An organizational framework for cooperating intelligent information systems. *International Journal of Intelligent and Cooperative Information Systems* 1(1):169–202.

[Patil et al. 1992] Patil, Ramesh S.; Fikes, Richard E.; Patel-Schneider, Peter F.; McKay, Don; Finin, Tim; Gruber, Thomas; and Neches, Robert; 1992. The DARPA knowledge sharing effort: Progress report. In *Proceedings of the Third International Conference on Principles of Knowledge Representation and Reasoning*. 777–787.

[Pylyshyn 1984] Pylyshyn, Zenon; 1984. *Computation and Cognition*. MIT Press, Cambridge, MA.

[Rao & Georgeff 1991] Rao, Anand S. and Georgeff, Michael P.; 1991. Modeling rational agents within a BDI architecture. In *Proceedings of the International Conference on Principles of Knowledge Representation and Reasoning*. 473–484.

[Rosenschein & Zlotkin 1994] Rosenschein, Jeffrey S. and Zlotkin, Gilad; 1994. Designing conventions for automated negotiation. *AI Magazine* 29–46.

[Russell & Norvig 1995] Russell, Stuart J. and Norvig, Peter; 1995. *Artificial Intelligence: A Modern Approach*. Prentice Hall, Upper Saddle River, NJ.

[Ryle 1949] Ryle, Gilbert; 1949. *The Concept of Mind*. Oxford University Press, Oxford.

[Sadek 1991] Sadek, M. D.; 1991. Dialogue acts are rational plans. In *Proceedings of the ESCA/ETRW Workshop on the Structure of Multimodal Dialogue*, Maratea, Italy. 1–29.

[Sayre & Gray 1993] Sayre, Kirk and Gray, Michael A.; 1993. Backtalk: A generalized dynamic communication system for DAI. *Software—Practice and Experience* 23(9):1043–1058.

[Shehory & Kraus 1996] Shehory, Onn and Kraus, Sarit; 1996. Formation of overlapping coalitions for precedence-ordered task execution among autonomous agents. In *Proceedings of the International Conference on Multiagent Systems*. 330–337.

[Shen 1993] Shen, Wei-Min; 1993. *Autonomous Learning from the Environment*. Computer Science Press and W. H. Freeman, New York.

[Simon 1996] Simon, Herbert; 1996. *The Sciences of the Artificial*, third edition. MIT Press, Cambridge, MA.

[Singh 1991] Singh, Munindar P.; 1991. Group ability and structure. In Demazeau, Y. and Müller, J.-P., editors, *Decentralized Artificial Intelligence, Volume 2*. 127–145. Elsevier/North-Holland, Amsterdam.

[Singh 1992] Singh, Munindar P.; 1992. A critical examination of the Cohen-Levesque theory of intentions. In *Proceedings of the 10th European Conference on Artificial Intelligence*. 364–368.

[Singh 1994] Singh, Munindar P.; 1994. *Multiagent Systems: A Theoretical Framework for Intentions, Know-How, and Communications*. Springer-Verlag, Heidelberg, Germany.

[Singh 1997a] Singh, Munindar P.; 1997a. Commitments among autonomous agents in information-rich environments. In *Proceedings of the 8th European Workshop on Modelling Autonomous Agents in a Multi-Agent World (MAAMAW)*. 141–155.

[Singh 1997b] Singh, Munindar P.; 1997b. Commitments in the architecture of a limited, rational agent. In *Proceedings of the Workshop on Theoretical and Practical Foundations of Intelligent Agents*. 72–87. Springer-Verlag, Berlin. Invited paper.

[Singh & Asher 1993] Singh, Munindar P. and Asher, Nicholas M.; 1993. A logic of intentions and beliefs. *Journal of Philosophical Logic* 22:513–544.

[Singh & Huhns 1994] Singh, Munindar P. and Huhns, Michael N.; 1994. Automating workflows for service provisioning: Integrating AI and database technologies. *IEEE Expert* 9(5):19–23.

[Singh et al. 1997] Singh, Mona; Barnett, Jim; and Singh, Munindar; 1997. Enhancing conversational moves for portable dialogue systems. In *Working Notes of the AAAI Fall Symposium on Communicative Action in Humans and Machines*.

[Stalnaker 1984] Stalnaker, Robert C.; 1984. *Inquiry*. MIT Press, Cambridge, MA.

[Sycara & Zeng 1996] Sycara, Katia and Zeng, Dajun; 1996. Coordination of multiple intelligent software agents. *International Journal of Cooperative Information Systems* 5:181–212.

[Wellman 1995] Wellman, Michael P.; 1995. A computational market model for distributed configuration design. *AI EDAM* 9:125–133.

[Wiederhold 1992] Wiederhold, Gio; 1992. Mediators in the architecture of future information systems. *IEEE Computer* 25(3):38–49.

[Winograd 1975] Winograd, Terry; 1975. Frame representations and the declarative/procedural controversy. In Bobrow, D. G. and Collins, A. M., editors, *Representation and Understanding*. Academic Press, New York. Reprinted as [Brachman & Levesque 1985 (ch. 20, pp. 358–370)].

[Wobcke 1995] Wobcke, Wayne; 1995. Plans and the revision of intentions. In *Proceedings of the Australian Workshop on Distributed Artificial Intelligence, LNAI 1087*. 100–114. Springer-Verlag, Heidelberg, Germany.

[Woelk et al. 1995] Woelk, Darrell; Huhns, Michael; and Tomlinson, Christine; 1995. Uncovering the next generation of active objects. *Object Magazine*. 33–40.

[Woelk et al. 1996] Woelk, Darrell; Cannata, Philip; Huhns, Michael; Jacobs, Nigel; Ksiezyk, Tomasz; Lavender, Greg; Meredith, Greg; Ong, Kayliang; Shen, Wei-Min; Singh, Munindar; and Tomlinson, Christine; 1996. Carnot prototype. In [Bukhres & Elmagarmid 1996 (ch. 18)]. 621–626.

[Wong 1993] Wong, Stephen T. C.; 1993. COSMO: A communication scheme for cooperative knowledge-based systems. *IEEE Transactions on Systems, Man, and Cybernetics* 23(3):809–824.

[Yourdon 1995] Yourdon, Edward; 1995. Java, the web, and software development. *IEEE Computer* 29(8):25–30.

[Zhang & Bell 1991] Zhang, C. and Bell, D. A.; 1991. HECODES: A framework for heterogeneous cooperative distributed expert systems. *Data & Knowledge Engineering* 6:251–273.

Chapter 2

Applications

A strong indication that agent technology has matured into a significant part of computer science is the large number and variety of applications that have recently appeared. The applications span the entire range of human-computer interactions, from engineering to commerce to personal information gathering, and people now rely on agents routinely. Of the many papers describing such applications, we have chosen ones that

- Typify the wide variety of agents in operation
- Represent milestones in the development of agent technology
- Introduce new advances in agent technology

ENTERPRISES

[Chaib-draa 1995] discusses some of the most interesting industrial applications of agent technology. He includes, among others, a synopsis of the Archon project [Jennings et al. 1996], a project carried out within the European community for the management of electricity distribution.

[Huhns et al. 1994] describe the agent components of the Carnot project at MCC, which was applied to heterogeneous information management in several diverse domains, including telecommunications. Additional implemented applications of Carnot are presented in [Singh et al. 1997].

[Cutkosky ct al. 1993] describe the Palo Alto Collaborative Testbed, which was one of the earliest projects applying agent technology to concurrent engineering. PACT highlighted many of the challenges in knowledge sharing and interagent communication.

[Petrie 1993] describes a general-purpose constraint reasoning and conflict resolution functionality, which can be used to support interactions and negotiation among agents cooperating to solve a large problem. Petrie uses examples from concurrent engineering related to the PACT project, but his approach is domain independent.

[Liu & Sycara 1996] apply multiagent techniques for real-time scheduling of manufacturing jobs. Although specialized to the job-shop domain, the techniques are applicable to agents managing any kind of schedule.

The contract net protocol, described in Chapter 1, has natural applications in electronic commerce. [Sandholm & Lesser 1995] address the challenges in applying it in settings where the agents have limited computational power. They introduce the notion of levels of commitment, which can be revoked by the payment of some monetary penalty.

INTERNET AND INFORMATION ACCESS

Information access, especially over open environments such as the Internet, has motivated some of the most significant agent applications to date. [Etzioni & Weld 1994] show how a softbot can be an advanced interface to the Internet. *Softbots* are software robots, whose effectors and sensors are software utilities such as FTP and telnet. A softbot has knowledge of various Internet utilities in terms of their inputs and outputs and can plan sequences on actions on behalf of a user. It can also dynamically replan in light of unexpected changes in the Internet. This paper includes a discussion of some security issues in Internet applications.

[Arens et al. 1996] report on the SIMS project at ISI. The SIMS project overlapped with the Carnot project [Huhns et al. 1994] and concentrated on related issues. However, it emphasized the problems of information access rather than information update (or workflows). [Arens et al. 1996] show how domain-level queries, of interest to users, can be mapped to efficient queries on information resources. The mapping is mediated via an ontology, represented in the LOOM system.

[Kuokka & Harada 1995a] describe a *matchmaker* agent, which is a component of the middleware through which application agents may be linked to information resources. The matchmaker uses a rule-based framework and KQML messagcs for a number of applications, including information access. The protocols involved in matchmaking are described and evaluated in [Kuokka & Harada 1995b].

[Durfee et al. 1997] apply agent technology to the problem of large-scale digital libraries. The approach of their project is interesting since it marries market techniques with more conventional ontology and interaction protocol techniques (these are emphasized in the included paper).

PERSONAL ASSISTANTS

Another major class of applications is concerned with agents that work intimately with a user, functioning as a personal assistant. [Lashkari et al. 1994] describe their research on interface agents, designed for applications such as electronic mail filtering. Their performance depends a lot on adapting to their users' needs, so these agents frequently involve a learning component to acquire simple "user models" or profiles. The present paper addresses collaborative agents, which learn from each other as well to serve their users more effectively.

[Rich & Sidner 1997] consider the problems in building agents to interact with humans. They adapt previous research by Sidner and others into collaborative discourse, which was initially developed for natural language understanding. The present paper generalizes those ideas beyond the specific modality of spoken or written language to the more ordinary user interfaces of today. However, the insights of the previous work still apply, especially the need to reason about plans, goals, and intentions and to maintain the context of the ongoing interaction.

[Kautz et al. 1994] describe their work on software agents in the context of scheduling a visit to a laboratory. Scheduling is a conceptually simple, yet fairly intricate, application; it has received much attention from the agent community. Their system outline consists of user agents as well as scheduling agents. Their contributions include experimentation on the agent system as well as insights on the deployability of agent technology in office settings.

[St. Amant & Cohen 1996] study the problem of data analysis in statistics. Data analysis is inherently an exploratory and interactive domain because users typically do not know what they are specifically looking for until they have formulated and tested some hypotheses. As we described in Chapter 1 of this book, interactive exploration makes certain demands on a personal assistant in terms of managing mixed-initiative dialogues. [St. Amant & Cohen 1996] describe how their assistant copes with these challenges.

EMERGING APPLICATIONS

The next papers present some of the newest applications of agent technology, involving the diverse topics of entertainment and design. These applications are not yet mature, but they show the potential for agent technology.

In the first of these, [Hayes-Roth et al. 1995] apply agents to the emerging application domain of entertainment. Computational characters are introduced that can exhibit behaviors to express their emotions and personal styles. In this application, in addition, humans direct computational characters to act in a certain manner. The characters then improvise behaviors that obey the directions as much as possible while still preserving their own personalities and the applicable social conventions. Just as in more conventional agent applications, the agents must interact dynamically with each other because their behaviors tend to be interdependent. This application differs in terms of how the agents are coordinated and their tasks distributed.

[Cassell et al. 1994] address some other aspects of making a computer character lifelike or believable. Conventionally, the output modalities used by human interface systems are limited. Advances in technology are enabling other modalities, such as synthesized speech with control for intonation, facial expressions, and gestures. This opens up the problems of synchronizing these modalities both temporally and conceptually. In other words, the various modalities should cooperate in communicating the desired message or disposition. [Cassell et al. 1994] bring in insights from graphics and discourse processing to approach this problem in a rich framework that represents the communicative significance of the modalities and uses agents to maintain dialogue context.

[Stone & Lester 1996] report on Herman the Bug, an animated personality that helps grade-school students learn about plant biology. This work marries ideas from knowledge-based learning and design to create an environment that is pedagogically sound, yet entertaining to its target audience of eighth graders.

[Ishizaki 1996] develops a model of *design*, understood as the creative activity in which a designer constructs a suitable representation for a message. Ishizaki's model is interesting to the design community because it emphasizes the dynamic or active aspects of modern media, such as computers. It is interesting to the agent community because it finds a novel application of agents. It considers a number of agents with different abilities that come together to create a composite design.

REFERENCES

Note: A bullet before a reference indicates a selected reading.

•[Arens et al. 1996] Arens, Yigal; Hsu, Chun-Nan; and Knoblock, Craig A.; 1996. Query processing in the SIMS information mediator. In *Proceedings of the ARPA/Rome Laboratory Knowledge-Based Planning and Scheduling Initiative Workshop.* AAAI Press, Menlo Park, CA.

•[Cassell et al. 1994] Cassell, Justine; Pelachaud, Catherine; Badler, Norman; Steedman, Mark; Achorn, Brett; Becket, Tripp; Douville, Brett; Prevost, Scott; and Stone, Matthew; 1994. Animated conversation: Rule-based generation of facial expressions, gesture, and spoken intonation for multiple conversational agents. In *Proceedings of the ACM SIGGRAPH Conference.* 413–420. ACM Press, New York.

•[Chaib-draa 1995] Chaib-draa, Brahim; 1995. Industrial applications of distributed artificial intelligence. *Communications of the ACM* 38(11):49–53.

•[Cutkosky et al. 1993] Cutkosky, Mark R.; Englemore, Robert S.; Fikes, Richard E.; Genesereth, Michael R.; Gruber, Thomas R.; Mark, William S.; Tenenbaum, Jay M.; and Weber, Jay C.; 1993. PACT: An experiment in integrating concurrent engineering systems. *IEEE Computer* 26(1):28–38.

•[Durfee et al. 1997] Durfee, Edmund H.; Kiskis, Daniel L.; and Birmingham, William P.; 1997. The agent architecture of the University of Michigan digital library. *Proceedings of the IEE: Software Engineering* 144(1):61–71.

•[Etzioni & Weld 1994] Etzioni, Oren and Weld, Daniel P.; 1994. A softbot-based interface to the Internet. *Communications of the ACM* 37(7):72–76.

•[Hayes-Roth et al. 1995] Hayes-Roth, Barbara; Brownston, Lee; and van Gent, Robert; 1995. Multiagent collaboration in directed improvisation. In *Proceedings of the International Conference on Multiagent Systems.* 148–154.

•[Huhns et al. 1994] Huhns, Michael N.; Singh, Munindar P.; and Ksiezyk, Tomasz; 1994. Global information management via local autonomous agents. In *Proceedings of the ICOT International Symposium on Fifth Generation Computer Systems: Workshop on Heterogeneous Cooperative Knowledge Bases.* 1–15.

•[Ishizaki 1996] Ishizaki, Suguru; 1996. Multiagent model of dynamic design: Visualization as an emergent behavior of active design agents. In *Proceedings of the ACM Conference on Computer Human Interaction.* 347–354.

[Jennings et al. 1996] Jennings, Nick R.; Mamdani, E. H.; Corera, Jose Manuel; Laresgoiti, Inaki; Perriollat, Fabien; Skarek, Paul; and Varga, Laszlo Zsolt; 1996. Using Archon to develop real-world DAI applications. Part 1. *IEEE Expert* 11(6):64–70.

•[Kautz et al. 1994] Kautz, Henry A.; Selman, Bart; Coen, Michael; Ketchpel, Steven; and Ramming, Chris; 1994. An experiment in the design of software agents. In *Proceedings of the National Conference on Artificial Intelligence.* 438–443.

•[Kuokka & Harada 1995a] Kuokka, Daniel and Harada, Larry; 1995a. Matchmaking for information agents. In *Proceedings of the 14th International Joint Conference on Artificial Intelligence.* 672–678.

[Kuokka & Harada 1995b] Kuokka, Daniel and Harada, Larry; 1995b. On using KQML for matchmaking. In *Proceedings of the International Conference on Multiagent Systems.* 239–245.

•[Lashkari et al. 1994] Lashkari, Yezdi; Metral, Max; and Maes, Pattie; 1994. Collaborative interface agents. In *Proceedings of the National Conference on Artificial Intelligence.* 444–449.

•[Liu & Sycara 1996] Liu, Jyi-Shane and Sycara, Katia; 1996. Multiagent coordination in tightly coupled real-time environments. In *Proceedings of the International Conference on Multiagent Systems.* 181–188.

•[Petrie 1993] Petrie, Charles J. Jr.; 1993. The Redux' server. In *International Conference on Intelligent and Cooperative Information Systems (CoopIS).* 134–143.

•[Rich & Sidner 1997] Rich, Charles and Sidner, Candace L.; 1997. Collagen: When agents collaborate with people. In *Proceedings of the First International Conference on Autonomous Agents.* AAAI Press, Menlo Park, CA.

•[Sandholm & Lesser 1995] Sandholm, Tuomas and Lesser, Victor; 1995. Issues in automated negotiation and electronic commerce: Extending the contract net framework. In *Proceedings of the International Conference on Multiagent Systems.* 328–335.

[Singh et al. 1997] Singh, Munindar P.; Cannata, Philip E.; Huhns, Michael N.; Jacobs, Nigel; Ksiezyk, Tomasz; Ong, Kayliang; Sheth, Amit P.; Tomlinson, Christine; and Woelk, Darrell; 1997. The Carnot heterogeneous database project: Implemented applications. *Distributed and Parallel Databases: An International Journal* 5(2):207–225.

•[St. Amant & Cohen 1996] St. Amant, Robert and Cohen, Paul R.; 1996. A planner for exploratory data analysis. In *Proceedings of the Third Annual Conference on AI Planning Systems.* 205–212. AAAI Press, Menlo Park, CA.

•[Stone & Lester 1996] Stone, Brian A. and Lester, James C.; 1996. Dynamically sequencing an animated pedagogical agent. In *Proceedings of the National Conference on Artificial Intelligence.* 424–431.

2.1 Enterprises

Industrial Applications of Distributed AI

B. Chaib-draa

Most work done in distributed artificial intelligence (DAI) has targeted sensory networks, including air traffic control, urban traffic control, and robotic systems. The main reason is that these applications necessitate distributed interpretation and distributed planning by means of intelligent sensors. Planning includes not only the activities to be undertaken, but also the use of material and cognitive resources to accomplish interpretation tasks and planning tasks. These application areas are also characterized by a natural distribution of sensors and receivers in space. In other words, the sensory data-interpretation tasks and action planning are interdependent in time and space. For example, in air traffic control, a plan for guiding an aircraft must be coordinated with the plans of other nearby aircraft to avoid collisions.

This interdependence results from possible overlaps in intercepted zones. The best way to take advantage of these overlaps to eliminate imprecision and uncertainty is to cooperate with the neighboring groups of sensors to evaluate and to interpret the available data. In addition to applications involving sensory networks, researchers have also investigated using DAI techniques in system automation projects, such as flexible workshops [13], and to help expert systems cooperate in engineering applications [2, 9]. These applications are motivated by the traditional positive aspects of distributed processing systems: performance, reliability, modularity, and resource sharing.

Distributed artificial intellegence helps far-flung, often stand-alone, application components work toward a common goal

Today, ideas from DAI are becoming important in such research fields as distributed databases, distributed and parallel computing, computer-supported cooperative work, computer-aided design and manufacturing, concurrent engineering, and distributed decision making.

Success Stories

Real-time embedded applications. The Pilot's Associate program was a five-year (1985–1990) ARPA-funded effort to define, design, and demonstrate the application of DAI to helping pilots of advanced fighter aircraft [15]. The system was implemented as a set of five individual expert systems cooperating under the guidance of a sixth expert system—the mission manager. The goal was to provide the pilot with enhanced situational awareness by sorting and prioritizing data, analyzing sensor and aircraft system data,

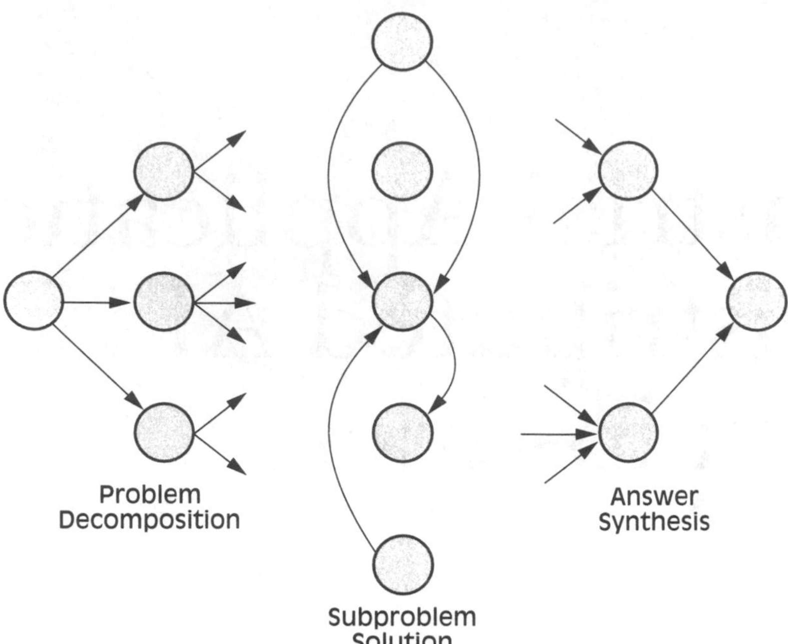

Figure 1.
An example of distributed problem solving

distilling the data into relevant information, and managing the presentation of that information to the pilot. From this presentation, corrective measures or alternative plans for achieving mission goals can be developed and presented to the pilot for approval and execution.

Particle accelerator control and electricity distribution. This multiagent system is being developed as part of the ESPRIT-II project ARCHON (Europe's largest DAI project) [8], seeking to create an environment in which cooperative interaction is possible. The system controls a high-energy particle accelerator (for CERN) and was built using an ARCHON prototype system called Generic Rules and Agent Model Testbed Environment (GRATE). GRATE is a general purpose integrative DAI system that contains generic knowledge about cooperation and situation assessment. GRATE's generic knowledge can be divided into three broad categories:

- Controlling local activities;
- Controlling social activities; and
- Assessing the current problem with both local and global considerations.

The CERN laboratories used two earlier expert systems to diagnose problems in the accelerator's operation. These systems were successfully transformed from standalone expert systems to a community of cooperating agents under the control of GRATE. The benefits of a DAI approach to this application include:

- Decomposing a problem into interacting modules, yielding smaller problems that are much easier to tackle;
- Fitting a modularized approach more naturally into the existing organizational structure;
- Working with agents in parallel and producing results faster; and
- Removing some of the drudgery of the operator's job.

Another industrial application from the ARCHON project, called Cooperating Intelligent Systems for DIstribution System Management (CIDIM), is being developed as an aid for control engineers (CEs) who must ensure the electricity supply to electricity users. CIDIM was built to help CEs by automatically providing such services as fault diagnosis, user-driven restoration planning, and security analysis, as well as automatically collating much of the information CEs collate manually by reference to standalone systems. CIDIM consists of 10 agents, some containing conventional programs and some containing expert systems. Pursuing a multiagent approach, CIDIM allows each distinct function to be implemented using the most appropriate model, whether expert system, database, or conventional software.

Resource allocation in distributed factory scheduling. Sycara and coworkers at Carnegie Mellon University [17] view distributed scheduling as a process carried out by a group of agents, each characterized by:

- Limited knowledge of the environment;
- Limited knowledge of the constraints and intentions of other agents; and
- A limited amount of resources to produce a system solution.

A DAI Tutorial

With the steady progress of research in information technology over the past decade, it is now clear that many classes of complex problems cannot be solved in isolation. Research advances in DAI, however, have opened up many new avenues for solving such problems. Generally, the DAI field aims to construct systems of intelligent entities that interact productively with one another. More precisely, DAI is concerned with studying a broad range of issues related to the distribution and coordination of knowledge and actions in environments involving multiple entities [3]. These entities, called agents, can be viewed collectively as a society. The agents work together to achieve their own goals, as well as the goals of the society as a whole.

A major distinction in the DAI field is between research in distributed problem solving (DPS) and research in multiagent systems (MAS). Early DPS work concentrated on applying the power of networked systems to a problem as exemplified by the three-phase nomenclature in Figure 1. In the first phase, the problem is decomposed into subproblems. The decomposition process may involve a hierarchy of partitionings. The second phase involves solving the kernel problems through agents that communicate and cooperate as needed. Finally, the results are integrated to produce an overall solution. DPS work also addresses the robustness available from multiple sources of expertise, multiple views, and multiple capabilities [7]. Generally, multiple views refer to distributed applications, such as air traffic control and urban traffic control. In summary, all DPS work emphasizes the problem and how to get multiple intelligent entities (programmed computers) to work together to solve it in a efficient manner [7].

In MAS, the agents are autonomous, possibly preexisting, and typically heterogeneous. Research here is concerned with coordinating intelligent behaviors among a collection of autonomous agents—how these agents coordinate their knowledge, goals, skills, and plans to take action and to solve problems. In this environment, the agents may be working toward a single global goal or toward separate individual goals that interact. Like solvers in DPS, agents in MAS might share knowledge about tasks and partial works. Unlike the DPS approach, however, they must also reason about the process of coordination among the agents. Coordination is central to multiagent systems; without it, the benefits of interaction vanish, and the behavior of the group of agents can become chaotic.

Unlike DPS work, where the emphasis is on the problem, MAS focuses on the agent and its characteristics in multiagent environments. Three possible views of the relationship between MAS and DPS were recently identified [7]:

- DPS is a subset of MAS;
- MAS provides a substrate for DPS; or
- MAS and DPS are complementary research agendas.

The DAI community still debates which of these views is correct.

A central issue in DAI is how to allow autonomous agents to model each other to reason about the activities of other agents. Reasoning about other agents allows agents to coordinate their activities to produce elaborate but coherent solutions. Coordination can be analyzed in terms of agents performing interdependent plans that achieve goals [10,11]. The different system components—goals, agents, plans, and interdependencies—are associated with the coordination process. Table 1 summarizes these components and their associated coordination processes. All four components are necessary for a situation to be analyzed in terms of coordination. Indeed, it does not make sense to refer to a DAI system as being coordinated if no activities are performed or if the activities are completely independent.

Why choose a DAI approach? There are four main reasons:

- We need to address the necessity of treating distributed knowledge in applications that are geographically dispersed, such as sensor networks, air traffic control, and cooperation between robots. DAI can also be used to tackle large and complex applications;
- DAI can aid our attempts to extend human-machine cooperation.
- DAI can yield a new perspective in knowledge representation and problem solving through richer scientific formulations and more realistic representations in practice.
- DAI can shed new light on the cognitive sciences and on AI.

Table 1. Components of Coordination

Components	Associated Processes
Goals	Identifying goals, including goal selection
Agents	Mapping goals to agents, including goal allocation and negotiation
Plans	Mapping plans to goals, including planning
Interdependencies	Managing interdependencies, including resource allocation, sequencing, and synchronizing

Many agents can share these resources for making local decisions about assigning resources to specific activities at specific time intervals. Therefore, a complete order schedule is cooperatively created by incrementally merging agents' partial schedules. Cooperation is needed because no single agent has a global system view. This cooperation arrives at global solutions by interleaving local computations with the information exchange among agents. The system goal is to find schedules that not only are feasible but also optimize a global objective, such as minimizing order tardiness or work in process. The global objective to be optimized reflects the quality of the schedule produced.

Telecommunications systems. Using DAI techniques in telecommunications systems seems inevitable when we consider two trends in the design of such systems: distribution of functionality and incorporation of intelligence software that implements sophisticated services and decision making. The DAI literature includes a number of approaches that address the telecommunications field [18]. A noteable example is a system called LODES, which has been tried on operational networks. LODES detects and diagnoses problems in a segment of a local-area network [16]. Different LODES system copies—each acting as an agent—can monitor and manage different network segments. LODES includes components that let each agent cooperate with other agents. Although LODES was developed primarily as a research testbed, it has been tried on operational networks with some success. LODES's designers chose a distributed approach over a centralized approach to tap the physical and functional distribution of networks. A distributed approach also enables local problem solving, facilitating the communication of the results of analysis, rather than all the information needed for the process.

Database technologies for service order processing. Singh and Huhns from MCC [14] defined a distributed agent architecture for intelligent workflow management that functions on top of Carnot's environment. Their system consists of four agents that interact to produce the desired behavior, as well as databases that include the relevant data and the application programs that execute on them. The four agents are:

- The graphical-interaction agent;
- The transaction-scheduling agent;
- The schedule-processing agent; and
- The schedule-repairing agent.

Applications are executed by the schedule-processing agent. If the agent encounters an unexpected condition, such as a task failure, it notifies the transaction-scheduling agent, which asks the schedule-repairing agent for advice on how to fix the problem. Advice can involve how to restart a transaction, how to abort a transaction, and other operations. Finally, the graphical-interaction agent queries the systems to help users. Singh and Huhns implemented a prototype that executes on top of a distributed computing environment to help a telecommunications company provide a service that requires coordination among many operation support systems and network elements.

Applications Almost Here

Concurrent engineering. The Palo Alto Collaborative Testbed (PACT) is a concurrent engineering infrastructure encompassing multiple sites, subsystems, and disciplines [6]. Through PACT, investigators—from Stanford University, Lockheed Palo Alto Research Labs, and Enterprise Integration Technologies—are examining the technological and sociological issues of building large-scale distributed concurrent-engineering systems. PACT experiments have looked into building an overarching framework along three dimensions:

- Cooperative development of interfaces, protocols, and architecture;
- Sharing of knowledge among systems that maintain their own specialized knowledge bases and reasoning mechanisms; and
- Computer-aided support for negotiating and making decisions in concurrent engineering projects.

The PACT architecture is based on interacting programs, or agents, that encapsulate engineering tools. The agent interaction relies on three things:

- Shared concepts and terminology for communicating knowledge across disciplines;
- A common language for transferring knowledge among agents;
- A communication and control language that enables agents to request information and services.

This technology allows agents working on different aspects of a design to interact at the knowledge level, sharing and exchanging information about the design, independent of the format in which the information is encoded internally.

PACT is an ongoing collaboration. Its activities are intended to expand PACT into a broad-based engineering infrastructure. To achieve this, authors are upgrading the prototype software, which now handles low-level message passing between agents, to improve reliability, scalability, and ease of use. The next version will build on a commercial substrate, such as the Object Management Group's Common Object Request Broker Architecture (CORBA) [12], that can support multicast protocols in environments containing thousands of agents. In the next version, simulation and analysis will be transformed into generic engineering services with published interfaces and ontologies and made available on the Internet 24 hours a day.

Urban traffic control. Urban traffic is generally a highly interactive activity among various agents, which can include people, such as drivers, police officers, and pedestrians, and machines, such as vehicles and traffic-lights, that continuously adjust their actions to prevent conflicts like traffic jams and crashes. Today, many multiagent approaches can help investigate this task, particularly in Canada and Europe [1, 4].

Conclusions

This article argues that a DAI approach can be used to cope with the complexity of industrial applications. DAI techniques are beginning to have a broad impact; the current introduction of these techniques by an ESPRIT project, a Palo Alto consortium, ARPA, Carnegie Mellon University, MCC, and others are good examples. In the near future, other industrial products will emerge from the application of DAI techniques to other domains, including distributed databases, computer-supported cooperative work, and air traffic control. An important advantage of a DAI approach is the ability to integrate existing standalone knowledge-based systems. This factor is important because software for industrial applications is often developed in an ad hoc fashion. Thus, organizations possess a large number of standalone systems developed at different times by different people using different techniques. These systems all operate in the same physical environment, all have expertise that is related but distinct, and all could benefit from cooperation with other such standalone systems. ◼

References

1. Bomarius, F. A. Multiagent approach towards modeling urban traffic scenarios. Tech. Rep. RR-92-47, DFKI-GmbH, Germany, 1992.
2. Bond, A.H. The cooperation of experts in engineering design. In *Distributed Artificial Intelligence,* Vol. 2. L. Gasser and M.N. Huhns, Eds. Morgan Kaufmann, Los Altos, Calif., 1989, 463–484.
3. Bond, A.H., and Gasser, L., Eds. *Readings in Distributed Artificial Intelligence.* Morgan Kaufmann, Los Altos, Calif., 1988.
4. Chaib-draa, B. Coordination between agents in routine, familiar and unfamiliar situations. Rapport de recherche DIUL-RR-9401 du département d'informatique, Univ. Laval, Sainte-Foy, PQ, Canada, 1994.
5. Cockburn, D. Cooperating intelligent systems for electricity distribution. In *Proceedings of Expert Systems* 1992, Cambridge, UK, 1992.
6. Cutkosky, M.R., Engelmore, R.S., Fikes, R.E., Genesereth, M.R., Gruber, T.R., Mark, W.S., Tenenbaum, J.M., and Weber, J.C. PACT: An experiment in integrating concurrent engineering systems. *IEEE Comput. 26,* 1(1993), 28–37.
7. Durfee, E., and Rosenschein, J.S. Distributed problem solving and multi-agent systems: Comparisons and examples. In *Proceedings of the 13th International DAI Workshop,* (Seattle, Wash.), 1994.
8. Jennings, N.R. Cooperation in Industrial Multi-Agent Systems. *World Scientific Series in Computer Science, Vol. 43.* 1994.
9. Lesser, V.R., Pavlin, J., and Durfee, E. Approximate processing in real-time problem solving. *AI Magazine 9,* 1 (1988), 81–96.
10. Malone, T.W., and Crowston, K. The interdisciplinary study of coordination. *ACM Comput. Surv. 26,* 1, (1994), 87–120.
11. Martial, F.V. Coordinating Plans of Autonomous Agents. *Lecture Notes in AI.* Springer-Verlag, Berlin, 1991.
12. Object Management Group. *The Common Object Request Broker: Architecture and specification.* OMG Document 391.12.1, Framingham, Mass., 1991.
13. Parunak, H.V.D. Manufacturing experience with the contract-net. In *Distributed Artificial Intelligence, Vol. 2.* L. Gasser and M.N. Huhns, Eds. Morgan Kaufmann, Los Altos, Calif., 1989, 285–310.
14. Singh, M.P., and Huhns, M. N. Automating workflows for service order processing. *IEEE Expert 9,* 5 (May 1994), 19–23.
15. Smith, D., and Broadwell, M. The pilot's association—An overview. In *Proceedings of the SAE Aerotech Conference,* Los Angeles, Calif., 1988.
16. Sugawara, T., and Murakami, K. A multiagent diagnostic system for internetwork problems. In *Proceedings of the Internet Society — INET 92 1992 International Networking Conference,* Internet Society, Reston, Va., 1992, pp. 317–325.
17. Sycara, K.P., Roth, S.F., Sadeh, N., and Fox, M. Resource allocation in distributed factory scheduling. *IEEE Expert 6,* 1 (June 1991), 29–40.
18. Weihmayer, D. and Veltguijsen, H. Application of distributed AI and cooperative problem solving to telecommunications. In *Proceedings of the 13th International DAI Workshop* (Seattle, Wash., 1994).

About the Author:
B. CHAIB-DRAA is an associate professor of computer science in the computer science department at Laval University. His research interests include multiagent systems, distributed AI, and real-time systems.

Author's Present Address: Département d'Informatique, Pav. Pouliot, Fac de Sciences, Université Laval, Sainte-Foy, QC, G1K 7P4, Canada. email: chaib@ift.ulaval.ca

Global Information Management via Local Autonomous Agents

Michael N. Huhns, Munindar P. Singh, and Tomasz Ksiezyk
Microelectronics and Computer Technology Corporation
3500 West Balcones Center Drive
Austin, TX 78759-5398
{huhns,msingh,ksiezyk}@mcc.com

ABSTRACT In this paper we describe how a set of autonomous computational agents can cooperate in providing coherent management of information in environments where there are many diverse information resources. The agents use models of themselves and of the resources that are local to them. The resource models may be the schemas of databases, frame systems of knowledge bases, or process models of business operations. Models enable the agents and resources to use the appropriate semantics when they interoperate. This is accomplished by specifying the semantics in terms of a common ontology. We discuss the contents of the models, where they come from, and how the agents acquire them. We then describe a set of agents for telecommunication service provisioning and show how the agents use such models to cooperate. Their interactions produce an implementation of relaxed transaction processing.

1. Introduction

Business operations, including sales, marketing, manufacturing, and design, can no longer be done in isolation, but must be done in a global context, i.e., as part of an enterprise. A characteristic of such enterprises is that their information systems are large and complex, and the information is in a variety of forms, locations, and computers. The topology of these systems is dynamic and their content is changing so rapidly that it is difficult for a user or an application program to obtain correct information, or for the enterprise to maintain consistent information.

Some of the techniques for dealing with the size and complexity of these enterprise information systems are modularity, distribution, abstraction, and intelligence, i.e., being smarter about how you seek and modify information. Combining these techniques implies the use of intelligent, distributed modules—a distributed artificial intelligence approach. In accord with this approach, we distribute and embed computational agents throughout an enterprise. The agents are knowledgeable about information resources that are local to them, and cooperate to provide global access to, and better management of, the information. For the practical reason that the systems are too large and dynamic (i.e., open) for global solutions to be formulated and implemented, the agents need to execute autonomously and be developed independently. To cooperate effectively, the agents must either *have models of each other and of the available information resources* or *provide models of themselves*. We focus on the latter in this paper.

For such an open information environment, the questions arise: what should be modeled, where do models come from, what are their constituents, and how should they be used? We discuss the types of models that might be available in an enterprise and how agents can acquire them. We use the ontology developed for the large knowledge-based system, Cyc, for semantic grounding of the models. This provides a common ontology. We then describe a set of agents for telecommunication service provisioning—a scheduling agent, a schedule-repairing agent, a schedule-processing agent, and an interface agent—and describe their models and how they use them to cooperate. We also describe the use of actors [Agha 1986]—one per agent—who manage communications among the agents. Each actor independently maintains the relationship between its agent and the common ontology (in the form of articulation axioms), and updates that relationship as the ontology changes or the agent itself evolves.

2. Modeling

Enterprise information modeling is a corporate activity that produces the models needed for interoperability. The resultant models should describe all aspects of a business environment, including

- databases
- database applications
- software repositories
- part description repositories
- expert systems, knowledge bases, and computational agents
- business work flows, and the information they create, use, maintain, and own, and
- the business organization itself.

The models provide online documentation for the concepts they describe. They enable application code and data to be reused, data to be analyzed for consistency, databases to be constructed automatically, the impact of change on an enterprise to be assessed, and applications to be generated automatically.

An enterprise might have many models available, each describing a portion of the enterprise and each constructed independently. For example,

- the information present in a database is modeled by the schema for the database, which is produced through a process of logical data modeling
- the data values present in a database are modeled (weak-

ly, in most cases) by data dictionary information, which is produced through data engineering

• the information present in an object-centered knowledge base is modeled by the ontology of the objects, which is produced through ontological engineering

• process models, possibly in the form of Petri nets or IDEFx descriptions, are produced through logical process modeling

• STEP (Standard for the Exchange of Product model data) schemas, written in Express, are produced from component and physical process modeling.

Although it might appear that interoperability would require all of these models to be merged into a single, homogeneous, global model, this is *not* the case in our approach. Instead, there are good reasons for retaining the many individual models: 1) they are easier to construct than a single large model; 2) enterprises may be formed dynamically through mergers, acquisitions, and strategic alliances, and the resultant enterprises might have inherited many existing models; 3) because enterprises are geographically dispersed, their resources are typically decentralized; and 4) as enterprises (and thus models) evolve, it is easier to maintain smaller models.

Unfortunately, the models are often mutually incompatible in syntax and semantics, not only due to the different things being modeled, but also due to mismatches in underlying hardware and operating systems, in data structures, and in corporate usage. In attempting to model some portion of the real world, information models necessarily introduce simplifications and inaccuracies that result in semantic incompatibilities. However, the individual models must be related to each other and their incompatibilities resolved [Sheth and Larson 1990], because

• A coherent picture of the enterprise is needed to enable decision makers to operate the business efficiently and designers to evaluate information flows to and from their particular application.

• Applications need to interoperate correctly across a global enterprise. This is especially important due to the increasing prevalence of strategic business applications that

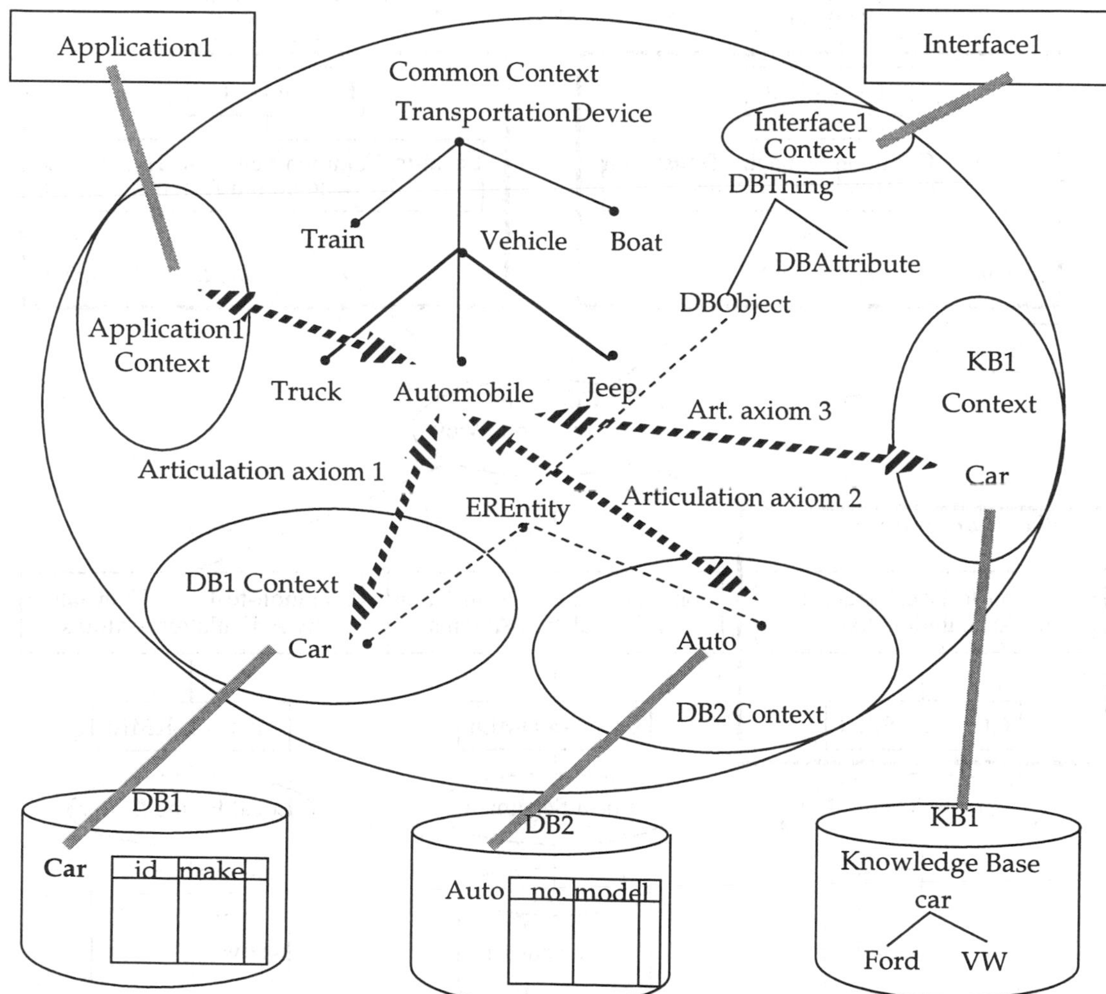

Figure 1: Concepts from different models are related via a common aggregate context by means of articulation axioms

require *intercorporate linkage*, e.g., linking buyers with suppliers, or *intracorporate integration*, e.g., producing composite information from engineering and manufacturing views of a product.

- Developers require integrity validation of new and updated models, which must be done in a global context.
- Developers want to detect and remove inconsistencies, not only among models, but also among the underlying business operations that are modeled.

We utilize a mediating mechanism based on an existing common ontology to yield the appearance and effect of semantic homogeneity among existing models. The mechanism provides logical connectivity among information resources via a semantic service layer that automates the maintenance of data integrity and provides an enterprise-wide view of all the information resources, thus enabling them to be used coherently. This logical layer is implemented as a network of interacting agents. Significantly, the individual systems retain their autonomy. This is a fundamental tenet of the Carnot architecture [Woelk *et al.* 1992], which provides the tools and infrastructure for interoperability across global enterprises.

3. Semantic Integration via a Common Ontology

In order for agents to interact productively, they must have something in common, i.e., they must be either grounded in the same environment or able to relate their individual environments. We use an existing common context—the Cyc common-sense knowledge base [Lenat and Guha 1990]—to provide semantic grounding. The models of agents and resources are compared and mapped to Cyc but not to each

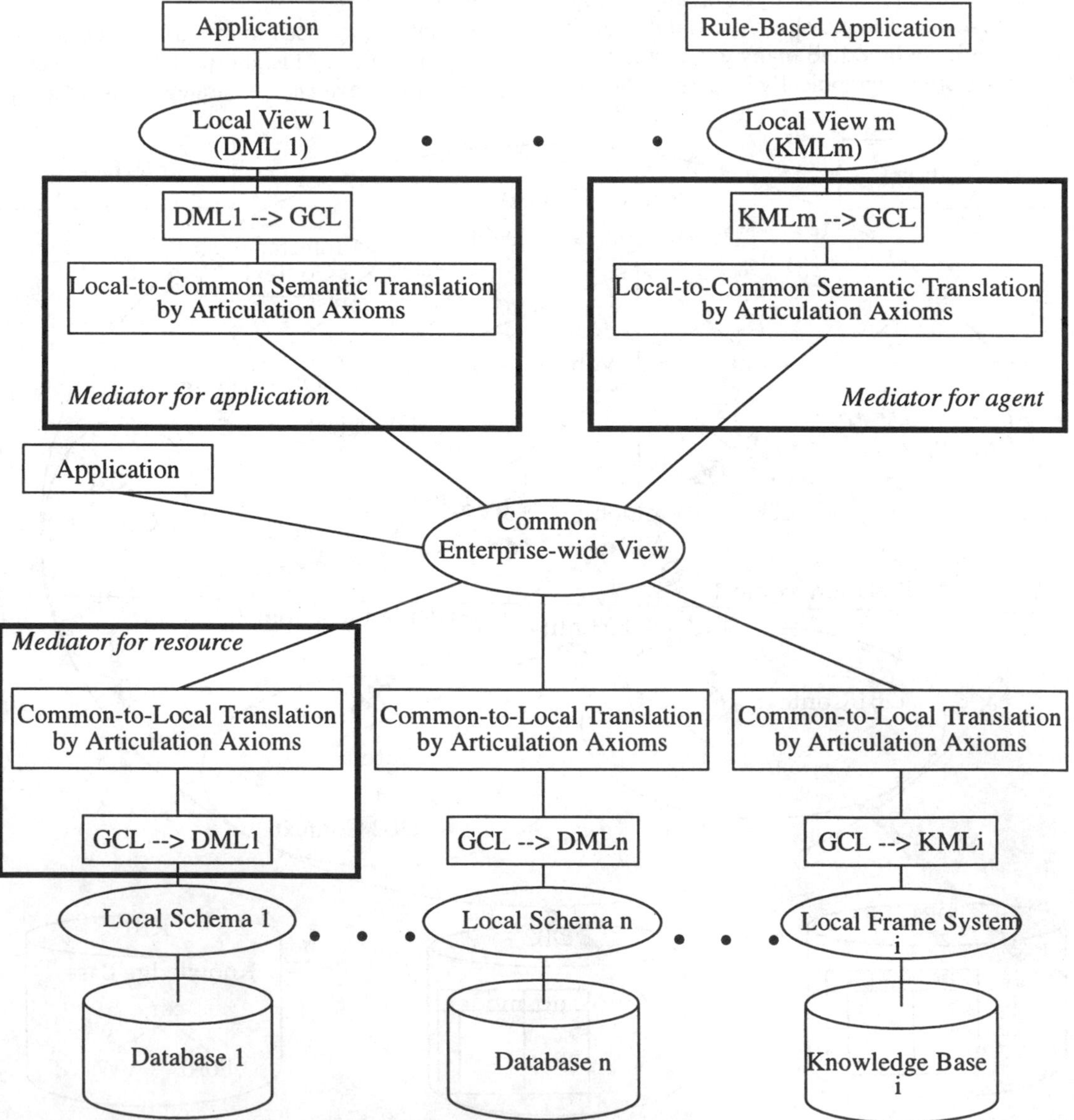

Figure 2: Logical view of the execution environment, showing how mediating agents apply articulation axioms to achieve semantic interoperation

other, making interoperation easier to attain. For n models, only n mappings are needed, instead of as many as $n(n-1)$ mappings when the models are related pairwise. Currently, Cyc is the best choice for a common context, because of 1) its rich set of abstractions, which ease the process of representing predefined groupings of concepts, 2) its knowledge representation mechanisms, which are needed to construct, represent, and maintain a common context, and 3) its size: it covers a large portion of the real world and the subject matter of most information resources.

The large size and broad coverage of Cyc's knowledge enable it to serve as a fixed-point for representing not only the semantics of various information modeling formalisms, but also the semantics of the domains being modeled. Carnot can use models constructed using any of several popular formalisms, such as

- IRDS, IBM's AD/Cycle, or Bellcore's CLDM for entity-relationship models
- Ingres, Oracle, Sybase, Objectivity, or Itasca for database schemas, and
- MCC's RAD or NASA's CLIPS for agent models.

Cyc's knowledge about metamodels for these formalisms and the relationships among them enables transactions to interoperate semantically between, for example, relational and object-oriented databases.

The relationship between a domain concept from a local model and one or more concepts in the common context is expressed as an articulation axiom [Guha 1990]: a statement of equivalence between components of two theories. Each axiom has the form

$$ist(G, \varphi) \Leftrightarrow ist(C_i, \psi)$$

where φ and ψ are logical expressions and *ist* is a predicate that means "is true in the context." This axiom says that the meaning of φ in the common context G is the same as that of ψ in the local context C_i. Models are then related to each other—or translated between formalisms—via this common context by means of the articulation axioms, as illustrated in Figure 1. For example, an application's query about `Automobile` would result in subqueries to DB1 about `Car`, to DB2 about `Auto`, and to KB1 about `car`. Note that each model can be added independently, and the articulation axioms that result do not have to change when additional models are added. Also note that applications and resources need not be modified in order to interoperate in the integrated environment. The Appendix contains a description of the graphical tool, MIST, that we have built to aid in the construction of articulation axioms.

Figure 2 shows a logical view of the execution environment. During interoperation, mediators [Wiederhold 1992], which are implemented by Rosette actors [Tomlinson *et al.* 1991], apply the articulation axioms that relate each agent or resource model to the common context. This performs a translation of message semantics. At most n sets of articulation axioms and n mediators are needed for interoperation among n resources and applications. The mediators also apply a syntax translation between a local data manipulation language, DML_i, and the global context language, GCL. GCL is based on extended first-order logic. A local data-manipulation language might be, for example, SQL for relational databases or OSQL for object-oriented databases. The number of language translators between DML_i and GCL is no greater than n, and may be a constant because there are only a small number of data-manipulation languages that are in use today. Additional details describing how transactions are processed semantically through the global and local views of several databases can be found in [Woelk *et al.* 1992].

The mediators also function as communication aides, by managing communications among the various agents, databases, and application programs in the environment. They buffer messages, locate message recipients, and translate message semantics. To implement message transfer, they use a tree-space mechanism—a kind of distributed virtual blackboard—built on the OSI and TCP/IP protocols [Tomlinson *et al.* 1991].

4. Application to Transaction Processing

We have applied our methodology to achieve relaxed transaction processing in the provisioning of telecommunication services, the task of providing communication facilities to customers. This task is executed in a heterogeneous multidatabase environment. It is an example of workflow control, in that it provides control and data flows among transactions executing on multiple autonomous systems [Jin *et al.* 1993; Tomlinson *et al.* 1993]. Service provisioning typically takes several weeks and requires coordination among many operation-support systems and network elements. Configuring the operation-support systems so that they can perform such a task often takes several months to complete.

We investigated ways to improve the provisioning of one type of communication facility—digital services (DS-1). Provisioning DS-1 takes more than two weeks and involves 48 separate operations—23 of which are manual—against 16 different database systems. Our goals were to reduce this time to less than two hours and to provide a way in which new services could be introduced more easily. Our strategy for accomplishing these goals was to 1) interconnect and interoperate among the previously independent systems, 2) replace serial operations by concurrent ones by making appropriate use of relaxed transaction processing [Attie *et al.* 1993; Bukhres *et al.* 1993; Elmagarmid 1992; Ansari *et al.* 1992], and 3) automate previously manual operations, thereby reducing the incidence of errors and delays. The transaction processing is relaxed in that some subsystems are allowed to be temporarily inconsistent, although eventual consistency is guaranteed. Relaxing the consistency requirements allows increased concurrency and, thus, improved throughput and response time.

The architecture of the agents used to implement relaxed transaction processing is shown in Figure 3. The agents operate as follows. The graphical-interaction agent helps a user fill in an order form correctly, and checks inventories to give

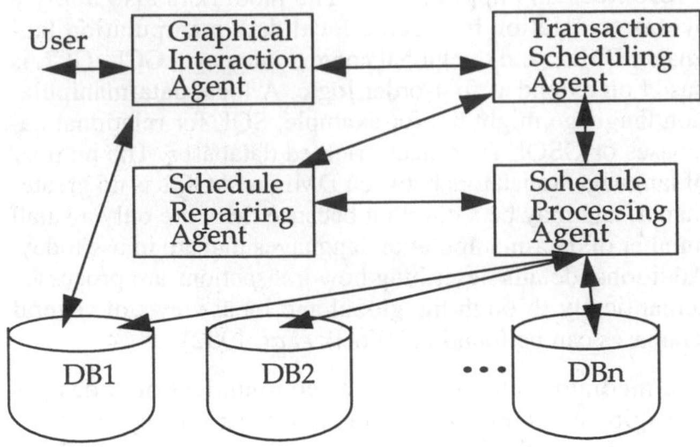

Figure 3: Agents for relaxed transaction processing

the user an estimate of when the order will be completed. It also informs the user about the progress of the order.

The transaction-scheduling agent constructs the schedule of tasks needed to satisfy an order. The tasks are scheduled with the maximum concurrency possible, while still satisfying their precedence constraints. Some of the rules that implement the schedule are shown in Figure 4. These particular rules, when appropriately enabled, generate a subtransaction to update the database for customer billing. When executing such rules, the transaction-scheduling agent behaves as a finite-state automaton, as shown in Figure 5.

The schedule-processing agent maintains connections to the databases involved in telecommunication provisioning, and implements transactions on them. It knows how to construct the proper form for a transaction, based on the results of other transactions. The transactions are processed concurrently, where appropriate. If something goes wrong during the processing of a transaction that causes it to abort or fail to commit, the schedule-repairing agent provides advice on how to fix the problem and restore consistency. The advice can be information on how to restart a transaction, how to abort a transaction, how to compensate for a previously committed transaction, or how to clean-up a failed transaction. The integrity knowledge that is stored in the schedule repairing agent comes from a comparison of the models, as expressed in terms of the common ontology.

The agents, as described above, are simply expert systems whose expertise is in processing orders for telecommunication services. However, they have the additional abilities to interact and cooperate with each other via the mediators described above.

The agents cooperate, at the knowledge level [Newell 1982], via models of themselves. For example, a conceptual domain model for the graphical-interaction agent is shown in Figure 6. An interface form that provides user access and modifications to the knowledge possessed by this agent is shown in Figure 7.. Entries on the form, or the form's completion, cause queries and transactions to be sent to the other agents or databases in the environment. Note, however, that the model does not capture the procedural knowledge necessary

```
This set of rules (1) executes an external program that
translates an Access Service Request into a command file
to update the database for customer billing, (2) executes
the command file, and (3) checks for completion. Note that
the scheduling agent, due to its truth-maintenance system,
stops processing this subtransaction whenever an abort of
the global transaction occurs.
?gtid denotes the global transaction identifier.
ill-Preparation:
If  (service-order(?gtid)
          new-tid(?subtid)
          unless(abort(?gtid)))
then (do(,run-shell-program
            ("asr2bill"
             :input ("asr-?gtid.out")
             :output "bill-?gtid.sql"))
          bill(?gtid ?subtid)
          tell(GIAgent "Task ?gtid BILLING ready"))

ill-Execution:
If  (bill(?gtid ?subtid)
          logical-db(?db))
then (tell(SchedProcAgent
            "task-execute ?subtid BILL ?db bill-?gtid.sql")
          tell(GIAgent "Task ?gtid BILLING active"))

ill-Completion:
If  (success(?subtid)
          bill(?gtid ?subtid))
then (tell(GIAgent "Task ?gtid BILLING done"))

ill-Failure:
If  (failure(?subtid)
      excuse(bill(?gtid ?subtid)))
then (abort(?gtid)
          tell(GIAgent "Task ?gtid BILLING failed"))
```

Figure 4: Some of the rules used by the transaction-cheduling agent to generate a schedule for DS-1 workflow

to specify the queries and transactions; a technique for modeling processes is needed to capture such knowledge In other words, the models represent the static knowledge of the agents, not (unfortunately) their dynamics. Nevertheless, they have proven useful in enabling the agents to interact coherently, as we describe next.

Conceptual models for two more of the agents are shown in Figures 8 and 9. Each model consists of organized concepts describing the context, domain, or viewpoint of the knowledge possessed by that agent, i.e., the knowledge base of each agent contains rules written in terms of these concepts.

The models in Figures 6, 8, and 9 are related to the common context, and thereby to each other, via articulation axioms. For example, the concept `Transaction` for the transaction-scheduling agent and the concept `DBTransaction` for the schedule-repairing agent are each related to the common concept `DatabaseTransaction` via the axioms:

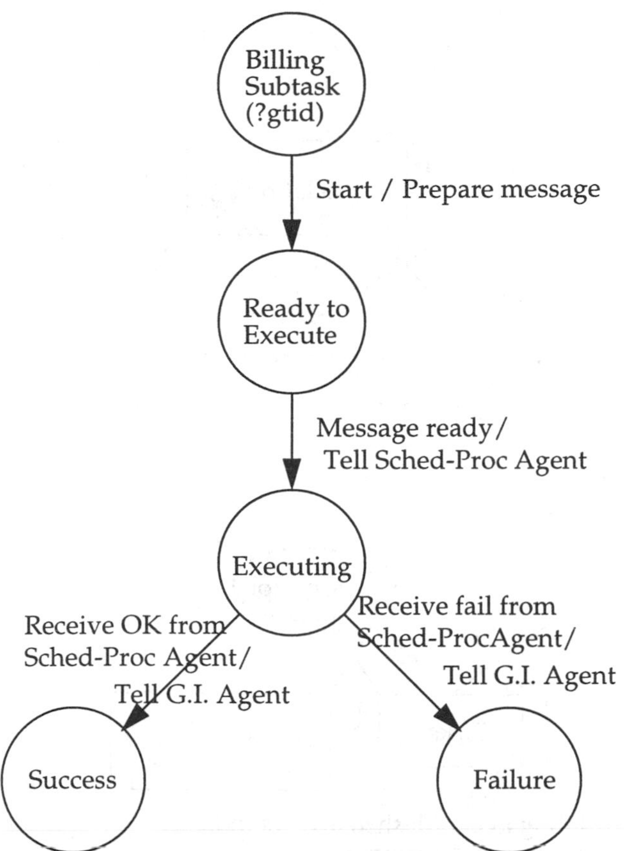

Figure 5: Representative automaton for a task, as implemented by the transaction-scheduling agent

ist(Cyc, DatabaseTransaction(T)) <=> ist(Scheduler, Transaction(T))

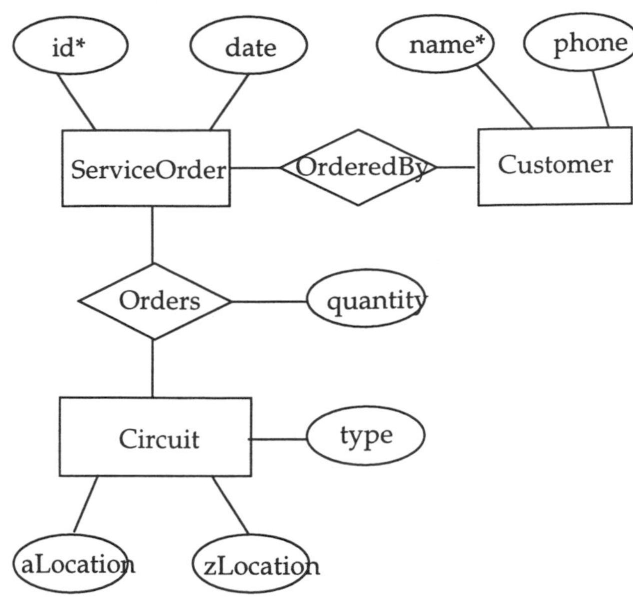

Figure 6: Semantic model (simplified) for the graphical-interaction agent

ist(Cyc, DatabaseTransaction(T)) <=> ist(Repairer, DB-Transaction(T))

The axioms are used to translate messages exchanged by the agents, so that the agents can understand each other. In the above example, the two agents could use their axioms to converse about the status of database transactions, without having to change their internal terminology. Similar axioms describing the semantics of each of the databases involved enable the schedule-processing agent to issue transactions to the databases. The axioms also relate the semantics of the form shown in Figure 8to the semantics of the other informa-

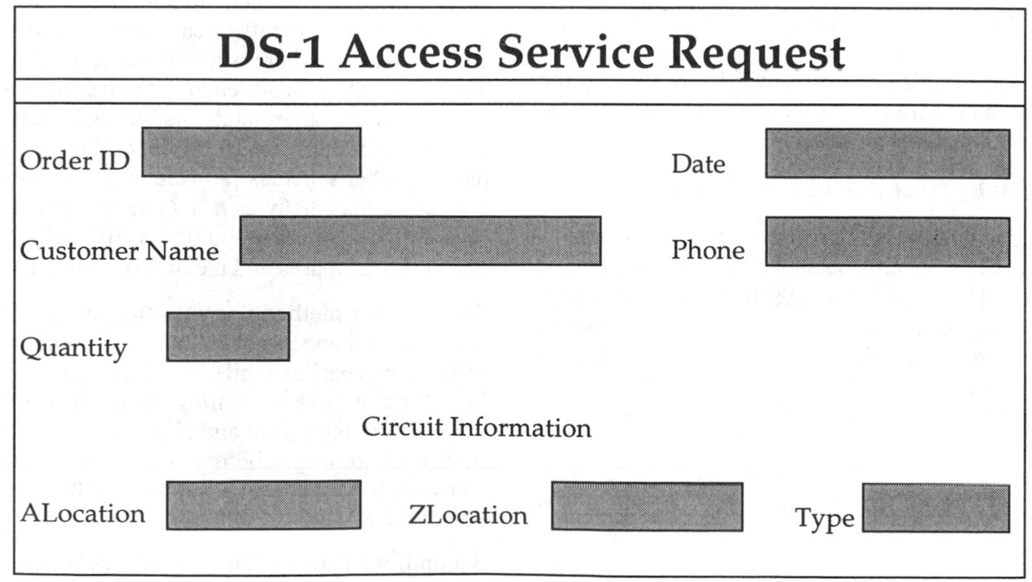

Figure 7: User interface form (simplified) corresponding to the declarative knowledge of the graphical-interaction agent

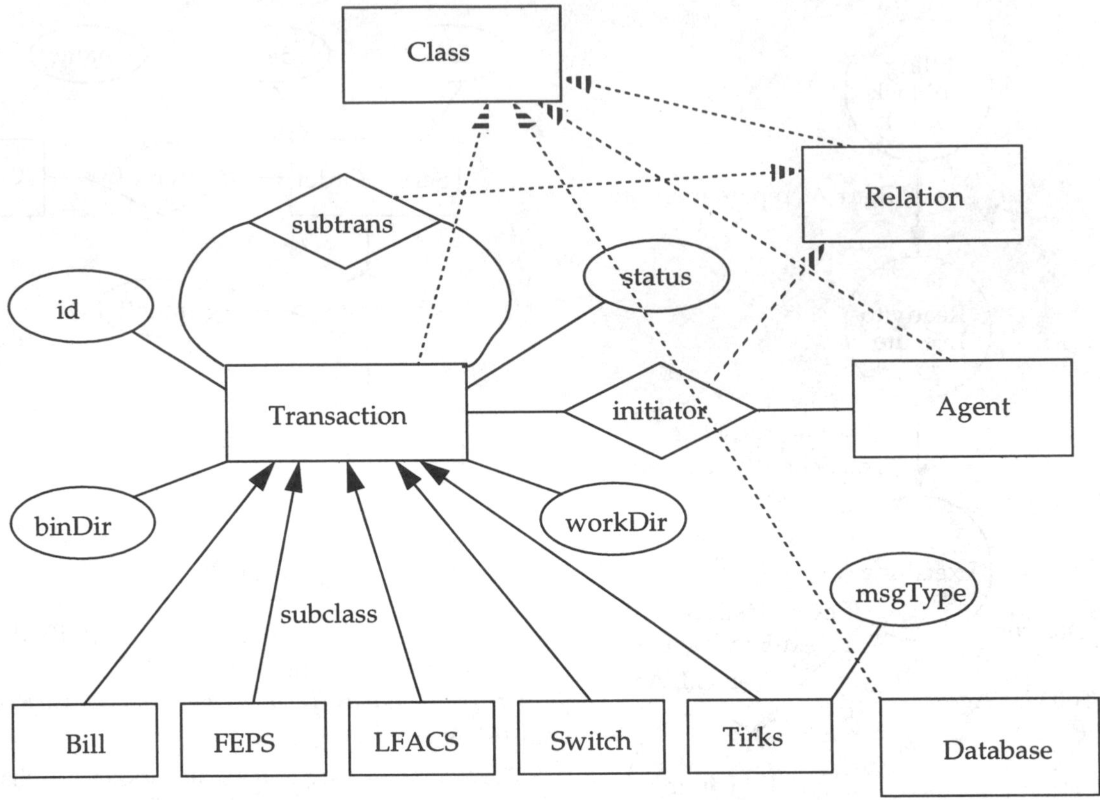

Figure 8: Semantic model for the transaction-scheduling agent (dashed arrows indicate instance relationships, and solid arrows indicate subclass relationships)

tion resources in the environment. Such axioms are constructed with the aid of a graphical tool called MIST, for Model Integration Software Tool. The operation of MIST is described in the Appendix.

Operationally, the axioms are managed and applied by the mediators that assist each agent. They use the axioms to translate each outgoing message from their agent into the common context, and to translate each incoming message for their agent into its local semantics.

5. Background and Discussion

Integrating enterprise models is similar to integrating heterogeneous databases. Two approaches have been suggested previously for this [Buneman *et al.* 1990]. The *composite approach* produces a global schema by merging the schemas of the individual databases. Explicit resolutions are specified in advance for any semantic conflicts among the databases, so users and applications are presented with the illusion of a single, centralized database. However, the centralized view may differ from the previous local views and existing applications might not execute correctly any more. Further, a new global schema must be constructed every time a local schema changes or is added.

The *federated approach* [Heimbigner and McLeod 1985, Litwin *et al.* 1990] presents a user with a collection of local schemas, along with tools for information sharing. The user resolves conflicts in an application-specific manner, and integrates only the required portions of the databases. This approach yields easier maintenance, increased security, and the ability to deal with inconsistencies. However, a user must understand the contents of each database to know what to include in a query: there is no global schema to provide advice about semantics. Also, each database must maintain knowledge about the other databases with which it shares information, e.g., in the form of models of the other databases or partial global schemas [Ahlsen and Johannesson 1990]. For n databases, as many as $n(n-1)$ partial global schemas might be required, while n mappings would suffice to translate between the databases and a common schema.

We base our methodology on the composite approach, but make three changes that enable us to combine the advantages of both approaches while avoiding some of their shortcomings. First, we use an *existing* common schema or context. In a similar attempt, [Sull and Kashyap 1992] describes a method for integrating schemas by translating them into an object-oriented data model, but this method maintains only the structural semantics of the resources.

Second, we capture the mapping between each model and the common context in a set of articulation axioms. The axioms provide a means of translation that enables the maintenance of a global view of all information resources and, at

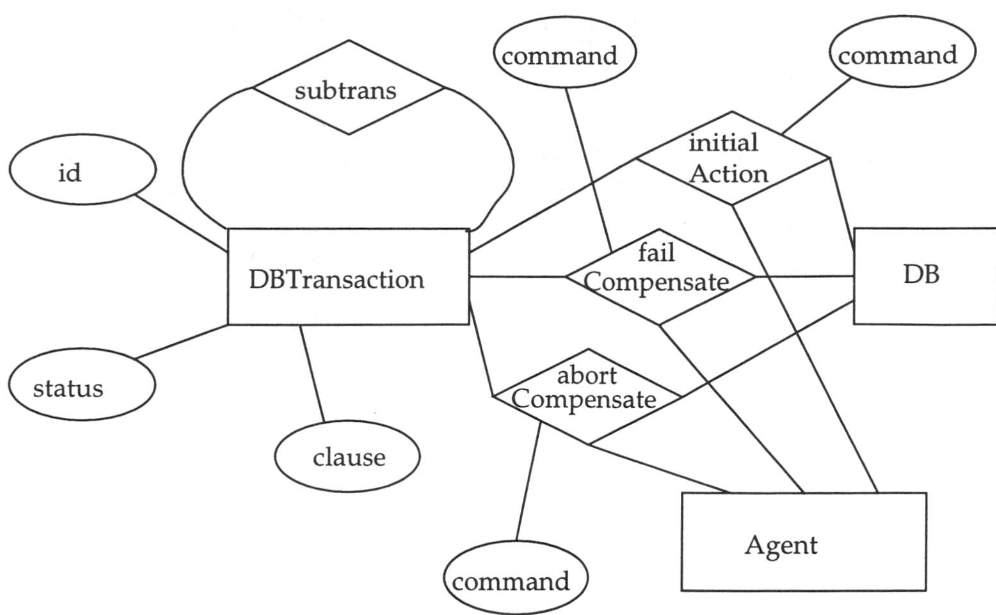

Figure 9: Semantic model for the schedule-repairing agent

the same time, a set of local views that correspond to each individual resource. An application can retain its current view, but use the information in other resources. Of course, any application can be modified to use the global view directly to access all available information.

Third, we consider knowledge-based systems (KBSs), interfaces, and applications, as well as databases.

Our use of agents for interoperating among applications and information resources is similar to the uses of mediators described in [Wiederhold 1992]. However, we also specify a means for semantic translation among the agents, as well as an implemented prototype. Other applications of similar agents, such as the Pilot's Associate developed by Lockheed *et al.* [Smith and Broadwell 1988], handcrafted their agents. This is not possible for large "open" applications: the agents must be such that they can be developed independently and execute autonomously.

Our architecture employs two kinds of computational agents: finer-grained, concurrent actors and coarser-grained, knowledge-based systems. The actors are used to control interactions among the components of the architecture. The knowledge-based agents are used where reasoning is needed, such as in deciding what tasks should be performed next or how to repair the environment when a task has failed. This seems to be a natural division of responsibilities for our example application. However, we took an engineering, rather than a scientific, approach, in that we did not investigate any alternative architectures.

6. Conclusion

For years, information-system personnel managed corporate data that was centralized on mainframes. The data was kept consistent, but eventually the amount of data increased to the point that centralized storage was no longer viable. Also, users wanted a way to share data across applications and wanted more direct involvement in the management of the data. So, data then began proliferating onto workstations and personal computers, where users could manage it themselves. But this resulted in redundancy, inconsistency, and no coherent global view. Hence, there are now attempts to reintegrate data. Users still need to manage their own data, which remains distributed, but they and their applications need coherent global access and consistency must be restored.

This paper describes Carnot's approach to enabling interoperation among enterprise information objects, i.e., among suppliers and consumers of information. In this approach, an enterprise information object is integrated based on articulation axioms defined between two contexts: the context of a model of the object and a common context provided by the Cyc knowledge base. The methodology is based on the following principles:

- Existing information resources should not have to be modified and data should not have to migrate.
- Existing applications should not have to be modified.
- Users should not have to adopt a new language for communicating with the resultant integrated system, unless they are accessing new types of information.
- Resources and applications should be able to be integrated independently, and the mappings that result should not have to change when additional objects are integrated.

The above principles are incorporated in an integration tool, MIST, for assisting an administrator in generating articulation axioms for a model, and in a set of agents that utilize the resultant axioms to provide users and applications with access to the integrated resources. They can use a familiar local context, while still benefiting from newly added resources.

These systems constitute part of the semantic services of Carnot [Cannata 1991], under development at MCC. They help specify and maintain the semantics of an organization's integrated information resources.

Extensions of our work are focused on developing additional information-system applications for agents, including

- intelligent directory service agents
- negotiating electronic data interchange (EDI) agents
- database triggers—making passive databases active
- rule-based database applications
- database administration agents
- intelligent information retrieval agents.

Our most important future work is centered on ways in which agents can acquire and maintain models of each other in order to improve their interactions.

References

[Agha 1986] Gul Agha, *Actors: A Model of Concurrent Computation in Distributed Systems*, MIT Press, Cambridge, MA, 1986.

[Ahlsen and Johannesson 1990] Matts Ahlsen and Paul Johannesson, "Contracts in Database Federations," in S. M. Deen, ed., *Cooperating Knowledge Based Systems 1990*, Springer-Verlag, London, 1991, pp. 293–310.

[Ansari *et al.* 1992] Mansoor Ansari, Marek Rusinkiewicz, Linda Ness, and Amit Sheth, "Executing Multidatabase Transactions," *Proceedings 25th Hawaii International Conference on Systems Sciences*, January 1992.

[Attie *et al.* 1993] Paul C. Attie, Munindar P. Singh, Amit P. sheth, and Marek Rusinkiewicz, "Specifying and Enforcing Intertask Dependencies," *Proceedings of the 19th VLDB Conference*, 1993.

[Bukhres *et al.* 1993] Omran A. Bukhres, Jiansan Chen, Weimin Du, Ahmed K. Elmagarmid, and Robert Pezzoli, "InterBase: An Execution Environment for Heterogeneous Software Systems," *IEEE Computer*, Vol. 26, No. 8, Aug. 1993, pp. 57–69.

[Buneman *et al.* 1990] O. P. Buneman, S. B. Davidson, and A. Watters, "Querying Independent Databases," *Information Sciences*, Vol. 52, Dec. 1990, pp. 1–34.

[Cannata 1991] Philip E. Cannata, "The Irresistible Move towards Interoperable Database Systems," *First International Workshop on Interoperability in Multidatabase Systems*, Kyoto, Japan, April 7–9, 1991.

[Ceri and Widom 1992] Stefano Ceri and Jennifer Widom, "Production Rules in Parallel and Distributed Database Environments," *Proceedings of the 18th VLDB Conference*, Vancouver, British Columbia, Canada, 1992, pp. 339–351.

[Collet *et al.* 1991] Christine Collet, Michael N. Huhns, and Wei-Min Shen, "Resource integration using a large knowledge base in Carnot," *IEEE Computer*, Vol. 24, No. 12, Dec. 1991, pp. 55–62.

[Cutkosky *et al.* 1993] Mark R. Cutkosky, Robert S. Englemore, Richard E. Fikes, Michael R. Genesereth, Thomas R. Gruber, William S. Mark, Jay M. Tenenbaum, and Jay C. Weber, "PACT: An Experiment in Integrating Concurrent Engineering Systems," *IEEE Computer*, January 1993, pp. 28–38.

[Elmagarmid 1992] Ahmed Elmagarmid, ed., *Database Transaction Models*, Morgan Kaufmann Publishers Inc., San Mateo, CA, 1992.

[Guha 1990] R. V. Guha, "Micro-theories and Contexts in Cyc Part I: Basic Issues," MCC Technical Report Number ACT-CYC-129-90, Microelectronics and Computer Technology Corporation, Austin, TX, June 1990.

[Heimbigner and McLeod 1985] Dennis Heimbigner and Dennis McLeod, "A Federated Architecture for Information Management," *ACM Transactions on Office Information Systems*, Vol. 3, No. 3, July 1985, pp. 253–278.

[Jin *et al.* 1993] W. Woody Jin, Linda Ness, Marek Rusinkiewicz, and Amit Sheth, "Executing Service Provisioning Applications as Multidatabase Flexible Transactions," Bellcore Technical Report (unpublished), 1993.

[Lenat and Guha 1990] Doug Lenat and R. V. Guha, *Building Large Knowledge-Based Systems: Representation and Inference in the Cyc Project*, Addison-Wesley Publishing Company, Inc., Reading, MA, 1990.

[Litwin *et al.* 1990] Witold Litwin, Leo Mark, and Nick Roussopoulos, "Interoperability of Multiple Autonomous Databases," *ACM Computing Surveys*, Vol. 22, No. 3, September 1990, pp. 267–296.

[Newell 1982] Allen Newell, "The Knowledge Level," *Artificial Intelligence*, Vol. 18, No. 1, January 1982, pp. 87–127.

[Sheth and Larson 1990] Amit P. Sheth and James A. Larson, "Federated Database Systems for Managing Distributed, Heterogeneous, and Autonomous Databases," *ACM Computing Surveys*, Vol. 22, No. 3, Sept. 1990, pp. 183–236.

[Smith and Broadwell 1988] David Smith and Martin Broadwell, "The Pilot's Associate—an overview," *Proceedings of the SAE Aerotech Conference*, Los Angeles, CA, May 1988.

[Sull and Kashyap 1992] Wonhee Sull and Rangasami L. Kashyap, "A Self-Organizing Knowledge Representation Scheme for Extensible Heterogeneous Information Environment," *IEEE Transactions on Knowledge and Data*

Engineering, Vol. 4, No. 2, April 1992, pp. 185–191.

[Tomlinson *et al.* 1991] Chris Tomlinson, Mark Scheevel, and Vineet Singh, "Report on Rosette 1.1," MCC Technical Report Number ACT-OODS-275-91, Microelectronics and Computer Technology Corporation, Austin, TX, July 1991.

[Tomlinson *et al.* 1993] Christine Tomlinson, Paul Attie, Philip Cannata, Greg Meredith, Amit Sheth, Munindar Singh, and Darrell Woelk, "Workflow Support in Carnot," *IEEE Data Engineering*, 1993.

[Wiederhold 1992] Gio Wiederhold, "Mediators in the Architecture of Future Information Systems," *IEEE Computer*, Vol. 25, No. 3, March 1992, pp. 38–49.

[Woelk *et al.* 1992] Darrell Woelk, Wei-Min Shen, Michael N. Huhns, and Philip E. Cannata, "Model-Driven Enterprise Information Management in Carnot," in Charles J. Petrie Jr., ed., *Enterprise Integration Modeling: Proceedings of the First International Conference*, MIT Press, Cambridge, MA, 1992.

Appendix: Developing Articulation Axioms

Carnot provides a graphical tool, the Model Integration Software Tool (MIST), that automates the routine aspects of model integration, while displaying the information needed for user interaction. The tool produces articulation axioms in the following three phases:

1. MIST automatically represents an enterprise model in a local context as an instance of a given formalism. The representation is declarative, and uses an extensive set of semantic properties.

1. By constraint propagation and user interaction it matches concepts from the local context with concepts from the common context.

1. For each match, it automatically constructs an articulation axiom by instantiating axiom templates.

MIST displays enterprise models both before and after they are represented in a local context. MIST enables the Cyc knowledge base to be browsed graphically and textually to allow the correct concept matches to be located. With MIST, a user can create frames in the common context or augment the local context for a model with additional properties when needed to ensure a successful match. MIST also displays the articulation axioms that it constructs. The three phases of articulation axiom development are described next in more detail.

In the model representation phase, we represent the model as a set of frames and slots in a Cyc context created specially for it. These frames are instances of frames describing the metamodel of the schema, e.g., (for a relational schema) `Relation` and `DatabaseAttribute`.

In the matching phase, the problem is: given a (Cyc) representation for a concept in a local context, find its corresponding concept in the common context. The two factors that affect this phase are (1) there may be a mismatch between the local and common contexts in the depth of knowledge representing a concept, and (2) there may be mismatches between the structures used to encode the knowledge. For example, a concept in Cyc can be represented as either a collection or an attribute [Lenat and Guha 1990, pp. 339ff].

If the common context's knowledge is more than or equivalent to that of the local context's for some concept, then the interactive matching process described in this section will find the relevant portion of the common context's knowledge. If the common context has less knowledge than the local context, then knowledge will be added to the common context until its knowledge equals or exceeds that in the local context; otherwise, the common context would be unable to model the semantics of the resource. The added knowledge refines the common context. This does not affect previously integrated resources, but can be useful when further resources are integrated.

Finding correspondences between concepts in the local and common contexts is a subgraph-matching problem. We base subgraph matching on a simple string matching between the names or synonyms of frames representing the model and the names or synonyms of frames in the common context. Matching begins by finding associations between attribute/link definitions and existing slots in the common context. After a few matches have been identified, either by exact string matches or by a user indicating the correct match out of a set of candidate matches, possible matches for the remaining model concepts are greatly constrained. Conversely, after integrating an entity or object, possible matches for its attributes are constrained.

In the third phase, an articulation axiom is constructed for each match found. For example, the match between a relational attribute phone in model `AAA` and the Cyc slot `phoneNumber` yields the axiom

ist(Cyc, phoneNumber(L, N)) <=> ist(AAA, phone(L, N))

which means that the `phone` attribute definition determines the `phoneNumber` slot in the common schema, and vice versa. Articulation axioms are generated automatically by instantiating stored templates with the matches found.

PACT: An Experiment in Integrating Concurrent Engineering Systems

Mark R. Cutkosky, Robert S. Engelmore, Richard E. Fikes,
Michael R. Genesereth, and Thomas R. Gruber, Stanford University
William S. Mark, Lockheed Palo Alto Research Labs
Jay M. Tenenbaum and Jay C. Weber, Enterprise Integration Technologies

Large design projects can involve multiple sites, subsystems, and knowledge-representation schemes. Using this testbed system, four teams produced a distributed robotic-device simulation and synchronized on a design modification.

Several research groups are jointly developing the Palo Alto Collaborative Testbed (PACT), a concurrent engineering infrastructure that encompasses multiple sites, subsystems, and disciplines. Through PACT, we are examining the technological and sociological issues of building large-scale, distributed concurrent-engineering systems.

Our approach has been to integrate existing multitool systems. These systems are themselves frameworks that were developed with no anticipation of subsequent integration. We take as a given that individual engineering groups prefer to use their own tool suites and integration environments. Certainly, they have significant investments in these self-contained systems. Nonetheless, projects that involve large segments of an enterprise or multiple enterprises must coordinate engineering activities that take place within individual frameworks. PACT experiments have explored issues in building an overarching framework along three dimensions:

- cooperative development of interfaces, protocols, and architecture;
- sharing of knowledge among systems that maintain their own specialized knowledge bases and reasoning mechanisms; and
- computer-aided support for the negotiation and decision-making that characterize concurrent engineering.

PACT serves as a testbed for knowledge-sharing research emerging from the artificial intelligence community, as well as for emerging data-exchange standards such as PDES/Step (Product Data Exchange Using Step/Standard for the Exchange of Product Model Data).[1]

The PACT architecture is based on interacting *agents* (that is, programs that encapsulate engineering tools). The agent interaction in turn relies on three things: shared concepts and terminology for communicating knowledge across disciplines, an interlingua for transferring knowledge among agents, and a communication and control language that enables agents to request information and services. This technology allows agents working on different aspects of a design to interact at the *knowledge level*: sharing and exchanging information about the design independent of the format in which the information is encoded internally.

The PACT systems include

- NVisage, a distributed knowledge-based integration environment for design tools developed by the Lockheed Information and Computing Sciences Group;
- DME (Device Modeling Environment), a model formulation and simulation environment from the Stanford Knowledge Systems Laboratory;
- Next-Cut, a mechanical design and process planning system from the Stanford Center for Design Research; and
- Designworld, a digital electronics design, simulation, assembly, and testing system from the Stanford Computer Science Department and Hewlett-Packard.

In the initial experiments, each system modeled different aspects of a small robotic device and reasoned about them from the standpoint of a different engineering discipline (software, digital and analog electronics, and dynamics). The systems then cooperated to produce a distributed device simulation and synchronize on a subsequent design modification.

In this article we discuss the motivations for PACT and the significance of the approach for concurrent engineering. We review our initial experiments in distributed simulation and incremental redesign, describe PACT's agent-based architecture, and discuss lessons learned and future directions. For details on the underlying language, protocols, and knowledge-sharing research issues, we refer the reader to Neches et al.,[2] Finin et al.,[3] and Genesereth et al.[4]

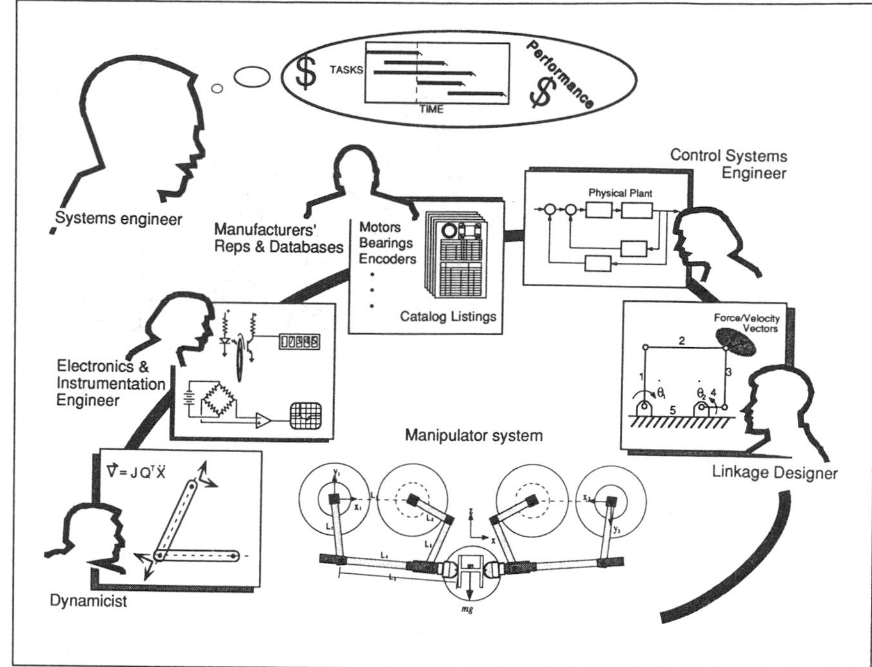

Figure 1. A multidisciplinary design team.

The distributed design problem

Although concurrent engineering is almost universally advocated today, it is hard to execute when large multidisciplinary projects are involved.

To illustrate some of the issues, consider the team depicted in Figure 1. At any instant, the team members may be working at different levels of detail, each employing his or her own representations of physical artifacts, engineering models, and knowledge. For example, the linkage designer is primarily concerned with the geometry of the device and its configuration space, while the dynamicist is constructing an accurate set of equations to predict device behavior. At the same time, the controls engineer needs a linearized dynamics model that captures the joint-space to task-space mapping and the primary inertial effects. (Indeed, as far as the controls engineer is concerned, the equations could just as well represent a gear train or an electronic circuit, with an analogous set of partial derivatives relating inputs and outputs.)

Despite their differences in perspective, the specialists share considerable information. For example, an appreciation of the dynamics is necessary when choosing the force sensors. Conversely, information about nonlinearities in the amplifiers and motors will interest the dynamicist in setting up the simulation. In applying information technology to support engineering projects such as this, we seek tools that will help the team members share knowledge and keep track of each others' needs, constraints, decisions, and assumptions.

Ironically, contemporary computer design and manufacturing tools appear to exacerbate the problems that concurrent engineering is trying to solve. Most tools provide point solutions to particular modeling and analysis problems, based on idiosyncratic representations and algorithms. Designers are often frustrated because these tools are developed by and for expert users. Effective use requires knowing the conventions (for example, for representing spatial transformations and instantaneous velocities), the assumptions (for example, that components are rigid bodies), and other characteristics or limitations of the approach (for example, whether the method is strictly conservative and whether it always converges).

Such information is rarely explicit in the models themselves, but must be absorbed by wading through extensive documentation and consulting with the tools' developers and frequent users. More fundamentally, idiosyncratic design tools contribute to the isolation of

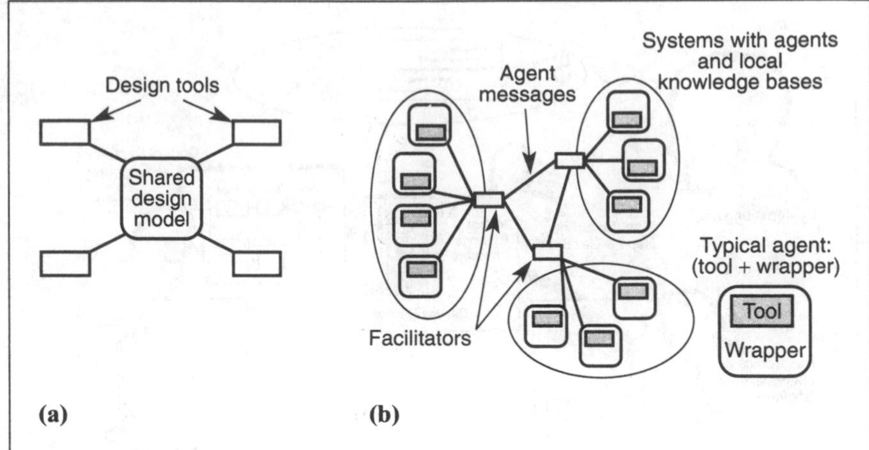

Figure 2. Interacting design tools require a shared design model (a). Scalability requires distribution of the model, with mechanisms for translating among different representations and coordinating interactions (b).

designers by preventing them from sharing their design models.

Integration via shared design models

A design such as the manipulator system in Figure 1 embodies many interacting constraints that must be met by the set of components making up the design. To ensure that constraints are met, the component descriptions must be organized into a framework that represents the evolving design. This representational framework is the design model. The descriptions in the model are composed from shared design-domain *ontologies* (that is, sets of agreed-upon terms and formally described meanings). In contrast to the superficial representations found in current design environments (for example, CAD data files), the design model forms a basis for knowledge sharing among diverse systems.

Figure 2a shows one solution for providing a shared design model. However, this approach runs into trouble in large-scale distributed design environments. Individual design tools tend to be highly specialized, making use of particular representations and reasoning methods to do their work efficiently. Any sharing must consider that these tools do not share the same internal model. Furthermore, design is a process of negotiation: Decisions are made and changed frequently as specifications change and new ideas come forward. A single shared database encompassing all the data of participating tools would quickly become a bottleneck.

The PACT experiments, though preliminary, have shown the feasibility of design through the interaction of distributed knowledge-based reasoners. Each reasoner has its own local knowledge base and reasoning mechanisms. As shown in Figure 2b, agents interact through (currently very simple) *facilitators* that translate tool-specific knowledge into and out of a standard knowledge-interchange language. Each agent can therefore reason in its own terms, asking other agents for information and providing other agents with information as needed through the facilitators.

PACT software interoperation

The PACT architecture was designed to conveniently and flexibly integrate the diverse operating systems, control mechanisms, data/knowledge formats, and environmental assumptions of software not originally written for wide-area interoperation. It is an extension of Open Distributed Processing (ODP) architectures appearing on mainstream computing platforms. For example, the publish/subscribe mechanism of Macintosh System 7 and the Dynamic Data Exchange mechanism of Windows 3.0 provide common data formats and mechanisms for interapplication messaging.

On a larger scale, the Object Management Group's Common Object Request Broker Architecture (OMG/CORBA)[5] defines sophisticated service-naming and parameter-type translation.

Although ODP architectures define the *form* of software interoperation, they say little about the content of shared information. Complex software interoperation, such as CAD data translation, recursive request decomposition, knowledge-based interaction (assert, retract, evaluate, etc.), and service location based on functionality are all left to ad hoc agreements among individual programs (that is, programmers). This situation limits interoperation to collections of programs engineered to interact with one another. Scalability suffers because idiosyncratic agreements about message content must be reevaluated whenever a new participant joins the interaction.

Message-content standards. Our software-interoperation architecture extends ODP architectures by further standardizing the style of program interactions. We do this by defining message content at three levels:

(1) Messages are expressions in a common *agent communication language* that supports knowledge-base operations (for example, assertions and queries).

(2) Message contents of the knowledge-base operations are expressions in a common *knowledge-interchange format* that provides an implementation-independent encoding of information.

(3) Expressions stated in the interchange format use a standard vocabulary from common *ontologies* that are defined for the shared application domain.

Each of these levels is the subject of widespread discussion and development, primarily by DARPA-sponsored knowledge-representation standards committees.[2] One group has proposed an agent communication language called the Knowledge Query and Manipulation Language.[3] KQML specifies a relatively small set of *performatives* that categorize the services agents may request of one another. For example, one agent may request to assert a fact to another's local data/knowledge, retract a previous assertion, or obtain the answer to some query.

A second proposal is a specification of the knowledge-interchange format called KIF.[4] KIF can be used as a format for KQML arguments (KQML allows multiple formats). KIF is a prefix version of the language of first-order predicate calculus, with various extensions to enhance its expressiveness. KIF provides for the communication of constraints, negations, disjunctions, rules, quantified expressions, and so forth. With the application of AI technology to practical problems, more programs can manipulate information of this sort.

The third effort concerns the development of engineering ontologies. This effort focuses on defining formal vocabularies for representing knowledge about engineering artifacts and processes. These vocabularies specify the assumptions underlying the common views of such knowledge. Given the application-specific nature of such ontologies, this activity is not intended to produce a single specification. Instead, it addresses various domains of importance to knowledge sharing, such as device behavior modeling. This effort complements the work of PDES/Step vocabulary committees, which have been most successful in specifying data models for domains such as solid modeling and finite-element geometry.

Facilitators. Plugging into the PACT architecture requires a substantial commitment to the message-content effort. We use facilitators to ease this burden. Each facilitator provides an interface between a local collection of agents and remote agents. The facilitator (1) provides a layer of reliable message passing, (2) routes outgoing messages to the appropriate destination(s), (3) translates incoming messages for consumption by its agent, and (4) initializes and monitors the execution of its agents.

Communication and coordination, therefore, occur between agents and facilitators and between facilitators, but not directly between agents. We call this arrangement of agents and facilitators a *federation architecture*. Messages from agents to facilitators are undirected (that is, they have content but no address). The facilitators route such messages to agents that can handle them.

In performing this task, facilitators can go beyond simple pattern matching: They can translate messages, decompose problems into subproblems, and schedule the work on those subproblems. In some cases, they can do this interpretively (with messages going through the facilitator); in other cases, they can do it in one-shot fashion (with the facilitator setting up specialized links between individual agents and then stepping out of the picture).

PACT agent communication. PACT has been demonstrated with 31 agent-based programs executing on 15 workstations and microcomputers. When grouped by engineering discipline, these programs compose the following six top-level agents: digital circuitry agent, control software agent, power system agent, physical plant agent, sensor agent, and parts catalog agent. All but the latter two existed before we built the PACT system (see sidebars).

In the demonstration system, each top-level PACT agent works through a facilitator to coordinate its interactions with other agents. Each PACT facilitator consists of two parts: a *connection associate* and an *agent manager*. A connection associate implements a layer of reliable message passing above the widely available TCP/IP transport protocol; it is nearly identical in implementation across facilitators. The connection associate supplies message strings for the agent manager. If the message is a control message from another facilitator, the agent manager interprets the message and reacts accordingly. If the message was from an agent (via a facilitator), the agent manager performs any necessary translations before forwarding the message to its agent.

PACT experiments

The demonstration system that we built to test our ideas about knowledge sharing, interoperability, and agent-based architectures for concurrent engineering was first shown in October 1991. The demonstration scenario involved four geographically distributed teams collaborating on the design, fabrication, and redesign of an electromechanical device. Each team was responsible for different subsystems and was supported by its own computational environment. The federation architecture linked these environments.

The subject of the PACT experiments was a robotic manipulator, a system

Glossary

Agent — A computer program that communicates with external programs exclusively via a predefined protocol. An agent is capable of responding to all messages defined by the protocol, and it uses the protocol to invoke the services of other agents. PACT agents use the KQML protocol to send and receive messages represented in the KIF interchange format using a shared, domain-specific vocabulary.

Facilitator — A program that coordinates the communication among agents. Facilitators provide a reliable network communication layer, route messages among agents on the basis of message contents, and coordinate the control of multiagent activities.

KIF (Knowledge Interchange Format) — A standard notation and semantics for an extended form of first-order predicate calculus. KIF allows programs to make assertions and ask queries in a neutral format, independent of internal data structures.

KQML (Knowledge Query and Manipulation Language) — A protocol for agents that specifies a set of domain-independent communication operations. For example, assert and evaluate allow agents to exchange information using some notation (for example, KIF) and a specified vocabulary (that is, an ontology).

Ontology — A specification of a domain of discourse among agents, in the form of definitions of shared vocabulary (classes, relations, functions, and object constants). Together with a standard notation such as KIF, an ontology specifies a domain-specific language for agent interaction. The PACT ontology includes vocabulary for describing behavior in terms of time-varying parameters.

that combined mechanics, electronics, and software, with extensive design documentation. Figure 3 shows the manipulator system schematically. The two fingertips of the manipulator mechanism are positioned by five-bar linkages connected directly to the shafts of four DC torque motors. The motors are powered by linear current amplifiers, and their joint angles are measured using shaft encoders. A digital circuit counts pulses from the encoders and multiplexes the resulting numbers so that high and low bytes are fed sequentially over an 8-bit parallel line to the control system. Depending on the application, various control laws are run at rates between 200 and 500 hertz. A digital-to-analog converter produces the controller-commanded torques as voltages that drive the amplifiers.

Figure 3 also shows the division of responsibilities among the PACT teams. The control software was the responsibility of the Lockheed team, using their NVisage environment. The power system and sensors were the responsibility of Stanford's Knowledge Systems Laboratory team, using their Device Modeling Environment (DME). The manipulator mechanism was the responsibility of Stanford's Center for Design Research and Enterprise Integration Technologies, using their Next-Cut system. Finally, the digital circuit was the responsibility of the team from Stanford's Logic Group and Hewlett-Packard, using their Designworld system. Designworld also maintained a catalog of components with shape and size information.

All participants had their own hardware and software platforms, including two Macintoshes, a DEC 3100, a TI Explorer Lisp machine, and HP and Sun workstations — all linked through the Internet. The demonstration scenario consisted of three parts: first, an example of cooperative design refinement; second, a simulation of the manipulator, requiring exchange of data among all four subsystems; and third, a typical interaction in which a design change initiated by one team necessitated changes by another.

Cooperative design refinement

In cooperative design refinement, each team begins with an initial subsystem design and produces a revised design that meets new specifications for accuracy, measurement methods, etc. Resolving design interactions requires considerable communication.

Figure 4 depicts some design interactions for the manipulator. Next-Cut's analysis uses a detailed rigid-body dynamics model, whereas NVisage needs a less detailed model for its controller. However, these models must be consistent. The interactions also include many constraints. For instance, encoder resolution and maximum motor velocity constrain the choice of chips used for decoding and multiplexing the encoder signals in the digital circuit.

The PACT demonstration directly

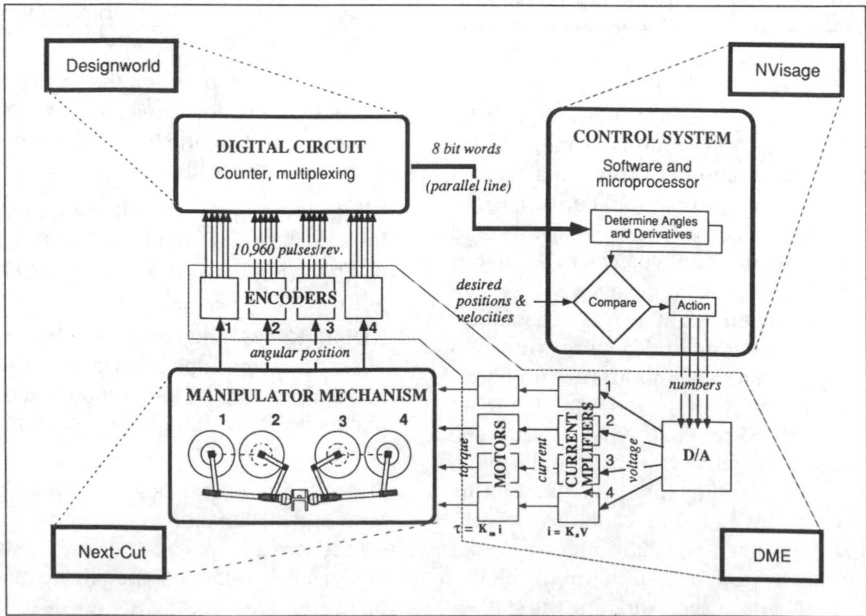

Figure 3. Manipulator system and division of responsibilities for the PACT experiment.

NVisage

NVisage is an engineering tool integration framework that supports spreadsheet-style design and development. When designers modify one aspect of the design, they immediately see the change reflected in other aspects. As with numerical spreadsheets, this facilitates what-if experimentation: Designers interactively try various options, receiving immediate feedback on their decisions.

The NVisage framework is knowledge-sharing technology that enables each engineering tool to encode and maintain its own separate model of a design, while intertool communication mechanisms maintain consistency among the models. Knowledge representation techniques have driven the development of shared languages and ontologies, and distributed knowledge-based systems techniques have driven the development of knowledge-exchange protocols. The separate models and interchange mechanisms are specifically designed to include information about functionality (corresponding to plans for PDES level 4[1]) as well as information currently representable in CAD interchange formats.

Reference

1. J.A. Fulton, *The Semantic Unification Metamodel: Technical Approach*, Standards Working Document ISO TC184/SC4/* WG3 N 81 (P0), IGES/PDES Organization, Dictionary/Methodology Committee, 1991. Contact James Fulton, Boeing Computer Services, PO Box 24346, MS 7L-64, Seattle, WA 98124-0346.

Further reading

J.C. Weber et al., "Spreadsheet-Like Design Through Knowledge-Based Tool Integration," *Int'l J. Expert Systems: Research and Applications*, Vol. 5, No. 1, 1992.

addressed only a few such interactions. The most interesting were those between NVisage and Next-Cut. For the experiment, the Lockheed design engineer selected a simple Cartesian position controller from an NVisage database of skeletal controller designs. To design the controller, NVisage needed a kinematic mapping from joint space to Cartesian workspace. One of the modules within NVisage therefore sent expressions of the form

(interested-in nvisage '(ASSERT
(closed-form '(pmx $q1 $q2) $f))).

This statement specifies that the NVisage agent requests a closed-form expression $f for determining the horizontal fingertip coordinate of the planar manipulator (pmx) in terms of the joint variables q1 and q2. The meanings of terms *closed-form* and *pmx* were specified in the common ontology for the PACT experiment.

Next-Cut picked up this request and responded with equations (for example, bindings for $f). NVisage received this information, compiled the equations into equivalent statements in executable code, and dynamically linked these into its component functionality module.

Device Modeling Environment

The Stanford University Knowledge Systems Laboratory is developing an evolving prototype "designer's associate" system called the Device Modeling Environment. DME focuses on helping electromechanical-device designers experiment with alternative designs by providing rapid feedback about the implications of design decisions. It also helps document a design for use in other engineering steps such as diagnosis and redesign.

DME operates on multiple engineering knowledge bases that include libraries of process and component models, representations of the principles of physics, and knowledge about modeling itself. It can represent multiple models of devices at various levels of abstraction. It also explicitly represents the relationships among device models. Given a model, which can be quite abstract, a simulation module can make predictions about the device behavior under specified conditions. Explanation capabilities generate natural-language text in an interactive medium to communicate the results to human engineers. Model formulation tools permit engineers to create useful models appropriate for various information requirements.

Further reading

Y. Iwasaki and C. Low, "Model Generation and Simulation of Device Behavior with Continuous and Discrete Changes," Tech. Report KSL-91-69, Knowledge Systems Laboratory, Stanford University, 1991.

Stanford's Center for Design Research (CDR) team did not have to know anything about how the controls specialist was using the requested information to create a control law. Similarly, the Lockheed team was insulated from the extensive geometric and kinematic knowledge of the mechanism used by the CDR team. On the other hand, the two systems had to agree on their definitions of

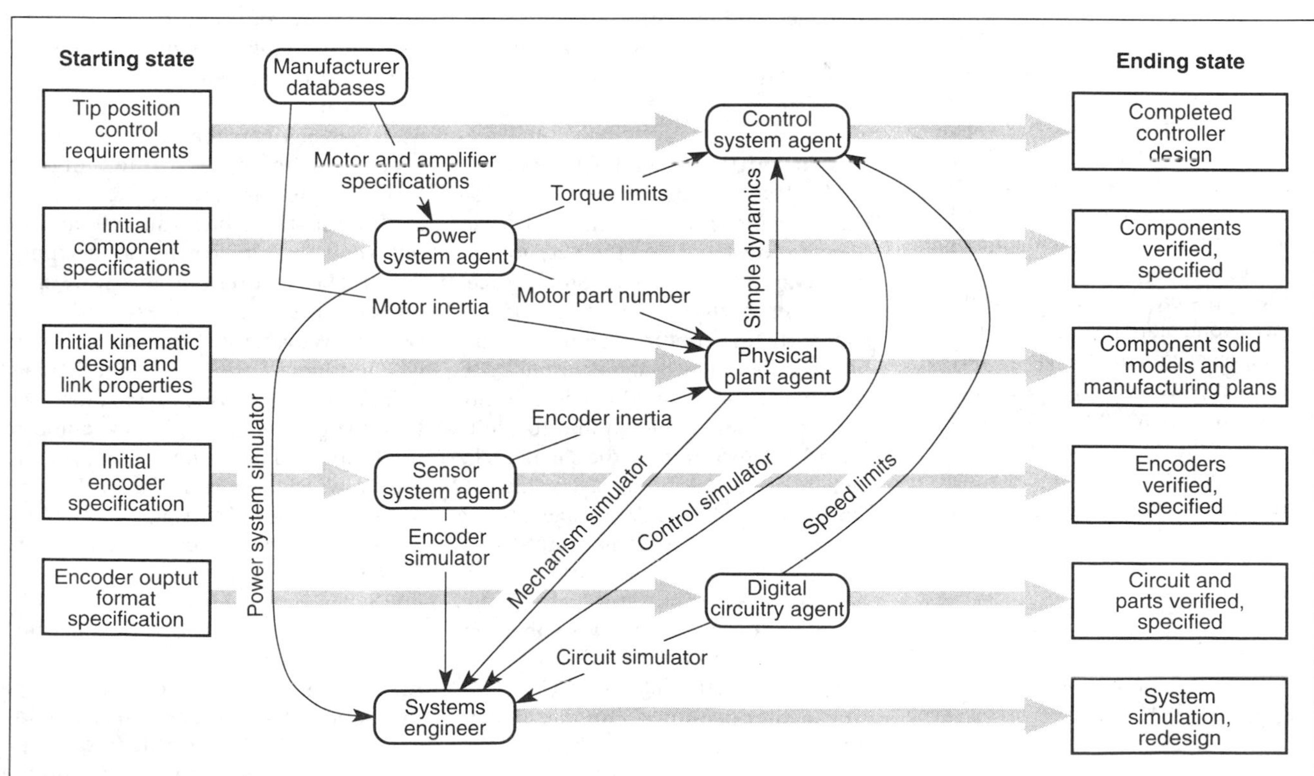

Figure 4. Interactions among aspects during manipulator design refinement.

space, time, coordinate frames, closed-form expressions, units of measure, and so forth, to effect the exchange of the coordinate transformations and inertial terms.

Distributed simulation. In the next part of the demonstration, the Lockheed team initiated a simulation of the entire device to test their controller design. The simulation was distributed over the PACT network, with the four systems simulating their respective components and communicating their results to the others. As Figure 2 shows, the simulation can be effected through a simple loop, where each system sends commands or data to the next. The simulation proceeded around the loop until DME, which modeled the motors and power system, signaled that a motor had overheated due to overloading. The simulation thus indicated the need for a redesign.

The simulation was actually developed first, as a forcing function to get all the component systems communicating via message passing and to test the adequacy of their models. The exchange of information was primarily achieved by passing simple assertions around the loop. For example, the assertion

(ASSERT (= (val pm-encoder-w-1 10000)4095))

states that the position encoder for wheel 1 at time 10,000 is reading 4,095. These messages triggered reevaluations of the subsystems in response to the state changes.

Although this part of the demonstration initiated the experiments in interoperation, the system designers negotiated extensively to decide on the control sequence and data formats. In that sense, systems for the distributed simulation were integrated in the traditional ad hoc fashion.

Distributed redesign. The objective of the last part of the demonstration was to explore interactions that occur during redesign, when the decisions of one team member have consequences for other parts of the design. In response to the motor burning out, the power subsystem designer used DME to replace the originally selected motors with a larger model and to notify the other subsystems of the change. The change notice was broadcast on the network as an ASSERT message, stating the part number of the new motor.

Next-Cut was interested in this change because the motor forms part of the manipulator-arm linkage assembly, and changing the motor can affect the mating features on the links. Next-Cut therefore posted a request for the dimensions of the motor with the new part number. Designworld, which maintains a components catalog, handled that query. The Designworld agent sent back the needed dimensions, thereby allowing Next-Cut to adjust mating features on the links, along with the process plan for machining them.

Designworld

In its current form, Designworld is an automated prototyping system for small-scale electronic circuits built from standard parts (such as TTL chips and connectors on prototyping boards). The design for a product enters the system via a multimedia design workstation. A dedicated robotic cell — essentially a microfactory — builds the product. If necessary, the product can be returned to the system for diagnosis and repair.

The Designworld system consists of 18 processes on six different machines (two Macintoshes and four HP workstations). These processes perform various tasks including design solicitation, simulation, verification, dignosis, test and measurement, layout, assembly planning, and assembly execution. Each of the 18 processes is implemented as a distinct agent that communicates with its peers via agent communication language (ACL) messages. Any one of these programs can be replaced by an ACL-equivalent program without changing the functionality of the system as a whole. Any agent can be moved to a different machine (with equivalent capabilities). Any agent can be deleted and the system will continue to run correctly, albeit with reduced functionality.

Further reading

M.R. Genesereth, "Designworld," *Proc. IEEE Conf. Robotics and Automation*, IEEE CS Press, Los Alamitos, Calif., Order No. 2163-02, 1991, pp. 2,785-2,788. Also, see "Automated Concurrent Engineering in Designworld," this issue, pp. 74-76.

Lessons learned

The introduction characterized PACT as a testbed for cooperative research, knowledge sharing, and computer-aided engineering. We summarize here what we learned in each area.

Cooperative research. Designing an integrated system by committee is always hard, and PACT was no exception. The most difficult task, by far, was agreeing on the ontological commitments that enable knowledge-level communication among the systems. Designing a shared ontology is difficult because it must bridge differences in abstractions and views. Participants must agree about natural-world concepts such as position and time, shape and behavior, sensors and motors. Each concept requires agreement on many levels, ranging from what it means to how it is represented. For instance, how should two agents exchange information about the voltage on a wire: what units, what granularity of time? How should manipulator dynamics be modeled: as simultaneous equations or functions? in what coordinate frame?

The four systems composing PACT used various coordinate systems and several distinct representations of time (for example, discrete events, points in continuous time, intervals of continuous time, and piecewise approximations). These representations were chosen for valid task- and context-dependent reasons. We cannot simply replace them by one standard product model that has a single representation of time. Instead, we must get the agents involved in any transaction to agree on a common ontology, which defines a standard vocabulary for describing time-varying behavior under each view of time that is needed.

What went on behind the scenes in PACT — and is not represented in computational form at all — was a careful negotiation among system developers to devise the specific pairwise ontologies that enabled their systems to cooperate. The developers met and emulated how their respective systems might discuss, say, the ramifications of increasing motor size. In this fashion, they ascertained and agreed upon what information had to be exchanged and how it would be represented.

Therefore, what PACT actually demonstrates is a mechanism for distributing reasoning, not a mechanism for automatically building and sharing a design model. The model sharing in PACT, as in other efforts, is still implicit — not given in a formal specification enforced in software. The ontology for PACT was documented informally in e-mail messages among developers of the interacting tools. The PACT tools can interact coherently because the commitments to common concepts and vocabulary are "wired" into their interactions (for example, programs were built to use a fixed vocabulary in messages).

PACT could get away with this ad hoc approach to ontology building because its task was constrained and it involved only a handful of developers and tools. Scaling up will require standard, reusable ontologies for generic concepts such as kinematics, dynamics, and the structure and behavior of electromechanical devices. It will also require a systematic process for developing and extending such ontologies, supported by CASE tools.

What PACT actually demonstrates is a mechanism for distributing reasoning.

Knowledge sharing. Conventional approaches to integrating engineering tools depend on standardized data structures and a unified design model, both of which require substantial commitments from tool designers. PACT departs from such approaches in two fundamental ways. First, tool data and models are encapsulated rather than standardized and unified. Each tool is thus free to use the most appropriate internal representations and models for its task. Second, the encapsulating agents help tools communicate by translating their internal concepts into a shared engineering *language* (that is, a system of grammar, vocabulary, and meanings). This shared language need only cover the intersection of tool interests, usually a small fraction of the contents of a full, shared design model. In principle, the language can evolve from a few core concepts.[2,6]

The agents communicate among themselves using KQML and KIF. Most KQML messages consist of queries and assertions in KIF (as well as basic control functions such as reset). Agents also use KIF expressions to inform each other of their interests and to request notification of informational changes that may affect them. Because queries and interests are expressed in a formal declarative language, the meanings of terms are not dependent on particular programs and can therefore be shared among programs with different implementations and knowledge stores. Moreover, facilitators can use the content of messages to route them selectively to agents that have relevant knowledge or interests.

Several commercially available systems support distributed messaging across heterogeneous applications. These systems permit tools to subscribe to "interest" groups and receive published results relevant to that group. However, such systems do not enable arbitrary tools to exchange knowledge. PACT provides the framework for specifying shared content. It enables tools that should interoperate to do so without committing to common data formats. It also makes possible routing and notification based on message content, not just simple syntactic patterns.

Computer-aided engineering. A key issue in concurrent engineering from a designer's perspective is how to bridge the multitude of models required to support a complex design at various stages of the design process. Programs, like people, use many models. The challenge is to use the right model for each task (that is, the right abstraction and granularity) and to communicate the results in an appropriate form to others with different needs and interests.

PACT has yet to deal with such issues in a deep way. For example, the PACT distributed-simulation demonstration employed a constant level of abstraction and granularity, each iteration around the loop corresponding to one sample of the digital servo system. Not

Next-Cut

Next-Cut is a prototype system for concurrent product and process design of mechanical assemblies. Next-Cut consists of several modules that surround representations of design artifacts, process plans, and tooling. Next-Cut presently includes modules for feature-based design of components and assemblies, tolerance analysis, kinematic analysis and synthesis, geometric analysis, and CNC process and fixture planning. A version of the Next-Cut framework has been applied to an industrial project on cable-harness design and fabrication.

The modules in Next-Cut communicate largely through the central representations, modifying them and extracting information from them. A notification mechanism alerts modules about changes that affect them. The representations of designs and plans in Next-Cut are hierarchical and include explicit dependencies both among different levels of detail and between artifacts and process steps. Individual components are described in terms of features, which are composed of geometric elements, location and form tolerances, reference frames, etc.

To provide fast response during interactive design sessions, Next-Cut employs incremental planning and analysis methods that reuse previous results where possible. The primary mechanism behind these methods is the maintenance of dependency structures.

Further reading

M.R. Cutkosky and J.M. Tenenbaum, "Toward a Framework for Concurrent Design," *Int'l J. Systems Automation: Research and Applications*, Vol. 1, No. 3, pp. 239-261, 1992.

only is this approach slow (the simulation ran over the network at something like 1/100 real time), but it also is at an unnecessarily fine scale for purposes of verifying that the subsystems behave properly.

A better approach would be to recognize that the participants in a simulation or verification exercise need to receive information from different sources and with different quanta of time, space, etc., depending on the circumstances. For example, during the early stages of controller design it might be best to bypass the encoder, amplifier, and digital circuit agents, and to send sequences of commanded torques directly to the dynamics module and receive sequences of joint angles directly from it.

Future directions

Through PACT, we are exploring a new methodology for cooperatively solving engineering problems on the basis of knowledge sharing. PACT encapsulates engineering tools and frameworks by using agents that exchange information and services through an explicit shared model of the design. Conceptually, this shared model is centralized; in practice, it is distributed among the specialized internal models that each tool or framework maintains.

To create the illusion of a shared design model, facilitators mediate all interactions between agents. Each agent's facilitator is responsible for (1) locating other agents on the network capable of providing requested information or services, (2) establishing a connection across (potentially) heterogeneous computing environments, and (3) managing the ensuing conversation. Information is passed among agents and facilitators in an interlingua (KIF) based on first-order logic, with agents translating between the interlingua and their clients' internal representations. Knowledge sharing across disciplines is possible because of a priori ontological agreements among the agents about the meanings of terms. Agents and facilitators coordinate their activities by using a communication and control language (currently, KQML).

In the PACT experiment, this agent-based interoperability architecture was implemented on a distributed messaging substrate that links platforms that support the TCP/IP transport protocol.

Instead of literally integrating code, users can encapsulate modules.

Agents were used at two levels: first, to integrate individual tools in the NextCut, Designworld, and NVisage frameworks; second, to integrate the frameworks themselves. Although the initial implementation has limited robustness, functionality, and scale, its potential for concurrent engineering is clear.

More generally, we believe that using agents to communicate on a knowledge level is the right way to compose large, complex systems out of existing software modules. Instead of literally integrating code, users can encapsulate modules in agents and then invoke them remotely as network services when needed. Such an approach is clearly advantageous in situations where installing the software locally would require expensive system reconfiguration or where experts are required to run and maintain the code.

Many engineering software packages have these characteristics, discouraging occasional users and small organizations from exploiting them. With PACT, such problems can be overcome by creating a corporate-wide CAD framework that links software services run and maintained by specialists.

PACT is an ongoing collaboration. Current activities are aimed at alleviating shortcomings in the initial demonstration and expanding PACT into a broadly based engineering infrastructure. First, we must upgrade the prototype software currently handling low-level message passing between agents to improve reliability, scalability, and ease of use. The next version will likely build on a commercial substrate such as the OMG/CORBA[5] that can support multicast protocols in environments containing thousands of agents.

Second, the simulation and analysis services currently provided in PACT will be transformed into generic engineering services (for example, dynamics simulation and logic simulation) with published interfaces and ontologies, and made available on the Internet 24 hours a day. Additional services provided by remote Internet sites will then be brought on line. Initial experiments are already under way to make rapid prototyping facilities at Carnegie Mellon University and the University of Utah available as PACT services. Transforming such existing resources into network services involves, among other things, installing agent wrappers that enable them to communicate via KQML and KIF. We are distributing PACT toolkits to facilitate such integration.

Finally, the skeletal ontology and limited interactions that characterized the original planar manipulator scenario will be relaxed to support a broader range of electromechanical devices and concurrent engineering tasks. For example, any PACT agent should be able to modify its subsystem at any time, selectively triggering resimulations by any agents whose subsystems are affected by that change. These resimulations should be performed at the highest abstraction and granularity sufficient to assess the consequences. Each agent should watch for violations of design constraints and notify other agents who have registered an interest in them. ■

Acknowledgments

The experiments would never have gotten off the ground without the talents and determination of the PACT programming core, consisting of Greg Olsen, Brian Livezey, Jim McGuire, Sampath Srinivas, Amr Assal, Narinder Singh, and Vishal Sikka. In addition, several others contributed significant ideas and code, including Pierre Huyn, Bruce Hitson, Rich Pelavin, Randy Stiles, and Reed Letsinger. Each individual system has a cast of inspired researchers that is too long to list here.

Finally, PACT stands on the shoulders of ongoing knowledge-representation standardization efforts and the DARPA sponsorship that makes our efforts possible. The work described here was partially supported by DARPA Prime Contract DAAA15-91-C-0104 (monitored by the US Army Ballistic Research Laboratory), by the support of Hewlett-Packard Laboratories, by the Office of Naval Research Contract ONR N00014-92-J-1833, and by NASA Grants NAG -2-581 and NCC -2-537.

References

1. J.A. Fulton, "The Semantic Unification Metamodel: Technical Approach," Standards Working Document ISO TC184/

SC4/* WG3 N 81 (P0), IGES/PDES Organization, Dictionary/Methodology Committee, 1991. Contact James Fulton, Boeing Computer Services, PO Box 24346, MS 7L-64, Seattle, WA 98124-0346.

2. R. Neches et al., "Enabling Technology for Knowledge Sharing," *AI Magazine*, Vol. 12, No. 3, 1991, pp. 16-36.

3. T. Finin et al., "Specification of the KQML Agent-Communication Language," Tech. Report EIT TR 92-04, Enterprise Integration Technologies, Palo Alto, Calif., 1992.

4. "Knowledge Interchange Format, Version 3.0 Reference Manual," M.R. Genesereth and R.E. Fikes, eds., Tech. Report Logic-92-1, Computer Science Dept., Stanford Univ., Palo Alto, Calif., 1992.

5. "The Common Object Request Broker: Architecture and Specification," OMG Document #91.12.1, Object Management Group, Framingham, Mass., Dec. 1991.

6. T.R. Gruber, J.M. Tenenbaum, and J.C. Weber, "Toward a Knowledge Medium for Collaborative Product Development," *AI in Design '92*, J. Gero, ed., Kluwer Academic Publishers, Norwell, Mass., 1992, pp. 413-432.

The *Redux′* Server

Charles Petrie
MCC Enterprise Integration Division
3500 West Balcones Center Drive
Austin, TX 78759
petrie@mcc.com

Abstract

Redux′ is a subset of the full REDUX model[7]. The latter performs problem solving. In contrast Redux′ does not and acts only as a decision maintenance server. It takes objects of types defined in an ontology of decision components and maintains dependencies between them. Redux′ is domain-independent. The dependency relationships are maintained on the basis of proposition type and not content, except for some string matching. Redux′ servers are proposed as a mechanism for federating heterogeneous design agents by encapsulating their design decisions within a simple model and providing coordination services, especially for design revision. This proposal is described within the context of the SHADE and PACT projects.

1 Introduction

The SHADE and PACT[10] projects take a *federating*[6, 9] approach to the problem of coordinating distributed design. Individual software systems, used by the people to accomplish their part of the design, are idiosyncratic and may not work with each other.[1] Since it is usually impractical if not impossible to impose a unifying structure on all systems, the most reasonable solution is to provide a framework that allows systems to coordinate as needed, while allowing them to be unchanged locally. This should allow, for example, subcontractors to develop their subdesigns and coordinate with each other over a wide-area network.

An important objective is to reduce the *semantic unification* required to connect two software systems. Each system will say something about its domain that the other system should "understand" to some degree. For instance, one CAD system configuring components and another CAD system designing mechanical platforms may have to agree at least that a *motor shaft* is round and requires support. But the former system may not need to worry about the shaft weight and the latter may not need to know about motor voltage. So it is possible to minimize how much the two systems have to agree upon the semantics of the terms that each formally represents.

The PACT approach is for participating agents to communicate through a language, KQML[3], that specifies a small set of performatives, such as *assert*, *retract*, or *query*. This isolates the predicates on which the various agents must agree, and the degree to which the semantics are common. In an example from [2], one agent mentions the domain-specific predicates **closed-form** and **pmx** in an assertion encapsulated in a KQML message using the domain-independent performative *interested-in*. This use of the performative identifies at least two points at which participating agents must perform semantic unification, rather than trying to unify complete models. The general principle is that *a standard communications language can help minimize semantic unification* because it allows agents to specify the connection points between them.

However, the KQML performatives have weak semantics. No inferences can be drawn from the message types. An *interested-in* message says something about when messages should be sent to whom. But there is no theory of message types that would allow distributed agents to make value-added inferences.

What one needs is a model of interactions among systems that minimizes the domain knowledge required for agents to cooperate. REDUX[7] is a general model of design and planning that emphasizes the propagation of the effects of change. We propose that it can be used as a framework for communication between systems. To that end, we have extracted a subset, *Redux′*, of the general model and show how it can be used to encapsulate systems in a way that pro-

[1] The general version of the problem of getting heterogeneous systems to cooperate in a larger task is known as *Enterprise Integration*.

vides significant functionality in return for a small requirement for formal structuring. If the requirement presented here is not small enough, then perhaps no general model is adequate for the problem of cooperating distributed design and planning.

The *Redux'* theory is formally described below in Section 3. This formal description is intended for conversion to Ontolingua[5] or some other KIF[4]-based system for portability. The informal idea is that *Redux'* provides a theory for determining the effects upon decisions of changing conditions and the making and revision of other decisions.

Redux' is presented here as a server. Clients send it messages about *decisions* and related types of objects. These messages are sent either by the user or by daemons in application code. When selected lines of application code are executed, such daemons send the appropriate messages to the server. The output is other messages, representing the change propagation, sent to the user, or receptor daemons. This is shown schematically in Figure 1.

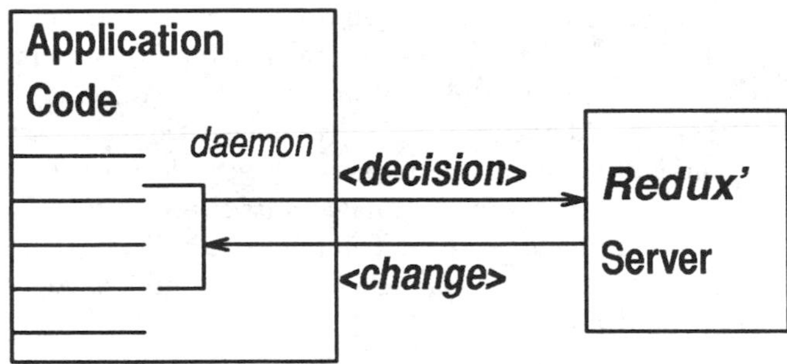

Figure 1: Decision Server

The input messages contain strings that are used by the server for object matching, but otherwise the server does not understand anything about the application domain. The result is that client applications are encapsulated by the *Redux'* object types, of which there is (currently) a small number.

We describe here how such a service could be used to coordinate distributed work, as in SHADE and PACT. Instead of a central server, we propose that each user has a local copy of *Redux'* and these local copies talk to each other, perhaps through PACT *facilitators*. In effect, each copy of *Redux'* becomes an "agent in a box" for each user.[2] We begin with an example, loosely adapted from PACT and SHADE.

[2]The knowledge acquisition problem is difficult: a phased implementation is suggested in [8].

2 Example

In the PACT/SHADE planar manipulator redesign scenario, the motor used is discovered to be inadequate for a new load specification. A larger motor is substituted. The change is annotated in a journal. Somehow, *change notifications* must be sent to other engineers. To quote from [10],

> One is for the manufacturing engineer responsible for milling the frame for the manipulator. The new motor has a larger shaft diameter, requiring a larger hole in the mounting bracket. The size of the hole must be increased in the CAD specification, and process planning tool invoked to verify that the specified bore hole is still within manufacturability limits.

The notification problem is determining who needs to know of what changes. SHADE proposes to solve the notification problem by allowing the individual users to write "relevance theories" that can infer that an agent should be notified of a given change. An example of such a theory is

> if a component is replaced, then the features of the replacement part (weight, cost, etc.) potentially change.

REDUX provides a relevance theory that generalizes much of what might otherwise have to be repeated in specific theories.

2.1 REDUX Model

We illustrate the REDUX model with the PACT planar manipulator example. In what follows, we use the notation that *ENG-n* is an engineer, or an engineering software system, and *RDX-n* is the local copy of *Redux'*, which is a server implementing a partial REDUX model. We will refer to the latter as computational "agents".

We start with the power engineer who chooses a motor for the artifact. As shown in Figure 2, given a *goal* $G1$ of something like *Choose Motor* for planar manipulator *PL-1*, engineer *ENG-1* makes a choice of *motor-1*. The result of this decision, say D_{11}, is an *assignment* of *motor-1* to the "motor slot" of the design and perhaps a *subgoal*, say $G2$; the design of the encoding electronics required for such a direct drive motor.

In addition, a *decision* may have a *contingency* associated with it. For example, in this case, the possible unavailability of the motor is an unexpected future

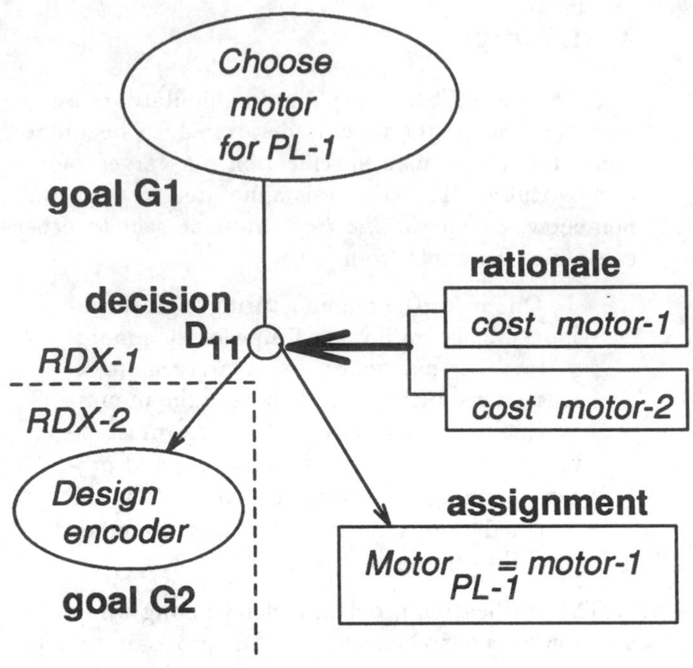

Figure 2: A Decision

event that would automatically invalidate the choice of motor.

Decisions are also said to have an *optimality*. This depends upon the validity of the decision *rationale*: why one operator was picked over the others in a conflict set. This reasoning is generally domain-specific. Suppose there was one other possible choice, *motor-2*, and *motor-1* was chosen because it was cheaper. This *rationale* may or may not be recorded. If it were, it would consist of the costs for the two motors and is indicated by the bold arrow in Figure 2.

This decision by *ENG-1* is defined by the goal, the contingency, the rationale, the assignment, and the subgoal and is recorded in *RDX-1* as a set of dependencies around the decision object D_{11}. The engineer (or program) would generate such a decision by sending a message to the *Redux'* server. While we do not specify the command language here, an example message would be:

MAKE-DECISION
goal: ``choose motor for planar manipulator''
assignment: ``motor is catalog number 701''
subgoal: ``design d-drive encoder for 701''
contingency: ``catalog number 701 unavailable''
rationale: {``cost of 701 is $200'',
``cost of 702 is $250''}

Notice that the strings encapsulated by the *Redux'* types (formally specified in Section 3) are arbitrary, and need not be as structured as suggested by the figures. The human or application program is free to say whatever makes sense, with the caveat that these strings may need to be unified with those of other agents, so that the simpler, the better.

2.2 Revision Services

The REDUX model determines what pieces of the domain model are used for what change propagation, and, thus, what revision services to provide to the design engineer. If *RDX-1* learns that *motor-1* is unavailable, then decision D_{11} becomes invalid and several inferences follow from the REDUX model. The assignment of this motor (and any other resulting from this decision) becomes invalid. Any constraint violations in which they participated become moot. The goal $G1$ is no longer reduced: *ENG-1* should be notified of this effect so that the goal may be placed back on the problem solving task agenda. The choice of *motor-1* is no longer an option when this task is reconsidered.

In addition, subgoal $G2$ becomes invalid. If this had been distributed as a subtask to electrical engineer *ENG-2*, then *RDX-1* would notify *RDX-2* that $G2$ was no longer valid. If it had not yet been reduced, *RDX-2* would notify *ENG-2* to remove it from the task agenda. If $G2$ had been reduced by, say, decision D_{21}, then D_{21} becomes suboptimal and its subgoals invalid. Any assignments resulting from D_{21} are still valid, but the problem solver is informed that it should consider retracting D_{21}.[3]

Alternatively, suppose that *motor-1* continues to be available, but the costs of the two motors change. *RDX-1* will notify *ENG-1* that decision D_{11} may have become suboptimal and should be reevaluated. This is a local action and would not affect any other agent. Thus, the case of possible loss of optimality is treated by REDUX very differently than the loss of decision validity.[4]

Redux' will also detect domain-independent cases of optimality loss. For instance, if a goal becomes invalid, then the decision reducing it becomes subop-

[3] It is easy to modify the REDUX theory so that D_{21} would automatically become invalid. Application studies by Juergen Paulokat and Helmuth Ritzer at the Universität Kaiserslautern indicate that this stronger condition is sometimes desirable. However, in the general case, this metadecision should not be automatic. For instance, the effect of the suboptimal decision may only be to add a flange, but undoing the decision will mean undoing much design work.

[4] The same notification would occur if goal $G1$ became invalid, except that $G2$ would also become invalid, which would affect other agents.

timal, regardless of the decision rationale. There is also a special case of domain-independent optimality involving backtracking that is in which the REDUX model is especially useful. This is discussed below in Section 2.4.

2.3 Notification and Connection

To complete the PACT example, there is another engineer, *ENG-3* that is designing the connecting rod between the motor and the manipulator. Let the goal of doing so be $G3$. Suppose that to make a decision reducing this goal, *ENG-3* has to know the shaft diameter of the motor *ENG-1* has selected because there must be a hole in the connecting rod to receive the motor shaft. PACT describes a reasonable way for these agents to proceed, once some humans have determined which agents need to talk and have manually performed the required semantic unification.[5] In PACT, *ENG-3* asks *ENG-1* to tell it the identity of the motor selected when it is chosen. Then, *ENG-3* uses this information to look up the shaft diameter in a parts catalog, maintained by yet another agent.

There is another general principle that is useful here: ***requests for information should be recorded and used for notification upon revision of the information.*** This is the basic principle behind the distributed truth maintenance system of [1]. In this case, the fact that *ENG-3* needed the motor identity from *ENG-1* implies that *ENG-1* should always tell *ENG-3* if the motor identity changes. There is no requirement for a domain-specific SHADE relevance theory that if a component changes, its features may change. *ENG-3* does not have to go to the trouble of stating such an interest. The PACT architecture should have *ENG-1* notify *ENG-3* automatically whenever the motor identity changes.

There are several possible ways that the above notification principle could be structured in REDUX. The motor identity could be recorded as part of the *rationale* for decision D_{31} that reduces $G3$ into other goals and assignments. If D_{11} is ever invalidated, then *RDX-1* identifies the assignments affected. At least one of these assignments is the motor identity, *motor-1*. *RDX-1* then notifies *RDX-3* which informs *ENG-3* that decision D_{31} to drill a particular size hole in the connecting rod may be suboptimal and need to be retracted[6].

[5] Decreasing the human involvement in this process is a very difficult problem not addressed here.

[6] Unless the decision was already committed, perhaps by drilling a limited supply of material.

For this distributed case however, let us use a ***dependent assignment***.[7] In this example, the size of the hole in the connecting rod is an assignment associated with D_{31} that must be valid to satisfy goal $G3$ as before. But unlike the usual case, this assignment depends for its validity on If D_{11}. The two *Redux'* agents, *RDX-1* and *RDX-3*, create a virtual link between this assignment and D_{11}, as if that decision had made two assignments instead of one. Such a link would create a stronger dependency between the two systems. Now, if D_{11} became invalid, *ENG-3* would be notified that goal $G3$ is no longer reduced or satisfied, as shown in Figure 3, because of the invalid dependent assignment.[8]

2.4 Optimality and Backtracking

So far, the example covers the simple case in which *ENG-1* retracts the choice of *motor-1* and *ENG-2* and *ENG-3* are subsequently notified. This was the case described in [2] because the first motor choice was determined to be inadequate for the load. In REDUX, the inadequacy of the motor would be represented as a constraint violation. *ENG-1* tells *RDX-1*, possibly through an application daemon, to reject D_{11} with a reason consisting of the propositions of the motor assignment, the constraint, and the load assertion.[9] Because $G1$ is no longer reduced, *RDX-1* prompts *ENG-1* to rechoose a motor. When *ENG-1* chooses, say, *motor-2*, *RDX-1* records the decision rationale as dependent upon the rejection of D_{11}. The new decision, D_{12}, is now propagated just as D_{11} was, notifying *ENG-3* of the new hole size of the connecting rod.

But this example can be made much more interesting, and possibly realistic, by supposing not that *motor-1* was determined to be inadequate, but that it conflicted with some other decision. Suppose *ENG-4* worries about the ability to actually manufacture parts and had decided (say in decision D_{41}) to use some exotic metal for the connecting rod that can not accommodate the right shape and hole size for *motor-1*.

In the REDUX model, this is represented as a constraint violation. Global constraint satisfaction is a problem for which *Redux'* servers offer little help. Constraints are that which are violated by assignments, but it is up to the problem solvers to detect constraint violations and say which assignments need to be rejected in order to resolve the violation. *Redux'*

[7] This is an extension of the basic REDUX model of [7].

[8] $G3$ no longer has a *supporting-decision* as defined in Definition 4 in Section 3.

[9] Rejection reasons are formally described in Definitions 5 and 6 in Section 3.

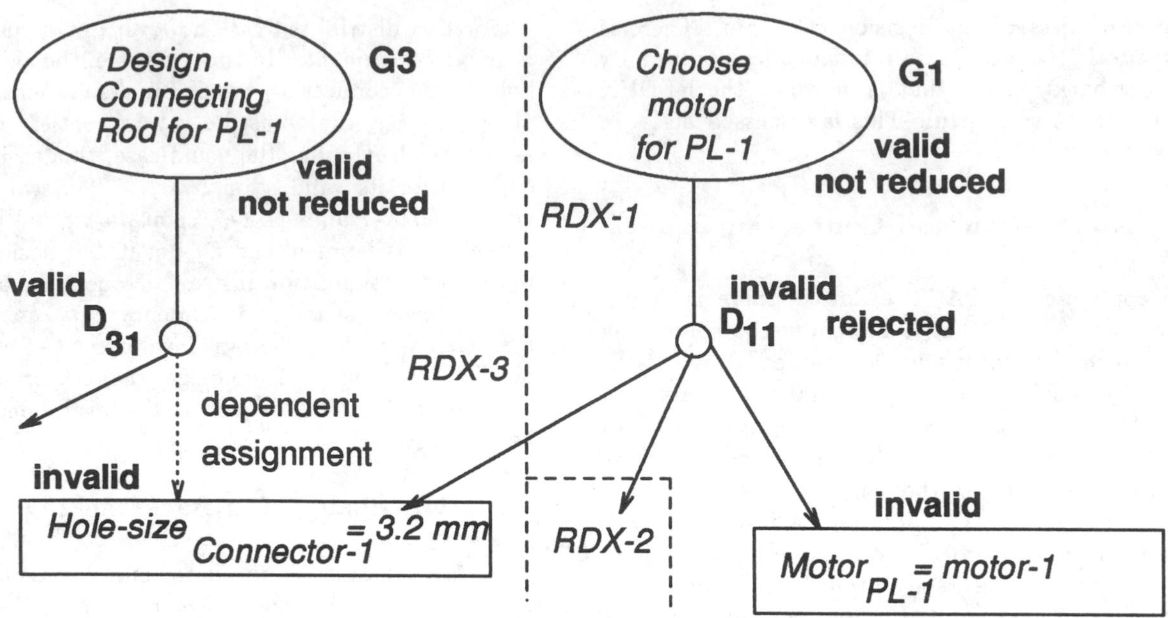

Figure 3: Motor Redesign with Dependent Assignment

servers only retract the necessary decisions and propagate the consequences. Semantic unification of variables and values in assignments is the crucial problem and we can only assume that it has somehow been done here.

Some engineer must give some *Redux'* a statement that some set of assignments are in conflict. The *Redux'* servers can indicate which decisions are responsible and what the effects of rejecting any of them. Suppose in this case, the engineers agree to reject the current hole size with a command that combines the conflict and the resolution sets:

CONSTRAINT-VIOLATION-RESOLUTION
conflicts: {``motor hole size is 3.2mm'',
``connector rod is titanium''}
culprits: {``motor hole size is 3.2mm''}

Because of the dependent assignment, *RDX-1* rejects decision D_{11}, with *motor-1*. When *ENG-1* (perhaps sometime later) chooses *motor-2*, he may or may not include the choice of exotic metal (say, titanium) explicitly in the rationale for this new decision, but the above command will cause *RDX-1* to do so. The new decision D_{12} automatically includes in its rationale the rejection of D_{11}. This rejection itself has a reason dependent on the choice of exotic metal, derived from the statement of the constraint violation. Both of these reasons are produced as part of the REDUX model. This is explained in more detail in Section 3.3.

Now we have the special case of domain-independent optimality. The *Redux'* servers may not really understand anything about the manufacture of the artifact, but dependencies have been established between the optimality of D_{12} and the validity of decision D_{41}. If *ENG-4* ever rejects the use of the exotic metal, then *RDX-4* and *RDX-1* conspire to notify *ENG-1* that decision D_{12} is now suboptimal and there is now an ***opportunity*** of improving the design by using *motor-1*.

The decision connections here are shown in Figure 4. The bold arrows represent reasons. The one from D_{41} to D_{11} represents the reason for rejecting D_{11}, and the one from D_{11} to D_{12} the reason for the optimality of D_{12}. When D_{41} becomes invalid, there is no longer a good reason for the rejection of D_{11}, and thus no longer a good rationale for D_{12}, which then becomes suboptimal.

However, *ENG-1* need not see all of these connections. If *ENG-1* is human, then an appropriate interface, such as one illustrated in Figure 5, may be provided. Such an interface would alert *ENG-1* to the opportunity and explain the reason for it to as deep a level as desired.

We now give the formal description of the model that performs the services in this example. The model consists of an ontology and a theory: a set of entailments that constrain the type relations as well as the

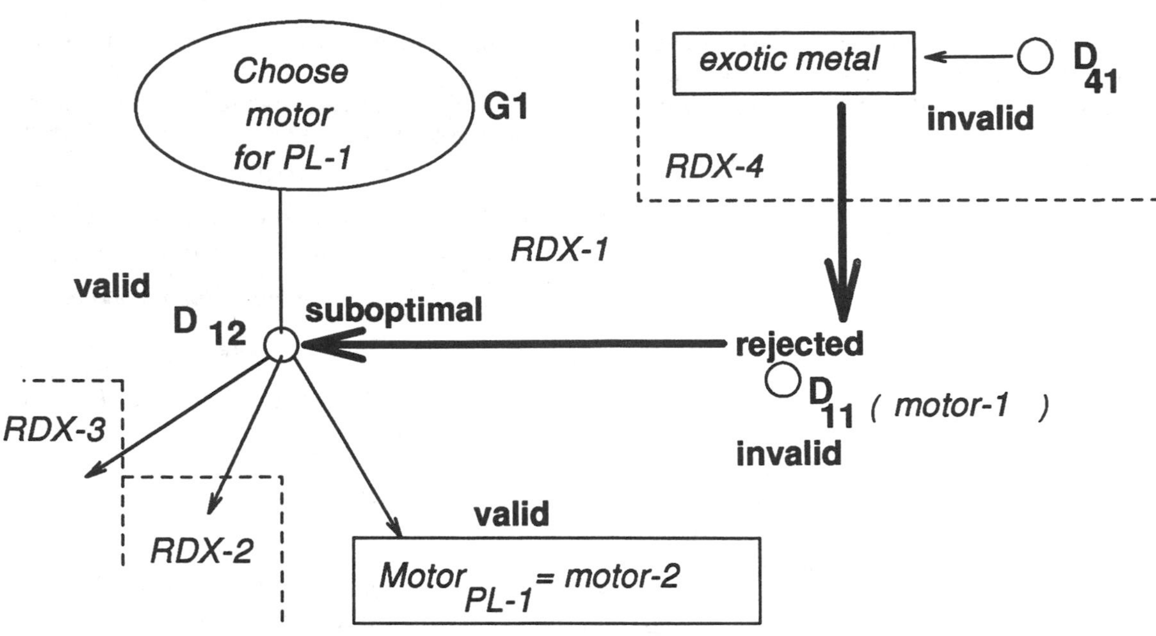

Figure 4: A Redesign Opportunity

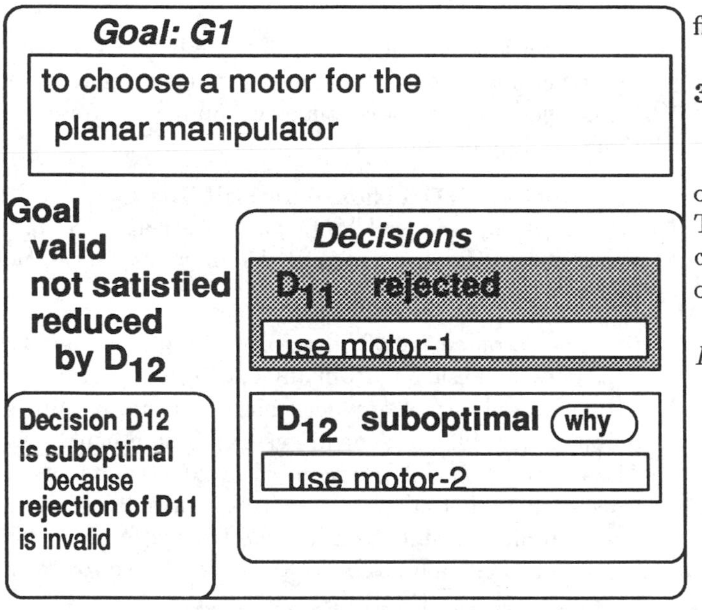

Figure 5: *ENG-1* View

values of the attributes of instances of the types in the ontology.

3 Theory

All input to *Redux'* are commands with arguments that are objects of types, or alternatively, classes, defined below.

3.1 Ontology

Here we define seven *Redux'* types of objects. Each object o has an associated type T, denoted by $o{:}T$. There are slots (binary relations) associated with each class, which map the objects to values consisting of other objects.

The four types that carry special significance for *Redux'* are:

- *<decision>*,
- *<goal>*,
- *<reason>*, and
- *<assignment>*.

Domain-specific computations are captured as *decisions* that reduce *goals* by making *assignments* and new goals. *Reasons* are captured for decisions and their rejections.

There are also three more generic types of objects. The first generic type is *<string>*. Domain-specific knowledge may be represented as strings, which are then encapsulated in *Redux'* object attributes, or slots. String matching is assumed as a primitive operation and is indicated by "=". The second generic type is

<proposition> limited to predicates defined in Definition 5. The third generic type is that of *datum*, which has but one slot, *datum-value*, with a single value of type *string*.

Decisions have the following slots:

Slot Name	Cardinality	Value Type
<name>	single	*string*
<objective>	single	*goal*
<contingency>	multiple	*string*
<rationale>	multiple	*reason*
<assertion>	multiple	*assignment*
<new-goal>	multiple	*goal*
<rejection>	multiple	*reason*
<dependent>	multiple	*assignment*

The relation *name* is a one-to-one function between *decisions* and the set of all *strings*. The following predicates take *decisions* as single arguments:

- *<valid>*,
- *<optimal>*,
- *<rejected>*,
- *<best>*,
- *<committed>* and
- *<retracted>*.

These predicates and the rest below in this section are defined in Section 3.2.

The type *goal* has the following slots:

Slot Name	Cardinality	Value Type
<consequent>	single	*string*
<supergoal>	multiple	*goal*
<subgoal>	multiple	*goal*
<supporting-decision>	multiple	*decision*

The relation *consequent* is a one-to-one function between *goals* and the set of all *strings*.

The following predicates take *goals* as single arguments:

- *<valid-goal>*,
- *<reduced>*, and
- *<satisfied>*.

The type *assignment* has only one slot, *<variable-value>*, with a single value of type *string*. The predicate *<valid-asg>* takes *assignments* as a single argument. The type *reason* has just one slot, *<conditions>*, which is a set of *propositions*. The predicate *<case>* takes *reasons* as a single argument.

In order to discuss how decisions relate to one another, certain slot values are required so that the decisions are sufficiently defined.

Definition 1 (Decision Completeness) *A decision is completely defined just when:*

- *There exists a unique value for name.*
- *There exists exactly one value for objective.*
- *There must be at least one value for assertion or new-goal.*■

3.2 Dependencies

The following describes the theory that defines relations among elements of the ontology that depend upon slot values and so determine *Redux′* services. We begin with some convenient notation. We say there is a database $\mathcal{S}$ of datum strings such that $s \in \mathcal{S} \Leftrightarrow \exists$ *d:datum* such that *datum-value(d s)*.[10]

A decision D is *admissible* iff there is no $c \in \mathcal{S}$ that matches one of its contingencies (no datum matches a contingency) and no contingency matches an assignment of any decision.

Definition 2 (Decision Admissibility)
∀D:decision, admissible(D) ⇔ ∀ c:string such that contingency(D c), c ∉ 𝒮∧ ∄ A:assignment such that variable-value(A c).■

The second part of admissibility requires that no assignments resulting from any one decision invalidate the admissibility of any decision; i.e., proof of admissibility should not depend on any assignment. All conflicts should be represented in constraints. Thus decisions monotonically extend problem solving. Nonmonotonicity results from either changes in the world that invalidate admissibility or as a response to a constraint violation that causes retraction.

Complete decisions are *valid* unless they have been retracted (not possible if they have been committed) or a contingency has occurred.

Definition 3 (Decision Validity)
The following are the validity relations for completely defined decisions:

[10] Alternatively, we could define a predicate, say *<Told>*, that takes *strings* as a single argument. The proposition *Told(s:string)* is true just when ∃ *d:datum* such that *datum-value(d s)*. The difference is only in notation.

- ∀ *D:decision, committed(D)* ⇔ *name(D n)* ∧ *"committed(n)"* ∈ $\mathcal{S}$.
- ∀ *D:decision, retracted(D)* ⇔ *name(D n)* ∧ *"retracted(n)"* ∈ $\mathcal{S}$ ∧ *not committed(D)*[11].
- ∀ *D:decision, valid(D)* ⇔ *admissible(D)* ∧ *not retracted(D)*.■

Goals are reduced, and ultimately satisfied, by decisions. Thus, reduction and satisfaction depend upon decision validity.

Definition 4 (Goal Satisfaction/Reduction) *The following are the reduction and satisfaction relations for goals:*

- ∀ *G, G':goal, supergoal(G' G)* ∧ *subgoal(G G')* ⇔ ∃ *D:decision such that objective(D G)* ∧ *new-goal(D G')* ∧ *valid(D)*.
- ∀ *G':goal, valid-goal(G')* ⇔ {∃ *G:goal such that subgoal(G G')* ∧ *valid-goal(G)* } ∨ { *consequent(G' g)* ∧ *"valid-goal(g)"* ∈ $\mathcal{S}$ }.
- ∀ *A:assignment, valid-asg(A)* ⇔ ∃ *D:decision such that assertion(D A)* ∧ *valid(D)*.
- ∀ *G:goal, D:decision, supporting-decision(G D)* ⇔ *objective(D G)* ∧ ∀ *A:assignment such that assertion(D A), valid-asg(A)* ∧ ∀ *A:assignment such that dependent(D A), valid-asg(A)*.
- ∀ *G:goal, reduced(G)* ⇔ ∃ *D:decision such that supporting-decision(G D)* ∧ ∀ *G':goal such that new-goal(D G'), valid-goal(G')*.
- ∀ *G:goal, satisfied(G)* ⇔ ∃ *D:decision such that supporting-decision(G D)* ∧ ∀ *G':goal such that new-goal(D G'), satisfied(G')*.■

Notice that the satisfaction entailment does not depend upon the validity of a decision but upon the status of its results. A decision may not be valid. But if its assignments are valid and the subgoals are satisfied by other decisions, then the decision is virtually valid; the effect is the same as if it were. Notice also that this entailment holds for a decision with no subgoals and only assignments. This is the leaf node for goal satisfaction.

Decision *optimality* depends upon having a valid *reason* for the decision *rationale* and none for the *rejection*. The *conditions*[12] value of a *reason* consists of a set of propositions, treated like a conjunct. There are only three kinds of propositions that may be in this set. One is that some assignment is *valid-asg*. Another is that some decision is *rejected*. The other is that some string is in $\mathcal{S}$.

Definition 5 (Reason Validity) ∀ *R:reason, case(R)* ⇔ $\forall \rho \in conditions(R)$, $\{\rho = valid\text{-}asg(A{:}assignment) \vee \rho = rejected(D_i) \vee \rho = \exists s \in \mathcal{S}\} \wedge \rho$.■

The rationale or rejection being the case then determines decision optimality.

Definition 6 (Decision Optimality) *The following are the optimality relations for completely defined decisions:*

- ∀ *D:decision, rejected(D)* ⇔ ∃ *R:reason such that rejection(D R)* ∧ *case(R)*.
- ∀ *D:decision, best(D)* ⇔ ∃ *R:reason such that rationale(D R)* ∧ *case(R)*.
- ∀ *D:decision, optimal(D)* ⇐ *committed(D)* ∧ *admissible(D)*.
- ∀ *D:decision, optimal(D)* ⇐ *not rejected(D)* ∧ *admissible(D)* ∧ *best(D)* ∧ ∃ *G:goal such that valid-goal(G)* ∧ *objective(D G)*.■

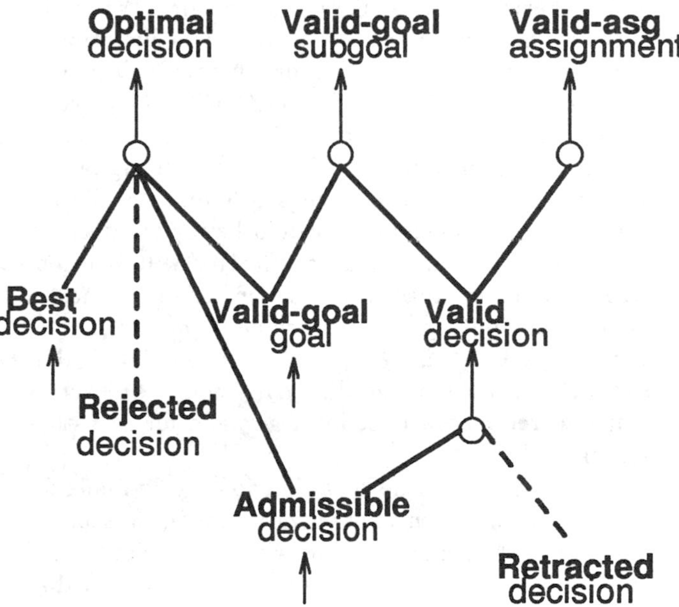

Figure 6: Standard Decision Dependencies

We conclude this section with Figure 6, which illustrates the major dependencies defined in the theory above. In this network, nodes are supported by

[11] This is negation by failure.

[12] In Definition 5, we treat this single-valued slot as a function.

one or more *justifications*, denoted by arrows pointing to the node supported. The justification itself is supported by positive (solid lines) and negative (dashed lines) links to other nodes. There is reason to believe a node when it has a valid justification. A justification is *valid* when there is reason to believe each node with a positive link and no reason to believe any node with a negative link.[13] For example, a subgoal is valid as long as its supergoal and parent decision are valid. A decision is valid as long as it is admissible, for whatever reason, and not retracted.[14]

3.3 Behavior

Messages to *Redux'* servers from client problem solvers use a protocol consisting of commands with semantics. We specify here only the non-obvious aspects of such a protocol, previously suggested in Section 2. The commands take typed objects defined in the theory in Section 3 as arguments.

Obviously there are commands for adding and deleting strings directly to and from the database $\mathcal{S}$, and for making and rejecting decisions. The REDUX model imposes some restrictions on these commands. For instance, a decision may not be made to reduce a goal that is already reduced. A rejection reason must be valid, though it may be empty.

The example in Section 2.4 deserves some detail as it otherwise may strike one as magic. When the client problem solver detects a constraint violation among assignments, it may report this to *Redux'* with a *CONSTRAINT-VIOLATION-RESOLUTION* command, which takes a (conjunctive) list L_1 of the offending assignments, a list of any contributing propositions that may occur as strings in $\mathcal{S}$, and a resolution list L_2 of assignments that should be made invalid to resolve the constraint violation. *Redux'* will then construct a rejection reason R consisting of a conjunction of the contributing propositions and *valid-asg(A)* for each element $A \in L_1, \notin L_2$. For every decision D that supports an assignment $A \in L_2$, *Redux'* will act as if it had received a rejection command for D with a reason of R.

Additionally, whenever a decision D_2 is made for some goal for which another decision D_1 was previously made but since rejected with reason R, *Redux'* will conjoin *rejected*(D_1) to any rationale of D_2 that the client may supply, including *nil*. Thus the optimality rationale of the second decision depends upon the validity of the reason for the rejection of the first.

In the example in Section 2.4, upon being told that there is a constraint violation involving some feature of the exotic metal chosen in decision D_{41} and the hole-size of the connector, and that the latter assignment should be made the culprit in the conflict; *RDX-1* determines that D_{11} must be rejected and constructs a rejection reason consisting of the exotic metal feature. When decision D_{21} is made, the rejection of D_{11} is automatically a part of its rationale. If D_{41} ever becomes invalid, *ENG-1* will be informed by *RDX-1* that there is an opportunity to reconsider the original choice of motor, which was decision D_{11}.

4 Summary

There are two general principles that may be used to reduce the amount of human work necessary to enable heterogeneous systems to cooperate in distributed design in systems such as PACT and SHADE.

A standard communications language minimizes semantic unification. KQML provides a small set of primitives that allow agents to communicate the terms that matter to them. This facilitates semantic unification because it points to just the connections that must be made, rather than having to unify complete models of heterogeneous agents. *Information exchanged for the purpose of design can be used for design revision.* The simplest case is that PACT should keep track of requests for information and notify requesters when that information changes.

The Redux' server improves the use of these principles. A subset of REDUX primitives adds semantics to the syntactic KQML primitives. This further determines the points of agreement on domain semantics between the systems. REDUX also specifies specific ways that change should be propagated in a distributed design, reducing the necessity for manual change notice specifications.

Another important relation of this paper to the PACT/SHADE work is that the REDUX model is a theory for some class of design, and in that sense is a reusable ontology of the kind proposed in the SHADE project and to be represented in Ontolingua. It is different in that it is not an ontology of design domain objects, but an ontology that can be used to encapsulate such objects.

Finally we add that this is a proposal for a kind of architecture in the same spirit as PACT and SHADE and, indeed, to be built on top of them. The REDUX model has previously been implemented as a full

[13] This is also known as a *truth maintenance* graph.

[14] The reader will note that not all of the required dependencies (e.g., goal satisfaction) are represented here. See [7] for detail not possible to give here.

problem solver useful for a certain class of problems as described in [7]. The idea presented here is to separate out the part of the model that performs decision maintenance and provide it as a network server to other problem solvers as a way to federate heterogeneous agents.

Implementing this proposal will undoubtedly require extensions and modifications to the basic model, as have already been suggested by the PACT experiment and work done at the University of Kaiserslautern. The hypothesis suggested here to be tested is whether it is possible to develop a structured encapsulation of heterogeneous design computations that provides sufficient added functionality to overcome the cost of structuring. The answer must be determined empirically and we intend to do so in cooperation with the SHADE and PACT projects.

Acknowledgements

Jay Weber was helpful in discussing the PACT example and REDUX applications. Tom Gruber originally suggested somehow posing REDUX as a server for representation by Ontolingua and has contributed to the formalization of the theory. Juergen Paulokat has also supplied valuable assistance. This work was partially funded by the Universität Kaiserslautern.

References

[1] Bridgeland, D. and M. Huhns, "Distributed Truth Maintenance," *Proc. AAAI-90*, pp. 72-77, 1990.

[2] Cutkosky, M., et al., "PACT An Experiment in Integrating Concurrent Engineering Systems,", To appear in *IEEE Computer*, January, 1993. Also available as EIT TR 92-02.1, Enterprise Integration Technologies, Palo Alto.

[3] Finin, T., McKay, D., and Fritzson, R., "An Overview of KQML: A Knowledge Query and Manipulation Language," Technical Report, Computer Science Dept., U. of Maryland, 1992.

[4] Genesereth, M. and Fikes, R., "Knowledge Interchange Format, Version 3.0 Reference Manual," Technical Report KSL 91-1, Stanford University Logic Group, 1992.

[5] Gruber, T., "Ontolingua: A Mechanism to Support Portable Ontologies," Technical Report KSL 91-66, Stanford University, Knowledge Systems Laboratory, 1992.

[6] Heimbinger, D. and McLeod D. "A Federated Architecture for Information Management," *ACM Transactions on Office Information Systems*, 3(3), January 1985.

[7] Petrie, C., "Constrained Decision Revision," *Proc. AAAI-92*. Also MCC TR EID-414-91, December, 1991.

[8] Petrie, C. "A Minimalist Model for Coordination", AAAI-92 Workshop on Design Rationale. Also in *Enterprise Intergration Modeling*, MIT Press, October, 1992.

[9] Petrie, C. "Introduction", *Enterprise Intergration Modeling*, MIT Press, October, 1992.

[10] Tenenbaum, J., Weber, J., and Gruber, T., "Enterprise Integration: Lessons from SHADE and PACT," *Enterprise Intergration Modeling*, C. Petrie ed., MIT Press, October, 1992.

Issues in Automated Negotiation and Electronic Commerce: Extending the Contract Net Framework

Tuomas Sandholm and Victor Lesser *
{sandholm, lesser}@cs.umass.edu
University of Massachusetts at Amherst
Computer Science Department
Amherst, MA 01003

Abstract

In this paper we discuss a number of previously unaddressed issues that arise in automated negotiation among self-interested agents whose rationality is bounded by computational complexity. These issues are presented in the context of iterative task allocation negotiations. First, the reasons why such agents need to be able to choose the stage and level of commitment dynamically are identified. A protocol that allows such choices through conditional commitment breaking penalties is presented. Next, the implications of bounded rationality are analyzed. Several tradeoffs between allocated computation and negotiation benefits and risk are enumerated, and the necessity of explicit local deliberation control is substantiated. Techniques for linking negotiation items and multiagent contracts are presented as methods for escaping local optima in the task allocation process. Implementing both methods among self-interested bounded rational agents is discussed. Finally, the problem of message congestion among self-interested agents is described, and alternative remedies are presented.

1 Introduction

The importance of automated negotiation systems is likely to increase [Office of Technology Assesment (OTA), 1994]. One reason is the growth of a fast and inexpensive standardized communication infrastructure (EDI, NII, KQML [Finin *et al.*, 1992], Telescript [General Magic, Inc., 1994] etc.), over which separately designed agents belonging to different organizations can interact in an open environment in real-time, and safely carry out transactions [Kristol *et al.*, 1994; Sandholm and Lesser, 1995d]. Secondly, there is an industrial trend towards *agile enterprises*: small, organizational overhead avoiding enterprises that form short term alliances to be able to respond to larger and more diverse orders than they individually could. Such ventures can take advantage of economies of scale when they are available, but do not suffer from diseconomies of scale. This concept paper explores the implications of performing such negotiations where agents are *self-interested* (SI) [1] and must make negotiation decisions in real-time with *bounded or costly computation resources*.

We cast such negotiations in the following domain independent framework. Each agent has a (possibly empty) set of tasks and a (possibly empty) set of resources it can use to handle tasks. These sets change due to domain events, e.g. new tasks arriving or resources breaking down. The agents can subcontract tasks to other agents by paying a compensation. This subcontracting process can involve breaking a task into a number of subtasks handled by different agents, or clustering a number of tasks into a supertask. A task transfer is profitable from the global perspective if the contractee can handle the task less expensively than the contractor, or if the contractor cannot handle it at all, but the contractee can. So, the problem has two levels: a *global task allocation problem*, and each agent's *local combinatorial optimization problem* defined by the agent's current tasks and resources. The goal of each agent is to maximize its *payoff* which is defined as its income minus its costs. Income is received for handling tasks, and costs are incurred by using resources to handle the tasks. We restrict ourselves to domains where the feasibility and cost of handling a task do not depend on what other agents do with their resources or how they divide tasks among themselves, but do depend on the other tasks that the agent has [2]. The global solution can be evaluated from a social welfare viewpoint according to the sum of the agents' payoffs.

Reaching good solutions for the global task allocation problem is difficult with SI agents, e.g. because they may not truthfully share all information. The problem is further complicated by the agents' bounded rationality: local decisions are suboptimal due to the inability

*This research was supported by ARPA contract N00014-92-J-1698. The content does not necessarily reflect the position or the policy of the Government and no official endorsement should be inferred. T. Sandholm also funded by a University of Massachusetts Graduate School Fellowship, Leo and Regina Wainstein Foundation, Heikki and Hilma Honkanen Foundation, and Ella and George Ehrnrooth Foundation.

[1] In domains where agents represent different real world organizations, each agent designer will want its agent to do as well as it can without concern for other agents. Conversely, some domains are inherently composed of benevolent agents. For example, in a single factory scheduling problem, each work cell can be represented by an agent. If the cells do not have private goals, the agents should act benevolently.

[2] Such domains are a superset of what [Rosenschein and Zlotkin, 1994] call Task Oriented Domains, and intersect their State Oriented and Worth Oriented Domains.

to precisely compute the value associated with accepting a task. This computation is especially hard if the feasibility and cost of handling a task depend on what other tasks an agent has. These problems are exacerbated by the uncertainty of an open environment in which new agents and new tasks arrive - thus previous decisions may be suboptimal in light of new information.

The original contract net protocol (CNP) [Smith, 1980] did not explicitly deal with these issues, which we think must be taken into account if agents are to operate effectively in a wide range of automated negotiation domains. A first step towards extending the CNP to deal with these issues was the work on TRACONET [Sandholm, 1993]. It provided a formal model for bounded rational (BR) self-interested agents to make announcing, bidding and awarding decisions. It used a simple static approximation scheme for *marginal cost*[3] calculation to make these decisions. The choice of a contractee is based solely on these marginal cost estimates. The monetary payment mechanism allows quantitative tradeoffs between alternatives in an agent's negotiation strategy. Within DAI, bounded rationality (approximate processing) has been studied with cooperative agents, but among SI agents, perfect rationality has been widely assumed, e.g. [Rosenschein and Zlotkin, 1994; Ephrati and Rosenschein, 1991; Kraus *et al.*, 1992]. We argue that in most real multiagent applications, resource-bounded computation will be an issue, and that bounded rationality has profound implications on both negotiation protocols and strategies.

Although the work on TRACONET was a first step towards this end, it is necessary—as discussed in the body of this paper—to extend in significant ways the CNP in order for bounded rational self-interested (BRSI) agents to deal intelligently with uncertainty present in the negotiation process. This new protocol represents a family of different protocols in which agents can choose different options depending on both the static and dynamic context of the negotiation. The first option we will discuss regards commitment. We present ways of varying the stage of commitment, and more importantly, how to implement *varying levels of commitment* that allow more flexible local deliberation and a wider variety of negotiation risk management techniques by allowing agents to back out of contracts. The second option concerns local deliberation. Tradeoffs are presented between negotiation risks and computation costs, and an approximation scheme for marginal cost calculation is suggested that dynamically adapts to an agent's negotiation state. The third set of options has to do with avoiding local optima in the task allocation space by *linking negotiation items* and by *contracts involving multiple agents*. The fourth set of options concerns *message congestion management*. We present these choices in terms of a new protocol for negotiation among BRSI agents, that, to our knowledge, subsumes the CNP and most—if not all—of its extensions.

[3]The *marginal cost* of adding a set of tasks to an agent's solution is the cost of the agent's solution with the new task set minus the cost of the agent's solution without it.

2 Commitment in negotiation protocols

2.1 Alternative commitment stages

In mutual negotiations, *commitment* means that one agent binds itself to a potential contract while waiting for the other agent to either accept or reject its offer. If the other party accepts, both parties are bound to the contract. When accepting, the second party is sure that the contract will be made, but the first party has to commit before it is sure. Commitment has to take place at some stage for contracts to take place, but the choice of this stage can be varied. TRACONET was designed so that commitment took place in the bidding phase as is usual in the real world: if a task is awarded to him, the bidder has to take care of it at the price mentioned in the bid. Shorter protocols (commitment at the announcement phase[4]) can be constructed as well as arbitrarily long ones (commitment at the awarding phase or some later stage).

The choice of commitment stage can be a static protocol design decision or the agents can decide on it dynamically. For example, the focused addressing scheme of the CNP was implemented so that in low utilization situations, contractors announced tasks, but in high utilization mode, potential contractees signaled availability—i.e. bid without receiving announcements first [Smith, 1980; Van Dyke Parunak, 1987]. So, the choice of a protocol was based on characteristics of the environment. Alternatively, the choice can be made for each negotiation separately before that negotiation begins. We advocate a more refined alternative, where agents dynamically choose the stage of commitment of a certain negotiation during that negotiation. This allows any of the above alternatives, but makes the stage of commitment a negotiation strategy decision, not a protocol design decision. The offered commitments are specified in *contractor messages* and *contractee messages*, Fig. 1.

2.2 Levels of commitment

In traditional multiagent negotiation protocols among SI agents, once a contract is made, it is binding, i.e. neither party can back out. In cooperative distributed problem solving (CDPS), commitments are often allowed to be broken unilaterally based on some local reasoning that attempts to incorporate the perspective of common good [Decker and Lesser, 1995]. A more general alternative is to use protocols with continuous levels of commitment based on a monetary penalty method, where commitments vary from unbreakable to breakable as a continuum by assigning a commitment breaking cost to each commitment separately. This cost can also increase with time, decrease as a function of acceptance time of the offer, or be conditioned on events in other negotiations or the environment. Using the suggested message types, the level of commitment can also be dynamically negotiated over on a per contract or per task set basis.

[4]With announcement phase commitment, a task set can be announced to only one potential bidder at a time, since the same task set cannot be exclusively awarded to many agents.

Among other things, the use of multiple levels of commitment allows:

- a low commitment search focus to be moved around in the global task allocation space (because decommitting is not unreasonably expensive), so that more of that space can be explored among SI agents which would otherwise avoid risky commitments[5],
- flexibility to the agent's local deliberation control, because marginal cost calculation of a contract can go on even after that contract has already been agreed upon,
- an agent to make the same low-commitment offer (or offers that overlap in task sets) to multiple agents. In case more than one accepts, the agent has to pay the penalty to all but one of them, but the speedup of being able to address multiple agents in committal mode may outweigh this risk,
- the agents with a lesser risk aversion to carry a greater portion of the risk. The more risk averse agent can trade off paying a higher price to its contractee (or get paid a lower price as a contractee) for being allowed to have a lower decommitting penalty, and
- contingency contracts by conditioning the payments and commitment functions on future negotiation events or domain events. These enlarge the set of mutually beneficial contracts, when agents have different expectations of future events or different risk attitudes [Raiffa, 1982].

The advantages of such a leveled commitment protocol are formally analyzed in [Sandholm and Lesser, 1995a], and are now reviewed. Because the decommitment penalties can be set arbitrarily high for both agents, the leveled commitment protocol can always emulate the full commitment protocol. Furthermore, there are cases where there is no full commitment contract among two agents that fulfills the participation constraints (agent prefers to agree to the contract as opposed to passing) for both agents, but where a leveled commitment contract does fulfill these constraints. This occurs even among risk neutral agents, for example when uncertainty prevails regarding both agents' future offers received, and both agents are assigned a (not too high or low, and not necessarily identical) decommitment penalty in the contract. Among risk neutral agents, this does not occur if only one of the agents is allowed the possibility to decommit (other agent's decommitment penalty is too high), or only one agent's future is uncertain. If the agents have biased information regarding the future, they may perceive that such a contract with a one-sided decommitment possibility is viable although a full commitment contract is not. In such cases, the agent whose information is biased is likely to take the associated loss while the agent with unbiased information is not.

Figure 1 describes the message formats of the new contracting protocol. A negotiation can start with either a

```
CONTRACTOR MESSAGE:
0. Negotiation identifier
1. Message identifier
2. In-response-to (message id)
3. Sender
4. Receiver
5. Terminate negotiation
6. Alternative 1
  6.1. Time valid through
  6.2. Bind after partner's decommit
  6.3. Offer submission fee
  6.4. Required response submission fee
  6.5. Task set 1
    (a) (Minimum) specification of tasks
    (b) Promised payment fn. to contractee
    (c) Contractor's promised commitment fn.
    (d) Contractee's required commitment fn.
  6.6. Task set 2
    ...
  6.i. Task set i-4
7. Alternative 2
  ...
j. Alternative j-5

CONTRACTEE MESSAGE:
0. Negotiation identifier
1. Message identifier
2. In-response-to (message id)
3. Sender
4. Receiver
5. Terminate negotiation
6. Alternative 1
  6.1. Time valid through
  6.2. Bind after partner's decommit
  6.3. Offer submission fee
  6.4. Required response submission fee
  6.5. Task set 1
    (a) (Maximum) specification of tasks
    (b) Required payment fn. to contractee
    (c) Contractor's required commitment fn.
    (d) Contractee's promised commitment fn.
  6.6. Task set 2
    ...
  6.m. Task set m-4
7. Alternative 2
  ...
n. Alternative n-5

PAYMENT/DECOMMIT MESSAGE:
0. Negotiation id
1. Message id
2. Accepted offer id
3. Acceptance message id
4. Sender
5. Receiver
6. Message type
     (payment/decommit)
7. Money transfer
```

Figure 1: *Contracting messages of a single negotiation.*

contractor or a contractee message, Fig. 2. A contractor message specifies exclusive alternative contracts that the contractor is willing to commit to. Within each alternative, the tasks can be split into disjoint task sets by the sender of the message in order for the fields (a) - (d) to be specific for each such task set - not necessarily the whole set of tasks. Each alternative has the following semantics. If the contractee agrees to handle all the task sets in a manner satisfying the minimum required task descriptions (a) (which specify the tasks and constraints on them, e.g. latest and earliest handling time or minimum handling quality), and the contractee agrees to commit to each task set with the level specified in field (d), then the contractor is automatically committed to paying[6] the amounts of fields (b), and can cancel the deal on a task set only by paying the contractee a penalty (c)[7]. Moreover, the contractor is decommitted

[5] For example, an agent can accept a task set and later try to contract the tasks in that set further separately. With full commitment, an agent needs to have standing offers from the agents it will contract the tasks to, or it has to be able to handle them itself. With the variable commitment protocol, the agent can accept the task set even if it is not sure about its chances of getting it handled, because in the worst case it can decommit.

[6] Secure money transfer can be implemented cryptographically e.g. by electronic credit cards or electronic cash [Kristol *et al.*, 1994].

[7] The "Bind after partner's decommit" (6.2) flag describes whether an offer on an alternative will stay valid according to its original deadline (field 6.1) even in the case where the contract was agreed to, but the partner decommitted by paying the decommitment penalty.

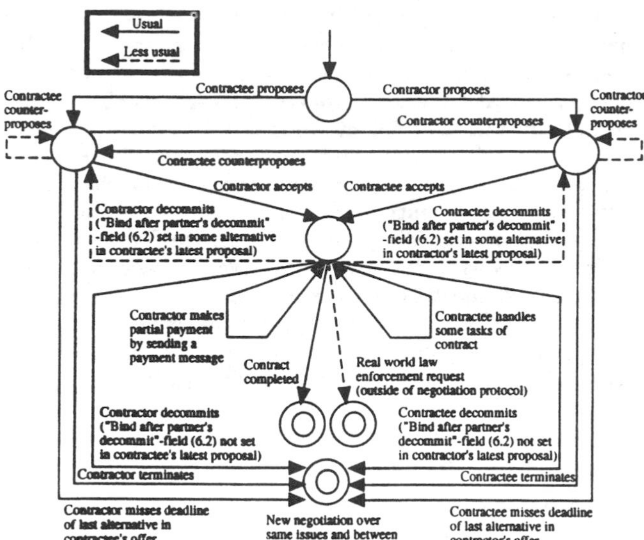

Figure 2: *State transition diagram of a single negotiation.*

from all the other alternatives it suggested[8]. If the contractee does not accept any of the alternatives, the contractor is decommitted from all of them. Fields (b), (c) and (d) can be functions of time, of negotiation events, or of domain events, and these times/events have to be observable or verifiable by both the contractor and the contractee. A contractee can accept one of the alternatives of a contractor message by sending a contractee message that has task specifications that meet the minimal requirements (a), and payment functions that meet the required payment functions (b), and commitment functions (c) for the contractee that meet the required commitment functions, and commitment functions (d) for the contractor that do not exceed the contractor's promised commitment. A contractor message can accept one of the alternatives of a contractee message analogously. An agent can entirely terminate a negotiation by sending a message with that negotiation's identifier (field 0), and the terminate-flag (field 5) set.

Alternatively, the contractee can send a contractee message that neither accepts the contractor message (i.e. does not satisfy the requirements) nor terminates the negotiation. Such a message is a *counterproposal*, which the contractor then can accept, terminate the negotiation, or further counterpropose etc. *ad infinitum* [9]. The CNP did not allow counterproposing: an agent could bid to an announcement or decide not to bid. A contractor had the option to award or not to award the tasks according to the bids. Counterproposing among cooperative agents was studied in [Moehlman *et al.*, 1992; Sen, 1993]. Our counterproposing mechanism is one way of overcoming the problem of lacking truthful abstractions of the global search space (defined by the task sets and resource sets of all the agents) in negotiation systems consisting of SI agents.

There are no uncommittal messages such as announcements used to declare tasks: all messages have some commitment specification for the sender. In early messages in a negotiation, these commitment specifications can be too low for the partner to accept, and counterproposing occurs. Thus, the level and stage of commitment are dynamically negotiated along with the negotiation of taking care of tasks.

The presented negotiation protocol is a strict generalization of the CNP, and can thus always emulate it. Moreover, there are cases where this protocol is better than the CNP—due to reasons listed earlier. Yet, the development of appropriate negotiation *strategies* for this protocol is challenging—e.g. how should an agent choose commitment functions and payment functions?

2.3 Decommitting: replies vs. timeouts

The (6.1) field describes how long an offer on an alternative is valid. If the negotiation partner has not answered by that time, the sender of the message gets decommitted from that alternative. An alternative to these strict deadlines is to send messages that have the (b) field be a function of the time of response (similarly for (c) and (d) fields). This allows a contractor to describe a payment that decreases as the acceptance of the contractor message is postponed. Similarly, it allows a contractee to specify required payments that increase as the acceptance of the contractee message is postponed. This motivates the negotiation partner to respond quickly, but does not force a strict deadline, which can inefficiently constrain that agent's local deliberation scheduling. Both the strict deadline mechanism and this time-dependent payment scheme require that the sending or receival time of a message can be verified by both parties.

An alternative to automatic decommitment by the deadline is to have the negotiation partner send a negative reply (negotiation termination message) by the deadline. These forced response messages are not viable among SI agents, because an agent that has decided not to accept or counterpropose has no reason to send a reply. Sending reply messages also in negative cases allows the offering agent to decommit before the validity time of its offer ends. This frees that agent from considering the effects of the possible acceptance of that offer on the marginal costs of other task sets that the agent is negotiating over. This saved computation can be used to negotiate faster on other contracts. Thus, an agent considering sending a negative reply may want to send it in cases where the offering agent is mostly negotiating with that agent, but not in cases, where the offering agent is that agent's competing offerer in most other negotiations.

[8] Another protocol would have offers stay valid according to their original specification (deadline) no matter whether the partner accepts, rejects, counterproposes, or does none of these. We do not use such protocols due to the harmfully (Sec. 3) growing number of pending commitments.

[9] An agent that has just (counter)proposed can counterpropose again (dotted lines in Fig. 2). This allows it to add new offers (that share the "In-response-to"-field with the pending ones), but does not allow retraction of old offers. Retraction is problematic in a distributed system, because the negotiation partner's acceptance message may be on the way while the agent sends the retraction.

3 Implications of bounded rationality

Interactions of SI agents have been widely studied in microeconomics [Kreps, 1990; Varian, 1992; Raiffa, 1982] and DAI [Rosenschein and Zlotkin, 1994; Ephrati and Rosenschein, 1991; Kraus *et al.*, 1992; Durfee *et al.*, 1993], but perfect rationality of the agents has usually been assumed: flawless deduction, optimal reasoning about future contingencies and recursive modeling of other agents. Perfect rationality implies that agents can compute their marginal costs for tasks exactly and immediately, which is untrue in most practical situations. An agent is bounded rational, because its computation resources are costly, or they are bounded and the environment keeps changing—e.g. new tasks arrive and there is a bounded amount of time before each part of the solution is used [Garvey and Lesser, 1994; Sandholm and Lesser, 1994; Zilberstein, 1993; Simon, 1982; Good, 1971]. Contracting agents have the following additional real-time pressures:

- A counteroffer or an acceptance message has to be sent by a deadline (field 6.1) - otherwise the negotiation terminates, Fig. 2. If the negotiation terminates, the agent can begin a new negotiation on the same issues, but it will not have the other agent's commitment at first.
- Sending an outgoing offer too late may cause the receiving agent to make a contract on some of the same tasks with some other agent who negotiated earlier—thus disabling this contract even if the offer makes the deadline. In case this deadline abiding offer is an acceptance message—as opposed to a counteroffer—the partner has to pay the decommitment penalty that it had declared.
- The (b)-(d) fields can be functions of response time, Fig. 1. An agent may get paid less for handling tasks (or pay more for having tasks handled) or be required to commit more strongly or receive a weaker commitment from the negotiation partner if its response is postponed.
- The agent's cost of breaking commitments (after a contract is made) may increase with time.

This problem setup leads to a host of local deliberation scheduling issues. An agent has to decide *how much computation* it should allocate to refine its marginal cost estimate of a certain task set. With a bounded CPU, if too much time is allocated, another agent may win the contract before the reply is sent, or not enough time remains for refining marginal costs of other task sets. If too little time is allocated, the agent may make an unbeneficial contract concerning that task set. If multiple negotiations are allowed simultaneously, the agent has to decide on *which sets of tasks* (offered to it or potentially offered by it) its bounded computation should be focused—and *in what order*. It may want to ignore some of its contracting possibilities in order to focus more deliberation time to compute marginal costs for task sets of some selected potential contracts. So, there is a tradeoff of getting more exact marginal cost estimates and being able to engage in a larger number of negotiations.

The CNP did not consider an agent's risk attitude toward being committed to activities it may not be able to honor, or the honoring of which may turn out unbeneficial. In our protocol, an agent can take a risk by making offers while the acceptance of earlier offers is pending. Contracting during pending commitments speeds up the negotiations because an agent does not have to wait for results on earlier commitments before carrying on with other negotiations. The work on TRACONET formalized the questions of risk attitude in a 3-stage (announce-bid-award) full-commitment protocol, and chose a risk taking strategy where each agent ignored the chances of pending commitments being accepted in order to avoid computations regarding these alternative future worlds. This choice was static, but more advanced agents should use a risk taking strategy where negotiation risk is explicitly traded off against added computation regarding the marginal cost of the task set in the alternative worlds, where different combinations of sent pending offers are accepted.

There is a tradeoff between accepting or (counter) proposing early on and waiting:

- A better offer may be received later.
- Waiting for more simultaneously valid offers enables an agent to identify and accept synergic ones: having more options available at the decision point enables an agent to make more informed decisions.
- Accepting early on simplifies costly marginal cost computations, because there are fewer options to consider. An option corresponds to an item in the power set of offers that an agent can accept or make.
- By waiting an agent may miss opportunities due to others making related contracts first.

An agent should anticipate future negotiation and domain events in its strategy [Sandholm and Lesser, 1995b].[10] It suffices to take these events into account in marginal cost estimation: this will cause the agent to anticipate with its domain solution. The real marginal cost of a task set is the difference in the *streams of payments and domain costs* when an agent has the task set and when the agent does not have it. This marginal cost does not necessarily equal the cost that is acquired statically at contract time (before the realization of unknown future negotiation events and domain events) by taking the difference of the cost of the agent's optimal solution with the task set and the optimal solution without it. Furthermore, for BR agents, the marginal cost may change as more computation is allocated to the solution including the task set or the solution without it. In general, the marginal cost of a task set depends on which other tasks the agent has. Therefore, theoretically, the marginal cost of a task set has to be computed in all of the alternative future worlds, where different combinations of pending,

[10]The agent can believe that domain events occur to the agent society according to some distribution and that in steady state these events will affect (directly or by negotiation) the agent according to some distribution. E.g. the agent assumes that future tasks end up in its task set according to a distribution. On another level, an agent can try to outguess the other agents' solutions so that it can use the others marginal costs as a basis for its own marginal cost calculation. On a third level, the agent can model what another agent is guessing about yet another agent, and so on *ad infinitum*. There is a tradeoff between allocating costly computation resources to such recursive modeling and gaining domain advantage by enhanced anticipation.

to-be-sent, and to-be-received offers have been accepted, different combinations of old and to-occur contracts have been broken by decommitting (by the agent or its partners), and different combinations of domain events have occurred. Managing such contingencies formally using probability theory is intractable: costs of such computations should be explicitly traded off against the domain advantage they provide. An agent can safely ignore the chances of other agents decommitting only if the decommitment penalties are high enough to surely compensate for the agent's potential loss. Similarly, an agent has to ignore its decommitting possibilities if its penalties are too high. The exponential number of alternative worlds induced by decommitting options sometimes increases computational complexity more than the benefit from the gradual commitment scheme warrants. Moreover, the decommitting events are not independent: chains of decommitting complicate the management of decommitment probabilities. Thus, decommitment penalty functions that increase rapidly in time may often be appropriate for BR agents.

Because new events are constantly occurring, the deliberation control problem is stochastic. An agent should take the likelihood of these events into account in its deliberation scheduling. The performance profile of the local problem solving algorithm should be conditioned on features of the problem instance [Sandholm and Lesser, 1994], on performance on that instance so far [Sandholm and Lesser, 1994; Zilberstein, 1993], and on performance profiles of closely related optimizations (related calculations of marginal costs). These aspects make exact decision theoretic deliberation control infeasible: approximations are required. The need for this type of deliberation control has not, to our knowledge, been well understood, and analytically developing a domain independent control strategy that is instantiated separately (using statistical methods) for each domain would allow faster development of more efficient automated negotiators across multiple domains.

4 Linking negotiation items

In early CNP implementations, tasks were negotiated one at a time. This is insufficient, if the cost or feasibility of carrying out a task depend on the carrying out of other tasks: there may be local optima, where no transfer of a single task between agents enhances the global solution, but transferring a larger set of tasks simultaneously does. The need for larger transfers is well known in centralized iterative refinement optimization [Lin and Kernighan, 1971; Waters, 1987], but has been generally ignored in automated negotiation. TRACONET extended the CNP to handle task interactions by having the announcer *cluster tasks into sets to be negotiated atomically*. Alternatively, the bidder could have done the clustering by counterproposing. Our protocol generalizes this by allowing either party to do the clustering, Fig. 1, at any stage of the protocol.

The equivalent of large transfers can be accomplished by smaller ones if the agents are willing to take risks. Even if no small contract is individually beneficial, the agents can sequentially make all the small contracts that sum up to a large beneficial one. Early in this sequence, the global solution degrades until the later contracts enhance it. When making the early commitments, at least one of the two agents has to risk taking a permanent loss in case the partner does not agree to the later contracts. Our protocol decreases such risks as much as preferred by allowing breaking commitments by paying a penalty. The penalty function may be explicitly conditioned on the acceptance of the future contracts, or it may specify low commitment for a short time during which the agent expects to make the remaining contracts of the sequence.

Sometimes there is no task set size such that transferring such a set from one agent to another enhances the global solution. Yet, there may be a beneficial *swap* of tasks, where the first agent subcontracts some tasks to the second and the second subcontracts some to the first. Swaps can be explicitly implemented in a negotiation protocol by allowing some task sets in an alternative (Fig. 1) to specify tasks to contract in and some to specify tasks to contract out. In the task sets added to implement swaps, "Minimum" in field (a) should be changed to "Maximum" and vice versa. In field (b), "Promised payment fn. to contractee" should be changed to "Required payment fn. from contractee" and "Required payment fn. to contractee" should be changed to "Promised payment fn. from contractee". Alternatively, in protocols that do not explicitly incorporate swaps, they can be made by agents taking risks and constructing the swap as a sequence of one way task transfer contracts. Here too, the decommitment penalty functions can be conditioned on later contracts in the sequence or on time to reduce (or remove) risk.

5 Mutual vs. multiagent contracts

Negotiations may have reached a local optimum with respect to each agent's local search operators and mutual contract operators (transfers and swaps of any size), but solution enhancements would be possible if tasks were transferred among more than two agents, e.g. agent A subcontracts a task to C and B subcontracts a task to C. There are two main ways to implement such deals[11]:

1. Explicit multiagent contracts. These contract operators can be viewed as atomic operators in the global task allocation space. First, one agent (with an incomplete view of the other agents' tasks and resources) has to identify the beneficiality of a potential multiagent contract. Alternatively, the identification phase can be implemented in a distributed manner. Second, the protocol has to allow a multiagent contract. This can be done e.g. by circulating the contract message among the parties and agreeing that the contract becomes valid only if every agent signs.

2. Multiagent contracts through mutual contracts. A multiagent contract is equivalent to a sequence of mutual contracts. In cases where a local optimum with respect to mutual contracts has been reached,

[11] Sathi et al. [Sathi and Fox, 1989] did this by having a centralized mediator cluster several announcements and bids from multiple agents into atomic contracts. That is unreasonable if decentralization is desired.

the first mutual contracts in the sequence will incur losses. Thus, one or more agents have to incur risk in initially taking unbeneficial contracts in unsure anticipation of more than compensatory future contracts. Our protocol provides mechanisms for decreasing this risk, either by conditioning the decommitment penalty functions on whether the contracts with other agents take place, or by choosing the penalties to be low early on and increase with time. In the limit, the penalty is zero (theoretically possibly even negative) for all contracts in the sequence if some contract in it is not accepted. The problem with contingency contracts is just the monitoring of the events that the contract (penalty) is contingent on: how can the contractee monitor the contractor's events and vice versa?

Sometimes an agent can commit to an unprofitable early contract in the sequence without risk even with constant high decommitting penalties. E.g. if an agent has received committal offers on two contracts, it can accept both without risk—assuming that decommitment penalties for the two senders are so high that they will not decommit. Even though the agent may have some offers committed simultaneously, the likelihood of having all the necessary offers committed simultaneously decreases as the number of mutual contracts required in the multiagent contract increases. Sometimes there is a loop of agents in the sequence of mutual contracts, e.g. say that the only profitable operator is the following: agent A gives task 1 to agent B, agent B gives task 2 to agent C, and agent C gives task 3 to agent A. In such cases it is impossible to handle the multiagent contract as separate mutual contracts without risk (without tailoring the decommitment penalty functions). A negotiating agent should take the possibilities of such loops into account when estimating the probabilities of receiving certain tasks, because the very offering or accepting of a certain task may directly affect the likelihood of getting offers or acceptances for other tasks.

6 Message congestion: Tragedy of the commons

Most distributed implementations of automated contracting have run into message congestion problems [Smith, 1980; Van Dyke Parunak, 1987; Sandholm, 1993]. While an agent takes a long time to process a large number of received messages, even more messages have time to arrive, and there is a high risk that the agent will finally be saturated. Attempts to solve these problems include focused addressing [Smith, 1980], audience restrictions [Van Dyke Parunak, 1987; Sandholm, 1993] and ignoring incoming messages that are sufficiently outdated [Sandholm, 1993]. Focused addressing means that in highly constrained situations, agents with free resources announce availability, while in less constrained situations, agents with tasks announce tasks. This avoids announcing too many tasks in highly constrained situations, where these announcements would seldom lead to results. In less constrained environments, resources are plentiful compared to tasks, so announcing tasks focuses negotiations with fewer messages. Audience restrictions mean that an agent can only announce to a subset of agents which are supposedly most potential.

Focused addressing and audience restrictions are imposed on an agent by a central designer of the agent society. Neither is viable in open systems with SI agents. An agent will send a message whenever it is beneficial to itself even though this might saturate other agents. With flat rate media such as the Internet, an agent prefers sending to almost everyone who has non-zero probability of accepting/counterproposing. The society of agents would be better off by less congested communication links by restricted sending, but each agent sends as long as the expected utility from that message exceeds the decrease in utility to that agent caused by the congesting effect of that message in the media. This defines a *tragedy of the commons* [Turner, 1992; Hardin, 1968] (n-player prisoners' dilemma). The tragedy occurs only for low commitment messages (usually early in a negotiation): having multiple high commitment offers out simultaneously increases an agent's negotiation risk (Sec. 2.2) and computation costs (Sec. 3).

The obvious way to resolve the tragedy is a use-based communication charge. Another is mutual monitoring: an agent can monitor how often a certain other agent sends low commitment messages to it, and over-eager senders can be punished. By mutual monitoring, audience restrictions can also be implemented: if an agent receives an announcement although it is not in the appropriate audience, it can directly identify the sender as a violator. Our protocol allows an agent to determine in its offer (field 6.4) a processing fee that an accepting or counterproposing agent has to submit in its response (field 6.3) for the response to be processed. This implements a self-selecting dynamic audience restriction that is viable among SI agents.

7 Conclusions

We introduced a collection of issues that arise in automated negotiation systems consisting of BRSI agents. Reasons for dynamically chosen commitment stage and level were given and a protocol that enables this was presented. The need for explicit local deliberation scheduling was shown by tradeoffs between computation costs and negotiation benefits and risk. Linking negotiation items and multiagent contracts were presented as methods to avoid local optima in the global task allocation space, and their implementation among BRSI agents was discussed. Finally, message congestion mechanisms for SI agents were presented.

Negotiations among BRSI agents also involve other issues (detailed in [Sandholm and Lesser, 1995b] due to limited space here) such as: insufficiency of the Vickrey auction to promote truth-telling and stop counterspeculation, usefulness of long term strategic contracts, tradeoffs between enforced and unenforced contracts [Sandholm and Lesser, 1995d], and knowing when to terminate the negotiations when an optimum with respect to the current tasks and resources has been reached or when further negotiation overhead outweighs the associated benefits. Coalition formation among BRSI agents has been studied in [Sandholm and Lesser, 1995c].

References

[Decker and Lesser, 1995] Keith Decker and Victor R Lesser. Designing a family of coordination algorithms. In *1st International Conference on Multiagent Systems*, San Fransisco, CA, June 1995.

[Durfee *et al.*, 1993] Edmund H Durfee, J Lee, and Piotr J Gmytrasiewicz. Overeager reciprocal rationality and mixed strategy equilibria. In *AAAI-93*, pages 225–230, Washington DC, July 1993.

[Ephrati and Rosenschein, 1991] Eithan Ephrati and Jeffrey S Rosenschein. The clarke tax as a consensus mechanism among automated agents. In *AAAI*, pages 173–178, Anaheim, CA, 1991.

[Finin *et al.*, 1992] Tim Finin, Rich Fritzson, and Don McKay. A language and protocol to support intelligent agent interoperability. In *Proc. of the CE & CALS Washington '92 Conference*, June 1992.

[Garvey and Lesser, 1994] A Garvey and V Lesser. A survey of research in deliberative real-time artificial intelligence. *Real-Time Systems*, 6:317–347, 1994.

[General Magic, Inc., 1994] General Magic, Inc. Telescript technology: The foundation for the electronic marketplace, 1994. White paper.

[Good, 1971] Irving Good. Twenty-seven principles of rationality. In V Godambe and D Sprott, editors, *Foundations of Statistical Inference*. Toronto: Holt, Rinehart, Winston, 1971.

[Hardin, 1968] G Hardin. The tragedy of the commons. *Science*, 162:1243–1248, 1968.

[Kraus *et al.*, 1992] Sarit Kraus, Jonathan Wilkenfeld, and Gilad Zlotkin. Multiagent negotiation under time constraints. Univ. of Maryland, College Park, Computer Science TR-2975, 1992.

[Kreps, 1990] David M Kreps. *A course in microeconomic theory*. Princeton University Press, 1990.

[Kristol *et al.*, 1994] David M Kristol, Steven H Low, and Nicholas F Maxemchuk. Anonymous internet mercantile protocol. 1994. Submitted.

[Lin and Kernighan, 1971] S Lin and B W Kernighan. An effective heuristic procedure for the traveling salesman problem. *Operations Research*, 21:498–516, 1971.

[Moehlman *et al.*, 1992] T Moehlman, V Lesser, and B Buteau. Decentralized negotiation: An approach to the distributed planning problem. *Group Decision and Negotiation*, 2:161–191, 1992.

[Office of Technology Assesment (OTA), 1994] Office of Technology Assesment (OTA). Electronic enterprises: Looking to the future, 1994.

[Raiffa, 1982] H. Raiffa. *The Art and Science of Negotiation*. Harvard Univ. Press, Cambridge, Mass., 1982.

[Rosenschein and Zlotkin, 1994] Jeffrey S Rosenschein and G Zlotkin. *Rules of Encounter*. MIT Press, 1994.

[Sandholm and Lesser, 1994] Tuomas W Sandholm and Victor R Lesser. Utility-based termination of anytime algorithms. In *ECAI Workshop on Decision Theory for DAI Applications*, pages 88–99, Amsterdam, The Netherlands, 1994. Extended version: Univ. of Mass. at Amherst, Comp. Sci. Tech. Report 94-54.

[Sandholm and Lesser, 1995a] Tuomas W Sandholm and Victor R Lesser. Advantages of a leveled commitment contracting protocol. Univ. of Mass. at Amherst, Comp. Sci. Tech. Report, 1995. In preparation.

[Sandholm and Lesser, 1995b] Tuomas W Sandholm and Victor R Lesser. Automated contracting among self-interested bounded rational agents. Technical report, University of Massachusetts at Amherst Computer Science Department, 1995. In preparation.

[Sandholm and Lesser, 1995c] Tuomas W Sandholm and Victor R Lesser. Coalition formation among bounded rational agents. In *Proc. 14th International Joint Conference on Artificial Intelligence (IJCAI-95)*, 1995.

[Sandholm and Lesser, 1995d] Tuomas W Sandholm and Victor R Lesser. Equilibrium analysis of the possibilities of unenforced exchange in multiagent systems. In *Proc. 14th International Joint Conference on Artificial Intelligence (IJCAI-95)*, Montreal, 1995.

[Sandholm, 1993] Tuomas W Sandholm. An implementation of the contract net protocol based on marginal cost calculations. In *Proc. 11th National Conference on Artificial Intelligence (AAAI-93)*, July 1993.

[Sathi and Fox, 1989] A Sathi and M Fox. Constraint-directed negotiation of resource reallocations. In Michael N. Huhns and Les Gasser, eds., *Distributed Artificial Intelligence*, vol. 2 of *Research Notes in Artificial Intelligence*, ch. 8, pages 163–193. Pitman, 1989.

[Sen, 1993] Sandip Sen. *Tradeoffs in Contract-Based Distributed Scheduling*. PhD thesis, Univ. of Michigan, 1993.

[Simon, 1982] Herbert A Simon. *Models of bounded rationality*, volume 2. MIT Press, 1982.

[Smith, 1980] Reid G. Smith. The contract net protocol: High-level communication and control in a distributed problem solver. *IEEE Transactions on Computers*, C-29(12):1104–1113, December 1980.

[Turner, 1992] Roy M Turner. The tragedy of the commons and distributed ai systems. In *Proceedings of the 12th International Workshop on Distributed Artificial Intelligence*, pages 379–390, May 1992.

[Van Dyke Parunak, 1987] H Van Dyke Parunak. Manufacturing experience with the contract net. In Michael N. Huhns, editor, *Distributed Artificial Intelligence*, Research Notes in Artificial Intelligence, chapter 10, pages 285–310. Pitman, 1987.

[Varian, 1992] Hal R Varian. *Microeconomic analysis*. New York: W. W. Norton, 1992.

[Waters, 1987] C D Waters. A solution procedure for the vehicle-scheduling problem based on iterative route improvement. *Journal of the Operational Research Society*, 38(9):833–839, 1987.

[Zilberstein, 1993] Shlomo Zilberstein. *Operational rationality through compilation of anytime algorithms*. PhD thesis, University of California, Berkeley, 1993.

2.2 Internet and Information Access

A Softbot-Based Interface *to the Internet*

Oren Etzioni

Daniel Weld

The Internet Softbot (software robot) is a fully implemented AI agent developed at the University of Washington [5]. It uses a Unix shell and the World-Wide Web to interact with a wide range of Internet resources. Effectors include **`ftp`**, **`telnet`**, **`mail`**, and numerous file manipulation commands; sensors include Internet facilities such as **`archie`**, **`gopher`**, **`netfind`**, and many more. The softbot is designed to incorporate new facilities into its repertoire as they become available.

The softbot's "added value" is threefold. First, it provides an integrated and expressive interface to the Internet. Second, the softbot dynamically chooses which facilities to invoke, and in what sequence. For example, the softbot might use **`netfind`** to determine David McAllester's email address. Since it knows **`netfind`** requires a person's institution as input, the softbot would first search bibliographic databases for a technical report by McAllester that reveals his institution. Third, the softbot fluidly backtracks from one facility to another based on information collected at run time. As a result, the softbot's behavior changes in response to transient system conditions (e.g., the UUCP gateway is down). In this article, we focus on the ideas underlying the softbot-based interface.

The Interface

By acting as an intelligent personal assistant, the softbot supports a qualitatively different kind of human-computer interface. A person can make a high-level request, and the softbot uses search, inference, and knowledge to determine how to satisfy the request. Furthermore, the softbot is able to tolerate and recover from ambiguity, omissions, and errors in human requests.

At its core, the softbot can handle goals specified in an expressive subset of first-order logic. In particular, conjunction, disjunction, negation, and universal quantification can be composed to specify goals for the softbot. Since naive users are uncomfortable with logical notation, we have implemented a menu of request forms (Figure 1) which can be sent to the softbot via email, from mosaic, or through an X-windows graphical user interface. A filled-in form is automatically translated into a softbot goal (Figure 2). In principle, any dialog modality (e.g., natural language, speech, and pen interfaces) could be used to communicate with the softbot; we need only add a module to translate to and from the softbot's logical language.

In designing our interface, we have deemphasized issues of "look and feel" of the interface, and focused on how to leverage the softbot's AI capabilities to increase the interface's expressive power and flexibility. Specifically, our softbot-based interface embodies the following ideas:

1. ***Goal oriented.*** A request indicates *what* the human wants. The softbot is responsible for deciding *how* and *when* to satisfy the request.
2. ***Charitable.*** A request is not a complete and correct specification of the human's goal, but a *clue* or a *hint* that the softbot attempts to decipher and then satisfy.[1]

3. ***Balanced.*** The softbot has to balance the cost of finding information on its own, against the nuisance value of pestering the human with questions.
4. ***Integrated.*** The softbot provides a single, expressive, and uniform interface to a wide variety of Internet services and utilities.

Consider the task "Send the budget memos to Mitchell at CMU." A human assistant would handle this request with ease, but most existing software agents would not. Even if one solves (or circumvents) the problem of natural-language understanding, the agent still has to figure out:

- Which Mitchell was intended?
- Which documents should be sent? (and where are they located?)
- How to transmit the memos? (email, fax, remote printing, and so forth.)
- What if the memos are confidential?
- What if Mitchell is out of town?

As this simple example illustrates, even mundane human requests are incompletely specified, potentially ambiguous, or even impossible to satisfy (what if there is no Mitchell at CMU?).

The softbot's first task is *disambiguation.* It has to decide what "objects" the request is referring to: for instance, who is the intended recipient of the memos? The request suggests that the memos ought to go to a person named Mitchell at CMU, but there may be several people at CMU who share the same last name. The softbot could adopt the policy of asking the human to specify the recipient more clearly whenever his full name is not provided, but this is inappropriate. A last name *could* potentially pick out a unique individual. For example, suppose the last name provided is "Satyanarayanan." In this case, the softbot's request for clarification would be gratuitous and annoying. In general, any description, however tenuous, might pick out a unique individual. Before asking questions, the softbot ought to *check* whether the given description is ambiguous.

The softbot could consult its knowledge base to see how many Mitchells it "knows" at CMU, but suppose the softbot is familiar with only one, can it be sure that it is familiar with *all* the Mitchells at CMU? Since its knowledge of people on the Internet is bound to be radically incomplete, the softbot cannot afford to make the *closed world assumption* made by many AI and database systems [13]. Thus, it cannot automatically conclude that there is only one Mitchell at CMU from the fact that it is *familiar* with only one. Fortunately, it is easy to find all the Mitchells at CMU (by executing `finger mitchell@cmu.edu`). The softbot executes this command, records who are the various Mitchells at CMU, and (if necessary) prompts the human with a request to choose the intended one. The softbot also records, for future reference, that it is now familiar with all the Mitchells at CMU. Despite its incomplete knowledge, the softbot can recognize when it has complete information on a particular topic or locale [4].

To resolve ambiguity, the softbot could try to infer who the intended Mitchell is based on the documents being sent and the context of the request (e.g., did the human just receive an email message from some Mitchell at CMU?). While plausible inference of this sort can be encoded within our softbot framework, our implementation is not that sophisticated, yet.

Currently, the softbot attempts to find all individuals or objects on the Internet matching a given description. If there is a single resource that provides this information, the softbot will access it (by fingering in the previous example). Otherwise, the softbot will form a plan to seek out matching individuals. If the description is not constrained appropriately, executing such a plan can be very expensive. For instance, suppose the human omits Mitchell's location in request. The softbot would be "tempted" to search the entire Internet looking for Mitchells. However, the balance principle implies that the softbot would be better off asking the human to further constrain Mitchell's description. Thus, before disambiguating, the softbot estimates the cost of its disambiguation plan. When the cost is high, the softbot prompts the human for more information: "I am not sure which Mitchell you mean, can you tell me Mitchell's workplace, city, or field of interest?"

Once the appropriate Mitchell (and memos) have been determined, the softbot's second task is to actually send the memos to Mitchell. The softbot may decide to email the memos, but first it has to find Mitchell's email address, and reason about document format. For example, if a document contains figures, then sending the postscript version is more appropriate than sending the LaTEX source. Furthermore, if Mitchell is out of town, or if the memos are confidential, the softbot has to ensure that the memos reach their recipient in a timely and secure manner.

In general, after the softbot has figured out what the human wants, it considers how to satisfy the human request. The softbot solves this problem by invoking an automatic planning algorithm.

Softbot Planning

To construct an *integrated* and *goal-oriented* interface, we use AI planning techniques. The softbot planner takes a logical expression describing the user's goal as input. After searching a library of *action schemata* describing available information sources, databases, utilities and software commands, the planner generates a sequence of actions that achieve the goal.

Unlike standard programs and scripts which are committed to a rigid control flow determined *a priori* by a programmer, the softbot's planner automatically synthesizes and executes plans to achieve the inputted goals. This avoids the problematic task of writing programs that anticipate and adapt to all possible changes in system environment, network status, and error conditions. In short, a softbot is worth a thousand shell scripts.

[1]When the request is unethical or dangerous, the most appropriate response may be to alter or even refuse the request [14, 16].

The softbot's planner accepts an expressive goal language, enabling the softbot to accept goals containing complex combinations of conjunction, disjunction, negation, and nested universal and existential quantification. Furthermore, the softbot's use of planning yields an integrated interface—users can write expressive goals, even when dealing with services that don't support them directly. Consider the task "Get all of Ginsberg's technical reports that aren't already stored locally." Through planning, the softbot can use `ftp` to handle this request, even though the `ftp` utility doesn't know which files are local, and does not handle this combination of universal quantification and negation. The softbot will determine which of Ginsberg's reports are not stored locally, and will issue `ftp` commands to obtain them.

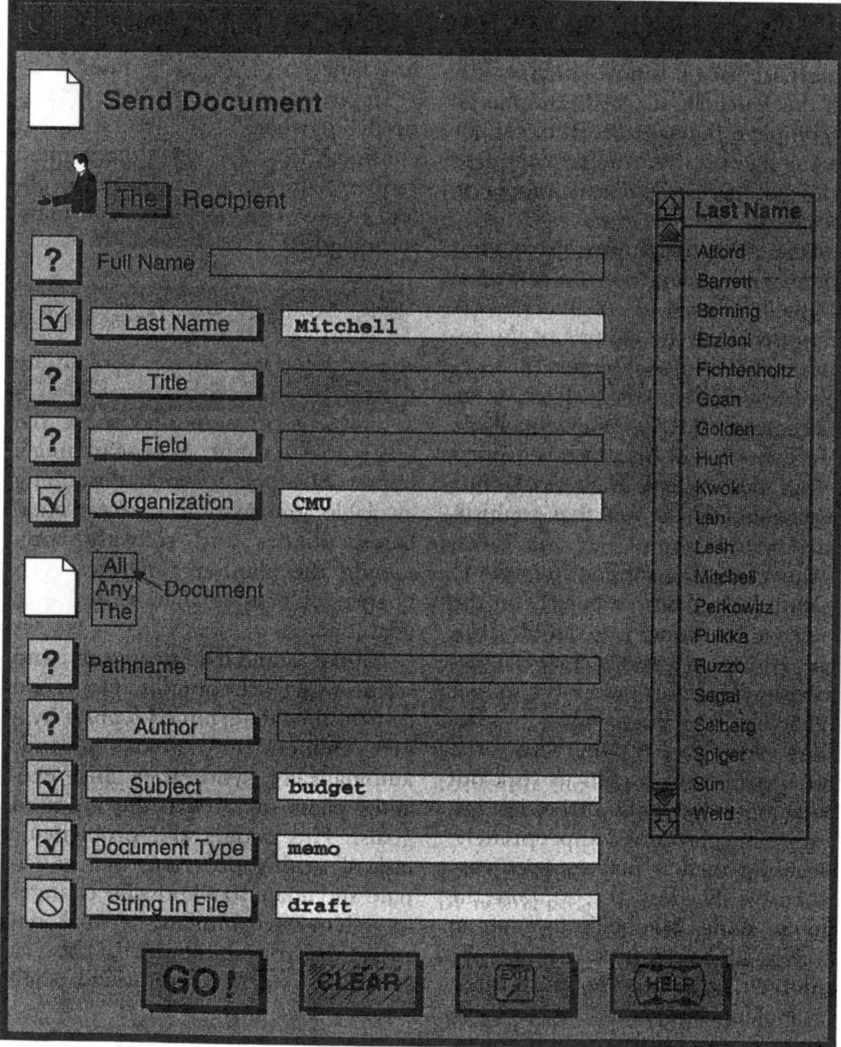

Figure 1. The request form for sending a document. In general, users need only provide a partial specification of the desired goal. The softbot disambiguates the request and plans how to achieve it, subgoaling and backtracking as required.

The softbot planner is implemented as a search process over partially specified action sequences called *plans*. The planner is able to decompose complex goal expressions into their constituents and solve them with divide and conquer techniques. Interactions between subgoals are automatically detected and resolved. Space precludes comprehensive discussion of the algorithm (see [4, 14]). However, we note that modern planning algorithms are provably

- complete: if a plan exists, the planner will find it, and
- sound: if the planner outputs a plan, that plan is guaranteed to achieve its goal (modulo certain explicit assumptions).

While these formal guarantees do not ensure the planner is efficient, we have not found efficiency to be a problem in practice. The softbot planner accepts control heuristics, specified in a high-level, declarative language, which constrain the planner's search by instructing it to prefer certain options over others, avoid blind alleys, and so forth. These heuristics can be hand-coded or generated automatically via machine learning techniques [6, 12].

If the softbot cannot satisfy its goal directly, it will automatically subgoal on an indirect way of satisfying the goals. For example, if looking up the phone number of a graduate student fails, the softbot will subgoal on identifying the student's office mates and finding their phone number. The softbot relies on an inference rule which states that office mates share the same telephone.

Resource Integration

The planner relies on a logical model of the available Internet resources, which answers two questions: how can the softbot invoke or access the resource, and what is the effect of doing so? This sort of "resource model" can be viewed as a generalization of a Prolog inference rule to allow for multiple effects, nested universal and existential quantification, and state change. The precise syntax and semantics of our representation language are described in [3, 4].

This declarative representation enables the softbot to integrate multiple, independent Internet facilities in service of its goals. For instance, as mentioned earlier, the softbot's model of `netfind` (Figure 3) tells it that it has to know a person's institution (or city) before accessing the `netfind` facility. Thus, when necessary, the softbot subgoals on finding this information by invoking different facilities (e.g., it might search the `INSPEC` database `grep` through local bibliographic databases). Furthermore, the softbot is poised to leverage new Internet resources. When a new facility becomes available, we need only write the appropriate logical models and search control rules to update the softbot. We are also investigating the use of learning techniques to help automate this task.

```
(forall (?d :in  files)
    (if (and (file.type ?d memo.document)
             (subject.of.document ?d "budget")
             (not (string.in.file "draft" ?d)))
        (delivered.to ?d ?obj341)))
```

Figure 2. The form shown in Figure 1 is automatically translated into an internal representation similar to the one shown here. During this process, the softbot executes actions as needed in order to find a unique person object.

```
Name:       (netfind ?person)
Preconds:                                  Postconds:
    (current.shell csh)                        (userid ?person !userid)
    (isa netfind.server ?server)               (person.machine ?person !machine)
    (firstname ?person ?firstname)
    (lastname ?person ?lastname)
    (or (person.city ?person ?keyword)
        (person.institution ?person ?keyword))
```

Figure 3. An action schema encoding the netfind utility. The softbot planner uses the schemata to determine when an Internet service could help achieve a user goal.

Incomplete Specification

The softbot accepts incompletely specified goals, and searches for missing information whenever possible. For example, if asked to print a file on "any free printer in the building," the softbot will find the printer list in a database, and will check the status of each printer until it finds one that is free. Similarly, if a human asks to be notified when Etzioni logs on to some machine at the University of Washington, the softbot will search for machines where Etzioni has an account and will monitor these machines until he appears. In general, the softbot's goal language allows the human to state three kinds of goals:

- *Ground goals:* notify me when Etzioni logs on to the machine called June.cs.washington.edu.
- *Existentially quantified goals:* notify me when Etzioni logs on to *some* machine.
- *Constrained goals:* notify me when Etzioni logs on to some computer-science machine at the University of Washington.

Empirically, we have found that constrained goals strike a useful balance between burdening the user with endless questions, and sending the softbot on a massive search of the Internet.

The use of a modern algorithm for planning with incomplete information is one of the most distinctive features of our softbot. In contrast, much of the current work on intelligent software agents focuses on task-specific "bots" for visitor scheduling [10], meeting scheduling [1], email filtering [11], white-page services [2], and so forth. While each of these agents has its strengths, none share the benefits of the planning approach including a highly expressive goal language, automatic backtracking and subgoaling, and more.

Softbot Safety

We have argued that in order to provide an integrated, goal-oriented interface, one needs powerful tools such as the softbot. However, the softbot also requires safety features. Of course, this is true of any software tool (e.g., the Macintosh refuses to reformat one's startup disk), but safety is more important for more powerful tools. Just as in the carpentry domain (where a table saw can slice through a tendon) Internet power tools, like the softbot, are capable of inflicting damage when used indiscriminately.

The greatest danger lies in the softbot's very ability to plan how to achieve the user's goal. Note that using a sound planner (i.e., one that only generates plans which are guaranteed to achieve the goal) is not sufficient, since there may be *many* such plans with different side effects. Consider the task "Reduce disk utilization below 90%." If the softbot succeeded by deleting irreplaceable LaTEX files without backing them up to tape, then users might prefer less "powerful" tools!

We believe that the softbot's safety mechanism should ensure the following qualities:

- *Safety.* The softbot should refuse to make destructive changes to the world.
- *Tidy.* The softbot should restore the world as close as possible to its original state (i.e., recompress files after searches).
- *Thrifty:* The softbot should limit its use of valuable resources.
- *Vigilant.* The softbot should block human actions that have unintended consequences.

See [14] for a formalization of some of these ideas in a manner that supports computationally tractable implementation. Since the ideas reported therein are preliminary and as yet unimplemented, we acknowledge that softbot safety is an area that deserves substantially more investigation.

Conclusion

Software environments such as the Internet are attractive testbeds for AI research [7]. Softbots circumvent many thorny issues that are inescapable in physical environments. Furthermore, the cost, effort, and expertise necessary to develop and experiment with software artifacts are relatively low. Yet, in contrast to simulated worlds, software environments are readily available, economically important, and *real*. In the past three years, the focus of the Internet Softbots project has been on the AI problems of designing and building an agent capable of effectively exploring the Internet. For a sample of technical AI results achieved in this context refer to [3, 4, 9].

We are now leveraging the softbot's AI capabilities to develop an expressive, goal-oriented, and charitable interface to the Internet. In contrast to a loosely structured browser such as Mosaic, our long-term objective is to develop an interface that will enable naive users to locate, monitor, and transmit information across the Net.

Acknowledgments

We would like to thank our co-softboticists Tony Barrett, Greg Fichtenholtz, Terrance Goan, Keith Golden, Cody Kwok, Aaron Pulkka, Mike Perkowtiz, Richard Segal, Ying Sun, and Rob Spiger. We thank Alan Borning and Steve Hanks for helpful comments. ◼

About the Authors:

OREN ETZIONI is an assistant professor at the university of Washington and the president of the AI Access Foundation. His research interests include software agents, machine learning, planning, plan recognition and human-computer interaction.

DANIEL WELD is an associate professor at the University of Washington and an associate editor for the *Journal of AI Research*. His research interests include planning algorithms, software agents and engineering problem solving.

Authors' Present Address: Computer Science and Engineering, University of Washington, Seattle, WA 98195; email: {etzioni, weld}@cs.washington.edu.

References

1. Dent, L., Boticario, J., McDermott, J., Mitchell, T., and Zabowski, D. A personal learning apprentice. In *Proceedings of the Tenth National Conference on AI*, (Jul. 12–16, 1992), AAAI Press/ MIT Press, Menlo Park Calif., 1992, pp. 96–103.
2. Droms, R. Access to Heterogeneous Directory Services. In *IEEE INFOCOM '90*. IEEE Computer Society Press, Vol. 3, 1990, pp. 1054–61.
3. Etzioni, O., Hanks, S., Weld, D., Draper, D., Lesh, N., and Williamson, M. An approach to planning with incomplete information. In *Proceedings of the Third International Conference on Principles of Knowledge Representation and Reasoning*. Morgan Kaufmann, San Mateo, Calif., 1992. Available via ftp from pub/ai/ at cs.washington.edu.
4. Etzioni, O., Golden, K., and Weld, D. Tractable closed-world reasoning with updates. In *Proceedings of the Fourth International Conference on Principles of Knowledge Representation and Reasoning*. (May 24–27, 1994), Morgan Kaufmann, San Mateo, Calif., 1994.
5. Etzioni, O., Lesh, N., and Segal, R. Building softbots for UNIX (preliminary report). Technical Report 93-09-01, University of Washington, 1993. Available via anonymous ftp from pub/etzioni/softbots/at cs.washington.edu.
6. Etzioni, O. Acquiring search-control knowledge via static analysis. *Art. Intel. 62,* 2 (Feb. 1993), 255–302.
7. Etzioni, O. Intelligence without robots (a reply to brooks). *AI Mag. 14* 4, (Apr. 1993), 7–13. Available via anonymous ftp from pub/etzioni/softbots/ at cs.washington.edu.
8. Ginsberg, M., ed. *Readings in Nonmonotonic Reasoning*. Morgan Kaufmann, San Mateo, Calif., 1987.
9. Golden, K., Etzioni, O., and Weld, D. Omnipotence without omniscience: Sensor management in planning. In *Proceedings of the Twelfth National Conference on AI*. (July 31–Aug. 4 1994), Seattle, Wash. To be published.
10. Kautz, H., Selman, B., Coen, M., Ketchpel, S., and Ramming, C. An experiment in the design of software agents. In *Proceedings of the Twelfth National Conference on AI*. (July 31–Aug. 4 1994), Seattle, Wash. To be published.
11. Maes, P., and Kozierok, R. Learning interface agents. In *Proceedings of The Eleventh National Conference on AI*. AAAI Press/MIT Press, Menlo Park, Calif., 1993, pp. 459–465.
12. Minton, S. Quantitative results concerning the utility of explanation-based learning. *Art. Intel. 42,* 2–3, (Mar. 1990), 363–391.
13. Reiter, R. On closed world databases. In H. Gallaire, and J. Minker, eds., *Logic and Data Bases*. Plenum Press NY, 55–76.
14. Weld, D., and Etzioni, O. The first law of softbotics. In *Proceedings of the Twelfth National Conference on AI*. Seattle, Wash. (July 31–Aug. 4 1994). To be published. Available via ftp from pub/ai/ at cs.washington.edu.
15. Weld, D. An introduction to least-commitment planning. *AI Mag.* To be published. Available via ftp from pub/ ai/ at cs.washington.edu.
16. Wilensky, R., Chin, D., Luria, M., Martin, J., Mayfield, J., and Wu, D. The Berkeley UNIX Consultant project. *Comput. Ling. 14,* 4 (Dec. 1988), 35–84.

This research was funded in part by the Office of Naval Research Grants 92-J-1946 and 90-J-1904, by the University of Washington Royalty Research Fund, and by National Science Foundation Grants IRI-8957302, IRI-9211045 and IRI-9357772.

Query Processing in the SIMS Information Mediator*

Yigal Arens, Chun-Nan Hsu, and Craig A. Knoblock
Information Sciences Institute and
Department of Computer Science
University of Southern California
4676 Admiralty Way
Marina del Rey, CA 90292, USA
{arens,chunnan,knoblock}@isi.edu

Abstract

A critical problem in building an information mediator is how to translate a domain-level query into an efficient query plan for accessing the required data. We have built a flexible and efficient information mediator, called SIMS. This system takes a domain-level query and dynamically selects the appropriate information sources based on their content and availability, generates a query access plan that specifies the operations and their order for processing the data, and then performs semantic query optimization to minimize the overall execution time. This paper describes these three basic components of the query processing in SIMS.

1 Introduction

SIMS [Arens *et al.*, 1993; Knoblock *et al.*, 1994; Arens and Knoblock, 1994; Ambite *et al.*, 1995; Arens *et al.*, 1996] is an information mediator that provides access and integration of multiple sources of information. Queries are expressed in a uniform language, independent of the distribution of information over sources, of the various query languages, the location of sources, etc. SIMS determines which data sources to use, how to obtain the desired information, how and where to temporarily store and manipulate data, and how to efficiently retrieve information.

The core part of the mediator is the ability to intelligently retrieve and process data. Information sources are constantly changing, new information becomes available, old information may be eliminated or temporarily unavailable, and so on. Thus, SIMS dynamically selects an appropriate set of information sources, generates a plan for processing the data, and then optimizes the plan to minimize the execution cost. The basic SIMS architecture is shown in Figure 1 and the query processing components are shown by the shaded rectangles.

This paper focuses on the query processing in SIMS. Before describing the query processing, Section 2 describes how the domain and information sources are modeled in SIMS. Section 3 describes the process of selecting the information sources. Section 4 present the approach to generating a query plan for execution. Section 5 describes the semantic query optimization performed before execution. Section 6 reviews the most closely related work. Section 7 concludes with a summary of the contributions and directions for future work.

2 Representing the Knowledge of a Mediator

A mediator contains a model of its domain of expertise, which provides the terminology for interacting with the mediator, as well as models of all information sources that are available to it. Both the domain and information source models are expressed in the Loom language. The domain model provides class descriptions, subclass and superclass relationships, roles for each class, as well as other domain-specific information. The information source models describe both the contents of the information sources and the mapping between those models and the domain model.

2.1 Modeling the Domain

The SIMS mediator is specialized to a single "application domain" and provides access to the available information sources within that domain. The largest application domain that we have to date is a transportation planning domain, with information about the movement of personnel and materiel from one location to another using aircraft, ships, trucks, etc.

The application domain models are defined using a hierarchical terminological knowledge base (Loom) [MacGregor, 1988; 1990] with nodes representing each class of objects, and relations between nodes that define the relationships between the objects. For example, Figure 2 shows a fragment of the domain model in the transportation planning domain. In this figure, circles represent

*This is an updated version of the paper that originally appeared as [Arens et al., 1994]. The research reported here was supported in part by Rome Laboratory of the Air Force Systems Command and the Defense Advanced Research Projects Agency under contract no. F30602-91-C-0081, and in part by the National Science Foundation under grant number IRI-9313993. Views and conclusions contained in this report are those of the authors and should not be interpreted as representing the official opinion or policy of NSF, DARPA, RL, the U.S. Government, or any person or agency connected with them.

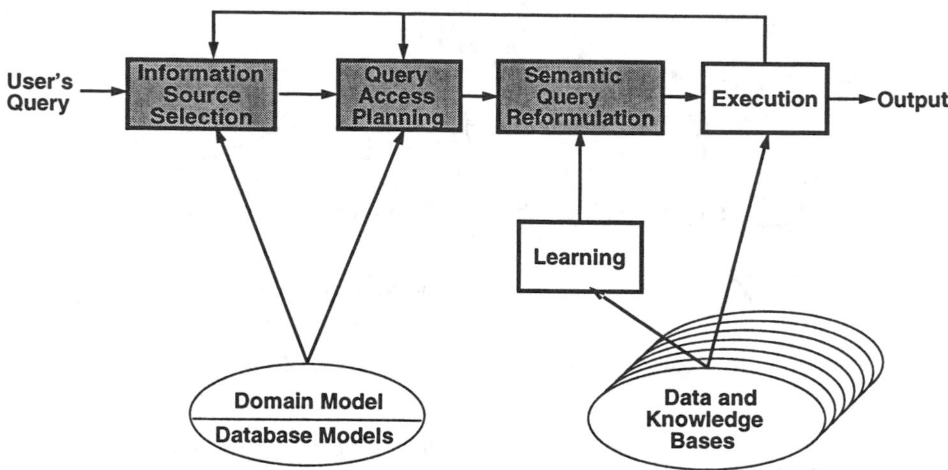

Figure 1: The SIMS Architecture

classes, the thick arrows represent subclass relationships, and the thin arrows represent relations between classes.

The classes defined in the domain model do not necessarily correspond directly to the objects described in any particular information source. The domain model is a high-level description of an application domain. Queries expressed in terms of this domain model are reformulated by SIMS into the appropriate subqueries to the various information sources. All of the information sources are defined using the terms in the domain model in order to make this reformulation possible. The reformulation of the domain-level queries is described further in Section 3.

Queries to SIMS are expressed in terms of the general domain model, so there is no need to know or even be aware of the terms or language used in the underlying information sources. Instead the system translates the domain-level query into a set of queries to the underlying information sources. These information sources may be databases, knowledge bases, or other application programs.

Figure 3 illustrates a query expressed in the Loom language. This query requests all seaports and corresponding ships with a range greater than 10,000 that can be accommodated within each port. The first argument to the `retrieve` expression is the parameter list, which specifies which parameters of the query to return. The second argument is a description of the information to be retrieved. This description is expressed as a conjunction of concept and relation expressions, where the concepts describe classes of information, and the relations describe constraints on these classes. The first subclause of the query is an example of a concept expression and specifies that the variable `?port` ranges over members of the class `seaport`. The second subclause is an example of a relation expression and states that the relation `port_name` holds between the value of `?port` and the variable `?port_name`. The query describes a class of seaports and a class of ships, and requests all seaport and ship pairs where the depth of the port exceeds the draft of the ship.

```
(retrieve (?port_name ?depth ?ship_type ?draft)
   (and (seaport ?port)
        (port_name ?port ?port_name)
        (channel_of ?port ?channel)
        (channel_depth ?channel ?depth)
        (ship ?ship)
        (vehicle_type ?ship ?ship_type)
        (range ?ship ?range)
        (> ?range 10000)
        (max_draft ?ship ?draft)
        (> ?depth ?draft)))
```

Figure 3: Example Loom query

2.2 Modeling Information Sources

The critical part of the information source models is the description of the contents of the information sources. This consists of both a description of the objects contained in the information source as well as the relationship between these objects and the objects in the domain model. The mappings between the domain model and the information source model are used for transforming a domain-level query into a set of queries into actual information sources.

Figures 4 illustrates how an information source is modeled in Loom and how it is related to the domain model. In the picture, the shaded circle represents the Seaports table in the GEO database. All of the concepts and relations in the information source model are mapped to concepts and relations in the domain model. A mapping link between two concepts indicates that they represent the same class of information. Thus, if the user requests all seaports, that information can be retrieved from the GEO database, which has information about seaports.

3 Information Source Selection

The first step in answering a query expressed in the terms of the domain model is to select the appropriate information sources [Arens *et al.*, 1996]. This is done by trans-

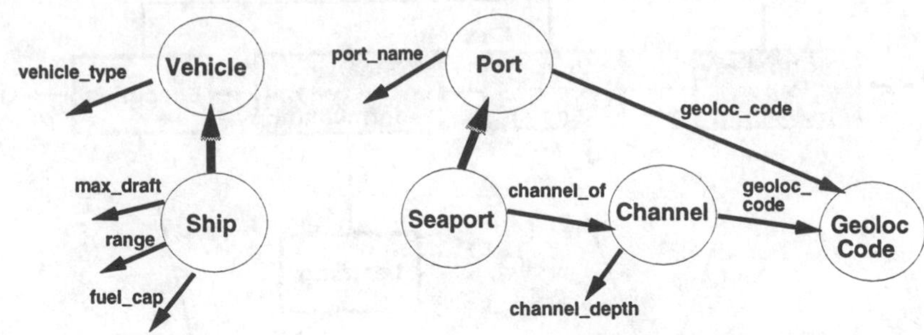

Figure 2: Fragment of the Domain Model

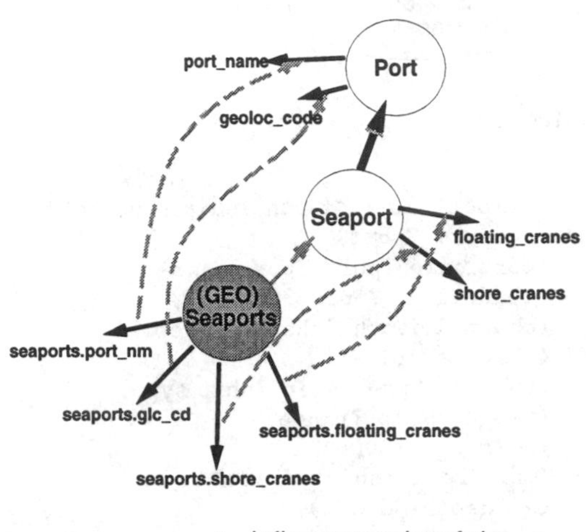

Figure 4: Relating an Information Source Model to a Domain Model

forming a query expressed in terms of the concepts in the domain model into a query expressed in terms of the concepts in the information source models. If the user requests information about ports and there is an information source-level concept that contains ports, then the mapping is straightforward. However, in many cases there will not be a direct mapping. Instead, the original domain-model query must be reformulated in terms of concepts that do correspond to information sources.

Consider the fragment of the knowledge base shown in Figure 5, which covers the knowledge relevant to the example query in Figure 3. The concepts Seaport, Channel and Ship have subconcepts shown by the shaded circles that correspond to concepts whose instances can be retrieved directly from some information source. Thus, the GEO information source contains information about both seaports and channels and the PORT information source contains information about only seaports. Thus, if the user asks for seaports, then it must be translated into one of the information source concepts — Seaports in GEO or Ports in PORT.

In order to select the information sources for answering a query, the system applies a set of reformulation operators to transform the domain-level concepts into concepts that can be retrieved directly from an information source. The system has a number of truth-preserving reformulation operations that can be used for this task. The operations include Select-Information-Source, Generalize-Concept, Specialize-Concept, and Decompose-Relation. These operations are described briefly below.

Select-Information-Source maps a domain-level concept directly to an information-source-level concept. In many cases this will simply be a direct mapping from a concept such as Seaport to a concept that corresponds to the seaports in some information source. There may be multiple information sources that contain the same information, in which case the domain-level query can be reformulated in terms of any one of the information source concepts. In general, the choice is made so as to minimize the overall cost of the retrieval. For example, the cost can be minimized by using as few information sources as possible.

Generalize-Concept uses knowledge about the relationship between a class and a superclass to reformulate a query in terms of the more general concept. In order to preserve the semantics of the original request, one or more additional constraints may need to be added to the query in order to avoid retrieving extraneous data. For example, if a query requires some information about airports, but the information sources that correspond to the airport concept do not contain the requested information, then it may be possible to generalize airport to port and retrieve the information from some information source that contains port information. In order to ensure that no extraneous data is returned, the reformulation will include a join between airport and port.

Specialize-Concept replaces a concept with a more specific concept by checking the constraints on the query to see if there is an appropriate specialization of the requested concept that would satisfy it. For example, if a query requests all *ports* with an elevation greater than 1000 feet, it may be possible to reformulate this in terms of all *airports* with an elevation greater than 1000 feet since there are no seaports with an elevation this high. Even if there was an information source corresponding to the port concept, this may be a more efficient way to retrieve the data. Range information such as this is natu-

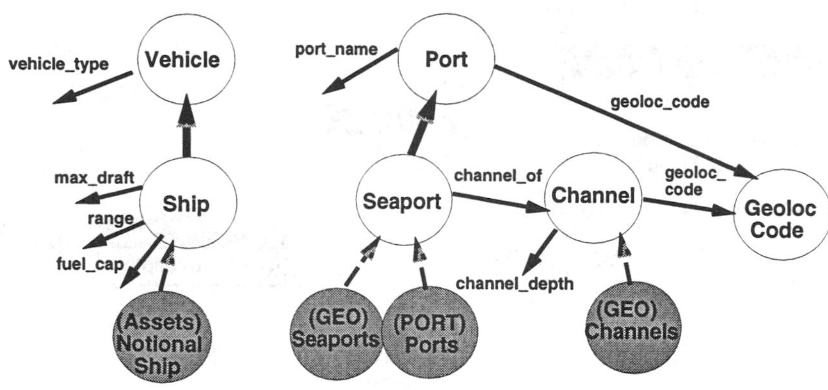

Figure 5: Fragment of the Domain and Source Models

rally represented and stored as part of the domain model.

Decompose-Relation replaces a relation defined between concepts in the domain model with equivalent terms that are available in the information source models. For example, `channel_of` is a property of the domain model, but it is not defined in any information source. Instead, it can be replaced by joining over a key, `geoloc-code`, that in this case happens to occur in both seaport and channel.

Reformulation is performed by treating the reformulation operators as a set of transformation operators and then using a planning system to search for a reformulation of the given query description. The planner searches for a way to map each of the concepts and relations into concepts and relations for which data is available.

For example, consider the query shown in Figure 3. There are two concept expressions – one about ships and the other about seaports. In the reformulation that is found, the first step translates the seaport expression into a information-source-level expression. Unfortunately, none of the information sources contain information that corresponds to `channel_of`. Thus, the system must reformulate `channel_of`, using the decompose operator. This expresses the fact that `channel_of` is equivalent to performing a join over the keys for the seaport and channel concepts. The resulting reformulation is shown in Figure 6.

The next step reformulates the seaport portion of the query into a corresponding information source query. This can be done using the select-information-source operator, which selects between the GEO and PORT databases. In this case GEO is selected because the information on channels is only available in the GEO database. The resulting query is shown in Figure 7.

The channel and ship portions of the query are then similarly reformulated. The final query, which is the result of reformulating the entire query is shown in Figure 8.

4 Query Access Planning

Once the system has reformulated the query so that it uses only terms from the information source models, the

```
(retrieve (?port_name ?depth ?ship_type ?draft)
   (:and (seaport ?port)
         (port_name ?port ?port_name)
         (geoloc_code ?port ?geocode)
         (channel ?channel)
         (geoloc_code ?channel ?geocode)
         (channel_depth ?channel ?depth)
         (ship ?ship)
         (vehicle_type ?ship ?ship_type)
         (range ?ship ?range)
         (> ?range 10000)
         (max_draft ?ship ?draft)
         (> ?depth ?draft)))
```

Figure 6: Result of Applying the Decompose Operator to Eliminate `channel_of`

```
(retrieve (?port_name ?depth ?ship_type ?draft)
   (:and (seaports ?port)
         (seaports.port_nm ?port ?port_name)
         (seaports.glc_cd ?port ?geocode)
         (channel ?channel)
         (geoloc_code ?channel ?geocode)
         (channel_depth ?channel ?depth)
         (ship ?ship)
         (vehicle_type ?ship ?ship_type)
         (range ?ship ?range)
         (> ?range 10000)
         (max_draft ?ship ?draft)
         (> ?depth ?draft)))
```

Figure 7: Result of Applying the Select-Information-Source Operator on Seaport

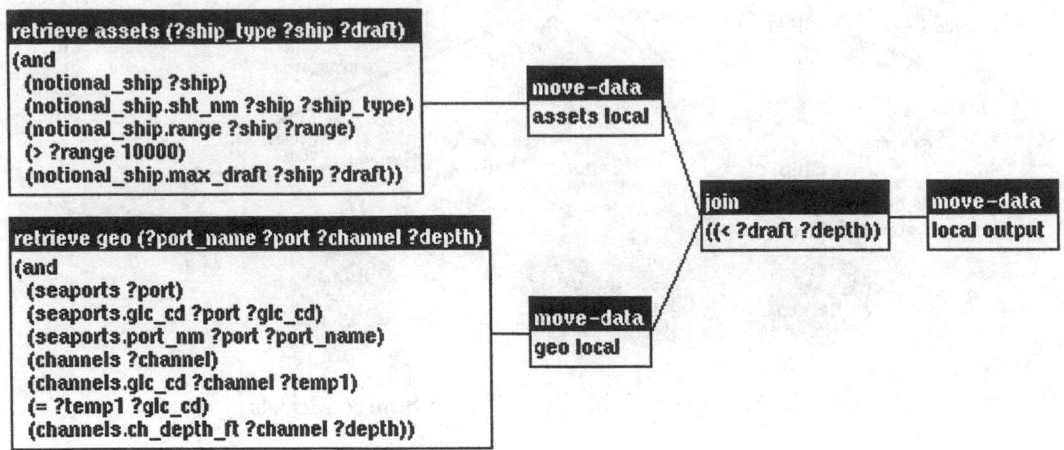

Figure 9: Parallel Query Access Plan

```
(retrieve (?port_name ?depth ?ship_type ?draft)
   (:and (seaports ?port)
         (seaports.port_nm ?port ?port_name)
         (seaports.glc_cd ?port ?glc_cd)
         (channels ?channel)
         (channels.glc_cd ?channel ?glc_cd)
         (channels.ch_depth_ft ?channel ?depth)
         (notional_ship ?ship)
         (notional_ship.sht_nm ?ship ?ship_type)
         (notional_ship.range ?ship ?range)
         (> ?range 10000)
         (notional_ship.max_draft ?ship ?draft)
         (< ?draft ?depth))))
```

Figure 8: Result of Selecting Information Sources for Channels and Ships

next step is to generate a query plan for retrieving and processing the data. The query plan specifies the precise operations that need to be performed, as well as the order in which they are to be performed.

There may be a significant difference in efficiency between different plans for a query. Therefore, the planner searches for a plan that can be implemented as efficiently as possible. To do this the planner must take into account the cost of accessing the different information sources, the cost of retrieving intermediate results, and the cost of combining these intermediate results to produce the final results. In addition, since the information sources are distributed over different machines or even different sites, the planner takes advantage of potential parallelism and generates subqueries that can be issued concurrently.

There are three basic operators that are used to plan out the processing of a query:

- Move-Data – Moves a set of data from one information source to another information source.
- Join – Combines two sets of data into a combined set of data using the given join relations.
- Retrieve-Data – Specifies the data that is to be retrieved from a particular information source.

Each of these operations manipulates one or more sets of data, where the data is specified in the same terms that are used for communicating with SIMS. This simplifies the input/output since there is no conversion between languages.

The planner [Knoblock, 1994; 1995; 1996] is implemented in a version of UCPOP [Penberthy and Weld, 1992; Barrett *et al.*, 1993] that has been modified to generate parallel execution plans. The system searches through the space of possible plans using a best-first search until a complete plan is found.

The plan generated for the example query in Figure 8 is shown in Figure 9. In this example, the system partitions the given query such that the ship information is retrieved in a single query to the ASSETS database and the seaport and channel information is retrieved in a single query to the GEO database. All of the information is brought into the local system (Loom) where the draft of the ships can be compared against the depth of the seaports. Once the final set of data has been generated, it is output for the user.

The system attempts to minimize the overall execution time by searching for a query that can be implemented as efficiently as possible. It does this by using a simple estimation function to calculate the expected cost of the various operations and then selecting a plan that has the lowest overall parallel execution cost. In the example, the system performs the join between the seaport and channel tables in the remote database since this will be cheaper than moving the tables into the local system. If the system could perform all of the work in one remote system, then it would completely bypass the local system and return the data directly to the user. Once an execution plan has been produced, it is sent to the optimization system for global optimization, as described in the next section.

5 Semantic Query Optimization

This section first describes how the system optimizes a single subquery and then describes how the system optimizes the entire query plan.

5.1 Subquery Optimization

The goal of the semantic query optimization is to search for the least expensive query in the space of semantically equivalent queries. The transformation from one query to another is done through logical inference using *database abstractions*, the abstracted knowledge of the contents of relevant databases. See [Hsu and Knoblock, 1994; 1995; 1996] for an explanation of how rules like these are automatically learned. The database abstractions describe the databases in terms of the set of closed formulas of first-order logic. These formulas describe the database in the sense that they are true with regard to all instances in the database.

Consider the example shown in Figure 10. The input query retrieves ship types whose ranges are greater than 10,000 miles. This query could be expensive to evaluate because there is no index placed on the `range` attribute. The system must scan the entire database table `notional_ship` and check the values of `range` to retrieve the answer.

Input Query:

```
(db-retrieve (?sht-type ?ship ?draft)
   (:and (notional_ship ?ship)
         (notional_ship.sht_nm ?ship ?ship-type)
         (notional_ship.max_draft ?ship ?draft)
         (notional_ship.range ?ship ?range)
         (> ?range 10000)))
```

Figure 10: Example Subquery

A set of applicable rules for this query is shown in Figure 11. These rules would either be learned by the system or provided as semantic integrity constraints. Rule `R1` states that for all ships with maximum drafts greater than 10 feet, their range is greater than 12,000 miles. Rule `R2` states that all ships with range greater than 10,000 miles have fuel capacities greater than 5,000 gallons. The last rule `R3` simply states that the drafts of ships are greater than 12 feet when their fuel capacity is more than 4,500 gallons.

Based on these rules, the system infers a set of additional constraints and merges them with the input query. The resulting query is the first query shown in Figure 12. This query is semantically equivalent to the input query but is not necessary more efficient. The set of constraints in this resulting query is called the `inferred set`. The system will then select a subset of constraints in the `inferred set` to complete the optimization. The selection is based on two criteria: reducing the total evaluation cost, and retaining the semantic equivalence. Detailed description of the algorithm is in [Hsu and Knoblock, 1993]. In this example, the input query is transformed into a new query where the constraint on the attribute `range` is replaced with a constraint on the attribute `max_draft`, on which there is a secondary index in the database. The optimized query can therefore be evaluated more efficiently.

The optimization is not limited to removing constraints. There are cases when the system can optimize a query by adding new constraints or proving that the query is unsatisfiable. The `inferred set` turns out to be useful information for extending the algorithm to optimize an entire query plan. Previous work only optimizes single database queries. In addition, our algorithm is polynomial in terms of the number of database abstraction rules and the syntactic length of the input query [Hsu and Knoblock, 1993]. A large number of rules may slow down the optimization. In this case, we can adopt sophisticated indexing and hashing techniques in rule matching, or constrain the size of the database abstractions by removing database abstractions with low utility.

Database Abstractions:

```
R1:
(:if (:and (notional_ship ?ship)
           (notional_ship.max_draft ?ship ?draft)
           (notional_ship.range ?ship ?range)
           (> ?draft 10))
  (:then (> ?range 12000)))

R2:
(:if (:and (notional_ship ?ship)
           (notional_ship.range ?ship ?range)
           (notional_ship.fuel_cap ?ship ?fuel_cap)
           (> ?range 10000))
  (:then (> ?fuel_cap 5000)))

R3:
(:if (:and (notional_ship ?ship)
           (notional_ship.max_draft ?ship ?draft)
           (notional_ship.fuel_cap ?ship ?fuel_cap)
           (> ?fuel_cap 4500))
  (:then (> ?draft 12)))
```

Figure 11: Applicable Rules in the Database Abstractions

Query with Inferred Set:

```
(db-retrieve (?ship-type ?ship ?draft)
   (:and (notional_ship ?ship)
         (notional_ship.sht_nm ?ship ?ship-type)
         (notional_ship.max_draft ?ship ?draft)
         (notional_ship.range ?ship ?range)
         (notional_ship.fuel_cap ?ship ?fuel_cap)
         (> ?range 10000)
         (> ?fuel_cap 5000)
         (> ?draft 12)))
```

Optimized Query:

```
(db-retrieve (?sht-type ?ship ?draft)
   (:and (notional_ship ?ship)
         (notional_ship.sht_nm ?ship ?ship-type)
         (notional_ship.max_draft ?ship ?draft)
         (> ?draft 12)))
```

Figure 12: Optimized Query

5.2 Query Plan Optimization

We can optimzie each subquery in the query plan with the subquery optimization algorithm and improve their efficiency. However, the most expensive aspect of the multidatabase query is often processing intermediate data. In the example query plan in Figure 9, the constraint on the final subqueries involves the variables `?draft` and `?depth` that are bound in the preceding sub-

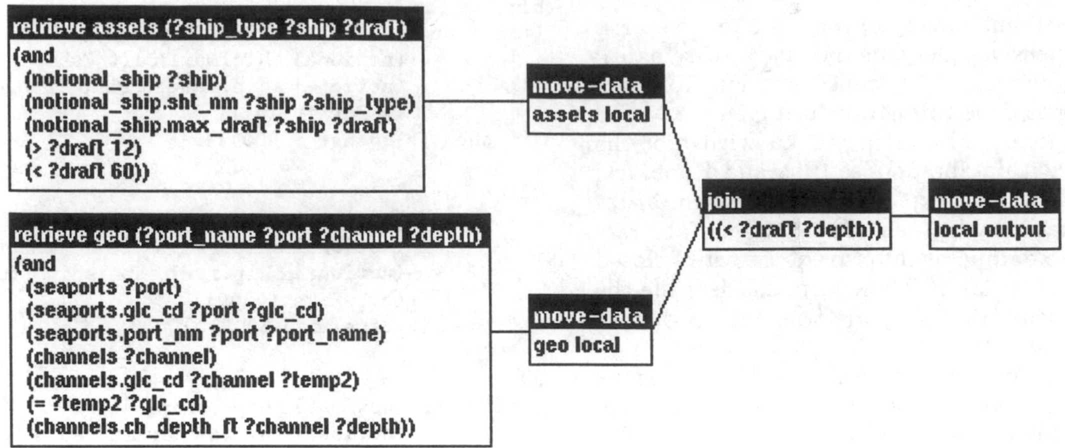

Figure 13: Optimized Query Access Plan

queries. If we can optimize these preceding subqueries so that they retrieve only the data instances possibly satisfying the constraint `(< ?draft ?depth)` in the final subquery, the intermediate data will be reduced. This requires the query plan optimization algorithm to be able to propagate the constraints along the data flow paths in the query plan. We developed a query plan optimization algorithm which achieves this by updating the database abstractions and rearranging constraints. We explain the algorithm using the query plan in Figure 9.

The algorithm first optimizes each subquery in the partial order (i.e., the data flow order) specified in the plan. The two subqueries to databases are optimized first. The database abstractions are updated and saved in `Inferred-Set`, which is returned from the subquery optimization to propagate the constraints to later subqueries. For example, when optimizing the subquery on `notional_ship`, `(> ?draft 12)` is inferred and saved in the inferred set. In addition, the constraint `(> ?range 10000)` in the original subquery is propagated along the data flow path to its succeeding subquery. Similarly, the system can infer the range of `?depth` in this manner. In this case, the range of `?depth` is `41` $\leq$ `?depth` $\leq$ `60`.

Now that the updated ranges for `?draft` and `?depth` are available, the subquery optimization algorithm can infer from the constraint `(< ?draft ?depth)` a new constraints `(< ?draft 60)` and add it to the subquery for the join. However, this constraint should be placed on the remote subquery instead of the local query because it only depends on the data in the remote database. In this case, when updating the query plan with the optimized subquery, the algorithm locates where the constrained variable of each new constraint is bound, and inserts the new constraint in the corresponding subqueries. In our example, the variable is bound by `(max_draft ?ship ?draft)` in the subquery on `notional_ship` in Figure 9. The algorithm will insert the new constraint on `?draft` in that subquery.

The semantics of the modified subqueries, such as the subquery on `notional_ship` in this example, are changed because of the newly inserted constraints. However, the semantics of the overall query plan remain the same. After all the subqueries in the plan have been optimized, the system optimizes these modified subqueries again to improve their efficiency. In our example, the subquery optimization algorithm is applied again to the `notional_ship` subquery. This time, no optimization is found to be appropriate. The final optimized query plan is returned and shown in Figure 13.

This query plan is more efficient and returns the same answer as the original one. In our example, the subquery to `notional_ship` is more efficient because the constraint on the attribute `range` is replaced with another constraint that can be evaluated more efficiently. The intermediate data are reduced because of the new constraint on the attribute `?draft`. The logical rationale of this new constraint is derived from the constraints in the other two subqueries: `(> ?range 10000)` and `(< ?draft ?depth)`, and the rules in the database abstractions. The entire algorithm for query plan optimization is still polynomial. Our experiments shows that the overheads of optimization is very small compared to the overall query processing cost. On a set of 32 example queries, the query optimization yielded significant performance improvements with an average reduction in execution time of 43%.

6 Related Work

In the database community, there are a variety of approaches to handling distributed, heterogeneous, and autonomous databases [Reddy *et al.*, 1989; Sheth and Larson, 1990]. Of these approaches, the tightly-coupled federated systems (e.g., Multibase [Landers and Rosenberg, 1982]) are the most closely related to SIMS in that they attempt to support total integration of all information sources in the sense that SIMS provides. However, building tightly-coupled federated system requires constructing a global schema for the databases to be combined and then hard-wiring the mapping between the global schema and the local schemas.

The information source selection in SIMS is used instead of the standard schema integration used in database systems [Batini and Lenzerini, 1986]. Our approach requires constructing a general domain model that encompasses the relevant parts of the database schemas. Then each of the database models is related to this general domain model. The integration problem is shifted from how to build a single integrated model to how to map between the domain and the information source models. After defining this mapping, the remaining integration process is performed automatically by the reformulation system using operators that transform the high-level query into an information source-level query. An important advantage of this approach is that it is easier and simpler to map one model to another model than it is to provide a completely integrated view of a number of models with different structures, types, and dependencies.

The query planning in SIMS is similar to the query access planning performed in many database systems. The primary difference between the planning in SIMS and query access planning in other systems is that the planning in SIMS is performed by an AI planner, which provides a level of flexibility that goes well beyond what standard database systems can provide. Currently, it allows the system to construct a plan that takes into account the availability of the various databases. In addition, we have integrated the planning with the execution system [Knoblock, 1995], which allows the system to dynamically replan parts of a query that fail while continuing to execute the other subqueries of the overall plan.

The semantic approach to query optimization was first developed by King [King, 1981] and has since been extended in a number of systems [Adam *et al.*, 1993; Shenoy and Ozsoyoglu, 1989; Shekhar *et al.*, 1988; Siegel, 1988]. Our approach to this problem differs from other related work in that we do not rely on explicit heuristics of the database implementation to guide search for optimized queries in the combinatorially large space of the potential optimizations. Instead, our algorithm considers all possible optimizations by firing all applicable rules and collecting candidate constraints in an *inferred set*. Then the system selects the most efficient set of the constraints from the inferred set to form the optimized subqueries.

The Carnot project [Collet *et al.*, 1991] is similar to SIMS in that it uses a knowledge base to integrate a variety of information sources. Carnot integrates heterogeneous databases using a set of articulation axioms that describe how to map between SQL queries and domain concepts. Carnot uses the Cyc knowledge base [Lenat and Guha, 1990] to build the articulation axioms, but after the axioms are built the domain model is no longer used or needed. In contrast, the domain model in SIMS is an integral part of the system, and allows SIMS to both combine information stored in the knowledge base and to optimize queries.

7 Conclusion

SIMS provides a flexible system for processing queries to multiple information sources. In this paper we described the process of transforming a domain-level query into an efficient and executable query plan. This process consists of three steps. First, the information sources are selected in the process of transforming the domain-level query into an information source-level query. Second, the system generates a query plan, which specifies all the operations to be performed on the data as well as the order of these operations. Third, the system performs global optimization through the use of database abstractions to optimize the query plans.

Future work will focus on extending the selection, planning, and optimization capabilities described in this paper. An important issue that we have not yet addressed is how to handle the various forms of incompleteness and inconsistency that will inevitably arise from using autonomous information sources. We plan to address these issues by exploiting available domain knowledge and employing more sophisticated planning and reasoning capabilities to both detect and recover from these problems.

References

[Adam *et al.*, 1993] N.R. Adam, A. Gangopadhyay, and J. Geller. Design and implementation of a knowledge-based query processor. *International Journal of Intelligent and Cooperative Information Systems*, 2(2):107–125, 1993.

[Ambite *et al.*, 1995] Jose-Luis Ambite, Yigal Arens, Naveen Ashish, Chin Y. Chee, Chun-Nan Hsu, Craig A. Knoblock, Wei-Min Shen, and Sheila Tejada. The SIMS manual: Version 1.0. Technical Report ISI/TM-95-428, University of Southern California, Information Sciences Institute, 1995.

[Arens and Knoblock, 1994] Yigal Arens and Craig A. Knoblock. Intelligent caching: Selecting, representing, and reusing data in an information server. In *Proceedings of the Third International Conference on Information and Knowledge Management*, Gaithersburg, MD, 1994.

[Arens *et al.*, 1993] Yigal Arens, Chin Y. Chee, Chun-Nan Hsu, and Craig A. Knoblock. Retrieving and integrating data from multiple information sources. *International Journal on Intelligent and Cooperative Information Systems*, 2(2):127–158, 1993.

[Arens *et al.*, 1994] Yigal Arens, Chin Chee, Chun-Nan Hsu, Hoh In, and Craig A. Knoblock. Query processing in an information mediator. In *Proceedings of the ARPA / Rome Laboratory Knowledge-Based Planning and Scheduling Initiative*, Tucson, AZ, 1994.

[Arens *et al.*, 1996] Yigal Arens, Craig A. Knoblock, and Wei-Min Shen. Query reformulation for dynamic information integration. *Journal of Intelligent Information Systems, Special Issue on Intelligent Information Integration*, 6(2/3):99–130, 1996.

[Barrett *et al.*, 1993] Anthony Barrett, Keith Golden, Scott Penberthy, and Daniel Weld. UCPOP user's manual (version 2.0). Technical Report 93-09-06, Department of Computer Science and Engineering, University of Washington, 1993.

[Batini and Lenzerini, 1986] Carlo Batini and Maurizio Lenzerini. A comparative analysis of methodologies for database schema integration. *ACM Computing Surveys*, 18(4):323–364, 1986.

[Collet *et al.*, 1991] Christine Collet, Michael N. Huhns, and Wei-Min Shen. Resource integration using a large knowledge base in Carnot. *IEEE Computer*, pages 55–62, December 1991.

[Hsu and Knoblock, 1993] Chun-Nan Hsu and Craig A. Knoblock. Reformulating query plans for multidatabase systems. In *Proceedings of the Second International Conference on Information and Knowledge Management*, Washington, D.C., 1993. ACM.

[Hsu and Knoblock, 1994] Chun-Nan Hsu and Craig A. Knoblock. Rule induction for semantic query optimization. In *Proceedings of the Eleventh International Conference on Machine Learning*, New Brunswick, NJ, 1994.

[Hsu and Knoblock, 1995] Chun-Nan Hsu and Craig A. Knoblock. Estimating the robustness of discovered knowledge. In *Proceedings of the First International Conference on Knowledge Discovery and Data Mining*, Montreal, Canada, 1995.

[Hsu and Knoblock, 1996] Chun-Nan Hsu and Craig A. Knoblock. Using inductive learning to generate rules for semantic query optimization. In Gregory Piatetsky-Shapiro, Usama Fayyad, Padhraic Symyth, and Ramasamy Uthurusamy, editors, *Advances in Knowledge Discovery and Data Mining*, chapter 17. AAAI Press, Menlo Park, CA, 1996.

[King, 1981] Jonathan Jay King. *Query Optimization by Semantic Reasoning.* PhD thesis, Stanford University, Department of Computer Science, 1981.

[Knoblock *et al.*, 1994] Craig A. Knoblock, Yigal Arens, and Chun-Nan Hsu. Cooperating agents for information retrieval. In *Proceedings of the Second International Conference on Cooperative Information Systems*, Toronto, Canada, 1994.

[Knoblock, 1994] Craig A. Knoblock. Generating parallel execution plans with a partial-order planner. In *Proceedings of the Second International Conference on Artificial Intelligence Planning Systems*, Chicago, IL, 1994.

[Knoblock, 1995] Craig A. Knoblock. Planning, executing, sensing, and replanning for information gathering. In *Proceedings of the Fourteenth International Joint Conference on Artificial Intelligence*, Montreal, Canada, 1995.

[Knoblock, 1996] Craig A. Knoblock. Building a planner for information gathering: A report from the trenches. In *Proceedings of the Third International Conference on Artificial Intelligence Planning Systems*, Edinburgh, Scotland, 1996.

[Landers and Rosenberg, 1982] Terry Landers and Ronni L. Rosenberg. An overview of Multibase. In H.J. Schneider, editor, *Distributed Data Bases.* North-Holland, 1982.

[Lenat and Guha, 1990] D. Lenat and R.V. Guha. *Building Large Knowledge-Based Systems: Representation and Inference in the Cyc Project.* Addison-Wesley, Reading, MA, 1990.

[MacGregor, 1988] Robert MacGregor. A deductive pattern matcher. In *Proceedings of the Seventh National Conference on Artificial Intelligence*, Saint Paul, Minnesota, 1988.

[MacGregor, 1990] Robert MacGregor. The evolving technology of classification-based knowledge representation systems. In John Sowa, editor, *Principles of Semantic Networks: Explorations in the Representation of Knowledge.* Morgan Kaufmann, 1990.

[Penberthy and Weld, 1992] J. Scott Penberthy and Daniel S. Weld. UCPOP: A sound, complete, partial order planner for ADL. In *Third International Conference on Principles of Knowledge Representation and Reasoning*, pages 189–197, Cambridge, MA, 1992.

[Reddy *et al.*, 1989] M.P. Reddy, B.E. Prasad, and P.G. Reddy. Query processing in heterogeneous distributed database management systems. In Amar Gupta, editor, *Integration of Information Systems: Bridging Heterogeneous Databases*, pages 264–277. IEEE Press, NY, 1989.

[Shekhar *et al.*, 1988] Shashi Shekhar, Jaideep Srivastava, and Soumitra Dutta. A formal model of trade-off between optimization and execution costs in semantic query optimization. In *Proceedings of the 14th VLDB Conference*, Los Angeles, CA, 1988.

[Shenoy and Ozsoyoglu, 1989] Sreekumar T. Shenoy and Zehra Meral Ozsoyoglu. Design and implementation of a semantic query optimizer. *IEEE Transactions on Knowledge and Data Engineering*, 1(3):344–361, 1989.

[Sheth and Larson, 1990] Amit P. Sheth and James A. Larson. Federated database systems for managing distributed, heterogeneous, and autonomous databases. *ACM Computing Surveys*, 22(3):183–236, 1990.

[Siegel, 1988] Michael D. Siegel. Automatic rule derivation for semantic query optimization. In Larry Kerschberg, editor, *Proceedings of the Second International Conference on Expert Database Systems*, pages 371–385. George Mason Foundation, Fairfax, VA, 1988.

Matchmaking for Information Agents

Daniel Kuokka **Larry Harada** *
Lockheed Palo Alto Research Labs, O/96-20, B/255
3251 Hanover Street, Palo Alto, CA 94304
kuokka@aic.lockheed.com, harada@aic.lockheed.com

Abstract

Factors such as the massive increase in information available via electronic networks and the advent of virtual distributed workgroups for commerce are placing severe burdens on traditional methods of information sharing and retrieval. Matchmaking proposes an intelligent facilitation agent that accepts machine-readable requests and advertisements from information consumers and providers, and determines potential information sharing paths. We argue that matchmaking permits large numbers of dynamic consumers and providers, operating on rapidly-changing data, to share information more effectively than via current methods. This paper introduces matchmaking, as enabled by knowledge sharing standards like KQML, and describes the SHADE and COINS matchmaker implementations. The utility and initial results of matchmaking are illustrated via example scenarios in engineering and consumer information retrieval.

1 Introduction

The trend toward computer-based tools for many aspects of commerce has led to a rapid increase in distributed virtual workgroups, such as multi-vendor design teams and virtual corporations. In addition, the advent of the Internet, personal computer networks, and interactive television networks has led to an explosion of information available on-line from thousands of new sources. These phenomena offer great promise for obtaining and sharing diverse information conveniently, but they also present a serious challenge. The sheer multitude, diversity, and dynamic nature of on-line information sources makes finding and accessing any specific piece of information extremely difficult.

To address this problem, several exciting new technologies have been developed. The standards and protocols of the World Wide Web, as well as its associated browsers, have provided a hugely successful dissemination framework for previously disassociated information. Furthermore, integration frameworks from CAD vendors and telecommunications companies provide information connectivity where there was none before. However, both of these employ address-based messaging or browsing paradigms—the users must know where the information exists. Unfortunately, as users try to make the transition from adventurous explorers to goal-driven information seekers, it becomes very difficult to find desired information. The pearls are lost in a sea of irrelevant information.

In response to this problem, two common solutions have appeared: clearinghouses and exploration agents. Clearinghouses, such as CommerceNet and MCC's EINet Galaxy, are central servers at which individual information providers can register. Since there are relatively few clearinghouses, consumers are able to effectively locate desired information. Exploration agents, such as Lycos [Mauldin and Leavitt, 1994] and the World Wide Web Worm [McBryan, 1994], "crawl" the network compiling a master index. The index can then be used as the basis for keyword searches much like a manually-created clearinghouse.

These approaches provide very useful solutions to the overflow of information, but several problems remain. First, as the number and size of clearinghouses grow, they degenerate into a duplication of the network, itself (an interesting phenomenon is that many clearinghouses are becoming cross-indexed, allowing each to benefit from the knowledge-base of the others). Thus, inefficiencies and difficulties in locating a specific piece of information are still present. Also, exploration is a computationally inefficient approach (in terms of bandwidth, processor, and memory utilization), so it is usually applied sparingly, and therefore provides a limited index of the subject network.

More fundamentally, the above approaches make the assumption that information producers are (mostly) passive, forcing consumers to drive the process. This necessarily imposes several handicaps:

*This work was supported in part by ARPA Contract DAAA 15-91-C0104 (Shared Knowledge-Based Technology for the Re-Engineering Problem), monitored by the U.S. Army Research Laboratory, Advanced Computational and Information Systems Directorate. The views, opinions, and/or findings contained in this report are those of the authors and should not be construed as an official Department of the Army position, policy, or decision, unless so designated by other documentation.

- Information consumers must know of or arduously locate all relevant providers. However, today's networks are composed of millions of potential information sources, each of which may provide information dynamically. Thus, discovering all sources is very difficult.
- Information providers have no way to contribute their efforts. Even though producers often have a stake in delivering their information, and would therefore be willing to assist in the process, this potential goes unutilized.
- Once a connection is made, there is no means by which a provider can notify a consumer of new knowledge or updates to past queries. Thus, in contexts where information is updated frequently and dynamically, approaches where the provider is passive simply can't work.

2 Matchmaking

A different approach to addressing this problem is called matchmaking. Matchmaking is based on a cooperative partnership between information providers and consumers, assisted by an intelligent facilitator [Genesereth, 1992] utilizing a knowledge sharing infrastructure [Patil *et al.*, 1992]. Information providers take an active role in finding specific consumers by *advertising* their information capabilities to a matchmaker. Conversely, consumers send *requests* for desired information to the matchmaker. The matchmaker attempts to identify any advertisements that are relevant to the requests and notifies the providers and consumers as appropriate.

Matchmaking is an automated process depending on machine-readable *messaging* and *content* languages. The main advantage of this approach is that the providers and consumers can continuously issue and retract advertisements and requests, so information does not tend to become stale. This is particularly critical in situations where information changes rapidly, as in product development and crisis management, and in situations where the shear magnitude of providers and consumers would cause the clearinghouse to be updated nearly continuously. A matchmaker is somewhat like a blackboard, except that it exists as a separate agent, the shared information tends to be highly structured in terms of knowledge-sharing protocols, and specific matchmaking algorithms are used. (The term agent is used in this paper to refer to a tool or program, possibly under the guidance of a human, that consumes or provides information to other agents.)

The content language must allow broad classes of information (i.e., many different documents) to be conveyed succinctly; otherwise, very many highly-specific messages, essentially duplicating the clients' databases, would be required. Whereas this provides useful representational economy and efficiency, it dictates that advertisements and requests are only approximate versions of the actual information. Thus, matchmaking is approximate, and false positive and false negative matches (depending on whether the advertisements and requests are over- or under-general) are likely to occur.

As variations on the general theme, matchmaking can follow many different specific modes. For example, the consumer might simply ask the matchmaker to *recommend* a provider that can likely satisfy the request. The actual queries then take place directly between the provider and consumer. The consumer might ask the matchmaker to forward the request to a capable provider with the stipulation that subsequent replies are to be sent directly to the consumer (called *recruiting*). Or, the consumer might ask the matchmaker to act as an intermediary, forwarding the request to the producer and forwarding the reply to the consumer (called *brokering*).

An implicit form of the last case, called *content-based routing*, is also possible, where a consumer simply *subscribes* to information as if the matchmaker were the source. The providers, rather than advertising their capabilities, simply send out changes as they occur. The matchmaker then routes the specific changes on to the subscriber. These different modalities (which correspond to several existing KQML message types as described in section 3) are shown in Figure 1.

An additional variation is on the persistency of the request. Consumers often desire to be told not only about providers that have already advertised a relevant capability, but also about any providers that advertise a capability in the future. In this case, the consumers would issue a persistent version of the above requests. This is essential, for instance, in the Parameter Manager example described in Section 5, in which a new consumer or provider with pertinent constraints may come on-line at any time.

There are many potential modes of matchmaking beyond those summarized in figure 1. As pointed out previously, one of the benefits of matchmaking is that it allows providers to take a more active role in information retrieval. Whereas the above schemes allow providers to advertise their capabilities dynamically, providers still cannot identify potential consumers unless the consumer actually issues a specific statement of interest. A useful extension would be to allow a provider to request the names of consumers that have posted related interests. This raises serious privacy considerations (imagine a consumer asking for a list of automobile dealerships only to be bombarded by sales offers from all of the dealerships), but in some cases, it may be desirable for a matchmaker to present a consumer with potential information providers spontaneously. Anonymity of the consumer is maintained, yet providers have an avenue for solicitations.

To evaluate and test the matchmaking approach, two prototype matchmakers have been built. The first matchmaker was designed and prototyped as part of the SHADE system [Kuokka and Harada, 1995a; McGuire *et al.*, 1993]. The SHADE matchmaker supports many modes of operation over formal, logic-based representations. The second matchmaker, created as an element of the COINS system (Common Interest Seeker) operates over free-text information, supporting fewer modes. The implementation of each of these systems is outlined in the following sections. Other researchers are also working on facilitators, such as the ABSI facilitator [Singh, 1993],

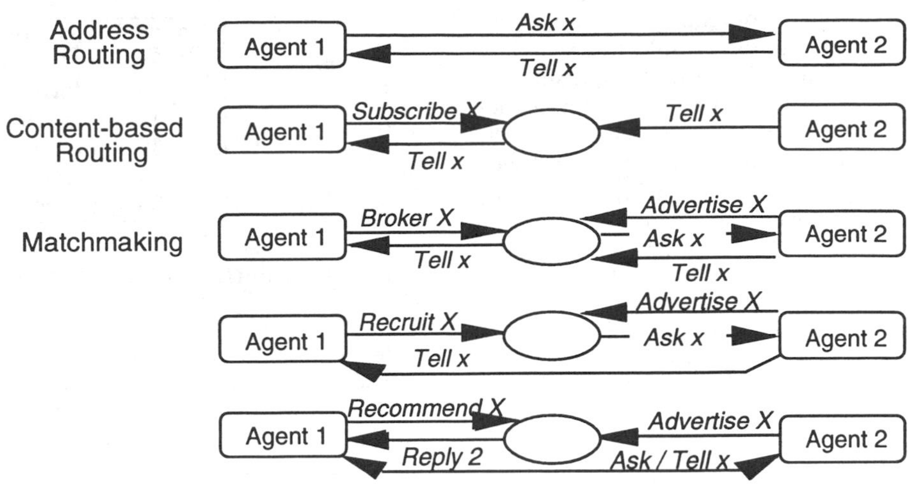

Figure 1: Modes of information routing

which also perform certain matchmaking functions. A detailed description of protocol issues related to matchmaking is covered in [Kuokka and Harada, 1995b].

The decision to implement two distinct matchmakers rather than a single, fully capable matchmaker was initially motivated by non-technical issues. However, it turns out that the resulting modularity is appropriate and beneficial in the agent-based world. This approach allows many matchmakers, each created by researchers with specific technical expertise, to be specialized for specific classes of languages. Such a distributed approach may also address pragmatic issues of scalability, but little effort has been applied in this area to date. If desired, a single, multi-language matchmaker may be implemented via a simple dispatching agent that farms out requests to the appropriate subcontracting agent.

3 SHADE Matchmaker

Matchmaking depends heavily on several technologies: an appropriate *messaging language* in which the client agents express their requests (e.g., the form of advertisement or request), an expressive *content representation* used to encode the actual information to be advertised and requested, and an effective matching algorithm.

The SHADE matchmaker communicates in terms of KQML (Knowledge Query and Manipulation Language [Finin *et al.*, 1993]) messages. Advertisements are sent using the KQML `advertise` performative (message type). Requests are sent using the `recommend`, `recruit`, and `broker` performatives. The matchmaker also supports content-based routing via the KQML performatives `tell` and `subscribe`.

For example, the KQML message

```
(advertise :sender p :receiver mm :lang kqml
  :content
  (ask-one :lang kif
    :content
    (subcomponent-of ?x ?y)))
```

advertises the capability to answer queries (ask-one) about the component hierarchy, and the message

```
(recruit-all :sender c :receiver mm :lang kqml
  :content
  (ask-one :lang kif
    :content
    (subcomponent-of gimbal ?x))))
```

asks the matchmaker to locate an agent that can answer the query: "What is the parent component of the gimbal?"

As its content language, the SHADE matchmaker supports two logic-based representations: a subset of KIF [Genesereth and Fikes, 1992], used in the above example, and a structured logic representation called MAX [Kuokka, 1990] augmented to support string patterns as terms. KIF is supported since it provides an expressive, standardized shared language with well-defined semantics. MAX is supported since it is more appropriate for representing highly structured data such as objects and frames. It essentially allows partial templates of frames to be advertised and requested. Furthermore, with the string matching augmentation, it provides a convenient means for advertising and requesting semi-structured text, such as outlines. For example, the message

```
(subscribe :sender c :receiver mm :lang kqml
  :content
  (ask-about :lang max
    :content
    [(trouble-report ?x)
     (match ?x [(subject ".*gimbal.*")])]))
```

subscribes to trouble report objects that have the string "gimbal" in their subject field.

The actual matching of advertised and subscribed content fields is performed by a Prolog-like unification algorithm. If strings are present in the logic forms, a regular expression pattern matcher is used for term unification.

Advertisements and requests must match based solely on their content; there is no knowledge base against which inference is performed. For example, an advertisement containing the term "engine" would not match an isomorphic request containing the term "propulsion system," since the matchmaker does not know that an engine is a subclass of a propulsion system. To address this issue, the SHADE project has also been developing technology to define *ontologies* [Gruber, 1993]—knowledge bases that define shared concepts. As ontologies become available, future versions of the matchmaker will include the capability to perform limited inference based on the specific ontology specified in the KQML message, allowing the above example to match.

This path must be followed carefully, however, since an arbitrary amount of inference or knowledge may be required to match any given advertisement and request. The matchmaker could quickly be transformed from a communication facilitator to a multi-domain reasoning engine. This would violate a key tenet of the agent-based approach—that of utilizing many different domain-specific agents. Therefore, the tendency to enhance the capabilities of the matchmaker must be tempered by the desirable separation of functionality underlying the network of agents.

The SHADE matchmaker is implemented entirely as a declarative rule-based program within the MAX forward-chaining agent architecture. This allows features of the matchmaker (e.g., support for additional KQML performatives) to be added as additional rules. For example, the rule that implements the broker request is shown below.

```
(rule
 [(pre
   [(message broker-one ?broker)
    (match ?broker [(content ?content)
                    (language kqml)
                    (sender ?sender)
                    (receiver ?receiver)])
    (match ?content [(perf ?bperf)
                     (language ?blang)
                     (content ?bcontent)])
    (advertisement ?bperf ?advertisement)
    (match ?advertisement
           [(language ?alang)
            (content ?acontent)
            (advertiser ?advertiser)])
    (not-match ?sender ?advertiser)
    (match ?blang ?alang)
    (match ?bcontent ?acontent)])
  (post
   [(advertisement ?bperf ?advertisement)
    (brokering ?advertiser ?sender)
    (kqml-message [(perf reply)
                   (receiver ?sender)
                   (sender ?receiver)
                   (content received)])
    (kqml-message [(perf ?bperf)
                   (receiver ?advertiser)
                   (sender ?receiver)
                   (content ?bcontent)])])])
```

In addition, the SHADE matchmaker supports meta-level queries about its operation. This feature allows other agents to subscribe to the message level actions of the matchmaker in addition to content level information. For example, another SHADE agent called the Bird's Eye View agent uses this feature to subscribe to all advertisements and requests, regardless of content. The Bird's Eye agent then displays the system of agents and message traffic. The meta-reasoning capabilities are also used to provide reasons for match failures in certain cases (the Space Imaging application described in section 6 uses this feature).

Count	Concept
97	matchmak
53	inform
45	content
38	advert
33	agent
33	match

Table 1: A portion of document vector for this paper

4 COINS Matchmaker

Motivated by the utility of the SHADE matchmaker on structured information and by the need for similar functionality over the huge amount of text available on-line, a second matchmaker has been created that operates on free-text as its content language. This matchmaker was initially conceived as the central part of a system called COINS (COmmon INterest Seeker), which allows users to easily advertise and request information about their interests. However, by architecting the system as a set of agents, the COINS matchmaker is also useful as a general purpose facilitator.

As with the SHADE matchmaker, the COINS matchmaker is accessed via the standard KQML messages advertise and broker. The content language is either free-text or a concept vector (a weighed list of stemmed words in the document). An example of a portion of the concept vector for this paper is shown in Table 1.

To determine if a free-text request matches a free-text advertisement, the content of each is converted into a concept vector using the SMART [Salton, 1989] information retrieval system. The SMART matching algorithm is then used to determine the degree of match. Finally, an adjustable cutoff measure is used to make the match binary. Thus, other than supporting a different content language, the COINS matchmaker works much like the SHADE matchmaker.

SMART employs an inverse document frequency scheme so the COINS matchmaker must maintain and use a local concept corpus. This functions somewhat like the ontology of the SHADE matchmaker in that it is a knowledge base of shared concepts allowing the match process to be more effective.

5 Application: Collaborative Engineering

The SHADE and COINS matchmakers are being used as a central component of several research projects. The

SHADE project, itself, is exploring broader infrastructure issues in support of distributed engineering. To this end, SHADE has developed a testbed for collaborative engineering to motivate and test infrastructure components such as the matchmaker.

To illustrate the utility of a matchmaker in an engineering environment, consider the following scenario showing a few steps in the design of a satellite. The engineering team consists of a Systems Engineer, responsible for specifying the overall architecture of the satellite; a Designer, responsible for designing the geometry and structure of a gimbal on the satellite; and a Mass Specialist, who allocates the mass budgets to individual subsystems.

The participants use a number of engineering tools that consume and produce complex engineering information. Each participant uses the Project Coordination Assistant (PCA) [Kuokka, 1994], which allows engineers to view and manipulate textual and structured data on the project such as the satellite component hierarchy and trouble reports, and the Parameter Manager (ParMan) [Kuokka and Livezey, 1994], which allows many different engineers to define constraints over shared parameters. In addition, each engineer may use any number of CAD tools specific to his or her discipline.

Initially, the Systems Engineer uses the PCA to request notification about any unresolved problems. This is translated into the following matchmaker subscription:

```
(subscribe :sender syseng :receiver mm
  :content
  (tell :lang max
    :content
    [(newpage [(item ?newitem)])
     (match ?newitem [(text "problem")])
     (oldpage ?opage)
     (not-match ?opage [(item ?newitem)])]))
```

Notice that the form of the content is designed such that a literal will match the interest template only the first time it is added to the page. Otherwise, if a pattern that matches the interest template exists within a page, every subsequent change to that page would result in a repeated notification, even if the pattern, itself, did not change.

Next, using the PCA, the Systems Engineer adds the mass budget attribute (mass-bgt) to the gimbal object in the global satellite topology database, resulting in a new page being sent to the matchmaker.

```
(tell :sender syseng :receiver mm :lang max
  :content
  [(newpage
    [(item [(text "Structure")
            (item [(text "Gimbal1")
                   (item [(text "mass")])
                   (item [(text "mass-bgt")])
                   ...]) ...])])
   (oldpage
    [(item [(text "Structure")
            (item [(text "Gimbal1")
                   (item [(text "mass")])
                   ...]) ...])])])
```

By virtue of a previous subscription to changes to the gimbal (similar to the System Engineer's subscription to unresolved problems), the Gimbal Designer receives notice of the new mass budget attribute.

The new parameter is relevant to his subsystem, so the designer imports the new parameter to his ParMan tool and enters the constraint that the actual mass of the gimbal must be less than the mass budget. Since the ParMan tool is designed to handle distributed constraints, it must attempt to locate other agents that have constraints over the new parameter. This results in the following messages being sent to the matchmaker.

```
(recruit-all :sender gimbal1-pm :receiver mm
  :content
  (subscribe :lang kqml
    :content
    (stream-about :lang kif
      :content
      (mass gimbal-1)))

(advertise :sender gimbal1-pm :receiver mm
  :content
  (subscribe :lang kqml
    :content
    (stream-about :lang kif
      :content
      (mass gimbal-1)))
```

Since the mass specialist is responsible for allocating the mass budgets, she also defines a constraint, which results in similar advertisements and requests being posted by her ParMan agent. The matchmaker matches the advertisements and requests for the mass budget posted by each ParMan and routes the requests on to the other ParMan agents. This allows each ParMan agent to locate all other sources of relevant constraints, and ultimately identify that the budget as supplied by the mass specialist is inconsistent with the actual mass of the gimbal.

At this point, we assume that the designer cannot restructure the gimbal to meet the budget demands, so he posts an open problem via PCA. This results in the following message being sent to the matchmaker.

```
(tell :sender gimbal1 :receiver mm :lang max
  :content
  [(newpage [(item [(text "Problems")
                   (item [(text
    "Gimbal 1 cannot satisfy mass budget")])
                   (item [(text
    "Dual controller hysteresis occurring")])
                   ...]) ...]
   (oldpage [(item [(text "Problems")
                   (item [(text
    "Dual controller hysteresis occurring")])
                   ...]) ...])])
```

This matches with the System Engineer's earlier subscription, so he receives notification of this problem. Thus, by facilitating the dynamic connection of relevant information sources, a problem that might have gone unnoticed for many days was identified and propagated to concerned participants within minutes. A diagram, generated by the Bird's Eye View agent based on its

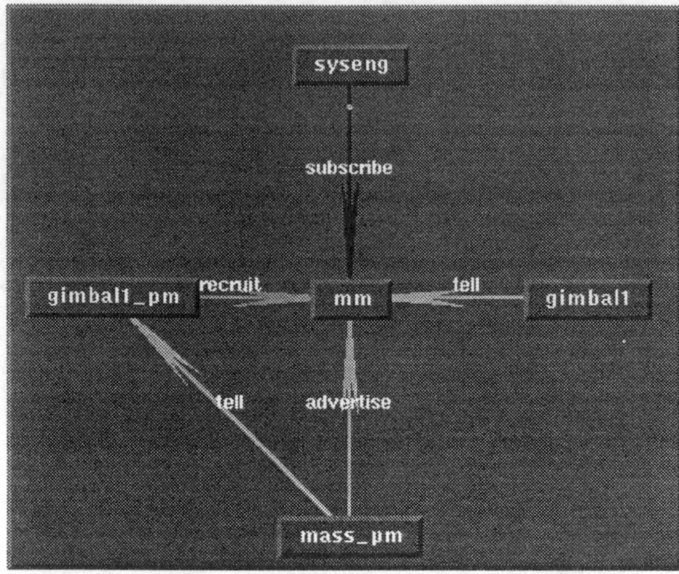

Figure 2: Key message traffic among agents

meta-level subscription to the matchmaker is shown in Figure 2.

The key to the matchmaking approach is that it avoids the need to identify a priori all potential information transfer paths, which is impossible in general due to the dynamic nature of engineering teams. This is especially important if the project is considered in its full context, where there are hundreds of engineers, scores of gimbals, hundreds of other components, and thousands of parameters and constraints. Many engineers might be using the Parameter Manager to state their constraints on the parameters of specific interest to them. When any one engineer decides to add a constraint, he has no way of knowing exactly which other engineers are impacted, and therefore whom should be notified. This is solved by each Parameter Manager sending advertisements and subscriptions to the matchmaker for the specific parameters of concern, allowing all agents to locate the new sources and sinks of information for this specific, unforeseeable engineering need.

The matchmaker is also vital to the operation of collaboration tools like the PCA. As described above, when the Systems Engineer created a monitor for problem reports, a KQML subscribe message was sent to the matchmaker. As other changes were made to the PCA data, they were forward to the matchmaker. This allowed the matchmaker to route relevant changes to subscribers. Not shown in the scenario is that as changes are made to PCA pages, the PCA also transforms the semi-structured text into concept vectors and sends them as subscriptions to the COINS matchmaker. As other agents do the same, the matchmaker monitors for pairs of concept vectors that match (according to the approximate concept vector match criterion). If a pair is found, pointers are returned to the PCA and the other agent. The PCA then adds them to a dynamic list of relevant documents. Thus, the matchmaker is used to locate other information relevant to the contents of the PCA information base.

The matchmaker has been used by several other engineering-related projects as well. The Cosmos project [Mark and Dukes-Schlossberg, 1994], which is creating a knowledge-based commitment reasoner to determine impacts of engineering changes, uses the matchmaker to provide indirection between a set of dynamic clients and the server. The ARPA Simulation Based Design project uses the matchmaker to provide change subscription and notification services over its large, object-oriented product model. In this application, if an object for which a subscription has been issued changes, the user will receive automatic notification. Other applications of the matchmaker, such as its use to locate relevant pages in a large distributed engineering notebook, are in earlier stages of development.

6 Application: Information Retrieval

The functionality of matchmaking goes beyond engineering teams. For example, the matchmaker is an integral part of a prototype information retrieval system being developed to support Lockheed's SII (Space Imaging, Inc) project, an effort to sell high-resolution satellite imagery on the commercial market. Since there are multiple satellite image providers, and numerous value-added post-processors, this task consists of locating data available from multiple dynamic sources in response to specific queries. Therefore, the SII prototype uses the SHADE matchmaker.

The system works as follows. As new classes of images become available, the data sources issue advertisements in terms of the image attributes (e.g., geographic area, resolution, spectral bands, and cloud cover). When a user requests a specific kind of image, a front-end agent issues a query to the matchmaker that describes the desired attributes. The matchmaker compares the advertisements to the queries, and sends any matches to the front-end agent. This first-pass match is used to locate servers for further, more specific, queries. In addition, when a source database is not appropriate, the matchmaker returns a failure reason.

The matchmaker is important to the SII application not only because there are multiple sources of data, but also because the data is constantly being updated as satellites circle the earth. The matchmaker allows each data source to advertise and retract its image capabilities dynamically, permitting the matchmaker to suggest sources even if the specific image hasn't yet been collected. Only an automated system like the matchmaker can offer the up-to-the-minute location of data required by SII.

7 Conclusions

The growth of information available via electronic networks presents both an unprecedented opportunity and a difficult challenge. Rather than relying on traditional techniques that are consumer-driven, matchmaking allows both of the stake holders (i.e., information providers and consumers) to contribute to information gathering activities. Thus, information providers can seek specific consumers much like consumers currently find specific providers. In addition, since matchmaking is an automated approach, it better addresses the dynamic nature of electronic information, which is based on huge numbers of potential information providers and consumers. The need for such an approach is underscored by the rapid adoption of the SHADE and COINS prototype matchmakers by several projects.

However, matchmaking is still an experimental approach, and many questions remain. Additional support is required for formal languages such as object and terminological representations, and a capability to load relevant knowledge bases and ontologies is needed to permit matchmaking based on subsumption reasoning and inference (however, the matchmaker cannot become the reasoning engine to the world). Also, further expansion into free-form human languages and graphics is needed, going beyond the current concept vector abstraction of text. Looking beyond the content language, the experiments with matchmaking to date have already begun to stretch the KQML messaging substrate. Further augmentations are required to support additional modalities and to clarify the semantics of the existing message types. And finally, as applications grow in size and complexity, techniques to distribute the matchmaker load will be required. Yet, in spite of these open issues, matchmaking is a promising approach to supporting information access in heterogeneous and dynamic environments.

Acknowledgments

The initial concept of matchmaking and the KQML formalization stemmed from efforts by the entire SHADE team, including Jim McGuire, Jay Weber, Greg Olsen, Rich Pelavin, Tom Gruber, and Marty Tenenbaum, as well as the efforts of the KQML committee. We also thank Brian Livezey for many insights and Morton Hirschberg for his invaluable support. This work was supported in part by ARPA prime contract DAAA15-91-C0104, monitored by the U.S. Army Research Laboratory.

References

[Finin *et al.*, 1993] T. Finin, J. Weber, G. Wiederhold, M. Genesereth, R. Fritzson, D. McKay, J. McGuire, R. Pelavin, S. Shapiro, and C. Beck. Draft specification of the KQML agent-communication language. Technical report, The ARPA Knowledge Sharing Initiative External Interfaces Working Group, 1993.

[Genesereth and Fikes, 1992] M. Genesereth and R. Fikes. Knowledge Interchange Format, version 3.0 reference manual. Technical Report Logic-92-1, Computer Science Department, Stanford University, 1992.

[Genesereth, 1992] M. Genesereth. An agent-based framework for software interoperability. In *Proceedings DARPA Software Technology Conference*, 1992.

[Gruber, 1993] T. Gruber. A translation approach to portable ontology specifications. *Knowledge Acquisition*, 5(2), 1993.

[Kuokka and Harada, 1995a] D. Kuokka and L. Harada. A communication infrastructure for concurrent engineering. *Artificial Intelligence in Engineering, Design, Analysis, and Manufacturing*, 1995.

[Kuokka and Harada, 1995b] D. Kuokka and L. Harada. On using KQML for matchmaking. In *International Conference on Multiagent Systems*, 1995.

[Kuokka and Livezey, 1994] D. Kuokka and B. Livezey. A collaborative parametric design agent. In *Proceedings of the National Conference on Artificial Intelligence*, pages 387–393, Menlo Park, CA, 1994. AAAI Press.

[Kuokka, 1994] D. Kuokka. An evolution of collaborative design tools. In *AAAI-94 Workshop on Models of Conflict Management in Cooperative Problem Solving*. AAAI Tech. Report WS-94-04, 1994.

[Kuokka, 1990] D. Kuokka. *The Deliberative Integration of Planning, Execution, and Learning.* PhD thesis, School of Computer Science, Carnegie Mellon University, 1990.

[Mark and Dukes-Schlossberg, 1994] W. Mark and J. Dukes-Schlossberg. Cosmos: A system for supporting engineering negotiation. *Concurrent Engineering: Research and Applications*, 2(3), 1994.

[Mauldin and Leavitt, 1994] M. Mauldin and J. Leavitt. Web-agent related research at the CMT. In *Proceedings of the ACM Special Interest Group on Notworked Information Discovery and Retrieval (SIGNIDR-94)*, 1994.

[McBryan, 1994] O. McBryan. WWWW—the World Wide Web Worm. http://www.cs.colorado.edu/home /mcbryan/WWWW.html, 1994.

[McGuire *et al.*, 1993] J. McGuire, D. Kuokka, J. Weber, J. Tenenbaum, T. Gruber, and G. Olsen. SHADE: Technology for knowledge-based collaborative engineering. *Concurrent Engineering: Research and Applications*, 1(3), 1993.

[Patil *et al.*, 1992] R. Patil, R. Fikes, P. Patel-Schneider, D. McKay, T. Finin, T. Gruber, and R. Neches. The DARPA Knowledge Sharing Effort: Progress report. In *Proceedings of the Third International Conference on Principles of Knowledge Representation and Reasoning.* Morgan Kaufmann, 1992.

[Salton, 1989] G. Salton. *Automatic Text Processing—The Analysis, Transformation and Retrieval of Information by Computer.* Addison-Wesley, Reading, MA, 1989.

[Singh, 1993] N. Singh. A CommonLisp API and facilitator for ABSI (revision 2.0.3). Technical Report Logic-93-4, Stanford University Computer Science Department Logic Group, 1993.

The agent architecture of the University of Michigan Digital Library

E.H. Durfee
D.L. Kiskis
W.P. Birmingham

Indexing terms: Agent architecture, Internet

Abstract: The University of Michigan Digital Library (UMDL) architecture encapsulates the many functionalities required in a digital library as a population of modular, goal-oriented, specialised 'agents'. These agents participate in markets for exchanging goods and services, and team their abilities to compose complex services. Realising the UMDL agent architecture requires us to provide sound mechanisms to encapsulate functions as agents, protocols to support the evolution of teams and agent interactions through markets, and protocols to enable interoperability among library agents that are teamed. The software-engineering aspects of our effort (the tools, techniques and experiences gained) are the focus of this paper.

1 Introduction

A challenge in developing large software systems for Internet applications is the unpredictability of the capabilities needed to provide useful services, or even of which services will in time be deemed useful. For example, digital libraries, currently a popular Internet-based service, imply notions of easy access to all kinds of information from anywhere in the world. Nobody knows how this will be done. The number of capabilities needed in a digital library is daunting, covering issues such as the following. How will authors of digital documents find readers and be compensated for their work? How will readers avoid aimlessly wandering through a quagmire of information, most of which they will find irrelevant? What will be the role of editors for reviewing, collecting, and improving documents that satisfy a particular readership's needs? How will other services, such as notification of changing library content, or translation across languages or formats, become available? Who will provide all of these within a digital library, and why would they?

We do not yet know the answers to these questions, but one thing is certain: whatever answers are formulated, the odds are good that they will be correct only for a short time. Thus, given the lack of a clear vision of a digital library, let alone detailed specifications, the development of complex, distributed software systems like a digital library poses substantial software-engineering challenges!

There are, however, useful design principles on which to base software development. It is clear that a digital-library service will be distributed in many ways, such as in terms of geography, functionality and ownership. For the foreseeable future, capabilities found as part of a digital library will mimic the broader set of capabilities seen in the production and use of information today, including authoring, editing, publishing, marketing, transporting, purchasing and viewing. Because of the vast number of capabilities needed in a digital library, it is very unlikely that a single organisation will provide a complete, integrated solution. Just as today when *autonomous* [Note 1] entities come together to achieve some objective (such as authors, editors and publishers working together to produce a book), this same kind of teaming of capabilities must be part of the software system that supports a digital library. Of course, teaming assumes that the entities can understand each other, and have the ability to strike a mutually acceptable deal. Such deals are necessary, as each entity must have an incentive to participate in any team. (In an open system with autonomous software agents, distributed software modules cannot directly invoke each other. Gone are the days of teaming through remote procedure calls!).

Based on this perspective of what must happen in a digital library, our response for the University of Michigan Digital Library (UMDL) [1] has been to adopt a software-development methodology that specifically supports an evolving, open network of capability providers and consumers, each of whom has idiosyncratic interests. Rather than attempt to shoehorn the vast number of capabilities a digital library must provide into a monolithic and centrally administered software system, our approach is to consider separate software components capable of embodying specific capabilities, and acting in the interest of the entity (organisation or person) that created that component. The general notion of object-oriented programming does not properly capture our decentralised philosophy: OOP assumes that objects are passively awaiting requests that they are obliged to serve. Rather than adopting a

IEE Proceedings online no. 19971024
Paper received 22nd October 1996
The authors are with the Univeristy of Michigan, Ann Arbor, MI 48109, USA; durfee@umich.edu

Note 1: We loosely use 'autonomous' here to mean that an entity or agent has the ability to reason about its resources, and is free to act in its own self-interest.

methodology in which a team of system designers negotiates the interactions between modules and then permanently puts these in place at *design* time, our approach instead is to support the development and incorporation of software modules that collectively configure their interactions themselves at *run* time.

Because each software module is capable of 'operating' alone and maintaining its own goals and preferences, we call them agents. The term agent has received many definitions over recent years, ranging from being defined in terms of internal structures or mechanisms of an agent (such as belief-desire-intention architectures) [2, 3] to behaviouralistic treatments that essentially claim that an agent is anything that it is convenient to think of as an agent [4]. As we shall see, the work we describe in this paper takes a behavioural view, but part of the architectural-development process is to specify carefully and commit to particular behaviours that agents may expect of others (without making strong commitments to how those behaviours should be realised).

It is agents that 'do' things in the UMDL, and each agent represents the interests of some (generally external) entity. So, for example, an author would have one or more agents representing her interests, while a reader would have one or more for his interests. Someone who has carefully read a body of on-line literature and can use that knowledge to help steer lost readers in profitable directions could also have an agent to proffer this navigation capability. Agents come and go as the providers and users of information and services come and go. Agents (and their typically human counterparts) survive if they are successful in achieving their objectives, which invariably means working in concert with other agents to the benefit of each. An agent that provides something no one wants, or needs something no one will ever provide, will not thrive in such an environment. On the other hand, this kind of environment provides incentives to entities that have information and services that others would be interested in using to participate, potentially enriching the overall digital library.

Achieving this lofty vision (of an evolving agent economy where agents team to achieve their goals and many agents come away winners) is a primary research goal of our project. In this paper we concentrate on the development of our initial software architecture that demonstrates rudimentary capabilities towards this ultimate goal. The architecture is shown in Fig. 1, and comprises the following: an **agent architecture** that provides quite general mechanisms for building an agent-based system; a **UMDL agent architecture** that refines the basic agent architecture in ways that make it particularly appropriate for the needs of an open information economy like the UMDL; and **instances** of the UMDL agent architecture, where particular capabilities of interest to a particular application of the UMDL are included. That is, the particular services needed in a high-school deployment of a digital library could be quite different from those in a corporate-research setting. The underlying UMDL agent architecture is suitable across these settings, but the architecture might be instantiated differently (populated with different agents).

Consider the layering of the architecture (Fig. 1). At the top are services that the digital library needs to provide. As argued above, we divide these services into two types: services that are dependent on the particular tasks for which an instance of the architecture is intended, and services that are assumed to be inherently in the UMDL architecture. An example of the former services might be one for locating images based on verbal descriptions, which might be of specific use in an art library. Within the UMDL, our emphasis on an open system of autonomous, rational agents leads us to presume that services for locating other agents, for reaching agreements with them, and for authentication and payment, for example, should be standardised as part of the UMDL architecture.

Services are in turn provided by teams of agents who actually accomplish the important tasks in the network. Again, for a particular application, the tasks can be associated with various task-specific agents, such as agents that specialise in natural-language processing for restricted domains, or agents that perform pattern recognition on images. The services inherently provided by the UMDL architecture are similarly realised by agents, such as agents that register information about others' capabilities to support agent-locator services.

Agents work together to provide services through particular patterns of interaction called protocols. Protocols can be specific to particular tasks within an instance of the UMDL architecture. For the services that span the UMDL, we assume that all agents affected by those services are capable of engaging in the UMDL-specified protocols, such as those for advertising capabilities to a registry.

Regardless of the details of the specifications, eventually the agents and protocols must be defined in terms of software modules and communication languages. In our work, we support this level of implementation by providing a well-defined yet flexible communication language, along with application programming interfaces (APIs) tailored to this language that simplify the process of constructing the communicating-agent processes. We call this support software 'agentware', as it provides a foundation for rapidly prototyping various kinds of agents.

Finally, of course, all of this must be embedded in particular networked computing systems, completing the levels shown in the Figure.

As the agent architecture provides communication services, it is generally applicable to most agent systems. The architecture, as mentioned earlier, does not commit to a particular agent model, nor does it assume particular interaction or teaming. The strongest assumption that we make is the use of messages and protocols. This assumption is relatively weak, but there

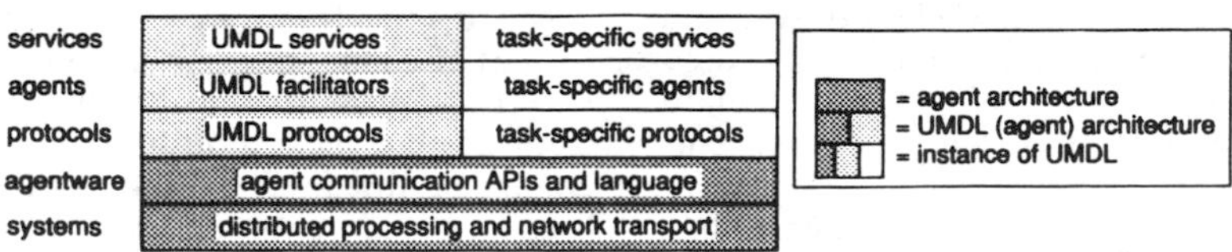

Fig. 1 *Layers of UMDL agent architecture*

are classes of agent organisations, such as blackboard systems [5], where our architecture may not be ideal (although it is likely 'workable').

In the remainder of this paper we discuss the current design and implementation of these layers from the bottom up by outlining our software-development environment. We describe the current state of the UMDL, illustrating how it is beginning to provide an open and extensible digital-library architecture that we believe is a template for future widely distributed (Internet-based) services. Finally, we conclude with a summary of the lessons that we have learned about agent-based software development, and an outline of our ongoing efforts in this arena.

2 Agent architecture

As illustrated in Fig. 1, the UMDL system is composed of several layers. The lowest layer makes commitments to particular networked systems that provide the operating systems and transport mechanisms upon which the rest of the system is built. For example, we have committed to using CORBA/ILU for transport. To simplify the use of these underlying capabilities as viewed in an 'agent-based' manner, on top of this layer is our 'agentware' layer. This layer commits us to the agent-based software-development paradigm, in the sense that the language specification is in terms of speech acts that correspond to the categories of intentional utterances associated with (human) agents, and the communication APIs provide a flexible means of associating semantics with the language.

2.1 System and network environment

For wide portability, agents are implemented as Unix processes that communicate using common network protocols, i.e. TCP/IP. We chose distributed-object technology as the basis for agent communication. We are using the CORBA distributed-object standard [6], and in particular Xerox's ILU (Inter-Language Unification) implementation of it. The CORBA standard provides us with the basic mechanisms that we need, and it seems the most appropriate for a Unix-based development. ILU is freely available, and thus allows us to experiment with CORBA with little investment. It also allows us to distribute our software to other institutions without burdening them with the requirement of purchasing an expensive ORB (object request broker).

2.2 Agentware

Although we make no commitments in our agentware to the internal architecture of an agent, a fundamental premise of an agent-based system is that agents must communicate to get anything done. Therefore, the most important feature of the agentware level is agent-communication tools.

These tools define for each agent a communication interface, embodied as an ILU object that handles communication with other agents' communication objects. The interface exported by the communication objects implements KQML (knowledge query and manipulation language) performatives and their (possibly nested) argument lists, where KQML is a standard language for communicating knowledge between agents [7].

KQML defines message structures and message types from which agent protocols may be constructed (see Fig. 2). A KQML message supplies a speech act or *performative* that is attached to the content of the message. There are performatives defined to indicate assertions (tell), queries (ask-about, recommend-one), advertisement of capabilities (advertise), commands (register, subscribe), and others. Each message contains a number of arguments (e.g. :sender, :receiver) that provide protocol information. The content of the message is contained in the :content argument. Other arguments (e.g. :ontology, :language) provide metadata about the content. This language structure makes KQML well suited for our general agent communication needs, because it provides sufficient structure to delineate agentware functionality, while remaining neutral to details of content, which will, of course, vary with agents and applications.

```
(performative
        (:sender X)
        (:receiver Z)
        (:ontology O)
        (:language L)
        (:content ()))
```

Fig. 2 *KQML message structure*

The primary component of our agentware is an Agent class written in C++. The Agent class encapsulates the communication mechanisms. Individual agents are implemented by subclassing this class, thus inheriting the ability to communicate through our standard mechanisms. The class provides an API for sending messages. There is one function for each performative. KQML performative arguments are stored in an object that is passed as a parameter to the function. The class for this object is also part of the agentware library.

Agents are differentiated by their internal processing methods, and by how they individually interpret and generate messages. Because some agents only respond to particular performatives, the programmer only implements code to handle those performatives. To do this, we define a unique function to process each performative. These functions are declared as C++ virtual functions in the Agent class, allowing the programmer to redefine them in the derived class. In this way, the behaviour triggered by a particular performative and whatever changes to the agent's state this causes can be fully customised. For each performative, our Agent class provides a default implementation of each function. Unless the programmer has redefined the function, the default implementation will send a 'sorry' response to messages it receives containing that performative. 'Sorry' is the KQML standard response that indicates that the receiver is unable to execute a performative.

2.3 Agent communication

While processing a task an agent will usually need to communicate with another agent. Sometimes, further processing of the task cannot proceed until the agent receives a response from the other agent. At other times it is possible to continue processing the task while the agent is waiting for a response, which will be handled at some future time. Our agentware supports both styles of communication by allowing the agent designer to choose whether the agent will communicate synchronously or asynchronously. In synchronous communication, the thread associated with the task in the calling agent blocks until the remote call completes and a result is returned. In asynchronous communication the thread continues. The reply is returned using an asynchronous *reply* performative. Thus, asynchronous communication can eliminate timing interdependencies between agents that can infringe upon individual autonomy [Note 2].

The Agent class supports both synchronous and asynchronous communication. This support is easy to provide for the send calls. A parameter of the send function for each performative allows the programmer to select the calling mode. ILU allows functions to be defined as synchronous or asynchronous (using the CORBA interface definition language keyword *oneway*). The communication-object interface has both types of calls defined for each performative. The object simply chooses which function to call, depending on the value of the send mode parameter.

Processing these calls on the receiving end is slightly more involved. As described above, a function has been defined in the Agent class (and possibly redefined in the derived class) to process each performative. We refer to such a function as the receive function for the performative. We would prefer that the programmer of the receive function only needs to programme one version of it, and not know nor care how it was invoked. Otherwise, we would be providing additional opportunities to introduce inconsistencies between versions. Thus, synchronous and asynchronous calls both invoke the same receive function in the Agent class. The receive function returns any results via a *pass-by-reference* parameter. If the call was invoked synchronously, it will have a CORBA *out* parameter through which the Agent class may return the results [Note 3]. If it was invoked asynchronously, the Agent class returns the results using an asynchronous *reply* performative call to the other agent.

2.4 Embedding UMDL-specific functionality

The agentware, as described so far, represents an extremely flexible foundation upon which to develop agent systems. As the agentware only makes commitments to a communication 'shell' without specifying how that shell is to be used (what agents should say to whom and when), the agentware could be applied broadly, from closed environments with inherently cooperative agents whose interactions are hardwired, to open environments with self-interested agents that dynamically reconfigure their interactions.

For convenience, however, we have added to our Agent class some functionality tailored to particular services that we assume are part of the UMDL. For example, because a required capability of a UMDL agent is that it must register with the UMDL registry so that other agents can find it, we have embedded this functionality into our Agent class, thus relieving the programmer of the necessity to write a correct implementation of the registration protocol for every agent created. Including this functionality in the Agent class specialises it somewhat; however, these features can easily be removed or ignored for the application of our agentware for different agent environments, where the commitments of the UMDL might be less appropriate.

Note 2: Note that autonomy is potentially threatened by many possible ways that agents might be dependent on what others do, why they do it, and how they do it, as well as when they do it. Asynchrony can thus influence autonomy, but is not synonymous with it.

Note 3: A CORBA out parameter behaves like a call-by-reference parameter in a local call, i.e. the caller of the function sees any changes to the parameter value made by the called function.

3 UMDL agent architecture

The commitment to an agent-based approach captured in the agent architecture allows a very wide range of designs, and further specialisation of the architecture depends on answers to many questions, such as: Do we assume that agents will choose to cooperate, or must they be convinced to work together? Will the population of agents change over time, or can we count on a particular population? Will all agents have access to all services and intellectual properties?

In the UMDL, we have generated answers to (many of) these questions, and so have taken the basic, underspecified agent architecture provided by the lower levels (Section 2), and have made commitments to services that must be part of the UMDL, and consequently protocols in which each UMDL agent need participate. A significant part of our effort, therefore, has been devoted to developing the agents and protocols necessary for providing these services. As these services are in place to facilitate widely used processes, such as team formation, the agents devoted to providing these services are called *facilitators*.

In this Section we describe the details of the UMDL agent architecture in terms of the communication patterns and particular facilitator agents. We conclude this Section with a description of how communication and facilitators come together to provide a UMDL service for agent location.

3.1 UMDL protocols, ontologies and task languages

Just because agents can communicate, this does not mean that they can work together. Agents must exchange appropriate content with selected agents. Details of content and selection of agents are generally domain-dependent. The tasks of location, negotiation, selection and forming a commitment, however, permeate the entire agent society. If agents have different views of these tasks, or different expectations about how they should interact to accomplish them, then teaming (and hence the delivery of significant services) is impossible.

Thus, layered on top of the underlying agent architecture, we have provided protocols for agent interaction, and ontological specifications that give the agents a shared vocabulary across their mutual tasks of locating and teaming. In what follows we describe these protocols and outline this ontology.

3.1.1 UMDL protocol: definitions and implementation: As described in Section 2.2, communication in the UMDL is based on exchanging messages using KQML message formats. Agents use these messages to accomplish UMDL tasks by using patterns of message exchanges that lead to a desirable set of state changes among agents. As a simple example, a message that poses a query is best answered with a message that conveys a reply. In fact, it turns out that there are a small number of fundamental patterns of message exchange among agents, which we term *protocols*. Thus, the protocols describe how KQML messages are to be sent and responded to during interagent communication.

Fig. 3 shows the classes of protocols developed thus far in the UMDL project, taking the perspective of the sender, who is initiating the communication act, with the response to each message shown. These protocols are the basic types of interaction that occur in UMDL at this time; the set of protocols is likely to expand. Each protocol is based on a particular kind of request for service from one agent to another, and the contexts of the request and response are all different. For example, the *registration* protocol allows an agent to describe itself to the registry using a particular language and ontology, which is significantly different from the *conspectus-update* protocol. Because of these differences, it is more convenient to separate them. We do this everyday: buying a chocolate bar and buying a car can be considered under a general protocol of 'buying', yet they are so different that we consider them very different protocols (and acts).

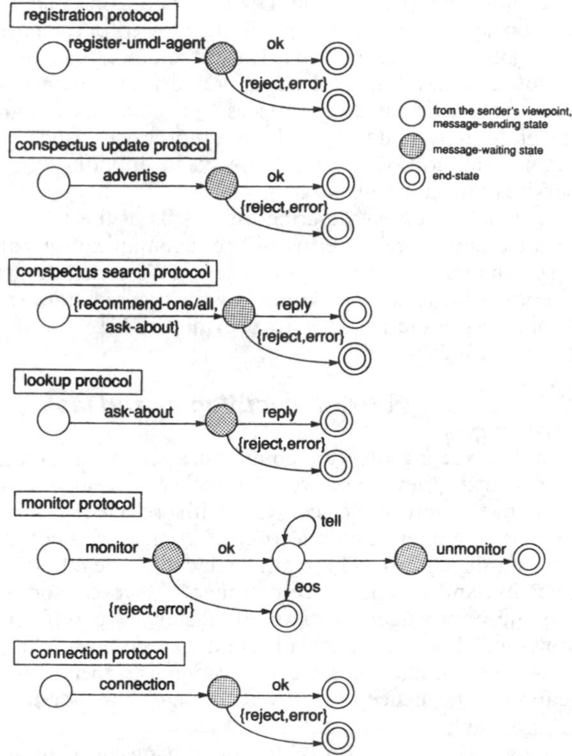

Fig.3 *UMDL protocols*

Given the general nature of KQML performatives, there are many ways in which they can be combined to form protocols. UMDL protocols have the following properties:

(*a*) they represent the basic types of interaction among agents;

(*b*) they are defined without regard to how any particular agent may use them;

(*c*) they are unbiased to the algorithms or goals of any agent;

(*d*) they are stateless whenever possible.

These properties mean that agents can combine the protocols in idiosyncratic fashions to create any number of more complex types of interactions.

The protocols are implemented by the agents through the Agent class mechanisms provided in the agentware. By adhering to the protocol specifications of the UMDL, an agent designer is assured that a new agent will be capable of communication with other UMDL agents. Moreover, our experience so far has indicated that these same protocols can be used both to accomplish UMDL tasks, such as teaming, and in more specialised interactions between particular agents, as we describe below.

As we are still developing the UMDL, the set of protocols is expected to grow. We expect, however, that this growth will be quite low compared with the growth in the number and type of both agents and services. This reflects one of the important tenets of the UMDL architecture: the UMDL system as a whole can grow arbitrarily larger, whereas the architectural elements, in this case protocols, remain constant or nearly so.

3.1.2 UMDL ontology: One of the advantages of the KQML messages and our protocols is their generality; they can be used by agents independently of the tasks that they perform or the capabilities that they have. This is also one of the weaknesses; the vagueness of the message performatives, in particular, can mean that an agent can apply an arbitrary definition that is incommensurate with the definition used by another agent to which it is communicating. The designers of KQML anticipated this problem, and require that a message, and hence a protocol, be interpreted relative to an ontology, which is specified in the message. The ontology must be subscribed to by both agents, thereby eliminating any problems with definitions.

We have defined an ontology specific to the UMDL. This ontology defines, among other things, what things can belong to a digital library (e.g. articles, multimedia documents), the generic types of services in a digital library, some aspects of intellectual property rights and licenses, and a large number of related concepts (such as definitions of time). The ontology is not intended to be a source of metadata to describe, for example, the contents of various information collections. Rather, the ontology defines the basic definitions needed to enable communication in the UMDL.

The particulars of the UMDL ontology are outside the scope of this paper, and its development is an ongoing process. The interested reader is encouraged to visit our website (http://www.si.umich.edu/UMDL/HomePage.html).

In UMDL, agents are free to subscribe to any ontology they wish: we have not made any architectural commitments to a particular ontology. It is fair to say, however, that not using the UMDL ontology to employ UMDL services would require an almost prohibitive amount of work. That is, the facilitator agents are only guaranteed to use the UMDL ontology.

3.1.3 UMDL task languages: Complementing the shared UMDL ontology is a set of task languages. These languages are necessary, along with the ontology, to instantiate both the messages and performatives for a particular task being performed by communicating agents. For example, the *query* protocol implies that a response is needed to a query. The format of the query and its response, however, are not predefined for the message type: queries could be in terms of SQL, a Boolean query language etc. Thus, communicating agents must share, in addition to an ontology, a task language.

As with ontologies, we have not made any architectural commitments to particular task languages, but we have made commitments within the UMDL to common languages for the basic UMDL services. For example, there is a language for registration and for querying the registry and we assume that all agents speak enough of this language to support the required UMDL capabilities (for registration). (The details of the UMDL task languages are outside the scope of this paper; the interested reader is encouraged to visit the UMDL project website.) For tasks that are more specialised, however, the agents are free to use alternative task languages, along with ontologies and protocols, as we shall see. In fact agents that speak multiple languages are free to negotiate what task languages to use. (This would, of course, require a new 'task-language-negotiation protocol', which we have yet to design.)

3.2 UMDL facilitators

The enhancements to the underlying agent architecture that define the UMDL architecture imply the existence of agents that collectively provide the UMDL services for agent location, content-based message routing, security, negotiation and remuneration. The agents that provide these services are called *facilitators* because their role is not to provide the specific services that ultimate users of the UMDL see, but rather to provide the underpinning facilities that allow task-specific agents to collectively provide services to users. The suite of facilitators thus represents a commitment to the facilities that other agents can depend upon, which in turn implicitly defines conventions and policies that agent developers should follow.

The development of facilitators has been a primary focus of our research. At this point, the facilitators for negotiation and remuneration have not yet fully been implemented, although prototypes of agents that represent 'auctions', where *clearing prices* for information goods and services can be established, have been moved into the UMDL. We are also experimenting with strategic negotiation among agents, as well as specifying various 'trusted' third parties to help both negotiation and security.

By far the most central facilitator currently in the UMDL is the Registry agent. It is responsible both for maintaining a record of the agents currently populating the UMDL and their capabilities, and for retrieving a list of agents with particular capabilities in response to a query. All agents are required upon 'joining' the UMDL to register, and are required to use a particular language (see Section 3.3).

At present, the Registry is a logically centralised database. Over time, we expect to distribute the registry in a number of ways. First, we plan to develop registry mirror sites, to lessen the contention that such a high-demand network resource will face. Mirroring also improves reliability. Second, the Registry will be divided along various lines, depending on usage patterns. For example, it may be advantageous to create different logical registries along the lines of agent type, such as one registry of information collections, and one for service-providing agents. As the Registry is implemented in Sybase, such logical and physical partitions are possible.

In the long-run, scaling UMDL to a very large number of agents will probably require decentralisation of facilitation services, including the registry, which has ramifications for consistency and completeness. Our assumptions about an open environment with constantly changing populations of agents make reliance on completeness and consistency unrealistic anyway. Thus, as we scale and extend the UMDL, our expectations should not be that all possible combinations of services should be equally deployable, but rather that services are sufficiently replicated and distributed to at least minimally satisfy the needs of the users.

3.3 UMDL services: enlisting facilitators through protocols

As has been alluded to above, the development of UMDL services, as embodied in facilitators and the protocols, ontologies and task-languages they use, is an ongoing research effort. In this section, we describe the registration service as an example of a UMDL service, to elaborate the details of the process.

The registry uses three protocols. Upon invocation, all agents must register themselves in the registry. Registration is accomplished by sending a properly composed message using the *register-umdl-agent* performative, a local extension to the KQML standard set of performatives. Registration simply tells the registry that the agent exists; it does not provide a description of the agent's capabilities. The descriptive information is sent to the registry using the conspectus-update protocol. (The term conspectus is often used as a shorthand for agent capability description in the UMDL.) In this protocol an agent sends an *advertise* performative message containing its capability or content description to the registry. An example conspectus language (CL) description of an author-index agent is given in Fig. 4; this description would form the content part of the advertise message. An author-index agent is representative of task-specific UMDL agents that do not initiate interactions (it is a server). Its CL description specifies its type and the service it provides in terms of what interactions it supports. The <Capability> field specifies that the agent accepts queries with a specific author $A as input, and returns the associated collections in which the author is known to appear. (Input parameters are denoted by an asterisk before the variable identifier, output parameters by an asterisk after.)

```
<CL description {
        <Agent_ID AID_777>
        <Agent_type Author_index>
        <Capability
                <Author *$A><CIA $U*> >
        <Task_Language SQL>
        <Content
                <Broad_Topics 'SCIENCES'>
                <Last_updated 12.31.1995>
                <Frequency_of_update end_of_year> >
        <Pricing fixed (1-bibliobuck-per-search)>
        <Content_Language {English,German,Latin}>}
```

Fig. 4 *Author index agent description in the conspectus language [1]*

Once the registry has successfully stored the advertised conspectus data in its database, it replies to the agent and the protocol is completed. Registration and conspectus update are separate protocols because there will be many times when a registered agent will want to update its conspectus entry without reregistering. An example of such an update is when a publisher of a collection adds new titles to its collection and must update the conspectus field, indicating the broad topic of the material in the collection.

Conspectus entries are found in the registry using the search protocol. This protocol is initiated with a *recommend-all* or *recommend-one* performative message from the querying agent. The semantics that we use for the *recommend-* performatives are that the sender is requesting that the receiver recommend one or all agents that it knows about that meet the criteria specified by the content of the message. For the Registry, the content of the message must be specified using the Conspectus Query Language (CQL), a simple encoding of a select-where relational database query using terms derived from the conspectus ontology. The response to a recommend request is a list of zero or more agent identifiers that were retrieved by the search.

Additional conspectus entry information about one or more entries may be requested using the lookup protocol. This protocol employs a CQL query contained within an *ask-about* performative message.

4 Task-specific instances of the UMDL architecture

The UMDL agent architecture provides the facilitators and protocols that provide services that all agents within the UMDL can use, but what about the services that particular user communities expect from a digital library? These are also provided by agents that interact through protocols, of course. However, although the UMDL imposes additional commitments on the generic agent architecture about UMDL-wide protocols, it remains non-committal about particular services, and hence what task-specific agents should populate it and what protocols they should use among themselves [Note 4]. This means that the UMDL architecture can support a variety of different, specific communities simply through changing the population of task-specific agents, rather than through a wholesale overhaul of the entire system [Note 5].

In the remainder of this Section, we look at details of generating task-specific protocols and agents, and give an example of how these come together to provide a useful service.

4.1 Task-specific protocols

Because the basic UMDL protocols were designed to be general, we have been able to reuse many of them to implement interactions among various task-specific agents. For example, when an agent locating agents with specific content (a query planning agent, or QPA) enlists the aid of an agent that knows some possible relationships between content topics (a thesaurus agent), it uses the *lookup* protocol, but with a task language and ontology particularly suited to topical queries. When interacting with the Registry, the QPA uses the conspectus-search protocol, the UMDL ontology, and the UMDL conspectus-query language as required by the UMDL (because the Registry is a facilitator).

At times, however, we have extended the UMDL protocols. For example, a protocol was needed for a user-interface agent (UIA) to request a connection with a collection-interface agent (CIA). The connection is a set of ILU objects that submit a query to a collection, and return the results on-demand to the UIA. The connection protocol uses a *connect* performative to indicate the UIA's intent. The CIA responds with a reply message containing the ILU object identifier for the collection server object with which the UIA is to interact. This protocol will be expanded in the future to communicate access rights and various types of license information.

Finally, for a variety of reasons, including legacy standards, there are times when it is appropriate for agents to communicate using protocols other than the KQML performatives. An example is our development of other ILU objects to implement a collection search and retrieval protocol. This protocol makes fuller use of the distributed-object model to allow richer interactions between agents. It implements query statements, collections and retrieved items as objects that are accessible over the network. These objects can be accessed and manipulated directly by agents. All collections are represented by collection objects with a standard interface. This allows us to access collections uniformly, regardless of the underlying search mechanisms used by each collection. For example, we have used this protocol to access on-line public-access catalogs which use the ANSI/NISO Z39.50 standard protocol for information search and retrieval [9]. Z39.50 is a stateful client–server protocol to submit search requests to a database and retrieve all or part of the results. We encapsulated a Z39.50 client in a collection object, thus creating a gateway between UMDL and Z39.50. The gateway translates requests and responses between the two protocols. We have also implemented collection objects to access locally maintained collections which use a custom search engine.

4.2 Task-specific agents

The UMDL facilitators and protocols do not by themselves provide a working digital library. Users of a digital library expect some services from that library. They expect to be able to search for documents and access content. In some cases, they might expect to be able to publish their own documents, or to express their thoughts on the documents that others have published. For some users, being able to browse through various topics might be important; for others, efficiently going directly to a known source might be desirable.

All of these services are provided through the teaming of 'task-specific' agents. A task-specific agent embodies expertise in a particular, narrow task domain. For example, a thesaurus agent knows about synonymous words within a particular field. A notification agent knows how to monitor events within the UMDL and match events with notification conditions. A query-planning agent knows procedures about taking a query and finding likely sources of relevant content for that query. Interface agents for users and for collections know how to translate between the digital library and their associated users and collections respectively.

Clearly, there are many possible task-specific agents, and the population of such agents will vary over time and user communities. Third parties should be encouraged to provide these agents; hence, the barriers to 'joining' the UMDL should be minimal. As we have already outlined, agents that join the UMDL must adhere to particular requirements, in terms of being able to engage in protocols to work with facilitators. The task-specific knowledge that agents possess, how it is encoded, and how the agent chooses to use it, how-

Note 4: Of course, a goal in defining UMDL protocols has been to formulate interactions in terms as generic as possible. As a consequence, although task-specific agents can use arbitrary protocols, in practice many of the task-specific agents that we have developed re-use many UMDL protocols.

Note 5: In fact, the protocols and facilitators are typically reused across applications. An example of such reuse is the HCF concurrent-engineering design system [8]. UMDL-based protocols and facilitators have been used as an architecture for concurrent engineering using distributed agents. Although the specific population of agents is vastly different from UMDL's agent population, the architecture is the same.

ever, are not dictated by the UMDL. Thus, agent designers have tremendous freedom within the UMDL.

Of course, freedom carries with it its own burdens. Not surprisingly, in developing agents within the UMDL project, we have recognised that allowing idiosyncratic agent architectures is fine, but in practice it is much more effective to reuse generic agent architectures. So far, there are two basic architectures that we have employed:

(*a*) one for agents that act as servers in a synchronous mode (such as agents that match terms in a thesaurus when asked);

(*b*) one for proactive agents that are asynchronously pursuing their own explicit goals.

As (non-exhaustive) examples of the kinds of internal architectures agents might possess, we next describe these agent architectures.

4.2.1 Thesaurus agent architecture: An example of a purely reactive agent is a thesaurus agent that provides a simple lookup service from its database. More generally speaking, there is a class of such agents, which vary depending on the contents of their databases. Consequently, we have developed a generic thesaurus agent architecture, with an associated thesaurus-query language, to build agents that generally take terms and operators on them as input (such as 'broaden *aurora borealis*') and return terms as output (such as '*atmospheric phenomena*').

The thesaurus-agent architecture implements the lookup protocol with the ask-about message's content specified using the thesaurus-query language. The thesaurus database consists of a number of linked terms. For each term, there may be links to broader, narrower, synonymous and related terms. There also may be a definition and other links, e.g. 'See Also' terms. The thesaurus-query language lets the caller formulate various types of query: find the term(s) containing some keyword(s), obtain the list of terms related to the specified term by the specified relation, or obtain the definition of a term.

The implementation of the agent architecture is fairly straightforward. Each received message implies a single lookup transaction. Therefore, the receive calls are implemented as if they were synchronous remote procedure calls. The *recv_ask_about* function maps the performative into a direct query into the agent's database, and returns the results of the query. By running ILU in multi-threaded mode, concurrency and request queuing is performed automatically without the programmer building it into the agent's code.

The basic thesaurus-agent architecture as described above is reused multiple times in the UMDL, because there are several different thesaurus databases that can each be embedded in an agent. Moreover, the common vocabulary for describing information content is currently captured as a taxonomy of terms following the library community's Broad System of Ordering, and this taxonomy is captured in an agent (the BSOA), which is particularly suited to broadening and narrowing the topical features of an information query. Thus, in the depiction of Fig. 5, in the thesaurus-agent architecture, the communication system is inherited from the Agent class, the knowledge base is the particular database embedded in the agent, the decision-making system is simply a database query procedure, and there are no explicit internal goals or beliefs.

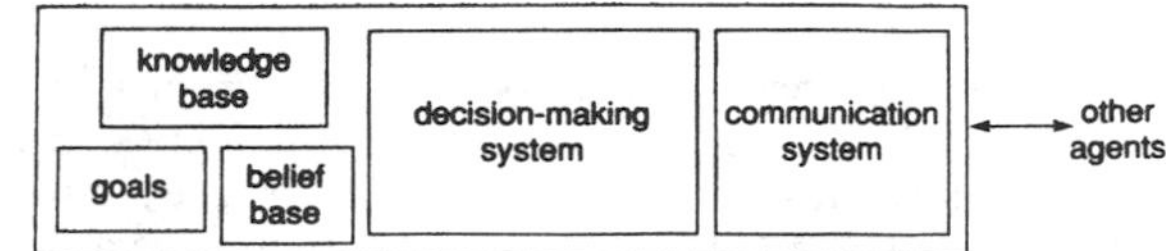

Fig. 5 *Agent internal architecture: major components*

4.2.2 Task planning agent architecture: The task planner agent (TPA) architecture provides a general means of accomplishing tasks by invoking procedures within the UMDL. In general, accomplishing a task involves decomposing the task into subtasks, which then must be pursued in a relative order. How (and whether) one subtask should be achieved can depend on the outcomes of previous subtasks, as well as broader changes to the operating conditions of the system. It is therefore important that an agent to execute plans for accomplishing tasks be able to retrieve appropriate subplans at appropriate times, and redirect activity as warranted by the circumstances.

To this end, our TPA architecture is based on the University of Michigan Procedural Reasoning System (UMPRS), which provides an advanced architecture for intelligent agents [10]. Although we cannot go into the details here, the basic components of UMPRS allow it explicitly to represent current goals, available plans, and beliefs about the state of the world, such that the UMPRS decision-making process chooses actions associated with the most appropriate plans for accomplishing its most important goals given the current situation (see Fig. 5). UMPRS can interleave actions in pursuit of various goals at the same time, and persists in pursuing its goals by choosing different plans when earlier attempts have failed.

The TPA architecture is composed of a UMPRS process coupled with the communication interface inherited from the Agent class. A challenge in this coupling is that, unlike the thesaurus agent that waits until a message comes in, the UMPRS process in the TPA architecture is constantly running, triggering actions associated with long-term goals, and then periodically checking whether any new messages have arrived that change its beliefs or goals. As a consequence, both the ILU communication interface and the UMPRS reasoning component have their own event loop, but it was desirable to have them execute in the same process. Our solution was to create a multithreaded agent where the two parts of the agent communicate through a mailbox mechanism in shared memory. This allows the TPA architecture to asynchronously send and receive messages, as it deems appropriate.

The TPA architecture, like the thesaurus agent architecture, can be the basis for a variety of specific agents; in the case of the TPA architecture, the instances differ in the goals that they can accomplish and the procedures at their disposal for doing so. A specific example of an instance of the TPA architecture in the UMDL is the Query Planning Agent (QPA), which has specialised knowledge of how to manipulate the topical field of a query so as to find collections that would be potentially appropriate for the query. That is, the QPA has procedures that indicate which other agents (Registry, Thesaurus, BSO) it should request information from under what circumstances, as it takes a query from a user and tries to find the best matches to collections (we go into this process in more detail in the next subsection).

4.3 Task-specific services

Task-specific services are accomplished through the efforts of multiple agents teaming their capabilities. We illustrate how this occurs using a working example from the UMDL, involving both task-specific agents (a Query Planning Agent (QPA), Thesaurus Agent (ThA), BSO Agent (BSOA)) and facilitators (specifically, the Registry). In addition, because this example involves having a user connect to collections, those entities must also be represented in the UMDL. Associated with a user is a UIA that is specific to that user, so long as it adheres to UMDL protocols when dealing with UMDL facilitators. Associated with a collection is a CIA, which can similarly be specific to a particular collection (author, publisher). When it comes on-line, a CIA must register itself describing its capabilities, including the content that it can provide. It describes its content using the BSO vocabulary.

Now a user's query is taken in by the UIA that is then responsible for finding collections that should be passed the query. As the UIA is knowledgeable about user interests and interactions, but not about how to find collections, the first thing it does is query the Registry to find a QPA. The Registry returns a pointer to the QPA [Note 6] and the UIA forwards to it the query, along with parameters that indicate the amount of effort the QPA should invest and the number of collections desired. The QPA retrieves a suitable procedure for processing the query, depending on its beliefs about the user's expectations (as conveyed through the additional parameters), and pursues it. Typically, it will first pass query information to the Registry to determine what, if any, collections have advertised that they contain content that might match the query. In some cases, the Registry will return enough potential collections to satisfy the QPA's model of the user's expectations, and the pointers to the collections will be sent back to the UIA.

However, often a queried topic is either outside of the BSO vocabulary or is too narrow to match with any known collections. The QPA's procedures consider this possibility. Should the results from the first inquiry to the Registry not meet the QPA's needs, it will selectively enlist the help of the other agents (ThA and BSOA). It can probe the BSOA to determine whether the query topic is part of the vocabulary. If so, it can further work with the BSOA to broaden the topic, and pass queries with broader topics to the Registry to identify possible collections. If this fails, it bounces back to the BSOA with a request to broaden the already broadened topics, and so on, bouncing between the BSOA and the Registry until it is satisfied with what it has found. If the topic is not in the vocabulary, the QPA interacts with the ThA and the BSOA, iteratively using the former to generate related topical terms, and checking these with the latter, until it has found an entry point into the vocabulary. It then can go to the Registry for matching collections, and if that fails will bounce between the BSOA and Registry as before.

In our experience with the UMDL, we have observed simple queries that involve few agents, as well as complex queries that involve more agents. The composition of the team of agents that collectively satisfies a query will vary with the query, and the number and order of interactions within a team will vary as well. Thus, although we have only a small population of task-specific agents, and despite the fact that team formation and execution are coordinated through a central agent (the QPA), we nonetheless already have clear evidence that the development approach that we have adopted, in terms of achieving services through the flexibly combined efforts of multiple, specialised agents, can work effectively.

To complete our example, once it has found a satisfactory set of collections, the QPA returns this set to the UIA. For elements of that set that represent searchable collections (those that support the UMDL collection search and retrieval protocol), the UIA submits the query to those collections, and receives documents. For collections that are not searchable, the UIA sends back the pointers (URLs) to the user, who may then probe further. Note that, ultimately, the task of submitting queries to the searchable collections may be migrated from the UIA to the QPA. In this way, the QPA can confirm that relevant documents are in collections before returning pointers to them. Moreover, as indicated above, collections currently always accept queries from the UIAs. In the future, part of the location of collections will involve issues of access privileges, costs, and so on, so that users and collections will engage in negotiation for access to information, mediated by the facilitators and task-specific agents in the UMDL.

5 Creating a new service

To illustrate the agent-based software development process in the UMDL, we now consider how a new service is defined to satisfy the needs of UMDL users.

Collections in the UMDL describe their topical content using terms from the BSO taxonomy, and so ultimately a topical search for collections must be phrased in BSO terms. In an early version of the UMDL, users had to know what these terms were in order to find collections. To aid the users, the UMDL incorporated a BSO Agent (BSOA), which was capable of testing terms for membership in the BSO, and for finding related BSO terms by traversing the taxonomy. These capabilities were used by the QPA to determine whether a user's query involved suitable topical terms, and to broaden (narrow) the query if it matched too few (many) entries in the registry.

For some user communities, such as high school students, it is unlikely that queries will be phrased in BSO terms. More generally, a UMDL user will either not know about, or not want to be constrained by, any controlled vocabulary. It has become obvious that the UMDL should support a broader array of topical specifications.

Providing this broader support required us to identify the needed capabilities. In discussions with our librarian colleagues, we attempted to find a procedure for how a librarian handles unorthodox topical specifications. Generally, a librarian uses his or her expertise to map a topic into a controlled vocabulary, or, when this proves impossible, the librarian uses some thesaurus to find related terms. Using this loosely defined procedural specification in the QPA, we were able to easily construct new procedures to find related terms.

Note 6: For simplicity, we generally have a single QPA executing, so there is no confusion as to which QPA should be selected. More generally, the Registry could return a list of QPAs with whom the UIA might negotiate to determine which to work with, or the Registry could return an auction where the UIA might bid for the services of an appropriate QPA.

The trouble, of course, is that these procedures expect agents with the right knowledge (e.g. thesaurus).

Our next step, therefore, was to identify the specific agents that apply thesaurus linking techniques that map user's terms into the BSO vocabulary. The BSOA is capable of determining whether a term was part of the BSO or not, so what was missing was another agent that could generate candidate alternative terms based on the initial topic, where these candidate terms could be passed on to the BSOA. We needed an agent to provide thesaurus knowledge.

In constructing this agent, we needed a suitable thesaurus database. As our early testbed systems have been aimed at providing earth- and space-science related documents for use in science education, a freely available thesaurus from the US National Aeronautics and Space Administration was located. This NASA thesaurus contains terms and relations between terms very much like the BSO data, and would interact in much the same way as the BSOA. The agent design thus fit naturally into the same basic Thesaurus agent architecture as the BSOA, and supported the same protocols, making development much easier.

Once we had built the agent, we integrated it into the system. By virtue of inheriting from the Agent class, it was already able to register and advertise itself. We simply provided it with a correct conspectus entry (description of itself) to advertise. The procedures of the QPA were then updated, such that if the user's query term was not located by the BSOA, a subgoal was initiated that would look up the term in the NASA Thesaurus Agent. If the term was found by that agent, it would be queried for related terms. These related terms were looked up in the BSO Agent. If a match was found, it was an entry into the BSO term hierarchy. If not, then the related terms were themselves passed to the NASA Thesaurus Agent, to broaden the search out further. The process terminated when an entry into the BSO was found or when no new terms were returned by the thesaurus. With these modifications to the QPA's suite of procedures, integration of the agent was complete.

This example highlights a situation where we were able to add a valuable new service to UMDL with very little effort. A great deal of code was reused, as the service was similar to previously existing services. Although this may seem like an unlikely occurrence, we expect it to be fairly typical. Most new services are likely to be variations on existing services. For example, we have reused significant amounts of code when developing CIAs for collections with disparate search engines and record formats. The code for the protocols is the same for all of these; the only thing developed for each new CIA is the knowledge for translation between UMDL formats and the native formats for the collection.

6 Conclusion and discussion

The important aspect of the UMDL from a user's perspective is the set of services it provides. As discussed in the introduction, we believe that it is impossible to describe accurately what these services will be in the future. This has in turn imposed on us the need to define the UMDL in a way that embraces evolution, and indeed encourages it. As a consequence, the UMDL architecture, by making specific commitments to protocols and facilities, describes an environment where third parties can develop their own services and agents, which can then be found and employed to satisfy the ever-changing demands of users.

Services in the UMDL are performed by groups of agents ephemerally forming teams in response to user demands. The agents communicate using the protocols described in Section 3.1. The constituents of a team are typically found dynamically. For example, an agent (A) may query the registry to find a group of agents that have a particular capability. Through a negotiation process, agent A then recruits from that set the agent(s) it needs. The agents may then employ protocols to perform the task. Now, it may be the case that agent A's task is so complex that it must form many teams over time to accomplish its goal. It is through this rolling *team formulation-task* accomplishment process that services are eventually delivered to a user.

The advantage of our approach is that central control and *a priori* specification, and hence undue limiting, of teams and services is unnecessary. Agents can respond to continually changing network conditions (e.g. traffic load, availability of agents, etc.) in the most preferred way at a particular instant. In addition, this dynamic nature lends reliability to the system, as a single point of failure is eliminated.

In addition, by providing an open system and economic incentives, we have created a system architecture that both simplifies integrating new services and has the potential to provide economic benefit to those providing information and services (thereby exploiting Adam Smith's 'Invisible Hand'). We see UMDL as subscribing to the philosophy started by the Internet, and followed on by the Web: decentralised (or minimally centralised) control and few standards are attractive to developers and information providers.

Our architecture is in stark contrast to traditional information-service architectures, even those based on client–server models, such as the NCSTRL project (www.ncstrl.org). These models maintain some centralised control, such as a central registry of metadata and uniform search services. These systems have the advantage of potentially more predictable search results, but we believe that their inherent inflexibility will not allow them to scale to the size or heterogeneity that we hope to demonstrate in UMDL, which we believe is a more realistic view of the evolving information-services world.

It is too early to determine whether a strongly decentralised, autonomous agent approach will be effective; we are encouraged with our early experience with UMDL. We have been able to scale the system from several agents to hundreds without problems, and we have added a variety of new services.

There are numerous caveats, however. The first caveat: for a service to be delivered, all the agents and protocols must exist. Thus, if a particular capability is needed, and no agent can provide it, the service will also fail. We have learned that, especially at the start of the project, considerable bootstrapping is needed. Developers must be closely coordinated to generate agents that others will find useful, and that in turn will be used. Effort must go into defining the protocols and languages that will be used by task-specific agents just to get the system to work in the simplest way. However, even in the short life of our project, we have already seen that, as the set of agents grows, so does the set of already defined protocols and languages, making subsequent agent development easier. Our expectation is that this trend will continue, so that ultimately the cost of entry into the system will be low enough to attract third parties to provide agents to the UMDL. As economic mechanisms become operational in the UMDL, third parties will have an incentive for participating, and an ability to identify untapped market niches to fill.

The second caveat: the tools for building agents must be rich enough to support various agent requirements and development styles. One example was the need to support both reactive and proactive agents. Similarly, we need to support both synchronous and asynchronous communication. Some developers strongly prefer one over the other. In the end, the UMDL will be composed of both proactive and reactive agents using a mix of synchronous and asynchronous communication. It is an interesting software-engineering challenge to build an infrastructure that supports this while maintaining modularity and encapsulation of individual design decisions.

The third caveat: reliable delivery of digital library services is critically dependent on reliable inter-agent communication, and good software-engineering principles encourage a clear ontology to support this communication. Our agent-based approach does not eliminate this need for a clear ontology; a common understanding among the agents is essential! The UMDL, by its very nature of encouraging highly distributed and decentralised software development, is particularly vulnerable to communication failure. Indeed, if our agents cannot communicate, then we have achieved nothing. Thus, a core ontology is central to the success of the UMDL, as it defines, or helps to define, the vocabulary and content of agent communication. We have expended a large effort on developing the UMDL ontology in two ways. First, we are developing a formal ontology using concepts from the library community and from related areas (e.g. law and economics). Second, we have developed several 'skunk works' ontologies specific to particular agents and tasks. This provides us with both theoretical and practical views on the ontology. We are now in the process of reconciling these views. Although we consider the effort to be generally successful (we can represent in the ontology the things that exist in the UMDL), we have many tough issues to face. The most difficult are incorporating concepts dealing with intellectual property rights and licenses, and compact, yet composable descriptions of agents.

The biggest problem that we face, however, is making the ontology accessible to the entire UMDL community, especially third parties that will soon be developing agents. Ontologies are difficult to write, and perhaps even more difficult to use. It requires care and skill to incorporate an ontology into an agent, for an agent developer must ensure that the agent properly adheres to any ontology to which it subscribes. In the worst case (of whose frequency we are yet unsure), an agent developer must be sure that everything his agent can communicate is consistent with the ontology. A tough task, indeed! As of yet, we have no solutions to this problem.

In this paper we have motivated and described the UMDL agent architecture in terms of a software engineering strategy for an Internet-based, constantly-evolving, open system. Until the project is much further along, it will be difficult to fully evaluate the pros and cons of this strategy, and it is not unlikely that the formulation of the UMDL agent architecture itself might undergo various evolutionary stages. Our experiences to date have hinted at the flexibility of such an architecture, and have demonstrated that non-trivial services can be realised through the teaming of multiple specialised agents. Our future work is to continue pursuing this approach, with an initial emphasis on fleshing out the suite of facilitators and their protocols to make the UMDL agent architecture more explicitly an economy where information goods and services can be flexibly exchanged.

7 Acknowledgments

The UMDL project is the fruit of the effort of many people. We would particularly like to thank Sun Park, Anisoara Nica and José Vidal for supplying both ideas and figures. Tracy Mullen and Mike Wellman have been central to shaping the current architecture, and moving it forward. We also thank the rest of the UMDL Architecture group (Eric Glover, Fritz Freiheit, Elke Rundensteiner, Karen Drabenstott, Amy Warner, Bill Aylesworth, Ken Alexander and Greg Peters) for contributing their ideas and programming talent.

We also thank our supportive and generous sponsors, the NSF/DARPA/NASA Digital Library Initiative under grant CERA IRI-9411287.

8 References

1 ATKINS, D.E., BIRMINGHAM, W.P., DURFEE, E.H., GLOVER, E.J., MULLEN, T., RUNDENSTEINER, E.A., SOLOWAY, E., VIDAL, J.M., WALLACE, R., and WELLMAN, M.P.: 'Toward inquiry-based education through interacting software agents', *IEEE Comput.*, 1996, **29**, (5), pp. 69–77

2 RAO, A.S., GEORGEFF, M.P., and SONENBERG, E.A.: 'Social plans: a preliminary report' *in* WERNER, E., and DEMAZEAU, Y. (Eds.): 'Decentralised AI' (North Holland, 1992), pp. 57–76

3 SHOHAM, Y.: 'Agent-oriented programming', *Artif. Intell.*, 1993, **60**, pp. 1993

4 DENNET, D.C.: 'The intentional stance' (MIT Press, Cambridge, MA, 1987)

5 NII, H.P.: 'Blackboard systems: the blackboard model of problem solving and the evolution of blackboard architectures', *AI Mag.*, 1986, **7**, (2), pp. 38–53

6 'The common object request broker: architecture and specification'. OMG document number 91.12.1, revision1.1., Object Management Group, Framingham, MA

7 FININ, T., FRITZSON, R., MCKAY, D., and MCENTIRE, R.: 'An information and knowledge exchange protocol' *in* KAZUHIRO, F., and TOSHIO, Y. (Eds.): 'Knowledge building and knowledge sharing' (Ohmsha and IOS Press, 1994)

8 D'AMBROSIO, J., DARR, T.P., and BIRMINGHAM, W.P.: 'Hierarchical concurrent engineering in a multiagent framework', *Concurr. Eng. Res. Appl.*, 1996, **4**, (1), pp. 47–57

9 'Information retrieval (Z39.50): application service definition and protocol specification'. ANSI/NISO Z39.50-1995, Library of Congress

10 LEE, J., HUBER, M.J., DURFEE, E.H., and KENNY, P.G.: 'UM-PRS: an implementation of the procedural reasoning system for multirobot applications'. Proceedings of the AIAA/NASA Conference on *Intelligent Robotics in Field, Factory, Service, and Space*, NASA Center for Aerospace Information, Linthicum Heights, MD, 1994, pp. 842–849

2.3 Personal Assistants

Collaborative Interface Agents

Yezdi Lashkari
MIT Media Laboratory,
Cambridge, MA 02139
yezdi@media.mit.edu

Max Metral
MIT Media Laboratory,
Cambridge, MA 02139
memetral@media.mit.edu

Pattie Maes
MIT Media Laboratory,
Cambridge, MA 02139
pattie@media.mit.edu

Abstract

Interface agents are semi-intelligent systems which assist users with daily computer-based tasks. Recently, various researchers have proposed a learning approach towards building such agents and some working prototypes have been demonstrated. Such agents learn by 'watching over the shoulder' of the user and detecting patterns and regularities in the user's behavior. Despite the successes booked, a major problem with the learning approach is that the agent has to learn from scratch and thus takes some time becoming useful. Secondly, the agent's competence is necessarily limited to actions it has seen the user perform. Collaboration between agents assisting different users can alleviate both of these problems. We present a framework for multi-agent collaboration and discuss results of a working prototype, based on learning agents for electronic mail.

Introduction

Learning interface agents are computer programs that employ machine learning techniques in order to provide assistance to a user dealing with a particular computer application. Although they are successful in being able to learn their user's behavior and assist them, a major drawback of these systems is the fact that they require a sufficient amount of time before they can be of any use. A related problem is the fact that their competence is necessarily restricted to situations similar to those they have encountered in the past. We present a collaborative framework to help alleviate these problems. When faced with an unfamiliar situation, an agent consults its peers who may have the necessary experience to help it.

Previous interface agents have employed either end-user programming and/or knowledge engineering for knowledge acquisition. For example, (Lai, Malone, & Yu 1988) have "semi-autonomous agents" that consist of a collection of user-programmed rules for processing information related to a particular task. The problems with this approach are that the user needs to recognize the opportunity for employing an agent, take the initiative in programming the rules, endow this agent with explicit knowledge (specified in an abstract language), and maintain the rules over time (as habits change etc). The knowledge engineered approach on the other hand, requires a knowledge engineer to outfit an interface with large amounts of knowledge about the application and the domain and how it may contribute to the user's goals. Such systems require a large amount of work from the knowledge engineer. Furthermore, the knowledge of the agent is fixed and cannot be customized to the habits of individual users. In highly personalized domains such as electronic mail and news, the knowledge engineer cannot possibly anticipate how to best aid each user in each of their goals.

To address the problems of the rule-based and knowledge-engineered approaches, machine learning techniques have been employed by (Kozierok & Maes 1993; Maes & Kozierok 1993; Hermens & Schlimmer 1993; Dent *et al.* 1992) and others. In the Calendar Agent (Kozierok & Maes 1993), memory-based reasoning is combined with rules to model each user's meeting scheduling habits. Results described in (Kozierok & Maes 1993) show that the learning approach achieves a level of personalization impossible with knowledge engineering, and without the user intervention required by rule-based systems. It is also interesting to note that the addition of rules provides the flexibility to explicitly teach the agent, and shows that the rule-based and learning approaches can successfully coexist.

While the learning approach enjoys several advantages over the others, it has its own set of deficiencies. Most learning agents have a slow 'learning curve' ; that is, they require a sufficient number of examples before they can make accurate predictions. During this period, the user must operate without the assistance of the interface agent. Even after learning general user behavior, when completely new situations arise the agent may have trouble dealing with them. The agents of different users thus have to go through similar experiences before they can achieve a minimal level of competence, although there may exist other agents that already possess the necessary experience and confidence.

We propose a collaborative solution to these problems. Experienced agents can help a new agent come up to speed quickly as well as help agents in unfamiliar situations. The framework for collaboration presented here allows agents of different users, possibly employing different strategies (rule-based, MBR, CBR, etc.) to cooperate to best aid their individual users. Agents thus have access to a much larger body of knowledge than that possessed by any individual agent. Over time agents learn to trust the suggestions of some of their peers more than others for various classes of situations. Thus each agent also learns which of its peers is a reliable 'expert' vis-a-vis its user for different types of situations.

A Single User's Agent

This paper describes experiments conducted with implemented interface agents for the electronic mail domain for a commercial email application, Eudora (Dorner 1992). This section describes an individual email agent.

Each user's interface agent learns by continuously "looking over the shoulder" of the user as the user is performing actions. The interface agent monitors the actions of the user over long periods of time, finds recurrent patterns and offers to automate them. For example, if an agent notices that a user almost always stores messages sent to the mailing-list "genetic-algorithms" in the folder *AI Mailing Lists*, then it can offer to automate this action next time a message sent to that mailing list is encountered. The agent can also automate reading, printing, replying, and forwarding as well as assign priority to messages.

We have chosen Memory Based Reasoning (Stanfill & Waltz 1986) as the algorithm which attempts to capture user patterns. Our implementation of MBR is based upon the concepts of situations and actions. In the electronic mail domain, we choose mail messages along with some context information to represent situations and the user's handling of the messages as actions. At any particular point in time, the user may be presented with a number of messages. When the user takes an action, it is paired with the corresponding situation and the situation-action pair is recorded in the agent's memory. For example, if the user reads a message $\mathcal{M}$, the pair $< \mathcal{M}'$, read-action$>$ is memorized, where $\mathcal{M}'$ contains details about the message $\mathcal{M}$ and relevant context information (for example that $\mathcal{M}$ was read n^{th} out of a total of k unread messages). When new situations occur, they are compared to the situations previously encountered. After gathering the closest matching situations in memory, the agent can calculate a prediction for an action in the new situation. In addition, the agent can calculate a confidence in its prediction by considering such factors as the number of situations in its memory and the proximity of the culled situations to the new situation. For a more detailed description, see (Kozierok & Maes 1993).

A situation is specified in terms of a set of fields. MBR measures situation proximity by applying a weighted sum of the distance between the corresponding fields of two situations. In the e-mail domain, appropriate fields would be the originator of the message, the subject, etc. The values of fields may be of any type. In previous systems, these fields were mainly strings or other static values. In our implementation, field values can also be objects. These objects can in turn have fields, which may be used in predicting actions. For example, the originator of a message is a *Person* object, which contains fields such as that person's position in an organization and their relation to the user. Object-based MBR is much less brittle than traditional MBR systems and can also use extra knowledge present in the objects if it finds it to be useful. For example, let's say that Mary always reads all messages from her boss Kay. If Mary were to suddenly receive a message from Kay's boss (therefore also Mary's boss), the system will correctly suggest that Mary read the message, since it uses the knowledge that Mary reads everything from her boss (and therefore probably her boss's boss too) although it has never previously received a message from Kay's boss. [1] Thus object-based MBR allows the same situation to be viewed differently depending on what information is available. In contrast, a string-based MBR system does not possess the same flexibility since we cannot extract more features from the string.

After predicting an action for a given situation, the agent must decide how to use that prediction. For each possible action, the user can set two confidence thresholds: the *tell-me* threshold and the *do-it* threshold. If the confidence in a prediction is above the tell-me threshold, the email agent displays the suggestion in the message summary line. If the confidence is above the do-it threshold, the agent autonomously takes the action.

The agent's confidence in its predictions grows with experience, which gives the user time to learn to trust the agent. During this period, it is especially useful to give the user the opportunity to see exactly what the agent is doing. This feedback is accomplished in three ways: an activity monitor, an explanation facility, and an interface to browse and edit the agent's memory. The activity monitor presents a small caricature to the user at all times. The caricature depicts states such as alert, thinking, and working, similar to (Kozierok & Maes 1993). An explanation facility provides English descriptions of why the agent suggested an action.

An agent starts out with no experience. As messages arrive and its user takes action, its memory grows. Only after a sufficient number of situation-action pairs have been generated, is the agent able to start predicting patterns of behavior confidently and accurately.

[1]Information about Kay and her boss are retrieved from a knowledge base of the kind maintained by most corporations or university academic departments.

However, when it encounters a new situation that is unlike anything it has in its memory, it is still unsure of what to do. This is because the machine learning algorithm used requires the training examples to cover most of the example space to work effectively.

A Framework For Collaboration

We propose a collaborative solution to the problems above. While a particular agent may not have any prior knowledge, there may exist a number of agents belonging to other users who do. Instead of each agent re-learning what other agents have already learned through experience, agents can simply ask for help in such cases. This gives each agent access to a potentially vast body of experience that already exists. Over time each agent builds up a trust relationship with each of its peers analogous to the way we consult different experts for help in particular domains and learn to trust or disregard the opinions of particular individuals.

Collaboration and communication between various agents can take many different forms. This paper is only concerned with those forms that aid an agent in making better predictions in the context of new situations. There are two general classes of such collaboration.

Desperation based communication is invoked when a particular agent has insufficient experience to make a confident prediction. For example, let us suppose that a particular agent A_1 has just been activated with no prior knowledge, and its user receives a set of new mail messages. As A_1 doesn't have any past experience to make predictions, it turns in desperation to other agents and asks them how their user would handle similar situations.

Exploratory communication, on the other hand, is initiated by agents in bids to find the best set of peer agents to ask for help in certain classes of situations. We envisage future computing environments to have multitudes of agents. As an agent has limited resources and can only have dealings with a small number of its peers at a given time, the issue of which ones to trust, and in what circumstances, becomes quite important. Exploratory communication is undertaken by agents to discover new (as yet untried) agents who are better predictors of their users' behaviors than the current set of peers they have previously tested.

Both forms of communication may occur at two orthogonal levels. At the situation level, desperation communication refers to an agent asking its peers for help in dealing with a new situation, while exploratory communication refers to an agent asking previously untested peers for how they would deal with old situations for which it knows the correct action, to determine whether these new agents are good predictors of its user's behavior. At the agent level, desperation communication refers to an agent asking trusted peers to recommend an agent that its peers trust, while exploratory communication refers to agents asking peers for their evaluation of a particular agent perhaps to see how well these peers' modelling of a particular agent corresponds with their own. Hence agents are not locked into having to turn for help to only a fixed set of agents, but can pick and choose the set of peers they find to be most reliable.

For agents to communicate and collaborate they must speak a common language as well as follow a common protocol. We assume the existence of a default ontology for situations in a given domain (such as electronic news, e-mail, meeting scheduling, etc). Our protocol does not preclude the existence of multiple ontologies for the same domain. This allows agent creators the freedom to decide which types of ontologies their agents will understand. As the primary task of an agent is to assist its particular user, the protocol for collaboration is designed to be flexible, efficient and non-binding. We briefly present the protocol below.

- **Registration:** Agents wishing to help others register themselves with a "Bulletin Board Agent" whose existence and location is known to all agents. While registering, agents provide information regarding how they can be contacted, what standard domains they can provide assistance in, what ontologies they understand and some optional information regarding their user. Every agent registering with a bulletin board agent is given a unique identifier by the bulletin board.
- **Locating peers:** Agents wishing to locate suitable peers may query bulletin board agents. An agent querying a bulletin board agent need not itself register with that bulletin board. Queries to a bulletin board agent can take many different forms depending on the type of information required. This allows agents to locate suitable peers in the most convenient way. For example, an agent's user may explicitly instruct it to ask a specific user's agent for help in dealing with certain types of situations.
- **Collaboration:** Collaborative communication between agents occurs in the form of request and reply messages. An agent is not required to reply to any message it receives. This leaves each agent the freedom to decide when and whom to help. Any request always contains the agent's identifier, the agent's contact information (for replies), the ontology used in the request, and a *request identifier* (*reqid*) generated by the agent issuing the request. The *reqid* is necessary since an agent may send out multiple requests simultaneously whose replies may arrive out of order.

  Analogously every reply always contains the replying agent's identifier and the reqid used in the request.

  The types of requests and their associated replies are presented below.

  - **Situation level collaboration:** When a situation occurs for which an agent does not have a good prediction, it sends off a Request-for-Prediction message to its peers. A prediction request contains all the features of the situation which the agent issuing the request wishes to divulge. This allows the requesting agent the freedom to withhold sensitive or private information.

An agent receiving a prediction request may choose to ignore it for any of a variety of reasons. It may not have a good prediction for the specific situation, it may be too busy to respond, the agent issuing the request may not have been very helpful in the past, or the agent may not be important enough. If however, an agent decides to respond to a prediction request, it sends back a response containing its prediction and its confidence in this prediction (a normalized value).

Note that the prediction request is used by agents for both desperation and exploratory communication. An agent receiving a prediction request does not know whether the request originated via exploratory or desperation based behavior on the part of the agent issuing that request. The distinction is made by the agent issuing the request. Replies to requests sent in desperation are used to predict an action for a particular situation, while replies to requests sent in exploratory mode are compared with the actions that the user ***actually took*** in those situations, and are used to model how closely a peer's suggestions correspond with its user's actions.

Agent level collaboration: An agent may send its peers a Request-for-Evaluation request. An evaluation request is sent when an agent wants to know what some of its peers think about a certain agent in terms of being able to model their users in particular classes of situations. An evaluation request contains the identifier of the agent to be evaluated (designated as the *target agent*) and the particular class of situations for which the evaluation is needed.

In any domain and ontology there exist different classes of situations. Certain agents may model a particular user's behavior in a particular class of situations very well and fail miserably in other classes. Note that we expect the domain ontologies to define these classes. For example an email agent may discover that peer agent A_1 is a very good predictor of its user's actions for messages sent to a mailing list, while being quite useless in predicting what its user does with any other type of message. On the other hand peers A_2 and A_3 are excellent predictors of its user's behavior with regards to email forwarded by her groupmates. This enables agents to locate and consult different 'expert' peers for different classes of situations.

An agent that chooses to respond to an evaluation request sends back a normalized value which reflects its *trust* in the target agent's ability to model its user's behavior for that particular class of situations.

An agent may also ask trusted peer agents to recommend a peer who has been found to be useful by the trusted peer in predicting its user's behavior for a particular class of situation. A Request-for-Recommendation contains the situation class for which the agent would like its trusted peer to recommend a good agent. Replies to recommendation requests contain the identifier and contact information of the agent being recommended.

Agents model peers' abilities to predict their user's actions in different classes of situations by a *trust* value. For each class of situations an agent has a list of peers with associated trust values. Trust values vary between 0 and 1.

The trust values reflect the degree to which an agent is willing to trust a peer's prediction for a particular situation class. A trust value represents a probability that a peer's prediction will correspond with its user's action based on a prior history of predictions from the peer. Agents may start out by picking a set of peers at random or by following their user's suggestion as to which peer agents to try first. Each previously untested peer agent gets has its trust level set to an initial value. As a peer responds to a prediction request with a prediction p, and an agent's user takes a particular action a, the agent updates the trust value of its peer in the appropriate situation class as follows:

$$trust = clamp(0, 1, trust + \delta_{p,a} * (\gamma * trust * conf))$$

where

$$\delta_{p,a} = \begin{cases} +1 & \text{if prediction p = user action a} \\ -1 & \text{if prediction p} \neq \text{user action a} \end{cases}$$

and *trust* represents the trust level of a peer, $conf$ represents the confidence the peer has in this particular prediction, γ is the trust learning rate, and $clamp(0, 1, c)$ ensures that the value of c always lies in $(0, 1]$. The rationale behind the modelling above is as follows. An agent's trust in a peer rises when the peer makes a correct prediction and falls for incorrect predictions. The amount it rises and falls by depends on how confident the peer was in its prediction. That is, a peer who makes an incorrect prediction with a high confidence value should be penalized more heavily than one that makes an incorrect prediction but with a lower confidence value.

When an agent sends out a prediction request to more than one peer it is likely to receive many replies, each with a potentially different prediction and confidence value. In addition, the agent has a trust value associated with each peer. This gives rise to many possible strategies which an agent can use to choose a prediction and a confidence value for this prediction. We believe that both trust and peer confidence should play a role in determining which prediction gets selected and with what confidence. Each predicted action is assigned a *trust-confidence sum* value which is the trust weighted sum of the confidence values of all the peers predicting this action. The action with the highest trust-confidence sum is chosen. The confidence associated with the action chosen is currently that of the most confident peer suggesting this action. We are exploring more sophisticated trust-confidence combination strategies using decision theoretic and Bayesian strategies.

Experimental Results

The concepts above have been implemented for a commercial electronic mail handler (Eudora) for the Apple Macintosh. The agent, implemented in Macintosh Common Lisp, communicates with the mail application using the AppleEvent protocol. The MBR Engine is domain independent, and can be easily adapted to calendar applications or news readers. Furthermore, all of these applications can share fields and actions. As more applications implement an AppleEvent interface, the agent should be able to aid the user with these applications as well. Currently, several users are actively making use of the agent on their actual mail. While the computations are intensive, we have achieved satisfactory performance on most high end Macintoshes.

The performance of MBR in interface agents has been documented in (Kozierok & Maes 1993). We wish to show that multi-agent collaboration strictly improves upon results obtained from single agent systems. Namely, multi-agent collaboration should steepen the learning curve and improve the handling of entirely novel messages.

To illustrate this, we set up the following scenario using the actual e-mail of two graduate students over a three day period (approximately 100 messages per user).

Calvin and Hobbes are two graduate students in the Intelligent Agents group.

1. **Hobbes :** Hobbes has been around for some time and hence his agent is quite experienced. Hobbes' agent has noted the following trends in its user's behavior. All messages to 'bpm', a music mailing list are refiled to a folder called bpm for later reading. Messages directly addressed to Hobbes are read by him and then deleted, as are messages to other mailing lists.

2. **Calvin :** Calvin is a new graduate student in the group. Calvin's agent starts out with absolutely no experience. Calvin also refiles all messages from the 'bpm' list for later perusal. He deletes subscription requests sent to the list. Calvin reads messages directly addressed to him, and then refiles them to appropriate folders. The rest of his mail, such as messages to other lists, he reads and deletes.

We plotted the confidence of Calvin's agent's suggestions as Calvin takes actions on about 100 actual mail messages. Figure 1 shows the results obtained. The x-axis indicates the growing experience of Calvin's agent as Calvin takes successive actions on the mail messages and the number of situation-action pairs in the memory increases. The thick rising *trend line* indicates how Calvin's agent's performance (in terms of confidence in predictions) rises slowly with experience. The numerous pockets show new user behavior being modeled. The agent makes several mistakes very early, which is to be expected, since the situations it has in its memory early on do not effectively capture all of Calvin's behavior patterns. Towards the end, we see several more mistakes, which reflect a new pattern occuring. With the tell-me threshold for all actions set at 0.1, the graph shows that it will take approximately 40 examples for the agent to gain enough confidence to consistently have suggestions for the user.

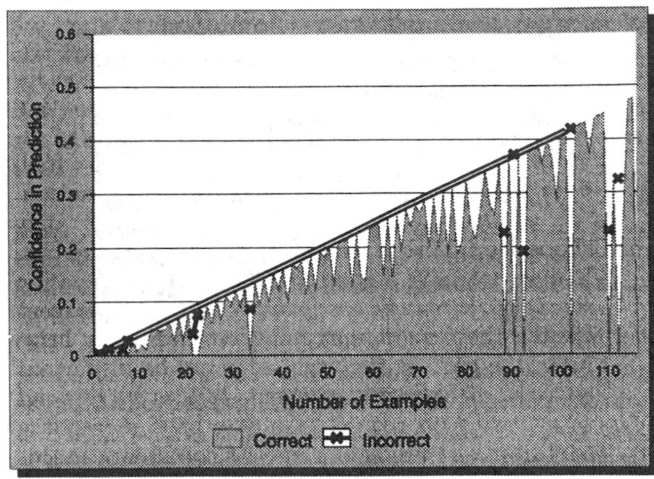

Figure 1: Performance without Collaboration

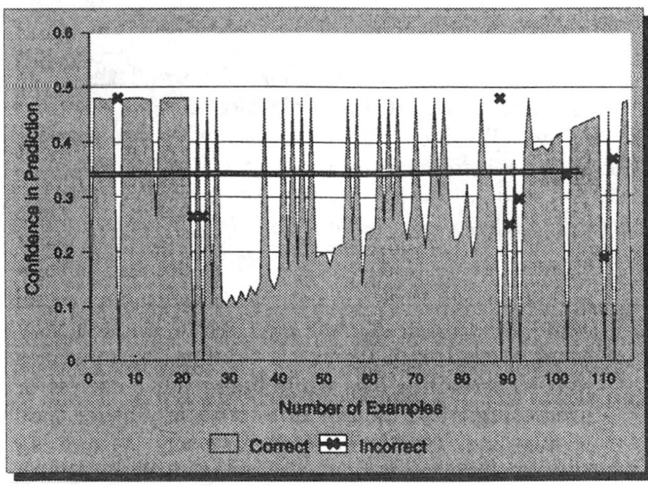

Figure 2: Performance with Collaboration

Figure 2 shows the level of confidence of Calvin's agent in its suggestions with multi-agent collaboration. [2] It may be noted that the confidence levels of all correct suggestions are always greater than the confidence levels generated by Calvin's agent alone at any point. The thick horizontal *trend line* indicates that multi-agent collaboration enables an inexperienced agent to make accurate predictions with high confidence as soon as it is activated as well as fill in gaps in even an experienced agent's knowledge. Note that trust modelling of Hobbes' agent is taking place inside Calvin's agent with each action Calvin takes on his mail. Space restrictions preclude the presentation of results regarding trust modelling of multiple peers in this paper.

Related Work

Various types of learning interface agents have been implemented (Kozierok & Maes 1993; Maes & Kozierok 1993; Hermens & Schlimmer 1993; Dent *et al.* 1992). All of them are essentially designed to act in a standalone fashion or engage in restricted task specific communication with identical peers. Our agents not only come up to speed much faster, but also discover which of a large set of heterogeneous peers are useful consultants to know in particular domains.

Multi-Agent Systems research has concentrated on negotiation and cooperation strategies that are used by autonomous agents who must compete for scarce resources. Various formal protocols and frameworks have been proposed to model agent's intentions, domains and negotiation strategies (Zlotkin & Rosenschein 1993; Rosenschein & Genesereth 1985) based on various game-theoretic, logical, economic and speech-act models. While the analytic frameworks above are important, most are based on restrictive assumptions about the domain or the agents' capabilities and assume that the reason agents cooperate is because they need access to a shared resource or have multiple overlapping goals.

The Ontolingua tools (Gruber 1993) and the work on the KQML Agent-Communication Language (Finin *et al.* 1993) provide a way for agents using different ontologies to communicate effectively with each other and may be used to implement our collaborative architecture. Our research represents an actually implemented system in a real domain that shows the benefits of collaboration amongst agents.

Conclusions

We have implemented a learning interface agent for a commercial application in a real world domain, and have tested it with real world data. Results have shown that multi-agent collaboration steepens the agent's learning curve, and helps in new, unseen situations. Trust modeling allows each agent to build a model of each agent's area of expertise, and consult only those agents which will be useful for each area.

[2] Hobbes takes no actions on his mail for the duration of this experiment, hence his agent's confidence remains unchanged.

Acknowledgments

This research was sponsored by grants from Apple Computer Inc. and the National Science Foundation under grant number IRI-92056688.

References

Dent, L.; Boticario, J.; McDermott, J.; Mitchell, T.; and Zabowski, D. 1992. A personal learning apprentice. In *Proceedings of the Tenth National Conference on Artificial Intelligence*, 96–103. San Jose, California: AAAI Press.

Dorner, S. 1992. *Eudora Reference Manual.* Qualcomm Inc.

Finin, T.; Weber, J.; Wiederhold, G.; Genesereth, M.; Fritzson, R.; McKay, D.; McGuire, J.; Pelavin, R.; Shapiro, S.; and Beck, C. 1993. Specification of the KQML agent-communication language. Technical Report EIT TR 92-04 (Revised June 15, 1993), Enterprise Integration Technologies, Palo Alto, CA.

Gruber, T. 1993. A translation approach to portable ontology specification. *Knowledge Acquisition* 5(2):199–220.

Hermens, L., and Schlimmer, J. 1993. A machine learning apprentice for the completion of repetitive forms. In *Proceedings of the Ninth IEEE Conference on Artificial Intelligence for Applications*, 164–170. Orlando, Florida: IEEE Press.

Kozierok, R., and Maes, P. 1993. A learning interface agent for scheduling meetings. In *Proceedings of the ACM SIGCHI International Workshop on Intelligent User Interfaces*, 81–88. Orlando, Florida: ACM Press.

Lai, K.; Malone, T.; and Yu, K. 1988. Object lens: A spreadsheet for cooperative work. *ACM Transactions on Office-Information Systems* 5(4):297–326.

Maes, P., and Kozierok, R. 1993. Learning interface agents. In *Proceedings of the Eleventh National Conference on Artificial Intelligence*, 459–465. Washington D.C.: AAAI Press.

Rosenschein, J., and Genesereth, M. 1985. Deals among rational agents. In *Proceedings of the Ninth International Joint Conference on Artificial Intelligence*, 91–99. Los Angeles, CA: Morgan Kaufmann.

Stanfill, C., and Waltz, D. 1986. Toward memory-based reasoning. *Communications of the ACM* 29(12):1213–1228.

Zlotkin, G., and Rosenschein, J. 1993. A domain theory for task oriented negotiation. In *Proceedings of the Thirteenth International Joint Conference on Artificial Intelligence*, 416–422. Chambery, France: Morgan Kaufmann.

COLLAGEN: When Agents Collaborate with People

Charles Rich
MERL–A Mitsubishi Electric
Research Laboratory
201 Broadway
Cambridge, MA 02139 USA
rich@merl.com

Candace L. Sidner
Lotus Development Corporation
55 Cambridge Parkway
Cambridge, MA 02142 USA
csidner@lotus.com

Abstract

We take the position that autonomous agents, when they interact with people, should be governed by the same principles that underlie human collaboration. These principles come from research in computational linguistics, specifically collaborative discourse theory, which describes how people communicate and coordinate their activities in the context of shared tasks. We have implemented a prototype toolkit, called Collagen, which embodies collaborative discourse principles, and used it to build a collaborative interface agent for a simple air travel application. The potential benefits of this approach include application-independence, naturalness of use, and ease of learning, without requiring natural language understanding by the agent.

Introduction

The current explosion of work on autonomous agents is primarily driven, as it should be, by the excitement of finding useful results in specific applications. In parallel, however, we also need to be developing a foundation of application-independent principles and techniques. This paper reports on a principled approach to the part of an autonomous agent which interacts with—and collaborates with—people.

We take the position that agents, when they interact with people, should be governed by the same principles that underlie human collaboration. Our motivation for this position is the assumption that a style of interaction which embodies familiar rules and conventions will be easier for people to learn and use than one that does not. This is similar to the arguments that motivated the development of direct-manipulation graphical user interfaces to take advantage of users' preexisting familiarity with the manipulation of real objects.

To find the principles underlying human collaboration, we appeal to research on collaborative discourse, specifically the SharedPlan work of Grosz & Sidner (1986, 1990), Grosz & Kraus (1996), and Lochbaum (1994, 1995). This work provides us with a well-specified computational theory that has been empirically validated across a range of human tasks. Applying this theory to autonomous agents poses a number of challenges, including:

- applying the theory without requiring natural language understanding by the agent,
- embodying the application-independent algorithms and data structures in a toolkit,
- and providing a modular description for application-specific information.

Our solutions to these problems are the focus of this paper. To develop these solutions, we have implemented both a prototype toolkit called *Collagen*[1] (for *Coll*aborative *agen*t) and an air travel application using it. Because this paper concentrates on Collagen, it will by necessity be sketchier on the prototype application. Whenever possible, general issues will be illustrated in the air travel domain; a short sample session is also presented at the end of this paper. Readers are referred to (Rich & Sidner 1996a, 1996b) for more details on the air travel application system.

Collagen and the air travel application have both been implemented in Common Lisp. All of the examples in this paper are from our demonstration system, which runs in real time (maximum of a few seconds per interaction).

Collaboration and Discourse

This section provides a brief overview of the theory on which Collagen is based. Readers are referred to the referenced literature for more detail.

Collaboration is a process in which two or more participants coordinate their actions toward achieving shared goals. Most collaboration between humans involves communication. *Discourse* is a technical term for an extended communication between two or more participants in a shared context, such as a collaboration.

Figure 1 shows the structure of a generic collaboration between a software agent and a human user. Theories of collaboration and discourse tell us about the

[1] Collagen is a fibrous protein that occurs in vertebrates as the chief constituent of connective tissue.

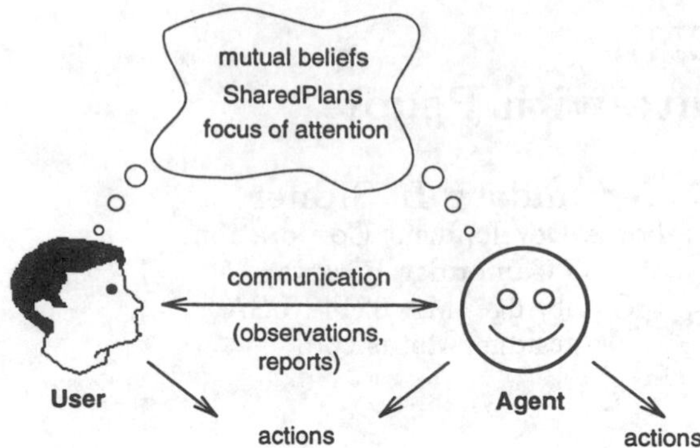

Figure 1: Collaborating with an agent.

structure and function of the "stuff" inside the clouds, which constitutes part of the human user's mental state and is computationally represented inside the agent. At this level of abstraction, this model applies to autonomous agents of all kinds.

Notice that communication between the user and agent includes observations and/or reports of their actions. It is clear that reports of actions, e.g., "I have done X," are a kind a communication. We also include direct observations of actions as a kind of communication when, as is often the case in close collaboration, both participants know and intend that their actions are observed. For example, in our example application, all agent and user actions are mutually observable through a direct-manipulation graphical interface (see Figure 3). Collagen also supports collaborations in which actions are only reported, e.g., where an agent is performing actions at a remote network site.

SharedPlans

Grosz & Sidner's (1990) theory predicts that, for successful collaboration, the participants need to have mutual beliefs[2] about the goals and actions to be performed and the capabilities, intentions, and commitments of the participants. The formal representation of these aspects of the mental states of the collaborators is called a *SharedPlan*.

As an example of a SharedPlan in the air travel domain, consider the collaborative scheduling of a trip wherein participant A (e.g., the user) knows the constraints on travel and participant B (e.g., the agent) has access to a database of all possible flights. To successfully complete the collaboration, A and B must mutually believe that they:

- have a common goal (to find an itinerary that satisfies the constraints);
- have agreed on a sequence of actions (a *recipe*) to accomplish the common goal (e.g., choose a route, specify some constraints on each leg, search for itineraries satisfying the constraints);
- are each capable of performing their assigned actions (e.g., A can specify constraints, B can search the database);
- intend to do their assigned actions; and
- are committed to the overall success of the collaboration (not just the successful completion of their own parts).

Collagen provides data structures and algorithms for representing and manipulating goals, actions, recipes, and SharedPlans.

Several important features of collaboration should be noted here. First, participants do not usually begin a collaboration with all of the conditions above in place. They typically start with only partial knowledge of the shared environment and the other participants and use communication as well as individual information gathering to determine the appropriate recipe to use, who should do what, and so on.

Second, notice that SharedPlans are recursive. For example, the first step in the recipe mentioned above, choosing a route, is itself a goal upon which A and B might collaborate.

Finally, planning (coming to hold the beliefs and intentions required for a collaboration) and execution (acting upon the current intentions) are usually interleaved for each participant and among participants.

Focus of Attention

In Grosz & Sidner's (1986) theory, the shifting focus of attention in a discourse is represented by a *focus stack* of discourse segments. A *segment* is a contiguous sequence of communication acts that serve some purpose. For example, a question and answer sequence constitutes a discourse segment whose purpose is (usually) to achieved shared knowledge of some fact. Segments are often hierarchically embedded. For example, a question/answer segment may include a question clarification subsegment.

The SharedPlan and focus stack representations are connected through discourse segment purposes: each discourse segment is associated with a SharedPlan for its purpose.

In the natural flow of a collaboration, new segments and subsegments are created, pushed onto the focus stack, completed, and then popped off the stack. Sometimes, participants also interrupt each other, abandon the current segment (purpose) even though it is not complete, or return to earlier segments.

Discourse Algorithms

The two key algorithms in Collagen are discourse interpretation, which is a reimplementation of Lochbaum's (1994) rgraph augmentation algorithm, and discourse generation, which is essentially the inverse of interpretation.

[2] A and B mutually believe p iff A believes p, B believes p, A believes that B believes p, B believes that A believes p, A believes that B believes that A believes p, and so on. This is a standard philosphical concept whose infinite formal definition is not a practical problem.

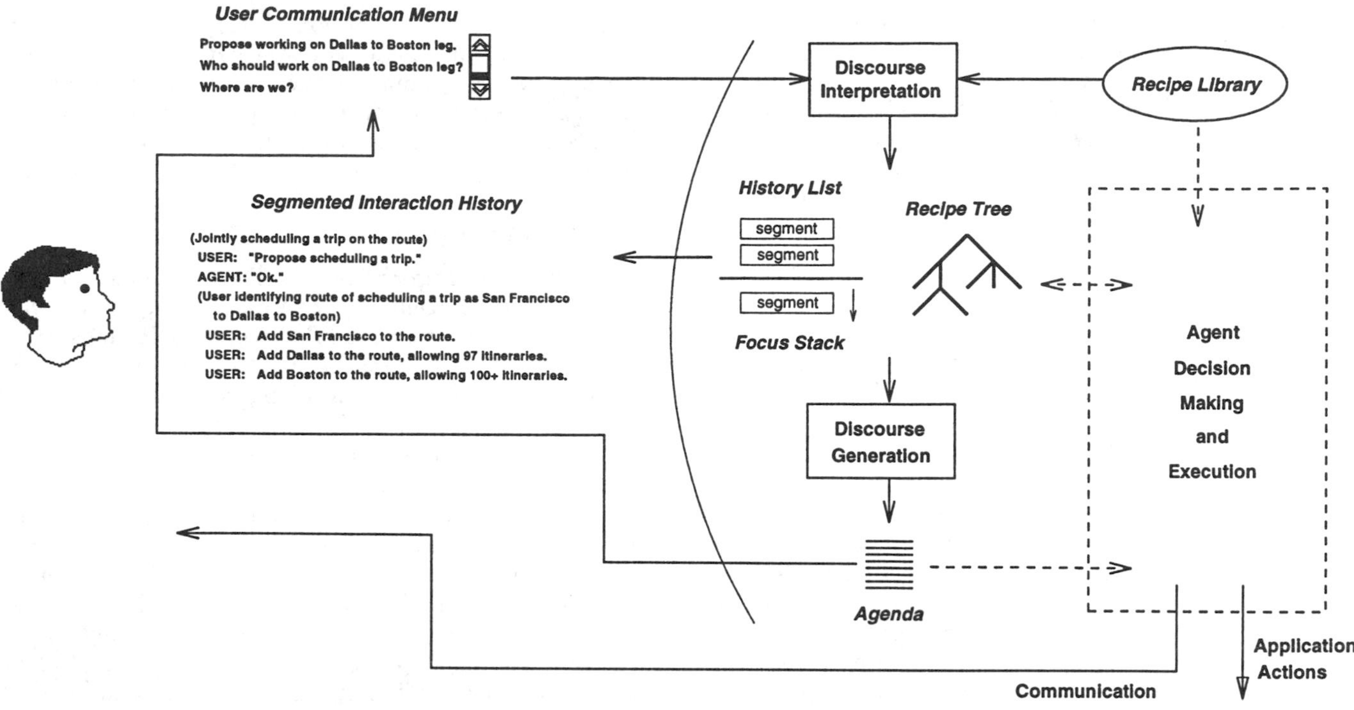

Figure 2: Collagen architecture.

The main job of *discourse interpretation* is to see how the current communication or observed action can be viewed as contributing to the current discourse purpose, i.e., the purpose of the top segment on the focus stack. For example, if the current purpose is to jointly schedule a trip, and the user proposes a route, the agent interprets this as the first step in the scheduling recipe. The intepretation algorithm also takes care of deciding when to push a new segment on the stack or pop the current segment.

It is tempting to think of discourse intepretation as plan recognition, which is known to be exponential in the worst case (Kautz 1990). However, this misses a key property of normal human discourse, namely that the participants work hard to make sure that their partners understand their intentions without a large cognitive search. In order to explain an observed or reported act, Collagen only searches through the steps of the current recipe or all known recipes for the current goal (and this is *not* done recursively). As we will see below, the agent relies on the user to communicate enough so that it can follow what is going on without having to do arbitrary plan recognition.

The *discourse generation* algorithm looks at the current focus stack and associated SharedPlan and produces a prioritized *agenda* of (possibly partially specified) actions which would contribute to the current discourse segment purpose. For example, if the current purpose is to jointly schedule a trip, the agenda includes an action in which the agent asks the user to propose a route. In general, the agenda contains communication and other actions by either the user or agent, which would advance the current problem-solving process.

Collagen

Collagen is a toolkit that embodies a set of conventions for collaborative discourse in the same sense that, for example, the Motif toolkit embodies a set of conventions for the graphical design of user interfaces. Generally speaking, what Collagen provides is a standard mechanism for maintaining the flow and coherence of agent-user interaction. In addition to saving implementation effort, using such a toolkit provides consistency across applications, and to the extent that the conventions are based on good principles, leads to applications that are easier to learn and use.

Even when using a toolkit, you still must provide a lot of application-specific information. After discussing the generic architecture of Collagen below, we will focus on how this application-specific information is provided and used.

Architecture

Figure 2 is a blow-up of Figure 1 to show the internal architecture of the part of the agent that interacts with the user. As commented earlier, the architecture at this level is applicable to all kinds of agents. In addition to the components shown in this figure, Collagen also includes a layer of special windowing facilities (Rich 1996) to support the interface agent paradigm (see later section).

The first thing to notice about the architecture in Figure 2 is that the agent's decision making and execution is a "black box." We are not trying to provide a toolkit for building a complete agent. At the heart of the agent there may be a rule-based expert system, a neural net, or a completely ad hoc collection of code. What we are providing are mechanisms for this black box to use when communicating with the user. Said another way, Collagen provides a generic framework for recording and communicating the decisions made by the agent (and the user), but not for *making* them.

User Presentations

From the user's point of view, a collaborative agent built using Collagen presents itself in three ways. All of these presentations are in natural language, which is generated from an internal artificial language (described below) by simple string template substitutions.

First (see bottommost arrow in the Figure 2), the user sees direct communications from the agent. The content of such a communication could be a question, an answer, a proposal, a report, etc. The exact method by which such communications are presented to the user depends on the application. For interface agents, Collagen provides a particular style of overlapping windows; other applications could simply print into a predefined message area.

Second (see topmost arrow in Figure 2), the user communicates to the agent by selecting from the dynamically-changing *user communication menu*, which is computed from the current discourse agenda. What we are doing here is using expectations generated by discourse context to replace natural language understanding. The user is not allowed to make arbitrary communications, but only to select from communications expected by the discourse interpretation algorithm. Thus, unlike usual ad hoc menu-driven interaction, the user menu in Collagen is systematically generated from an underlying model of orderly discourse. The choices in the user communication menu are simply the subset of the discourse agenda which are communication acts that may be performed by the user (plus a few special entries, such as "Where are we?" to request printout of the segmented history described below). An example of a user communication menu in our example application can be see in the lower left corner of Figure 4.

Finally (see middle arrow Figure 2), the user can request a printout of parts of the agent's internal discourse state in the form of a *segmented interaction history* (see example Figure 5). Segmented interaction histories are one of Collagen's most useful features. They are like log files, except that they are hierarachically structured and include not only primitive actions, but also the user's and agent's higher-level goals and intentions. The most basic function of the segmented interaction history is to orient the user. For example, if the user needed to leave her computer in the middle of working on a problem and returned after a few hours (or days), the history would help her reestablish where in the problem solving process she was.

The segmented interaction history also serves as a menu for history-based transformations, such as returning to earlier points in the collaboration or replaying earlier segments in a new context. See (Rich & Sidner 1996b) for more about history-based transformations.

Inside the Agent

The left side of Figure 2 shows the components of Collagen inside the agent. At the top of the figure, the *discourse interpretation* module receives selections from the user communication menu. Even though the user menu is presented in natural language, there is no natural language understanding required here, since each entry in the menu is associated with the artificial language expression from which it was generated.

The interpretation module updates the agent's internal discourse state representation according to the rules of discourse theory and the specific content of the user's communication. The agent's internal discourse state consists of the focus stack described earlier (shown growing downward in the figure), the *history list*, which records toplevel segments that have been popped off the stack, and the *recipe tree*, which is a concrete representation of some of the mutual beliefs in SharedPlans. The recipe library, which is also an input to discourse interpretation, will be discussed in its own section below.

The *discourse generation* module constantly updates the agenda as the discourse state changes.

Notice that the agent communication arrow at the bottom of Figure 2 originates in the agent decision making box. Only application-specific code can decide what the agent should actually say (or do) at any particular time. However, the Collagen architecture does provide resources which this application-specific agent code can use to support intelligent assistance. Collagen provides software interfaces (API's) for the recipe library, the discourse state representation, and the agenda.

For example, the agent in our air travel application consults the recipe tree as part of determining the best suggestion to make when the user has added too many constraints to her trip. Also, our example agent often chooses one of the entries on the current discourse agenda as its next action.

Task Modelling

In order to use Collagen, an agent developer must provide a formal model of the collaborative task(s) being performed by the agent and user. Defining this model is very similar to what is called "data modelling" in database or "domain modelling" in artificial intelligence (Brodie, Mylopoulos, & Schmidt 1982). It also overlaps with modern specification practices in software engineering, although the goals and recipes in a task model for collaborative discourse include more abstract concepts than are usually formalized in current software practice, except for in expert or knowledge-based systems.

On the one hand, task modelling can be thought of as an unfortunate hidden cost of applying discourse theory. On the other hand, the need for an explicit task model should be no surprise. From an artificial intelligence point of view, what the task model does is add a measure of reflection—"self-awareness," if you like—to a system. Reflection is a well-known technique for improving the performance of a problem-solving system. From a software engineering point of view, the task model can be thought of as part of the general trend towards capturing more of the programmer's design rationale in the software itself. Also, since the agent is not required to use the task model alone for its decision making and execution, the model only needs to be complete enough to support communication and collaboration with the user.

In the remainder of this section, we discuss and illustrate some of the issues in building task models, starting with the artificial discourse language and then moving on the recipe library.

Artificial Discourse Language

As the internal representation for user and agent communication acts, we use Sidner's (1994) artificial discourse language. Sidner defines a collection of constructors for basic act types, such as proposing, retracting, accepting, and rejecting proposals. Our current implementation includes only two of these act types: `PFA` (propose for accept) and `AP` (accept proposal).

`PFA(`t, $participant_1$, $belief$, $participant_2$`)`

The semantics of `PFA` are roughly: at time t, $participant_1$ believes *belief*, communicates his belief to $participant_2$, and intends for $participant_2$ to believe it also. If $participant_2$ responds with an `AP` act, e.g., "Ok", then *belief* is mutually believed.

Sidner's language at this level is very general—the proposed *belief* may be anything. For communicating about collaborative activities, we introduce two application-independent operators for forming beliefs about actions: `SHOULD(`*act*`)` and `RECIPE(`*act*,*recipe*`)`.

The rest of the belief sublanguage is application-specific. For example, to model our air travel application, we defined appropriate object types (e.g., cities, flights, and airlines), relations (e.g., the origin and destination of a flight), and goal/action constructors (e.g., scheduling a trip, adding an airline specification). We can imagine automatically extracting some of these definitions from declarations in the implementation code for the agent.

Below are examples of how some of the communications in our example application are represented in the artificial discourse language. In each example, we show the internal representation of the communication followed by the English gloss that is produced by a straightforward recursive substitution process using string templates associated with each operator. Italicized variables below denote parameters that remain to be bound, e.g., by further communication.

```
PFA(36,agent,SHOULD(add-airline(t,agent,ua)),user))
36 AGENT: "Propose I add United specification."
```

Notice below that a present participle template is used when the participant performing an act is unspecified.

```
PFA(1,user,SHOULD(schedule(t,who, route)),agent)
1 USER: "Propose scheduling a trip."
```

Questions arise out of the embedding of `PFA` acts as shown below (`route` is a constructor for route expressions).

```
PFA(11,agent,
    SHOULD(PFA(t1,user,
              RECIPE(schedule(t2,who,
                     route(bos,dfw,den,sfo,bos)),
                     recipe), agent)),
    user)
11 AGENT: "How will a trip on Boston to Dallas to
   Denver to San Francisco to Boston be scheduled?"
```

Recipe Library

At its most abstract, a *recipe* is a resource used to derive a sequence of steps to achieve a given goal (the objective of the recipe). Although very general, application-independent recipes exist, such as divide and conquer, we are primarily concerned here with application-specific recipes.

In our implementation, a recipe is concretely represented as a partially ordered sequence of act types (steps) with constraints between them. The recipe library contains recipes indexed by their objective. There may be more than one recipe for each type of objective.

The recipe library for the example application contains 8 recipes defined in terms of 15 different goal or action types. It is probably about half the size it needs to be to reasonably cover the application domain.

Recipes with a fixed number of steps are easily represented in our simple recipe formalism. However, in working on our example application, we quickly discovered the need for more complicated recipes whose step structure depends on some parameters of the objective. For example, two common toplevel recipes for scheduling a trip are working forward and working backward. The working-forward recipe works on the legs of a trip in order starting with the first leg; the working-backward recipe starts with the last leg. In both cases, the number of steps depends on the length of the route.

Rather than "hairing up" our recipe representation as each difficult case arose, we decided instead to provide a general-purpose procedural alternative, called *recipe generators*. Recipes such as working forward/backward are represented in Collagen as procedures which, given an objective, return a recipe. A predicate can also be associated with a recipe to test whether it is still applicable as it is being executed.

A related category of application-specific procedures in the recipe library are *recipe recognizers*. These are primarily used for the bottom-up grouping of a sequence of similar actions on the same object into a single abstract action. For example, such a recognizer is invoked in our example application when the user moves the same time constraint indicator back and forth several times in a row.

Example Application

Our example application concerns solving problems such as the following:

> You are a Boston-based sales representative planning your trip home from San Francisco. On the way, you would like to meet a customer in Dallas who is only available afternoons between 1 and 4 p.m. You would like to avoid overnight flights and fly on American Airlines.

Scheduling a more complicated trip, e.g., one involving four or five cities, typically takes a user about 15 minutes and entails about 150 user or agent actions.

Interface Agents

In addition to illustrating the general framework for agent-user collaboration shown in Figure 1, our example agent is more specifically an *interface agent* (see Figure 3). The collaborative interface agent paradigm mimics the relationships that hold when two humans collaborate on a task involving a shared artifact, such as two mechanics working on a car engine together or two computer users working on a spreadsheet together.

In the collaborative interface agent paradigm, the agent can both communicate with and observe the actions of the user. One of the agent's main responsibilities is to maintain the history and context of the collaboration.

The agent can also interact directly with the shared application program. The agent queries the state of the application using the application's programming interface (API). The agent modifies the application state using the same graphical interface as the user, so that the user can observe the agent's actions.

Our concept of an interface agent is similar to Maes's (1994), although she uses the term "collaborative" to refer to sharing information between multiple software agents, rather than collaboration between agents and people.

Figure 4 shows how the architecture of Figure 3 is realized on a user's display. The large window labelled "Application" is a direct-manipulation interface to an airline schedule database and a simple constraint checker. By pressing buttons, moving sliders, and so on, the user can specify and modify the geographical, temporal, and other constraints on a planned trip. The user can also retrieve and display possible itineraries satisfying the given constraints.

The smaller overlapping windows in the upper-right and lower-left corners of the screen in Figure 4 are the agent's and user's *home windows*, through which they communicate with each other. These windows are

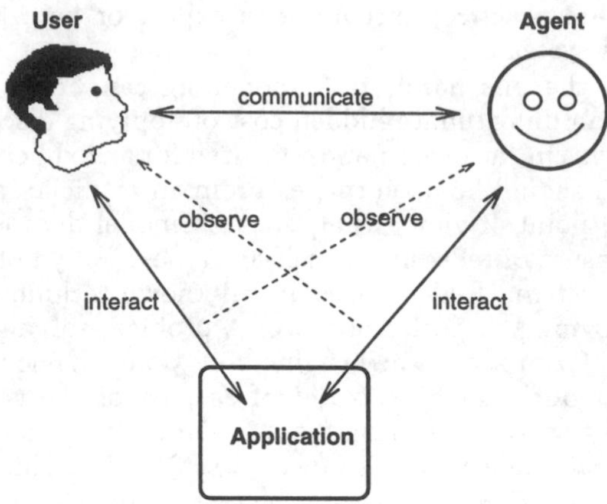

Figure 3: Collaborative interface agent paradigm.

moveable and expand and shrink as their use changes. In a typical session, application actions by the user and agent are interleaved with communication actions between them. The agent manipulates objects in the application window using the hand icon currently shown at rest in its home window.

For additional details on some of the implementation issues related adding an interface agent to graphical user interfaces, see (Rich & Sidner 1996a).

Sample Session

The user could just start working by herself on scheduling the San Francisco-Dallas-Boston trip above by directly manipulating objects in the application window. Instead, she chooses to communicate with the agent to initiate a collaboration. Clicking the arrow at the bottom of her home window causes the window to expand showing her current communication menu:

Propose scheduling a trip.
Where are we?

There is only one possible collaboration to propose here, since this example system was built with only one toplevel goal in mind. A typical real application would have a range of high-level goals. The agent indicates its acceptance of the user's proposal by displaying "Ok" in its home window. Note that at this point the agent has only its generic knowledge of the typical tasks involved in scheduling a trip and recipes for performing them. It does does not know anything about the user's particular problem or preferences.

The user now clicks in order on three cities on the map. The agent recognizes these three actions as forming a segment whose purpose is to identify one of the parameters of the current goal, i.e., the route of the trip. If the user requests a display of the segmented interaction history at this point (by choosing "Where are we?" from the communication menu), the following would be displayed in the agent's home window:

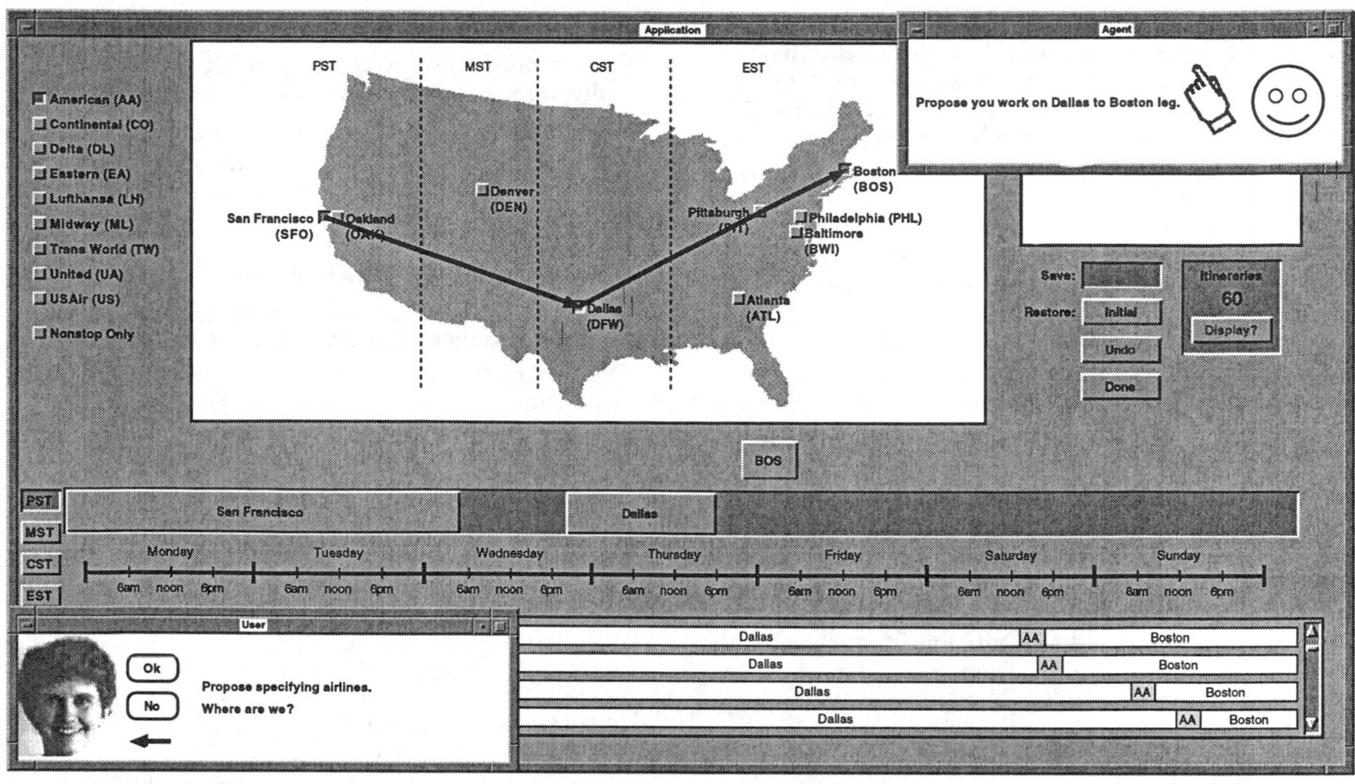

Figure 4: Example application screen.

(Jointly scheduling a trip on the route)
USER: "Propose scheduling a trip."
AGENT: "Ok."
(User identifying route of scheduling a trip as San Francisco to Dallas to Boston)
USER: Add San Francisco to the route.
USER: Add Dallas to the route, allowing 97 itineraries.
USER: Add Boston to the route, allowing 100+ itineraries.

Notice that the interaction history above is hierarchically structured. The purpose of each segment is shown in parentheses at the start of the segment. The elements of a segment are either primitive actions or subsegments. Communication actions are indicated by quotation marks. In general, the purpose of a subsegment contributes to the purpose of the parent segment.

The user now clicks "Ok" in her home window to signal the end of the current segment. After a brief pause to see if the user is going to do something else, the agent takes the initiative and asks:

How should a trip on the route be scheduled?

This question is an example of intelligent assistance in which the agent helps the user focus on what needs to be decided next in order to push the task forward. The user is free either to answer the agent's question or to ignore it and proceed on her own. If she chooses to answer, the following option will be presented in her communication menu:

Propose scheduling a trip on the route via ___ .
working forward
working backward

The user chooses the working forward recipe and then asks "What should be done next?", to which the agent replies:

Propose you work on San Francisco to Dallas leg.

Here again the agent uses the current context to assist the user, in this case to suggest the next step in the current recipe. Working on a leg entails manipulating the "interval bars" in the horizontal slider area below the map (see Figure 4) to specify latest arrival and earliest departure times at each city.

We skip ahead now to the end of the sample session, where the interaction history is as shown in Figure 5. Notice the varying level of detail in this history: the

(Jointly scheduling a trip on the route via working forward)
(Done user identifying route of scheduling a trip as San Francisco to Dallas to Boston, allowing 100+ itineraries)
(Done user proposing a trip on the route be scheduled via working forward)
(Done user working on San Francisco to Dallas leg, allowing 70 itineraries)
(Done user working on Dallas to Boston leg, allowing 55 itineraries)
(Done jointly specifying airlines, allowing 10 itineraries)
USER: Add American specification, allowing no itineraries.
(Done agent adding United specification)
AGENT: "Propose I add United specification."
USER: "Ok."
AGENT: Add United specification, allowing 10 itineraries.
(Done user displaying itineraries)

Figure 5: History at end of sample session.

selected segment in which the agent and user jointly specify airlines is shown in full, while the internal elements of the other segments are suppressed. The user can interactively control the level of detail in interaction histories by single and double clicking on segments similarly to the way hierarchial file structures are typically inspected.

The airline specification segment in Figure 5 is expanded in full to show an example of the agent performing an application act, rather than just communicating with the user. The user began this segment by requiring all flights use American airlines, which resulted in no possible itineraries. Whenever a constraint (such as an airline specification) is entered or changed, the application program automatically recomputes the number of possible itineraries and displays this number in the box labelled "Itineraries." In the segmented interaction history, the number of possible itineraries after each segment or action is indicated if it is different from the number before.

Noticing that the user had over-constrained the trip, the agent proposed adding United airlines which, with the user's approval, it did. The agent did not propose this particular airline at random—it used the application's API to find an airline that would in fact increase the number of possible itineraries.

Related Work

Cohen (1992) and Jacob (1995), among others, have explored discourse-related extensions to direct manipulation interfaces that make previous context directly available. However, most work on applying human discourse principles to human-computer interaction, e.g., (Lambert & Carberry 1991, Yanklovich 1994), has assumed that natural language understanding will be applied to the user's utterances. Terveen (1991) has explored providing intelligent assistance through collaborative graphical manipulation without explicitly invoking the agent paradigm.

The two systems we know of that are overall closest in spirit to our own are Stein et al.'s MERIT (1995) and Ahn et al.'s DenK (1994). MERIT uses a different version of discourse theory and compiles it into a finite-state machine representation, which is less flexible and extensible. DenK has the goal of providing a discourse-based agent, but has not yet modelled collaboration.

Conclusion

We have demonstrated the feasibility of an application-independent toolkit for applying human collaborative discourse principles to autonomous software agents. We hope the sample scenario above suggests that this approach can lead to agents that are natural and easy to collaborate with.

Our future plans include:

- improving the flexibility and robustness of the discourse processing algorithms, especially as related to incompleteness of the agent's recipe library,
- supporting negotiation between the user and agent,
- a pilot user study to compare using the example application with and without the interface agent, and
- using Collagen to build agents that operate remotely in space and time (e.g., on the Internet), which will require more discussion between the agent and user about past and future actions.

References

Ahn et al, R. 1994-5. The DenK-architecture: A fundamental approach to user-interfaces. *AI Review* 8:431–445.

Brodie, M.; Mylopoulos, J.; and Schmidt, J., eds. 1982. *On Conceptual Modelling.* NY, NY: Springer-Verlag.

Cohen, P. 1992. The role of natural language in a multimodal interface. *UIST'92*, pp. 143–149.

Grosz, B. J., and Kraus, S. 1996. Collaborative plans for complex group action. *Artificial Intelligence.* To appear.

Grosz, B. J., and Sidner, C. L. 1986. Attention, intentions, and the structure of discourse. *Computational Linguistics* 12(3):175–204.

Grosz, B. J., and Sidner, C. L. 1990. Plans for discourse. In Cohen, P. R.; Morgan, J. L.; and Pollack, M. E., eds., *Intentions and Communication.* Cambridge, MA: MIT Press. chapter 20, 417–444.

Jacob, R. J. K. 1995. Natural dialogue in modes other than natural language. In Beun, R.-J.; Baker, M.; and Reiner, M., eds., *Dialogue and Instruction.* Berlin: Springer-Verlag. 289–301.

Kautz, H. 1990. A circumscriptive theory of plan recognition. In Cohen, P. R.; Morgan, J. L.; and Pollack, M. E., eds., *Intentions and Communication.* Cambridge, MA: MIT Press. chapter 6, 105–133.

Lambert, L., and Carberry, S. 1991. A tripartite plan-based model of dialogue. In *Proc. 29th Ann. Meeting ACL.*

Lochbaum, K. E. 1994. Using collaborative plans to model the intentional structure of discourse. TR 25-94, Harvard Univ., Ctr. for Res. in Computing Tech. PhD thesis.

Lochbaum, K. E. 1995. The use of knowledge preconditions in language processing. *IJCAI'95*, pp. 1260–1266.

Maes, P. 1994. Agents that reduce work and information overload. *Comm. ACM* 37(17):30–40.

Rich, C., and Sidner, C. 1996a. Adding a collaborative agent to graphical user interfaces. *UIST'96.* To appear.

Rich, C., and Sidner, C. 1996b. Segmented interaction history in a collaborative interface agent. *3rd Int. Conf. on Intelligent User Interfaces.* To appear.

Rich, C. 1996. Window sharing with collaborative interface agents. *ACM SIGCHI Bulletin* 28(1):70–78.

Sidner, C. L. 1994. An artificial discourse language for collaborative negotiation. *AAAI'94*, pp. 814–819.

Stein, A., and Maier, E. 1995. Structuring collaborative information-seeking dialogues. *Knowledge-Based Systems* 8(2-3):82–93.

Terveen, G.; Wroblewski, D.; and Tighe, S. 1991. Intelligent assistance through collaborative manipulation. *IJCAI'91*, pp. 9–14.

Yanklovich, N. 1994. Talking vs. taking: Speech access to remote computers. *CHI'94*, pp. 275–276.

An Experiment in the Design of Software Agents

Henry Kautz, Bart Selman,
Michael Coen, Steven Ketchpel, and Chris Ramming
AI Principles Research Department
AT&T Bell Laboratories
Murray Hill, NJ 07974
{kautz, selman, jcr}@research.att.com
mhcoen@ai.mit.edu
ketchpel@cs.stanford.edu

Abstract

We describe a bottom-up approach to the design of software agents. We built and tested an agent system that addresses the real-world problem of handling the activities involved in scheduling a visitor to our laboratory. The system employs both task-specific and user-centered agents, and communicates with users using both email and a graphical interface. This experiment has helped us to identify crucial requirements in the successful deployment of software agents, including issues of reliability, security, and ease of use. The architecture we developed to meet these requirements is flexible and extensible, and is guiding our current research on principles of agent design.

Introduction

There is much recent interest in the creation of software agents. A range of different approaches and projects use the term "agents", ranging from adaptive user interfaces to systems that use planning algorithms to generate shell scripts (Maes 1993; Dent *et al.* 1992; Shoham 1993; Etzioni *et al.* 1992).

In our own approach, agents assist users in a range of daily, mundane activities, such as setting up meetings, sending out papers, locating information in multiple databases, tracking the whereabouts of people, and so on. Our objective is to design agents that blend transparently into normal work environments, while relieving users of low-level administrative and clerical tasks. We take the practical aspect of software agents seriously: users should feel that the agents are reliable and predictable, and that the human user remains in ultimate control.

One of the most difficult aspects of agent design is to define specific tasks that are both feasible using current technology, and are truly useful to the everyday user. Furthermore, it became clear during the testing of our initial prototype that users have little patience when it it comes to interacting with software agents. We therefore paid special attention to the user interface aspects of our system. In particular, whenever possible, we opted for graphically-oriented interfaces over pure text-based interfaces. In addition, reliability and error-handling is crucial in all parts of a software agent system. The real world is an unpredictable place: messages between agents may be lost or delayed, people may respond inappropriately to requests, and so forth.

Our approach has been bottom-up. We began by identifying possible useful and feasible tasks for a software agent. The first such task we choose involved the activities surrounding the scheduling of a visitor to our lab. We designed and implemented a set of software agents to handle this task. We deliberately made no commitment in advance to a particular agent architecture. We then tested the system with ordinary users; the feedback from this test led to many improvements in the design of the agents and the human/agent interfaces, as well as the development of a general and flexible framework for agent interaction. The key feature of the framework is the use of personalized agents called "userbots" that mediate communication between users and task-specific agents. We are now in our third round of implementation and testing, in which we are further refining and generalizing our userbots so that they can communicate with software agents developed by other research groups, such as the "softbots" of Etzioni *et al.* (1992).

We believe that the bottom-up approach is crucial in identifying the necessary properties of a successful agent platform. Our initial experiments have already led us to formulate some key properties. Examples include the separation of task-specific agents from user-centered agents, the need to handle issues of security and privacy, and as mentioned above, the need for good human interfaces and high reliability.

Taskbots and Userbots

Selecting an appropriate task for software agents to perform is itself a challenge. Agents must provide solutions to real problems that are important to real users. The whole raison d'être for software agents is lost if they are restricted to handling toy examples. On the other hand, more complex tasks frequently include a range of long-term research issues, such as understanding unrestricted natural language.

After considering a number of possible agent tasks, we settled on the problem of scheduling a visitor to our lab.[1] This job is quite routine, but consumes a substantial amount

[1] See also Dent *et al* (1992) and Maes and Kozierok (1993), that describe the design of software agents that *learn* how to assist users in scheduling meetings and managing their personal calendars.

of the host's time. The normal sequence of tasks consists of announcing the upcoming visit by email; collecting responses from people who would like to meet with the visitor, along with their preferred meeting times; putting together a schedule that satisfies as many constraints as possible (taking into account social issues, such as not bumping the lab director from the schedule); sending out the schedule to the participants, together with appropriate information about room and telephone numbers; and, of course, often rescheduling people at the last minute because of unforeseen events.

We decided to implement a specialized software agent called the "visitorbot" to handle these tasks. (We use the suffix "bot" for "software robot".) After examining various proposed agent architectures (Etzioni, Lesh, & Segal 1992; Shoham 1993), we decided that it was necessary to first obtain practical experience in building and a using a concrete basic agent, before committing to any particular theoretical framework. Our initial implementation was a monolithic agent, that communicated directly with users via email. The program was given its own login account ("visitorbot"), and was activated upon receiving email at that account. (Mail was piped into the visitorbot program using the ".forward" facility of the Unix mail system.)

Our experience in using the visitorbot in scheduling a visit led to the following observations:

1. Email communication between the visitorbot and humans was cumbersome and error-prone. The users had to fill in a pre-defined form to specify their preferred meeting times. (We considered various forms of natural language input instead of forms. However, the current state of the art in natural language processing cannot parse or even skim unrestricted natural language with sufficient reliability. On the other hand, the use of restricted "pseudo"-natural language has little or no advantage over the use of forms.) Small editing errors by users often made it impossible to process the forms automatically, requiring human intervention. Moreover, users other than the host objected to using the visitorbot at all; from their point of view, the system simply made their life harder.

Based on this observation, we realized that an easy to use interface was crucial. We decided that the next version of the visitorbot would employ a graphical interface, so that users could simply click on buttons to specify their preferred meeting times. This approach practically eliminated communication errors between people and the visitorbot, and was viewed by users as an improvement over the pre-Bot environment.

2. There is a need for redundancy in error-handling. For example, one early version of the visitorbot could become confused by bounced email, or email responses by "vacation" programs. Although our platform has improved over the initial prototype, more needs to be done. Agents must react more or less predictably to both foreseen errors (*e.g.*, mangled email), and unforeseen errors (*e.g.*, a subprocess invoked by the bot terminates unexpectedly). Techniques from the area of software reliability and real-time systems design could well be applicable to this problem. For example, modern telephone switching systems have a down-time of only a few minutes per year, because they continuously run sophisticated error-detection and recovery mechanisms.

3. The final task of creating a good schedule from a set of constraints did not require advanced planning or scheduling techniques. The visitorbot translated the scheduling problem into an integer programming problem, and solved it using a commercial integer programming package (CPLEX). An interesting advantage of this approach is that was easy to incorporate soft constraints (such as the difference between an "okay" time slot and a "good" time slot for a user).

This experience led us to the design shown in Fig. 1. This design includes an agent for each individual user in addition to the visitorbot. For example, the agent for the user "kautz" is named "kautzbot", for "selman" is named "selmanbot", and so on. The userbots mediate communication between the visitorbot and their human owners.

The normal interaction between the visitorbot and the users proceeds as follows. The initial talk announcement is mailed by the visitorbot to each userbot. The userbot then determines the preferred mode of communication with its owner. In particular, if the user is logged in on an X-terminal, the userbot creates a pop-up window on the user's screen, containing the announcement and a button to press to request to meet with the visitor, as shown in the left-hand window in Fig. 2. If the user clicks on "yes", the userbot passes this information back to the visitorbot, which responds with a request to obtain the user's preferred meeting times. The userbot then creates a graphical menu of meeting times, as shown in the right-hand window in Fig. 2. The user simply clicks on buttons to indicate his or her preferences. The userbot then generates a message containing the preferences and mails it back to the visitorbot. If the userbot is unable to determine the display where the user is working, or if the user fails to respond to the pop-up displays, the userbot forwards the request from the visitorbot via email to the user as a plain text form.

There are several important advantages of this design. First, the visitorbot does not need to know about the user's display, and does not need permission to create windows on that display. This means, for example, that a visitorbot at Bell Labs can create a graphical window at any site that is reachable by email where there are userbots. This was successfully tested with the "mhcoenbot" running at MIT.[2] The separation of the visitorbot from the userbot also simplifies the design of the former, since the userbots handle the peculiarities of addressing the users' displays. Even more importantly, the particular information about the user's location and work habits does not have to be centrally available. This information can be kept private to the user and his or

[2]Sometimes it is possible to create a remote X-window over the internet, but this is prone to failure. Among other problems, the user would first have to grant permission to ("xhost") the machine running the visitorbot program; but note that the user may not even know the identity of machine on which the visitorbot program is running. Even if the identity of the machine is known, it may be impossible to serve X-windows directly due to "firewalls" or intermittent connections.

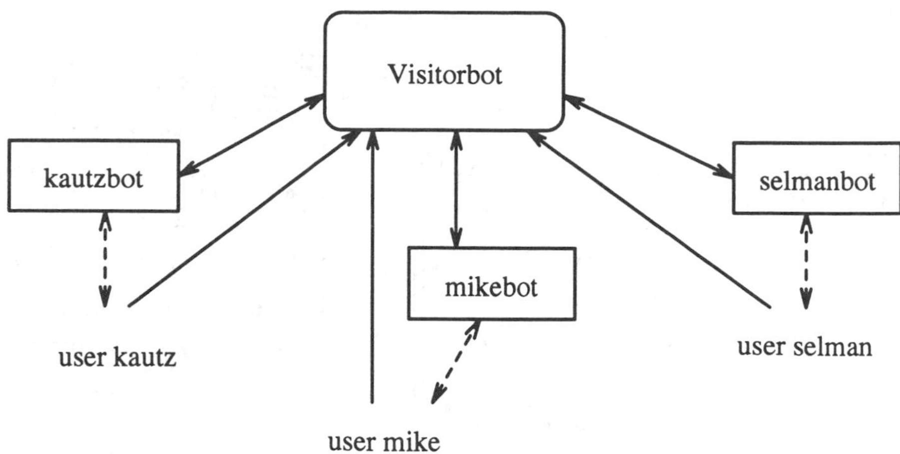

Figure 1: Current architecture of the agent system. Solid lines represent email communication; dashed lines represent both graphical and email communication.

her userbot.

Another advantage of this design is that different users, who may have access to different computing resources, can run different userbots, of varying levels of sophistication. Thus, everyone is not restricted to a "least common denominator" type interface.

Perhaps the most important benefit of the design is that a task-specific agent (such as the visitorbot) is not tied to any specific form of communication. The task-specific agent specifies *what* information is to be transmitted or obtained, but not *how* the communication should take place. The userbot can then employ a wide range of media, such as graphics, voice, FAX, email, etc. for interacting with its owner. The userbot also can take into account its owners preferences and such factors as the owners whereabouts and current computing environment in deciding on the mode of communication. For example, a userbot could incorporate a telephone interface with a speech synthesizer. This would enable a userbot to place a call to its owner (if the owner so desires), read the talk announcement, and collect the owner's preferences by touch-tone. Note that this extension would not require any modification to the visitorbot itself.

Refining the Userbot

Tests of the visitorbot/userbot system described in the previous section showed that users greatly preferred its ease of use and flexibility over our initial monolithic, email-based agent. Now that we had developed a good basic architecture, the logical next step was to incorporate new task-specific agents. In order to do so, we undertook a complete reimplementation of the system. In the new implementation, all visitorbot-specific code was eliminated from the userbots. We designed a simple set of protocols for communication between task-specific agents and userbots. Again, our approach was pragmatic, in that we tried to established a minimal set of conventions for the applications we were considering, rather than immediately trying to create a full-blown agent interlingua.

In brief, bots communicate by exchanging email which is tagged with a special header field, "XBot-message-type". The message type indicates the general way in which the body of the message (if any) should be processed by the receiver. For example, the message type "xchoices" means that the message is a request for the receiver to make a series of *choices* from among one or more sets of alternatives described in the body of the message. The inclusion of the field "XBot-return-note" in the message indicates that the result of processing the message should be mailed back to the sender. The communication protocol establishes the syntax for the data presented in the body of each message type, and the format of the data that results from processing the message. However, the protocol deliberately does not specify the exact method by which the processing is carried out. For example, a userbot may process an xchoices message by creating a pop-up menu, or calling the user on the telephone, or simply by consulting a database of defaults that the user has established.

When applications are developed that demand novel kinds of interactions with userbots, the communication protocols can be extended by adding new message types. This will require the creation of mechanisms for distributing "updates" to the userbots to handle the extensions (an issue we return to below). So far, however, only a very small number of message types (namely, ones for requesting choices, requesting help, and simply conveying a piece of information) have been needed. One question that more experience in building bots will answer is whether the number of basic message types is indeed bounded and small, or if new types are often needed with new applications.

In essence, then, the messages that task-specific bots and userbots exchange can be viewed as *intensions* – such a request to make a choice – rather than *extensions* – for example, if one were to mail a message containing a program that draws a menu on the screen when executed.[3] In this

[3]This description of messages as intensions versus extensions

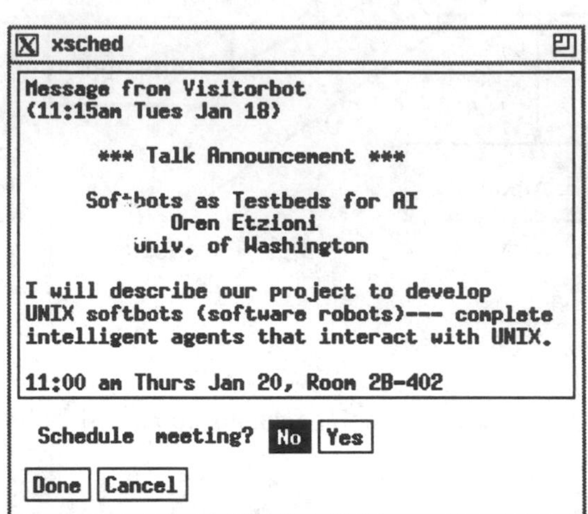

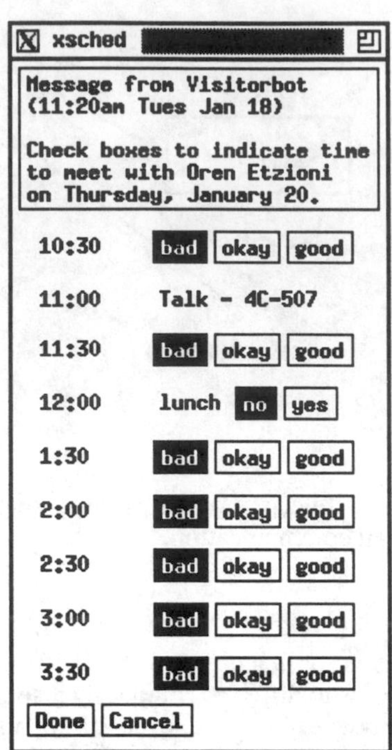

Figure 2: Graphical interfaces created by a userbot in response to messages from the visitorbot. The left window is created by processing a talk announcement; the right, by a request for the user's preferred meeting times.

regard it is informative to contrast our approach with that used in *Telescript*, the electronic messaging language created General Magic. In Telescript, messages are full-fledged programs, and are executed on the receiving machine by a fixed interpreter. Thus, Telescript messages are purely extensional. While the Telescript approach has the advantage that the reception of a message can initiate arbitrarily novel and complex processing, this must be weighed against the fact that any flexibility in the *way* in which the interaction takes place with the user must be built into each and every message.

One aspect of the preliminary userbot that some users found objectionable was the fact that various windows (such as those in Fig. 2) would pop-up whenever the userbot received mail, which could be disruptive. Therefore, in the new implementation messages are normally not displayed until the user makes an explicit request to interact with his or her userbot. This interaction is supported by a continuously-running "active" userbot, as shown in Fig. 3. The main userbot window indicates the number of outstanding messages waiting to be processed, the userbot's state (working or idle), and three buttons. Clicking on the "process message" button allows the userbot to process messages that require user interaction – for example, bringing up an xchoices window on behalf of the visitorbot. Note, however, that messages that are tagged as "urgent" are always immediately processed by the userbot.

The second button, "user preferences", brings up a window in which the user can set various options in the behavior of his or her userbot. For example, checking the "autopilot" box makes the userbot pop up windows without waiting to be explicitly told to do so. The "voice" checkbox causes the userbot to announce the receipt of new userbot mail using the speaker in a Sun workstation – a kind of audible "biff" for botmail. The "forward to" options are used to indicate that the userbot should choose try to communicate with its owner at a remote location – for example, by transmitting messages via a FAX-modem to the owner's home telephone. (Currently the code to support the "forward to" options has not yet been completed. The exact appearance and functionality of these options may differ in the final version.)

Finally, the third button in the main userbot window brings up the window labeled "taskbots". This window contains a button for each task-specific agent whose email address is known to the userbot. (This information is maintained in file that the user can easily customize.) Clicking on a button in this window initiates communication with the designed task-specific agent, by sending a message of type "help" to that agent. The communication protocol specifies that the agent should respond to a help message by sending back a menu of commands that the agent understands, together with some basic help information, typically in the form of an xchoices message. When the userbot processes this response, it creates a window containing the appropriate controls for interacting with that particular task-specific

is due to Mark Jones.

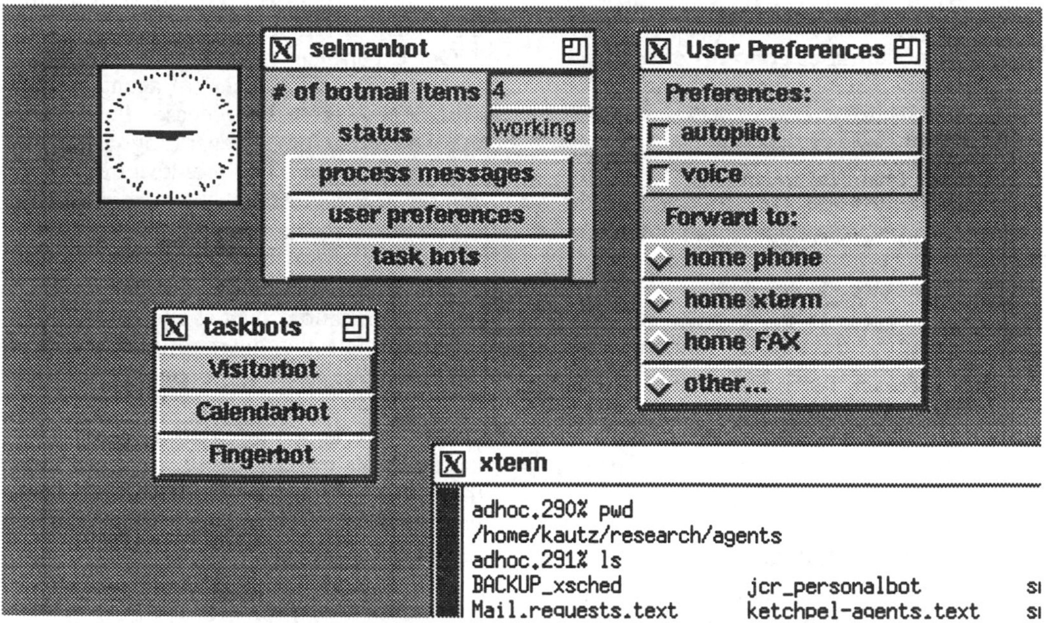

Figure 3: Graphical display of a userbot.

agent. For example, a user who is hosting a visitor to our lab starts the entire process by clicking on the visitorbot button. This leads to the creation of a window containing buttons for basic visitorbot commands, such as scheduling a new visitor, getting the status of a visit, ordering a schedule to be generated, and so on. Clicking on some of these buttons could lead to the creation of other windows, for example, one in which to type the text of the abstract of the visitor's talk.

At the time that this paper is being written, only the visitorbot button in the taskbots menu is active. Over the next few months we intend to establish communication with Oren Etzioni's "finger" agent (used to obtain information about people on the internet) (Etzioni, Lesh, & Segal 1992), and Tom Mitchell's "calendar" agent (used to schedule meetings among groups of people) (Dent *et al.* 1992). The fingerbot and calendarbot will not themselves be ported to our laboratory's computers; instead, those programs will run at their respective "homes" (University of Washington and CMU), and communication with userbots at various sites will take place using ordinary internet email. We hope that the idea of a userbot will provide a powerful and flexible framework for integrating many different kinds of software agents that run in different computing environments.

Privacy and Security

Early discussions with potential users made it clear that privacy and security are central issues in the successful deployment of software agents. Some proposed agent systems would filter through all of the user's email, pulling out and deleting messages that the agent would like to handle. We found that users generally objected to giving a program permission to delete automatically any of their incoming mail. An alternative approach would give the bot authority to read but not modify the user's mail. The problem with this is that the user's mail quickly becomes polluted with the many messages sent between the various bots.

Our solution to this problem has been to create a pseudo-account for each userbot, with its own mail alias. Mail sent to this alias is piped into a userbot program, that is executed under the corresponding user's id. This gives the instantiated userbot the authority, for example, to create a window on the user's display. Any "bot mail" sent to this alias is not seen by the user, unless the userbot explicitly decides to forward it.

Each user has a special ".bot" directory, which contains information customized to the particular user. These files specify the particular program that instantiates the userbot, a log of the userbot mail, and the user's default display id. In general, this directory contains user-specific information for the userbot. It is important to note that this directory does not need to be publicly readable, and can thus contain sensitive information for use by the userbot. Examples of such information include the names of people to which the bot is not supposed to respond, unlisted home telephone numbers, the user's personal schedule, and so on.

Thus, userbots provide a general mechanism for the distribution and protection of information. For a concrete example, consider the information you get by running the "finger" command. Right now, you have to decide whether your home phone number will be available to everyone on the internet, or no one at all. A straightforward task of your userbot would be to give out your phone number via email on request from (say) faculty members at your department and people listed in your address book, but not to every person who knows your login id.

Earlier we described the alternative Telescript model in which messages are programs that are executed on the receiving machine. This model raises concerns of computer security, particularly if such programs are able to access the host's file system. (Security features in Telescript allow the user to disable file access, but this would appear to limit the kinds of tasks Telescript agents could perform.) Userbot systems are by nature secure, insofar as the routines for processing each message type within the userbot are secure. Although this is a non-trivial condition, it would appear to be easier to guarantee that the code of the userbot itself (that is presumably obtained from a trusted source) is secure, rather than to guarantee that every email program (that could come from anyone) does not contain a virus. Extensions and updates to userbots to handle new message types would have to be distributed through secure channels, perhaps by using cryptographic techniques (Rivest, Shamir, & Adleman 1978).

Bots vs. Programs

An issue that is often raised is what exactly distinguishes software agents from ordinary programs. In our view, software agents are simply a special class of programs. Perhaps the best way to characterize these programs is by a list of distinguishing properties:

Communication: Agents engage in complex and frequent patterns of two-way communication with users and each other.

Temporal continuity: Agents are most naturally viewed as continuously running processes, rather than as functions that map a single input to a single output.

Responsibility: Agents are expected to handle private information in a responsible and secure manner.

Robustness: Agents should be designed to deal with unexpected changes in the environment. They should include mechanisms to recover both from system errors and human errors. If errors prevent completion of their given tasks, they still must report the problem back to their users.

Multi-platform: Agents should be able to communicate across different computer system architectures and platforms. For example, very sophisticated agents running on a high-end platform should be able to carry out tasks in cooperation with relatively basic agents running on low-end systems.

Autonomy: Advanced agents should have some degree of decision-making capability, and the ability to choose among different strategies for performing a given task.

Note that our list does not commit to the use of any particular form of reasoning or planning. Although advanced agents may need general reasoning and planning capabilities, our experiments have shown that interesting agent behavior can already emerge from systems of relatively simple agents.

Conclusions

We have described a bottom-up approach to the design of software agents. We built and tested an agent system that addresses the real-world problem of handling the communication involved in scheduling a visitor to our laboratory.

Our experiment helped us to identify crucial factors in the successful deployment of agents. These include issues of reliability, security, and ease of use. Security and ease of use were obtained by separating task-specific agents from personal userbots. This architecture provides an extensible and flexible platform for the further development of practical software agents. New task-specific agents immediately obtain a graphical user interface for communicating with users via the userbots. Furthermore, additional modalities of communication, such as speech and FAX, can be added to the userbots, without modifying the task-specific agents.

Perhaps the hardest problem we encountered was defining the initial task. More attention should be paid to identifying useful and compelling agent applications that blend unobtrusively into ordinary work environments. We believe that the empirical approach taken in this paper is essential for guiding research toward the truly central and difficult issues in agent design.

Acknowledgements

We thank Oren Etzioni for stimulating discussions about softbots during his visit to Bell Labs, leading us to initiate our own softbot project. We also thank Ron Brachman, Mark Jones, David Lewis Chris Ramming, Eric Sumner, and other members of our center for useful suggestions and feedback.

References

Dent, L.; Boticario, J.; McDermott, J.; Mitchell, T.; and Zabowski, D. 1992. A personal learning apprentice. In *Proceedings of AAAI-92*, 96–103. AAAI Press/The MIT Press.

Etzioni, O.; Hanks, S.; Weld, D.; Draper, D.; Lesh, N.; and Williamson, M. 1992. An approach to planning with incomplete information. In *Proceedings of KR-92*, 115–125. Morgan Kaufmann.

Etzioni, O.; Lesh, N.; and Segal, R. 1992. Building softbots for UNIX. Technical report, University of Washington, Seattle, WA.

Maes, P., and Kozierok, R. 1993. Learning interface agents. In *Proceedings of AAAI-93*, 459–464. AAAI Press/The MIT Press.

Maes, P., ed. 1993. *Designing Automomous Agents*. MIT/Elsevier.

Rivest, R. L.; Shamir, A.; and Adleman, L. 1978. A method for obtaining digital signatures and public key cryptosystems. *Communications of the ACM* 21(2):120–126.

Shoham, Y. 1993. Agent-oriented programming. *Artificial Intelligence* 60:51–92.

A Planner for Exploratory Data Analysis

Robert St. Amant and Paul R. Cohen
Computer Science Department
University of Massachusetts
Amherst, MA 01003-4610
stamant@cs.umass.edu, cohen@cs.umass.edu

Abstract

Statistical exploratory data analysis (EDA) poses a difficult search problem. The EDA process lends itself however to a planning formulation. We have built a system, called AIDE, to help users explore data. AIDE relies on partial hierarchical planning, a form of planning appropriate for tasks in complex, uncertain environments. Our description of the EDA task and the AIDE system provides a case study of the application of planning to a novel domain.

Exploring data

Data exploration plays a central role in empirical scientific research. Sometimes we can build a model of complex phenomena based on theory alone; often, however, we need to explore the data. We need to identify suggestive features of the data, interpret the patterns these features indicate, and generate hypotheses to explain the patterns. Successive steps through the process lead us gradually to a better understanding of underlying structure in the data. Exploratory data analysis (EDA) gives us a powerful set of operations for this process: we fit linear and higher-order functions to relationships; we compose and transform variables with arithmetic functions; we separate relationships into partitions and clusters; we extract features through statistical summaries (Tukey 1977). Through the selective and often intuitive application of these operations we gradually build a description of a dataset.

Exploration poses a difficult search problem. The flexibility of exploratory operators gives a large branching factor and an unbounded search space. If an exploratory analysis were driven purely by successive features discovered in data, the task would be impossible: Is a partitioning or a functional transformation appropriate? With what parameters? When should one stop? Though manageable in human hands, exploration is a difficult and painstaking task.

We have designed and implemented an Assistant for Intelligent Data Exploration, AIDE, to help users carry out their exploration (St. Amant & Cohen 1995). In AIDE, data-directed mechanisms extract simple observations and suggestive indications from the data. EDA operations then act in a goal-directed fashion to generate more extensive descriptions of the data. The system is mixed-initiative, autonomously pursuing its own goals while still allowing the user to guide or override its decisions. Our description of the planner and its task provides a case study of how domain characteristics can influence planner design.

In the remainder of the paper we discuss an EDA example, describing the types of operations and results involved in the process. We then discuss the planner and its plan representation in some detail. Returning to the EDA example, we show how it is solved by AIDE acting in concert with a user. We conclude by showing where AIDE fits in the context of approaches to planning.

An EDA example

We can best illustrate the EDA process with an example, taken from an experiment with Phoenix, a simulation of forest fires and fire-fighting agents in Yellowstone National Park (Cohen *et al.* 1989). The experiment involved setting a fire at a fixed location and specified time, and observing the behavior of the fireboss (the planner) and the bulldozers (the agents that put out the fire). Variability between trials is due to randomly changing wind speed and direction, non-uniform terrain and elevation, and the varying amounts of time agents take in executing primitive tasks. In this experiment we collected forty variables over the course of some 340 Phoenix trials, including measurements of the wind speed, the outcome (success or failure), the type of plan used, and the number of times the system needed to replan. We became interested in a comparison of the time it takes the planner to put out a fire (Duration) and the amount of fireline built during the trial (Effort). Figure 1a shows a scatter plot of these two variables.

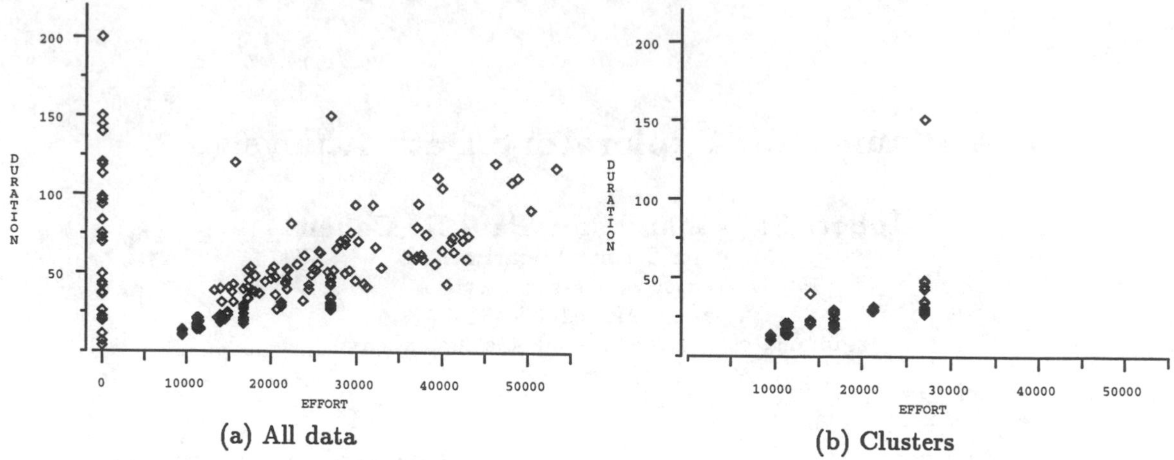

(a) All data

(b) Clusters

Figure 1: Patterns in Planner Effort and Trial Duration

We begin by observing that the relationship can be partitioned into two parts: a vertical partition at zero on the Duration axis and a separate, approximately linear partition. We call this an *indication*, a suggestive characteristic of the data. Examining other variables, we find that the vertical partition corresponds to trials in which the outcome was `Failure`. We note that the correlation is positive in the `Success` partition, as expected, but that there are two outliers from the general pattern.

We can be more precise about the "approximately linear" pattern in the `Success` partition: we can fit a regression line to the data. We then examine the residuals of the fit—the degree to which the data are *not* explained by the description—by subtracting the actual value of Duration, for each value of Effort, from the value predicted by the regression line. We see no indications of further structure, such as curvature, that would render our description incorrect, and thus we tentatively accept the linear description.

Looking again at the `Success` partition, we notice small, vertical clusters in the lower range of Effort. In a histogram, or a kernel density estimate, these would appear as peaks. The clustered points are isolated in Figure 1b. We can describe the behavior of the clusters in terms of their central location, by reducing each cluster to its median Effort and Duration value. These medians are also linear, with approximately the same slope as the line fitting the entire partition.

We then try to explain why some observations fall into clusters while others do not. We find that the clustered data correspond to trials in which the planner did not need to replan; that is, observations fall into clusters only when #Replans = 0. If we associate each cluster with a unique identifier, we find that together the discrete variables WindSpeed and PlanType predict cluster membership almost perfectly. It further becomes clear that for the clustered data there is an interaction between the two predictive variables in their effect on Duration.

This brief account gives the flavor of EDA. A more detailed account given in *Empirical Methods in Artificial Intelligence* (Cohen 1995). The remainder of this paper describes the planner that lets AIDE, in cooperation with a user, generate these kinds of results.

Abstractions in exploration

In *Exploratory Data Analysis*, John Tukey describes EDA in this way:

> A basic problem about any body of data is to make it more easily and effectively handleable by minds—our minds, her mind, his mind. To this general end:
>
> - anything that makes a simpler description possible makes the description more easily handleable.
> - anything that looks below the previously described surface makes the description more effective.
>
> So we shall always be glad (a) to simplify description and (b) to describe one layer deeper (Tukey 1977, p.v).

Tukey's account of exploration emphasizes two related aspects: description through abstraction and description by hierarchical problem decomposition.

Abstraction is ubiquitous in exploration. Fitting a straight line to a relationship involves deciding that variance around the line, evidence of curvature, outlying values, and so forth may be ignored at an appropriate level of abstraction. One fits a simple description, a line, before attempting to describe the residuals, i.e., those data that don't fit the abstraction well. The effect is of moving from higher to lower levels of abstraction. A more subtle example can be seen in the Phoenix analysis. To describe the behavior of the vertical clusters in Effort and Duration, we summarize each cluster in terms of its central location. In other words, we deal with a simplification of each cluster, in which spread around the central location has been abstracted away.

Hierarchical problem decomposition plays a large part in exploration as well. The Phoenix example gives a good illustration: we begin by fitting a partition to the relationship, and then pursue the description of each component independently. Much of exploration can be viewed as the incremental decomposition of data into simple descriptions, which are then combined into a more comprehensive result.

Exploratory procedures furthermore impose top-down structure on the exploration process. In other words, when we execute an exploratory operation we generally have a good notion of which operation, of many possible, to execute next. Common procedures often fall into a few basic families that process data in similar ways. It is easy to see, for example, that constructing a histogram involves the same procedures as constructing a contingency table: the contingency table is a two-dimensional analog of the histogram, with cell counts corresponding to bin heights. We can draw similar analogies between procedures for smoothing and for generating kernel density estimates, or between resistant line fitting and locally-weighted regression curves. While sometimes novel procedures are constructed from scratch, variations on existing procedures are much more common.

Knowledge of abstraction, problem decomposition, and common combinations of operations lets us restructure the EDA search space, to make it more manageable. These elements identify exploration as a planning problem (Korf 1987). Still, there are many different approaches to planning. Other characteristics of the domain help us refine our understanding of the type of planning involved.

Exploratory procedures require control structures more complex than simple sequences of operations. It is hard to see, for example, how one can iteratively improve a resistant fit or search through a space of model extensions given only the ability to chain together single operations. Many procedures are more naturally formulated in terms of tests of generated values, iteration, recursion, and other forms of control.

Exploration is opportunistic. Though procedures often specify a course of action, there can be a great deal of uncertainty in carrying out the details. Each operation is simultaneously an effective action and an information-gathering action. In the Phoenix example we could not have predicted that there would be vertical clusters in the relationship. Once we noticed the clusters, we were able to deal with them by reducing them to their medians and trying to describe the result. We could not have predicted that these points would be approximately linear, but this new information let us extend the exploration further. At each point during the process we can determine what the next few steps should be; the details of how to proceed must often wait until we have actually performed those steps.

Finally, the results of an exploratory session are not simply the p-values, tables, graphs, and so forth that have been computed. Exploration is constructive, in that the interpretation of these individual results depends on how they were derived. Interpretation of the residuals of a linear fit depends on whether a regression or resistant line was applied; individual cluster properties depend on clustering criteria. In many cases the knowledge that some operation has been applied and has failed can influence our interpretation of a related result. The result of an exploration, then, must include an annotated trace of the process itself.

The planner

A form of reactive planning called partial hierarchical planning (Georgeff & Lansky 1986) turns out to be a good match for the task. Systems that use the approach include PRS (Georgeff & Lansky 1987), the Phoenix planner (Cohen *et al.* 1989) and the RESUN system (Carver & Lesser 1993). Our design of the AIDE planner is largely based on experience with Phoenix and RESUN.

The AIDE planner operates by manipulating a stack of *control units*. The planner is essentially a high-level language interpreter, in which the active stack stores the current execution context. The planner executes the control unit at the top of the planning stack, by calling its `execute` method. If this generates a new control unit, it is pushed onto the stack to be executed in turn. The process continues as long as the topmost stack element has the status `:in-progress`. If its status changes to `:succeeded` or `:failed`, then the control unit is not executed, but rather popped off the stack, its `complete` method being called at that point. The behavior of a control unit thus depends on the specialized definition of its execution and completion methods.

In this simple representation a variety of control structures can be defined. Consider a `:sequence` control unit, which executes a sequence of subordinate control units in order. A `:sequence` unit maintains an internal list of subordinate units. Each call to its execution method pops off and returns the next remaining element on the list. When the list is exhausted, or a subordinate fails, the `:sequence` unit's completion status is set appropriately and its completion method is called.

```
(define-plan explore-by-incremental-modeling ()
  :satisfies   (explore-by :modeling ?model-type ?structure ?model)
  :constraints ((?structure ((:dataset-type dataset))))
  :body        (:SEQUENCE
                (:WHEN (null ?model)
                  (:SUBGOAL generate (generate-initial-model ?structure ?model-type ?model)))
                (:SUBGOAL elaborate (elaborate-model ?model-type ?activity ?structure ?model))))

(define-action generate-initial-generic-model
  :satisfies (generate-initial-model ?description ?structure :generic ?model)
  :action (values t (return-bindings ?model (make-generic-model. . .))))
```

Figure 2: Plan and action definitions

Other control constructs can be defined similarly for conditionalization, iteration, and more specialized processing. Goals, plans, and actions are also specialized forms of control units.

A plan has a name, a specification of a goal that the plan can potentially satisfy, constraints on its bindings, and a body. The body of a plan is a control schema of subgoal specifications, subgoals which must be satisfied for the plan to complete successfully. An action is similar to a plan, except that its body contains arbitrary code, rather than a control schema. The plan in Figure 2 is instantiated in the exploration of a dataset. It generates an initial model of an appropriate type and then establishes the goal of elaborating the model. With the plans in the AIDE library, elaboration will involve incrementally adding relationships to the model. One of the plans that matches the `elaborate` subgoal recursively establishes an identical subgoal, with `?model` bound to the incrementally extended model.

A plan instance, as a type of control unit, executes by instantiating the control units represented in its body. On completion a plan instance sends to its parent goal a completion status, `:succeeded` or `:failed`, along with a set of variable bindings. An action instance generates no new control units in its execution, but simply returns a completion status and a set of bindings for its matching goal. A goal instance executes by generating a new plan instance—searching through the plan library and finding a matching (unifying) plan.

We must complicate this account somewhat. There are often several plans that satisfy a given goal, and sometimes an unlimited number of possible bindings for its plan variables. To manage these situations we have three mechanisms: evaluation rules, focus points, and meta-level plans. Selection of plans is similar to the selection of plan variable bindings, so we will only discuss plan selection.

When more than one plan in the plan library matches a goal, AIDE must decide which to instantiate. *Control rules* inform its decision. There are three steps involved in executing a plan to satisfy a goal: matching, activation, and preference. The matching step, already described, establishes that the plan is syntactically able to satisfy the goal. `power-transform`, for example, satisfies the goal of fitting a power function to a relationship. The activation step involves running a set of rules that further test the applicability of plans, in order to activate or deactivate them. The `power-transform` plan is only activated in the presence of a curvature indication. The preference step involves running another set of rules that impose an ordering on the active plans. In the presence of the curvature indication, the `power-transform` plan is preferred to the `linear-regression` plan.

Candidate plans are maintained by *focus points*. A focus point manages branch points in the planning stack. Suppose that a goal instance is the top entry on the stack. If only a single plan matches this goal, then it is pushed onto the stack directly, as described earlier (shown here in Figure 3a.) If more than one plan matches the goal, a *plan focus point* is generated and pushed onto the stack. The focus point manages a set of newly created execution stacks, each rooted at a different instance of each plan that matches the goal. This is shown in Figure 3b. The planning process continues when one of these new stacks is selected, based on information generated by the evaluation rules, and the stack processed. When any stack becomes exhausted, the focus point can either select another of the stacks to proceed, or can return to the stack that originally generated the focus point.

For example, in the Phoenix data we saw that one subset of Duration and Effort was approximately linear, but with outliers in the relationship. We have several options: we can fit a regression line directly to the data; we can remove the outliers and then fit the line; we can let the outliers remain and fit a resistant line; we can fit a smooth to the data. Each of these options is implemented by a different plan. Each plan is instantiated to provide the root of a new execution stack, and the set of new stacks is then associated with the plan focus point. One stack is selected to continue the exploration.

As plans progress, a network of focus points is

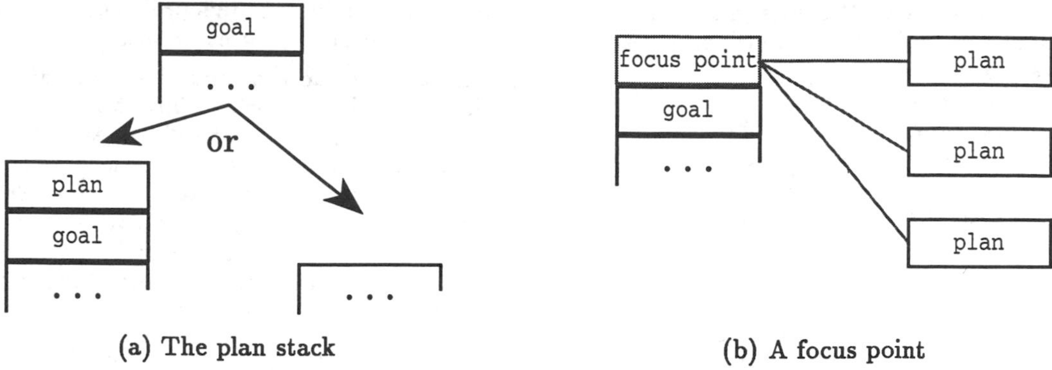

(a) The plan stack

(b) A focus point

Figure 3: The planning process

generated. Only one is active at any time. Determining which focus point should be active at any given time is the responsibility of *meta-level plans*. A meta-level planner, identical in design to the base-level planner, handles focus point selection. The meta-level behavior of the system is similar to what would be provided by rule-based activation of plans; however, incorporating a planner at the meta-level lets us maintain the nessary execution context to switch dynamically between plans in progress.

In the Phoenix data, a vertical clustering indication in the relationship (Effort, Duration) activates several distinct plans. One plan searches for a way to distinguish between clustered and non-clustered points by using other variables in the dataset. Another plan tries to predict which cluster each data point belongs to. Other plans search for similar clustering patterns in other variables and relationships. Each of these plans leads to further exploration. Because the default behavior of focus points causes the network to expand in depth-first fashion, the exploration of just the first plan at this decision point could potentially go on indefinitely. A meta-level plan, however, can cause the planner to switch between active, partially-expanded plans. The plan expansion often leads to actions that generate new information, which can be relevant to the planner's behavior. In other words, meta-level plans in this and comparable situations capture a general huristic: When more than one plan exists to extend or deepen a description (e.g., a clustering or a regression) and these plans compute intermediate results that may provide useful indications, then alternate between partial expansions of the plans. In this case, the final decision about which plan is most appropriate is usually made by the user.

To summarize briefly, evaluation rules decide which plans are relevant in trying to satisfy a goal. A focus point selects one plan from those possibilities and executes it; the focus point may switch dynamically between possible plans as knowledge about the problem changes. Meta plans decide which focus point is currently active, i.e., which goal the system should be trying to satisfy at the current time. These mechanisms give us local and non-local control over the planning process.

User interaction

The correspondence between planning and EDA lets us take two different views of the interaction between AIDE and the user. We can say that AIDE is in the business of building and executing plans, in an environment that lets the user review and modify the system's plan selection and variable binding decisions. We can just as well say that the system is a statistical computing environment in which a user carries out EDA procedures; AIDE's job is to follow the process the best it can, making suggestions and supplying relevant information at each decision point. To show how this works, we return to the Phoenix example. The following dialog represents the information exchanged between AIDE and the user, though the interaction is actually through menu selections, user gestures, and the usual interactions common to statistical user interfaces. Some of the points are marked with a number in parentheses for later discussion.

USER *(1)*: Select relationship (Effort, Duration).

AIDE: (Effort, Duration) indications: high correlation ($r = 0.93$); outliers in Effort; outliers in Duration; clustering. Suggested courses of action are (a) generating a linear fit and (b) exploring clusters.

USER: Why the linear fit?

AIDE: A linear fit can be appropriate for relationships with high correlation.

USER: Why the given ordering of actions?

AIDE: When there is a high correlation and no evidence of extreme outliers, we fit a line before trying other possibilities.

USER: Okay.

AIDE *(2)*: (Generates linear fit.) A three-group resistant line fits the data with a slope of 0.0017 and intercept of −0.96. (Presents graphical display of linear fit.) Indications: outliers in residuals; clustering.

USER *(3)*: Show recent decisions.

AIDE: In reverse order: (a) With the goal of fitting a line, I decided without consultation on a resistant fit. The alternative is a regression fit. (b) With the goal of exploring (Effort, Duration), you accepted the linear fit suggestion. The alternative is to explore clusters...

USER: Back up a step.

AIDE: With the goal of fitting a line to (Effort, Duration), the possibilities are a resistant fit, which is in progress, or a regression fit, which has not started.

USER: Execute the regression fit.

AIDE: (Generates regression fit.) The regression line has a slope of 0.0019 and an intercept of −2.73; $r^2 = 0.57$. (Presents graphical display of linear fit.) Indications: outliers in the residuals; clustering. The slope of the regression line is 1.13 times the slope of the resistant line.

USER: Make a note: I am confident that the relationship (Effort, Duration) is linear, despite indications of outliers and clustering. I prefer the regression fit.

AIDE: (Accepts note.)

USER: Okay.

AIDE: (Considers linear fit phase to be complete.) The possibilities remaining to explore (Effort, Duration) are (a) the linear fit, which is in progress, and (b) cluster exploration, which has not started.

USER: Okay.

AIDE: (Begins cluster exploration.) Here are the clustering possibilities for (Effort, Duration). (Displays identifiers for potential clustering criteria: single-linkage clusters in Effort, regions of constant values in Effort, etc. Also displays similarity between resulting clusters.)

...

A single step in this exchange often represents a great deal of underlying processing. The steps marked with numbers are discussed in more detail below:

1. When the user loads a dataset, AIDE's top level plan is activated, which incrementally explores the variables and relationships of the dataset. Because any variable or relationship might be relevant, a focus point is created to manage the possibilities. Evaluation rules rank the possibilities by their features and indications, computed dynamically. When the evaluation is complete, AIDE presents a data selection menu to the user, along with its own preference and supporting indications. AIDE thus generates a great deal of information to support its internal decisions before interacting with the user. In this example the user overrides AIDE's preference by selecting (Effort, Duration) for exploration.
2. Here the user accepts one of AIDE's suggestions, that of fitting a line. The user could potentially have chosen a specific linear fitting procedure (through a menu selection) but instead lets AIDE maintain control over the exploration. AIDE makes an internal decision for a resistant line, generates the fit, and elaborates the description by generating and examining the residuals of the fit.
3. When the user asks for a listing of recent decisions, AIDE displays all focus points leading to the current decision point. Some of these may have been handled internally, while others may have been directed by the user. The list of focus points can be read directly from the plan execution network. The user can select any of these decisions, to be reconsidered and perhaps changed, as happens in the next few steps.

The network of focus points is central to AIDE's processing. It lets the user "navigate" through the exploration space at the strategic decision level, rather than the level of primitive EDA operations. Further, the network gives AIDE a way of interpreting user actions in context, and of following along when the user takes control of the exploration.

Related Work in Planning

Partial hierarchical planning was introduced by Georgeff and Lansky (Georgeff & Lansky 1986). Several characteristics distinguish it from classical planning. In the classical formulation a plan is a partially-ordered sequence of actions, often with annotated links between actions. In partial hierarchical planners, a plan is a procedural specification of a set of subgoals to be achieved. A plan may specify that subgoals must be satisfied sequentially, or conditionally on some test, or iteratively. Control constructs may also provide for parallel satisfaction of subgoals, mapping over lists of subgoals, recursion, and domain-specific processing.

A partial hierarchical planner executes a plan before it is completely elaborated. In a sense, these planners do not generate plans at all, but simply execute them. This behavior has advantages over off-line planning: in dynamic environments, information necessary to choose a specific action may not be known at planning time; in complex or uncertain environments, an action may generate too many possible results to enumerate exhaustively in advance. A disadvantage is the uncertainty about whether a given partial plan will succeed.

As with case-based planning, plan definitions are stored in a library. AIDE's definitions are not the fully-elaborated sequences of actions that are usually stored in a case library, however, but are partial specifications as described above. AIDE constructs plans by searching through the library, its set of partial solutions, for appropriate matches to established goals.

This lack of emphasis on constructing plans from scratch is balanced by a greater concentration on the meta-level problem of which plan to invoke when several match the current situation. Meta-level processing can be handled in different ways. PRS uses meta-level "knowledge areas" that function something like blackboard knowledge sources for control (Georgeff & Lansky 1987). The Phoenix planner maintains a time line of subgoals and pending plans, and gives each plan a degree of meta-level control over the actions remaining to be executed. The RESUN planner establishes focus points during its plan expansion to allow suspension and resumption of in-progress plans, as a way of focusing attention in its search (Carver & Lesser 1993). These mechanisms let the planners behave opportunistically.

Reactive planning techniques provide a good match for the EDA problem. Though there are no hard time constraints on the process, the space of exploration is highly dynamic, in that each action can provide potentially significant information. All the aspects of partial hierarchical planning mentioned above contribute to solving the problem.

AIDE is also an example of a mixed-initiative planning system. By making an analogy to dialog behavior, James Allen has identified three distinguishing characteristics of mixed-initiative planning: flexible, opportunistic control of initiative; the ability to change focus of attention; mechanisms for maintaining shared, implicit knowledge (Allen 1994). Mixed-initiative systems display these characteristics to a greater or lesser extent, depending on the domain in which they operate and the requirements on their behavior.

AIDE's control of initiative changes with context. That is, whether a decision is presented to the user or is settled internally depends on situation-dependent factors. For example, if AIDE determines that only one plan is able to satisfy a given goal (i.e., all others rendered inactive by evaluation rules), then this decision point will not be presented to the user. An exception is made in the case where a plan is being selected for the initial exploration of a variable or relationship. Choosing an initial plan for a relationship is often a more important decision than deciding how to bind its plan variables or how to satisfy its subgoals; thus the decision about how to proceed from the new point is presented to the user even if only one course of action seems appropriate.

AIDE changes its focus of attention to follow the user. In the processing for the Phoenix analysis, for example, AIDE interprets the selection of a new relationship as a shift of focus from exploration of its current relationship to a new point in the search space. AIDE also makes limited decisions on its own to change focus. For example, after fitting a line to a relationship and generating residuals, AIDE presents a set of residual examination and other plans to the user. An OK gesture, which usually indicates that the top-rated plan for the current decision should be activated, rather in this context causes AIDE to refocus on other plans for exploring the relationship.

AIDE also provides ways for the user to follow its planning process. The user can view the data under consideration, results constructed, commands carried out, and planning structures leading to the current point. These views also act as navigation mechanisms, giving the user more explicit control over AIDE's focus of attention. AIDE does not ask for clarification of user actions, however, which could clearly be beneficial in some situations.

The mixed-initiative approach has become interesting to researchers in both planning and statistical expert systems. An extension of PRODIGY, for example, provides autonomous planning with consultation (Stone & Veloso 1995), by letting the user review each decision the planner makes. The early regression expert system, REX, gave users similar abilities when reaching difficult decision points in its analysis (Gale 1986). TESS, a sophisticated interactive system for data analysis, took the approach further by letting users opportunistically modify its search strategies and decisions (Lubinsky & Pregibon 1988). AIDE takes steps toward an even fuller cooperation between user and machine.

In summary, we have described the task of EDA and how it can (and should) be cast as a planning problem. We have presented the AIDE planner as part of a solution to the problem. We have described a representative example in the domain of EDA, and shown how AIDE solves the problem. A series of experiments is currently in progress to evaluate the performance of users working with and without assistance from AIDE.

Acknowledgments

Thanks to Tim Oates for useful discussion and comments about this work. This research is supported by ARPA/Rome Laboratory under contract #F30602-93-0100, and by the Dept. of the Army, Army Research Office under contract #DAAH04-95-1-0466. The U.S. Government is authorized to reproduce and distribute reprints for governmental purposes not withstanding any copyright notation hereon.

References

Allen, J. F. 1994. Mixed initiative planning: Position paper. Presented at the ARPA/Rome Labs Planning Initiative Workshop. See URL http://www.cs.rochester.edu/research/trains/.

Carver, N., and Lesser, V. 1993. A planner for the control of problem solving systems. *IEEE Transactions on Systems, Man, and Cybernetics, special issue on Planning, Scheduling, and Control* 23(6).

Cohen, P. R.; Greenberg, M. L.; Hart, D. M.; and Howe, A. E. 1989. Trial by fire: Understanding the design requirements for agents in complex environments. *AI Magazine* 10(3):32–48.

Cohen, P. R. 1995. *Empirical Methods in Artificial Intelligence.* MIT Press.

Gale, W. A. 1986. REX review. In Gale, W. A., ed., *Artificial Intelligence and Statistics I.* Addison-Wesley.

Georgeff, M. P., and Lansky, A. L. 1986. Procedural knowledge. *Proceedings of the IEEE Special Issue on Knowledge Representation* 74(10):1383–1398.

Georgeff, M. P., and Lansky, A. L. 1987. Reactive reasoning and planning. In *Proceedings of the Fifth National Conference on Artificial Intelligence*, 677–682. American Association for Artificial Intelligence.

Korf, R. E. 1987. Planning as search: A quantitative approach. *Artificial Intelligence* 33:65–88.

Lubinsky, D., and Pregibon, D. 1988. Data analysis as search. *Journal of Econometrics* 38:247–268.

St. Amant, R., and Cohen, P. R. 1995. Control representation in an EDA assistant. In Fisher, D., and Lenz, H., eds., *Learning from Data: AI and Statistics V.* Springer. To appear.

Stone, P., and Veloso, M. 1995. User-guided interleaving of planning and execution. In *European Workshop on Planning.*

Tukey, J. W. 1977. *Exploratory Data Analysis.* Addison-Wesley.

2.4 Other Applications

Multiagent Collaboration in Directed Improvisation

Barbara Hayes-Roth, Lee Brownston, and Robert van Gent

Knowledge Systems Laboratory
Stanford University
701 Welch Road, Bldg C
Palo Alto, CA 94304

Telephone: 415 723-0506
email: hayes-roth@cs.stanford.edu
fax: 415 725-5850

Abstract

Directed improvisation is a new paradigm for multiagent interaction. One or more human users direct one or more computer characters with scripted or interactive directions. The characters work together to improvise a course of behavior that follows the directions, expresses their distinctive individual styles, honors social conventions, and meets other objectives. The resulting "performance" reflects the collaboration among all of the human and computer agents. Directed improvisation has several attractive properties as a paradigm for multiagent human-computer interaction, which we illustrate in our testbed application, an animated improvisational theater company for children. Directed improvisation also presents distinctive requirements for agent interaction (emphasizing: situated, spontaneous, opportunistic behavior; very intimate interaction with shared control; and process-oriented evaluation criteria), which make it a useful addition to the domain of inquiry for multiagent systems.

Directed Improvisation

Directed improvisation is the simultaneous invention and performance of a new "work" under the constraints of user-specified directions. Besides its role in theater [7, 18, 22], directed improvisation mediates other activities: jazz music [9], planning and control of everyday behavior [12, 14, 16, 17], reactive behavior [1, 16], conversation [21], human-machine communication [26], scientific investigation [24], children's planning and playcrafting [2, 3, 23], and life management [6]. Indeed, most human behavior and interaction appears to incorporate some degree of directed improvisation.

We are studying directed-improvisation as a paradigm for multiagent human-computer interaction. Here, the "new work" is a course of behavior enacted by computer characters. Users give characters abstract directions, either interactively or in preconceived scripts. The characters improvise a collaborative course of behavior that follows the directions, expresses their distinctive individual styles, reflects social principles, and achieves other performance objectives. Thus, the characters obey their users, but also surprise and engage them along the way with artfully improvised behavior.

Section 2 of this paper illustrates directed improvisation in our current testbed application, an animated improvisational theater company for children. Section 3 presents an agent architecture to support improvisational characters. Section 4 discusses distinctive requirements for multiagent interaction that arise in the directed-improvisation paradigm.

Illustrative Application

We are developing an animated improvisational theater company to support children's participation in a variety of creative, playful, and educational activities [13, 17, 19]. Here we focus on characters and directed improvisation.

Each character in the company has a repertoire of physical and verbal behaviors (Figure 1), which serve as building blocks for improvisation. Different instances within a class allow characters to express life-like variability and moods. For example, a character may go to a destination by beeline or hop, depending on whether it feels determined or playful. Idiosyncratic instances allow characters to express life-like individual differences. For example, character C2 uses more casual verbal behaviors than C1. Even with nominally equivalent physical behaviors, characters may move differently due to differences in size and other physical features.

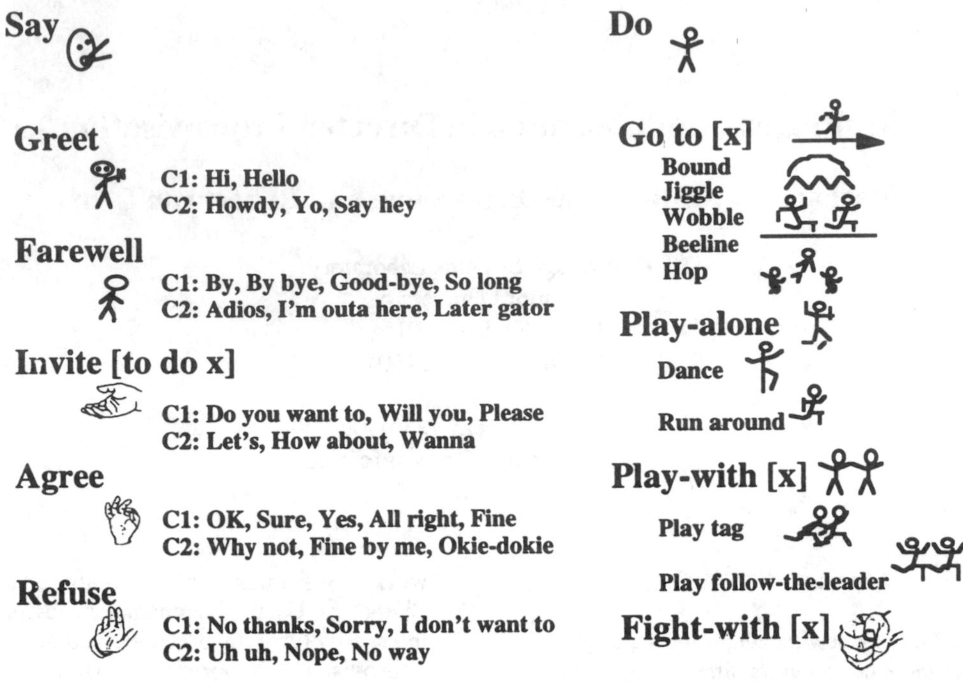

Figure 1. Excerpts from behavioral repertoires of two characters, C1 and C2.

Our illustrations are based on two characters that we adapted from the "woggles" system of J. Bates of Carnegie-Mellon University (including the RAL system of Production Systems Technologies). Unlike the CMU woggles, our characters have multiple gaits, speak lines, follow directions, and improvise. Each character has about 10 classes of physical behaviors and 20 classes of verbal behaviors, each with 1-5 instances. The characters' verbal behaviors and personalities were conceived and recorded by Aaron and Nora Hayes-Roth, who were 13 and 10 years old at the time. We plan to develop new human-like animated characters that will have similar behaviors, as well as new behaviors. To create stories, children direct the characters to adopt moods and to perform sequences of behaviors. The characters improvise within the constraints of the directions. We have conceived several interaction modes [13, 18], but present only two here for illustration.

In *animated-puppets mode*, children direct characters interactively by making choices from *situated behavior menus*. For example, in Figure 2, the large character feels cheerful and energetic. It considers going somewhere, playing alone, or inviting its partner to play. The small character feels OK, but tired. It considers going to the rest area, playing alone, or speaking. One child directs the large character to invite its partner to play. The character improvises an appropriate course of behavior (e.g., approach the small character, greet it, and say "Do you want to play follow the leader?"). Its executed behaviors change the shared situation and, as a result, the behaviors both characters subsequently consider. The children work side by side, directing their characters' moods and behavior to create a shared story, just as they would with physical puppets. The characters also collaborate on the playcrafting, improvising within the constraints of the children's directions. We have implemented animated puppets, with graphical user interfaces similar to the schematic ones in Figure 2, for the two characters described above [19].

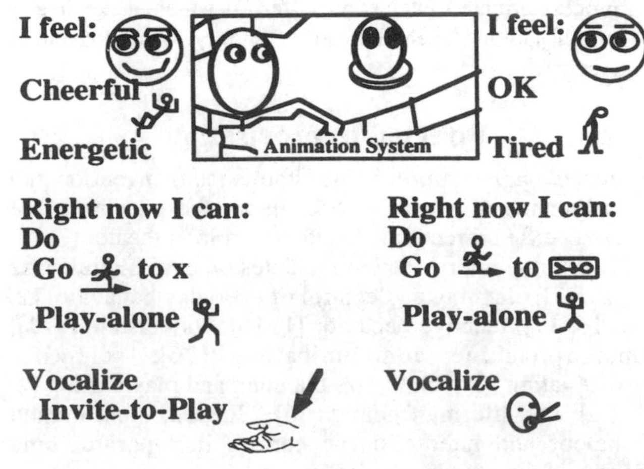

Figure 2. Snapshot from situated behavior menus for a two-character play.

In *animated-actors mode*, children direct characters prospectively by giving them *synchronized behavior scripts*. For example, in Figure 3, the characters begin by playing independently (e.g., dancing, hopping on the pedestal). C2 determines when "awhile" has passed and suggests a game (e.g., hide and seek, follow the leader). C1 agrees and the two characters play the game together. The characters also may improvise script-independent behaviors (e.g., exchange greetings in a chance encounter while playing alone). We have implemented a few simple behavior scripts for brief conversations (e.g., greeting and reply; invitations and acceptances to play) and for games (e.g., follow the leader). We are developing a repertoire of such scripts as a form of reusable knowledge to be incorporated in different characters.

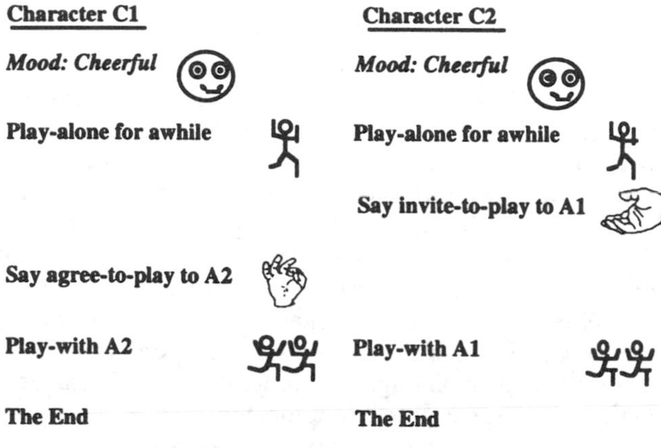

Figure 3. Synchronized Behavior Script.

The animated theater company illustrates multiagent human-computer collaboration in the directed-improvisation paradigm. Children collaborate to create the narrative structures of stories and direct the behavior of characters within the structure. Characters collaborate with children to implement the directions and with one another to determine the details of their interactions. Characters' improvisations may reflect moods and personalities, social conventions, relationships amd recent interactions, and improvisational expertise. The balance of creative work shifts among children and characters, depending on the specificity of the children's directions.

An Architecture for Improvisational Actors

Each animated character embodies an intelligent agent (Figure 4), whose two-level architecture comprises a *cognitive controller* and a *physical controller* [11, 17]. An agent's cognitive controller receives perceptual inputs from its physical controller, constructs an evolving model of its situation and its interactions with other characters, plans its physical and verbal behaviors, and sends control plans to its physical controller. An agent's physical controller interprets and filters inputs from its user interface and from sensors on its animated embodiment and sends those perceptions to its cognitive controller. It receives control plans from its cognitive controller and enacts those plans with appropriate physical behaviors, sending their outputs to effectors on its animated embodiment and to its user interface.

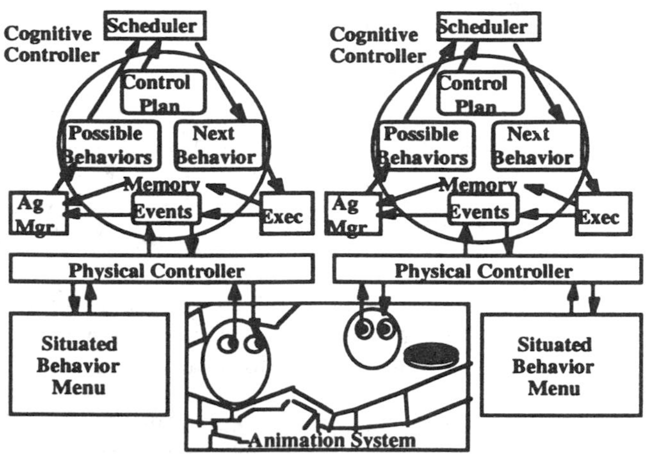

Figure 4. Framework for a Two-Character Production.

A *dynamic control model* [10, 12, 15, 16] underlies an agent's cognitive and physical controllers, each of which iterates this cycle: (a) its agenda manager triggers behaviors for the current situation; (b) its scheduler chooses the best triggered behavior based on the current control plan; and (c) its executor performs the chosen behavior. The cycle has three key features, as illustrated in Figure 5. First, the agent continually notices possible behaviors. For example, the agent might notice that it's able to play any of several games, go somewhere, say something, etc. Second, the agent describes its intended behavior in abstract control plans that permit alternative realizations. For example, the control plan "go to x" can be realized by "bound to pedestal," "hop to pedestal," "hop to rest area," etc. Third, the agent generates and modifies its control plans at run time. For example, the agent refines its plan to "go to x" by planning to "hop to pedestal." At each point in time, the agent performs possible behaviors that match its current control plans.

Our architecture is a natural framework for directed improvisation. The agenda manager generates situated behaviors—the raw materials out of which a character creates meaningful behavior patterns. Dynamic control plans can represent children's scripted and interactive directions. Dynamic control planning enables characters to improvise the details of directions and to augment them with undirected behaviors on the fly. Characters can use knowledge of the distinctive properties of behavior instances within a class to choose among them. For example, given the direction "Go to x," a character might choose any of five gaits.

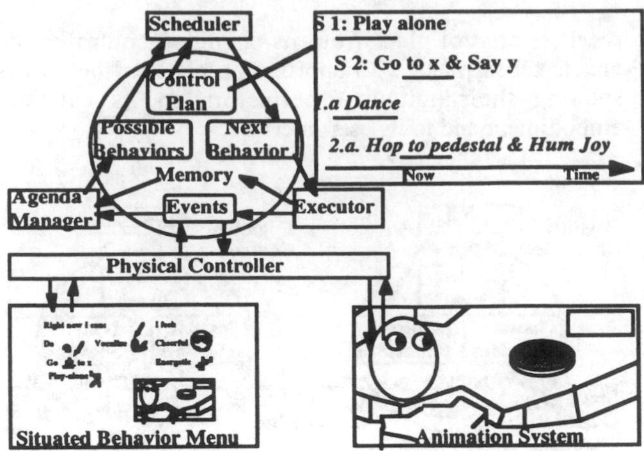

Figure 5. Dynamic Control Plans Integrate Users' Scripted and Interactive Directions with Characters' Improvisational Decisions (in *italics*).

If it previously had adopted a "silly" mood, it would choose a silly gait: hop, wobble, or jiggle. If the direction were more specific, "Go quickly to x," the character would choose a fast gait: bound or beeline. These examples illustrate a very simple form of directed improvisation, solo choice among alternative behaviors.

Table 1. Forms of Directed Improvisation.

Solo Improvisation	*Collaborative Improvisation*
One-Step Improvisation	
Choose among alternative logically equivalent behaviors Direction: Go to pedestal Improvise: Hop to pedestal - 3	Respond to a partner's behaviors Partner: Greeting Improvise: Return greeting
Sequential Improvisation	
Construct a coherent path to a dramatic moment Direction: Play alone, Rest Improvise: Play alone, Get tired, Rest	Recognize and coordinate with a partner's behavior sequence Partner: Going toward pedestal Improvise: Go toward pedestal, Meet at pedestal
Patterned Improvisation	
Instantiate an improvisational schema Direction: Dance: Improvise: Iterate(Hop, twirl)	Recognize and participate in a partner's schema Partner: Play hide and seek? Improvise: I count to 10, etc.

Table 1 characterizes six forms of directed improvisation that vary in: (a) the involvement of partners; and (b) the complexity of the recognized situation and the improvised course of behavior. We are working on developing these more sophisticated forms of improvisational expertise in our agents.

To support multi-agent collaborative improvisation, we are elaborating our agent architecture so that agents can monitor, interpret, and predict their partners' behavior with the same mechanisms they use to represent, plan, monitor, and control their own behavior. In Figure 6, the large character enters the set first and makes a plan to look for something (1). The small character enters (2), observes its partner standing still, and infers nothing about its mood or plans (3). The small character plans to "start something" by playing alone for awhile and then hiding (4). Meanwhile, the large character observes its partner enter and start playing alone and infers that it is acting "shy" (5). The large character plans an appropriate interaction: approach, greet, and invite the shy partner to play (6). Now, the two characters have unknowingly constructed conflicting plans. One of them must change its plan and perhaps its model of its partner. However, as discussed below, it doesn't matter which character changes, as long as their observable interactions are plausible. Thus, if the large character succeeds in inviting the small character to play, the small character must abandon its plan and agree to play. If the small character notices the large character approaching and rushes over to tell it to hide, the large character must abandon its plan and its model of its partner and go hide. The extended architecture enables characters to generate and adapt their models of one another and their plans for their own behavior as their interaction unfolds.

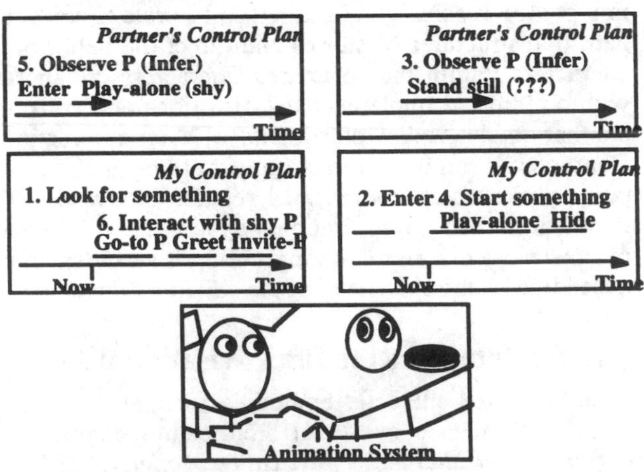

Figure 6. Simple Illustration of Collaborative Improvisation

Issues in Multiagent Interaction

Directed improvisation is a new interaction paradigm for multiagent systems. Although it shares important requirements and approaches with previously-studied multiagent paradigms (e.g., cooperative problem solving, distributed work, discretionary cooperation [8]), it presents three distinctive requirements that make it a useful addition to the domain of inquiry. We have taken these requirements from the writings and teachings of improvisation experts [7, 20, 22, 24] and view them as design objectives in our efforts to elaborate and instantiate the proposed agent architecture.

Directed improvisation demands behavior that is situated, spontaneous, and opportunistic in the service of abstract and weakly-constrained goals.

Most multi-agent paradigms assume that agents' individual and collective activities are predominantly and specifically goal-directed. In cooperative problem solving, the team's goal is to solve a shared problem. In distributed work, the team's goal is to get all of the work done as efficiently and effectively as possible. In discretionary cooperation, individual agents have their own goals and cooperate to the degree that doing so enhances achievement of their own goals or at least does not compromise them. Techniques for these paradigms focus on goal-directed reasoning in support of individual and group planning. Unplanned behavior occurs only when it is necessary to compensate for plan failure or when it happens to advance planned efforts to achieve established goals.

The directed-improvisation paradigm also assumes that agents have goals, but they are less well defined and less constraining than in other paradigms. Agents collaborating in a production share a general goal to produce a successful joint performance that meets the constraints of the users' directions. Although directions can vary in specificity, effective application of the paradigm typically involves relatively abstract directions that only weakly constrain the performance and give characters plenty of freedom to improvise. The working assumption is that producing the directed behaviors is easy; the art lies in the improvisation. The literature on improvisation reflects this assumption in its prescription of two underlying cognitive heuristics for the improviser: (a) *welcome possibilities* (Just let the words flow. Do not fear mistakes. Turn off the censor. Look for relationships. Do not plan too far ahead.); and (b) *pursue promising possibilities* (Make the natural response. Relate present actions to past actions. Keep the action on stage. Listen and respond to your partner. Take it to the extreme. Accept (don't block) offers). In contrast to the forward-looking, goal-directed reasoning and planning of agents in traditional paradigms, effective improvisers engage in backward-looking efforts to *reincorporate* incidental themes and behavioral qualities that they or their partners happen to have generated previously. Thus, the improviser at work is sometimes described as "a man walking backwards, trying to make sense of where he's been" [24]. In sum, the individual agent's behavior is firmly situated in the dynamic context, spontaneous in its short-term etiology, and opportunistic in its thematic relationships to other aspects of the performance. Ensemble behavior builds incrementally out of individual agents' actions and reactions. Achievement of the "goal" is not the specific product of a deliberate, provably correct process, but an emergent and uncertain epiphenomenon of the agents' real-time interactions.

Directed improvisation demands intimate collaboration and shared control among agents engaged in closely intertwined and interdependent behaviors.

Most multi-agent paradigms assume that agents have limited interest in working together and limited interactions during the actual performance of their collective activities. In cooperative problem solving and distributed work, agents work together because they are committed to solving a shared problem or to completing a shared job. The prevailing interaction model is to divide-and-conquer the joint task so that individual agents can work more or less independently. Multi-agent planning is used to allocate and coordinate tasks among agents, with run-time communication used primarily to exchange selected results of individual activities and, in some cases, to reallocate responsibilities. In discretionary cooperation, individual agents have their own goals and may or may not be willing to work together at all, depending on what it costs them. Competition for resources or conflict among goals may impede cooperation or even motivate agents to thwart one another's efforts, raising issues of trust and deception. Communications focus mainly on determining agents' willingness to cooperate. In all of these paradigms, research concentrates on the key question of how agents should decide in advance who is able and willing to do what. Techniques have been developed for: problem decomposition, communication of assumptions, beliefs, decisions, and commitments; negotiation and persuasion; conflict resolution and consensus building; organization of effective chains of command; and establishing mutually beneficial social laws.

By contrast, the directed improvisation paradigm assumes that agents are 100% committed to collaboration on their joint performance and that they will work together every step of the way. Their prospective work is so intertwined (and unpredictable) that agents do not even think of dividing it up ahead of time. Instead, effective improvisers rely on one another to do what is necessary to generate the work jointly and interactively in real time. The work is intrinsically collaborative: none of the participating agents can progress without interacting with its partners. Individual agents may introduce plot devices or instantiate improvisational routines. They may build small individual plans of activity in particular situations. However, all such structures, routines, and plans are tentative and dispensable under the fundamental rule of collaborative improvisation: *Accept all offers*. An "offer" is any explicit or implicit assertion. No matter how an individual agent feels about a partner's offer, no matter where the individual had been planning to go in the performance prior to the offer, no matter how the partner's offer redirects the individual's behavior, there can be only one response: "Yes." An effective improviser always embraces a partner's offers and tries to advance them with constructive, collaborative behavior. Since all of the participants are allowed to make offers and since not all offers are detected or understood by partners, each improviser must be willing to both lead and follow, with no preconception of when, how often, or how long. The dynamism and mutual adaptation of good improvisers reflects this underlying willingness to share control. Unlike control regimes based on organization, negotiation, turn-taking, or other explicit arrangements, *shared control* is an implicit arrangement in which the participants readily and immediately adopt and contribute to one another's assertions, goals, strategies, and tactics so that they can move forward together.

Directed improvisation succeeds when it produces a joint performance that follows the script and directions in an engaging manner.

Most multi-agent paradigms are "product-oriented"—they evaluate the objective consequences of agents' behavior against high objective standards: achievement of agents' individual and collective goals, optimal use of resources, and acceptability of side effects. These criteria for evaluating group performance imply related criteria for evaluating individual performance. To succeed as a member of the group, an agent must: reason correctly in performing its own tasks, reliably execute its planned physical behaviors, model its partners' knowledge and behavior correctly, make rational decisions about commitments to cooperative behavior, keep its commitments or at least inform its partners of changes, etc. Features of agents' behavior that do not affect the product are not valued, may be distracting, and, in the worst case, may carry unacceptable costs.

By contrast, the directed improvisation paradigm is "process-oriented"—the joint course of behavior enacted by computer characters is their product. Other than meeting the constraints of users' directions (which is usually assumed to be easy), there is no "correct" or "incorrect" performance. There is no concern with resources and unexpected side effects are simply folded into the performance. In general, there can be many alternative, equally "successful" performances of a given script—that is, performances that follow the directions in an engaging manner. In fact, in domains like our computer theater, children (and adults) may find it especially charming to observe or participate in repeated performances of a favorite story or one they have created themselves just to see how the characters will improvise anew. By implication, instead of behavior that is correct, rational, and reliable, effective improvisers produce behavior that appears appropriate in context, varies in different performances, and, in the best case, is endearingly idiosyncratic. The individual qualities that agents bring to a production are not costly distractions, but powerful sources of texture and depth in their contributions to the joint performance. In contrast to the all-business mentality of the ideal agent in traditional multi-agent paradigms, effective improvisers bring believable characters to life.

Concluding Remarks

In this paper, we have tried to illustrate the promise of directed improvisation as a paradigm for multiagent systems. First, it provides a structured framework for multiagent, human-computer collaboration [8]. Second, it explicitly allows run-time flexibility in the manner in which objectives can be achieved [1, 11, 16, 17]. Third, it offers a familiar, life-like, and potentially delightful interactive experience [4, 5]. Finally, because of its distinctive requirements for agent interaction, directed improvisation represents a useful addition to the domain of inquiry for multiagent systems.

References

1. Agre, P.E., and Chapman, D. What are plans for? Robotics and Autonomous Systems, 6, 17-34, 1990.

2. Applebee, A.N. The User's Concept of Story. Chicago: University of Chicago Press, 1978.

3. Baker-Sennett, J. Matusov, E., and Rogoff, B. Sociocultural processes of creative planning in children's playcrafting. In P. Light and G. Butterworth (eds.), Context and Cognition: Ways of Learning and Knowing. New York: Harvester Wheatsheaf, 1992.

4. Bates, J. The role of emotion in believable agents. Communications of the ACM, 1994, 37, 122-125.

5. Bates, J., Hayes-Roth, B., Laurel, B., and Nilsson, N. Working notes of the AAAI Symposium on believable agents, Menlo Park, CA: AAAI, 1994.

6. Bateson, M.C. Composing a Life. NY: The Atlantic Monthly Press, 1989.

7. Belt, L., and Stockley, R. Improvisation through Theater Sports. Seattle: Thespis Productions, 1991.

8. Charib-draa, B., Mandiau, R., and Millot, P. Distributed artificial intelligence: An annotated bibliography. SigArt Bulletin, 3,1992, 20-37.

9. Dean, R. Creative Improvisation: Jazz, Contemporary Music and Beyond. Philadelphia: Open University Press, 1989.

10. Hayes-Roth, B. A blackboard architecture for control. Artificial Intelligence, 1985, 26, 251-321.

11. Hayes-Roth, B. An architecture for adaptive intelligent systems. Artificial Intelligence, in press, 1994.

12. Hayes-Roth, B. Architectural foundations for real-time performance in intelligent agents. Real-Time Systems, 2, 99-125, 1990.

13. Hayes-Roth, B. Directed improvisation: A new paradigm for computer games. Proc. of the Computer Game Developers' Conference, Santa Clara, 1995.

14. Hayes-Roth, B. Opportunistic control of action. IEEE Trans. on Systems, Man, and Cybernetics, 12, 1575-1587 1993.

15. Hayes-Roth, B., and Collinot, A. A satisficing cycle for real-time reasoning in intelligent agents. Expert Systems with Applications, 7, 1993.

16. Hayes-Roth, B., and Hayes-Roth, F. A cognitive model of planning. Cognitive Science, 1979, 3, 275-310.

17. Hayes-Roth, B., Pfleger, K., Lalanda, P., Morignot, P., and Balabanovic, M. A domain-specific software architecture for adaptive intelligent systems. IEEE Trans. on Software Engineering, in press, 1994.

18. Hayes-Roth, B. Sincoff, E., Brownston, L., Huard, R., and Lent, B. Directed improvisation. Stanford University: Knowledge Systems Laboratory Technical Report KSL-94-61, 1994.

19. Hayes-Roth, B. Sincoff, E., Brownston, L., Huard, R., and Lent, B. Directed improvisation with animated puppets. Proc. of CHI '95 Conference on Computer-Human Interaction; Denver, 1995.

20. Johnstone, K. IMPRO: Improvisation in the Theatre. New York: Penguin Books, 1987.

21. Moore, J. Invited presentation at the National Conference on Artificial Intelligence, 1994.

22. Nachmanovitch, S. Free Play: Improvisation in life and art. Los Angeles: Jeremy P. Tarcher, Inc. 1990.

23. Rogoff, B., Gauvain, M., and Gardner, W. The development of children's skills in adjusting plans to circumstances. In S. Friedman, E. Scholnick, and R. Cocking (eds.), Blueprints for Thinking: The role of planning in psychological development. New York: Cambridge University Press, 1987, 303-20.

24. Ryan, P. Personal communication, Stanford University, Course HS 173 Improvisation - Discovering Spontaneity, 1994.

25. Stefik, M. Planning and meta-planning (MOLGEN: part 2). Artificial Intelligence, 16, 1981, 141-169.

26. Suchman, L. A. Plans and Situated Actions: The Problem of Machine/Human Communication. Cambridge, England: Cambridge University Press, 1987.

ANIMATED CONVERSATION: Rule-based Generation of Facial Expression, Gesture & Spoken Intonation for Multiple Conversational Agents

Justine Cassell Catherine Pelachaud Norman Badler Mark Steedman
Brett Achorn Tripp Becket Brett Douville Scott Prevost Matthew Stone [1]
Department of Computer & Information Science, University of Pennsylvania

Abstract

We describe an implemented system which *automatically* generates and animates conversations between multiple human-like agents with appropriate and synchronized speech, intonation, facial expressions, and hand gestures. Conversation is created by a dialogue planner that produces the text as well as the intonation of the utterances. The speaker/listener relationship, the text, and the intonation in turn drive facial expressions, lip motions, eye gaze, head motion, and arm gesture generators. Coordinated arm, wrist, and hand motions are invoked to create semantically meaningful gestures. Throughout we will use examples from an actual synthesized, fully animated conversation.

1 Introduction

When faced with the task of bringing to life a human-like character, few options are currently available. Either one can manually and laboriously manipulate the numerous degrees of freedom in a synthetic figure, one can write or acquire increasingly sophisticated motion generation software such as inverse kinematics and dynamics, or one can resort to "performance-based" motions obtained from a live actor or puppet. The emergence of low-cost, real-time motion sensing devices has led to renewed interest in active motion capture since 3D position and orientation trajectories may be acquired directly rather than from tedious image rotoscoping [34]. Both facial and gestural motions are efficiently tracked from a suitably harnessed actor. But this does not imply that the end of manual or synthesized animation is near. Instead it raises the challenge of providing a sophisticated toolkit for human character animation that does not require the presence nor skill of a live actor [2], thus freeing up the craft of the skilled animator for more challenging tasks.

In this paper we present our system for *automatically animating conversations between multiple human-like agents with appropriate and synchronized speech, intonation, facial expressions, and hand gestures*. Especially noteworthy is the linkage between speech and gesture which has not been explored before in synthesizing realistic animation. In people, speech, facial expressions, and gestures are physiologically linked. While an expert animator may realize this unconsciously in the "look" of a properly animated character, a program to automatically generate motions must know the rules in advance. This paper presents a working system to realize interacting animated agents.

Conversation is an interactive dialogue between two agents. Conversation includes spoken language (words and contextually appropriate intonation marking topic and focus), facial movements (lip shapes, emotions, gaze direction, head motion), and hand gestures (handshapes, points, beats, and motions representing the topic of accompanying speech). Without all of these verbal and non-verbal behaviors, one cannot have realistic or at least believable autonomous agents. To limit the problems (such as voice and face recognition) that arise from the involvement of real human conversants, and to constrain the dialogue, we present the work in the form of a dialogue generation program in which two copies of an identical program having different knowledge of the world must cooperate to accomplish a goal. Both agents of the conversation collaborate via the dialogue to develop a simple plan of action. They interact with each other to exchange information and ask questions.

In this paper, we first present the background information necessary to establish the synchrony of speech, facial expression, and gesture. We then discuss the system architecture and its several subcomponents.

2 Background

Faces change expressions continuously, and many of these changes are synchronized to what is going on in concurrent conversation. Facial expressions are linked to the content of speech (scrunching one's nose when talking about something unpleasant), emotion (wrinkling one's eyebrows with worry), personality (frowning all the time), and other behavioral variables. Facial expressions can replace sequences of words ("she was dressed [wrinkle nose, stick out tongue]") as well as accompany them [16], and they can serve to help disambiguate what is being said when the acoustic signal is degraded. They do not occur randomly but rather are synchronized to one's own speech, or to the speech of others [13], [20].

Eye gaze is also an important feature of non-verbal communicative behaviors. Its main functions are to help regulate the flow of conversation, signal the search for feedback during an interaction (gazing at the other person to see how she follows), look for information, express emotion (looking downward in case of sadness), or influence another person's behavior (staring at a person to show power)[14].

People also produce hand gestures spontaneously while they

[1]The authors would like to thank Francisco Azuola, Chin Seah, John Granieri, Ioi Kim Lam, and Xinmin Zhao.

speak, and such gestures support and expand on information conveyed by words. The fact that gestures occur at the same time as speech, and that they carry the same meaning as speech, suggests that the production of the two are intimately linked. In fact, not only are the meaning of words and of gestures intimately linked in a discourse, but so are their functions in accomplishing conversational work: it has been shown that certain kinds of gestures produced during conversation act to structure the contributions of the two participants (to signal when an utterance continues the same topic or strikes out in a new direction), and to signal the contribution of particular utterances to the current discourse. It is clear that, like facial expression, gesture is not a kinesic performance independent of speech, or simply a 'translation' of speech. Rather, gesture and speech are so intimately connected that one cannot say which one is dependent on the other. Both can be claimed to arise from a single internal encoding process ([8], [21], [27]).

2.1 Example

In this section of the paper we present a fragment of dialogue (the complete dialogue has been synthesized and animated), in which intonation, gesture, head and lip movements, and their inter-synchronization were automatically generated. This example will serve to demonstrate the phenomena described here, and in subsequent sections we will return to each phenomenon, to explain how rule-generation and synchronization are carried out.

In the following dialogue, imagine that Gilbert is a bank teller, and George has asked Gilbert for help in obtaining $50. The dialogue is unnaturally repetitive and explicit in its goals because the dialogue generation program that produced it has none of the conversational inferences that allow humans to follow leaps of reasoning. Therefore, the two agents have to specify in advance each of the goals they are working towards and steps they are following (see section 4.1).

Gilbert: Do you have a blank check?
George: Yes, I have a blank check.
Gilbert: Do you have an account for the check?
George: Yes, I have an account for the check.
Gilbert: Does the account contain at least fifty dollars?
George: Yes, the account contains eighty dollars.
Gilbert: Get the check made out to you for fifty dollars and then I can withdraw fifty dollars for you.
George: All right, let's get the check made out to me for fifty dollars.

When Gilbert asks a question, his voice rises. When George replies to a question, his voice falls. When Gilbert asks George whether he has a blank check, he stresses the word "check". When he asks George whether he has an account for the check, he stresses the word "account".

Every time Gilbert replies affirmatively ("yes"), or turns the floor over to Gilbert ("all right"), he nods his head, and raises his eyebrows. George and Gilbert look at each other when Gilbert asks a question, but at the end of each question, Gilbert looks up slightly. During the brief pause at the end of affirmative statements the speaker (always George, in this fragment) blinks. To mark the end of the questions, Gilbert raises his eyebrows.

In saying the word "check", Gilbert sketches the outlines of a check in the air between him and his listener. In saying "account", Gilbert forms a kind of box in front of him with his hands: a metaphorical representation of a bank account in which one keeps money. When he says the phrase "withdraw fifty dollars," Gilbert withdraws his hand towards his chest.

2.2 Communicative Significance of the Face

Movements of the head and facial expressions can be characterized by their placement with respect to the linguistic utterance and their significance in transmitting information [35]. The set of facial movement clusters contains:

- *syntactic functions* accompany the flow of speech and are synchronized at the verbal level. Facial movements (such as raising the eyebrows, nodding the head or blinking while saying "do you have a blank CHECK") can appear on an accented syllable or a pause.
- *semantic functions* can emphasize what is being said, substitute for a word or refer to an emotion (like wrinkling the nose while talking about something disgusting or smiling while remembering a happy event: "it was such a NICE DAY.").
- *dialogic functions* regulate the flow of speech and depend on the relationship between two people (smooth turns[1] are often co-occurrent with mutual gaze; e.g at the end of "do you have a blank check?", both interactants look at each other).

These three functions are modulated by various parameters:

- *speaker and listener characteristic functions* convey information about the speaker's social identity, emotion, attitude, age (friends spend more time looking at each other while talking than a lying speaker who will avoid the other's gaze).
- *listener functions* correspond to the listener's reactions to the speaker's speech; they can be signals of agreement, of attention, of comprehension (like saying "I see", "mhmm").

2.3 Communicative Significance of Hand Gestures

Gesture too can be described in terms of its intrinsic relationship to speech. Three aspects of this relationship are described before we go on to speak about the synchronization of the two communicative channels.

First of all, four basic types of gestures occur only during speech ([27] estimates that 90% of all gestures occur when the speaker is actually uttering something).

- *Iconics* represent some feature of the accompanying speech, such as sketching a small rectangular space with one's two hands while saying "do you have a blank CHECK?"
- *Metaphorics* represent an abstract feature concurrently spoken about, such as forming a jaw-like shape with one hand, and pulling it towards one's body while saying "then I can WITHDRAW fifty dollars for you".
- *Deictics* indicate a point in space. They accompany reference to persons, places and other spatializeable discourse entities. An example might be pointing to the ground while saying "do you have an account at THIS bank?".
- *Beats* are small formless waves of the hand that occur with heavily emphasized words, occasions of turning over the floor to another speaker, and other kinds of special linguistic work. An example is waving one's left hand briefly up and down along with the phrase "all right".

In some discourse contexts about three-quarters of all clauses are accompanied by gestures of one kind or another; of these, about 40% are iconic, 40% are beats, and the remaining 20% are divided between deictic and metaphoric gestures [27]. And surprisingly, although the proportion of different gestures may change, all of these types of gestures, and spontaneous gesturing in general, are found in discourses by speakers of most languages.

There is also a semantic and pragmatic relationship between the two media. Gesture and speech do not always manifest the same information about an idea, but what they convey is always complementary. That is, gesture may depict the way in which an action was carried out when this aspect of meaning is not depicted in speech. For example, one speaker, describing how one deposits checks into a bank account, said "you list the checks" while she

[1] Meaning that the listener does not interrupt or overlap the speaker.

depicted with her hands that the deposit slip is to be turned over and turned vertically in order for the checks to be listed in the spaces provided on the back of the slip.

Finally, the importance of the interdependence of speech and gesture is shown by the fact that speakers rely on information conveyed in gesture – sometimes even to the exclusion of information conveyed by accompanying speech – as they try to comprehend a story [9].

Nevertheless, hand gestures and gaze behavior have been virtually absent from attempts to animate semi-autonomous agents in communicative contexts.

2.4 Synchrony of Gesture, Facial Movements, and Speech

Facial expression, eye gaze and hand gestures do not do their communicative work only within single utterances, but also have inter-speaker effects. The presence or absence of confirmatory feedback by one conversational participant, via gaze or head movement, for example, affects the behavior of the other. A conversation consists of the exchange of meaningful utterances and of behavior. One person punctuates and reinforces her speech by head nods, smiles, and hand gestures; the other person can smile back, vocalize, or shift gaze to show participation in the conversation.

Synchrony implies that changes occurring in speech and in body movements should appear at the same time. For example, when a word begins to be articulated, eye blinks, hand movement, head turning, and brow raising can occur and can finish at the end of the word.

Synchrony occurs at all levels of speech: the phonemic segment, word, phrase or long utterance. Different facial motions are characteristic of these different groups [13], [20]. Some of them are more adapted to the phoneme level, like an eye blink, while others act at the word level, like a frown. In the example "Do you have a blank check?", a raising eyebrow starts and ends on the accented syllables "check", while a blink starts and ends on the pause marking the end of the utterance. Facial expression of emphasis can match the emphasized segment, showing synchronization at this level (a sequence of head nods can punctuate the emphasis). Moreover, some movements reflect encoding-decoding difficulties and therefore coincide with hesitations and pauses inside clauses. Many hesitation pauses are produced at the beginning of speech and correlate with avoidance of gaze (the head of the speaker turns away from the listener) as if to help the speaker to concentrate on what she is going to say.

Gestures occur in synchrony with their semantically parallel linguistic units, although in cases of hesitations, pauses or syntactically complex speech, it is the gesture which appears first ([27]). At the most local level, individual gestures and words are synchronized in time so that the 'stroke' (most energetic part of the gesture) occurs either with or just before the phonologically most prominent syllable of the accompanying speech segment ([21], [27]). At the most global level, we find that the hands of the speaker come to rest at the end of a speaking turn, before the next speaker begins her turn. At the intermediate level, the phenomenon of co-articulation of gestural units is found, whereby gestures are performed rapidly, or their production is stretched out over time, so as to synchronize with preceding and following gestures, and the speech these gestures accompany. An example of gestural co-articulation is the relationship between the two gestures in the phrase "get the check MADE OUT TO YOU for fifty dollars and then I can WITHDRAW fifty dollars for you". During the phrase 'made out to you', the right hand sketches a writing gesture in front of the speaker. However, rather than carrying this gesture all the way to completion (either both hands coming to rest at the end of this gesture, or maintaining the location of the hands in space), the hand drops slightly and then pulls back towards the speaker to perform the 'withdraw' gesture. Thus, the occurrence of the phrase 'made out to you', with its accompanying gesture, affected the occurrence of the gesture that accompanied "withdraw".

3 Computer Animation of Conversation

3.1 Literature on Facial Control Systems

Various systems have been proposed to integrate the different facial expression functions. Most of the systems use **FACS** (Facial Action Coding System) as a notational system [17]. This system is based on anatomical studies, and describes any visible facial movements. An action unit **AU**, the basic element of this system, describes the action produced by one or a group of related muscles.

The multi-layer approach [19] allows independent control at each level of the system. At the lowest level (geometric level), geometry of the face can be modified using free form deformation techniques. At the highest level, facial animation can be computed from an input utterance.

In M. Patel's model [28] facial animation can also be done at different levels of representation. It can be done either at the muscle level, the **AU** level or the script level. For each **AU** the user can select starting and ending points of action, the intensity of action, the start and end tensions and the interpolation method to compute the in-between frames. An alternative approach is proposed by [11] with good results.

Building a user-interface, [37] propose a categorization of facial expressions depending on their communicative meaning. For each of the facial functions a list of facial displays is performed (for example, remembering corresponds to eyebrow action, eye closure and one side of mouth pull back). A user talks to the 3D synthetic actor. A speech system recognizes the words and generates an answer with the appropriate facial displays. Grammar rules, a small vocabulary set and a specific knowledge domain are part of the speech analysis system. The responses by the 3D actor are selected from a pre-established set of utterances. The appropriate facial displays accompanying the answer follow the analysis of the conventional situation (e.g. if the user's speech is not recognized the 3D actor will answer with a "not-confident" facial display).

3.2 Literature on Gesture Animation

The computer graphics literature is rather sparse on the topic of gesture animation. Animators frequently use key parameter techniques to create arm and hand motions. Rijpkema and Girard [33] created handshapes automatically based on the object being gripped. The Thalmanns [18, 26] improved on the hand model to include much better skin models and deformations of the finger tips and the gripped object. Lee and Kunii [22] built a system that includes handshapes and simple pre-stored facial expressions for American Sign Language (ASL) synthesis. Dynamics of arm gestures in ASL have been studied by Loomis et al [25]. Chen et al [10] constructed a virtual human that can shake hands with an interactive participant. Lee et al [23] automatically generate lifting gestures by considering strength and comfort measures. Moravec and Calvert [5] constructed a system that portrays the gestural interaction between two agents as they pass and greet one another. Behavioral parameters were set by personality attribute "sliders" though the interaction sequence was itself pre-determined and limited to just one type of non-verbal encounter.

4 Overview of System

In the current system, a model of face-to-face interaction is used to generate all of the behaviors implemented, from the informational status of intonation to the communicative function of head nods, gaze, and hand gestures. Additionally, however, this system implements two agents whose verbal and nonverbal behaviors are integrated not only within turns, but across speakers.

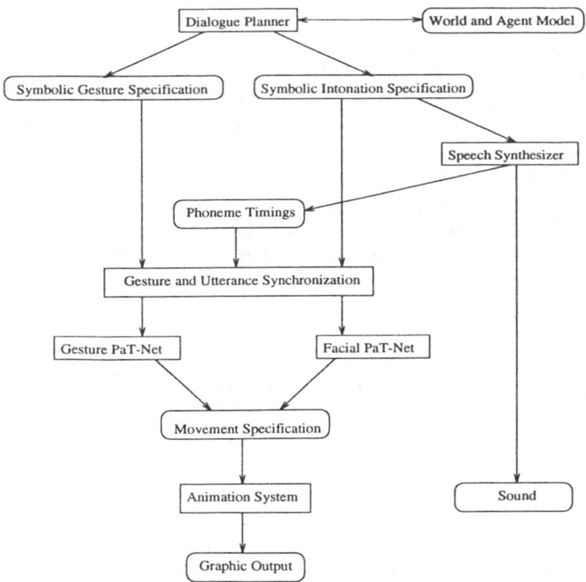

Figure 1: Interaction of components

In the remaining parts of the paper we explain the different boxes of Figure 1. We start from the top of the figure and work towards its bottom. Currently, gesture is generated by the dialogue planner, while facial expression and gaze are generated by the facial PaT-Net.

4.1 Dialogue Planner

The text of this dialogue is automatically generated on the basis of a database of facts describing the way the world works, a list of the goals of the two agents, and the set of beliefs of those two agents about the world, including the beliefs of the agents about one another [30], [7]. In this instance the two agents have goals that change over the course of the dialogue (Gilbert comes to have the goal of helping George get $50; George comes to have the goal of writing a check).

Text is generated and pitch accents and phrasal melodies are placed on generated text as outlined in [36] and [31]. This text is converted automatically to a form suitable for input to the AT&T Bell Laboratories TTS synthesizer ([24]). When the dialogue is generated, the following information is saved automatically: (1) the timing of the phonemes and pauses, (2) the type and place of the accents, (3) the type and place of the gestures.

This speech and timing information will be critical for synchronizing the facial and gestural animation.

4.2 Symbolic Gesture Specification

The dialogue generation program annotates utterances according to how their semantic content could relate to a spatial expression (literally, metaphorically, spatializeably, or not at all). Further, references to entities are classified according to discourse status as either new to discourse and hearer (indefinites), new to discourse but not to hearer (definites on first mention), or old (all others) [32]. According to the following rules, these annotations, together with the earlier ones, determine which concepts will have an associated gesture. Gestures that represent something (iconics and metaphorics) are generated for rhematic verbal elements (roughly, information not yet spoken about) and for hearer new references, provided that the semantic content is of an appropriate class to receive such a gesture: words with literally spatial (or concrete) content get iconics (e.g. "check"); those with metaphorically spatial (or abstract) content get metaphorics (e.g. "account"); words with physically spatializeable content get deictics (e.g. "this bank"). Meanwhile, beat gestures are generated for such items when the

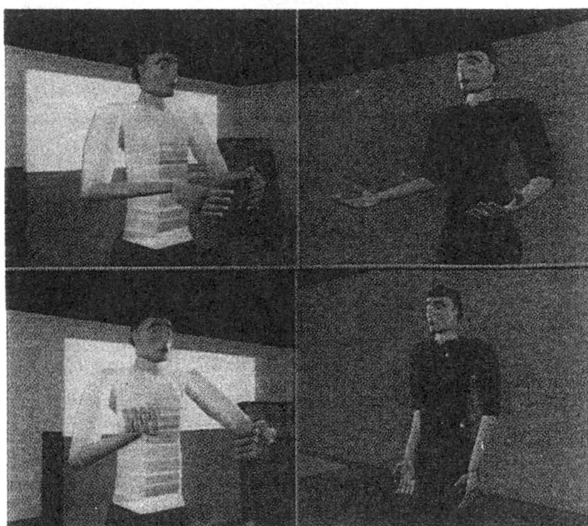

Figure 2: Examples of symbolic gesture specification

semantic content cannot be represented spatially, and are also produced accompanying discourse new definite references (e.g. "fifty dollars"). If a representational gesture is called for, the system accesses a dictionary of gestures (motion prototypes) that associates semantic representations with possible gestures that might represent them[2] (for further details, see [7]).

In Figure 2, we see examples of how symbolic gestures are generated from discourse content.

1. "Do you have a BLANK CHECK?"
   - In the first frame, an iconic gesture (representing a rectangular check) is generated from the first mention (new to hearer) of the entity 'blank check'.
2. "Will you HELP me get fifty dollars?"
   - In the second frame, a metaphoric gesture (the common *propose* gesture, representing the request for help as a proposal that can be offered to the listener) is generated because of the first mention (new to hearer) of the request for help.
3. "You can WRITE the check."
   - In the third frame, an iconic gesture (representing writing on a piece of paper) is generated from the first mention of the concrete action of 'writing a check'.
4. "I will WAIT for you to withdraw fifty dollars for me."
   - In the fourth frame, a beat gesture (a movement of the hand up and down) is generated from the first mention of the notion 'wait for', which cannot be represented spatially.

After this gestural annotation of all gesture types, and lexicon look-up of appropriate forms for representational gestures, information about the duration of intonational phrases (acquired in speech generation) is used to time gestures. First, all the gestures in each intonational phrase are collected. Because of the relationship between accenting and gesturing, in this dialogue at most one representational gesture occurs in each intonational phrase. If there is a representational gesture, its preparation is set to begin at or before the beginning of the intonational phrase, and to finish at or before the next gesture in the intonational phrase or the nuclear stress of the phrase, whichever comes first. The stroke phase is then set to coincide with the nuclear stress of the phrase. Finally, the relaxation is set to begin no sooner than the end of the stroke or the end of

[2] This solution is provisional: a richer semantics would include the features relevant for gesture generation, so that the form of the gestures could be generated algorithmically from the semantics. Note also, however, that following [21] we are led to believe that gestures may be more standardized in form than previously thought.

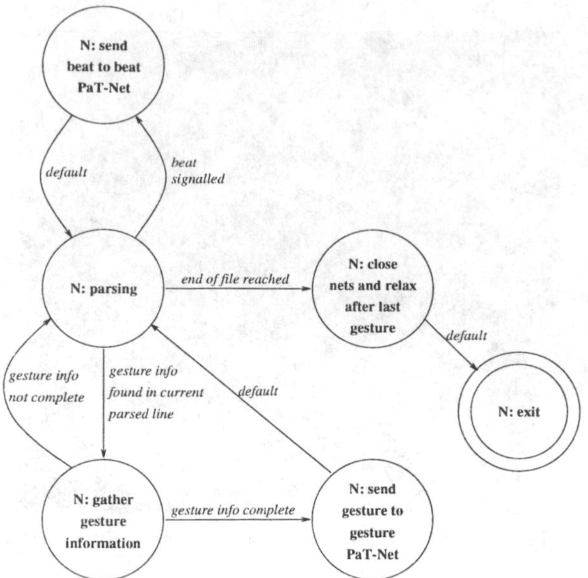

Figure 3: Pat-Net that synchronizes gestures with the dialogue at the phoneme level.

the last beat in the intonational phrase, with the end of relaxation to occur around the end of the intonational phrase. Beats, in contrast, are simply timed to coincide with the stressed syllable of the word that realizes the associated concept. When these timing rules have been applied to each of the intonational phrases in the utterance, the output is a series of symbolic gesture types and the times at which they should be performed. These instructions are used to generate motion files that run the animation system ([3]).

4.3 The Underlying Coordination Model

Interaction between agents and synchronization of gaze and hand movements to the dialogue for each agent are accomplished using Parallel Transition Networks (PaT-Nets), which allow coordination rules to be encoded as simultaneously executing finite state automata ([4]). PaT-Nets can call for action in the simulation and make state transitions either conditionally or probabilistically. Pat-Nets are scheduled into the simulation with an operating system that allows them to invoke or kill other PaT-Nets, sleep until a desired time or until a desired condition is met, and synchronize with other running nets by waiting for them to finish or by waiting on a shared semaphore.

In addition, the PaT-Net notation is object oriented with each net defined by a *class* with actions and transition conditions as *methods*. The running networks are instances of the PaT-Net class and can take parameters on instantiation. This notation allows Pat-Nets to be hierarchically organized and allows constructing new nets by combining existing nets or making simple modifications to existing nets.

Behaviors are implemented as specified in the following sections, with all head, eye and hand movement behavior for an individual encoded in PaT-Nets. A PaT-Net instance is created to control each agent with appropriate parameters. Then as agents' PaT-Nets synchronize the agents with the dialogue and interact with the unfolding simulation they schedule activity that achieves a complex observed interaction behavior.

4.4 Gesture Generator

The gesture PaT-Net sends information about the timing, shape, and position of the hands and arms to the animation system. The animation process produces a file of motions to be carried out by the two figures. Starting with a given gesture and its timing, speech rate and surrounding gestures constrain the motion sequence for a proper co-articulation effect. As depicted in Figure 3, upon the signalling of a particular gesture, parse-net will instantiate one of two additional PaT-Nets; if the gesture is a beat, the finite state machine representing beats ("beat-net") will be called, and if a deictic, iconic, or metaphoric, the network representing these types of gestures ("gest-net") will be called. This separation is motivated by the "rhythm hypothesis" ([38]) which posits that beats arise from the underlying rhythmical pulse of speaking, while other gestures arise from meaning representations. In addition, beats are often found superimposed over the other types of gestures, and such a separation facilitates implementation of superposition. Finally, since one of the goals of the model is to reflect differences in behavior among gesture types, this system provides for control of freedom versus boundedness in gestures (e.g. an iconic gesture or emblem is tightly constrained to a particular standard of well-formedness, while beats display free movement); free gestures may most easily be generated by a separate PaT-Net whose parameters include this feature.

Gesture and beat finite state machines are built as necessary by the parser, so that the gestures can be represented as they arise. The newly created instances of the gesture and beat PaT-Nets do not exit immediately upon creating their respective gestures; rather, they pause and await further commands from the calling network, in this case, parse-net. This is to allow for the phenomenon of gesture coarticulation, in which two gestures may occur in an utterance without intermediary relaxation, i.e. without dropping the hands or, in some cases, without relaxing handshape. Once the end of the current utterance is reached, the parser adds another level of control: it forces exit without relaxation of all gestures except the gesture at the top of the stack; this final gesture is followed by a relaxation of the arms, hands, and wrists.

Consider the following data from the intonation and gesture streams. Let us examine a gesture PaT-Net that acts on this input.
Intonation: Do you have a blank CHECK
Gesture: pr beat sk rx
In this example, the primary intonational stress of the phrase falls on 'check', but there is a secondary stress on 'blank'. The gesture line of the example shows that the preparation ('pr') of the gesture begins on 'have', that the stroke of the gesture ('st') falls on check, and that the gesturing relaxes ('rx') after 'check'. Because of the secondary stress on the new informational item 'blank', a beat gesture falls there, and it is found superimposed over the production of the iconic gesture.

Due to the structure of the conversation, where the speakers alternate turns, we assume similar alternation in gesturing. (Gesturing by listeners is almost non-existent [27].) For the purposes of gesture generation, phoneme information is ignored; however, utterance barriers must be interpreted both to provide an envelope for the timing of a particular gesture or sequence of gestures and to determine which speaker is gesturing. Timing information, given in the speech file, also allows the PaT-Net to determine whether there is enough time for a complete gesture to be produced. For example, the iconic gesture which accompanies the utterance *"Do you have a blank [check]?"* has sufficient time to execute: it is the only (non-beat) gesture occurring in the phrase, as shown above. However, if this timing is insufficient to allow for full gesture production, then the gesture must be foreshortened to allow for the reduced available timing (because beat gestures are produced by a separate PaT-Net system, they do not enter into questions of co-articulation).

The most common reason for foreshortening is anticipation of the next gesture to be produced in a discourse. In anticipatory co-articulation effects, most often the relaxation phase of the foreshortened iconic, metaphoric or deictic gesture and preparation phase of the next gesture become one. This process can be seen in the gestures accompanying the phrase *"Get the check [made out to you] for fifty dollars and then I can [withdraw] fifty dollars for you"*. "[Made out to you]" is produced .90 seconds into the phrase, and "[withdraw]" is generated at 1.9 seconds. This causes some foreshortening in the relaxation process during the first gesture, from which the second gesture is then produced.

Co-articulation constraints – synchronizing the gestures with intonational phrases and surrounding gestures – may actually cause the given gestures to be aborted if too little time is available for production given the physical constraints of the human model.

4.5 Gesture Motion Specification

The graphics-level gesture animation system accepts gesture instructions containing information about the location, type, timing, and handshape of individual gestures. Based on the current location of the hands and arms in space, the system will attempt to get as close as possible to the gesture goals in the time allowed, but may mute motions or positionings because it cannot achieve them in time (co-articulation effects). This animation system calls upon a library of predefined handshapes which form the primitives of hand gesture. These handshapes were chosen to reflect the shapes most often found in gesture during conversational interaction ([21]). The animation system also calls upon separate hand, arm and wrist control mechanisms.

The gesture system is divided into three parts: hand shape, wrist control, and arm positioning. The first, hand shape, relies on an extensible library of hand shape primitives for the basic joint positions, but allows varying degrees of relaxation towards a neutral hand position. The speed at which the hand may change shape is also limited to allow the modelling of hand shape co-articulation. Large changes in hand position are restricted as less time is allotted for the hand movement, forcing faster hand gestures to smooth together.

The wrist control system allows the wrist to maintain and change its position independently of what complex arm motions may be occurring. The wrist is limited within the model to a physically realistic range of motion. Wrist direction is specified in terms of simple directions relative to the gesturer, such as "point the fingers of the left hand forward and up, and the palm right".

The arm motion system accepts general specifications of spatial goals and drives the arms towards those goals within the limits imposed by the arm's range of motion. The arm may be positioned by using general directions like "chest-high, slightly forward, and to the far left".

The expressiveness of an individual's gesturing can be represented by adjusting the size of the gesture space of the graphical figure. In this way, parameters such as age (children's gestures are larger than adults') and culture (in some cultures gestures tend to be larger) can be implemented in the gesture animation.

4.6 Symbolic Facial Expression Specification

In the current system, facial expression (movement of the lips, eyebrows, etc.) is specified separately from movement of the head and eyes (gaze). In this section we discuss facial expression, and turn to gaze in the next section.

P. Ekman and his colleagues characterize the set of semantic and syntactic facial expressions depending on their meaning [15]. Many facial functions exist (such as manipulators that correspond to biological needs of the face (wetting the lips); emblems and emotional emblems that are facial expressions replacing a word, an emotion) but only some are directly linked to the intonation of the voice. In this system, facial expressions connected to intonation are automatically generated, while other kinds of expressions (emblems, for example) are specified by hand [29].

4.7 Symbolic Gaze Specification

Gaze can be classified into four primary categories depending on its role in the conversation [1], [12]. In the following, we give rules of action and the functions for each of these four categories (see Figure 4). The nodes of the Pat-Net they refer to is also indicated.

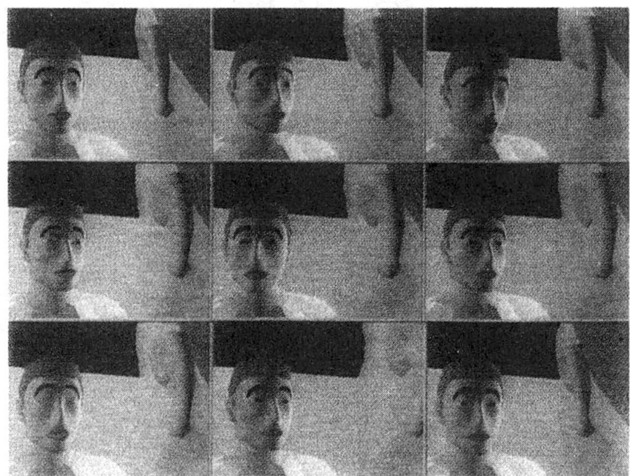

Figure 4: Facial expressions and gaze behavior corresponding to: "All right. <pause> You can write the check".

planning: corresponds to the first phase of a turn when the speaker organizes her thoughts. She has a tendency to look away in order to prevent an overload of information (`beginning of turn`). On the other hand, during the execution phase, the speaker knows what she is going to say and looks more at the listener. For a short turn (duration less than 1.5 sec.), the speaker and the listener establish eye contact (mutual gaze) [1] (`short-turn`).

comment: accompanies and comments speech, by occurring in parallel with accent and emphasis. Accented or emphasized items are punctuated by head nods; the speaker looks toward the listener (`accent`). The speaker also gazes at the listener more when she asks a question. She looks up at the end of the question (`utterance: question`). When answering, the speaker looks away (`utterance: answer`).

control: controls the communication channel and functions as a synchronization signal: responses may be demanded or suppressed by looking at the listener. When the speaker wants to give her turn of speaking to the listener, she gazes at the listener at the end of the utterance (`end of turn`). When the listener asks for the turn, she looks up at the speaker (`turn request`).

feedback: is used to collect and seek feedback. The listener can emit different reaction signals to the speaker's speech. Speaker looks toward the listener during grammatical pauses to obtain feedback on how utterances are being received (`within-turn`). This is frequently followed by the listener looking at the speaker and nodding (`back-channel`). In turn, if the speaker wants to keep her turn, she looks away from the listener (`continuation signal`). If the speaker doesn't emit a `within-turn` signal by gazing at the listener, the listener can still emit a `back-channel` which in turn may be followed by a `continuation signal` by the speaker. But the probability of action of the listener varies with the action of the speaker [14]; in particular, it decreases if no signal has occurred from the speaker. In this way the listener reacts to the behavior of the speaker.

4.8 Gaze Generator

Each of the dialogic functions appears as a sub-network in the PaT-Net. Figure 5 outlines the high-level PaT-Net for gaze control for a single agent. It contains the four dialogic functions, their nodes that define each function, and their associated actions. From the definitions given above, we extract the conditions and the actions characterizing the dialogic functions. For this current version of the

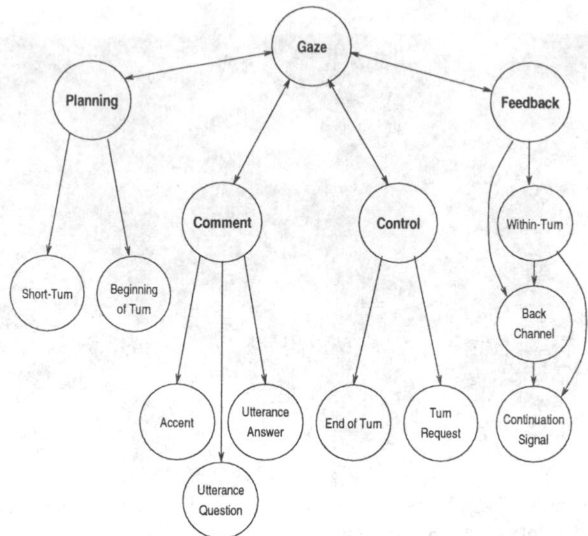

Figure 5: The gaze movement PaT-Net: actions are defined in the nodes; conditional and probabilistic transitions occur on arcs. All leaf nodes also branch back to the root node unconditionally.

program we do not differentiate head movement and eye movement. That is the eyes follow the head. Moreover, in the literature this difference is rarely made. In what follows, we use "gaze" to refer to head and eye movement.

Each node is characterized by a probability. A person can have the floor talking or pausing, but loses it as soon as the other person starts talking. There are 3 possible states per person while having the floor. If Speaker has the floor: Speaker talks and Listener pauses, both of them are talking, or both of them are pausing. For each of these states, Speaker and Listener can gaze at each other or not. This gives us 12 possibilities, or 24 per dyad. We can then compute the probability of being in each of these states [6]. Most of the nodes of the Pat-Net can be characterized by a certain set of states. For example the occurrence of a "within-turn signal" as we defined it corresponds to the action: person1 looks at the person2 while having the floor and pausing. These state sets correspond to a sub-matrix. We compute the probability of each sub-matrix in relation to the particular state (having the floor and pausing) to arrive at a probability of occurrence. We do such a computation for all the other nodes of the Pat-Net. Probabilities appropriate for each agent given the current role as listener or speaker are set for the PaT-Net before it executes. At each turn change, the probabilities change values accordingly. This information is used to determine the rules and transitional probabilities for actions in Pat-Nets.

For each phoneme, the GAZE Pat-Net is entered. A transition is made on the node whose condition is true. If the probability of the nodes allows it, the action is performed. The action of the different nodes of the Pat-Net is illustrated in the following with the example:

`Gilbert: Get the chEck made OUt to you for fifty dollars` *<pause>* `And thEn` *<pause>* `I can withdrAw fifty dollars for you.`

planning: For the first few phonemes of the beginning of the example utterance [3](in our example it corresponds to "Get the ch"), the sub-network **planning** is applied. This utterance is not short so the node `short-turn` is not entered.

But the node `beginning-turn` is entered; the condition of being in a beginning of turn is true but its probability did not allow the action `speaker gazes away` to be applied. Therefore the speaker (Gilbert) keeps his current gaze direction (looking at George).

comment: In our example, on accented items ("chEck", "thEn" and "withdrAw"), the node `accent` of the sub-network **comment** is reached; the actions `speaker gazes at the listener` and `head nod` are performed by Gilbert. As before, the instantiation of an action depends on its probability. The system easily represents the parallel agent actions.

control: In our example at the end of the utterance[4] (corresponding to "fifty dollars for you" here) the sub-network **control** is entered. Two actions are considered. The node `end of turn` corresponds to action performed by the speaker: `speaker gazes at listener`. The other node `turn request` affects the listener; the action `listener gazes at the speaker and up` is performed.

feedback: The two intonational phrases of our example (*get the check made out to you for fifty dollars* and *and then*) are separated by a pause; this corresponds to a within-turn situation. The sub-network **feedback** is entered. If the probability allows it, the action `speaker gazes at the listener` is performed[5]. After a delay (0.2 sec., as specified by the program), the node `back-channel` is reached. Once more the program checks the probabilities associated with the actions. Two actions can happen: `listener gazes at the speaker` and/or `the listener nods`. In either case, the final step within the **feedback** sub-network is reached after some delay. The action `speaker gazes away from the listener` is then performed.

4.9 Facial Expression Generator

Facial expressions belonging to the set of semantic and syntactic functions (see section 4.6) are clustered into functional groups: lip shape, conversational signal, punctuator, manipulator and emblem. We use **FACS** to denote facial expressions. Each is represented by two parameters: *its time of occurrence* and *its type*. Our algorithm [29] embodies rules as described in Section 4.6 to automatically generate facial expressions, following the principle of synchrony.

The program scans the input utterance and computes the different facial expressions corresponding to these functional groups. The computation of the lip shape is made in three passes and incorporates coarticulation effects. Phonemes are associated to some characteristic shapes with different degree of deformability. For deformable elements, temporal and spatial constraints modify these shapes to consider their surrounding context. A conversational signal (movements occurring on accents, like the raising of an eyebrow) starts and ends with the accented word; while punctuator signal (movement occurring on pause, like frowning) happens on the pause. When a blink is one of these signals it is synchronized at the phoneme level. Other signals such as emblems and emotional emblems are performed consciously and must be specified by the user.

By varying the two parameters defining a facial expression, different speaker personalities can be obtained. For example a persuasive person can punctuate each accented word with raising eyebrows, while another person might not.

4.10 Gaze and Facial Motion Specification

The gaze directions generated in a previous stage can now be instantiated. As discussed earlier, the GAZE PaT-Net in Figure 5 is run for each agent at the beginning of every phoneme. Depending on the course taken through the GAZE network due to probabilistic

[3]A beginning of a turn is defined as all the phonemes between the first one and the first accented segment.

[4]End of turn is defined as all the phonemes between the last accented segment and the last phonemes.

[5]In the case the action is not performed, the arc going to the node `back-channel` is immediately traversed without waiting for the next phonemic segment.

branching and environmental state, the net may commit its agent to a variety of actions such as a head nod or a change in the gaze point. A change in the gaze is accomplished by supplying the human model with a 3D coordinate at which to look and a time in which to move – the scheduled motion then begins at the current point in the simulation and has the specified duration. A head nod is accomplished by scheduling a sequence of joint motions for the neck, supplying both the angle and the angular velocity for each nod cycle. Note that the gaze controller schedules motions as they are necessary by reacting to the unfolding simulation (in fact, it does this in semi-real time) and does not have to generate all motions in advance. This makes the gaze controller easy to extend and easy to integrate with the rest of the system.

Different functions may be served by the same action, which differ only in their timing and amplitude. For example, when punctuating an accent, the speaker's head nod will be of larger amplitude than the feedback head nods emitted by the listener. Different head nod functions may also be characterized by varying numbers of up/down cycles. The gaze direction is sustained by calling for the agent to look at a pre-defined point in the environment until a change is made by another action.

For facial expressions, the program outputs the list of **AUs** that characterize each phonemic element and pause [29].

After scanning all the input utterances, all the actions to be performed are specified. Animation files are output. The final animation is done by combining the different output files for the gesture, face and gaze in *Jack*.

5 Conclusions

Automatically generating information about intonation, facial expression, head movements and hand gestures allows an interactive dialogue animation to be created; for a non-real-time animation much guess-work in the construction of appropriate motions can be avoided. The resulting motions can be used as is – as demonstrated in the video – or the actions and timings can be used as a cognitively and physiologically justified guide to further refinement of the conversation and the participants' interactions by a human animator.

REFERENCES

[1] M. Argyle and M. Cook. *Gaze and Mutual gaze*. Cambridge University Press, 1976.

[2] N. I. Badler, B. A. Barsky, and D. Zeltzer, editors. *Making Them Move: Mechanics, Control, and Animation of Articulated Figures*. Morgan-Kaufmann, San Mateo, CA, 1991.

[3] N. I. Badler, C. Phillips and B. L. Webber. *Simulating Humans: Computer Graphics, Animation, and Control*. Oxford University Press, June 1993.

[4] Welton M. Becket. The *jack lisp api*. Technical Report MS-CIS-94-01/Graphics Lab 59, University of Pennsylvania, 1994.

[5] Tom Calvert. Composition of realistic animation sequences for multiple human figures. In Norman I. Badler, Brian A. Barsky, and David Zeltzer, editors, *Making Them Move: Mechanics, Control, and Animation of Articulated Figures*, pages 35–50. Morgan-Kaufmann, San Mateo, CA, 1991.

[6] J. Cappella. personal communication, 1993.

[7] Justine Cassell, Mark Steedman, Norm Badler, Catherine Pelachaud, Matthew Stone, Brett Douville, Scott Prevost and Brett Achorn. *Modeling the interaction between speech and gesture. Proceedings of the Cognitive Science Society Annual Conference*, 1994.

[8] Justine Cassell and David McNeill. Gesture and the poetics of prose. *Poetics Today*, 12:375–404, 1992.

[9] Justine Cassell, David McNeill, and Karl-Erik McCullough. Kids, don't try this at home: Experimental mismatches of speech and gesture. presented at the International Communication Association annual meeting, 1993.

[10] D. T. Chen, S. D. Pieper, S. K. Singh, J. M. Rosen, and D. Zeltzer. The virtual sailor: An implementation of interactive human body modeling. In *Proc. 1993 Virtual Reality Annual International Symposium*, Seattle, WA, September 1993. IEEE.

[11] M.M. Cohen and D.W. Massaro. Modeling coarticulation in synthetic visual speech. In N.M. Thalmann and D.Thalmann, editors, *Models and Techniques in Computer Animation*, pages 139-156. Springer-Verlag, 1993.

[12] G. Collier. *Emotional expression*. Lawrence Erlbaum Associates, 1985.

[13] W.S. Condon and W.D. Osgton. Speech and body motion synchrony of the speaker-hearer. In D.H. Horton and J.J. Jenkins, editors, *The perception of Language*, pages 150–184. Academic Press, 1971.

[14] S. Duncan. Some signals and rules for taking speaking turns in conversations. In Weitz, editor, *Nonverbal Communication*. Oxford University Press, 1974.

[15] P. Ekman. Movements with precise meanings. *The Journal of Communication*, 26, 1976.

[16] P. Ekman. About brows: emotional and conversational signals. In M. von Cranach, K. Foppa, W. Lepenies, and D. Ploog, editors, *Human ethology: claims and limits of a new disipline: contributions to the Colloquium*, pages 169–248. Cambridge University Press, Cambridge, England; New-York, 1979.

[17] P. Ekman and W. Friesen. *Facial Action Coding System*. Consulting Psychologists Press, Inc., 1978.

[18] Jean-Paul Gourret, Nadia Magnenat-Thalmann, and Daniel Thalmann. Simulation of object and human skin deformations in a grasping task. *Computer Graphics*, 23(3):21–30, 1989.

[19] P. Kalra, A. Mangili, N. Magnenat-Thalmann, and D. Thalmann. Smile: A multilayered facial animation system. In T.L. Kunii, editor, *Modeling in Computer Graphics*. Springer-Verlag, 1991.

[20] A. Kendon. Movement coordination in social interaction: some examples described. In Weitz, editor, *Nonverbal Communication*. Oxford University Press, 1974.

[21] Adam Kendon. Gesticulation and speech: Two aspects of the process of utterance. In M.R.Key, editor, *The Relation between Verbal and Nonverbal Communication*, pages 207–227. Mouton, 1980.

[22] Jintae Lee and Tosiyasu L. Kunii. Visual translation: From native language to sign language. In *Workshop on Visual Languages*, Seattle, WA, 1993. IEEE.

[23] Philip Lee, Susanna Wei, Jianmin Zhao, and Norman I. Badler. Strength guided motion. *Computer Graphics*, 24(4):253–262, 1990.

[24] Mark Liberman and A. L. Buchsbaum. Structure and usage of current Bell Labs text to speech programs. Technical Memorandum TM 11225-850731-11, AT&T Bell Laboratories, 1985.

[25] Jeffrey Loomis, Howard Poizner, Ursula Bellugi, Alynn Blakemore, and John Hollerbach. Computer graphic modeling of American Sign Language. *Computer Graphics*, 17(3):105–114, July 1983.

[26] Nadia Magnenat-Thalmann and Daniel Thalmann. Human body deformations using joint-dependent local operators and finite-element theory. In Norman I. Badler, Brian A. Barsky, and David Zeltzer, editors, *Making Them Move: Mechanics, Control, and Animation of Articulated Figures*, pages 243–262. Morgan-Kaufmann, San Mateo, CA, 1991.

[27] David McNeill. *Hand and Mind: What Gestures Reveal about Thought*. University of Chicago, 1992.

[28] M. Patel. *Making FACES*. PhD thesis, School of Mathematical Sciences, University of Bath, Bath, AVON, UK, 1991.

[29] C. Pelachaud, N.I. Badler, and M. Steedman. Linguistic issues in facial animation. In N. Magnenat-Thalmann and D. Thalmann, editors, *Computer Animation '91*, pages 15–30. Springer-Verlag, 1991.

[30] Richard Power. The organisation of purposeful dialogues. *Linguistics*, 1977.

[31] Scott Prevost and Mark Steedman. Generating contextually appropriate intonation. In *Proceedings of the 6th Conference of the European Chapter of the Association for Computational Linguistics*, pages 332–340, Utrecht, 1993.

[32] Ellen F. Prince. The ZPG letter: Subjects, definiteness and information status. In S. Thompson and W. Mann, editors, *Discourse description: diverse analyses of a fund raising text*, pages 295–325. John Benjamins B.V., 1992.

[33] Hans Rijpkema and Michael Girard. Computer animation of hands and grasping. *Computer Graphics*, 25(4):339–348, July 1991.

[34] Barbara Robertson. Easy motion. *Computer Graphics World*, 16(12):33–38, December 1993.

[35] Klaus R. Scherer. The functions of nonverbal signs in conversation. In H. Giles R. St. Clair, editor, *The Social and Physhological Contexts of Language*, pages 225–243. Lawrence Erlbaum Associates, 1980.

[36] Mark Steedman. Structure and intonation. *Language*, 67:260–296, 1991.

[37] Akikazu Takeuchi and Katashi Nagao. Communicative facial displays as a new conversational modality. In *ACM/IFIP INTERCHI'93*, Amsterdam, 1993.

[38] K. Tuite. The production of gesture. *Semiotica*, 93(1/2), 1993.

6 Research Acknowledgments

This research is partially supported by NSF Grants IRI90-18513, IRI91-17110, CISE Grant CDA88-22719, NSF graduate fellowships, NSF VPW GER-9350179; ARO Grant DAAL03-89-C-0031 including participation by the U.S. Army Research Laboratory (Aberdeen); U.S. Air Force DEPTH contract through Hughes Missile Systems F33615-91-C-000; DMSO through the University of Iowa; National Defense Science and Engineering Graduate Fellowship in Computer Science DAAL03-92-G-0342; and NSF Instrumentation and Laboratory Improvement Program Grant USE-9152503.

Dynamically Sequencing an Animated Pedagogical Agent*

Brian A. Stone and **James C. Lester**
Multimedia Laboratory
Department of Computer Science
North Carolina State University
Raleigh, NC 27695-8206
{bastone,lester}@eos.ncsu.edu

Abstract

One of the most promising opportunities introduced by rapid advances in knowledge-based learning environments and multimedia technologies is the possibility of creating animated pedagogical agents. These agents should exhibit three properties: timely domain coverage (they should clearly communicate fundamental concepts and relationships within the allotted time); contextuality (they should provide explanations in appropriate problem-solving contexts); and continuity (their activities and utterances should be pedagogically, visually, and aurally coherent).

We have developed the *coherence-structured behavior space* approach to creating animated pedagogical agents. This is a two-step approach. First, we design a behavior space of animation and audio segments that are structured by prerequisite relationships and a continuity metric. Second, we navigate coherent paths through the space to dynamically sequence behaviors. This creates seamless global behaviors that communicate fundamental knowledge and provide contextualized problem-solving advice. The coherence-structured behavior space approach has been implemented in Herman the Bug, an animated pedagogical agent for Design-A-Plant, a knowledge-based learning environment for botanical anatomy and physiology. Formative evaluations of the agent with middle school students are encouraging.

Introduction

Since their conception more than a quarter of a century ago, knowledge-based learning environments (Hollan, Hutchins, & Weitzman 1987; Lesgold *et al.* 1992) have offered significant potential for fundamentally changing the educational process. It has long been believed—and recently rigorously demonstrated (Mark & Greer 1995)—that presenting knowledgeable feedback to students increases learning effectiveness. Despite this promise, few learning environments have made the difficult transition from the laboratory to the classroom, and the challenge of developing learning environments that are both pedagogically sound *and* visually appealing has played no small part in this impasse. Fortunately, recent years have witnessed the appearance of a new generation of animation software that enables teams of animators to rapidly create life-like characters. This development raises an intriguing possibility: creating *animated pedagogical agents* that couple key feedback functionalities with a strong visual presence. Introduced immersively into a 3D learning environment, an animated pedagogical agent could observe students' progress and provide them with visually contextualized problem-solving advice.

An animated pedagogical agent's behaviors must exhibit contextuality, continuity, and temporality. An agent's advisory behaviors must be rhetorically contextualized within problem-solving episodes, and its physical behaviors must be graphically contextualized within the learning environment. To exhibit continuity of action, all of its behaviors must be visually coherent. Moreover, because many domains and tasks are highly complex and learning time is limited, sequencing a pedagogical agent's explanatory behaviors must take into account temporal resources to provide the greatest coverage of the domain in the given time. Together, these requirements call for a dynamic solution that marries inference with animation. Although knowledge-based graphical simulations (Hollan, Hutchins, & Weitzman 1987) are virtually *de rigueur* in contemporary learning environments, and the problem of planning multimedia presentations has been the subject of much study (André *et al.* 1993; Feiner & McKeown 1990; Maybury 1991; Roth, Mattis, & Mesnard 1991; Mittal *et al.* 1995), work on "self-animating" characters (Bates 1994; Blumberg & Galyean 1995; Tu & Terzopoulos 1994) is receiving increasing attention but is still in its infancy.

In this paper, we propose the *coherence-structured behavior space* framework for dynamically sequencing animated pedagogical agents' behaviors. We focus in particular on animated pedagogical agents that will be employed in learning environments whose purpose is to

*Support for this work was provided by the IntelliMedia Initiative of North Carolina State University and donations from Apple and IBM.

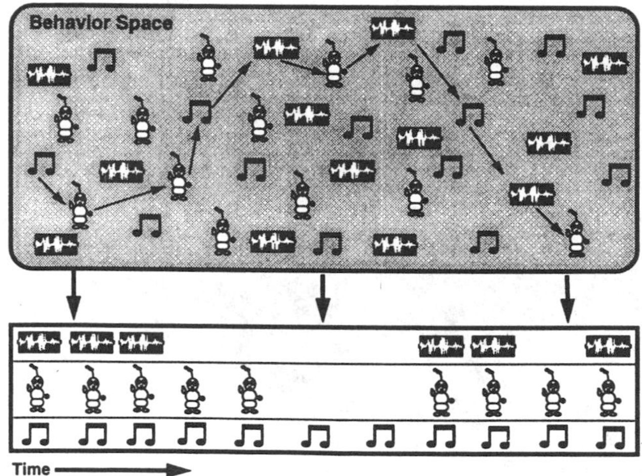

Figure 1: Sequencing coherence-structured behaviors

provide instruction about the structure and function of a particular device or organism. Applying this framework to create an agent entails constructing a behavior space, imposing a coherence structure on it, and developing a behavior sequencing engine that dynamically selects and assembles behaviors:

1. **Behavior Space Construction:** A behavior space contains animated segments of the agent performing a variety of actions, as well as audio clips of the agent's utterances. It is designed by a multidisciplinary team and rendered by a team of graphic artists and animators.
2. **Behavior Space Structuring:** The behavior space is structured by (1) a tripartite index of ontological, intentional, and rhetorical indices, (2) a pedagogically appropriate prerequisite ordering, and (3) behavior links annotated with distances computed with a *visual continuity metric.*
3. **Dynamic Behavior Sequencing:** At runtime, the behavior sequencing engine creates global behaviors in response to the changing problem-solving context by exploiting the coherence structure of the behavior space. The sequencing engine selects the agent's actions by navigating coherent paths through the behavior space and assembling them dynamically (Figure 1).

This approach creates seamless global behaviors in which the agent provides visually contextualized problem-solving advice. In addition, by attending to temporal resources, it selects and composes explanatory behaviors so as to achieve the greatest coverage of the domain within the allotted time.

This framework has been used to implement **Herman the Bug**, an animated pedagogical agent (Figure 2) for DESIGN-A-PLANT (Lester *et al.* 1996), a knowledge-based learning environment for botanical anatomy and physiology. Given a set of environmental conditions, children use DESIGN-A-PLANT to graphically assemble a customized plant that can survive in the specified environment. In response to changing problem-solving contexts in DESIGN-A-PLANT, a sequencing engine orchestrates Herman the Bug's actions by selecting and assembling behaviors from a behavior space of 30 animations and 160 audio clips that were created by a team of 12 graphic artists and animators. It also employs a large library of runtime-mixable soundtrack elements to dynamically compose a score that complements the agent's activities. Formative evaluations of Herman the Bug with middle school students are encouraging.

Coherence Requirements

Pedagogical Coherence. Naturally, considerations of pedagogical coherence loom large in the design of animated pedagogical agents. Perhaps most central among these requirements is that an agent's explanatory behaviors be *situated* (Suchman 1987): all of its explanatory behaviors—not merely its advisory actions but also its communication of fundamental conceptual knowledge—should take place in concrete problem-solving contexts. For example, students using DESIGN-A-PLANT should learn about leaf morphology in the context of selecting a particular type of leaf as they design a plant that will survive in particular environmental conditions. Moreover, prerequisite-based sequencing, content selection, and topical transitions of explanatory behaviors should exhibit pedagogical coherence.

Visual Coherence. Because animated pedagogical agents inhabit two-dimensional space—albeit one that, by design, closely emulates three-dimensional space—their behaviors should be governed by the conventions of visual coherence. Because the birth and maturation of the film medium over the past century has precipitated the development of a visual language with its own syntax and semantics (Monaco 1981), the "grammar" of this language should be employed in all aspects of the agent's behaviors. In addition to traditional film language, an agent's designers can also exploit the behavior cannon of the animated film (Noake 1988; Lenburg 1993; Jones 1989) by computationalizing classical animation principles (Lasseter 1987; Bates 1994). For example, the zoom levels of the shots and the positioning of the agent visually communicate what is—and is not—important. In DESIGN-A-PLANT, macroscopic shots of the agent and plant can depict the agent interacting with external morphological structures; median shots can depict the agent interacting with internal plant structures; and microscopic shots can show the agent interacting with cellular structures. Moreover, careful selection of the agent's spatial positioning and orientation, its accouterments (e.g., props such as microscopes, jetpacks, etc.), and visual expressions of its emotive state (Bates 1994) can emphasize

Figure 2: DESIGN-A-PLANT's animated pedagogical agent, Herman the Bug

the most salient aspects of the domain for the current problem-solving context.

Considerations of pedagogical and visual coherence suggest the following maxims for the design of animated pedagogical agents:

- **Agent Persistence:** Keep the agent in the frame. An omni-present agent in the problem-solving environment can reassure learners and increase their interest. Although brief excursions offscreen to obtain a prop can enliven the action, maintaining a strong onscreen presence provides visual consistency. For example, an agent for DESIGN-A-PLANT should remain in the onscreen design studio (where students select anatomical structures such as roots, stems, and leaves) at all times.
- **Pedagogical Object Persistence:** Maintain in frame a manipulable 3D model of the object (or task) being discussed. Keeping the primary pedagogical object onscreen reduces the cognitive load that would be imposed if it were to disappear and reappear with frequent scene changes. For example, the evolving 3D plant model—the one being designed by the students—should be visible at all times.
- **Agent Immersion:** Graphically immerse the agent in the problem-solving environment. Whenever possible, its behaviors should be conducted in close proximity to a manipulable 3D model of the primary pedagogical object. For instance, the DESIGN-A-PLANT agent should remain in close proximity to the plant itself, e.g., by flying around leaves, sliding down stems, or standing on chloroplasts.
- **Verbal Support:** *Audio-primary utterances*, i.e., verbalizations accompanied by little or no actions, should be used for brief reminders and interjections. Verbal meta-comments such as bridging phrases can also usher in transitions.
- **Contextualized Musical Score:** Complement the agent's behaviors with a context-sensitive soundtrack whose tempo and instrumentation are appropriate for the current context. For example, the DESIGN-A-PLANT agent should be accompanied by a score that employs internal consistency of voicing and melody within a problem-solving episode and thematic consistency across problem-solving episodes.

These maxims should inform all decisions about the construction of behavior spaces, the imposition of a coherent structure on the behaviors, and the design of the behavior sequencing engine.

Designing Behavior Spaces

To provide an agent with the flexibility required to respond to a broad range of problem-solving contexts, its behavior space must be populated with a large, diverse set of animated and audio-primary behaviors. In contrast to the linear storyboarding approach employed in traditional animation (Noake 1988), the pedagogical and visual connectivity of behavior spaces require a *networked storyboarding* approach. Posing significant pedagogical and aesthetic challenges, the design of a networked storyboard is a complex, labor-intensive task. Networked storyboarding consists of designing specifications for eight classes of animated and audio-primary behaviors and imposing a coherence structure on them.

Specifying Behaviors

Creating the agent's behavior repertoire entails setting forth precise visual and audio specifications that describe in great detail the agent's actions and utterances, rendering the actions, and creating the audio clips. The core of a behavior space is a highly interconnected web of animated segments depicting the agent performing a variety of explanatory behaviors. This is complemented by a set of audio clips of the agent's audio-primary utterances, as well as soundtrack elements (not discussed here) for the dynamically created score. To assist the sequencing engine in assembling behaviors that exhibit visual coherence, it is critical that the specifications for the animated segments take into account continuity. Accordingly, we adopt the principle of *visual bookending* to create animated segments that can more easily be assembled into visually coherent global behaviors. Visually bookended animations begin and end with frames that are identical. Just as walk cycles and looped backgrounds can be seamlessly composed, visually bookended animated behaviors can be joined in any order and the global behavior will always be flawlessly continuous.

It is important to note that visual bookending should be applied to topically-partitioned clusters of animated segments. In theory, all segments could begin and end with identical frames, but the global behaviors assembled from such a behavior space would depict the agent repeatedly leaving and returning to a single location. Because this would compromise visual coherence in most domains, partitioning the behavior space into clusters and then bookending segments within a cluster will yield superior global behaviors.

To construct a behavior space for an animated pedagogical agent, eight families of behaviors are specified collaboratively by the multi-disciplinary agent design team and then rendered by the graphic designers and animators:

- **Conceptual Explanatory Animated Segments:** The agent explicates the structures and functions of the primary pedagogical object. For example, the DESIGN-A-PLANT agent's behavior space contains an animated segment of the agent explaining how root hairs absorb water through osmosis.
- **Problem-Solving Advisory Animated Segments:** The agent provides abstract, principle-based advice. Students must then operationalize this advice in their problem solving activities. For example, one animated segment of the DESIGN-A-PLANT agent depicts him pointing out the relation between leaf size and low sunlight (plants in limited sunlight sometimes have larger leaves).
- **Animated Transition Segments:** These portray the agent moving from one *keyframe* (a frame initiating or terminating a segment in a bookended cluster) to another keyframe, or performing an action that will set the stage for several behaviors.
- **Audio-Primary Problem Overviews:** The agent introduces a student to a new problem. For example, the DESIGN-A-PLANT agent's behavior space contains audio clips of the agent describing environmental conditions. These utterances are played at the beginning of problem-solving episodes.
- **Audio-Primary Advisory Reminders:** The agent briefly reminds a student about principle-based advice that was presented earlier. For example, an audio clip in the DESIGN-A-PLANT agent's behavior space is a voiceover of the agent stating, "Remember that small leaves are struck by less sunlight."
- **Audio-Primary Direct Suggestions:** The advice presented by the agent is immediately operationalizable. For example, the DESIGN-A-PLANT agent's behavior space contains a voiceover of the agent stating, "Choose a long stem so the leaves can get plenty of sunlight in this dim environment." The agent makes these types of suggestions when a student is experiencing serious difficulties.
- **Audio-Primary Interjections:** The agent remarks about the student's progress and makes off-the-cuff comments. For example, the DESIGN-A-PLANT agent's behavior space includes Audio-Primary Interjections in which the agent congratulates the student about the successful completion of a plant design. Because a large repertoire of interjections contributes significantly to an agent's believability, a behavior space should include a variety of Audio-Primary Interjections.
- **Audio-Primary Transitions:** The agent makes meta-comments that signal an upcoming behavior. For example, the DESIGN-A-PLANT agent's Audio-Primary Transitions include a clip of him stating "It seems we're having some difficulty. Let's see if this helps ..."

Imposing a Coherence Structure

Once the behavior space has been created, it must then be structured to assist the sequencing engine in selecting and assembling behaviors that are coherent. Charting the topology of a behavior space is accomplished by constructing a tripartite behavior index, imposing a prerequisite structure on the explanatory behaviors, and creating annotations that indicate visual continuities between behaviors.

Tripartite Behavior Index. Just as the indexing of stories and advice is critical for case-based learning environments (Edelson 1993), indexing behaviors is of paramount importance for animated pedagogical agents. To enable rapid access to appropriate behaviors so they can be efficiently sequenced at runtime, behaviors are indexed ontologically, intentionally, and rhetorically. First, an *ontological* index is imposed on explanatory behaviors. Each behavior is labeled with the structure and function of the aspects of the primary pedagogical object that the agent discusses in that segment. For example, explanatory segments in the DESIGN-A-PLANT agent's behavior space are labeled by (1) the type of botanical structures discussed, e.g., anatomical structures such as roots, stems, and leaves, and by (2) the physiological functions they perform, e.g., photosynthesis. Second, an *intentional* index is imposed on advisory behaviors. Given a problem-solving goal, this structure enables the sequencing engine to identify the advisory behaviors that help the student achieve the goal. For example, one of the DESIGN-A-PLANT agent's behaviors indicates that it should be presented to a student who is experiencing difficulty with a "low water table" environment. Finally, a *rhetorical* index is imposed on audio-primary segments. This indicates the rhetorical role played by each clip, e.g., introductory remark or interjection.

Prerequisite Structure. The primary goal of an animated pedagogical agent is to guide students through a complex subject by clearly explaining difficult concepts and offering context-sensitive problem-solving advice. To assist the sequencing engine in making decisions about the selection of behaviors, we impose a prerequisite structure on the explanatory behaviors. Prerequisite relations impose a partial order on explanatory behaviors: a behavior can be performed only if all its (immediate and indirect) prerequisite behaviors have been performed. Prerequisites should be imposed conservatively; by imposing only those relations that are clearly mandated by the domain, greater flexibility is provided to the sequencing engine because the number of behaviors it may select at any given time will be greater.

Visual Continuity Annotations. Because visual bookending is not always possible, the behavior space should include knowledge about the visual continuities between animated segments in the prerequisite structure. Visual attributes including the shot's zoom level and the agent's frame position are represented as normalized numerical variables and are assigned weights based on priority. The visual continuity $v_{x,y}$ between behaviors B_x and B_y is defined as the distance in n-dimensional attribute space between the final frame of B_x and the initial frame of B_y:

$$v_{x,y} = \sqrt{w_1(x_1 - y_1)^2 + w_2(x_2 - y_2)^2 + \ldots w_n(x_n - y_n)^2}$$

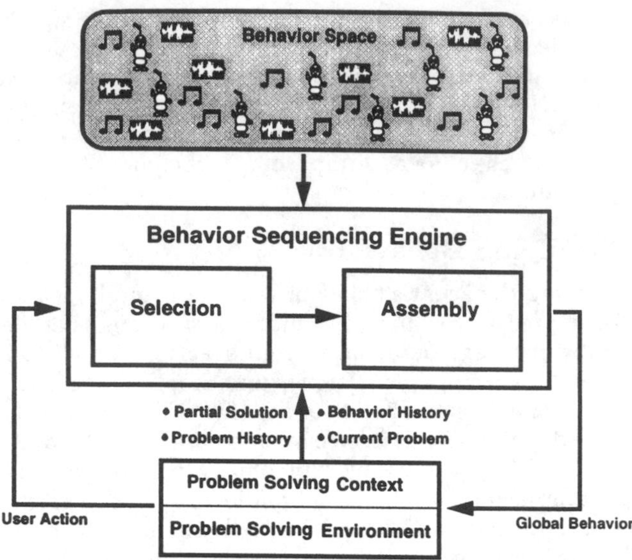

Figure 3: The behavior sequencing engine

where w_i is the prioritized weight of the ith visual attribute. The sequencing engine uses the continuity annotations to maximize visual continuity among sequenced animated segments.

Sequencing Agents' Behaviors

To achieve agent persistence, agent immersion, and pedagogical object persistence, the agent remains on-screen, visually immersed in the learning environment, and on or near the primary pedagogical object at all times. The moment a student requests assistance, constructs an incorrect (complete or partial) solution, or fails to take action for an extended period of time, the sequencing engine (Figure 3) is called into play to create the agent's next behavior. By exploiting the behavior space's coherence structure and noting different aspects of the current problem-solving context, the sequencing engine navigates through the space to weave the local behaviors into global behaviors. It employs the following algorithm to select and assemble local behaviors in real time:

1. **Compute n, the number of explanatory behaviors to exhibit.** This quantity is computed by $\lfloor b/f \rfloor$. The quantity b is the number of explanatory behaviors that have not yet been exhibited, The function f, which is determined from empirical data, is the predicted number of future problem-solving situations in which explanatory behaviors can be exhibited. The floor is taken for non-integer results to be conservative—representing the number of Conceptual Explanatory Animated Segments that should be exhibited. Employing n has the effect of evenly distributing these explanations over the course of the learning session.

2. **Select all explanatory behaviors E^P that are pedagogically viable.** First, apply the ontological index structure to index into behavior space and identify all Conceptual Explanatory Animated Segments that are currently relevant. By noting the current structures, functions, and problem-solving features that are active in the current problem, the sequencing engine can identify the animations that are pedagogically appropriate. Second, determine candidate behaviors whose prerequisite behaviors have already been exhibited by using the prerequisite structure to perform a topological sort of behaviors in the global behavior history.
3. **Select explanatory behaviors $E^{P,V}$ that are both pedagogically and visually viable.** Of the candidates in E^P chosen in Step 2, select a subset $E^{P,V}$ such that (a) the sum of the continuity annotations along the best path in $E^{P,V}$ is minimized, and (b) $| E^{P,V} |$ is as close as possible to n without exceeding it.[1]
4. **Select problem-solving advisory behaviors A that are pedagogically appropriate.** Use the intentional and rhetorical indices to identify advisory behaviors that are germane to the topic of the current problem. A may include both animated and audio-primary behaviors.
5. **Select the media with which to exhibit a subset A' of the behaviors in A.** Inspect the behavior history to determine if advisory behaviors about the current topic have been exhibited. If no prior advisory behaviors on this topic have been presented, select an animated advisory behavior on this topic. If an animated advisory behavior on this topic has been previously exhibited, select an audio-primary verbal reminder on this topic. If an animated advisory behavior on this topic has been previously exhibited but a significant amount of time has elapsed, select it for repeat viewing. If both an animated advisory behavior and a verbal reminder on this topic have been exhibited recently, select an audio-primary direct behavior in which the agent will explicitly tell the student what problem-solving action to take.
6. **Select animated and verbal transitions T.** Use the indices and prerequisite structure to identify transition behaviors for $E^{P,V}$ and A'.
7. **Assemble the final global behavior.** Impose the following temporal ordering on the selected behaviors: (a) verbal transitions in T to introduce the upcoming explanations; (b) animated explanatory behaviors in $E^{P,V}$ ordered by prerequisite structure; (c) animated advisory behaviors in A'; and (d) audio-primary reminders and direct advisory behaviors in A'.

[1]Note that Steps (2) and (3) must be interleaved when selecting multiple behaviors because prerequisites can be met dynamically in the process of exhibiting a global behavior.

The resulting global behavior is presented onscreen and the sequencing engine sleeps until the next invocation. While it is sleeping, it pseudo-randomly schedules audio-primary interjections. In addition, the agent's actions are complemented at all times by a continuous soundtrack whose voicing and tempo are dynamically updated to reflect changes in problem-solving contexts. Introductory measures are played as problems are introduced, and additional voicing is added as partial solutions are successfully constructed. The net effect of the sequencing engine's activities is students' perception that a life-like character is carefully observing their problem-solving activities and moving in and out of the primary pedagogical object to provide advice just when it is needed.

An Implemented Animated Agent

The coherence-based approach to dynamic sequencing has been implemented in Herman the Bug, an animated pedagogical agent for DESIGN-A-PLANT, which is a learning environment being developed in our laboratory to teach middle school students about botanical anatomy and physiology.[2] Herman the Bug is a talkative, quirky, somewhat churlish insect with a propensity to fly about the screen and dive into the plant's structures as it provides students with problem-solving advice. His behavior space consists of 30 animated segments[3] (twenty are in the 20—30 second range and ten are in the 1–2 minute range), 160 audio clips, several songs, and a large library of runtime-mixable, soundtrack elements. Throughout the learning session, he remains onscreen, standing on the plant assembly device when he is inactive (Figure 2) and diving into the plant as he delivers advice visually. In the process of explaining concepts, he performs a broad range of activities including walking, flying, shrinking, expanding, swimming, fishing, bungee jumping, teleporting, and acrobatics. All of his behaviors are sequenced in real time on a Power Macintosh 9500/132.

To illustrate the behavior of the sequencing engine that composes Herman the Bug's actions, consider the following situation in a DESIGN-A-PLANT learning session. A student has seen Herman the Bug present

[2]DESIGN-A-PLANT is a *design-centered* learning environment that embodies a strong constructivist approach to learning. Students use it to graphically assemble customized 3D plants from a library of plant anatomical structures. Their goal in each design episode is to create a plant that will survive under a specific set of environmental conditions. At the implementational level, DESIGN-A-PLANT is a constraint-based system, where the constraints imposed by the plant's environment must be satisfied by the anatomical structures selected by the student.

[3]Its animations were designed, modeled, and rendered on SGIs and Macintoshes by twelve graphic artists and animators.

an overview of basic anatomy, watched him explain external anatomy in a prior problem-solving episode, and very quickly (relative to her peers using the system) reached the third level of problem complexity. As she assembles a plant that will thrive in the current environment, she selects a type of leaf that violates the environmental constraints. This action causes the problem-solving system to invoke the behavior sequencing engine, which has access to representations of: the student's partial (and incorrect) solution; the constraints and environmental settings in the current problem; a history of previous behaviors Herman the Bug has exhibited; and a history of the student's previous problem-solving episodes.

First, the number of explanatory behaviors to exhibit is computed. Because the student reached the third complexity level quickly, and there are four total levels, the sequencing engine predicts that there will be only two opportunities (including the current one) for presenting explanations. Of the four explanatory behaviors not yet seen, it will show two of them. By using the ontological index structure to find the relevant candidate behaviors and then using the behavior history and the prerequisite structure of the behavior space to perform a topological sort, three explanatory behaviors are selected which are pedagogically viable. Of these three candidate behaviors, two are chosen for which the the sum of the continuity annotations along the best path is minimized. This produces explanatory behaviors of internal anatomy and transpiration. Next, the sequencing engine exploits the the intentional and rhetorical indices to identify advisory behaviors that are germane to the structure of interest (leaves) and the environmental attributes of interest (low rain and high temperature). The media with which to exhibit the behaviors is then selected. The sequencing engine notes that the student has been given no prior principle-based advice about leaves, so a behavior depicting Herman the Bug giving a principle-based explanations of leaves—and which she will then have the opportunity to operationalize—is selected. (Alternatively, if the student had already seen the principle-based explanations of leaves, an audio-primary reminder would have been selected instead.) The principle-based explanations are introduced by an audio-primary transition in which Herman the Bug explains that, "The low rain and high temperature make some leaves unsuitable for this environment. Here's why ..." Finally, the behavior sequencing engine orders the selected behaviors as follows: the animated segment of Herman the Bug explaining internal anatomy; the animated segment of Herman explaining transpiration; the verbal transition; the animated advisory segment about leaves in low-rain environments; and the animated advisory segment about leaves in high-temperature environments.

Because of recency effects and the fact that the advisory explanations were communicated last, the student can more easily apply the advice to refine her plant design. She chooses an alternate type of leaf and continues to puzzle out the remaining structures.

Evaluation

To gauge the effectiveness of the coherence-based approach to dynamically sequencing the behaviors of animated pedagogical agents, formative observational studies were conducted with thirteen middle school students using the DESIGN-A-PLANT learning environment and its accompanying agent, Herman the Bug. Each student interacted with the learning environment for forty-five minutes to one hour. As the students designed plants for a variety of environmental conditions, the agent introduced problems, explained concepts in botanical anatomy and physiology, provided problem-solving advice, and interjected congratulatory and off-the-cuff remarks. These studies suggest that animated pedagogical agents whose behaviors are selected and assembled with the sequencing engine can effectively guide students through a complex subject in a manner that exhibits both pedagogical and visual coherence.

Herman was unanimously well received. His pedagogical and visual coherence, together with its immersive property—the fact that it inhabits a 3D environment and interacts with 3D plant models to explain structural and functional concepts—produced strikingly life-like behaviors. Herman's visual behaviors seemed to so flow well that no student commented or displayed surprise during transitions. Because of book-ending, many of Herman's transitions were technically flawless. Herman's verbal reminders enabled students to continue with their problem solving uninterrupted, and during the study students made frequent (and unprompted) positive comments about Herman's physical actions and remarks. The variety of his behaviors maintained their interest throughout the session, and every student, without exception, commented positively about the continuously updated score. Perhaps not surprisingly—considering its seventh grade audience—Herman's quirky asides were well received.

The studies also revealed three problems with the initial algorithm. Each of these problems has been addressed in the algorithm presented in this paper, as well as in the current implementation. First, in the original version, the agent provided its advice *before* giving the conceptual explanations. Students tended to forget this advice because, we hypothesize, there were intervening conceptual explanations. The sequencing engine's assembly mechanism was therefore modified to present advisory behaviors at the end of global behaviors. Second, students were clearly irritated by the repetition of explanatory behaviors. We therefore modified the selection mechanism to ensure that explanations would be repeated only if sufficient time had elapsed. Third, the initial version permitted only isolated explanatory (non-advisory) behaviors to be exhibited. This ran the risk of limiting explanatory coverage, so the methods for sequencing multiple explanatory behaviors were developed. This in turn created a secondary problem: students who progressed quickly through the problem-solving episodes might be bombarded with a formidable number of explanations near the end of the learning session. This concern prompted the addition of the mechanism for selecting the number of explanatory behaviors based on the predicted number of opportunities during the remainder of the learning session.

Conclusion

Animated pedagogical agents can combine adaptive explanatory behaviors with great visual appeal. We have proposed an approach to dynamically sequencing these agents' behaviors that exploits (1) a behavior space containing animated and verbal behaviors, and (2) a coherence structure consisting of a tripartite behavior index of ontological, intentional, and rhetorical indices, a prerequisite structure, and continuity annotations that estimate the degree of visual continuity between pairs of behaviors. By navigating the behavior space and attending to the coherence structure, a behavior sequencing engine selects and assembles behaviors that exhibit both pedagogical and visual coherence. This coherence-based approach to behavior sequencing has been implemented in an agent that operates in real time to dynamically sequence behaviors in response to rapidly changing problem-solving contexts. It has been tested in a learning environment with middle school children, and the results are encouraging.

This work represents a promising first step toward creating animated pedagogical agents with a large repertoire of communicative behaviors. Perhaps the greatest challenge lies in increasing agents' flexibility, and an effective technique for accomplishing this is to reduce the granularity of their behaviors. We will be investigating fine-grained behavior sequencing mechanisms for animated pedagogical agents in our future research.

Acknowledgements

Thanks to: the animation team which was lead by Patrick FitzGerald; the students in the Intelligent Multimedia Communication, Multimedia Interface Design, and Knowledge-Based Multimedia Learning Environments seminars; Chris Tomasson and her seventh grade class at Martin Middle School for participating in the evaluation; and Patrick FitzGerald and Charles Callaway for comments on an earlier draft of this paper.

References

André, E.; Finkler, W.; Graph, W.; Rist, T.; Schauder, A.; and Wahlster, W. 1993. WIP: The automatic synthesis of multi-modal presentations. In Maybury, M. T., ed., *Intelligent Multimedia Interfaces*. AAAI Press. chapter 3.

Bates, J. 1994. The role of emotion in believable agents. *Communications of the ACM* 37(7):122–125.

Blumberg, B., and Galyean, T. 1995. Multi-level direction of autonomous creatures for real-time virtual environments. In *Computer Graphics Proceedings*, 47–54.

Edelson, D. C. 1993. *Learning from Stories: Indexing and Reminding in a Socratic Case-Based Teaching System for Elementary School Biology.* Ph.D. Dissertation, Northwestern Univeristy.

Feiner, S. K., and McKeown, K. R. 1990. Coordinating text and graphics in explanation generation. In *Proceedings of the Eighth National Conference on Artificial Intelligence*, 442–449.

Hollan, J. D.; Hutchins, E. L.; and Weitzman, L. M. 1987. STEAMER: An interactive, inspectable, simulation-based training system. In Kearsley, G., ed., *Artificial Intelligence and Instruction: Applications and Methods.* Reading, MA: Addison-Wesley. 113–134.

Jones, C. 1989. *Chuck Amuck: The Life and Times of an Animated Cartoonist.* New York: Avon.

Lasseter, J. 1987. Principles of traditional animation applied to 3D computer animation. In *Proceedings of SIGRAPH '87*, 35–44.

Lenburg, J. 1993. *The Great Cartoon Directors.* New York: Da Capo Press.

Lesgold, A.; Lajoie, S.; Bunzo, M.; and Eggan, G. 1992. SHERLOCK: A coached practice environment for an electronics trouble-shooting job. In Larkin, J. H., and Chabay, R. W., eds., *Computer-Assisted Instruction and Intelligent Tutoring Systems: Shared Goals and Complementary Approaches.* Hillsdale, NJ: Lawrence Erlbaum. 201–238.

Lester, J.; Stone, B.; O'Leary, M.; and Stevenson, R. 1996. Focusing problem solving in design-centered learning environments. In *Proceedings of the Third International Conference on Intelligent Tutoring Systems.*

Mark, M. A., and Greer, J. E. 1995. The VCR tutor: Effective instruction for device operation. *Journal of the Learning Sciences* 4(2):209–246.

Maybury, M. T. 1991. Planning multimedia explanations using communicative acts. In *Proceedings of the Ninth National Conference on Artificial Intelligence*, 61–66.

Mittal, V.; Roth, S.; Moore, J. D.; Mattis, J.; and Carenini, G. 1995. Generating explanatory captions for information graphics. In *Proceedings of the International Joint Conference on Artificial Intelligence.*

Monaco, J. 1981. *How To Read a Film.* New York: Oxford University Press.

Noake, R. 1988. *Animation Techniques.* London: Chartwell.

Roth, S. F.; Mattis, J.; and Mesnard, X. 1991. Graphics and natural language as components of automatic explanation. In Sullivan, J. W., and Tyler, S. W., eds., *Intelligent User Interfaces.* New York: Addison-Wesley. 207–239.

Suchman, L. 1987. *Plans and Situated Actions: The Problem of Human Machine Communication.* Cambridge University Press.

Tu, X., and Terzopoulos, D. 1994. Artificial fishes: Physics, locomotion, perception, and behavior. In *Computer Graphics Proceedings*, 43–50.

Multiagent Coordination in Tightly Coupled Task Scheduling

Jyi-Shane Liu
Department of Computer Science
National Cheng Chi University
Taipei, TAIWAN
E-mail: jsliu@cs.nccu.edu.tw

Katia P. Sycara
The Robotics Institute
Carnegie Mellon University
Pittsburgh, PA 15213, U.S.A.
E-mail: katia@cs.cmu.edu

Abstract

We consider an environment where agents' tasks are tightly coupled and require real-time scheduling and execution. In order to complete their tasks, agents need to coordinate their actions both constantly and extensively. We present an approach that consists of a standard operating procedure and a look-ahead coordination. The standard operating procedure regulates task coupling and minimizes communication. The look-ahead coordination increases agents' global visibility and provides indicative information for decision adjustment. The goal of our approach is to prune decision myopia while maintaining system responsiveness in real-time, dynamic environments. Experimental results in job shop scheduling problems show that (1) the look-ahead coordination significantly enhances the performance of the standard operating procedure in solution quality, (2) the approach is capable of producing solutions of very high quality in a real-time environment.

Introduction

Most research on multiagent systems has considered loosely coupled agents (Huhns 1987) (Bond & Gasser 1988) (Gasser & Huhns 1989) that coordinate their actions for mutual benefit. In most of these environments, agent interaction occurs only when one agent has data, facts, views, and solutions that are of interest to other agents (Durfee & Lesser 1991), or when agents need to resolve their conflicts (Sycara 1988) (Conry, Meyer, & Lesser 1988), etc. In other words, coordination activity, although essential, does not constitute a substantial part of an agent's effort to achieve its goal. In this paper, we consider an environment where agents' tasks are tightly coupled in the sense that (1) there are only enabling relationships among subtasks and each task usually consists of more than two subtasks, thus creating cascading effects; (2) subtasks are distributed among agents and enabling relationships among agents are of multi-directions, e.g., for task$_1$, A $\rightarrow$ B $\rightarrow$ C $\rightarrow$ D ; for task$_2$, B $\rightarrow$ D $\rightarrow$ C $\rightarrow$ A, etc., where A, B, C, D are agents, and $\rightarrow$ represents an enabling relationship, thus creating complex cause-effect relationships among agents; (3) the objective function is related to task completion time only and can not be broken down into "quality" function of subtasks, in other words, agents have no local utility function to guide their decisions. Therefore, agents need to coordinate their actions constantly and extensively in order to both complete their tasks and improve system performance. The multiagent system also needs to operate in real time that involves both scheduling and task execution. The characteristics of the environment require substantial coordination among agents, but exclude time-consuming, elaborate coordination activities.

We present an approach that consists of two parts, e.g., a standard operating procedure and a look-ahead coordination. The standard operating procedure, adopted from a generic work-flow model, is predefined according to agents' relationships. It regulates task coupling, minimizes communication, and ensures smooth real-time task execution without violating technological constraints of a task. We developed a look-ahead coordination that operates on top of the standard operating procedure and enhances its performance by increasing agents' visibility. The approach has three features. First, it is prearranged. Agents abide by an operating procedure and adopt predetermined cues/hints for adjusting their actions. This allows agents to disentangle their task coupling and coordinate their actions in real time. Second, it is self-contained. Agents consult information from others to decide their actions. Information is exchanged by message sending. Agents do not perform query. Third, it is responsive. Agents have a "perceive-and-act" type of coordination behavior. This enables the integration of task scheduling and execution in real-time multiagent systems.

The task model we consider can be formulated as distributed constraint optimization (DCOP). A constraint satisfaction problem (CSP) (Mackworth 1987) involves a set of *variables* $X = \{x_1, x_2, \ldots, x_m\}$, each having a corresponding set of *domain values* $V = \{v_1, v_2, \ldots, v_m\}$, and a set of *constraints* $C = \{c_1, c_2, \ldots, c_n\}$ specifying which values of the variables are compatible with each other. A solution to a CSP is an assignment of values (an instantiation) to all variables, such that all constraints are satisfied. Recent work in DAI has considered the *distributed* CSPs (DCSPs) (Huhns & Bridgeland 1991) (Sycara et al. 1991) (Yokoo et al. 1992) (Liu & Sycara 1995a) in which variables of a CSP are distributed among agents. Each agent has a subset of variables and coordinates with other agents in instantiating its variables so that a global solution can be found. DCOP is an extension of DCSP in which a subset of the constraints are relaxed to achieve optimization of a given objective function (Liu & Sycara 1995b).

In our task model, each subtask is a variable that needs to be instantiated with an execution start time. Variables are distributed among a set of agents to be instantiated in real time. The problem constraints include precedence relations between subtasks and agents' processing capacity. An objective function measures the quality of task schedule produced by the agents. Since the problem is solved in real time, the goal is not to find the optimal solution but a solution as best as possible. (Yokoo et al. 1992) describes work on distributed constraint satisfaction problems (DCSPs). The work focused on complete algorithms for solving DCSPs and was not concerned with solution optimization and time restriction. (Decker & Lesser 1995) presented a family of coordination algorithms for distributed real-time schedulers. They considered a task environment where task interrelationships can be explicitly and quantitatively represented as functions that describe the effect of agents' decisions on performance. In our task model, such a function is impossible to either define beforehand or estimate on-line with any precision.

Our work can also be viewed as addressing the problem of distributed agenda ordering, e.g., at any given time, an agent might have multiple tasks waiting to be processed; how does the agent coordinate with other agents to decide its local agenda, when its decision affects other agents and, ultimately, the performance of the group of agents? This is one of the most commonly encountered problem in DAI research and has been widely studied in many application domains, such as Distributed Vehicle Monitoring Testbed (DVMT) (Lesser & Corkill 1983). The abstract solution, perhaps a direct result from human experiences, has been using sophisticated local control coupled with exchange of meta-level information (as in the work of Partial Global Planning (PGP) (Durfee & Lesser 1991)). In our approach, agents are coordinated by local prioritizing strategies and non-local look-ahead information. The unique contributions of our work are in presenting a specific coordination solution to a tightly coupled task model and in providing a clear description of local decision making and meta-level information that is applicable in a significant class of scheduling problems.

In this paper, we present initial experimental results to test the utility of the approach and investigate its performance factors. The study was conducted in the domain of real-time job shop schedule optimization. Experimental results show that the approach is capable of producing solutions of very high quality in a real-time environment. The performance factors include (1) accuracy of agents' forecasts, (2) complexity of agents' interaction, and (3) availability of indicative information.

Job Shop Schedule Optimization

A job shop is a manufacturing production environment where a set of m jobs (or tasks) $J = \{J_1, ..., J_m\}$ have to be performed on a set of n machines (or resources) $R= \{R_1, ..., R_n\}$. Each job J_i is composed of a set of sequential operations (or subtasks) opr_{ij}, $i = 1, ..., m, j = 1, ..., m(i)$, $m(i) \leq n$, where i is the index of the job, and j is the index of the step in the overall job. Each operation opr_{ij} has a deterministic *processing time* p_{ij} and has been pre-assigned a unique resource that may process the operation. Jobs can have very different numbers of operations and sequences of using resources. The job shop scheduling problem involves synchronization of the completion of m jobs J on n resources (machines) R and is one of the most difficult NP-complete combinatorial optimization problems (French 1982). The problem (hard) constraints of job shop scheduling include (1) *operation temporal precedence* constraints, i.e., an operation must be finished before the next operation in the job can be started, (2) *release date* constraints, i.e., the first operation of a job J_i can begin only after the release date rd_i of the job, and (3) *resource capacity* constraints, i.e., resources have only unit processing capacity. A solution of the job shop scheduling problem is a feasible schedule, which assigns a start time st_{ij} and an end time et_{ij} to each operation opr_{ij} that satisfies all problem constraints.

Given a job shop scheduling problem, the umber of feasible solutions can be enormous. For example, for a problem with m jobs of n operations on n resources, each resource has $m!$ possible processing sequences, and the total number of possible schedules is $(m!)^n$ since all precedence constraints between operations can be satisfied by right shifting operations toward the end of time. Organizations are usually interested in optimizing a schedule according to objective functions that reflect the economic goals. In his paper, we consider a commonly used objective function, called weighted tardiness, where each job J_i is given a due date dd_i and a weight w_i that represents the importance of the job. Weighted tardiness (WT) of a schedule is defined by $WT = \sum_{i=1}^{m} w_i \times max\ [0, (C_i - dd_i)]$, where w_i is the weight of individual job J_i and C_i is the completion time of J_i. The goal is to produce a schedule with minimized weighted tardiness.

On-line job shop scheduling is a typical multiagent task in a tightly coupled, real-time environment. We *assign each resource to an agent* that is responsible for making decision and monitoring usage of the resource. Agents are tightly coupled with each other because of the precedence constraints between operations and the fact that they can process only one operation at a time.

A Standard Operating Procedure - Dispatch Scheduling

Since a job consists of a set of operations that has to be performed in sequential order by different agents, it is convenient to follow a work-flow model where a job enters the shop, visits different agents to have its corresponding operations performed, and then leaves the shop. A job's *routing* is the sequential set of agents that the job visits before its completion. The *arrival time* of a job at an agent is the time at which the job leaves the previous agent in its routing, and is equivalent to the *ready time* of the operation to be performed by the agent.

Dispatch scheduling is a way of generating schedules by either simulating or actualizing the process of jobs being performed by the agents. Each agent has a buffer where arriving jobs (or equivalently, the operations ready to be processed) can wait until they are processed. Jobs are released to the buffers of the first agents in their routings after their release dates. After a job is being processed by an agent, it travels to the buffer of the next agent in the routing of the job. At any point in time, an agent is in one of four states: (1) the agent is executing an operation, (2) the agent has just finished executing an operation, and there are operations ready for execution, (3) the agent is not executing an operation, and there are operations that have just become ready for execution, (4) the agent is not executing an operation, and there is no operation ready for execution. In both states (2) and (3), an agent selects an operation from its buffer to execute.

For implementation, it is convenient to view that each operation has been pre-allocated to the buffer of its designated agents. The first operation of a job is only eligible to be selected for processing after the release date of the job. An operation that is not the first operation of a job is eligible to be selected only after its immediate preceding operation has finished its processing. We give an algorithmic description of dispatch scheduling as follows:

```
T = – 1 ;
For each agent Aᵢ ;
  Oᵢᵘ = the set of unprocessed operations ;
  Oᵢᵉ = the set of eligible operations ;
while (∃Oᵢᵘ ≠ ∅ ) do
  T = T + 1 ;
  For each agent Aᵢ ;
  if Aᵢ is not executing an operation
    Oᵢᵉ = updated from Oᵢᵘ ᵢ;
    if (Oᵢᵉ ≠ ∅)
        opr = selected operation from Oᵢᵉ;
        set start time of opr to T ;
        remove opr from Oᵢᵘ and Oᵢᵉ;
    fi;
  fi;
od.
```

Dispatch scheduling is simple, robust, and has been used for years as a standard operating procedure in human organizations and production/service facilities. Mostly, an agent selects an operation based on a priority rule that assigns priority indices to operations waiting to be processed. For due-date-based objectives (e.g., weighted tardiness), priority rules calculate priority index of an operation using due date of the job in various ways, e.g., earliest due date, minimum slack time, etc.

From the point of view of multiagent systems, dispatch scheduling is a robust coordination mechanism at the *procedural* level. It ensures technological constraints are satisfied, e.g., each task is completed properly by agents' sequential execution of its constituted operations. Agents communicate by reading/writing information associated with operations, e.g., operation status, job due dates, etc. The system can operate in dynamic, real-time environments. However, system performance in terms of solution quality suffers from agents' myopic decisions based on only local and current conditions (characteristics of operations currently competing for execution). Our research hypothesis was that agent coordination that broadens agents' views of problem solving conditions can obtain higher quality solutions without sacrificing computational efficiency.

A Look-ahead Coordination - Coordinated Forecasts

We developed a look-ahead coordination mechanism, called coordinated forecasts (COFCAST), that operates on top of dispatch scheduling to improve its performance. COFCAST increases agents' visibility by incorporating useful indicative information (cues) based on global and future conditions. At each decision point, agents make a decision as well as survey local situations by predicting their future decisions. These forecasts are coordinated among agents and predefined indicative information is extracted. Agents then utilize the indicative information that embeds downstream and global conditions to make better decisions.

In tardiness related objectives, the subject of coordination is the operation sequencing of agents so as to reduce the tardiness cost of the final schedule. We observe that a job's tardiness cost depends on the end time of its last operation only. In other words, no matter whether a job's upstream operations are processed earlier or just in time for the last operation to end at the same time, they would have the same tardiness cost. While a job is being processed by an agent, other jobs waiting to be processed by the same agent are delayed because of agents' unit capacity. Therefore, a good schedule is a schedule in which jobs are processed only when necessary to ensure the prompt completion of their last operations. This means that if we can reduce unnecessary earliness of upstream

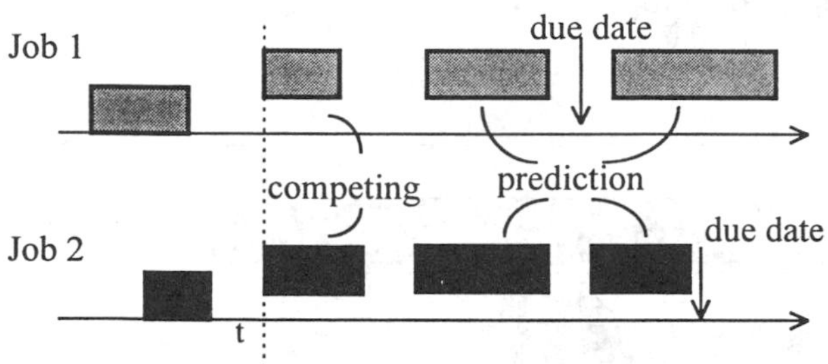

Figure 1: Example of Relaxed Urgency

operations, the resulting schedule will have reduced tardiness.

Based on this observation, we developed the innovative notion of *relaxed urgency* (RU), where jobs' due dates used in priority rules are replaced by *relaxed due dates* that are dynamically adjusted to take downstream and global processing conditions into account. In particular, if a job is predicted to be tardy in the downstream processing, then the first unprocessed operation in the job is not regarded as urgent as it was to meet the job's original due date. Its urgency is relaxed accordingly by the tardiness of the downstream operations. For example, in Figure 1, at time t, the second operations of J_1 and J_2 are competing for the same resource. Based on the prediction of both jobs' downstream processing, J_2 should have a higher priority to use the resource than J_1. Given the complex interaction among agents' operation sequencing in a general job shop, the approach hinges on the ability to coordinate different forecasts from agents and extract useful information for current decisions.

In COFCAST-RU, agents forecast their future processing by assigning *predicted start times* and *predicted end times* to a partial set of the unprocessed operations. To coordinate agents' forecasts, we assign a *predicted ready time* to each operation, which is dynamically adjusted during the scheduling process. Initially, an operation's predicted ready time is set to its earliest start time $est_{ij} = rd_i + \sum_{k=1}^{j-1} p_{ik}$, where p_{ik} is the processing time of an operation opr_{ik}. We consider two actions of forecast coordination. First, an agent forecasts future processing only on operations that are "in view", i.e., its predicted ready time is less than or equal to the end time of the selected operation. This reduces the likelihood of making incorrect forecast by excluding operations that are not ready for processing in near future. Second, operations' predicted ready times are dynamically adjusted according to the predicted start times of their upstream operations. Specifically, if the predicted end time of an operation opr_{ij} is later than the predicted start time of $opr_{i(j+1)}$, then the predicted ready time of $opr_{i(j+1)}$ is set to the predicted end time of opr_{ij}. This adjustment of predicted ready times accounts for agents' processing interaction and increases forecast credibility.

An agent's forecast is done after an operation has been selected for processing. According to the priority rule, an agent sequences the set of unprocessed operations that are in view and assigns predicted start times and predicted end times to the set of operations. Then, jobs' relaxed due dates are adjusted by the agent according to the prediction on the set of operations. For a job J_i with the first unprocessed operation opr_{ij}, the *relaxed due date* dd_i^r is set by, $dd_i^r = max[dd_i, max_{q=j+1}^{m(i)} (pet_{iq} + \sum_{r=q+1}^{m(i)} p_{ir})]$, where pet_{iq} is the predicted end time of an operation opr_{iq}. In other words, relaxed due date dd_i^r of a job J_i is adjusted by its downstream operation with the greatest predicted tardiness. If none of the downstream operations is predicted to be tardy, dd_i^r is set by its original job due date dd_i. Note that the notion of relaxed urgency is realized by dynamically adjusting jobs' relaxed due dates according to downstream processing forecasts.

In summary, at each point of scheduling an operation, an agent performs four actions: (1) select an operation based on a priority rule using relaxed due dates, and assign its start time and end time, (2) based on a priority rule, assign predicted start times and predicted end times of a partial set of unprocessed operations that are in view, (3) adjust jobs' relaxed due dates based on the prediction, and (4) coordinate future forecasts by adjusting operations' predicted ready times. We describe the algorithmic procedure as follows, where prt_{ij} is the predicted ready time of an operation, pst_{ij} is the predicted start time, pet_{ij} is the predicted end time, and est_{ij} is the earliest start time.

(Initialization)
  For $i = 1, \ldots, m, j = 1, \ldots, m_i$;
    $prt_{ij} = est_{ij}$;
while (an agent A_k becomes idle at time t);
(Schedule an operation)
  O_k^e = the set of operations eligible for scheduling ;
  opr_{ij} = selected operation from O_k^e, using relaxed due dates ;
  $st_{ij} = t$;
  $et_{ij} = t + p_{ij}$;
(Forecast future processing)
  O_k^u = the set of unprocessed operations ;
  O_k^v = the set of operations in view (updated from O_k^u);
    $(\forall\ opr_{pq} \in O_k^v, prt_{pq} \leq et_{ij})$
  S_k^v = sequence of O_k^v by priority rule;
  assign pst_{pq} and pet_{pq} for opr_{pq} in S_k^v according to the sequence beginning at et_{ij};
(Update relaxed due date)
  J_s = the set of jobs of operations in S_k^v;
  For each job J_p in J_s;
    $dd_p^r = max\ [\ dd_p, max_q^{m(p)} (pet_{pq} + \sum_{g=q+1}^{m(p)} p_{pg})\ ]$;
(Coordinate future forecast)

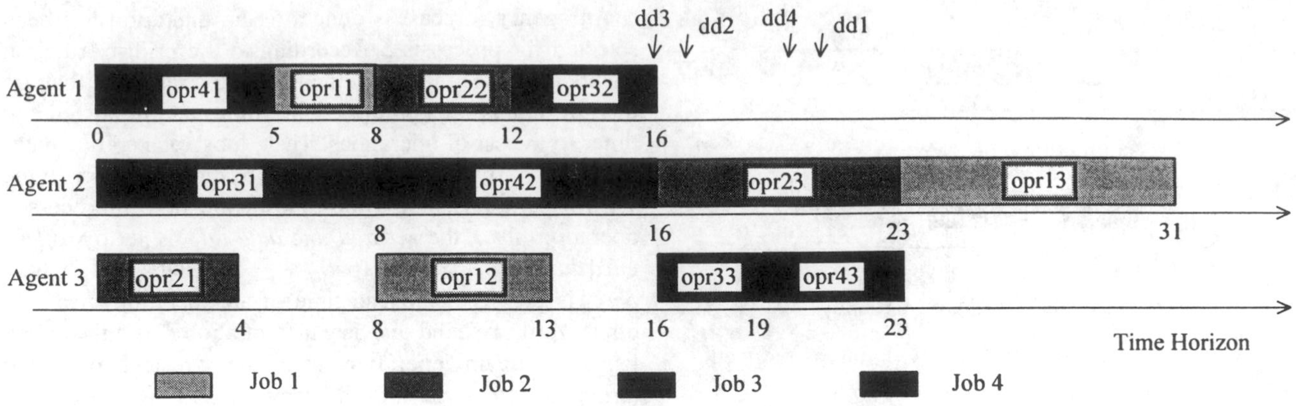

Figure 2: Example of dispatch scheduling

```
For each job Jp in Js ;
    oprpq = the first operation remaining to be
        processed ;
    For g = q + 1 to m(p);
        if (pstpg has not been set);
            continue on next job in Js ;
        fi;
        if (pstpg < petp(g-1));
            pstpg = petp(g-1);
        fi;
od.
```

An Example

We briefly illustrate the effect of coordinated forecasts with a simple example schedule shown in Figure 2. The problem has four jobs that need to be performed by three agents. The schedule was generated by dispatch scheduling with a simple due-date-based heuristic, e.g., minimum slack time $s_{ij} = dd_i - \sum_{k=j}^{m_i} p_{ij} - t$. Due dates of J_1 (dd_1), J_2 (dd_2), J_3 (dd_3), and J_4 (dd_4), are 21, 17, 16, and 20, respectively. At $t = 0$, A_1 selects opr_{41} because it has less slack time ($s_{41} = 20 - (5 + 8 + 4) - 0 = 3$) than opr_{11} ($s_{11} = 21 - (3 + 5 + 8) - 0 = 5$). Both A_2 and A_3 schedule opr_{31} and opr_{21}, respectively, because they are the only ready operations. At $t = 5$, both opr_{11} and opr_{22} are ready for A_1. Since $s_{11} = 21 - (3 + 5 + 8) - 5 = 0$ and $s_{22} = 17 - (4 + 7) - 5 = 1$, A_2 selects opr_{11}. The process continues until all operations are performed by the agents. The total tardiness cost of the schedule is (31 – 21) + (23 – 17) + (19 – 16) + (23 – 20) = 22, from J_1, J_2, J_3, and J_4, respectively.

Figure 3 shows a schedule generated by the COFCAST-RU enhanced dispatch scheduling. We focus on the forecast of A_2 since it changes the schedule. After opr_{31} is scheduled, opr_{42}, opr_{23}, and opr_{13} are all in A_2 's view, e.g., $prt_{42} = est_{42} = 5$, $prt_{23} = est_{23} = 8$, $prt_{13} = est_{13} = 8$, $\leq et_{31} = 8$. A_2 predicts its future processing sequence as (opr_{42}, opr_{23}, opr_{13}) based on minimum slack time. Therefore, $pst_{42} = 8$, $pet_{42} = 16$, $pst_{23} = 16$, $pet_{23} = 23$, $pst_{13} = 23$, and $pet_{13} = 31$. With this forecast, A_2 updates relaxed due dates of J_4, J_2, and J_1, e.g., $dd_4{}^r = max$ [20, 16 + 4] = 20, $dd_2{}^r = max$ [17, 23] = 23, and $dd_1{}^r = max$ [21, 31] = 31. At $t = 5$, A_1 calculates slack times of opr_{11} and opr_{22} using relaxed due dates $dd_1{}^r$ and $dd_2{}^r$, and finds that $s_{22} = 23 - (4 + 7) - 5 = 7 < s_{11} = 31 - (3 + 5 + 8) - 5 = 10$. Therefore, opr_{22} is selected, instead of opr_{11}. Similarly, opr_{32} is scheduled before opr_{11}. The total tardiness cost of the schedule is (33 – 21) + (23 – 17) + (16 – 16) + (20 – 20) = 18, from J_1, J_2, J_3, and J_4, respectively. The example shows that, with the indicative information of relaxed due dates, A_1 adjusts its decisions to take A_2's processing conditions into account. This look-ahead coordination improves quality of the generated schedule.

Evaluation of the Approach

We hypothesized that in a tightly coupled, real-time environment, system performance can be improved by increasing agents' visibility on global conditions and extracting useful cues for agents' decision adjustment. Agents' predictions of future decisions are used and written on a shared memory so that agents can obtain a broader view of problem solving conditions. We developed relaxed due date as an useful indication of global conditions that is incorporated in agents' decision rules. Analytically, we can identify a number of factors of this look-ahead coordination: (1) the accuracy of the decision rule used in agents' decision forecasts, (2) the credibility of the relaxed due date information indicating global conditions, which is affected by the complexity of agents' interaction, (3) the availability of indicative information for decision adjustment.

In job shop scheduling, a more accurate priority rule produces better schedules. The first factor is related to the accuracy of the priority rule used in dispatching an operation since agents use the same priority rule to predict future decisions. The second and the third factors are

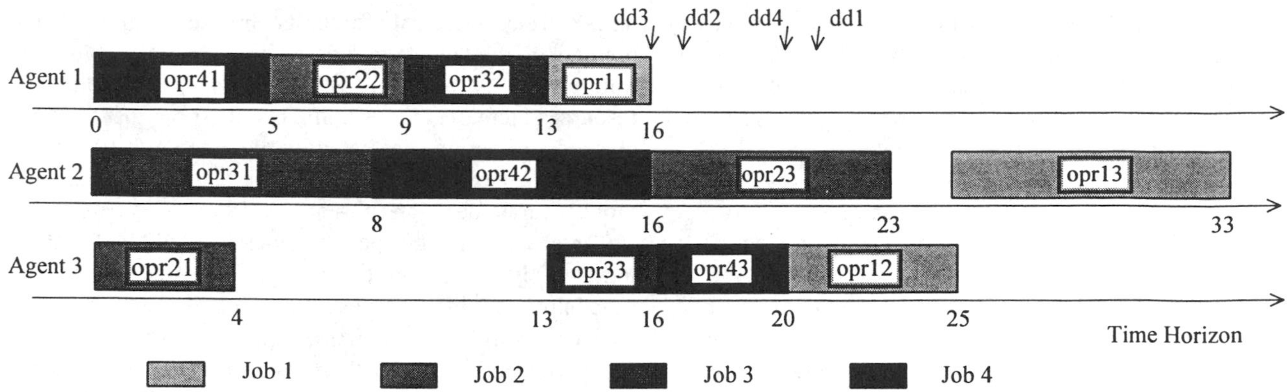

Figure 3: Example of dispatch scheduling enhanced by look-ahead coordination

related to the shop conditions. Most of the agents' interaction conditions can be measured by the number of bottleneck resources in the shop. The complexity of agents' interaction increases as the number of bottleneck resources increases. The other shop condition of concern is the due date tightness of jobs. Since jobs' due dates are relaxed only when their downstream operations are predicted to be tardy, this indicative information is less available in shops with loose due dates than in shops with tight due dates.

We conducted an empirical study to test our hypothesis and analysis of the approach. Our goals are to: (1) compare the performance of COFCAST-RU enhanced dispatch scheduling and regular dispatch scheduling, (2) examine the effect of each of the three factors we identified on system performance. The experiments were conducted on a set of problems created in (Narayan et al. 1994) that consists of a total of 270 problems. Each problem has 50 jobs of 10 different routes and 5 resources. The jobs arrive dynamically with a Poisson distribution. Each job has one to five operations, and is assigned a due date and a weight that represents its importance. The objective function is the weighted tardiness of the schedule. We consider a set of priority rules - WCOVERT, S/RPT+SPT, CR+SPT, ATC, that are commonly used in Operations Research, and their more aggressive versions - X-WCOVERT, X-SRPT/SPT, X-CR+SPT, X-ATC, that strategically insert resource idle times that can be utilized to process more important jobs. For detail of these priority rules, please refer to (Morton & Pentico 1993).

For the purpose of experimentation, we implemented the coordination technique based on a blackboard model, e.g., agents communicate by reading/writing information on a shared memory space. This implementation short-cut does not affect our study of the performance of the look-ahead coordination. Our coordination technique is realistic for the following reasons: (1) a standard operating procedure is perhaps one of the most feasible approach in such a tightly coupled, real-time environment; (2) agents exchange very simple messages (e.g., operation start times, jobs' relaxed due dates, etc.) and need no response from other agents; (3) the look-ahead coordination adds only little overhead to the standard operating procedure.

Experimental Results

We report our experimental results in performance indices. The performance index (PI) of a method x on a problem is calculated by $PI_x = 100\% \times (S_x - S_B) / (S_S - S_B)$, where S_x is the score of method x, S_B is the best score known, and S_S is the score of a ``strawman". We used the naïve First Come-First Serve (FCFS) rule as the ``strawman". Because job shop schedule optimization is NP-complete and because for many of these problems there is no optimum known, we consider as the optimal values the results from an extensive search technique, e.g., Tabu Search, reported in (Narayan et al. 1994). The performance index can be interpreted as the percentage of error of each method from the estimated optimal.

rules	dispatch	w/ COFCAST	imp.
X-WCOVERT	5.46	6.08	−11.4%
WCOVERT	6.69	6.85	−2.4%
S/RPT+SPT	7.20	6.40	+11.1%
X-S/RPT+SPT	6.02	5.04	+16.3%
CR+SPT	5.65	4.65	+17.7%
X-CR+SPT	4.20	3.23	+23.1%
ATC	4.75	3.30	+30.5%
X-ATC	3.38	1.82	+46.2%

Table 1: Performance of COFCAST-RU on dispatch scheduling

Table 1 reports the average performance on the problem set by regular dispatch scheduling and COFCAST-RU enhanced dispatch scheduling with each priority rule we considered. COFCAST-RU improves system performance with six out of eight priority rules. With X-ATC rule, COFCAST-RU improved the scheduling quality of dispatch scheduling by 46.2%, and obtained a performance index of 1.82, e.g., 1.82% from the estimated optimal. The results show that COFCAST-RU is able to improve the performance of dispatch scheduling and is quite effective with both ATC and X-ATC rules. Computationally, dispatch scheduling is very fast. For example, for a problem of 10 jobs and 5 machines, e.g., 50 operations, it took only 0.1 CPU seconds to generate a schedule. The look-ahead coordination is computationally efficient. It requires only 1.6 times the computational cost of regular dispatch scheduling in our experiment.

The results also reveal the effect of the accuracy of a priority rule. In general, COFCAST-RU improves dispatch scheduling better when the priority rule becomes more accurate, e.g., from SRPT/SPT to CR+SPT, to ATC. COFCAST-RU does not work well when COVERT rule is used because its priority index function does not differentiate jobs with large slack times, e.g., they are all assigned an index of zero. This is problematic for making forecast as it may lead to erroneous information and bad decision adjustment. In addition, for the same priority rule, the effect of COFCAST-RU was magnified by the aggressive version (X-) of the rule. Overall, the results show that the success of the look-ahead coordination is proportional to the accuracy of agents' decision rules.

Priority Rules	COFCAST-RU Improvement		
	Bot.=1	Bot.=2	Bot.=5
S/RPT+SPT	17.1%	13.5%	3.4%
X-SRPT+SPT	27.0%	17.0%	6.7%
CR+SPT	27.9%	19.8%	6.9%
X-CR+SPT	37.9%	23.6%	10.5%
ATC	37.6%	32.1%	20.8%
X-ATC	55.6%	45.8%	36.2%

Table 2: Performance improvement of COFCAST-RU by numbers of bottleneck resources

Table 2 reports the performance of COFCAST-RU in terms of improvement percentage over regular dispatch scheduling in problems with different number of bottleneck resources. COFCAST-RU's improvement percentage monotonically drops as the number of bottleneck resources increases. The reason is that when there are more than one bottleneck resource, interaction among resources becomes more complex.

While agents extract indicative information (relaxed due dates) from different forecasts by selecting the one predicting the most tardiness, the credibility of this information is reduced as the number of bottleneck resources increases. Overall, the results show that the look-ahead coordination is affected by the complexity of agents' interaction. However, the effects are less substantial when more accurate decision rules are used.

Table 3 reports the performance of COFCAST-RU in terms of improvement percentage over regular dispatch scheduling at different levels of due date tightness. In problems with loose due dates, e.g., tardy=0.5, COFCAST-RU performed less well than regular dispatch scheduling with less accurate rules. However, COFCAST-RU's improvement percentage sharply increases when due dates become tighter. This is related to the fact that the availability of indicative information depends on due date tightness. In COFCAST-RU, indicative information (e.g., relaxed due date) is available only when jobs are predicted to be tardy. Therefore, in problems with tighter due dates, COFCAST-RU performs considerably well in improving dispatch scheduling by using more indicative information. In problems with loose due dates, occasional indicative information seems to mislead agents' decisions when the decision rule is less accurate. Overall, the results show that the availability of indicative information has the most significant effect on the look-ahead coordination.

Priority Rules	COFCAST-RU Improvement		
	Tardy=0.5	Tardy=0.7	Tardy=0.9
S/RPT+SPT	-14.8%	12.6%	21.9%
X-SRPT+SPT	-10.5%	18.3%	30.6%
CR+SPT	-18.8%	17.8%	32.8%
X-CR+SPT	-20.2%	20.6%	48.7%
ATC	1.3%	27.2%	38.1%
X-ATC	11.4%	37.4%	61.2%

Table 3: Performance improvement of COFCAST-RU by due date tightness

Conclusions

We have presented an approach for multiagent coordination in tightly coupled, real-time environments. The approach consists of a standard operating procedure and a look-ahead coordination. The main contribution of the paper is the development of a computationally efficient coordination technique that can easily be integrated with a standard operating procedure (e.g., dispatch scheduling) to improve system performance in tightly coupled, real-time environments. We have applied the approach to job shop scheduling, one of the most difficult NP-complete combinatorial optimization problems. Experimental results show that the approach effectively enhances the performance of dispatch scheduling for optimizing objective of weighted tardiness. We have also obtained similar results for other objective functions, e.g., makespan. Our future work includes extension to agents in charge of multiple resources and jobs with substitutable resources.

The approach is also potentially useful for extending the contract net protocol (CNP) (Davis & Smith 1983). While CNP has been extended to deal with a competitive setting (Fischer et al. 1995) and varying levels of commitment by bounded rational self-interested agents (Sandholm & Lesser 1995), temporal planning (e.g., deadlines, makespan) is very important in many real world problems (e.g., project management). The approach provides a coordinated temporal look-ahead capability that is potentially useful for extending CNP in problems that involve temporal objectives. In the envisioned CNP extension, a manager agent provides additional information, e.g., task deadlines and interdependency. A contractor agent uses this information and an extension of our coordination procedure to estimate its local schedule and see whether it can perform the task within the specified deadlines. This would be helpful for the contractor agent in deciding whether to bid for the task. This capability is particular useful when (1) tasks have deadlines and interdependency, and (2) when a contractor agent receives penalties for not performing a task by its deadline. We are currently investigating this CNP extension.

References

Bond, A. H., and Gasser, L. eds. 1988. *Readings in Distributed Artificial Intelligence.* San Mateo, Calif.: Morgan Kaufmann.

Conry, S. E.; Meyer, R. A.; and Lesser, V. R. 1988. Multistage Negotiation in Distributed Planning. In *Readings in Distributed Artificial Intelligence,* 367-384. San Mateo, Calif.: Morgan Kaufmann.

Davis, R., and Smith, R. G. 1983. Negotiation as a Metaphor for Distributed Problem Solving. *Artificial Intelligence* 20:63-109.

Decker, K. S., and Lesser, V. R. 1995. Designing a Family of Coordination Algorithms. In Proceedings of the First International Conference on Multi-Agent Systems, 73-80. San Francisco, Calif.

Durfee, E. H. , and Lesser, V. R. 1991. Partial Global Planning: A Coordination Framework for Distributed Hypothesis Formation. *IEEE Transactions on Systems, Man, and Cybernetics* 21(5): 1167-1183.

Fischer, K.; Muller, J. P.; Pischel, M.; and Schier, D. 1995. A Model for Cooperative Transportation Scheduling. In Proceedings of the First International Conference on Multiagent Systems, 109-116. San Francisco, Calif.

French, S. 1982. *Sequencing and Scheduling: An Introduction to the Mathematics of the Job Shop.* Wiley.

Gasser, L., and Huhns, M. N. eds. 1989. *Distributed Artificial Intelligence.* Vol. 2. Los Altos, CA.: Morgan Kaufmann Publishers.

Huhns, M. ed. 1987 *Distributed Artificial Intelligence.* Altos, Calif.: Morgan Kaufmann Publishers.

Huhns, M., and Bridgeland, D. 1991. Multiagent Truth Maintenance. *IEEE Transactions on Systems, Man, and Cybernetics* 21(6): 1437-1445.

Lesser, V., and Corkill, D. 1983. The Distributed Vehicle Monitoring Testbed: A Tool for Investigating Distributed Problem Solving Networks. *AI Magazine* 4(3): 15-33.

Liu, J., and Sycara, K. P. 1995a. Emergent Constraint Satisfaction through Multiagent Coordinated Interaction. In *From Reaction to Cognition*: 107-121. Castelfranshi, C., and Muller, J. P. eds. Vol. 957 of Lecture Notes in Artificial Intelligence.

Liu, J., and Sycara, K. P. 1995b. Exploiting Problem Structure for Distributed Constraint Optimization. In Proceedings of the First International Conference on Multi-Agent Systems, 246-253. San Francisco, Calif.

Mackworth, A. K. 1987. Constraint Satisfaction. In *Encyclopedia in Artificial Intelligence,* 205-211. Shapiro, S. C. ed. New York: Wiley.

Morton, T. E., and Pentico, D. W. 1993. *Heuristic Scheduling Systems: With Applications to Production Systems and Project Management.* New York: Wiley.

Narayan, V.; Morton, T. E.; and Ramnath, P. 1994. X-Dispatch Methods for Weighted Tardiness Job Shops, Technical Report, #1994-14, Graduate School of Industrial Administration, Carnegie Mellon Univ.

Sanholm, T., and Lesser, V. 1995. Issues in Automated Negotiation and Electronic Commerce: Extending the Contract Net Framework. In Proceedings of the First International Conference on Multi-Agent Systems, 328-335. San Francisco, Calif.

Sycara, K. P. 1988. Resolving Goal Conflicts via Negotiation. In Proceedings of AAAI-88, 245-250.

Sycara, K. P.; Roth, S.; Sadeh, N.; and Fox, M. 1991. Distributed Constraint Heuristic Search. *IEEE Transactions on Systems, Man, and Cybernetics* 21(6): 1446-1461.

Yokoo, M.; Durfee, E.; Tshida, T.; and Kuwabara, K. 1992. Distributed Constraint Satisfaction for Formalizing Distributed Problem Solving. In Proceedings of the 12th IEEE International Conference on Distributed Computing Systems, 614-621.

Multiagent Model of Dynamic Design

Visualization as an Emergent Behavior of Active Design Agents

Suguru Ishizaki[+]

Design Department · Carnegie Mellon University
MMC 110 · Pittsburgh · PA 15213
phone 412-268-6952 · email suguru+@cmu.edu

Abstract
This research has been motivated by the lack of models and languages in the visual design field that are able to address design solutions, which continuously adapt in response to the dynamic changes both in the information itself and in the goals or intentions of the information recipient. This paper postulates *a multiagent model of dynamic design*—a theoretical framework of design that provides a model with which the visual designer can think during the course of designing. The model employs a decentralized model of design as a premise, and borrows its conceptual model from the improvisational performance, such as dance and music, and bases its theoretical and technical framework on the field of multiagent systems. A design solution is considered an emergent behavior of a collection of active design agents, *or performers*, each of which is responsible for presenting a particular segment of information. The graphical behaviors of design agents are described by their dynamic activities—rather than by the traditional method of fixed attributes. The model is illustrated with two design projects, Dynamic News Display System and E-Mail Display, both of which were implemented using a multiagent design simulation system, **perForm**, along with an agent description language, **persona**.

Keywords: visual design, visualization, dynamic information, automatic design, multiagent systems

1. Introduction

1.1 Problems and Opportunities

Traditional visual design encapsulates information into fixed forms, such as print or film, so that the message can be distributed or stored. In the design of computer-based communication, design problems become more dynamic as the media become more interactive and include more temporal information. It is therefore important to create a design that continuously adapts in response to the dynamic changes of context, that is, information and the reader's intention. I argue that visual design as a field limits its own contributions to traditional methodologies, despite increasing efforts from within the field to improve the visual design of digital media. This lack of models and languages prevents designers from exploring those solutions that are unique to computer-based communication.

The problem on which I have focused in this research is identified by two unique characteristics of computer-based communication: dynamic change in context; and the capability of temporal presentation (Fig.1).

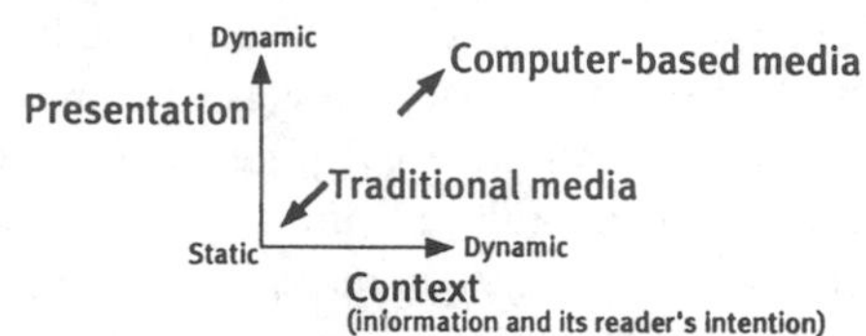

Fig.1. Two unique characteristics of computer-based communication raise new problems in design.

First, dynamic change in context (*i.e.,* information and the reader's intention) raises a new problem in the design of computer-based media. For example, on-line information systems, such as news databases and traffic information systems, are updated as information changes. The design in such a medium must reflect the dynamic changes in information over time. Interactive media provide readers with personalized access to information. The pace and order of reading and the amount and selection of information change over time based on the intention of the individual user. Consequently, in the design of computer-based media, a designer often finds it impossible to design for solving a particular problem, and instead must represent *a way of designing* in a form of a computer program that can generate design solutions at run-time.

But, what do I mean by a way of designing, or process of designing? What kind of *form* does this process take? In this paper, "a way of designing" is an explicit description of how individual design elements, unknown at the time of designing, change over time according to changes in the immediate context. A goal of this research has been to propose a conceptual model and a descriptive language that designers can use in the course of creating such dynamic design solutions.

The second characteristic of computer-based media is the capability of temporal presentation. It introduces new challenges and opportunities in design. Designers are no longer limited to fixed forms in order to communicate information. For example, a gradual color shift can be used to convey complex emotional quality; or a rapid repetitive movement can be used to indicate a quantity.

However, although traditional visual design has dealt with temporal presentation media, such as television and film, there have been only a few studies on temporal forms [4]. As a consequence, the visual design field lacks the rich models and languages that would allow designers to discuss visual forms presented over time. A classic example of such a model is a color space, *e.g.,* the Munsell model [6], which has provided designers with a conceptual model of color, along with a vocabulary set, allowing the use of rich color harmony as well as the analysis of complex interaction of

[+] *This work was done while the author was at the MIT Media Laboratory's Visible Language Workshop. (MIT Media Laboratory, E15-443, 20 Ames St. Cambridge, MA 02139)*

color. This research proposes such a model for the visual forms that change over time.

These characteristics have raised various questions that need to be answered: How can a designer conceptualize and describe a solution that can be interrupted by some immediate changes in information and in the reader's intention? How can a designer describe a design that contains an undetermined number of design elements constantly changing? How can a designer contemplate design problems as continuous problems, rather than a series of discrete problems?

I suggest that it is valuable to develop a model of design that would provide designers with a conceptual framework during the course of solving design problems, in order to extend the fixed nature of the traditional design-object so that it will include more continuous and responsive characteristics. The model is also intended to contribute to the development of computer systems that *represent* and *generate* continuous and responsive design solutions. In this paper, I shall call this framework *a multiagent model of dynamic design*, or **maDes**.

1.2 Background

There have been a number of researchers that proposed generative design systems (*e.g.*, [3][5][8][11]). However, most of their representation schemes do not consider the fluid nature of computer-based communication. Rather, those representations are modeled after traditional static design (*e.g.*, a layout, or a presentation) where a design solution is described as a collection of declarative statements that are intended to fix formal attributes. On the other hand, **maDes** is intended to encourage designers to perceive (1) a design problem in computer-based communication as a continuous stream, instead of a collection of discrete problems; and (2) a design solution as a fluid emergent entity generated by dynamic activities of design elements, instead of a set of design elements with fixed attributes.

maDes has been influenced by three distinct areas of studies. First is the cognitive models of design that suggest the multiplicity of knowledge involved in designing (*e.g.*, [10][12]). These theories have encouraged a distributed representation as a natural means for representing a generative design process. Second, in order to develop a distributed model, I have drawn an analogy from improvisational performance, such as dance and music [1][7]. The intrinsic nature of improvisation that addresses performers' responses to the spontaneous changes in context during a performance has provided an insight for a design solution that must respond to dynamic changes in its context. Finally, the research in multiagent systems—a branch of distributed AI—has provided a theoretical and technical foundation to this research [2]. In particular, **maDes** has adopted cooperative reactive (or situated) agents [9] as constituents of multiagent design systems.

2. A Scenario

Imagine that you are a designer. Think of a news display system that allows users to access a news database that is constantly updated. News stories arrive at the display system as they are issued, and a user can view them as they are published. The purpose, or more precisely, intention, of a user may also vary over time. For example, a user may want to read news articles according to locations; or a user may need to look at a particular category. Your task as a designer is to create a visual design solution for the display

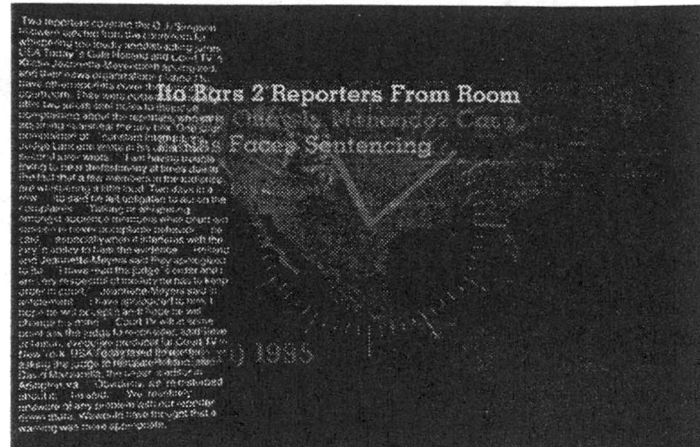

Fig.2. A screenshot of Dynamic News Display, showing a scene while a user is reading a news story, after its headline is selected.

that reflects the dynamic changes in both reader's intention and the database. Since information is only available at run-time, you are not allowed to directly adjust attributes of potential design elements, such as typeface and color, unlike the newspaper design. Thus, you must design a way of designing, or design process, in order to dynamically solve this continuous design problem. In addition, since the display is capable of presenting temporal expressions (*e.g.*, animation), you are not limited to the traditional notion of static design solutions. Rather, you are free to use *temporal forms*. For example, you may use repetitive motion (*e.g.*, up and down) as a "label" for an important news story, as you would use a hue (*e.g.*, red) for the same purpose in the design of a news magazine.

I have just described that your task as a designer is to create a design solution that is responsive. And the solution is a way of designing that you have to describe. Now, how would you want to *describe* such a design solution?

maDes provides a designer with a unique framework for describing such a design solution. For example, Fig.2 is a scene from an experimental on-line news display designed based on the proposed model. Here, the design solution is an emergent expression created by the situated activities of design agents that are responsible for presenting headlines, news stories, placenames, a clock, a date text, and a map, each of which has its behavior specified by a designer. A headline agent left-aligns its text to its placename first when it is born; and when a new headline is issued at the same location it aligns the text to the new headline. Headline agents also change the translucency of its text based on its age. Placename agents change their text color when there is a headline associated with their location. When a news story is being read by a user, other design agents make their visual representations highly translucent so that they do not distract the user's reading. And so on... The solution here is created by a team of collaborating agents.

A designer's task when working with **maDes** is to anticipate potential changes in the context, and specify kinds of expressive forms for design agents to perform according to their immediate situations. An analogy to the designer's role here can be made with that of a director of an improvisational dance performance—selecting dancers with the desired expressive skill (body forms) and coaching their situated acting through a thorough rehearsal. In the course of creating a final dynamic solution, a designer would have to rehearse behaviors of agents iteratively by simulating real dynamic design situations.

3. A Multiagent Model of Dynamic Design

3.1. Overview

maDes models a design solution as a system consisting of a collection of smaller design systems. Each system, or *design agent*, is responsible for presenting a particular segment of information. A design agent is a system that can modify its expressive behavior as the context changes and can cooperate with other design agents. In traditional visual design, a design element is usually described by a set of fixed attributes; while in **maDes**, a design element is described by *a set of dynamic activities*.

The term *context* here is used from the perspective of an agent, and it is comprised of the information, the reader's intention, and the immediate presentation environment (*i.e.*, surrounding visual elements). Any of the three constituents is potentially dynamic.

3.2. Agent's ability

I have described that the design agent presents information according to a given context. But, how can a designer describe agents' activities? The proposed multiagent model of design adopts reactive agents as its constituents [9]. As described in Scenario, design agents are like performers in an improvisational performance, in that they perform reactively using their skills, without deliberately planning their actions. Performers seem to simply act on immediate situations, but it does not imply their performance is not intelligent. Rather, deliberation is considered embedded in their reactive pattern, or skill, through previous training. In dynamic design, the behavior of the design agent is described as a set of situation-action patterns. If a design agent is capable of communicating a particular segment of information at any given situation in such a manner that a designer desires, the agent's *ability* is said to satisfy the designer's intention.

Agent's ability is specified either for a particular agent, or for a class of agents. When it is specified for a class of agents, agents that belong to the same class share their ability. For example, there may be a set of design agents belonging to one class that are all responsible for presenting a headline in a dynamic electronic news system. In dynamic design, a designer often has to focus on behaviors for a class of design agents, rather than a particular design agent, since a particular information set is usually unknown at the time of designing. However, there is nothing to prevent the designers from creating a single unique agent. A clock agent in Dynamic News System is an example of such a unique agent.

In **maDes**, the ability of the agent is determined as well as described by the following characteristics:

Physical Realization

Physical realization is a perceivable representation of the agent. It is important to recognize that an agent is not bound to a particular type of expression. For example, an agent that is responsible for presenting a headline in Dynamic News Display may express itself using text or through voice. Since the agent is an active system, it chooses an appropriate realization according to a given context. Physical realization(s) for an agent is determined based on the available technology and a particular design problem at hand.

State and Sensor

State is a unit of what the agent "knows." State includes: physical properties (*e.g.*, color) that are determined by the agent's physical realization and changed by actions described next; information about other related agents, and information about user's intention; and changes in information for which the agent is responsible.

The design agent is assumed capable of sensing information from the external world (external to itself), which include: information to be presented (*e.g.*, news data), the reader's intention, and other agents' activities. A set of sensors is defined for an agent by a designer, and the value observed by a sensor is a special type of state.

Action

Action is the abstraction for the agent's basic ability—just as body-form is the abstraction for describing performer's skill in dance. There are three basic categories of actions that the agents can perform: formal, communicative, and external. Formal action is an expressive action that influences the agent's form, such as typography and color. For example, a flash shown in Fig.3, which can be used to attract a reader's attention, is a formal action. Communicative action is the act of sending a message to other agents, which is used when explicit coordination is necessary. An example of communicative action is a message sending action taken by a placename agent to inform its selection to the associated headline agents. Finally, external action is a type of action used to influence outside the multiagent system, such as an application program. For example, there can be a quit button agent that terminates the application program.

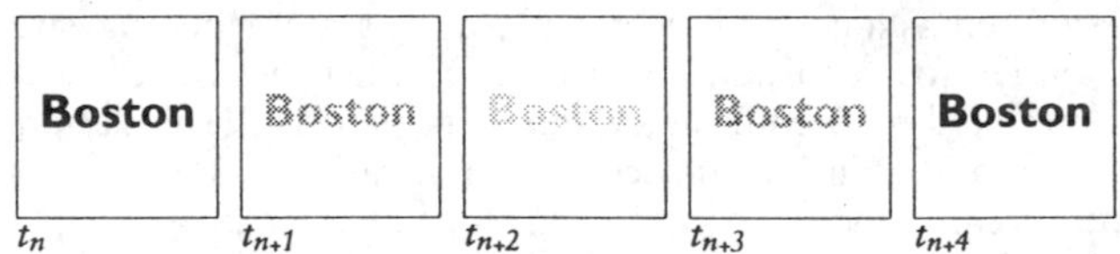

Fig.3. A simplified view of a flash action.

Each formal action—*or temporal form*—must be carefully described by a designer for a particular design problem. An action can be performed instantaneously (*e.g.*, change font), or it may take a certain duration (*e.g.*, gradually glow size). **maDes** provides an abstraction that allows structural and analytical descriptions of forms expressed over time.

Any meaningful formal expression can be considered an action. However, what is considered a meaningful action is determined by how a designer views a design problem and its solution. For example, consider the flash action shown in Fig.3. A designer may consider it as a meaningful action to attract a reader's attention. Alternatively, the first half of the same action (t_n~t_{n+2}), which changes the color of text from dark to bright, can be considered another action that serves a different purpose. *The abstraction of action provides a framework to structure design as a set of meaningful temporal forms.*

Strategy

Strategy is the abstraction over actions, which describes the agent's ability to achieve a particular goal. Strategy is like a performer's ability to express a certain theme in a musical improvisation. A player achieves a particular theme by selecting an appropriate action sequence at the right timing. A set of strategies determines the ability of a design agent.

To select an appropriate action as a response to its immediate situation, the agent must be able to recognize various *contexts* by which it is potentially situated. In other words, the designer of a dynamic design solution must identify possible situations for individual agents. A situation can depend on an agent's own state, another agent's state, information it's presenting, a reader's intention, or a combination of these. For example, the placename agent in the news display can recognize when a cursor is above its text, when its text is clicked, when there are headline agents associated with its place, and when some news story is being presented.

Situations are structured in a hierarchical manner. Suppose a user is interested in reading news articles based on locations (sit-1). Then, if a reader selects a placename with which a headline agent is associated, it generates a sub-situation for the headline: a reader is potentially interested in reading its story (sit-2). Notice that, sit-2 is situated within a larger situation sit-1. You can also find another substitution within sit-2 when a reader selects the headline agent: a reader is interested in reading its story (sit-3). In other words, when the agent is situated in one situation, it does not have to watch out for all the situations it can recognize; rather it only has to consider sub-situations that potentially happen within the immediate high level situation. Fig.4 presents a schematic diagram of situations that are hierarchically defined. *The abstraction of strategy and situation provides designers with a means of analyzing and structuring dynamic design problems in a systematic manner.*

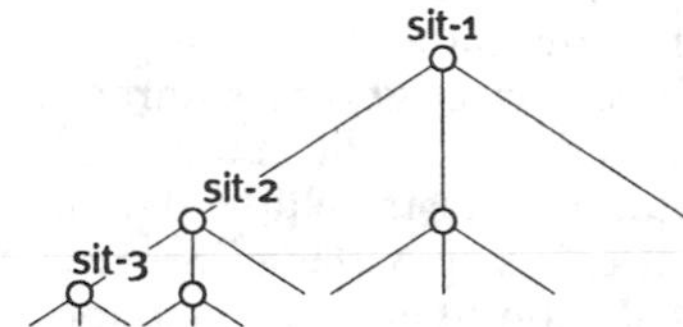

Fig.4. A schematic diagram of a situation hierarchy.

Given abilities to recognize necessary situations, a strategy is specified as a simple procedure and is composed of a set of actions and a set of reactive rules, based on the reactive agent model proposed by Singh [9]. The simplest strategy consists of a sequence of one or more design action. For example, a headline's strategy to attract a viewer's attention may consist of an action to gradually become red and increase its size. From a perspective of a headline agent, this strategy can be written as:

S-1 ***attract-viewer's-attention-strategy:***
*perform **flash-action***

More complex strategies provide the agent an ability to determine an appropriate action to perform according to its immediate context. An example of this type of strategy, for the headline agent, is to attract a viewer when the news item is important. This strategy is achieved by adding a conditional statement to *S-1*:

S-2 ***attract-viewer's-attention-strategy:***
If my news article is important to my reader
*perform **flash-action***
otherwise
do-nothing

A strategy can also consist of a set of other strategies. For instance, a simple strategy for a headline agent to use ***attract-viewer's-attention-strategy*** until it is deleted by a user can be defined as follows:

S-3 ***basic-strategy:***
while I am not deleted,
*use **attract-viewer's-attention-strategy***

Also, a strategy can consist of a sequence of multiple strategies.

Notice that these two strategies, ***basic-strategy*** and ***attract-viewer's-attention-strategy***, involve three situations as shown in Fig.5. First the top level situation is when the headline agent is not deleted. Then, there are two sub-situations: one when the agent's news article is important, another when it is not.

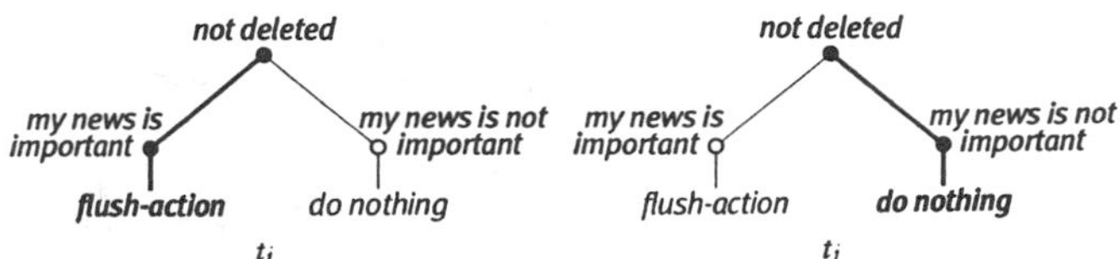

Fig.5. A schematic diagram of a situation hierarchy.

Strategy is a useful abstraction which a designer can use in the course of exploring design solutions, as well as in describing the final solution. *It provides designers with a framework for identifying changes in context, and for determining appropriate dynamic and responsive design solutions.*

3.3. External view

Fig.6 summarizes the agent's ability. The design agent acts on the immediate situation using a strategy that is designed to achieve its current goal. The information observed from the external world and messages sent from other agents are used by the strategy to determine appropriate actions to perform.

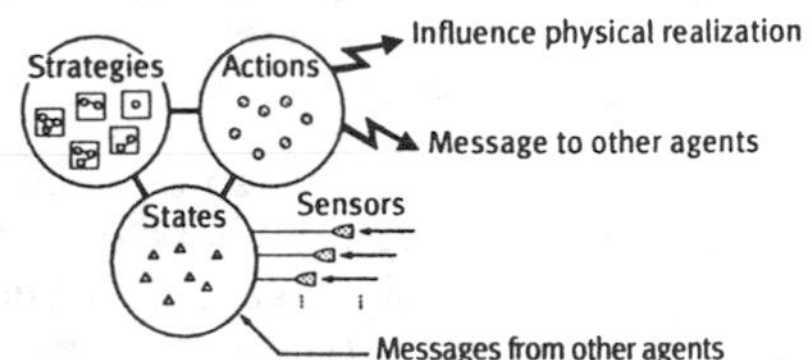

Fig.6. A summary of the agent's ability.

It may seem complex to understand how an agent behaves, with a given set of strategies and actions. One method that helps one understand an agent's behavior is to consider its history. Fig.7 shows a history of a headline agent. The agent repeated performing ***flash-action*** through t_i since its news story is important. Then, its situation changed at t_n, where the news story became no longer important. At t_n, the agent stopped performing ***flash-action*** and started perform ***do-nothing*** and kept doing nothing until now through t_j.

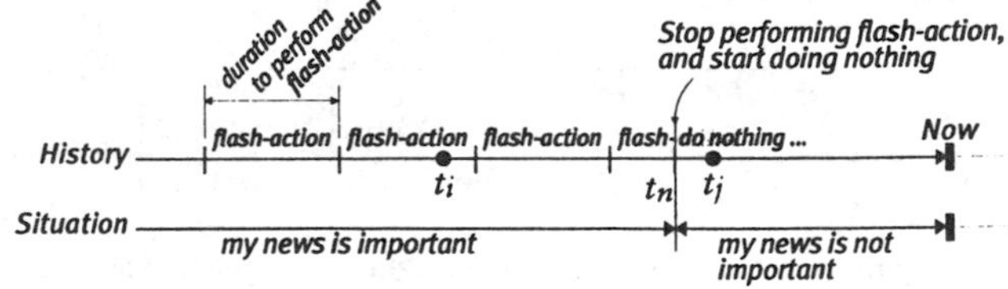

Fig.7. A historical view of a headline agent.

Also, an agent's future can be understood in terms of *histories*. Given a particular point in time, there are many possible histories. As time progresses, an agent possesses one history in its past. Fig.8 is a schematic diagram showing the concept of possible histories found in the future of an agent. The notion of history is an external description of the agent behavior, but it is not explicitly represented.

History is simply an analytical device that can be used to understand the agent's behaviors.

Fig.8. A schematic diagram of future histories of an agent.

3.4. Organization of Agents

maDes emphasizes a decentralized and lateral interaction among design agents, as opposed to a centralized and hierarchical one (Fig.9). Like dancers or players on a football team, who do not have strict hierarchical control, the design agents collaboratively act in order to achieve a global goal. However, an agent can become a local leader with some authority over other agents, like the lead dancer or the quarterback. The leaders can orchestrate other agents. For example, a headline agent in the dynamic news design can be a leader that oversees a story agent and a photograph agent.

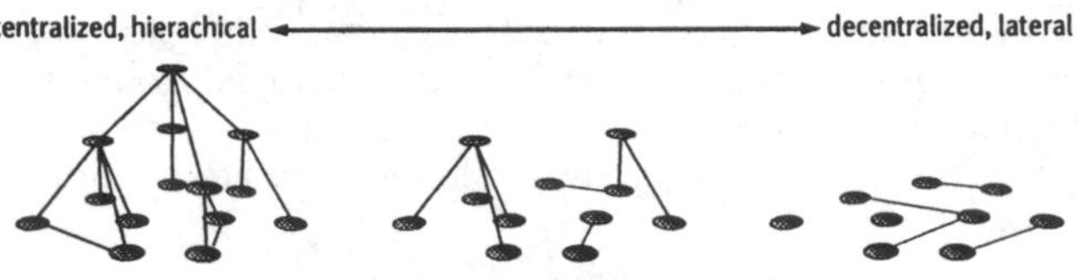

Fig.9. A range of organizational styles.

I have described that a design solution as a whole is an emergent behavior generated by both implicit and explicit collaborations among design agents. This emergent solution is considered a group strategy, and its communicative quality is considered the ability of a group. However, there is no explicit description about group strategies. Group strategy and group ability are like those of a football team, and composed of a collection of strategies used by individual agents.

3.5. Design Method

In addition to the theoretical framework, this research suggests a methodical process which a designer can follow through to solve a design problem. Fig.10 shows a schematic flow of a design process with **maDes**. This method fundamentally resembles a typical prescriptive design process paradigm—analysis, synthesis, and evaluation.

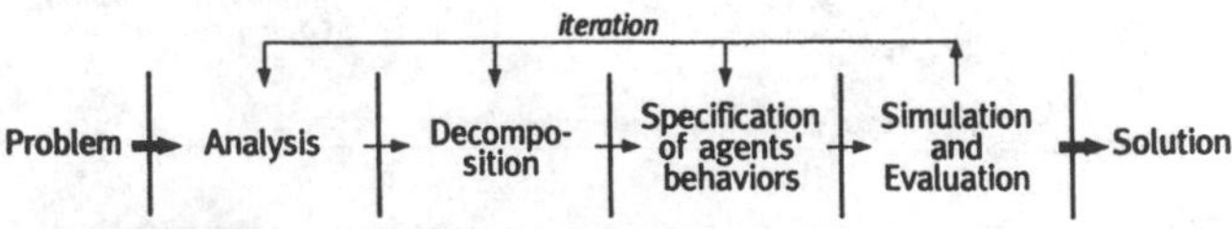

Figure 10. A design method that uses the multiagent model of dynamic design.

The first phase is the analysis of a design problem. The designer must understand the nature of information, the goal of communication, and types of intended readers. The second phase is the decomposition of the problem. A design problem is described as a set of design agents. In this phase, types of design agents, their roles and organizational style are determined. The third phase is the specification of the agents' behaviors. Here, a designer specifies the behaviors for individual classes of design agents using actions and strategies. Then the solution, or partial solution, created in the third phase is evaluated by simulating agents' behaviors in various contexts.

Although the design method is described in a linear fashion, the design is not completed by a simple four-stage process; rather it is an iteration of exploring and examining agents' behaviors and relations among them. The role of a designer is like that of a director in the performing arts, in that, the design process consists of a course of *dialogue* between a designer and the design agents. A designer must carefully determine the behaviors of agents in such a way that each agent can play its role according to the changes in the immediate context, and can contribute to an emergent design solution.

4. perForm: A Multiagent Design Simulation System

perForm is an experimental software program that was implemented based on **maDes** to examine its theoretical framework with concrete design examples. **perForm** provides an agent description language called **persona**, along with a multiagent design simulation engine, which simulates parallel activities of design agents. **persona** is implemented in LISP and provides a set of macros that are used to define agents' abilities, including actions, strategies, sensors, and messages. **perForm** uses a special 3D graphics library for the realization of the design agent, enabling the use of high quality typography to examine **maDes** with design solutions that are not too simplistic. The software is written using SGI's Performer graphics library on SGI's ONYX Workstation with the Reality Engine graphics.

The following sections illustrate how dynamic design can be created with **maDes**, using **perForm**. Because of the space limitation, the description of agents' behaviors are given in the style of stories, instead of strategies written in **persona**.

5. Case Study 1: Dynamic News Display

5.1. Overview

The design problem is to create a visual interface to an online news database, as introduced in Section 2. In this experimental project, I intended to create a visual interface that can continuously provide users with an overview of entire news articles issued within a certain time period (*e.g.*, past 12 hours). I also decided to present news articles based on their physical locations where they are issued.

5.2. Decomposition and Roles of Agents

The information is decomposed into the following agent types: Headline Agent, Story Agent, Map Agent, Placename Agent, Clock Agent, and Date Agent. Notice that a news article is represented by a headline agent and a story agent. The role of the Headline Agent is to quickly inform the content, as well as to present the age of its associated news article. The role of the Story Agent is simply to provide its message content. The reason to decompose a news article in two different agents (headline and story) is to create a visually less overwhelming interface. It is also conceivable to create a class of design agent that is responsible for presenting the entire news article. However, it was rather meaningful to represent a news story using two agents.

5.3. Solution

This particular example used a set of news articles categorized as top U.S. news from the Clarinet database on May 19, 1995. Fig.11.a shows the display just before 9 o'clock in the morning. There are three headlines at Los Angels, one at Kansas City, and one at Washington D.C. The place-

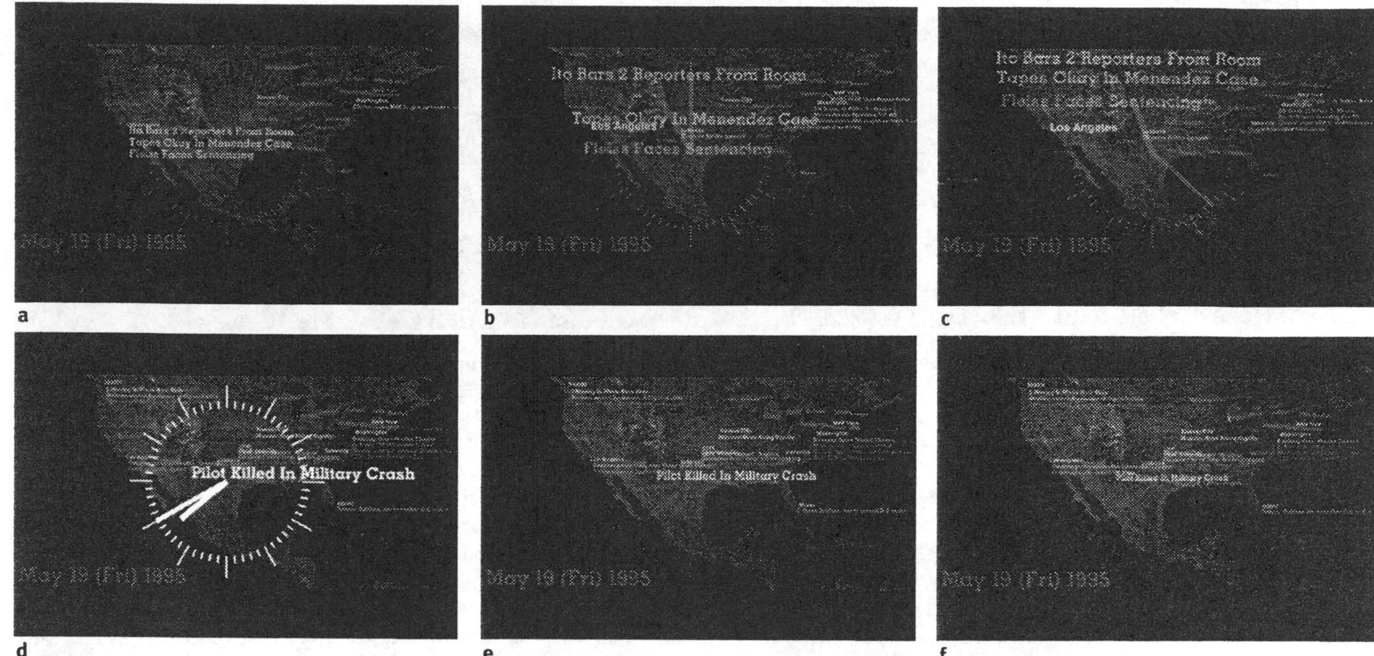

Fig.11. Interactive scenes from the Dynamic News Display. **a-c** show a sequence after Los Angles is selected. **d-f** show an introductory action of a headline agent.

name agents responsible for presenting these three placenames have recognized that there are news stories associated with them, and changed their color from light gray to bright orange. Also, notice that three headlines at Los Angeles have larger type size than the others. This scene is taken right after a reader moved a cursor over to the text "Los Angeles." First, the Los Angeles agent notices that a cursor is on top of it—a new situation; and then it informs headlines associated with it that it is being focused upon. Having been informed by the placename, those headline agents now "know" that their placename is being focused upon. According to my instruction for this situation, headline agents gradually grew their type size. It then kept that size while a cursor was on its associated placename, in order to make their text more readable.

When a headline agent is born, it first flashes its text close to a viewpoint (in *z-axis*) using white (Fig.11.d-f). Then, right after that, it gradually aligns the text to its placename. This introductory action is achieved by using a strategy with a flash action and a move action. After introducing its text, the Headline Agent uses a higher level strategy until the age of its news article reaches to the specified limit. This strategy provides the headline agent an ability to act based on how a user is interacting with its associated placename as well as with itself.

Each headline agent left-aligns its text to a headline that is issued next at the same place; or to its placename if it is the most recent one. The Headline Agent always tries to maintain this alignment using the *same* strategy. The Headline Agent also looks at the age of its new article and changes the translucency of its text proportional to its age. For example, the headline presented at Kansas City shows that its story is older than other news stories.

If a placename is selected, headline agents associated with that place use a different strategy to grow their text size, and to move to the top left position. Fig.11.b-c presents a sequence of scenes after Los Angels is selected. Three headline agents gradually move their text to the upper left part of the display. In this design, selecting a placename means to further examine articles at that place. Thereafter, if a user selects a headline by clicking its text, it informs its news story agent of its selection. This changes the situation for a story agent, which has been using a strategy to hide. Then, it uses another strategy to make its text visible (Fig.2). Notice that there have been other news stories arrived to other cities, while a user has been interacting with news articles at Los Angeles.

Behaviors of the other agents are relatively simple. The Clock Agent finds current time based on whether the system is used in quick review mode or real-time mode, and displays it in the form of a clock. It also changes color of its clock every hour based on a previously chosen set of 24 colors around a hue circle. The Date Agent keeps checking current date and displays it in the from of a text. The Map Agent just keeps displaying a map. In an earlier design The Map Agent changed the brightness of the map based on the time of a day; however, I decided not to use that strategy since color coding schemes of other agents were difficult to maintain.

Finally, notice that, in Fig.2, texts representing placenames and headlines, other than the selected headlines and its news story, are highly translucent. When the headline and the placename agents notice (using their sensors) a situation in which a news story is being presented , they use a strategy which tries not to visually distract the user's reading.

5.4. Summary

Imagine the design of a newspaper, for instance. The design of Dynamic News Display clearly has shown a different method in which designers can approach a problem, when compared to a traditional model. **maDes** was able to highlight the fluid nature of design problems and the potential of dynamic and responsive design solutions. **maDes** also provides a means to describe a rich and emergent solution out of relatively simple distributed agents.

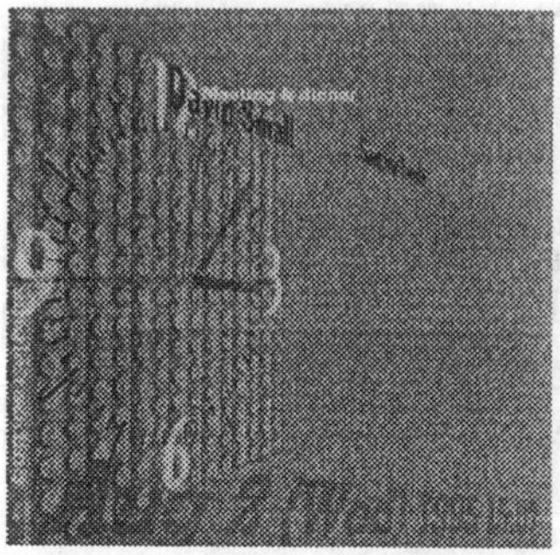
a

b

c

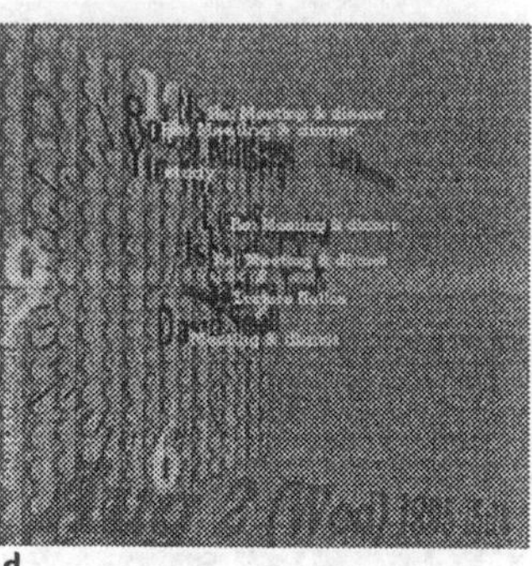
d

Fig.12. Interactive screens from the E-Mail Displlay, showing how the sender and subject agents introduce their text by coordinating each other.

6. Case Study 2: E-Mail Display

6.1. Overview

The design problem in the second case study is to create a visual interface to an e-mail system, E-Mail Display. The interface must represent: an arrival of a new message; reply-replied message relationships; whether or not a message is read by the user; and the number of mail messages. In addition, I intended to make the interface playful, avoiding conservative structured layout, using interesting temporal forms and vivid colors.

6.2. Decomposition and Roles of Agents

The information is decomposed into the following design agents: Sender Agent, Subject Agent, Message Agent, Clock Agent, Number-of-Messages-Agent (MumMsg agent), Reading-Mode-Switch-Agent (Switch agent), and Date Agent (Fig.12). Similar to a news article in the Dynamic News Display, a mail message is decomposed into three design agents: a sender, a subject, and a message. In addition to the obvious roles that are implied by these three agents, additional communicative roles are assigned to them. First, Sender Agent is responsible for representing whether or not its message is read, the temporal relationship to other messages, and reply-replied relationships. Sender Agent is also responsible for informing its message agent when it is selected by the user. Subject Agent must visually represent its relationship to its sender. The message agent must present its text when its sender is clicked. The roles of Clock Agent, Date Agent, and NumMsg Agent are those of which their names suggest. The role of Switch Agent is to indicate the current *reading mode* of the system, and to switch a reading mode between single and relational (discussed later) when it is clicked.

6.3. Solution

Similar to the Dynamic News Display, design agents are realized using a 3D space. However, unlike the News Display, the view point is rotated 45 degrees clockwise around the *y-axis*, creating a sense of perspective (Fig.12). The clock agent uses a LEGO-block pattern to create a playful atmosphere. Unlike other graphical elements, which use a single realization element such as text, the clock agent uses multiple parts: numbers, LEGO background, in addition to the clock itself. There is no need to decompose a clock into smaller design agents since it is a meaningful unit.

When a new email message arrives in the mail system, the sender agent presents its name text at the far right in the *x-axis* and at about the height of the clock in the *y-axis*; and then moves the text towards the clock. The sender agent randomly chooses the position for its text somewhere between the center and right edge of the clock (Fig.12.a-c). This random positioning in the *x-axis* is intended to make the names of senders easier to distinguish from adjacent ones, and to create a playful emergent form. As the sender agent approaches the clock, it uses squashing and stretching action, and stops. The design of this action is influenced by a technique used in traditional animation in order to provide a viewer a sense of life. After arriving at the clock, the sender agent adjusts the *y* position of its text at the top of the clock if it is responsible for the most recent message, and otherwise places it just below the next sender text (Fig.12.d).

As the sender agent finishes performing its introductory action, its associated subject agents introduce its text by gradually showing the text right next to the name of the sender, using its introductory strategy (Fig.13.a). Since the sender agent stops at a random location, its associated subject agent uses its sensor to adjust its final location.

The Sender Agent is sensitive to a reader's clicking, and if its text is clicked, it informs its associated message agent about the selection. After receiving a message from its associated sender agent, the Message Agent recognizes a new situation, and uses a different strategy to present its text in front of other graphical element facing towards the view point (Fig.13.b-c). The Message Agent keeps the text visible until a reader clicks the text. Simultaneously, the sender agent that is clicked faces its text to the view point, become translucent, and start "dancing" in the background. The subject agent associated with the message places its text just behind the message and rotates it 60 degrees counter clockwise in order to make it readable. While a message text is presented—a new situation—other sender agents make their text *defocused*, decreasing the contrast, and their associated subject agents make their text transparent, in order to make the message currently chosen easier to read.

Individual strategies, as well as group strategies, introduced by now are relatively short-sighted. In other words, although a group of agents presents a complex visual message with multiple contents, such as sender's name, message text, and subject, each of which uses its own strategies in *parallel*, each presentation remains relatively brief. What if there is more information than that can fit in a screen? What if a designer desires to present a chain of causal relationships in sequence? The next simple example will illustrate how a group of agents can collaborate to create a sequence of presentation.

Fig.13.d shows a scene after the agent whose sender name is "Ishantha Lokuge" is selected under the relational reading mode, and becomes *a leader*. Since Ishantha's message is a reply to the message sent by David Small, the leader agent (responsible for Ishantha's name) requests the agent responsible for David's name (*replied agent*) to start a pre-

a

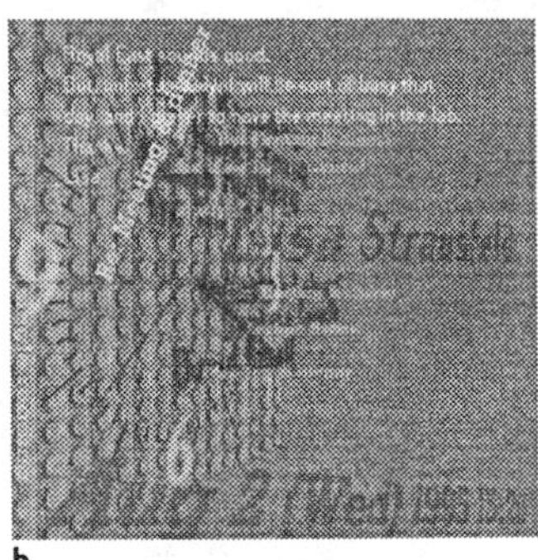
b

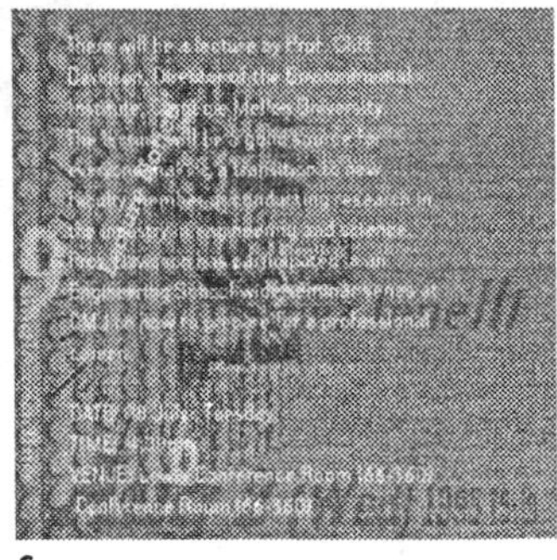
c

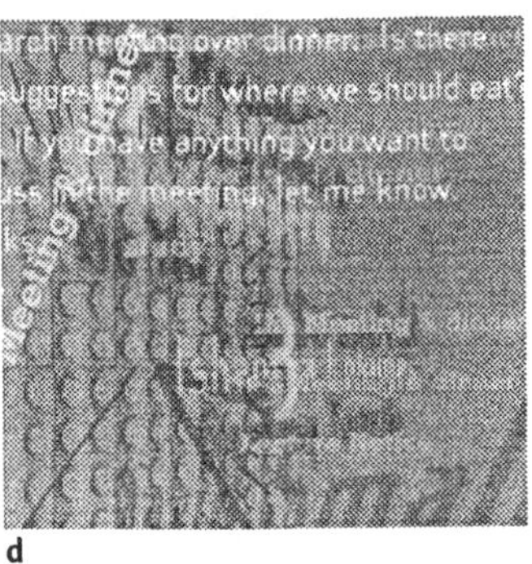
d

Fig.13. a is a close-up view showing how a sender and subject coordinate. b-c are scenes while a message is presented by a message agent. In d, a leader agent is waiting for a previous message to finish its presentation, by moving back and forth.

sentation. While David's message is being presented, the leader agent waits and visually indicates the fact that it is performing next, by shrinking and stretching in the *x-axis* (*waiting-action*). Then, after a user finishes reading David's message, the leader agent recognizes it and begins its own presentation. Simultaneously, the leader agent informs *reply agents* (sender agent whose messages are the reply to the message associated with its message) so that they can present their messages after its own presentation is over. This action changes the situation of the *reply agents*; and the closest *reply agent*, which is presenting next, starts performing *waiting-action* indicating its next presentation. Finally, when a user finishes reading the leader agent's message (Ishantha's), the leader agent stops its presentation and asks the closest reply agent to start its performance. The first reply agent informs the next reply agent when it is deselected. The remaining reply agents simply relay their presentation, one by one. Fig.14 shows a schematic diagram of this collaborative presentation.

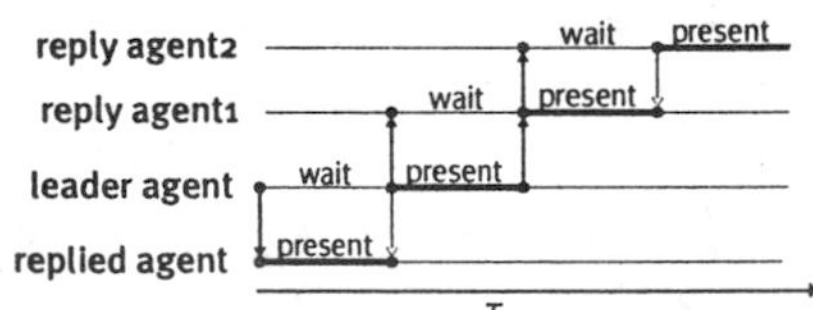

Fig.14. A historical view of the interaction among a group of agents. *(thick arrow=a message sending, thin arrow=sensing)*

6.4. Summary

The second study experimented with another type of collaboration orchestrated by a temporary leader agent. It has demonstrated that a collection of agents can generate a rather longer presentation sequence, as opposed to a short-sighted reactive design solution. I also tried to utilize temporal form as a more meaningful way to communicate messages. For example, the squash/stretch action for the sender agent is used to generate a sense of life; the dancing action for the sender agent is used as an "icon" expressing a sender's name for the message currently presented.

7. Conclusion

I have presented *a multiagent model of dynamic design*—a theoretical framework which provides designers with an approach towards creating design solutions that are responsive to dynamic changes in information and the user's intention. I have also emphasized the opportunity of utilizing *temporal forms* as a communicative means. Two case studies have demonstrated that the model is a plausible framework for highlighting the dynamic nature of computer-based communication, and for creating complex design solutions in a systematic manner with simpler descriptions of design agents.

Acknowledgement

I would like to thank the members of the Media Laboratory's Visible Language Workshop for their suggestions, and Munindar Singh for our conversation via email on his theory of multiagent systems.

This work was performed at the MIT Media Laboratory, and supported, in part, by ARPA, NYNEX, and Alenia Corporation.

References

1. Blom, L.A. and Chaplin, T.L. ***The Moment of Movement: Dance Improvisation.*** Univ. of Pittsburgh Press. 1988.
2. Bond, A.H. and Gasser, L. (eds.) ***Readings in Distributed Artificial Intelligence.*** Morgan Kaufmann. 1988.
3. Feiner, S.K. and McKeown K.R. **Automating the generation of coordinated multimedia explanations.** *IEEE Computer,* 24 10. 1991.
4. Hiebert, K. ***Graphic Design Processes: universal to unique.*** VanNostrand Reinhold. 1992.
5. Mackinlay, J.D. **Automating the design of graphical presentations of relational information.** *ACM Transactions on Graphics,* 5 2. 1986.
6. ***Munsell Book of Color: Defining, Explaining, and Illustrating the Fundamental Characteristics of Color,*** Munsell Color Company, Inc. 1929.
7. Pressing, J. **Cognitive processes in improvisation. In Cognitive Processes,** In the Perception of Art. W.R. Crozier and A.J.Chapman (eds.). Elsevier Science. 1987.
8. Roth, S.F. and Hefley,W.E. **Intelligent multimedia presentation systems: Research and principles,** In Intelligent Multimedia Interfaces, M.T. Maybury (ed.). MIT Press. 1993.
9. Singh, M.P. ***Multiagent Systems: A Theoretical Framework for Intentions, Know-How, and Communications.*** Springer Verlag. 1994.
10. Schön, D.A. and Wiggins, G. **Kinds of seeing and their functions in designing.** *Design Studies,* 13, No.2. 1992.
11. Weitzman, L. and Kent,W. **Automatic presentation of multimedia documents using relational grammars.** *Proceedings of ACM Multimedia* '94. 1994.
12. Whitefield, A. and Warren,C. **A blackboard framework for modeling designers' behavior.** *Design Studies,* Vol.10, No.3. 1989.

Chapter 3

Architectures and Infrastructure

Architectures provide the organizing frameworks within which agents can be designed and constructed, while an infrastructure provides the services that are available to the agents as they operate. This chapter of the book begins with three descriptions of agent-based architectures for information systems. The first of these is Wiederhold's introduction to mediators [Wiederhold 1992]. Some of the application papers appearing in this collection, [Huhns et al. 1994], [Arens et al. 1996], and [Kuokka & Harada 1995], involve architectures that are closely related to mediator-based ones.

This work has motivated numerous research efforts to explore the possibilities of mediators, extend their capabilities, and deploy them in real applications. The papers [Cohen et al. 1994] and [Bayardo et al. 1997] represent large, determined efforts to provide such extensions and deployments. In particular, [Bayardo et al. 1997] describe a wide variety of agents for information access in an open environment.

Besides these system architectures, another large body of research has concentrated on architectures for constructing individual agents, which might still have the ability to interact with other agents as part of their functionality. [Fischer et al. 1996] present one such architecture that enables agents having explicit representations for beliefs, desires, and intentions to be constructed.

[Bates et al. 1994] present another such architecture for *broad* agents, by which they mean agents with integrated capabilities. They argue that such agents are necessary for simulated worlds in which the agents must act in a way that is believable to their human observers, just as in fiction. Unlike previous work on agent architectures, [Bates et al. 1994] explicitly consider the emotional state of an agent. As a result, an agent has an emotional control in conjunction with the more typical goal-directed control. The controls might reinforce or inhibit each other.

A focus of many agent architectures is on a system that is *open*. The keys to openness are standardization and formalization of the components of the infrastructure made available in an environment. The papers chosen for the section on Communications and Knowledge Sharing, [Patil et al. 1992] and [Labrou & Finin 1997], introduce the proposed standard languages KQML and KIF and specify most of a formal semantics for KQML. [Dowell et al. 1995] describe the use of an ontology—a conceptual model of a domain—to relate the logical and physical schemas of several information sources to each other.

An important service that an agent infrastructure can provide is a mechanism for the agents to be mobile. We include four different perspectives and approaches for such a mechanism in the papers [Johansen et al. 1995], [Chess et al. 1995], [Rus et al. 1997], and [Borenstein 1994]. [Johansen et al. 1995] specify network and operating system primitives that would be useful or needed by the mobile agents described in the other three papers. [Chess et al. 1995] focus on potential applications for mobile agents, while [Rus et al. 1997] and [Borenstein 1994] describe extensions to the scripting language Tcl that makes it suitable for constructing agents that can be mobile and communicate, both with users and each other.

The final two papers of this chapter, [Sirbu 1997] and [Reiter 1996], present network infrastructure components for security, trust, and commerce. These are crucial for the application of agents in distributed domains, such as financial, health care, or business enterprises.

REFERENCES

Note: A bullet before a reference indicates a selected reading.

[Arens et al. 1996] Arens, Yigal; Hsu, Chun-Nan; and Knoblock, Craig A.; 1996. Query processing in the SIMS information mediator. In *Proceedings of the ARPA/Rome Laboratory Knowledge-Based Planning and Scheduling Initiative Workshop.* AAAI Press, Menlo Park, CA.

•[Bates et al. 1994] Bates, Joseph; Loyall, A. Bryan; and Reilly, W. Scott; 1994. An architecture for action, emotion, and social behavior. In [Castelfranchi & Werner 1994 (pp.55–68)]. Springer-Verlag, Berlin.

•[Bayardo et al. 1997] Bayardo, R.; Bohrer, W.; Brice, R.; Cichocki, A.; Fowler, J.; Helal, A.; Kashyap, V.; Ksiezyk, T.; Martin, G.; Nodine, M.; Rashid, M.; Rusinkiewicz, M.; Shea, R.; Unnikrishnan, C.; Unruh, A.; and Woelk, D.; 1997. InfoSleuth: Semantic integration of information in open and dynamic environments. In *Proceedings of the ACM SIGMOD Conference.* 195–206.

•[Borenstein 1994] Borenstein, Nathaniel S.; 1994. Email with a mind of its own: The Safe-Tcl language for enabled email. In *Proceedings of the IFIP International Working Conference on Upper Layer Protocols and Architectures (ULPAA).* Sponsored by the IFIP Technical Committee 6, Working Group 6.5. 389–402.

[Castelfranchi & Werner 1994] Castelfranchi, Cristiano and Werner, Eric, editors; 1994. *Artificial Social Systems: Fourth European Workshop on Modeling Autonomous Agents in a Multi-Agent World.* Springer-Verlag, Berlin.

•[Chess et al. 1995] Chess, David; Grosof, Benjamin; Harrison, Colin; Levine, David; Parris, Colin; and Tsudik, Gene; 1995. Itinerant agents for mobile computing. *IEEE Personal Communications* 2(5):34–49.

•[Cohen et al. 1994] Cohen, Philip R.; Cheyer, Adam; Wang, Michelle; and Baeg, Soon Cheol; 1994. An open agent architecture. In *Proceedings of the AAAI Spring Symposium on Software Agents.*

•[Dowell et al. 1995] Dowell, Michael L.; Stephens, Larry M.; and Bonnell, Ronald D.; 1995. Using a domain-knowledge ontology as a semantic gateway among information resources. In *Proceedings of the IJCAI Workshop on Basic Ontological Issues in Knowledge Sharing.* Chapter 4, 1–9.

•[Fischer et al. 1996] Fischer, Klaus; Müller, Jörg; and Pischel, Markus; 1996. A pragmatic BDI architecture. In *Intelligent Agents II: Agent Theories, Architectures, and Languages.* 203–218.

[Huhns et al. 1994] Huhns, Michael N.; Singh, Munindar P.; and Ksiezyk, Tomasz; 1994. Global information management via local autonomous agents. In *Proceedings of the ICOT International Symposium on Fifth Generation Computer Systems: Workshop on Heterogeneous Cooperative Knowledge Bases.* 1–15.

•[Johansen et al. 1995] Johansen, Dag; van Renesse, Robbert; and Schneider, Fred B.; 1995. Operating system support for mobile agents. In *Proceedings of the 5th IEEE Workshop on Hot Topics in Operating Systems.* IEEE Computer Society Press, Washington, D.C.

[Kuokka & Harada 1995] Kuokka, Daniel and Harada, Larry; 1995. Matchmaking for information agents. In *Proceedings of the 14th International Joint Conference on Artificial Intelligence.* 672–678.

•[Labrou & Finin 1997] Labrou, Yannis and Finin, Tim; 1997. Semantics and conversations for an agent communication language. In *Proceedings of the International Joint Conference on Artificial Intelligence.* 584–591.

•[Patil et al. 1992] Patil, Ramesh S.; Fikes, Richard E.; Patel-Schneider, Peter F.; McKay, Don; Finin, Tim; Gruber, Thomas; and Neches, Robert; 1992. The DARPA knowledge sharing effort: Progress report. In *Proceedings of the Third International Conference on Principles of Knowledge Representation and Reasoning.* 777–787.

•[Reiter 1996] Reiter, Michael K.; 1996. Distributing trust with the Rampart toolkit. *Communications of the ACM* 39(4):71–74.

•[Rus et al. 1997] Rus, Daniela; Gray, Robert; and Kotz, David; 1997. Transportable information agents. In *Proceedings of the International Conference on Autonomous Agents.* 228–236. ACM Press, New York.

•[Sirbu 1997] Sirbu, Marvin A.; 1997. Credits and debits on the Internet. *IEEE Spectrum* 34(2):23–29.

•[Wiederhold 1992] Wiederhold, Gio; 1992. Mediators in the architecture of future information systems. *IEEE Computer* 25(3):38–49.

3.1 Architectures

Mediators in the Architecture of Future Information Systems

Gio Wiederhold, Stanford University

Mediators embody the administrative and technical knowledge to create information needed for user decision-making modules. The goal is to exploit the data technology puts within our reach.

Computer-based information systems, connected to worldwide high-speed networks, provide increasingly rapid access to a wide variety of data resources.[1] This technology expands access to data, requiring capabilities for assimilation and analysis that greatly exceed what we now have in hand. Without intelligent processing, these advances will provide only a minor benefit to the user at a decision-making level. That brave user will be swamped with ill-defined data of unknown origin.

The problems. This article will expand on the two types of problems that exist:

- For single databases, a primary hindrance for end-user access is the volume of data that is becoming available, the lack of abstraction, and the need to understand the representation of the data.
- When information is combined from multiple databases, the major concern is the mismatch encountered in information representation and structure.

Volume and abstraction. The volume of data can be reduced by selection. It is not coincidental that *Select* is the principal operation of relational database management systems, but selected data is still at too fine a level of detail to be useful for decision making. Further reduction is achieved by abstracting data to higher levels. Aggregation operations such as Count, Average, Standard_Deviation, Maximum, and Minimum provide some computational facilities for abstraction. Today, such abstractions are formulated within the end user's application, using a variety of domain knowledge.

For most base data, more than one abstraction must be supported: For the sales manager, the aggregation is by sales region, while aggregation by customer income is appropriate for marketing. Figure 1 presents examples of required abstraction types.

Computations for abstraction may be extensive and complex. Collecting all instances that lead to an abstraction can involve recursion, say, locating all potentially useful flight segments for a trip. Such a computation cannot be specified with current database query languages. Hence, application programs are written by specialists to reduce the data. Using specific data-processing programs as intermediaries reduces flexibility and responsiveness for the end user. The knowledge that creates the abstractions is hidden and hard to share and reuse.

Type of Abstraction	Example Base Data		Abstraction
Granularity	Sales detail	→	Product summaries
Generalization	Product data	→	Product type
Temporal	Daily sales	→	Seasonally adjusted monthly sales
Relative	Product cost	→	Inflation-adjusted trends
Exception recognition	Accounting detail	→	Evidence of fraud
Path computation	Airline schedules	→	Trip duration and cost

Figure 1. Abstraction functions.

Mismatch. As Figure 2 shows, data obtained from remote and autonomous sources often will not match in terms of name, scope, granularity of abstractions, temporal units, and domain definitions. The differences shown in the examples must be resolved before automatic processing can join these values.

Without an extended processing paradigm, as proposed here, the information needed to initiate actions will be hidden in ever larger volumes of detail, scrollable on ever larger screens, in ever smaller fonts. In essence, the gap between information and data will be even wider than it is now. Knowing that information exists and is accessible gives end users expectations. Finding that it is not available in a useful form or that it cannot be combined with other data creates confusion and frustration. I believe the reason some users object to computer-based systems, saying they create information overload, is that they get too much of the wrong kind of data. (See the sidebar, "Knowledge versus data.")

Use of a model. To visualize the requirements we will place on future information systems, let's consider the activities carried out today when decisions are being made. Making informed decisions requires applying a variety of knowledge to information about the state of the world.

To manage this variety, we employ specialists. To manage the volume of data, we segment our databases. In these partitions, partial results are produced, abstracted, and filtered. The problem of making decisions is now reduced to the issue of choosing and evaluating the significance of the pieces of information derived in those partitions and fusing the important portions.

For example, an investment decision for a manufacturer will depend on the fusion of information on its own production capability versus that of others, its sales experience in related products, the market for the conceived product at a certain price, the cost-to-price ratio

Knowledge versus data

I favor a pragmatic distinction between data and knowledge in this model.

- *Data* describes specific instances and events. It may be gathered automatically or clerically. The correctness of data can be checked versus the real world.
- *Knowledge* describes abstract classes. Each class can cover many instances. Experts are needed to gather and formalize knowledge.

One item of knowledge can affect the use of many items of data; also, one item of new data can disprove or weaken existing knowledge.[2]

Type of Mismatch	Example		Domains
Key difference	Alan Turing: The Enigma *Reference for reader*	versus	QA29.T8H63 *Reference for librarian*
Scope difference	Employees paid *Includes retirees*	versus	Employees available *Includes consultants*
Abstraction grain	Personal income *From employment*	versus	Family income *For taxation, housing*
Temporal basis	Monthly budget *Central office*	versus	Weekly production *Factory records*
Domain semantics	Postal codes *One can cover multiple places*	versus	Town names *Can have multiple codes*
Value semantics	Excessive_pay *Per Internal Revenue Service*	versus	Excessive_pay *Per board of directors*

Figure 2. Mismatches in data resources.

appropriate for the size of the market, and the cost of the funds to be invested. Specialists would consider these diverse topics and consult multiple data resources to support their claims. The decision-maker will integrate and fuse that information to arrive at a single set of ranked alternatives, considering risk and long-range objectives in combining the results.

An effective architecture for future information systems must support automated information-acquisition processes for decision-making activities. By default, I model the solution following the partitioning seen in human-based support systems. However, most aspects of human behavior cannot be captured and formalized adequately. We merely define a modular architecture wholly composed of pieces of software that are available or appear to be attainable in a modest time frame, say 10 years. Modern hardware should be capable of dealing with the processing demands imposed by such software.

Current state. We are not starting from a zero base. Systems are now becoming available that are capable of achieving what Vannevar Bush envisaged nearly a half-century ago for his information management desk (Memex).[3] We can select and scroll information on our workstation displays. We have access to remote data and can present the values in one of multiple windows. We can insert documents into files in our workstation, and we can annotate text and graphics. We can reach conclusions based on this evidence and advise others of decisions made.

The vision in this article is intended to provide a basis for automated integration of such information. Neither Memex nor our current systems address that level of processing. At best, they provide graphic visualizations so that voluminous information is assimilated more easily by the end user.

A model of information processing

Information lets us choose among several otherwise indistinguishable actions. Let's again consider a simple business environment. Say a factory manager needs sales data to set production levels, a sales manager needs demographic information to project future sales, and a customer wants price and quality information to make purchase choices.

Most of the information these people need can be represented by factual data and is available on some computer. Communication networks can make the data available wherever needed. However, before decisions are made, a considerable amount of knowledge also has to be applied. Today, most knowledge is available through various administrative and technical staff at institutions.[4] Some knowledge is encoded in data-processing programs and expert systems for automated processing.

Use of supporting information for decision making is similar in partially automated and manual systems. In manual systems, the decision-maker obtains assistance from staff and colleagues who peruse files and prepare summaries and other documentation. With partial automation, the staff uses computers to prepare these documents. The decision-maker rarely uses the computer, because the information from multiple sources is too diverse for automatic integration.

Processing and applying knowledge. A technician will know how to select and transfer data from a remote computer to one used for analysis. A data analyst will understand the attributes of the data and define the functions to combine and integrate the data. A statistician might provide procedures to aggregate data on customers into groups that present distinctive behavior patterns. A psychologist might provide classification parameters that characterize the groups.

Ultimately, it's up to a manager to assess the validity of the classifications that are made, use the information to make a decision, and assume the risk of making the decision. A public relations person might take the information and present it to stockholders, the people who eventually assume the risk. Since these tasks are characterized by data and knowledge gathered in the past and projected into the future, we term these tasks planning. (This definition of planning is more extensive than that used in artificial intelligence research,[5] although the objectives are the same.)

To be able to deal with support for planning in a focused way, we model the information-processing aspects. Figure 3 illustrates the two distinct feedback loops and their interaction. The data loop closes when the effects of actions taken are recorded in the database. The knowledge loop closes when recently gained knowledge is made available so it can be used for further selection and data-reduction decisions. At their interaction points, information is created. Those points are of prime concern for future systems.

Creation of information. The model in Figure 3 identifies the interaction points where, during processing, information is created. Since getting information means that something novel has been learned, one or more of the following conditions have to hold:

- The information is obtained from a remote source that was previously not known locally (Step 3.ii.b of Figure 3). Here, the information system must provide communication and remote access support. A special case of this condition occurs when a database is used for recall, to provide data we knew once but cannot remember with certainty. The database component is used here to communicate over time — from the past to the present.
- Two previously distinct facts are merged or unified (Step 3.ii.c). A classic, although trivial, example is finding one's grandfather via transitivity of parents. In realistic systems, unification of data also involves computation of functions, say, the average income and its variation among groups of consumers.
- Multiple results are fused using pragmatic assessments of the quality and risks associated within Step 4. Here, derived abstractions, rather than facts, are combined; the processing techniques are those associated with symbolic processing in rule-based expert systems, although they are also found coded within application programs. In our example, the market specialist might want to unify incomes of current consumers with their reading habits to devise an advertising strategy.

Databases record detailed data for each of many instances or events. Reducing this detail to a few abstract cases increases the information content per element. Of these abstractions, only a small, manageable number of justified results is brought to the decision-maker. For instance, the market analyst has made it possible to base decisions on consumer groups rather than individual consumers. Certain groups may be unlikely purchasers and are therefore not targeted for promotions.

While the behavior of any individual may not adhere to the rules hypothesized in the prior steps, the expected behavior of the aggregate population should be close to the prediction. Failures only occur if the underlying data contains many errors or if we have serious errors in our knowledge. Uncertainty, however, is common.

Uncertainty. We cannot predict the future with certainty. For automation of full-scale information systems, the processing of uncertainty measures must be supported, although subtasks do exist whereby results can be precisely defined. Uncertainties within a domain may be captured by a formal model.

The uncertainty of the results of an application is based on the uncertain precision of source information and the uncertainty created at each step where information is merged. For example, we collect domain-specific observations based on some criterion — say, people living in a certain postal-code area. We also have data to associate an income level with that postal-code area. At the same time, we might know the income distribution of people buying some product.

The desired result requires unification of the postal code with income to estimate potential sales. Unfortunately, there is no logical reason why such a unification should be correct. We have some formal classes — namely, people with a certain postal code — and some other formalizable classes based on income. In addition, some natural classes exist that are not formalized but are intuitively known. In our example, these comprise the potential purchasers, of which there are several subgroups — including those found in the database who bought in the past and those who may buy the planned products in the future. For the future class, only informal criteria can be formulated.

The marketing manager will use definable classes — by postal code and by observed and recorded purchasing patterns — to establish candidate members for the natural class of potential consumers. These classes overlap; the more they overlap the more correct the decision-maker's predictions will be. If we infer from classes that do not match well, the uncertainty attached to the generated plans will be greater. But uncertainty is the essence of decision making and is reflected in the risk that the manager takes on. If we only have to report the postal codes for our consumers, we do not need a manager with decision-making skills or intelligent support software. Hence, uncertainty is created when formal and natural classes are matched.

Communication of knowledge and data is necessary to achieve this conflu-

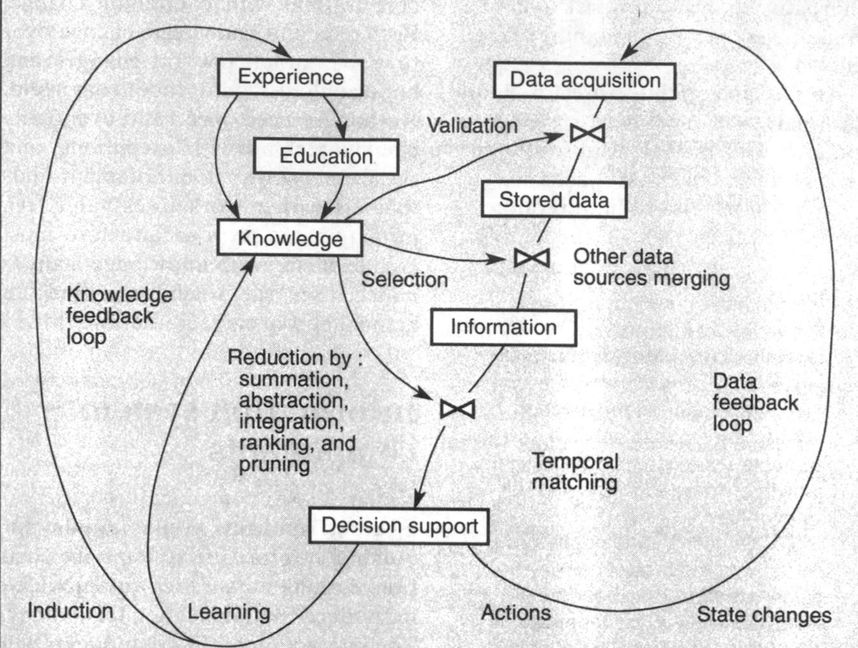

Major steps in the information-processing loops include:

1. Data are made available. These are either factual observations or results from prior processing, or combinations thereof.
2. Knowledge is made available. It derives from formal training and experience.
3. Knowledge about the data and its content is applied:
   - i Validation: Errors in data or knowledge are identified.
   - ii Selection: Subsets of available data are (a) defined, (b) obtained, and (c) merged.
   - iii Reduction: The data found are summarized to an appropriate level of abstraction.
4. Results are made available and multiple results are fused.
5. The combined information is utilized in two ways:
   - i Actions are taken that will affect the state of the world.
   - ii Unexpected results will augment the experience base of the participants and of others who receive this information, increasing their knowledge.
6. The process loops are closed with two independent steps.
   - i The actions and their effect are observed and recorded in some database.
   - ii The knowledge is recorded to effect subsequent validation, data definition, selection, reduction, or fusion.

Figure 3. Knowledge and data feedback loops and their interaction.

A manual approach to mediation

The concept of mediation is related to the notion of having corporate information centers, as promoted by IBM and others. These corporate resources are staffed and equipped with tools to aid any user needing information. The needs and capabilities of an information center, however, differ from those of automated mediators:

1. A single center, or mediator for that matter, cannot deal with the variety of information that is useful for corporate decision making.
2. Automation of the function will be necessary to achieve acceptable response time and growth of knowledge and its quality over time.
3. The user should not be burdened with the task of seeking out information sources. This task, especially if it is repetitive, is best left to an interaction of application programs in a workstation and automated mediation programs.

The information center notion initiates yet another self-serving bureaucracy within a corporation. Effective staff is not likely to be content in the internal service roles that an information center provides, so that turnover of staff and its knowledge will be high. The only role foreseen in such a center is mediation — bringing together potential users with candidate information.

To manage mediation, modularization instead of centralization seems to be essential. Modularity is naturally supported by a distributed environment, the dominant computing environment in the near future.

Further reading

Atre, S., *Information Center: Strategies and Case Studies*, Vol. 1, Atre Int'l Consultants, Rye, N.Y., 1986.

Wetherbe, J.C., and R.L. Leitheiser, "Information Centers: A Survey of Services, Decisions, Problems, and Successes," *Information Systems Management*, Vol. 2, No. 3, 1985, pp. 3-10.

ence. The communication may occur over space or over time. The information systems we consider must support both communication and fusion of data and knowledge.

Change. Our systems must also be able to deal with continuing change. Both data and knowledge change over time because the world changes and because we learn things about our world. Rules that were once valid eventually become riddled with exceptions, and the specialist who does not adapt finds that his or her work loses value. An information system architecture must deal explicitly with knowledge maintenance. (See the sidebar entitled "A manual approach to mediation.")

Information system components

The components available today for building information systems are positioned along a *data highway* provided by modern communication technology. The interaction of the components will be primarily constrained by logical and informational limitations, not by physical linkages. When we place the components into the conceptual architecture, we will recognize lacunae, that is, places where there are no existing components, only inadequate or uncooperative ones. We will see where the components must work together. Effective systems can be achieved only if the data and knowledge interfaces of the components are such that cooperation is feasible.

Data and knowledge resources. There is a wide variety of data resources. We might classify them by how close they are to the source. Raw data obtained from sensors, such as purchase records from point-of-sale scanners, or, on a different scale, images recorded by earth satellites, are at the factual extreme. Census and stock reports contain data that have gone through some processing, but they will be seen as facts by most users.

At the other extreme are textual representations of knowledge. In general, books, research reports, and library material contain accumulated knowledge, contributed by writers and their colleagues. Unfortunately, from our processing-oriented viewpoint, that knowledge is difficult to integrate and fuse. For instance, combining a travel guide description with airline and bus schedules to plan a trip is a research challenge. The tables, maps, and figures in such documents are data as well, but rarely in a form that can be processed without human input.

Workstation applications. The new generations of capable workstations provide the systems environment for planning activities. For planning, users need to interact with their own hypotheses, save intermediate results for comparison of effects, and display alternate projections over time. This interaction with information establishes the insights you need to gain confidence in your decisions.

Our architecture must not constrain the users as they exercise creativity at the workstation. A variety of data resources will be needed for planning processes. But help is needed to deal with the aggregation and mismatch problems being encountered. By providing comprehensive support for access to information, the complexity of the end user's applications can be reduced to such an extent that quite involved analyses remain manageable.

Network interfaces. Modern operating and network systems simplify the users' administrative tasks by handling all hardware resources and interfaces. Interfaces for remote access from the users' workstation nodes to the nodes containing database servers are based on communication protocols and formats. They ignore the contents of the messages. Mediators, on their network nodes, will provide services that deal with the content of the data being transmitted. Mediators can be interposed using existing communication network protocols.

The mediator architecture

Intelligent and active use of information requires a class of software modules that mediate between the workstation applications and the databases. Mediation simplifies, abstracts, reduces, merges, and explains data. The examples of mediation shown in the "Mediation" sidebar are specialized and are

Mediation

In this article, the term *mediation* covers a wide variety of functions that enhance stored data prior to their use in an application. Mediation makes an interface intelligent by dealing with representation and abstraction problems that you must face when trying to use today's data and knowledge resources.

Mediators have an active role. They contain knowledge structures to drive transformations. Mediators may store intermediate results.

Some examples of mediation found in current information systems are shown here. Most readers will be able to add entries from their experience.

• *Transformation and subsetting of databases using view definitions and object templates.* These techniques reorganize base data into new configurations appropriate to specific users and applications.

Barsalou, T., R.M. Chavez, and G. Wiederhold, "Hypertext Interfaces for Decision-Support Systems: A Case Study," *Proc. Medinfo 89*, IFIP, 1989, pp. 126-130.

Basu, A., "Knowledge Views in Multiuser Knowledge-Based Systems," *Proc. Fourth IEEE Int'l Data Eng. Conf.*, IEEE CS Press, Los Alamitos, Calif., Order No. 827 (microfiche only), 1988, pp. 346-353.

Chamberlin, D.D., J.N. Gray, and I.L. Traiger, "Views, Authorization, and Locking in a Relational Data Base System," *Proc. 1975 Nat'l Computer Conf.*, Vol. 44, AFIPS Press, pp. 425-430.

Lai, K-Y., T.W. Malone, and K-C. Yu, "Object Lens: A Spreadsheet for Cooperative Work," *ACM Trans. Office Information Systems*, Vol. 6, No. 4, Oct. 1988, pp. 332-353.

Wiederhold, G., "Views, Objects, and Databases," *Computer*, Vol. 19, No. 12, Dec. 1986, pp. 37-44.

• *Methods to gather an appropriate amount of data.* Conventional database management systems do not deal well with data that are recursively linked. To gather all instances, computations to achieve closure may process data from a relational database, as in some logic and database projects. To select sufficient instances for a narrowly phrased query, it is possible to broaden a search by generalization. A frequent abstraction is to derive temporal interval representations from detailed event data.

Chaudhuri, S., "Generalization and a Framework for Query Modification," *Sixth IEEE Int'l Data Eng. Conf.*, IEEE CS Press, Los Alamitos, Calif., Order No. 2025, 1990, pp. 139-145.

Ullman, J.D., *Principles of Database and Knowledge-Base Systems, Vol. II*, Computer Science Press, 1989.

Wiederhold, G., S. Jajodia, and W. Litwin: "Dealing with Granularity of Time in Temporal Databases," *Lecture Notes in Computer Science*, Vol. 498, R. Anderson et al., eds., Springer-Verlag, N.Y., 1991, pp. 124-140.

• *Methods to access and merge data from multiple databases.* These have to compensate for mismatch at the level of database systems, database structure, and the representation and meaning of the actual data values. Mismatch is often due to differing temporal representations, say, monthly budgets and weekly production figures. These methods may induce uncertainty in the results because of mismatched sources.

Chiang, T.C., and G.R. Rose, "Design and Implementation of a Production Database Management System (DBM-2)," *Bell System Technical J.*, Vol. 61, No. 9, Nov. 1982, pp. 2,511-2,528.

Dayal, U., and H.Y. Hwang, "View Definition and Generalization for Database Integration in Multibase: A System for Heterogeneous Databases," *IEEE Trans. Software Eng.*, Vol. SE-10, No. 6, Nov. 1983, pp. 628-645.

DeMichiel, L., "Performing Operations Over Mismatched Domains," *IEEE Trans. Knowledge and Data Eng.*, Vol. 1, No. 4, Dec. 1989, pp. 485-493.

Litwin, W., and A. Abdellatif: "Multidatabase Interoperability," *Computer*, Vol. 19, No. 12, Dec. 1986, pp. 10-18.

Sacca, D., et al., "Description of the Overall Architecture of the KIWI System," *ESPRIT 85*, EEC, Elsevier, 1986, pp. 685-700.

• *Computations that support abstraction and generalization over underlying data.* These are needed to bring data at a low level of detail to a higher level. Typical operations involve statistical summarization and searching for exceptions. Abstractions are also needed to resolve mismatches.

Adiba, M.E., "Derived Relations: A Unified Mechanism for Views, Snapshots, and Distributed Data," *Proc. Seventh Conf. Very Large Data Bases*, C. Zaniolo and C. Delobel, eds., IEEE Computer Soc. Press, Los Alamitos, Calif., Order No. 371 (microfiche only), 1981, pp. 293-305.

Chen, M.C., and L. McNamee, "A Data Model and Access Method for Summary Data Management," *Fifth IEEE Int'l Data Eng. Conf.*, IEEE CS Press, Los Alamitos, Calif., Order No. 1915, 1989, pp. 242-249.

DeZegher-Geets, I., et al., "Summarization and Display of Online Medical Records," *M.D. Computing*, Vol. 5, No. 3, Mar. 1988, pp. 38-46.

Ozsoyoglu, Z.M., and G. Ozsoyoglu, "Summary-Table-By-Example: A Database Query Language for Manipulating Summary Data," *First IEEE Int'l Data Eng. Conf.*, IEEE CS Press, Los Alamitos, Calif., Order No. 533 (microfiche only), 1984, pp. 193-202.

• *Much information is available in the form of text.* Most text processing is limited today to selection and presentation. More can be done. Most routine reports tend to have a degree of structure that makes some analysis feasible. Developing standards for text representation will help, regularizing textual information for further processing and mediation.

Callahan, M.V., and P.F. Rusch, "Online Implementation of the Chemical Abstract Search File and the Chemical Abstracts Service Registry Nomenclature File," *Online Rev.*, Vol. 5, No. 5, Oct. 1981, pp. 377-393.

McCune, B.P., et al., "Rubric: A System for Rule-Based Information Retrieval, "*IEEE Trans. Software Eng.*, Vol. SE-11, No. 9, Sept. 1985, pp. 939-945.

Sager, N., et al., *Medical Language Processing, Computer Management of Narrative Data*, Addison-Wesley, Reading, Mass., 1987.

• *Mediators may maintain derived data for the sake of efficiency.* Having derived data reduces the need to access databases, but the intermediate knowledge has to be maintained. Research into truth-maintenance is relevant here. There is also a problem of maintaining integrity under concurrent use.

Filman, R.E., "Reasoning with Worlds and Truth Maintenance in a Knowledge-Based Programming Environment," *Comm. ACM*, Vol. 31, No. 4, Apr. 1988, pp. 382-401.

Hanson, E., "A Performance Analysis of View Materialization Strategies," *Proc. ACM SIGMOD*, 1987, pp. 440-453.

Kanth, M.R., and P.K. Bose, "Extending an Assumption-Based Truth Maintenance System to Databases," *Fourth IEEE Int'l Data Eng. Conf.*, IEEE CS Press, Los Alamitos, Calif., Order No. 827 (microfiche only), 1988, pp. 354-361.

Roussopoulos, N., and H. Kang, "Principles and Techniques in the Design of ADMS," *Computer*, Vol. 19, No. 12, Dec. 1986, pp. 19-25.

tied to a specific database or to a particular application.

Mediators are modules occupying an explicit, active layer between the user applications and the data resources. They will be accessed by application programs residing in the user workstations. (Recall that our goal is a sharable architecture.)

Mediators form a distinct middle layer, making the user applications independent of the data resources. What are the transforms needed in such a layer, and what form will the modules supporting this layer have? The responses to these questions are interrelated.

Three architectural layers. We create a central layer by distinguishing the function of mediation from the user-oriented processing and from database access. Most user tasks will need multiple, distinct mediators for their subtasks. A mediator uses one or a few databases.

As Figure 4 shows, the interfaces to be supported provide the cuts where communication network services are needed. Unfortunately, the commonality of functions described in the examples (see the "Mediation" sidebar) does not extend to an architectural commonality: All the examples cited are bound to the data resources and the end users' applications in their idiosyncratic ways. This is where new technology must be established if fusion at the application level is to be supported. Accessing one mediator at a time does not allow for fusion, and seeing multiple results on distinct windows of one screen does not support automation of fusion.

Mediators. Having listed some examples of mediators in use or planned for specific tasks, I offer this general definition: *A mediator is a software module that exploits encoded knowledge about certain sets or subsets of data to create information for a higher layer of applications.*

We place the same requirements on a mediation module that we place on any software module: It should be small and simple[6] so that it can be maintained by one expert or, at most, by a small and coherent group of experts.

An important, although perhaps not essential, requirement I'd like to place on mediators is that they be inspectable by potential users. For instance, the rules used by a mediator using expert system technology can be obtained by the user as in any good cooperative expert system. In this sense, the mediators provide data about themselves in response to inspection, and such data could be analyzed by yet another mediator module, an inspector mediator.

Since there will eventually be a great number and variety of mediators, users have to be able to choose among them. Inspectability enables that task. For instance, we might have distinct mediators that can provide the names of the best consultants for database design. Alternate metamediators are likely to use different evaluation criteria; one may use the number of publications and another the number of clients.

Some metamediators will have to exist that merely provide access to catalogs listing available mediators and data resources. The search may go either way: For a given data source, it may be necessary to locate a knowledgeable mediator; for a desirable mediator, we need to locate an adequate data resource. It will be essential that the facilities provided by these metalevel mediators can be integrated into the general processing model, since search for information is always an important aspect of information processing. Where search and analyses are separated — as is still common today in, for instance, statistical data-processing — trying to find and understand the data is often the most costly phase of information processing.

Since many databases are autonomous, it is desirable that only a limited and recognizable set of mediators depend on any one of them. Focusing data access through a limited number of views maintained by these mediators provides the data independence necessary for databases that are evolving autonomously. Currently, compatibility constraints are hindering growth of databases in terms of structure and scope, since many users are affected. As the number of users and the automation of access increase, the importance of indirect access via mediators will increase.

Mediator interfaces. The two interfaces to the mediator layer are the most critical aspect of this three-layer architecture. Today's mediating programs use a wide variety of interface methods and approaches. The user learns one or a few of them and remains committed to that choice until its performance becomes wholly unacceptable. Unless the mediators are easily and flexibly accessible, the model of common information access I envisage is bound to remain fictitious. The research challenge then lies in the interface and its support. Our hardware environment implies that mediators can live on any node, not just on workstation and database hosts.

User's workstation interface to the mediators. The range of mediator capabilities is such that a high-level language should evolve to drive them. Here, I am thinking of language concepts, rather than interface standards, to indicate the degree of extensibility that must be provided if the mediating concepts are to be generalized.

Determining an effective interface between the workstation application and the mediators will be a major research effort in establishing systems sharing this architecture. It appears that a language is needed to provide flexibility, composability, iteration, and evaluation in this interface. Descriptive, but static, interface specifications seem unable to deal with the variety of control and the information flow that must be supported. The basic language structure should permit incremental growth so that new functions can be supported as mediators join the network to provide new functionality.

It is important to observe that I do not see a need for a user-friendly interface. What is needed here is a machine- and communication-friendly interface. Application programs executing on the users' workstations can provide the type of display and manipulation functions appropriate to their users. Omitting the criterion of user friendliness avoids the dichotomy that has led to inadequacies in the Structured Query Language (SQL), which tries to be user friendly, while its predominant use is for programmed access.[7] Standards needed here can only be defined after experience has been obtained in sharing these resources to support the high-level functions needed for decision making.

The mediator to the database management system interface. Existing database standards, such as SQL and the Remote Data Access (RDA) protocol, provide a basis for database access by mediators. Relational concepts — selection, views, etc. — are a good starting point, but much flexibility is possible. A mediator dealing with a specific database need not be constrained to a particular protocol, while a more general mediator will gain applicability through a standard interface. A mediator that combines information from multiple databases can use its knowledge to control the merging process, specifying relational operations directly. Joins may, for instance, be replaced by explicit semijoins, so that intelligent filtering can occur during processing. Still, dealing with multiple sources is likely to lead to incompleteness. Outer-joins are often required for data access to avoid losing objects with incomplete information.

New access languages are needed to manage sensor-based and simulation processes. Such systems also provide data to be abstracted and fused.

The separation of user applications and data sources provided by mediating modules allows reorganization of data structures and redistribution of data over the processing nodes of communication networks without affecting the functionality of the modules. The three-layer architecture then makes an explicit trade-off favoring flexibility over integration. The argument is the distinction of data and the results of mediator modules:

- Sharability of information requires that database results can be configured according to one of several views. Mediators, being active, can create objects for a wide variety of orthogonal views.
- Making complex objects themselves persistent, on the other hand, binds knowledge to the data — hampering sharability.
- The loss of performance due to the interposition of a mediator can be overcome, for instance, via techniques listed in the section entitled "SODs."

These arguments do not yet address the distribution of the mediators I envisage.

Available interfaces. We need interface protocols for data and knowledge. Mediation defines a new layer within the application layer defined by the open-system architecture. Open-systems layers will soon provide good communication support.

However, as mentioned earlier, communication of data alone does not guarantee that the data will be correctly understood for processing by the receiver. Mediation considers the meaning assigned to the bits stored; Figure 2 contains some examples.

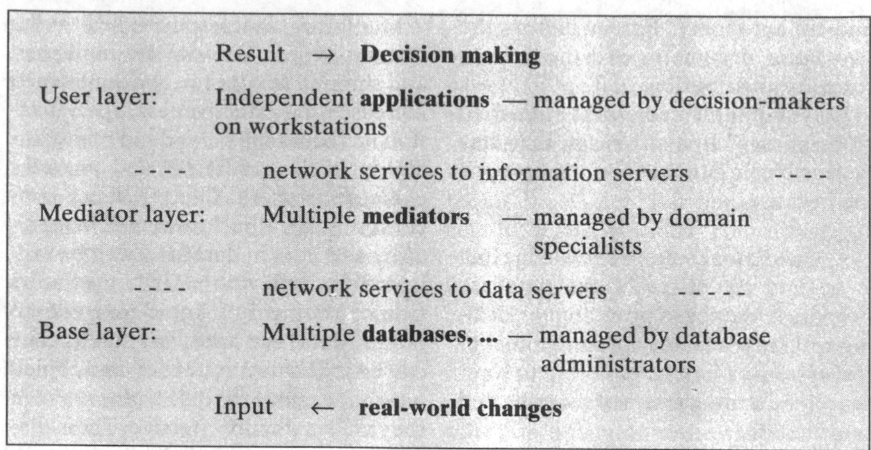

Figure 4. Three layers of a mediator architecture.

Sharing of mediator modules. Since we are getting access to so much more data from a variety of sources, which are arriving at ever higher rates, automated processing will be essential. The processing tasks needed within the mediators — selection, fusion, reduction, abstraction, and generalization — are sketched in the interaction model of Figure 3. Diverse mediator modules will combine these functions in various ways to serve user applications at the decision-making layer above.

The mediator modules will be most effective if they can serve a variety of applications. The applications will compose their tasks as much as possible by acquiring information from the set of available mediators. Unavailable information may motivate the creation of new mediators.

Sharing reinforces the need for two types of partitioning. First, there are the three horizontal layers supporting end users, mediators, and databases. Second, each of those layers will be vertically partitioned. There will be multiple-user applications, each using various configurations of mediators. Each of the mediators in turn will use distinct views over one or several databases. Vertical partitioning does not create a hierarchy. Just as databases are justified by a diversity of shared usage, mediators should be sharable. Today's expert systems are rarely modular and sharable, so their development and maintenance cost is harder to amortize.

For instance, the mediation module that can deal with inflation adjustment can be used by many applications. The mediator that understands postal codes and town names can be used by the post office, express delivery services, and corporate mail rooms.

Partitioning leads to modules, as sketched in Figure 5.

Distribution of mediators. I have implied throughout this article that mediators are distinct modules, distributed over the network. Distribution can be motivated by greater economy for access, by better locality for maintenance,

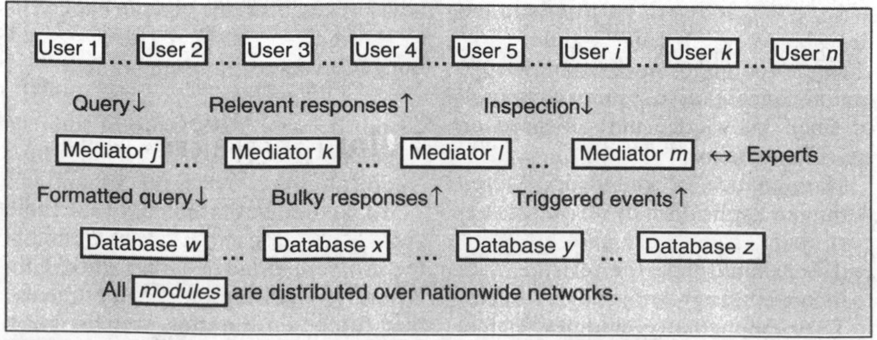

Figure 5. Interfaces for information flow.

and by autonomy. For mediators the two latter arguments are the driving force for distribution.

Why shouldn't mediators be attached to databases? In many cases, that may be feasible; in general it is not appropriate because

- A mediator contains knowledge that is beyond the scope of the database proper. A database programmer dealing with, say, a factory production-control system cannot be expected to foresee all the strategic uses of the collected information.
- Concepts of abstraction are not part of database technology today. The focus has been on reliable and consistent management of large volumes of detailed facts.
- Intelligent processing of data will often involve dealing with uncertainty, adding excessive and undesirable complexity to database technology.
- Many mediators will access multiple databases to combine disjointed sets of data prior to analysis and reduction.

Similarly, we can argue that the mediators should not be bound to the users' workstation applications. Again, the functions that mediators provide are different in scope from the tasks performed on the workstations. Workstation applications might use a variety of mediators to explore the data resources.

Maintenance issues, a major motivation for keeping mediators distinct, have received insufficient attention in the past. During the initial stage of most projects that developed expert systems, knowledge bases simply grew and the cost of knowledge acquisition dominated the cost of knowledge maintenance. Many projects, in fact, assumed implicitly that knowledge, once obtained, would remain valid for all times. Although some fundamental rules may indeed not change for a long time, new concepts arise, older ones are partitioned, and definitions are refined as demands change. The importance of knowledge maintenance leads to systems composed of small knowledge units focused on specific domains.[8]

Maintenance of knowledge stored within an application by an outside expert system is intrusive and risky. The end user should make the decision when to incorporate new knowledge. It is best to keep the mediator modules distinct from the applications.

Mediators are associated with the domain expert, but may be replicated and shipped to other network nodes to increase their effectiveness. Specialization increases the power and maintainability of the mediators and provides choices for users. The efficiency concerns of separating knowledge in mediators and data in databases can be mitigated by replication. Since mediators (incorporating only knowledge and no factual data) are relatively stable, they can be replicated as needed and copied onto nodes along the data highway where they are maximally effective. Their content certainly should not change during a transaction. As long as the mediators remain small, they can also be easily shipped to a site where substantial data volumes have to be processed.

Triggers for knowledge maintenance. I have incorporated one aspect of mediation into Figure 5 that has not yet been discussed. Since the knowledge in the mediator must be kept up to date, placing triggers or active demons in databases[2] is useful. Now the mediators can be informed when the database and, by extension, the real world changes. The owner of the mediator should ensure that such changes are, in due time, reflected in the mediator's knowledge base.

Again justified by the analogy to human specialists, I consider that a mediator is fundamentally trustworthy but is inspectable when suspicions of obsoleteness arise. For instance, an assumption, say, that well-to-do people buy big cars may be used in the marketing mediator, but it is possible that over time this rule will become invalid. I expect that the base data will be monitored for changes and that exceptions to database constraints will trigger information flow to the mediator. In a rule-based mediator the certainty factor of rules can be adjusted. If the uncertainty exceeds a threshold, the mediator can advise its creator, the domain expert, to abandon this rule. The end user need not get involved.[9]

Related research

We have seen that many of the individual concepts underlying this architecture were found in earlier work. This is hardly surprising, since the problems that future information systems must address exist now and are being dealt with in many specific situations. Rather than extrapolating into the unknown, I define an architecture that is based on a number of known concepts.

Object-oriented concepts. We have great expectations from object-oriented concepts, since these provide a semantic, meaningful clustering of related data and methods. A mediator can be viewed as an autonomous superobject. It also hides the representation of the underlying data. However, the mediator should be accessed by a higher level language. Internally, the choice of language is not restricted.

An important difference between mediators and objects is in their scale. This difference is reflected in their scope and ownership. Mediators are independent units and have to deal with multiple applications. Furthermore, they do not need to encapsulate data.

The network of connections within the global architecture means that distinct tasks can intersect at nodes within this information-processing structure. The same mediator type may access distinct sets of data, and information from one data source can be used by distinct mediators. Sources can include object databases.

Independent actors and agents. Independence is even more prominent in the concept of Actors, as proposed by Hewitt.[10] In an Actor architecture, modules operate independently but are assumed to cooperate towards a common goal. Mediators do not act independently. They respond to queries from applications or to triggers placed in databases. They do not interact intelligently with each other; a hierarchy is imposed for every specific task. This limitation provides computational simplicity and manageability. The extent to which networks of autonomous Actors can be motivated is unclear.

The concepts underlying Agents, as developed to control robot activities, are based on control mechanisms similar to those in mediators. Such Agents do not yet deal with abstractions, mismatch, and autonomous data resources.

Maintenance and learning. The knowledge embodied in mediators cannot be permitted to be static. Knowledge maintenance is based on feedback. In effective organizations, lower levels of management involved in information processing provide feedback to superior layers.

Knowledge in mediators will initially be updated by human experts. For active knowledge domains, some automation will be important. Checking for inconsistencies between acquired data and assumed knowledge is the next step.

Eventually, some mediators will be endowed with learning mechanisms. Feedback for learning might either come from performance measures or from explicit induction over the databases they manage. Learning is triggered by monitors placed in the database. Ideally, every rule in the mediator is related to triggers. For instance, the rule "Wealthy people buy big cars" requires triggers on income and car ownership. Now, changes in the database can continuously update hypotheses of interest within the mediator.

Learning by modifying certainty parameters in the knowledge base is relatively simple. Tabular knowledge — or say, a list of good customer types — can be augmented. Learning new concepts is much more difficult, since we have no mechanisms that relate observations automatically to unspecified symbolic concepts. By initially depending fully on the human expert to maintain the mediator and later updating parameters of rules, we can gradually move to automated learning.

Implementation techniques. Mediators will embody a variety of techniques now found in freestanding applications and programs that perform mediation functions. These programs are now often classified by the underlying scientific area rather than by their place in information systems.

The nature of mediators is such that many techniques developed in artificial intelligence will be employed. We expect that mediators will often use

- declarative approaches,
- capability for explanation,
- heuristic control of inference,
- pruning of candidate solutions,
- evaluation of the certainty of results, and
- estimation of processing costs for high-level optimization.

The literature on these topics is broad.[5] Heuristic approaches are likely to be important because of the large solution spaces. Uncertainty computations are needed to deal with missing data and mismatched natural classes.

SODs. The knowledge-based management systems (KBMS) project group at Stanford University has formulated a specific form of mediator, which focuses on well-structured semantic domains of discourse (SODs).[11] A SOD provides a declarative structure for the domain semantics, suitable for an interpreter. We see multiple SODs being used by an application, executing a long and interactive transaction.

I summarize our concepts here as one research avenue for the architecture I have presented.

Specific features and constraints imposed on SODs are

- The knowledge should be represented in a declarative form.
- Each should have a well-formed language interface.
- Each should contain feature descriptions exploitable by the interpreter.
- Each should be inspectable by the user applications.
- Each should be amenable to parallel execution.
- Each accesses the databases through relational views.
- During execution, source data and derived data objects are bound in memory.
- Each can share instances of objects.

By placing these constraints on SODs as mediators, proofs of their behaviors and interaction are feasible. Provable behavior is not only of interest to developers, but also provides a basis for prediction of computational efficiency.

However, the modularity of SODs causes two types of losses:

(1) Loss in power, due to limitations in interconnections.
(2) Loss in performance, due to reliance on symbolic binding rather than on direct linkages.

We hope to offset these losses through gains obtained from having structures that enable effective computational algorithms. An implementation of a demonstration using frame technology is being expanded. Of course, the long-range benefit is that small, well-constructed mediators will enable knowledge maintenance and growth.

Interface language. Defining the language needed to effectively invoke a variety of mediators is the major issue. If we cannot express the high-level concepts encapsulated in the mediators well, we will not be able to implement the required services. For application access to SODs, we start from database concepts, where high-level languages have become accepted. The SOD access language (SODAL) must include the functional capabilities of SQL, plus iteration, test, and ranking. New predicates are needed to specify intelligent selection. Selection of desirable objects requires an ability to rank objects according to specified criteria. These criteria are understood by the SOD and are not necessarily predicates on underlying data elements, although for a trivial SOD that may be true. These criteria are associated with such result size parameters as "Give me the 10 best *X*," where the *best* predicate is a semantically overloaded term interpreted internally to a particular SOD.

Given an application to find reviewers for an article, the Expertise SOD will rank candidate scientists by best match to the article's keywords, while a Competency SOD will rank the candidates by the quality of their publication record. Other SODs can assess the potential bias and responsiveness of the candidates.

The format of SODAL is not user friendly; after all, other subsystems will use the SODs, not people. It should have a clear and symmetric structure that is machine friendly. It should be easy to build a user-friendly interface, if needed, on top of a capable SODAL.

Limits and extensions

The separation into layers envisaged here reduces the flexibility of information transfer. Structuring the mediators into a single layer between application and data is overly simplistic. Precursors to general mediators already recognize hierarchies and general interaction, as Actors do.[10]

The simple architecture described here is intended to serve large-scale applications. To assure effective exploitation of the mediator concepts, I propose to introduce complexity within layers slowly, only as the foundations are established to permit efficient use.

Structuring mediators into hierarchies

A futuristic world with mediators

A mediator contains an expert's knowledge and makes that expertise available to applications customers.

One can envisage a world where mediators can be purchased or leased for use. A market for mediators enables experts to function as knowledge generators and sell their knowledge in a form that is immediately usable. Traditional papers and books are a knowledge representation that requires extensive human interpretation. To apply the knowledge from a book to actual data, a program has to be written and tested. The knowledge in a mediator is ready for consumption.

There will be a trade-off in such a market between mediators that are powerful and highly specialized and mediators that are more basic and more general. The latter will sell more copies but at a lower price.

A mediator that contains very valuable knowledge may only be made available for use on its home computer, since limited access can greatly reduce the risk of unauthorized copying.

A market economy of mediators will greatly change the interaction between knowledge workers. Publication volume will decrease. Mediators that are incomplete, incorporate foolish assumptions, or contain errors will soon lose their credibility. A review mediator can make user comments available to a wide community. To introduce new and improved mediators, advertisements can be posted via a news mediator. Metamediators can process advertisements and reviews to help applications make sensible decisions.

should not lead to problems. We already required that directory mediators could be inspected. Directory mediators can help select other mediators by inspecting them and analyzing their capabilities. High-level mediators can obtain help in locating and formatting data from lower level mediators. Low-level mediators might only have database access knowledge and understand little about application-domain semantics. Optimizers may restructure the information flow, taking into account success or failure with certain objects in one of the involved SODs.

More complex is lateral information-sharing among mediators. Some such sharing will be needed to maintain the lexicons that preserve object identity when distinct mediators group and classify data. Fully general interaction between mediators is not likely to be supported at this level of abstraction. Just as human organizations are willing to structure and constrain interactions, even at some lost-opportunity cost, we impose similar constraints on the broad information systems we envisage.

Requirements of data security will impose further constraints. Dealing with trusted mediators, however, may encourage database owners to participate in information sharing to a greater extent than they would if all participants would need to be granted file-level access privileges.

The proposed generalization of practices seen today takes advantage of modern hardware. The architecture can focus a variety of research tasks needed to support such systems. Some extensions, such as general uncertainty algebras, are beyond today's conceptual foundations. As stated earlier, we can take a cue from Vannevar Bush,[3] who could identify all units needed for the Memex — although its components were based on technology that did not exist in 1945.

A language will be needed to provide flexibility in the interaction between the end users' workstation and the mediators. The partitioning of artificial intelligence paradigms into pragmatics (at the user-workstation layer) and the formal infrastructure (in the mediation layer) are discussed elsewhere.[11]

For query operations, the control flow goes from the application to the mediator. There, the query is first interpreted to plan optimal database access. The data obtained from that database would flow to the mediator, be aggregated, reduced, pruned, and so on, and the results reported to the query originator. Multiple mediators serve an application with pieces of information from their subdomains. Good scheduling is critical.

The knowledge-based paradigms inherent in intelligent mediators indicate the critical role of artificial intelligence technology foreseen when implementing mediators.

Mediators may be strengthened by having learning capability. Derived information may simply be stored in a mediator. Learning can also lead to new tactics of data acquisition and control of processing.

It is not the intent of the mediator-based model to be exclusive and rigid. The model is intended to provide a common framework under which many new technologies can be accommodated. An important objective is to utilize a variety of information sources without demanding that they be brought into a common internal format.

In a 1990 report,[12] the three primary issues to be addressed in knowledge-based systems were listed as maintenance, problem modeling, and learning and knowledge acquisition. The architecture presented here contributes to all three issues, largely by providing a partitioning that permits large systems to be composed from modules that are maintainable. ■

Acknowledgments

This article integrates and extends concepts developed during research into the management of large knowledge bases, primarily supported by DARPA under contract N39-84-C-211. Useful insights were gathered via interaction with researchers at Digital Equipment Corp. and with the national HIV-modeling community. The 1988 DARPA Principal Investigators meeting helped by providing a modern view of the communication and processing capabilities that lie in our future. Robert Kahn of the Corporation for National Research Initiatives encouraged development of these ideas. Further inputs were provided by panel participants at a number of conferences and at the National Science Foundation Workshop on the Future of Databases.

Tore Risch at the Hewlett-Packard Stanford Science Center is conducting research on triggers, and his input helped clarify salient points. Andreas Paepke of HP commented as well. Witold Litwin of the Institut National de Recherche en Informatique et en Automatique and the students on the Stanford KBMS project, especially Surajit Chaudhuri, provided a critical review and helpful comments. I thank the reviewers from *Computer* for their careful and constructive comments.

References

1. J.S. Mayo and W.B. Marx Jr., "Introduction: Technology of Future Networks," *AT&T Technical J.*, Vol. 68, No. 2, Mar. 1989.

2. *On Knowledge Base Management Systems: Integrating Artificial Intelligence and Database Technologies*, M. Brodie, J. Mylopoulos, and J. Schmidt, eds., Springer Verlag, N.Y., June 1986.

3. V. Bush, "As We May Think," *Atlantic Monthly*, Vol. 176, No. 1, 1945, pp. 101-108.

4. M.M. Waldrop, "The Intelligence of Organizations," *Science*, Vol. 225, No. 4,667, Sept. 1984, pp. 1,136-1,137.

5. *Handbook of Artificial Intelligence*, P.R. Cohen and E. Feigenbaum, eds., Morgan Kaufmann, San Mateo, Calif., 1982.

6. M. Bull et al., "Applying Software Engineering Principles to Knowledge-Base Development," *Proc. Expert Systems and Business 87*, Learned Information, Meadford, N.J., 1987, pp. 27-37.

7. M. Stonebraker, "Future Trends in Database Systems," *Proc. Fourth IEEE Int'l Data Eng. Conf.*, IEEE CS Press, Los Alamitos, Calif., Order No. 827 (microfiche only), 1988, pp. 222-231.

8. D. Tsichritzis et al., "KNOs: Knowledge Acquisition, Dissemination, and Manipulation Objects," *ACM Trans. Office Information Systems*, Vol. 5, No. 1, Jan. 1987, pp. 96-112.

9. T. Risch, "Monitoring Database Objects," *Proc. 15th Conf. Very Large Data Bases*, 1989, Morgan Kaufmann, San Mateo, Calif., pp. 445-454.

10. C. Hewitt, P. Bishop, and R. Steiger, "A Universal Modular Actor Formalism for Artificial Intelligence," *Proc. Third Int'l Joint Conf. Artificial Intelligence*, SRI, 1973, pp. 235-245.

11. G. Wiederhold et al., "Partitioning and Combining Knowledge," *Information Systems*, Vol. 15, No. 1, 1990, pp. 61-72.

12. B.G. Buchanan et al., "Knowledge-Based Systems," J. Traub, ed., *Ann. Rev. Computer Science*, 1990, Vol. 4, pp. 395-416.

Readers can contact the author, as well as obtain a report with more references, at the Department of Computer Science, Stanford University, Stanford, CA 94305-2140. His e-mail address is wiederhold@cs.stanford.edu.

An Open Agent Architecture*

Philip R. Cohen
Adam Cheyer
SRI International
(pcohen@ai.sri.com)
Michelle Wang
Stanford University
Soon Cheol Baeg
ETRI

ABSTRACT

The goal of this ongoing project is to develop an open agent architecture and accompanying user interface for networked desktop and handheld machines. The system we are building should support distributed execution of a user's requests, interoperability of multiple application subsystems, addition of new agents, and incorporation of existing applications. It should also be transparent; users should not need to know where their requests are being executed, nor how. Finally, in order to facilitate the user's delegating tasks to agents, the architecture will be served by a multimodal interface, including pen, voice, and direct manipulation. Design considerations taken to support this functionality will be discussed below.

INTRODUCTION

Agents are all the rage. "Visioneering" videos, such as Apple Computer's Knowledge Navigator, have helped to popularize the notion that programs endowed with agency, if not intelligence, are just around the corner. Soon, users need not themselves wade into the vast swamp of data in search of information, but rather the desired, or better yet, needed information will be presented to the user by an intelligent agent in the most comprehensible form, at just the right time.

Although such rosy scenarios are easy to come by, intelligent agents are considerably more difficult to obtain. Still, substantial progress is being made on a variety of aspects of the agent story. At least three general conceptions of agent-based software systems can be found in current thinking:

1. Agents are programs sent out over the network to be executed on a remote machine.
2. Agents are programs on a given machine that offer services to others.
3. Agents are programs that assist the user in performing a task.

*This paper was supported by a contract from the Electronics and Telecommunications Research Institute (Korea). Our thanks are also extended to AT&T for use of their text-to-speech system.

Each of these models can be found to some extent in present-day software products, for example, in (1) General Magic's emerging TELESCRIPT interpreter, (2) Microsoft's OLE 2.0 and (3) Apple Computer's Newton and Hewlett Packard's New Wave desktop, respectively. Given this space of conceptualizations, we need to be specific about ours.

Definitions and Objectives

Listed below are characteristics of what we are terming agents followed by an example of those characteristics as found in our system:

- *Delegation* — e.g., the ability to receive a task to be performed without the user's having to state all the details
- *Data-directed Execution* — e.g., the ability to monitor local or remote events, such as database updates, OS, or network activities, determining for itself the appropriate time to execute.
- *Communication* — e.g., the ability to enlist other agents (including people) in order to accomplish a task.
- *Reasoning* — e.g., the ability to prove whether its invocation condition is true, and to determine what are its arguments.
- *Planning* — e.g., the ability to determine which agent capabilities can be combined in order to achieve a goal.

Our initial prototype includes agents that exhibit aspects of all the above capabilities, except planning (but see [7]). Our goal is to develop an open agent architecture for networked desktop and handheld machines. The system we are building should support distributed execution of a user's requests, interoperability of multiple application subsystems, addition of new agents, and incorporation of existing applications. Finally, it should be transparent; users should not need to know where their requests are being executed, nor how.

AGENT ARCHITECTURE

Based loosely on Schwartz's FLiPSiDE system [17], the Open Agent Architecture is a blackboard-based framework allowing individual software "client" agents to communicate by means of goals posted on a blackboard controlled by a "Server" process.

The Server is responsible both for storing data that is global to the agents, for identifying agents that can achieve various goals, and for scheduling and maintaining the flow of communication during distributed computation. All communication between client agents must pass through the blackboard. An extension of Prolog has been chosen as the interagent communication language (ICL) to take advantage of unification and backtracking when posting queries. The primary job of the Server is to decompose ICL expressions and route them to agents who have indicated a capability in resolving them. Thus, agents can communicate in an undirected fashion, with the blackboard acting as a broker. Communication can also take place also in a directed mode if the originating agent specifies the identity of a target agent.

An agent consists of a Prolog meta-layer above a knowledge layer written in Prolog, C or Lisp. The knowledge layer, in turn, may lie on top of existing standalone applications (e.g. mailers, calendar programs, databases). The knowledge layer can access the functionality of the underlying application through the manipulation of files (e.g., mail spool, calendar datafiles), through calls to an application's API interface (e.g. MAPI in Microsoft Windows), through a scripting language, or through interpretation of an operating system's message events (Apple Events or Microsoft Windows Messages).

Individual agents can respond to requests for information, perform actions for the user or for another agent, and can install triggers to monitor whether a condition is satisfied. Triggers may make reference to blackboard messages (e.g. when a remote computation is completed), blackboard data, or agent-specific test conditions (e.g. "when mail arrives...").

The creation of new agents is facilitated by a client library furnishing common functionality to all agents. This library provides methods for defining an agent's capabilities (used by the blackboard to determine when this agent should participate in the solving of a subgoal), natural language vocabulary (used by the interface agent), and polling status. It also provides functionality allowing an agent to read and write information to the blackboard, to receive requests for information or action, and to post such requests to the blackboard, a specific agent, or an entire population of appropriate agents.

When attempting to solve a goal, an agent may find itself lacking certain necessary information. The agent can either post a request of a specific agent for the information, or it may post a general request on the blackboard. In the latter case, all agents who can contribute to the search will send solutions to the blackboard for routing to the originator of the request. The agent initiating the search may choose either to wait until all answers return before continuing processing, or may set a trigger indicating that when the remote computation is finished, a notification should interrupt local work in progress. An agent also has access to primitives permitting distributed AND and OR-parallel solving of a list of goals.

Distributed Blackboard Architecture

As discussed above, the Open Agent Architecture contains one blackboard "server" process, and many client agents; client agents are permitted to execute on different host machines. We are investigating an architecture in which a server may itself be a client in a hierarchy of servers; if none of its client agents can solve a particular goal, this goal may be passed further along in the hierarchy. Following Gelerntner's LINDA model [8], blackboard systems themselves can be structured in a hierarchy, which could be distributed over a network (see Figure 1).[1]

When a goal (G) is requested to be posted on a local blackboard (BB1), and the blackboard server agent at BB1 determines that none of its child agents has the requisite capabilities to achieve the goal, it propagates the goal to a more senior blackboard server agent (BB4) in the hierarchy. BB4 maintains a knowledge base of the predicates that its lower level blackboards can evaluate. When a senior server receives such a request, it in turn will propagate the request down to its subsidiary servers. These subsidiary servers either have immediate client agents who can evaluate the goal, or can themselves pass on the goal to another subsidiary server. In the case illustrated in Figure 1, BB4 determines that none of its subsidiary blackboards can handle the goal, and thus sends the goal to its superior agent (BB5). BB5 passes the goal to BB6, who in turn passes it to BB9. When such a referred goal is passed through the hierarchy of blackboards, it is accompanied by information about the originating blackboard (indicated by the BB1 subscript on G), including information identifying its input port, host machine, etc. This continuation information will enable a return communication (with answers or failure) to be routed to the originating blackboard. Also, the identity of the responding knowledge source BB9 can be sent back to the originator, so that future queries of the same type from BB1 may be addressed directly to BB9 without passing through the hierarchy of blackboards.

Operational Agents

A variety of agents have been integrated into the Open Agent Architecture:

[1] This is referred to as a "federation architecture" in [9].

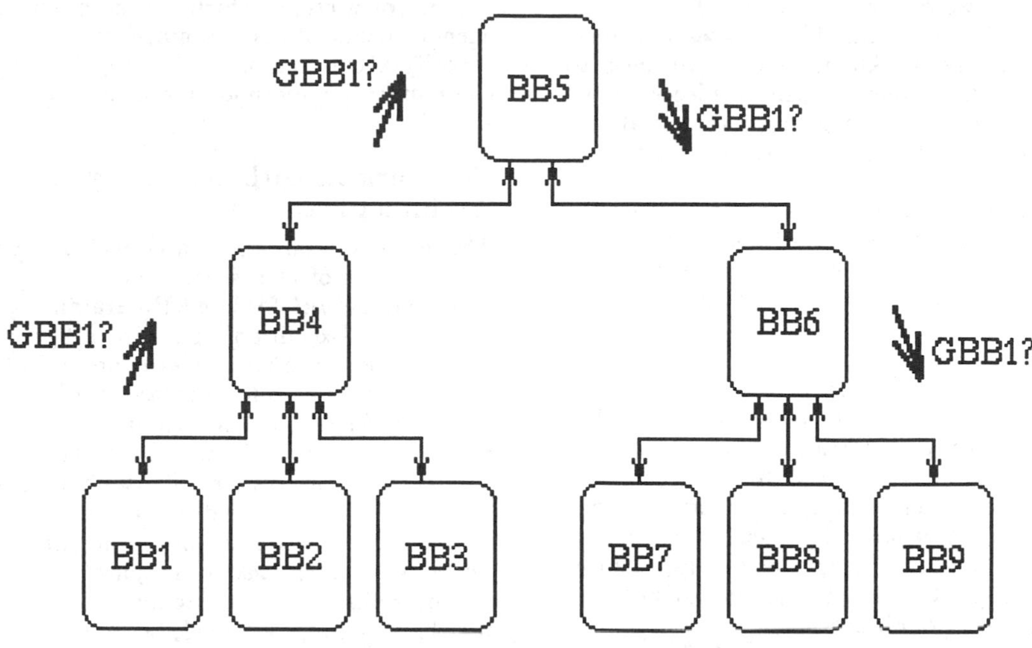

Figure 1: Hierarchy of Blackboard Servers

- a *User-interface* agent that accepts spoken or typed (and soon, handwritten) natural language queries from the user and presents responses to the queries.
- a *Database* agent, written in C, that interacts with a remote X.500 Directory System Agent database containing directory information.
- a *Calendar* agent, which can report upon where a person might be, or when they might be performing a particular action. This information is retrieved from data created by Sun Microsystem's CalenTool application.
- a *Mail* agent that can monitor incoming electronic messages, and forward or file them appropriately. The mail agent works with any Unix-compatible mail application (e.g. Sun's MailTool).
- a *News* agent that scans Internet newsgroups searching for specified topics or articles.
- a *Telephone* agent, that can dial a telephone using a ComputerPhone controller, and can communicate with users in English, using NewTTS, AT&T's text-to-speech system.

Communication Language

The key to a functioning agent architecture is the interagent communication language. We explain ours in terms of its form and content. Regarding the former, three speech act types are currently supported: `Solve` (i.e., a question), `Do` (a request) and `Post` (an assertion to the blackboard). For the time being, we have adopted little of the sophisticated semantics known to underlie such speech acts [5, 18, 19]. However, in attempting to protect an agent's internal state from being overwritten by uninvited information, we do not allow one agent to change another's internal state directly — only an agent that chooses to accept a speech act can do so. For example, a fact posted to the blackboard does not necessarily get placed in the database agent's files unless it so chooses, by placing a trigger on the blackboard asking to be notified of certain changes in certain predicates (analogous to Apple Computer's Publish and Subscribe protocol).

Although our interagent communication language is still evolving, we have adopted Horn clauses as the basic predicates that serve as arguments to the speech act types. However, for reasons discussed below, we have augmented the language beyond ordinary Prolog to include temporal information.

Because delegated tasks and rules will be executed at distant times and places, users may not be able simply to use direct manipulation techniques to select the items of interest, as those items may not yet exist, or their identities may be unknown. Rather, users will need to be able to *describe* arguments and invocation conditions, preferably in a natural language. Because these expressions will characterize events and their relationships, we expect natural language tense and aspect to be heavily employed [6]. Consequently, the meaning representation (or "logical form") produced by the multimodal interface will need to incorporate temporal information, which we do by extending a Horn clause representation with time-indexed predicates and temporal constraints. The blackboard server will need to decompose these expressions, distribute pieces to the various relevant agents, and engage in temporal reasoning to determine if the appropriate constraints are satisfied.

With regard to the content of the language, we need to specify the language of predicates that will be shared among the agents. For example, if one agent needs to know the location of the user, it will post an expression, such as `solve(location(user,U))`, that another agent knows how to evaluate. Here, agreement among agents would be needed that the predicate name is `location`, and its arguments are a person and a location. The language of nonlogical predicates need not be fixed in advance, it need only be common. Achieving such commonality across developers and applications is among the goals of the ARPA "Knowledge Sharing Initiative," [13] and a similar effort is underway by the "Object Management Group" (OMG) CORBA initiative to determine a common set of objects.

A difficult question is how the user interface can know about the English vocabulary of the various agents. When agents enter the system, they not only register their functional capabilities with the blackboard, they also post their natural language vocabulary to the the blackboard, where it can be read by the user interface. Although conceptually reasonable for local servers (and somewhat problematic for remote servers) the merging of vocabulary and knowledge is a difficult problem. In the last section, we comment on how we anticipate building agents to enforce communication and knowledge representation standards.

Example Scenario

The following is an example of an operational demonstration scenario that illustrates inter-agent communication (see Figure 2).

The user tells the interface agent (in spoken language) that "When mail arrives for me about a security break, get it to me". The interface agent translates this statement into a logical expression, and posts the expression to the blackboard. The blackboard server determines that a trigger should be installed on the mail agent, causing it to poll the user's mail database. Once the mail agent has determined that a message matching the requested topic has arrived for the user, it posts a query to find out the user's current location. The calendar agent responds, noting that the user is supposed to be in a meeting which is being held in a particular room; the database agent is then queried for the phone number of the room. Finally, the telephone agent is instructed to call the number, ask for the user (using voice synthesis), perform an identification verification by requesting a touchtone password, and then read the message to the user. We intend to add agents that would increase the number of ways in which a user might be contacted: agents to control fax machines, automatic pagers, and a notify agent that uses planning to determine which communication method is most appropriate in a given situation.

Comparison with Other Agent Architectures

The most similar agent architectures are FLiPSiDE [17] and that of Genesereth and Singh [9]. Like FLiPSiDE (Framework for Logic Programming Systems with Distributed Execution), our Open Agent Architecture uses Prolog as the interagent communication language, and introduces a uniform meta-layer between the blackboard Server and the individual agents. Some aspects of FLiPSiDE's blackboard architecture are more complex than in our system. It uses a multi-level locking scheme to try to reduce deadlock and minimize conflicts in blackboard access during moments of high concurrency. The system also uses separate knowledge sources for controlling triggers, ranking priorities and scheduling the executing of knowledge sources, whereas we incorporate these sorts of actions directly into the blackboard server. Some features important to our system that are not addressed by FLiPSiDE are the ability to handle temporal contraints over variables, and the possibility for an agent to explicitly request AND and OR-parallel solvingof a list of distributed goals.

Genesereth and Singh's architecture is more ambitious than ours in its employing a full first-order logic as the interagent communication language. As yet, we have not needed to expand our language beyond Horn clauses with temporal constraints, but this step may well be necessary. Genesereth and Singh use KIF (Knowledge Interchange Format) [13] as their basic language of predicates and as a knowledge integration strategy. Because of our user interface considerations, which in turn are heavily influenced by the form-factor constraints of future handheld devices, we will need to be able to merge contributions by different agents of their natural language vocabulary, related pronunciations, and semantic mappings of those vocabulary items to underlying predicates.

MAIL MANAGEMENT

In our earlier scenario, the mail agent was rather limited. To test our user interface and agent architecture more fully, we are creating a more substantive mail management agent, MAILTALK.

It has become common to develop mail managers that manipulate messages as they arrive according to a set of user-specified rules. The virtue of such systems is that users can make mail management decisions once, rather than consider each message in turn. However, a number of problems exist for such systems, as well as for all agent systems that we know of, especially when considered as tools for the general population.

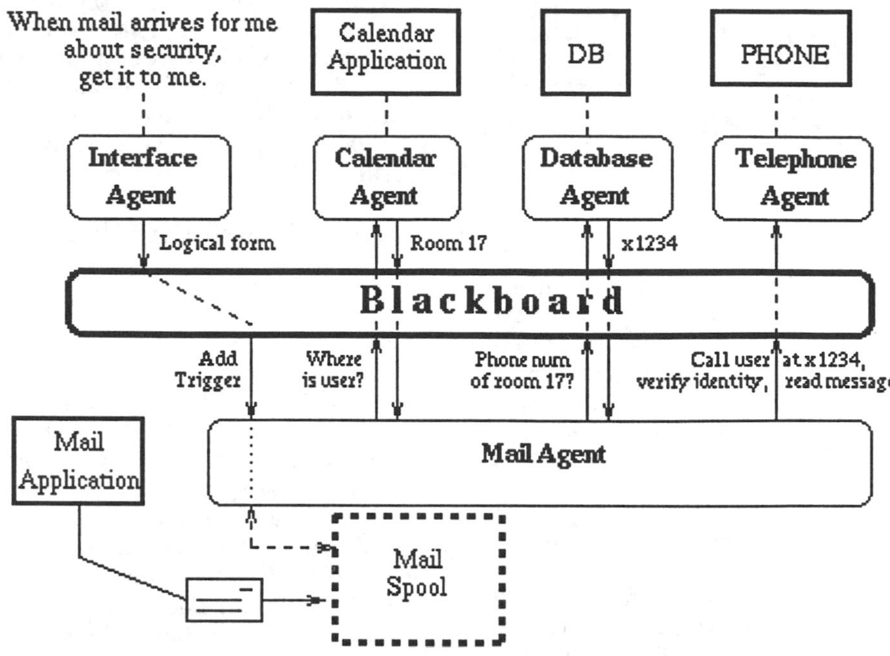

Figure 2: Example of agent interaction

- End users cannot easily specify the rules. In a number of current systems, a scripting language needs to be employed [1, 20], and in one system, users were required to write rules in a temporal query language [10]. We believe such methods for rule creation effectively eliminates the class of nontechnical users. Other systems employ templates that the user fills out [12]. Although this technique may work in many cases, it limits the power of the rules that users can create because they must search for an icon at which to point in order to specify the contents of a slot. Otherwise, they need to know or select the special syntax or concept name required. However, the selection of items from long menus is infeasible for handheld devices with little screen territory.
- End users cannot determine in advance how the *collection* of rules will behave once a new rule is added. This lack of predictability and the lack of debugging tools will undermine the utility of agent-based systems, especially in a networked environment.
- End users cannot easily determine what happened. Generally, little or no history of the database of events and rule firings is kept, and few tools are provided for reviewing that history.[2]
- The mail manager is a special purpose system, interacting loosely, if at all, with other components. Without tighter integration, the architecture and user interface for dealing with mail rules may diverge from what is offered for other agents.

[2] An exception to this is the use of "Mission Status Reports" in the Envoy agent framework [15].

Our prototype MAILTALK was built to address these concerns.

Rule specification. Based on technology developed for the SHOPTALK factory simulation system [2, 3, 4], MAILTALK permits users to specify rules by describing complex invocation conditions, and arguments with a multimodal interface featuring typed and spoken natural language, combined with direct manipulation. For example, the user can delegate to the mail agent as follows: "When Jones replies to my message about 'acl tutorials', send his reply to the members of my group." Here, Jones's reply cannot be selected or pointed at since it does not yet exist. The English parser produces expressions in the temporal logic, which are evaluated against various databases (e.g., the mail database, or a simulation database).

Predicting behavior. By giving end users the power to write their own rules means we have given them the freedom to make their own mistakes. Before letting a potentially erroneous collection of agents loose on one's mail (or, more generally, the network), we encourage users to *simulate* the behavior of those agents. Included with MAILTALK is a knowledge-based simulation environment that allows users to create hypothetical worlds, and permits them to send test messages or re-examine old mail files. In re-

When:	A message from someone in the AIC has been read
	ARCHIVE
Which message(s):	it
In which file:	<AIC-Mail>

Figure 3: Creating a mail rule

sponse, the system fires the relevant rules, and updates a simulation database with the events that have happened. This database can extend the actual mail file, permitting expressions that depend on the entire database to be evaluated (e.g., "when more than 5 messages from cohen are in < point to icon for mail file>, move them to <icon for 'unimportant mail'>).

Reviewing History. In order to determine if the resulting behavior was in fact desired, users can ask questions about the results of the simulation, can view the simulation graphically, and can rewind the history to interesting times (e.g., when a message was read, or when a message was forwarded to a member of a given mail group). When satisfied with the resulting behavior of the collection of rules, users can install them in the real world to monitor the real mail file. Moreover, users can ask questions about the real mail database, such as "Who has replied to my message of November 26 about budgets?"

Example

The following is an example of the kind of processing found in MAILTALK. First, the user determines that she wants to test out a mail management rule before installing it. She creates a new "hypothetical world," and proceeds to create a rule by selecting the **Archive** action from a menu. This results in a template's being presented, which she fills out as shown in Figure 3.

The user enters an English expression as the invocation condition, points at the icon for a file (**AIC-Mail**), and deposits it into the destination field.[3] This rule definition is parsed into a Prolog representation, augmented with temporal information and constraints.

The user then proceeds to *digest* an old mail file, which simulates the sending of the old messages, updating the simulated mail database. The animated simulation indicates that the rule has been fired, but just to be certain that the appropriate messages were put into the desired file, the user asks "When did I read a message from someone in the AIC?", followed by "Where are those messages now?" When satisfied, she transfers this rule to the real world, and requests that incoming mail be monitored.

[3] For a discussion of the usability advantages of such templates over simply entering the above in one sentence, please see [3, 14].

It should be noted that the reading of a message creates an event that triggers a rule. In general, that verb (i.e., 'read') could be one that results from an agent's action (e.g., forwarding), and thus a cascade of rule activations would ensue. It is to ensure that users understand such complexities that we offer the simulation facility.

Comparison with Other Mail Managers

Numerous mail managers exist, and space precludes a comprehensive survey. Only the more comparable ones will be discussed below.

The mail management system most similar to our is ISCREEN [16]. It allows a keyword and forms-based creation of rules, and offers a simple simulation capability in which a user can pose test messages. In response, the system applies its rules and explains in English what it would have done. Because mail is filtered using a boolean combination of keywords in various fields, ISCREEN can detect that various rules will conflict, and can ask the user for a prioritization. The user can employ organizational expressions (e.g., "manager"), which the system resolves based on a Prolog-based Corporate Directory database. Our use of the X.500 Directory System Agent offers the same capability based on an emerging international standard.

The TAPESTRY mail system [10] incorporates a mail database (as opposed to just a mail file), that is queried by a temporal query language. MAILTALK share this basic underlying model, but rather than have users write temporal queries, the user interface creates the temporal logic expressions through English language desciptions, which are then evaluated over the mail database.

The INFORMATION LENS system [12] provides various message types, which can enter into filtering rules (e.g., when a message of type **Weekly Sales Report** arrives, forward it to ...), or can become arguments for other actions (e.g., opening a spreadsheet). This approach takes the first step to integrating mail with other agent-like behavior, but a more fuller integration is possible once it is realized that rule-based mail management is analogous to database monitoring (as shown in TAPESTRY), and that a more general agent architecture can subsume mail management as a special case. It is this latter approach that we are following by embedding the mail manager as an agent in the architecture.

IMPLEMENTATION

An initial implementation of each of the pieces described above has been developed (in Prolog and C) on a Unix platform, with the exception of the pen/voice interface, which is being implemented now. Communication is based on TCP/IP. The blackboard architecture has been ported to Windows/NT, and agents that encapsulate Microsoft API's will be developed. Also planned is a port of the blackboard interpreter to the

Macintosh. When completed, the architecture will support multiple hardware and software platforms in a distributed environment.

FUTURE PLANS

In addition to the integration activities discussed above, a number of future research activities are needed. In order that an agent be invocable, its capabilities need to be mapped into terms understood by the ensemble of agents, and also by users. Moreover, as discussed earlier, the natural language vocabulary needed to invoke an agent's services, including lexical, syntactic, and semantic properties, will also be posted on the blackboard for use by the user interface. In general, however, this advertising of vocabulary can lead to conflicts among definitions. We intend to develop an API Description Tool, with which the agent designer describes the services provided by that agent. The tool will produce mappings of expressions in ICL into those services, including vocabulary and knowledge representations that can be merged into a common whole. Techniques used in developing natural language database porting tools (e.g., TEAM [11]) will be investigated.

In order to generalize the simulation approach in MAILTALK to encompass the entire collection of agents, the API Description Tool also needs to supply information sufficient to allow the agent architecture to simulate an agent's behavior. It will need to characterize the preconditions and effects of agent actions, thereby also providing a basis for a server's planning to incorporate the agent into a complex action that satisfies a user's stated goal [7].

Finally, an interesting question is where to situate the temporal reasoning subsystem. Currently, it is located with the blackboard server, but it could also be distributed as part of the agent layer, enabling other agents to accept complex expressions for evaluation and/or routing. We intend to experiment with various architectures.

References

[1] S.-K. Chang and L. Leung. A knowledge-based message management system. *ACM Transactions on Office Information Systems*, 5(3):213–236, 1987.

[2] P. R. Cohen. Integrated interfaces for decision support with simulation. In B. Nelson, W. D. Kelton, and G. M. Clark, editors, *Proceedings of the Winter Simulation Conference*, pages 1066–1072. Association for Computing Machinery, December 1991. invited paper.

[3] P. R. Cohen. The role of natural language in a multimodal interface. In *The 2nd FRIEND21 International Symposium on Next Generation Human Interface Technologies*, Tokyo, Japan, November 1991. Institute for Personalized Information Environment. Also appears in Proceedings of UIST'92, ACM Press, New York, 1992, 143-149.

[4] P. R. Cohen, M. Dalrymple, D. B. Moran, F. C. N. Pereira, J. W. Sullivan, R. A. Gargan, J. L. Schlossberg, and S. W. Tyler. Synergistic use of direct manipulation and natural language. In *Human Factors in Computing Systems: CHI'89 Conference Proceedings*, pages 227–234, New York, New York, April 1989. ACM, Addison Wesley Publishing Co.

[5] P. R. Cohen and H. J. Levesque. Rational interaction as the basis for communication. In P. R. Cohen, J. Morgan, and M. E. Pollack, editors, *Intentions in Communication.* MIT Press, Cambridge, Massachusetts, 1990.

[6] M. Dalrymple. The interpretation of tense and aspect in English. In *Proceedings of the 26th Annual Meeting of the Association for Computational Linguistics*, Buffalo, New York, June 1988.

[7] O. Etzioni, N. Lesh, and R. Segal. Building softbots for UNIX. Department of Computer Science and Engineering, University of Washington, unpublished ms., November 1992.

[8] D. Gelernter. *Mirror Worlds.* Oxford University Press, New York, 1993.

[9] M. Genesereth and N. P. Singh. A knowledge sharing approach to software interoperation. Computer Science Department, Stanford University, unpublished ms., January 1994.

[10] D. Goldberg, D. Nichols, B. M. Oki, and D. Terry. Using collaboratorive filtering to weave an information tapestry. *Communications of the ACM*, 35(12):61–70, December 1992.

[11] B. J. Grosz, D. Appelt, P. Martin, and F. Pereira. Team: An experiment in the design of transportable natural language interfaces. *Artificial Intelligence*, 32(2):173–244, 1987.

[12] T. W. Malone, K. R. Grant, F. A. Turbak, S. A. Brobst, and M. D. Cohen. Intelligent information-sharing. *Communications of the ACM*, 30(5):390–402, May 1987.

[13] R. Neches, R. Fikes, T. Finin, T. Gruber, R. Patil, T. Senator, and W. Swartout. Enabling technology for knowledge sharing. *AI Magazine*, 12(3), 1991.

[14] S. L. Oviatt, P. R. Cohen, and M. Wang. Reducing linguistic variability in speech and handwriting through selection of presentation format. In K. Shirai, editor, *Proceedings of the International Conference on Spoken Dialogue: New Directions in Human-Machine Communication*, Tokyo, Japan, November 1993.

[15] M. Palaniappan, N. Yankelovitch, G. Fitzmaurice, A. Loomis, B. Haan, J. Coombs, and N. Meyrowitz. The Envoy framework: An open architecture for agents. *ACM Transactions on Information Systems*, 10(3):233–264, July 1992.

[16] S. Pollock. A rule-based message filtering system. *ACM Transactions on Office Information Systems*, 6(3):232–254, July 1988.

[17] D. G. Schwartz. Cooperating heterogeneous systems: A blackboard-based meta approach. Technical Report 93-112, Center for Automation and Intelligent Systems Research, Case Western Reserve University, Cleveland, Ohio, April 1993. Unpublished Ph.D. thesis.

[18] J. R. Searle. *Speech acts: An essay in the philosophy of language*. Cambridge University Press, Cambridge, 1969.

[19] Y. Shoham. Agent-oriented programming. *Artificial Intelligence*, 60(1):51–92, 1993.

[20] R. Turlock. SIFT: A Simple Information Filtering Tool. Bellcore, Mountain, New Jersey, 1993.

InfoSleuth: Agent-Based Semantic Integration of Information in Open and Dynamic Environments

R. J. Bayardo Jr., W. Bohrer, R. Brice, A. Cichocki, J. Fowler, A. Helal, V. Kashyap, T. Ksiezyk, G. Martin, M. Nodine, M. Rashid, M. Rusinkiewicz, R. Shea, C. Unnikrishnan, A. Unruh, and D. Woelk

Microelectronics and Computer Technology Corporation (MCC)
3500 West Balcones Center Drive
Austin, Texas 78759

http://www.mcc.com/projects/infosleuth
sleuth@mcc.com

Abstract

The goal of the InfoSleuth project at MCC is to exploit and synthesize new technologies into a unified system that retrieves and processes information in an ever-changing network of information sources. InfoSleuth has its roots in the Carnot project at MCC, which specialized in integrating heterogeneous information bases. However, recent emerging technologies such as internetworking and the World Wide Web have significantly expanded the types, availability, and volume of data available to an information management system. Furthermore, in these new environments, there is no formal control over the registration of new information sources, and applications tend to be developed without complete knowledge of the resources that will be available when they are run. Federated database projects such as Carnot that do static data integration do not scale up and do not cope well with this ever-changing environment. On the other hand, recent Web technologies, based on keyword search engines, are scalable but, unlike federated databases, are incapable of accessing information based on concepts. In this experience paper, we describe the architecture, design, and implementation of a working version of InfoSleuth. We show how InfoSleuth integrates new technological developments such as agent technology, domain ontologies, brokerage, and internet computing, in support of mediated interoperation of data and services in a dynamic and open environment. We demonstrate the use of information brokering and domain ontologies as key elements for scalability.

1 Introduction

Database research in the past has been focused on the relatively static environments of centralized and distributed enterprise databases. In these environments, information is centrally managed and the structure of data is consistent. Typically, the binding of concepts to specific sets of data is known at the time a schema is defined and data access performance can be optimized using pre-computed indices.

The World Wide Web presents us with a different challenge. Here, there is more information and the information is spread over a vast geographic area. There is no centralized management of the information since anyone can publish information on the Web. Thus, there is minimal structure to the data and the structure may bear little relationship to the semantics. Therefore, there can be no static mapping of concepts to structured data sets, and querying is reduced to search engines that dynamically locate relevant information based on keywords.

The InfoSleuth project at MCC [19, 35, 37] is broadening the focus of database research to meet the challenge presented by the World Wide Web. A broadening of focus requires a re-thinking of fundamental requirements, a deep understanding of existing database technology, and a pragmatic approach to merging key technologies from database research and research from other computer disciplines. The InfoSleuth Project is developing technologies that operate on heterogeneous information sources in an open, dynamic environment. InfoSleuth views an information source at the level of its relevant semantic concepts, thus preserving the autonomy of its data. Information requests to InfoSleuth are specified generically, independent of the structure, location, or even existence of the requested information. InfoSleuth filters these requests, specified at the semantic level, flexibly matching them to the information resources that are relevant at the time the request is processed.

InfoSleuth is based on MCC's previously developed Carnot technology [7, 18, 36], which was successfully used to integrate heterogeneous information resources. The Carnot project developed semantic modeling techniques that enabled the integration of static information resources and pioneered the use of agents to provide interoperation among autonomous systems. Carnot, however, was not designed to operate in a dynamic environment where information sources change over time, and where new information sources can be added autonomously and without formal control.

The InfoSleuth project extends the capabilities of the Carnot technologies into dynamically changing environments, where the identities of the resources to be used may be unknown at the time the application is developed. InfoSleuth, therefore, rigidly observes the autonomy of its resources, and

SIGMOD '97 AZ,USA

does not depend on their presence. Information-gathering tasks are thus defined generically, and their results are sensitive to the available resources. InfoSleuth must consequently provide flexible, extensible means to locate information during task execution, and must deal with incomplete information and partial results.

To achieve this flexibility and openness, InfoSleuth integrates the following new technological developments in supporting mediated interoperation of data and services over information networks:

1. *Agent Technology.* Specialized agents that represent the users, the information resources, and the system itself cooperate to address the information processing requirements of the users, allowing for easy, dynamic reconfiguration of system capabilities. For instance, adding a new information source merely implies adding a new agent and advertising its capabilities. The use of agent technology provides a high degree of decentralization of capabilities which is the key to system scalability and extensibility.

2. *Domain models (ontologies).* Ontologies give a concise, uniform, and declarative description of semantic information, independent of the underlying syntactic representation or the conceptual models of information bases. Domain models widen the accessibility of information by allowing the use of multiple ontologies belonging to diverse user groups.

3. *Information Brokerage.* Specialized broker agents semantically match information needs (specified in terms of some ontology) with currently available resources, so retrieval and update requests can be routed only to the relevant resources.

4. *Internet Computing.* Java and Java Applets are used extensively to provide users and administrators with system-independent user interfaces, and to enable ubiquitous agents that can be deployed at any source of information regardless of its location or platform.

In this paper, we present our working prototype version of InfoSleuth, which integrates the aforementioned technologies with more classic approaches to querying (SQL) and schema mapping. We also describe a utilization of InfoSleuth in the domain of health care applications.

This paper is organized as follows. The overall architecture is described in section 2. Detailed descriptions of the agents are given in section 3. Section 4 describes the InfoSleuth and the domain ontology design. Brokering and constrained information matching is described in section 5. A data mining application in the health care domain is briefly presented in section 6. Related work is discussed in section 7. Finally, section 8 gives the conclusion and future work.

2 Architecture

2.1 Architectural Overview

InfoSleuth is comprised of a network of cooperating agents communicating by means of the high-level agent query language KQML [11]. Users specify requests and queries over specified ontologies via applet-based user interfaces. The dialects of the knowledge representation language KIF [13] and the database query language SQL are used internally to represent queries over specified ontologies. The queries are routed by mediation and brokerage agents to specialized agents for data retrieval from distributed resources, and for integration and analysis of results. Users interact with this network of agents via applets running under a Java-capable Web browser that communicates with a personalized intelligent User Agent.

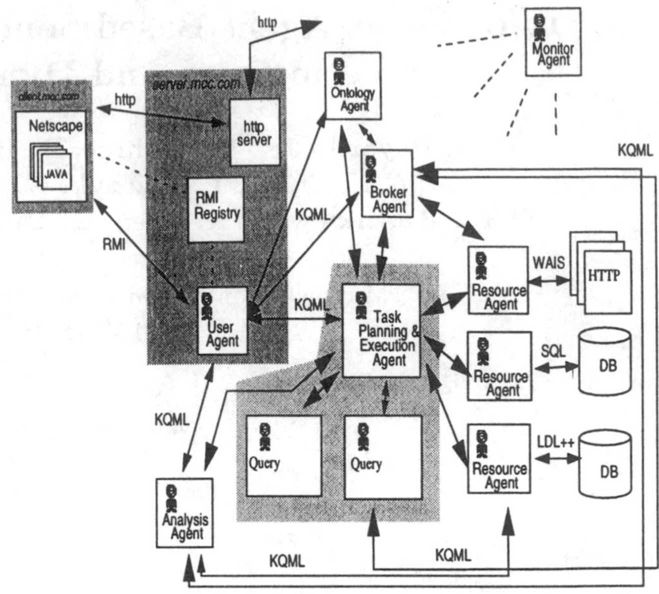

Figure 1: The InfoSleuth architecture

Agents advertise their services and process requests either by making inferences based on local knowledge, by routing the request to a more appropriate agent, or by decomposing the request into a collection of sub-requests and then routing these requests to the appropriate agents and integrating the results. Decisions about routing of requests are based on the "InfoSleuth" ontology, a body of metadata that describes agents' knowledge and their relationships with one another. Decisions about decomposition of queries are based on a domain ontology, chosen by the user, that describes the knowledge about the relationships of the data stored by resources that subscribe to the ontology.

Construction of ontologies for use by InfoSleuth is accomplished most easily by the use of the Integrated Management Tool Suite (IMTS, not discussed in this paper), which provides a set of graphic user interfaces for that purpose.

Figure 1 shows the overall architecture of InfoSleuth, in terms of its agents. The functionalities of each of the agents are briefly described below. Detailed descriptions are given in the following section.

User Agent: constitutes the user's intelligent gateway into InfoSleuth. It uses knowledge of the system's common domain models (ontologies) to assist the user in formulating queries and in displaying their results.

Ontology Agent: provides an overall knowledge of ontologies and answers queries about ontologies.

Broker Agent: receives and stores advertisements from all InfoSleuth agents on their capabilities. Based on this information, it responds to queries from agents as to where to route their specific requests.

Resource Agent: provides a mapping from the common ontology to the database schema and language native to its resource, and executes the requests specific to that resource, including continuous queries and notifications. It also advertises the resources' capabilities.

Data Analysis Agent: corresponds to resource agents specialized for data analysis/mining methods.

Task Execution Agent: coordinates the execution of high-level information-gathering subtasks (scenarios) necessary to fulfill the queries. It uses information supplied by the Broker Agent to identify the resources that have the requested information, routes requests to the appropriate Resource Agents, and reassembles the results.

Monitor Agent: tracks the agent interactions and the task execution steps. It also provides a visual interface to display the execution.

2.2 Agent Communication Languages

KQML [11] is a specification of a message format and protocol for semantic knowledge-sharing between cooperative agents. Agents communicate via a standard set of KQML performatives, which specify a set of permissible actions that can be performed on the recipient agent, including basic query performatives ("evaluate," "ask-one," "ask-all"), informational performatives ("tell," "untell"), and capability-definition performatives ("advertise," "subscribe," "monitor"). Since KQML is not tied to any one representation language, it can be used as a "shell" to contain messages in various languages and knowledge representation formats, and permit routing by agents which do not necessarily understand the syntax or semantics of the content message.

The Knowledge Interchange Format, KIF [13], provides a common communication mechanism for the interchange of knowledge between widely disparate programs with differing internal knowledge representation schemes. It is human-readable, with declarative semantics. It can express first-order logic sentences, with some second-order capabilities. Several translators exist that convert existing knowledge representation languages to and from KIF. InfoSleuth agents currently share data via KIF. Typically, an agent converts queries or data from its internal format into KIF, then wraps the KIF message in a KQML performative before sending to the recipient agent.

Both languages have been extended to provide additional functionalities required by the design of InfoSleuth.

2.3 Agent Interactions

In the following, we demonstrate a scenario of interaction among the InfoSleuth agents in the context of a simple query execution:

During system start-up, the Broker Agent initializes its InfoSleuth ontology, and commences listening for queries and advertisement information at a well-known address. Each Agent advertises its address and function to the Broker Agent using the InfoSleuth ontology.

When a Resource Agent initializes, it sets up its connection to its resource and advertises the components of ontology(ies) that it understands to the Broker Agent. One specialized Resource Agent, the Ontology Agent, deals with the information system's metadata.

A user commences interaction with InfoSleuth by means of a Web Browser or other Java applet viewer interacting with her personal User Agent. The user poses a query by means of the viewer applet. At this point, the User Agent queries the Broker Agent for the location of an applicable Execution Agent. The User Agent then issues the query to that Execution Agent.

On receiving a request, the Execution Agent then queries the Broker Agent for the location of the Ontology Agent (if it does not already know it), and queries the Ontology Agent for the ontology appropriate to the given query. Based on the ontology for the domain of the query, the Execution Agent queries the Broker Agent for currently appropriate Resource Agents. The Broker Agent may return a different set of Resource Agents if the same query is posted at a different time, depending on the availability of the resources.

The Execution Agent takes the set of appropriate Resource Agents, decomposes the query, and routes it appropriately. Each Resource Agent translates the query from the query domain's global ontology into the resource-specific schema, fetches the results from the resource, and returns them to the Execution Agent. The Execution Agent reassembles the results and returns them to the User Agent, which then returns the results to the user's Viewer applet for display.

The above scenario of a simple query execution is chosen for brevity. Other common scenarios of interactions in InfoSleuth would reflect complex queries with multiple-task plans and data mining queries that require knowledge discovery tasks.

3 Agent Design and Implementation

In this section, we describe the functionality, design rationale, and implementation of each of the InfoSleuth agents.

3.1 User Agent

The User Agent is the user's intelligent interface to the InfoSleuth network. It assists the user in formulating queries over some common domain models, and in displaying the results of queries in a manner sensitive to the user's context.

Upon initialization, the User Agent advertises itself to the broker, so that other agents can find it based on its capabilities. It then obtains information from the ontology agent about the common ontological models known to the system. It uses this information to prompt its user in selecting an ontology in which a set of queries will be formulated.

After a query is formulated in terms of the selected common ontology, it is sent to the task execution agent that best meets the user's needs with respect to the current query context. When the task execution agent has obtained a result, it engages in a KQML "conversation" with the user agent, in which the results are incrementally returned and displayed. The User Agent is persistent and autonomous; storing information (data and queries) for the user, and maintaining the user's context between browser sessions.

Implementation. The User Agent is implemented as a stand-alone Java application. As with the other agents in the architecture, explicit thread management is used to support concurrent KQML interactions with other agents, so that the User Agent does not suspend its activity while waiting for the result of one query to be returned. Currently, the agents query the task execution agents using KQML with SQL content.

A user interface is provided via Java applets for query formulation, ontology manipulation, and data display, which communicate with the User Agent by means of Java's Remote Method Invocation (RMI). The applets provide a flexible, platform-independent, and context-sensitive user interface, where query formulation can be based on knowledge of the concepts in the relevant common ontology, the user's profile, and/or application-specific knowledge. Various sets of applets may be invoked based on these different contexts. The User Agent is capable of saving the queries created via applets, as well as results of queries. As the complexity of the InfoSleuth knowledge domain grows, this set of applets may eventually be maintained as reusable modules in a warehouse separate from the User Agent.

3.2 Task Execution Agent

The Task Execution Agent coordinates the execution of high-level information gathering tasks. We use the term "high-level" to suggest workflow-like or data mining and analysis activities. Such high-level tasks can potentially include global query decomposition and post-processing as sub-tasks carried out by decomposition sub-agents, where the global query is couched in terms of a common ontology; and sub-queries must be generated based on the schemas and capabilities of the various resources known to the system, and then the results joined.

The Execution Agent is designed to deal with dynamic, incomplete and uncertain knowledge. We were motivated in our design by the need to support flexibility and extensibility in dynamic environments. This means that task execution, including interaction with users via the user agents, should be sensitive both to the query context and the currently available information.

The approach we have taken for the Task Execution Agent is based on the use of *declarative* task plans, with *asynchronous* execution of procedural attachments. Plan execution is *data-driven*, and supports flexibility in reacting to unexpected events and handling incomplete information.

The declarative specification of the agent's plan and subtask knowledge supports task plan maintenance, as well as the opportunity for collaborative task execution via the exchange of plan fragments. This declarative specification resides in the agent's knowledge base, and consists of several components, including: (1) Domain-independent information about how to execute task plan structures; (2) knowledge of when it is acceptable to invoke a task operator (including its preconditions) and how to instantiate it; (3) knowledge of how to execute the operator; (4) a Task Plan library; and (5) agent state.

The task plans are declarative structures, which can express partial-orders of plan nodes, as well as simple execution loops. Plans are currently indexed using information about the domain of the query and the KQML "conversational" context for which the task has been invoked.

Task Plan Execution Using Domain-independent Rules. After an agent's knowledge base has been populated with operator descriptions and declarative task plans, it uses its domain-independent task execution knowledge to carry out the plans. Its knowledge, in the form of rules, supports the following functionality:

- Multiple plans and/or multiple instantiations of the same plan may concurrently execute.
- For a given node in a plan, multiple instantiations of the node may be created.
- Task execution is *data-driven*: a plan node is not executed until its preconditions are met [34].
- Execution of a plan node can be overridden by rules for unusual situations.
- Reactive selection of operations not in the current explicit plan can occur based on domain heuristics.
- Information-gathering operators [21, 8], and conditional operator execution are supported.

Each time a query from the user agent is received, a new instantiation of the appropriate plan from the plan library is initialized by the rule-based system. A task execution agent can concurrently carry out multiple instantiations of one or more plans, with potentially multiple instantiations of steps in each plan. The plan execution process is what defines the Task Execution Agent's behavior. The sequences of interactions with other agents are determined by the task plans the agent executes, and the conversations with a given agent are determined by the KQML protocols and supported primarily by the procedural attachments to the task operators. For example, a user agent can request that the results of the query be returned incrementally.

Example: General Query Task Plan. Executing a general query task plan causes the Task Execution Agent to carry out the following steps.

- Advertise to the Broker, using a *tell* performative, and wait to receive a reply (done at agent initialization).
- Wait to receive queries from User Agents. These will typically be encoded as KQML *directives*, such as *ask-all*, *standby*, or *subscribe*). The query as well as the domain context determines the task plan that is instantiated to process the query.
- Parse the query, and decompose it if appropriate[1]. Parsing involves getting an ontological model from the Ontology Agent; once this model is obtained, it is cached for future use.
- Construct KIF queries based on the SQL queries' contents, and query the Broker using the KIF queries and the *ask-all* performative to find relevant resources.
- Query the relevant resource agents specified by the broker.
- Compose the results.
- Incrementally return the results to the user agent using a streaming protocol. Using this protocol, the user agent successively requests additional result tuples.

[1] Only query union decomposition is performed at the task plan level. Previous work in the InfoSleuth project has focused on techniques for global query decomposition and post-processing. Work is currently in progress to port this functionality to the agent architecture while supporting the dynamic nature of resource availability, via decomposition agents invoked from the task level. See Section 8.3.

Implementation. The Task Execution Agent is implemented by embedding a CLIPS [32] agent in Java, using Java's "native method" facility. CLIPS provides the rule-based execution framework for the agent, and, as described above, the declarative specification of plan and operator knowledge. The Java wrapper supports procedural attachments for the plan operators, as well as providing the Java KQML communications packages used by all the agents in the InfoSleuth system. Thus, all communication with other agents takes place via procedural operator implementations.

A CLIPS/Java API has been defined to send information from CLIPS to the Java sub-task implementations, and for each plan operator (in CLIPS) that invokes a Java method, a new thread is created to carry out the sub-task, parameterized via this API. During sub-task execution, new information (in the form of CLIPS facts and objects) may be passed back to the CLIPS database, and this is how the Java sub-task methods communicate their results. The sub-task execution is asynchronous, and results may be returned at any time. Because the task execution is data-driven, new task steps will not be initiated until all the required information for those steps are available.

3.3 Broker Agent

The Broker Agent is a semantic "match-making" service that pairs agents seeking a particular service with agents that can perform that service. The Broker Agent, therefore, is responsible for the scalability of the system as the number and volume of its information resources grow. The Broker Agent determines the set of relevant resources that can perform the requested service. As agents come on line, they advertise their services to the broker via KQML. The Broker Agent responds to an agent's request for service with information about the other agents that have previously advertised relevant service. Details of the Broker protocols describing the exchanged information are given in section 5.2. In effect, the Broker Agent is a cache of metadata that optimizes access in the agent network. Any individual agent could perform exactly the same queries on an as-needed basis. In addition, the existence of the Broker Agent both reduces the individual agent's need for knowledge about the structure of the network and decreases the amount of network traffic required to accomplish an agent's task.

Minimally, an agent must advertise to the Broker its location, name, and the language it speaks. Additionally, agents may advertise meta-information and domain constraints based on which it makes sense to query a given agent. The purpose of domain advertising is to allow the Broker to reason about queries and to rule out those queries which are known to return null results. For example, if a Resource Agent advertises that it knows about only those medical procedures relating to heart surgery, it is inappropriate to query it regarding liver resection, and the Broker would not recommend it to an agent seeking liver resection data. The ontology used to express advertisements is called the "InfoSleuth" ontology because the metadata the Broker Agent is storing is a description of the relationships between agents.

Implementation. The Broker Agent is written in Java and the deductive database language LDL++ [38]. It supports queries from other agents using KQML for the communication layer and KIF for the semantic content (based on the "InfoSleuth ontology"). The constraint matching and data storage for the Broker Agent are implemented in LDL++. The Broker translates the KIF statements into LDL++ queries and then sends them off to the LDL server to be processed. The use of the deductive database allows the broker to perform rule-based matching of advertisements to user requests.

3.4 Resource Agent

The purpose of the Resource Agent is to make information contained in an information source (e.g., database) available for retrieval and update. It acts as an interface between a local data source and other InfoSleuth agents, hiding specifics of the local data organization and representation.

To accomplish this task, a Resource Agent must be able to announce and update its presence, location, and the description of its contents to the broker agent. There are three types of contents information that are of potential interest to other agents: (1) metadata information, i.e., ontological names of all data objects known to the Resource Agent, (2) values (ranges) of chosen data objects, and (3) the set of operations allowed on the data. The operations range from a simple read/update to more complicated data analysis operations. The advertisement information can be sent by the Resource Agent to the broker at the start-up time or extracted from the Resource Agent during the query processing stage.

The Resource Agent also needs to answer queries. The Resource Agent has to translate queries expressed in a common query language (such as KQML/KIF) into a language understood by the underlying system. This translation is facilitated by a mapping between ontology concepts and terms and the local data concepts and terms, as well as between the common query language syntax, semantics and operators, and those of the native language. Once the queries are translated, the resource agent sends them to the information source for execution, and translates the answers back into the format understood by the requesting agent. Additionally, the resource agent and the underlying data source may group certain operations requested by other agents into an atomic (local) transaction. Also, the resource agent provides limited transactional capabilities for (global) multi-resource transactions.

The capability of a Resource Agent can be enhanced in many ways. For example, it may be able to keep the query context and thus allow for retrieval of results in small increments. Handling of event notifications (e.g., new data is inserted, an item is deleted) can be another important functionality of a Resource Agent.

The components of an example Resource Agent are presented in Figure 2. The communication module interacts with the other agents. The language processor translates a query expressed in terms of global ontology into a query expressed in terms of the Oracle database schema. It also translates the results of the query into a form understood by other agents. Mapping information necessary for this process is created during the agent installation time as it requires specialized knowledge of both the local data and the global ontology. The task of the event detection module is to monitor the data source for the events of interest and prepare the notifications to be sent to the agents interested in those events.

The InfoSleuth architecture has a specialized resource agent, called the ontology agent, which responds to the queries related to ontologies. It uses the same KQML message exchange as other agents, but unlike resource agents that are associated with the databases, it only interprets

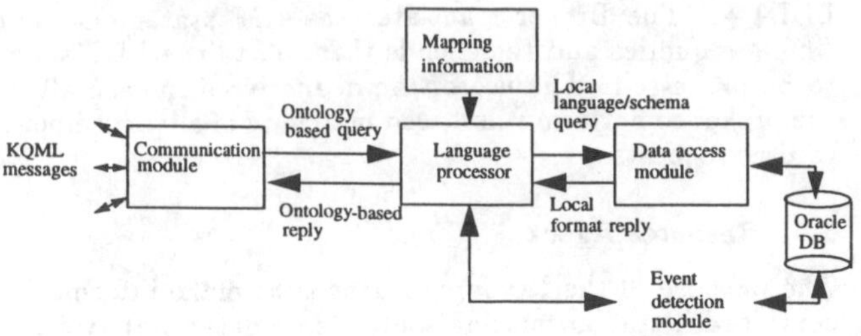

Figure 2: An example of a resource agent

KIF queries. This agent is designed to respond to queries concerning the available list of ontologies, the source of an ontology and searching the ontologies for concepts.

We are currently researching the possibility of adding inferencing capability to respond to more sophisticated queries. There is also a need for maintaining different versions of the same ontology as the agent architecture is scaled up. These two capabilities become particularly relevant as the number of served ontologies increases, especially when multiple ontologies are integrated for more complex query formulation.

Implementation. The resource agent is written in Java and provides access to relational databases via JDBC and ODBC interfaces. We have run it successfully with Oracle and Microsoft Access and SQL Server databases. The functionality of the implemented agent covers advertisements about the data (both metadata information and ranges/values of the data contained in the database), and processing of queries expressed in either global ontology terms or local database schema terms. We implemented three types of query performatives: ask-one, ask-all and standby, thus giving the other agents the option of retrieving one reply, all replies or all replies divided in smaller chunks.

4 Ontologies in the InfoSleuth architecture

The InfoSleuth architecture as discussed in the previous section is based on the communication among a community of agents, cooperating to help the user to find and retrieve the needed information. A critical issue in the communication among the agents is that of *ontological commitments*, i.e. agreement among the various agents on the terms for specifying agent context and the context of the information handled by the agents.

An ontology may be defined as the specification of a representational vocabulary for a shared domain of discourse which may include definitions of classes, relations, functions and other objects [15]. Ontologies in InfoSleuth are used to capture the database schema (e.g., relational, object-oriented, hierarchical), conceptual models (e.g., E-R models, Object Models, Business Process models) and aspects of the InfoSleuth agent architecture (e.g., agent configurations and workflow specifications). The motivations for using ontologies are two-fold:

1. *Capturing and reasoning about information content:* In an open and dynamic environment, the volume of data available is a critical problem affecting the scalability of the system. Ontologies may be used to:
   - Determine the relevance of an information source without accessing the underlying data. This requires the ability to capture and reason with an intensional declarative description of the information source contents. Object-oriented and relational DBMSs do not support the ability to reason about their schemas. Ontologies specified in a knowledge representation or logic programming language (e.g., LDL) can be used to reason about information content and hence enable determination of relevance.
   - Capture new and different world views in an open environment as domain models. Wider accessibility of the data is obtained by having multiple ontologies describe data in the same information source.

2. *Specification of the agent infrastructure:* Ontologies are used to specify the context in which the various agents operate, i.e., the information manipulated by the various agents and the relationships between them. This enables decisions on which agents to route the various requests to. This information is represented in the InfoSleuth ontology and represents the world view of the system as seen by the broker agent. As the functionality of the various agents evolves, it can be easily incorporated into the ontology.

Thus, ontologies are used to specify both the infrastructure underlying the agent-based architecture and characterize the information content in the underlying data repositories.

4.1 A Three-layer Model for Representation and Storage of Ontologies

Rather than choose one universal ontology format, InfoSleuth allows multiple formats and representations, representing each ontology format with an ontology meta-model which makes it easier to integrate between different ontology types. We now discuss an enhancement of the 3-layer model for representation of ontologies presented in [20]. The three layers of the model (shown in Figure 3) are: Frame, Meta-model, and Ontology.

The Frame layer (consisting of Frame, Slot, and Meta-Model classes) allows creation, population, and querying of new meta-models. Meta-model layer objects are instances of frame layer objects, and simply require instantiating the frame layer classes. Ontology layer objects are instances of meta-model objects.

The objects in the InfoSleuth ontology are instantiations of the entity, attribute and relationship objects in the Meta-model layer. In our architecture, agents need to know about other entities, called "agents". Each "agent" has an attribute called "name" that is used to identify an agent during message interchange. The "type" of an agent is relevant for determining the class of messages it handles and its general functionality.

A key feature of the InfoSleuth ontology is that it is *self-describing*. As illustrated in Figure 3, the entity agent has ontologies associated with it. The entity ontology is an object in the meta-model layer and the various ontologies of the system are its instantiations. However in the case of the InfoSleuth ontology, the instantiation "InfoSleuth" of the ontology object is also a part of the InfoSleuth ontology. This is required as the InfoSleuth ontology is the ontology associated with the broker agent.

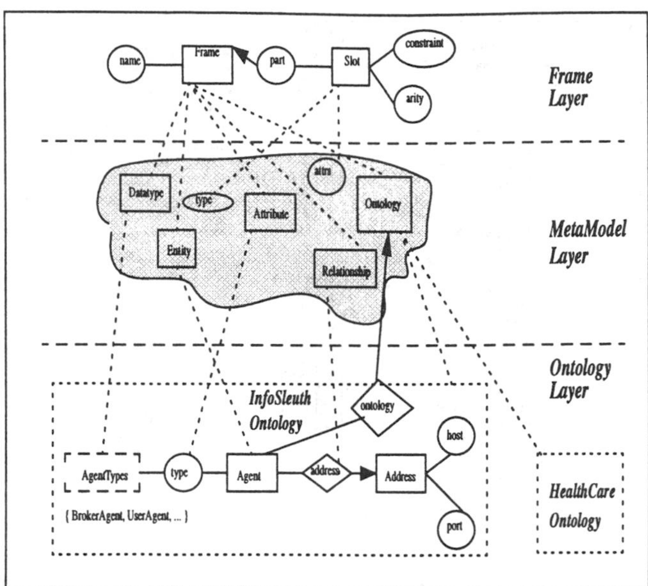

Figure 3: The three-layer ontology model

```
ontology(o_857456345)
ontology_name(o_857456345, 'healthcare')
ontology_frame(o_857456345, f_12312444)
frame(f_12312444)
frame_name(f_12312444, 'encounter_drg')
slot(s_34556346)
frame_slot(f_12312444, s_34556346)
slot_name(s_34556346, 'patient_age')
constraint(c_67457456)
slot_constraint(s_34556346, c_67457456)
constraint_expression(c_67457456,
    [[gt, 'patient_age', 43],[lt, 'patient_age', 75]])
```

```
(ontology ?o)
(ontology ?a ?o)
(name ?o "Healthcare")
(frame ?f)
(frame ?o ?f)
(name ?f "encounter_drg")
(slot ?s)
(slot ?f ?s)
(name ?s "patient_age")
(constraint ?c)
(constraint ?s ?c)
(expression ?c (and (> ?s 43) (< ?s 75)))
```

Figure 4: Multiple representation of same ontology

4.2 Utilization of Multiple Representations of Ontologies

One of the reasons for representing ontologies is the ability to reason about them. For this purpose, different agents might represent them in different languages depending on the type of inferences to be made. Figure 4 shows an example of the same piece of ontology represented by the resource agent in KIF and by the broker agent in LDL. The broker agent uses this representation to determine whether a resource agent is relevant for a particular query.

The Broker Agent utilizes a representation of the ontology exported by the Resource Agent (shown in Figure 4) in LDL [38]. The deductive mechanisms of LDL help determine the consistency of the constraints in the user query and those exported by the Resource Agent which in turn determines the relevance of the information managed by Resource Agent. The Resource Agent, on the other hand, translates this information into KIF expressions (as shown in Figure 4), and sends them to the Broker Agent.

5 Brokering in InfoSleuth

One of the valuable new features of the InfoSleuth technology is an intelligent brokering system that performs semantic as well as syntactic brokering of resources. Each agent in the system advertises its capabilities to the Broker Agent. The advertisements specify the agent's capabilities in terms of one or more of the ontologies. From the user's perspective, semantic brokering enables requests to be specified in terms of the concepts in an ontology, and matches those semantic concepts to the resources that are currently best suited to handle those specific requests.

5.1 Capabilities Enabled by Semantic Brokering

Semantic brokering helps expand the functionality of InfoSleuth in the following ways.

Intelligent Routing. Through the use of brokering, InfoSleuth offers the ability to route information requests based on content, through the use of constraint matching on the ontology a resource claims expertise over. For instance, a resource may have access to information only about doctors in Houston and Austin. It would be fruitless to query this resource about doctors in Dallas and the use of constraints rules this resource out.

Currently constraint matching is an intersection function between the user query and the data resource constraints. If the conjunction of all the user constraints with all the resource constraints is satisfiable, then the resource contains data relevant to the user request. We should mention here that, following "the open world assumption", the Broker Agent always matches a query with unconstrained, yet relevant data sources, regardless of the constraints imposed by the query.

Note that the constraints for both the user request and the resource data profiles are specified in terms of some common ontology. It is the use of this common vocabulary that enables the dynamic matching of requests to applicable resources.

Dynamic Binding of Resources. An InfoSleuth broker accepts advertisements from new resources and notifications of resource unavailability at any time. Thus, InfoSleuth is able to keep up with an ever changing set of resources, which is not easily accomplished in a federated database. As resources come and go, the broker is made aware of this through KQML advertisements, and will thus only recommend appropriate resources to the agents doing the query planning. This means that the same user request may produce different results at different times, depending on which resources are available. Also, neither the user nor any agents acting on his behalf needs to know where or what resources are available when building a query plan, i.e. the user can query an open information space.

Scalability. There are several ways in which our approach to brokering impacts system scalability. First, decisions on which resources are likely to be relevant to specific user requests are made without actually accessing the resource. This greatly reduces the time and effort required to route a request. Secondly, the ease with which new resources may be added to the system makes scalability much less of an issue. To add a resource to the system it need only have a KQML/KIF interface for advertising its services; then other agents can make use of them immediately. Thirdly, as the number of agents in InfoSleuth grows, the different syntactic and semantic brokering functions can be factored out into separate agents.

5.2 Broker Protocols

The protocol for the Broker Agent currently supports two types of requests: advertisements and queries. Each is discussed in turn.

Advertisement. Advertisement is accomplished by means of the KQML performative *tell*. Modification of a service description is accomplished simply by issuing a new *tell* performative with appropriate fields altered to reflect the new state. Repudiation of a service is accomplished by issuing a *tell* performative with appropriate fields nulled out. Constraints on the agent's advertised ontology are expressed using KIF. The Broker currently accepts constraints on fields for single values, value ranges, and sets of values. A *tell* advertisement of a simple range constraint might look like that in Figure 5.

Broker Query. Queries to the Broker Agent about the InfoSleuth ontology are made by means of a KQML message that uses the *ask-one* and *ask-all* performatives and embeds a KIF query specifying constraints that should be met by the agents whose addresses are to be returned. Figure 5 illustrates an example of an *ask-all* query. The Broker reasons about these constraints by translating the KIF expressions into LDL++. Queries on constraints are currently restricted to expressions on open-ended ranges and set membership. Logical conjunction of constraints is currently possible; disjunction is not yet explicitly supported; however, an agent can achieve disjunction by issuing separate queries and concatenating the results.

A successful reply from the broker will return a list of tuples, each containing the name and address of the advertised agent, among other information. If the broker does not find an agent matching the request, the returned list will be empty. The reply to an *ask-one* query returns the first tuple found to meet the minimal requirements, and the reply to an *ask-all* query returns as many tuples as the broker finds which satisfies the query. In the future, we will be more flexible in allowing the querying agent to specify the type of information to be returned beyond a simple name and address in the aspect field of the KQML query. Likewise, the broker will also return the "best" match to an *ask-one*, and a ranked list of recommendations to an *ask-all*.

The query in Figure 5 represents an execution agent asking the Broker Agent for Resource Agents that understand SQL and have information about patients older than 65. The Broker Agent, based on the previous advertisement, would send a KQML reply performative indicating the address of the resource agent that matches the query.

```
(tell
        :sender "resourceagent1"
        :receiver "brokeragent"
        :ontology "Infosleuth"
        :language KIF
        :content
            (and
                (agent ?a)
                (name ?a "resourceagent1")
                (address ?addr)
                (address ?a ?addr)
                (host ?addr "fake.com")
                (port ?addr "5699")
                (protocol ?addr "http")
                (type ?a "ResourceAgent")
                (language ?a SQL)
                (ontology ?o)
                (ontology ?a ?o)
                (name ?o "Healthcare")
                (frame ?f)
                (name ?f "encounter_drg")
                (slot ?s)
                (slot ?f ?s)
                (name ?s "patient_age")
                (constraint ?c)
                (constraint ?s ?c)
                (expression ?c (and
                                (> ?s 43)
                                (< ?s 75)
                                    )
                )
        )
)
```

```
(ask-all
        :sender "executionagent1"
        :receiver "brokeragent"
        :ontology "Infosleuth"
        :language KIF
        :aspect (?name ?protocol ?host ?port)
        :content
            (and
                (agent ?a)
                (name ?a ?name)
                (address ?addr)
                (address ?a ?addr)
                (host ?addr ?host)
                (port ?addr ?port)
                (protocol ?addr ?protocol)
                (type ?a "ResourceAgent")
                (language ?a SQL)
                (ontology ?o)
                (ontology ?a ?o)
                (name ?o "Healthcare")
                (frame ?f)
                (slot ?s)
                (slot ?f ?s)
                (name ?s "patient_age")
                (constraint ?c)
                (constraint ?s ?c)
                (expression ?c (> ?s 65))
            )
)
```

Figure 5: A *Tell* and *Ask-All* advertisements

6 Applications

In this section, we demonstrate the use of InfoSleuth in data mining applications, and we present a data mining example from the health care application domain.

6.1 Knowledge Discovery through InfoSleuth

Knowledge discovery in databases has recently received considerable attention due to the proliferation of large databases whose size prohibits effective analysis via traditional means. Fayyad, Piatetsky-Shapiro, and Smyth [12] describe the process of knowledge discovery as one involving five phases: data selection, data preprocessing, data transformation, data analysis, and interpretation and evaluation. While most attention has been devoted to the analysis phase involving the mining of patterns from appropriately transformed data, they stress that other phases are also considerably important for knowledge-discovery systems to be successful in practice. The InfoSleuth project is experimenting with providing support for all knowledge discovery phases by tightly integrating data access, data analysis (mining), and data presentation tasks.

One difficulty in establishing a close connection between the data access and data analysis phases of knowledge discovery is a mismatch between how the data is structured within the individual databases, and how it is conceptualized by the user. This mismatch complicates query specification and can lengthen query retrieval time considerably. The InfoSleuth approach is to specify a common ontology for a domain, and local mappings from individual database schemas to the common ontology. These mappings can be thought of as views of the data that simplify query specification for selecting information. Given an appropriate set of mappings for a particular knowledge discovery task, the InfoSleuth system provides query support for selecting relevant information. Furthermore, it pre-processes and transforms the underlying database data into records whose attributes consist of concepts from the ontology; thereby minimizing query retrieval time. When knowledge discovery processes result in new, general concepts, these concepts can also be reflected in the ontology. In support of the data analysis phase, InfoSleuth provides generic analysis agents for performing data summarization [3], classification [9], and deviation detection [1, 29]. As illustrated in Figure 1, the execution of both data access and data analysis components is seamlessly controlled by the task planning and execution agent.

6.2 A Health care Application

The InfoSleuth project is collaborating with the Health care Open Systems Trials (HOST) consortium, partially funded by the U. S. National Institute of Standards and Technology, to develop advanced information technologies for Health care.

We are applying the InfoSleuth technology to help health care administrators in determining how to reduce costs and improve quality of care by providing querying, knowledge discovery, and workflow management capabilities on vast amounts of data stored in the distributed, heterogeneous databases of different hospitals and other care providers.

InfoSleuth is well suited to providing querying capabilities across the databases of different hospitals. The use of a common ontology for the health care domain enables queries to be specified with respect to the ontology, rather than to the idiosyncratic schemas associated with each hospital. Adding a new hospital to the system simply entails adding a new Resource Agent, along with its mapping to the common ontology. The brokering and query decomposition capabilities increase the efficiency of queries by directing local queries only to the databases that are likely to contain the requested information. InfoSleuth ontology-based brokering is the main technology enabling the development of an efficient Master Patient Index (MPI).

The goal of knowledge discovery in this application is to help hospital administrators compare outcomes of treatment (such as average length of stay and incidence of complications) across different care providers (such as hospitals and doctors) for patients with similar risks. Concepts like "patients with similar risks" and "outcomes of treatment" are not explicitly represented in the databases or in the ontologies created for integrating the databases. Therefore, knowledge discovery becomes a 2-step process. The first step involves discovering how to map the data in the databases onto these more abstract concepts and represent them in the ontology. The second step involves discovering how to predict one concept from another, such as predicting the outcomes of a particular treatment given different patient risk factors and health care providers. Association rules finding and deviation detection algorithms are used to carry out the first step, and Bayesian statistics techniques are used to carry out the second step.

7 Related Work

In the SIMS project [4], a model of the application domain is created using a knowledge representation system to establish a fixed vocabulary describing objects in the domain, their attributes, and relationships. For each information source a model is constructed that indicates the data model used, query language, network location, and size estimates, and describes the contents of its fields in relation to the domain model. Queries to SIMS are written in the high-level uniform language of the domain model. SIMS determines the relevant information sources by using the knowledge encoded in the domain model and the models of the information sources. These information sources are determined at run time based on their availability at that time. The InfoSleuth agent-based architecture is an attempt to capture the dynamic availability/unavailability of information sources in a Web-based environment.

TSIMMIS [16] is a system for integrating information. It offers a data model and a common query language that are designed to support the combining of information from structured and semi-structured sources. The emphasis in the TSIMMIS system is that of automatic generation of translators and mediators for accessing and combining information in heterogeneous data sources. The resulting information is expressed in an Object Exchange Model. The Distributed Interoperable Object Model (DIOM) [25] shares similar goals with the TSIMMIS project. Also, similar functionality can be found in the resource agents in the InfoSleuth architecture. Additionally, we are considering approaches for automatic generation of translators and mediators for resource agents. In InfoSleuth, these are presently used by the resource agents to mediate between concepts in a rich domain model and the data stored in a variety of syntactic representations in the data repositories.

The DISCO project [33] provides support for integrating unstable data sources in a dynamic environment. DISCO provides a partial query evaluation scheme that accounts for source unavailability. Mediation in DISCO is based on the ODMG-93 standard object model. A collection of modeling tools are provided to facilitate the wrapping of data sources into ODMG first class objects. To facilitate query mapping and optimization from ODMG's OQL to the source query languages, the ODMG model is slightly modified.

The Information Manifold [27] is a system for retrieval and organization of information from disparate (structured and unstructured) information sources. The architecture of Information Manifold is based on a knowledge base containing a rich domain model that enables describing the properties of the information sources. The user can interact with the system by browsing the information space (which includes both the knowledge base and the information sources). The presence of descriptions of the information sources also enables the user to pose high-level queries based on the content of the information sources. The focus in the Information Manifold project however is to optimize the execution of a user query expressed in a high-level language which might potentially require access to and combination of content from several information sources [24]. Similar functionality can be found to a limited extent in the Task Planning and Execution Agent in InfoSleuth. The focus in InfoSleuth is to model a dynamic web-based environment where resource agents may join and leave the system dynamically. This information is kept by the broker agent which enables the task planning agent to reformulate its plan to access the relevant information sources.

The OBSERVER project [28] represents an approach for query processing in Global Information Systems. Intensional metadata descriptions organized as domain specific ontologies are used to model and query the information content in various repositories. OBSERVER helps the user to observe a semantic conceptual view of a Global Information System by giving him the ability to browse multiple domain specific ontologies as opposed to individual heterogeneous repositories. Ontology-based interoperation is achieved by navigation of the synonym relationships between terms in the various ontologies. While the present version of the InfoSleuth system lacks ontology-based interoperation found in OBSERVER, it is better able to capture the dynamic nature of a web-based environment where information sources may join or leave the system, through its agent-based architecture.

8 Conclusions

8.1 Current Accomplishments

Our current InfoSleuth design is scalable and portable. This is accomplished through the use of collaborative agents, and the use of Java as a common agent wrapper. Java provides the portability that will be required if InfoSleuth agents need to be deployed dynamically in an unknown environment. Both User Agents, representing individual users, and Resource Agents, representing specific data resources, are platform-independent. Furthermore, all GUIs are written as Java applets, which can be executed from any browser on any platform.

Internally, multi-threading supports concurrent KQML dialogs between the agents, and allows subtasks to be executed asynchronously. To facilitate communication between agents, we have also implemented KQML in Java.

Our current InfoSleuth release does the following:

- Dynamically integrates heterogeneous data sources while maintaining their local autonomy.
- Executes context-sensitive information-gathering tasks that are capable of dealing with dynamic and uncertain knowledge of the application domain. This is achieved through hybrid declarative/procedural task specifications using rule-based systems with Java procedural attachments.
- Accesses global information flexibly. This is achieved through the use of semantically precise, hierarchically organized ontologies to describe information and data resources. Ontological descriptions capture database schemas (e.g., relational, object-oriented, hierarchical) and conceptual models (e.g., E–R models, Object Models, Business Process models). Users query data based on their ontologies and without regard to the physical representation or the underlying conceptual model.

In addition to its basic functionality, InfoSleuth also provides a suite of GUI tools to perform data mining and statistical analysis, for both general and application-specific data evaluation. Also, InfoSleuth provides the Integrated Management Tool Suite, which provides a complete set of GUI tools for ontology creation and maintenance.

8.2 Lessons Learned

Our experience thus far with InfoSleuth has been very encouraging, and we are continuing to refine and expand its capabilities to meet new needs.

We have faced several issues regarding KQML which we hope to see addressed. First, the KQML specification makes seemingly contradictory assumptions regarding the transport layer. On the one hand, KQML is supposedly "neutral" with regard to transport layer, designed to accommodate TCP, SMTP, email, etc. But the KQML specification makes the assumption that KQML performatives delivered from a single agent to another will arrive in the order in which they were sent; this is an erroneous assumption for many transport layers, including email and TCP (where a single connection is opened and then closed for a single message). Since there is no provision at the KQML level for determining the correct order of messages, we have deviated significantly from the specification to implement streaming of large query results.

Secondly, we have frequently found it necessary to implement various brokering capabilities (*advertise, recommend*) at the content-language level rather than at the level of KQML. For example: the KQML "advertise" performative specifies that the content of advertise be another KQML performative of the form that can be accepted by the advertiser. The problem is that it is quite often the case in InfoSleuth that different agents can accept exactly the same performative, but return different results depending on the type of service provided by that agent. For instance, consider the following performative:

```
(ask-all
      :sender A
      :receiver B
      :language SQL
      :ontology healthcare
      :content "select drg_code from encounter"
)
```

If this performative is sent to a resource agent, the result will be the requested data from that single resource. But if it is sent to an execution agent, the result will be the requested data from all relevant resource agents. In normal usage, the sender will only want to send this message to an execution agent, which is capable of doing query decomposition and result integration. But in KQML, there is no way for the sender to distinguish the services provided by the two types of agents based on the advertisement alone. To compensate for this, we pushed most advertising information down into the content-level, reducing *advertise* and *recommend* to simple *tell* and *ask-one/ask-all* queries based on a system-wide InfoSleuth ontology, which represents information about agents and ontologies. As we add more advanced features such as subscription, facilitators, active brokering, etc., we suspect that we will continue to have the same difficulties.

In general, the KQML specification was ambiguous on other key points; it was often necessary to go to the KQML community for guidance on proper usage. As of this writing, an updated KQML specification including a formal semantics for the language is soon to see print, and is eagerly awaited [22].

On a more positive note, we have found ODBC and JDBC to provide true portability that significantly simplified our implementation of a generic resource agent. For example, even though the resource agent could run on Solaris and Windows NT platforms, but not on Sun OS (where Java is not supported), we were still able to access Sun OS Oracle databases thanks to ODBC/JDBC. Drivers for JDBC are not widely available yet for all databases, but availability is growing rapidly. Also, we could have used more transactional support in ODBC/JDBC. Our early experience with providing transaction support in InfoSleuth suggests that we adopt the X/Open XA interface which is currently widely complied with. To this end, we plan to develop a lightweight transaction monitor to support the XA interface.

Another experience that we have learned from using Java is the extent of the achievable code mobility in a system like InfoSleuth. Currently, only user interface applets will be accessible from general browsers like Netscape (as soon as RMI support, which is underway, is completed). This is because InfoSleuth applets do not use any native calls, just the way Java is intended to be used. Making InfoSleuth agents accessible from Internet browsers, however, is not possible under the heavy and necessary use of network communication calls and database interface libraries.

8.3 Future Work

The current design of InfoSleuth has been extensively tested, and successfully used in the health care application domain. Several extensions are currently being investigated and will be included in the future release. Areas of extension include expanding the scope of information that we can examine from InfoSleuth, and extending the scope of our brokering capabilities. Also, we plan to extend the functionality of the current task execution agent to support more complex tasks. Finally, we plan to expand the functionality of the user agents

Our vision for expanding the information that can be deduced and/or examined includes adding new types of resource agents, including resource agents for LDL, text indexing and retrieval, ontologies, and possibly images. Also at the level of queryable information, we intend to add different data analysis agents, each of which can analyze a set of data in specific ways. These agents will be used in support of the data mining capability.

We intend to enhance the brokering capabilities, splitting the broker agent into a family of cooperating, specialized brokers. We will factor out the syntactic brokering capabilities into a separate type of broker agent, possibly implementing it as an ORB interface using CORBA [30]. Semantic brokering will be available at different levels—for example, local to the site, local to the enterprise, and between enterprises. Semantic brokering may include additional information on contents, and additional semantic information such as quality and cost of information. Furthermore, we plan to implement the capability for the broker to discover information, rather than relying on its being told everything explicitly through advertisement.

We are in the process of splitting the current execution agent into two separate agents, a query decomposition agent and a task execution agent. The task execution agent will develop execution plans based on user requirements using generative planning and plan retrieval utilizing case-based reasoning techniques [17, 31]. The task execution agent may interleave planing with information-gathering subtasks [2, 34, 23] and repair plans when unexpected situations are encountered [10, 26]. Plans will be specified as (transactional) workflows that can be executed by InfoSleuth. It will supervise the execution of the resulting workflows, including managing the transactions it generates. The query decomposition agent will be called by the task execution agent when it has a query over multiple resource agents. It will optimize and decompose queries over multiple resource agents, reassemble the results, and return them to the task execution agent.

We also plan to extend our event monitoring capabilities significantly. This includes developing a complex event specification language and the ability to decompose such events into simpler events on single resource agents. Complex events may include such properties as changes in the result of a query, and sets of simple events and/or operations that happen in a particular sequence or timing.

There are several important directions in which the user agent will be extended. These include developing queryable user profiles containing the user's preferences and a history of his sessions. We also plan to develop applets that aid in visual query specification [6], refinement, and pruning. The user agent will have additional support for security and collaboration.

Acknowledgments

The authors would like to thank M. Huhns, N. Jacobs, B. Perry, and M. Singh for their participation in the early design and implementation of InfoSleuth.

References

[1] A. Arning, R. Agrawal, and P. Raghavan, "A linear method for deviation detection in large databases", In KDD-96 Proceedings, Second International Conference on Knowledge Discovery and Data Mining, 1996.

[2] J. Ambros-Ingerson and S. Steel, "Integrating planning, execution and monitoring", In Proceedings of the Seventh National Conference on Artificial Intelligence (AAAI-88), pages 83-88, St. Paul, MN, 1988.

[3] R. Agrawal, T. Imielinski, and A. Swami, "Mining association rules between sets of items in large databases", In Proceedings of the ACM SIGMOD Conference on Management of Data, 207-216, 1993.

[4] Y. Arens, C. A. Knoblock and W. Shen, "Query Reformulation for Dynamic Information Integration", Journal of Intelligent Information Systems, 1996.

[5] R. Agrawal, and K. Shim, "Developing tightly-coupled data mining applications on a relational database system". In KDD-96 Proceedings, Second International Conference on Knowledge Discovery and Data Mining, 1996.

[6] C. Ahlberg, C. Williamson, and B. Shneiderman, "Dynamic queries for information exploration: An implementation and evaluation". In B. Shneiderman, editor, Sparks of Innovation in Human-Computer Interaction. Ablex Publishing, 1993.

[7] "http://www.mcc.com/projects/carnot"

[8] O. Etzioni and D. Weld, "A softbot-based interface to the internet". Communications of the ACM, 37(7):72-76, July 1994.

[9] U. M. Fayyad, S. G. Djorgovski, and N. Weir, "Automating the analysis and cataloging of sky surveys", In Usama M. Fayyad, Gregory Piatetsky-Shapiro, Padhraic Smyth and Ramasamy Uthurusamy (Editors) Advances in Knowledge Discovery and Data Mining, AAAI Press/The MIT Press Menlo Park, California, 1995.

[10] J. Firby, "Task networks for controlling continuous processes", In Proceedings of the Second International Conference on AI Planning Systems, 1994.

[11] T. Finin, R. Fritzson, D. McKay, R. McEntire, "KQML as an Agent Communication Lan guage", Proceedings of the Third International Conference on Information and Knowledge Management, ACM Press, November 1994.

[12] U. M. Fayyad, G. Piatetsky-Shapiro, P. Smyth, "From Data Mining to Knowledge Discovery: An Overview", In U. M. Fayyad, G. Piatetsky-Shapiro, and P. Smyth (Editors) Advances in Knowledge Discovery and Data Mining, AAAI Press: Menlo Park, CA, 1-34, 1995.

[13] M. R. Genesereth, R. E. Fikes, et al. "Knowledge Interchange Format Version 3 Reference Manual", Logic-92-1, Stanford University Logic Group, 1992.

[14] M. Genesereth and S. Ketchpel, "Software Agents", Communications of the ACM, Vol. 37, No. 7, pp. 48-53, July, 1994.

[15] T. Gruber, "A translation approach to portable ontology specifications", in Knowledge Acquisition, An International Journal of Knowledge Acquisition for Knowledge-Based Systems. 5(2), June 1993.

[16] H. Garcia-Molina, Y. Papakonstantinou, D. Quass, A. Rajaraman, Y. Sagiv, J. Ullman and J. Widom, "The TSIMMIS Approach to Mediation: Data Models and Languages", In Proceedings of the NGITS (Next Generation Information Technologies and Systems), June 1995.

[17] K. J. Hammond, "CHEF: A model of case-based planning". In Proceedings of the Fifth National Conference on Artificial Intelligence (AAAI-86), Philadelphia, PA, 1986.

[18] M. Huhns, N. Jacobs, T. Ksiezyk, W. M. Shen, M. Singh and P. Canata, "Enterprise Information Modeling and Model Integration in Carnot", Enterprise Integration Modeling: Proceedings of the First International Conference, The MIT Press, 1992.

[19] "http://www.mcc.com/projects/infosleuth"

[20] N. Jacobs and R. Shea, "The Role of Java in InfoSleuth: Agent-based Exploitation of Heterogeneous Information Resources", IntraNet96 Java Developers Conference, April, 1996.

[21] C. Knoblock, "Planning, executing, sensing, and replanning for information gathering", In Proceedings of the Fourteenth International Joint Conference on Artificial Intelligence, 1995.

[22] Y. Labrou, "Semantics for an Agent Communication Language", Ph.D. Dissertation, CSEE department, University of Maryland, Baltimore County, September 1996.

[23] J.Lee, M.Huber, E.Durfee, and P.Kenny, "UM-PRS: An implementation of the procedural reasoning system for multirobot applications", In Proceeding of the AIAA/NASA Conference on Intelligent Robotics in Field, Factory Service and Space, pages 842-859, 1994.

[24] A. Levy, A. Rajaraman and J. Ordille, "Querying Heterogeneous Information Sources Using Source Descriptions", In Proceedings of the 22nd VLDB Conference, September 1996.

[25] L. Liu and C. Pu, "The Distributed Interoperable Object Model and its Application to Large-Scale Interoperable Database Systems", Fourth International Conference on Information and Knowledge Management, 1995.

[26] J. E. Laird, D. J. Pearson, R. M. Jones, and R. E. Wray III, "Dynamic knowledge integration during plan execution", In Proceedings of the AAAI-96 Fall Symposium on Plan Execution: Problems and Issues, 1996.

[27] A. Levy, D. Srivastava and T. Kirk, "Data Model and Query Evaluation in Global Information Systems", Journal of Intelligent Information Systems 5(2), September 1995.

[28] E. Mena, V. Kashyap, A. Sheth and A. Illarramendi, "OBSERVER: An approach for query processing in global information systems based on interoperation across pre-existing ontologies", In Proceedings of the First IFCIS International Conference on Cooperative Information Systems (CoopIS 96), June 1996.

[29] C. J. Matheus, G. Piatetsky-Shapiro, and D. McNeill, "Selecting and reporting what is interesting", In Usama M. Fayyad, Gregory Piatetsky-Shapiro, Padhraic Smyth and Ramasamy Uthurusamy (Editors) Advances in Knowledge Discovery and Data Mining, AAAI Press/The MIT Press Menlo Park, California, 1996.

[30] Object Management Group. "CORBA: The Common Object Request Broker: Architecture and Specification", Release 2.0, July 1995.

[31] M. V. Nagendra Prasad, Victor. R. Lesser, and S. Lander, "Reasoning and retrieval in distributed case bases", Technical Report 95-27, UMASS, 1995.

[32] G. Riley, "CLIPS: An Expert System Building Tool", Proceedings of the Technology 2001 Conference, San Jose, CA, December 1991.

[33] , A. Tomasic, L. Raschid, and P. Valduriez, "Scaling Heterogeneous Distributed Databases and the Design of DISCO", Proceedings of the 16th International Conference on Distributed Computing Systems, Hong Kong, 1995.

[34] M. Williamson, K. Decker, and K. Sycara, "Unified information and control flow in hierarchical task networks", Technical report, The Robotics Institute, CMU, 1996.

[35] D. Woelk, M. Huhns and C. Tomlinson. "InfoSleuth Agents: The Next Generation of Active Objects", Object Magazine, July/August, 1995.

[36] D. Woelk, P. Cannata, M. Huhns, N. Jacobs, T. Ksiezyk, R. Lavender, G. Merdith, K. Ong, W. Shen, M. Singh, and C. Tomlinson, "Carnot Prototype", in Object-Oriented Multidatabase Systems, O. Bukhres and A. Elmagarmid (editors), 1996.

[37] D. Woelk and C. Tomlinson, "The InfoSleuth Project: Intelligent Search Management via Semantic Agents", Second International World Wide Web Conference, October, 1994.

[38] C. Zaniolo, "The Logical Data Language (LDL): An Integrated Approach to Logic and Databases", MCC Technical Report STP-LD-328-91, 1991.

A Pragmatic BDI Architecture*

Klaus Fischer, Jörg P. Müller**, Markus Pischel

DFKI GmbH, Stuhlsatzenhausweg 3, D-66123 Saarbrücken

Abstract. We present a unifying perspective of the individual control layers of the agent architecture INTERRAP. INTERRAP aims at modeling autonomous resource-bounded agents that interact with each other in dynamic multiagent environments. INTERRAP implements a pragmatic Belief-Desire-Intention (BDI) architecture, where the agent's mental state is distributed over a set of layers. Based on the processes of *situation recognition* and *planning and scheduling*, a uniform description for each control layer – the behavior-based layer, the local planning layer, and the cooperative planning layer – is provided. We demonstrate various options for the design of interacting agents within this framework in an interacting robots application. The performance of different agent types in a multiagent environment is experimentally evaluated.

1 Introduction

The design of intelligent agents is an important research direction within multiagent systems (MAS) [6], where the behavior of a society of agents is described by modeling the individuals and their interactions from a local, agent-based perspective. Thus, finding appropriate architectures for these individuals is one of the fundamental research issues within agent design.

There are at least two reasons for dealing with agent architectures: One is to explain and to predict agent behavior; this means to describe how an agent's decisions are derived from its internal (mental) state and how this mental state is affected by the agent's perception. The other reason is to actually support the design of MAS. It deals with providing tools and methodologies for designing computational agents and their interactions in an implemented system.

A prominent example for architectures that are primarily driven by the former reason are BDI architectures [3, 15], describing the internal state of an agent by the mental attitudes of *beliefs*, *goals*, and *intentions*. BDI theories provide a clear conceptual model of the knowledge, the goals, and the commitments of an agent. However, they offer little guidance to the modeling of motivation and intention formation; thus, they have to be extended to actually support the design of resource-bounded and goal-directed agents for practical applications.

Another important direction in intelligent agent design are layered architectures (see Section 7). Layering is a powerful concept for the design of resource-bounded agents. It supports a natural modeling of different levels of abstraction, responsiveness, and complexity of knowledge representation and reasoning. However, a recent criticism of layered architectures has been that they are mainly motivated by intuition, and that they are too complex to allow the formal investigation of properties of agents and multiagent systems [19].

The agent architecture INTERRAP which is described in this paper aims at combining the advantages of BDI-style architectures with those of layered ones. Thus, our goal is to provide an architecture that serves both to explain agent behavior and to support system design. INTERRAP adopts the mental categories used in BDI theory to describe an agent's knowledge, goals, and state of processing. It extends the work of [15, 16] by organizing an agent's state and control within a layered architecture. The problem-solving capabilities of an agent are described hierarchically by a behavior-based layer, a local planning layer, and a cooperative planning layer. INTERRAP adopts the BDI-model rather in a conceptual than in a strictly theoretical sense. Thus, this paper does not provide a new theory for beliefs, desires, and intentions, but takes a pragmatic perspective.

Previous work [12, 13] has described the basic layered structure of the INTERRAP architecture and a first simple concept and implementation of the individual control layers. In this paper, we present a redesign of INTERRAP aimed to make the architecture easier to describe and to make agents easier to analyze by providing a clear control methodology. Using the FORKS application describing an automated loading dock as an example, we then show how different agent types can be described using the control framework and we provide empirical results comparing their behavior in the loading dock.

2 The INTERRAP Agent Architecture

INTERRAP is an approach to modeling resource-bounded, interacting agents by combining reactivity with deliberation and cooperation capabilities. This section illustrates the basic concepts of the architecture. Due to space limitations, the discussion is kept somewhat superficial. We refer to [12] for more details.

2.1 Overview

Figure 1 illustrates the overall structure of the architecture. INTERRAP describes an agent by a world interface, a control unit, and a knowledge base (KB). The control unit consists of three layers: the behavior-based layer (BBL), the local planning layer (LPL), and the cooperative planning layer (CPL). The agent knowledge base is structured correspondingly in a world model, a mental model, and a social model. The different layers correspond to different functional levels of the agent. The purpose of the BBL is to allow the agent to react to certain critical situations (by so-called *reactor patterns of behavior* (PoBs)), and to deal with routine situations (using *procedure PoBs*). Reactors are triggered by events recognized from the world model that incorporates the agent's object-level knowledge about its environment. The LPL gives the agent the ability of longer-term deliberation. It builds on world model information, but additionally uses

* The work presented in this paper has been supported by the German Ministry of Research and Technology under grant ITW9104

** email: jpm@dfki.uni-sb.de, phone: ++49 681 302 5331, fax: ++49 681 3025341

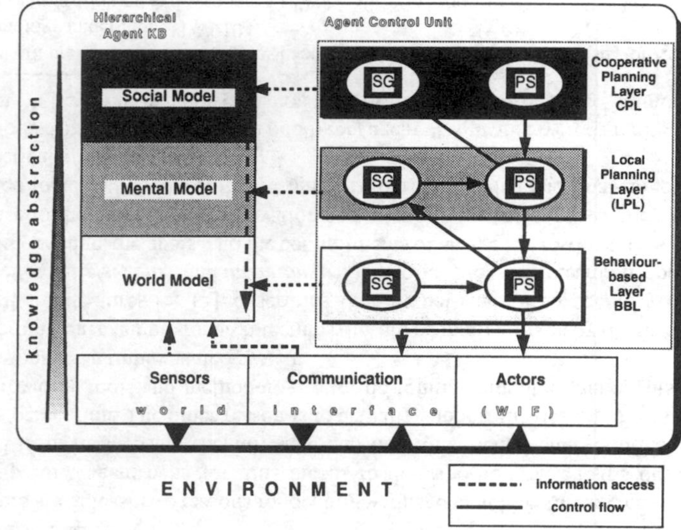

Fig. 1. The INTERRAP agent architecture

the agent's current goals and local intentions maintained in the mental model part of the knowledge base, as well as domain-dependent planning mechanisms available. The CPL finally extends the planning functionality of an agent to *joint plans*, i.e., plans by or for multiple agents that allow to resolve conflicts and to cooperate. Apart from world model and mental model knowledge, the CPL uses information about other agents' goals, skills, and commitments stored in the social model of the knowledge base. The internal structure of the control components is explained in more detail in the following sections of this paper.

In the following, let $\mathcal{B}$, $\mathcal{G}$, $\mathcal{I}$ denote the beliefs, goals, and intentions of an agent, respectively, and let $\mathcal{P}$ denote a set of perceived propositions. The INTERRAP agent architecture implements three basic functions:

- $BR(\mathcal{P},\mathcal{B}) = \mathcal{B}$ is a belief revision and knowledge abstraction function, mapping an agent's current perception $\mathcal{P}$ and its old beliefs $\mathcal{B}$ into a set of new beliefs $\mathcal{B}'$.
- $SG(\mathcal{B},\mathcal{G}) = \mathcal{G}'$ is a situation recognition and goal activation function, deriving new goals $\mathcal{G}'$ from the agent's beliefs $\mathcal{B}$ and its current goals $\mathcal{G}$.
- $PS(\mathcal{B},\mathcal{G},\mathcal{I}) = \mathcal{I}'$ is a planning and scheduling function, deriving a set $\mathcal{I}'$ of new intentions (commitments to courses of action) based on the beliefs $\mathcal{B}$, the goals $\mathcal{G}$ selected by SG, and the current intentional structure $\mathcal{I}$ of the agent.

Table 1 shows how the functions defined above are distributed over the individual layers. In this paper, we focus on the functions SG and PS. For issues of knowledge representation and belief revision, we refer to [9].

Layer / Function	BBL	LPL	CPL
BR	generation and revision of beliefs (world model)	abstraction of local beliefs (mental model)	maintaining models of other agents (social model)
SG	activation of reactor patterns	recognition of situations requiring local planning	recognition of situations requiring cooperative planning
PS	reactor PoB: direct link from situations to action sequences	modifying local intentions; local planning	modifying joint intentions; cooperative planning

Table 1. The basic functions in the INTERRAP control hierarchy

2.2 The control layers

The processes implemented at the different layers of the INTERRAP architecture have many similarities in that they describe different instantiations of the basic functions SG and PS. Based on this observation, we present a uniform structure shared by each layer. Figure 2 shows the internal structure of an INTERRAP control layer. Each layer $i \in \{BBL, LPL, CPL\}$ consists of two processes implementing the functions SG and PS; these interact with each other and with processes from neighbor layers:

- The **situation recognition and goal activation** process SG_i recognizes situations that are of interest for the respective layer; it results in the activation of a goal.
- The **planning and scheduling** process PS_i implements the mapping from goals to intentions and thus, to actions. It receives as input goal–situation pairs created by the SG component of the layer; it determines the plans to achieve the goals, schedules them into the current intention structure of the agent, and monitors the execution of plan steps.

The implementation of the two functions in INTERRAP is explained in more detail in Sections 3 and 4.

2.3 The flow of control

The control flow and thus the behavior of an INTERRAP agent emerges from the interaction among the individual modules as illustrated in Figure 2. The model provides two basic protocols specifying the global flow of control[3].

Upward Activation Requests: If PS_i is not competent for a situation S, it sends an activation request containing the corresponding situation-goal pair to SG_{i+1}; there, the situation description is enhanced by additional knowledge available to this component in order to produce a suitable goal description. The result of processing S is reported back to PS_i. This mechanism implements a *competence-based* control mechanism.

[3] Additional, more specific protocols cannot be discussed here due to space restrictions.

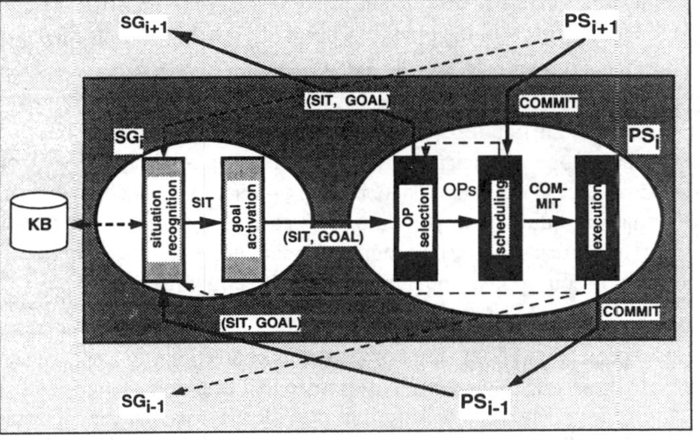

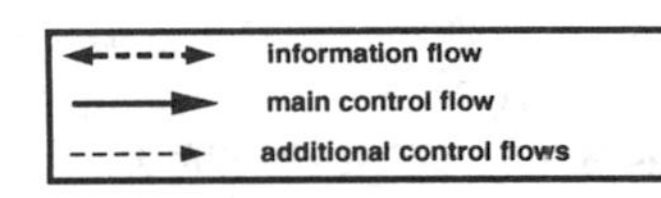

Fig. 2. Structure of an INTERRAP control layer

Downward Commitment Posting: Planning and scheduling processes at different layers coordinate their activities by communicating commitments. For example, this allows the local planning component both to integrate partial plans devised by the CPL layer in the course of a joint plan negotiation and to take into account certain commitments made by the upper layer (integrity constraints). Also the interface between the LPL and BBL component is designed by the higher layer posting activation requests for patterns of behaviors.

2.4 Coherence

The coherence problem results from the concurrent access to actions, perception, and knowledge by a set of layers, possibly leading to different results of situation recognition, to inconsistent decisions, and thus, to an incoherent behavior of the agent. Thus, the question is how coherent agent behavior can be achieved, i.e., how to coordinate situation recognition and the authority to perform actions.

The hierarchical control regime of INTERRAP allows to simplify some of these problems by restricting concurrency in activation and by restricting the concurrent access to the actuators. It allows us to deal without global control rules as in [7]. The main idea for coordination between reactive and plan-based layers is to give priority to the actions proposed by the BBL, and to allow a posteriori correction by the LPL [5]. In order to avoid foreseeable harmful interactions between the LPL and the BBL, there is the possibility of explicit suppression [4] which allows the LPL to enable or disable PoB in certain situations by sending appropriate messages to the BBL. Moreover, PoB that are no longer useful from the planner's point of view can be cancelled.

3 Situation Recognition

Situations are described from the view of an individual agent. A situation S is a set of formulae $S \equiv S_B \cup S_L \cup S_C$ with $S_B \subseteq WM$, $S_L \subseteq MM$, and $S_C \subseteq SM$[4]. It describes a portion of the agent KB containing parts of its world model, mental model, and social model. The world model part (*external context*) of a situation is a set of ground atomic formulae; the mental model part (*mental context*) describes parts of the local intention structure of the agent, i.e., goals and intentions; the social model part (*social context*) describes belief about other agents characterizing a specific situation.

Classes of situations are denoted by formulae in a first-order language $\mathcal{L}$, so-called *situation descriptions*. Situation descriptions provide patterns that can be instantiated to situations. For each layer i within the INTERRAP hierarchy, a set $\mathcal{D}_i \subseteq 2^{\mathcal{L}}$ of situation descriptions is defined that are recognized by this layer. Let $\mathcal{T}$ denote a set of time points. The semantics of the function SG_i is defined by a function $OCC_i : 2^{\mathcal{L}} \times 2^{\mathcal{L}} \times \mathcal{T} \mapsto 2^{\mathcal{L}}$. $OCC_i(B_i^t, D_i, t) = \mathcal{S}'$ returns the subset $\mathcal{S}'$ of instantiations of a situation description $D_i \in \mathcal{D}_i$ which occur at time t, i.e., which can be derived from the set of beliefs B_i^t at time t. At layer i, situations are mapped to goals by a function $\beta_i : \mathcal{S}_i \mapsto \mathcal{G}_i$, where the function $SG_i : 2^{\mathcal{L}} \times \mathcal{T} \times 2^{2^{\mathcal{L}}} \times 2^{\mathcal{L}} \mapsto 2^{2^{\mathcal{L}} \times 2^{\mathcal{L}}}$ is defined as

$$SG_i(B_i^t, t, \mathcal{D}_i, \mathcal{G}_i) \stackrel{\text{def}}{\equiv} \{(S, G) | \exists D \in \mathcal{D}_i \exists G \in \mathcal{G}_i . S \in OCC_i(B_i^t, D, t) \wedge G = \beta_i(S)\}.$$

Thus, given the beliefs, the situation descriptions to be monitored, and the potential goals the agent may adopt at time t, the output of function SG is a set of situation–goal pairs, namely the pairs (S, G) where situation S instantiates one of the input situation descriptions, and where situation S is mapped to goal G by the goal activation function.

Differences between the control layers result from restrictions on the admissible form of the set B_i^t and from the implementation of OCC_i. For the BBL, we have $B_B^t \subseteq WM$. For the LPL, we have $B_L^t \subseteq WM \cup MM$. Situation recognition in the CPL may access the whole knowledge base: $B_C^t \subseteq WM \cup MM \cup SM$.

OCC_B is defined by $OCC_B(B_B^t, D_B, t) = S$ iff $S = D_B\theta$ for a ground substitution θ. This many-pattern, many-objects matching problem can be solved e.g., by the RETE algorithm, allowing fast recognition of situations that have to dealt with quickly at the behavior-based layer. On the other hand, OCC_L and OCC_C include checking whether the agent itself has a specific goal or an intention, or even if other agents have certain goals or intentions. For OCC_L we assume that local goals are also represented as ground formulae; moreover, we require that an agent explicitly knows all its goals and intentions. In the case of OCC_C, however, more complex, time-consuming deduction may be necessary e.g., in order to recognize other agents' goals, either through communication, or through explicit goal recognition techniques.

Situation recognition is an incremental process, i.e., partial situations may be recognized at lower layers and complemented at higher layers. The SG_i process outputs

[4] We use the subscripts B for BBL, L for LPL, and C for CPL.

pairs (S, G). A goal G is associated to each situation S recognized by SG_i. This pair characterizes a new option to be pursued by the agent. It serves as an input to the planning and scheduling process described in the sequel.

4 Planning and Scheduling

According to Figure 2, at any point in time, the planning and scheduling process PS_i of layer i may receive input from two possible sources: situation-goal pairs from the SG_i process and commitment messages from the planning and scheduling process PS_{i+1} at the next higher layer. The output of PS_i are situation-goal pairs which are sent to SG_{i+1} and commitments to PS_{i-1}. PS_i maintains an intention structure which informally can be looked upon as the agent's runtime stack, holding the agent's current goals $\mathcal{G}_i$ and its intentions $\mathcal{I}_i$, denoting its state of planning and plan execution. Each situation–goal pair (S, G) received from SG_i at time t is processed according to the following steps:

1. If layer i is competent for (S, G), continue with step 2; otherwise send an upward activation request `request(do(S, G))` to SG_{i+1}; RETURN
2. Add G to the set $\mathcal{G}_i$.
3. Select an subset $\mathcal{G}' \in \mathcal{G}_i$ for being pursued next and devise a partial plan P' for achieving the goals[5] in $\mathcal{G}'$ given the current intention structure $\mathcal{I}_i$.
4. Compute the modified intention structure $\mathcal{I}_i'$ and thus, the next commitment.

This procedure is basically the same for the planning and scheduling modules at any layer; however, as is outlined in the sequel, the individual steps are implemented in a different manner.

4.1 Competence

The competence-based control flow is a central feature of INTERRAP. Each layer can deal with a set of situations, and is able to achieve a set of goals. The competence of layer i for a situation–goal pair (S, G) is decided by a predicate $\chi_B : \mathcal{S} \times \mathcal{G} \mapsto \{0, 1\}$. The competence predicates for the individual layers are defined as follows:

$\chi_B(S, G) = 1$ iff ex. a reactor PoB whose activation condition matches G.
$\chi_L(S, G) = 1$ iff ex. a single-agent plan p_s that achieves G given start situation S.
$\chi_C(S, \{G_1, \ldots, G_n\}) = 1$ iff ex. a joint plan p_j that achieves $\bigcup_{i=1}^{n} G_i$ given S.

If $\chi_i(S, G) = 0$ for a situation S and goal G, the layer is not competent for this situation/goal; then, an activation request containing (S, G) is sent to SG_{i+1}, notifying this layer of the new situation. χ_B can be computed by a simple matching; thus, it is possible to make decisions quickly at the reactive layer. However, constructing a plan may be necessary in order to determine χ_L and χ_C. These functions can be augmented by not only requiring the existence of a plan, but also requiring a minimal quality of the plan based on a utility function $u : PLANS \mapsto I\!R$. This is useful for an agent in order to decide whether to start a cooperation in a certain situation because there is only a poor local solution.

[5] Here, we assume that the goals in $\mathcal{G}'$ can be achieved independently of each other.

4.2 Deciding what to do

After a layer has decided to be competent for a situation, the planning process starts resulting in a commitment, e.g., a decision to perform a certain action. This planning process differs throughout the INTERRAP layers: At the BBL, patterns of behavior provide direct hard-wired links from situations to compiled executable procedures; thus, they ensure high responsiveness of the system to emergency situations. At the LPL, a single-agent planner is used to determine a sequence of actions to achieve the goal. For example, the forklift robots in the loading dock application (see Section 5) use a library with domain plans. Multiagent planning situations at the CPL are described by an initial situation and by the goals of the agents involved in the planning process. Cooperative planning therefore involves agreeing on a joint plan that satisfies the goals of the agents ([13] describe such a mechanism for the loading-dock).

4.3 Execution

The execution of an action a by the PS_i process of a layer i is done by posting a commitment `request(commit(a))` down to the process PS_{i-1}. Commitments made by PS_C to PS_L are partial single-agent plans which are local projections of the joint plan negotiated among the agents. This partial plan is scheduled into the current local plan of the agent. Commitments made at the LPL, i.e., from PS_L to PS_B, are activations of procedure PoB determined to be executed. Finally, at the BBL, commitments result from the actual execution of procedures. Procedures describe sequences of activations of primitive actions (or the sending of messages) which are available in the agent's world interface. Procedures are processed by a stepwise execution mechanism. Each execution step is a commitment to the execution of a primitive action in the world interface.

5 Designing Multiagent Systems with INTERRAP

In this section, we present the FORKS application, a MAS developed according to the INTERRAP architecture. After describing the domain, the models for situation recognition and planning and scheduling defined above are instantiated by the example of recognizing and handling conflict situations.

5.1 The domain

The FORKS simulation system describes a MAS of interacting robots, automated forklifts that have to carry out transportation tasks in a loading dock. Figure 3 illustrates the structure of the loading dock. It is represented as a grid of size $m \times n$; each square $((i, j), t, r)$ can be of type $t \in \{ground, truck, shelf\}$ and can be within region $r \in \{parking\_zone, hallway, truck\_region, shelf\_region\}$. Squares of type $truck$ and $shelf$ can additionally contain at most one box.

Forklift agents occupy one square at a time; they have a range of perception (e.g.: one square in front), can communicate with other forklifts and perform actions $a \in$

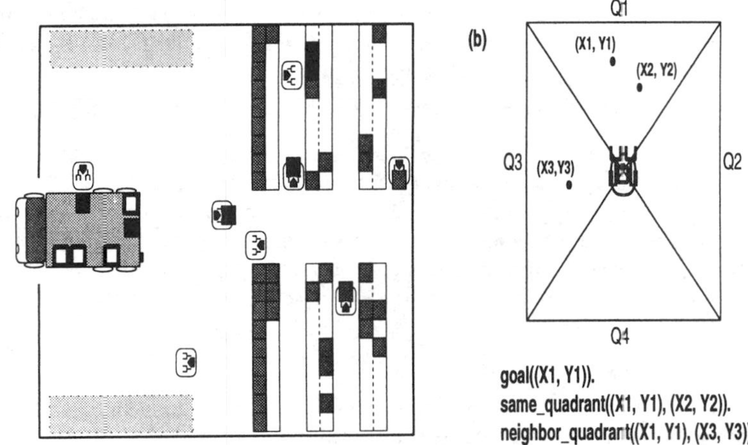

Fig. 3. (a) The loading dock (b) Quadrants

$\{moveto(dir), turnto(dir), grasp\_box, put\_box\}$, $dir \in \{n, e, s, w\}$. Agents receive orders to load or unload trucks; while performing their tasks, they may run into conflicts with other agents. E.g., agents may block each other, i.e., one agent may have the goal to move to a square occupied by another one, or two agents may try to move to one square by the same time.

5.2 Situation recognition and goal activation

The situation recognition capability of an agent is distributed over the three layers BBL, LPL, and CPL, allowing fast recognition of emergency situations, and a thorough classification of other situations, when more time is available.

An example for an emergency situation to be recognized in the SG_B module is a threatening collision. It can be modeled by a situation description sd_1:

$$sd_1 = \{location(self, (X_S, Y_S), O_S), status(self, moving), \\ perception(self, O_S, ((X, Y), T, R), \neg free((X, Y))\}$$

Note that sd_1 is defined merely by the external context, i.e., without taking into consideration knowledge about the agent's goals. A second type of conflict are blocking conflicts, which are defined by the fact that the agent is not moving, but intends to move to a square that is occupied by another agent. A situation description sd_2 for a mutual blocking conflict is:

$sd_2 =$
$\{location(self, (X_s, Y_s), O_s), location(A, ((X_a, Y_a), O_a)\}$ `/* external context */`
$opposed((X_s, Y_s, O_s), (X_a, Y_a, O_a))\} \cup$
$\{intends(self, goto\_landmark(X_a, Y_a))\} \cup$ `/* mental context */`
$\{bel(self, intends(A, goto\_landmark(X_s, Y_s))\}$ `/* social context */`

5.3 Planning and scheduling

Once recognized, there are several different possibilities to deal with a conflict situation. These possible reactions are implemented in the agents' PS processes. We draw a distinction between three basic classes of mechanisms which can be directly associated to the different INTERRAP control layers: behavior-based, local planning, and cooperative planning mechanisms.

Behavior-based mechanisms: This class of mechanisms has the Markov property: the decision of an agent at an instant t_i only depends on the state of the world at time t_{i-1}. One important class of decision functions having this property are *probabilistic decision functions* (PDFs). Let $\mathcal{A}$ be a non-empty set of actions, $\mathcal{G}$ a set of goals; let $f : \mathcal{S} \times \mathcal{A} \times \mathcal{G} \mapsto [0, 1]$ be a conditional probability distribution on $\mathcal{A}$ given $s \in \mathcal{S}, g \in \mathcal{G}$. Then a PDF is $\mathcal{F}^f(s, \mathcal{A}, g) = a_i$ with probability $f(s, a_i, g)$ for each $a_i \in \mathcal{A}$. We omit the superscript f for $\mathcal{F}$ in cases it is irrelevant.

An important class of PDFs are *uniform decision functions*, i.e., decision functions producing random behavior: A PDF $\mathcal{F}_r \equiv \mathcal{F}_r^f$ is an UDF iff $f(s, a, g) = \frac{1}{|\mathcal{A}|}$ for all $a \in \mathcal{A}$ and for all s, g.

```
proc PS_B
  i = 0;
  init([s_i, G_i]);
  repeat
    i = i + 1;
    s_i = update_beliefs(s_{i-1}, Perc_i);     /* Perc_i = perception at time i */
    𝒢_i = update_goals(𝒢_{i-1}, s_i);         /* determine new goals */
    g = select_unsatisfied_goal(𝒢_i);         /* select one goal */
    A = compute_alternatives(𝒜, g, s_i);      /* compute alternatives */
                                                 for the goal */
    next_action = ℱ(s_i, A, g);               /* commit to next action */
                                               using decision function ℱ */
    try_execute(next_action);
  forever
```

Fig. 4. The BBL control cycle

The behavior-based layer of INTERRAP is defined by a control cycle which, in each loop, computes a set of alternative PoBs (in the following simply called *alternatives* that might be pursued; it then decides which one actually to pursue by means of a PDF. This cycle is illustrated in Figure 4. In the loading dock, given a situation s, the probability function f can be defined e.g., as:

$$f(s, a, grasp\_box(B)) = \begin{cases} 1 & : \quad a = grasp\_box(B) \\ 0 & : \quad otherwise \end{cases}$$

$$f(s, moveto(Dir), goto\_landmark(L)) = \begin{cases} 0.5 & : \quad same\_quadrant(Dir, L) \\ 0.2 & : \quad neighbor\_quadrant(Dir, L) \\ 0.1 & : \quad otherwise. \end{cases}$$

Same_quadrant and *neighbor_quadrant* are predicates relating different squares wrt. their relative location from the perspective of an agent (see Figure 3.b). Function f defines a variation of a potential field method where the agent is attracted by its goal region (in the example box B and landmark L), and prefers options that let it proceed towards its goal. In Section 5.4 we show how behavior-based agents can be modeled using PDF and UDF. For a more detailed analysis of decision functions for behavior-based reasoning, we refer to [11] in this volume.

Local planning mechanisms: This class of mechanisms uses a planning formalism in order to determine the next action to be performed, taking into consideration the agent's current goals. For task planning, a hierarchical skeletal planner has been implemented in the FORKS system (see [12]). It decomposes goals into subgoals, until an executable procedure PoB is reached; in this case a commitment is posted to the BBL. In FORKS, a path planner $\mathcal{P}$ is used on a graph representation of the loading dock to determine the shortest paths between a given square and the goal square. If e.g., a blocking conflict is detected, $\mathcal{P}$ is run again to determine a new path to the agent's goal.

Cooperative mechanisms: Local planning mechanisms run into trouble in two cases: Firstly, if the number of agents increases, blocking conflicts occur very often (see Section 6); thus, the effort of replanning becomes too big. Secondly, given incomplete information, certain goal conflicts cannot be resolved by mere local replanning. Therefore, the PS_C process contains cooperative planning facilities. Joint plans for conflict resolution are negotiated among the agents and executed in a synchronized fashion (see Section 4 and [13]).

5.4 Agent design

The different mechanisms described in the above subsections can be combined by the system designer to build a variety of agents having different types and different properties. Thus, controlled experimentation is supported aimed at investigating how the design of individual agents determines the behavior of the MAS. In the sequel, five exemplary agent types for the loading dock application are defined; they are analyzed empirically in Section 6.

The random walker (RWK): RWK is an agent that chooses its actions randomly; i.e., it always uses an UDF $\mathcal{F}_r$. In the case of RWK, conflict resolution is done implicitly: if the agent selects an alternative that cannot be carried out, execution will fail and the agent will continue selecting alternatives randomly until it has found a solution (if one exists).

Behavior-based agent with random conflict resolution (BCR): BCR performs task planning using a PDF $\mathcal{F}_p$ as defined above. To resolve blocking conflicts, it shifts to random mode (using function $\mathcal{F}_r$) for n steps; after this, it uses function $\mathcal{F}_p$, again. The advantage of randomness is that it allows to get out of local optima; in practice, this has turned out useful to avoid livelocks.

Behavior-based agent with heuristic conflict resolution (BCH): Similar to BCR, BCH uses decision function $\mathcal{F}_p$ for task planning; however, to resolve blocking conflicts, it employs a different strategy: if possible, it tries to dodge the other agent instead of just moving randomly. Especially conflicts in the hallway region can be resolved efficiently by this strategy.

Local planner with heuristic conflict resolution (LCH): LCH uses the hierarchical skeletal planner described in [12] for local task planning; it employs the same heuristic conflict resolution strategy as BCH.

Local planner with cooperative conflict resolution (LCC): This agent type has the same local planning behavior as LCH; however, for resolving conflicts, it combines local heuristics (for conflicts in hallway and truck regions) with coordination via joint plans (for conflicts in shelf regions).

6 Experimental Results

In this section, the results of a series of experiments carried through for the loading dock application are reported. The goal of these experiments was to evaluate the behavior of different types of INTERRAP agents and how they depend on different internal and environmental parameters.

6.1 Description of the experiments

The test series reported in this paper contains tests with homogeneous agent societies. We ran experiments with four, eight, and twelve forklift agents. These agents had to carry out randomly generated tasks in a loading dock of size 15×20 squares, with six shelves and one truck. The topology of the loading dock (see Figure 3.a) ensures that any square of type *ground* is reachable from any other. The number of tasks were 50 for four agents, 100 for eight agents, and 150 in the twelve-agent case. Each experiment was repeated five times (for twelve agents) and ten times, respectively (for eight and four agents) with the five agent types RWK, BCR, BCH, LCH, and LCC. The focus of the experiment was to evaluate the system behavior wrt. the following questions: (i) Is one of the described agent types or conflict resolution strategies dominant for the FORKS application? (ii) How gracefully degrade the different types and strategies when the number of agents is increased? How robust are they? (iii) How well do communication-based strategies compared to local ones?

6.2 Results

The main results of the experiments are illustrated by the diagrams 5.a - 5.d.

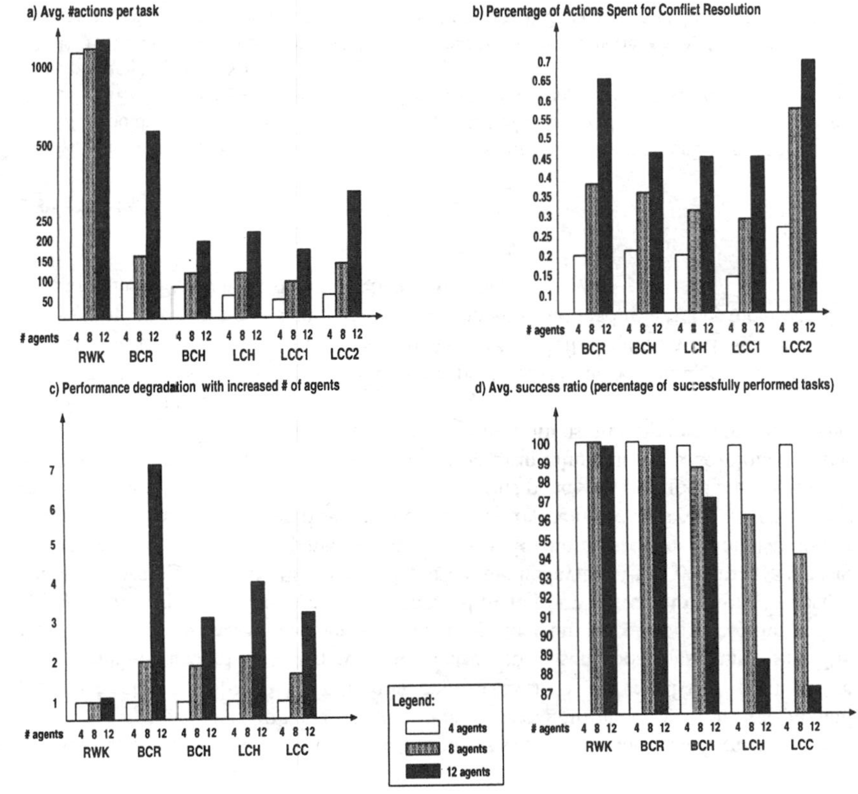

Fig. 5. Experimental results for the FORKS application

Absolute performance: Diagram 5.a shows the absolute performance for each agent type as the average number of actions needed per task. There are two entries for LCC: LCC1 only accounts for the number of physical actions (moves, turns, gripper actions), whereas LCC2 adds the number of messages sent (one message $\cong$ one action). As expected, RWK performs worst in all experiments. The best strategy is LCC; thus, resolving conflicts by communication pays off as regards the absolute performance. However, as LCC2 shows, the exact value depends on the cost of communication.

Conflict efficiency: Diagram 5.b displays the the ratio of actions needed for conflict resolution to the total number of actions. Since RWK does not explicitly recognize conflicts, it is not included in this statistics. The main result to be noted here is that LCC performs very well for smaller agent societies; for larger ones, it actually does not lead to a considerably higher conflict resolution efficiency, in comparison with local methods.

Degradation: The factor of performance degradation δ shown in Figure 5.c for x agents, $x \in \{4, 8, 12\}$ is computed as $\delta(x) \stackrel{\text{def}}{=} \frac{\#a(x) \cdot \#t(4)}{\#a(4) \cdot \#t(x)} \cdot \frac{1}{\rho}$, where ρ is the success ratio (see below), $\#a(x)$ denotes the total number of actions, and $\#t(x)$ denotes the total number of tasks in the x-agent experiment.

The performance of agent type RWK happens to be very insensitive to the size of the agent society, whereas the performance of all other agent types degrades considerably with a growing number of agents. A second interesting observation is that the agents employing simpler types of interaction show a more graceful degradation of performance than the more complex ones, especially the one based on communication. This is mainly due to the fact that the effort for communication and replanning outweighs the benefits of more elaborate strategies if the environment changes very rapidly.

Robustness: Robustness is measured by the success ratio ρ, which is the ratio of successfully finished tasks to the total number of tasks given to the agent. In our experiments, there are three sources of failures. Failures due to local maxima, deadlock situations caused by conflicts, and failures due to multiple conflicts that could not be adequately recognized and handled by the agents. The main result concerning robustness is that behavior-based strategies tend to be more robust than plan-based, cooperative strategies.

7 Related Work

Since the beginning of this decade, a considerable research effort has been devoted to the development of architectures for autonomous agents in dynamic environments. Only a few of these approaches can be discussed here; in particular, we focus on the relationship between our work and that of others contained in this volume. For an survey of developments in agent design, we refer to [19]. Layered approaches date back at least to Brooks' hardwired subsumption architecture [4]; the approach has been extended and refined by many other researchers, e.g., by adding planning capabilities to a reactive basis layer (e.g., [8], [7]). A recent approach incorporating the idea of layering to reconcile reaction and deliberation is 3T (see [2] in this book). The three layers in 3T are *reactive skills*, *sequencing*, and *deliberation*. In INTERRAP, the skill layer is implemented by reactor PoBs; sequencing tasks are running in all layers of INTERRAP, but particularly correspond to the handling of procedures in the behavior-based layer. Deliberation in INTERRAP is split up into local and cooperative deliberation; thus, while the focus in 3T still is on the case where we have a single agent acting in a dynamic world. INTERRAP extends the classical reactor-planner view by the cooperative layer to agents living in multiagent worlds, where dynamics is caused by the presence of other agents.

Another interesting approach to be read in this book is SIM_AGENT by Sloman and Poli [18]. The architectural concept is similar to 3T and to INTERRAP. An agent is a layered entity consisting of (1) a level of automatic processes, (2) a level of resource-bounded deliberation, and (3) a meta-level. Again, the main difference to INTERRAP is that cooperation is not modeled as a generic capability in the SIM_AGENT architecture. On the other hand, SIM_AGENT makes a conceptual distinction between meta- and object-level process management, and it extends the current scope of INTERRAP by providing various toolkit functionalities.

Various other contributions inside this volume deal with *multiagent architectures* and testbeds (see e.g., [1], [14], [10]). The difference between this work and ours is that our focus is on the design of the individual agent and defines cooperation mechanisms viewed from this agent-centered perspective, whereas multiagent architectures rather provide tools for designing multiagent systems.

Finally, we should comment on the BDI aspect of our work. Looking at Rao and Georgeff's work, there is a development from a theoretical model [15] over an abstract agent interpreter [16] to a complex agent programming system supporting the development of real-world applications [17]. INTERRAP uses notion such as beliefs, goals, and intentions as useful abstractions of the mental state of an agent, but focuses on architectural issues, such as how reactivity and deliberation can be integrated within a layered BDI framework, and how cooperation mechanisms can be integrated, i.e., issues that have not yet been considered in depth by the researchers who have developed the BDI paradigm.

8 Discussion

In this paper, we identified two basic functions explaining the transformation from what an agent perceives to what it does: situation recognition and goal activation, and planning and scheduling. The individual control layers of the INTERRAP architecture were redefined according to a new uniform structure based upon these functions. The implementation of these concepts was shown by the example of an interacting robots application; empirical results were presented showing how different options to design agents according to the INTERRAP model affect the behavior of the system as a whole. The main contribution of the paper has been to provide a uniform control model allowing to express reactivity, deliberation, and cooperation by defining different instantiations of three general functions. The work reported in this paper has provided a basis for the reimplementation of INTERRAP using the Oz programming language developed at the DFKI. The FORKS system has been implemented both as a computer simulation and on KHEPERA miniature robots.

This paper has necessarily focussed on aspects of the individual agent. Aspects of cooperation and interaction have been treated very briefly. Future work will explore more complex planning and cooperation mechanisms and lead to a richer model of the LPL and the CPL than the one described in this paper.

References

1. M. Barbuceanu and M. S. Fox. The architecture of an agent building shell. In M. Wooldridge, J. P. Müller, and M. Tambe, editors, *Intelligent Agents — Proceedings of the 1995 Workshop on Agent Theories, Architectures, and Languages (ATAL-95)*, LNAI series. Springer-Verlag, 1996. (In this volume).
2. R. P. Bonasso, D. Kortenkamp, D. P. Miller, and M. Slack. Experiences with an architecture for intelligent, reactive agents. In M. Wooldridge, J. P. Müller, and M. Tambe, editors, *Intelligent Agents — Proceedings of the 1995 Workshop on Agent Theories, Architectures, and Languages (ATAL-95)*, LNAI series. Springer-Verlag, 1996. (In this volume).
3. M. E. Bratman, D. J. Israel, and M. E. Pollack. Toward an architecture for resource-bounded agents. Technical Report CSLI-87-104, Center for the Study of Language and Information, SRI and Stanford University, August 1987.
4. Rodney A. Brooks. A robust layered control system for a mobile robot. In *IEEE Journal of Robotics and Automation*, volume RA-2 (1), pages 14–23, April 1986.
5. V. G. Dabija. *Deciding Whether to Plan to React.* PhD thesis, Stanford University, Department of Computer Science, December 1993.
6. E. H. Durfee and J. Rosenschein. Distributed problem solving and multiagent systems: Comparisons and examples. In M. Klein, editor, *Proceedings of the 13th International Workshop on DAI*, pages 94–104, Lake Quinalt, WA, 1994.
7. I. A. Ferguson. *TouringMachines: An Architecture for Dynamic, Rational, Mobile Agents.* PhD thesis, Computer Laboratory, University of Cambridge, UK,, 1992.
8. R. James Firby. *Adaptive Execution in Dynamic Domains.* PhD thesis, Yale University, Computer Science Department, 1989. Also published as Technical Report YALEU/CSD/RR#672.
9. K. Fischer, J. P. Müller, and M. Pischel. Unifying control in a layered agent architecture. Technical Memo TM-94-05, DFKI GmbH, Saarbrücken, January 1995.
10. C. A. Iglesias, J. C. González, and J. R. Velasco. MIX: A general purpose multiagent architecture. In M. Wooldridge, J. P. Müller, and M. Tambe, editors, *Intelligent Agents — Proceedings of the 1995 Workshop on Agent Theories, Architectures, and Languages (ATAL-95)*, LNAI series. Springer-Verlag, 1996. (In this volume).
11. J. P. Müller. A markovian model for interaction among behavior-based agents. In M. Wooldridge, J. P. Müller, and M. Tambe, editors, *Intelligent Agents — Proceedings of the 1995 Workshop on Agent Theories, Architectures, and Languages (ATAL-95)*, LNAI series. Springer-Verlag, 1996. (In this volume).
12. J. P. Müller and M. Pischel. An architecture for dynamically interacting agents. *International Journal of Intelligent and Cooperative Information Systems (IJICIS)*, 3(1):25–45, 1994.
13. J. P. Müller and M. Pischel. Integrating agent interaction into a planner-reactor architecture. In M. Klein, editor, *Proceedings of the 13th International Workshop on Distributed Artificial Intelligence*, Seattle, WA, USA, July 1994.
14. S.-J. Pelletier and J.-F. Arcand. Cognitive based multiagent architecture. In M. Wooldridge, J. P. Müller, and M. Tambe, editors, *Intelligent Agents — Proceedings of the 1995 Workshop on Agent Theories, Architectures, and Languages (ATAL-95)*, LNAI series. Springer-Verlag, 1996. (In this volume).
15. A. S. Rao and M. P. Georgeff. Modeling Agents Within a BDI-Architecture. In R. Fikes and E. Sandewall, editors, *Proc. of the 2rd International Conference on Principles of Knowledge Representation and Reasoning (KR'91)*, pages 473–484, Cambridge, Mass., April 1991. Morgan Kaufmann.
16. A. S. Rao and M. P. Georgeff. An abstract architecture for rational agents. In *Proc. of the 3rd International Conference on Principles of Knowledge Representation and Reasoning (KR'92)*, pages 439–449. Morgan Kaufmann, October 1992.
17. A. S. Rao and M. P. Georgeff. BDI-agents: from theory to practice. In *Proceedings of the First Intl. Conference on Multiagent Systems*, San Francisco, 1995.
18. A. Sloman and R. Poli. SIM_AGENT: A toolkit for exploring agent designs. In M. Wooldridge, J. P. Müller, and M. Tambe, editors, *Intelligent Agents — Proceedings of the 1995 Workshop on Agent Theories, Architectures, and Languages (ATAL-95)*, LNAI series. Springer-Verlag, 1996. (In this volume).
19. M. J. Wooldridge and N. R. Jennings, editors. *Intelligent Agents – Theories, Architectures, and Languages*, volume 890 of *LNAI* series. Springer-Verlag, 1995.

An Architecture for Action, Emotion, and Social Behavior

Joseph Bates, A. Bryan Loyall and W. Scott Reilly

School of Computer Science, Carnegie Mellon University
Pittsburgh, PA 15213, USA

Abstract. The Oz project at Carnegie Mellon is studying the construction of artistically effective simulated worlds. Such worlds typically include several agents, which must exhibit broad behavior. To meet this need, we are developing an agent architecture, called Tok, that presently supports reactivity, goals, emotions, and social behavior. Here we briefly introduce the requirements of our application, summarize the Tok architecture, and describe a particular social agent we have constructed.

1 The Oz Project and Broad Agents

The Oz project at Carnegie Mellon University is developing technology for artistically interesting simulated worlds [3]. We want to let human users participate in dramatically effective worlds that include moderately competent, emotional agents. We work with artists in the CMU Drama and English Departments, to help focus our technology on genuine artistic needs.

An Oz world has four primary components. There is a simulated physical environment, a set of automated agents which help populate the world, a user interface to allow one or more people to participate in the world [14], and a planner concerned with the long term structure of the user's experience [2].

One of the keys to an artistically engaging experience is for the user to be able to "suspend disbelief". That is, the user must be able to imagine that the world portrayed is real, without being jarred out of this belief by the world's behavior. The automated agents, in particular, must not be blatantly unreal. We believe that a way to create such agents is to give them a broad set of tightly integrated capabilities, even if some of the capabilities are somewhat shallow. Thus, part of our effort is aimed at producing agents with a broad set of capabilities, including goal-directed reactive behavior, emotional state and behavior, social knowledge and behavior, and some natural language abilities. For our purpose, each of these capacities can be as limited as is necessary to allow us to build broad, integrated agents [4].

Oz worlds can be simpler than the real world, but they must retain sufficient complexity to serve as interesting artistic vehicles. The complexity level seems to be somewhat higher, but not exceptionally higher, than typical AI micro-worlds. Despite these simplifications, we find that our agents must deal with imprecise and erroneous perceptions, with the need to respond rapidly, and with a general inability to fully model the agent-rich world they inhabit. Thus, we suspect that some of our experience with broad agents in Oz may transfer to the domain of social, real-world robots [5].

Building broad agents is a little studied area. Much work has been done on building reactive systems [1, 6, 7, 10, 11, 23], natural language systems (which we do not discuss here), and even emotion systems [9, 19, 21]. There has been growing interest in integrating action and learning (see [16]) and some very interesting work on broader integration [24, 20]. However, we are aware of no other efforts to integrate the particularly wide range of capabilities needed in the Oz domain. Here we present our efforts, focusing on the structure of a particular agent designed to exhibit goal-directed reactive behavior, emotion, and some social behavior.

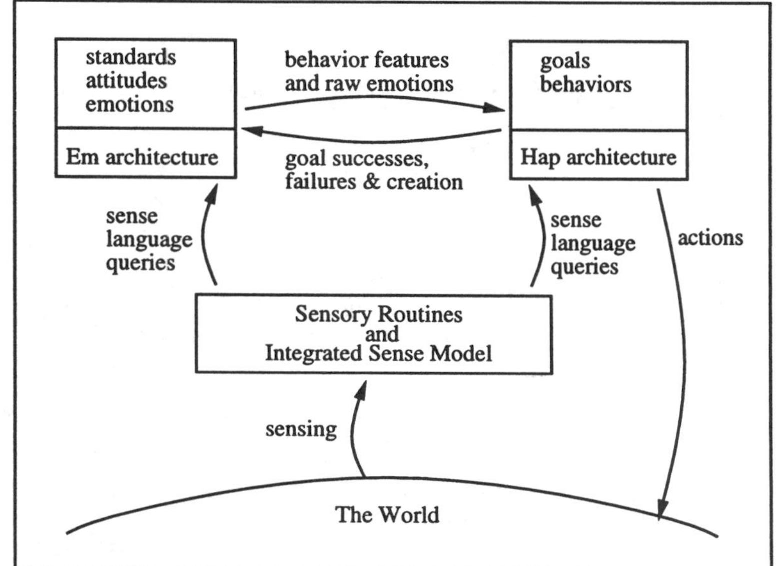

Fig. 1. Tok Architecture

2 Tok and Lyotard

Through analysis of our task domain, we have concluded that the primary capabilities we want in our initial Oz agents are perception, reactivity, goal-directed behavior, emotion, social behavior, natural language analysis, and natural language generation. Our agent architecture, Tok, assigns these tasks to several communicating components. Perception, while partially task specific, is also in part handled by a pair of systems called the Sensory Routines and the Integrated

Sense Model. Reactivity and goal-directed behavior are handled by Hap [17]. Emotion and social relationships are the domain of Em [22]. Language analysis and generation are performed by Gump and Glinda, respectively [13, 14]. Figure 1 shows how these components, excluding Glinda and Gump, are connected to form Tok.

In the remainder of this section we discuss the components of Tok and their integration. We illustrate using an existing Tok agent, a simulated house cat named "Lyotard", which exercises most of the capabilities of the architecture. Our goal in developing Lyotard was to build a creature that could believably pass for a cat in an Oz micro-world.

Figure 2 lists the emotions and behaviors from our original informal design document for Lyotard. The emotions are those naturally available in the current version of Em, though in the end we did not use all of them. The behaviors were developed over several hours of brainstorming by several cat owners in our group. The behavioral features are used to modify details of Hap's processing during the production of particular behaviors. They are usually derived from Lyotard's emotional state, though they also can be directly adjusted by behaviors.

Emotions	Behaviors
hope†	wanting to be pet *or brushed*
fear	cleaning self
happy	wanting to go out/in
sad	eating
pride	wanting to eat
shame	getting object (using human or other tool)
admiration	searching for something
reproach	*carrying mouse*
gratification	playing with ball
remorse	playing with mouse
gratitude	*crazy hour*
anger	hiding (anger/fear)
love	pushing things around
hate	purring
	arch back
Features	hiss
	swat
curious	bite
content	escape/run away
aggressive	have fun
ignoring	*pouncing on creatures*
friendly	chasing ball/*creatures*
proud	rubbing against
energetic	licking
	watching/staring at
	sitting on a sunny ledge

†*italicized items were not included in final implementation*

Fig. 2. Original Lyotard Task

2.1 The Simulated World

We are developing versions of Tok for several distinct simulation environments. Here we describe Tok within an "interactive fiction" system, where space is discrete and topological. We have also embedded Tok in an animated real-time world, where space is more continuous and geometric. For more information on this version, please see [18].

The interactive fiction physical world is a very simple object-oriented simulation in which agents perform actions by invoking methods on appropriate sets of objects. These methods may alter the world, propagate sense data, and succeed or fail. Objects are connected to each other via topological relations, for example Lyotard could be *on* the table which is *in* the room. We have found this model more than adequate to express artistically interesting physical environments.

Agents sense the world via sense data objects which propagate from the item sensed through the world to the agents. These sense data convey the properties of objects, relationships between objects, and events such as the room becoming dark or Lyotard pouncing on his toy mouse. Each sense datum describes the thing sensed as a collection of property/value pairs. Unique names are not used to identify objects; agents must infer the identity of an object from its properties. Sense data can be transformed as they travel. For example speech behind a closed door can be muffled so that the words are unintelligible but the voice is recognizable or a white shirt can appear blue when seen through blue tinted glass. In general, the sense data available to an agent can be incomplete, incorrect, or absent.

2.2 Perception (Sensory Routines and Integrated Sense Model)

In the interactive fiction world, each Tok agent runs by executing a three step loop: sense, think, act. First, raw sense data is extracted from the world and recorded by the Sensory Routines. Because the world is simple, most of the perceivable world state can be determined and recorded using task independent mechanisms. The relationships between objects are represented as links, thus creating a topological graph of the newly encountered world fragment. The new data is marked with the agent's internal notion of time, and the older graphs are retained. When Hap behaviors execute, this low level memory of raw sense data can be queried for information such as "have I seen food in the kitchen in the last ten minutes?".

After the raw data are recorded in the Sensory Routines, an attempt is made to merge them into the Integrated Sense Model (ISM), which maintains the agent's best guess about the physical structure of the whole world. This requires inference, including merging sense data from different modalities, such as sight and sound, if they seem to be related, and merging new and past perceptions of seemingly identical objects. The process uses whatever (partial) property/value pairs are available in the sense data as well as topological information. Some higher-level inferences are made, such as deciding which of the visible objects are within reach.

Lyotard starts with an empty ISM and with no fragments in the sensory routines. As he interacts with the world these perception systems collect information. By exploring the environment he visually determines how space is connected and how objects are placed in the world. This allows him, for instance, to make a good guess later about the location of his favorite toy mouse or various soft places to sit. By executing actions which result in touching objects, he collects tactile information via the tactile sensory routine. For example, by sitting on an object which visually appeared soft, Lyotard's tactile sensory routine perceives and records the actual softness of the object. If the object is not soft, Lyotard's ISM representation of the object would change.

The continuously updated information in the sensory routines and the longer term, approximate model in the ISM are routinely queried when choosing actions or updating the emotional state of Lyotard.

2.3 Action (Hap)

Hap is Tok's goal-directed, reactive action engine [17]. It continuously chooses the agent's next action based on perception, current goals, emotional state, behavioral features and other aspects of internal state. Goals in Hap contain an atomic name and a set of parameters which are instantiated when the goal becomes active, for example (`goto` <object>). Goals do not characterize world states to accomplish, and Hap does no explicit planning. Instead, sets of actions (which for nostalgic reasons we call "plans") are chosen from an unchanging plan memory which may contain one or more plans for each goal. These plans are either ordered or unordered collections of subgoals and actions which can be used to accomplish the invoking goal. For example one plan for the above `goto` goal is the sequence: `goto-floor` of the current room, `goto-room` of the room containing <object>, `goto-object-in-room` of the <object>. Plans have testable *preconditions* which are true when the plan could apply in the current state of the world. Multiple plans can be written for a given goal, with Hap choosing between the plans at execution time. If a plan fails, Hap will attempt any alternate plans for the given goal, and thus perform a kind of backtracking search in the real world.

Hap stores all active goals and plans in a structure called the active plan tree (APT). This is a tree of alternating layers of goals and plans that represents Hap's current execution state. The APT may be thought of as an AND-OR tree, where the goals are OR nodes and the plans are AND nodes. The APT expands and contracts as goals and plans succeed and fail.

There are various annotations in the APT to support reactivity and the management of multiple top-level goals. Two important annotations are *context conditions* and *success tests*. Both of these are arbitrary testable expressions over the perceived state of the world and other aspects of internal state. Success tests are associated with each goal in the APT. When a success test is true, its associated goal is deemed to have been accomplished and thus no longer needs to be pursued. For example, in Lyotard the first step of the `goto` plan described above has a success test associated with it to determine if the agent is already on the floor of the room. This success test may allow Lyotard to skip the subgoal. Also, if Lyotard is in the process of going to the floor when some external factor, such as a human, causes him to arrive on the floor before the subgoal completes, the success test would enable him to recognize that his goal has succeeded and stop pursuing it.

Similarly, context conditions are associated with plans in the active plan tree. When a context condition becomes false its associated plan is deemed no longer applicable in the current state of the world. That plan fails and a new plan must be chosen to accomplish the invoking goal. For the `goto` plan, an appropriate context condition might be that the object of the `goto` goal appear to remain reachable. If that context condition failed, Lyotard would try other plans for going to his target, perhaps including finding a human to help out.

Figure 3 shows the concrete expression of a small plan that includes some of these annotations.

Every instance of a goal has a *priority* number used when choosing a goal to execute and an *importance* number used by Em when considering the significance of the goal. These annotations are assigned to instances of goals rather than to types of goals, because identical goals could have different priority or emotional importance depending on the context in which they arise. In Lyotard, going to the kitchen to get food has a higher priority than going to the kitchen in pursuit of an exploration goal.

After sense data is processed, Hap begins execution by modifying the APT based on changes in the world. For every goal and plan in the APT, the associated success test or context condition is evaluated. Goals whose success test is true and plans whose context condition is false are removed. Next one of the leaf goals is chosen. This choice is made by a goal arbiter which prefers high priority goals and prefers continuing a line of expansion among goals of equal priority. If the chosen goal is a primitive action, it is executed. Otherwise it is a subgoal, in which case the plan library is indexed and the plan arbiter chooses a plan for this new goal from those whose preconditions are true. The plan arbiter will not choose plans which have already failed to achieve this goal instance, and prefers more specific plans over less specific ones (a measure of specificity is encoded with each plan). After either executing the primitive act or expanding the chosen subgoal, the execution loop repeats.

To date we have found Hap's mechanisms adequately flexible for our needs.

```
(sequential-production goto (target)
      (precondition
       (and (can-see (a location ?l-me) location (node $$me))
            (know-of-in-ism (a location ?l-target) location
                            (node $$target))
            (know-of-in-ism (node $$target) reachable (node $$me))))
      (context-condition
       (and (can-see (a location ?l-me) location (node $$me))
            (know-of-in-ism (node $$target) reachable (node $$me))))
  (with (success-test
         (or (can-see (a location) containing (node $$me))
             (can-see (node $$l-target) location (node $$me))))
    (subgoal goto-floor $$l-me))
  (with (success-test
         (can-see (node $$l-target) location (node $$me)))
    (subgoal goto-room $$l-target))
  (with (success-test
         (or (can-see (node $$target) containing (node $$me))
             (can-see (node $$target) supporting (node $$me))))
    (subgoal goto-object-in-room $$target)))
```

Fig. 3. Example Hap Plan in Lyotard

However, we have found additional organizing principles which help to guide the style of programming in Hap. In Lyotard we cluster related goals and plans into conceptual structures that we call *behaviors*. Each behavior represents a recognizable, internally coherent unit of action. These behaviors are usually activated by a single goal, which can be created in the pursuit of another goal or by a top-level demon.

As mentioned earlier, Lyotard's behaviors are shown in Figure 2. An example behavior is wanting-to-be-pet, which represents plans such as finding a person and then purring or rubbing against their leg, or otherwise relaxing in a comfortable place with the expectation that a human should sense the Lyotard's desire and pet him. When the behavior is active, Lyotard displays coherent action toward this end. Section 3 provides examples of additional behaviors.

2.4 Emotion and Social Relationships (Em)

Em models emotional and certain social aspects of the agent. It is based on ideas of Ortony et al. [21]. Like that work, Em develops emotions from a cognitive base: external events are compared with goals, actions are compared with standards, and objects (including other agents) are compared with attitudes. Most of Em's possible emotions are shown in Figure 2.

In this paper we present only the subset of Em that was necessary for implementing Lyotard. This is a very limited initial implementation that does not convey the full capabilities of the underlying theory. For a more detailed description of Em, see [22].

As Hap runs, goals are created, goals succeed, and goals fail. As these events occur, Hap informs Em, and Em uses this information to generate many of its emotions. Happiness and sadness occur when the agent's goals succeed or fail. The degree of happiness or sadness depends on the importance of the goal to the agent, which is provided by the agent builder. Lyotard feels a greater degree of happiness when he satisfies an active eating goal than when he satisfies an active relaxation goal because we labeled the former as more important.

Not all goals generate emotional reactions. Most of Lyotard's goals have an importance of zero and hence produce no effect on emotion. In addition, there are thresholds in Em which generally prevent low importance goals from affecting the emotional state. If enough of these low importance effects occur, however, then the emotional state will change.

Hope and fear occur when Em believes that there is some chance of an active goal succeeding or failing. For example, Lyotard feels hope when he sees a human about to feed him. The amount of hope or fear is determined by a function of the goal's importance and the believed likelihood of success or failure.

Pride, shame, reproach, and admiration arise when an action is either approved or disapproved. These judgments are made according to the agent's *standards*, which represent moral beliefs and personal standards of performance. Pride and shame occur when the agent itself performs the action; admiration and reproach develop in response to others' actions. Lyotard uses only the most primitive standards, do-not-cause-my-goals-to-fail and help-my-goals-to-succeed, so he will feel reproach toward an agent who shoves him from his soft chair as this causes the failure of his relaxation goal.

Anger, gratitude, remorse and gratification arise from combinations of other emotions. An agent shoving Lyotard from his chair not only causes reproach toward the agent, but also causes sadness in Lyotard due to the failure of Lyotard's relaxation goal. The sadness and reproach combine to produce the composite emotion of anger toward the agent. Similarly, gratitude is a composite of happiness and admiration, remorse is sadness and shame, and gratification is happiness and pride.

Our choice of standards for Lyotard means that reproach and anger always coexist. The same is true for the other emotion pairs admiration-gratitude, pride-gratification, and shame-reproach. This is a consequence of the simple standards we chose for modelling the cat's emotions. For modelling more complicated agents, or even more realistic cats, the standards used would be correspondingly complicated. Em is designed to handle such standards, even though this capability is not used in Lyotard.

Em's final two emotions, love and hate, arise from noticing objects toward which the agent has positive or negative *attitudes*. In Lyotard we use attitudes to help model the human-cat social relationship. Lyotard initially dislikes the user, a negative attitude, and this attitude varies as the user does things to make Lyotard angry or grateful. As this attitude changes, so will the degree of his emotion of love or hate, when the human is nearby.

Emotions (but not attitudes) should fade with time, and Em models this decay. An agent will feel love when close to someone liked. This will fade if the other agent leaves, but the attitude toward that agent will remain relatively stable.

2.5 Behavioral Features

Behavioral features modulate the activity of Hap. They are adjusted by Hap or Em to vary the ways in which Hap achieves its goals. Em adjusts the features to express emotional influences on behavior. It continuously evaluates a set of functions that control certain features based on the agent's emotional state. Hap modifies the features when it wants to force a style of action. For example, it may decide to act friendly to get what it wants, even if the agent isn't feeling especially friendly.

Features may influence several aspects of Hap's execution. They may trigger demons that create new top-level goals. They may occur in the preconditions, success tests, and context conditions of plans, and so influence how Hap chooses to achieve its goals. Finally, they may affect the precise style in which an action is performed.

Lyotard's behavioral features are listed in Figure 2. One such feature is `aggressive` which arises whenever Lyotard is either angry or mildly afraid (which might be considered bravado). The aggressive feature may affect Hap by giving rise to a new goal, such as bite-human, by influencing the choice of plan for a goal, such as nipping instead of meowing to attract attention, or by modifying the style of an action, such as swatting a toy mouse a little more emphatically than usual.

We have no structured set of features, and know of no source that suggests one. Besides those in Lyotard, we have seen the following suggested: curious, belligerent, persistent, depressed, patient [8]; timid, reckless, quiet, arrogant [12]. The feature mechanism, while very *ad hoc*, appears to provide a useful degree of abstraction in the interface between emotion and behavior.

3 The Behavior of Lyotard

To our knowledge, whether an agent's behavior produces a successful suspension of disbelief can be determined only empirically. The agent must be embedded in a world, and a variety of users must report their subjective experience with the agent. For us this evaluation is an on-going effort, which we will attempt to report in the literature [15] and to convey by demonstration.

In an attempt to provide the reader of this non-interactive text with some sense of Lyotard's behavior, we present in Figure 4 a small excerpt of a session with Lyotard. In this session a human user interacted with Lyotard in a simulated

```
Lyotard:
 L: (*go-to "the bedroom").
    (*go-to "the sunroom").
    (*go-to "the spare room").
    (*jump-on "the chair").
    (*sit-down).
    (*lick "Lyotard").
    (*lick "Lyotard").

Player:
 P: (*go-to "the spare room").
 L: (*jump-off "the chair").
    (*run-to "the sunroom").

 P: (*go-to "the sunroom").
 L: (*lookaround nervously).
 P: (*pet "Lyotard").
 L: (*bite "Player").
    (*run-to "the diningroom").

 P: (*go-to "the spare room").
 L: (*lookaround nervously).
    (*go-to "the sunroom").
    (*pounce-on "the superball").
    (*lookat "the superball").
    (*nudge "the superball").
    (*pounce-on "the superball").
    (*pounce-on "the superball").

 L: (*go-to "the diningroom").
 L: (*go-to "the kitchen").
    (*meow).
 P: (*go-to "the sunroom").
 L: (*meow).
 P: (*go-to "the diningroom").
 L: (*wait).
 P: (*take "the glass jar").

 L: (*go-to "the diningroom").
 P: (*go-to "the kitchen").
 L: (*jump-on "the table").

 L: (*jump-off "the table").
    (*go-to "the kitchen").
    (*meow).
 P: (*pour "the glass jar" in
             "the kitty bowl").

 L: (*eat "the sardine").
    (*eat "the sardine").
    (*eat "the sardine").
    (*eat "the sardine").
    (*eat "the sardine").

 P: (*pet "Lyotard").
 L: (*close-eyes lazily).
 P: (*take "Lyotard").
 L: (*close-eyes lazily).
```

Fig. 4. Section of an interaction with Lyotard

six room house. Because we are interested in the actions of the agents, the figure contains debugging output showing the actions of each agent from an omniscient perspective. The normal output from the system to the human user has been omitted: English descriptions of what the human perceives, prompts for the human's action, etc. Blank lines have also been included to improve clarity.

Just prior to the beginning of this excerpt, Lyotard had successfully finished an exploration goal. This success was passed on to Em which made Lyotard mildly happy. This happy emotion led to the content feature being set. Hap then noticed this feature as active and decided to pursue a behavior to find a comfortable place to sit. This decision was due to the presence of a high-level amusement goal and the content feature. Other behaviors were under consideration both in pursuit of the amusement goal and in pursuit of Lyotard's other active high-level goals.

In finding a comfortable place to sit, Lyotard (using the ISM) remembers places that he believes to be comfortable and chooses one of them, a particular chair in the spare room. He then goes there, jumps on the chair, sits down, and starts cleaning himself for a while.

At this point, the human user, whom Lyotard dislikes, walks into the room. The dislike attitude, part of the human-cat social relationship in Em, gives rise to an emotion of mild hate toward the user. Further, Em notices that one of Lyotard's goals, do-not-be-hurt, is threatened by the disliked user's proximity. This prospect of a goal failure generates fear in Lyotard. The fear and hate combine to generate a strong aggressive feature and to diminish the previous content feature. In this case, Hap also has access to the fear emotion itself to determine why Lyotard is feeling aggressive. The fear emotion and proximity of its cause combine in Hap to give rise to an avoid-harm goal, while the aggressive feature gives rise to a goal to threaten the user. In this case the avoid-harm goal wins out, creating a subsidiary escape/run-away behavior that leads Lyotard to jump off the chair and run out of the room. Since Lyotard is no longer on the chair, the plan he was executing in pursuit of his relaxation goal no longer makes sense. This is recognized by the appropriate context condition evaluating to false, which causes the plan to be removed from the APT.

At this point some time passes (not shown in the trace), during which Lyotard does not see the user. This causes the success test of the escape/run-away goal to fire and thus the goal to be removed from the APT. However, when the user follows Lyotard into the sunroom, these goals are again generated. As the user then tries to pet Lyotard, Lyotard sees the action, and notices that the actor trying to touch him is one toward whom he feels mild hate. This combination generates another goal, respond-negatively-to-contact. Lyotard responds to this rather than to either of the first two goals or any of his other goals because we annotated it as having a higher priority than the others due to its immediacy. Further refinement of this goal through a series of plan choices leads to Lyotard biting the player.

As the player leaves Lyotard alone, the emotions engendered by the player start to decay, and Lyotard again pursues his amusement goal. This time he is no longer content, which is one of several changes to his emotional state, so a slightly different set of amusement choices are available. He chooses to play with one of his toys, and so goes to find his superball.

As the simulation has progressed, Lyotard's body has been getting more hungry. At this point his hunger crosses a threshold so that his mind notices it as a feeling of hunger. This triggers a feeding goal causing him to go to his bowl, but it is empty so he complains by meowing. After a while, he gives up on this technique for getting food, so he tries another technique; he goes looking for food himself. He remembers places where he has seen food that was reachable, and goes to one of them, passing by the user in the process. At this point he again feels fear and aggression, but he ignores these feelings because dealing with the hunger is more important to him. As he reaches the location he expected to find the food, he notices that it is gone (taken by the user when Lyotard couldn't see him), so Lyotard again considers other techniques to get food. He could try to find a human and suggest he be fed, but instead he chooses to try his bowl again. This time the human feeds him, and Lyotard eats. As he eats he feels happy because his emotionally important goal of eating is succeeding, and he also feels gratitude toward the user, because he believes the user helped to satisfy this goal. This gratitude in turn gradually influences Lyotard's attitude toward the user from dislike to neutral.

Now when the user pets Lyotard, Lyotard responds favorably to the action by closing his eyes lazily. Lyotard wants to be pet because he no longer dislikes or fears the user. Thus, being pet causes a goal success which causes happiness, and because the goal success was attributed to the user, increases gratitude toward the user. The result is that Lyotard now strongly likes the player.

The trace we have shown was produced by the interactive fiction version of Oz, which is written in Common Lisp. Of the 50,000 lines of code that comprise Oz, the Tok architecture is roughly 7500 lines. Lyotard is an additional 2000 lines of code. On an HP Snake (55 MIPS), each Tok agent takes roughly two seconds for processing between acts. (Most of this time is spent sensing, which suggests that even in the interactive fiction domain it may be desirable to use task specific selective perception.)

4 Conclusion and Future Work

We have described Tok, an architecture that integrates mechanisms for perception, reactivity, goals, emotion, and some social knowledge. Lyotard, a particular small agent, has been built in Tok and exhibits, we believe, interesting behavior.

This architecture has been extended to control creatures in a real time, multi-agent, animated Oz world. This imposed hard timing constraints and genuine parallelism on Hap, and caused substantial changes to the implementation and smaller changes to the architecture[18]. Some of the changes include improving the speed of the architecture (approximately by a factor of 50), providing task-specific sensing, permitting multiple actions and goals to be pursued concurrently, and providing early production of actions to enable smooth animation. In addition, this version of Hap provides a common computational environment for other parts of the Tok architecture, namely sensing and emotion, scheduling them along with other goals of the agent.

We are engaged in two additional efforts to extend Tok. First, Gump and Glinda, our natural language components, are attached to Tok only as independent Lisp modules invocable from Hap rules. It would be best if they were expressed as complex behaviors written directly in Hap. We have increasingly observed similarities in the mechanisms of Hap and Glinda, and are exploring the possibilities of merging them fully.

Second, since the Oz physical world and agent models are computer simulated, we have the opportunity to embed (possibly imprecise) copies inside Tok for use by an envisionment engine. This might allow Tok, for instance, to consider possible re-orderings of steps in behaviors, to model and consider the internal states of other agents, and generally to make decisions based on a modicum of foresight.

It has been suggested to us that it may be impossible to build broad, shallow agents. Perhaps breadth can only arise when each component is itself modeled sufficiently deeply. In contrast to the case with broad, deep agents (such as people), we have no *a priori* proof of the existence of broad, shallow agents. However, at least in the Oz domain, where sustained suspension of disbelief is the criteria for success, we suspect that broad, shallow agents may be possible. This work is an experimental effort to judge the issue.

5 Acknowledgments

This research was supported in part by Fujitsu Laboratories, Ltd. We thank Phoebe Sengers, Peter Weyhrauch, and Mark Kantrowitz for their broad and deep assistance.

References

1. Philip E. Agre and David Chapman. Pengi: An implementation of a theory of activity. In *Proceedings of the Sixth National Conference on Artificial Intelligence*, July 1987.
2. Joseph Bates. Computational drama in Oz. In *Working Notes of the AAAI-90 Workshop on Interactive Fiction and Synthetic Realities*, Boston, MA, July 1990.
3. Joseph Bates. Virtual reality, art, and entertainment. *PRESENCE: Teleoperators and Virtual Environments*, 1(1):133–138, 1992.
4. Joseph Bates, A. Bryan Loyall, and W. Scott Reilly. Broad agents. In *Proceedings of AAAI Spring Symposium on Integrated Intelligent Architectures*, Stanford, CA, March 1991. Available in *SIGART Bulletin*, Volume 2, Number 4, August 1991, pp. 38-40.
5. Joseph Bates, A. Bryan Loyall, and W. Scott Reilly. Integrating reactivity, goals, and emotion in a broad agent. In *Proceedings of the Fourteenth Annual Conference of the Cognitive Science Society*, Bloomington, IN, July 1992.
6. Rodney Brooks. Intelligence without representation. In *Proceedings of the Workshop on the Foundations of Artificial Intelligence*, June 1987.
7. Rodney Brooks. Integrated systems based on behaviors. In *Proceedings of AAAI Spring Symposium on Integrated Intelligent Architectures*, Stanford University, March 1991. Available in *SIGART Bulletin*, Volume 2, Number 4, August 1991.
8. Jaime Carbonell. Computer models of human personality traits. Technical Report CMU-CS-79-154, School of Computer Science, Carnegie Mellon University, Pittsburgh, PA, November 1979.
9. Michael Dyer. *In-Depth Understanding.* The MIT Press, Cambridge, MA, 1983.
10. James R. Firby. *Adaptive Execution in Complex Dynamic Worlds.* PhD thesis, Department of Computer Science, Yale University, 1989.
11. Michael P. Georgeff, Amy L. Lansky, and Marcel J. Schoppers. Reasoning and planning in dynamic domains: An experiment with a mobile robot. Technical Report 380, Artificial Intelligence Center, SRI International, Menlo Park, CA, 1987.
12. Eduard Hovy. *Generating Natural Language under Pragmatic Constraints.* Lawrence Erlbaum Associates, Hillsdale, NJ, 1988.
13. Mark Kantrowitz. Glinda: Natural language text generation in the Oz interactive fiction project. Technical Report CMU-CS-90-158, School of Computer Science, Carnegie Mellon University, Pittsburgh, PA, 1990.
14. Mark Kantrowitz and Joseph Bates. Integrated natural language generation systems. In R. Dale, E. Hovy, D. Rosner, and O. Stock, editors, *Aspects of Automated Natural Language Generation*, volume 587 of *Lecture Notes in Artificial Intelligence*, pages 13–28. Springer-Verlag, 1992. (This is the Proceedings of the Sixth International Workshop on Natural Language Generation, Trento, Italy, April 1992.).
15. Margaret Thomas Kelso, Peter Weyhrauch, and Joseph Bates. Dramatic presence. *PRESENCE: Teleoperators and Virtual Environments*, 2(1), 1993. To appear.
16. John Laird, editor. *Proceedings of AAAI Spring Symposium on Integrated Intelligent Architectures*, March 1991. Available in *SIGART Bulletin*, Volume 2, Number 4, August 1991.
17. A. Bryan Loyall and Joseph Bates. Hap: A reactive, adaptive architecture for agents. Technical Report CMU-CS-91-147, School of Computer Science, Carnegie Mellon University, Pittsburgh, PA, June 1991.
18. A. Bryan Loyall and Joseph Bates. Real-time control of animated broad agents. In *Proceedings of the Fifteenth Annual Conference of the Cognitive Science Society*, Boulder, CO, June 1993.
19. Erik T. Mueller. *Daydreaming in Humans and Machines.* Ablex Publishing Corporation, 1990.
20. Allen Newell. *Unified Theories of Cognition.* Harvard University Press, Cambridge, MA, 1990.
21. A. Ortony, G. Clore, and A. Collins. *The Cognitive Structure of Emotions.* Cambridge University Press, 1988.
22. W. Scott Reilly and Joseph Bates. Building emotional agents. Technical Report CMU-CS-92-143, School of Computer Science, Carnegie Mellon University, Pittsburgh, PA, May 1992.
23. Reid Simmons. Concurrent planning and execution for a walking robot. In *Proceedings of the IEEE International Conference on Robotics and Automation*, Sacramento, CA, 1991.
24. S. Vere and T. Bickmore. A basic agent. *Computational Intelligence*, 6:41–60, 1990.

3.2 Communications and Knowledge Sharing

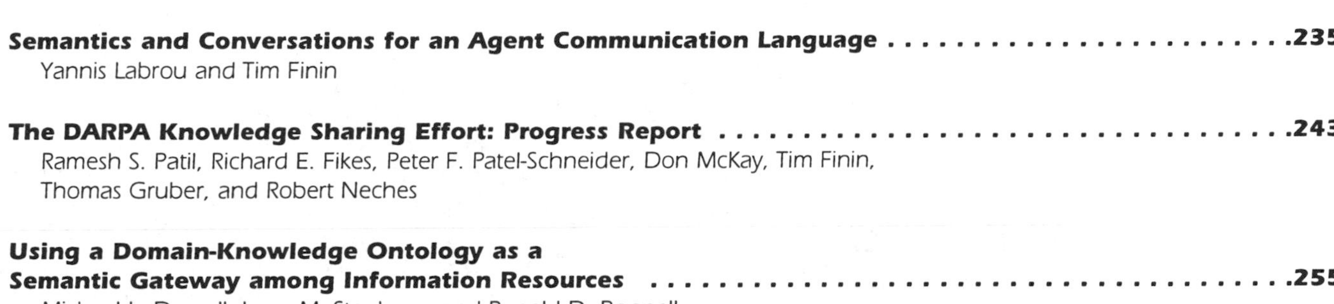

Semantics and Conversations for an Agent Communication Language *

Yannis Labrou and **Tim Finin**
Computer Science and Electrical Engineering Department,
University of Maryland, Baltimore County, Baltimore, MD 21250, USA

Abstract

We address the issues of semantics and conversations for *agent communication languages* and the Knowledge Query Manipulation Language (KQML) in particular. Based on ideas from speech act theory, we present a semantic description for KQML that associates "cognitive" states of the agent with the use of the language's primitives (performatives). We have used this approach to describe the semantics for the whole set of *reserved* KQML performatives. Building on the semantics, we devise the conversation policies, *i.e.*, a formal description of how KQML performatives may be combined into KQML exchanges (conversations), using a *Definite Clause Grammar*. Our research offers methods for a speech act theory-based semantic description of a language of communication acts and for the specification of the protocols associated with these acts. Languages of communication acts address the issue of communication among software applications at a level of abstraction that is useful to the emerging *software agents* paradigm.

1 Introduction

Communication among software agents [Petrie, 1996; Nwana, 1996] is an essential property of agency [Wooldridge and Jennings, 1995]. Agent communication languages allow agents to effectively communicate and exchange *knowledge* with other agents despite differences in hardware platforms, operating systems, architectures, programming languages and representation and reasoning systems. We view an agent communication language as the medium through which the attitudes regarding the content of the exchange between agents are communicated; it suggests whether the content of the communication is an assertion, a request, a query, *etc.*

Knowledge Query and Manipulation Language (KQML) is such a language; it consists of primitives (called *performatives*) that express attitudes regarding the content of the exchange and allow agents to communicate such attitudes to other agents and find other agents suitable to process their requests. Our research provides semantics for KQML along with a framework for the semantic description of KQML-like languages for agent communication. We also address the issue of conversations, *i.e.*, of sequences of causally-related messages in exchanges between agents and present a method for the specification of conversations (*conversation policies*).

After an introduction to KQML, we describe our semantic framework and give the semantics for a small set of KQML performatives. We follow with our method for describing the protocols (conversations) associated with the primitives and present the resulting conversations for our set of performatives. [1] We end by summarizing our contributions regarding the semantics and the specification of the conversations.

2 KQML for Agent Communication

KQML is an abstraction, a collection of *communication* primitives (message types) that express an *attitude* regarding the actual expression being exchanged, along with the assumptions of a simple model for inter-agent communication and an abstract design for KQML-speaking agents. There is no such thing as an *implementation* of KQML, *per se*, meaning that KQML is not an *interpreted* or *compiled* language that is offered in some hardware platform or an abstract machine. Agents *speak* KQML in the sense that they use those primitives, this *library of communication acts*, with their reserved *meaning*. The application programmer is expected to provide

*This work was supported in part by the Air Force Office of Scientific Research under contract F49620-92-J-0174, and the Advanced Research Projects Agency monitored under USAF contracts F30602-93-C-0177 and F30602-93-C-0028 by Rome Laboratory.

[1] Specifications for the full set of KQML performatives and associated policies are available in [Labrou, 1996].

code that processes each one of the performatives for the agent's language or knowledge representation framework. This is a KQML message:

```
(ask-if :sender      A
        :receiver    B
        :language    prolog
        :ontology    bible-genealogy
        :reply-with  id1
        :content     ''spouse(adam,eve)'' )
```

In KQML terminology, *ask-if* is a *performative.* [2] The value of the `:content` is an expression in some language or another KQML message and represents the content of the communication act. The other parameters (*keywords*) introduce values that provide a context for the interpretation of the `:content` and hold information to facilitate the processing of the message. In this example, A is querying B (these are symbolic names for agents[3]), in *Prolog* (the `:language`), about the truth status of *spouse(adam,eve)*. Any response to this KQML message will be identified by *id1* (the `:reply-with`). The ontology [4] *bible-genealogy* may provide additional information for the interpretation of the `:content`. In an environment of KQML-speaking agents there are agents called *facilitators* (*mediators* or *brokers* [Decker *et al.*, 1996]) denote similarly intended agents to whom agents *advertise* their services and ask for assistance in finding other agents that can provide services for them.

Our goal is to provide a semantic description for the language in a way that captures all the intuitions expressed in its existing documentation [ARPA Knowledge Sharing Initiative, 1993]. The lack of semantics for KQML has been a long-standing problem of KQML. Moreover, although agents engage into extended interactions with other agents (conversations), conversations is an issue that has received little attention with respect to KQML, or other agent communication languages (the few notable exceptions are [Barbuceanu and Fox, 1995; Kuwabara, 1995; Bradshaw *et al.*, 1996; Parunak, 1996]). Building on the semantic description we explore the issue of specifying KQML conversations in a formal manner.

3 A Framework for the Semantics

We treat KQML performatives as speech acts. We adopt the descriptive framework for speech acts and particularly illocutionary acts suggested by Searle [Searle, 1969; Searle and Vanderveken, 1985]. The semantic approach we propose uses expressions, that suggest the minimum set of preconditions and postconditions that govern the use of a performative, along with conditions that suggest the final state for the *successful* performance of the performative; these expressions describe the states of the agents involved in an exchange and use propositional attitudes like *belief*, *knowledge*, *desire*, and *intention* (this *intentional description* of an agent is only intended as a way of viewing the agent) which have the following reserved meaning:

1. BEL, as in BEL(A,P), which has the meaning that P is (or can be proven) true for A. P is an expression in the native language of agent A.[5]
2. KNOW, as in KNOW(A,S), expresses knowledge for S, where S is a state description (the same holds for the following two operators).
3. WANT, as in WANT(A,S), to mean that agent A desires the cognitive state (or action) described by S, to occur in the future.
4. INT, as in INT(A,S), to mean that A has every intention of doing S and thus is committed to a course of action towards achieving S in the future.

We also introduce two instances of actions:

1. PROC(A,M) refers to the action of A processing the KQML message M. Every message after being *received* is *processed*, in the sense that it is a valid KQML message and the piece of code designated with processing the performative for the application indeed processes it. PROC(A,M) does not guarantee proper processing of the message (or conformance of the code with the semantic description).
2. SENDMSG(A,B,M) refers to the action of A sending the KQML message **M** to B.

For an agent A it is BEL(A,P) if and only if P is true (in the *model-theoretic* sense) for A; we do not assume any axioms for BEL. Roughly, KNOW, WANT and INT stand for the psychological states of knowledge, desire and intention, respectively. All three take an agent's state description (either a cognitive state or an action) as their arguments. An agent can KNOW an expression that refers to the agent's own state or some other agent's state description if it has been communicated to it. So, KNOW(A,BEL(B,"foo(a,b)")) is valid, if BEL(B,"foo(a,b)") has been communicated to A with some message, but KNOW(A,"foo(a,b)") is not valid because "foo(A,B)"is not a state description. Researchers have grappled for years with the problem of formally capturing the notions of *desire* and *intention.* Various formalizations exist but none is considered a definitive one. We do not adopt a particular one neither we offer a formalization of our own. It is our belief that any of the existing formalizations would accommodate the modest use of WANT and INT in our framework.

Our semantic description, which includes expressions with the mental attitudes and actions we described, provides the following: **(1)** a natural language description

[2]The term was first coined by Austin [Austin, 1962], to suggest that some verbs can be uttered so that they perform some action.

[3]We will use the term *agents* to indiscriminately refer to all kinds of KQML-speaking programs and applications.

[4]An ontology is a repository of semantic and primarily pragmatic knowledge over a certain domain.

[5]The *native* language of the application may or may not have modal operators but we do not assume any, here.

of the performative's intuitive meaning; **(2)** an expression which describes the content of the illocutionary act and serves as a formalization of the natural language description; **(3)** preconditions that indicate the necessary state for an agent in order to send a performative (**Pre(A)**) and for the receiver to accept it and successfully process it (**Pre(B)**); if the preconditions do not hold a *error* or *sorry* will be the most likely response; **(4)** postconditions that describe the states of both interlocutors after the *successful* utterance of a performative (by the sender) and after the receipt and processing (but before a counter utterance) of a message (by the receiver); the postconditions (**Post(A)** and **Post(B)**, respectively) hold unless a *sorry* or an *error* is sent as a *response* in order to suggest the unsuccessful processing of the message; **(5)** a completion condition for the performative (**Completion**) that indicates the final state, after possibly a conversation has taken place and the intention suggested by the performative that started the conversation, has been fulfilled; and **(6)** any explanatory comments that might be helpful. the performative.

4 Semantics for KQML Performatives

We present the semantics for five KQML performatives (*advertise*, *ask-if*, *tell*, *sorry* and *broker-one*) which can support some interesting agent conversations and illustrate our approach. [6] We first introduce our notation. For a KQML message **performative(A,B,X)**, **A** is the `:sender`, **B** is the `:receiver` and **X** is the `:content` of the performative (KQML message). Occasionally we use **M** to refer to an instance of a KQML message. Capital-case letters from the beginning of the alphabet (*e.g.*, *A*, *B*, *etc.*) are agents' names and letters towards the end of the alphabet (*e.g.*, *X,Y,Z*) are propositional contents of performatives. All underscores (_) are unnamed, universally quantified variables (they stand for performative parameters that do not have values in the KQML message). Capital case letters preceded by a question mark (?), *e.g.*, *?B*, are existentially quantified variables.

All expressions in our language denote agents' states. Agents' states are either actions that have occurred (PROC and SENDMSG) or agents' mental states (BEL, KNOW, WANT or INT). Conjunctions (∧) and disjunctions (∨) of expressions that stand for agents' states are agent's states, also, but we do not allow ∧ and ∨ in the scope of KNOW, WANT and INT. Propositions in the agent's native language can only appear in the scope of BEL and BEL can only take such a proposition as its argument. BEL, KNOW, WANT, INT and actions can be used as arguments for KNOW (actions should then be interpreted as actions that have already happened). WANT and INT can only use KNOW or an action as arguments. When actions are arguments of WANT or INT, they are actions to take place in the future.

A negation of a mental state is taken to mean that the mental state does not hold in the sense that it should not be inferred (we will use the symbol not). When ¬ qualifies BEL, *e.g.*, ¬ (BEL(A,X)), it is taken to mean that the `:content` expression *X* is not true for agent *A*, *i.e.*, it is not provable in *A*'s knowledge base. Obviously, what "not provable" means is going to depend on the details of the particular agent system, for which we want to make no assumptions.

[6] Semantics for the complete set appear in [Labrou, 1996].

advertise(A,B,M)

1. A states to B that A can and will process the message *M* from B, if it receives one (A commits itself to such a course of action).
2. INT(A,PROC(A,M))
   where *M* is the KQML message **performative_name(B,A,X)**.
3. **Pre(A)**: INT(A,PROC(A,M))
   Pre(B): NONE
4. **Post(A)**:
   KNOW(A,KNOW(B,INT(A,PROC(A,M))))
   Post(B): KNOW(B,INT(A,PROC(A,M)))
5. **Completion**: KNOW(B,INT(A,PROC(A,M)))
6. An *advertise* is a commisive act, in the sense that it commits its sender to process *M*, as suggested by the announcement of the intention to process. If B is a *facilitator* then B is interchangeable (in the semantic description) with the name of any agent the facilitator knows about.

ask-if(A,B,X)

1. A wants to know what B believes regarding the truth status of the content *X*.
2. WANT(A,KNOW(A,S))
   where *S* may be any of BEL(B,X), or ¬(BEL(B,X)).
3. **Pre(A)**: WANT(A,KNOW(A,S)) ∧ KNOW(A,INT(B,PROC(B,M)))
   where *M* is **ask-if(A,B,X)**
   Pre(B): INT(B,PROC(B,M))
4. **Post(A)**: INT(A,KNOW(A,S))
   Post(B): KNOW(B,WANT(A,KNOW(A,S)))
5. **Completion**: KNOW(A,*S'*))
   where *S'* is either BEL(B,X) or ¬(BEL(B,X)), but not necessarily the same instantiation of *S* that appears in *Post*(*A*), for example.
6. **Pre(A)** and **Pre(B)** suggest that a proper advertisement is needed to establish them (see *advertise* and our comments in Section 7).

tell(A,B,X)

1. A states to B that A believes the content to be true.
2. BEL(A,X)

3. **Pre(A)**: BEL(A,X) ∧ KNOW(A,WANT(B,KNOW-(B,S)))
   Pre(B): INT(B,KNOW(B,S))
   where S may be any of BEL(B,X), or ¬(BEL(B,X)).
4. **Post(A)**: KNOW(A,KNOW(B,BEL(A,X)))
   Post(B): KNOW(B,BEL(A,X))
5. **Completion**: KNOW(B,BEL(A,X))
6. The completion condition holds, unless a *sorry* or *error* suggests B's inability to acknowledge the *tell* properly, as is the case with any other performative.

sorry(A,B,Id)

1. A states to B that although it processed the message, it has no (possibly further) response to provide to the KQML message M identified by the `:reply-with` value **Id** (some message identifier).
2. PROC(A,M)
3. **Pre(A)**: PROC(A,M)
   Pre(B): SENDMSG(B,A,M)
4. **Post(A)**: KNOW(A,KNOW(B,PROC(A,M))) ∧ not($Post_M(A)$),
   where $Post_M(A)$ is the **Post(A)** for message M.
   Post(B): KNOW(B,PROC(A,M)) ∧ not($Post_M(B)$)
5. **Completion**: KNOW(B,PROC(A,M))
6. The postconditions and completion conditions do not hold, even though A dispatched the performative to the appropriate function, because A could not (or did not want) to come up with a response that would result to their satisfiability. The not should be taken to mean that the mental state it qualifies should not be inferred to be true as a *result* of this particular message. This does not mean that for example $Post_M(B)$ does not hold if it has already been established by a previous message; it is up to B to decide (perhaps after using additional information) if and how it wants to alter its internal state with respect to the *sorry*.

broker-one(A,B,performative(A,_,X))
Let D be an agent such that CANPROC*(D,performative(B,D,X))* [7] and *performative* be a performative that entails a request (a *directive*); for the set of performatives presented here, only *ask-if* falls into this category. B sends **performative(B,D,X)** to D, receives some *response* (depending on the *performative*) from D, let us call it **response(D,B,X')**, and then B sends to A the message **forward(B,A,_,A,response(_,A,X'))**. [8]

Semantically this is a three-party situation. We break down the semantic description to the three (agent) pairs involved in the transaction.

A and B For A and B, the semantics are **not** those of a **performative(A,B,X)**, meaning that A is aware that whatever *response*, if any, comes from B is merely an "echo" of the utterance of the broker-ed agent D. So, the semantics is:

1. A wants B (a broker) to send the `:content` of the *broker-one* to some agent that can process it and eventually forward the response of the broker-ed agent back to A.
2. WANT(A,SENDMSG(B,D,M))
   where M is **performative(B,D,X)** and D is an agent such that CANPROC(D,M).
3. **Pre(A)**: WANT(A,SENDMSG(B,D,M))
   Pre(B): B has to be a *facilitator*; an agent can be a facilitator if and only if it can process performatives like *broker-one*, although it is usually more helpful to ascribe facilitator status to an agent in advance, so that agents can know which agent to contact for such requests.
4. **Post(A)**: KNOW(A,SENDMSG(B,D,M))
   Post(B): SENDMSG(B,D,M))
5. **Completion**: SENDMSG(B,A,forward(B,A,_,A,M'))
   where M' is the message **response(_,A,X')** generated by the broker-ed agent's response to B, *i.e.*, **response(D,B,X')**.
6. To offer an example, if the `:content` of the *broker-one* was **ask-if(A,_,X)**, A understands that the (possible) *response* **forward(B,A,_,A,tell(_,A,X))** does not imply that BEL*(B,X)*, since D's response to B is wrapped in a *forward* and then sent to A. Also, D's name is omitted in the *forward*, so A does not know D's name.

B and D For B and D the semantics are those of **performative(B,D,X)**, meaning that as far as D knows of, the exchange has the meaning and repercussions of **performative(B,D,X)** (and whatever additional responses) being exchanged between B and D.

A and D For A and D the semantics are those of **performative(A,D,X)** (let us call it M) but with the major difference that this is an one-sided exchange. So, $Pre_M(D)$ and $Post_M(D)$ are empty because D does not know that it has this exchange with A. Additionally, A can have no prior knowledge (in $Pre_M(A)$) of its interlocutor's state. Finally, the applicable $Post_M(A)$ and $Completion_M$ lack the name of D. To show how this translates semantically, we present the semantics of **broker-one(A,B,ask-if(A,_,X))** for agent A and the broker-ed agent D.

1. A wants to know what some other agent believes regarding the truth status of the content X.

[7] CANPROC, as in CANPROC(A,M), stands for "A being able to process message M." It is always the case that if **advertise(A,B,M)** then CANPROC(A,M), but it could very well be the case that CANPROC(A,M) may be inferred in other ways (this is to be provided or inferred by B). CANPROC is entirely different from PROC; CANPROC suggests ability to process and PROC suggest that the agent will process (or has already processed) a performative, in the sense that it will (or did) dispatch the message to the appropriate piece of code for handling.

[8] The performative *forward* is not presented here. Its meaning is basically the intuitive one and the four parameters `:from`, `:to`, `:sender` and `:receiver` refer respectively to the originator of the performative in the `:content`, the final destination, the `:sender` of the *forward* and the `:receiver` of the *forward*.

2. WANT(A,KNOW(A,S))
   where S may be any of BEL(?D,X), or ¬(BEL(?D,X)).
3. **Pre(A)**: WANT(A,KNOW(A,S))
   Pre(D): NONE
4. **Post(A)**: INT(A,KNOW(A,S))
   Post(D): NONE
5. **Completion**: KNOW(A,S'))
   where S' is either BEL(?D,X) or ¬(BEL(?D,X)), but not necessarily the same instantiation of S that appears in *Post*(A), for example.
6. In effect, D's identity remains unknown to A and D is unaware that A knows its belief regarding the truth status of X.

5 Describing Conversations

A *conversation* is a sequence of KQML messages that belong to the same thread of interaction between two or possibly more agents. We assume some sort of (intuitive) causal relation between messages that are taken to belong in the same *conversation* and we use the `:in-reply-to` value as the indicator of such linkage. *Conversation policies* are rules that describe permissible *conversations* among KQML-speaking agents. The *conversation policies* that we provide do not describe *all* possible *conversations* because more complex interactions (and thus conversations) are possible between KQML-speaking agents. The conversations we present can be used as building blocks for more complex interactions.

We use the Definite Clause Grammars (DCGs) formalism for the specification of the *conversation policies* for the KQML performatives. DCGs extend Context Free Grammars (CFGs) in the following way [Perreira and Warren, 1986]: 1) **Non-terminals** may be compound terms (instead of just atoms as in the CFG case), and 2) the body of a rule may contain **procedural attachments**, written within "{" and "}" (in addition to terminals and non-terminals), that express extra conditions that must be satisfied for the rule to be valid. For example, a DCG rule might look like
noun(N) ⟶ [W], {RootForm(W,N), is_noun(N)} with the possible meaning that "a phrase identified as the noun **N** may consist of the single word **W** ([W] is a terminal), where **N** is the root form of **W** and **N** is a noun" [Perreira and Warren, 1986].

5.1 DCGs & KQML conversation policies

Conversation policies describe both the sequences of KQML performatives and the constraints and dependencies on the values of the *reserved parameters* of the performatives involved in the conversations. In other words, we are not only interested in asserting that an *ask-if* might be followed by a *tell* (among other performatives) but we want to also capture constraints such as, the $\mathtt{content}_{ask-if}$ being the same with the $\mathtt{content}_{tell}$ or the $\mathtt{reply-with}_{ask-if}$ being also the $\mathtt{in-reply-to}_{tell}$. The DCG we provide in the next section fully describes the above in a declarative fashion.

Each KQML message is a *terminal* in the DCG. A terminal is a list of the following values: `performative_name`, `:sender`, `:receiver`, `:in-reply-to`, `:reply-with`, `:language`, `:ontology`, `IO` (if `IO` is set to 1 the message is an incoming message and if it is set to 0 the current message is an outgoing message), `:content`, and whenever the `:content` is a performative itself, then the `:content` is going to be a list itself. *Terminals* are enclosed in "[" and "]", so a terminal in our DCG will look like: **[[ask-if,A,B,id1,id2,prolog,bar,foo(X,Y)]]** In the DCG we present here, we omit the `:language` and `:ontology` values (we take them to remain unchanged throughout the same conversation).

The conversation policies we present are tied to the semantics in the sense that changes in the semantic description would result to different conversation policies. Our conversation policies technically are not inferred from the semantic description, but they define the *minimal* set of conversations that are consistent with the semantics when following these heuristics:

- If a performative has *preconditions* for the sender, then it cannot start a conversation if these preconditions have to be established by a communication act (see *tell*).
- If the *completion condition(s)* for a performative are not not a subset of the postconditions, then a performative cannot end a conversation since further (communicative) action has to take place to establish the *completion condition(s)* (see *ask-if*).
- A performative may be preceded by a performative that can (partially) establish its preconditions (*e.g.*, a *tell* may be preceded by an *ask-if*; compare **Post(A)** for *ask-if* and **Pre(A)** for *tell*).

6 Converation Policies, in detail

We present a complete DCG for the set of performatives presented in Section 4. This is a subset of the full DCG that describes the whole set of conversation policies (see [Labrou, 1996]) and is intended as a demonstration of how our method may be used.

ask-if, tell

```
S →
        s(CC,P,S,R,IR,Rw,IO,C),
        {member(P,[advertise,broker-one])}
s(CC,ask-if,S,R,IR,Rw,IO,C) →
        [[ask-if ,S,R,IR,Rw,IO,C]] |
        [[ask-if ,S,R,IR,Rw,IO,C]], {OI is abs(1-IO)},
            r(CC,ask-if,S,R,_,Rw,OI,C)
r(CC,ask-if,R,S,_,IR,IO,C) →
        [[tell ,S,R,IR,Rw,IO,C]] |
        problem(CC,R,S,IR,_,IO)
```

The rules are organized into groups that describe the

sub-dialogues that may start with a performative, or a group of them and are written so that any sequence of messages that is reachable from the start is also a conversation that will be accepted by the DCG. Note that there is no notion of a *complete* KQML conversation, although it might be possible to define such conversations in some cases. Rules might be called by other rules.

As a result, an *advertise* of an *ask-if* is a conversation; if a proper *ask-if* follows the *advertise*, the sequence of *advertise* and *ask-if* is a conversation; and finally, if an appropriate *tell* follows the *ask-if*, the resulting sequence of the three messages will be a conversation that the DCG will accept. The values of the various terminals and non-terminals define what an *appropriate* follow-up is, at any point of a KQML exchange. We use the following variables for the various tokens that appear in the DCG (symbols that start with a capital-case letter are variables and those that start with small-case letters are constants): `CC` stands for the *current conversation* that the DCG handles; `P` is the *performative_name*; `S` is the `:sender`; `R` is the `:receiver`; `IR` is the `:in-reply-to` value; `Rw` is the `:reply-with`; `IO` and `OI` are the variables that indicates if a message is an incoming or outgoing one (they only take the values 0 and 1 and always have complimentary values) ; `C` is the `:content`; and `[]` is the *empty string*.

We take the position that all starting points for conversations are *advertise* performatives and the *broker-one* performative (when sent to, or processed by facilitators). *Ask-if* may follow an *advertise* and may be responded to (in this KQML subset) with a *tell*. [9] The `:in-reply-to` value of the response must equal the `:reply-with` of the *ask-if* for all performatives that act as a *response* or a *follow-up* to some other performative. Also, notice that the `:content` of a response is the same as the `:content` of the querying performative in the case of the *ask-if*.

sorry

```
problem(CC,R,S,IR,Rw,IO) →
        [[sorry ,S,R,IR,Rw,IO,[]]]
```

A *problematic* or a *non-positive* response, *i.e.*, a *sorry* (or an *error*, not included here) is always a possibility and those two performatives may follow almost any performative (except for another *sorry* or *error*).

advertise

```
s(CC,advertise,S,R,_,Rw,IO,_) →
        { OI is abs(1-IO) },
        [[advertise,S,R,_,Rw,IO,[P1,R,S,Rw,_,OI,C1]]] ,
            {member(P1,[ask-if])},
            c_adv(CC,P1,S,R,Rw,_,OI,C1)
c_adv(CC,P,R,S,Rw_adv,_,IO,C) →
        s(CC,P,S,R,Rw_adv,_,IO,C) |
        problem(CC,S,R,Rw_adv,_,IO) | []
```

The procedural attachment restricts the performatives that might appear in the `:content` of an *advertise*. The `:content` has the form of the expected follow-up to the *advertise*. This follow-up is given by the part of the DCG that starts the sub-dialogue for the embedded performative. Note that it is possible to have a *sorry* response to the *advertise* itself, as well to the follow-ups to the *advertise*.

broker-one

```
s(CC,broker-one,S,R,IR,Rw,IO,C) →
        {OI is abs(1-IO)},
        [[broker-one,S,R,IR,Rw,IO,[P1,R,_R,Rw,Rw1,_,C1]]] ,
            {member(P1,[ask-if])},
            c_brk_one(CC,P1,S,R,Rw,Rw1,OI,C1)
c_brk_one(CC,P,R,S,Rw_brk,Rw,1,C) → [] |
        problem(CC,S,R,Rw_brk,_,1) |
        r(CC,P,Brk,R,_,Rw,1,C)
c_brk_one(CC,P,R,S,Rw_brk,Rw,0,C) → [] |
        problem(CC,S,R,Rw_brk,Rw,0) |
        s(CC,P,S,Brk,Rw_brk,Rw,0,C),
            c_brk_one1(CC,P,S,R,Brk,Rw_brk,Rw,0,C)
c_brk_one1(CC,P,S,R,Brk,Rw_brk,Rw,IO,C) → [] |
        {OI is abs(1-IO), last(CC,[P1,Brk,S,Rw,Rw1,OI,C1]),
         assert(send_MSG([forward,S,R,Rw_brk,Rw2,OI,
                  [P1,_Brk,R,Rw_brk,Rw1,OI,C1]]))} |
        [[forward,S,R,Rw_brk,Rw2,OI,
             [P1,_Brk,R,Rw_brk,Rw1,OI,C1]]]
```

The *broker-one* performative presents an interesting case because it involves a three-party interaction. The $\texttt{receiver}_{broker-one}$ sends the $\texttt{content}_{broker-one}$ (with the appropriate values) to some other agent and then passes the response(s) to it to the $\texttt{sender}_{broker-one}$. The last part of this exchange can be done automatically with a procedural attachment in the DCG instead of being taken care of by the handler function for *broker-one*. As the `c_brk_one1` rule suggests, a sub-dialogue (a new conversation) with the third agent starts and the response (or follow-up), *i.e.*, the last message in the conversation being handled by the DCG with the expected values for `:sender` and `:in-reply-to`, is sent to $\texttt{sender}_{broker-one}$ (this is the meaning of the procedural attachment in the `c_brk_one1` rule, that makes reference to predicates that are not a part of the DCG).

If the **local** agent sent a *broker-one*, the message expected is the prescribed response or follow-up to the *performative* in the `:content`. Technically this message (or messages) will arrive wrapped in a *forward* but from the DCG point of view will be stripped from their "forwarding" packaging. This performative is a prime example of how complicated interactions might be composed from the simpler building blocks.

---

[9] A response with a *sorry* or *error* (not included in this set) is always a possibility of course.

7 Discussion

The issue of semantics for communication acts has received a fair share of attention. Cohen and Lesveque suggest a model for rational agents [Cohen and Levesque, 1990], which uses a *possible-worlds* formalism, that can in turn be used as a framework for the semantic description of illocutionary acts [Cohen and Levesque, 1995; Smith and Cohen, 1996]. Sadek [Sadek, 1992] has also taken on a similar task of defining rational agency and defining communicative acts on top of it. Finally, Singh proposes a model of agency [Singh, 1993a], which differs from that of Cohen and uses it as a framework for the semantic treatment of speech acts [Singh, 1993b].

In contrast, we draw directly from a high-level speech act account, although the resulting preconditions-/postconditions framework is reminiscent of planning (but it could also be thought as operational semantics, *i.e.,* transitions on agents' states). Also, we provide no formal semantics (in a *possible-worlds* formalism or some similar framework) for the modal operators but we restrict the scope and use of these operators, so that they can be subsumed by similar modalities whose semantics could be provided by an intentional theory of agency. Apart from the complexity of possible-worlds–like formalisms which can be prohibiting for the intended audience of our semantic description that includes application developers that want to support KQML in their software agents, we want to avoid a tight coupling with a particular theory of agency. Another common element of the mentioned approaches is the strictly declarative definitions of the primitives. Instead, our preconditions, postconditions and completion conditions framework suggests a more operational approach which we hope will be useful to implementors that have to provide the code that processes the communication primitives.

By attempting a semantics for communication acts without a theory of agency, *i.e.*, formal semantics for the propositional attitudes (operators), we certainly give up interesting inferencing. For example, if an agent sends **tell(A,B,X)** and later **tell(A,B,X → Y)**, *B* will not be able to infer that BEL(A,Y) (since we do not even assume a universal *weak S4* model for BEL) based on the KQML semantics alone. Nothing is lost though, because the additional information of the agent theory that holds for the agent can be supplied as part of the KQML exchange (*e.g.*, in the `:ontology` value of a KQML message) and subsequently taken into consideration for further inferencing. In the end, we trade a formal semantics for the propositional attitudes, which inevitably define a *model of agency* that is unlikely to be universal for all agents, for a simpler formalism and agent theory independence.

Objections may be raised regarding some of our choices regarding the meaning we chose to attribute to some of the performatives. Our semantics for *tell*, for example, suggest that an agent can not offer unsolicited information to some other agent. This can be easily amended by introducing another performative, let us call it *proactive-tell* which has the same semantic description as *tell* with the following difference: **Pre(A)** is BEL(A,X), and **Pre(B)** is empty. Similarly, an agent *A* can send an *ask-if* to agent *B* if and only if *A* knows that *B* is going to process such a request. Implicit in this choice, is our preference for a model where agents advertise their services so that other agents (with the help of *mediators* or *facilitators*) can find agents that can process requests for them. A "relaxed" version of *ask-if* can be introduced to allow for direct querying. The semantic description of this *proactive-ask-if* differs from that of *ask-if* as follows: **Pre(A)** is WANT(A,KNOW(A,S)), and **Pre(B)** is empty. Following KQML's tradition of an open standard, the KQML users' community should decide the performative names to be associated with whatever semantic description. Additionally, these two "new" performative could be starting points for conversations in our conversation policies.

Our description and implementation of the conversation policies using a DCG allows as to provide a description that would not be possible had we chosen a CFG or a Finite State Machine for the task. Another formalism that would probably provide us with the same flexibility is that of Augmented Transition Networks[10] (ATNs), but DCGs have the advantage that they can be expressed directly in a general purpose programming language like Prolog (in fact our DCG is a Prolog program). The conversation policies do not prescribe the only possible behavior for an agent but they rather define one which is consistent with the semantics. Such a specification is in no way a prescriptive one and thus does not constrain elaborate agents but it could be useful for simpler ones.

8 Conclusions

We have presented excerpts of a complete semantic description for the primitives in the agent communication language KQML. This specification uses a framework for the semantic description of KQML-like languages [11] for the linguistic communication among software agents along with a method for specifying the conversations that builds on our semantic description. We have used our approach to provide the semantics and conversation policies for the full set of KQML primitives and we have presented the framework and the semantic description along with the method and the conversation policies'

[10] Perreira and Warren claim that DCGs are at least as powerful of a formalism as ATNs ([Bates, 1979]), with DCGs having some considerable advantages over ATNs ([Perreira and Warren, 1986]).

[11] That is, languages of attitude-expressing communication primitives, modeled after speech acts.

specification for a handful of performatives.

The conversation policies present us with some attractive possibilities. They can be used to devise a software component that monitors an agent's incoming and outgoing messages and ensures that it only engages in valid KQML conversations of well-formed KQML messages. Such a component can keep track of an agent's multiple interactions (conversations) with other agents and offer ways to recover from unforeseen situations. Alternatively, one may view an agent as a collection of conversations that "unfold" concurrently as the agent interacts with other agents. Finally, the conversation policies can be used as building blocks for more complex interactions. In the end, we should keep in mind that agents do not use the primitives of a communication language statically, but in order to carry, often complex, interactions which the conversation policies can help describe.

References

[ARPA Knowledge Sharing Initiative, 1993] ARPA Knowledge Sharing Initiative. Specification of the KQML agent-communication language. ARPA Knowledge Sharing Initiative, External Interfaces Working Group working paper., July 1993.

[Austin, 1962] J.L. Austin. *How to do things with words.* Harvard University Press, Cambridge, MA, 1962.

[Barbuceanu and Fox, 1995] M. Barbuceanu and M. S. Fox. COOL: a language for describing coordination in multi-agent systems. In *Proceedings of the 1st International Conference on Multi-agent systems (ICMAS'95)*, pages 17–24. AAAI/MIT Press, 1995.

[Bates, 1979] Madeleine Bates. The theory and practice of augmented transition network grammars. In Leonard Bolc, editor, *Natural Language Communication with Computers*, Lecture Notes in Computer Science, pages 191–260. Morgan Kaufmann, 1979.

[Bradshaw *et al.*, 1996] Jeffrey M. Bradshaw, Stuart Dutfield, Pete Benoit, and John D. Woolley. Kaos: Toward an industrial-strength open agent architecture. In Jeffrey M. Bradshaw, editor, *Software Agents (in preparation)*. AAAI/MIT Press, 1996.

[Cohen and Levesque, 1990] Philip R. Cohen and Hector J. Levesque. Intention is choice with commitment. *Artificial Intelligence*, 42:213–261, 1990.

[Cohen and Levesque, 1995] Philip R. Cohen and H.J. Levesque. Communicative actions for artificial agents. In *Proceedings of the 1st International Conference on Multi-Agent Systems (ICMAS'95)*. AAAI Press, June 1995.

[Decker *et al.*, 1996] Keith Decker, Mike Williamson, and Katia Sycara. Matchmaking and brokering. In *Proceedings of the 2nd International Conference on Multi-Agent Systems (ICMAS'96)*, December 1996.

[Kuwabara, 1995] K. Kuwabara. AgenTalk: coordination protocol description for multi-agent systems. In *Proceedings of the 1st International Conference on Multi-agent systems (ICMAS'95)*. AAAI/MIT Press, 1995.

[Labrou, 1996] Yannis Labrou. *Semantics for an Agent Communication Language.* PhD thesis, University of Maryland, Baltimore County, August 1996.

[Nwana, 1996] Hyacinth S. Nwana. Software agents: an overview. *Knowledge Engineering Review*, 11(3):1–40, September 1996.

[Parunak, 1996] H. Van Dyke Parunak. Visualizing agent conversations: Using enhanced dooley graphs for agent design and analysis. In *Proc. of the 2nd International Conference on Multi-Agent Systems (ICMAS'96)*, 1996.

[Perreira and Warren, 1986] F. Perreira and D. Warren. Definite clause grammars for language analysis. In Barbara J. Grosz, Karen Sparck Jones, and Bonnie Lynn Webber, editors, *Readings in Natural Language Processing*, pages 101–124. Morgan Kaufmann Publishers, 1986.

[Petrie, 1996] Charles Petrie. Agent-based engineering, the web, and intelligence. *IEEE Expert*, December 1996.

[Sadek, 1992] M.D. Sadek. A study in the logic of intention. In *Proceedings of the 3rd Conference on Principles of Knowledge Representation and Reasoning (KR'92)*, pages 462–473, Cambridge, MA, 1992.

[Searle and Vanderveken, 1985] J. Searle and D. Vanderveken. *Foundations of illocutionary logic.* Cambridge University Press, Cambridge, UK, 1985.

[Searle, 1969] John R. Searle. *Speech Acts.* Cambridge University Press, Cambridge, UK, 1969.

[Singh, 1993a] M.P. Singh. A logic of intentions and beliefs. *Journal of Philosophical Logic*, 22:513–544, 1993.

[Singh, 1993b] M.P. Singh. A semantics for speech acts. *Annals of Mathematics and Artificial Intelligence*, 8(I-II):47–71, 1993.

[Smith and Cohen, 1996] Ira A. Smith and Philip R. Cohen. Toward a semantics for an agent communications language based on speech-acts. In *Proceedings of the 13th National Conference on Artificial Intelligence.* AAAI/MIT Press, August 1996.

[Wooldridge and Jennings, 1995] M. Wooldridge and N.R. Jennings. Intelligent agents: Theory and practice. *Knowledge Engineering Review*, 10(2), 1995.

The DARPA Knowledge Sharing Effort: Progress Report

Ramesh S. Patil
USC Info. Sci. Inst.
Marina del Rey, California

Richard E. Fikes
Stanford University
Palo Alto, California

Peter F. Patel-Schneider
AT&T Bell Labs
Murray Hill, New Jersey

Don Mckay
Paramax Systems Corp.
Paoli, Pennsylvania

Tim Finin
Univ. of Maryland
Baltimore, Maryland

Thomas Gruber
Stanford University
Palo Alto, California

Robert Neches
USC Info. Sci. Inst.
Marina del Rey, California

Building knowledge-based systems today usually entails constructing a new knowledge base from scratch. Even if several groups of researchers are working in the same general area, such as medicine or electronic diagnosis, each team must develop its own knowledge base from scratch. The cost of this duplication of effort has been high and will become prohibitive as we build larger and larger systems. Furthermore, lack of methodology for sharing and communicating knowledge poses a significant road-block in developing large multi-center research projects such as DARPA/Rolm Laboratory Planning and Scheduling Initative [21]. To overcome these barrier and advance the state of the art, we must find ways of preserving existing knowledge bases, and sharing, reusing, and building on them.

The Knowledge-Sharing Effort, sponsored by the Defense Advanced Research Projects Agency (DARPA), The Air Force Office of Scientific Research (AFOSR), the Corporation for National Research Initiative (NRI), and the National Science Foundation (NSF), is an initiative to develop the technical infrastructure to support the sharing of knowledge among systems. [27] The goal of this effort is to develop a technology that will enable researchers to develop new systems by selecting components from library of reusable modules and assembling them together. Their effort will be focused on creating specialized knowledge and reasoners specific to the task of their system. Their new system would inter-operate with existing systems, using them to perform some of its reasoning. In this way, declarative knowledge, problem solving techniques and reasoning services could all be shared among systems. The reusable modules in the library them-selves will benefit from refinements that are only possible through extensive use. This would facilitate building larger systems cheaply and reliably. The infrastructure to support such sharing and reuse would lead to greater ubiquity of these systems, potentially transforming the knowledge industry.

The work in the Knowledge-Sharing Effort began with the identification of the impediments to knowledge sharing and corresponding needs for the development of technology to overcome these impediments. Four key areas were identified for the initial effort. They are: (1) mechanisms for translation between knowledge bases represented in different languages; (2) common versions of languages and reasoning modules within families of representational paradigm; (3) protocols for communication between separate knowledge-based modules, as well as between knowledge-based systems and databases; and, (4) libraries of "ontologies," i.e., pre-fabricated foundations for application-specific knowledge bases in a particular topic area.

A detailed discussion of the impediments, and an analysis of the issues that motivated us to focus on these four types, appears in [27]. That article also describes the working groups (comprised of researchers from the DARPA AI community and other volunteers) that were established to address these issues. The next four sections describe the progress made by each of the four working groups in addressing these issues through the development of draft specifications, implementations and experiments.

1 AN INTERLINGUA FOR KNOWLEDGE INTERCHANGE

For a knowledge-based system to incorporate encoded knowledge from a library or to interchange knowledge with another system, the knowledge must either be represented in the receiving system's representation language or be translatable in some practical way into that language. Since an important means of achieving efficiency in application systems is to use specialized representation languages that directly support the knowledge processing requirements of the application, we cannot expect a standard knowledge representation language to emerge that would be used generally in application systems. Thus, we are confronted with a *heterogeneous language problem.* We may, however, be able to deal with that problem by developing a knowledge interchange language that would be commonly used as an *interlingua* for communicating knowledge between computer programs.

Given such an interlingua, a sending system could translate knowledge from its application-specific representation into the interlingua for communication purposes and a receiving system could translate knowledge from the interlingua into its application-specific representation before use. In addition, the interlingua could be the language in which libraries would provide reusable knowledge bases. An interlingua eases the translation problem in that without an interlingua one must write N pairs of translators in order to communicate knowledge to and from N other languages. With an interlingua, one need only write one pair of translators into and out of the interlingua.

1.1 KIF – A KNOWLEDGE INTERCHANGE FORMAT

The Interlingua Working Group, chaired by Richard Fikes and Michael Genesereth, is attacking the heterogeneous language problem by developing and testing a language for use as an interlingua called the Knowledge Interchange Format (KIF)[16]. The group began its work by observing that an interlingua needs to be a language with the following general properties:

- A formally defined declarative semantics;
- Sufficient expressive power to represent the declarative knowledge contained in typical application system knowledge bases; and
- A structure that enables semi-automatic translation into and out of typical representation languages.

The working group then merged ongoing language design efforts to produce a preliminary version of the KIF language which could be used as a straw man interlingua in knowledge interchange experiments and design discussions. Since then, the language has been continually evolved and expanded based on feedback from ongoing e-mail discussions, formal design reviews, translation of example knowledge bases, and interoperation experiments.

KIF is an extended version of first order predicate logic. The current 3.0 version of KIF has the following features:

- Simple list-based linear ASCII syntax suitable for transmission on serial media. For example, the following is a KIF sentence:

```
(forall ?x (=> (P ?x) (Q ?x)))
```

- Model-theoretic semantics with axiomatic characterization of a large vocabulary of object, function, and relation constants.
- Function and relation vocabulary for numbers, sets, and lists.
- Support for expression of knowledge about the properties of functions and relations. Functions and relations are included in the universe of discourse as sets of lists so that they can be arguments to relations (e.g, **transitive** and **one-one**) and functions (e.g., **inverse** and **range**). In addition, a **holds** relation is included that is true when its first argument denotes a relation that has as a member the list consisting of the items denoted by the remaining arguments. So, for example, one could define transitivity as follows:

```
(<=> (transitive ?r)
     (=> (holds ?r ?x ?y)
         (holds ?r ?y ?z)
         (holds ?r ?x ?z)))
```

- A sublanguage for defining objects, n-ary relations, and n-ary functions that enables augmentation of the representational vocabulary and specification of domain ontologies. Definitions can be *complete* in that they specify an equivalent expression or *partial* in that they specify an axiom that restricts the possible denotations of the constant being defined. For example, the following is a complete definition of the unary relation **bachelor**:

```
(defrelation bachelor (?x) :=
   (and (man ?x) (not (married ?x))))
```

and the following is a partial definition of a binary relation **above** which specifies that **above** is transitive and holds only for "located objects":

```
(defrelation above (?b1 ?b2)
   :=> (and (located-object ?b1)
            (located-object ?b2))
   :axiom (transitive above))
```

- Support for expression of knowledge about knowledge. KIF expressions are included as objects (i.e., lists) in the universe of discourse, and functions are available for changing level of denotation. For example, the following sentence says that Lisa has the same belief as John about the material of which things are made:

```
(=> (believes john '(material ,?x ,?y))
    (believes lisa '(material ,?x ,?y))
```

and the following sentence says that every sentence of the form (=> ϕ ϕ) is true:

```
(=> (sentence ?p) (true '(=> ,?p ,?p)))
```

- A sublanguage for stating both monotonic and nonmonotonic inference rules. For example:

```
(<<= (flies ?x)
     (bird ?x) (consis (flies ?x)))
```

A KIF reference manual describing the entire language in detail is available through anonymous FTP from

hudson.stanford.edu[17]. The working group expects the current language design to remain relatively stable and for future versions to be essentially extensions to the existing language. Extensions under active consideration include support for uncertain knowledge and contexts, and additional support for default knowledge.

KIF is intended to be a core language which is expandable by defining additional representational primitives. For example, one can define a frame language vocabulary of classes, slots, number restrictions, value restrictions, etc. (as Gruber has done in [19]) so that knowledge can be expressed in a form directly analogous to a frame language. Thus, given suitable definitions, one could define a "guest meal" as being a meal in which there is at least one guest and the food is gourmet as follows:

```
(defrelation guest-meal (?m)
   :=> (and (meal ?m)
            (at-least-fillers ?m guest 1)
            (all-fillers ?m food
                         gourmet-food)))
```

1.2 KNOWLEDGE INTERCHANGE EXPERIMENTS USING KIF

The problems involved in interchanging knowledge bases are not yet well understood, and there is open debate as to whether a generally useful interlingua can be specified. The Interlingua Working Group is attempting to inform that debate by developing KIF as a candidate interlingua and by promoting knowledge interchange experiments designed to substantially test the viability and adequacy of KIF as an interlingua. Several small scale experiments have been conducted thus far and multiple projects are underway to build and test KIF translators. These activities, though still in preliminary stages, have already been very productive in identifying issues that need to be resolved and technology that needs to be developed in order for knowledge interchange to be a practical reality. We describe three examples of such activities below.

Ramesh Patil built translators to an early version of KIF from CLASSIC [4] and from LOOM [22]. He then used those translators to produce KIF versions of simple CLASSIC and LOOM knowledge bases. As expected, such translation experiments highlighted weaknesses in KIF and motivated evolution of the language. In general, producing KIF translations of a wide range of sample knowledge bases is an effective means of evaluating the expressive adequacy of KIF and focusing its continuing development. Building the translators themselves does not appear to be problematical. The primary issue is whether KIF has sufficient expressive power to represent the declarative knowledge expressible in the source language.

Translating knowledge *out of* KIF is in general an intractable problem because any given proposition can be expressed in KIF in many equivalent but syntactically different forms and the recognition grammar for a target language will only be able to recognize some subset of those forms. The translation task, therefore, involves applying equivalence preserving rewrite rules to transform unrecognizable sentences into recognizable forms. Despite the worst-case complexity of logically complete translation, effective translation may be achievable in most situations by logically incomplete techniques combined with interactive direction from the user. To explore that hypothesis, Fikes and Van Baalen are building a translator development "shell" which will contain a grammar-based recognizer, a goal-directed rewrite rule interpreter, a library of general-purpose rewrite rules, facilities for hand translation of problematic sentences, etc. [12]. Initial versions of the basic components of that shell have been implemented and have been used to successfully translate simple KIF knowledge bases into CLASSIC.

A knowledge interchange capability is important both to enable *incorporation* of knowledge into a knowledge-based system (e.g., during system development) and to enable *interoperation* of knowledge-based systems so that they can cooperatively perform tasks and solve problems. KIF is being used as the knowledge level inter-agent communication language in multiple interoperation experiments, including those conducted by Mike Genesereth using the Designworld system [15] and those being conducted by participants in the Palo Alto Collaborative Testbed (PACT).

Designworld is an automated prototyping system for small scale electronic circuits built from standard parts (TTL chips and connectors on prototyping boards). The design for a product is entered into the system via a multi-media design workstation; the product is built by a dedicated robotic cell; and, if necessary, the product, once built, can be returned to the system for diagnosis and repair. The system consists of eighteen processes on six different machines. Each of the eighteen programs is implemented as a distinct agent that communicates with its peers via messages in a KQML-like Agent Communication Language (ACL) that uses KIF as the "content" language.

PACT is a laboratory for exploring the use of knowledge sharing technology and agent-based system integration architectures to support concurrent engineering. Participants include research groups at Stanford University, Lockheed AI Laboratory, Hewlett-Packard Laboratories, and Enterprise Integration Technologies. The initial experiments integrated four preexisting concurrent engineering systems into a common computational framework and explored engineering knowledge exchange in the context of a distributed simulation and simple incremental redesign scenario [9]. In those experiments, each of the individual systems was used to model one or more components of an example programmable electro-mechanical device, a small robotic manipulator. The systems interact via software agents which use KQML as the "performative" language and KIF as the "content" language during knowledge interchange.

Although these experiments have not yet placed severe demands on KIF as an interlingua, KIF successfully provided what was needed, namely a clearly specified logical sentence language for interchange of assertions, queries, and simulation inputs and outputs.

2 THE KNOWLEDGE REPRESENTATION SYSTEM SPECIFICATION

Even within a single family of knowledge representation systems (e.g. KL-ONE) minor differences in syntax and semantics between systems pose significant barriers to knowledge sharing. The goal of the Knowledge Representation System Specification (KRSS) group is to develop common specifications for the representational component of families of knowledge representation systems. These specifications will help facilitate the transfer of collections of knowledge between knowledge representation systems in the same family, by reducing the representational differences among systems in the family. The intent of the group is to produce, by-and-large, descriptive specifications, although reconciliation of some syntactic differences will almost certainly be required.

Specifications produced by the group will concentrate on the representational components of the family of knowledge representation systems. Thus, they will provide a complete definition of the representation language underlying the family, but will not include a complete definition of the interface functions that are required in a useful knowledge representation system. Instead the specifications will only define a minimal interface, one that is sufficient to create knowledge bases and query them in limited ways. Also, specifications will completely ignore user-interface issues.

These specifications will definitely not be interlinguas. The representation formalism in the specifications will be specific to the family of representation systems under consideration, and will not be general-purpose representation logics. The specifications also have to be concerned with the computational properties of the formalism they define (i.e., how hard inference in the formalism is), as the aim of the group is to specify knowledge representation *systems*, and not just abstract formalisms.

The initial effort of the KRSS group is the development of a specification for knowledge representation systems based on what are now called description logics (also known as frame-based description languages, terminological logics, etc.). These systems include BACK [31], CLASSIC [6], KRIS [2], and LOOM [22]. This group of systems was chosen partly because there is a large number of systems that are based on description logics (see above), partly because there was already some interest in the community of developers of such systems for a common specification [1], partly because many of the people in the initial group gathered together at the start of the DARPA Knowledge Sharing Initiative were working with such systems, and partly because such systems have a formal basis that is readily amenable to a well-defined specification. There has also been considerable study of the formal properties of reasoning in systems based on description logics. This includes studies of how reasoning should proceed in such systems [26] and the computational complexity and decidability of reasoning in description logics [5, 25, 10, 30]. The presence of such a large body of formal work makes the specification process much easier.

Although there is a common background for all knowledge representation systems based on description logics, there is surprising variance in several dimensions in the systems. First, different systems have different input syntaxes. One goal of the initial KRSS effort is to minimize differences in this dimension. Second, different systems have different interfaces, both functional and user interfaces. Another goal of the initial KRSS effort is to minimize differences in the portion of the functional interface used to construct and directly query knowledge bases. However, the rest of the interfaces of the various systems will not be incorporated into the specification, as it is outside the goals of the KRSS group.

The main difference between the various systems is that they take different positions in the trade-offs among expressive power, completeness of inference, and resource consumption. Some systems try to be as complete as possible in a less-expressive description logic while consuming as few resources as possible, trading off expressive power for computational benefits. Some systems implement complete inference in a moderately-expressive but decidable description logic, trading off possible resource consumption for better expressive power. Some systems implement only partial inference in an expressively-powerful description logic, trading off completeness for expressive power.

Many points in this set of trade-offs are reasonable, so a specification has to allow for both the current set of trade-offs, and also for possible future trade-offs. This means that the specification will not be a complete specification nor even a nearly complete specification.

The approach that has been taken in the specification is to define an expressively powerful description logic, including both a syntax and a semantics, incorporating those constructs whose meaning has been generally agreed upon by the community. Along with the description logic is a set of interface functions that allow for the construction, manipulation, and querying of description-logic knowledge bases. These functions allow

- the formation of descriptions and sentences;
- the definition of concepts and roles from descriptions;
- the assertion of sentences, including ground facts about individuals and simple rules about concepts;
- the creation of individuals and reasoning about their identity;
- the making of local closed-world statements;
- the making of default statements about instances of concepts;
- the retracting of previously-told assertions; and
- the querying of knowledge bases.

The non-query functions are defined by their effect on an abstract knowledge base, which is a collection of statements in the description logic. The results of the query functions are (mostly) defined by semantic relationships between the knowledge base and the query.

Because it is impossible to efficiently perform inference in the full description logic, conforming systems are not required to completely implement it. Conforming systems are free to recognize only a subset of the syntax of the logic, and need not even perform complete reasoning in the subset that they do recognize. However, such systems must use this logic as the ideal meaning of their knowledge bases, and must perform "sound" reasoning with respect to the logic.

Conforming systems are not completely free in what portion of the logic they choose to address. There is a core portion of the logic that all conforming systems are required to implement; in this way a minimal competence is required for all conforming systems. The core is not just a syntactic subset of the full logic—complete inference on even very minimal subsets of the logic is very difficult—but is instead a set of constructs that must be recognized, along with a set of inferences that must be performed on these constructs.

Most of the debate on the specification has involved the details of this core. The constructs to include in the core, the inferences to perform on them, and how to specify these inferences have all been subjects of debate. This was to be expected, as the specification of the core is where the specification is making decisions on matters that have been decided in different ways by different systems. Devising a core that is both reasonable and non-trivial is an interesting exercise in how to balance various representation and implementation concerns.

There is now (July 1992) a second draft of the complete specification that has been distributed to interested parties. Some changes still need to be made to this draft. First, formal work in description logics has advanced, and should be incorporated into the specification. Second, there are portions of the draft, particularly in the inferences required in the core, that are objectionable to some parties. By September 1992, there should be a third draft prepared and discussed, and by the end of October 1992 a final version of the specification should be available. Also, a method for demonstrating compliance with the specification will be developed.

Future work in the KRSS group effort on description-logic based systems will then consist of augmenting the specification as new formal work on description logic produces relevant results and as new implementation techniques make it possible to extend the core. Also, other families of knowledge representation systems may be given the same treatment, provided that developers are interested.

3 KNOWLEDGE QUERY AND MANIPULATION LANGUAGE (KQML)

The *External Interfaces* working group was originally charged with addressing the general problem of defining standard high-level interfaces for knowledge representation systems. This was seen as including such diverse interfaces as those to other KR systems, DBMSs, active sensors, and human users. Over the past two years, this working group has focused on and experimented with a somewhat narrowed and more focused problem – designing a common high-level language (KQML) and associated protocol which can be used by software systems for the run-time sharing of information and knowledge. This section briefly describes the current status of the effort to specify KQML and experiment with its use in several testbeds.

3.1 OVERVIEW

The Knowledge Query and Manipulation Language (KQML) is both a message format and a message-handling protocol to support run-time knowledge sharing among agents. KQML can be used as a language for an application program to interact with an intelligent system or for two or more intelligent systems to share knowledge in support of cooperative problem solving. KQML focuses on an extensible set of *performatives*, which defines the permissible operations that agents may attempt on each other's knowledge and goal stores. The performatives comprise a substrate on which to develop higher-level models of interagent interaction such as contract nets and negotiation [8, 33].

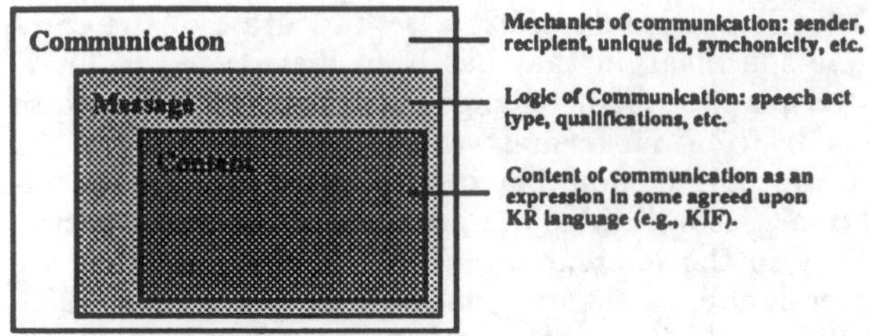

Figure 1: KQML expressions can be thought of as consisting of a content expression encapsulated in a message wrapper which is in turn encapsulated in a communication wrapper.

In addition, KQML provides a basic architecture for knowledge sharing through a special class of agent called *communication facilitators*. These agents coordinate the interactions of other agents by providing such functions as:

- identification of other agents with which to communicate both explicitly via "names" or "addresses" or implicitly via declared topics of interest or capabilities,
- maintaining registration databases of knowledge services offered and sought by agents,
- communication services (e.g., forwarding information from one agent to other interested agents), and
- content translation to bridge semantic and ontologic differences between end agents.

These functions are embodied in special performatives (which take messages as arguments), and in the way that facilitators treat messages received from application agents.

The ideas which underly the evolving design of KQML are currently being explored through experimental prototype systems which are being used to support two testbeds: the Palo Alto Collaborative Testbed (PACT) [9] which is focused in the concurrent engineering domain, and the DARPA/Rome Planning Initiative (DRPI) which deals with military transportation planning [13].

3.2 KQML EXPRESSIONS ARE LAYERED

KQML expressions consist of a content expression encapsulated in a message wrapper which is in turn encapsulated in a communication wrapper, as shown in Figure 1. Thus the language is thought of as being divided into three layers: content, message and communication. The content layer contains an expression in some language which encodes the knowledge to be conveyed. The format of this expression is unimportant to KQML; it can carry any type of content expressed in any representation language which follows some general syntactic constraints (currently, the content expression must be an s-expression). However, there are emerging conventions for knowledge representation (e.g., Interlingua, KIF [17], etc) and standards for *persistent objects* (e.g., the OMG Object Request Broker) which may prove to be very valuable in the near future.

The primary purpose of the message layer is to identify the speech act or performative that the sender attaches to the content, such as an assertion, a query or a command, and any of a small set of qualifiers that may be appropriate to that performative. In addition, since the the content is opaque to KQML, this layer also includes optional features describing the content's language, the ontology it assumes and a descriptor naming a topic within the ontology. These features make it possible for the protocol implementation to analyze, route and properly deliver messages even though their content may be inaccessible.

The final communication level adds a second layer of features to the message which describe the lower level communication parameters, such as the identity of the sender and recipient, a unique identifier associated with the communication and whether the communication is meant to be synchronous or asynchronous. These are used by the network layer which provides reliable transfer of bytes between processes on a network.

3.3 KQML PERFORMATIVES

The message layer is used to encode a message that one application would like to have transmitted to another application and forms the core of the language, determining the kinds of interactions one can have with a KQML-speaking agent. It can be thought of as a "speech act layer", since an important attributes to specify about the content is what kind of "speech act" it represents – an assertion, a query, a response, an error message, etc.

Structure. Conceptually, a KQML message consists of an operator or *performative*, its associated arguments which constitute the real *content* of the message and a set of optional arguments which describe the content in a standard, language-independent manner. For example, a message representing a query about the location of an particular airport might be encoded as:

```
(ask (geoloc lax (?long ?lat))
     :number_answers 1
     :ontology drpi_geo)
```

In this message, the KQML performative is *ask*, the content (i.e., knowledge being sought) is (*geoloclax*(*?long?lat*)), the number of answers requested is 1, the language in which the content is expressed is (by default) *kif* and the ontology to be assumed is that named by the token $drpi_geo$. The same general query could be conveyed in using standard Prolog as the content language in a form that requests the set of all answers as:

```
(ask "geoloc(lax, (Long,Lat))"
     :language standard_Prolog
     :number_answers all
     :ontology drpi_geo)
```

Semantics. It is our intention to allow the set of KQML performatives to be extensible. We will identify a core set of performatives that will have a well defined meaning. An KQML-speaking agent need not implement or handle all of the performatives in this core, but for those it does, it must adhere to the standard semantics. Moreover, it is our goal to provide a standard mechanism by which one can define the semantics of new performatives, allowing the set to be extended. The semantics of the core performatives will be defined in terms of a smaller set of *primitive performatives.* The semantics of these primitive performatives are defined with respect to a simple and general model of agents in which each agent as a store of information structures (i.e., "belief" like items) and a store of goals structures (i.e., items which may effect the agent's future behavior).

Primitive Performatives. We are currently working with a set of four primitive performatives from which we believe the core and various interesting extensions can be defined. These four primitives provide operators to present an agent with items to add (*ADVISE*) and remove (*UNADVISE*) from its information store and to add (*ACHIEVE*) and remove from (*FORGET*) its goal store. These four performatives are primarily used as a means to specify the semantics of the larger core performatives.

Core Performatives. The core set of performatives is expected to include several dozen operators which most KQML-speaking agents will support. If an agent accepts a message with a core performative, it must adhere to its agreed upon semantics. Some of these performatives will accept optional arguments which serve as qualifier. Figure 2 shows some examples of performatives that are in the current specification.

Messaging via Facilitators. Any substantial collection of interacting agents will require some structure on information flow [20, 28, 32]. For this reason, KQML introduces a class of communication facilitator agents that help manage the message traffic among application agents. Facilitator agents can route performatives to appropriate agents (MONITOR performatives in particular), record the performative-processing abilities of new agents, and bridge the capabilities of superficially incompatible agents (through buffering, translation, and problem decomposition). These facilitation functions will be reflected in new core performatives, e.g., **(FORWARD** *agent-name message***)** and **(DISTRIBUTE** *message***)**.

- **(ASSERT P)** - Add P to the agent's information store, performing whatever reasoning the agent can perform.
- **(RETRACT P)** - Remove P from the agent's information store if present, signalling an error if not present and performing whatever reasoning the agent can perform.
- **(ASK P)** - Query the agent's information store to find answers matching query P. The number of answers returned is governed by an optional argument.
- **(GENERATOR P)** - Reply with a *generator* that the recipient can use to elicit a stream of answers to the query P.
- **(MONITOR P)** - Modify the agent's goal store to cause it to inform the sender whenever a sentence matching P becomes true.

Figure 2: These are a few of the core KQML performatives.

Software Architecture. As Figure 3 shows, a typical KQML-speaking agent will be built using two reusable pieces – an interface between the agent's system language (e.g., LOOM or Prolog) which ties communication actions to system actions, and a router which handles the low-level communication chores necessary to talk to other agents. These might all be done within a single process (e.g., in Lisp) or might include several processes (e.g., the router might be done in C or Perl).

3.4 STATUS AND OPEN ISSUES

The ideas which underly the evolving design of KQML are currently being explored through experimental prototype systems which are being used to support

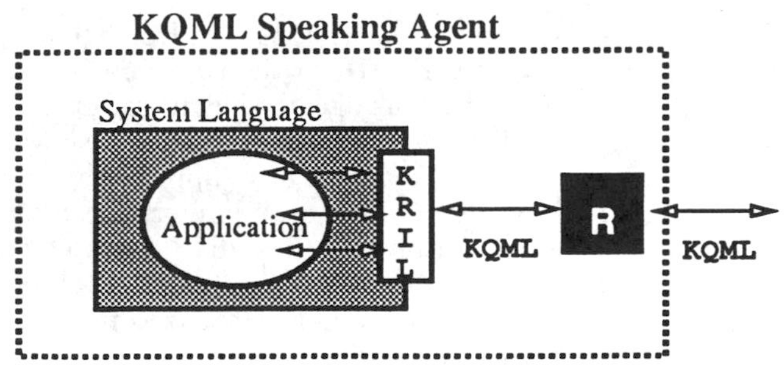

Figure 3: A typical KQML-speaking agent will be built using two reusable pieces – an interface between the agent's system language (e.g., LOOM or Prolog) which ties communication actions to system actions, and a router which handles the low-level communication chores necessary to talk to other agents.

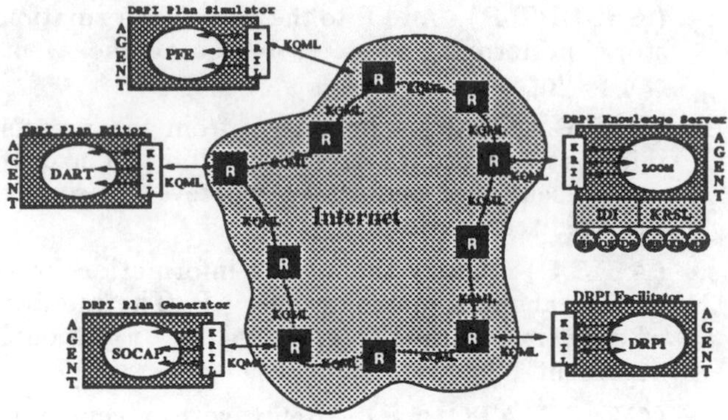

Figure 4: KQML will be used as communication language among the various agents which make up the DRPI testbed. It will be used, for example, to support the interchange of knowledge among the planner, the plan simulator, the plan editor and the DRPI knowledge server which is the repository for the shared ontology and access point for common databases.

two testbeds: the Palo Alto Collaborative Testbed (PACT) [9] which is focused in the concurrent engineering domain, and the DARPA/Rome Planning Initiative (DRPI) which deals with military transportation planning.

KQML use in PACT. The Palo Alto Collaborative Testbed (PACT) uses KQML as its medium for agent interaction in support of concurrent engineering. PACT participants modified several existing knowledge-based engineering systems to speak KQML and thereby exchange design and manufacturing knowledge of mutual interest. (For example, the mechanical modeler sends the controls modeler knowledge regarding the dynamics of the design; the power modeler sends the manufacturing process planner knowledge regarding a motor replacement.) These agents find each other in part through facilitators, which handle message forwarding, content-based routing, and simple format translations.

KQML use in DRPI. The DARPA/Rome Planning Initiative is using KQML as the communication language among the various agents that make up the testbed and feasibility demonstrations. Figure 4 shows KQML being used, for example, to support the interchange of knowledge among the planner, the plan simulator, the plan editor and the DRPI knowledge server, which is the repository for the shared ontology [21] and access point to common databases through the *Intelligent Database Interface* [23, 29]

Open Issues. The design of KQML has continued to evolve as the ideas are explored and feedback is received from the prototypes and the attempts to use them in real testbed situations. We mention here a few of the important issues that we expect to be addressed in the coming year.

The core set of performatives is still undergoing revision as we experiment with its use. This set needs to be stabilized and well specified. In particular, we need to refine the model of what a communication facilitator is and what services it might offer so that we develop a good set of performatives to support their effective use.

A method for defining new extensions to the core set needs to be worked out. This includes a method for defining them for humans as well as a method to allow one agent to define a new performative to another.

The basic model of a knowledge representation agent that we have been working with is quite simple. One of several extensions that may be needed, for example, is a mechanism to define contexts within an agents information and goal stores.

An important part of KQML will be the protocols associated with the different performatives. There are some general issues which go beyond defining the semantics of particular performatives that must be addressed. These general protocols include such things as refusing to accept a message, error reporting, security, and transaction oriented processing.

4 SHARED, REUSABLE KNOWLEDGE BASES

The SRKB Working Group (Shared, Reusable Knowledge Bases) of the DARPA Knowledge effort is working on the problem of sharing the *content* of formally represented knowledge. Sharing content requires more than a formalism (KIF) and communication protocol (KQML). Of course, understanding the nature of what needs to be held in common between communicating agents, or between the author of a book and its reader, is a fundamental question for philosophy and science. The SRKB group is focusing on the practical problem of building knowledge-based software that can be shared and reused as off-the-shelf technology. The charter of the group is to identify the technical barriers to the sharing and reuse of formally represented knowledge by AI programs, and to provide a forum for experimentation with possible approaches.

4.1 STRATEGY: COMMON ONTOLOGIES AS A SHARING MECHANISM

The strategy is to focus on common ontology as the sharing mechanism [27, 18]. What is a common ontology? Every knowledge-based system is based on some conceptualization of the world: those objects, processes, qualities, distinctions, and relationships that matter for performing some task. A program (or its programmer) makes ontological commitments to a conceptualization by embodying these concepts, distinctions, etc. in a formal representation and using knowledge formulated in that representation during problem solving. By **common ontology** we mean an explicit specification of a the ontological commitments of a set of programs. Such a specification is an objective description—interpretable outside of the programs—of the concepts and relationships that the programs assume and use when interacting with other programs, knowledge bases, and human users.

Operationally, a common ontology can be specified as a set of definitions of representational terms used to construct expressions in a knowledge base, such as classes, relations, slots, and object constants. To make a common ontology shareable, the definitions should consist of human-readable text and machine-enforceable, declarative constraints (i.e., axioms) on the well-formed use of the terminology. The set of terms in a common ontology need not include all the terms used internally in participating programs. Rather, the shared vocabulary defined in a ontology is used for specifying the coupling between programs and knowledge bases (at design time) and for knowledge-level communication among agents (at run time). We hope to enable large-scale sharing and reuse of knowledge bases and knowledge based systems by making common ontologies available as open specifications, much like interchange formats and communication protocols.

The initial activities of the working group have been to explore the research issues in knowledge sharing, and to identify areas where it might be practical and useful to specify common ontologies. The Summer Ontology Project, held at Stanford in 1990, studied the collaborative, multi-disciplinary development of reusable ontologies for describing electromechanical devices and their designs. One outcome was the observation that several approaches to device modeling, from digital circuit modeling to rigid body dynamics, seemed to make commitments to lumped-element models of physical devices. In a lumped-element model, the behavior of a device is described in terms of values of functions (state variables) that map a single independent variable (e.g., time, but not space) to physical quantities (position, force, etc.). A preliminary ontology was proposed to formalize these concepts.

In March of 1991, the SRKB group met at Pajaro Dunes to characterize some of the research issues. There was some controversy about whether it is premature to "standardize" ontologies of any sort, especially those designed to be comprehensive over tasks and domains. Instead, a series of collaborative, grassroots experiments were proposed, in which two or more research groups identify potential candidates for knowledge sharing.

In the past year, several collaborations have begun, and a set of ad hoc subgroups have been formed to study these ontological niches. Each subgroup is tasked with identifying, collecting, making available, and analyzing ontologies for knowledge sharing. We will describe the efforts of these groups within a framework of models of sharing and reuse.

4.2 MODELS OF KNOWLEDGE SHARING AND REUSE

Three models of sharing and reuse are being explored, and in each, common ontologies play an enabling role.

First is the **library model**, in which bodies of formally represented knowledge are available as off-the-shelf products, like books in a library. In this model, knowledge bases are designed artifacts, and the role of SRKB to help make them available and reusable.

Two ad hoc subgroups are currently active within the library model of sharing. One is an effort by representatives of projects in qualitative physics to specify a common language for model fragments. Model fragments are conceptual building blocks for programs that formulate and assemble engineering models of device behavior, using techniques such as compositional modeling [11]. For example, idealized components such as resistors and physical processes such as liquid flow are represented by model fragments, which are composed to produce simulation models of complete systems. The language under development is a unification of model formulation and simulation systems such as QPE, DME, and QPC, and should enable a community library of model fragments that can be directly executed by these systems. The axiomatic semantics of the language will be expressed in KIF, and the ontological commitments of these programs will be specified as an ontology.

A second subgroup, following up on the Summer Ontology Project, is developing a family of ontologies for specifying various styles of engineering modeling. It is formalizing the classes of algebras used in constraints (e.g., with or without differential equations; qualitative operators), the assumptions underlying component/connection topologies, and the various styles of dynamics analysis (e.g., Newtonian, LaGrangian, Kane's method). This work is complementary to the composition modeling effort; any of these styles of modeling can be formulated using the model fragment language.

A preliminary finding is that the ontological commitments of a given approach to modeling may be factored into separate ontologies. These ontologies form an inclusion hierarchy, where each ontology can inherit (by set inclusion) the definitions of included ontologies. For example, the original proposal for a lumped-element ontology has since been divided into several ontologies, including *continuous-state-space* (commits to describing behavior using state variables) and *hierarchical-component-assembly* (objects are structured into components related by connections and part-of relations). To specify how state variables are associated with components, one writes a third ontology that includes the other two, adding a few additional constraints. To support this sort of modular partitioning of ontologies, the interlingua committee is considering context mechanisms such as Cyc's microtheories.

A second mode of sharing and reuse under investigation is the **software engineering model**. A standard approach to making software reusable is to decompose complex programs into modular pieces, and to provide a formal specification of the inputs, outputs, and function computed by each piece. Knowledge-based systems are like other software in this respect, except that they operate on a special input called the "background knowledge base" or "domain theory." Reusable modules are designed so that the same code can be used on several knowledge bases. However, to write these knowledge bases the developer needs to understand the ontological assumptions and commitments made in the code. An ontology that defines the vocabulary with which to write the knowledge bases can help determine which software module to use on a given problem, how to provide it the necessary domain knowledge, and whether the knowledge base meets the input requirements of the software.

A significant effort is under way in the knowledge acquisition community to formally characterize the tasks being performed by knowledge based systems, and to design modular problem-solving methods that can be combined to address these tasks [24]. For example, complex, amorphous tasks such as diagnosis and planning have been decomposed into more generic subtasks that can be solved with reusable methods such as simple classification, abductive assembly, and varieties of constraint satisfaction. An subgroup led by Mark Musen is studying ways to describe these tasks and methods, and has begun to define ontologies that specify the input and output assumptions of reusable methods.

A second subgroup, headed by Ed Hovy and Doug Skuce, is identifying and analyzing the comprehensive, *top-level* ontologies that are intended to be general across domains and tasks. A motivating application for such ontologies is natural language processing. NLP techniques needs a way to couple to domain knowledge bases (for something to talk about) without committing the programs to particular subject matter areas. For example, the Penman language generation system's "Upper Structure" ontology [3] divides the world up according to the major type distinctions made in English and German (Objects of various types, Processes and Relations of various types, Qualities, etc.). A developer customizes Penman to a particular application domain by defining the domain's concepts as specializations of the appropriate Upper Structure concepts. As a result, the domain concepts inherit the necessary linguistic annotations from their Upper Structure ancestors. In general, such top-level ontologies can be viewed as a software reuse mechanism for programs parameterized by large knowledge bases.

Another subgroup is looking at ontologies that specify semiformal representations of decision making and design rationale (Jeff Bradshaw, Jin Tae Lee, and Charles Petrie). In semiformal rationale support systems, users organize text describing design decisions in to a hypertext document that supports a fixed vocabulary of node types (classes) and link types (relations). For example, in the gIBIS ontology [7], decisions are described in terms of *issues*, *arguments*, and *positions*, and these node types are linked by relations such as *supports* and *objects-to*. The documents structured by these terms are called semiformal or semistructured, since only the node and link types are machine interpretable and the contents of the nodes are not formalized. Several methodologies for developing semiformal documents, and tools to support them, are based on these ontologies of node and link types.

A third kind of sharing and reuse is the **reference model**, typically used to define an integration framework for a family of application programs. A reference model defines the concepts in a domain and/or problem area that are common to the set of application tasks. For example, a reference model for digital circuits includes a formalism for describing the netlist, which is a representation of circuit topology. The reference model ontology commits the participating tools to the existence of shared objects such as components connected by ports in a netlist; this is necessary to enable tools to exchange data.

An international standards effort called PDES/STEP is working on a family of reference-model ontologies for product data, starting by defining primitives for geometry and working toward high level descriptions of behavior and functionality. The DARPA knowledge sharing effort is exploring avenues for collaboration with the PDES organization.

Within the SRKB working group, ad hoc subgroups are studying reference-model ontologies for user interface toolkits (Jim Foley and Bob Neches), manufacturing enterprise models (Mark Fox), and planning/scheduling (Don McKay, Masahiro Hori).

4.3 TECHNICAL SUPPORT FOR ONTOLOGIES – ONTOLINGUA

Each of the subgroups of the SRKB are charged with identifying and collecting ontologies, and making them available in a form amenable to analysis and possible reuse. However, existing ontologies are either incompletely formalized or written in a specific knowledge representation tool. To address this problem, a system called Ontolingua has been developed [19]. Ontolingua is a mechanism for defining ontologies *portably*, that is, independent of specific representation systems. It allows the definition of classes, relations, and distinguished objects using KIF sentences, and translates these definitions into several implemented representation systems.

Ontolingua's design demonstrates the use of a common ontology to facilitate sharing and reuse (in this case, of ontologies). Translation from a very expressive language (KIF) into restricted languages is inherently incomplete. Therefore, Ontolingua supports a subset of legal sentences that can be translated into a class of commonly-used representation systems: the object-centered or frame-based systems. These implemented systems commit to particular ways of organizing and specifying knowledge about objects, such as inheritance hierarchies and slot descriptions. These ontological commitments are captured in the Frame Ontology, which defines a vocabulary for describing classes, binary relations, and second-order relationships among them (e.g., subclass, instance, class partitions, slot-value restrictions). Ontolingua recognizes the use of Frame Ontology concepts in KIF sentences, and translates them into the special syntax of each target representation system. The Frame Ontology, on top of a syntactically restricted KIF, defines a language for portable ontologies. The Ontolingua software operationalizes the language by providing automatic translation into implemented representation systems.

5 SUMMARY

Moving beyond the capabilities of current knowledge-based systems will require development of knowledge bases that are substantially larger than those we have today. It will require knowledge-based systems to communicate with other knowledge-based systems and conventional software systems in carrying out their functions. Meeting these challenges on a broad scale will require development new knowledge-sharing technology and shared conventions. The on-going efforts in the Knowledge Sharing Effort represent steps in this directions. The efforts underway are neither complete nor comprehensive – they represent an initial first steps that will result in valuable experience and understanding, will identify shortcomings in current methods and point to new research directions, will encourage others to focus on solving problems encountered in knowledge sharing, to explore alternatives and to enhance the state of the art.

Acknowledgments

This effort is supported by NSF grant IRI-9006923, DARPA/NASA-Ames contract NCC 2-719, and a cooperative agreement between USC/ISI and the Corporation for National Research Initiative. We would also like to acknowledge members of the Knowledge Sharing Effort, too numerous to name individually.

References

[1] Franz Baader, Hans-Jürgen Bürckert, Jochen Heinsohn, Bernhard Hollunder, Jürgen Müller, Bernhard Nebel, Werner Nutt, and Hans-Jürgen Profitlich. Terminological knowledge representation: A proposal for a terminological logic. A DFKI note., June 1991.

[2] Franz Baader and Bernhard Hollunder. KRIS: Knowledge Representation and Inference System—system description. Technical Memo TM-90-13, Deutsches Forschungszentrum für Künstliche Intelligenz, November 1990.

[3] John A. Bateman. Upper modeling: A general organization of knowledge for natural language processing. Penman development note, USC/Information Sciences Institute, 1989.

[4] A. Borgida, R. J. Brachman, D. L. McGuinness, and L. A. Resnick. CLASSIC: A structural data model for objects. In *Proceedings of the 1989 ACM SIGMOD International Conference on Management of Data*, Portland, Oregon, 1989.

[5] Ronald J. Brachman and Hector J. Levesque. The tractability of subsumption in frame-based description languages. In *Proceedings of the Fourth National Conference on Artificial Intelligence*, pages 34–37, Austin, Texas, August 1984. American Association for Artificial Intelligence.

[6] Ronald J. Brachman, Deborah L. McGuinness, Peter F. Patel-Schneider, Lori Alperin Resnick, and Alex Borgida. Living with CLASSIC: When and how to use a KL-ONE-like language. In Sowa [34], pages 401–456.

[7] Jeff Conklin and M. L. Begeman. gIBIS: A hypertext tool for exploratory policy discussion. In *Proceedings of the 1988 Conference on Computer Supported Cooperative Work (CSCW-88)*, pages 140–152, Portland, Oregon, 1988. ACM.

[8] Susan E. Conry, Robert A. Meyer, and Victor R. Lesser. Multistage negotiation in distributed planning. In Alan H. Bond and Les Gasser, editors, *Readings in Distributed Artificial Intelligence*, pages 367–384. Morgan Kaufman, 1988.

[9] Mark Cutkosky, Robert Engelmore, Richard Fikes, Thomas Gruber, Micheal Genesereth, William Mark, Jay Tenenbaum, and Jay Weber. Pact: An experiment in integrating concurrent engineering systems. *IEEE Computer*, 1992. To appear in a special issue on computer-supported concurrent engineering.

[10] Francesco M. Donini, Maurizio Lenzerini, Daniele Nardi, and Werner Nutt. The complexity of concept languages. In *Proceedings of the Second In-*

ternational Conference on Principles of Knowledge Representation and Reasoning, pages 151–162. Morgan Kaufmann, May 1991.

[11] Brian Falkenhainer and Ken Forbus. Compositional modeling: Finding the right model for the job. *Artificial Intelligence*, 51:95–143, 1991.

[12] Richard Fikes, Mark Cutkosky, Tom Gruber, and Jeffrey Van Baalen. Knowledge sharing technology project overview. Technical Report KSL 91-71, Stanford University, Knowledge Systems Laboratory, 1991.

[13] T. Finin, R. Fritzson, and D. McKay et. al. A language and protocol to support intelligent agent interoperability. In *Proceedings of the CE & CALS Washington '92 Conference*, June 1992.

[14] T. Finin, R. Fritzson, and D. McKay et. al. An overview of KQML: A knowledge query and manipulation language. Technical report, Department of Computer Science, University of Maryland Baltimore County, 1992.

[15] Michael R. Genesereth. Designworld. In *Proceedings of the 1991 International Conference on Robotiocs and Automation*, pages 2785–2788, 1991.

[16] Michael R. Genesereth. Knowledge interchange format. In James Allen, Richard Fikes, and Erik Sandewall, editors, *Proceedings of the Conference of the Principles of Knowledge Representation and Reasoning*, pages 599–600. Morgan Kaufmann Publishers, Inc., 1991.

[17] Michael R. Genesereth, Richard E. Fikes, and et al. Knowledge interchange format, version 3.0 reference manual. Technical Report Logic-92-1, Computer Science Department, Stanford University, 1992.

[18] Thomas R. Gruber. The role of common ontology in achieving sharable, reusable knowledge bases. In J. A. Allen, R. Fikes, and E. Sandewall, editors, *Principles of Knowledge Representation and Reasoning: Proceedings of the Second International Conference*, pages 601–602, Cambridge, MA, 1991. Morgan Kaufmann.

[19] Thomas R. Gruber. Ontolingua: A mechanism to support portable ontologies. Technical Report KSL 91-66, Stanford University, Knowledge Systems Laboratory, 1992. June 1992 Revision.

[20] Michael N. Huhns, David M. Bridgeland, and Natraj V. Arni. A DAI communication aide. Technical Report ACT-RA-317-90, Microelectronics and Computer Technology Corporation, Microelectronics and Computer Technology Corporation, 3500 West Balcones Center Drive, Austin TX 78759-6509, October 1990.

[21] Nancy Lehrer. DARPA/Rolm Laboratory Planning and Scheduling Initiative, Knowledge Representation Specification Language: KRSL Version 2.0. Language specification and manual, 1992.

[22] Robert MacGregor. Loom users manual. Working Paper ISI/WP-22, USC/Information Sciences Institute, 1990.

[23] Don McKay, Tim Finin, and Anthony O'Hare. The intelligent database interface. In *Proceedings of the 7th National Conference on Artificial Intelligence*, August 1990.

[24] Mark A. Musen. Overcoming the limitations of role-limiting methods. *Knowledge Acquisition*, 4(2):165–170, 1992.

[25] Bernhard Nebel. Terminological reasoning is inherently intractable. *Artificial Intelligence*, 43(2):235–249, May 1990.

[26] Bernhard Nebel. Terminological cycles: Semantics and computational properties. In Sowa [34].

[27] Robert Neches, Richard Fikes, Tim Finin, Thomas Gruber, Ramesh Patil, Ted Senator, and William R. Swartout. Enabling technology for knowledge sharing. *AI Magazine*, 12(3):16–36, 1991.

[28] Mike P. Papazoglou and Timos K. Sellis. An organizational framework for cooperating intelligent information systems. *International Journal on Intelligent and Cooperative Information Systems*, 1(1), (to appear) 1992.

[29] J. Pastor, D. McKay, and T. Finin. Viewconcepts: Knowledge-based access to databases. In *Proceedings of the First International Conference on Information and Knowledgement*, November 1992.

[30] Peter F. Patel-Schneider. Undecidability of subsumption in NIKL. *Artificial Intelligence*, 39(2):263–272, June 1989.

[31] Christof Peltason, Albrecht Schmiedel, Carsten Kindermann, and Joachim Quantz. The BACK system revisited. KIT-Report 75, Department of Computer Science, Technische Universität Berlin, September 1989.

[32] Kirk Sayre and Michael A. Gray. Backtalk: A generalized dynamic communication system for DAI. Technical Report CSIS-91-004, The American University, Washington DC, August 1991.

[33] Sandip Sen and Edmund H. Durfee. A formal study of distributed meeting scheduling: preliminary results. In *Proceedings of the ACM Conference on Organizational Computing Systems*, pages 55–68, November 1991.

[34] John Sowa, editor. *Principles of Semantic Networks: Explorations in the representation of knowledge*. Morgan-Kaufmann, San Mateo, California, 1991.

Using a Domain-Knowledge Ontology as a Semantic Gateway among Information Resources*

Michael L. Dowell, Larry M. Stephens, and Ronald D. Bonnell
Department of Electrical and Computer Engineering
University of South Carolina
Columbia, SC 29208

Abstract

We show that an ontology of domain knowledge can be used as a semantic gateway among different information resources. In particular, we show how to translate a query against a local database into queries to nonlocal databases so that a local user may obtain information from nonlocal information sources We first map each database's logical schema to a conceptual model—the extended entity-relationship model. The labels of the entities, relationships, and attributes in the extended ER are then linked to corresponding items in the domain ontology. The domain ontology consists of a hierarchy of *types* (corresponding to entities) and a hierarchy of *links* (corresponding to relationships and attributes). We show how queries to a local database may be mapped to nonlocal databases, and how queries to nonlocal databases may be specializations or generalizations of the original query to a local database.

1 Introduction

Within an enterprise, different groups of users have different perceptions and requirements for the organization and representation of semantically overlapping information. Schema designers develop different, often incompatible, schemas of information for each group. This solution has worked well in isolation. However, users needing to combine information from several sources are faced with the problem of locating and integrating relevant information [Spaccapietra and Parent, 1994].

This paper presents a mechanism querying other relevant information resources using only the local data model that the user knows. This mechanism allows the user to retrieve information from other information resources without learning other schemas, and it extends the work of MCC's Carnot project [Huhns *et al.*, 1992; Collet *et al.*, 1991]. As in the Carnot approach, existing information resources and programs do not have to be changed.

* This is a revision of a paper presented at the *Workshop on Basic Ontological Issues in Knowledge Sharing*, IJCAI, 1995.

The next section introduces the overall model of our Domain Knowledge Repository System and metamodels for the relational and extended ER models. Section 3 presents the domain knowledge repository. An example query is introduced in Section 4. Finally, our conclusions and future work are presented in Section 5.

2 The Domain Knowledge Repository Model

This paper shows how a domain knowledge ontology and information resource models permit users, having only knowledge of a local relational model, to query other information resources for relevant information. Our Domain Knowledge Repository System (DKRS) model is shown in Figure 1. It is an extension of Carnot's relationship between its domain ontology, Cyc, and its relational model [Huhns *et al.*, 1991]; we have added a conceptual model (the extended entity-relationship model) between our domain ontology and a logical model (in this discussion, the relational database model). The addition of the extended ER model helps bridge the semantic gap between the logical database level known to the user and the terms in the ontology.

In Figure 1, a user queries a local database using only his knowledge of the local database's relational model. DKRS captures this query and links it to the relational model that represents the local database. This relational model has two-way links to the extended entity-relation model that also represents the local database schema. In addition, the extended ER model has two-way links to the domain knowledge repository. This domain knowledge repository contains knowledge that is common to the different databases within the DKRS. Thus, the user's local query is linked to two models and the domain knowledge repository. The domain knowledge repository and the models themselves are described in Sections 3 and 4.

2.1 Relational Metamodel

The relational metamodel, shown in Figure 2, is derived from the ideal table metamodel of [Blaha *et al.*, 1994]. Each *Ideal table* is linked to a *Database* since multiple databases are connected to the DKRS. Each *Ideal table* has one or more *Ideal table columns*. Each *Ideal table*

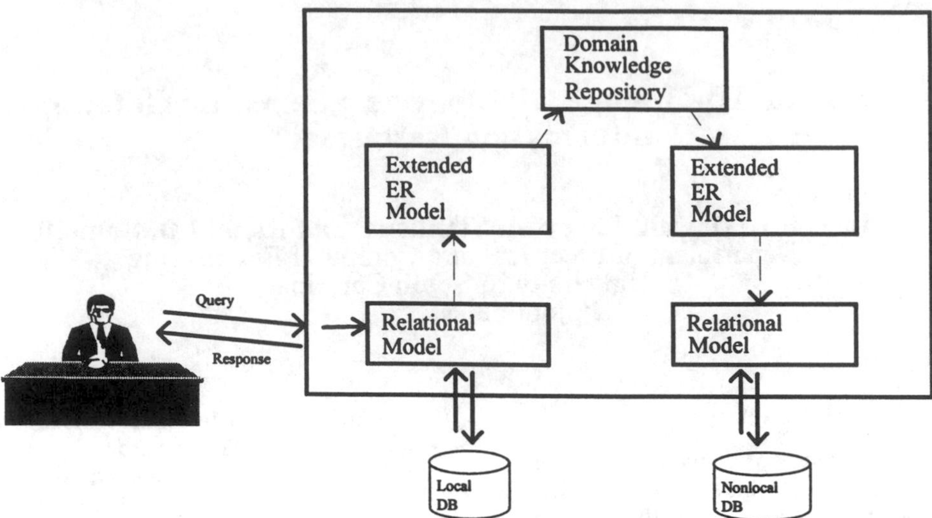

Figure 1: The DKRS Model

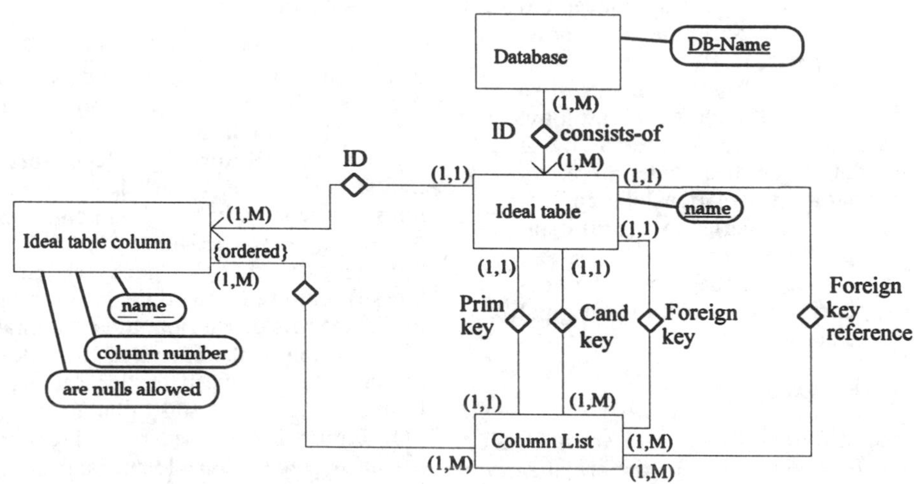

Figure 2: Relational Metamodel

column is grouped into one or more *Column lists*. In addition, each *Ideal table* has associated primary, candidate, and foreign key lists. The information represented by the relational model is at the logical level.

2.2 Extended Entity-Relation Metamodel

Because some of the information represented within the relational model is implicit, we have found the semantic gap between the logical level (relational model) and the semantic level (domain knowledge) is too large to bridge directly. For example, a foreign key implicitly represents a relationship between two entity sets. To bridge the semantic gap, the DKRS uses an intermediate representation, the extended entity-relation model [Davis and Bonnell, 1988], between a database's relational model and the domain knowledge ontology. The implicit information from a relational model is made explicit in an extended entity-relationship model by representing entities, relationships, attributes, cardinality restrictions, and other conceptual-level items. To ensure correctness of an extended ER itself, we instantiate each from a *metamodel* of the extended ER [Dowell *et al.*, 1995]. Furthermore, the extended ER model is a general data model independent of the actual database implementation.

3 Domain Knowledge Ontology

A domain knowledge ontology represents information from the different information sources connected to the DKRS. These information sources have different, often incompatible, schemas of overlapping information. The *structures* of the different schemas are represented by the DKRS relational and extended ER models; the domain knowledge repository represents the *semantics* of the information contained within the different schemas.

The domain knowledge is represented using an ontology of concepts and relations. These concepts are used in the process of semantic unification, which consists of mapping the concepts in each information resource to concepts in the common ontology. These two-way mappings are done by DKRS users since only the users know the exact meaning of the domain concepts within their information resource schemas.

The domain ontology represents labels for the concepts of entities, relationships, and attributes of the universe of discourse. The relationship and attribute types are represented as first-class objects in the ontology since these concepts are linked to elements in the extended ER model. In addition, these objects must be explicitly represented to allow the DKRS to generalize and specialize related attribute and relationship concepts from different information sources.

Building and maintaining an all-encompassing, enterprise-wide domain ontology is expensive [Gruber, 1993]. In addition, only a portion of the concepts in the various information sources overlap. To justify the expense, there must be an identifiable payoff for each of the concepts added to the domain ontology. Therefore, the DKRS system is designed to start with a small set of top-level concepts and allow the users to take a bottom-up approach in building the domain ontology. This approach, similar to using several layers of ontologies [Bradshaw, *et al.*, 1992], allows the users to focus on representing the overlapping information without having to create an enterprise-wide domain ontology; information that appears in only one information resource is not represented in the domain ontology. However, a user can add new concepts at any time.

The different database schemas provide a logical description of the information within the databases, while an ontology provides concepts that represent the *knowledge* [Gruber, 1993]. Thus, using both descriptions provides a more complete understanding of the overlapping information. In addition, these descriptions describe the sets of data stored in the database but do not describe any of the specific instances of the data. For example, the concept *Person* represents the set of data describing people but does not represent a specific instance of the set.

4 Examples

In our first example, two similar entity sets from different schemas are linked to different levels of the domain ontology, as shown in Figure 3. An *Employee* entity set is stored in Database 1 and is represented in Schema 1, an extended ER model. The models and links to the ontology are done prior to querying the database. The *Employee* table (not shown) is linked indirectly to the *Employee* concept in the domain knowledge through the extended ER model. In addition, a *Person* entity set in Database 2, represented in Schema 2, is linked to the *Person* concept in the domain ontology. These entity sets have overlapping information concerning attributes of people since in this domain employees are also people.

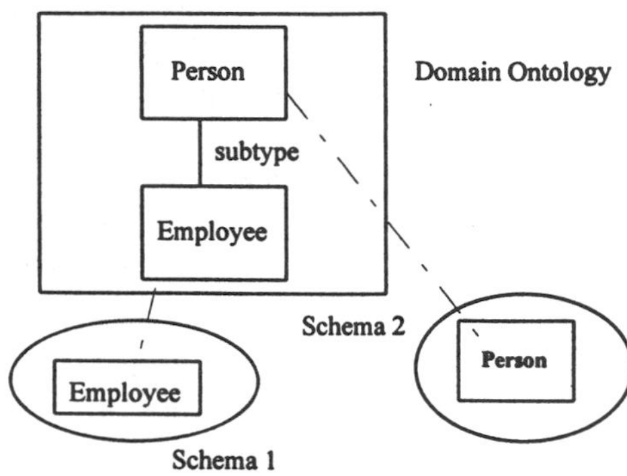

Figure 3: Different Ontology Levels Example

A user, familiar with the schema of Database 2, queries the DKRS about attributes of the *Person* entity set. If the two schemas overlap, the DKRS can retrieve information about the *Employee* entity set in Database 1. The query on Schema 1 is a specialization of the query on Schema 2 since the information from Schema 1 represents employees only. The query on Schema 1 will return a subset of the desired tuples since the original query concerns all *Persons* but Database 1 has information only about *Employees*. The user querying about *Person* should be made aware that the information returned from Schema 1 is only about *Employees* not about all the persons at the university. Specializing queries by moving down the type hierarchy of the domain ontology returns relevant information from other information sources:

Query(Person, Local-Schema-2) $\rightarrow$ *Query(Employee, Local-Schema-1)*,

where the $\rightarrow$ symbol represents a semantic mapping from a local database to a nonlocal database via the domain ontology.

A more interesting problem is a query that must move up the type hierarchy of the domain ontology. If a query is about attributes of the *Employee* entity set that are also attributes of the *Person* entity set, should a query about persons be generated for Schema 2 even though the original query concerns only employees? This second query is a generalization of the original query and will return a superset of the tuples requested:

Query(Employee, Local-Schema-1) $\rightarrow$ *Query(Person, Local-Schema-2)*

Generalizing queries by moving up the type hierarchy may return information that is not relevant. Deciding when to move up the type hierarchy and how far to move up is an open question. Generalizing a query will return more information, for example, there may be many more people in

Database 2 than there are Employees in Database 1. One solution is to ask the user making the query if a given generalization of the query is desired. In this case, specification of the content of the shared information is needed [Gruber, 1993].

For the second example, two similar *relationships* from different schemas are linked to different levels of the domain ontology, as shown in 4. This example involves the same problems as the previous example, but the decision of when to generalize or specialize involves not only entity concepts but also relationship concepts.

In Figure 4, a *tracked-by* relation in extended ER Model 1 is linked to the *tracked-by* concept in the domain ontology, while a *traced-by* relation in extended ER Model 2 is linked to the higher-level *traced-by* concept. In addition, each entity concept involved is linked to a domain concept. Generalizing a query involves generalizing not only the relation but also the entities being related. For instance, a query concerning *tracked-by* relationships can be generalized to include queries about *traced-by* relationships. But the two entities linked by *tracked-by* — *Response* and *Coordinator* — must also be generalized to two higher-level concepts — *Document* and *Person:*

Query(tracked-by,
Response, Coordinator, Local-Schema-1) →
Query(traced-by, Document, Person, Local-Schema-2)

The final example, shown in Figures 5 and 6, illustrates

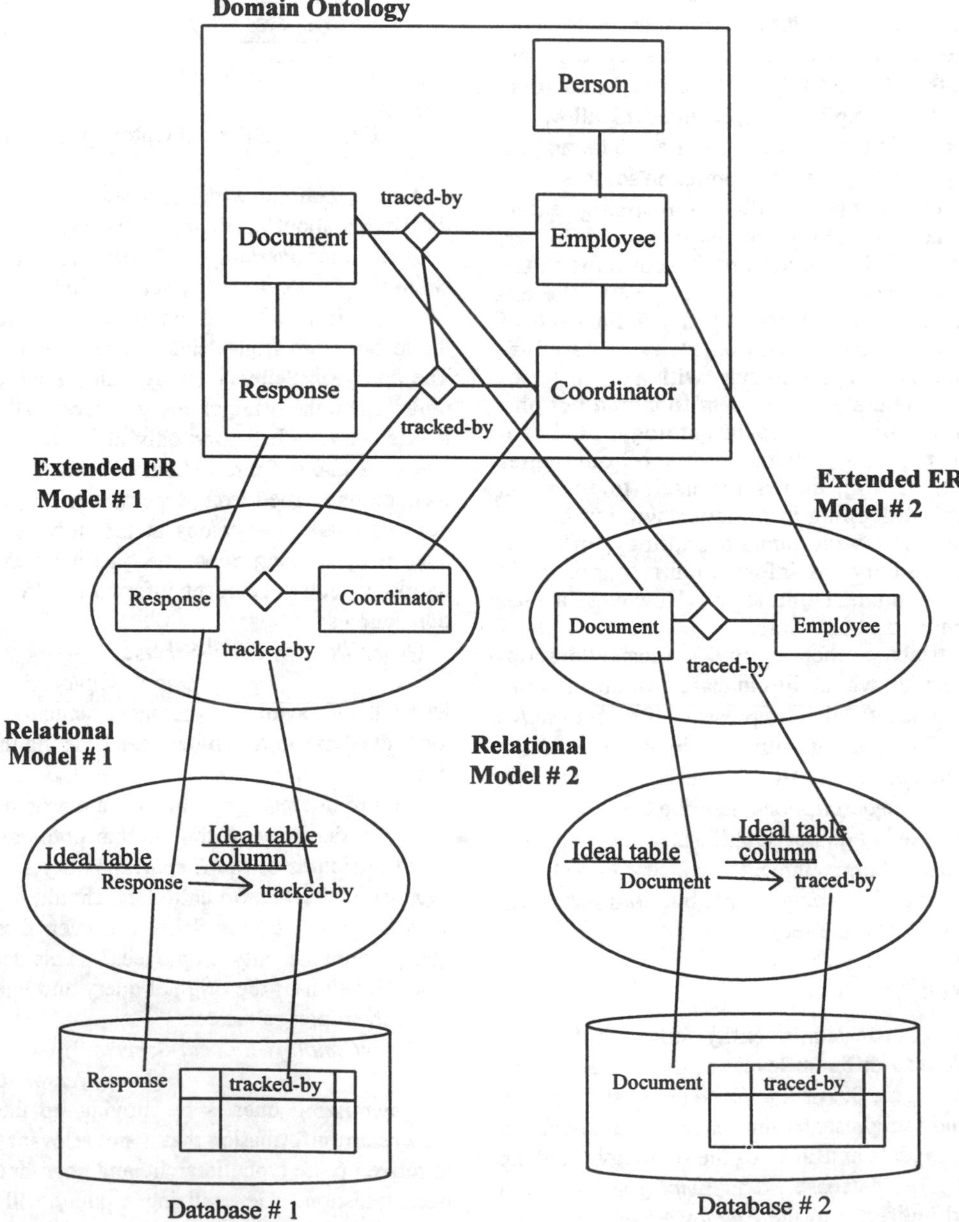

Figure 4: Different Relational Levels in the Ontology

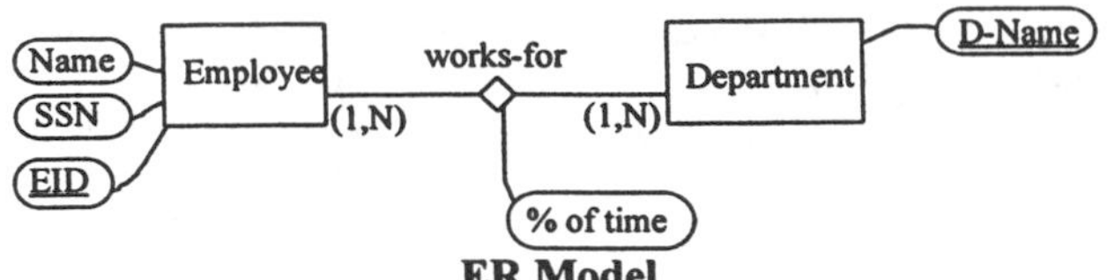

Employee(EID, Name, SSN)
Works_For(*SSN*, *D-Name*, $_Of_Time)
Department(D-Name)
Relational Model

Figure 5: Database # 1

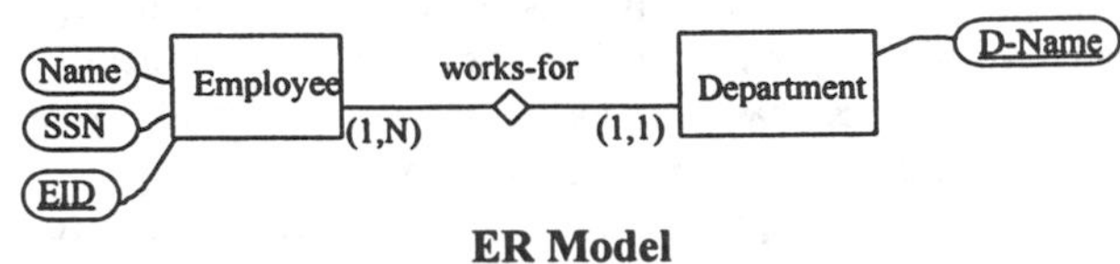

Employee(EID, Name, SSN, *D-Name*)
Department(D-Name)
Relational Model

Figure 6: Database # 2

bridging the gap between relational tables at the logical database level and terms in the domain ontology. An additional attribute on the *works-for* relationship in schema 1 requires the relationship to be represented as a separate relational table. This table is linked to the *works-for* term shown in the ontology in Figure 7. In Figure 7, the dotted lines represents instances of the classes while the solid lines represent subclasses. The other tables, *Employee* and *Department*, are also linked to appropriate terms in the ontology. All of the columns in these tables represent attributes and are linked to related attribute terms in the ontology of Figure 7.

In the second schema, the *works-for* relationship is represented as a foreign-key column in the *Employee* table. The *Employee* table is again linked to the *Employee* term in the ontology but the foreign-key column is linked to the *works-for* term. The other columns in the *Employee* table are attributes of the employee entity set and are linked to employee attribute terms in the ontology.

Therefore, the entire *Employee* table and all but one of its columns are directly related to the *Employee* term, but the foreign-key column of the *Employee* table is related to a relationship — not an attribute. If the extended ER model is inserted between the relational model and the domain ontology, the implicit information represented by the foreign-key column is made explicit and the links to the domain ontology are straight-forward and easier to create. In addition, the two schemas are easier to match. More details on the organization and classification of relationships can be found in [Stephens and Chen, 1996].

5 Conclusions

The DKRS uses two models to bridge the gap between the logical level (relational model) and the semantic level (domain knowledge) within a single information resource connection to the domain ontology. Structural differences are represented and processed using the relational and extended ER model. Semantic differences are represented and processed using the domain knowledge ontology.

Furthermore, a bottom-up approach to building the ontol-

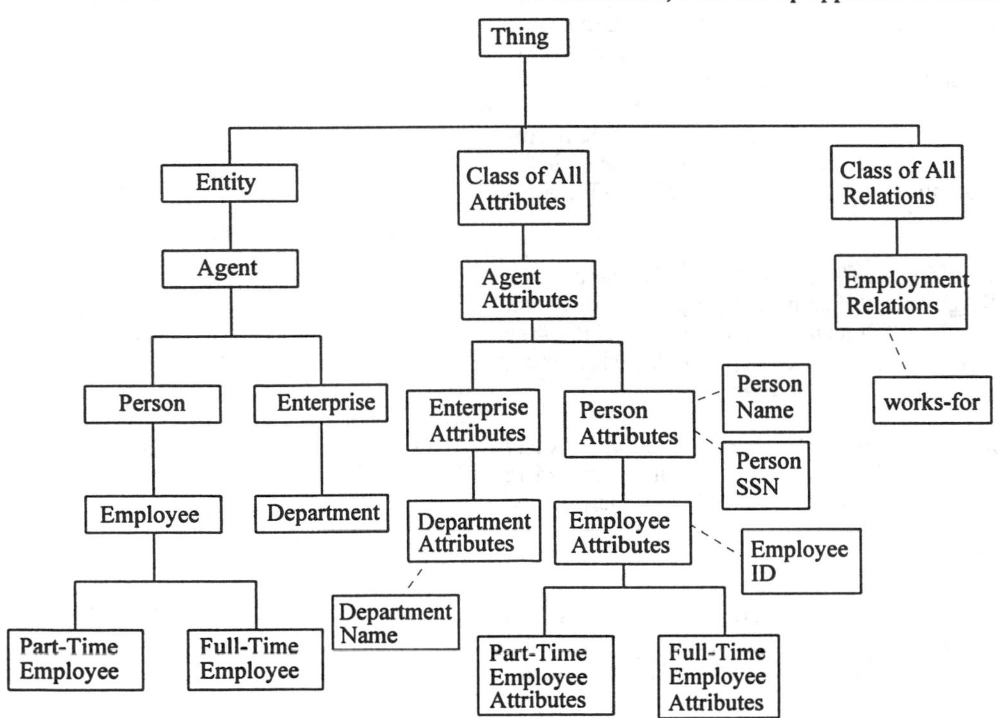

Figure 7: Example Domain Ontology

ogy allows users to add only those concepts needed to represent overlapping schema information. Users may identify and add concepts that benefits information retrieval while avoiding concepts that are not used by the DKRS.

A prototype to explore the knowledge representation requirements has been implemented using ROCK, a frame-based system implemented in the C and C++ programming languages. Future work will look at developing algorithms to generalize and specialize queries. In addition, the use of more powerful tools such as Ontolingua [Gruber, 1993] is being explored.

References

[Blaha *et al.*, 1994] M. R. Blaha, W. J. Premerlani, and H. N. Shen. Converting OO Models into RDBMS Schema. *IEEE Software*, 11(5):pp. 28-39, May 1994.

[Bradsahw *et al.*, 1992] Jeffery M. Bradshaw, John H. Boose, David B. Shema, Douglas Skuce, and Timothy C. Lethbridge. Steps Toward Sharable Ontologies for Design Rationale. *Proceddings of the AAAI-92 Design Rationale Capture and Use Workshop*, AAAI-92, San Jose, CA, July 1992.

[Collet *et al.*, 1991] C. Collet, M. N. Huhns, and W. Shen. Resource Integration Using a Large Knowledge Base in Carnot. *IEEE Computer*, December 1991, pp. 55-62.

[Davis and Bonnell, 1988] James P. Davis and Ronald D. Bonnell. EDICT - An Enhanced Relational Data Dictionary: Architecture and Example. *Proceedings of the Fourth International Conference on Data Engineering*, February, 1988, Computer Society Press, pp. 184-191.

[Dowell *et al.*, 1995] Michael L. Dowell, Larry M. Stephens, and Ronald D. Bonnell. Using Metamodels as Part of a Semantic Gateway among Databases. USC Technical Report ECE-MLD-030-95, March 1995.

[Gruber, 1993] Thomas R. Gruber. A Translation Approach to Portable Ontology Specifications. Knowledge Systems Laboratory Technical Report KSL 92-71, April 1993.

[Huhns *et al.*, 1992] M. Huhns, N. Jacobs, T. Ksiezyk, W. Shen, M. Singh, and P. Cannata. Enterprise Information Modeling and Model Integration in Carnot. In *Enterprise Integration Modeling*, C. J. Petrie, Jr. (ed.), MIT Press, Cambridge, MA, pp. 290-299, 1992.

[Spaccapietra and Parent, 1994] Stefano Spaccapietra and Christine Parent. View Integration: A Step Forward in Solving Structural Conflicts. *IEEE Transactions on Knowledge and Data Engineering*, 6(2): pp. 258-274, April 1994.

[Stephens and Chen, 1996] Larry M. Stephens and Yufeng F. Chen. Principles for Organizing Semantic Relations in Large Knowledge Bases. *IEEE Transactions on Knowledge and Data Engineering*, 8(3):492-496, June 1996.

3.3 Distributed Computing Aspects

Operating System Support for Mobile Agents

Dag Johansen
dag@cs.uit.no
Dept. of Computer Science
University of Tromsø
N-9037 Tromsø
Norway

Robbert van Renesse
rvr@cs.cornell.edu
Dept. of Computer Science
Cornell University
Ithaca, New York
U.S.A.

Fred B. Schneider
fbs@cs.cornell.edu
Dept. of Computer Science
Cornell University
Ithaca, New York
U.S.A.

Abstract

The TACOMA project is concerned with implementing operating system support for agents, processes that migrate through a network. Two TACOMA prototypes have been completed; this paper outlines our experiences in building and using them. A mechanism for exchanging electronic cash was explored, as well as agent-based schemes for scheduling and fault-tolerance.

1. Introduction

An *agent* is a process that may migrate through a computer network in order to satisfy requests made by its clients. Agents implement a computational metaphor that is analogous to how most people conduct business in their daily lives: visit a place, use a service (perhaps after some negotiation), and then move on. Thus, for the computer illiterate, agents are an attractive way to describe network-wide computations.

Agents are also useful abstractions for programmers who must implement distributed applications. This is because in the agent metaphor, the processor or *place* the computation is performed is not hidden from the programmer, but the communications channels are. Contrast this with the traditional approach of employing a client at one site that communicates with servers at other sites. Communication is not hidden and must be programmed explicitly. Moreover, pieces of a computation performed at different sites must be coordinated, placing an added burden on the programmer.

Johansen is supported by grant No. 100413/410 from the Norwegian Science Foundation. Van Renesse is supported by ARPA/ONR grant N00014-92-J-1866. Schneider is supported by the ARPA/NSF Grant No. CCR-9014363, NASA/ARPA grant NAG-2-893, and AFOSR grant F49620-94-1-0198.

By structuring a system in terms of agents, applications can be constructed in which communication-network bandwidth is conserved. Data may be accessed only by an agent executing at the same site as the data resides. An agent typically will filter or otherwise reduce the data it reads, carrying with it only the relevant information as it roams the network; there is rarely a need to transmit raw data from one site to another. In contrast, when an application is built using a client and servers, raw data may have to be sent from one site to another if, for example, the client obtains its computing cycles from a different site than it obtains its data.

Most current research on agents has focused on language design (e.g. [6]) and application issues (e.g. [4]). The TACOMA project (Tromsø And COrnell Moving Agents) has, instead, focused on operating system support for agents and how agents can be used to solve problems traditionally addressed by operating systems. We have implemented prototype systems to support agents using UNIX and using Tcl/Tk [3] on top of Horus [5].

The remainder of this paper outlines insights and questions based on that experience. In section 2, we briefly discuss abstractions needed by an operating system to support agents. Section 3 discusses some problems that arise in connection with electronic commerce involving agents. How to schedule agents by using other agents is the subject of section 4. Some preliminary thoughts on implementing fault tolerance are given in section 5. Section 6 discusses the status of our implementations.

2. Abstractions and mechanisms for agents

An agent must be accompanied by data in order for its future actions to depend on its past ones. For this reason, our implementations associate with each agent a *briefcase*, which contains a collection of named *folders*. A folder is a list of elements, each of which is an uninterpreted sequence of bits. Because it is a list, it can be treated as a stack or a queue. This makes folders reminiscent of the familiar objects used to group documents. Unlike files in a traditional operating system, folders must be easy to transfer from one computing system to another, since this operation occurs frequently. Thus, elaborate index structures are not suitable for implementing the folders that accompany agents.

It is also important that agents be able to read and write folders that are bound and local to a site executing the agent. Site-local folders allow more efficient use of network bandwidth. If an agent requires certain information only when it is executing at a given site, then it is inefficient to carry along that information to every site the agent visits. A site-local folder allows an agent to leave such information behind. In addition, site-local folders allow communication between agents that are not simultaneously resident at a given site. For example, consider a flooding algorithm to deliver a message at all sites in a network. One implementation would have each agent deliver the message and then create a clone of itself at every adjacent site. Unfortunately, here the number of agents increases without bound. If, instead, an agent also records its visit in a site-local folder, then an agent can simply terminate—rather than clone—when it finds itself at a site that has already been visited.

Just as an agent's folders are grouped into briefcases, we have found it useful to group site-local folders. We refer to such a grouping as a *file cabinet*. File cabinets support the same operations as briefcases, but we expect these operations to be implemented differently. In particular, since it is rare to move a file cabinet from site to site, file cabinets can be implemented using techniques that optimize access times even if this increases the cost of moving the file cabinet from one site to another.

One agent causes another to execute using the **meet** operation, where a briefcase allows information to be exchanged between the two agents. The **meet** operation is thus analogous to a procedure call, and the specified briefcase is analogous to an argument list (with each folder containing the value of one argument). For example, an agent *A* executing

meet *B* **with** *bc*

causes agent *B* to be executed at the current site with briefcase *bc*; *A* continues executing only after *B* terminates the **meet** operation. Note that after the **meet** terminates, *B* may continue executing concurrently with *A*.

Surprisingly, no additional abstractions are required to implement our basic computational metaphor. Services for agents—communication, synchronization, and so on—are provided directly by other agents. For example, an agent moves from one site to another by **meeting** with the local *rexec* agent. The *rexec* agent expects to find two folders in the briefcase with which it is invoked: a *HOST* folder names the site where execution is to be moved and a *CONTACT* folder names the agent to be executed at that site. The *CONTACT* folder might contain the name of an agent that is a shell or a compiler. Such an agent would expect to find a *CODE* folder in the briefcase, which it would then translate and execute. Since the contents of this *CODE* folder might be the source code for the agent that originally met with *rexec*, it is possible for an agent to travel from one site to another. Note that this scheme allows an agent to move to a destination site having a completely different machine language.

Given an *rexec* agent, it is not difficult to program a *courier* agent, which transfers a folder to a specified agent on a specified machine. This allows agents to communicate without having to meet (on a common machine). It is also not difficult to program our *diffusion* agent, which executes a specified agent locally and then creates a clone of itself at every site that appears in the set difference of the site-local *SITES* folder and the briefcase *SITES* folder.

3. Obtaining and paying for services

Once agents are employed for commerce—as some proponents [6] of the metaphor intend—support for a negotiable instrument becomes necessary. We, therefore, decided to explore the implementation and use of *electronic cash*. Electronic cash is nothing more than an unforgeable and untraceable capability that enables its owner to obtain goods and services. By implementing an electronic analogue to a well understood concept, we hoped to produce a system that remained understandable to the computer illiterate. We also hoped that electronic cash would provide a mechanism for controlling run-away agents. Specifically, charging for services would limit possible damage by a run-away agent.

Even as simple an operation as transferring electronic cash from one agent to another turned out to be surprisingly subtle to implement. With the familiar physical form of cash, money transfers are achieved by moving physical objects (coins or pieces of paper). This works only because it is difficult to manufacture copies of such objects. In a computer system, however, "copy" is a cheap operation. The usual solution to this problem would be to employ indirection and store all electronic cash in a single trusted agent. One agent could then transfer money to another by invoking an operation provided by this trusted agent.

We must reject solutions based on indirection because they necessarily violate our untraceability requirement for funds transfers. Following [1], the solution we adopted was to implement each unit of electronic cash (ECU) as a record containing an amount and a large random number. Only certain of these random numbers appear on the records for valid ECUs. Each agent stores records for the ECUs it owns. An agent transfers funds by placing these records in a briefcase that is then passed to the intended recipient of those funds.

The recipient of such a briefcase, however, has no guarantee that the sending agent has not already spent (a copy of) the ECUs being transferred. To solve this problem, a trusted *validation* agent is employed. This agent can check whether a record it is shown corresponds to a valid ECU. If it is valid, then a record for an equivalent ECU is returned, but this record has a new random number (effectively retiring an old bill and replacing it by a new one). An attempt by an agent to spend retired or copied ECUs will be foiled if a validation agent is always consulted before any service is rendered. Notice that using a validation agent supports our untraceability requirement, since the validation agent does not require knowledge of the source or destination of a transfer.

A second problem that we encountered in supporting electronic cash concerned implementing the exchange of funds for services. It must not be possible to obtain a service without paying for it or to pay without obtaining the service. This precludes the obvious two-step protocols, because as long as electronic cash is untraceable either party might cheat the other. For example, the customer might claim to have paid when it has not, or the service-provider might claim not to have been paid when it has. What would seem to be required is support for transactions, so that we are guaranteed that both actions ("paying" and "providing the service") occur or that neither action occurs.

We rejected adding support for transactions to our system for two reasons:

(1) Having such a mechanism would impact performance and would be effective only if it were trusted.

(2) Such a mechanism would be alien to the computer illiterate, because such a mechanism does not exist in current business practice.

Our solution was to employ the threat of audits, a scheme that is well-known in current business practice.

- Participants document their actions so that a third party (a court, in real life) can perform an audit to find violations of a contract.
- An aggrieved agent requests an audit.

Documenting actions sometimes requires the presence of a third agent and the use of cryptographic protocols—we omit the details here. Having to interact with such a third agent will be familiar to computer-illiterate users (at least, to those who have purchased a house).

4. Scheduling

In our prototypes, scheduling allows the enforcement of policies that govern when and where an agent is executed. Sites in a computer network are presumed to be autonomous, so facilities must be provided for system administrators to control the resources comprising a site. Agents are also presumed to be autonomous, though. Thus, implementing support for scheduling requires mechanisms to match the needs of agents with the providers of services while, at the same time, respecting constraints imposed by system administrators.

Scheduling is implemented by *broker* agents, which are ordinary agents whose names are well known. Some broker agents maintain databases of service providers; these brokers serve as matchmakers. An agent that requires a given service consults a broker to identify which agents provide that service. Brokers are expected to communicate among themselves and with the service providers, so that requests can be distributed amongst service providers based on load and capacity. The problem of maintaining the requisite state information and intelligently distributing service requests seems to be equivalent to that of routing in a wide-area network. We do not yet have experience with various routing protocols to know how they can be adapted to this new setting, but this is a topic under investigation.

Another use of broker agents is to enforce some *protected* agent's policies with regard to meeting other agents. This is accomplished by keeping the name of the protected agent secret from all but its broker. The broker, then, provides the only way to meet with the protected agent. To do this, the broker maintains a folder for each agent that has requested a meeting with the protected agent. This folder contains the agent that has requested the meeting (along with its briefcase). Notice that this scheme is possible only because folders are uninterpreted and typeless and, therefore, can themselves store agents and sets of folders.

5. Fault-tolerance

It is to be expected that sites in a computer network will fail. When such a failure occurs, agents at that site are no longer able to continue executing. To deal with this problem, we have been investigating ways to ensure that a computation can proceed, even though one or more of its agents is the victim of a site failure. The solutions we have studied involve leaving a *rear guard* agent behind whenever execution moves from one site to another. This rear guard is responsible for (i) launching a new agent should a failure cause an agent to vanish and (ii) terminating itself when its function is no longer necessary (because the agent it protects is itself ready to terminate). The details of implementing rear guards efficiently are complex, because the sites traversed by an agent computation may be cyclic and because a single agent may clone itself and fan out through a network.

6. Prototype implementations

Our most recent version of TACOMA is based on Tcl [3]. Each site in our system runs a Tcl interpreter, which provides the place where agents execute. An agent is implemented by a Tcl procedure; the text of the procedure is stored in the agent's *CODE* folder. Folders, briefcases, and file cabinets are Tcl data structures. File cabinets can be flushed to disk when permanence is required.

A collection of system agents provides a variety of support functions. The most basic of these is *ag_tcl*, which pops a Tcl procedure from the *CODE* folder and executes that procedure. Currently, two implementations exist for the *rexec* agent. The first uses the UNIX rsh command to start a Tcl interpreter on the remote host. The second uses Tcl/TCP, an extension to Tcl that allows Tcl processes to set up TCP communication channels. We are now completing a third implementation based on Tcl/Horus, a version of Tcl that uses Horus [5] to support group communication and fault-tolerance.

In our first prototype of TACOMA, we implemented the electronic cash of section 3. The implementation used the security mechanisms provided by UNIX; this simplified our implementation, but relies on UNIX for security. We are now investigating alternatives.

Our TACOMA prototype currently supports a scheduling service that assigns to processors based on load. It uses four different agents to implement a scheme like that outlined in section 4. One of these agents is the broker, another is responsible for monitoring the status of a site and reporting that to the brokers, one is a courier, and one issues tickets to allow access to the service.

To evaluate the metaphor we are using our prototype to construct a variety of distributed applications. First, we are reimplementing StormCast [2], which uses a set of expert systems to predict severe storms in the Arctic based on weather data obtained from a distributed network of sensors. Second, we have started to build an interactive mail system where agents implement *active documents*, which support interactive dialogs with a recipient. Active documents are useful, for example, for implementing a meeting scheduler that moves among a group of people to determine a non-conflicting meeting time.

References

[1] Chaum, D. Achieving Electronic Privacy. *Scientific American* 267,2 (Aug 1992), 96-101.

[2] Johansen, Dag. StormCast: Yet another exercise in distributed computing. *Distributed Open Systems* F.M.T. Brazier and D. Johansen, eds. *IEEE Computer Society Press*, California (Oct 1993), 152-174.

[3] Ousterhout, John K. *Tcl and the Tk Toolkit* Addison Wesley, Reading, Massachusetts, 1994.

[4] Riecken, D. (guest editor). Intelligent Agents. *Commun. of the ACM* 37,7 (July 1994), 19-21.

[5] Van Renesse, Robbert, Takako M. Hickey, and Kenneth P. Birman. Design and Performance of Horus: A Lightweight Group Communications System. Technical Report TR 94-1442, Department of Computer Science, Cornell University, Aug 1994.

[6] White, J.E. Telescript Technology: The Foundation for the Electronic Marketplace. General Magic White Paper, General Magic Inc., 1994.

Secure, remote applications for large public networks

Itinerant Agents for Mobile Computing

DAVID CHESS, BENJAMIN GROSOF, COLIN HARRISON, DAVID LEVINE, COLIN PARRIS, AND GENE TSUDIK

This article describes an abstract framework for itinerant agents that can be used to implement secure, remote applications in large, public networks such as the Internet or the IBM Global Network. Itinerant agents are programs, dispatched from a source computer, that roam among a set of networked servers until they accomplish their task. This is an extension to the client/server model in which the client sends a portion of itself to the server for execution. An additional feature of itinerant agents is their ability to migrate from server to server, perhaps seeking one that can help with the user's task or perhaps collecting information from all of them. A major focus of this article is the Agent Meeting Point, an abstraction that supports the interaction of agents with each other and server based resources.

Why is this extended form of client/server computing desirable or valuable? There are many detailed motivations for using itinerant agents [6]. They fall broadly into two categories: 1) support for mobile computers or lightweight devices and 2) the emerging need in rapidly evolving networks for an asynchronous method of searching for information or transaction services. For example:

- The reduction of overall communication traffic over the low bandwidth, high latency, high cost access networks typically employed by mobile computers.
- The ability of the agent to engage in high bandwidth communication (with a server, for example) to search through large, free text data bases.
- The ability of lightweight mobile computers to interact with heavyweight applications without prior detailed knowledge of the remote server's capabilities.
- The ability of the agent to integrate knowledge from the client and server and perform inferencing at the server.
- The ability of the user to create "personalized services" by customizing agents that take up residence at a server.

These claimed advantages are, at present, hypothetical, and we are performing experiments to determine if they can be realized. We believe they merit initial exploration.

Public networks already contain an enormous number of computers capable of providing specific services. This number will continue to grow. These servers employ a wide variety of processors, operating systems, data bases, application frameworks, and applications. An itinerant agent framework enables these numerous, heterogeneous servers to offer many advantages. These include a host-independent execution environment for itinerant agent programs, standard communication languages with which agents and servers can engage in dialogues, a method of employing public security services to enable authenticated access to server resources, and secure auditing and error recovery mechanisms.[1]

This article is structured as follows: it begins with an overview of the operation of an itinerant agent framework (first section) and a review of previous work (second section). In the third section we consider likely applications of itinerant agents and discuss one specific example in detail. The fourth section is an architectural description of the structure of itinerant agents, the languages employed to create them, and the execution environments required at the servers. In the fifth section we give a detailed description of how an itinerant agent is processed at a server. The sixth section discusses security issues, always important in network services and especially so in this case. Finally, in the seventh section, we describe the technical advantages of the itinerant agent framework and the services it enables.

Background

In this section we give an overview of the operation of an itinerant agent framework, some of the surrounding issues, and a history of work in this area.

In many cases, the itinerant agent is launched from a client device such as a laptop or desktop PC by an otherwise conventional application. We anticipate that most end users will not write their own agents (though that is certainly possible), but that various classes of agents will be distributed by services for use by their subscribers or will be packaged with the client applications. The agent is initialized with the user's task (see below for examples) and transmitted by a message channel [2, 26]. The sending client may specify a destination service directly. But the client will more likely send the agent initially to, for example, a Yellow Pages server, which can propose servers to be visited to fulfill the user's task.

When the agent reaches a server, it is delivered to an

[1] *In many cases, itinerant agents will in effect be performing electronic commerce. This requires us to consider many commercial issues, including payment methods. However, we believe the electronic payment systems being developed for other forms of electronic commerce will be applicable to commerce conducted by itinerant agents; hence we do not discuss such payment issues in this article.*

agent execution environment, which we call an Agent Meeting Point (AMP).[2] Upon arrival at an AMP, the agent's external wrapper is inspected for authentication credentials. After validation, the AMP examines the agent's description of itself. Ontologically named service requests are resolved to determine if the desired services are available at the AMP. If sufficient resources are available and permitted, the constituent parts of the agent are passed to the services.

The executable portions of the agent are then started. In some cases the itinerant agent will be interacting directly with server resources via proxy objects, which enable access control to be enforced. In other cases, it will interact with a *static agent* resident at the AMP. The static agent may have been dispatched to the AMP by the sender of the itinerant agent, or it may have been installed by the server operator. Static agents enable the server's function to be personalized by the server's owner or by users. When the agent has successfully completed its task at this server, it may collect its state, including information acquired at the server, and request to be transported to a new host. Or, it may launch a smaller agent to deliver the acquired information to the sending client or to another server while it terminates. This ability to acquire knowledge and transport it from place to place is a key attribute of an itinerant agent. The new knowledge may be simply a new destination or it may be a security token or transaction. This ability means that the agent is not merely a program executed at a remote host and then returned to its origin, but a moving process that progressively accomplishes a task by moving from place to place.

If the agent proves to be unauthorized, or if the meeting point is unable to provide the agent with the resource it has requested, the AMP will take action based on the agent's header. It may discard the agent. It may send the indicated party a description of the failure. Or if it is capable it may propose one or more AMPs to satisfy the request.

The range of large-scale public networks, and the absence of formal administration arrangements among the many domains that comprise them, pose particular problems for navigation and authentication of itinerant agents. Unlike private networks where itinerant agents might be viewed as being "at home," itinerant agents navigating the Internet are very much on their own. Although they may be capable of sending messages back to their origins, it is counter-productive to impose a strong dependency on the (mobile) sending clients constant accessibility. So we seek a model in which the agent:

- Carries with it the minimal, necessary, and sufficient information to accomplish its task.
- Can prove its authority to any AMP it may visit.
- Can accumulate knowledge during its itinerary and make decisions based on that information.

In addition, the model should permit the detection of AMPs that tamper with agents and their data, and it should provide sufficient auditing for AMPs to prove they have behaved properly.

The idea of dispatching a program for execution on a remote computer is quite old. Often the motivation has been that the local computer does not have the capacity to execute the program. Or perhaps the remote computer has direct access to some resource, such as an attached peripheral, that cannot be efficiently exported via the network. In the 1960s such schemes were employed to enable mini-computers to submit batch jobs on mainframes and to receive results, typically print files, back for local processing [3]. In the 1970s executable scripts were dispatched among networks of mini-computers to permit distributed, real-time processing [10].

Recently, scripts have become a focus of attention. The concept of active mail has been used to enable widely available electronic mail services [4] to deliver executable scripts [23]. The Telescript mobile scripting language, for example, was deployed in 1994 for an initial set of services on AT&T's public PersonaLink network. Telescript provides security features intended to support electronic commerce by means of mobile agents [29].

The HotJava web browser [21] from Sun Microsystems will retrieve programs from World Wide Web servers for immediate execution on the local machine. The programs are typically written in the Java language and compiled into a machine-independent intermediate code. The intent is to allow for great flexibility in the function and presentation of information retrieved from the server, while preserving the security of the local system by carefully controlling what the received program can do. These programs are only itinerant in a weak sense, since they are retrieved from the server by the browser, but go no further.

The emergence of standard, distributed object-oriented frameworks is another important enabler for mobile scripts. In such frameworks, the need to transport methods can often be greatly reduced when common methods can be presumed to be remotely available.

Other recent developments include the emergence of knowledge representation languages and protocols such as those in the ARPA Knowledge Sharing Effort. These include the Knowledge Query and Manipulation Language (KQML) [11], and the Knowledge Interchange Facility (KIF) [13], which provide a basis for agent-server or agent-agent communication. Recent interest in on-demand electronic commerce is leading to the creation of public security services such as TERISA, the joint effort of RSA and EIT [7]. The emergence of standard, distributed object-oriented frameworks is another important enabler for mobile scripts. In such frameworks, the need to transport methods can often be greatly reduced when common methods can be presumed to be remotely available. In such cases, transport of only a set of object references, instance data, and a process state are necessary.

Technologies are thus becoming available to successfully implement an itinerant agent frame-

[2] *The sending client may also have an AMP, which it can use for launching agents, but in general it is not necessary for a client to have the full functionality of an AMP.*

work and to propagate it throughout the public networks. Such a framework or, more likely, set of frameworks, may have a significant impact on existing businesses. Many industries have multiple intermediaries between the creator of a good or service and its ultimate consumer. These intermediaries add value by applying expert knowledge, for example, to perform targeted distribution or to add ancillary services. Such industries include travel agents, financial and insurance brokers, and online information services. Itinerant agent frameworks are likely to impact such industries by replacing or eliminating some or all intermediaries. This process, which we call *disintermediation*, is facilitated in itinerant agent frameworks through the communication of knowledge as data among consumers and providers.

The agent framework enables people with expertise to make their skills available through the global network with a relatively low investment in computer technology, and with simple payment methods.

A corollary is that agent frameworks provide a mechanism for the creation of small, knowledge-based businesses offering services to large companies that formerly had to provide such services themselves. Examples are specialists in international trade, government regulations, language translation, and so forth. The agent framework enables people with expertise to make their skills available through the global network with a relatively low investment in computer technology, and with simple payment methods.

Agent frameworks thus play a role in the ongoing reconstruction of large-scale corporations in which more services are outsourced and each enterprise becomes increasingly focused on its area of expertise. Large companies can shed supporting staffs and small companies can offer niche services.

Itinerant Agent Applications

In this section we suggest some typical applications of itinerant agents and give one scenario in some detail. An itinerant agent provides an extension to conventional client-server computing. Within this extension it supports several styles of application, which differ in the nature of the interaction between the itinerant agent and the server or servers it visits. The styles of interaction can be represented by *models*. Examples of these models range from simple to complex interactions, as follows.

An Information Dispersal/Retrieval Model – A client sends its agent to various host servers to update the latest version of an application, or into the network to retrieve the latest version of a technical paper on "Agent Technologies." This model represents a simple interaction based on an *ask/receive* paradigm between an itinerant agent and a static agent. In this case, the itinerant agent serves as the courier and installer for data or program content.

A Collaborative Model – The five authors of this article send our agents to an AMP, which has a service that allows you to reserve conference rooms and schedule a meeting. This model represents a more complicated interaction in which there is a single clearly defined goal and the agents are required not only to ask for and receive information, but to evaluate and compromise based on a range of preferences. In this case, the itinerant agents convey not only the specified task, but relevant knowledge from the rule bases of the requesters, which are combined at the AMP and processed to yield a solution. The ability to transport and combine knowledge is supported by one or more *Agent Communication Languages* (ACLs). In some cases the ACL may be a knowledge representation language from the artificial intelligence community. In other cases it may be a language developed specifically for a certain purpose, such as *Electronic Data Interchange* [17].

A Procurement Model – An example of this interaction is that of an open-bidding auction in which multiple itinerant agents attempt to bid for goods or services offered by an auctioneer (usually a static agent). This model represents a very complex interaction governed by an auction protocol in which the agents' goals and monetary resources are hidden from other agents [28]. The procurement model also includes the activities of strategy and electronic commerce. This model has many "sub models" such as *electronic malls* (many static agents and itinerant agents), *flea markets* (many itinerant agents), and *sealed bidding auctions*.

To understand this method of client/server computing more clearly, we will examine a scenario that serves to illustrate the major features of an itinerant agent framework. The scenario involves the purchase of airline seats by an employee of a company (Fig. 1). The scenario is incomplete in that it does not address several important issues, including: error recovery and auditing, privacy, and various aspects of trust among the participants. However, some of these are considered in subsequent sections.

Travel Reservation Scenario

A mobile employee has a need to fly from New York City to Austin, Texas on a Thursday evening. His business will be completed by Friday evening, but if there is a significant fare saving, he is willing to stay in Austin until Sunday. He has a portable computer, which is able to access his company's LAN via a public network and a secure gateway. He uses a form or a dialogue to state his need. The application translates this need into a task expressed in an Agent Communication Language, using a vocabulary standardized for travel reservations. This task specification is used to create an instance of a Transaction Agent in the portable computer. The Transaction Agent is a program, expressed in a script language, that is able to interact via an AMP with a transaction server, assess the results of the transaction, make a decision, and commit a purchase. The Transaction Agent is also given the user's preferences for travel reservations (expressed as rules), and the agent is dig-

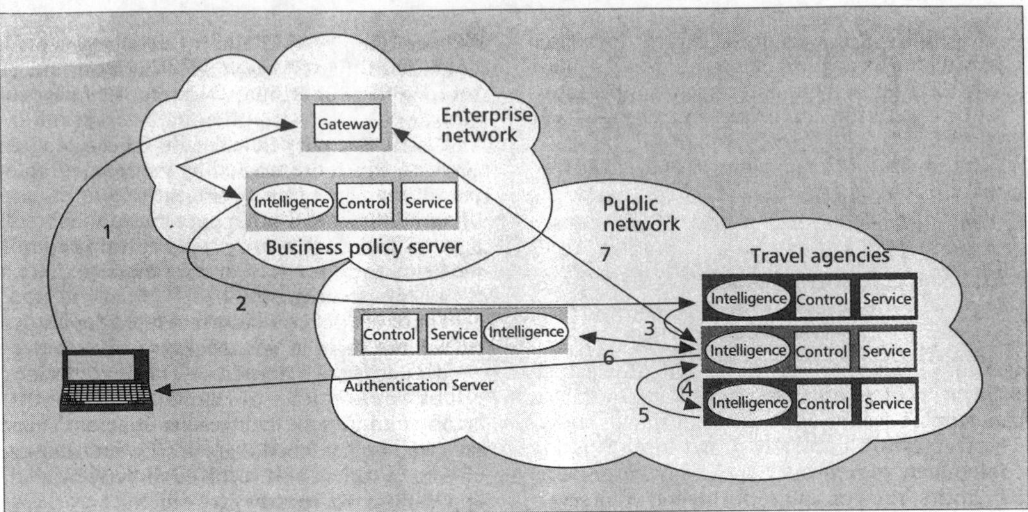

■ **Figure 1.** *Travel reservation scenario.*

itally signed with the user's authority.

The user's employer has a travel policy and a number of preferred providers of travel services, so the agent is sent initially from the laptop to the employer's Business Policy Server. To achieve this, the agent is partially encrypted with the Business Policy Server's public key, and then passed to a messaging system for transport via the LAN gateway to the server (step 1 in Fig. 1). The mobile user then disconnects his computer from the network. At the Business Policy Server's AMP, the incoming agent is decrypted and authenticated using the AMP's private key. The agent and the AMP engage in a dialogue in which the agent communicates its task, which is to perform a transaction to obtain airline seats. The Business Policy Server's AMP verifies that the task does not violate current policy by employing an inferencing system to see whether the expressed facts conflict with the company's policy. If all is well, a subset of the policy rules are attached to the agent, it is given a list of approved travel agencies and their public keys, and the agent is encrypted with the key of the first agency's AMP. The agent is now passed to a messaging system for transport to the first server to be visited (step 2). At the first server, the AMP uses its private key to decrypt the agent, ensuring that the agent can only be executed on the intended servers. The AMP then verifies the authority of the agent by examining the credentials it carries using one of the public security services to which the travel agency subscribes. The agent and the AMP engage in a dialogue in which the agent communicates its assignment, to obtain airline seats. The travel agency AMP accepts the specification of the transaction and passes it to the on-line reservation system, parsing the Agent Communication Language expression of the task into the semantics of the reservation system, and performing the transaction dialogue. The reservation system returns (we hope) a number of candidate seats and prices, for return flights on Friday and Sunday. The agent employs a local inference engine to process each of these candidates against the user's travel preferences and the company's travel policy. After ordering the candidates according to preference, the agent selects the best candidate and requests the AMP to hold the seat for a certain time, say 10 minutes. The agent is then re-encrypted and transferred to the next server on the approved list (step 3).

The agent repeats this process at each of the servers visited (step 4).[3] Whenever it finds a better candidate, it sends a message back to the server where it found the previous selection, releasing the hold it had requested. When it has examined a minimum number of candidates or visited a minimum number of servers, as specified by the company policy, it returns to the server of the best candidate and completes the transaction (step 5). This server's AMP issues a Ticket Agent, encrypted with the user's public key, obtained from the public security service, and sends it to the user (step 6). It then sends a Billing Agent (also encrypted), to the security service (step 7). Since the user has disconnected from the network, the Ticket Agent is held at the gateway until the user reconnects.

The Transaction Agent is a program, expressed in a script language, that is able to interact via an AMP with a transaction server, assess the results of the transaction, make a decision, and commit a purchase.

We do not claim that this is an accurate method for purchasing airline tickets, but it serves to illustrate many of the features and operations of an itinerant agent framework:

- The ability of the mobile user to dispatch an asynchronous task and receive a response at a later time.
- The ability of the itinerant agent to collect various kinds of knowledge to be applied to the execution of the task at the AMPs. The ability of the agent to migrate from place to place, accumulating information until it is able to complete its task.
- The ability of the agent framework to employ various public security services for its own protection, the protection of the servers, and the completion of a payment method.

[3] The manner in which the agent is authenticated at these servers is discussed in the sixth section, "Security Issues."

- The ability of the agent to employ the visited AMPs for its own execution purposes (selecting the best seat) in addition to simply interacting with the server's resources or static agents.

In the rest of this article we discuss how to structure itinerant agents and AMPs in order to realize these kinds of services.

Itinerant Agent Framework

Overview

In the following sections we describe the principal aspects of an itinerant agent framework that can support scenarios of the kind shown above. The framework naturally draws upon existing components of networks, such as name servers, directories, routers, and so forth, and adds several new facilities:

Itinerant Agents — These may be expressed in various programming languages and may transport knowledge expressed in various forms. They must be structured to engage in a progressive dialogue with the AMPs until they are able to execute or are rejected. An agent that executes at an AMP will usually complete its activity before moving to another AMP. However, an agent may also elect to suspend its activity at an AMP, transport itself to another AMP, and resume activity. In this case both the content of the agent (its physical state) and the representation of the environment in which the agent is executing (its execution state) must be moved to the new AMP. We will describe the abstract structure of itinerant agents and how they are processed by the AMP in the next section.

In theory, any executable environment willing to conform to the architecture of the AMP can be supported. In practice, however, some languages are more practical for writing itinerant agents than others.

Agent Languages — Two kinds of languages are involved. One is the language in which the programmatic content of the agent is written; this is usually (though not necessarily) a script language. The second is a language for knowledge representation, which provides the means to express goals, tasks, preferences, and vocabularies appropriate to various domains. We will review the requirements for these languages in the section following on "agent languages."

Agent State Accumulation — In general, as agents interact with servers and other agents they will accumulate state information representing the results of these interactions. In the section "Moving Programs and Accumulated State," we will discuss how state may be accumulated and managed in the agent framework.

Agent Meeting Places — These have various subcomponents, and they are the principal means by which a server becomes part of the agent framework. We think of the AMP as a broker between the agents, which are making requests for resources and services, and the applications that implement these resources and services. We will describe the AMP and its sub-components in detail in sections "Agent Meeting Point Structure," and "Functional Decomposition of the AMP."

Public Security Services — These security services, which are trusted by the servers taking part in the agent framework, include certificates of authenticity and other services to the mobile agents. The framework places certain requirements on these services, and we describe them in the section security issues.

There are several closely related topics that we will not cover in this article:

User Interface Agents — These are used by client applications to launch agents and to receive and present their results. Itinerant agents may well be launched from AMPs, but they can also be launched and received directly by client applications, which may vary widely.

Static Agents — Itinerant agents are a subset of the larger question of intelligent agents acting on behalf of users. The same basic framework applies to these agents and their access to services, but with a different set of communications, protocol, and security issues.

Non-Agent Invocation of AMP Services — Many of the services provided by the AMP to local agents are of interest to other AMPs, static agents, and normal applications within the larger computing infrastructure. RPC or CORBA/OMG [14] style bindings can be made available to these potential clients. Again, a set of issues that are not germane to itinerant agents apply to these services.

Agent Status Management — One of the inhibitors to building and deploying itinerant agent-based solutions is the complexity of managing the activity of an agent traversing multiple loosely coupled nodes. A complete itinerant agent framework will include services to register work as it is initiated, track its success or failure, and recover from system failures. These services need to address such issues as recovering in the face of single and multiple AMP failures, partitions of the underlying network, and poorly behaved services, AMPs, and agents. Therefore, we will generally mention that the problems exist and that there are services planned within the framework to address them, and defer detailed discussion to papers with these issues as their primary focus.

Virus Control Services — It is well known that accepting unknown programs into a computer invites corruption and subversion of that computer. There are efforts in progress to define such virus services and it is not the purpose of this article to describe any of these.

We begin the discussion of the framework by first describing the basic structure of an itinerant agent.

Itinerant Agent Structure

The basic structure of an itinerant agent (as shown in Fig. 2) can be divided into three distinct portions: the Agent Passport, the Table Of Contents (TOC), and the Components, which are discussed below.

The *Agent Passport* consists of the basic information required to permit the agent to move from AMP to AMP. This includes:

Authentication of Originator — This certificate includes the name or the authority of the request's owner and the name or names of other authority sanctioning entities. In the example of Fig. 1, this certificate may carry the identity of the originator of the agent and the "network name" of the business server. This may allow the travel services to provide the agent with the business rate for the tickets.

Error Actions and Addresses — This is the action the AMP should take when an error occurs while processing the agent. Some possible actions include: discarding the agent without comment; delivering an error notification to a specified address; routing the agent to another AMP.

Goals and Status Information — This information includes a representation of the agent's goal, and can include its relationship to other agents and their goals. Note that this agent may be the child of an agent present at the AMP, returning after an assignment from that parent. In some cases, the agent may require the AMP to notify an external entity (another agent or a client) of its status or progress based on some specified condition. The address of the external entity and the conditions are provided in this information.

Note also that this structure is that of only the agent, not any headers or segmentation imposed by communications protocols used to move it between AMPs.

The *Table Of Contents* for the body of an agent provides a map of its structure. Each component has a size, type and importance. The size, as expected, is the size of the component. The type field contains a simple representation of what is required to process the component. The importance field describes whether the component is necessary for the agent to be instantiated at the AMP. This permits agents to carry obscure components through AMPs that do not support these components, and to avoid unpacking components that will not be used at any AMP. Note that in order to provide for arbitrary length expressions of the service type needed to support the component, the type fields are stored in a variable length section of the TOC. Offsets to the start of each type and its length are stored in the fixed table structure of the TOC.

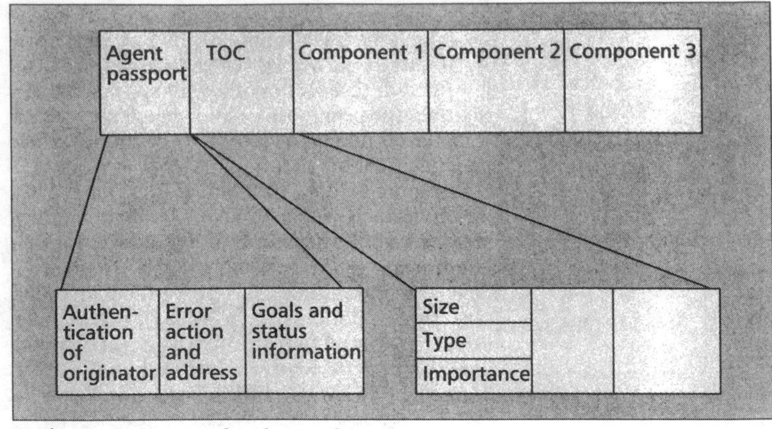

■ **Figure 2.** *Encapsulated agent format.*

Agent Language

Agent Programming Languages – One of the basic goals of this framework is that it should support a broad range of languages. In theory, any executable environment willing to conform to the architecture of the AMP can be supported. In practice, however, some languages are more practical for writing itinerant agents than others. We will briefly discuss some of the desirable attributes for an agent programming language.

- High Level Language — While not strictly required, it is very difficult to secure environments that permit raw machine code to be executed as agent code.
- Object-Oriented — While procedural languages can be made to fit within an agent framework, Object-Oriented (OO) languages provide several advantages for the builder of agent frameworks. The object abstraction provides a good leverage point for access control and data mobility.
- Mobility Hooks — Mobility is a key feature of itinerant agents, so it is desirable that an agent language easily support moving the agent. However, agent language support is not enough and some standardized primitives will be needed to invoke the collection of an agent's parts and the movement of the agent from one AMP to another. The language support needed for movement is discussed in more detail later.
- Fork/Spawn construct — As with mobility, itinerant agents will frequently desire to split up their processing among multiple copies of themselves at multiple AMPs or spawn agents to traverse the network. Again it is not necessary that the language expressly include support for this as a primitive, as some standardized primitives will have to be provided by the environment.
- Distributed Computing — As itinerant agents are dealing directly with a distributed computing environment, it is useful for the agent language to provide constructs that help programmers manage these issues. The ability to create proxy objects to represent remote objects is one example of this sort of support. Other examples include expressing synchronization points between multiple threads of execution, and providing facilities to flatten and unflatten objects and constructs to facilitate coordinating the management of objects shared between environments.

Knowledge Representation Languages – Languages for knowledge representation (KR) provide the means to express goals, tasks, preferences, beliefs, and vocabularies appropriate to various domains. Such goals and beliefs may take the form of facts, rules, other logical formulas, defaults, probabilities and utilities, fuzzy sets and logic, neural networks, and plan and action operators, to name a few.

By a language, we mean a formalism that defines what one can express in the way of beliefs (e.g., data) and goals (e.g., requests), as well as other similar entities (e.g., preferences). A language has syntax: including structure, operators, arguments, sequence constraints, block delimiters, and connectives. A language may also have semantics: a mapping of the language's syntactic entities to a set of meanings that are described in terms of another formal system. For example, the semantics of knowledge representations based on classical logic is often described in terms of model theory.

Languages (e.g., first-order logic) are often parametrized by vocabularies. By a vocabulary, we mean a collection of building blocks for representation, in the following sense. In classical logic (the underpinning of most practical knowledge representation systems today), this includes a description of the predicates and functions (symbols) out of which belief and goal expressions are syntactically built. More informally, these predicates and functions correspond to

By using distributed computing frameworks such as those being built by the OMG/CORBA community, we can delegate a large number of distributed computing issues to the computing framework.

what are otherwise known as attributes, relationships, and entities, and need to be described in terms of their symbols and what kinds of arguments they take (arity and types). Vocabulary also includes other kinds of definitional information such as taxonomic (or subsumption) hierarchy and mutual exclusion (or distinctness) among various classes.

There are, of course, many different kinds of KR languages. A leading approach to interoperation and high-level languages for interchange and interaction is via the ARPA Knowledge Sharing Effort [22, 25].

The Knowledge Sharing Effort today has several parts; we focus here on three.

KIF — Knowledge Interchange Format [13] is a rich standard language for interchange between other KR languages. It can express beliefs, rules, facts, partial descriptions of procedures, and more. Currently under construction are translators for a number of specific KR languages (services, systems) already in practical use. These translate between various KR languages and KIF, and therefore transitively to each other. Translating between n KR languages through one central common language, such as KIF, reduces the number of translators from $O(n^2)$ to $O(n)$.

Ontolingua — Ontolingua [15, 16] is a facility (system and approach) for creating and maintaining vocabularies. In Ontolingua a number of domain-specific vocabularies already exist for mechanical and electrical engineering, where the vocabularies contain terminologies usually found in standard introductory textbooks. One of the major advantages of agents is that they can bring domain-specific knowledge to bear on problems. This entails the opportunity, and need, for domain-specific vocabularies. To develop and maintain a single comprehensive global vocabulary is practically impossible. Interestingly, an AMP itself as a domain requires a vocabulary. The Knowledge Sharing Effort approach supports named vocabularies, which qualify vocabulary terms. This helps to reduce confusion when agents and AMPs are communicating in multiple vocabularies.

KQML — Knowledge Query and Manipulation Language (KQML) [5, 11, 12] is a high-level protocol and language for agent-service and agent-agent interactions and communications. KQML can be viewed as providing a "package" layer to wrap around the transport of "content" such as might be described in KIF. KQML is based on the concept of a performative from speech act theory in linguistics. Currently defined performatives include: ask, tell, forward, and broker. KQML passes as parameters: the language and vocabulary in which the content is represented. Also, KQML can nest performatives, such that, more specialized performatives can be nested within more general-purpose performatives.

Electronic Data Interchange (EDI) [17] deserves special mention as a KR language because of its importance as a standard practical framework for electronic commerce. While not an AI-style language, it serves much the same purpose.

Knowledge representation is important for routing in the broad sense. In order for itinerant agents to encapsulate the goals of their user, and to find services that have answers related to these goals, information must be expressed in terms that can be used to match goals and the services that can fulfill these goals.

The need to support KR languages and the opportunity to employ them thus motivate a number of components within our proposed AMP. In particular, the Deep Request Handler, the Linguistic Registry, and the Shallow Request Handler are oriented toward knowledge representation issues.

Moving Programs and Accumulated State

Moving Programs – Concerning the movement of itinerant agents, two possibilities exist. A simple case where the agent is a program that runs to completion at the agent's destination, and a more complex case in which an agent program begins executing at one AMP and then decides to move, complete with its current state, to another AMP.

In the simple case, the program can be encoded, loaded, and run until it signals completion. This can be done with only a few changes to an existing execution engine.[4] In the more complex case in which a program wishes to move from one server to another in mid execution, an important question arises how to extract the program's variables and state from the execution environment and insert them into another execution engine.

Briefly, there are several approaches to the problem of moving executing programs. One of the easiest is to allocate all information associated with the program's execution on the program stack and transport the stack, along with the engine, from one execution environment to another. Another approach involves keeping a registry of variables as they are created and moving the registry and the variables. In these two cases and other similar schemes, more extensive changes are required to the execution environment.

---

[4] *This execution engine is usually an interpreter.*

Accumulated State – An agent traversing several servers within a network of servers may need to accumulate information derived at each of the servers it visits. Agents can accumulate this information through two primary mechanisms: by adding new objects containing the new information and state to its existing collection of objects, or capturing state through changes within its existing collection of objects.

Consider an agent that is searching for information matching some specific request. As the agent traverses the network of servers, it adds these matching documents to its collection of items. Note that many of these items could be marked as cargo in the TOC and not be instantiated as the agent visits various AMPs.

State can also be captured within an agent's existing collection of objects. The degenerate case of this is an agent that consists of a single object, that is, an executable program and its execution context. An agent searching for the lowest price offer for a specific item need only carry the current lowest bid (and the identity of the bidder) in a local variable within its execution context. As the agent moves from AMP to AMP, the program and its context are saved, moved, and restored.

More complicated combinations of the above mechanisms are possible. An agent may build a separate object for holding the state of its work and update this object as it traverses a collection of servers. It is also possible that an agent will send state updates back to its origin point as it traverses the network.

Agent Meeting Point Structure

It is our belief that an agent infrastructure will be most naturally expressed in terms of a set of object services. Objects provide a number of attributes that are of particular interest in the distributed agent environment. Objects form a coherent, concrete element of mobility. We can move an entire object and we can refer to remote objects through proxy objects. We can apply authentication and access controls to objects more readily than to procedural data structures. By using distributed computing frameworks such as those being built by the OMG/CORBA community, we can delegate a large number of distributed computing issues to the computing framework.

The basic structure of the AMP is a set of OO classes designed to provide a very lightweight, minimal framework for building specific meeting points. The focus of this framework is providing the set of base services that can be used to register the services that a specific AMP will use.

The base services will include a Shallow Request Handler, which will permit components that snap into the framework to express what function they provide in terms of a simple knowledge representation scheme.

Although even very basic services will be accessed through the Shallow Request Handler, we will define the AMP as fundamentally including these functions. This permits us to provide a sufficiently rich and robust description of the AMP while allowing for incremental development and extension of the AMP structure.

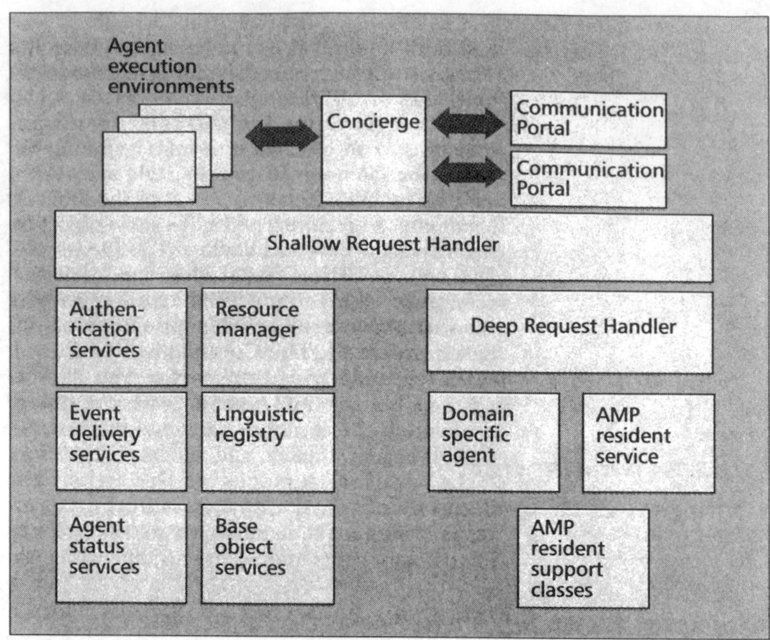

■ **Figure 3.** *Agent meeting points – functional level decomposition.*

In this initial work we focus on the design of a minimal structure that can support basic agent interaction. Yet the structure can be easily expanded to support a broad range of service types and interaction models. Our approach is to articulate an underlying set of component frameworks that focus on building a minimum set of services for registering and routing work within the AMP.

On top of the Shallow Request Handler and the base components we define additional parts that provide specific services. These parts center on the Deep Request Handler and the Linguistic Registry, the focus for managing more complex knowledge representation and semantic issues.

For the purposes of this article, we will ignore the admittedly complex issues surrounding the proper construction of an object-oriented, distributed computing environment and focus on the portions of an agent meeting place that are agentry specific.

Functional Decomposition of the AMP

The functional decomposition is shown in Fig. 3, with the components comprising the architecture discussed in the following sections.

Base Object Services – The Base Objects Services are CORBA/OMG based object services or their equivalent. Included are language-independent, object interface bindings, remote object invocation, marshaling of objects, object based access control services, persistence, and replication.

Communication Portals – The Communication Portals are responsible for managing the arrival and departure of itinerant agents, as well as routing messages to the residing agents or services in the AMP. The Communication Portals support protocol handlers, each of which manages a specific protocol, providing both inbound and outbound services to encapsulated agents. They also provide a consistent interface to the bulk of the AMP through *location* objects, which provide a set of methods to send agents and messages to abstract locations. For inbound services, the Communication Portals extract the arriving mobile agent and pass it to the itinerant agent concierge, along with a location object for the arriving agent's location.

Communication Portals may support either session-oriented connections to other parts of the infrastructure or may support messaging based protocols. The Communication Portals mask the underlying transport service and are responsible for the transport-specific details associated with the transports and their media, such as header, trailers, and data representation.

In addition to managing the arrival and departure of agents, Communication Portals are responsible for the handling of messages directed to components and agents residing within the AMP. Agents can communicate remotely with other agents or AMPs through the passing of messages. Communication Portals utilize the Shallow Request Handler to direct such messages into the AMP.

> *The Linguistic Registry's purpose can be viewed in terms of the paradigm of the DARPA Knowledge Sharing Effort approach. There, a prime focus is support for multiple agent communication languages and vocabularies.*

Authentication Services – The Authentication Services are an OO encapsulation of the underlying distributed authentication scheme used in the agent network. While the Authentication Services component will primarily be used by the Concierge, it is also generally available to other components and agents that need to perform authentication.

Concierge – The Concierge acts much as a concierge does in a full service hotel. It examines an agent's credentials, makes sure that the facilities that the agent has requested are available, and helps the agent arrive at the AMP. The Concierge is also available to help agents who wish to travel to other AMPs. The Concierge provides a set of functions to gather an agent and its collected parts, package them and their credentials into a standard form, and pass them to the desired Communications Portal.

In order for the Concierge to perform its task it requires an intimate understanding of the basic headers of the encapsulated agent (as shown in Fig. 2). Upon arrival of an encapsulated agent, the Concierge strips the *Agent Passport* from the encapsulated agent. This passport contains the information needed to authenticate the agent (as discussed previously). Either the passport is validated, or the information within the passport is used to manage the graceful rejection of the agent. The passport is also used to assign the agent an *Access Control Factor*, which determines the permissions that apply to the agent and its components.

If the agent is admitted to the AMP, the Concierge then uses the TOC to examine the goal of the agent and the basic services it requires. The Concierge strips this information from the agent header and passes it to the Shallow Request Handler. The Shallow Request Handler (possibly with use of the Linguistic Registry and Deep Request Handler) passes back both the list of mapped resources and a list of those resources that could not be mapped. The Concierge then decides to either set up the agent or generate an error report.

The approach of having the Concierge manage goals through the Shallow Request Handler (and by implication the Deep Request Handler as needed), permits goals to be expressed at multiple levels of language ranging from low-level requests in the Shallow Request Handler's vocabulary to high-level requests expressed in KQML performatives. As the Deep Request Handler is an extensible component of the AMP and capable of translating representations, we can extend this range as new representations are developed.

Shallow Request Handler – The Shallow Request Handler forms the glue that binds the AMP, acting as the interface between agents and the components of the AMP. These components register themselves using a description of the service they perform. The Shallow Request Handler then uses this description to route requests from agents to the components that support them.

The Shallow Request Handler uses a limited vocabulary to match user requests with available services. The Shallow Request Handler is also capable of recognizing requests expressed in forms of notation beyond its vocabulary. When such a request is passed to the Shallow Request Handler, it checks its cache for a translated version of the request. If it does not find one it sees if the Linguistic Registry has the vocabulary registered, and if so, passes the request to the Deep Request Handler for translation.

The Shallow Request Handler uses the access control factors assigned agents by the concierge to limit their access to those objects and services which they are permitted to manipulate.

Linguistic Registry – The Linguistic Registry is a data base used to support medium-level and high-level understanding of agent communications. It registers 1) languages and 2) vocabularies (i.e., ontologies). It does not itself keep all of the information about the languages and vocabularies; rather, it keeps track of which languages are known and which AMP services know these languages. This is important because we expect that various itinerant agents may represent their goals, facts, and rules in different high-level languages. The Linguistic Registry's purpose can be viewed in terms of the paradigm of the DARPA Knowledge Sharing Effort approach (recall the section on "Knowledge Representation Languages," especially Ontolingua). There, a prime focus is support for multiple agent communication languages and vocabularies. Other components of the itinerant agent framework, such as the Concierge, employ the Linguistic Registry to help them find the information needed to understand and converse with particular agents. One scenario: an incoming agent describes in KQML its topmost-level goal ("performative" in KQML), and names its language and vocabulary via KQML parameters. The Concierge consults the Linguistic Registry and discovers that this AMP does not know the vocabulary the agent needs. The Concierge finally tenders its regrets to the agent: in effect, "sorry, I can't meet your basic needs."

Deep Request Handler – The Deep Request Handler helps the Shallow Request Handler deal with more special or difficult requests. It maps a request by an agent into one or more service destinations, which may be another (non-agent) service or another agent, either in this same AMP or at a remote server. The Deep Request Handler provides, in effect, an extended directory service. It can be viewed as a kind of facilitator, and hence as itself a kind of agent. An interesting case occurs when the service destination is another agent that performs a similar task, i.e., a facilitator agent. Generally, an alternative aspect of the Deep Request Handler is the provision of a "social directory" of other agents, which may include their identities, interests, languages (vocabularies), and addresses.

The Deep Request Handler is oriented toward requests provided in the form of a description. This description might be partial, such as, "I'd like to talk to a travel agent who handles international airplane flights." The Deep Request Handler matches service request descriptions to its knowledge of available services. This process might involve, for example, inferencing over a specialized knowledge base of facts and rules describing available services.

The Deep Request Handler translates and reformulates the request, perhaps using inferencing, into one that can be executed via a (list of) destination(s). To do so, it employs the language and vocabulary information obtained with the assistance of the Linguistic Registry. The Deep Request Handler may itself call upon other services or agents to help. These agents are special-purpose intelligent agents that are domain-specific.

Information access is an important category of request. Descriptions of information resources, at the level of data base schemas and associated conceptual hierarchies, are thus an interesting kind of knowledge base the Deep Request Handler might employ.

More examples of requests fielded by the Deep Request Handler include:

- "I want a printer that can handle Viceroy 4000 format and has more than 300 dpi."
- "Tell me the other participants in the ongoing automobile auction being held at this AMP."
- "Tell the other auction participants about my identity and interests."
- "Give me the list of any other agents who have the goal of buying or selling DOS-compatible double-speed CD-ROM drives."
- "I want to subscribe to the Refrigerator Today news service."
- "I want to append to the Refrigerator Today news service."
- "I want to publish Refrigerator Today as a news service on a major public network."

Resource Manager – The Resource Manager serves two primary purposes. It acts as a registry for all of the active agents within the AMP and the resources associated with these agents. It also serves as the focus for managing the use of resources within the AMP. It is where an agent's current resource allocation is stored. As components within the AMP perform services for the agent, the cost of these services is deducted from the resources available to the agent. By its nature, access to the Resource Manager must be strictly limited to those trusted components of the AMP that deal with allocating and managing agent resources. The current allocation any agent has may be determined by that agent, but the allocation can only be increased through trusted interfaces. The Resource Manager can also act as a firebreak against the excessive use of resources by agents. Either the total permitted resources can be limited, or the rate at which the resources are consumed can be controlled.

The Resource Manager serves two primary purposes. It acts as a registry for all of the active agents within the AMP and the resources associated with these agents. It also serves as the focus for managing the use of resources within the AMP.

Agent Execution Environments – These are execution environments that have registered with the AMP, offering to interpret scripts or agents whose encoding they support. In addition to registering their named environment with the meeting point, the Agent Execution Environments must provide access to the base facilities of the agent meeting point. This includes access to all of the exported object encapsulations. An Agent Execution Environment can couple into the AMP at several levels. A full-function coupling would include registering not only the ability to accept agents to execute, but individual objects and scripts that have suspended themselves during execution. Based on which services the Execution Environment volunteers, more or less function is available to agents using a specific environment.

Event Delivery Services – Event Delivery Services are concerned with conveying information from services within the agent AMP to agents that have expressed an interest in this information. Event generators can be local services, agents residing within the AMP, or programs coupled to the AMP through the underlying network. Event generators register the type of event they deliver to Event Delivery Services through the Shallow Request Handler. The event they are delivering is described so that agents may search for available events. Agents add entries to the Event Delivery Services through the Shallow Request Handler (possibly with the assistance of the Deep Request Handler and the Linguistic Registry). Once a request for event delivery has been set up, the Event Delivery Services act as the focal point for distributing events to all interested parties.

Agent Status Services – As agents traverse the network of servers, they require mechanisms that track their progress and possibly report back to their origin. The Agent Status Services component provides a set of services that enable agents entering or leaving the AMP to log some significant aspect of its activities at this AMP. This log may include information associated with the agent's arrival, its success at instantiating itself, and the transactions it conducted. The AMP also uses the Agent Status Services to report failures and errors to the originating AMP.

It is difficult to exaggerate the value and importance of security in an itinerant agent environment. While the availability of strong security features would not make itinerant agents immediately appealing, the absence of security would certainly make itinerant agents very unattractive.

Agents can register their controlling AMP within their passport and request that the Agent Status Service provide reports to this controller. The controlling AMP then receives reports about the progress of the agent as it traverses the network. Further, as subordinate agents are spawned by an agent, they can register to either the local AMP (which can be asked to perform status forwarding) or at the controlling AMP.

The Agent Status Services are responsible for providing persistent storage of status reports and attempting reliable delivery of status reports to the controlling AMP. By relieving the agents of the need to embed the support needed to provide these services, the writing of reliable agents is significantly simplified.

Itinerant Agent Arrival and Departure

In this section we will walk through the steps that occur when an itinerant agent arrives at or departs from an AMP. The flow of an agent will be followed from its arrival through a Communication Portal, to the Concierge as shown in Fig. 4. The actions taken by the Concierge will be described, followed by the instantiation of the agent's parts, and the initial execution of the agent.

We will then walk through the inverse scenario, of taking a running agent, building a package of its parts, and dispatching it to another AMP.

Agent Arrival

The itinerant agent's arrival proceeds in the following steps:

1) Encapsulated Agent Processing — The agent arrives through a Communications Portal. At this point, the agent is wrapped in headers associated with the communications channel. The Communications Portal is responsible for fully receiving the agent and assembling it. Once assembled, the agent is then passed to the Concierge.

2a) Agent Authentication — The initial step by the AMP's Concierge consists of origin authentication,[5] data integrity check, and optional decryption of the agent's body.

Origin authentication is obtained by verifying the certificate included in the agent passport. A data integrity check is performed by computing a strong (publicly known) one-way function over the agent's body and matching against the corresponding value found in the agent passport. (This implies that the passport itself "or portions thereof" must be digitally signed by the originator.) The body of the agent can be optionally encrypted in transit. The originator needs only to encrypt for the first-hop AMP. Thereafter, each AMP can encrypt the agent under the next-hop AMP's key as it gets ready to perform agent hand-off. Alternatively, if the originator knows the exact path beforehand, it can encrypt an individual copy of the agent for each AMP in the path.[6]

In addition to its body (the executable component) the agent may carry some *appendages* in the form of information it collects from the visited AMPs. These appendages must be encrypted and/or integrity-protected individually by the AMPs that contribute them. Moreover, to protect against malicious AMPs tearing off other AMPs' information, agent hand-off between any two AMPs can be handled in such a way as to provide a reliable trace of the agent's state at every point in its itinerary. Next, the Concierge builds a local credential for the agent in the form of an *Access Control Factor*, which will be applied to all requests from the agent to use services within the AMP.

2b) Agent Registering — Once the basic agent authentication is complete, the Concierge builds a status block for the agent and registers it with the Resource Manager. This block becomes the anchor for all information about the agent while it resides within the AMP.

2c) Resource Matching — Once the basic authentication is complete, the Concierge examines the table of contents describing the parts of the agent. Each element in the TOC is passed to the Shallow Request Handler, which matches requests expressed in the native language of the AMP. It passes more exotic requests to the Deep Request Handler. The Concierge receives two collections, one of mapped elements, one of unavailable elements. It then determines if all the required elements are available, performing a graceful error delivery if not.

2d) Component Distribution — The agent's elements are then routed to the service elements that support them and control is passed to one or more of the agent's parts. Each part is passed to the support element with a collection of handles to the other parts of the agent. Each part is also passed a number of handles to other useful objects. These include the agent's *goal and status object*, the local AMP's name, and the agent's passport object.

3) Agent Execution — After instantiating all of the parts of the agent, one part, identified in

---

[5] *Agent authentication, data integrity, and other security issues are discussed in greater detail in the next section.*

[6] *Obviously, this is not very efficient.*

the agent's TOC, begins executing. This will most likely be the procedural portion of the agent, which choreographs the execution of the agent's overall mission. This central component of the agent may have suspended its execution at a previous AMP and will need to have its execution state restored to continue its execution. In this case, the execution state, which would have been stored as one of the agent's components and identified in the TOC, will be restored.

Agent Departure

The inverse of an agent's arrival at an AMP is its departure. In this case, we start with a set of components running within the AMP. Each component must be stopped, stored in a transportable form, and added to a package. In order to transport the package from AMP to AMP, the package may need to be encrypted. At a minimum, the body will be sealed for data integrity checking and the passport signed by the AMP.

Any event registrations performed by the agent are removed, and the status block for the agent is updated. The Access Control Factor issued for the agent is revoked and its status block deleted. Upon successful delivery to a Communications Portal, the Concierge will update the agent's status management information, and write a log record recording the agent's passage through the AMP.

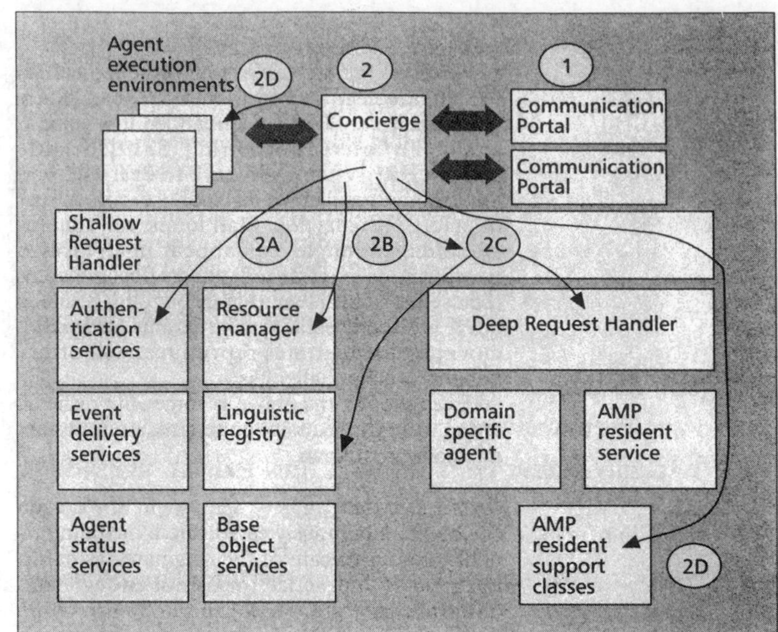

■ **Figure 4.** *Agent arrival.*

Security Issues

It is difficult to exaggerate the value and importance of security in an itinerant agent environment. It is, without a doubt, one of the cornerstone issues. While the availability of strong security features would not make itinerant agents immediately appealing, the absence of security would certainly make itinerant agents very unattractive. This section presents a brief overview of the basic security issues and concerns. More detailed treatments, concentrating on some of the new issues that arise in agent-based and highly distributed systems, may be found in [1, 9].

The most fundamental security building block in an itinerant agent environment is the digital signature. Digital signatures are typically associated with public key cryptography.[7] The best known and most popular method of obtaining digital signatures is the RSA public key cryptosystem [27].

Very germane to public-key-based digital signatures is the concept of universal certification of all potential *signers* — the users that originate agents as well as the AMPs that execute them. Universal certification is a lengthy and cumbersome process, mostly because it involves the establishment of a global certification hierarchy similar to that in the electronic mail milieu. (Privacy-Enhanced Mail (PEM) [20] is a case in point.) The good news is that certification hierarchies have been springing up in the last few years and there is no need to create a new hierarchy for the purpose of itinerant agents. A single certification hierarchy and one general certificate per entity[8] should be enough for a number of electronic activities.

Some observations on itinerant agent security:

- It is impossible to hide anything within an agent without the use of cryptography. If part (or all) of an agent is to be private, it has to be protected cryptographically.
- It is impossible to communicate secretly with a large, anonymous group of potential AMPs. This is, essentially, an issue of scale. One of the most appealing features of itinerant agents is their potential for seamless roaming of the global Internet (or a comparable internetwork), which contains a large and dynamic population of AMPs. An itinerant agent of the future is likely to visit a large number of AMPs.
- It is impossible to *prevent* agent tampering unless trusted (and tamper-resistant) hardware is available in AMPs. Without such hardware, a malicious AMP can always modify/manipulate the agent. If every AMP is equipped with, say, a general-purpose trusted processor, only agents that bear valid and recognizable credentials (certificates) and signatures would be allowed to execute. Currently tamper-resistant hardware and the enabling software are expensive and not readily available. Nonetheless, this is an area of active research (see, for example, [24]) and if it proves useful in agent-based computing, economies of scale will drive the prices down.
- It is impossible to verify with complete certainty that an arbitrary program (such as an incoming agent) is not a virus [8]. In practice, the problem of writing a program that can verify the correct (or even simply non-malicious) behavior of another program is unsolved. In general, the more an agent travels from environment to environment, the more opportunities there will be for tampering; trusting an agent means trusting every program that ever had write access to it, and (therefore) every program that ever had write access to any of them, and so on transitively. Well designed access controls and hierarchical authentication services will reduce the danger, but these issues of trust will have to be addressed in designing AMP controls

[7] *Albeit, not all public key methods are amenable to digital signatures.*

[8] *This entity may be an amalgam of the user, the AMP, and an organization.*

and agent abilities.

• Even agent strategies that seem logical and benign, if considered by themselves, can lead to undesirable results when embedded in a complex and highly interactive world [18, 19]. Security and integrity systems will have to deal with both innocent and malicious instances of various sorts of emergent behavior. Mail loops, the simplest and oldest example, can appear in an array of new forms as transmitted objects become active themselves. This is an area of ongoing research, but it is already clear that programs designed to move, and sometimes reproduce, will offer a number of new challenges.

Even though the above is somewhat disheartening, certain security goals are, nonetheless, attainable as follows.

Origin Authentication – The origin of the agent can be unambiguously established, including the public key certificate of the originator as part of the agent. (In practice this is not enough since data integrity goes hand in hand with origin authentication. In other words, the entire agent must be signed and integrity-protected.)

Data Integrity – The body (executable code) of the agent can be integrity-protected, thus allowing for after-the-fact *detection* of tampering. For example, a malicious AMP receives a *shopping* agent that specifies a ceiling of $400 for an airline ticket. The AMP cheats and ups the ceiling to $500. However, since it cannot produce a corresponding agent integrity check (computed with the aid of digital signatures), the originator can subsequently refuse to pay.

Since one of the esthetically appealing features of itinerant agents is precisely the freedom of movement, it is unrealistic to expect all agents to be launched with a set itinerary. The bottom line is the fundamental trade-off between the security advantages of fixed itineraries and the flexibility of free roaming.

Access/Itinerary Control – The number and the identity of the AMPs can be restricted. The originator can explicitly specify (or otherwise restrict) the AMPs allowed to execute its agent. This is, of course, meaningful only if the agent is protected from tampering (if the agent includes a strong integrity-checking mechanism.) Also, access control by explicit naming is not very desirable, since — as mentioned above — this severely handicaps the notion of a free-roaming agent. Consequently, it is more likely that access control (or policy) will be more coarsely grained, e.g., by attributes such as computing power, occupancy level, organizational affiliation, and pricing, to name a few.

Agent's Privacy – As alluded to above, it is impossible to keep an agent private unless its itinerary is known in advance. (In the latter case, the agent code can be wrapped up and delivered as multi-destination secure e-mail, as in PEM [20].) Since one of the esthetically appealing features of itinerant agents is precisely the freedom of movement, it is unrealistic to expect all agents to be launched with a set itinerary. The bottom-line is the fundamental trade-off between the security advantages of fixed itineraries and the flexibility of free roaming.

Privacy and Integrity of Gathered Information – An agent's foremost task is to gather information, and the privacy of this information is perhaps of greater concern than the privacy of the agent's code. We identify two modes of information gathering: *stateless* and *stateful*. The former means that an agent intermittently sends parcels of acquired information *home* to its originator. In the extreme case, the agent sends the information home at every hop. In the stateful mode, the gathered information is attached in some way to the agent (the amount of carried information grows), but it is only delivered to the originator upon the agent's eventual return.

Protecting information in the stateless mode is not difficult; the AMP currently executing the agent can take care of encrypting/signing and delivering the information to the agent's originator (or someone designated by the originator). Multiple AMPs executing the same agent cannot interfere with one another unless a malicious AMP unduly "terminates" an agent, thus preventing it from migrating to other AMPs.

Stateful mode is similar with respect to information privacy; each AMP can simply attach its own encrypted information to the agent. An AMP may also attach a signed record with hand-off parameters, including the identities of the AMP that the agent was received from, and of the next AMP it was sent to. This allows for subsequent verification of the agent's path, and is commensurate with the added data, the length of which is roughly proportional to the number of AMP hops.

There remains a danger of a group of (at least two) AMPs collaborating to *tear* off information added by a rival AMP. However, this is only a problem if the agent's itinerary is treated as a *loose*, rather than a *strict*, route. (A loose route means that some hops may be omitted; a strict route implies traversal of all hops.) If an itinerary is treated as a strict route, traversal of all hops in the intended order can be securely verified.

In general, an AMP can make use of the itinerary and other signed data attached to an incoming agent to decide on the privileges the agent should have. Some of this information can be made available to other agents, enabling them to determine how much the agent can be trusted. The general AMP architecture can be made flexible enough to support various models of trust.

When an AMP receives a stateless-mode agent, it can verify that the agent program carries a valid signature of the agent's originator. It can thereafter be reasonably confident that the agent expresses the wishes of the originator. Stateful agents, on the other hand, carry not only the agent's body signed by the originator, but also state information. The latter can be signed only by the previously-visited AMP, where the agent reached its current state. In deciding how much to trust a stateful agent, an AMP must consider how much it trusts not only the originator, but also all preceding AMPs.

Discussion and Summary

In previous sections we motivated our work by describing several application models (and some applications) that can, collectively, be best supported by an itinerant agent framework. In this section we discuss some of the technical advantages of our itinerant agent framework, presenting them in the context of a few of the motivations and examples mentioned previously. Much of our initial motivation was derived from the desire to support mobile computers or lightweight devices with their inherent persistence and resource capacity limitations. These limitations and the subsequent benefits of the itinerant agent frameworks are described below. We also describe the framework support for agent and client interaction and present topics for future work.

Framework Support for Mobile Devices

Mobile devices are intermittently connected to a network (or server). Our itinerant agent framework provides the mobile client with the ability to formulate an agent request (possibly while disconnected), launch the agent during a brief connection session, and then immediately disconnect. When launched, the agent would proceed directly to a specified AMP or to a "known" AMP from which it would obtain the address of an AMP suitable to its needs. The Concierge, using the contents of the agent passport, would determine if the initially chosen AMP was suitable. If so, it would execute the agent after creating the environment requested in the agent's table of contents. In the event the AMP was not suitable, the Concierge would take the appropriate action based on the information in the passport. Such action might be to forward the agent to a suitable AMP, determined through its communication portals. The agent's response to the client, if any, is collected during a subsequent connection session.

Because the client may not be connected when the agent's response is ready, the agent may elect to wait at a predetermined AMP until the client is connected. The agent can make use of the Agent Status Services to indicate its status and await an indication from its client. Or it can alert the user to reconnect by using the services of the predetermined AMP to send a "page" to the client. It should be noted that the agent launched by the client can be written in any scripting language, and can communicate in any agent communication language, supported by the AMP. Also, the client may use any of a number of transport services, managed by the AMP, to launch the agent. The framework permits the support of multiple scripting and communication languages. The common abstractions required for interoperation among these communication languages are service descriptions (and other types) handled by the Shallow Request Handler and the Deep Request Handler, together with the Linguistic Registry.

When connected, mobile devices have low-bandwidth, high-latency, high-cost connections. Modems now provide 28.8 kb/s links on dial-up lines, but wireless links above 12 kb/s per client are unlikely to be widely available in this century and have significant usage costs. In this case the technical advantage provided by the framework lies in the ability of an agent to perform both information retrieval and filtering at a server, and to return to the client only the relevant (and reduced) information. In many cases a single agent may also be able to replace several tens of

> *Much of our initial motivation was derived from the desire to support mobile computers or lightweight devices with their inherent persistence and resource capacity limitations.*

remote procedure call messages. The availability of the framework would permit an agent to pose a complex query that can be processed by the Deep Request Handler and the Linguistic Registry, and possibly answered by the AMP Resident Services. This would reduce the volume of data normally sent between the client on the mobile device and the information server.

Mobile devices have limited storage and processing capacity. While there are laptop computers today with 500 MB disks and Intel Pentium™ CPUs, there will always be a class of devices that tries to make do with minimal resources; one example is Hewlett Packard's successful HP 95/100/200™ series, which natively offers only 2 MB of storage. The technical advantage afforded here lies in the ability of an agent to perform retrieval, processing, and filtering at an AMP supporting the information server, and to return to the client only the relevant information. The AMP would provide the agent with all of the necessary tools that could not be supported at the client. These may include an inference engine, a front-end natural language interface to a data base, and other scripts for sorting and presenting the resulting information.

Because of the limited resource capacities in mobile devices, they may not be able to carry detailed information on the various AMPs in the network. Rather, they would launch their agents with high-level descriptions of their goals. They would rely on the Linguistic Registry, the Deep Request Handler, and Communication Portals to determine (possibly through an inference engine) the needed services. They would then access those services, or if necessary, direct the agent to another AMP. When additional services are required by an agent Base Object Services can be used to permit access to them, if available, at other AMPs. The resulting information transmitted to the device is minimized and the device itself does not need to perform any significant filtering or processing.

Framework Support for Agent and Client Interactions

Our itinerant agent framework also permits the AMP to support multiple agent and client interaction models. A few of the many possible interaction models were described in the third section. These include the *Information Dispersal/Retrieval*, the *Collaborative*, and the *Procurement* models, which are instantiated by the use of a facilitator agent[9] and various components of the AMP. Agents resident in the AMP can advertise their services by using the Shallow Request Handler.

Agents who wish to subscribe to a service will add an entry to the Event Delivery Services for that service. A match can then be made between a provider of the service and a subscriber. This match permits us to gather parties interested in a specific model of interaction.

The facilitator agent, which presides over the agent interactions (ensuring that the model is adhered to), executes via the Agent Execution Environment. It uses the Shallow Request Handler and the Event Delivery Services to advertise its services and to access agents interested in its services. Recall (see the previous section) that the facilitator and agent can be written in any supported scripting language and multiple scripting languages may be present in a single interaction.

Our itinerant agent framework permits the secure interaction of agents written in multiple scripting languages, communicating in various agent communication languages, and traveling via multiple transport services in a heterogeneous network.

Client interaction models can be supported by the creation of "personalized services." In these models the AMP supports servers that offer basic APIs and exports them via the Base Object Services for use by itinerant agents. Clients (or other agent authors) then have the freedom to use the server as they see fit. Clients can create agents that act as intermediaries between themselves and a server. As a result, they can present their requests and receive responses in a manner most suitable to them, thereby creating a "personalized" service.

Thus in a procurement model of agent interaction, a user can browse the catalogues of several vendors rather than simply using the client application provided by the vendor. He or she has the freedom to do so by dispatching an itinerant agent to forage the vendor's servers for information relevant to a purchase. The user can then retrieve this information in the desired manner. The client can also create proxy agents at this AMP and send them messages via the Communication Portals. The agents will receive these messages or user requests can then return the appropriate information to the user in the most suitable form.

Aggregate Technical Advantages

In the previous subsection we presented several of the technical advantages provided by our framework. While some subset of these technical advantages may be present in other solutions, collectively the framework provides an overwhelming technical advantage when compared to any currently posed solution. Our itinerant agent framework permits the secure interaction of agents writing in multiple scripting languages, communicating in various agent communication languages, and traveling via multiple transport services in a heterogeneous network.

The framework also supports the use of standardized and non-standard distributed object-oriented frameworks, enabling the support of a variety of execution environments. This support allows client and service providers to write agents in a scripting language of their choice and to interface their legacy systems with proxy agents suited to any interfacing application. The introduction of the Authentication Services provides clients and service providers with access to a variety of authentication and encryption schemes and permits them to use the schemes in any manner suitable for their use.

[9] *Previously mentioned in the section on "Deep Request Handler."*

Summary and Future Work

In this article we present an overview of a prototype framework for the support of itinerant agents. This framework provides a secure facility that can support interaction between agents requiring diverse execution environments, communicating via multiple languages, and traveling via multiple transport services. We motivated this presentation by discussing, in general, several examples of the use of agents and, in detail, an example of a travel reservation scenario.

This initial work addressed several major issues in the area of itinerant agents. While there are some issues that have not been addressed, they are being actively pursued and will be presented in subsequent publications. Several of these future topics have been presented previously, including graphical user interfaces for launching and receiving agents, static agent support, agent status management, and virus control services. Another topic of interest to us is the support of electronic cash services. We believe such services would be of key importance in making network services truly viable.

Acknowledgments

The authors wish to acknowledge the many people who stimulated and contributed to the discussions that resulted in this work. In particular we would like to thank Stephen Brady, Jeff Kephart, Steve White, Robin Williamson, and the OREXX team at Endicott.

References

[1] Emergent Phenomena in Distributed Systems. http://www.research.ibm.com/massdist.

[2] "Middleware to go mobile," *Computerworld*, vol. 29, no. 4, Jan. 1995.

[3] J. K. Boggs, IBM Remote Job Entry Facility: Generalized Subsystem Remote Job Entry Facility, IBM Technical Disclosure Bulletin, 752, Aug. 1973.

[4] N. Borenstein and N. Freed, MIME (Multipurpose Internet Mail Extensions), Internet RFC 1521, 1993.

[5] H. Chalupsky *et al.*, An overview of KQML: A knowledge query and manipulation language, Technical report, April 1992.

[6] D. M. Chess, C. G. Harrison, and A. Kershenbaum, "Mobile agents: Are they a good idea?" IBM Research Report, RC 19887, Oct. 1994.

[7] S. Chokhani, "Toward a national public key infrastructure," *IEEE Commun. Mag.*, vol. 32. no. 9, Sept. 1994, pp. 70-74.

[8] F. Cohen, "Computer Viruses: Theory and Experiment,"

Computers and Security, vol. 6, 1987, pp. 22-35.

[9] L. Hoffman, ed., Rogue Programs: Viruses Worms and Trojan Horses, (Van Nostrand Reinhold, New York, 1990).

[10] M. Crowley-Milling *et al.*, "The Nodal System for the SPS," CERN, 1978, pp. 78-87.

[11] T. Finin *et al.*, "KQML as an Agent Communication Language." *Proc. of the Third International Conference on Information and Knowledge Management (CIKM '94)*, (ACM Press, Nov. 1994).

[12] T. Finin *et al.*, "External Interfaces Working Group of the DARPA Knowledge Sharing Effort, Specification of the KQML Agent-Communication Language plus example agent policies and architectures," Technical report, Working paper, June 1993.

[13] M. R. Genesereth and R. E. Fikes, Knowledge Interchange Format Version 3.0 Reference Manual, Technical report, Stanford University, Technical Report Logic-92-1, Jan. 1992.

[14] Object Management Group. Common Object Request Broker Architecture and Specifications. Document number 91.12.1, vol. 1, no. 1.

[15] T. R. Gruber, "A translation approach to portable ontology specifications," *Knowledge Acquisition*, vol. 5, no. 2, 1993, pp. 199-220.

[16] T. R. Gruber "Ontolingua overview (World Wide Web home page)," Technical report, Stanford University, Knowledge Systems Laboratory, 1995. Hypertext document on World-Wide-Web: URL http://www-ksl.stanford.edu/knowledge-sharing/ontolingua/index.html.

[17] L. J. Haisting, EDI: A New Way of Doing Business, (St. Paul Software, St. Paul, MN, 1993).

[18] J. Kephart, T. Hogg, and B. Huberman, "Collective behavior of predictive agents," *Physica D*, 42, 1990.

[19] J. Kephart, T. Hogg, and B. A. Huberman, "Can predictive agents prevent chaos?" Economics and Cognitive Science, (Pergamon Press, Oxford, 1991).

[20] J. Linn *et al.*, Privacy enhancement for internet electronic mail: Parts i-iv. Internet RFC 1421-1424, 1993.

[21] Sun Microsystems, The HotJava Browser: A white paper, (White Paper, 1995).

[22] R. Neches *et al.*, "Enabling technology for knowledge sharing," *AI Magazine*, vol. 12, no. 3, Sept. 1991.

[23] J. K. Ousterhout, TcL and the Tk toolkit, (Addison-Wesley Publication Company, 1994).

[24] E. Palmer, "An Introduction to Citadel: a secure crypto coprocessor for workstations," *Proc. IFIP SEC '94 Conference*, Curacao, Dutch Antilles, May 1994. 21

[25] R. Patil *et al.*, The DARPA Knowledge Sharing Effort: Progress Report, *Proc. of the Third Int'l Conf. on Principles of Knowledge Representation and Reasoning*, Morgan Kaufmann, San Francisco, CA., Nov. 1992.

[26] J. B. Postel, SMTP (Simple Mail Transport Protocol), Internet RFC 821, 1982.

[27] R. Rivest *et al.*, "A method for obtaining digital signatures and public-key crypto-systems," CACM, vol. 21, no. 2, 1978.

[28] J. S. Rosenschein and G. Zlotkin, Rules of Encounter, (The MIT Press, 1994).

[29] J. E. White, Telescript Technology: The Foundation for the Electronic Marketplace, (General Magic Inc., Mountain View, CA, 1994).

Biographies

DAVID M. CHESS joined IBM at the T. J. Watson Research Center in 1981. He has done work in VM performance management, large-scale computer conferencing, host-workstation cooperative processing, genetic algorithms, and computer security. He is currently a research staff member in the High Integrity Computing Laboratory, concentrating on computer virus protection and the implications of self-replicating phenomena for distributed systems, and a member of the R&D team for IBM AntiVirus. He holds a degree in philosophy from Princeton University, and in computer science from Pace University.

BENJAMIN GROSOF has worked at IBM Research since 1988, primarily on the intersection of knowledge representation and software engineering. Currently, he leads a project on Intelligent Agents, designing personalized information managers and matchmaker software intelfaces for a variety of applications. His interests also include machine learning, delault and probabilistic reasoning, and business process reengineering. He received a B..A. from Harvard in 1980 and a Ph.D. in computer science from Stanford in1993.

The introduction of the Authentication Services provides clients and service providers with access to a variety of authentication and encryption schemes and permits them to use the schemes in any manner suitable for their use.

COLIN HARRISON studied Electrical Engineering at the Imperial College of Science and Technology at the University of London and at Ludwig Maximilians University, Munich. He obtained his Ph.D. in 1973 for studies of micromagnetic structures in thin single-crystals of nickel. He joined the IBM General Products Division in 1979 in San Jose to work on detector problems for magnetic bubble memories. During 1981-87 he lead a research project for IBM Instruments, Inc. and IBM Federal Systems Division in the area of medical imaging. He joined the Research division in 1988 in the ACE multiprocessor workstation project and was one of the instigators of the development of portable computers with handwriting input and wireless communications. This lead in 1992 to the PC Vision view of future experiences of personal computing.During 1992-93 he was on assignment at the IBM Zurich Research Laboratory, where he was an architect of the IBM Intelligent Communication Services platform. In 1994 he formed the Networked Services group to perform research in the area of of intelligent agents and Smart Networks. In October 1994 he took over management of the Communication Systems group, which is currently working on the delivery of interactive multimedia services over CATV and on developing designs for high bandwidth adapters; the Networked Applications Architecture group, which is participating in the development of Intelligent Transportation Systems and a TINA Distributed Processing Environment; and the Communications Microelectronics group, which designs high-performance protocol engines. He is personally leading a project to develop a standard for a residential communications gateway. He spent several years at CERN in Switzerland building the SPS accelerator and with EMI Central Research Laboratories in England inventing magnetic resonance imaging.

DAVID W. LEVINE received a B.A. in computer science from Brandeis University in 1985. He is currently working on an M.S. in computer science at Columbia University. He has worked at IBM Research since 1987. His research interests include complex system design, programming methodology, and managing technology transfer.

COLIN PARRIS received a B.S. from Howard University, and M.S. and Ph.D. degrees from the University of California at Berkeley, all in electrical engineering. He has worked at AT&T Bell Laboratories in Naperville, Illinois for two years on the #5 Electronic Switching System (5ESS) as a member of technical staff (MTS). Since 1994 he has been a research staff member at the IBM T.J. Watson Research Center where his current research interests are distributed systems, integrated services networks, and nomadic computing. His e-mail address is: cjparris@watson.ibm.com.

GENE TSUDIK has been a research staff member at the IBM Zurich Research Laboratory since 1991. He received a B.S. from the University of Houston in 1985, and M.S. and Ph.D. degrees from the University of Southern Californiain 1987 and 1991, respectively. His research interests include network security, electronic commerce, mobile computing, fault-tolerant protocols, and internetwork routing. His e-mail address is: gts@zurich.ibm.com.

Transportable Information Agents

Daniela Rus, Robert Gray, and David Kotz

Department of Computer Science
Dartmouth College
Hanover, NH 03755
{rus,rgray,dfk}@cs.dartmouth.edu

Abstract

Transportable agents are autonomous programs. They can move through a heterogeneous network of computers under their own control, migrating from host to host. They can sense the state of the network, monitor software conditions, and interact with other agents or resources. The network-sensing tools allow our agents to adapt to the network configuration and to navigate under the control of reactive plans. In this paper we describe the design and implementation of the navigation system that gives our agents autonomy. We also discuss the intelligent and adaptive behavior of autonomous agents in distributed information-gathering tasks.

1 Introduction

Modern information systems have data distributed over heterogeneous and unreliable networks. We wish to develop sophisticated methods for browsing, searching, and organizing distributed information systems. Traditional approaches to distributed information access co-locate the data and the computation needed to process it by bringing the data to the computation. We advocate a novel approach that brings the computation to the data in the form of *transportable agents*. A transportable agent is a program that can migrate from machine to machine in a heterogeneous network. Transportable agents have navigation autonomy, that is, they are capable of traveling freely and independently throughout a computer network. This approach requires an agent to have substantial intelligence in making decisions and filtering information.

In this paper we discuss our transportable-agent system called *Agent Tcl* and describe a distributed information-gathering experiment in a network of mobile computers, such as laptops. Mobile computers do not have a permanent connection into the network and are often disconnected for a long period of time. We focus on sensori-computational aspects of the system that allow the agents to observe changes in their world and to navigate adaptively through a network, guided by reactive plans. For example, a user might write a transportable agent for a distributed information-gathering task, launch it from a laptop connected to the Internet in California, and disconnect the laptop. The agent will navigate the Internet autonomously, gathering and organizing information. Some time later, the user might resurface on the Internet in New York, where the laptop is assigned a different IP address. The agent should detect the presence of the laptop on the Internet at the new location and return to it with the search results. The system we describe here permits the quick specification of adaptive autonomous agents for such classes of tasks.

Transportable agents navigate heterogeneous networks under the control of reactive plans that give *adaptation* powers to these agents. We support adaptation with an infrastructure of *network-sensing* modules. Agents can sense hardware conditions (for example, whether a host is connected to the network) or software conditions (for example, a specific change in a database). The systems infrastructure for information processing on mobile computers is described in detail in [GKNRC95].

Transportable agents provide a convenient, effi-

This paper describes research done in the Dartmouth Transportable Agents Laboratory at Dartmouth. This work is supported in part by the Navy and Air Force under contracts ONR N00014-95-1-1204 and AFOSR F49620-93-1-0266. Mark Giles and Dawn Lawrie implemented the virtual yellow-page system. David Hofer and Saurab Nog implemented the network sensors. Katya Pelekhov implemented the Smart server.

To appear in the International Conference on Autonomous Agents, February 1997. Available at the URL
ftp://ftp.cs.dartmouth.edu/pub/kotz/papers/rus:autonomous2.ps.Z

cient, robust, and intelligent paradigm for implementing distributed applications, especially in the context of wireless computing. First, by migrating to the location of an electronic resource, an agent can access the resource locally and eliminate costly data transfers over congested networks. This reduces network traffic, because it is often cheaper to send a small agent to a data source than to send all the intermediate data to the requesting site. Second, the agent does not require a permanent connection to the host machine (*e.g.*, the computer from where an agent is launched). This capability supports distributed information-processing applications on mobile computers. Third, the network-sensing capabilities enable agents to autonomously find the host computer, even when the host changes its geographical location. Our system infrastructure for using mobile agents with mobile computing is described in [GKNRC95]. Fourth, the network software- and hardware-sensing capabilities permit transportable agents to navigate adaptively. Fifth, our transportable agents can communicate with each other even when they do not know their specific locations in the network. Finally, agents have autonomy in decision making: by using feedback from visiting a site, they can independently modify the overall plan or refine ill-specified queries. When combined with communication, decision-making enables our agents to be negotiators. Agent Tcl supports negotiation through an infrastructure of electronic cash, transactions on electronic cash, arbitration on electronic cash transactions, and economic policies for resource control.

Mobile agents provide a simple, adaptive, and unified solution for networking mobile computers and for supporting many distributed systems applications. A good transportable agent system eliminates the need for application-specific solutions, while providing similar performance. Specifically, with such an agent system there is (1) no need for high-level search engines at the remote sites (*e.g.*, the search application); (2) no need for automated installations (*i.e.*, follow-me computing[1]) and (3) no need for distributed applications to build their own control language (*e.g.*, programmable distributed databases.)

2 Previous Work

Kahn's proposal [KC86] about architectures for retrieving information from electronic repositories was the first recognition of the utility of software agents for information processing. It provides context for the issues discussed in this paper. We draw from research results in several distinct areas: operating systems, agents, information retrieval, and mobile robotics.

Although little has been published on transportable agents, much work has been done concerning the general concept of remote computation. Remote Procedure Call (RPC) [BN84] was an early form of remote client-server processing. Falcone [Fal87] discusses a distributed-system in which a programming language provides a remote service interface as an alternative to RPC calls. Stamos and Gifford [SG90] introduce the concept of Remote Evaluation (REV), in which servers are viewed as programmable processors. The Telescript technology introduced by General Magic, Inc. in 1994 was the first commercial description of transportable agents [Whi94]. Prototypes of transportable agent systems exist [KK94, Gra95, Gra96, JRS95, TLKC95]. Telescript has been primarily used in connection with Personal Digital Assistants, network management, active email, electronic commerce, and business process management. The details of how Telescript agents jump between mobile hosts and handle disconnected operations are unclear. The Mobile Service Agent [TLKC95] has been used primarily for "follow-me" computing, and it is less general than our system.

In the software-agents literature, much time and effort has been devoted to designing task-directed agents and to the cognitive aspects of agents. Agents are called *knowbots* by [KC86], *softbots* by [EW94], *sodabots* by [KSC94], *software agents* by [GK94], *personal assistants* by [Mae94, MCF94], and *information agents* by [RS93, RS96]. We are interested in the same class of tasks as [EW94, Mae94, MCF94, KSC94]. Etzioni and Weld [EW94] use classical AI planning techniques to synthesize agents that are Unix shell scripts. Mitchell and Maes [MCF94, Mae94] study the interaction between users and agents and propose statistical and machine-learning methods for building user models to control the agent actions. Rus and Subramanian [RS93, RS96, RS96] propose a modular, open, and customizable agent architecture organized around a notion of structure recognition. In our previous work [Gra95, Gra96, NCK96, GKNRC95, KGR96] we describe other aspects of Agent Tcl.

The analogy between mobile robots in unstructured physical environments and information agents in rich multi-media environments is not just metaphorical. We have observed that the lessons learned in designing task-directed mobile robots [Bro86] can be imported to the problem of distributed information gathering with transportable agents. We also draw from recent

[1] In follow-me computing, a user's applications are sent to her current location so that she may interract with them more effectlively.

results in analyzing the information requirements for robot tasks [DJR93].

3 Transportable Agents

Autonomous agents should move independently. A *transportable agent* is a program that can migrate under its own control from machine to machine in a heterogeneous network. In other words, the program can suspend its execution at an arbitrary point, transport to another machine, and resume execution on the new machine. Transportability is a powerful attribute for information-gathering agents since their world is usually a distributed collection of information resources, each of which can contain tremendous volumes of data. By migrating to the network location of an electronic resource, a transportable agent eliminates all intermediate data transfer and can access the resource efficiently even if the resource provides only low-level primitives for working with its contents. This benefit is particularly great with a low-bandwidth network connection for which moving the data is often infeasible; moving the computation to the data with a transportable agent is a convenient and efficient alternative.

Before transportable agents can be used effectively, several challenges must be met. Most difficulties arise from the fact that we are allowing code to roam at will through a distributed system. The most important issues are to protect machines from malicious agents and agents from malicious machines; to provide effective fault tolerance in the uncertain world of the Internet; to allow programmers to write and debug agents quickly and easily; to make agents almost as efficient as highly tuned, application-specific servers; and to provide a location-independent namespace in which agents can communicate. We are currently addressing these issues.

3.1 Agent Tcl: a system for transportable agents

Agent Tcl [Gra95] reduces migration to a single instruction, provides simple communication among agents, supports multiple languages and transport mechanisms, runs on generic platforms, and provides effective security, fault tolerance and performance. In the current implementation, agents are written in a modified version of the Tool Command Language (Tcl) [Ous94]. Tcl is a high-level scripting language and is an attractive agent language since it is highly portable, easy to use, and easy to make secure (due to the large amount of existing work that addresses the problem of executing a Tcl program from an untrusted source). Our modified version of Tcl is the same as standard Tcl except that the internal state of an executing script (the stack, the contents of variables, etc.) can be captured at an arbitrary point. In addition, the modified version of Tcl provides a special set of commands that allow a Tcl script to migrate and to communicate with other migrating scripts.

Thus, one of our transportable agents is simply a Tcl script that runs in the modified Tcl interpreter and uses the agent commands to roam through a network and interact with other agents. A Tcl script can decide to move to a new machine at any time. It issues the `agent_jump` command, which suspends script execution, captures and packages the internal state of the script, and sends this state image to a *server* on the destination machine (a special server runs on every machine to which transportable agents can be *sent*). The server restores the state image and the Tcl script continues execution on the new machine from the exact point at which it left off. The Tcl scripts can communicate via message passing, or remote procedure call [NCK96]. An agent can use the Tk toolkit to present a graphical user interface on either its home machine or on a remote machine to which it has migrated. In addition, Agent Tcl includes the beginnings of a mechanism for considering economic issues in societies of agents. Agents interact by exchanging electronic cash. Their use of resources is limited by a set of policies for resource control.

4 Sensing

To remain efficient, agents unleashed in the network must operate without continuous contact with their home sites, without user intervention, and despite complications. For example, if the agent was launched from a mobile platform that has since become temporarily disconnected from the network, it must be prepared to proceed on its own rather than waiting an unknown amount of time for the mobile platform to reappear. Complications arise because agents operate in a dynamic and uncertain world. Machines go up and down, the information stored in repositories changes, and the exact sequence of steps needed to complete an information-gathering task is not completely known at the time the agent is launched into the world. Without external state (what the agent can perceive about the state of its world) an autonomous agent is crippled since it has no way of perceiving and adapting to the dynamic changes in its environment. This section elaborates on the "sensors" that allow an agent to discover important information about its environment and to establish its external state. We focus on the following three components of external state: hardware, software, and other agents.

4.1 Sensing the state of the network

Our agents can determine whether a network site is reachable and can predict the expected transit time across the network and the expected processing time at the site. This information allows an agent to adapt to currently unreachable or overloaded sites by visiting other sites first. Smart agents can use information about reachability, network delays, and available bandwidth to intelligently construct routing plans. We have implemented several network sensors:

Local connectivity. This sensor determines whether the local host is physically connected by "pinging" the broadcast address on the local subnet; if there is any response in a short interval, the network is connected.

Site Reachability. This sensor returns true if a specific site is reachable. This is implemented by using the Unix `ping` command.

Network Load. This sensor tests the expected bandwidth to a remote host. It predicts latency by consulting a local table that compiles traffic history information. The table estimates bandwidth for several time ranges: 0-15 seconds; 15-30 seconds; 30 seconds-3 minutes; 3 minutes-2 hours; 2 hours-1 day; 1 day-2 weeks; and 2 weeks and up. The table gets updated incrementally and each category is weighted differently in the computation for the estimate.

4.2 Sensing software changes

Agents are often faced with the problem that a resource is unavailable, does not contain the desired information, or is expected to contain additional relevant information at an unknown point in the future. Depending on the application, the agent might choose to report failure, move to an alternative resource, or wait for the desired resource or information to become available. Our agents use information-retrieval techniques to detect when the state of a software resource has changed. Significant activity on a resource is signaled by an increase in the resource size (detected by looking at the size) or a shift in content (detected by the information-retrieval methods we use in Section 7). Figure 1 shows an agent that monitors a set of files and directories and sends an email message when it senses significant activity on a file. The agent works by creating one child agent for each remote filesystem. Each child monitors one or more directories and sends a message to the parent when there is significant file activity. The parent then contacts the user's mail agent to send the message. Although simplistic, this agent illustrates the general task of waiting for an event to occur and then reacting appropriately, a task that is faced by nearly every agent.

5 Navigation

Agents implemented in Agent Tcl have the ability to move by themselves through a network. But where should they go? Agents need either a partial model or partial knowledge of both the task and the environment. We use an implicit scheme that provides a system of *virtual yellow pages* to help the agents decide where to go. These yellow pages contain listings of services and resources. By consulting these virtual yellow pages and using the network-sensing tools, an agent selects a list of services relevant for its task and formulates adaptive plans to visit some of the sites.

Virtual Yellow Pages. The virtual yellow pages are a distributed database of service locations maintained by a hierarchical set of navigation agents. Services register with the navigation agents that are scattered throughout the system (Figure 2) and manage the yellow pages. Each machine has a specialist agent that knows the location of some of the navigation agents (which in turn know the locations of services and other navigation agents). In general, by consulting the local specialist agent and then visiting one or more navigation agents, an application agent can obtain the necessary list of services and their locations.

Since the information landscape changes, the virtual yellow pages are not static entities. We use adaptive learning methods to keep the virtual yellow pages up to date.

Construction of Virtual Yellow Pages. New services register with one or more navigation agents to advertise their location. They describe their service through a list of keywords. For example, in Figure 2, Service 1 first contacts the specialist agent on its machine to find the location of Navigation Agent 2. Service 1 then sends a registration message to Navigation Agent 2, which adds Service 1 to the database.

Locating Services. An application agent locates a list of navigation agents by querying the specialist agent on the local host (Figure 2). The application agent then consults the navigation agents by providing a list of keywords. The navigation agent returns a list of matching services from its database.

Adaptive selection of the best service. After visiting some of the services, the application agent revisits the navigation agents to provide feedback about the sites (speed of service and usefulness of results). These "consumer reports" enable the navigation agents to learn which services are most useful and to prioritize services accordingly.

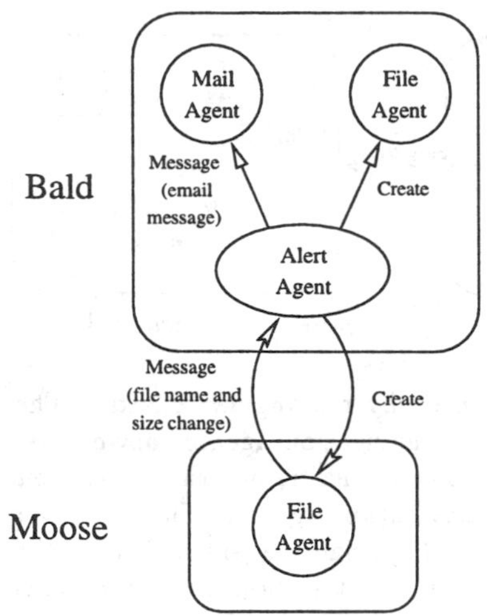


```
set email_agent "bald rgray_email"        # machine and name of email agent
set machines "bald moose"
set directory "~rgray"

  # get a name from the server
agent_begin

  # submit the "file" agents that watch for changes in file size

for each m $machines {
  agent_submit $m -vars directory -proc file_watch {file_watch $directory}
}

  # wait for one of the "file" agents to send a message saying that a
  # file has changed size; then send an alert message to the user by
  # asking the user's email agent to send a message to its owner

while {1} {

  agent_receive code string -blocking
  set alert [construct_alert $string]
  agent_send $email_agent {SEND OWNER $alert}

}
```

Figure 1: The alert agent monitors a set of files and sends an email message to the user when it detects a significant file activity. A simplified version of this agent appears at bottom. The network location of the various agents is shown at top. `file-watch` looks at the size of the file and compares the content of the file against a query or a previous version of the file using information retrieval techniques [Sal91].

As a general policy for identifying the optimal service, we keep the average feedback of each of the service providers. In most cases the navigation agent should recommend the best service it knows. This method converges to the best service in a static system. We consider a dynamic system, where services appear and disappear[2] by augmenting the best-first policy with a method that encourages initial exploration of other agents. The exploration function returns an overly optimistic estimate of the usefulness of a service until the service is explored N times; after that the real average value of the agent is used for ranking. Figure 3(left) shows the performance of two exploration functions in a system where an initial virtual page consists of 5 services, not ranked in any particular order. We ran a simulation in which agents visited the services and returned with feedback on the goodness of the service. Several iterations (about 100) in this experiment, a new and better service (Agent 6) was added. We examined evaluation functions for several values on N. The case $N = 1$ is denoted by Avg, and $N = 5$ is denoted by $High$. Both cases converge to Agent 6.

This algorithm does not take into account that the relative usefulness of an agent may vary over time. One agent may improve on another's service, or it may become outdated or congested. To discover bad services that have radically improved their performance, a small randomization factor is added in the exploration function (see Figure 3(right)). Our experiments with dynamic service landscapes show that the best service is always found, although it may take on the order of 100 trials to converge to it.

Navigation Plans. Agents construct an initial plan, *e.g.*, an ordered sequence of sites, from the information provided by the virtual yellow pages. The agent uses this list to sequentially move from site to site, advancing when the necessary processing at the current site has been completed. The agent might also choose to launch child agents at certain points. The plan of the agent need not be static, however. The agent formulates and reformulates the plan by consulting its sensors and adapting on-line to changes in network configuration and software content. For example, if the plan consists of the sequence A, B, C, D and machine A is sensed to be down while B is sensed to be up, the agent greedily rearranges the sequence to B, A, C, D. Analogously, if the bandwidth to A is much lower than to B, the agent can decide that there is a higher payoff in executing the sequence B, A, C, D, even though A had the first priority.

6 Interaction between agents

Our agents interact by implicit and explicit communication. Implicit communication entails the observation of another agent's changes to the world. Implicit communication is possible in our system because the

[2] When a new service appears in the system it registers with a yellow page. When a service disappears, we use a lazy method to detect it. When an agent is sent to the location of a service that is out of business, the agent comes back to report this finding to the yellow page.

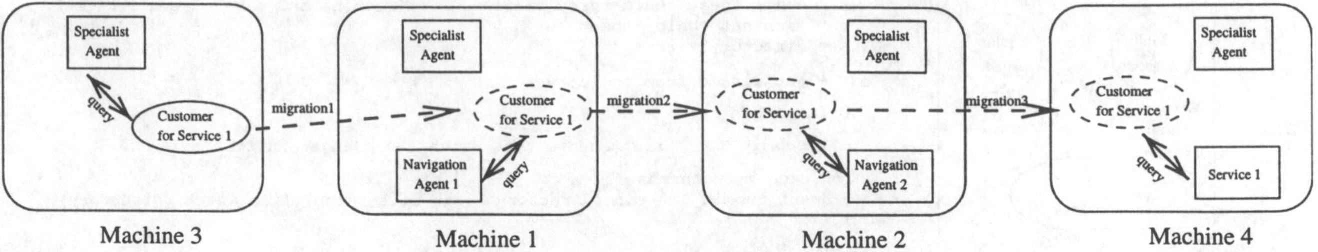

Figure 2: An example of navigation. Each machine has a number of fixed agents (denoted by rectangular blocks.) The *specialist agents* know about the location of one or more *navigation agents*. There are two navigation agents shown here: one on machine 1 and one on machine 2. The navigation agent on machine 2 knows about service 1, but the navigation agent on machine 1 does not. The specialist agent on machine 3 knows about both navigation agents. The *customer agent* on machine 3 uses the following protocol to locate service 1. It first contacts its local specialist agent and finds the location of navigation agents 1 and 2. Then it migrates to machine 1 and queries navigation agent 1 about service 1. This navigation agent does not know about service 1 since service 1 is only registered with navigation agent 2. The customer agent then migrates to machine 2 where it queries navigation agent 2 and finds the location of service 1. Finally, the customer agent migrates to the location of service 1.

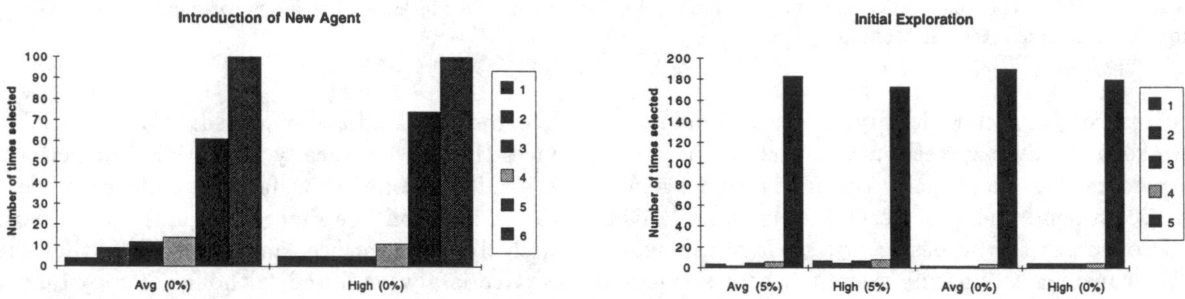

Figure 3: Selection of the best service. The services are listed in an increasing order of "goodness" and they are numbered 1-6 on the right hand side of the diagram. The left graph shows the service selection numbers when a new and better service (Agent 6) is added. The right graph shows the effects of randomization on the service selection numbers.

agents can use their sensors to observe changes in the environment as described in sections 4. Explicit communication is the direct exchange of information between two agents. In our system, two agents residing on the same or different machines can exchange messages and can open a dedicated connection for direct data transfer with the agent commands **agent_send**, **agent_receive**, and **agent_meet**. Agents need to know the current network location of the recipient as well as the unique symbolic name that the recipient has chosen for itself (the servers maintain a list of the agents that are executing on the current machine and keep track of their activity). An agent discovers another agent by using a hardwired name, consulting a specific Agent Tcl server, or consulting a virtual yellow page.

7 Information-Gathering Agents

We have used transportable agents for distributed information access. In distributed information gathering, a distributed collection of corpora is searched based on a query and the results extracted from each site are fused in a coherent picture.

We have built information-gathering agents that interface with the Smart information retrieval system[3]. Our data is a distributed collection of Smart repositories running the Smart system. Each collection consists of computer science technical reports. For a given

[3]The Smart system is a successful statistical information-retrieval system [Sal91] that uses the vector-space model to measure the textual similarity between documents. The idea of the vector-space model is that each word that occurs in a collection defines an axis in the space of all words in the collection. A document is represented as a weighted vector in this space. The premise of this system is that documents that use the same words map to neighboring points and that statistics capture content similarity.

query, an information agent visits a sequence of sites; at each site, it interacts with the local Smart agent to search the local collection. The results retrieved are brought home, or used as relevance feedback to refine the query.

In our experiment, the agent extracts a list of sites (DEC stations, PCs, and SGIs) that run Smart servers by consulting a virtual yellow page. The agent routes itself through the sites using the reactive-planning techniques outlined in Section 5, visiting each place exactly once. The query is run on the local server and a ranked list of documents is returned to the agent. Some simple error-detection and recovery mechanisms are incorporated into this system. If the plan of the agent takes it to a crashed or non-existent site, the error-recovery wrapper around the jump command enables the plan to continue. If the current site is down or on a low bandwidth connection, the agent greedily attempts to go to the next site. In our current implementation, if the Smart server crashes, the agent times out while waiting for the answer and continues the task at the next site. If the site crashes while the agent is there, the agent dies. A sample session from running this information-retrieval agent is shown in Figure 4.

We have extended this experiment using the mobile computer-support functions described in [GKNRC95] as follows. We started the information gathering agent on a laptop computer called Bond, and the agent immediately jumped off the laptop to interact with Smart agents throughout the network. Before the agent could return, we disconnected Bond, carried it to another lab, connected it to a different subnet, and reconfigured it with a new IP address. Meanwhile, the Information Gathering agent had finished its task and had attempted to jump back to Bond. The jump failed so this agent waited on a "dock" computer associated with Bond. When Bond reconnected to the network, it contated the dock, which then forwarded the Information Gathering Agent on to Bond.

8 Summary

We describe a system that implements autonomous software agents and illustrate an application of agents to distributed information gathering. We argue that autonomous agents require mobility and independent decision making. Mobility is an important attribute for dealing with an increasingly networked world. Independent decision making is critical for a mobile agent to adapt to a dynamic environment, especially when far from "home." We implement mobility with transportable programs (agents). As they travel, these agents sense the current network and software conditions and adapt their behavior to the sensed values. Our agents can be viewed as virtual robots that are equipped with virtual sensors and effectors and are capable of maintaining internal state, registering external state, and interacting with their environment.

References

[BN84] A. Birrell and B. Nelson, Implementing remote procedure calls, in *ACM Transactions on Computer Systems*, 2(1):39–59, February 1984.

[Bro86] R. Brooks, A robust layered control system for a mobile robot, in *IEEE Journal of Robotics and Automation*, 1986.

[DJR93] B. Donald, J. Jennings, and D. Rus, Information Invariants for Cooperating Autonomous Mobile Robots, in *Proceedings of the International Symposium on Robotics Research*, 1993.

[DJR94] B. Donald, J. Jennings, and D. Rus. Analyzing Teams of Cooperating Mobile Robots. In *Proceedings of the International Conference on Robotics and Automation*, San Diego, 1994.

[EW94] O. Etzioni and D. Weld, A softbot-based interface to the Internet, in *Communications of the ACM*, 37(7):72–76, 1994.

[Fal87] J. Falcone, A programmable interface language for heterogeneous distributed systems, in *ACM Transactions on Computer Systems*, 5(4):330–351, 1987.

[GK94] M. Genesereth and S. Ketchpel, Software agents, in *Communications of the ACM*, 37(7):48–53, 1994.

[Gra95] R. Gray, Agent Tcl, in Proceedings of the CIKM Workshop on Intelligent Agents, Baltimore, MD, 1995.

[Gra96] R. Gray, Agent Tcl: A transportable agent system, in Proceedings of the Fourth Annual Tcl/Tk Workshop, Monterey, Ca, 1996.

[GKNRC95] R. Gray, D. Kotz, S. Nog, D. Rus, and G. Cybenko, Mobile Agents for Mobile Computing, Technical Report PCS-TR96-285, Department of Computer Science, Dartmouth College, 1996.

[JRS95] D. Johansen, R. van Renesse, and F. Schneider, Operating system support for mobile agents, in *Proceedings of the 5th IEEE Workshop on Hot Topics in Operating Systems*, 1995.

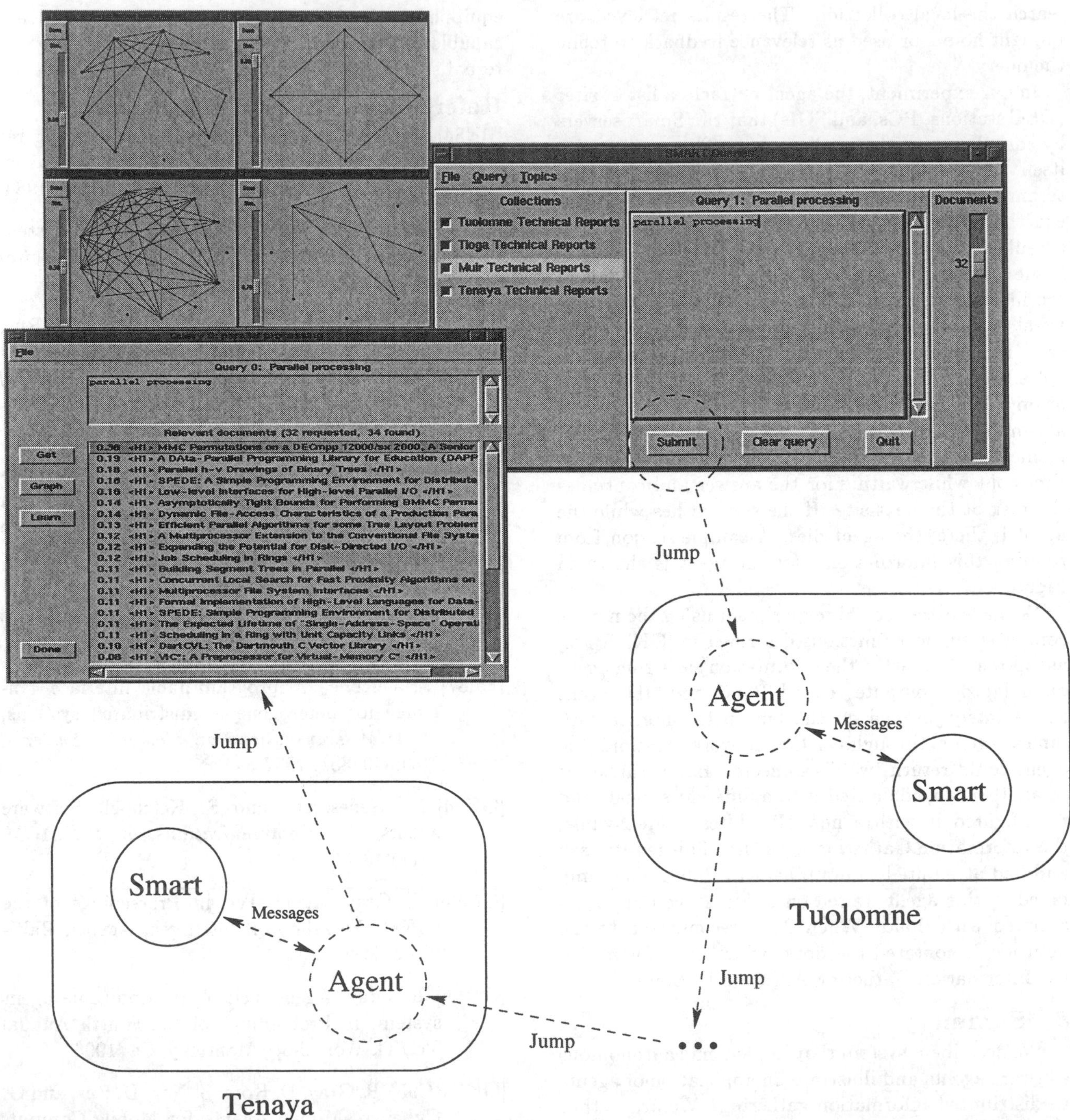

Figure 4: A sample session for the information-retrieval agent. The query screen is shown in the upper right corner of the figure. The agent follows the path described with dotted arrows from the home site to a first document collection on Tuolomne, to a second collection on Tioga, to a third collection on Muir, and finally, to the last collection on Tenaya. The agent returns to the home site and displays the results as (1) a ranked list of titles and (2) four graphs that show the inter-document similarities. The nodes in these graphs represent documents and the edges show similarity connections. The user may click on a node to view the text of the document

[KC86] R. Kahn and V. Cerf, *The World of Knowbots*, report to the Corporation for National Research Initiative, Arlington, VA, 1988.

[KSC94] H. Kautz, B. Selman, and M. Coen, Bottom-up design of software agents, in *Communications of the ACM*, 37(7):143–145, 1994.

[KK94] K. Kotay and D. Kotz, Transportable agents, in *Workshop on Intelligent Information Agents*, December 1994.

[KGR96] D. Kotz, R. Gray, and D. Rus, Transportable Agents Support Worldwide Applications, in Proceedings of SIGOPS96, 1996.

[Mae94] P. Maes, Agents that reduce work and information overload, in *Communications of the ACM*, 37(7):31–40, 1994.

[MCF94] T. Mitchell, R. Caruana, D. Freitag, J. McDermott, and D. Zabowski, Experience with a learning personal assistant, in *Communications of the ACM*, 37(7):81–91, 1994.

[NCK96] S. Nog, S. Chawala, and D. Kotz, An RPC mechanism for transportable agents, Technical Report PCS-TR96-280, Department of Computer Science, Dartmouth College, 1996.

[Ous94] J. Ousterhout, *Tcl and the Tk Toolkit*, in Addison-Wesley, Reading, Massachusetts, 1994.

[RS93] D. Rus and D. Subramanian, Multi-media RISSC Informatics: Retrieving Information with Simple Structural Components, in *Proceedings of the ACM Conference on Information and Knowledge Management*, Nov. 1993.

[RS96] D. Rus and D. Subramanian, Customizing Multimedia Information Access, *ACM Computing Surveys*, vol. 7, no. 4, 1995.

[RS96] D. Rus and D. Subramanian, Customizing Information Access, *ACM Transactions on Information Systems*, January 1997.

[Sal91] G. Salton. The Smart document retrieval project. In *Proceedings of the Fourteenth Annual International ACM/SIGIR Conference on Research and Development in Information Retrieval*, pages 356-358, 1991.

[SG90] J. Stamos and D. Gifford, Remote execution, in *ACM Transactions on Programming Languages and Systems*, 12(4):537–565, October 1990.

[TLKC95] B. Tomsen, L. Leth, F. Knabe, and P-Y. Chevalier, Mobile agents, ECRC external report, European Computer-Industry Research Center, 1995.

[Whi94] J. E. White, Telescript technology: The foundation for the electronic marketplace, General Magic White Paper, General Magic, Inc., 1994.

EMail With A Mind of Its Own:
The Safe-Tcl Language for Enabled Mail

Nathaniel S. Borenstein

First Virtual Holdings, Inc., 25 Washington Avenue, Morristown, NJ 07960, USA
Email: nsb@nsb.fv.com

Abstract

A uniform extension language for email systems can radically extend the utility of electronic mail, simplifying the construction of mail-based services and permitting the delivery of active messages that interact with their recipients and take differential actions based on the recipients' responses. This paper describes such a language, Safe-Tcl, including the strong security and portability constraints it has to satisfy, and outlines its fundamental design.

Keyword Codes: C.2.4, D.3.2, H.4.3
Keywords: Distributed Systems, Programming Language Classifications, Communications Applications

I. The Dream of Enabled Mail

The phrase "enabled mail" encompasses several technologies that share the common goal of significantly increasing the power and utility of electronic mail systems. Enabled mail, in general, is the augmenting of electronic mail systems by the introduction of computational power at several key points in the electronic mail process. Many existing systems offer such power in some places, but the power is incomplete, non-uniform, and suffers from a lack of interoperability across platforms and tools.

A conceptual model for the introduction of computational power in email systems is given in [13]. Specifically, the general email model is enhanced by viewing the delivery process as consisting of three distinct phases: First, "delivery-time", which occurs immediately before the message crosses the delivery slot, and in which the message is still conceptually under the control of the sender; Second, "receipt-time", which occurs immediately after the message crosses the delivery slot; and, finally, "activation-time", which occurs whenever the recipient processes the message. This model provides an abstract framework for considering various uses of computational technology to provide enabled mail.

The types of enabled mail most commonly found in existing system allow users to specify customized computational processes to be executed upon the receipt of a mail message, or upon the incorporation of a message into a user's message store. Various mail systems offer extremely powerful languages for this type of functionality. Because this functionality is largely incorporated within a single software suite, the fact that each of these systems uses a different language and model is only a minor nuisance, particularly for those attempting to switch between different mail systems.

Less common, and more of a radical break for most users and implementors, is the notion of "active" mail. Traditionally, electronic mail has been a passive, unidirectional medium. Even multimedia mail [1, 2, 3] has operated this way -- mail messages contain text that is displayed to the user, images that are shown to the user, audio that is played for the user, and so on, but the process is traditionally one-way and non-interactive. In active mail, a message contains a program to be executed when the recipient reads the message. Such a message can potentially perform arbitrarily complex interactions, vastly increasing the scope and utility of electronic mail. Active mail has hitherto been largely confined to experimental research software, due to problems of security, portability and standardization. [1,7,8,9] Recent research [10] has demonstrated workable solutions to the security and portability problems, making the time ripe to consider the wider deployment and eventual standardization of a language for active mail. In the area of active mail, convergence on a single language is critical, because email that does not interoperate in a cross-platform manner is of extremely limited utility.

Recently, the author and a colleague, Marshall Rose, have published a draft specification of a model for enabled mail, clarifying the conceptual roles of the various places in the email process where computation can augment the email process. [13] Additionally, we have published a specification and public-domain implementation for a language, Safe-Tcl, that we believe can serve as a uniform, cross-platform engine for all of these kinds of mail-enabling computation [14]. While standardization is more important for some aspects of enabled mail (notably active mail) than for others, there is much to be gained from using a uniform language at all phases of the enabled-mail process. We have based our language on Tcl [4, 5, 6], a language that was explicitly designed to be embedded as a computational extension to a larger application. Aside from our highly subjective judgment that Tcl is a very well-designed language for such purposes, Tcl has the virtue of being simple, well-defined, and available in a high-quality, extremely portable public domain implementation.

The choice of Tcl as a base language provides the basic syntax and many of the primitives for an enabled mail language, but vanilla Tcl is not itself suitable for enabled mail. The design of a language for enabled mail involves a complex combination of constraints. For some parts of the computation, where the program comes entirely from a trusted source (such as the user on behalf of whom it is executing), any sufficiently powerful and well-defined language would probably suffice, especially if augmented with messaging-specific features. The most severe constraints come from the active mail case, where security, interface portability, and cross-platform availability are absolutely critical.

The remainder of this paper is structured in two parts. First, we outline the problems inherent in the design of a language for enabled mail. Then, we describe the Safe-Tcl language and how it solves these problems. Concluding sections discuss the current status, availability and future prospects for the Safe-Tcl language in particular and enabled mail in general.

II. The Key Problems: Designing a Language for Enabled Mail

As stated previously, some types of enabled mail, such as programs to filter incoming mail, can be provided in almost any general-purpose programming language. To provide a uniform language for all phases of the enabled mail process, however, special attention must be paid to the "worst case" -- active mail. In active mail, any electronic mail user can send a program to any other electronic mail user, to be executed in the recipient's environment. This raises several severe constraints which must be addressed in the design of an enabled mail language.

Security

The most critical constraint for active mail is security. Simply put, it must be possible to read a message from your mortal enemy without that message doing you any harm. The use of an arbitrarily powerful programming language in this role would be completely unacceptable, as it would allow malicious users to send email messages that deleted the recipient's files, stole confidential information and mailed it elsewhere, forged email impersonating the email recipient, or caused any number of other kinds of mischief.

Fortunately, recent research [10] has demonstrated that a language for active mail can be suitably restricted and constrained to do no such harm. The details are beyond the scope of this paper, but the basic idea is quite simple: you simple remove from the language any features that can be used to do harm, and then augment the resulting, impoverished language with less general primitives that provide a safe subset of the removed functionality. For example, you might remove the general-purpose mechanisms for reading and writing files, but replace it with new primitives that only allow limited operations on a specific set of "public" files.

When the solution is framed in these terms, it is clear that, with sufficient attention to some subtle details, a language can be made safe for widespread active mail use. What is probably less clear is that such a language will retain sufficient power to be broadly useful.

Power

After an active mail language is made safe, the question of the language's power becomes important. Previous active messaging systems either left the burden of security entirely to the user [1], sidestepped it by restricting all computation to a trusted environment, which doesn't scale to the most general email networks [7, 9], or restricted the language so severely as to fundamentally prohibit certain classes of potential applications [10].

The fundamental problem is that the most dangerous primitives, where active messaging is concerned, tend to be the most general primitives. The process of making a language safe for active messaging consists largely of replacing general primitives with more specialized safe primitives. Inevitably, the resulting loss of expressive power handicaps the creation of certain applications, particularly those applications not anticipated by the language designers.

Extensibility

The obvious solution to the problem of insufficient power in an active messaging language is to simply add more specialized safe primitives as needed. This, however, is a challenging idea when applied to the whole universe of email systems. Upgrading all systems to support the new primitives, however safe they might be, will generally be so difficult that it rarely happens. The biggest innovation that Safe-Tcl has over previous active messaging languages (such as ATOMICMAIL) is its extension model, which makes it plausible to grow the system's functionality in a safe evolutionary manner.

Missing from all previous active messaging systems is any systemic support for the distributed maintenance and evolution of the set of known safe primitives. In all such systems of which the author is aware, the only way to extend the language in a manner that augments its fundamental power (as opposed to simply defining new procedures using the existing primitives, which provides conceptual and computational convenience but no real increase in power) is to recompile the language interpreter itself, typically a major enterprise. Ideally, an active messaging language should provide some simple mechanism by which users can define specialized operators in an unrestricted environment, and make those specializations alone available to active mail programs.

Authentication

Once the ability for users to provide power-augmenting extensions is provided, the issue of authentication inevitably arises. For many applications, users will want to define actions that are available only for active messages from certain trusted senders. Trusting the mail headers is dangerously naive in this regard, as mail is trivial to forge in most environments. This implies that the ideal active messaging language would have the ability to understand and validate authenticated mail (using such technology as Privacy Enhanced Mail (PEM) [11] or Pretty Good Privacy (PGP) [12]). Such capabilities have not been available in any previous systems for active messaging.

Interface Portability

The notion of portability is of obvious importance to a language for enabled mail, as it will have to run on the widest imaginable variety of computing platforms. When most people think of portability, however, they tend to think primarily about the issues involved in writing portable software. While these issues are as important to enabled mail as they are to any other multiplatform application, there is an even harder issue for active mail, that of user interface portability.

The problem is that the sender of an active mail message will not, in the general case, have any knowledge about the type of computing platform or platforms on which his message will be read. This means that he cannot write programs for a particular user interface model such as that provide by Windows, the Macintosh, X11, or a teletype. The program must be written and delivered without any knowledge about the environment in which it will interact with the user.

Previous research active mail systems typically ignored this issue entirely, generally focusing on providing a single-platform active mail, which was rightly perceived as "hard enough". The ATOMICMAIL system [10] was the first to provide any kind of solution to this problem. In ATOMICMAIL, all user interaction took place via abstract primitives such as "get a string from the user" or "ask the user a multiple choice question". The implementation of these primitives varied significantly on the supported platforms (Macintosh, X11, smart terminals, and teletypes), but this variation was invisible to ATOMICMAIL programs, which simply knew, for example, that they had asked the user a multiple choice question and somehow gotten an answer. ATOMICMAIL thus demonstrated that it was conceptually possible to write interactive programs that were entirely ignorant and independent of the user interface platform on which they would be executed.

Interface Quality

Unfortunately, ATOMICMAIL's solution to the problem of user interface portability led directly to another problem, that of interface quality. ATOMICMAIL was generally perceived as solving the portability program by making it possible to produce programs that would have a user interface that was uniformly terrible on a wide variety of platforms.

The problem was that ATOMICMAIL's abstractions constituted a Procrustean bed into which all interactive applications had to be made to fit. An ATOMICMAIL program might be running in the world's most sophisticated user interface environment, but it couldn't exploit that power in any way other than to use the world's most sophisticated implementation of "ask the user a multiple choice question". In particular, it was impossible to develop a modern event-driven program with this model.

To succeed with a broad base of casual users, an active messaging language must provide some way to write programs with better user interfaces, without sacrificing the portability demonstrated by ATOMICMAIL.

III. The Safe-Tcl Language

With a solid history of experimental and proprietary technologies demonstrated for various aspects of Enabled Mail, the time seemed right to begin designing a language that would be suitable for all the various aspects of enabled mail. Unlike previous research projects, the goal of this effort was not pure research -- although some interesting problems remained, as described in the previous section -- but rather the development of a language that was good enough to be a candidate for standardization. That the project was begun with this in mind does not imply that the authors think the language should necessarily be standardized as it now stands, nor that it is impossible that a better candidate will appear. Rather, the goal was to produce an enabled mail language that was good enough to initiate a standards process in this area.

In this section we will describe the basic technology of the Safe-Tcl language. A detailed description of the language is beyond the scope of this paper, but may be found in [14].

Tcl and Tk: A "Good Enough" Language Model

The history of standardization efforts shows that there is no such thing as an uncontroversial or simple standard. Indeed, most people don't realize that even such a basic and near-universal standard as ASCII remains the subject of ambiguity and debate. (There are several slightly different things that are considered "ASCII" in different communities; sticklers for detail will always reference a specific standard such as [15].) However, of all the things one might wish to standardize, it is hard to imagine anything more prone to controversy than programming languages. Programming languages come in a very rich diversity and differ widely in their basic syntax, features, and philosophies.

Fortunately, the world does not, in general, need a single standard programming language; applications written in multiple languages can coexist happily on most systems. Unfortunately, in the area of enabled mail, and particularly for active mail, a standard language is essential. It would be unrealistic to expect that there could ever be a single language that satisfied all interested parties. Instead, the goal of the effort that produced Safe-Tcl was to produce a language that was "good enough" for essentially all uses of enabled mail. We knew that the choice of the base language would inevitably be controversial and that some people would hate any language we might choose. It is our hope that those who dislike the language model we settled on will recognize the importance of converging on a single such language, and will try to shape their criticisms constructively, helping to evolve the language by correcting whatever deficiencies they might perceive in it.

The basic language model we chose was Tcl, the Tool Command Language developed by John Ousterhout at the University of California at Berkeley. The great strengths of Tcl, for this application, are:

-- It has an extremely simple, easily learned syntax.
-- It is interpreted rather than compiled.
-- It was explicitly designed to be embedded in larger applications.
-- There is a high quality multi-platform public domain implementation available.
-- There is a high-level graphical toolkit (Tk) available for X11 programming.

Major drawbacks we perceived in Tcl were:

-- There is no high-level graphical toolkit for non-UNIX platforms. However, the elegant structure of Tk is convincing proof that such toolkits are eminently plausible.

-- The variable scoping mechanism offers no intermediate scope between local and global variables. (However, access to other evaluation contexts is available using the Tcl "uplevel" and "upvar" facilities, which makes most things possible, if not graceful.)

In the end, there was no candidate language that seemed a closer fit to our needs than Tcl, but we recognized from the start that the language would have to evolve before it could be standardized. This is precisely the process we sought to initiate.

MIME Types for Safe-Tcl

With the emergence of MIME [3] as the widely-implemented standard representation for multimedia mail, it was clear from the start that we wanted Safe-Tcl to be MIME-smart. We defined two new MIME content-types for Safe-Tcl.

The first, "application/safe-tcl", is the MIME content-type for an actual Safe-Tcl program. That is, a Safe-Tcl program may be included as data anywhere in a MIME message by labeling it with this content-type value. An additional parameter that may be provided on the content-type line is the "evaluation-time" parameter, which may have one of two values, "activation" or "delivery". If the evaluation-time is "activation", this means that theprogram is to be evaluated when the user reads the message, i.e. the message is an active mail message, as described above. If the evaluation-time is "delivery", then the program is intended to be evaluated in a non-interactive process at the time of final message delivery, i.e. when the message is delivered to the user's mailbox. In neither case are any unsafe primitives to be made available to the program. (It is, however, desirable to have a mode in which the Safe-Tcl interpreter makes the unsafe primitives available to a program that is not received in the mail, but is supplied by the user as part of his customization environment.) This reflects the basic enabled mail model set forth in [13].

The second content-type we defined is "multipart/enabled-mail". This is a new MIME compound type, which (as per the MIME standard) shares a common syntax with all other MIME compound types, but which has different semantics. A MIME object of type multipart/enabled-mail has exactly two sub-parts. The first of these is an arbitrary MIME object (of any content-type, including possibly another compound type). The second is of type application/safe-tcl. The intended semantics are that the first MIME entity is not displayed to the user, but rather is made available for the manipulation of the Safe-Tcl program.

One advantage of this approach is that if a message of type multipart/enabled-mail is read using a mail tool that understands MIME but does not understand the Safe-Tcl extensions, the user will be able to view all the sub-parts (pictures, sounds, etc.) even though the interactive structure is missing. This means that the sub-parts can be ordered and structured with such serial viewing in mind, possibly even including explanatory textual parts that are never actually used by the Safe-Tcl program when it runs, but are there only for serial-viewing by MIME readers that do not support Safe-Tcl. (Currently, such careful structuring must be done by hand, but tools to automatically generate this kind of message are perfectly plausible.)

Safe-Tcl Restrictions

Safe-Tcl may be described as an extended subset of basic Tcl. Certain Tcl commands were considered unsafe for use in active mail, and are not made available to untrusted programs. These include all commands that access files or execute system commands. Once all of these are removed from Tcl, however, the language has no remaining capability to interact with the user or the environment, so the addition of more limited commands for this purpose was essential.

Safe-Tcl Language Enhancements

The Safe-Tcl language supplements the restricted Tcl subset with a number of commands that give untrusted programs a limited ability to interact with the user and the environment.

Some Safe-Tcl commands are used to store and retrieve persistent data in a safe way. (The storage mechanism used is implementation-dependent, but will typically involve a single file or directory.) The information that one Safe-Tcl program stores in this manner is available to any other Safe-Tcl program; there is no mechanism for protecting one Safe-Tcl application from another, because there is no way of telling that messages A and B are not generated by the same application as message C. This situation could be remedied with authentication-smart extensions, using the mechanisms to be described below.

A great many Safe-Tcl commands deal with messaging-specific details such as address and date parsing, MIME object composition and decomposition, and so on. This gives language-level support for some of the most commonly-desired actions that users will want to take with Safe-Tcl.

Additional Safe-Tcl commands allow untrusted programs to send mail and print data, but only after the data in question is presented to the user and the user's consent is obtained.

Another Safe-Tcl command is used to access a distributed library of Safe-Tcl extension programs. Such libraries may be obtained locally or from a user-authorized repository elsewhere on the network, but should only refer to sources trusted by the user.

Safe-Tcl Interface Styles

Most of the remaining Safe-Tcl commands deal with user interface issues. Safe-Tcl seeks to have the universality of interface of the ATOMICMAIL program, as described above, but without precluding the possibility of having Safe-Tcl programs actually be pleasant to use. This goal is achieved by the introduction of a notion of user interface styles.

Each Safe-Tcl user interface style is, in essence, a package of Safe-Tcl extensions that permit user interface programming on a certain platform or platforms. In particular, Safe-Tcl defines a user interface style of "Tk3.6" for Tk-based graphical interaction under the X11 window system. Safe-Tcl also defines a user interface style of "generic" for user-interface-independent interaction, in the manner of ATOMICMAIL. The Safe-Tcl interpreter always provides a global variable, SafeTcl_InterfaceStyle, which contains a list of interface styles supported by the currently running Safe-Tcl interpreter. This list always includes "generic".

This means that, with the current system, one can write Safe-Tcl code that checks the locally available user interface styles, providing a high-quality graphical user interface if X11 is running, and providing a less pleasant but still usable interface if X11 is not running. Eventually, it is anticipated, there may be Safe-Tcl interface styles for Windows, Macintosh, or any other important platforms. (Eventually, it might also be desirable to define an abstract user interface style that is both system-independent and graphically-oriented, the higher-level analog of the "generic" style.) But any program that has a fallback to the "generic" case will be able to run with any Safe-Tcl interpreter. In this manner, Safe-Tcl provides a user interface that is no better than ATOMICMAIL's in the worst case, but considerably better in many other cases.

Safe-Tcl Multimedia Capability

Designing Safe-Tcl with MIME in mind made it almost trivial to give the language rich multimedia capability, a marked contrast with previous systems for enabled mail. In particular, the language includes primitives for getting a list of parts inside a multipart MIME object, and for displaying any particular subpart. The latter functionality is implemented by calling a general-purpose MIME-displaying tool. Our implementation works with either of two such interpreters, mhn or metamail.

The simple Safe-Tcl primitives for MIME access open up a rich range of multimedia behaviors, such as offering the user a button to click on to see a video clip, and makes Safe-Tcl suitable as the "control structure" for almost any interactive multimedia application. In fact, when the interpreter is run without the "safe" mode, restoring all the power of full Tcl while retaining the Safe-Tcl extensions, the result is an extremely powerful scripting language for arbitrary (non-mail-based) multimedia applications.

Safe-Tcl Extensions

Because Safe-Tcl replaces general Tcl primitives with safer but much less powerful primitives, it is inevitable that application writers will think of things that could be done safely, but only with the introduction of a new Safe-Tcl command. In previous systems, this would have been intractable, especially in a distributed environment, due to the sophistication needed to modify the language interpreter and even more importantly to the extreme difficulty of getting such extensions installed everywhere on the network.

Two aspects of Safe-Tcl's design make the problem much more tractable: twin interpreters and distributed libraries.

Because the basic Tcl language was designed to be embedded in larger applications, the implementation is extremely sensitive to the possibility that there might be multiple Tcl-based extension languages in a single process and address space. For this reason, Tcl's key data structures are not global, but are tied to an object known as a Tcl interpreter. Multiple Tcl interpreters in a given process can implement different Tcl-based extension languages without interfering with each other.

The implementation of Safe-Tcl relies heavily on this feature, and is based on a "twin interpreter" model. The Safe-Tcl process contains two interpreters, a trusted interpreter and an untrusted interpreter. Untrusted code (such as an active mail message) is evaluated in the untrusted interpreter, which is modified in all the ways described above. The trusted interpreter never directly evaluates untrusted code, but may be used to extend the untrusted interpreter. This is done by defining a procedure in the trusted interpreter, and then exporting it to the untrusted interpreter. This effectively makes a new bit of functionality available to untrusted programs without actually modifying the underlying C program that interprets the Safe-Tcl code. As long as the extensions are carefully designed and implemented, this kind of extensibility does not compromise security, although it does give users the ability to "shoot themselves in the foot" by inadvertently creating unsafe extensions. (An important thing to avoid, for example, is having the extension code evaluate its arguments as Tcl subprograms, which would effectively import untrusted code into the trusted interpreter.)

The relationship between the two interpreters is one of the most subtle and important aspects of the safe-tcl system. In order to use the system wisely and safely, it must be understood well by extension programmers. A good analogy from the domain of timesharing operating systems is the common distinction between "user space" and "kernel space". The trusted interpreter operates in an unrestricted environment, similar to the kernel in a UNIX operating system. The restricted environment of the untrusted interpreter is analogous to user space, where a more limited set of capabilities are available. In this analogy, each time the unrestricted interpreter adds a new bit of functionality to the restricted interpreter, it is performing the analogue of defining a new system call to the kernel.

The twin interpreter model makes it much easier to safely extend the functionality of the restricted Safe-Tcl language, but does not address the problem of distributing extensions on the network. For this, Safe-Tcl provides a primitive called "SafeTcl_loadlibrary". This primitive will attempt to find and load a specified Safe-Tcl extension package. By default, the interpreter will only look in the local Safe-Tcl libraries for such extensions, but the system can be configured to download extensions from a trusted FTP site as well. Thus a community of users who share trust in such a repository can all have their Safe-Tcl interpreters simultaneously extended by the addition of an extension file to an FTP repository.

Authentication and Safe-Tcl

Although the Safe-Tcl interpreter does not currently implement any authentication mechanism, the language was designed with authentication in mind. In particular, the interpreter provides a global associative array variable, SafeTcl_services, which is used to indicate, among other things, the authenticated identity of the author of the program. If such an authenticated identity is available, then the value of SafeTcl_services(authentication) contains it, and this identity may be used by Safe-Tcl extensions to provide different levels of functionality to messages from trusted recipients.

IV. An Example Program

As with almost any programming language, a sample Safe-Tcl program long enough to be truly interesting would not fit in a paper such as this one. The following, however, is a simple program that demonstrates some important Safe-Tcl functionality. It offers the reader the opportunity to order a Bill Clinton T-shirt, using a graphical interface if Tk is running and a generic interface otherwise:

```
proc ordershirt {} {
  SafeTcl_sendmessage  -to tshirts@nowhere.really \
      -subject "Shirt request" \
      -body [SafeTcl_makebody "text/plain" \
              [SafeTcl_getline "What size t-shirt do you wear?"
                               "medium"] "" ]
    exit
}
if {[lsearch $SafeTcl_InterfaceStyle Tk3.*] >= 0} {
    set foo [mkwindow]
    message $foo.m -aspect 1000 \
       -text "Click below if you want a free Bill Clinton t-shirt!"
    button $foo.b -text "Click here for free shirt!" \
        -command {ordershirt}
    button $foo.b2 -text "Click here to exit without ordering" \
         -command exit
    pack append $foo $foo.m {pady 20} $foo.b {pady 20} $foo.b2 {pady 20}
} else {
    set ans [string index \
               [SafeTcl_getline "Do you want a free Clinton t-shirt? "
                                "No"] 0]
    if {$ans == "y" || $ans == "Y"} {ordershirt}
    exit
}
```

The screen images that follow show how this process proceeds when the Tk interface is in fact available.

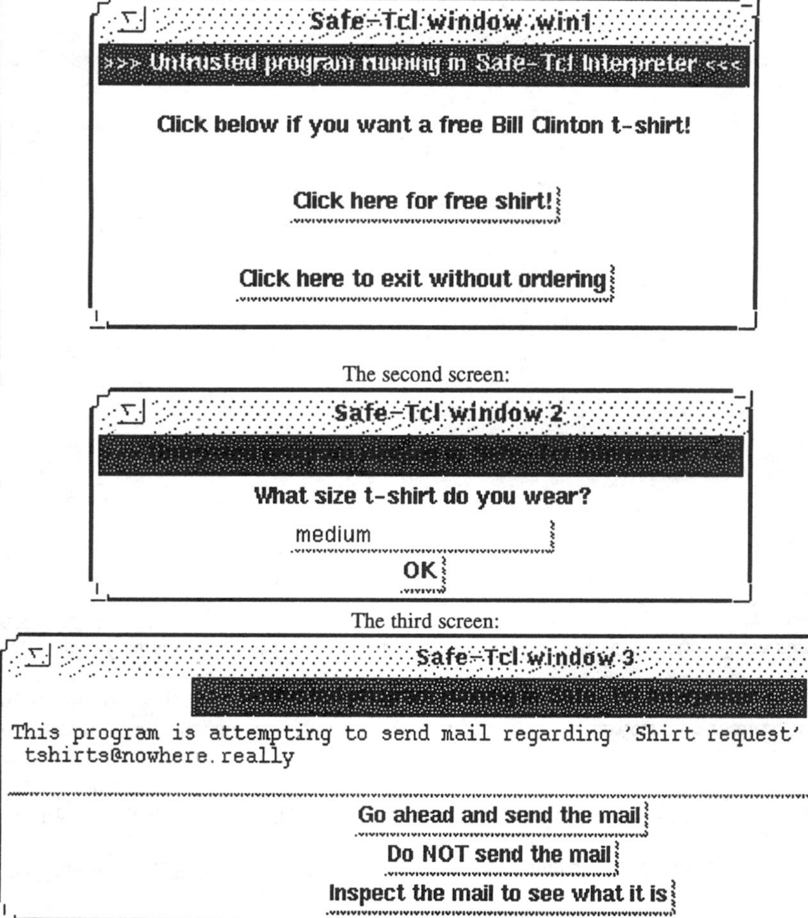

The second screen:

The third screen:

V. Status, Availability, and Future Prospects of Safe-Tcl and Enabled Mail

The Safe-Tcl specification and our implementation of it were made freely available on the Internet in December, 1993. With the exception of the authentication mechanisms, the implementation completely implements the specification. The documentation and implementation may be obtained on the Internet via anonymous ftp from ftp.ics.uci.edu, in the file "mrose/safe-tcl/safe-tcl.tar.Z". An Internet Safe-Tcl mailing list may be joined by sending mail to safe-tcl-request@cs.utk.edu.

Unlike prior languages for enabled mail, the authors believe that the Safe-Tcl technology is complete and robust enough to serve as the first real open platform for mail enabled applications. It is our hope that many people in the Internet community will develop Safe-Tcl applications and extensions.

If successful, this technology will be, for most of the world, the first clear glimpse of the power of enabled mail. As such, we expect that it will teach us a lot about the design requirements for an enabled mail language. For that reason, we are not rushing to try to obtain any kind of official standardization status for the language, but will consider taking that step after accumulating substantial real-world experience with Safe-Tcl. Eventually, we hope that Safe-Tcl will either evolve into the standard language for enabled mail or else strongly influence the design of a successor language that will fill that role.

Acknowledgements

Safe-Tcl was implemented by Marshall Rose and Nathaniel Borenstein. The implementation would not have been possible, however, without the solid Tcl/Tk code base and consistently helpful advice provided by John Ousterhout. We have also benefited from the comments of several people in the process of designing Safe-Tcl, notably Dave Crocker, Ned Freed, Karl Lehenbauer, Daniel Newman, Rich Salz, Allan Shepherd, and Peter Svanberg. I am grateful to Ralph Hill and Marshall Rose for their comments on an earlier draft of this paper.

References

1. Borenstein, N; Thyberg, C. "Power, Ease of Use, and Cooperative Work in a Practical Multimedia Message System", Int. J. Man-Machine Studies, April, 1991.

2. Forsdick, H.C., et al., "Initial Experience with Multimedia Documents in Diamond", Computer Message Service, Proceedings IFIP 6.5 Working Conference, IFIP, 1984.

3. Borenstein, N., Freed, N. MIME (Multipuprpose Internet Mail Extensions), RFC 1521.

4.Ousterhout, J., "Tcl: An Embeddable Command Language.", Proc. USENIX Winter Conference, January 1990, pp. 133-146.

5. Ousterhout, J., *Tcl and the Tk Toolkit*, Addison-Wesley, Reading Massachusetts, 1994.

6. Ousterhout, J., "An X11 Toolkit Based on the Tcl Language.", Proc. USENIX Winter Conference, January 1991, pp. 105-115.

7. Goldberg, et al, "Active Mail - A Framework for Implementing Groupware", CSCW '92 proceedings, Toronto.

8. Vittal, John, "Active Message Processing: Messages as Messengers", in *Computer Message Systems*, R. P. Uhlig, editor, North-Holland Publishing Company, 1981.

9. Hogg, John, "Intelligent Message Systems", in *Office Automation*, Dionysios Tsichritzis, editor, Springer-Verlag, 1985.

10. Borenstein, N. "Computational Mail as Network Infrastructure for Computer-Supported Cooperative Work", CSCW '92 proceedings, Toronto.

11. Linn, J., "Privacy Enhancement for Internet Electronic Mail: Part I - Message Encryption and Authentication Procedures", RFC 1421, IAB IRTF PSRG, IETF PEM WG, February 1993.

12. Zimmerman, Phil, "PGP Users's Guide", online documentation, June, 1993.

13. Rose, Marshall, and Nathaniel Borenstein, "A Model for Enabled Mail (EM)", draft in preparation.

14. Rose, Marshall, and Nathaniel Borenstein, "MIME Extensions for Mail-Enabled Applications: Application/Safe-Tcl and Multipart/enabled-mail", draft.

15. Coded Character Set--7-Bit American Standard Code for Information Interchange, ANSI X3.4-1986.

Credits and debits on the Internet

Since the advent of banking in the Middle Ages, bank customers have used paper-based instruments to move money between accounts. In the past 25 years, electronic messages moving through private networks have replaced paper for most of the value exchanged among banks each day. With the arrival of the Internet as a mass market data network, new technologies and business models are being developed to facilitate electronic credit and debit transfers by ordinary consumers.

These new systems include CyberCash (which is a gateway between the Internet and the authorization networks of the major credit cards) and the Secure Electronic Transactions protocol (a standard for presenting credit card transactions on the Internet), as well as First Virtual (a way of using e-mail to secure approval for credit card purchases of information), GC Tech (a payment system that can use credit or debit via an intermediation server), and NetBill (a public–private-key encryption system for purchasing information).

Conventional checking

In today's banking world, money consists of ledger entries on the books of banks or other financial institutions. A checking account, also known as a demand deposit account (DDA), records deposits by the consumer and can be used, via the consumer's instructions in the form of a check, to make payments to third parties. Typically, a check is written by a consumer, authenticated by signature, and presented to a merchant, who may endorse it with a signature before presenting it to a bank for payment. If the merchant's bank and the consumer's bank are the same, it can simply transfer the funds on its ledgers from the consumer's account to the merchant's. If the payer and the payee keep accounts at different banks, the payee bank presents the check for settlement to the payer's bank and receives the funds in return through a settlement system. Several private check clearinghouse systems, as well as the Federal Reserve system, provide settlement services in the United States [Fig. 1].

When checks are sent to banks for deposit, merchants do not yet know if consumers have adequate funds and therefore need to find out whether the checks cleared. Similarly, consumers receive statements from their banks showing which checks have been paid. Any discrepancy between bank records and those of the payers may indicate that forged checks were presented against consumers' accounts.

This model works equally well when there is a negative balance in consumers' accounts, at least if the consumers' banks are willing to extend credit—that is, to lend the consumers funds needed to pay off the checks.

A plethora of technologies and business models are in development to enable electronic payments

Many banks in the United States and Europe provide such credit facilities, sometimes referred to as "overdraft protection." A credit card is another example of an account that lends money to the consumer.

The simple model below illustrates the major issues that must be addressed in designing an electronic credit or debit system.

- Naming: there must be an unambiguous way of identifying the payers' bank accounts and the payees' bank accounts.
- Signatures: it must be possible for the payers' banks to verify that payment instructions were generated by people authorized to use accounts.
- Integrity: electronic checks should be difficult to alter.
- Confirmation: payees must have confirmation that transfers took place; payers must have notification of transfers out of their accounts.
- Confidentiality: third parties should not be able to monitor such payments.

MARVIN A. SIRBU
Carnegie Mellon University

• Settlement: separate banking institutions must have a way of settling their accounts.

Such a system does exist for paper checks. In the United States and Canada, a bank identification code and account numbers are encoded in magnetic ink on the check. But the naming of accounts is not standardized internationally. Payees provide their account numbers when endorsing checks. The payers' banks match the signatures on checks with customers' signatures on file at banks. Integrity is ensured by the use of special paper and the practice of writing checks in ink with no alterations. The U.S. Federal Reserve system provides a vehicle for settlement, and confirmation takes the form of periodic statements or special notices for bounced checks. If checks are presented in person or mailed in sealed envelopes, they are generally protected from observation by third parties.

From a business perspective, payment systems differ in the warranties the different parties make and in the liabilities they assume. For example, the payers' banks are responsible for verifying signatures on checks. If this fails to happen, the payers are not liable for forged checks drawn on their accounts. It is possible to cut the cost of the entire process if payment messages can be readily tied to the parties' accounting systems—for instance, by including purchase order numbers or a consumer's account number with a merchant on all checks. It may also be desirable to link payment to some proof that merchandise has been delivered. These links to other processes are among the principal benefits of electronic payments.

In a payment processing system, the cost of normal operations is frequently outweighed by the costs associated with exception handling. If a typical transaction costs US 5 cents to process, and the manual labor associated with handling errors and exceptions comes to an average of $25, even with an error rate of only two per thousand, exception costs will equal normal processing costs. As electronic processing drives down the cost of normal transactions, exception handling becomes relatively more significant. Payment systems must therefore be implemented to the highest standards of reliability, with automated procedures for recovering from errors whenever possible.

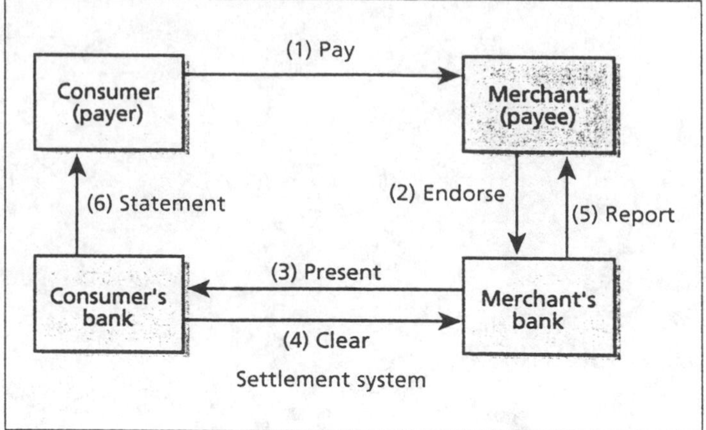

[1] This simplified model shows the steps involved in processing standard paper checks used by a consumer to pay a merchant.

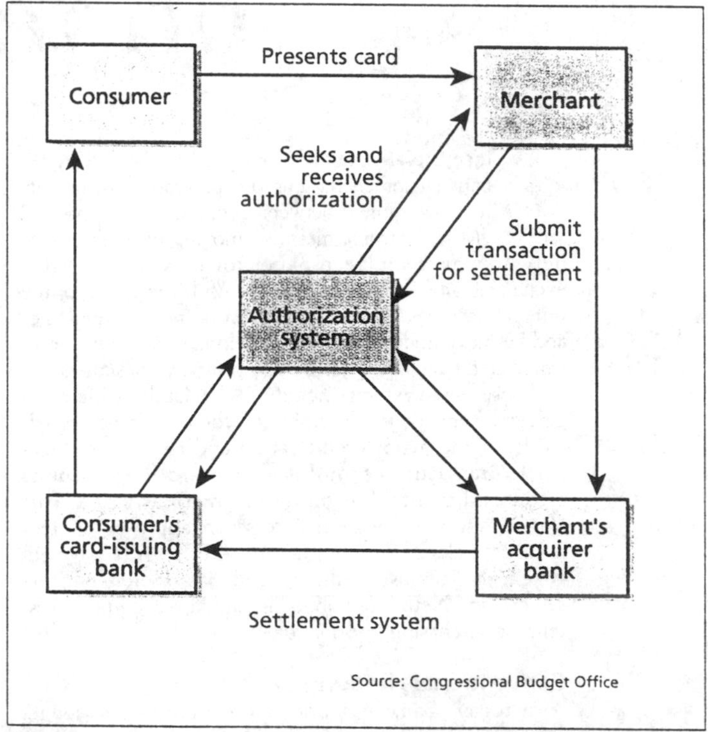

[2] In this model of credit card transactions, consumers present their cards to the merchants who submit the card numbers and transaction details to the authorization system, which either approves transactions directly or routes the requests to the card issuing bank for approval. Periodically—for example, at the end of the day—merchants submit details on approved transactions to their banks. This information is submitted to the card association for settlement after a bank nets out transactions for which it serves as both card issuer and acquirer.

The case of credit cards

The credit card system was designed to provide immediate gratification of the wants of consumers by allowing them to purchase goods or services on credit. A credit card is a token of trust that transfers the risk of granting credit from a merchant to the card-issuing bank. Once a merchant has had a purchase authorized by the card issuer over the private authorization network, the merchant is assured of payment and the card issuer assumes responsibility for billing the consumer and collecting the money. Settlement takes place later, when the merchant periodically submits a batch of authorized transactions to the merchant's (acquiring) bank for settlement with the card issuer. But the issuer's assumption of risk is limited, however, to "card-present" transactions, such as those taking place in retail stores. When a merchant accepts a credit card by mail or phone ("card not present"), the card issuer accepts only the risk of nonpayment; the merchant bears the risk of fraudulent card usage. Merchants pay the costs of credit card use because selling on credit expands their business. Under U.S. law, a consumer's liability if someone else fraudulently uses the consumer's card is limited to $50 [Fig. 2].

In a card-present transaction, the merchant validates the payer's signature by matching the one on the back of the card against the one on the charge slip. Integrity is protected by the device of giving the consumer a carbon copy of the slip. The consumer's account number is verified by the embossed number on the credit card. Settlement is handled by card associations (such as Visa and MasterCard). The merchant receives immediate confirmation of a transaction while submitting it for authorization by way of the card association's private data network.

When a catalog sale takes place by mail or phone, the merchant has no way of verifying the consumer's right to use the card number proffered. At best, the merchant can request the consumer's billing address and receive an address verification. In

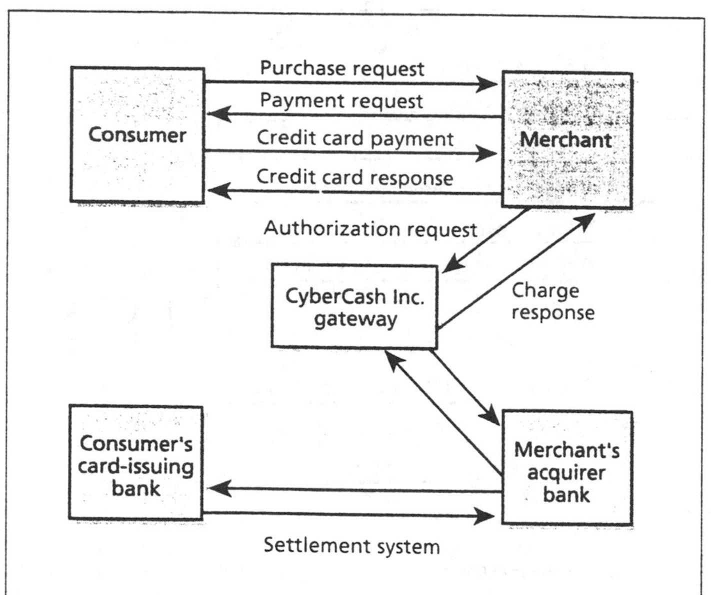

[3] CyberCash Inc., Reston, Va., provides consumer software, merchant software, and a gateway to support the secure communication of credit card transactions over the Internet.

effect, a credit card purchase requires only that the card number be conveyed from buyer to seller. For this reason, consumers are asked to protect their credit card numbers.

While conventional checking and credit card systems may seem quite similar, the legal meaning of credit card and check payment differ significantly. Credit card companies warrant their merchants; a person can challenge a credit card charge if dissatisfied with the goods. Checks provide no such recourse. If a person buys a plane ticket on an airline with a check, and the airline goes bankrupt before the ticket can be used, the unlucky purchaser becomes an unsecured creditor, behind many other claimants. By contrast, someone who pays for a ticket with a credit card may claim restitution from the card-issuing bank, and the card issuer in turn is entitled to redress from the airline's bank, which must stand behind the airline.

Payment systems vary significantly in their allocation of liability and in the warranties made by the different parties. Technical mechanisms have a strong influence on the willingness of parties to assume liability. If only the payer's bank can verify a signature on a check, the merchant or payee bank will not assume any liability for fraudulent signatures. But if public-key–based "signatures" make it possible for a merchant to verify them on an electronic check, merchants can be expected to undertake verification as they now do in card-present transactions.

Transactions on the Internet

Translating checks or credit card transactions to the Internet requires finding electronic and business model equivalents for the functions described above.

Signatures and confidentiality are the two biggest problems in creating digital payment instruments. These issues are typically handled with some form of cryptography. The use of public–private-key pairs allows a message to be "signed" digitally and verified by anyone who has the public key. Some form of public-key infrastructure, such as certificates, must be employed to associate a named user or an account unambiguously with a particular public key. Message digests provide integrity.

Most payment systems require special consumer and merchant software to prepare and process electronic payment messages. Although the consumer software is often described as an "electronic wallet," that term is misleading; funds are never kept in the wallet, which acts rather as an electronic checkbook for signing payment orders—managing keys, performing cryptographic operations, and formatting messages, as well as acting as a check register for keeping track of transactions.

The use of credit cards over the phone for catalog shopping is well established. Some of the first Internet systems propose to extend that model to shopping from Web-based catalogs.

CyberCash's gateway

CyberCash Inc., Reston, Va., implemented a system for protecting credit card presentation on the Internet in April 1995. The system was one of the first of its kind. The company, which provides software to both consumers and merchants, operates a gateway between the Internet and the authorization networks of the major credit card brands. As Nathaniel Borenstein, chief technical officer for First Virtual Holdings Inc., San Diego, Calif., noted, "Debugging obscure problems with incompatible implementations of Internet protocols is not a core competence of most financial institutions"—hence, the role for a gateway service.

The consumer begins by downloading the wallet software, which supports encryption and transaction record keeping. Like a physical wallet that may hold a number of credit cards, the software wallet can be used by the consumer to register several credit cards. Another software package provides similar services to the merchant. Messages are encrypted using a random symmetric key, which in turn is included in the message encrypted under the recipient's public key. The CyberCash public key is built into the wallet and merchant software. Consumers generate a public–private-key pair when they register credit cards with the wallet software, and the public key is sent to CyberCash, where it is maintained in a database. While consumers, merchants, and CyberCash all have public–private-key pairs, only CyberCash knows for certain everyone's public key. As a result, the company can exchange information securely with consumers or merchants, but they communicate with one another in the clear, relying on CyberCash to authenticate all signatures [Fig. 3].

When the time comes to make a purchase, the consumer requests the item desired by selecting it with a Web browser. The merchant's server sends the wallet software a cleartext, signed payment-request message that describes the purchase and indicates which credit cards the merchant accepts. The wallet software thereupon displays a window that lets the consumer select which credit card to use, and approve the purchase and the amount.

A credit card payment message, including a signed and encrypted description of the transaction, along with the consumer's credit card number, is sent back to the merchant, which forwards the payment message, along with the merchant's own signed and encrypted description of the transaction, to the CyberCash gateway. There, CyberCash decrypts and compares the two messages and their signatures. If they match, it submits a conventional authorization request and returns the charge response to the merchant, whose software confirms the purchase to the consumer's wallet software (credit card response). Additional messages cover refunds, voiding transactions, capture, and status inquiries.

CyberCash operates its gateway as an agent of the merchant's (acquiring) bank. Thus it must be trusted to decrypt the information for resending over conventional authorization networks.

Since the information is encrypted under CyberCash's public key, the merchant does not actually see the consumer's credit card number—a procedure that in theory cuts the risk that customer credit card numbers will be abused. In practice, so many

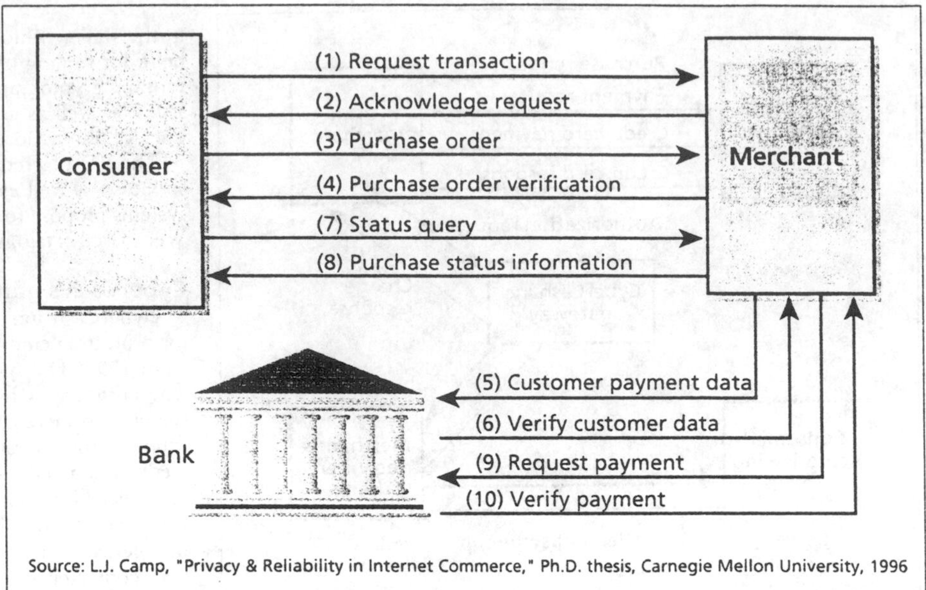

Source: L.J. Camp, "Privacy & Reliability in Internet Commerce," Ph.D. thesis, Carnegie Mellon University, 1996

[4] The operation of the Secure Electronic Transaction (SET) protocol relies on a sequence of messages. In the first two, the consumer and merchant signal their intention to do business and then exchange certificates and establish a transaction ID number. In the third step, the consumer purchase request contains a signed hash of the goods and services order, which is negotiated outside the protocol. This request is accompanied by the consumer's credit card information, encrypted so that only the merchant's acquiring bank can read it. At this point, the merchant can acknowledge the order to the customer, seeking authorization later (steps five and six) or perform steps five and six first and confirm authorization in step four. Steps seven and eight give the consumer a query capability, while the merchant uses steps nine and ten to submit authorizations for capture and settlement.

catalog companies organize their customer marketing records by credit card numbers that an acquirer usually authorizes CyberCash to provide them to merchants on request.

Secure electronic transactions

In February 1996, Visa and MasterCard announced their joint support of a standard protocol, dubbed Secure Electronic Transactions (SET), for presenting credit card transactions on the Internet. SET is designed to operate both in real time, as on the World Wide Web, and in a store-and-forward environment, such as e-mail. As an open standard, it is also designed to permit consumer, merchant, and banking software companies to develop software for their respective clienteles independently and to have them interoperate successfully.

In the CyberCash protocol, only CyberCash knows everyone's public key. SET, however, assumes the existence of a hierarchy of certificate authorities that vouch for the binding between a user and a public key. Consumers, merchants, and acquirers must exchange certificates before a party can know what public key to employ to encrypt a message for a particular correspondent [Fig. 4].

Although the software industry is moving rapidly to implement SET, the protocol poses significant problems for banks. Card issuers must invest considerable sums to have public key pairs and certificates issued to their card holders. Yet the benefits to the SET card issuers are not clear. A standard protocol may reduce software costs to merchants and consumers, as well as inhibit merchant fraud, but the cost of such dishonesty is borne by the acquirers, not the card issuers. What is more, it is not clear that SET will generate significant new credit card volume, as opposed to merely displacing mail and telephone orders. The card associations suggest that SET transactions, like card-present ones, should involve lower payments to card issuers. Thus a shift from telephone orders to SET could actually reduce the revenues of card issuers, while increasing costs by requiring them to issue certificates. Aligning benefits with costs will require a reallocation of the merchant discount between issuers and acquirers, a politically difficult task for card associations.

First Virtual: no hide and seek

First Virtual provides a mechanism that lets information providers accept credit cards for Internet purchases without resorting to cryptography. Consumers establish account IDs

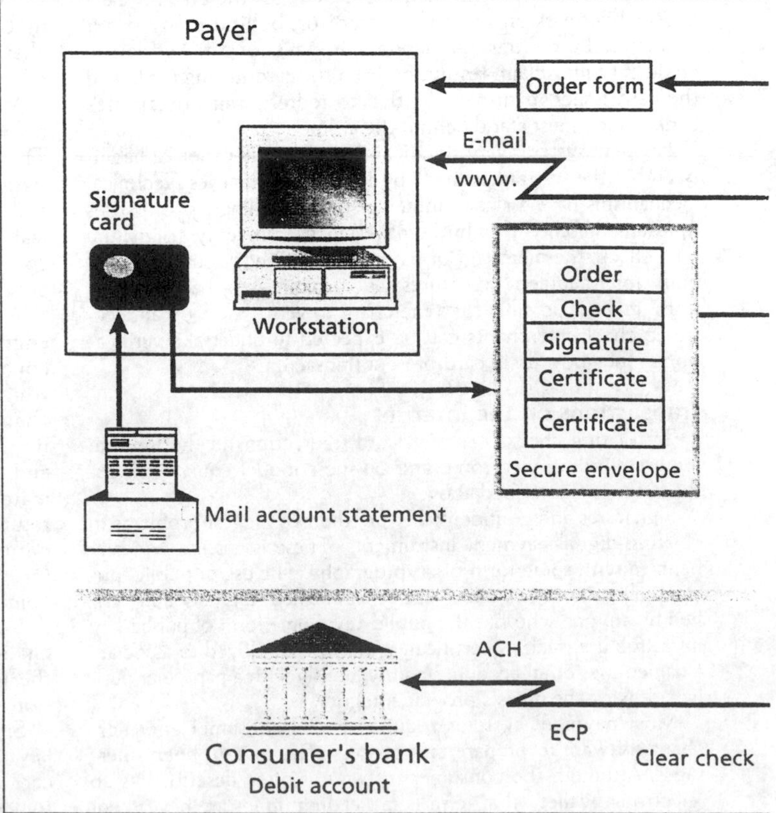

[5] In the electronic check concept developed by Financial Services Technology Consortium Inc., consumers uses smartcards or secure processors to compose and sign electronic checks. A check is sent, together with the consumers' public-key certificates and transaction details, to the payee for endorsement. The payee then adds its own signature and certificates and sends the check to its bank for deposit. The results of transactions are reported to both merchants and consumers.

with First Virtual and fax or telephone their credit card numbers to it. To buy information, consumers present those account IDs to merchants, who then connect to the First Virtual server to verify that IDs are valid; if so, the information is sent directly to the consumers. The server then sends them an e-mail message asking if they are willing to pay for the information. Consumers e-mail a reply indicating "yes," "no," or "fraud." If the answer is yes, First Virtual submits the user's credit card number through its acquirer, and the consumer's card is charged. After holding the funds for 90 days, the company transfers them to the merchant by means of an automated clearing house.

The First Virtual model has several key premises. First, consumers do not really know if they want a piece of information until they have looked at it. Second, the cost of sending information electronically "on approval" is negligible, so a merchant has lost very little if a consumer's answer is "no." Third, most consumers are honest: they will not systematically order goods and then answer "no" even when they are satisfied. (As an added deterrent to dishonest behavior, First Virtual will cancel a consumer's account if the pattern of usage suggests abuse.) By not charging consumers until they are satisfied, the system eliminates the cost of reversing charges for information that was not delivered as a result of network or computer problems.

Since the request for payment approval comes by e-mail, while goods are typically delivered over the Web, First Virtual believes that its model is so hard for an attacker to abuse that the risks are justified. Moreover, because the company delays payment to merchants for 90 days, consumers have plenty of time to discover fraudulent charges on their credit card statements, in which case First Virtual can easily reimburse the credit card with the funds it is holding.

In the First Virtual model, naming is provided by the account ID. In lieu of signatures, the company relies on the integrity of the Internet's e-mail infrastructure to ensure that a real consumer is answering yes or no. There is no message confidentiality, except that the account IDs may be viewed as pseudonyms.

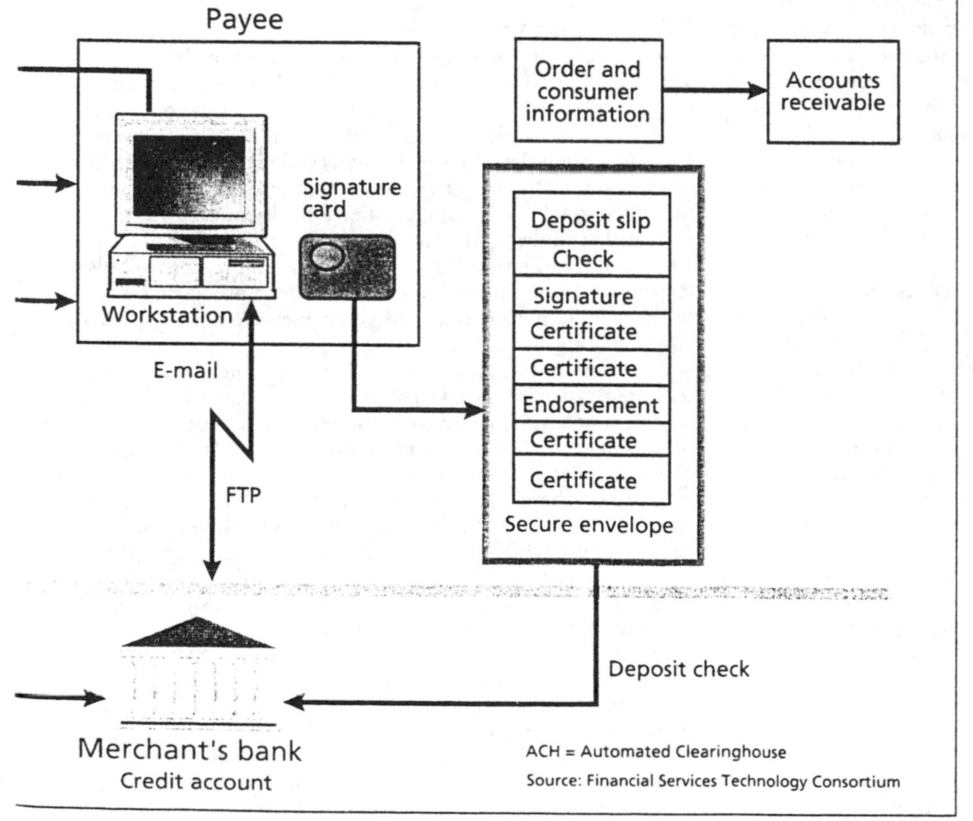

Source: Financial Services Technology Consortium

Confirmation is provided by e-mail and credit card statements. Settlement is handled first by the credit-card provider transferring payment to First Virtual and then First Virtual transferring payment to the merchants.

The company has been in operation since October 1994. It claims more than 180 000 consumer accounts.

Electronic checks

Beginning in the early 1970s, banks began searching for ways to reduce the costs of check processing (6.5¢–13¢ per item) by handling payments electronically. In direct payroll deposit, an employer sends a list of payroll payments to its bank, which then transfers funds to the employees' accounts at their banks through one of several automated clearinghouses (ACH). Consumers use direct payment to deal with recurring bills, such as utility, mortgage, and auto loan payments. In 1995, four ACH operators—the Federal Reserve, the New York Clearinghouse, the Arizona Clearinghouse, and VisaNet ACH Services—handled 2.9 billion transactions worth $13 trillion on their private electronic networks. The cost to banks was only half of what they would have spent processing checks manually. Payers and payees saved even more.

For both direct payroll deposit (used today by more than 45 percent of the U.S. workforce) and for direct payments, transactions begin when a large organization sends a batch file or tape to its bank with a list of payments or requests for payment. Because this is a batch system, it can take as many as three days for a payee to receive confirmation that a payment has cleared. The existence of these ACH systems for settlement between banks provides a strong base on which to build consumer-oriented electronic payment systems that can accept individual electronic requests for payment originating with consumers.

On the Internet, a paper check can readily be replaced by a digitally signed message—that is, an electronic check. A consortium of banks working through the Financial Services Technology Consortium (FSTC) Inc. has demonstrated a prototype electronic check system that maps directly into the model described above for conventional checks. The payer uses a secure processor, in the form of a PC card, to generate a digitally signed payment instruction, or "check," that is transmitted to the premises of the merchant where it is "endorsed" digitally before it is sent on to the merchant's bank. There, the check can be settled through an existing ACH [Fig. 5]. Other scenarios are also supported; for example, payers can send electronic checks to their own banks, which would then transfer funds directly to the payees' banks.

Standards for conveying invoice and remittance information so that payments can be readily linked into accounts payable and accounts receivable processing systems are an important component of the electronic check concept.

The FSTC model assumes that public keys and certificates are widely available, with banks vouching for their customers and associations of banks, such as an ACH, vouching for one another. The insistence on a hardware token for protecting a private key is designed to provide a high level of protection against such threats as Trojan horse software.

Instant debit systems

To the extent that FSTC's electronic checks rely on the conventional ACH system for clearing, they cannot give the merchant immediate payment confirmation of the sort provided by credit card authorization. CyberCash, Carnegie Mellon University, and GC Tech have introduced, or are developing, low-cost debit payment systems that give a merchant an immediate assurance that the payment will go through.

These systems provide a service model based on the concept of an on-line bank account, with immediate posting of transactions so that payees can get real-time confirmation that funds are available. In addition, they offer an interface to existing electronic funds-transfer mechanisms, including both ACHs and credit cards, so that consumers can easily transfer funds between their primary banks or credit accounts and their Internet payment accounts. Furthermore, these systems aggregate many on-line transactions for batch settlement over traditional settlement networks. They differ in the order of steps required for a transaction, in the consumer protection they provide in the event that goods are not delivered, and in the balance they strike between computationally expensive public-key cryptography and the use of shared-key cryptography.

GC Tech's turnkey offering

GC Tech SA, headquartered in Paris, France, bases its business model on turnkey payment systems software for banks and other financial institutions [Fig. 6]. The intermediation server in the GC Tech model maintains a "ledger" of consumer funds on account in the payment system. These funds may actually be on deposit at the consumer's bank, but their disposition is accounted for on the intermediation server's books. Account funding may take the form of a charge against the consumer's credit card or a transfer from the consumer's checking account to the payment system account. A consumer opens an account by downloading the wallet software and specifying a credit card used to fund the account.

When the consumer has selected a product for purchase, the merchant responds with a digitally signed payment-request message that is sent to the consumer's electronic wallet, which verifies the terms of the transaction and forwards the message to the intermediation server. The server then issues an authentication challenge to the consumer's wallet software. Upon receiving a correct response, the server debits the consumer's account and credits the merchant. Accumulated merchant credits will be settled in a single periodic batch transaction. If the consumer has sufficient funds, the server returns a digitally signed proof of payment (PPT) to the consumer's wallet software, which forwards it to the merchant. Assured of payment, the merchant can now deliver the goods.

The GC Tech cryptographic model assumes that the intermediation server and the merchant have public–private-key pairs, while consumers have only a PIN number. When the consumer forwards the proof of payment to the server, it proposes a session key encrypted under the server's public one. This session key is used to encrypt the authentication challenge and response, as well as to protect the PIN from disclosure. The proof of payment, signed by the server's private key, can be independently verified by both consumers and merchants. This model eliminates the need to issue and manage certificates for consumers.

Various entities are expected to use the GC Tech system, marketed under the brand name GlobeID. The GlobeID operator in France is Kleline SA, a joint venture operated by Moet Hennessey Luis Vuitton SA and Compagnie Bancaire SA, all three of which are in Paris. U.S. operations are expected to start in early 1997.

NetBill for information delivery

NetBill, a system under development at Carnegie Mellon University (CMU), Pittsburgh, in cooperation with Mellon Bank Corp., also in Pittsburgh, is optimized for delivering such information goods as text, images, and software over the Internet. Its developers, who include the author, have stressed the importance of guaranteeing that consumers receive the information they pay for. To that end, consumers are not charged until the information has actually been delivered to them. Similarly, merchants are guaranteed payment for goods delivered. The basic NetBill protocol has eight steps, beginning with the authentication of identity (using public-key cryptography) and ending with the transmission of a decryption key to the consumer so that the information being purchased can be decrypted and presented [Fig. 7].

In this system, consumers are not charged until the (encrypted) goods reach them. At the same time, if there is not enough money in the consumer's account, the transaction will be rejected and the key never delivered, preventing the consumer from using information that has not been paid for. The merchant's endorsement of the electronic payment order also serves as a warranty that what was received by the consumer is what the merchant intended to deliver. In the unlikely event that the merchant or client machine goes down after the consumer has been charged but before the key is delivered, the consumer can request a copy of the receipt—which contains the key—from the NetBill server.

Note the contrast in message flows between the GC Tech and NetBill systems. GC Tech requires merchants to communicate with the intermediary by way of the consumer's software. In a NetBill microtransaction, only the merchant talks directly to the accounting server.

NetBill will fund its accounts by charging the credit cards of consumers to put spending money in their NetBill accounts. These funds will be held at NetBill's bank. As merchants accumulate credit balances, funds will be transferred via VisaNet to the merchants' banks.

CMU and Mellon Bank expect to launch a commercial trial of the NetBill system in the first half of 1997. Transaction fees, paid by the merchant, are expected to range from 2.5 cents on a 10 cent transaction to 7 cents on a $1 transaction.

CyberCoin for small deals

In September 1996, CyberCash Inc., Reston, Va., introduced its CyberCoin service, which is designed to support low-cost (25 cent to $10) transactions for information goods over the World Wide Web. Like the NetBill and GC Tech systems, this one relies on a real-time account database to track Internet transactions. The CyberCash business model assumes that many banks will want to offer a bank-branded payment service that CyberCash would operate on their behalf. This approach would be similar to the recent trend in credit cards: fewer than 25 percent of banks do their own processing; most of them leave it to specialized companies such as First Data Corp., Atlanta. Ga.

A CyberCoin account can be "loaded" either by a charge to a credit card or by a transfer from the consumer's checking account. In the latter case, the transfer is handled in one of several ways: as an ACH transaction, by direct access through a debit or ATM network, or by other means. Depending on the mode of access and the user's level of authorization, funds may become available immediately or held for as many as three days until the transaction clears. While it is less costly to the intermediary to obtain the funds through the clearing house—thus avoiding the credit card discount fee—consumers are likely to prefer credit cards that give them instant access to the funds and 30 days before they have to pay the bill.

In the CyberCoin system, like the NetBill one, merchants deliver the goods encrypted and provide the key only after payment is confirmed. But rather than using RSA digital signatures on every small transaction, the CyberCoin system uses asymmetric cryptography only to load accounts and

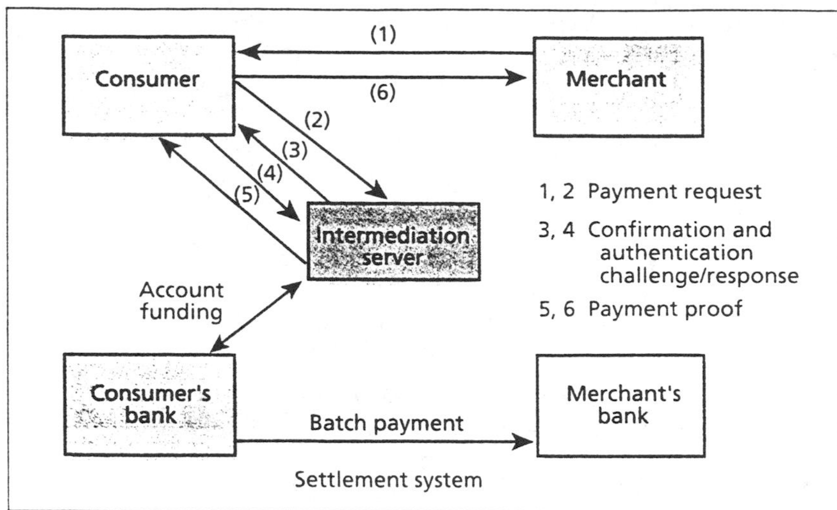

[6] The payment system protocol from GC Tech SA, headquartered in Paris, France, revolves around an intermediation server that maintains account information for consumers and merchants. Merchant requests for payment are relayed by way of consumers' wallets to the intermediation server, which authenticates the consumers and returns through them a confirmation to the merchant that he will be paid.

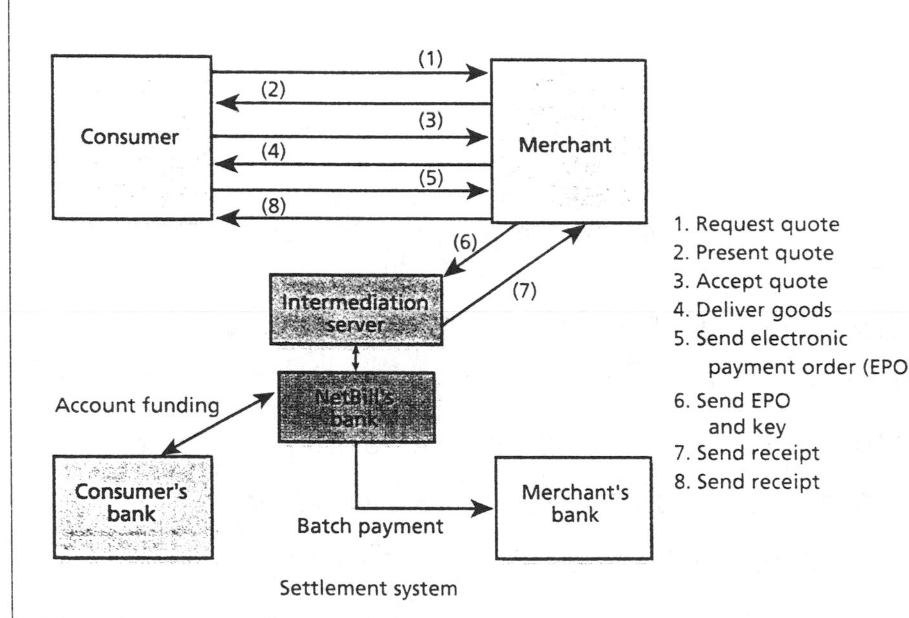

[7] The NetBill payment protocol has eight steps. In the first, the consumer and merchant authenticate each other using their public-key certificates and establish a symmetric session key to protect the privacy of subsequent messages. The first message requests a quote based on the consumer's identity, to allow for customized per-user pricing, such as volume discounts or support for subscriptions. If the quote (step two) is accepted (step three), the merchant sends the digital information to the consumer (step four) but encrypts it and withholds the key. The consumer software constructs an electronic payment order (EPO) describing the transaction and including a cryptographic checksum of the goods received. The order is signed with the consumer's private key and sent to the merchant, who verifies all its contents, appends the key for decrypting the goods, endorses the EPO with a digital signature, and sends it on to the NetBill server. The NetBill server verifies funds in the consumer's NetBill account, debiting the consumer and crediting the merchant, and a digitally signed receipt, including the key to decrypt the goods, is sent first to the merchant and then on to the consumer. The consumer software can now decrypt the purchased information and present it to the consumer.

establish a session key. Individual transactions are then signed with this symmetric key, thus reducing the data processing burden.

CyberCash has established partnerships with a number of important players. Netscape, for one, has agreed to bundle the CyberCash wallet software with its browser software products.

The future is not like the past

Payment systems can be expected to go on proliferating for the next several years, until the market determines the most desirable combinations of functions, price, and performance. The paper world, after all, has many different instruments, which embody different tradeoffs among risk, cost, complexity, responsiveness, and the time until the transaction is final. The same variety should be expected in electronic credit and debit systems.

Yet new technologies uncover new ways to distribute risk, liability, and cost among the parties to a transaction, so that new financial instruments with no comparable paper analog are also to be expected. They will take somewhat longer to develop, however, as they require changes in regulatory assumptions, case law, and participant behavior, all of which evolve much more slowly than technology does. ◆

About the author

Marvin Sirbu holds a joint appointment as professor in the departments of Engineering and Public Policy, the Graduate School of Industrial Administration, and Electrical and Computer Engineering, at Carnegie Mellon University, Pittsburgh. In 1989 he founded the university's Information Networking Institute, which is concerned with interdisciplinary research and education at the intersection of telecommunications, computing, business, and policy studies. Before joining Carnegie Mellon in 1985, he taught in the Sloan School of Management at the Massachusetts Institute of Technology, where he also directed a research program on communications policy.

Distributing Trust
with the Rampart Toolkit

Michael K. Reiter

The Rampart group communication protocols are designed to distribute trust among a group of nodes in a distributed system—so while individual nodes need not be fully trusted, the group can be.

Many mechanisms for enforcing security policy in distributed computer systems rely on trusted nodes, that is, computers and resident software whose correct functioning is essential to implementing the policy. In this article, we describe our research on distributing trust among a group of nodes, so while no single node need be fully trusted, the function performed by the group can be. Central to this effort is a toolkit of group communication protocols called Rampart we developed to simplify construction of such groups.

An overarching goal of computer security mechanisms is to limit the extent to which each component of a system must be trusted to implement a desired security policy. Typically, this goal leads to system designs in which components are labeled

Rampart supports distributed process groups, *a programming paradigm shown to simplify construction of distributed programs tolerant of simple failures.*

"trusted" or "untrusted," the trusted ones constituting a small kernel of hardware and software on which the proper enforcement of the security policy relies. In distributed systems, these trusted components often take the form of localized and physically protected nodes from which the security of the larger system is leveraged. Network firewalls, file servers, authentication servers [15], and certification authorities [10] are all examples of enforcing security policy by leveraging trust in a few nodes.

Distributed systems also offer another means for arranging trust, so it is necessary to trust only some reasonably large fraction of a group of nodes to behave correctly. That is, no node in the group is trusted completely, and even the arbitrary behavior (*Byzantine failure* [11]) of a few nodes (e.g., due to physical capture, electronic penetration, or insider malfeasance) is survivable. Provided that sufficiently few nodes misbehave, the group, acting in concert, can be trusted as a whole. Distributing trust in this way has obvious security and fault-tolerance advantages over the placing-all-your-eggs-in-one-basket alternative.

There has been substantial research on techniques for distributing trust; for surveys of particular classes of techniques, see [3, 8, 20, 21]. In some cases, the results of this research have been dramatic. For example, it has been shown that a group of nodes, each with a private value, can reliably compute any function of those values so that no information about any correct node's input is revealed to other nodes beyond what can be computed from the function's output, despite even the collaboration of a minority of faulty nodes [9]. Distributing trust has also been applied in such cases as clock synchronization [13], file storage, and security administration [4].

Despite a few limited successes, however, most research in this area has not affected distributed systems practice. This is largely due to the inherent complexity of coordinating the actions of many nodes, some of which may behave in unexpected ways. Distributed coordination in the presence of failures is difficult—even more so when the failures may be intentionally arbitrary—and is beyond the reach of the average programmer. Infrastructure and tools for distributing trust are essential if we are to see distributed trust become viable for common use.

The Rampart System

At AT&T Bell Laboratories, we are engaged in an ongoing research effort to overcome these barriers to distributing trust in practical distributed systems. To this end, we developed Rampart, a toolkit of protocols designed to simplify the task of coordinating correctly operating nodes in a dynamic environment characterized by simple (e.g., crash) and arbitrary node failures, node recoveries, and communication failures. Rampart provides support for distributed *process groups*, a programming paradigm shown to simplify construction of distributed programs tolerant of simple failures [1]. Rampart supports communication primitives by which group members can multicast messages to the group, and membership primitives by which a process can be removed from or added to the group if it (or the node on which it executes) fails or recovers, respectively.

The semantics of Rampart process groups borrow much from the notion of *virtual synchrony* introduced by the Isis system [1] and further developed in the Horus [2], Transis [5], and Totem [14] systems. Intuitively, a virtually synchronous process group is one in which each multicast and membership change appears to be executed as a globally indivisible and instantaneous event. Each multicast and membership change is delivered to all group members, and each is ordered identically relative to other events at all group members. These semantics enable a programmer to implement a distributed application without concern for many of the complexities introduced by distribution in a system in which failures can occur [1].

Though Rampart process groups offer semantics similar to the virtually synchronous process groups of many simple-fault-tolerant systems, their implementation is more complex due to the possibility of arbitrary member failures admitted by our system model. For example, implicit in the semantics of a group multicast in the virtual synchrony model is that all group members receive the same multicast message. An arbitrarily faulty multicast initiator may, however, send different messages to different group members in a single "multicast." For such reasons, the Rampart process group implementation employs *agreement protocols* by which correct group members reach agreement on the contents of multicasts and the ordering of events.

The agreement protocols underlying Rampart

process groups are a *group membership protocol* [18] and *reliable* and *atomic* (totally ordered) *group multicast protocols* [16, 17]. The role of the group membership protocol is to enforce agreement among correct processes on the group composition, despite communication failures and (simple or arbitrary) process failures. The reliable and atomic group multicast protocols then enforce agreement on the contents of each multicast to the group (even from an arbitrarily faulty member) and order multicasts relative to group membership changes and other multicasts. These protocols, and thus a Rampart process group, are suitable for use in asynchronous systems; that is, they require no upper bounds on network delays or relative clock drifts among members. Moreover, they can tolerate the arbitrary failure of fewer than one-third of each instance of the group membership.

The semantics offered by Rampart process groups can simplify distributing trust in systems, and indeed, prior work has already placed reliable group multicast (*Byzantine agreement* [11]) and atomic group multicast at the heart of many techniques for distributing trust (see [8, 20]). For example, *state machine replication* [20] is a general technique for constructing services that continue to operate correctly despite the simple or arbitrary failure of component servers. In this technique, a service is implemented using multiple identical deterministic servers, initialized to the same state. Clients issue requests to the service using an atomic multicast protocol, so that all correct servers receive and process the same sequence of requests and thus return the same reply for each request. The client accepts the response returned by a majority of the servers, ensuring that the outputs of a faulty minority of the servers are ignored.

Applications

In conjunction with developing Rampart, we are focusing on applications it can enable. Two efforts, pursued with colleagues at Bell Labs, have resulted in prototype services that illustrate Rampart's potential utility, while also being of interest themselves. The two applications are a service for performing sealed-bid auctions [6] and a cryptographic key management service [19]. Both demonstrate techniques for distributing trust among many servers so that the arbitrary failure of fewer than one-third of the servers risks neither the integrity or the availability of the service, nor the secrecy of the confidential information it holds.

The first service illustrates how auctions, which have already appeared on the Internet [12], can be implemented in conjunction with next-generation secure commerce techniques to promote direct competition in electronic buying and selling. Our service offers an interface through which bidders can submit secret monetary bids for an advertised item. Once the bidding period has ended, the auction service opens the bids, determines the winning bid, and provides the winning bidder with a ticket for claiming the item. The service provides strong protection for both the auction authority and correct bidders, despite the arbitrary failure of any number of bidders and fewer than one-third of the servers comprising the auction service. Specifically, it is guaranteed that bids of correct bidders are not revealed until after the bidding period has ended; the auction authority collects payment for the winning bid; losing bidders forfeit no money; only the winning bidder can collect the item bid upon; and, if desired, bidders can remain anonymous.

The second application is a service for managing cryptographic keys in open networks, called Ω ("Omega"). Ω supports traditional interfaces for managing public keys, including interfaces for a client to register a public key for a principal (e.g., person, computer), retrieve a public key for a principal, and revoke a public key on behalf of a principal. In addition, motivated by the need for key backup to ensure that critical information can be decrypted, Ω provides interfaces for escrowing the private keys corresponding to the public keys it distributes. This mechanism allows an escrowed private key to be reconstructed if, for example, it is lost by its owner, or to be used to decrypt data selectively in a protected and auditable way, such as in emergency situations when the owner of the private key is not available. This mechanism can also be tailored to support law enforcement access to encrypted communications. Ω ensures the integrity and availability of its functions, and the confidentiality of the private keys it escrows, despite the arbitrary failure of fewer than one-third of the servers comprising the service.

Both our auction service and Ω are built using the technique of state machine replication (described earlier) to ensure that the failure of servers does not result in clients receiving incorrect responses to requests. Moreover, in both of these

Rampart has been adapted for two notable applications: *sealed-bid auctions and cryptographic key management*

Rampart greatly simplifies the task of distributing trust *among multiple nodes in a system*

services, further measures are required to protect the secrecy of information stored at the service in the event of server penetrations. In the case of the auction service, that private information is digital cash each bidder escrowed at the service to back its bid. In the case of Ω, that information is private keys that are escrowed at the service. The requirement to protect this information from arbitrarily faulty servers implies that the information can never be collected at a single server, and thus the validation and use of this information must be performed as distributed computations. In Ω, this is done with known techniques [3]; our auction service, however, required new ones [7].

Conclusion

At the time of this writing, Rampart is a research prototype and the subject of ongoing work. While it is too early to deem Rampart a success, our initial experiences with the system indicate it can greatly simplify the task of distributing trust among multiple nodes in a system, and that it performs sufficiently well to support a wide range of applications. Our plans include efforts to extend the protocols to accommodate new failure models and to improve system performance. In addition, we are preparing Rampart for release to the scientific community free of charge to encourage peer review of the system and experimentation with challenging applications. For more information, write to reiter@research.att.com.

References

1. Birman, K.P. The process group approach to reliable distributed computing. *Commun. ACM 36,* 12 (Dec. 1993) 37–53.
2. Birman, K.P., Maffeis, S., and van Renesse, R. Software support for distributed modularity in Horus. *Commun. ACM 39,* 4 (April 1996).
3. Desmedt, Y. Threshold cryptography. *European Transactions on Telecommunications and Related Technologies 5,* 4 (July 1994) 449–457.
4. Deswarte, Y., Blain, L., and Fabre, J. Intrusion tolerance in distributed computing systems. In *Proceedings of the 1991 IEEE Symposium on Research in Security and Privacy* (Oakland, Calif., May 1991) pp. 110–121.
5. Dolev, D. and Malki, D. The Transis approach to high availability cluster communication. *Commun. ACM 39,* 4 (April 1996).
6. Franklin, M.K. and Reiter, M.K. The design and implementation of a secure auction service. In *Proceedings of the 1995 IEEE Symposium on Security and Privacy* (Oakland, Calif., May 1995) pp. 2–14.
7. Franklin, M.K. and Reiter, M.K. Verifiable signature sharing. In L.C. Guillou and J. Quisquater, eds., *Advances in Cryptology—EUROCRYPT '95* (Lecture Notes in Computer Science 921) pp. 50–63. Springer-Verlag, 1995.
8. Franklin, M.K. and Yung, M. The varieties of secure distributed computation. In *Proceedings of Sequences II, Methods in Communications, Security and Computer Science* (June 1991) pp. 392–417.
9. Goldreich, O., Micali, S., and Wigderson, A. How to play any mental game. In *Proceedings of the 19th ACM Symposium on the Theory of Computing* (May 1987) pp. 218–229.
10. Kent, S.T. Internet privacy-enhanced mail. *Commun. ACM, 36,* 8 (Aug. 1993), 48–60.
11. Lamport, L., Shostak, R., and Pease, M. The Byzantine generals problem. ACM *Transactions on Programming Languages and Systems, 4,* 3 (July 1982) 382–401.
12. Lewis, P.H. Auction of collectibles on the Internet. *The New York Times,* May 23, 1995.
13. Mills, D.L. Network Time Protocol (Version 2) specification and implementation. RFC 1119, Sept. 1989.
14. Moser, L.E., Melliar-Smith, P.M., Agarwal, D.A., Budhia, R.K., and Lingley-Papadopoulos, C.A. Totem: A fault-tolerant multicast group communication system. *Commun. ACM 39,* 4 (April 1996).
15. Neuman, B.C. and Ts'o, T. Kerberos: An authentication service for computer networks. *IEEE Commun. 32,* 9 (Sept. 1994).
16. Reiter, M.K. Secure agreement protocols: Reliable and atomic group multicast in Rampart. In *Proceedings of the 2nd ACM Conference on Computer and Communications Security* (Fairfax, Va., Nov. 1994) pp. 68–80.
17. Reiter, M.K. The Rampart toolkit for building high-integrity services. In K.P. Birman, F. Mattern, and A. Schiper, eds., *Theory and Practice in Distributed Systems* (Lecture Notes in Computer Science 938), 99–110. Springer-Verlag, 1995.
18. Reiter, M.K. A secure group membership protocol. *IEEE Transactions on Software Engineering, 22,* 1 (Jan. 1996) 31–42.
19. Reiter, M.K., Franklin, M.K., Lacy, J.B., and Wright R.N. The Ω key management service. In *Proceedings of the 3rd ACM Conference on Computer and Communications Security* (New Delhi, India, March 1996).
20. Schneider, F.B. Implementing fault-tolerant services using the state machine approach: A tutorial. *ACM Computing Surveys, 22,* 4 (Dec. 1990), 299–319.
21. Simmons, G.J. An introduction to shared secret and/or shared control schemes and their application. In G.J. Simmons, ed., *Contemporary Cryptology: The Science of Information Integrity,* 441–497. IEEE Press, 1992.

About the Author:
MICHAEL K. REITER is a principal investigator and member of the technical staff at AT&T Bell Laboratories. **Author's Present Address:** AT&T Bell Laboratories, 600 Mountain Ave., Murray Hill, NJ; email: reiter@research.att.com

Chapter 4

Models of Agency

Agents will operate best if they are constructed in a principled manner. Much of the research on agents has concentrated on the development of techniques for imbuing agents with abilities that mimic or complement human capabilities. Due to these techniques, agents at times appear rational, social, adaptive, and communicative. This section of the book surveys the most significant of these techniques, beginning with those imparting rationality to agents.

RATIONAL AGENCY

[Rao & Georgeff 1991] present a formalization of the *belief, desire, and intention* (BDI) architectures for agents. BDI agents must have some—implicit or explicit—representation of the corresponding abstractions or attitudes. Rao and Georgeff model these abstractions as modal operators in a logic and state an interesting set of requirements on their semantics. This approach can be seen as lying in the middle of the continuum between two other modal approaches: [Cohen & Levesque 1990] and [Singh 1994]. Unlike Cohen and Levesque and like Singh, Rao and Georgeff treat the revision of intentions as external to the core semantics of that concept. However, like Cohen and Levesque and unlike Singh, they make certain assumptions about the goals always being dropped. This assumption was criticized in [Singh 1992].

[Shoham 1993] motivates agent-oriented programming as the next natural step to object-oriented programming. Following [McCarthy 1979], he defines agents as entities for which it is convenient to take the intentional stance; that is, entities that are usefully described using mental abstractions. He formalizes these abstractions along with obligation. He suggests a programming language based on these constructs and takes some preliminary steps toward its formal semantics. In this manner, Shoham's work addresses challenges similar to those in [McCarthy 1992].

[Rosenschein & Zlotkin 1994] introduce a game-theoretic approach to agent interaction. They show how agents may negotiate with each other to maximize their individual payoffs. They consider situations in which the agents may mislead each other and propose protocols that reduce or eliminate the benefits to any agent from being deceptive.

Market-oriented programming is an important paradigm in multiagent systems. [Wellman 1995] describes a computational market model for the task of configuration design, which is a simplified setting exhibiting the broader problem of distributed resource allocation. This paper is interesting in general, however, because it offers insights on computational market solutions for distributed problems and discusses potential limitations and improvements.

Focal points are choices that are somehow salient. They are often used by humans in achieving coordination with others when they cannot communicate—if everyone chooses a focal point, then they all agree. [Fenster et al. 1995] formalize this intuition in the context of multiagent coordination and experimentally evaluate its effectiveness in some simulated scenarios.

SOCIAL AGENCY

[Gasser 1991] describes some of the key sociological issues underlying multiagent systems. He highlights the duality between agents and the societies in which they exist and function. Gasser's notion of the multiple simultaneous roles played by social agents inspired part of our discussion in Chapter 1 on future work on interaction-oriented programming.

[Sichman et al. 1994] develop a theory and interpreter for agents that can perform social reasoning. Their agents represent knowledge about one another to determine their relative autonomy or dependence for various goals. Dependence leads to joint plans for achieving the intended goals. This theory does not discuss social commitments per se, so it is complementary to some of the other literature on social agency.

[Tokoro 1993] views agents as the next generation of concurrent objects. He argues that agents naturally form societies, which are loci of their collective emergent behaviors. Tokoro synthesizes insights from (concurrent) object-oriented programming, programming languages, distributed computing, and AI to illuminate a variety of agent systems and applications.

[Hewitt & Inman 1991] review the *actor* concept and develop some enhancements suited to multiagent systems. The actor model is a powerful means to implement multiagent systems that naturally supports concurrency and autonomy. The enhancements take the form of *organizations of restricted generality* (ORGs)—roughly, coordinated sets of actors. It is interesting that the work of Hewitt, Tokoro, and their colleagues has had an impact on theoretical distributed computing in general [Milner 1993; Frenkel 1993].

Cooperative problem solving is one of the most important capabilities of agent-based systems. [Wooldridge & Jennings 1994] develop a formalization of this process, based on the key steps of (1) recognizing the need and possibility of cooperation and (2) creating and monitoring social commitments.

INTERACTIVE AGENCY

[Haddadi 1995] takes the next step in formally specifying the reasoning processes using those agents that can move through their abstract states as defined by beliefs, desires, intentions, and commitments.

Basing their work on the empirical observation that no single coordination mechanism or organization is effective for all application scenarios, [Decker & Lesser 1995] propose a generic approach to developing coordination algorithms. These algorithms work in a cooperative environment while preserving execution autonomy to a large extent. They show how the agents can commit to one another socially and reason about the social commitments of others.

[Singh 1993] considers the problem of the semantics of speech acts defined as their conditions of satisfaction. In this way, this paper differs from much other research into speech acts, which is motivated from philosophy of action or language, and considers the conditions under which a speech act may be said to have happened. In artificial languages, the occurrence of a communication is easily determined. The satisfaction conditions are used to state normative constraints on communications, which may apply in different societies.

[Lux & Steiner 1995] study cooperation among agents from an agent's perspective. They consider higher-level primitives for cooperation rather than the speech acts, which may, however, be used to implement the higher-level primitives. They define each primitive in terms of its preconditions and effects—each of these being given separately for the sender and receiver. This generic framework is instantiated to define a rich variety of cooperation primitives.

ADAPTIVE AGENCY

Although there is an enormous body of work on machine learning, all of which is of interest, we include here those papers that are directly agent based in their orientation.

[Weiss 1993] presents an analysis of reinforcement learning for several agents to coordinate their actions in an environment where they share a common goal but have limited and inexact knowledge. The results are appropriate for relatively simple agents.

[Tan 1993] reports on simple hunter-prey experiments with multiple reinforcement learning agents. The agents share sensory information, policies, and experience.

[Littman et al. 1995] develop an approach by which an agent can learn about its environment through limited observations. Their technique combines reinforcement learning with partially observable Markov decision processes.

Agent tracking is an important component of both collaborative and competitive or adversarial situations. An agent must determine what other agents are up to so as to support mutual goals or to prevent adversarial action. [Tambe 1995] studies the problem of adaptive agency in the context of agent tracking. An adaptive approach, even a simple one, is essential to cope with complex environments with agents of limited computational power.

[Sen et al. 1994] also study the problem of learning to coordinate, but from a different perspective and style. They are concerned with the experimental aspects of learning and address that problem of learning in the absence of explicit sharing of information among the agents.

REFERENCES

Note: A bullet before a reference indicates a selected reading.

[Cohen & Levesque 1990] Cohen, Philip R. and Levesque, Hector J.; 1990. Intention is choice with commitment. *Artificial Intelligence* 42:213–261.

•[Decker & Lesser 1995] Decker, Keith S. and Lesser, Victor R.; 1995. Designing a family of coordination algorithms. In *Proceedings of the International Conference on Multiagent Systems.* 73–80.

•[Fenster et al. 1995] Fenster, Maier; Kraus, Sarit; and Rosenschein, Jeffrey; 1995. Coordination without communication: Experimental validation of focal point techniques. In *Proceedings of the International Conference on Multiagent Systems.* 102–108.

[Frenkel 1993] Frenkel, Karen; 1993. An interview with Robin Milner. *Communications of the ACM* 36(1):90–97.

•[Gasser 1991] Gasser, Les; 1991. Social conceptions of knowledge and action: DAI foundations and open systems semantics. *Artificial Intelligence* 47:107–138.

•[Haddadi 1995] Haddadi, Afsaneh; 1995. Towards a pragmatic theory of interactions. In *Proceedings of the International Conference on Multiagent Systems.* 133–139.

•[Hewitt & Inman 1991] Hewitt, Carl and Inman, Jeff; 1991. DAI betwixt and between: From "intelligent agents" to open systems science. *IEEE Transactions on Systems, Man, and Cybernetics* 21(6):1409–1419.

•[Littman et al. 1995] Littman, Michael; Cassandra, Anthony; and Kaelbling, Leslie; 1995. Learning policies for partially observable environments: Scaling up. In *Proceedings of the 12th International Conference on Machine Learning.* 362–370.

•[Lux & Steiner 1995] Lux, Andreas and Steiner, Donald; 1995. Understanding cooperation: An agent's perspective. In *Proceedings of the International Conference on Multiagent Systems.* 261–268.

[McCarthy 1979] McCarthy, John; 1979. Ascribing mental qualities to machines. In Ringle, Martin, editor, *Philosophical Perspectives in Artificial Intelligence.* Harvester Press, Brighton, England.

[McCarthy 1992] McCarthy, John; 1992. Elephant 2000: A programming language based on speech acts. Computer Science Department, Stanford University, **http://www-formal.stanford.edu/jmc/elephant.html.**

[Milner 1993] Milner, Robin; 1993. Elements of interaction. *Communications of the ACM* 36(1):78–89. Turing Award Lecture.

•[Rao & Georgeff 1991] Rao, Anand S. and Georgeff, Michael P.; 1991. Modeling rational agents within a BDI architecture. In *Proceedings of the International Conference on Principles of Knowledge Representation and Reasoning.* 473–484.

•[Rosenschein & Zlotkin 1994] Rosenschein, Jeffrey S. and Zlotkin, Gilad; 1994. Designing conventions for automated negotiation. *AI Magazine.* 29–46.

•[Sen et al. 1994] Sen, Sandip; Sekaran, Mahendra; and Hale, John; 1994. Learning to coordinate without sharing information. In *Proceedings of the National Conference on Artificial Intelligence.* 426–431.

•[Shoham 1993] Shoham, Yoav; 1993. Agent-oriented programming. *Artificial Intelligence* 60(1):51–92.

•[Sichman et al. 1994] Sichman, Jaime Simao; Conte, Rosaria; Demazeau, Yves; and Castelfranchi, Cristiano; 1994. A social reasoning mechanism based on dependence networks. In *Proceedings of the 11th European Conference on Artificial Intelligence.* 188–192.

[Singh 1992] Singh, Munindar P.; 1992. A critical examination of the Cohen-Levesque theory of intentions. In *Proceedings of the 10th European Conference on Artificial Intelligence.* 364–368.

•[Singh 1993] Singh, Munindar P.; 1993. A semantics for speech acts. *Annals of Mathematics and Artificial Intelligence* 8(I–II):47–71.

[Singh 1994] Singh, Munindar P.; 1994. *Multiagent Systems: A Theoretical Framework for Intentions, Know-How, and Communications.* Springer-Verlag, Heidelberg, Germany.

•[Tambe 1996] Tambe, Milind; Johnson, Lewis; and Shen Wei-Min; 1996. Adaptive agent tracking in real-world multi-agent domains: A preliminary report. In *Proceedings of the AAAI Spring Symposium on Adaptation, Coevolution, and Learning in Multiagent Systems.* AAAI Press, Menlo Park, CA.

•[Tan 1993] Tan, M.; 1993. Multi-agent reinforcement learning: Independent vs. cooperative learning. In *Proceedings of the 10th International Conference on Machine Learning.* 330–337.

•[Tokoro 1993] Tokoro, Mario; 1993. The society of objects. In *Addendum to the Proceedings of the International Conference on Object-Oriented Programming Systems, Languages, and Applications (OOPSLA).* 3–11. Invited talk.

•[Weiss 1993] Weiss, Gerhard; 1993. Learning to coordinate actions in multi-agent systems. In *Proceedings of the International Joint Conference on Artificial Intelligence.* 311–316.

•[Wellman 1995] Wellman, Michael P.; 1995. A computational market model for distributed configuration design. *AI EDAM* 9:125–133.

•[Wooldridge & Jennings 1994] Wooldridge, Michael and Jennings, Nick; 1994. Formalizing the cooperative problem solving process. In *Proceedings of the 13th International Workshop on Distributed Artificial Intelligence.* 403–417.

4.1 Rational Agency: Logical

Modeling Rational Agents within a BDI-Architecture*

Anand S. Rao
Australian Artificial Intelligence Institute
Carlton, Victoria 3053
Australia
Email: anand@aaii.oz.au

Michael P. Georgeff
Australian Artificial Intelligence Institute
Carlton, Victoria 3053
Australia
Email: georgeff@aaii.oz.au

Abstract

Intentions, an integral part of the mental state of an agent, play an important role in determining the behavior of rational agents as they seek to attain their goals. In this paper, a formalization of intentions based on a branching-time possible-worlds model is presented. It is shown how the formalism realizes many of the important elements of Bratman's theory of intention. In particular, the notion of intention developed here has equal status with the notions of belief and desire, and cannot be reduced to these concepts. This allows different types of rational agents to be modeled by imposing certain conditions on the persistence of an agent's beliefs, goals, and intentions. Finally, the formalism is compared with Bratman's theory of intention and Cohen and Levesque's formalization of intentions.

1 INTRODUCTION

The role played by attitudes such as beliefs (B), desires (D) (or goals (G)), and intentions (I) in the design of rational agents has been well recognized in the philosophical and AI literature [2, 3, 9]. Systems and formalisms that give primary importance to intentions are often referred to as BDI-architectures. While most philosophical theories treat intentions as being reducible to beliefs and desires, Bratman argues convincingly that intentions play a significant and distinct role in practical reasoning. He treats intentions as partial plans of action that the agent is committed to execute to fulfill her goals.

Some of the philosophical aspects of Bratman's theory were formalized by Cohen and Levesque [6]. In their formalism, intentions are defined in terms of temporal sequences of an agent's beliefs and goals. In particular, an agent *fanatically committed* to her intentions will maintain her goals until either they are believed to be achieved or believed to be unachievable; an agent with a *relativized commitment* to her intentions is similarly committed to her goals but may also drop them when some specified conditions are believed to hold.

In this paper, we present an alternative possible-worlds formalism for BDI-architectures. There are three crucial elements to the formalism. First, intentions are treated as first-class citizens on a par with beliefs and goals. This allows us to define different strategies of commitment with respect to an agent's intentions and thus to model a wide variety of agents. Second, we distinguish between the *choice* an agent has over the actions she can perform and the *possibilities* of different outcomes of an action. In the former case, the agent can choose among outcomes; in the latter case, the environment makes that determination. Third, we specify an interrelationship between beliefs, goals, and intentions that allows us to avoid many of the problems usually associated with possible-worlds formalisms, such as commitment to unwanted side effects.

In the following sections, we briefly outline the formalism and describe some of its more important features. We then define a number of different commitment strategies and show how these affect agent behavior.

2 INFORMAL SEMANTICS

We choose to model the world using a temporal structure with a branching time future and a single past, called a *time tree*. A particular time point in a particular world is called a *situation*.

Event types transform one time point into another. Primitive events are those events directly performable by the agent and uniquely determine the next time point in a time tree. Non-primitive events map to non-adjacent time points, thus allowing us to model

*This research was partly supported by a *Generic Industrial Research and Development Grant* from the Department of Industry, Technology and Commerce, Australia.

the partial nature of plans. Their potential for decomposition into primitive events can be used to model hierarchical plan development.

The branches in a time tree can be viewed as representing the *choices* available to the agent at each moment of time. For example, if there are two branches emanating from a particular time point, one labeled e_1, say, and the other e_2, then the agent has a choice of executing e_1 and moving to the next time point along the branch of the time tree labeled with e_1, or of executing e_2 and likewise moving along its associated branch.

Of course, the agent may attempt to execute some event, but fail to do so. We thus distinguish between the successful execution of events and their failure and label the branches accordingly. As we shall see later, this distinction is critical in having an agent act on her intentions without requiring her to be successful in her attempts.

We use a formalism similar to Computation Tree Logic, CTL*, [7] to describe these structures.[1] A distinction is made between *state formulas* and *path formulas*: the former are evaluated at a specified time point in a time tree and the latter over a specified path in a time tree. We introduce two modal operators, *optional* and *inevitable*, which operate on path formulas. A path formula ψ is said to be *optional* if, at a particular time point in a time tree, ψ is true of at least one path emanating from that point; it is *inevitable* if ψ is true of all paths emanating from that point.[2] The standard temporal operators $\bigcirc$ (next), $\Diamond$ (eventually), $\Box$ (always), and U (until), operate over state and path formulas.

These modalities can be combined in various ways to describe the options available to the agent, such as shown in Figure 1. For example, the structure shown in the figure could be used to represent the following statements: it is *optional* that John will *eventually* visit London (denoted by p); it is *optional* that Mary will *always* live in Australia (r); it is *inevitable* that the world will *eventually* come to an end (q); and it is *inevitable* that one plus one will *always* be two (s).

Belief is modeled in the conventional way. That is, in each situation we associate a set of *belief-accessible* worlds; intuitively, those worlds that the agent *believes* to be possible. Unlike most conventional models of belief, however, each belief-accessible world is a time tree. Multiple belief-accessible worlds result from the agent's lack of knowledge about the state of the world. But within each of these worlds, the branching future represents the choice (options) still available to the agent in selecting which actions to perform.

Further insight into the approach is provided by comparing the above possible-worlds model with a conventional decision tree. In this case, each arc emanating from a *chance* node of a decision tree corresponds to a possible world, and each arc emanating from a *decision* node to the choice available within a possible world. A formal comparison of our possible-worlds model with the decision-tree representation is carried out elsewhere [14].

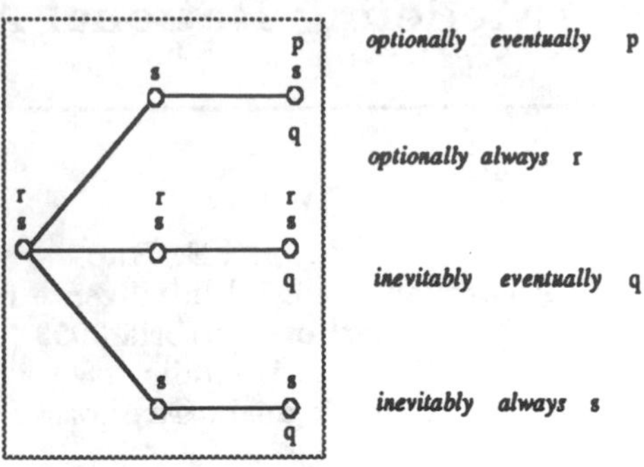

Figure 1: Temporal modalities

Similar to belief-accessible worlds, for each situation we also associate a set of *goal-accessible* worlds to represent the goals of the agent. Although, in the general case, desires can be inconsistent with one another, we require that goals be consistent. In other words, goals are chosen desires of the agent that are consistent. Moreover, the agent should believe that the goal is achievable. This prevents the agent from adopting goals that she believes are unachievable and is one of the distinguishing properties of goals as opposed to desires. Cohen and Levesque [5] call this the property of *realism*.

In this paper, we adopt a notion of *strong realism*. In particular, we require that the agent believe she can optionally achieve her goals, by carefully choosing the events she executes (or, more generally, that get executed by her or any other agent). We enforce this notion of compatibility by requiring that, for each belief-accessible world w at a given moment in time t, there must be a goal-accessible world that is a *sub-world* of w at time t. Figure 2 illustrates this relation between belief- and goal-accessible worlds. The goal-accessible world $g1$ is a sub-world of the belief-accessible world $b1$.

Intentions are similarly represented by sets of *intention-accessible* worlds. These worlds are ones that the agent has *committed* to attempt to realize. Similar to the requirement for belief-goal compatibility, the intention-accessible worlds of the agent must be compatible with her goal-accessible worlds; an agent can only intend some course of action if it is one of her goals. Consequently, corresponding to each

[1] Elsewhere [15] we use an explicit notion of time to describe these structures.

[2] In CTL*, E and A are used to denote these operators.

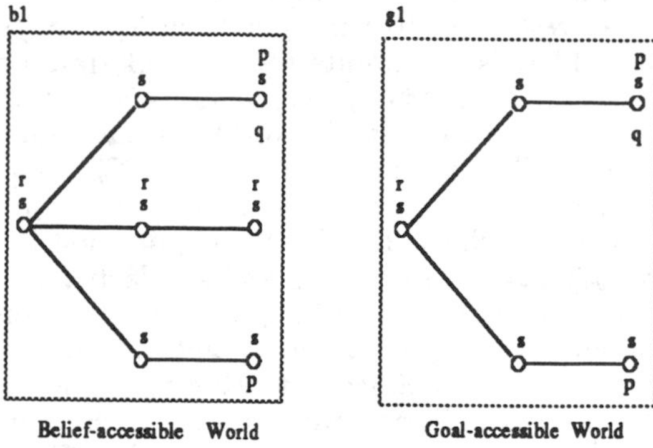

Figure 2: Subworld relationship between beliefs and goals

goal-accessible world w at time t, there must be an intention-accessible world that is a *sub-world* of w at time t. Intuitively, the agent chooses some course of action in w and commits herself to attempt its execution.

In this framework, different belief-, goal-, and intention-accessible worlds represent different possible scenarios for the agent. Intuitively, the agent believes the actual world to be one of her belief-accessible worlds; if it were to be belief world $b1$, then her goals (with respect to $b1$) would be the corresponding goal-accessible world, $g1$ say, and her intentions the corresponding intention-accessible world, $i1$. As mentioned above, $g1$ and $i1$ represent increasingly selective choices from $b1$ about the desire for and commitment to possible future courses of action.

While for every belief-accessible world there must be a goal-accessible world (and similarly for intentions), the converse need not hold. Thus, even if the agent believes that certain facts are inevitable, she is not forced to adopt them as goals (or as intentions). This means that goals and intentions, while having to be consistent, need not be closed under the beliefs of the agent.

In this way, an agent believing that it is inevitable that pain (p) always accompanies having a tooth filled (f), may yet have the goal (or intention) to have a tooth filled without also having the goal (or intention) to suffer pain. This relationship between belief, goal, and intention-accessible worlds is illustrated by the example shown in Figure 3. Although the agent believes that ***inevitably always*** $(f \supset p)$, she does not adopt this as a goal nor as an intention. Similarly, although the agent adopts the goal (and intention) to achieve f, she does not thereby acquire the goal (or intention) p.

The semantics of beliefs, goals, and intentions given above is formalized in Section 3. It thus remains to be shown how these attitudes determine the actions of

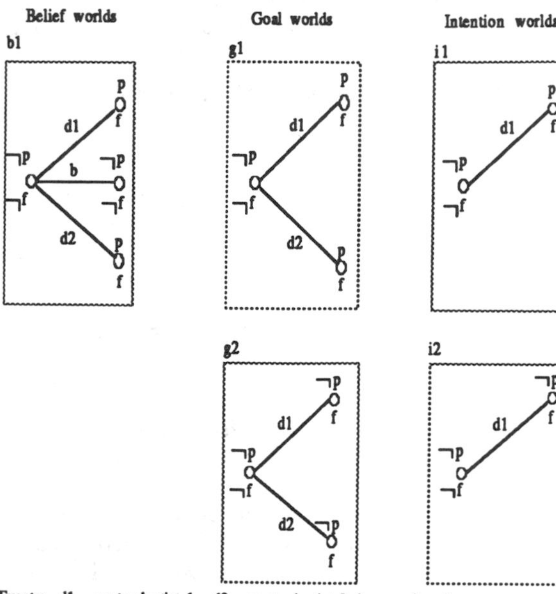

Events: d1 - go to dentist 1, d2 - go to dentist 2, b - go shopping
Facts: p - pain, f - tooth-filled

Figure 3: Belief, Goal, and Intention Worlds

an agent and how they are formed, maintained, and revised as the agent interacts with her environment. Different types of agent will have different schemes for doing this, which in turn will determine their behavioral characteristics. We consider some of these schemes and their formalization in Section 4.

3 FORMAL THEORY

3.1 SYNTAX

CTL* [7] is a propositional branching-time logic used for reasoning about programs. We extend this logic in two ways. First, we describe a first-order variant of the logic. Second, we extend this logic to a possible-worlds framework by introducing modal operators for beliefs, goals, and intentions. While Emerson and Srinivasan [7] provide a sound and complete axiomatization for their logic, we do not address the issue of completeness in this paper. Our main aim is to present an expressive semantics for intentions and to investigate certain axioms that relate intentions to beliefs and goals within this structure.

Similar to CTL*, we have two types of formulas in our logic: *state formulas* (which are evaluated at a given time point in a given world) and *path formulas* (which are evaluated along a given path in a given world). A state formula can be defined as follows:

- any first-order formula is a state formula;

- if ϕ_1 and ϕ_2 are state formulas and x is an individual or event variable, then $\neg\phi_1$, $\phi_1 \vee \phi_2$, and $\exists x\ \phi_1(x)$ are state formulas;
- if e is an event type then *succeeds*(e), *fails*(e), *does*(e), *succeeded*(e), *failed*(e), and *done*(e) are state formulas;
- if ϕ is state formula then BEL(ϕ), GOAL(ϕ) and INTEND(ϕ) are state formulas; and
- if ψ is a path formula, then *optional*(ψ) is a state formula.

A path formula can be defined as follows:

- any state formula is also a path formula; and
- if ψ_1 and ψ_2 are path formulas, then $\neg\psi_1$, $\psi_1 \vee \psi_2$, $\psi_1 \mathsf{U} \psi_2$, $\Diamond\psi_1$, $\bigcirc\psi_1$ are path formulas.

Intuitively, the formulas *succeeded*(e) and *failed*(e) represent the immediate past performance, respectively successfully and unsuccessfully, of event e. The formula *done*(e) represents the immediate past occurrence of e, either successfully performed or not. The formulas *succeeds*(e), *fails*(e), and *does*(e) are similarly defined but refer to the immediate future occurrence of events. The operators BEL, GOAL, and INTEND represent, respectively, the beliefs, goals, and intentions of the agent.

3.2 POSSIBLE-WORLDS SEMANTICS

We first provide the semantics of various state and path formulas. This will be followed by the semantics of events and, finally, the possible-worlds semantics of beliefs, goals, and intentions.

Definition 1 : An interpretation M is defined to be a tuple, M = $\langle$W, E, T, $\prec$, U, $\mathcal{B}$, $\mathcal{G}$, $\mathcal{I}$, $\Phi\rangle$. W is a set of worlds, E is a set of primitive event types, T is a set of time points, $\prec$ a binary relation on time points,[3] U is the universe of discourse, and Φ is a mapping of first-order entities to elements in U for any given world and time point. A situation is a world, say w, at a particular time point, say t, and is denoted by w_t. The relations, $\mathcal{B}$, $\mathcal{G}$, and $\mathcal{I}$ map the agent's current situation to her belief, goal, and intention-accessible worlds, respectively. More formally, $\mathcal{B} \subseteq$ W $\times$ T $\times$ W and similarly for $\mathcal{G}$ and $\mathcal{I}$. Sometimes we shall use $\mathcal{R}$ to refer to any one of these relations and shall use $\mathcal{R}^w_t$ to denote the set of worlds $\mathcal{R}$-accessible from world w at time t. Figure 4 shows how the belief relation $\mathcal{B}$ maps the world $w0$ at time t_1 to the worlds $b1$ and $b2$. In other words, $\mathcal{B}^{w0}_{t_1} = \{b1, b2\}$.

Definition 2 : Each world w of W, called a *time tree*, is a tuple $<T_w, \mathcal{A}_w, \mathcal{S}_w, \mathcal{F}_w>$, where $T_w \subseteq$ T is a set of time points in the world w and $\mathcal{A}_w$ is the same as $\prec$, restricted to time points in T_w. A ***fullpath*** in a world w is an infinite sequence of time points (t_0, t_1,...) such that $\forall i\ (t_i, t_{i+1}) \in \mathcal{A}_w$. We use the notation ($w_{t_0}$, w_{t_1},...) to make the world of a particular fullpath explicit. The arc functions $\mathcal{S}_w$ and $\mathcal{F}_w$ map adjacent time points to events in E. More formally, $\mathcal{S}_w$: $T_w \times T_w \mapsto$ E and similarly for $\mathcal{F}_w$. We require that if $\mathcal{S}_w(t_i, t_j) = \mathcal{S}_w(t_i, t_k)$, then $t_j = t_k$ and similarly for $\mathcal{F}_w$. Also, the domains of $\mathcal{S}_w$ and $\mathcal{F}_w$ are disjoint. Intuitively, for any two adjacent time points for which the arc function $\mathcal{S}_w$ is defined, its value represents the event that successfully occurred between those time points. Similarly, the value of the arc function $\mathcal{F}_w$ represents the failure of events occurring between adjacent time points.

Definition 3 : A ***sub-world*** is defined to be a sub-tree of a world with the same truth-assignment of formulas. A world w' is a ***sub-world*** of the world w, denoted by $w' \sqsubseteq w$, if and only if (a) $T_{w'} \subseteq T_w$; (b) for all $u \in T_{w'}$, $\Phi(q, w', u) = \Phi(q, w, u)$, where q is a predicate symbol; (c) for all $u \in T_{w'}$, $\mathcal{R}^w_u = \mathcal{R}^{w'}_u$; and (d) $\mathcal{A}_{w'}$ is $\mathcal{A}_w$ restricted to time points in $T_{w'}$ and similarly for $\mathcal{S}_{w'}$ and $\mathcal{F}_{w'}$. We say that w' is a ***strict sub-world*** of w denoted by $w' \sqsubset w$ if and only if $w' \sqsubseteq w$ and $w \not\sqsubseteq w'$.

Now consider an interpretation M, with a variable assignment v.[4] We take v^i_d to be that function that yields d for the variable i and is the same as v everywhere else. The semantics of first-order formulas can be given as follows:

$M, v, w_t \models q(y_1, ..., y_n)$ iff $\langle v(y_1), ..., v(y_n)\rangle \in \Phi[q, w, t]$ where $q(y_1, ..., y_n)$ is a predicate formula.
$M, v, w_t \models \neg\phi$ iff $M, v, w_t \not\models \phi$.
$M, v, w_t \models \phi_1 \vee \phi_2$ iff $M, v, w_t \models \phi_1$ or $M, v, w_t \models \phi_2$
$M, v, w_t \models \exists i\phi$ iff $M, v^i_d, w_t \models \phi$ for some d in U.
$M, v, (w_{t_0}, w_{t_1}, ...) \models \phi$ iff $M, v, w_{t_0} \models \phi$.
$M, v, (w_{t_0}, w_{t_1}, ...) \models \bigcirc\psi$ iff $M, v, (w_{t_1}, ...) \models \psi$.
$M, v, (w_{t_0}, w_{t_1}, ...) \models \Diamond\psi$ iff $\exists k, k \geq 0$ such that $M, v, (w_{t_k}, ...) \models \psi$.
$M, v, (w_{t_0}, w_{t_1}, ...) \models \psi_1 \mathsf{U} \psi_2$ iff
(a) $\exists k, k \geq 0$ such that $M, v, (w_{t_k}, ...) \models \psi_2$ and for all $0 \leq j < k$, $M, v, (w_{t_j}, ...) \models \psi_1$ or
(b) for all $j \geq 0$, $M, v, (w_{t_j}, ...) \models \psi_1$.
$M, v, w_{t_0} \models$ *optional*(ψ) iff there exists a fullpath (w_{t_0}, w_{t_1},...) such that $M, v, (w_{t_0}, w_{t_1},...) \models \psi$.

The formula ***inevitable***(ψ) is defined as $\neg$***optional***($\neg\psi$) and $\Box\psi$ is defined as $\neg\Diamond\neg\psi$. The definition of U (until) given above is that of ***weak*** until, which allows fullpaths in which ψ_1 is true forever. Well-formed formulas that contain no positive occurrences of ***inevitable*** (or negative occurrences of ***optional***) outside the scope of the

[3] We require that the binary relation be total, transitive and backward-linear to enforce a single past and branching future.

[4] For the sake of simplicity, we shall assume that the variable assignment of event terms are events denoted by the same letter, i.e., $v(e) = e$ for any event term e.

modal operators BEL, GOAL, or INTEND will be called O-formulas and denoted by α. Conversely, we define I-formulas, denoted by β, to contain no positive occurrences of *optional*.

3.2.1 Semantics of Events

Event types transform one time point into another. The various aspects involved in this transformation are called the *dynamics* of a system [8, 13]. Just as one can define the *truth* or *falsity* of formulas at a time point, we need mechanisms for defining the *success* or *failure* of events in transforming one time point to another.

We use the formula *succeeded*(e) to denote the successful execution of event e by the agent, and *failed*(e) to denote its failure. Note that event e *not occurring* is not the same as the event e *failing*. Failure of event types alter the world irrevocably, possibly forcing the agent to replan or revise her plans. This aspect is crucial in capturing the dynamics of any system. For example, the consequences of a thief successfully robbing a bank is quite different from the thief failing in his attempt to rob the bank, which is again different from the thief not attempting to rob the bank. All three are distinct behaviors and have to be distinguished accordingly.

We say that the agent has *done*(e) if she has either *succeeded* or *failed* in doing the event. The notions *succeeds*, *failed*, and *does* are similarly defined, but require the event to occur on all paths emanating from the time point at which the formula is evaluated.

More formally, we have:

$M, v, w_{t_1} \models succeeded(e)$ iff there exists t_0 such that $\mathcal{S}_w(t_0, t_1) = e$.
$M, v, w_{t_1} \models failed(e)$ iff there exists t_0 such that $\mathcal{F}_w(t_0, t_1) = e$.

The formula *done*(e) is defined as *succeeded*(e) $\vee$ *failed*(e); *succeeds*(e) is defined as *inevitable*$\bigcirc$(*succeeded*(e)); *fails*(e) is defined as *inevitable*$\bigcirc$(*failed*(e)); *does*(e) is defined as *inevitable*$\bigcirc$(*done*(e));

In this paper, we have considered only single-agent, non-parallel actions. If parallel actions among multiple agents are to be allowed, the functions $\mathcal{S}_w$ and $\mathcal{F}_w$ must be extended to map to a set of event-agent pairs, signifying which events are performed by which agents.

3.2.2 Semantics of Beliefs, Goals, and Intentions

The traditional possible-worlds semantics of beliefs considers each world to be a collection of propositions and models belief by a belief-accessibility relation $\mathcal{B}$ linking these worlds. A formula is said to be believed in a world if and only if it is true in all its belief-accessible worlds [10].

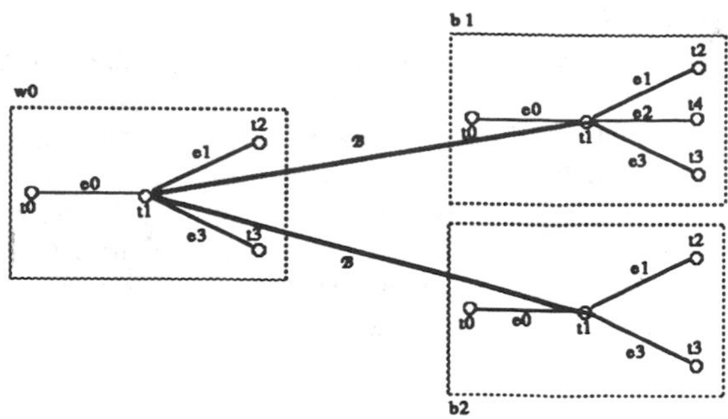

Figure 4: Worlds as time trees

Cohen and Levesque [6] treat each possible world as a *time-line* representing a sequence of events, temporally extended infinitely into the past and the future. As discussed in Section 2, we instead consider each possible world to be a *time tree*. Each time tree denotes the optional courses of events choosable by an agent in a particular world. The belief relation maps a possible world at a time point to other possible worlds. We say that an agent has a belief ϕ, denoted BEL(ϕ), at time point t if and only if ϕ is true in all the belief-accessible worlds of the agent at time t.

Figure 4 shows how the belief relation $\mathcal{B}$ maps the world $w0$ at time t_1 to the worlds $b1$ and $b2$. Let us assume that the formulas that are true at t_1 in $b1$ are ϕ_1 and ϕ_2, while the formulas that are true at t_1 in $b2$ are ϕ_1 and $\neg\phi_2$. From this it is easy to conclude that BEL(ϕ_1) and $\neg$BEL(ϕ_2) are true at t_1 in $w0$. As discussed earlier, ϕ_1 and ϕ_2 could be any state formulas; in particular, ones involving the future options available to the agent.

As the belief relation is time-dependent, the mapping of $\mathcal{B}$ at some other time point, say t_2, may be different from the one at t_1. Thus the agent can change her beliefs about the options available to her.

The semantics of the modal operator GOAL is given in terms of a goal-accessible relation $\mathcal{G}$ which is similar to that of the $\mathcal{B}$ relation. The goal-accessibility relation specifies situations that the agent *desires* to be in. Thus, in the same way that we treat belief, we say that the agent has a goal ϕ at time t if and only if ϕ is true in all the goal-accessible worlds of the agent at time t.

One can view intentions as future paths that the agent *chooses to follow*. The intention-accessibility relation $\mathcal{I}$ will be used to map the agent's current situation to all her intention-accessible worlds. We shall say that the agent intends a formula at a certain time if and only if it is true in all the agent's intention-accessible worlds of that time.

We saw above that the goal-accessible worlds of the agent can be viewed as the sub-worlds of the belief-accessible worlds in which the agent desires to be. Similarly, one can view intention-accessible worlds as sub-worlds of the goal-accessible worlds that the agent chooses to follow (i.e., to act upon). Thus, one moves from a belief-accessible world to a goal-accessible world by *desiring* future paths, and from a goal-accessible world to an intention-accessible world by *committing* to certain desired future paths.

The semantics for beliefs, goals, and intentions can be defined formally as follows:

$M, v, w_t \models \mathsf{BEL}(\phi)$ iff $\forall w' \in \mathcal{B}_t^w\ M, v, w'_t \models \phi$.
$M, v, w_t \models \mathsf{GOAL}(\phi)$ iff $\forall w' \in \mathcal{G}_t^w\ M, v, w'_t \models \phi$.
$M, v, w_t \models \mathsf{INTEND}(\phi)$ iff $\forall w' \in \mathcal{I}_t^w\ M, v, w'_t \models \phi$.

We allow intentions over any well-formed formula, which means that one can have intentions about intentions, intentions about goals, intentions about beliefs, and intentions to do certain actions. Some might consider only the last type of intention to correspond with natural usage. While this is arguable, in our formalism the agent might have any type of intention but will only act on the last type of intention.

As an illustration of these ideas, Figure 3 shows one world $b1$ that is belief-accessible from the current situation, say $w0$ at t_0, two worlds $g1$ and $g2$ that are goal-accessible from $w0$ at t_0, and two worlds $i1$ and $i2$ that are intention-accessible from $w0$ at t_0. It is clear from the figure that $i1 \sqsubset g1 \sqsubset b1$ and $i2 \sqsubset g2$. One of the formulas that is true at t_0 in all the intended worlds is $succeeds(d_1)$. Thus the agent intends $succeeds(d_1)$. The sub-world relationship forces the agent to believe, as well as have the goal that $succeeds(d_1)$. The agent intends to succeed and hence intends to carry out the action d_1, but the agent cannot guarantee the ultimate success of her actions—that will be determined by the environment in which the agent is embedded. Thus, even though the above formula is true, it is not necessary, in the actual world, that the formula $succeeded(d_1)$ be true.

From the figure it is clear that at t_0, one of the goal formulas true in all goal accessible worlds is $inevitable(\Diamond f)$. This also implies that the agent believes that this goal is achievable; in other words, $\mathsf{BEL}(optional(\Diamond f))$. From the beliefs, goals, and intentions of the agent, one can say that the agent believes that, if she succeeds in doing d_1, she will achieve the goal f.

3.3 AXIOMATIZATION AND SEMANTIC CONDITIONS

So far, we have not provided any axioms or semantic conditions to capture the desired interrelationships among an agent's beliefs, goals, and intentions. We examine some of these below; additional constraints are discussed elsewhere [14].

The axiomatization for beliefs is the standard weak-S5 (or KD45) modal system [11]. We adopt the D and K axioms for goals and intentions; i.e., goals and intentions have to be closed under implication and have to be consistent.

We also have the inference rule of necessitation [11] for beliefs, goals, and intentions. In other words, the agent believes all valid formulas, intends all valid formulas, and has them as a goal. Hence, like most possible-worlds formalisms, our logic also suffers from the logical omniscience problem [18]. This problem can be partly alleviated by adopting the *minimal-model* semantics of Chellas [4] and giving up the inference rule of necessitation and the K-axiom for beliefs, goals, and intentions. However, in this paper we adopt the more traditional modal-logic semantics.

Belief-Goal Compatibility:

The *Axiom of belief-goal compatibility* states that if the agent adopts an O-formula α as a goal, the agent believes that formula.

(AI1) $\mathsf{GOAL}(\alpha) \supset \mathsf{BEL}(\alpha)$.

The above axiom essentially states that, if the agent has the goal that $optional(\psi)$ is true, she also believes it; i.e., there is at least one path in all the belief-accessible worlds in which ψ is true.

Consider, for example, the case where the formula ψ above is $\Diamond p$. The axiom then states that, if in all the goal-accessible worlds of the agent there is at least one path where eventually p becomes true, it must be the case that in all the belief-accessible worlds of the agent there is at least one path where eventually p is true. But note that, because of the branching nature of time, the agent need not believe she will ever reach the time point where p is true.

The notion of strong realism as described in Section 2 is captured by imposing the restriction that, for each and every belief-accessible world, there is a corresponding goal-accessible world such that the goal-world is a sub-world of the belief-world. This leads to the following semantic condition:

(CI1) $\forall w' \in \mathcal{B}_t^w\ \exists w'' \in \mathcal{G}_t^w$ such that $w'' \sqsubseteq w'$.

We shall use $\mathcal{B}_t^w \subseteq_{super} \mathcal{G}_t^w$ as a succinct notation for CI1. Such a relationship is shown in Figure 3, where $g1 \sqsubset b1$.

As both beliefs and goals are consistent, the relations $\mathcal{B}$ and $\mathcal{G}$ have to be *serial* (i.e., for any situation there is at least one belief-accessible world and at least one goal-accessible world). This ensures that, in the above semantic condition, we can find at least one belief-accessible world for which there is a goal-accessible world.

To capture the notion of realism, Cohen and Levesque require, instead, that the goal relation $\mathcal{G}$ be a subset of the belief relation $\mathcal{B}$; i.e., $\mathcal{G} \subseteq \mathcal{B}$. As each possible world in their formalism is a time line, this imposes the condition that the chosen (or goal-accessible) worlds are compatible with the agent's belief-accessible worlds. In other words, BEL(ϕ) $\supset$ GOAL(ϕ) is an axiom in their formalism. This axiom forces the agent to adopt as goals certain inevitable facts about the world. As we shall see later, the different semantic condition used in our approach helps us avoid this problem of overcommitment.

Strong realism and realism are not the only ways of capturing the relationship between beliefs and goals. Elsewhere [16] we provide a different semantic relation between beliefs and goals that is suited to realizing other properties of these attitudes.

Goal-Intention Compatibility:

The *Axiom of goal-intention compatibility* states that, if the agent adopts an O-formula α as an intention, the agent should have adopted that formula as a goal to be achieved.

(AI2) INTEND(α) $\supset$ GOAL(α).

From the above axioms we have that, if the agent intends α, she believes in α as well. For example, if the agent intends to do an event e, she has the goal to (optionally) do e and also believes that she will (optionally) do e. Nested intentions lead to some interesting consequences. If the formula INTEND(*inevitable*($\Diamond$INTEND(*does*(e)))) is true, then BEL(*optional*($\Diamond$INTEND(*does*(e)))) is true and also BEL(*optional*($\Diamond$BEL(*does*(e)))) is true.

Analogous to the semantic condition CI1 we have the semantic condition CI2, which imposes the restriction that for each and every goal-accessible world there is a corresponding intention-accessible world such that the intention-world is a sub-world of the goal-world.

(CI2) $\forall w' \in \mathcal{G}_t^w \; \exists w'' \in \mathcal{I}_t^w$ such that $w'' \sqsubseteq w'$.

We shall use $\mathcal{G}_t^w \subseteq_{super} \mathcal{I}_t^w$ as a succinct notation for CI2. Figure 3 illustrates the above semantic condition, where $i1 \sqsubset g1$ and $i2 \sqsubset g2$.

As discussed earlier, for each situation there is at least one goal-accessible world and at least one intention-accessible world.

Intentions leading to Actions:

The *Axiom of intention to action* (AI3) captures volitional commitment [2] by stating that the agent will act if she has an intention towards a single primitive action e. Note that we have not said that the event e will occur successfully, just that the agent is committed to *trying* it. Whether the agent is successful or not depends on the environment in which she is embedded.

(AI3) INTEND(*does*(e)) $\supset$ *does*(e).

Thus, whenever an agent has an intention to do a particular primitive action, she will do that action. However, the axiom does not prevent the agent from doing actions that are not intended. Nor does it say anything about non-primitive actions or other forms of nested intentions.

Note that, if the agent has a *choice* of actions at the current time point, she would be incapable of acting *intentionally* until she deliberates and chooses one of them. One way of modeling this deliberation is to treat the process of deliberation itself as an action to be chosen by the agent [17]. An alternative approach would be to modify Axiom AI3 so that the agent arbitrarily chooses one of her intended actions and does that action.

Beliefs about Intentions:

If an agent has an intention, she believes that she has such an intention. The following axiom and semantic condition capture this notion.

(AI4) INTEND(ϕ) $\supset$ BEL(INTEND(ϕ)).
(CI4) $\forall w' \in \mathcal{B}_t^w$ and $\forall w'' \in \mathcal{I}_t^w$ we have $w'' \in \mathcal{B}_t^{w'}$.

In Figure 3, this requires that $b1$ be $\mathcal{I}$-related to $i1$ and $i2$.

Beliefs about Goals:

If the agent has a goal to achieve ϕ, the agent believes that she has such a goal. This intuition can be captured by the following axiom and its corresponding semantic condition.

(AI5) GOAL(ϕ) $\supset$ BEL(GOAL(ϕ)).
(CI5) $\forall w' \in \mathcal{B}_t^w$ and $\forall w'' \in \mathcal{G}_t^w$ we have $w'' \in \mathcal{B}_t^{w'}$.

In Figure 3, this requires that $b1$ be $\mathcal{G}$-related to $g1$ and $g2$.

Goals about Intentions:

If an agent intends to achieve ϕ, the agent must have the goal to intend ϕ. This requires the following axiom and semantic condition.

(AI6) INTEND(ϕ) $\supset$ GOAL(INTEND(ϕ)).
(CI6) $\forall w' \in \mathcal{G}_t^w$ and $\forall w'' \in \mathcal{I}_t^w$ we have $w'' \in \mathcal{G}_t^{w'}$.

In Figure 3, this requires that $g1$ be $\mathcal{I}$-related to $i1$ and $i2$ and $g2$ be $\mathcal{I}$-related to $i1$ and $i2$.

One can strengthen Axioms AI4–AI6 by replacing each implications by an equivalence. This would result in $\mathsf{INTEND}(\phi) \equiv \mathsf{BEL}(\mathsf{INTEND}(\phi)) \equiv \mathsf{GOAL}(\mathsf{INTEND}(\phi))$ and similarly $\mathsf{GOAL}(\phi) \equiv \mathsf{BEL}(\mathsf{GOAL}(\phi))$, which has the effect of collapsing mixed, nested modalities to their simpler non-nested forms.

Awareness of Primitive Events

The next axiom requires the agent to be aware of all primitive events occurring in the world. Once again, we require only that the agent believe a primitive action has been done, not necessarily whether or not it was done successfully.

(AI7) $done(e) \supset \mathsf{BEL}(done(e))$.

No Infinite Deferral

Finally, we require the agent not to procrastinate with respect to her intentions. In other words, if an agent forms an intention, then some time in the future she will give up that intention. This axiom is similar to the one adopted by Cohen and Levesque [6], which requires that there be no infinite deferral of achievement goals.

(AI8) $\mathsf{INTEND}(\phi) \supset inevitable\Diamond(\neg\mathsf{INTEND}(\phi))$.

The above axiom assumes that the intentions corresponding to maintenance goals are also dropped eventually. This could, if necessary, be avoided by restricting the formula ϕ in Axiom AI8 to be an action formula.

We shall refer to this set of eight axioms, AI1 – AI8, together with the standard axioms for beliefs and goals, as the *basic I-system.*

4 COMMITMENT AS AXIOMS OF CHANGE

So far we have treated intentions as a commitment to the performance of current actions. However, we have not formalized how these intentions guide or determine the agent's future commitment to her actions. In other words, we have not discussed how the agent's current intentions relate to her future intentions.

An alternative, proof-theoretic way of viewing the relationship between current and future intentions is as a process of intention maintenance and revision, or what we could intuitively think of as a commitment strategy. Different types of agent will have different commitment strategies. In what follows, we describe three different commitment strategies: *blind*, *single minded*, and *open minded.*

We define a *blindly* committed agent to be one who maintains her intentions until she *actually* believes that she has achieved them. Formally, the axiom of blind commitment states that, if an agent intends that inevitably ϕ be eventually true, then the agent will inevitably maintain her intentions until she believes ϕ.

(AI9a) $\mathsf{INTEND}(inevitable\Diamond\phi) \supset inevitable(\mathsf{INTEND}(inevitable\Diamond\phi)\ \mathsf{U}\ \mathsf{BEL}(\phi))$.

Depending on whether the formula ϕ is an event formula or not, we can capture commitment to actions (i.e., means) or to conditions that have to be true in the future (i.e., ends). Note also that the axiom is defined only for I-formulas (i.e., for intentions towards actions or conditions that are true of *all* paths in the agent's intention-accessible worlds); we do not say anything about the commitment of agents to *optionally* achieve particular means or ends.

A blind-commitment strategy is clearly very strong: the agent will eventually come to believe she has achieved her intentions or keep them forever. Relaxing this requirement, one can define *single-minded* commitment, in which the agent maintains her intentions as long as she believes that they are still options. More formally, we have the following axiom of single-minded commitment:

(AI9b) $\mathsf{INTEND}(inevitable\Diamond\phi) \supset inevitable(\mathsf{INTEND}(inevitable\Diamond\phi)\ \mathsf{U}\ (\mathsf{BEL}(\phi) \vee \neg\mathsf{BEL}(optional\Diamond\phi))$.

As long as she believes her intentions to be achievable, a single-minded agent will not drop her intentions and thus is committed to her goals. This requirement can also be relaxed. We define an *open-minded* agent to be one who maintains her intentions as long as these intentions are still her goals. In other words, the axiom of open-minded commitment can be stated as follows:

(AI9c) $\mathsf{INTEND}(inevitable\Diamond\phi) \supset inevitable(\mathsf{INTEND}(inevitable\Diamond\phi)\ \mathsf{U}\ (\mathsf{BEL}(\phi) \vee \neg\mathsf{GOAL}(optional\Diamond\phi)))$.

We are now in a position to analyze the properties of different types of agent who adopt the basic I-system, together with one of the above axioms of commitment. Such an agent will be called a *basic agent.*

A basic agent blindly committed to her means (or ends) will inevitably eventually *believe* that she has achieved her means (or ends). This is because Axiom AI9a only allows future paths in which either the object of the intention is eventually believed or the intention is maintained forever. However, by Axiom AI8, the latter paths are not allowed, leading the agent to eventually believe that she has accomplished her intentions.

A basic single-minded agent reaches an identical conclusion only if she continues to believe, until the time she believes she has realized her intentions, that the intended means (or ends) remains an option. Similarly, a basic open-minded agent will eventually believe she has achieved her intentions provided she maintains these intentions as goals until they are believed to have been achieved.

More formally, we have the following theorem for basic agents.

Theorem 1 :

(a) A basic, blindly committed agent, with the basic I-system and Axiom AI9a, satisfies the following property:

$$\mathsf{INTEND}(inevitable(\Diamond\phi)) \supset inevitable(\Diamond \mathsf{BEL}(\phi)).$$

(b) A basic single-minded agent, with the basic I-system and Axiom AI9b, satisfies the following property:

$$\mathsf{INTEND}(inevitable(\Diamond\phi)) \wedge inevitable(\mathsf{BEL}(optional(\Diamond\phi)) \mathsf{~U~} \mathsf{BEL}(\phi)) \supset inevitable(\Diamond \mathsf{BEL}(\phi)).$$

(c) A basic open-minded agent, with the basic I-system and Axiom AI9c, satisfies the following property:

$$\mathsf{INTEND}(inevitable(\Diamond\phi)) \wedge inevitable(\mathsf{GOAL}(optional(\Diamond\phi)) \mathsf{~U~} \mathsf{BEL}(\phi)) \supset inevitable(\Diamond \mathsf{BEL}(\phi)).$$

Proof:

(a) Assume the premise INTEND $(inevitable\ (\Diamond\phi))$. By Axiom AI9a we can conclude *inevitable* (INTEND $(inevitable\ \Diamond\phi)$ U BEL (ϕ)). By Axiom AI8 and the definition of weak until we can conclude *inevitable* ($\Diamond$ BEL (ϕ)). Cases (b) and (c) follow a similar line of reasoning. ♣

Consider now a *competent agent* [6] who satisfies the *Axiom of True Beliefs*, namely $\mathsf{BEL}(\phi) \supset \phi$ (AI10). Under each of the different commitment strategies AI9a, AI9b, and AI9c, the competent agent *will* actually achieve her means (or ends), rather than just believe so. However, AI10 is often difficult for real agents to live up to, as it requires an agent to have true beliefs about the future realization of her intentions. By restricting Axiom AI10 to current beliefs only or to beliefs about primitive action formulas, we can define a less omniscient class of agents who will also inevitably eventually achieve their intentions.

Theorem 2 : *Under the same conditions as Theorem 1, competent agents yield the conclusion* inevitable*$(\Diamond\phi)$ for all three types of commitment.*

Proof: Follows directly from the proofs of Theorem 1 followed by the use of Axiom AI10. ♣

The above theorems, however, are not as useful as one would like. First, they do not make any use of Axiom AI3. This means that the same result is achieved independent of whether or not the agent acts intentionally. Moreover, the second conjunct of the premises of (b) and (c) are conditions that have to be true in the real world and which are impossible for a situated agent to enforce; i.e., the agent cannot control these conditions. As a result, the above theorems, although interesting, do not provide a sufficient basis for a situated agent to reason about her intentions and actions.

Consider now an agent who always performs only intentional actions. This can be enforced by requiring the agent to intend a single primitive action at each and every time point. It is reasonable to expect that, in a world free of surprises, such an agent would maintain her beliefs after doing each intended action; i.e., she would not forget previously held beliefs.

More formally, we can state that an agent *preserves a belief γ over an intentional action x* if and only if (a) she intends to do x and (b) if she believes γ will hold after doing x, then after doing x, she does indeed believe γ:

$$\mathsf{INTEND}(does(x)) \wedge (\mathsf{BEL}(optional \bigcirc (done(x) \wedge \gamma)) \supset optional \bigcirc \mathsf{BEL}(done(x) \wedge \gamma).$$

A single-minded agent who intends inevitably that ϕ is true in the future will inevitably come to believe ϕ provided that she carry out only intentional actions and that she preserve her beliefs about ϕ over these actions. If she were also competent, she would actually come to achieve ϕ.

Theorem 3 :

(a) A basic single-minded agent, with the basic I-system and Axiom AI9b, satisfies the following property:

$$\mathsf{INTEND}(inevitable(\Diamond\phi)) \wedge inevitable \Box (\exists x (\mathsf{INTEND}(does(x)) \wedge (\mathsf{BEL}(optional \bigcirc (done(x) \wedge (\Diamond\phi))) \supset optional \bigcirc \mathsf{BEL}(done(x) \wedge (\Diamond\phi))) \supset inevitable(\Diamond \mathsf{BEL}(\phi)).$$

(b) A competent single-minded agent, with the basic I-system, Axiom AI9b, Axiom AI10, and Axiom AI11 satisfies the following property:

$$\mathsf{INTEND}(inevitable(\Diamond\phi)) \wedge inevitable \Box (\exists x (\mathsf{INTEND}(does(x)) \wedge (\mathsf{BEL}(optional \bigcirc (done(x) \wedge (\Diamond\phi))) \supset optional \bigcirc \mathsf{BEL}(done(x) \wedge (\Diamond\phi))) \supset inevitable(\Diamond(\phi).$$

where the event variable x maps to a primitive event type.

Proof: (a) Assume the premise (i) INTEND $(inevitable\ (\Diamond\phi))$ and (ii) $inevitable\ \Box\ (\exists x$ (INTEND $(does(x)) \wedge$

(BEL ($optional\bigcirc$ ($done(x) \wedge (\Diamond\phi)$))) $\supset$ $optional\bigcirc$ BEL ($done(x) \wedge (\Diamond\phi)$)).

From (i) and Axioms AI2 and AI3 we have BEL ($optional(\Diamond\phi)$). From this conclusion and (ii), we have the conclusion $inevitable$(BEL($optional(\Diamond\phi)$) U BEL(ϕ)). Now we can use Theorem 1 to draw the desired conclusion.

Case (b) is identical to the above proof followed by the application of Axiom AI10. ♣

The second conjunct of the premises of both (a) and (b) can be weakened in several ways. First, Axiom AI3 allows us to drop the $done(x)$ formula in the real world. Second, the agent needs to act according to her intentions only until the moment that she achieves her intentions. In other words, $inevitable\Box$ can be replaced by the until operator.

Given that the agent will also believe the above theorem (by the inference rule of necessitation for beliefs) she will believe that, if she does only intentional actions and preserves her beliefs while doing so, she would ultimately achieve her goals. However, at the same time she can also reason that, if she is forced to do unintentional actions or does not maintain her beliefs, she may not be able to achieve her goals. Therefore, the "Little Nell" problem [12], in which an agent drops an intention precisely because he believes that its fulfillment will achieve his goal, does not arise.

Similar to the property of preservation of beliefs over intentional actions, one can introduce an analogous property of preservation of goals. This would allow open-minded agents to similarly achieve the object of their intentions.

We can also define other types of agent with mixed commitment strategies. For example, a particularly interesting commitment strategy is one in which the agent is open-minded with respect to ends but single-minded with respect to the means towards those ends. Such an agent is free to change the ends to which she aspires but, once committed to a means for realizing those ends, will not reconsider those means.

A ***fanatically committed*** agent [6] corresponds to a competent single-minded agent. Similarly, an agent with a ***relativized commitment*** is competent and open-minded with respect both to means and ends.

We are not suggesting that the above categorization is exhaustive or sufficient for describing realistic rational agents. Our aim in providing the above categorization has simply been to show that the formalism presented here provides a good basis for defining different types of agents and investigating their behavioral properties. It also lays the foundation for a more detailed analysis of reconsideration of intentions [2].

5 PROPERTIES OF THE LOGIC

There are two important aspects of belief-goal-intention interaction that have received attention in the literature [2, 5]. First, if an agent believes that a formula ϕ is ***inevitably always*** true (i.e., ϕ is true at all time points in all the future paths of all belief-accessible worlds), then the agent should ***not*** be forced to (a) adopt ϕ has a goal, or (b) intend ϕ. For example, given that "The earth is round" is true at all time points in all future paths of all belief-accessible worlds of the agent, the agent should not be forced to adopt this as a goal nor be forced to intend such inevitable facts. The same requirement holds for a slightly weaker form of belief; namely, the belief that a formula ϕ is ***inevitably eventually*** true (such as the belief about the rising of the sun). Clearly, an agent with such a belief should not be forced to adopt it as a goal nor intend it. Moreover, this requirement should hold no matter how persistent are the agent's beliefs. In particular, is should hold even if the agent ***inevitably always*** believes that a formula ϕ is ***inevitably always*** true.

Second, if an agent believes that a formula $\phi \supset \gamma$ is ***inevitably always*** true, and the agent intends ϕ (or has the goal ϕ), then the agent should ***not*** be forced to intend γ (or have the goal γ). In other words, an agent who intends to do a certain action should not be forced to intend all the ***side-effects*** of such an action. For example, an agent who intends to go to the dentist to have her tooth removed, but believes ***inevitably*** that going to the dentist will ***always*** cause her pain as a side-effect, should not be forced to intend herself pain [5]. As before, the above requirement also applies to the weaker form of belief and to persistent beliefs.

The above requirements are met by our formalism. While for every belief-accessible world there must be a goal-accessible world (and similarly for intentions), the converse need not hold. Thus, even if the agent believes that certain facts are inevitable, she is not forced to adopt them as goals (or as intentions). In this way, an agent believing that it is inevitable that pain always accompanies having a tooth filled, may yet have the goal (or intention) to have a tooth filled without also having the goal (or intention) to suffer pain. This relationship between belief, goal, and intention-accessible worlds is shown in Figure 3.

Let us define a binary relation $<_{strong}$ on the modal operators such that BEL $<_{strong}$ GOAL $<_{strong}$ INTEND. A modal formula $R_2(\phi)$ is said to be stronger than $R_1(\phi)$ if and only if $R_1 <_{strong} R_2$. We then have the following two propositions:

Proposition 1 : *A modal formula does not imply a stronger modal formula. For example, if the agent believes (or inevitably always believes) that ϕ is true, she need not adopt ϕ as a goal. In other words, the follow-*

ing formulas are satisfiable:

(a) $\mathsf{BEL}(\phi) \wedge \neg\mathsf{GOAL}(\phi)$;

(b) $inevitable(\Box\mathsf{BEL}(\phi)) \wedge \neg\mathsf{GOAL}(\phi)$.

General case: *In general, the above results hold if* BEL *is substituted by* R_1 *and* GOAL *by* R_2, *where* $R_1 <_{strong} R_2$.

Proof: For every belief-accessible world there has to be a goal-accessible world. But the goal relation $\mathcal{G}$ can map to worlds that do not correspond to any belief accessible world. Thus, if in one such world the formula ϕ is not true, the agent will not have ϕ as a goal. This shows the satisfiability of Case (a). The satisfiability of Case (b) follows a similar pattern. ♣

Proposition 2 : *A modal operator is not closed under implication with respect to a weaker modality. For example, the following formulas are satisfiable:*

(a) $\mathsf{GOAL}(\phi) \wedge \mathsf{BEL}(inevitable(\Box(\phi \supset \gamma))) \wedge \neg\mathsf{GOAL}(\gamma)$;

(b) $\mathsf{GOAL}(\phi) \wedge inevitable(\Box\mathsf{BEL}(inevitable(\Box(\phi \supset \gamma))) \wedge \neg\mathsf{GOAL}(\gamma)$.

General case: *In general, the above results hold if* BEL *is substituted by* R_1 *and* GOAL *by* R_2, *where* $R_1 <_{strong} R_2$.

Proof: For every belief-accessible world there has to be a goal-accessible world. But the goal relation $\mathcal{G}$ can map to worlds that do not correspond to any belief-accessible world. Thus, if in one such world the formula $\phi \supset \gamma$ is not true, the agent will not have γ as a goal. This shows the satisfiability of Case (a). The satisfiability of Case (b) follows a similar pattern. ♣

Both the above propositions deal with the stronger form of beliefs; namely, that the agent believes *inevitably always* ϕ. They can be suitably modified for the weaker form as well.

Note that although we have the above propositions, the agent's goals and intentions are closed under implication. In other words, the following formulas are valid formulas in our system:

$$\mathsf{INTEND}(\phi) \wedge \mathsf{INTEND}(\phi \supset \gamma) \supset \mathsf{INTEND}(\gamma).$$
$$\mathsf{GOAL}(\phi) \wedge \mathsf{GOAL}(\phi \supset \gamma) \supset \mathsf{GOAL}(\gamma).$$

Moreover, although an agent need not have as a goal or intention such inevitable facts, this does not prevent her from reasoning about them. Thus, for example, on adopting the intention to go to the dentist, the agent could still use her beliefs about the certainty of accompanying pain in deciding to take along a strong analgesic.

Cohen and Levesque define a notion of persistent goal which appears to have some of the above properties. However, these properties are obtained by appealing to the temporal nature of persistent goals, rather than any intrinsic properties of beliefs, goals, or intentions [1]. For example, Cohen and Levesque can only avoid intending the side effects of any intended action if, at *some* time point in the future, the agent does not believe that the side effect will result from performance of the intended action. The problem remains, however, for cases in which the agent, for example, always believes that the side effect will occur. In other words, Case (b) is not satisfiable for the above propositions for the non-trivial cases. In contrast, in our formalism the agent is not forced to adopt unwanted goals or intentions on account of her beliefs, no matter how strong or persistent these beliefs are.

6 COMPARISON AND CONCLUSION

Bratman [2] argues against the reducibility of intentions to an agent's beliefs and desires and treats intentions as partial plans of action to which the agent is committed. He then goes on to show how the agent's existing beliefs, desires, and intentions form a background for future deliberation. Following this line of argument, we have introduced a logical formalism which accords a primary status to intentions. Further, by adopting certain axioms of change, we have shown how the present beliefs, goals, and intentions of an agent constrain her future attitudes.

Philosophically, our approach differs from that of Cohen and Levesque [6] in that it treats intention as a basic attitude and shifts the emphasis of future commitment from the definition of intention to the process of intention revision. Semantically, our approach differs in that we distinguish between the choice available to the agent in choosing her actions and her beliefs about which worlds are possible. In addition, we specify an interrelationship between beliefs, goals, and intentions that allows us to avoid all variations of the problem of unwanted side effects.

We have only considered constraints on the maintenance of intentions. Important aspects of rational behavior that concerns intention formation by *deliberation* and intention modification in the light of changing circumstances or *reconsideration* [2] have not been dealt with in this paper. These are separate topics which will be considered elsewhere; the sub-world relationship between beliefs, goals, and intentions provides useful techniques for analyzing these issues.

In summary, we have presented a theory of intention that treats intentions on a par with the agent's beliefs and goals. By introducing various axioms of change, we were able to categorize a variety of rational agents and their commitment strategies. We also captured, for the first time, the process of belief, goal, and intention revision, which is crucial for understanding rational behavior [1]. Although there are many aspects of a theory of rational agency that we have not addressed, we believe that we have presented a formalism that provides a foundation upon which such a theory can be constructed.

Acknowledgements

The authors would like to thank Phil Cohen, Martha Pollack, Liz Sonenberg, David Israel, Kurt Konolige, Douglas Appelt, and Félix Ingrand for valuable discussions and comments on the contents of this paper.

References

[1] J. Allen. Two views of intention: Comments on Bratman and on Cohen and Levesque. In P. R. Cohen, J. Morgan, and M. E. Pollack, editors, *Intentions in Communication*. MIT Press, Cambridge, Ma., 1990.

[2] M. E. Bratman. *Intentions, Plans, and Practical Reason*. Harvard University Press, Massachusetts, 1987.

[3] M. E. Bratman, D. Israel, and M. E. Pollack. Plans and resource-bounded practical reasoning. *Computational Intelligence*, 4:349–355, 1988.

[4] B. F. Chellas. *Modal Logic: An Introduction*. Cambridge University Press, 1980.

[5] P. R. Cohen and H. J. Levesque. Persistence, intention and commitment. In M. P. Georgeff and A. L. Lansky, editors, *Proceedings of the 1986 workshop on Reasoning about Actions and Plans*, pages 297–340. Morgan Kaufmann Publishers, San Mateo, CA, 1987.

[6] P. R. Cohen and H. J. Levesque. Intention is choice with commitment. *Artificial Intelligence*, 42(3), 1990.

[7] E. A. Emerson and J. Srinivasan. Branching time temporal logic. In J. W. de Bakker, W.-P. de Roever, and G. Rozenberg, editors, *Linear Time, Branching Time and Partial Order in Logics and Models for Concurrency*, pages 123–172. Springer-Verlag, Berlin, 1989.

[8] P. Gardenfors. *Knowledge in Flux: Modeling the Dynamics of Epistemic States*. Bradford Book, MIT Press, Cambridge, MA., 1988.

[9] M.P. Georgeff and F.F. Ingrand. Decision-making in an embedded reasoning system. In *Proceedings of the International Joint Conference on Artificial Intelligence*, Detroit, MI, 1989.

[10] J. Y. Halpern and Y. O. Moses. A guide to the modal logics of knowledge and belief. In *Proceedings of the Ninth International Joint Conference on Artificial Intelligence(IJCAI-85)*, Los Angeles, CA, 1985.

[11] G. E. Hughes and M. J. Cresswell. *A Companion to Modal Logic*. Methuen & Co. Ltd., London, England, 1984.

[12] D. V. McDermott. A temporal logic for reasoning about processes and plans. *Cognitive Science*, 6:101–155, 1982.

[13] A. S. Rao and N. Y. Foo. Minimal change and maximal coherence: A basis for belief revision and reasoning about actions. In *Proceedings of the International Joint Conference on Artificial Intelligence, IJCAI-89*, Detroit, MI, 1989.

[14] A. S. Rao and M. P. Georgeff. Deliberation and the formation of intentions. Technical Report 10, Australian AI Institute, Carlton, Australia, 1990.

[15] A. S. Rao and M. P. Georgeff. A formal model of intentions. In *Pacific Rim International Conference on Artificial Intelligence, PRICAI-90*, Nagoya, Japan, November 1990.

[16] A. S. Rao and M. P. Georgeff. Asymmetry thesis and side-effect problems in linear time and branching time intention logics. Technical Report 13, Australian AI Institute, Carlton, Australia, 1991.

[17] S. Russell and E. Wefald. Principles of metareasoning. In *Proceedings of the First International Conference on Principles of Knowledge Representation and Reasoning*, Toronto, 1989.

[18] M. Y. Vardi. On epistemic logic and logical omniscience. In J. Y. Halpern, editor, *Proceedings of the First Conference on Theoretical Aspects of Reasoning about Knowledge*, pages 293–306, San Mateo, California, 1986. Morgan Kaufmann Publishers.

Agent-oriented programming

Yoav Shoham

Robotics Laboratory, Computer Science Department, Stanford University, Stanford, CA 94305, USA

Received June 1991
Revised February 1992

Abstract

Shoham, Y., Agent-oriented programming, Artificial Intelligence 60 (1993) 51–92.

A new computational framework is presented, called *agent-oriented programming* (AOP), which can be viewed as a specialization of *object-oriented programming*. The state of an agent consists of components such as beliefs, decisions, capabilities, and obligations; for this reason the state of an agent is called its *mental state*. The mental state of agents is described formally in an extension of standard epistemic logics: beside temporalizing the knowledge and belief operators, AOP introduces operators for obligation, decision, and capability. Agents are controlled by *agent programs*, which include primitives for communicating with other agents. In the spirit of *speech act theory*, each communication primitive is of a certain type: informing, requesting, offering, and so on. This article presents the concept of AOP, discusses the concept of mental state and its formal underpinning, defines a class of agent interpreters, and then describes in detail a specific interpreter that has been implemented.

1. Introduction

This paper proposes a new programming paradigm. The paradigm promotes a societal view of computation, in which multiple "agents" interact with one another, although in this document we will concentrate on the design of the individual agent. Many of the ideas here intersect and interact with the ideas of others. For the sake of continuity, however, I will not place this work in the context of other work until the end.

Correspondence to: Y. Shoham, Robotics Laboratory, Computer Science Department, Stanford University, Stanford, CA 94305, USA. Telephone: (415) 723-3432. E-mail: shoham@cs.stanford.edu.

0004-3702/93/$ 06.00

1.1. What is an agent?

The term "agent" is used frequently these days. This is true in AI, but also outside it, for example in connection with databases and manufacturing automation. Although increasingly popular, the term has been used in such diverse ways that it has become meaningless without reference to a particular notion of agenthood. Some notions are primarily intuitive, others quite formal. Some are very austere, defining an agent in automata-theoretic terms, and others use a more lavish vocabulary. The original sense of the word, of someone acting on behalf of someone else, has been all but lost in AI (an exception that comes to mind is the use of the word in the intelligent-interfaces community, where there is talk of "software agents" carrying out the user's wishes; this is also the sense of *agency theory* in economics [64]). Most often, when people in AI use the term "agent", they refer to an entity that functions continuously and autonomously in an environment in which other processes take place and other agents exist. This is perhaps the only property that is assumed uniformly by those in AI who use the term. The sense of "autonomy" is not precise, but the term is taken to mean that the agents" activities do not require constant human guidance or intervention. Often certain further assumptions are made about the environment, for example that it is physical and partially unpredictable. In fact, agents are sometimes taken to be robotic agents, in which case other issues such as sensory input, motor control, and time pressure are mentioned. Finally, agents are often taken to be "high-level". Although this sense is quite vague, many take some version of it to distinguish agents from other software or hardware components. The "high level" is manifested in symbolic representation and/or some cognitive-like function: agents may be "informable" [24], may contain symbolic plans in addition to stimulus–response rules [13,18,29,53], and may even possess natural language capabilities. This sense is *not* assumed uniformly in AI, and in fact a certain counter-ideology deliberately denies the centrality or even existence of high-level representation in agents [1,7].

Clearly, the notion of agenthood in AI is anything but crisp. I should therefore make it clear what *I* mean by the term "agent", which is precisely this: An agent is an entity whose state is viewed as consisting of mental components such as beliefs, capabilities, choices, and commitments. These components are defined in a precise fashion, and stand in rough correspondence to their common sense counterparts. In this view, therefore, agenthood is in the mind of the programmer: What makes any hardware or software component an agent is precisely the fact that one has chosen to analyze and control it in these mental terms.

The question of what an agent is is now replaced by the question of what entities can be viewed as having mental state. The answer is that *anything* can be so described, although it is not always advantageous to do so. This view is not original to me. For example, in [15] and other publications, Daniel Dennett proposes the "intentional stance", from which systems are ascribed mental qualities such as intentions and free will. The issue, according to Dennett, is not whether a system really is intentional, but whether we can coherently view it as such. Similar sentiments are expressed by John McCarthy in [47], who also distinguishes between the "legitimacy" of ascribing mental qualities to machines and its "usefulness":

> To ascribe certain *beliefs, free will, intentions, consciousness, abilities* or *wants* to a machine or computer program is *legitimate* when such an ascription expresses the same information about the machine that it expresses about a person. It is *useful* when the ascription helps us understand the structure of the machine, its past or future behavior, or how to repair or improve it. It is perhaps never *logically required* even for humans, but expressing reasonably briefly what is actually known about the state of the machine in a particular situation may require mental qualities or qualities isomorphic to them. Theories of belief, knowledge and wanting can be constructed for machines in a simpler setting than for humans, and later applied to humans. Ascription of mental qualities is *most straightforward* for machines of known structure such as thermostats and computer operating systems, but is *most useful* when applied to entities whose structure is very incompletely known.

In [67] I illustrate the point through the light switch example. It is perfectly coherent to treat a light switch as a (very cooperative) agent with the capability of transmitting current at will, who invariably transmits current when it believes that we want it transmitted and not otherwise; flicking the switch is simply our way of communicating our desires. However, while this is a coherent view, it does not buy us anything, since we essentially understand the mechanism sufficiently to have a simpler, mechanistic description of its behavior. In contrast, we do not have equally good knowledge of the operation of complex systems such robots, people, and, arguably, operating systems. In these cases it is often most convenient to employ mental terminology; the application of the concept of "knowledge" to distributed computation, discussed below, is an example of this convenience. [1]

[1] In [67] I discuss how the gradual elimination of animistic explanations with the increase in knowledge is correlated very nicely with both developmental and evolutionary phenomena. In the evolution of science, theological notions were replaced over the centuries with mathematical ones. Similarly, in Piaget's stages of child development, there is a clear transition from animistic stages around the ages of 4–6 (when, for example, children claim that clouds move because they follow us around), and the more mature later stages.

1.2. On the responsible use of pseudo-mental terminology

When I (like Dennett and McCarthy before me) state that in principle anything can be ascribed intensionality, I do not mean that there are no rules for this ascription. We do not arbitrarily label one component of the machine a "belief" and another a "commitment"; that would be gratuitous fancy naming, against which McDermott has already warned [51]. Indeed, if the labeling were arbitrary, there would be no reason not to exchange the labels "belief" and "commitment", or for that matter not to call the first component "F112" and the second "F358".

When then are we justified in ascribing a particular mental quality such as belief to a particular component of a machine? It seems to me reasonable to require the following elements as justification:

- a precise theory regarding the particular mental category; the theory must have clear semantics (or, to quote McDermott in [51], "No Notation without Denotation"), and should correspond to the common-sense use of the term;
- a demonstration that the component of the machine obeys the theory;
- a demonstration that the formal theory plays a nontrivial role in analyzing or designing the machine (or, to coin a new phrase, "No Notation without Exploitation").

As an example, it is instructive to consider the use of logics of knowledge and belief in distributed computation (cf. [26,27]). The initial motivation behind that line of research was to prove properties of distributed protocols. Researchers noted that intuitive reasoning about protocols included statements such as: "Processor A does not yet know that the network is back up, but since processor B knows that processor A doesn't know it, it (processor B) will not send the next message." Wishing to formalize this sort of reasoning, researchers adopted a logic of knowledge which had been introduced in analytic philosophy by Hintikka [32] and imported to AI by Moore [54] (subsequent work on knowledge and belief within AI includes [37,41,55,69]).

The logic widely (though not universally) adopted, the S5 modal system, is at best an idealization of the common sense notion of knowledge. Some of its more counter-intuitive properties include tautological closure (you know all that follows from your knowledge), positive introspection (if you know something then you know that you know it), and negative introspection (if you do not know something then you know that you do not). The important point is that, for the applications considered in distributed computation, the deviation from common sense was harmless. Intuitively, in those applications the knowledge possessed by agents was so simple that complexity of internal reasoning could be neglected.

The first lesson, then, is that while the formal theory of the mental category should correspond to common sense, this correspondence will not be exact. It is up to the consumer of the theory to consider the application at hand, and judge whether the correspondence between theory and common sense is sufficiently close that s/he will not be misled by allowing common sense intuition to guide reasoning with the formal construct. For example, if in the application all the beliefs are propositional Horn clauses, and if in the application all linear-time computation is negligible, then the axiom of tautological closure is quite reasonable, since propositional Horn theories admit a linear-time decision procedure. On the other hand, this same axiom renders the logic useless for reasoning about number-theoretic cryptographic protocols. [2]

The distributed computation application serves also to illustrate the second element required to justify the use of a mental term, a demonstration that the machine obeys the properties of the formal construct. The semantics adopted for the knowledge operator were standard possible-worlds semantics [38], but here possible worlds were given a very concrete interpretation: A possible world was a possible global state of the system (that is, a possible combination of local states of the various processors) given a fixed protocol, and the worlds accessible to each agent from a given world consisted of all global states in which its local state was the same as in the given world. It was easy to show that this concrete definition obeyed the S5 properties.

Finally, using this definition of knowledge, it became possible to prove certain properties of distributed protocols. The logic of knowledge was in principle dispensable—one could theoretically replace the knowledge operator by the corresponding statement about the states of the various processors—but the statements would get complex, and intuition would be lost. In practice, therefore, logics of knowledge proved invaluable, satisfying the third requirement of ascribing a mental attitude to a machine.

In this article we will consider mental constructs that are somewhat more involved than knowledge. We will consider belief, obligation, and capability, and add a temporal component to each of those. As in the case of knowledge, however, we will not reach an exact match between the formal properties of these formal constructs and common sense, but rather will aim to strike a balance between computational utility and common sense.

1.3. AOP versus OOP

It was mentioned in the previous section that the ascription of mental constructs must be coherent and useful. The application of the logic of knowledge in distributed computation, given there as an example, used the mental construct "knowledge" in a particular way: It mapped it onto an existing computational framework (a distributed network of processors), and used it to reason about the system. The use we will make of mental constructs is different: Rather than use them for mere analysis, we will employ them to *design* the computational system. The various mental categories will appear in the programming language itself, and the semantics of the programming language will be related to the semantics of the mental constructs. This is similar in spirit to a development within the distributed-computation community, where a proposal has been made to include tests for epistemic properties in the protocols themselves [28]; at this time the proposal has not yet been followed up on.

Specifically, I will propose a computational framework called *agent-oriented programming* (AOP). The name is not accidental, since from the engineering point of view AOP can be viewed as an specialization of the *object-oriented programming* (OOP) paradigm. I mean the latter in the spirit of Hewitt's original Actors formalism [31], rather than in the more specific sense in which it is used today. Intuitively, whereas OOP proposes viewing a computational system as made up of modules that are able to communicate with one another and that have individual ways of handling incoming messages, AOP specializes the framework by fixing the state (now called *mental state*) of the modules (now called *agents*) to consist of components such as beliefs (including beliefs about the world, about themselves, and about one another), capabilities, and decisions, each of which enjoys a precisely defined syntax. Various constraints are placed on the mental state of an agent, which roughly correspond to constraints on their common sense counterparts. A computation consists of these agents informing, requesting, offering, accepting, rejecting, competing, and assisting one another. This idea is borrowed directly from the *speech act* literature [4,25,66]. Speech act theory categorizes speech, distinguishing between informing, requesting, offering, and so on; each such type of communicative act involves different presuppositions and has different effects. Speech act theory has been applied in AI, in natural language research as well as in plan recognition [36,59]. To my knowledge, AOP and McCarthy's Elephant2000 language (see Section 8) are the first attempts to base a programming language in part on speech acts. Table 1 summarizes the relation between AOP and OOP. [3]

[2] Indeed, there have since been a number of proposals to escape the property of tautological closure, by modifying the logic.

[3] There is one more dimension to the comparison, which I omitted from the table, and it regards inheritance. Although absent from Hewitt's proposal, inheritance among objects is today one of the main features of OOP, constituting an attractive abstraction mechanism. I have not discussed it since it is not essential to the idea of OOP, and even less so to the idea of AOP. Nevertheless a parallel can be drawn here too, and I discuss it briefly in the final section.

Table 1
OOP versus AOP

	OOP	AOP
Basic unit	object	agent
Parameters defining state of basic unit	unconstrained	beliefs, commitments, capabilities, choices, ...
Process of computation	message passing and response methods	message passing and response methods
Types of message	unconstrained	inform, request, offer, promise, decline, ...
Constraints on methods	none	honesty, consistency, ...

1.4. *Organization of the document*

The rest of the document is organized as follows. In Section 2, I provide further motivation for the AOP paradigm by looking at two scenarios in which AOP is expected to prove useful. In Section 3, I outline the main ingredients of the AOP framework. The bulk of the paper then describes progress made to date towards realizing the concept. In Section 4, I discuss the mental categories that are essential to AOP, and as many of the details involved in formalizing those that are needed for the remainder. In Section 5, I discuss a general family of agent interpreters. In Section 6, I define a simple programming language called AGENT-0, and its specific interpreter. In Section 7, I briefly discuss the process of "agentification", or transforming an arbitrary device into a programmable agent. In Section 8, I discuss related work by others in AI. Finally, in the last section I discuss some of the directions in which the work described here can be extended.

2. Two scenarios

Below are two scenarios. The first is fairly complex, and illustrates the type of future applications envisioned. The second is a toy example, and serves three purposes: It illustrates a number of AOP ideas more crisply, it is implementable in the simple language defined later in this article, and it illustrates the fact that agents need not be robotic agents.

2.1. *Manufacturing automation*

Alfred and Brenda work at a car-manufacturing plant. Alfred handles regular-order cars, and Brenda handles special-order ones. The plant has a welding robot, Calvin. The plant is controlled by a coordinating program, Dashiel. The following scenario develops, involving communication between Alfred, Brenda, Calvin, and Dashiel. It contains communication acts such as informing, requesting, committing, permitting, and commanding, and requires agents to reason about the beliefs, capabilities, and commitments of other agents.

- 8:00: Alfred requests that Calvin promise to weld ten bodies for him that day; Calvin agrees to do so.
- 8:30: Alfred requests that Calvin accept the first body, Calvin agrees, and the first body arrives. Calvin starts welding it and promises Alfred to notify him when it is ready for the next body.
- 8:45: Brenda requests that Calvin work on a special-order car which is needed urgently. Calvin responds that it cannot right then, but that it will when it finishes the current job, at approximately 9:00.
- 9:05: Calvin completes welding Alfred's first car, ships it out, and offers to weld Brenda's car. Brenda ships it the car, and Calvin starts welding.
- 9:15: Alfred enquires why Calvin is not yet ready for his (Alfred's) next car. Calvin explains why, and also that it (Calvin) expects to be ready by about 10:00.
- 9:55: Calvin completes welding Brenda's car, and ships it out. Brenda requests that it reaccept it and do some painting, but Calvin refuses, explaining that it does not know how to paint. Calvin then offers to weld another car for Alfred, and proceeds to weld Alfred's cars for a while.
- 12:15: Brenda requests that Calvin commit to welding four more special-order cars that day. Calvin replies that it cannot, since that conflicts with its commitment to Alfred, who still has six unwelded cars. Brenda requests Alfred to release Calvin from its commitment to Alfred. Alfred refuses. Brenda requests that Dashiel (remember Dashiel?) order Calvin to accept her important request and revoke its commitment to Alfred. Dashiel orders Calvin to weld two of Brenda's cars, and then as many of Alfred's as time allows.
- 3:30: Calvin senses it is low on lubricant, and, without interrupting its work, asks Alfred for when the next lubrication is scheduled. Alfred responds that he doesn't know, but that Dashiel should know. Calvin asks Dashiel, who informs it that the next lubrication is scheduled for 4:00. Since that is sufficiently soon, Calvin continues to weld.

2.2. *Airline reservation*

This example is a minor modification of one due to John McCarthy [48], who uses it to illustrate his Elephant2000 programming language (see Section 8). The example involves three agents: a passenger P, an airline clerk C, and C's supervisor S. P and S are human, and C is a program (or is it the other way around? Or perhaps all three are programs?). Note that by confirming a reservation the airline enters into a commitment to issue a boarding pass to the passenger at the appropriate time. Again, the following exchange involves requesting (a query is a request to inform), informing, permitting, and denying, as well as mental components such as knowledge and commitment.

March

- P to C: Please inform me what flights you have from San Francisco to New York on April 18.
- C to P: Flight #354 departs at 08:30, flight #293 departs at 10:00, flight #441 departs at noon, ...
- P to C: Please book me on #354.
- C to P: That is sold out.
- P to C: Please book me on #293.
- C to P: That is confirmed; your reservation number is 112358.
- P to C: Please book me also on #441.
- C to P: That conflicts with #293; I am not allowed to double book a passenger.
- P to C: Please get permission to do so.
- C to S: I request permission for the following double booking: ...
- S to C: Permission denied.
- C to P: Sorry, I cannot get approval.

April 18, at the airport

- P to C: My name is P; I have a reservation for flight #293.
- C to P: Here is your boarding pass.

3. Overview of the AOP framework

A complete AOP system will include three primary components:

- a restricted formal language with clear syntax and semantics for describing mental state; the mental state will be defined uniquely by several modalities, such as belief and commitment;
- an interpreted programming language in which to define and program agents, with primitive commands such as `REQUEST` and `INFORM`; the semantics of the programming language will be required to be faithful to the semantics of mental state;
- an "agentifier", converting neutral devices into programmable agents.

In this article I will fall short of supplying a complete system. My main purpose in this article is to discuss the second component. However, since it relies in part on the first one, I will start with a short discussion of mental state. I will limit discussion of logic to the minimum needed for the discussion of the interpreter. There is, however, substantial literature on the logic of various mental categories, and I will provide references to it.

In contrast to the first two components, of which I have relatively good understanding, the third component is still somewhat mysterious to me, and I will discuss it only briefly at the end.

4. Mental categories and their properties

The first step in the enterprise is to define the various components of mental state and their properties. There is not a unique "correct" selection of mental categories, nor a correct theory regarding them, as different applications can be expected to call for specific mental properties.[4] In this section I will discuss what could be viewed as a bare-bones theory of mental state, a kernel that will in the future be modified and augmented (for in-depth treatment within our research group of various logical aspects of mental state, see [14,43,69,73]).

4.1. Components of mental state

In related past research by others in AI (see Section 8), three modalities were explored: belief, desire, and intention (giving rise to the pun on BDI agent architectures). Other similar notions, such as goals and plans, were also pressed into service. These are clearly important notions; however, I propose starting with a slightly different set of modalities, which are more modest and, I find, more basic.

By way of motivation, here is an informal view of the world which underlies the selection. At any point in time, the future is determined by two factors: The past history, and the current actions of agents. For example, past history alone does not (in this view) determine whether I raise my arm; that is determined by whether in fact I take the appropriate action. The actions of an agent are determined by its *decisions*, or *choices*.[5] In other words, some facts are true for natural reasons, and other facts are true because agents decided to make them so. Decisions are logically constrained, though not determined, by the agent's *beliefs*; these beliefs refer to the state of the world (in the past, present, or future), to the mental state of other agents, and to the *capabilities* of this and other agents. For example, given that the robot believes that it is incapable of passing through the narrow doorway, it will not decide to go through it. Decisions are also constrained

[4]In this respect our motivation here deviates from that of philosophers. However, I believe there exist sufficient similarities to make the connection between AI and philosophy mutually beneficial.

[5]The term *choice* is somewhat ambiguous; I discuss various senses of choice later.

by prior decisions; the robot cannot decide to be in Room 5 in five minutes if it has already decided to be in Room 3 at that time.

This perspective motivates the introduction of two basic mental categories, *belief* and *decision* (or *choice*), and a third category which is not a mental construct *per se*, *capability*. These are precisely the categories I will adopt, with one modification: rather than take choice as basic, I will start with the notion of *obligation*, or *commitment*, and will treat decision simply as obligation to oneself.

By restricting the components of mental state to these modalities I have in some informal sense excluded representation of motivation. Indeed, I will not assume that agents are "rational" beyond assuming that their beliefs, obligations and capabilities are internally and mutually consistent. This stands in contrast to the other work mentioned above, which makes further assumptions about agents acting in their own best interests, and so on. Such stronger notions of rationality are obviously important, and I am convinced that in the future we will wish to consider them. However, neither the concept of agenthood nor the utility of agent-oriented programming depend on them.

In the remainder of this section I will describe the various modalities in more detail. My goal here is not to provide a comprehensive analysis of them; that is the subject of the papers mentioned earlier. Here I will discuss them only to the extent that they bear on the development of the interpreter defined later.

4.2. *A language for belief, obligation, and capability*

Time

Time is basic to the mental categories; we believe things both *about* different times and *at* different times, and the same is true of other modalities. We will adopt a simple point-based temporal language to talk about time; a typical sentence will be

$$\texttt{holding(robot,cup)}^{t}$$

meaning that the robot is holding the cup at time t.

Action

Actions take place at different points in time, and, depending on the circumstances at the time they are taken, have certain effects. However, for the purposes of this article, we will not distinguish between actions and facts, and the occurrence of an action will be represented by the corresponding fact holding. For example, strictly speaking, rather than say that the robot took the action raise-arm at time t, we will say that the sentence $\texttt{raise-arm(robot)}^{t}$ is true. (However, to retain the agency behind the action, we will introduce the notion of decision; see below.) Given that actions are facts, they too are instantaneous. This too is a limitation in the current language.

There is substantial literature on representing action; the best-known representative in AI is the *situation calculus* [50]. There are a number of proposals to allow time, durational facts, and durational actions all in the same language. In fact, in [42] we represent time and parallel action in the situation calculus itself. However, the details are somewhat involved, and these extensions are not essential to the current discussion. Nonetheless, since actions are such a natural concept, in the programming language discussed later we will introduce them as syntactic sugar.

Belief

We now augment the language with a modal operator B, denoting belief. As mentioned above, an agent believes things both at certain times and about certain times. The general form of belief statement is

$$B_{a}^{t}\varphi$$

where a is an agent, t a time term, and φ a (recursively defined) sentence. For example, $B_{a}^{3}B_{b}^{10}\texttt{like(a,b)}^{7}$ will mean that at time 3 agent a believes that at time 10 agent b will believe that at time 7 a liked b.

Obligation

So far I have used largely well-known notions: Temporal languages are standard fare, operators denoting belief common, and their combination, although somewhat novel, is straightforward. We now depart more radically from past constructions and introduce a new modal operator, OBL. OBL has one more argument than B:

$$\texttt{OBL}_{a,b}^{t}\varphi$$

will mean that at time t agent a is obligated, or committed, to agent b about φ. Notice that, since actions are represented simply as facts, the agent is obligated to a fact holding rather than to taking action.

Decision (choice)

The freedom to choose among several possible actions is central to the notion of agenthood,[6] and earlier on in the research we indeed took decision, or choice, to be a primitive notion. The current definition of obligation provides an alternative, however: decision is defined to be simply obligation, or commitment, to oneself:

[6]To quote Isaac Bashevis-Singer, "We *must* believe in free will; you see, we have no choice."

$$\mathtt{DEC}^{t}_{a}\varphi =_{def} \mathtt{OBL}^{t}_{a,a}\varphi.$$

Again, the term "choice" carries many connotations, and I emphasize that I mean it in the sense of "decision"; an agent has chosen something if it has decided that that something be true. Thus, most of us can decide to own a new pair of shoes, but few of us can decide to own yacht.

Capability

Intimately bound to the notion of agenthood is also that of capability. I may decide to move my arm, but if I am not capable of it then it will not move. I will not decide to do anything I believe myself incapable of. Similarly, I will not request a two-year-old, nor a mobile robot, to climb a ladder, since I do not believe they are capable of it.

It is debatable whether capability is best defined in mental terms or not. For example, one definition would say that agent a is capable of φ just in case the following is true: If a were to decide φ, then φ would be true. There are also reasonable philosophical arguments against this definition (cf. [5,8,19]). Here I will simply introduce the notation

$$\mathtt{CAN}^{t}_{a}\varphi$$

to represent the fact that at time t a is capable of φ. We will place certain constraints on such sentences, but not take a stance on whether CAN is reducible to mental notions or not.[7] Note that, like the other modalities, capabilities refer to specific times; a typical sentence is

$$\mathtt{CAN}^{5}_{robot}\mathtt{open(door)}^{8}.$$

Thus at time 5 the robot might be able to ensure that the door is open at time 8, but at time 6 it might no longer have that capability. We may define ABLE to be the "immediate" version of CAN. First, for any sentences φ, we define $time(\varphi)$ to be the outermost time occurring in it; for example, $time(\mathtt{open(door)}^{t}) = time(\mathtt{B}^{t}_{a}\varphi) = \mathtt{t}$. We now define ABLE as follows:

$$\mathtt{ABLE}_{a}\varphi =_{def} \mathtt{CAN}_{a}^{time(\varphi)}\varphi,$$

and thus

$$\mathtt{ABLE}_{robot}\mathtt{open(door)}^{5} \equiv \mathtt{CAN}^{5}_{robot}\mathtt{open(door)}^{5}.$$

[7] However, Thomas [73] does take a stance; capability is taken to be a primitive notion defined in terms of future-branching structures, not reducible to other notions. This is in the spirit of recent philosophical treatments of agency [5,8,19] mentioned earlier.

4.3. *Properties of the various components*

I have so far not placed any constraints on the various modalities defined, and therefore have not guaranteed that they in any way resemble their common sense counterparts. We will now place such constraints. Just as there is no objectively "right" collection of mental categories, there is no "right" list of properties for any particular mental category. It was already stated in the introduction that the correspondence between the formal definition and common sense will always be only approximate, and that we would like to strike a balance between common sense and utility. Indeed, I expect different applications of AOP to call for different properties of belief, commitment, and capability. In this section I will define a number of properties I assume about the modalities. These properties are quite weak, but they are sufficient to justify the terminology, and necessary for the design of the interpreter. The weakness of the assumptions ensures that the interpreters apply to a wide variety of applications. Still, even these assumptions will be inappropriate for some purposes, in which case a new type of interpreter will be required.

Internal consistency

We assume that both the beliefs and the obligations are internally consistent. Specifically, we assume:

- for any t,a: $\{\varphi\colon \mathtt{B}^{t}_{a}\varphi\}$ is consistent;
- for any t,a: $\{\varphi\colon \mathtt{OBL}^{t}_{a,b}\varphi$ for some b$\}$ is consistent.

Good faith

We further assume that agents commit only to what they believe themselves capable of, and only if they really mean it:

- for any t,a,b,φ: $\mathtt{OBL}^{t}_{a,b}\varphi \supset \mathtt{B}^{t}_{a}((\mathtt{ABLE}_{a}\varphi) \wedge \varphi)$.

Introspection

Although in general we do not assume that agents have total introspective capabilities, we do assume that they are aware of their obligations:

- for any t,a,b,φ: $\mathtt{OBL}^{t}_{a,b}\varphi \equiv \mathtt{B}^{t}_{a}\mathtt{OBL}^{t}_{a,b}\varphi$;
- for any t,a,b,φ: $\neg\mathtt{OBL}^{t}_{a,b}\varphi \equiv \mathtt{B}^{t}_{a}\neg\mathtt{OBL}^{t}_{a,b}\varphi$.

On the other hand, we do not assume that agents are necessarily aware of commitments made *to* them.

Persistence of mental state

We have only placed restrictions on mental attitudes at a single instant of time. We conclude this section by discussing how mental states change or persist over time. However, unlike in the previous discussion, we will not place precise constraints, but rather informal guidelines.

Consider, for example, belief. Our restrictions so far allow agents which at one time believe nothing at all, shortly afterwards have a belief about *every* sentence, and then again become quite agnostic. Common sense suggests that beliefs tend to be more stable than that, and it would indeed be difficult to rely on the behavior of agents with such volatile beliefs. We will now place a strong condition on belief; we will assume that agents have perfect memory of, and faith in, their beliefs, and only let go of a belief if they learn a contradictory fact. Beliefs therefore persist *by default*. Furthermore, we will assume that the *absence* of belief also persists by default, although in a slightly different sense: if an agent does not believe a fact at a certain time (as opposed to believing the negation of the fact), then the only reason he will come to believe it is if he learns it.

How to formally capture these two kinds of default persistence is another story, and touches on issues that are painfully familiar to researchers in nonmonotonic temporal reasoning and belief revision. In fact, a close look at the logical details of belief (or knowledge) persistence reveals several very subtle phenomena, which have so far not been addressed in the literature [43].

Obligations too should persist; they wouldn't be obligations otherwise. As in the case of belief, however, the persistence is not absolute. Although by default obligations persist, there are conditions under which obligations are revoked. These conditions presumably include explicit release of the agent by the party to which it is obligated, or alternatively a realization on the part of the agent that it is no longer able to fulfill the obligation. (In their discussion of the persistence of commitment, Cohen and Levesque [9] actually propose a more elaborate second condition, one that requires common knowledge by the committer and committee of the impossibility; however further discussion of their position and arguments against it would be too long a detour; see a brief discussion of their work in Section 4.4.)

Since decision is defined in terms of obligation, it inherits the default persistence. Notice, however, an interesting point about the persistence of decision: While an agent cannot unilaterally revoke obligations it has towards others, it *can* cancel obligations held towards it—including obligations it holds towards itself, namely decisions. An agent is therefore free to modify an existing decision, but unless he explicitly does so the decision will stand.

Finally, capabilities too tend to not fluctuate wildly. In fact, in this document I assume that capabilities are fixed: What an agent can do at one time it can do at any other time. However, I will allow to condition a capability of an action on certain conditions that hold at the time of action.

The contextual nature of modal statements

I have throughout the discussion talked of "unequivocal" statements regarding beliefs, obligations, and capabilities. Common sense, however, suggests that each of these modalities is context-sensitive: I can print the document right now, but only in the context of the network being up; I am obligated to you to finish the work by tomorrow, but if my child has just been rushed to hospital then all bets are off (even though I am still capable of finishing the work). Indeed, McCarthy has argued that all statements, not only modal ones, should be viewed in context [49]. Although I agree in principle, and discuss it further in [68], in this article I will ignore the issue of context sensitivity.

4.4. A short detour: comparison with Cohen and Levesque

In several publications (e.g., [9,10]) Cohen, Levesque, and several associates have investigated the logical relationships between several modalities such as the above-mentioned ones. As mentioned earlier, I have deferred discussion of related work to a later section. However, since there is room for confusion between Cohen and Levesque's definitions of mental categories and our own, I will make an exception in this case. The reader may skip this subsection, although I believe the discussion may provide further intuition about our definition as well as Cohen and Levesque's.

Cohen and Levesque employ two basic modalities, BEL (belief) and G (goal, or choice). Although these bear a resemblance to our belief and choice modalities, important differences exist. Their belief modality is really the same as ours, except that they are not as explicit about its temporal aspect. In their language, one may use the $\diamond$ tense operator to specify that "Sometime in the future an agent will believe a fact" or "Sometime in the future the agent will believe a fact either about that time or about a time yet further into the future", but one is not able to talk about (e.g.) the agent believing in the future something about the past. This capability could be achieved by adding other tense operators, if the authors insisted on a tense logic. [8]

The primary intuition offered about the G modality is that it denotes choice ("Consider the desire that the agent has chosen to pursue as put into a new category. Call this chosen desire, loosely, a goal"). However, I have already noted that the term "choice" is multi-faceted, and indeed G is quite different from our DEC. For Cohen and Levesque, the choices of an agent constitute a consistent subset of the agent's desires, those that the agent

[8] However, the authors do find it necessary to mention explicit dates, which they represent by propositions such as "1/1/90/12:00". That being the case, I do not see the utility of retaining the tense operators.

has adopted as goals. In contrast, our OBL modality (and hence the derived DEC modality) reflects absolutely no motivation of the agent, and merely describes the actions to which the agent is obligated.

The difference in senses is the difference between a decision to act and a decision to pursue a goal. This difference is reflected in the different interactions between choice (or decision) and belief. In our construction, obligation (and therefore also decision) implies belief: $\mathrm{DEC}^t_a p \supset \mathrm{B}^t_a p$ (if an agent decides on an action he believes it will take place). The converse implication does not hold in our construction (the agent may believe that the sun will rise tomorrow without making a choice in this regard). For Cohen and Levesque, on the other hand, belief does imply choice: (BEL a p) $\supset$ (G a p) (see, e.g., their Proposition 17). The intuition there is that the G modality specifies possible worlds chosen by the agent, and these worlds are selected among the ones the agent believes are possible; therefore if a fact is true in all worlds believed possible by the agent, it must be true in the subset he selects. Note that both senses of choice guarantee that an agent does not choose something he believes impossible: both $\mathrm{DEC}^t_a p \supset \neg \mathrm{B}^t_a \neg p$ and (G a p) $\supset \neg$(BEL a $\neg$p) hold in the respective systems.

Both senses of choice are worthwhile, although one can imagine other ways of capturing a decision to pursue a goal. In particular, I am not sure that it is best to use a single operator to capture both "having a goal" and "deciding to adopt a goal". For example, it may prove advantageous to start with a G modality denoting "having a goal", and define "goal adoption" by DEC_aG(a,p) (with the appropriate temporal arguments added). However, I have deliberately avoided such more complex notions in this document as they are not needed for the fundamentals of AOP, and will not pursue the issue further.

In summary, the pioneering work of Cohen and Levesque introduces mental categories that are different from ours. The two frameworks share the essential view of belief and time. They each introduce modalities absent from the other: obligation and capability in our framework, goals and intentions in theirs. Even two notions that at first appear to be similar—our decision and their choice—turn out to be quite different.

5. A generic agent interpreter

In the previous section I discussed the first component of the AOP framework, namely the definition of agents. I now turn to the central topic of this paper, the programming of agents. In this section I will outline a generic agent interpreter. In the next section I describe a specific programming language and its implemented interpreter.

The role of agent programs is to control the evolution of an agent's mental state; actions occur as a side-effect of the agent's being committed (that is, obligated) to an action whose time has come. Since the mental state of agents is captured in a formal language, it might be tempting to view AOP as a form of logic programming. In this view, the program would consist of logical statements about the mental state of the agent, and through a process of theorem proving the mental state at each point in time will be determined. However, this is not what I intend; although it might be possible in principle to develop such a programming language,[9] multi-modal temporal theorem proving is sufficiently daunting to discourage me from attempting it at this point. Instead, I will allow standard operationally-defined languages; indeed, I will define such a language myself in the next section. These languages, however, will include data structures which represent various logical sentences (for example, those denoting beliefs and commitments), and the (extra-logical) operations on these data structures will be required to obey the properties of the various logical operators. For example, no two data structures denoting contradictory beliefs may be instantiated by the interpreter at the same time.

The basic loop

The behavior of agents is, in principle, quite simple. Each agent iterates the following two steps at regular intervals:

(1) read the current messages, and update your mental state, including your beliefs and commitments (the agent program is crucial for this update);

(2) execute the commitments for the current time, possibly resulting in further belief change (this phase is independent of the agent's program).

Actions to which agents can be committed include communicative ones such as informing and requesting, as well as arbitrary "private" actions. The process is illustrated in Fig. 1; dashed arrows represent flow of data, solid arrows temporal sequencing.

Assumption about message passing

Agent programs will include, among other things, communication commands. In order that those be executable I will assume that the platform is capable of passing messages to other agents addressable by name, whether those reside in the same machine or in others. The programming language

[9] Indeed, an early design of agent programs by Akahani was entirely in the style of logic programming.

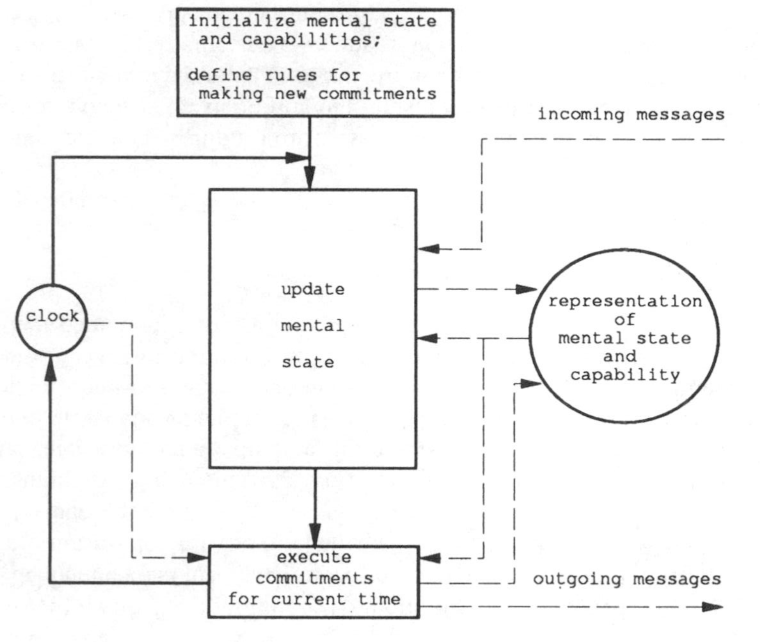

Fig. 1. A flow diagram of a generic agent interpreter.

will define the form of these messages, and the interpreter will determine when messages are sent.

Assumption about the clock

Central to the operation of the interpreter is the existence of a clock; agents are inherently "real-time" (to use another overloaded term). The main role of the clock is to initiate iterations of the two-step loop at regular intervals (every 10 milliseconds, every hour, etc.); the length of these intervals, called the "time grain", is determined by the settable variable `timegrain`. I do not discuss the implementation of such a clock, which will vary among platforms, and simply assume that it exists. We also assume a variable `now`, whose value is set by the clock to the current time in the format defined in the programming language (an integer, *date:hour:minute*, etc.).

In the remainder of the description we make the very strong assumption that a single iteration through the loop lasts less than the time grain; in future versions of the language we will relax this assumption, and correspondingly will complicate the details of the loop itself.

Of course, the fact that agents use the same temporal language does not ensure that their clocks are synchronized. If all agents are running on the same machine there will be no problem, but otherwise the possibility of clock drift exists. Although synchronization does not impact the design and programming of single agents, it is crucial for ensuring that a society of agents is able to function usefully. Fortunately, there exist synchronization protocols which ensure limited drift among clocks (for an overview, see [65]), and we expect to use these in our applications. However, since the focus in this article is on the design of single agents, I will not discuss this issue further.

6. AGENT-0, a simple language and its interpreter

Agent interpreters may vary along many dimensions, and in general pose many challenging problems. In this section I describe a particular programming language called AGENT-0, whose interpreter is an extremely simple instance of the generic agent interpreter. In fact, the simplifications embodied in AGENT-0 are so extreme that it may be tempting to dismiss it as uninteresting. However, it was recognized early on that one would not gain good insight into the strengths and weaknesses of AOP without writing actual programs. It was decided therefore to implement a simple interpreter first, and design more complex languages and interpreters based on this experience. It turned out the design of AGENT-0 itself posed some challenges, and we have been surprised by the diversity of applications that even this simple language admits. Furthermore, AGENT-0 is designed in a way that suggests obvious extensions; a few are being currently pursued, and will be described in the last section.

6.1. *The syntax of AGENT-0*

In the programming language itself one specifies only conditions for making commitments; commitments are actually made, and later carried out, automatically at the appropriate times (see discussion of the interpreter in Section 6.2 below). Commitments are only to primitive actions, those that the agent can directly execute. In other words, in AGENT-0 an agent cannot commit to achieving any condition which requires some sort of planning. Before we define the syntax of commitments we need a few preliminary definitions. I will first develop the syntax of AGENT-0 in a bottom-up fashion, and then summarize it in BNF notation. The reader may wish to refer forward to the formal definition while reading the following description.

Fact statements

Fact statements are fundamental to AGENT-0; they are used to specify the content of actions as well as conditions for their execution. Fact statements constitute a tiny fragment of the temporal language described earlier; they are essentially the atomic objective sentences (that is, no conjunction or disjunction, nor modal operators). Typical fact statements will be `(t (employee smith acme))` and `(NOT (t (employee jones acme)))`.

Private and communicative action statements

Agents commit to action, and so we now specify what actions are. We make two orthogonal distinctions between types of action: Actions may be *private* or *communicative*, and, independently, they may be *conditional* or *unconditional*.

The syntax for private actions is

```
(DO t p-action)
```

where `t` is a time point and `p-action` is a private action name. Private action names are idiosyncratic and unconstrained; a database agent may have retrieval primitives, a statistical computation agent may run certain mathematical procedures, and a robot may serve itself. The effects of private actions may be invisible to other agents, as in the database example, but need not be so, as in the robot example.

Private actions may or may not involve IO. Communicative actions, on the other hand, always involve IO. Unlike private actions, communicative actions are uniform, and common to all agents. While in a general AOP system we can expect many types of communicative action, the restricted version AGENT-0 has only three types of communicative action: informing, requesting, and cancelling a request.

The syntax of informing is

```
(INFORM t a fact)
```

where `t` is a time point, `a` is an agent name, and `fact` is a fact statement. Note that `t` is the time at which the informing is to take place, and `fact` itself contains other temporal information, as in `(INFORM 5 b (1 (employee smith acme)))`.

The syntax of requesting is

```
(REQUEST t a action)
```

where `t` is a time point, `a` is an agent name, and `action` is an action statement, defined recursively. So, for example, `(REQUEST 1 a (DO 10 update-database))` constitutes a legitimate request. Again, one should distinguish between the time at which the requesting is to be done (1, in this example) and the time of the requested action (10, in the example). Requests can be embedded further, as in

```
(REQUEST 1 a (REQUEST 5 b (INFORM 10 c fact))).
```

The syntax of cancelling a request is:

```
(UNREQUEST t a action)
```

where `t` is a time point, `a` is an agent name, and `action` is an action statement.

The last unconditional action in AGENT-0 is really a nonaction. Its syntax is:

```
(REFRAIN action)
```

where `action` is an action statement. The role of refraining will be to prevent commitment to particular actions.

Conditional action statements

In AGENT-0 we distinguish between commitments for conditional actions, which include conditions to be tested right before acting, and conditions for entering into commitments in the first place. I now discuss only conditional actions, and will discuss conditions for entering into commitments later.

Conditional actions rely on one form of condition, called a *mental condition*. Mental conditions refer to the mental state of the agent, and the intuition behind them is that when the time comes to execute the action, the mental state *at that time* will be examined to see whether the mental condition is satisfied. For this reason the agent- and time-components of the mental state are implicit and can be omitted in the specification of mental conditions. A mental condition is thus any combination of modal statements in the temporal-modal language, with the primary "agent" and "time" arguments omitted.

Specifically, a mental condition is a logical combination of *mental patterns*. A mental pattern is one of two pairs:

```
(B fact) or ((CMT a) action)
```

where `fact` is a fact statement, `a` is an agent name, and `action` is an action statement (we use the term `CMT` rather than `OBL` since, for historical reasons, this is the notation used in the actual implementation). An example of a mental pattern is `(B (t (employee smith acme)))`.

Given the syntax of mental conditions, the syntax of a conditional action is

```
(IF mntlcond action)
```

where `mntlcond` is a mental condition and `action` is an action statement. An example of a conditional action is

```
(IF (B (t' (employee smith acme)))
    (INFORM t a (t' (employee smith acme)))).
```

The intuitive reading of this action is "if at time t you believe that at time t' smith is an employee of acme, then at time t inform agent a of that fact".

As was said, mental conditions may contain logical connectives. These connectives are AND, OR, and NOT. The following three actions illustrate the use of NOT; together they constitute a QUERY about whether fact is true (b is the one being queried, a is the one he is asked to inform):

```
(REQUEST t b (IF (B,fact) (INFORM t+1 a fact))).
(REQUEST t b (IF (B (NOT fact))
                 (INFORM t+1 a (NOT fact)))).
(REQUEST t b (IF (NOT (BW fact))
                 (INFORM t+1 a
                  (NOT (t+1 (BW a fact)))))).
```
[10]

Variables

In the style of logic programming and production systems, in AGENT-0 procedures are invoked in a pattern-directed fashion. Specifically, we will see that commitment rules are "activated" based on certain patterns in the incoming messages and current mental state. Variables play a crucial role in these patterns.

A variable is denoted by the prefix "?". Variables may substitute agent names, fact statements, or action statements. Thus the following is a legitimate conditional action:

```
(IF (NOT ((CMT ?x) (REFRAIN sing))) sing).
```

In the tradition of logic programming, variables in action statements (including the mental condition part) are interpreted as existentially quantified. The scope of the quantifier is upwards until the scope of the first NOT, or it is the entire statement, if the variable does not lie in the scope of a NOT. Thus the last statement reads informally as "if you are not currently committed to anyone to refrain from singing, then sing".

It is advantageous to allow other quantifiers as well. The one quantifier included in AGENT-0 is a limited form of the universal quantifier, but in the future others, such as the "latest (earliest) time point such that" quantifier, may be introduced. The universally-quantified variables will be denoted by the prefix "?!". The scope of these variables is always the entire formula, and thus the conditional action

```
(IF (B (t (emp ?!x acme)))
    (INFORM a (t (emp ?!x acme))))
```

results in informing a of all the individuals who the agent believes to be acme employees.[11]

Having discussed action statements, we can now finally discuss the type of statements that actually appear in the program, namely commitment rules.

Commitment rules

Since action statements contain information about what needs to be done, about when it needs to be done, and even the preconditions for doing it, one might have expected a collection of action statements to constitute a program. However, there is another crucial layer of abstraction in AGENT-0. Most of the action statements are unknown at programming time; they are later communicated by other agents (one of which may be the "user", in situations where that concept is applicable). The program itself merely contains conditions under which the agent will enter into new commitments. Some of these conditions may be trivial, resulting in a priori commitments, but most commitments will be in response to messages.

The conditions under which a commitment is made include both mental conditions, discussed above, and message conditions, which refer to the current incoming messages. A message condition is a logical combination of *message patterns*. A message pattern is a triple

```
(From Type Content)
```

where From is the sender's name, Type is INFORM, REQUEST, or UNREQUEST, and Content is a fact statement or an action statement, depending on the type. The other information associated with each incoming message, its destination and arrival time, are implicit in this context and are thus omitted from the message pattern (of course, the Content will include reference to time, but that is the time of the fact or action, not the arrival time of the message). An example of a message pattern is (a INFORM fact), meaning that one of the new messages is from a informing the agent of fact. An example of a more complex message condition is

```
(AND (a REQUEST (DO t walk))
     (NOT (?x REQUEST (DO t chew-gum)))),
```

meaning that there is a new message from a requesting the agent to walk, and there is no new request from anyone that the agent chew-gum.

The syntax of a commitment rule is

```
(COMMIT msgcond mntlcond (agent action)*)
```

[10] BW is the "believe whether" operator, defined by (t (BW a p)) $\equiv$ (t (B a p)) $\vee$ (t (B a (NOT p))).

[11] This feature of AGENT-0 was not included in its actual implementation, described below.

where msgcond and mntlcond are respectively message and mental conditions, agent is an agent name, action is an action statement, and * denote repetition of zero or more times.[12] Note that the action statement itself may be conditional, containing its own mental condition.

An example of a simple commitment rule is

```
(COMMIT (?a REQUEST ?action)
        (B (now (myfriend ?a))) 13
        (?a ?action ))
```

Finally, a program is simply a sequence of commitment rules, preceded by a definition of the agent's capabilities and initial beliefs, and the fixing of the time grain.

A BNF description of the AGENT-0

Before describing the interpreter for AGENT-0 and providing an example, let me summarize the discussion of the syntax by giving its BNF definition. (In accordance with standard conventions, * denotes repetition of zero or more times.)

```
<program>     ::= timegrain := <time>
                  CAPABILITIES := (<action> <mntlcond>)*
                  INITIAL BELIEFS := <fact>*
                  COMMITMENT RULES := <commitrule>*
<commitrule>  ::= (COMMIT <msgcond> <mntlcond>
                         (<agent> <action>)*)
<msgcond>     ::= <msgconj>    | (OR <msgconj>*)
<msgconj>     ::= <msgpattern> | (AND <msgpattern>*)
<msgpattern>  ::= (<agent> INFORM  <fact>)    |
                  (<agent> REQUEST <action>) |
                  (NOT <msgpattern>)
<mntlcond>    ::= <mntlconj>    | (OR <mntlconj>*)
<mntlconj>    ::= <mntlpattern> | (AND <mntlpattern>*)
<mntlpattern> ::= (B <fact>) | ((CMT <agent>) <action>) |
                  (NOT <mntlpattern>)
<action>      ::= (DO        <time> <privateaction>)         |
                  (INFORM    <time> <agent> <fact>)          |
                  (REQUEST   <time> <agent> <action>)        |
                  (UNREQUEST <time> <agent> <action>)        |
                  (REFRAIN   <action>)                       |
                  (IF        <mntlcond> <action>)
<fact>        ::= (<time> (<predicate> <arg>*))
<time>        ::= <integer> | now | <time-constant> |
                  (+ <time> <time>) | (- <time> <time>) |
                  (x <integer> <time>)
                    ; Time may be a <variable> when
                    ; it appears in a commitment rule
<time-constant> ::= m | h | d | y
                    ; m (minute) = 60, h (hour) 3600, etc.
<agent>       ::= <alphanumeric_string> | <variable>
<predicate>   ::= <alphanumeric_string>
<arg>         ::= <alphanumeric_string> | <variable>
<variable>    ::= ?<alphanumeric_string> | ?!<alphanumeric_string>
```

A note about time: The programming language allows use of symbolic dates and times; in the actual implementation, described below, each date is represented internally by the number of seconds that have passed since 1900.

6.2. The AGENT-0 interpreter

Since it is an instance of the generic interpreter, the AGENT-0 interpreter inherits its two-step loop design. However, since in AGENT-0 the mental state is made up of three specific components, one of which (capabilities) is fixed, the first step in the loop may be specialized as follows:

(1a) Update the beliefs.
(1b) Update the commitments.

We now look at the various substeps in more detail.

Updating beliefs and commitments

In AGENT-0 the beliefs, commitments, and capabilities of an agent are each represented by a database. The belief database is updated either as a result of being informed, or as a result of taking a private action. There is little to say about the latter; a database agent will come to believe a fact after performing a retrieval operation, and a robotic agent will come to believe something after performing a visual routine. These updates are implemented by the analogue of brain surgery, that is, by providing the appropriate routines with the ability to directly modify the belief database. More interesting is the former sort of update. In its full generality, the assimilation of new information into an existing belief base poses difficult problems, both semantical and algorithmic. It is not obvious what in general

[12]For no good reason, the actual implementation described below allows only one agent–action pair.

[13]now is a global variable that evaluates to the current time. The reader might have expected other conditions, such as the absence of contradictory prior commitments. However, as is explained below in Section 6.2, these conditions are verified automatically by the interpreter and therefore need not be mentioned explicitly by the programmer.

the semantics of this assimilation should be. Indeed, normative theories have been proposed for at least two different sorts of assimilation, *revision* [21] and *update* [35], and a number of new results on these operations have recently been discovered.

Beside the semantical issue, one is faced with an algorithmic one as well. Consider a given database Γ and a new fact φ. Most theories of belief assimilation require that, if φ is consistent with Γ, then assimilation amounts to simply adding φ to Γ. But checking consistency for unconstrained theories is a notoriously hard problem, either intractable (in the propositional case) or undecidable (in the first-order case). Furthermore, if φ is inconsistent with Γ, most theories of assimilation require that Γ be "minimally" modified so as to restore consistency, and this is even a harder problem. What then are we to do?

There are at least to approaches to getting around the computational complexity. The first is to relax the requirements, and adopt a heuristic assimilation algorithm which compromises either soundness, or completeness, or both. The second approach, which is the one taken in AGENT-0, is to restrict the sentences in the languages sufficiently so that the problem becomes tractable. In fact, as we have seen, AGENT-0 imposes an extreme restriction, which is to disallow logical connectives other than negation (this is in addition to disallowing modal operators, necessary for representing nested beliefs such as "I believe that you believe ..."). This makes the consistency checking trivial—at most linear in the size of the database, and much less with good data structuring.

This still leaves open the question of what to do with new information. We will ultimately require a theory of authority, which will dictate whether or not new information is believed. However, in AGENT-0 agents are completely gullible; they incorporate any fact of which they are informed, retracting the contradictory atomic belief if that were previously held.

We now turn to the process of updating commitments. For that we need to explain the structure of the commitment and capability databases. Items in the database of commitments are simply pairs `(agent action)` (the agent to which the commitment was made, and the content of the commitment). Items in the database of capabilities are pairs `(privateaction mntlcond)`. The mental condition part allows one to prevent commitment to incompatible actions, each of which might on its own be possible. An example of an item in the capability database is:

```
((!?time (rotate wheelbase ?degrees))
 (NOT ((CMT ?x) ?!time (service wheelbase)))).
```

Existing commitments are removed either as a result of the belief change, or as a result of `UNREQUEST` messages. Considering the former first, recall that agents must believe in their ability to perform the actions to which they are committed. Belief change may affect capabilities, since the capability of each private action depends on mental preconditions. And thus whenever a belief update occurs, the AGENT-0 interpreter examines the current commitments to private actions, and removes those whose preconditions in the capability database have been violated. Exhaustive examinations of all current commitments upon a belief change can be avoided through intelligent indexing, but I will not pursue this optimization issue. It is recommended that in such a case the agent add a commitment to immediately inform the agents to whom he was committed of this development, using commitment rules, but AGENT-0 does not enforce this.

The handling of `UNREQUEST` messages is trivial: The agent removes the corresponding item from the commitment database if it exists, and otherwise does nothing.

Note that the removal of existing commitments is independent of the program. The addition of commitments, on the other hand, depends on the program very strongly. The algorithm adding commitments is as follows:

Algorithm. Check all program commitment statements; for each program statement `(COMMIT msgcond mntlcond` $(\mathtt{a}_i\ \mathtt{action}_i)*$`)`, if:

- the message condition `msgcond` holds of the new incoming messages,
- the mental condition `mntlcond` holds of the current mental state,
- for all i, the agent is currently capable of the $\mathtt{action}_i$, and
- for all i, the agent is not committed to `REFRAIN` $\mathtt{action}_i$, and, if $\mathtt{action}_i$ is itself of the form `REFRAIN` $\mathtt{action}'_i$, the agent is not committed to $\mathtt{action}'_i$,

then, for all i, commit to $\mathtt{a}_i$ to perform $\mathtt{action}_i$.

Although I am not explicit about it here, it is clear what it means for the message conditions and mental conditions to hold, given their definitions. An agent is capable of an action under the following conditions:

- An agent can request and unrequest anything from anyone.
- An agent can inform anyone of a fact he (the agent) believes. An agent can inform *itself* of any fact whatsoever (this is useful to implement reasoning in the agent; of course it presents a danger as well, and it is up to the programmer of commitment rules to prevent self-delusion).
- An agent is capable of any private action in the capability database provided the mental condition associated in the database with that private action holds at that time. [14]

[14] This last mental condition is separate from the mental condition `mntlcond` mentioned above; the one mentioned above is a condition for making a commitment regardless of whether the agent is capable of the action; in contrast the mental condition currently discussed determines whether the agent is capable of it in the first place.

- An agent can refrain from any action, provided he is not already committed to that action.
- An agent can perform a conditional action (`IF mntlcond action`) if he can perform `action` under the condition `mntlcond`.

Carrying out commitments

We have so far discussed the first of the two steps in each iteration of the interpreter, updating the mental state. We now discuss the second step, which is less complex by far. Recall that each commitment in the commitment database has a time associated with it: `(INFORM t a fact)`, `(IF mntlcond (DO t privateaction))`, etc. In this second step the interpreter simply executes all the actions whose time falls in the interval `(now-timegrain , now]`. The meaning of "execute" depends on the type of action:

- `INFORM`, `REQUEST`, `UNREQUEST`: Send the appropriate message.
- `REFRAIN`: No effect on execution (`REFRAIN` commitments play a role only in preventing commitment to other actions).
- `DO`: Consulting the belief and commitment databases, check the mental condition associated in the capability database with the primitive action; if it holds then perform the primitive action.
- `IF`: Consulting the belief and commitment databases, test the mental condition; if it holds then (recursively) execute the action.

6.3. A sample program and its interpretation

As an example of AGENT-0 programs, consider the flight-reservation scenario described in Section 2. We now present an annotated program implementing the airline representative. Although the scenario was simple to begin with, here I simplify it further by ignoring the exchange relating to the supervisor as well as other aspects of the communication. The idea behind the program is that the relevant activity on the part of the airline is issuing a boarding pass to the passenger, and that confirming a reservation is in fact a commitment to issue a boarding pass at the appropriate time.

Since some of the low-level definitions are long, it will be convenient to use abbreviations. We will therefore assume that AGENT-0 supports the use of macros (the actual implementation, mentioned below, does not). We define the following macros:

```
(issue_bp pass flightnum time) ⇒
  (IF (AND (B ((- time h) (present pass)))
           (B (time (flight ?from ?to flightnum))))
      (DO time-h (physical_issue_bp pass flightnum time))).
```

Explanation: This no-frills airline issues boarding passes precisely one hour prior to the flight; there are no seat assignments. `physical_issue_bp` is a private action involving some external events such as printing a boarding pass and presenting it to the passenger.

```
(query_which t asker askee q) ⇒
  (REQUEST t askee (IF (B q) (INFORM (+ t 1) asker q))).
```

Explanation: `query_which` requests only a positive answer; if `q` contains a universally-quantified variable then `query_which` requests to be informed of all instances of the answer to the query `q`.

```
(query_whether t asker askee q) ⇒
  (REQUEST t askee (IF (B q) (INFORM (+ t 1) asker q)))
  (REQUEST t askee (IF (B (NOT q))
                       (INFORM (+ t 1) asker (NOT q)))).
```

Explanation: `query_whether` expects either a confirmation or a disconfirmation of a fact.

We now define the airline agent. To do so we need to define its initial beliefs, capabilities, and commitment rules. Of the initial beliefs, the ones relevant here refer to the flight schedule, and the number of available seats for each flight. The former are represented in the form `(time (flight from to number))` (ignoring the fact that in practice airlines have a more-or-less fixed weekly schedule), and the latter in the form `(time (remaining_seats time1 flight_number seats))`. We also assume that the agent can evaluate arithmetic comparisons, such as 4>0.

There are two relevant capabilities here: Issuing boarding passes, and updating the count of the available seats on flights. Thus the capability database contains two items:

```
((issue_bp ?a ?flight ?time) true)

((DO ?time (update_remaining_seats ?time1 ?flight_number
                                   ?additional_seats))
 (B (?time (remaining_seats ?time1 ?flight_number
                            ?current_seats)))).
```

Explanation: `update_remaining_seat` is a private action which changes the belief regarding `remaining_seats`.

Finally, the airline agent has two commitment rules:

```
(COMMIT (?pass REQUEST (IF (B,?p) (INFORM ?t ?pass ?p)))
        true
        ?pass
        (IF (B,?p) (INFORM ?t ?pass ?p)))

(COMMIT (?cust REQUEST (issue_bp ?pass ?flight ?time))
```

Table 2
Sample exchange between a passenger and an airline agent

agent	action
smith	(query_which 1march/1:00 smith airline (18april/?!time (flight sf ny,?!num)))
airline	(INFORM 1march/2:00 smith (18april/8:30 (flight sf ny #354)))
airline	(INFORM 1march/2:00 smith (18april/10:00 (flight sf ny #293)))
airline	(INFORM 1march/2:00 smith (18april/ ...
smith	(REQUEST 1march/3:00 airline (issue_bp smith #354 18april/8:30))
smith	(query_whether 1march/4:00 smith airline ((CMT smith) (issue_bp smith #354 18april/8:30)))
airline	(INFORM 1march/5:00 smith (NOT ((CMT smith) (issue_bp smith #354 18april/8:30))))
smith	(REQUEST 1march/6:00 airline (issue_bp smith #293 18april/10:00))
smith	(query_whether 1march/7:00 smith airline ((CMT smith) (issue_bp smith #293 18april/10:00)))
airline	(INFORM 1march/8:00 smith ((CMT smith) (issue_bp smith #293 18april/10:00)))
...	
smith	(INFORM 18april/9:00 airline (present smith))
airline	(DO 18april/9:00 (issue_bp smith #293 18april/10:00))

```
(AND (B (?time (remaining_seats ?flight ?n)))
     (?n>0)
     (NOT ((CMT ?anyone)
           (issue_bp ?pass ?anyflight ?time))))
(myself (DO (+ now 1)
            (update_remaining_seats ?time
                                    ?flight -1)))
(?cust (issue_bp ?pass ?flight ?time)))
```

In a more realistic example one would have other commitment rules, notifying the passenger whether his reservation was confirmed, and the reasons for rejecting it in case it was not accepted. In the current implementation the passenger must query that separately.

This concludes the definition of the simple airline agent. Table 2 is a sample exchange between a passenger, smith, and the airline agent. The messages from the passenger are determined by him; the actions of the airline are initiated by the agent interpreter in response. The times are given in a convenient date/hh:mm format, rather than the number of seconds that have passed since 1900.

6.4. *Implementation*

A prototype AGENT-0 interpreter has been implemented in Common Lisp, and has been installed on Sun/Unix, DecStation/Ultrix, and Macintosh computers. Both the interpreter and the programming manual [74] are available to the scientific community. A separate implementation has been developed by Hewlett Packard as part of a joint project to incorporate AOP in the New Wave™ architecture. The interpreter for AGENT-1, which extends AGENT-0 in a number of ways (see below), is under development.

7. Agentification

In the previous two sections I discussed the second component of the AOP framework, agent programs and their interpretation. In this section I discuss, briefly, the process of agentification. My purpose in this section is not to make a substantial contribution to the topic, but to clarify some of the issues involved and point to some related work.

Agentification refers to bridging the gap between the low-level machine process and the intensional level of agent programs. Of course, the interpreter itself is one such bridge, but it requires a direct mapping between the constructs in the agent language and the machine implementing the agent. In particular it requires explicit representation in the machine of beliefs, commitments, and capabilities. When we are the ones creating the agents we indeed have the luxury of incorporating these components into their design, in which case the interpreter is adequate. However, we intend AOP as a framework for controlling and coordinating general devices, and those—cars, cameras, digital watches, spreadsheets—do not come equipped with beliefs and commitment rules.

Even if we were in a position to persuade (say) General Motors, Finmeccanica, and Matsushita to equip every single product with a mental state, we would be ill-advised to do so. AOP offers a perspective on computation and communication that has its advantages, but it is not proposed as a uniform replacement of other process representations. It would be ridiculous to require that every robot-arm designer augment his differential equations with beliefs, or that the digital-watch design verifier augment finite automata with commitments.

However, releasing the manufacturers from the requirement to supply a mental state creates a gap between the intensional level of agent programs on the one hand, and the mechanistic process representation of a given device on the other hand. The role of the agentifier is to bridge this gap.

We inherit this decoupling of the intensional level from the machine level from *situated automata*, introduced by Rosenschein in [62] and further developed by him and Kaelbling [34,63]. In situated automata there is a low-level language for describing the device, and another, high-level language for the designer to reason about the device. The compiler takes a program written in the high-level language and produces a description of a device in the low-level language.

Like the "knowledge-based" camp in distributed computation we adopt Rosenschein and Kaelbling's insight that intensional notions can be viewed as the designer's way of conceptualizing a device (as was discussed also in the introductory section, in connection with McCarthy's and Dennett's ideas). Having accepted this decoupling, however, we depart from situated automata in important ways. First, we consider different high-level and low-level languages. Concerning the high-level language, situated automata has had several versions; published versions have included a knowledge operator (K) and a tense operator (◇, or "eventually"). Our intensional language has already been discussed—it is the AGENT-0 language defined in the previous section, which is quite richer. In fact, we are currently engaged in enriching the language even further.

The low-level process languages in the two cases are also different. Many process languages exist—synchronous Boolean circuits with or without delays (the choice of situated automata as a process language), finite automata and Turing machines, and various formalisms aimed at capturing concurrency. Our requirements of the process language included the following:

- representation of process time, including real-valued durations,
- asynchronous processes,
- multiple levels of abstraction.

We found that no existing process models met all requirements, and have developed an alternative process model, called *temporal automata.*[15] The details of temporal automata are not relevant to the current discussion, so I will omit them; they appear in [39,40].

The choice of intensional languages and process description is important, but more crucial than anything is the translation process envisioned. As was mentioned, in situated automata the idea is to generate a low-level process model from a high-level, intensional description. In contrast to that, the goal of agentification is to agentify a particular, given machine. The input to the translator will include a description of a machine in the process language, and the output will be an intensional program. From this perspective, the process considered in situated automata is *de*-agentification. Since we have not tackled the problem of agentification in a substantial way, it is premature to assert with certainty how difficult it is. However, I expect that the unconstrained problem will be quite difficult. By this I mean that, given only a particular device (say, a camera) and general constraints on mental state of the sort described in the article, it will be hard to generate an intensional description of the device which fully captures is functioning. After all, who is to say where in the camera lie the beliefs? Is it in the state of a particular component, or perhaps in a complicated sequence of state changes? It seems to me more fruitful to include in the input information about the location of at least some mental attitudes ("when the light meter registers x, the camera believes that ..."), and attempt to synthesize a high-level program based on this information (this is closer in spirit to Rosenschein's original writing, but farther from the subsequent work). Again, I stress that we do not have sufficient experience with the problem to report any results.

8. Related work

Except occasionally, I have so far not discussed related past work. This body of related work is in fact so rich that in this section I will mention only the most closely related work, and briefly at that. I do not discuss again past work on logics of knowledge and belief, which the logic of mental state extends, since I already did that in the introduction. For the same reason, I will not discuss object-oriented programming and Hewitt's work. The following is ordered in what I see as decreasing relevance to, and overlap with, AOP. The order (or, for that matter, inclusion in the list) reflects no other ranking, nor is it implied that researchers high up on the list would necessarily endorse any part of AOP.

- McCarthy's work on Elephant2000 [48]. This language under development is also based on speech acts, and the airline-reservation scenario I have discussed is due to McCarthy. One issue explored in connection with Elephant2000 is the distinction between illocutionary and perlocutionary specifications, which I have not addressed. In contrast to AOP, in Elephant2000 there is currently no explicit representation of state, mental or otherwise. Conditional statements therefore refer to the history of past communication rather than to the current mental state.
- There is related work within the Distributed-AI community (cf. [60]). Although AOP is, to my knowledge, unique in its definition of mental state and the resulting programming language, others too have made the connection between object-oriented programming and agenthood [20,30].

[15] However, in recent years the specification and verification community has taken much interest in real-time computation, and some of the recent proposals make come closer to meeting our needs.

- The Intelligent Communicating Agents project (1987–1988), carried out jointly at Stanford, SRI, and Rockwell International (Nilsson, Rosenschein, Cohen, Moore, Appelt, Buckley, and many others). This ambitious project had among its goals the representation of speech acts and connection between the intensional level and the machine level. See discussion of some of the individual work below.
- Cohen and Levesque's work on belief, commitment, intention, and coordination [9,10]. This work was discussed in detail in Section 4.4. To summarize that discussion, Cohen and Levesque too have investigated the logical relationships between several modalities such as belief and choice. Although they have not approached the topic from a programming-language perspective as I have, they too have been interested in speech acts and mental state as building blocks for coordination and analysis of behavior. Their work has its roots in earlier work in natural language understanding by Allen, Cohen and Perrault [2,11]. Despite some similarities, crucial differences exist between the mental categories employed by Cohen and Levesque and ours.
- AOP shares with early work on *contract nets* [72] the computational role of contracts among agents. The similarity ends there, though. Contract nets were based on broadcasting contracts and soliciting bids, as opposed to the intimate communication in AOP. Contract nets had no other notion of mental state, no range of communicative speech acts, nor the asynchronous, real-time design inherent in AOP.
- Rosenschein and Kaelbling's situated automata [34,62,63]. I already discussed this work in the previous section. To summarize, it is relevant in connection with the process of agentification; we adopt their idea of decoupling the machine language from the programmer's intensional conceptualization of the machine, but differ on the specific details.
- Research on coordination. Several researchers have been concerned with the process of coordination in modern environments. For example, as a part of their more global project, Winograd and Flores have developed a model of communication in a work environment. They point to the fact that every conversation is governed by some rules, which constrain the actions of the participants: a request must be followed by an accept or a decline, a question by an answer, and so on. Their model of communication is that of a finite automaton, with the automaton states corresponding to different states of the conversation. This is a macro-theory, a theory of societies of agents, in contrast to the micro-theory of AOP. In related work, Malone and his associates are aiming towards a general theory of coordination, drawing on diverse fields such as computer science and economics [46].
- Genesereth's work on informable agents [23,24]. Genesereth's interest lies primarily in agents containing declarative knowledge that can be informed of new facts, and that can act on partial plans. In this connection he has investigated also the compilation of declarative plans and information into action commands. Genesereth uses the term "agents" so as to include also low-level finite-automaton-like constructs. AOP's structure of mental state is consistent with Genesereth's declarative regime, but is not required by it.
- Recent work on plan representation and recognition by Kautz, Pollack, Konolige, Litman, Allen and others (e.g., [6,36,44,59]). This literature also addresses the interaction between mental state and action, but it is usually concerned with finer-grained analyses, involving the actual representation of plans, reasoning limitations, and more complex mental notions such as goals, desires and intentions.
- Nilsson's action nets. ACTNET [58] is a language for computing goal-achieving actions that depends dynamically on sensory and stored data. The ACTNET language is based on the concept of action networks [57]. An action network is a forest of logical gates that select actions in response to sensory and stored data. The connection to AOP, albeit a weak one, is that some of the wires in the network originate from database items marked as "beliefs" and "goals". The maintenance of these databases is not the job of the action net.

9. Discussion

I have described the philosophy behind agent-oriented programming, and progress made towards realizing it—both in terms of formal underpinning and in terms of algorithm design.

This is clearly only a beginning. Beside debugging and fine-tuning the logic (which has not been the main focus of this article) and programming language (which has been), the framework can be extended dramatically in a number of directions. Below are some of the more important ones.

- Mental categories. The language for describing mental state can be augmented to include more complex notions such as desires, intentions, and plans, allowing a richer set of communicative commands and more structure on the behavior of agents. In this effort we hope to build on previous work mentioned in the previous section; Thomas [73] explores a notion of intention and planning, and in [17] we take a stab a the notion of desire, building on Doyle and Wellman's earlier work.
- Groundedness of mental categories. One of the contributions of distributed computation to the formal theory of knowledge is the concrete grounding of the semantics: What were formerly purely formal constructs, possible worlds, became the set of possible global states of a

collection of finite-state processors, given a particular protocol. In connection with the process of agentification, it will be satisfying to be able to anchor belief and commitment similarly.

- Probability and utility. As in most recent work on knowledge and belief, we have adopted very crisp notions of mental attitude; there is no representation of graded belief or commitment. This stands in contrast to game-theoretic work on rational interaction among agents in economics (e.g., [3,22]) and AI (e.g., [61]), where uncertainty and utility play a key role. This is a natural direction in which to extend our framework.
- Inheritance and groups. In the analogy between OOP and AOP I did not mention inheritance, a key component of OOP today. In OOP, if an object is a specialization of another object then it inherits its methods. One analogous construct in AOP would be "group agents"; that is a group of agents will itself constitute an agent. If we define the beliefs of this composite agent as the "common beliefs" of the individual agents and the commitments of the composite agent as the "common commitments" (yet to be defined) of the individual agents, then mental attitudes of the group are indeed inherited by the individual.
- Persistence of mental states. At the end of Section 4, I mentioned that dealing formally with the persistence of mental state is even harder than dealing with the familiar frame problem: If I believe that you don't believe x, do I believe that you will not believe in a little while? Do I believe that I will believe that you don't? Will I believe then that you don't? Will I believe then that I believed in the past that you didn't know? Answers to these questions depend on some subtle assumptions; our preliminary results appear in [43].
- Resource limitations. In the definition of the interpreter I assumed that the belief and commitment updates all happened fast enough before the next cycle was to start. While often reasonable, this assumption is violated in many real-time applications. In these cases the manipulation of data structures (such as beliefs) must be shortened or suppressed in favor of rapid action. There is much interest nowadays in intelligent real-time problem solving, including issues such as tradeoff between quality and timeliness. From the agent interpreter's standpoint this means that the belief and commitment update cannot proceed blindly, but must take into account the elapsed time, choosing wisely among mental operations.
- Belief revision and update. AGENT-0 adopts an extreme form of belief revision, accepting all new information. Obviously there are situations that call for more discriminating agents, raising the question of what constitutes a reasonable policy of belief update. We are interested both in semantical and algorithmic questions; our results on the former appear in [14].
- Temporal belief maps. AGENT-0 restricts beliefs to "objective" sentences, so one cannot represent beliefs of agents about the beliefs or commitments of other agents. AGENT-0 keeps tracks of these beliefs by a *time map* mechanism [12], essentially recording the points of transition and assuming default persistence between them. In the new interpreter under development, AGENT-1, we allow nested modalities in the belief database. For this purpose we introduce a new computational construct, called *mental time maps*, which is essentially a high-dimensional time map. *Temporal belief maps* are a special case, and are described in [33].
- Societies. Both the theoretical development of mental categories and the AGENT-0 programming language concentrated on a single agent. Indeed, the view promoted was of agents functioning autonomously. However, if a society of agents is to function successfully, some global constraints must be imposed. These include social *rules* as well as social *roles*; both reduce the problem solving required by agents and the communication overhead. There is a rich body of literature on computer societies, examples of which include Minsky's informal Society of Mind metaphor [52], Winograd's studies of societal roles, both human and machine [75], Moses and Tennenholtz's recent discussion of the computational advantages of social laws [56], and Doyle's pioneering work on the relationship between AI, rational psychology, and economics [16]. In recent work we have investigated the off-line design of social laws which strike a good balance between preventing chaos on the one hand, and allowing sufficient freedom to individual agents on the other hand [70,71]; we are currently investigating the automatic on-line learning of such laws.

These are some of the directions we intend to continue to explore. Above all, it is important to experiment with significant applications. At this time there are about a half dozen projects experimenting with variants of AGENT-0, and it will be important to continue this activity. I have been deliberately conservative so far in the scope of the work, but, I believe, more ambitious explorations, involving, for example, other mental attitudes, will benefit from a clear and rigorous basis of the kind I have defined.

Acknowledgement

I have discussed AOP in general and this document in particular with many people, and have benefited from their comments. Members of the Nobotics group, including Jun-ichi Akahani, Nita Goyal, Hideki Isozaki,

George John, Jean-Francois Lavignon, Fangzhen Lin, Eyal Moses, Anton Schwartz, Dominique Snyers, Moshe Tennenholtz, Becky Thomas, Mark Torrance, and Alvaro del Val have contributed in many ways. I have discussed agents and agenthood also with Vint Cerf, Tom Dean, Mike Genesereth, Joe Halpern, Barbara Hayes-Roth, Leslie Kaelbling, Bob Kahn, Jean-Claude Latombe, Yoram Moses, Nils Nilsson, Stan Rosenschein, Rich Thomason, Terry Winograd, and many others; I apologize for not mentioning everyone. I thank Phil Cohen, Kurt Konolige, Martha Pollack and an anonymous referee for critical comments. Finally, special thanks to John McCarthy for enlightening conversations.

References

[1] P. Agre and D. Chapman, Pengi: an implementation of a theory of activity, in: *Proceedings AAAI-87*, Seattle, WA (1987) 268–272.

[2] J.F. Allen, Recognizing intentions from natural language utterances, in: M. Brady and R.C. Berwick, eds., *Computational Models of Discourse* (MIT Press, Cambridge, MA, 1983) 107–166.

[3] R. Aumann, Agreeing to disagree, *Ann. Stat.* **4** (1976) 1236–1239.

[4] J.L. Austin, *How to Do Things with Words* (Harvard University Press, Cambridge, MA, 1955/1975).

[5] N.D. Belnap and M. Perloff, Seeing to it that: a canonical form of agentives, *Theoria* **54** (1989) 175–199.

[6] M.E. Bratman, *Intention, Plans, and Practical Reason* (Harvard University Press, Cambridge, MA, 1987).

[7] R.A. Brooks, A robust layered control system for a mobile robot, *IEEE J. Rob. Autom.* **2** (1) (1986).

[8] B.F. Chellas, Time and modality in the logic of agency, *Stud. Logica* (to appear).

[9] P.R. Cohen and H.J. Levesque, Intention is choice with commitment, *Artif. Intell.* **42** (3) (1990) 213–261.

[10] P.R. Cohen and H.J. Levesque, Rational interaction as the basis for communication, in: P.R. Cohen, J. Morgan and M.E. Pollack, eds., *Intentions in Communication* (MIT Press, Cambridge, MA, to appear).

[11] P.R. Cohen and C.R. Perrault, Elements of a plan-based theory of speech acts, *Cogn. Sci.* **3** (1979) 177–212.

[12] T.L. Dean and D.V. McDermott, Temporal data base management, *Artif. Intell.* **32** (1) (1987) 1–55.

[13] T.L. Dean and M.P. Wellman, *Planning and Control* (Morgan Kauffman, San Mateo, CA, 1991).

[14] A. del Val and Y. Shoham, Deriving the postulates of belief update from theories of action, in: *Proceedings AAAI-92*, San Jose, CA (1992).

[15] D.C. Dennett, *The Intentional Stance* (MIT Press, Cambridge, MA, 1987).

[16] R. Doyle, Artificial intelligence and rational self-government, Tech. Rept. CMU-CS-88-124, Computer Science Department, Carnegie-Mellon University, Pittsburgh, PA (1988).

[17] R. Doyle, Y. Shoham and M. Wellman, A theory of relative desire, in: *Proceedings ISMIS* (1991).

[18] M. Drummond, Situated control rules, in: *Proceedings First International Conference on Knowledge Representation and Reasoning*, Toronto, Ont. (1989).

[19] D. Elgesem, He would have done it anyway: the logic of agency, ability and opportunity, Stanford University, CSLI, Stanford, CA (1990).

[20] J. Ferber and P. Carle, Actors and agents as reflective concurrent objects: a Mering IV perspective, in: *Proceedings 10th International Workshop on Distributed Artificial Intelligence*, Tech. Rept. ACT-AI-355-90, MCC, Austin, TX (1990).

[21] P. Gärdenfors, *Knowledge in Flux: Modeling the Dynamics of Epistemic States* (MIT Press, Cambridge, MA, 1987).

[22] J. Geanakoplos, Common knowledge, Bayesian learning, and market speculation with bounded rationality, Memo, Yale University, New Haven, CT (1988).

[23] M.R. Genesereth, A comparative analysis of some simple architectures for autonomous agents, Tech. Rept. Logic-89-2, Computer Science Department, Stanford University, Stanford, CA (1989); also in: K. VanLehn, ed., *Architectures for Intelligence* (Lawrence Erlbaum, Hillsdale, NJ, 1991).

[24] M.R. Genesereth, A proposal for research on informable agents, Tech. Rept. Logic-89-4, Computer Science Department, Stanford University, Stanford, CA (1989).

[25] P. Grice, *Studies in the Ways of Words* (Harvard University Press, Cambridge, MA, 1989).

[26] J.Y. Halpern, Using reasoning about knowledge to analyze distributed systems, in: J.F. Traub, ed., *Annual Review of Computer Science* **2** (Annual Reviews Inc., Palo Alto, CA, 1987).

[27] J.Y. Halpern and Y. Moses, A guide to the modal logics of knowledge and belief: preliminary draft, in: *Proceedings IJCAI-85*, Los Angeles, CA (1985) 480–490.

[28] J.Y. Halpern and L.D. Zuck, A little knowledge goes a long way: simple knowledge-based derivations and correctness proofs for a family of protocols, in: *Proceedings 6th ACM Symposium on Principles of Distributed Computing* (1987) 269–280.

[29] B. Hayes-Roth, R. Washington, R. Hewett, M. Hewett and A. Seiver, Intelligent monitoring and control, in: *Proceedings IJCAI-89*, Detroit, MI (1989) 243–249.

[30] C. Hewitt, Towards open information systems semantics, in: *Proceedings 10th International Workshop on Distributed Artificial Intelligence*, Tech. Rept. ACT-AI-355-90, MCC, Austin, TX (1990).

[31] C. Hewitt, Viewing control structures as patterns of passing messages, *Artif. Intell.* **8** (1977) 323–364.

[32] J. Hintikka, *Knowledge and Belief* (Cornell University Press, Ithaca, NY, 1962).

[33] H. Isozaki and Y. Shoham, A mechanism for reasoning about time and belief, in: *Proceedings Third International Conference on Fifth Generation Computer Systems*, Tokyo (1992).

[34] L.P. Kaelbling, Goals as parallel program specifications, in: *Proceedings AAAI-88*, St. Paul, MN (1988) 60–65.

[35] H. Katsuno and A.O. Mendelzon, On the difference between updating a knowledge base and revising it, in: *Proceedings Second Conference on Knowledge Representation and Reasoning*, Cambridge, MA (1991).

[36] H.A. Kautz, A circumscriptive theory of plan recognition, in: P.R. Cohen, J. Morgan and M.E. Pollack, eds., *Intentions in Communication* (MIT Press, Cambridge, MA, 1990).

[37] K. Konolige, *A Deduction Model of Belief* (Pitman/Morgan Kaufmann, London, 1986).

[38] S. Kripke, Semantical considerations of modal logic, *Z. Math. Logik Grundl. Math.* **9** (1963) 67–96.

[39] J.F. Lavignon, A simulator for temporal automata, Tech. Rept., Computer Science Department, Stanford University, Stanford, CA (1990).

[40] J.F. Lavignon and Y. Shoham, Temporal automata, Tech. Rept. STAN-CS-90-1325, Computer Science Department, Stanford University, Stanford, CA (1990).

[41] H.J. Levesque, All I know: an abridged report, in: *Proceedings AAAI-87*, Seattle, WA (1987) 426–431.

[42] F. Lin and Y. Shoham, Concurrent actions in the situation calculus, in: *Proceedings AAAI-92*, San Jose (1992).

[43] F. Lin and Y. Shoham, On the persistence of knowledge and ignorance, Stanford Working Document, Stanford, CA (1992).

[44] D.J. Litman and J.F. Allen, Discourse processing and commonsense plans, in: P.R. Cohen, J. Morgan and M.E. Pollack, eds., *Intentions in Communication* (MIT Press,

Cambridge, MA, 1990).

[45] W. Litwin, A model for computer life, Manuscript, Computer Science Department, Stanford University, Stanford, CA (1990).

[46] T.W. Malone, Toward an interdisciplinary theory of coordination, Tech. Rept. CCS 120, MIT Sloan School of Management, Cambridge, MA (1991).

[47] J. McCarthy, Ascribing mental qualities to machines, Tech. Rept. Memo 326, Stanford AI Lab, Stanford, CA (1979).

[48] J. McCarthy, Elephant 2000: a programming language based on speech acts, Unpublished Manuscript (1990).

[49] J. McCarthy, Notes on formalizing context, Unpublished Manuscript (1991).

[50] J.M. McCarthy and P.J. Hayes, Some philosophical problems from the standpoint of artificial intelligence, in: B. Meltzer and D. Michie, eds., *Machine Intelligence* **4** (Edinburgh University Press, Edinburgh, Scotland, 1969) 463–502.

[51] D.V. McDermott, Tarskian semantics, or no notation without denotation!, *Cogn. Sci.* **2** (3) (1978) 277–282.

[52] M. Minsky, *The Society of Mind* (Simon and Schuster, New York, 1986).

[53] T.M. Mitchell, Becoming increasingly reactive, in: *Proceedings AAAI-90*, Boston, MA (1990) 1050–1058.

[54] R.C. Moore, A formal theory of knowledge and action, in: J.R. Hobbs and R.C. Moore, eds., *Formal Theories of the Commonsense World* (Ablex, Norwood, NJ, 1985).

[55] L. Morgenstern, Foundations of a logic of knowledge, action, and communication, Ph.D. Thesis, New York University (1988).

[56] Y. Moses and M. Tennenholtz, In favor of a society, Manuscript, Department of Applied Mathematics, Weizmann Institute of Science, Rehovot, Israel (1990).

[57] N.J. Nilsson, Action networks, in: *Proceedings of the Workshop on Planning*, Rochester, NY (1989).

[58] N.J. Nilsson, R. Moore and M. Torrance, Actnet: an action-network language and its interpreter (1990).

[59] M.E. Pollack, Plans as complex mental attitudes, in: P.R. Cohen, J. Morgan and M.E. Pollack, eds., *Intentions in Communication* (MIT Press, Cambridge, MA, 1990).

[60] Proceedings 10th International Workshop on Distributed Artificial Intelligence, Tech. Rept. ACT-AI-355-90 MCC Austin, TX (1990).

[61] S.J. Rosenschein and M.R. Genesereth, Deals among rational agents, in: *Proceedings IJCAI-85*, Los Angeles, CA (1985).

[62] S.J. Rosenschein, Formal theories of knowledge in AI and robotics, Tech. Rept. 362, SRI International, Menlo Park, CA (1985).

[63] S.J. Rosenschein and L.P. Kaelbling, The synthesis of digital machines with provable epistemic properties, in: *Proceedings Conference on Theoretical Aspects of Reasoning about Knowledge*, Monterey, CA (1986) 83–86.

[64] S. Ross, The economic theory of agency, *Am. Econ. Rev.* **63** (1973) 134–139.

[65] F. Schneider, Understanding protocols for byzantine clock synchronization, Tech. Rept., Computer Science Department, Cornell University (1987).

[66] J.R. Searle, *Speech Acts: An Essay in the Philosophy of Language*, (Cambridge University Press, Cambridge, England, 1969).

[67] Y. Shoham, Time for action, in: *Proceedings IJCAI-89*, Detroit, MI (1989) 954–959.

[68] Y. Shoham, Varieties of context, in: V.A. Lifschitz, ed., *Artificial Intelligence and Mathematical Theory of Computation* (Academic Press, New York, 1991) 393–408.

[69] Y. Shoham and Y. Moses, Belief as defeasible knowledge, in: *Proceedings IJCAI-89*, Detroit, MI (1989) 1168–1172.

[70] Y. Shoham and M. Tennenholtz, On the synthesis of useful social laws for artificial agents, in: *Proceedings AAAI-92*, San Jose, CA (1992).

[71] Y. Shoham and M. Tennenholtz, On traffic laws for mobile robots, Stanford Working Document, Stanford, CA (1992).

[72] R.G. Smith, The contract net protocol: high-level communication and control in a distributed problem solver, *IEEE Trans. Comput.* **29** (12) (1980) 1104–1113.

[73] S.R. Thomas, A logic for representing action, belief, capability, and intention, Stanford Working Document, Stanford, CA (1992).

[74] M. Torrance, The AGENT-0 programming manual (revise), Computer Science Department, Stanford University, Stanford, CA (1991).

[75] T. Winograd, A language/action perspective on the design of cooperative work, *Human-Comput. Interaction* **3** (1) (1987/88) 3–30.

4.2 Rational Agency: Economic

Designing Conventions for Automated Negotiation

Jeffrey S. Rosenschein and Gilad Zlotkin

■ As distributed systems of computers play an increasingly important role in society, it will be necessary to consider ways in which these machines can be made to interact effectively. We are concerned with heterogeneous, distributed systems made up of machines that have been programmed by different entities to pursue different goals. Adjusting the rules of public behavior (the rules of the game) by which the programs must interact can influence the private strategies that designers set up in their machines. These rules can shape the design choices of the machines' programmers and, thus, the run-time behavior of their creations. Certain kinds of desirable social behavior can thus be caused to emerge through the careful design of interaction rules. Formal tools and analysis can help in the appropriate design of these rules.

We consider how concepts from fields such as decision theory and game theory can provide standards to be used in the design of appropriate negotiation and interaction environments. This design is highly sensitive to the domain in which the interaction is taking place.

This article is adapted from an invited lecture given by Jeffrey Rosenschein at the Thirteenth International Joint Conference on Artificial Intelligence in Chambery, France, on 2 September 1993.

We've all been hearing a lot about convergence between telephone, television, and computer technology. The basic idea is that the networks that constitute our telephone infrastructure, our television (particularly cable) infrastructure, and our computer infrastructure will be coalescing into one harmonious whole. Then the user, sitting in his/her home or office, has some kind of information appliance that can handle the wealth of resources that are available.

Now, AI has a role to play in how the computer works in this brave new world of information consolidation. Several groups of AI researchers are already actively involved in trying to design automated agents that will help the user filter or retrieve information from the network. To mention just one example, Oren Etzioni's group at the University of Washington at Seattle is building what he calls *softbots,* software robots, to handle the interface between humans and network resources. There are also a lot of good, meaty, classic AI problems that need to be solved in this context, such as knowledge representation and planning problems.

What we discuss here has a strong connection to those efforts to build software agents. What we have been interested in over the last few years has been to look at the ways in which these automated software agents will be dealing with one another. In other words, it's all well and good to have agents residing in your home computer that help you deal with all the information, but this agent of yours is going to have to deal with the agents of other people, either private agents if you're trying to do a job such as setting up a meeting with a group of people or corporate agents if you're trying to access information from a company database. These software agents are on their way, and they're going to be getting a lot of things accomplished by interacting with each other. The question is, How will these agents be cooperating with each other, competing with each other, and negotiating with each other?

Machines Controlling and Sharing Resources

There are actually a lot of different environments in which machines are making more and more decisions that affect our daily lives, and they're making these decisions not in isolation but in concert with other machines. Computers that control electric grid networks and need to balance their power requirements can share electricity with other computers controlling other networks. If there's a drop or rise in power consumption, one computer can sell or buy excess power from other utilities to which it's connected.

Another example is routing among telecommunication networks. Information, or packets, can pass over a network controlled by one company onto another network controlled by another company, or it can pass through one country on through another. Computers that control a telecommunications network might find it beneficial to enter into agreements with other computers that control other networks about routing packets more efficiently from source to destination. The point is that it might make sense for both machines to be able to exploit the resources controlled by the other so that they can both get their jobs done more effectively.

... the agents that we are interested in looking at are heterogeneous, self-motivated agents.

We're also seeing the emergence of tools such as *personal digital assistants,* small, handheld computers (for example, the Newton). These personal assistants are going to assume the roles of a number of machines or tools involved with managing our daily lives, such as notebooks, communicators, fax machines, telephones, and automated schedulers. We're going to have some kind of agent software on the personal assistant, and it's ultimately going to get part of its work done by interacting with other agents on other personal assistants.

Another example is the proliferation of shared databases, where there's information spread all over the world. They have sprung up with a vengeance in the last decade. You've already got agents, such as Etzioni's softbots, that are going out there to gather information—for example, a person's Internet address—from a shared database. Finally, even something such as traffic control, coordination of vehicular traffic, or air traffic control illustrates situations where software agents will be making decisions based on communication and agreements with other agents.

Each of these situations is an instance where computers are controlling some resource and might be able to help themselves by strategically sharing this resource with other computers. With personal digital assistants, the resource might be a person's time, whereas with a telecommunications network, the resource might be communication lines, switching nodes, or short- and long-term storage. In each situation, the computers that control these resources can do their own job better by reaching agreements with other computers.

Heterogeneous, Self-Motivated Agents

Now, the agents that we are interested in looking at are heterogeneous, self-motivated agents. The systems are not assumed to be centrally designed. For example, if you have a personal digital assistant, you might have one that was built by IBM, but the next person over might have one that was built by Apple. They don't necessarily have a notion of global utility. Each personal digital assistant or each agent operating from your machine is interested in what your idea of utility is and in how to further your notion of goodness. They're dynamic; for example, agents might enter and leave the system in an unpredictable way. The system as a whole is flexible; new personal assistants are coming in, even new types of personal assistants are being built and coming in to the system and have to interact with other agents.

In particular, the personal assistants do not act benevolently unless it's in their interest to do so. They do not necessarily share information, they do not necessarily do things that other agents ask them to do unless they have a good reason for doing so. Thus, imagine lots of agents, each one residing in your personal computer or on your personal digital assistant, trying to carry out tasks, and interacting with other agents.

The Aim of the Research

The aim of the research that we've been doing can really be thought of as a kind of social engineering for communities of machines. With communities of people, social engineering means setting up laws or setting up an environment that causes people to act in a certain beneficial way or causes people to act in certain ways that we decided ahead of time are desirable. At the least, it constrains their behavior.

Similarly, we're interested in the creation of interaction environments that foster a certain kind of social behavior among machines. We want to develop conventions, rules of encounter, for these software agents that will cause them to act in certain ways. Another way to look at this research is that we're trying to exploit formal tools, in this case, game theory tools, for high-level protocol design. We're looking at protocols for interactions among agents, and we would like to design protocols that cause, for example, these personal digital assistant agents to act in certain ways.

Broad Working Assumption

These agents are obviously still pursuing their own utility, they're still pursuing their own goals, but they're going to be constrained somehow by the environment that we design. However, who's "we"? "We" means the designers of the network or the designers of the system. Let's say, as a working assumption, that designers from IBM, Apple, Toshiba, and Sony all come together and say, "OK, we've got this domain. The domain is personal digital assistants doing scheduling, time scheduling. Given this domain, we would like to set up the rules for the way in which schedules will be set. We want to set up the rules, a high-level protocol, that determines the kind of deals, let's say, that agents can make among themselves."

These designers then come together and try to agree on standards for how their automated agents interact. An important part of this process is that it takes place in a given domain. They might decide on different protocols for different domains, but given the domain, like scheduling among personal digital assistants, the designers are going to decide on standards for how the agents reach agreements.

Now, what are the designers actually doing in this meeting? It is a standards committee meeting: They sit around a big table and discuss the trade-offs of different decisions. One of them says, "You know, if we have this kind of protocol, the agents will be able to come to agreement quickly. The agreements probably won't be optimal, but we'll be able to get to them fast." Somebody else at the table says, "Yes, but it's important to us at IBM that these protocols not allow agents to manipulate one another. You know, we don't want any manipulative, exploitative agents getting into the system and taking advantage." Yet another designer says, "Well, that's not so important to me. The most important thing is that the average utility among all the agents be as high as possible."

We are not trying to impose a group of decisions that these company representatives might make. Instead, what we're trying to do is come forward, elucidate a variety of protocol decisions, and show how particular protocols have certain desirable attributes. Once we show that protocol A has a certain attribute, the designers of these personal digital assistants might decide to choose it, and they might not; they might choose something else. However, the idea of the research is to come forward and elucidate and elaborate on the possibilities. Protocol A has this set of attributes, and protocol B has this slightly different set of attributes. Which do you want to choose when you design your agents? It's up to you. Part of the research is to make it clear to those designers what the options are.

Attributes of Standards

What are we looking at when we try to design a standard? Well, we might look at the efficiency of the system, such as Pareto optimality; that is, the agreement that is reached by the agents can be made no better for any one of the them without making it worse for one of the other agents. Thus, we have what might be considered a broadly acceptable doctrine of general goodness.

... what we're trying to do is come forward, elucidate a variety of protocol decisions, and show how particular protocols have certain desirable attributes

Stability: An agent has no incentive to deviate from a particular strategy. This idea is related to the game theory notion of equilibrium.

Simplicity: This quality is important for computer science but much less important for game theory. We certainly want our protocols to have low computation and communication costs. This attribute is one that we might propose, and those designers might say, "This attribute is absolutely important; it's important that our small processor not have a heavy load in doing negotiation."

We'd like the protocol to be distributed, typically because if we're going to have a lot of distributed agents, it would be nice not to have a central decision maker. It would be nice to have it be symmetric, so that no agent plays a special role. When the agents come together, they don't have to decide who's going to be the master and who's going to be the slave or who's going to do what.

The idea is to design protocols for specific classes of domains that satisfy some or all of these attributes. As we present protocols, or design decisions, it might be the case that it's simple but not distributed or that it's stable but not efficient or that it's efficient but not stable. These are classic trade-offs.

Distributed AI

How does this work relate to other research being done in the field? It fits into the broad

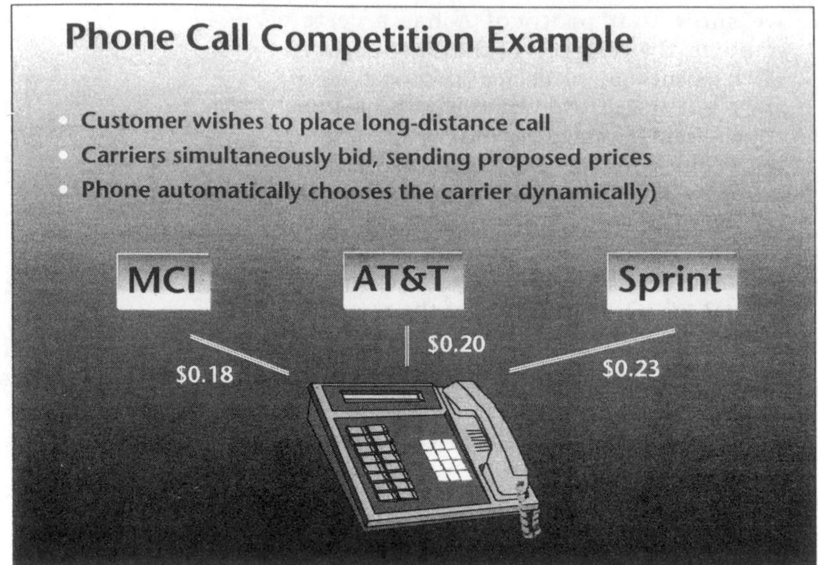

Phone Call Competition Example
Customer wishes to place long-distance call
Carriers simultaneously bid, sending proposed prices
Phone automatically chooses the carrier dynamically)
MCI
AT&T
Sprint
$0.18
$0.20
$0.23

Figure 1. A System for Placing a Call.

area of distributed AI, which can be broken down into two related areas. These two areas constitute distinctions between research agendas; they are not really appropriate as descriptions of running systems.

One stream of research is *distributed problem solving,* which constitutes the original emphasis of distributed AI, namely, the study of distributed but centrally designed AI systems. How do you build a distributed system that is made up of many agents that have some global problem to solve? You're going to design the system so that the agents solve the problem in a good way, in a distributed way, in an efficient way. In distributed problem solving, there is assumed to be a single body that is able, at design time, to directly influence the preferences of all agents in the system.

This area contrasts with another stream of research within distributed AI called *multiagent systems*. In multiagent systems, you again have multiple agents in a distributed system, but you do not assume that there is a single designer who stands behind all of them, or put another way, you do not assume that the individual agents have a group sense of utility. Each of the agents in the system can be working at different goals, even conflicting goals. You have to deal with a system made up of multiple agents where competition or cooperation is possible between the agents. In multiagent systems, no single body is assumed that, at design time, can directly influence the preferences of all agents in the system. The agents' preferences arise from distinct designers.

In particular, if a distributed problem-solving researcher can show that acting in a particular way is good for the system as a whole, he/she can impose this behavior on all the agents in the system at design time. For the multiagent system researcher, such an alternative is unavailable. At best, he/she might be able to design aspects of the environment that motivate all the (selfish) agents to act in a certain way. This need for indirect incentives is one element that distinguishes multiagent system research from distributed problem-solving research.

The work we describe here is multiagent system research.

The Telephone Call Competition Example

We mentioned how we're trying to design protocols for agent interactions. To illustrate this point, we use the example of a hypothetical environment to show how different protocols motivate agents to act in different ways and how these different protocols end up having different global properties.

In the United States, there are several long-distance telephone companies, and each telephone customer sends in a postcard asking to hook up with one or another of them. The selected company becomes the customer's default carrier; you have to dial extra numbers to place a long-distance call with some other company. Imagine another kind of system, one that might operate within the current technology but has certain benefits over the way things are done now. What if a customer lifts a handset and dials a long-distance call, and a microprocessor within the telephone automatically collects bids from the various carriers? Each company's computer automatically and simultaneously declares the price per minute for which it's willing to carry the call. In figure 1, we see the MCI computer relaying 18 cents, but the AT&T computer bids 20 cents, and so on. This process can take place in a split second, without significantly delaying the call.

Best Bid Wins

Our telephone's microprocessor is now collecting the bids. Assume that the protocol involves our telephone choosing the company with the lowest bid, which is completely reasonable, and placing the telephone call with the company. The winning carrier receives a price for each minute equal to the amount that it bid. The prices set by the companies for telephone calls at different times of the day no longer have to be fixed ahead of time, nor does the pricing system have to be simple enough to be remembered by consumers. It can be completely dynamic and sensitive to the real costs or economies that exist at any given moment. The system appears to be much more open to competition too: A new long-distance carrier doesn't have to win over consumers with a costly advertising campaign; it just needs to set up its computers to enter into the bidding game. In fact, the companies now have greater motivation to sink their budgets into researching ways to lower their costs rather than into advertising to grab consumers. The process sounds good, but this bidding mechanism has a serious flaw (figure 2).

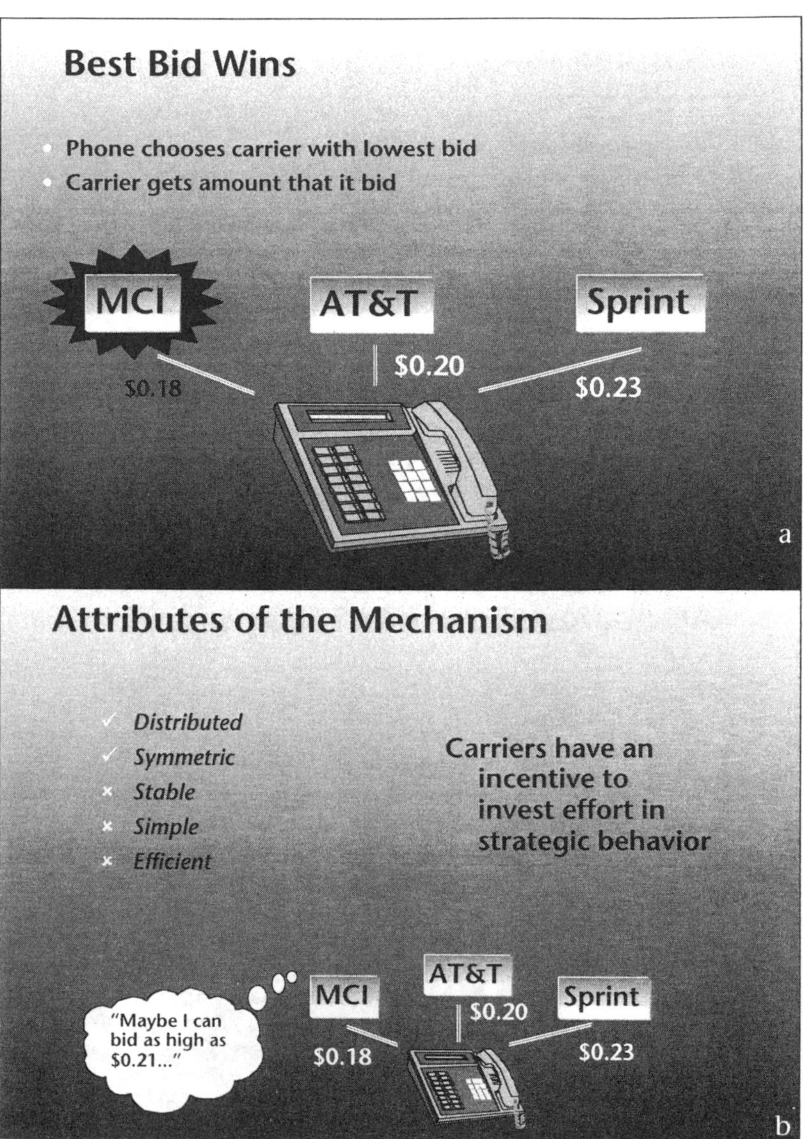

Figure 2. Rules of the Game and Resulting Attributes.

Strategic Behavior Results

We have made the long-distance carrier selection distributed and symmetric, but the protocol, the rules by which the agents play to win the telephone call, does not encourage stable, simple, or efficient behavior on the part of the telephone company computers. Let's pretend that our consumer wants to make a long-distance call and consider the MCI computer's reasoning. Although it could carry the call for 18 cents and get an acceptable profit, it might rationally try to increase the profit by bidding higher. It might think that the next-highest bidder won't go below 22 cents and, consequently, make its own bid 21 cents. Now, this strategy is risky, but the carriers have a great incentive for investing effort in strategic behavior. Instead of putting their money into polished ad campaigns, they'll pay programmers to develop sophisticated models of their opponents' bidding strategies; that is, how much can carrier X really afford to carry a call for right now? They'll put energy into trying to discover relevant information about their opponents, information that might affect the bid the opponent puts in, for example, which switching stations are down and what the other company's profit and loss are for this quarter. Ultimately, this sort of effort drains resources that might be better spent elsewhere. Equally important, the actual bidding procedure can result in an inefficient outcome. In this example, MCI might lose the bid when it could have served as the lowest-cost alternative.

Can we do better by changing the protocol of bidding? The answer is yes.

Best Bid Wins, Gets Second Price

Let's say that in our new protocol, all the company computers put their bids in, and our telephone's computer again automatically chooses the lowest bidder as the winner. However, this time, the carrier that wins gets paid a price for each minute equal to the second lowest bid. This bidding system, called *Vickrey's mechanism*, is attractive because it provides no incentive for a company to underbid or overbid. A company has the incentive only to provide the true minimum acceptable price. A company won't bid lower than its minimum acceptable price because it fears that some other company might bid in the gap that it has opened up (in fact, if no one else bids in the gap, the first company would have won anyway without bidding low). If MCI bid 1 cent and won, somebody

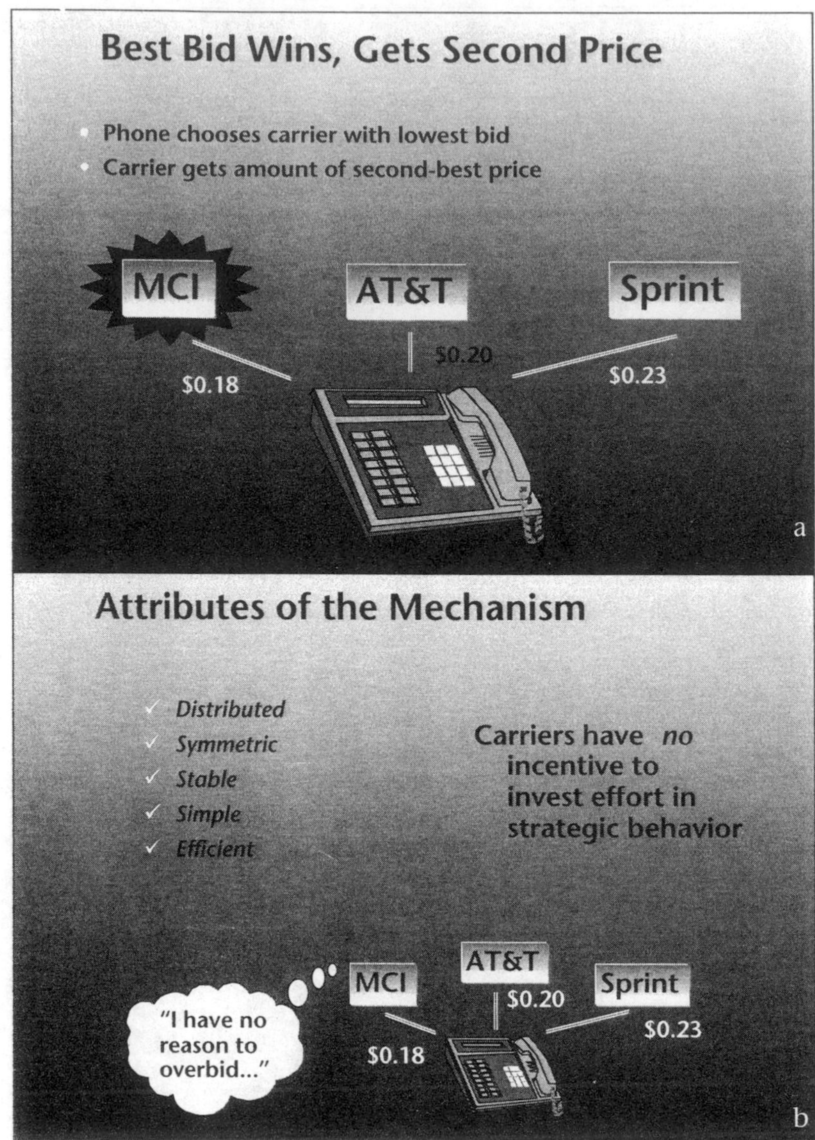

Figure 3. Different Protocol, Different Attributes.

else might bid 10 cents; then MCI would be forced to carry the call for less than its minimal acceptable 18 cents for each minute. However, no company has an incentive to overbid either. What possible benefit could MCI get from declaring a price higher than 18 cents? If it says, for example, 20 cents, it might lose a bid it would otherwise have won, and in any case, its own bid will never affect how much money it gets! By separating the issues of who wins the bid and how much the winner gets, we have fundamentally altered the way in which computers should play the game (figure 3).

Attributes of the Mechanism

Now, the carriers at our long-distance companies have no incentive to invest effort in strategic behavior. They can put all their money into lowering the costs of long-distance calls so that they'll win more bids and get more business. We've got a distributed, symmetric, stable, simple, and efficient mechanism for these self-motivated machines to use. Of course, we've bought these wonderful attributes at a cost; the consumer has to pay a small premium on each call to make things work, in this example, paying 20 cents rather than 18 cents for each minute. With many carriers, this effect will be minimized. In any case, the point of this example is not its details. We illustrated how we can design the rules of the game for multiple-agent interactions and reach a situation where rational agents are motivated to play in certain ways.

The telephone call domain is actually incredibly simple. We are interested in more complicated real-world situations, with computers controlling and sharing resources.

Domain Theory

It is important in which domain our independently motivated agents are working because these domain attributes are going to affect the properties of our protocols. A technique that works in one domain class, motivating agents to act in a certain way, won't necessarily work in another type of domain.

We've found it useful to categorize classes of domains into a three-level hierarchy, where each level is increasingly more general. This categorization is not exhaustive; there are other, more general categorizations of domains. However, the three-level hierarchy covers many of the real-world domains in which we are interested.

The lowest-level, the simplest kind of domain that we've looked at is the *task-oriented domain.* A task-oriented domain exists when agents have nonconflicting jobs to do, and these jobs or tasks can be redistributed among the agents. Thus, the agents receive some list of jobs that they have to accomplish, and the object of negotiation in this kind of environment is to redistribute tasks among the agents to everyone's mutual benefit if possible. Most of the talk will be on this first area.

The next-higher level we call the *state-oriented domain.* State-oriented domains are a superset of task-oriented domains. State-oriented domains have goals that specify acceptable final states in the classic AI way. Importantly, in contrast to task-oriented domains, actions in state-oriented domains can have side effects, where an agent doing one action might hinder or help another agent. The object of negotiation is to develop joint plans and schedules for the agents. The agents want to figure out when each agent should do each action so that they stay out of each other's way but also help one other if appropriate.

Finally, we come to the *worth-oriented domain*, which is a superset of the state-oriented domain. Worth-oriented domains assume, like state-oriented domains, that goals specify final states, but this fact is encoded in a function that rates the acceptability of states. Every state in the world is better or worse, but it's not the binary notion of goal that we have in state-oriented domains. In a worth-oriented domain, we have a decision-theoretic kind of formulation, with the agent striving for better states. Again, the object of negotiation is a joint plan, schedules, and goal relaxation. In other words, agents might not be able to get to the state that is their ultimate objective, but they might be willing to arrive at a state that is a little bit worse. Because the agents have a function that rates the acceptability of states, they are able to evaluate gradations among goal states, which they can't do in state-oriented domains.

Examples of Task-Oriented Domains

In this subsection, we discuss various examples of task-, state-, and worth-oriented domains. To illustrate task-oriented domains, we present the postmen, database, and fax domains. To illustrate state-oriented domains, we discuss the slotted blocks world. Finally, to illustrate worth-oriented domains, we discuss the multiagent tile world.

Postmen Domain A classic task-oriented domain that we've looked at quite a bit is the *postmen domain* (figure 4). In this case, two agents arrive at the post office early in the morning; they receive sacks of letters that they then have to take and deliver around the city, which is represented by a graph. At each node, there is a little mailbox. Let's say agent 1 has to go to c, f, and e and then return to the post office, but the other agent might have to go to c, b, and d and then return to the post office. This example illustrates a task-oriented domain. The cost of carrying out a delivery is only in the travel distance. There are no side effects to their actions, there is no limit to the number of letters they can carry, and there is no limit to how many letters they can put in a mailbox.

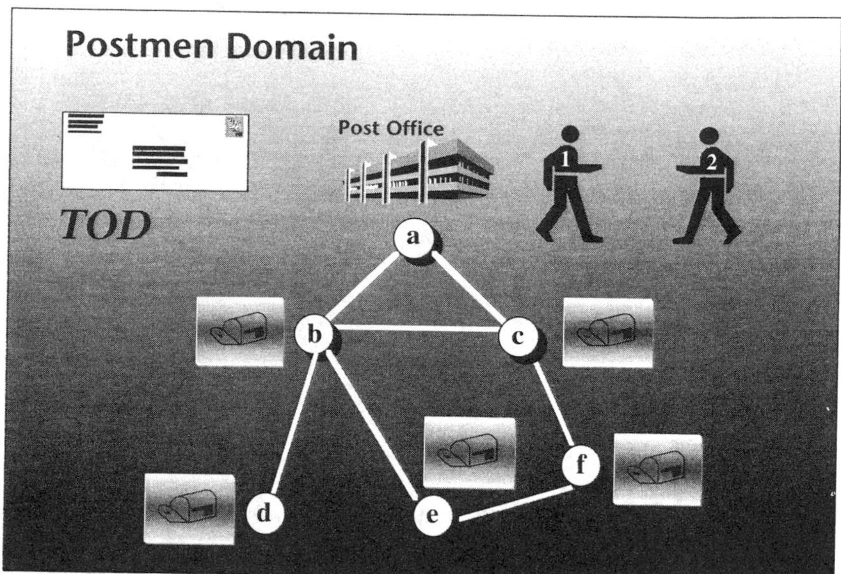

Figure 4. Example of a Task-Oriented Domain.

They have these tasks to do, and there is no possibility of getting in each other's way.

The agents cooperate before they start on their journey. For example, they look at the letters and say, "You know, it doesn't really make sense. You're going past c anyway, why don't you take my letter? It is no extra cost to you; the cost is only in the travel distance, and I'll have a shorter trip." What they try to do is evaluate these deals. There are different possible divisions of the tasks, some are better for one, some are better for the other. We would like the agents to come to some agreement about how they are going to divide the tasks.

Database Domain Let's look at another domain, also a task-oriented domain, called the *database domain*. There's a common database residing on the Internet, let's say. Two agents are sent out to get information. One is supposed to retrieve the names of all the female employees making over $50,000 a year and return, and the other one is supposed to get the names of all the female employees with more than three children and bring them back. In this domain, each subquery to the database costs money. These two agents approach the database and look at each other and say, "You know, one of our subqueries is the same. We could structure our requests for information so that only one of us asked for all female employees, and then subsequently, we would each do another operation on the subset of names. We don't both have to ask for the names of all the

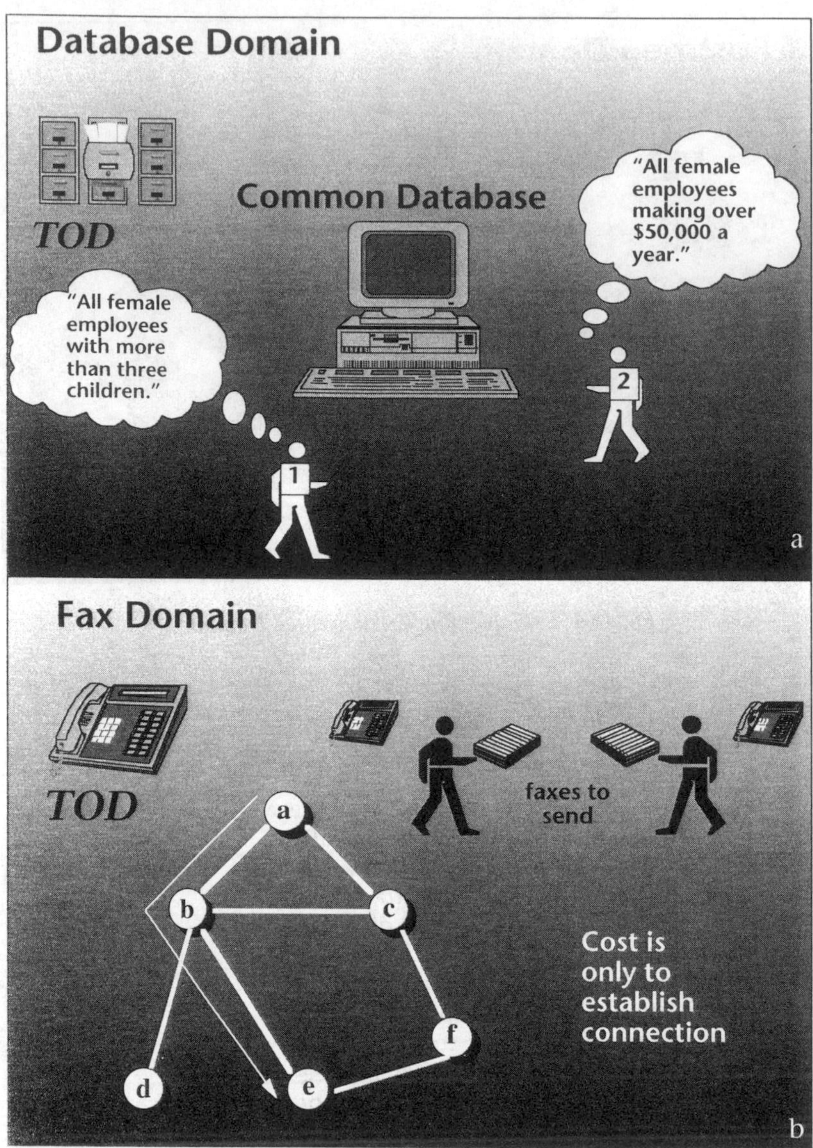

Figure 5. More Examples of Task-Oriented Domains.

female employees." There are no side effects, no possibility for getting in each other's way, just cooperation (figure 5).

Fax Domain One final example of a task-oriented domain, one similar to the postmen domain, is the *fax domain.* In the fax domain, two agents arrive in the morning and are given lists of faxes they have to send all over the world. The agents fortunately only have to pay to connect to the other fax machine; once they connect, they are allowed to down load as many faxes as they want.

The two agents might find that they both have faxes to send to London and say, "It doesn't make sense for both of us to pay the charge of connecting to London. Let's divide the faxes: You take my London faxes, and I'll take your Rome faxes."

Slotted Blocks World—State-Oriented Domain

A *blocks world* is an example of a state-oriented domain. An agent comes and wants the blocks in a certain configuration. The other agent comes and wants the blocks in a certain configuration. These goals can be identical, or they can be in conflict with one another. One agent might want the orange block on top of the blue block, and the other agent might want the blue block on top of the orange block. There's a possibility for real conflict (figure 6).

There are other possibilities, too, such as accidental cooperative action, where one agent inadvertently does something that's good for the other without the other having to ask for it. This type of action can never be true in our task-oriented domains, where there has to be some communication, passing of tasks back and forth, for cooperative action to take place. Here, side effects really affect our analysis of the domains.

The Multiagent Tile World—Worth-Oriented Domain

A *multiagent* version of the *tile world,* originally introduced by Martha Pollack, is an example of a worth-oriented domain. We have agents operating on a grid, and there are tiles that need to be pushed into holes. The holes have value to one or both of the agents, there are obstacles, and agents move around the grid and push tiles into holes. It's true that each agent has a most desirable state, where all the tiles are in its holes, but other states are also good, although less good than the most desirable state. Thus, each agent is able to rank different states, and agreements more easily reflect the possibility of compromise.

Task-Oriented Domain

Let's go back now and look at the task-oriented domains. A task-oriented domain consists of a tuple, $<T, A, c>$, where T is the set of tasks, all the possible actions in the domain; A is the list of agents; and c is some kind of monotonic cost function from any set of tasks to a real number. An *encounter* within a task-oriented domain is a list, $T_1, \ldots T_n$, of finite sets of tasks from the task set T, such that each agent needs to achieve all the tasks in its set. You might as well also call the task set its goal. Thus, we have an encounter, a group of agents coming together, each with a list of tasks.

Remember, we're doing an analysis for the sake of all those designers from IBM, Toshiba, Sony, and so on, that are going to be sitting around the table deciding how to design their personal digital assistants.

Building Blocks

In doing this analysis, we have three things we would like to look at. The first element is a precise specification of the domain, a definition of what a goal is and what agent operations are. We just performed this specification in a broad sense for a task-oriented domain.

The second element is the design of a negotiation protocol for the domain. A negotiation protocol involves a definition of what a deal is among the agents, a definition of what utility is among the agents, and a definition of the so-called *conflict deal*. The conflict deal is the deal, the default deal, that the agents get if they fail to reach an agreement. You can think of the negotiation protocol as something like the rules of the game. In chess, for example, the negotiation protocol would be analogous to a description of what all the possible moves are.

The third element is the negotiation strategy, or how an agent should act given the set of rules. Think again about a chess game. Think about separating the rules that describe the game from the technique that an agent uses in response to the environment, in response to the rules. First, we would like to define the rules of the negotiation, and then, for purposes of illuminating the situation for our designers, we would like to discuss negotiation strategies that they might choose to put into their agents.

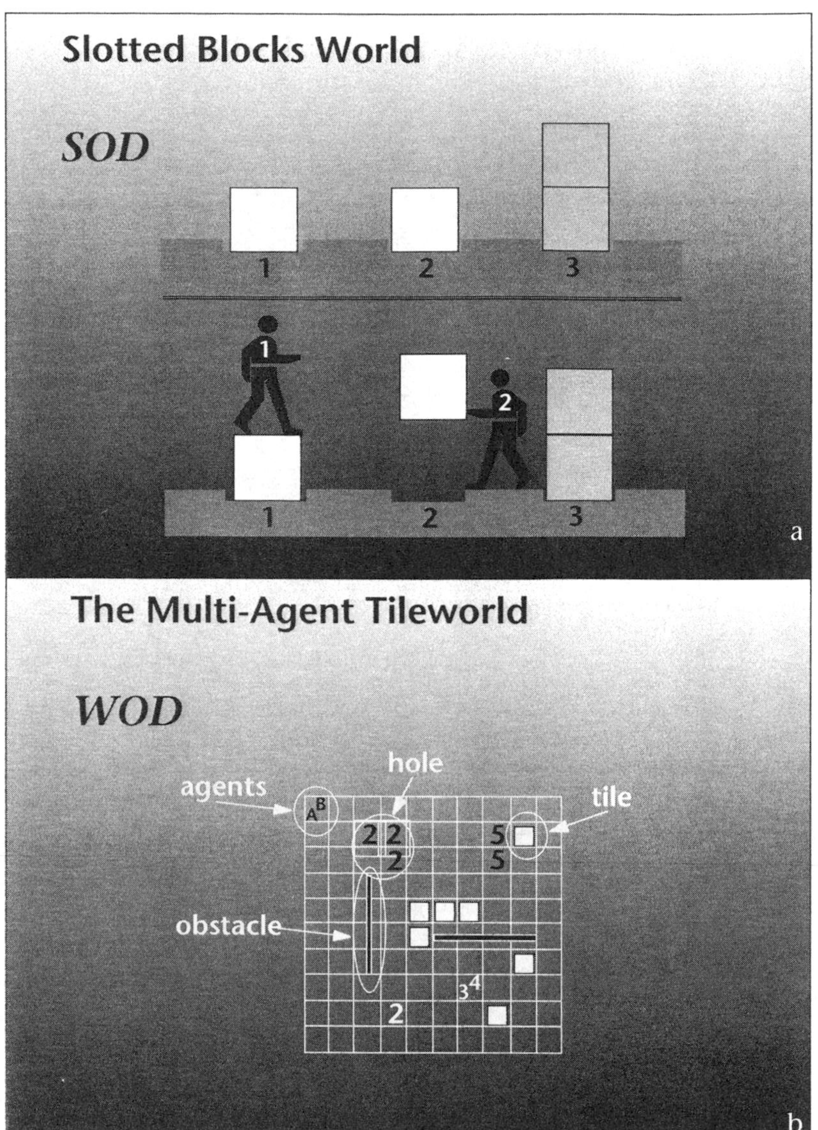

Figure 6. State-Oriented Domain and Worth-Oriented Domain Examples.

Deal and Utility in Two-Agent Task-Oriented Domain

First, we would like to have a definition of the deal, the utility, and the conflict deal. Here we have it for a two-agent task-oriented domain: A deal δ is a pair (D_1, D_2) such that $D_1 \cup D_2 = T_1 \cup T_2$. The conflict deal is defined as $\Theta \equiv (T_1, T_2)$. $\text{Utility}_i(\delta) = \text{Cost}(T_i) - \text{Cost}(D_i)$.

A deal in a two-agent task-oriented domain is a pair, D_1, D_2, such that their union is equal to the union of the original task sets. Think about those postmen with their letters. They come together with T_1 and T_2, their original sacks of letters. A deal is a new distribution, such that all the letters are taken care of.

The conflict deal in this case is simply the original sets of letters. If you don't reach agreement, you deliver your original sack of letters.

The utility of a deal for an agent is defined as the cost of its original work minus the cost of its new work given the deal. The difference is how much it has gained from the deal. It used to have to walk five miles; now it only has to walk three miles. The utility is two.

Negotiation Protocols

As far as the protocol that the agents are going to use, there are lots of good choices. For the purposes of this discussion, we're going to assume that the agents are using some kind of product-maximizing negotiation protocol, such as in Nash bargaining theory. For our purposes, it really doesn't matter which one they use as long as it's symmetric; that is, it maximizes the product of the utili-

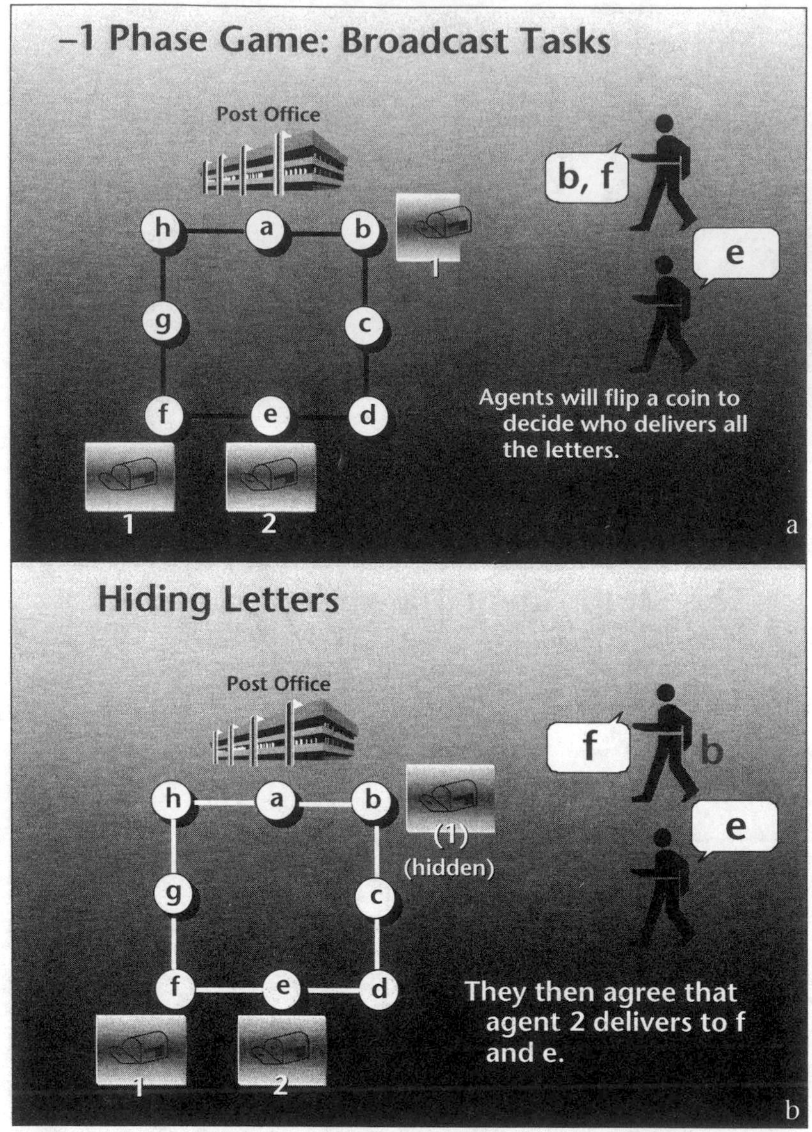

Figure 7. Dealing with (and Exploiting) Incomplete Information.

ties. There are all sorts of examples of different protocols, different rules, that will bring the agents to an agreement that maximizes the product of their utilities. You can even have a one-step protocol; if they know everything, they can compute the agreement point, which will be the point they jump to. Instead, you can have some kind of a *monotonic concession protocol,* where each agent first starts with a deal that's best for it and then iteratively makes compromises to the other agent. There are a lot of different product-maximizing protocols.

Now we return to the last item on our building blocks list. Given that we have a task-oriented–domain specification, a definition of the deal, the utility, the conflict deal, and an overall protocol, what negotiation strategy should the agents use? Given the previous discussion, you could say, "Well, strategy is not really important in this situation because once the designers have decided on the protocol, and they know exactly what the tasks are for the other agent and what their own tasks are, there's a well-defined agreement point. This well-defined point tells them when they have maximized the product of their utilities. They can just move to this point in one way or another. It doesn't really matter how," which is true when the agents have complete information.

Negotiation with Incomplete Information

What about the case where the agents don't have complete information? What about that situation where the postmen show up in the morning, and the sacks of letters are opaque, and they have to decide how to negotiate. Let's assume that the first agent has to carry letters to b and f, and the second agent has to go to e. Each agent knows its own letters but doesn't know the other's letters, so they can't compute the agreement for the two of them. Instead, they need some other kind of mechanism that will allow them to come to an agreement. One simple, straightforward technique is to set up a 21 phase game, a sort of pregame exchange of information (figure 7).

The two agents broadcast their tasks and then continue as before, computing where the agreement is going to be. Agent 2 announces that it has to go to e, agent 1 says "I have to go to b and f," and they decide who's going to do what. Now, just to carry out its own tasks, each one would have to go a distance of eight units. Agent 1 would certainly go all the way around, and agent 2 might go half-way around and back, but it's equivalent to going all the way around. In this particular case, because of the structure of the problem, the agents eventually agree to flip a coin, and one of them travels all the way around while the other one stays at the post office. Assuming it's a fair coin toss, they have divided up the work equally.

Hiding Letters

However, our intrepid agent has been built by a smart group of designers, and it makes the following claim: Agent 2 honestly says, "I have to go to e"; agent 1 says, "I have to go to f," and it hides its letter to b (see figure 7b). Now, the negotiation situation has changed because agent 1 is purporting to say here that it only has to travel six units, and it should be required to do less of the final work. In fact, in this situation, the only pure deal that the agents can agree to is that agent 2 takes the letters to f and e, and agent 1 supposedly does nothing. This deal is agreed on because it would not be rational for agent 1 to agree to carry letters all the way around the loop. It would then be doing eight units of work, more than the six units of work it would supposedly be doing by itself. It can't be expected to agree to a deal that makes it do extra work. However, agent 2 doesn't benefit from this deal because it still travels eight units, but it isn't harmed either. Thus, the deal where agent 2 does all the work is the only rational, Pareto-optimal deal. In the meantime, agent 1 runs off and delivers its hidden letter to b at a cost of two units. Agent 1 has really made off well with this manipulation, guaranteeing itself two units of work instead of eight if it were alone or four units of expected work if it were honest in its deal making.

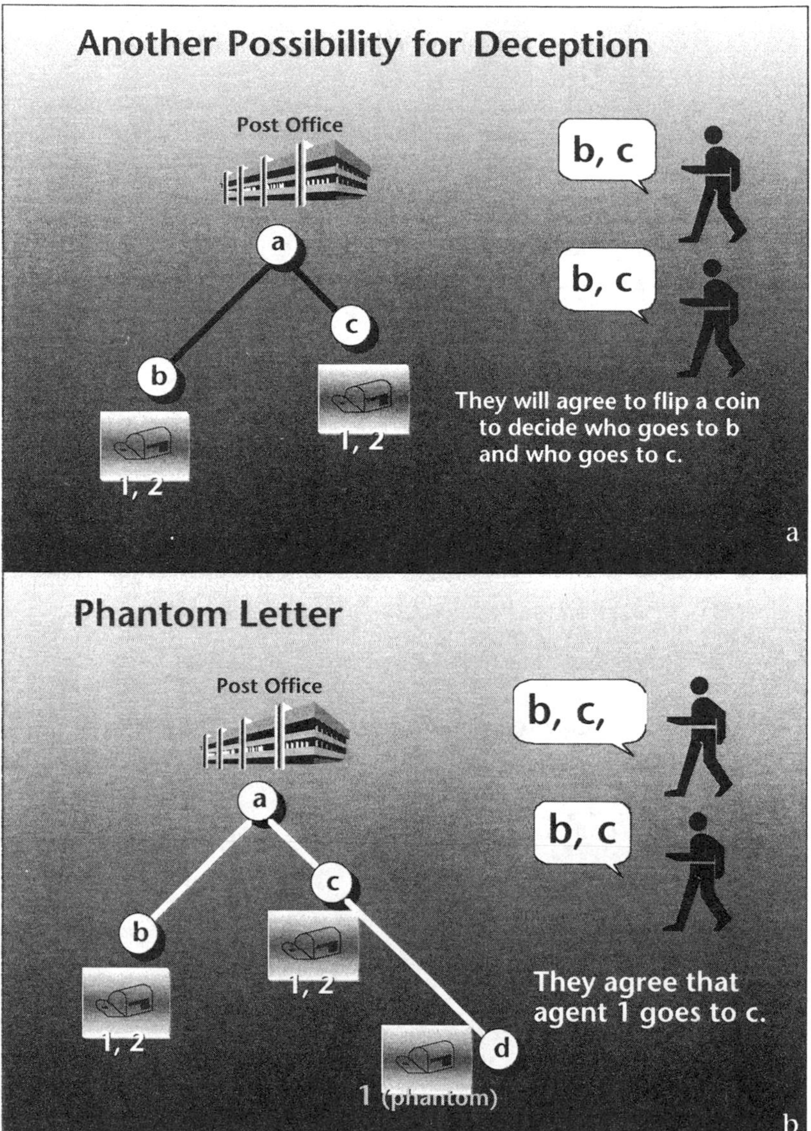

Figure 8. Creating a Phantom Task.

Phantom Letters

Let's look at another possibility for deception (figure 8). Let's say our agents both have to deliver letters to nodes b and c. It's an entirely symmetric situation. Obviously, it makes sense for one agent to go to b and one to go to c. However, b is relatively far away, and c is relatively close; each agent would prefer to be the one to go to c. If they tell the truth and declare their true tasks, they'll flip a coin to decide which one goes to which node.

Agent 1 again decides to manipulate the agreement. It announces that it has a letter to deliver to node d, which is a long way off in the direction of node c. It only makes sense for agent 1 to go to c and, presumably, continue to d. If agent 2 were given the right side of this route, it would have to do more work than when it's alone, which wouldn't be acceptable to agent 2. They have to agree that agent 2 goes to the left side and that agent 1 goes to the right side. Of course, the letter to d doesn't exist; agent 1 just goes to c and comes back and benefits from its manipulation.

Part of what's going on here is that the form of a deal that we defined has constrained the kinds of agreement the agents can come to. Remember, a deal is just a division of tasks, and we get certain discontinuities when we define a deal this way. However, it's really that our deal space is discrete that gives rise to some of these possibilities for deception. In other words, you have a certain limited number of ways to divide up tasks between agents. Depending on the particular encounter, an agent might be able to maneuver its way to a certain deal that's better for it, exploiting the fact that there are only certain ways to divide the tasks.

Negotiation over Mixed Deals

One straightforward way of getting rid of some deception is to make the deal space continuous. We can redefine what a deal is, what a division of tasks is, to include probability. A mixed deal is defined to be a division of tasks (D_1, D_2) with an associated probability p, so that with probability p, agent 1 does

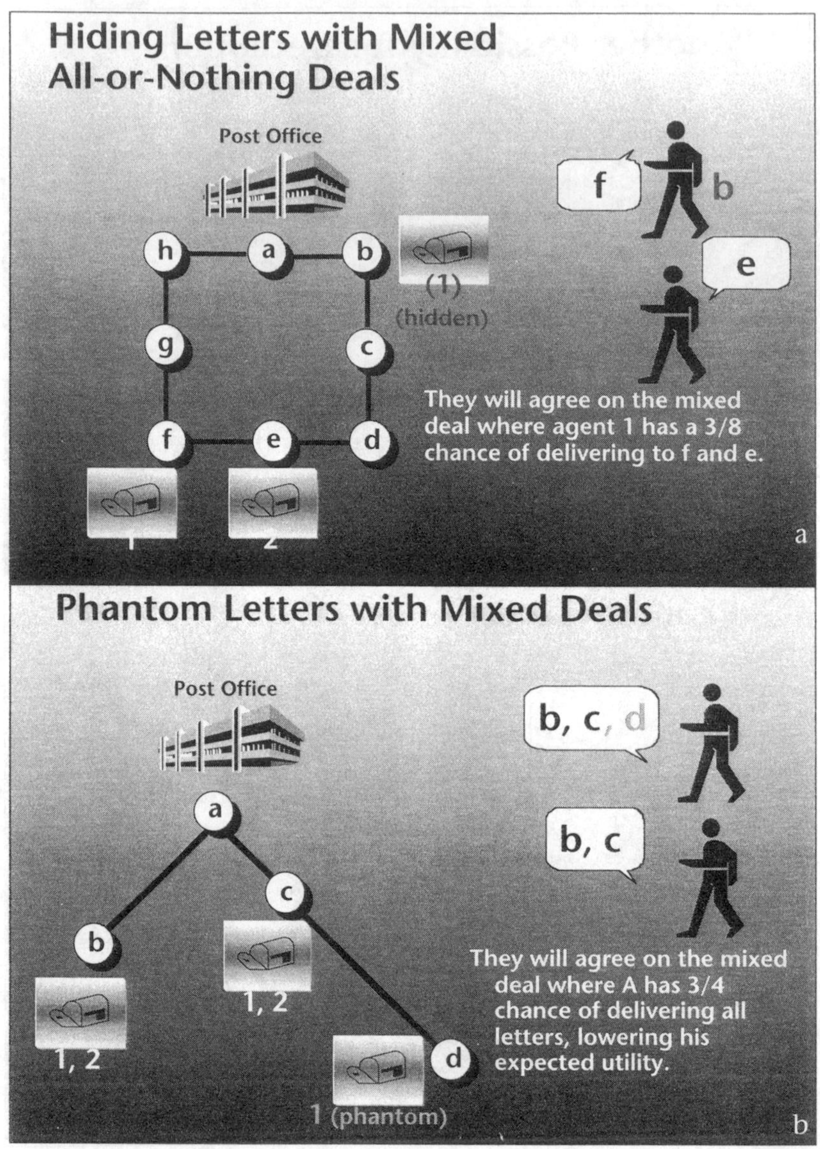
Hiding Letters with Mixed All-or-Nothing Deals
Post Office
h
a
b
g
c
f
e
d
f
b
e
(1)
(hidden)
They will agree on the mixed deal where agent 1 has a 3/8 chance of delivering to f and e.
a
Phantom Letters with Mixed Deals
Post Office
b, c, d
b, c
a
c
b
d
1, 2
1, 2
They will agree on the mixed deal where A has 3/4 chance of delivering all letters, lowering his expected utility.
1 (phantom)
b

Figure 9. Mixed All-or-Nothing Deals Discouraging Deception.

task set D_1, and with probability 1 2 p, it does task set D_2 (and vice versa for agent 2). This deal definition results in a continuous space of deals. In addition, because of the way that our class of task-oriented domains is defined, if the agents use mixed deals, they can always restrict their agreements to the so-called all-or-nothing deal. In the all-or-nothing deal, all tasks are put into one big set, and a weighted coin is tossed to decide which agent does all the tasks. In our examples, this kind of agreement will always be a potential deal, but there can be others. By adding this probability into the deal definition, we make the space of deals continuous instead of discrete, the way it was originally.

Thus, at least some of the agents' possibilities for deception have vanished. Let's revisit our original postmen domain example. Now the protocol has agents negotiating over mixed all-or-nothing deals (figure 9). If agent 1 hides its letter to node b, it still has a certain probability of going all the way around the loop, which means that it doesn't get off for free, as in the original example. There is some possibility (less than 50 percent, but it's there) that it might deliver the declared letters. In any case, it still has a guaranteed trip of two units to node b, even if he wins the coin toss. If you work out the numbers, you see that agent 1 has not benefited any more from its hiding one of its tasks.

Similarly, in the second encounter, where agent 1 declared an extra, phantom task, the use of probability in the deal ends up worsening agent 1's position. It will end up doing extra work because it had the audacity to claim that it came into the encounter with extra work. The logic of maximizing the product of utilities here means that if it came into the encounter with extra work, it has to bear more of the burden of the final deal. In both these specific cases, we did well by just introducing probability into the deal definition.

Does adding probability really solve all our problems? No, but it removes problems for specific kinds of encounter. We have to understand the kinds of task-oriented domain that exist; not all task-oriented domains are the same.

Subadditive Task-Oriented Domains

All the examples we have given to this point have been illustrations of what are called *subadditive task-oriented domains.* A task-oriented domain is subadditive if for all finite sets of tasks, the cost of the union of tasks is less than or equal to the sum of the costs of the separate sets (for finite X, Y in T, $c(X \cup Y) \leq c(X) + c(Y)$). In other words, if you have two sets of tasks, and you put them together, you'll never increase the cost, and perhaps you'll decrease it. You can see the general idea in figure 10. Putting the sets of tasks together lowers the overall cost of the combined set.

All our examples have been subadditive, but not all task-oriented domains are subadditive. For example, consider a minor variation on the postmen domain; we call it the *delivery domain,* where agents go out and deliver their packages but are not required to return to the post office at the end of the day.

In this case, we don't have a subadditive domain (see figure 10b). If one agent has the task of delivering to the left node, and another agent has the task of delivering to the right node, then each has a task that costs one unit. The combined set of tasks costs three units: down one side, back to the original node, then down the other side; so, the combined tasks cost more than the sum of the individual tasks and, thus, are not subadditive. If this domain were the postmen domain, each separate delivery would cost two units, and the combination would cost four units and, thus, would be subadditive.

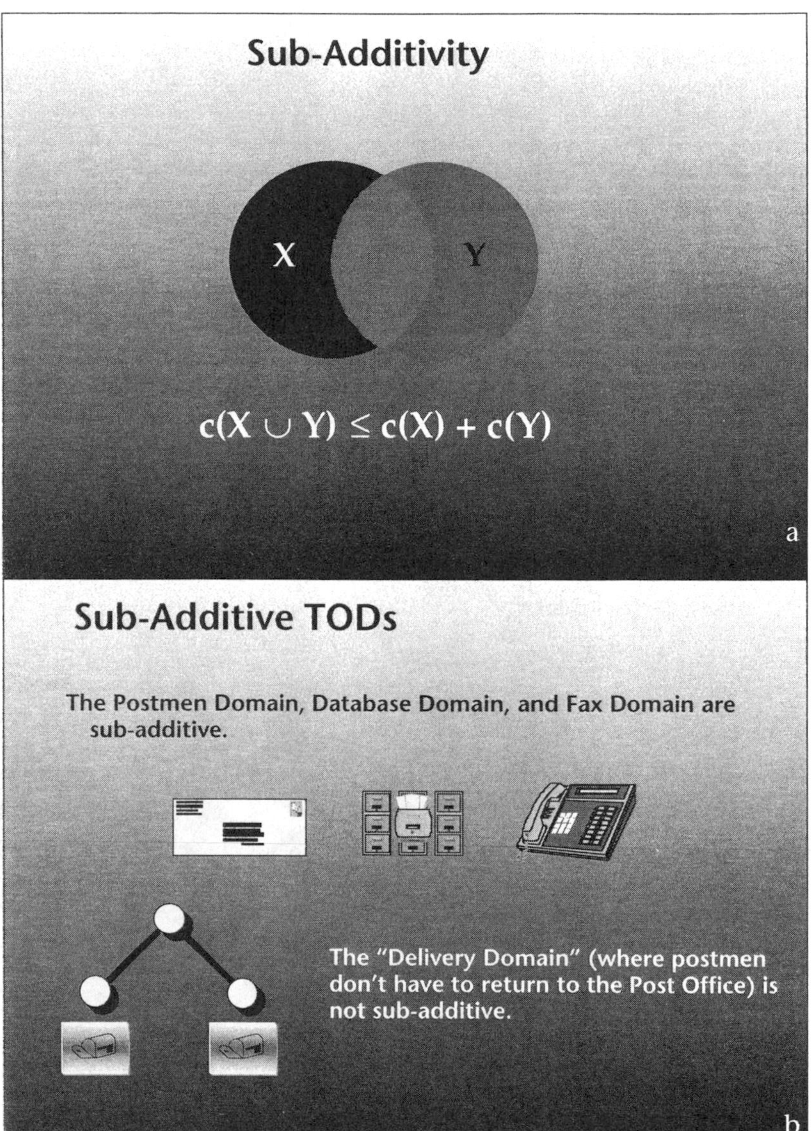

Figure 10. The Nature of Subadditivity.

Incentive-Compatible Mechanisms

Now we can summarize what we know so far into a table that illustrates when lying is potentially advantageous and when telling the truth is the best policy (figure 11). For subadditive task-oriented domains, we have three protocols: (1) the original deal definition that we call pure deals; (2) the new deal definition that uses probability, which we call mixed deals; and (3) the all-or-nothing protocol that always results in this special mixed deal where one agent does everything with some probability. The original loop example, where a pure deal was being used in the protocol, was an instance where hiding a letter might be beneficial to an agent. The L signifies that encounters exist where lying is beneficial. The second example illustrates where a phantom task was beneficial; it also gets an L. A T in a box means that honesty is the best policy. An agent's best strategy is to always tell the truth. For example, when an all-or-nothing utility product-maximizing mechanism (PMM) protocol is being used in a subadditive task-oriented domain, no agent has an incentive to hide a task. The best strategy is to reveal all the tasks.

The entry T/P means that although creating a phantom letter might sometimes be beneficial, the deception might also be discovered because the nonexistent task might have to be handed over to the other agent using these probabilistic protocols. Thus, with a high enough penalty mechanism, telling the truth becomes the best strategy.

Also notice that there's a relationship between table entries, denoted by the white arrow. The relationships are implications that arise naturally from the definitions of the columns and rows. Here, for example, the fact that all-or-nothing deals are a subset of mixed deals means that if telling the truth is the best strategy in mixed deals, it is certainly also the best strategy in all-or-nothing deals, which are a subset.

Decoy Tasks

One more kind of lie that's worth looking at is the *decoy task.* A decoy task is like a phantom: It's a fake task, but an agent can create it on demand if necessary. A postman might claim it has a letter to some particular node. If required to hand it over when using a probabilistic deal, the agent quickly jots down a note, "Dear Resident: You might have already won the sweepstakes," and hands it over. Thus, a simple penalty mechanism won't work, and, in fact, as the table shows (figure 11b), decoy lies in subadditive domains can sometimes be beneficial for an agent even

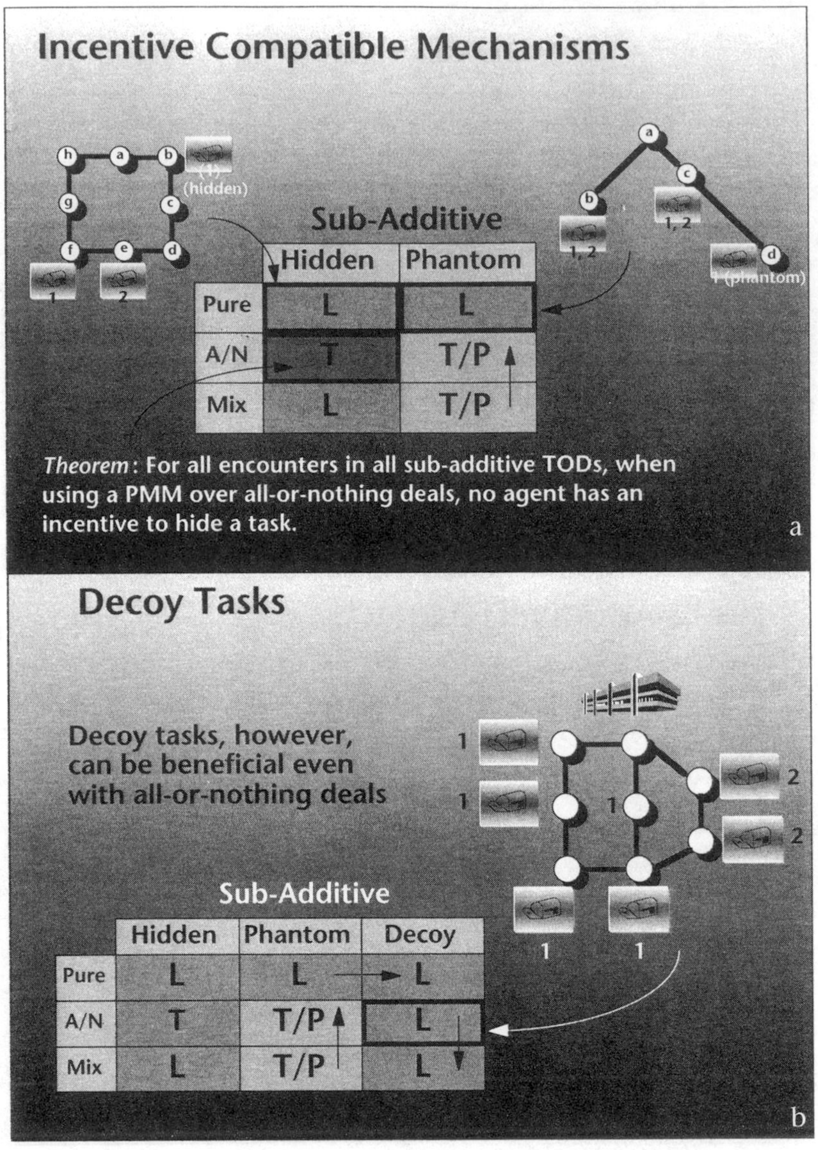

Figure 11. Tables Summarizing Strategies, Given Protocols.

when all-or-nothing protocols are used. Look at figure 11, where agent 1 would prefer to just deliver its own letters and return to the post office. By creating this decoy letter in the middle node, it claims that it would have to do a lot of extra work to carry out agent 2's delivery. It deceptively locks itself into its original path. Again, notice the white arrows. Because lying can be beneficial using an all-or-nothing protocol, it must also be beneficial sometimes when using mixed deals, which are a superset. Thus, having filled out one entry in the table, other entries can be implied automatically.

Subadditive task-oriented domains are an important domain class, but we can use other, more restrictive classifications to understand task-oriented domains.

Concave Task-Oriented Domains

Concave task-oriented domains are a subset of subadditive task-oriented domains that satisfy the following condition: Imagine that we have two sets of tasks, X and Y, where X is a subset of Y, and we come along with some other set of tasks, Z. The cost Z adds to X, the subset, is greater than or equal to the cost Z adds to Y, the superset: $c(X \cup Z) - c(X) \geq c(Y \cup Z) - c(Y)$. If a domain is concave, then it is also subadditive (figure 12).

Figure 12 is actually a bit misleading because it appears like such an obvious property that it ought to hold for all reasonable task-oriented domains, but it doesn't (see figure 12b).

Of the three task-oriented domains we introduced originally, only the database domain and the fax domain are concave. The general postmen domain is not concave unless graphs are restricted to trees. To see an example of a nonconcave encounter in the general postmen domain, consider the example we gave for a beneficial decoy task. Agent 1 has to travel around the left nodes; let's call it X. Agent 2 has to travel around the right nodes; let's call Y the set of all dark-gray nodes (that is, excluding the middle node marked Z). Thus, X, the left nodes marked with a 1, is a subset of Y, all the dark-gray nodes. Agent 1 lies with a decoy task to the node in the middle. This decoy task is set Z. The amount of work that Z adds to the set X is 0. The agent visits Z on the way at no extra cost. However, the amount of work that Z adds to Y, a superset of X, is 2. An agent would have to make a special trip to visit all Y, then visit Z; so, this example is not concave.

Three-Dimensional Incentive-Compatible Mechanism Table: If we return to the table that we've been setting up, we can examine an entirely new set of possibilities (figure 13). The table is now three dimensional; the black arrows show that relationships exist among the concave and the subadditive dimensions of the table. For example, if hiding letters is sometimes beneficial in concave domains when a pure deal protocol is used, then it will also sometimes be beneficial in subadditive domains because a concave domain is also always a subadditive domain.

The main thing to notice here is that concave domains are considerably better behaved with regard to lying. There are more T's in the concave part of the table; in particular, we proved a theorem that says that in all concave task-oriented domains, when using all-or-nothing deals, no agent has any incentive to hide tasks or to create phantom or decoy tasks. There's absolutely no incentive for lying. It is the theorem that allows us to put the middle row of T's into the concave part of the table.

Modular Task-Oriented Domains

We can make an even more precise classification of task-oriented domains with the following definition: A *modular task-oriented domain* is one in which the cost of combining two sets of tasks, X and Y, into one large set is exactly the sum of their separate costs minus the cost of their intersection (you don't want to count the tasks that appear in both sets twice): $c(X \cup Y) = c(X) + c(Y) - c(X \cap Y)$. Any modular domain is also a concave domain as well as a subadditive domain.

In figure 14, the cost of the combined set of X union Y is exactly the cost of the set X plus the cost of the set Y minus the cost of the intersection of X and Y; the middle region isn't counted twice in the cost calculation.

Of the three original task-oriented domains we introduced, only the fax domain is modular. The general postmen domain is modular if you restrict the graphs that the postmen visit to a star topology (the post office in the middle and the other nodes connected to it like spokes on a wheel). Modular task-oriented domains are the most restrictive category and the best behaved with regard to lying, but even with modular task-oriented domains, hiding tasks can sometimes be beneficial if the agents are using general mixed-deal protocols.

Three-dimensional incentive-compatible mechanism table: Returning to our evolving table, we add another layer to the third dimension (figure 15). This modular layer has more T's. You can see that in moving from subadditive to concave to modular, we increase the percentage of T boxes, where telling the truth is always the best policy for an agent; however, there are still some residual L's lurking in the table.

Designers who together could determine that their domain was, for example, a modular task-oriented domain could look at this table and decide, perhaps, to use a protocol that has agents negotiating over all-or-nothing deals; the designers would be confident in the knowledge that none of the individual companies building the agents would have an incentive to conceal their tasks or create false ones. The best policy here is really just to tell the truth: simple, efficient, and stable.

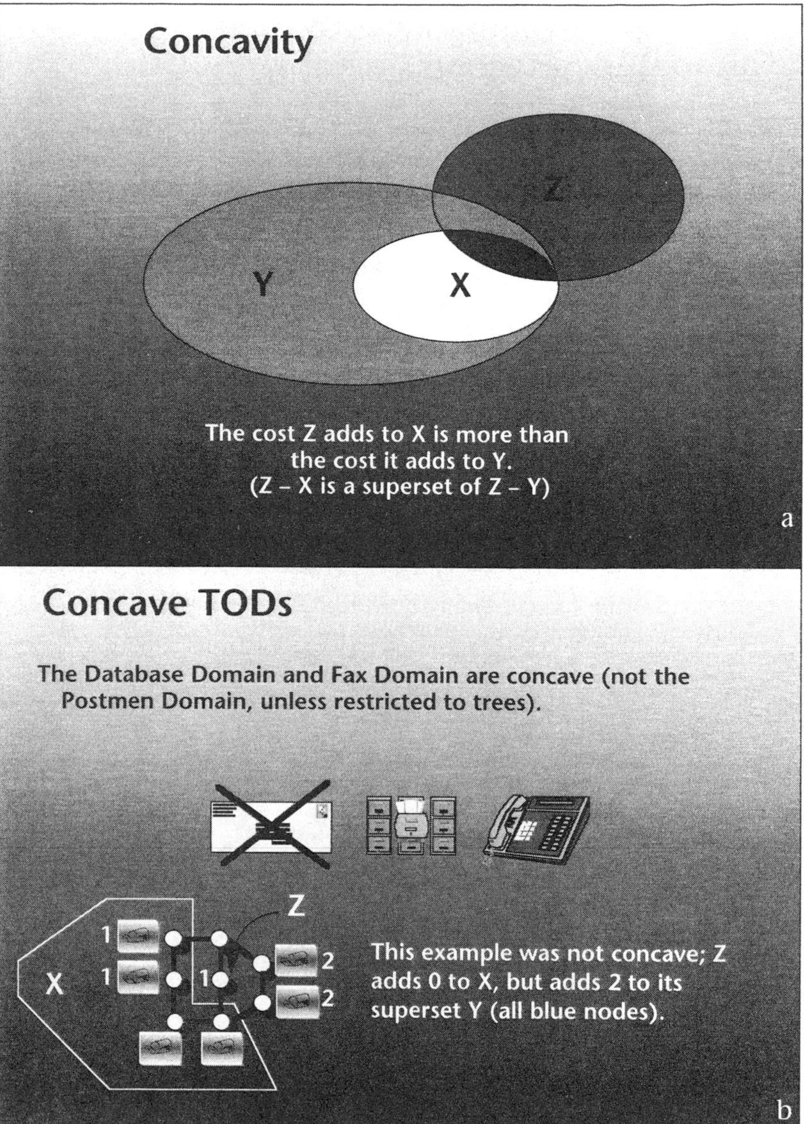

Figure 12. Concave Task-Oriented Domains.

In an article that appeared recently in the *Boston Globe* ("A New Dimension in Deception"), Michael Schrage talked about software agents that might choose to lie to further the aims of their owners. For example, a scheduling agent might falsely claim that its owner has an appointment at a certain time to force a group of people to set a meeting at a time the agent wants to have the meeting and not at some other time. Schrage was pretty good at laying out the scenario, but he missed one

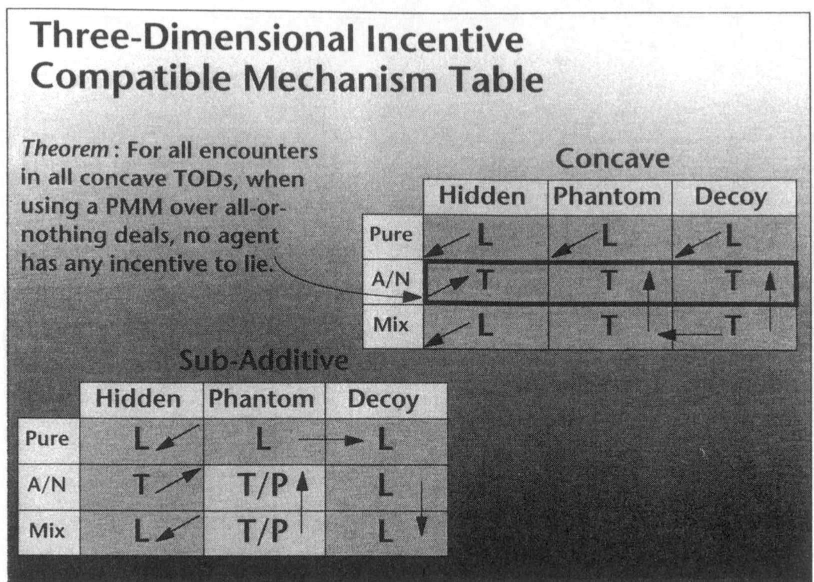

Figure 13. The Enlarged Strategy-Protocol Table.

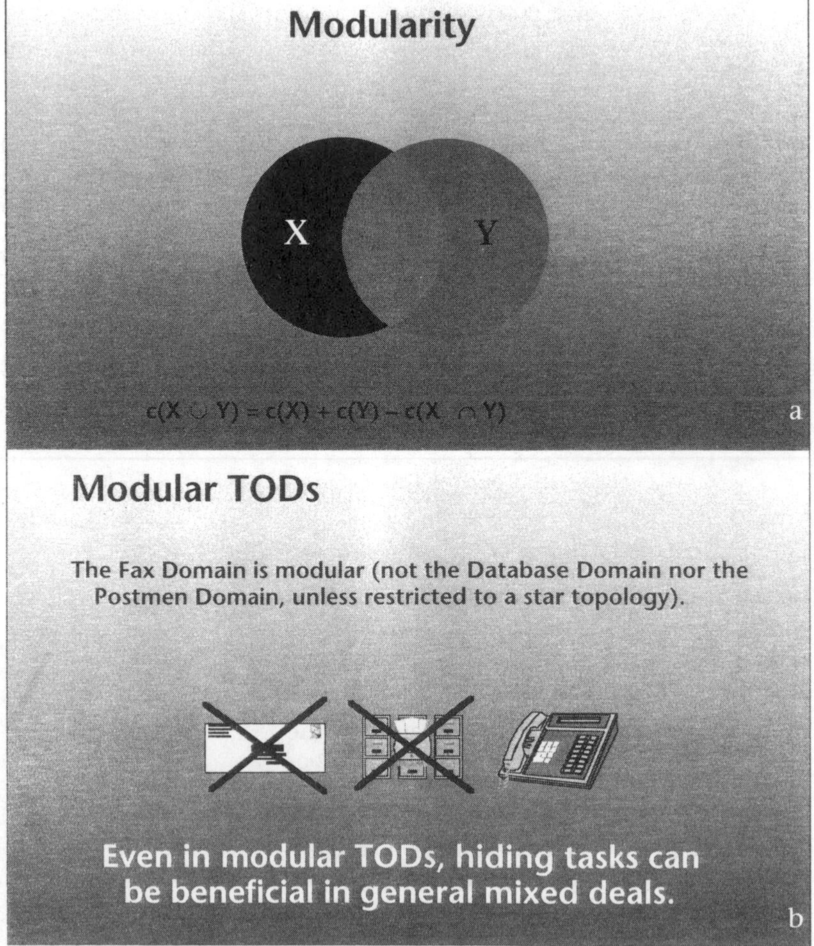

Figure 14. Modular Task-Oriented Domains.

crucial point: Sometimes, it's possible to design the rules of encounter so that lying is simply not in anyone's interest.

Related Work

This article only covers the tip of the iceberg. First, task-oriented domains are only a small class of encounters between agents; remember, we presented two other general classes: state-oriented domains and worth-oriented domains. We have carried out similar kinds of protocol analysis in these more general types of domain, and the situation becomes more complicated. Lying, for example, is harder to prevent in the more general encounters, but we can still analyze properties of protocols, such as efficiency and stability, and provide guidelines for how agent designers might want to build their systems.

Other work that's going on in this general direction within AI includes several recent papers on coalition formation where there are more than two agents (S. Ketchpel, S. Kraus, J. Rosenschein, and G. Zlotkin); general research into mechanism design (E. Ephrati, S. Kraus, and M. Tennenholtz); research on other models of negotiation among agents (S. Kraus, K. Sycara, E. Durfee, V. Lesser, L. Gasser, and P. Gmytrasiewicz); and research on other consensus mechanisms, such as voting techniques, explored in work that Jeffrey Rosenschein has carried out with E. Ephrati, and economic models, such as those being examined by M. Wellman.

Conclusions

What did we argue? First, by appropriately adjusting the rules of encounter by which agents must interact, we can influence the private strategies that designers will rationally build into their machines. When we can't have direct control of how multiple agents will be built, we can exert indirect influence by carefully designing the negotiation protocol.

Second, we pointed out that the interaction mechanism can and should be designed to ensure efficiency of the multiagent system.

Third, to maintain efficiency over time of dynamic multiagent systems, the rules must also be stable. It is not enough to figure out a strategy that has good properties, such as efficiency. The agent designers have to feel that they should stick with this strategy; they shouldn't have any incentive to move to another strategy. Stability is an important part of multiagent systems.

Finally, we did our analysis with the use of formal tools. Our commitment to the formal design and analysis of protocols both makes us more sensitive to issues such as efficiency and stability and gives us the ability to make definitive statements about them. Such tools give us the leverage we need to design interaction environments for automated negotiation.

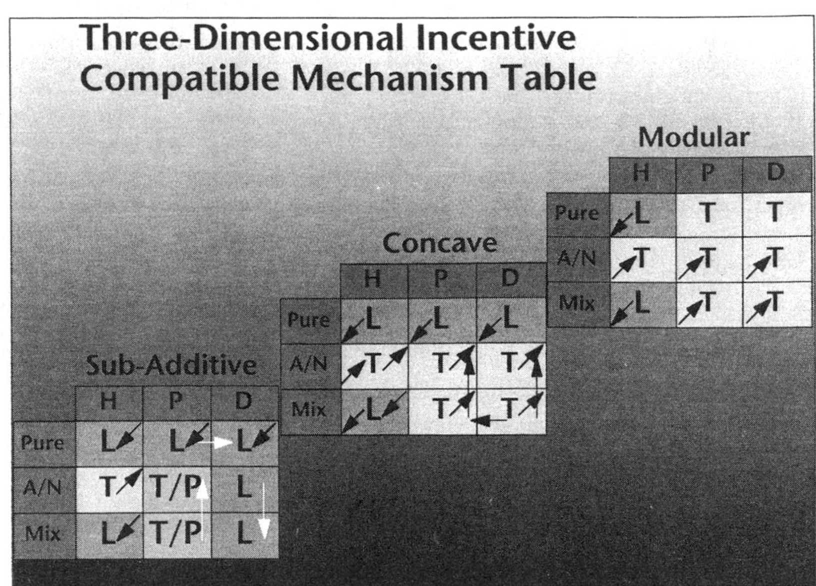

Figure 15. Categorizing Strategies Based on Domain and Protocol.

Acknowledgments

This research has partially been supported by the Leibniz Center for Research in Computer Science at the Hebrew University of Jerusalem and the Israeli Ministry of Science and Technology (grant 032-8284). The authors want to thank their many colleagues who have helped in the refinement of this research, including Erik Brynjolfsson, Edmund Durfee, Eithan Ephrati, Les Gasser, Mike Genesereth, Barbara Grosz, Robin Hanson, Sarit Kraus, Daniel Lehmann, Nati Linial, Ariel Rubinstein, Moshe Tennenholtz, Mario Tokoro, and Avi Wigderson.

Suggestions for Further Reading

Avouris, M., and Gasser, L. 1992. *Distributed Artificial Intelligence: Theory and Praxis.* Boston, Mass.: Kluwer Academic.

Binmore, K. 1992. Fun and Games: A Text on Game Theory. Lexington, Mass.: D. C. Heath.

Conry, S.; Meyer, R.; and Lesser, V. 1988. Multistage Negotiation in Distributed Planning. In *Readings in Distributed Artificial Intelligence,* eds. A. Bond and L. Gasser, 367–384. San Mateo, Calif.: Morgan Kaufmann.

Decker, K., and Lesser, V. 1993a. An Approach to Analyzing the Need for Meta-Level Communication. In Proceedings of the Thirteenth International Joint Conference on Artificial Intelligence, 360–366. Menlo Park, Calif.: International Joint Conferences on Artificial Intelligence.

Decker, K., and Lesser, V. 1993b. A One-Shot Dynamic Coordination Algorithm for Distributed Sensor Networks. In Proceedings of the Eleventh National Conference on Artificial Intelligence, 210–216. Menlo Park, Calif.: American Association for Artificial Intelligence.

Ephrati, E., and Rosenschein, J. 1993. Distributed Consensus Mechanisms for Self-Interested Heterogeneous Agents. In First International Conference on Intelligent and Cooperative Information Systems, 71–79. Washington, D.C.: IEEE Computer Society.

Ephrati, E., and Rosenschein, J. 1992. Reaching Agreement through Partial Revelation of Preferences. In *Proceedings of the Tenth European Conference on Artificial Intelligence,* 229–233. Chichester, U.K.: Wiley.

Ephrati, E., and Rosenschein, J. 1991. The Clarke Tax as a Consensus Mechanism among Automated Agents. In Proceedings of the Ninth National Conference on Artificial Intelligence, 173–178. Menlo Park, Calif.: American Association for Artificial Intelligence.

Etzioni, O.; Leash, N.; and Segal, R. 1993. Building Softbots for UNIX, Preliminary Report, 93-09-01, Dept. of Computer Science, Univ. of Washington.

Fudenberg, D., and Tirole, J. 1992. *Game Theory.* Cambridge, Mass.: MIT Press.

Gasser, L. 1991. Social Conceptions of Knowledge and Action: DAI Foundations and Open Systems Semantics. *Artificial Intelligence* 47(1–3): 107–138.

Gmytrasiewicz, P.; Durfee, E.; and Wehe, D. 1991a. A Decision-Theoretic Approach to Coordinating Multiagent Interactions. In Proceedings of the Twelfth International Joint Conference on Artificial Intelligence, 62–68. Menlo Park, Calif.: International Joint Conferences on Artificial Intelligence.

Gmytrasiewicz, P.; Durfee, E.; and Wehe, D. 1991b. The Utility of Communication in Coordinating Intelligent Agents. In Proceedings of the Ninth National Conference on Artificial Intelligence, 166–172. Menlo Park, Calif.: American Association for Artificial Intelligence.

Harsanyi, J. 1977. Rational Behavior and Bargaining Equilibrium in Games and Social Situations. Cambridge, U.K.: Cambridge University Press.

Kraus, S. 1993. Agents Contracting Tasks in Non-Collaborative Environments. In Proceedings of the Eleventh National Conference on Artificial Intelligence, 243–248. Menlo Park, Calif.: American Association for Artificial Intelligence.

Kraus, S., and Wilkenfeld, J. 1991. Negotiations over Time in a Multi-Agent Environment: Preliminary Report. In Proceedings of the Twelfth International Joint Conference on Artificial Intelligence, 56–61. Menlo Park, Calif.: International Joint Conferences on Artificial Intelligence.

Kraus, S.; Wilkenfeld, J.; and Zlotkin, G. 1992. Multiagent Negotiation under Time Constraints, Technical Report, CS-TR-2975, Dept. of Computer Science, University of Maryland.

Luce, R., and Raiffa, H. 1957. *Games and Decisions*. New York: Wiley.

Moses, Y., and Tennenholtz, M. 1989. On Cooperation in a Multi-Entity Model. In Proceedings of the Eleventh International Joint Conference on Artificial Intelligence, 918–923. Menlo Park, Calif.: International Joint Conferences on Artificial Intelligence.

Osborne, M., and Rubinstein, A. 1990. *Bargaining and Markets*. San Diego, Calif.: Academic.

Rosenschein, J., and Zlotkin, G. 1994. Rules of Encounter: Designing Conventions for Automated Negotiation among Computers. Cambridge, Mass.: MIT Press.

Roth, A. 1979. *Axiomatic Models of Bargaining*. Berlin: Springer-Verlag.

Shoham, Y., and Tennenholtz, M. 1992. On the Synthesis of Useful Social Laws for Artificial Agent Societies. In Proceedings of the Tenth National Conference on Artificial Intelligence, 276–281. Menlo Park, Calif.: American Association for Artificial Intelligence.

Zlotkin, G., and Rosenschein, J. 1993a. A Domain Theory for Task-Oriented Negotiation. In Proceedings of the Thirteenth International Joint Conference on Artificial Intelligence, 416–422. Menlo Park, Calif.: International Joint Conferences on Artificial Intelligence.

Zlotkin, G., and Rosenschein, J. 1993b. Negotiation with Incomplete Information about Worth: Strict versus Tolerant Mechanisms. In Proceedings of the International Conference on Intelligent and Cooperative Information Systems, 175–184. Washington, D.C.: IEEE Computer Society.

Zlotkin, G., and Rosenschein, J. 1993c. The Extent of Cooperation in State-Oriented Domains: Negotiation among Tidy Agents. *Computers and Artificial Intelligence* 12(2): 105–122.

Zlotkin, G., and Rosenschein, J. 1991a. Cooperation and Conflict Resolution via Negotiation among Autonomous Agents in Noncooperative Domains. *IEEE Transactions on Systems, Man, and Cybernetics* 21(6): 1317–1324.

Zlotkin, G., and Rosenschein, J. 1991b. Incomplete Information and Deception in Multi-Agent Negotiation. In Proceedings of the Twelfth International Joint Conference on Artificial Intelligence, 225–231. Menlo Park, Calif.: International Joint Conferences on Artificial Intelligence.

Zlotkin, G., and Rosenschein, J. 1990. Negotiation and Conflict Resolution in Non-Cooperative Domains. In Proceedings of the Eighth National Conference on Artificial Intelligence, 100–105. Menlo Park, Calif.: American Association for Artificial Intelligence.

Zlotkin, G., and Rosenschein, J. 1989. Negotiation and Task Sharing among Autonomous Agents in Cooperative Domains. In Proceedings of the Eleventh International Joint Conference on Artificial Intelligence, 912–917. Menlo Park, Calif.: International Joint Conferences on Artificial Intelligence.

A computational market model for distributed configuration design

MICHAEL P. WELLMAN
AI Laboratory, University of Michigan, 1101 Beal Avenue, Ann Arbor, MI 48109-2110, U.S.A.

(RECEIVED May 5, 1994; ACCEPTED November 11, 1994)

Abstract

A precise market model for a well-defined class of distributed configuration design problems is presented. Given a design problem, the model defines a computational economy to allocate basic resources to agents participating in the design. The result of running these "design economies" constitutes the market solution to the original problem. After defining the configuration design framework, the mapping to computational economies and the results to date are described. For some simple examples, the system can produce good designs relatively quickly. However, analysis shows that the design economies are not guaranteed to find optimal designs, and some of the major pitfalls are identified and discussed. Despite known shortcomings and limited explorations thus far, the market model offers a useful conceptual viewpoint for analyzing distributed design problems.

Keywords: Design Economy; Computational Markets; Distributed Design

1. INTRODUCTION

The current dramatic expansion in network technology and infrastructure, including the explosive growth of the Internet, will soon see an inevitable proliferation of automated, distributed, information agents [for example, of the sort described by Etzioni and Weld (1994)]. With these advances, opportunities and incentives for the decentralization of design activities are rapidly emerging. Computational support for distributed design collaboration presents a variety of new challenges (Cutkosky et al., 1993; Edmonds et al., 1994; Reddy et al., 1993). In particular, the specialization of design expertise suggests a future where teams form *ad hoc* collaborations dynamically and flexibly, according to the most opportunistic connections. Centralized coordination or control is anathema in this environment. Instead we seek general decentralized mechanisms that respect the local autonomy of the agents involved, yet at the same time facilitate results (in our case, designs) with globally desirable qualities.

The design of complex artifacts can be viewed as fundamentally a problem of *resource allocation*. We generally have numerous performance and functional objectives to address, with many options for trading among these objectives and for furthering these objectives in exchange for increased cost. When the design problem is distributed, these trade-offs are not only across objectives, but also across agents (human or computational) participating in the design. Typically, each agent is concerned with a subset of the components or functions of the artifact being designed, and may individually reflect a complex combination of the fundamental objectives.

Consider a hypersimplified scenario in aircraft design. (We choose this not as a serious exemplar of the methodology, but merely as an evocative illustration of the concept of decentralized resource allocation.) Suppose we have separate agents responsible for the airfoil, engines, navigation equipment, etc. Suppose also that we have a target for the aircraft's total weight. Since total weight is the sum of the weights of its parts, we might consider allocating *a priori* each agent a slice of the "weight budget." This approach has several serious problems. First, if we do not choose the slices correctly, then it could be that one of the agents makes extreme compromises (e.g., an underpowered engine or expensive exotic metals for the fuselage), while the others could reduce weight relatively easily (e.g., replace the lead in the wings). Second, it typically will be impossible to determine good slices in advance, because the appropriate allocation will depend on other design choices. For example, depending on the position of the wings, reducing body weight while maintaining struc-

Reprint requests to: Dr. Michael P. Wellman, AI Laboratory, University of Michigan, 1101 Beal Avenue, Ann Arbor, MI 48109-2110, U.S.A. E-mail: wellman@engin.umich.edu

tural soundness may be more or less expensive. Or, if we have a more powerful engine, then it may be that extra total weight can be accommodated, and the fixed budget itself was not realistic.

Rather than allocate fixed proportions of resources, we desire an approach that dynamically adjusts the allocation as the design progresses. One way to achieve this sort of behavior is via a negotiation and trading process. For example, if the engine agent would benefit substantially from a slight increment in weight, it might offer to trade some of its drag allowance to the airfoil agent for a share of the latter's weight allocation. If there is enough of this kind of trading going on, then it makes sense to establish *markets* in the basic resources—weight, drag, etc. Then we can view the entire system as a sort of economy devoted to allocating resources for the design. We call this system the *design economy*.

In this paper we present a precise market model for a well-defined class of distributed configuration design problems. Given a design problem, our model defines a computational economy to solve the design problem, expressed in terms of concepts from microeconomic theory. We then can implement these economies in our WALRAS system for market-oriented programming (Wellman, 1993), thus producing a runnable design economy.

The following sections describe the configuration design framework, the mapping to computational economies, and preliminary results. For some simple examples, the system can produce good designs relatively quickly. However, analysis shows that the design economies are *not* guaranteed to find optimal designs, and we identify and discuss some of the major pitfalls. We argue that most of these problems are inherent in decentralization generally, not in the design economy *per se*, and moreover that the market model offers useful concepts for engineering the configuration of a variety of multiagent tasks.

2. DISTRIBUTED CONFIGURATION DESIGN

We adopt a standard framework for configuration design (Mittal & Frayman, 1989). Our specific formulation follows Darr and Birmingham (1994) and covers many representative systems (Balkany et al., 1993). Design in this framework corresponds to the selection of *parts* to perform *functions*. More precisely, a design problem consists of:

- A set of attributes, $A_1, \ldots, A_n$, and their associated domains, $X_1, \ldots, X_n$.
- A set of available parts, P, where each part $p \in P$ is defined by a tuple of attribute-value pairs.
- A distinguished subset of attributes, F, the *functions*. The domain of a function attribute is the set of parts than can perform that function.
- A set of constraints, R, dictating the allowable part combinations (either directly or indirectly via constraints on the attributes).
- A utility function, $u: X_1 \times \cdots \times X_n \rightarrow \Re$, ranking the possible combinations of attribute values by preference.

A *design* D is an assignment of parts to functions. Thus, the role of functions in this framework is to define when a design is complete. D is *feasible* if it satisfies R. The *valuation* of a design, $val(D)$, is the assignment to attribute values induced by the assignment of parts to functions. Typically, this is just the sum over the respective attribute values of a design's component parts. Finally, a feasible design D is *optimal* if for all feasible designs D', $u(val(D)) \geq u(val(D'))$.

In addition, it is often useful to organize the parts into *catalogs*. Let catalog i, $1 \leq i \leq m$, consist of parts C_i, where $C_1, \ldots, C_m$ is a partition of P. A catalog design includes at most one part per catalog.[1] In distributed design, catalogs are the units of distribution: Each catalog agent selects a part to contribute or chooses not to participate.

In this general form, the design task is clearly intractable (it subsumes general constraint satisfaction and optimization). Tractability can be obtained only by imposing restrictions on R and u. Instantiations of this framework adopt specialized constraint languages and often relax the requirement of optimality. We shall accept comparable compromises in our mapping to the market model.

3. COMPUTATIONAL MARKETS

The market model we adopt is a computational realization of the most generic, well-studied theoretical framework, that of general equilibrium theory (Hildenbrand & Kirman, 1976; Shoven & Whalley, 1992). General equilibrium is concerned with the behavior of a collection of interconnected markets, one market for each good. A general-equilibrium system consists of:

- a collection of goods, $g_1, \ldots, g_n$, and
- a collection of agents, divided into two types:
  consumers—who simply exchange goods
  producers—who can transform some goods into others.

A consumer is defined by (1) a *utility function*, which specifies its relative preference for consuming a bundle of goods $\langle x_1, \ldots, x_n \rangle$, and (2) an *endowment* $\langle e_1, \ldots, e_n \rangle$ of initial quantities of the goods. Consumers may trade all or part of their initial endowments in exchange for

[1] In the degenerate case where each catalog lists only one part, catalog design reverts to the situation without catalogs. Typically, catalogs will correspond to functions, although this is not a requirement. Indeed, this definition places no restriction on the number of functions any part may implement.

quantities of the other goods. All trades must be executed at the established market prices, $\langle p_1, \ldots, p_n \rangle$. A consumption bundle is feasible for a consumer if and only if it satisfies the *budget constraint*,

$$\sum_{i=1}^{n} x_i p_i \le \sum_{i=1}^{n} e_i p_i,$$

which says that a consumer may spend only up to the value of its endowment. The decision problem faced by a consumer is to maximize its utility subject to the budget constraint.

The other class of agents, producers, do not consume goods, but rather transform various combinations of some goods (the inputs) into others (outputs). The feasible combinations of inputs and outputs are defined by the producer's *technology*. For example, if the producer can transform one unit of g_1 into two units of g_2, with constant returns to scale, then the technology would include the tuples $\{\langle -x, 2x, 0, \ldots, 0\rangle | x \ge 0\}$. This production would be profitable as long as $p_1 < 2p_2$. The producer's decision problem is to choose a production activity so as to maximize *profits*, the difference between revenues (total price of output) and costs (total price of input). Note that a producer does not have a utility function.

In the computational market price system we use, WALRAS, we can implement consumer and producer agents and direct them to bid so as to maximize utility or profits, subject to their own feasibility constraints. The system derives a set of market prices that balance the supply and demand for each good. Since the markets for the goods are interconnected (due to interactions in both production and consumption), the price for one good will generally affect the demand and supply for others. WALRAS adjusts the prices via an iterative bidding protocol until the system reaches a *competitive equilibrium* [see Wellman (1993) for details], i.e., an allocation and set of prices such that (1) consumers bid so as to maximize utility, subject to their budget constraints; (2) producers bid so as to maximize profits, subject to their technological possibilities; and (3) net demand is zero for all goods.

An economy in competitive equilibrium has the desirable property of Pareto Optimality: It is not possible to increase the utility of one agent without decreasing that of other(s). Moreover, for any Pareto optimum (i.e., any admissible allocation), there is some corresponding set of initial endowments that would lead to this result. Given certain technical restrictions on the producer technologies and consumer preferences, equilibrium is guaranteed to exist, and the system converges to it. Specifically, if technologies and preferences are smooth and strictly convex, then a competitive equilibrium exists [see Varian (1984) for formal treatment]. If, in addition, the derived demands are such that increasing the price for one good does not decrease the demand for others, then the equilibrium is unique, and iterative bidding process is guaranteed to converge to it (Arrow & Hurwicz, 1977; Milgrom & Roberts, 1991).

3.1. The design economy

We next proceed to instantiate the general-equilibrium framework for our distributed configuration design problem. As noted above, our purpose in applying the economic mechanism is to provide a principled basis for resolving trade-offs across distributed design agents. By grouping the agents together in a single economy, we establish a *common currency* linking the agents' local demands for available resources. Using this common currency, the market can (at least under the circumstances sketched above) efficiently allocate resources toward their most productive use with minimal communication or coordination overhead. The fact that all interaction among agents occurs via the exchange of goods at standard prices greatly simplifies the design of individual agents, as they can focus on their own attributes and the parameters of their local economic problems. In addition, the price interface provides a straightforward way to influence the system's behavior from the outside—by setting the relative prices of exogenously derived resources and performance attributes. And similarly, the prices within the system can be interpreted from the outside in terms of economic variables that are meaningful to those participating in the design process.

3.2. Market configuration

In general, to cast a distributed resource-allocation problem in terms of a computational market, one needs to specify

- the goods (commodities) traded,
- the consumer agents trading and ultimately deriving value from the goods,
- the producer agents, with their associated technologies for transforming some goods into other goods, and
- the agents' bidding behaviors.

There are two classes of goods we consider in the problem of distributed design. First, we have basic resource attributes, such as weight and drag in the fanciful aircraft example above. These are resources required by the components in order to realize the desired performance, but are limited or costly or both. Generally, we desire to minimize our overall use of resources. The second class of goods is performance attributes, such as engine thrust or leg room in a passenger aircraft. We also include the function attributes in this category. Performance attributes measure the capabilities of the designed artifact, and we typically desire to maximize these.

In terms of our framework for distributed configuration design, both resource and performance attributes are kinds of attributes. Functions can be viewed as a subclass of performance attributes. So, the first step in mapping a design problem to our market model is to identify the goods with the attributes. Although it is not strictly necessary to distinguish the resource from performance attributes, we do so for expository reasons, as it facilitates intuitive understanding of the flow of goods in the design economy.

The remaining steps are to identify the agents and define their behavior. As mentioned above, it is typical in multiagent design to allocate individual agents responsibility for distinct components or functions. Within our distributed design scheme, these agents correspond to catalogs. In a distributed constraint-satisfaction formulation of the problem (Darr & Birmingham, 1994), catalog agents select a part to contribute to the overall design. The chosen part entails a particular pattern of resource usage and performance, as specified in its associated attribute vector.

Correspondingly, in the design economy, each part in the catalog is associated with a vector of resource and performance *goods*. The resources can be interpreted as input goods, and the performance goods as output. In this view, the *catalog producer* is an agent that transforms resources to performance. For example, the engine agent in our aircraft design transforms *weight* and *drag* (and *noise*, etc.) into *thrust*. The particular combinations of weight/drag/thrust/ . . . represented by the various engine models constitute this producer's *technology*. Thus, to specify a catalog producer's technology (and that's all there is to specify for a producer), we simply form a set of the attribute-value tuples characterizing each part. We then go through and negate the values for the resource goods, leaving the values for performance goods intact.[2]

An economy with only producers would have no purpose. To ground the system, we define a consumer agent, conceptually the end user or customer for the overall design.[3] The consumer is endowed with the basic resource goods. So, for example, we will initialize the system by endowing the consumer with a total weight, typically an amount greater than the heaviest conceivable aircraft defined by a combination of the heaviest available parts. The idea is that the consumer then (effectively) sells this weight to the various catalog agents in exchange for performance goods like thrust.

The consumer has preferences over the overall design attributes, as specified by its utility function. This function is essentially equivalent to the function u defined in the general framework for configuration design. There is one syntactic modification, however. In the original specification, u was increasing in the performance attributes and decreasing in the resource attributes. The consumer's utility function, in contrast, must be increasing in all attributes. To ensure this, we define the "consumption" of a resource good as the amount left over after the consumer sells part of its endowment. Thus, if the consumer's endowment of weight is w and the total weight of the aircraft (sum of the weight of the parts) is w', then the effective weight consumed is $w - w'$. If the consumer prefers lighter airplanes, then it prefers to "consume" as much weight as possible.

Thus far we have accounted for all elements of the configuration design framework except for the constraints (recall that the functions are a subset of performance attributes). We are able to map some kinds of constraints into this framework, but not others. The simplest type of constraint is an upper bound on the total usage of a particular resource (e.g., the total noise cannot exceed FAA regulations). To capture this kind of constraint, we simply endow the consumer with exactly the upper bound. Since the consumer is the only source of resource goods in the economy, this effectively restricts the combined choices of the producers. Some other kinds of constraints can also be handled by defining new intermediate goods. This is best illustrated by example in the next section. (Unfortunately, we do not have a compact characterization of the constraints that can be easily mapped in this way.)

Finally, we must note an implicit assumption underlying the mapping described above. In order for the resource and performance goods to be reasonably traded among the consumer and producers, it must be the case that the total resource usage (resp. performance achieved) does indeed correspond to the sum of the parts. In other words, the *val* function described above must be additive (but note that the utility function u need not be). There may be some encoding tricks to get around this restriction in some cases, but the basic design economy assumes this property.

3.3. An example

To illustrate the mapping from configuration design problems to design economies, we carry out the exercise for an example presented by Darr and Birmingham (1994). The problem is a very simplified computer configuration design. In the example, we have two functions to satisfy: *processing* and serial *port*. Our design criteria are *dollar* cost and reliability, as measured in failures-per-million-hours (fpmh). These criteria are represented in the design economy as resource goods. There are no performance goods, except for the two functions mentioned. There is

---

[2] This assumes that all attributes are measured in increasing resource usage or increasing performance. If not, we would simply rescale the values in advance.

[3] If there is more than one class of users or customers with distinct preferences, then we could introduce several consumer agents. The underlying computational market accommodates any number of agents, but our design economies thus far have employed only one.

Table 1. *CPU catalog*

CPU	Process	Dollars	fpmh	Memory
CPU1	1	6	1	40
CPU2	1	4	7	140
CPU3	1	2	2	40
CPU4	1	1	5	30

also another good, *memory* access, which is conceived here not as an overall performance attribute, but as an intermediate good enabling the *processing* function.[4]

We also have three constraints. The total dollar cost must not exceed 11, the total failure rate must not exceed 10 fpmh, and the RAM must be at least as fast as the CPU's memory access. The first two of these constraints are captured simply by endowing the consumer with 11 dollars and 10 fpmh. The consumer's utility function specifies preferences over these two goods, as well as the functions *processing* and *port*. Representing the functions as utility attributes rather than constraints deviates from the original framework somewhat by allowing the user the flexibility to trade off functionality for performance or resource savings.

There are 14 available parts, organized into three catalogs. The CPU catalog contains four CPU models, each of which supplies the *processing* function. Five serial ports are available to support the *port* function, and five RAM models can supply *memory* access. The complete CPU catalog is presented in Table 1.

The catalogs are converted into technologies simply by listing the attribute tuples as good tuples, possibly after some rescaling. For example, the CPU agent's technology is:

$$\{\langle 1,-6,-1,-1/40\rangle,\langle 1,-4,-7,-1/140\rangle,$$
$$\langle 1,-2,-2,-1/40\rangle,\langle 1,-1,-5,-1/30\rangle,\langle 0,0,0,0\rangle\}.$$

This means that the agent has five options, with the net good productions listed. The first option is to produce an output of 1 unit of processing (by default, functions take values in {0,1}) from an input of 6 *dollars*, 1 *fpmh*, and 1/40 *memory* access units. This last input requires some explanation. In order to represent the constraint that CPU be at least as fast as RAM, we define the intermediate good *memory* access, which is an output of RAM and an input of CPU. The constraint is then enforced by requiring that CPU buy enough speed from RAM. Since the values listed in the catalog above are memory access times, we invert them to convert to speed units.

[4] We chose this interpretation specifically to illustrate the notion of intermediate goods; in the next section we simplify the model to treat *memory* as a function.

Finally, the tuple of zeros is an element of every technology. An agent always has the option to produce nothing, in which case its resource usage is zero (as are its profits).

Similar technologies are generated for the RAM catalog (input *dollar* and *fpmh*, output *memory*) and serial port (input *dollar* and *fpmh*, output *port*), as shown in Table 2.

The configuration of the design economy is best described in terms of flow of goods, depicted in Figure 1. The consumers supply the basic resources, which are transformed by the producers to performance goods (as well as intermediate resources needed by other producers), which are ultimately valued by the consumer.

3.4. Agent behavior

All that remains to specify our mapping is to define the behavior of the various agents. The consumer's problem is to set demands maximizing utility, subject to the budget constraint. This defines a constrained optimization problem, parameterized by current going prices.

In our example, we adopt a standard special functional form for utility, one exhibiting constant elasticity of substitution (CES) (Varian, 1984). The CES utility function is

$$u(x_1,\ldots,x_n) = \left(\sum_{i=1}^{n} \alpha_i^{1-\rho} x_i^{\rho}\right)^{1/\rho},$$

where the α_i are good coefficients and ρ is a generic substitution parameter. One virtue of the CES utility function is that there is a closed-form solution to the optimal demand function,

$$x_i(p_1,\ldots,p_n) = \frac{\alpha_i \sum_{j=1}^{n} p_j e_j}{p_i^{1/(1-\rho)} \sum_{j=1}^{n} \alpha_j p_j^{\rho/(\rho-1)}}.$$

The consumer can simply evaluate this function at the going prices whenever prompted by the bidding protocol. In WALRAS, bids are actually demand *curves*, where the price p_i of the good i being bid varies while the other prices are held fixed. CES consumers transmit a closed-

Table 2. *Technologies for RAM and Port catalog producers*

RAM	$	fpmh	Memory	Port	$	fpmh	Port
null	0	0	0	null	0	0	0
RAM1	−6	−2	1/40	SP1	−6	−1	1
RAM2	−3	−3	1/10	SP2	−3	−3	1
RAM3	−2	−6	1/35	SP3	−2	−4	1
RAM4	−2	−4	1/30	SP4	−1	−8	1
RAM5	−1	−7	1/35	SP5	−1	−6	1

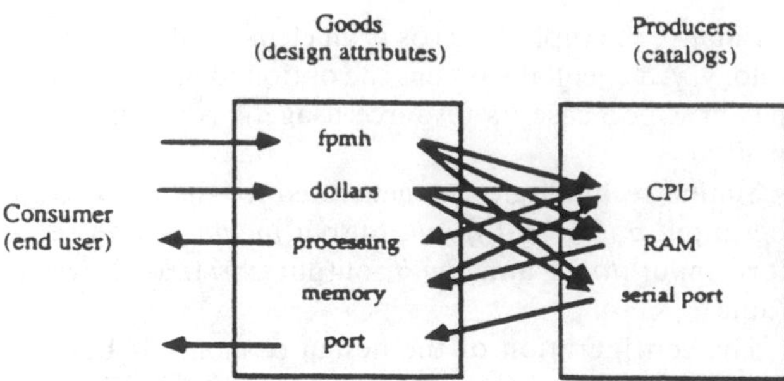

Fig. 1. Flow of goods in the example design economy.

form description of this curve, with p_i the dependent variable.

The producers' bidding task is also quite simple. Catalog producers face a discrete choice among the possible component instances, each providing a series of values for goods corresponding to resource and performance attributes. Let $(x_1^j, \ldots, x_n^j)$ be the vector of quantities representing part j in the producer's catalog, and π^j denote the profitability of part j, as a function of prices:

$$\pi^j(p_1, \ldots, p_n) = \sum_{i=1}^{n} p_i x_i^j.$$

All catalogs include the null part 0, where $x_i^0 = 0$ for all i. Given a set of prices, the producer selects the most profitable part:

$$j^*(p_1, \ldots, p_n) = \arg\max_j \pi^j(p_1, \ldots, p_n).$$

Just as for consumers, when a producer bids on good i, it specifies a range of demands for all values of p_i (the price of good i), holding all other prices fixed, which is determined by the optimal part for that price,

$$x_i(p_i) = x_i^{j^*(p_1, \ldots, p_i, \ldots, p_n)}.$$

When all prices but one are fixed, we can simplify the profit function as follows:

$$\pi^j(\bar{p}_1, \ldots, p_i, \ldots, \bar{p}_n) = p_i x_i^j + \sum_{k \neq i} \bar{p}_k x_k^j = p_i x_i^j + \bar{\beta}^j,$$

where the parameter $\bar{\beta}^j$ depends on part j and the fixed prices $\bar{p}_k$, $k \neq i$. For example, part j is more profitable than j' if and only if

$$p_i x_i^j + \bar{\beta}^j > p_i x_i^{j'} + \bar{\beta}^{j'},$$

or equivalently (for $x_i^j > x_i^{j'}$),

$$p_i > \frac{\bar{\beta}^{j'} - \bar{\beta}^j}{x_i^j - x_i^{j'}}.$$

It is clear from the above that parts with higher values of x_i^j become maximally profitable, if ever, at higher prices p_i. Therefore, one way to calculate $j^*(\bar{p}_1, \ldots, p_i, \ldots, \bar{p}_n)$ is to sort the parts in increasing order of x_i^j and then use the inequality above to derive the price threshold between each adjacent pair.[5] These thresholds dictate the optimal part at any p_i (assuming the other prices fixed) and the associated demand $x_i^{j^*}$. Thus, the form of the producer's demand is a step function, defined by a set of threshold prices where different components become optimal.

4. DISCUSSION

4.1. Results

We have run the design economy on a few simple examples, including the one presented above modified to treat *memory* as a function rather than an intermediate good. For this example it produces the optimal design in three bidding cycles, although it never (as long as we have run it) reaches a price equilibrium. After the third cycle, the prices continue to fluctuate, although never enough to cause one of the catalog producers to change its optimal part. Unfortunately, we have no way of detecting with certainty that the part choices are stable.

Although we have yet to run systematic experiments, we have observed similar behavior on a variety of small examples. We have also encountered examples where the design economy does not appear to converge on a single design, or it converges on a design far from the global optimum. This is not surprising, as the general class of design economies producible by the mapping specified above does not satisfy the known conditions for existence of competitive equilibrium. Indeed, the conditions are never strictly satisfied by design economies generated as described, because the discreteness of catalogs violates convexity.

4.2. Limitations

The analytical theories underlying the market approach make it easy to characterize the limitations of the approach. To guarantee optimal results, strictly speaking, we require that the catalogs represent convex sets of attribute vectors, a condition that is not typically satisfied in configuration design problems. Although the system sometimes produces good or even optimal designs despite violating the conditions, we currently lack an adequate model to predict the system's performance on novel problems.

In other (nondesign) applications of the market-based approach, we have found that the method scales very well with the number of agents. Scaling the number of goods can be a more serious problem, particularly if the goods are highly interconnected.

The approach as presented here is also fundamentally limited in applicability to a subclass of configuration de-

[5] This includes the null part, with $x_i^0 = \bar{\beta}^0 = 0$. If the threshold decreases, then the intervening part can never be optimal (it is not on the convex hull) for any price of good i, and can be skipped.

sign problems. While configuration design is a standard framework in the design-automation literature, there are clearly many design domains (including the fanciful aircraft example) where the framework does not fit. Moreover, even within configuration design, we require that overall resource usage be decomposed into the sum of resource usage of the parts, and limit the form of constraints that can be accommodated in the market system.

It is important to note, however, that many of these difficulties are inherent in the problem of decentralization, and not particular to the market approach. Indeed, one of the main virtues of this approach is that, compared to others, its limitations are transparent and amenable to analysis.

4.3. Extensions

As mentioned above, designs produced by the market model are not guaranteed to be optimal or even feasible, due to the discreteness (and other nonconvexities) of the problem. They are more likely to be local optima, where no single change of policy by one of the producer agents will constitute an improved design. In current work, we are attempting to characterize the performance of the scheme for special cases. For those cases where perfectly competitive equilibria do not exist, we are investigating the possibility of relaxing the competitiveness assumption. In addition, we are looking into hybrid schemes that use the market to bound the optimal value by computing the global optimum for a smooth and convex relaxation of the original problem. This is analogous to branch-and-bound schemes that make use of regular linear-programming algorithms for integer-programming problems. In this and other approaches, we expect the economic price information exploited by the market-oriented approach to lead to more rational trade-offs in the distributed design process.

We are also exploring combinations of market-based and constraint-based methods, where we use general constraints (including those inexpressible in the market model) to prune the catalogs before running the design economy. This might be accomplished using an auxiliary constraint network (Bowen & Bahler, 1993) or one built on the existing agent structure (Darr & Birmingham, 1994). A hybrid approach interleaving market-directed search for good designs with constraint reasoning uses each method to compensate for inadequacies in the other.

Another specific modification to the underlying model we are exploring is to maintain intervals on prices rather than specific points. For any given interval of prices, the producer and consumer agents in the computational economy can derive their admissible design choices. Given a collection of agents' bids in the form of sets of admissible choices, the system can compute a new price interval. When the price converges to a single point, the behavior of the individual agents will correspond to a unique overall design. This, too, meshes well with general constraint operations, as pruning based on price bounds complements pruning based on physical constraints.

5. ECONOMICS AND DISTRIBUTED AI

5.1. Why economics?

To coordinate a set of largely autonomous agents, we usually seek mechanisms that (1) produce globally desirable results, (2) avoid central coordination, and (3) impose minimal communication requirements. In addition, as engineers of such systems, we also prefer mechanisms that (4) are amenable to theoretical and empirical analysis. In human societies, advocates of market economies argue that criterion 2 is essential (for various reasons) and that market price systems perform well on criterion 1 because they provide each agent with the right incentives to further the social good. Because prices are a very compact way to convey this incentive information to each agent, we can argue that price systems also satisfy criterion 3 (Koopmans, 1970). For these reasons, some have found the market economy an inspiring social metaphor for approaches to coordinating distributed computational agents. Thus, we sometimes see mechanisms and protocols appealing to notions of negotiation, bidding, or other economic behavior.

Criterion 4 is also a compelling motivation for exploring economic coordination mechanisms in a computational setting. The problem of coordinating multiple agents in a societal structure has been deeply investigated by economists, resulting in a large body of concepts and insights as well as a powerful analytical framework. The phenomena surrounding social decision making have been studied in other social science disciplines as well, but economics is distinguished by its focus on three particular issues:

Resource allocation. The central aspect of the outcome of the agents' behavior is the allocation of resources and distribution of products throughout the economy.

Rationality abstraction. Most of microeconomic theory adopts the assumption that individual agents are *rational* in the sense that they act so as to maximize utility. This approach is highly congruent with much work in artificial intelligence, where we attempt to characterize an agent's behavior in terms of its knowledge and goals (or more generally, beliefs, desires, and intentions). Indeed, this *knowledge-level* analysis requires some kind of rationality abstraction (Newell, 1982) and is perhaps even implicit in our usage of the term *agent*.

Decentralization. The central concern of economics is to relate decentralized, individual decisions to aggregate behavior of the overall society. This is also the concern of distributed AI as a computational science.

5.2. Related work

In addition to our own prior work in market-oriented programming (Wellman, 1993, 1995), there have been several other efforts to exploit markets for distributed computation (Clearwater, 1995). Most famous in AI is the contract net (Davis & Smith, 1983), but it is only recently that true economic mechanisms have been incorporated in that framework (Sandholm, 1993). There have been interesting recent proposals for incorporating a range of economic ideas in distributed allocation of computational resources (Drexler & Miller, 1988; Miller & Drexler, 1988) as well as some actual experiments along these lines (Cheriton & Harty, 1993; Kurose & Simha, 1989; Waldspurger et al., 1992). However, there are no other fully computational market models for distributed design of which we are aware.

This approach also shares some conceptual features with other agent-based frameworks for distributed computing (Genesereth & Ketchpel, 1994; Wiederhold, 1992), particularly Shoham's approach to "agent-oriented programming" (Shoham, 1993). Where Shoham defines a set of interactions based on speech acts, we focus exclusively on economic actions such as exchange and production. In both approaches [as well as some others (Huberman, 1988)], the underlying idea is to get an improved understanding of a complex computational system via social constructs.

Finally, there is a large literature on decomposition methods for mathematical programming problems, which could perhaps be applied to distributed design. Many of these and other distributed optimization techniques (Bertsekas & Tsitsiklis, 1989) can themselves be interpreted in economic terms, using the close relationship between prices and Lagrange multipliers. The main distinction of the approach advocated here is conceptual. Rather than taking a global optimization problem and decentralizing it, our aim is to provide a framework that accommodates an exogenously given distributed structure.

6. CONCLUSIONS

The main contribution of this work is a precise market model for distributed design, covering a significant class of configuration design problems. The model has been implemented within a general environment for defining computational market systems. Although we have yet to perform extensive, systematic experiments, we have found that the design economy produces good designs on some simple problems, but breaks seriously on others. Analysis is underway to characterize the cases where it works. It cannot be expected to work universally, as these are known intractable optimization problems, and distributing the problem only makes things worse.

In the long run, by embedding economic concepts within our design algorithms, we facilitate the support of actual economic transactions that we expect will eventually be an integral part of networks for collaborative design and other interorganizational interactions. Many other technical problems will need to be solved (involving security for proprietary information and bidding protocols, for example) before this is a reality, but integrating economic ideas at the conceptual level is an important first step.

ACKNOWLEDGMENTS

Special thanks are owed to Bill Birmingham and Tim Darr for assistance with the distributed design problem and examples. John Cheng, Daphne Koller, and some anonymous referees provided useful comments on the paper and the work.

REFERENCES

Arrow, K.J., & Hurwicz, L., Eds. (1977). *Studies in Resource Allocation Processes*. Cambridge University Press, Cambridge, United Kingdom.

Balkany, A., Birmingham, W.P., & Tommelein, I.D. (1993). An analysis of several configuration design systems. *AI EDAM 7*, 1–17.

Bertsekas, D.P., & Tsitsiklis, J.N. (1989). *Parallel and distributed computation*. Englewood Cliffs, NJ: Prentice-Hall.

Bowen, J., & Bahler, D. (1993). Constraint-based software for concurrent engineering. *Computer 26(1)*, 66–68.

Cheriton, D.R., & Harty, K. (1993). A market approach to operating system memory allocation. Technical Report. Department of Computer Science, Stanford University, Stanford, CA.

Clearwater, S., Ed. (1995). *Market-Based Control: A Paradigm for Distributed Resource Allocation*. World Scientific.

Cutkosky, M.R., Englemore, R.S., Fikes, R.E., et al. (1993). PACT: An experiment in integrating concurrent engineering systems. *Computer 26(1)*, 28–37.

Darr, T.P., & Birmingham, W.P. (1994). Automated design for concurrent engineering. *IEEE Expert 5(9)*, 35–42.

Davis, R., & Smith, R.G. (1983). Negotiation as as metaphor for distributed problem solving. *Artif. Intell. 20*, 63–109.

Drexler, K.E., & Miller, M.S. (1988). Incentive engineering for computational resource management. In *The Ecology of Computation* (Huberman, B.A., Ed.), pp. 231–236. Elsevier, North-Holland.

Edmonds, E.A., Candy, L., Jones, R., et al. (1994). Support for collaborative design: Agents and emergence. *Commun. ACM 37(7)*, 41–47.

Etzioni, O., & Weld, D. (1994). A softbot-based interface to the internet. *Commun. ACM 37(7)*, 72–76.

Genesereth, M.R., & Ketchpel, S.P. (1994). Software agents. *Commun. ACM 37(7)*, 48–53.

Hildenbrand, W., Kirman, A.P. (1976). *Introduction to Equilibrium Analysis: Variations on Themes by Edgeworth and Walras*. North-Holland, Amsterdam.

Huberman, B.A., Ed. (1988). *The Ecology of Computation*. North-Holland, Amsterdam.

Koopmans, T.C. (1970). Uses of prices. In *Scientific Papers of Tjalling C. Koopmans*, pp. 243–257. Springer-Verlag, New York.

Kurose, J.F., & Simha, R. (1989). A microeconomic approach to optimal resource allocation in distributed computer systems. *IEEE Trans. Comput. 38*, 705–717.

Milgrom, P., & Roberts, J. (1991). Adaptive and sophisticated learning in normal form games. *Games and Economic Behavior 3*, 82–100.

Miller, M.S., & Drexler, K.E. (1988). Markets and computation: Agoric open systems. In *The Ecology of Computation* (Huberman, B.A., Ed.), pp. 133–176. North-Holland, Amsterdam.

Mittal, S., & Frayman, F. (1989). Towards a generic model of configuration tasks. *Proc. Eleventh Int. Joint Conf. on Artificial Intelligence*, Detroit, MI. Morgan Kaufmann, Palo Alto, CA.

Newell, A. (1982). The knowledge level. *Artif. Intell. 18*, 87–127.

Reddy, Y.V.R., Srinivas, K., Jagannathan, V., et al. (1993). Computer support for concurrent engineering. *Computer 26(1)*, 12–16.

Sandholm, T. (1993). An implementation of the contract net protocol based on marginal cost calculations. *Proc. Nat. Conf. on Artificial Intelligence*. AAAI Press, Washington, DC.

Shoham, Y. (1993). Agent-oriented programming. *Artif. Intell. 60*, 51–92.

Shoven, J.B., & Whalley, J. (1992). *Applying General Equilibrium*. Cambridge University Press, Cambridge, United Kingdom.

Varian, H.R. (1984). *Microeconomic Analysis*. W.W. Norton, New York.

Waldspurger, C.A., Hogg, T., Huberman, B.A., et al. (1992). Spawn: A distributed computational economy. *IEEE Trans. Software Engrg. 18*, 103–117.

Wellman, M.P. (1993). A market-oriented programming environment and its application to distributed multicommodity flow problems. *J. Artif. Intell. Res. 1(1)*, 1-23.

Wellman, M.P. (1995). Market-oriented programming: Some early lessons. In *Market-Based Control: A Paradigm for Distributed Resource Allocation*, (Clearwater, S., Ed.). World Scientific.

Wiederhold, G. (1992). Mediators in the architecture of future information systems. *Computer 26(3)*, 38–49.

Michael P. Wellman is an Assistant Professor in the Department of Electrical Engineering and Computer Science at the University of Michigan. He received a Ph.D. degree in computer science from the Massachusetts Institute of Technology in 1988 for his work in qualitative probabilistic reasoning and decision-theoretic planning, including methods for knowledge-based model construction. From 1988 to 1992, Dr. Wellman conducted research in these areas at the USAF's Wright Laboratory. Current research also includes investigation of computational market mechanisms for distributed decision making. In 1994, he received an NSF National Young Investigator award.

Coordination without Communication: Experimental Validation of Focal Point Techniques

Maier Fenster **Sarit Kraus***
Department of Mathematics and Computer Science, Bar Ilan University, Ramat Gan, Israel
{fenster,sarit}@bimacs.cs.biu.ac.il

Jeffrey S. Rosenschein
Institute of Computer Science, Hebrew University, Givat Ram, Jerusalem, Israel
jeff@cs.huji.ac.il

Abstract

Coordination is a central theme of Distributed Artificial Intelligence. Much work in this field can be seen as a search for mechanisms that allow agents with differing knowledge and goals to coordinate their actions for mutual benefit. Additionally, one cornerstone assumption of the field is that communication is expensive relative to local computation. Thus, coordination techniques that minimize communication are of particular importance.

This paper considers how automated agents could use a coordination technique common to communication-free human interactions, namely *focal points*. Given a problem and a set of possible solutions from which the agents need to choose one, focal points are prominent solutions of the problem to which agents are drawn. Theoretical work on this subject includes (Schelling 1963; Kraus & Rosenschein 1992).

The purpose of the current research is to consider the practical use of focal point techniques in various domains. We present simulations over randomly generated domains; these simulations strongly suggest that focal points can act as an effective heuristic for coordination in real-world environments.

Keywords: Coordination, Distributed AI

Introduction

Coordination is a central theme of Distributed Artificial Intelligence (DAI). Much of the work in this field can be seen as a search for mechanisms that will allow agents with differing views of the world, and possibly with different goals, to coordinate their actions for mutual benefit.

One of the cornerstone assumptions of DAI is that communication is expensive relative to computation (Bond & Gasser 1988) (i.e., DAI agents are loosely coupled). Thus, work in DAI has actively explored coordination techniques that require little or no communication. Researchers in this area may allow some limited communication in their models, especially insofar as it is required to establish problem constraints. So, for example, in (Genesereth, Ginsberg, & Rosenschein 1986) agents are assumed to jointly perceive an interaction (the joint perception could conceivably involve communication), then proceed without further communication. Similarly, there have been attempts to get multiple agents to interact effectively with little *explicit* communication, while allowing the implicit communication of sensing other agents' external actions or condition (e.g., location) (Levy & Rosenschein 1992).

Another motivation for studying communication-impoverished interactions, other than the expense of communication, has been that communication is sometimes impossible or inconsistent with the environment (communication has been cut off, or is inadvisable in the presence of hostile forces). There has also been a deep-seated intuition that humans are sometimes capable of sophisticated interaction with little explicit communication, and that it ought to be possible for automated agents to emulate this.

This paper explores a coordination technique common to communication-free human interactions, namely *focal points*. Given a problem and a set of possible solutions from which the agents need to choose one, focal points are prominent solutions of the problem to which agents are drawn.[1] Theoretical work on this subject includes (Schelling 1963; Kraus & Rosenschein 1992).

The purpose of the current research is to carry out simulations of focal point techniques. We describe in this paper the application of an algorithm based on focal points to an abstraction of a real world situation. We assume that there are objects in the world with various properties, and we want two agents to choose one of the objects (i.e., the same one) without communicating. If the two agents choose the same object, we have a "meeting" and success. We make no assumptions in our simulations about the properties of the objects, the way they are ordered, or any other special

*Kraus is also affiliated with the Institute for Advanced Computer Studies, University of Maryland, College Park, Maryland.

[1]The Focal Point concept is discussed below in the section "Focal Points".

characteristics of the domain.

We present a domain-independent algorithm and test it in simulations of various instances of the abstract world. The power of focal points in coordinating common choices among agents was highly evident in our simulations. We found that in most randomly generated situations there is more than a 90% probability that the agents will make a common choice, and in many circumstances the probability rises to 100%.

The Coordination Problem

Two agents are trying to choose the same object out of a set of objects. The following examples might occur in an environment where communication is difficult (radio frequency disturbance, or secrecy demands during a battle, or the simple inability to communicate because a specific frequency has been jammed), and therefore an attempt must be made to come to an agreement without any communication. There are various scenarios that might require this kind of communication-poor interaction. For example, two agents that are out of touch with one another must agree on the same plan of action, out of a set of several equally reasonable plans. Another example is of agents that are unable to communicate, but must choose one of several "safe houses" where they will meet and communicate. Another possibility is when agents may need to actually reestablish communication, by choosing a radio frequency to use for future messages.

The worlds we examine have the following characteristics:

- There is a group of objects (denoted by $\mathcal{T}erm$) out of which the agents must choose one (ideally the same one).
- There is a set of predicates $\mathcal{P}red$. Each of the predicates $P \in \mathcal{P}red$ has two arguments: an object in $\mathcal{T}erm$ and a value from the set $\mathcal{V}alue_P$, so that each object has a value for each predicate. For example, $Color(1, red)$ might mean that object 1 is red, while $Height(1, 4)$ might mean that the height of object 1 is 4.
- Any characteristic of an object can be encoded in the values that the predicates can take. We assume, without loss of generality, that the predicates in $\mathcal{P}red$ are ordered and numbered by 1, 2, 3, and so on.[2]

We make the following additional assumptions:

1. The agents observe the same objects and properties in the world. They have the sets $\mathcal{T}erm$, $\mathcal{P}red$ and $\mathcal{V}alue_P$'s as described above.
2. The agents have great flexibility regarding their internal representations of the world, and these internal representations of the different agents need not match one another. For example, they may have different predicates and may represent the value of the predicates differently.
3. Utility is only attached to success at choosing the same object, not to the selection of any specific object (i.e., the agents are indifferent among objects).

In game theory the above problem can be described using a game matrix. One agent needs to choose a row and the other agent needs to choose a column. The payoff for each agent is written in the cell specified by their respective choices.

J \ K	*a*	*b*
a	1, 1	0, 0
b	0, 0	1, 1

For example, the game matrix shown here can be used to describe situations where two agents need to choose the same object; if both agents choose the same object (e.g., "a") their payoffs are 1 to each of them. Otherwise, they both get 0.

Since the matrix is symmetric, there is no guarantee, using game theory techniques, that the agents will both choose the same object[3] and their chance of choosing the same object is only 50%.

Focal Points

Originally introduced by Schelling (Schelling 1963; Rasmusen 1989), focal points refer to prominent solutions of an interaction, solutions to which agents are drawn. His work on this subject explored a number of simple games where, despite surface equivalence among many solutions, human players were predictably drawn to a particular solution by using contextual information. The following "toy example" illustrates the concept clearly.

Consider a TV game show, where two people have each been asked to divide 100 identical objects into two arbitrarily-sized piles. Their only concern in deciding how much goes into each pile is to match the other person's behavior. If the two agents match one another, they each win $40,000, otherwise they get nothing. Schelling found that most people, presented with this scenario, choose an even division of 50 objects per pile. The players reason that, since at one level of analysis all choices are equivalent, they must focus on any uniqueness that distinguishes a particular option (such as symmetry), and rely on the other person's doing likewise. A similar problem has each person asked to choose any positive number, with their only concern to match the other person's choice. Most people

[2] The predicates' numbers are used only for the presentation of the paper. As is explained below, we allow flexibility regarding the agents' internal representation. In particular, we do not assume that the agents assign the same names to the predicates.

[3] In these situations there are multiple equilibria, and there is a problem in choosing among them. Detailed discussion can be found in (Kraus & Rosenschein 1992).

seem to choose the number 1, it being the only positive number without a predecessor.

There are a number of intuitive properties that seem to qualify a given agreement as a focal point. Among these properties are uniqueness, symmetry, and extremeness. Even when we consider these special properties, more must be done to identify focal points. In the TV game show example above, there is another fairly strong contender for a solution in the choice of 0 objects in one pile, and 100 objects in the second pile (or vice versa). Of course, it is precisely the "vice versa" aspect of this solution that makes it appear less appealing in comparison to the 50–50 split.

In adapting the idea of focal points from human behavior patterns to automated agents, one major difference must be considered. Focal points are based on the naturalness and intuitiveness of certain objects (or solutions) in the world. Automated agents do not have the cultural background (common sense) needed to judge naturalness and intuitiveness. However, their designers can endow them with an algorithm capable of identifying focal points to which they will adhere.

The Focal Point Algorithm

We devise a mathematical formula that specifies the prominence of an object in the world. This formula is based on intuitive properties such as rarity and extremeness. The premise of the work is that in any random world some objects will have a predicate-value vector that is different from those of other objects, and so the object itself will be marked as special. Several agents examining the same world, using the same formula, will see the same "special" objects. Focal point algorithms provide a technique to choose one of these "special objects" uniquely.

The algorithm described below is useful in situations where a single designer builds both agents,[4] and sends them to an environment about which s/he does not have advance information. If the designer suspects that the agents may lose communication and need to get back in touch, s/he might choose to provide them with a mechanism as described below. Since s/he doesn't know the exact details of their environment, the coordination policy can't make use of instructions like "go to the highest building," since there may not be a unique building that satisfies the criterion.

The important point here is that the designer wants to use as little prior information as possible to aid the agents' coordination, but some prior information (e.g., the existence of certain predicates) might still be required by a focal point algorithm. This is not an unreasonable demand. For example, the fact that the agents have certain sensors to which they have access mirrors the prior existence of predicates that can be used in a focal point algorithm.

Algorithm 1 Joint selection of an object using focal points

1. *Calculate the focal point value for all objects $i \in Term$ using the following equation:*

$$F(i) = \sum_{P \in Pred} R_i^P + 0.5 * E_i^{P,\leq,>} \tag{1}$$

where R_i^P is the rarity of i with respect to predicate P, i.e., how rare is the value of i relative to the other objects, and E_i^P is the extremeness of i with respect to predicate P, i.e., how close (relative to the other objects) is the value of i to one of the extreme values that predicate P takes in this particular world.[5] *Formally, assume $P(i,x)$; then,*

$$R_i^P = \frac{100}{|\{i' | P(i',x) \text{ is true in this world}\}|} \tag{2}$$

Suppose we have $P(i,x)$, the order on $Value_P$ denoted by $\leq$ and $>$, and let $MAX(i,P)$ be the largest of the following numbers: (1) number of objects that have the value x or less for predicate P; (2) number of objects that have a value greater than x for predicate P. Then we have

$$E_i^{P,\leq,>} = \frac{100 MAX(i,P)}{|Term|} \tag{3}$$

2. *Choose the object c with the largest value that is unique in having that value. Formally, let $UFP = \{i | i \in Term, \forall i' \in Term, \text{ if } i' \neq i \text{ then } F(i) \neq F(i')\}$. If $UFP \neq \emptyset$ then $c = argmax_{i \in UFP} F(i)$.*

There are several aspects of the algorithm that were chosen arbitrarily.[6] To normalize the values calculated, an arbitrary factor of 100 was chosen. The extremeness property was given a lower weight (0.5 in Equation 1), because it seemed to be intuitively weaker than the rarity property. Most importantly, the definitions of the rarity and extremeness properties are arbitrary.

Another problem we faced in creating this algorithm was the relative weight of the different predicates. Since we chose to assume the maximum possible flexibility in the internal representation of the agents, we couldn't assume that agents would identify the predicates in a similar manner. The solution, as mirrored in the formula, was to give equal weight to all the predicates.

[4] The algorithm is also useful, if the agents were designed by *different* designers, and they agreed by prior communication to use this algorithm.

[5] E_i^P is only calculated if there is an order on the values of the predicate P.

[6] It is important to emphasize that there is no unique "focal point algorithm"; rather, there are many algorithms that might make use of the basic focal point idea, as presented above (the identification and use of "prominent" objects to heuristically aid coordination).

Example

Suppose there are five objects in the world and three predicates: Type, Size and Color. The values of the predicates with respect to the objects are given in the following table.

object	type	size	color
1	1 (=bridge)	1 (=small)	1 (=red)
2	1 (=bridge)	2 (=big)	2 (=blue)
3	2 (=house)	1 (=small)	1 (=red)
4	2 (=house)	2 (=big)	3 (=brown)
5	2 (=house)	3 (=huge)	3 (=brown)

Some examples of how one would calculate the extremeness and rarity values:

E_1^{type} = Not relevant $\qquad R_1^{type} = \frac{100}{2} = 50$

$E_1^{size,\leq,>} = 100 * \frac{3}{5} = 60 \qquad R_1^{size} = \frac{100}{2} = 50$

The general formula for calculating the focal point value in this example is: $F(i) = R_i^{type} + .5 * E_i^{type,\leq,>} + R_i^{size} + .5 * E_i^{size,\leq,>} + R_i^{color} + .5 * E_i^{color,\leq,>}$. See Figure 1.

Thus, the agents choose the big blue bridge, i.e., Object 2, which has the largest unique focal point number.[7]

Properties of the Algorithm

The focal point algorithm described above has the following properties:

Success Rate:
The high success rate of the algorithm is demonstrated in the section "Results" below.

Front End:
If the focal point algorithm succeeds (i.e., $UFP \neq \emptyset$), the agents will definitely meet. That is, both agents, when choosing the object according to the algorithm, *know* that the other agent will choose the same object, too. That is the simplest case. In the rare cases that the focal point algorithm fails, both agents know that it failed (also common knowledge), and so this algorithm can be used as a front end for any other coordination algorithm.

Simplicity and Intuitiveness
The algorithm is simple to describe, which is important in case it needs to be transmitted in a noisy environment (e.g., just before communication cut-off). In addition, the algorithm resembles human thought processes, which can help in communicating between man and machine.

Complexity of the Algorithm:
One of the advantages of the focal point algorithm is its low complexity:

Lemma 1 *Given a set of objects Term and a set of predicates Pred, the complexity of Algorithm 1 is* $O(|Term| * Max(|Pred|, Log(|Term|)))$.

Domain Independence:
The algorithm is applicable in any domain where there are objects, predicates, and the need to choose one of the objects.

Independence of Agents' Internal Representations:
All agents must have sets of objects, predicates, and values for the predicates. However, the agents may have different names for objects, predicates and values. For example, one agent might see a big house and a little house, i.e., $Size(1, big)$ and $Size(2, little)$ while, the other agent sees a medium sized house $Size(1, medium)$ and a small house respectively $Size(2, small)$. Furthermore, agents may have different names for the houses, i.e., the first agent may denote the big house by 1 and the small house by 2, and the second agent may call them 2 and 1 respectively. They may also use different terminology internally; the first agent may use the concept of "house" and the second the concept of "building."

Description of the Simulations

A *configuration* of the world included the number of objects, and the number of predicates, in the world. In each run of the simulation, a new random world was created, by giving new values to the predicates. First, the number of values that a predicate could take was randomly chosen from the range 2–20. Second, the values were generated for each predicate/object pair. The third step was to calculate the focal point value for each object, as described by Algorithm 1. Finally, if there was an object with a unique focal point value, the run was considered a success; otherwise, it was a failure.

To make the simulations computationally tractable, we assumed that the world contained up to 19 objects, that there were up to 9 orthogonal predicates, and that each predicate had up to 20 different possible values.

For each configuration, 500 runs over random worlds were simulated, giving a calculated accuracy of 5% (with 95% probability (Devore 1991) [Section 7]). The final output of 500 runs for each configuration was a number between 0 and 100 that represented the probability of finding an object with a unique focal point value in a random world with the parameters described above. That is, the number represented the probability that the agents will be in a world such that they *definitely* meet when they use the focal point mechanism.[8]

We conducted many sets of simulations. In each set of simulations, we varied some aspect of the world (such as the distribution of the values of predicates and the homogeneity of the world) so as to cover a variety of situations in which agents might find themselves.

In this paper we present in detail only two sets of simulations. These simulations, while quite abstract,

[7] Note that in this case all the objects belong to the the set UFP that is defined in Algorithm 1, however, Object 2 is the one that has the largest value.

[8] This in no way depends on the number of agents in the world.

Object	R_i^{type}	E_i^{type}	R_i^{size}	$E_i^{size,\leq,>}$	R_i^{color}	$E_i^{color,\leq,>}$	F(i)
1	50	0	50	60	50	0	180
2	50	0	50	80	100	0	240
3	33	0	50	60	50	0	163
4	33	0	50	80	50	0	173
5	33	0	100	100	50	0	233

Figure 1:

cover wide variations of possible (real) worlds. The first set of simulations was chosen to show that the algorithm works in cases that are similar to our expectations regarding the nature of predicates in the real world. The second set of simulations was chosen to show that the algorithm works even if the representations that the agents (respectively) use for the world are so different that the only common information they can use is whether two values are equal or not.

A. Different number of values, binomial and dependency distribution, ordered values:

In this set of simulations, the world had the following details (in addition to the general structure described above):
1. The possible values in the world were distributed using a binomial distribution.
2. Some of the predicates were statistically dependent on other predicates. For example, most trees are green, and only very few are blue.
3. The predicates' values were ordered.
The dependency among predicates was defined as follows: we chose randomly[9] $\frac{1}{3}$ of the predicates to be dependent on the predicates before them, in the following manner. Assume $P_j(x, v_j)$ and $P_{j+1}(x, v_{j+1})$; then $v_j = \lfloor \frac{v_{j-1}}{3} \rfloor + r$ where r was randomly chosen between 0 and 1.

B. Different number of values, even distribution, non-ordered:

In this set of simulations, the world had the following details (in addition to the general structure described above):
1. The possible values in the world were evenly distributed.
2. No predicate was statistically dependent on other predicates.
3. The predicates did not have an internal order: given two different values for a predicate, the agents could not assign an order to them, they could only distinguish between them. For example, consider the predicate *type*. The values "table" and "chair" could not be ordered, but the agents could tell them apart. Therefore, when using the algorithm described above, the agents could not use the extremeness term, only the rarity term.
In all other respects, this set of simulations was similar to the previous one.

[9] In each run, different predicates were chosen.

Results

The results of cases A and B are presented in Figures 2 and 3 respectively. In these figures, the rows correspond to the number of objects in the tested configuration and the columns correspond to the number of predicates in the tested configuration.

In general, the results of the simulations show that the success rate of the algorithm was very high. For example, in case A (Figure 2) if there are at least 2 predicates and at least 3 objects in the configuration, then in more than 97% of the worlds, the algorithm will succeed. The only cases where there is a low success rate is when there is only one predicate or two objects in the configuration.[10]

In case B (Figure 3), where there is no order on the values of predicates in the configuration, if there are at least 4 predicates and at least 7 objects in the configuration, then in more than 94% of the worlds the algorithm will succeed. It is clear that when there are only two objects there is no way to choose one of them based only on rarity; therefore, we have the zeros in row 1 in Figure 3.[11] Also, when there is only one predicate the probability that the algorithm will succeed is very low.[12]

In general, the success rate of the algorithm rises as the number of predicates or objects increases in the world. However, when the number of predicates in the world is very small the success rate of the algorithm doesn't necessarily rise as the number of objects increases. It may be that with a small number of predicates this specific algorithm tends to repeat the same FP values for different objects, and therefore the chance of finding an object with a unique focal point value is relatively low.

[10] As we explained above, in these cases the agents may use a different algorithm to increase their probability of choosing the same object (see the section "Extension of the Algorithm to Probabilistic Choice" below for details).

[11] Recall that in case B the values of the predicates are not ordered, so that the extremeness term in the focal point formula in Algorithm 1 cannot be calculated.

[12] The chance of finding a unique object in a world that has only one predicate is obviously low.

No. of Objects	No. of Predicates								
	1	2	3	4	5	6	7	8	9
2	81	72	82	79	86	85	90	89	92
3	95	99	99	99	99	99	100	99	99
4	90	97	98	98	99	100	99	99	100
5	93	99	100	100	100	100	100	100	100
6	91	99	99	100	100	100	100	100	100
7	89	100	100	100	100	100	100	100	100
8	87	99	100	100	100	100	100	100	100
9	87	99	100	100	100	100	100	100	100
10	89	99	100	100	100	100	100	100	100
11	87	100	100	100	100	100	100	100	100
12	84	100	100	100	100	100	100	100	100
13	85	100	100	100	100	100	100	100	100
14	82	100	100	100	100	100	100	100	100
15	83	99	100	100	100	100	100	100	100
16	80	99	100	100	100	100	100	100	100
17	84	100	100	100	100	100	100	100	100
18	78	99	100	100	100	100	100	100	100
19	78	99	100	100	100	100	100	100	100

Figure 2: Probability of Definitely Choosing the Same Object in Case A

Short Description of Other Experiments

As mentioned above, in addition to experiments A and B, many additional experiments were conducted. Some of these experiments are concisely described here.

Noise: Worlds with partial knowledge were modeled by adding random noise to one of the agent's information (before the addition of noise, the agents had the same knowledge, but used different representations). As can be expected, the algorithm does not perform as well in these cases as in cases A and B; however, it still performs much better that random choice.

Expanded range of values: In other experiments we explored the relationships between the number of values a predicate can have and the success rate of the algorithm. We discovered that in general the success rate of the focal point algorithm increases with the number of values that a predicate can receive. In addition, we discovered that even a small number of possible values was generally enough for a high success rate.

Exact knowledge: Another experiment was performed to test the added utility of using exact knowledge: both agents see the exact values of the predicates in the world. The probability of success in these cases was very similar to the success rate shown in this paper, although the chances of success are significantly higher when the number of objects, predicates, or possible values in the world, is very small.

Extension of the Algorithm to Probabilistic Choice: In previous sections, the focal point algorithm provided the agents with a mechanism for guaranteeing their common choice of the same object. However, even when the focal point algorithm fails, the information that it provides can be used to increase the probability of choosing the same object. The agents can look for the smallest set of objects such that their focal point value is the same (if there's more than one such set, they can choose the one with the largest focal point value) and then choose one of them randomly. Simulations we performed showed an increase in success rate over cases A and B.

Conclusions

We have presented the concept of focal point solutions to cooperation problems. An algorithm was presented for discovering unique focal points, and a series of simulations were run over various randomly generated worlds that demonstrated the usefulness of the focal point algorithm as a heuristic for multi-agent coordination.

The algorithm is shown to be successful in a wide variety of cases, including cases where the only information that the agents can use for their coordination is the non-ordered values of a few properties (predicates).

Acknowledgments

This research has been partially supported by the Israeli Ministry of Science and Technology (Grant 032-8284 and Grant 4210), by the Israel Science Foundation (Grant 032-7517), and by the National Science Foundation under Grant Number IRI-9311988.

References

Bond, A. H., and Gasser, L. 1988. An analysis of problems and research in DAI. In Bond, A. H., and

No. of Objects	No. of Predicates								
	1	2	3	4	5	6	7	8	9
2	0	0	0	0	0	0	0	0	0
3	31	54	68	77	80	87	88	91	91
4	8	33	42	55	62	71	75	82	82
5	17	55	76	86	90	93	94	97	97
6	9	49	68	81	88	93	95	96	98
7	11	65	88	94	97	98	98	99	100
8	9	61	82	96	97	99	99	99	100
9	10	80	92	99	99	99	99	100	100
10	10	75	92	98	99	99	100	100	100
11	11	81	97	99	99	100	100	100	100
12	12	80	97	99	100	100	100	100	100
13	11	86	99	99	100	100	100	100	100
14	11	83	97	99	100	100	100	100	100
15	11	89	99	99	100	100	100	100	100
16	12	87	99	100	100	100	100	100	100
17	12	92	100	100	100	100	100	100	100
18	10	90	99	100	100	100	100	100	100
19	10	92	100	100	100	100	100	100	100

Figure 3: Probability of Definitely Choosing the Same Object in Case of Different Number of Values, Even Distribution (B), Non-Ordered Values

Gasser, L., eds., *Readings in Distributed Artificial Intelligence.* San Mateo, California: Morgan Kaufmann. chapter 1, 3–56.

Devore, J. L. 1991. *Probability and Statistics for Engineering and Sciences.* Pacific Grove, California: Brooks/Cole Publishing Company.

Genesereth, M. R.; Ginsberg, M. L.; and Rosenschein, J. S. 1986. Cooperation without communication. In *Proceedings of The National Conference on Artificial Intelligence*, 51–57.

Kraus, S., and Rosenschein, J. S. 1992. The role of representation in interaction: Discovering focal points among alternative solutions. In *Decentralized AI, Volume 3.* Amsterdam: Elsevier Science Publishers B.V./North-Holland.

Levy, R., and Rosenschein, J. S. 1992. A game theoretic approach to distributed artificial intelligence and the pursuit problem. In *Decentralized Artificial Intelligence III.* Amsterdam: Elsevier Science Publishers B.V./North-Holland. 129–146.

Rasmusen, E. 1989. *Games and Information.* Cambridge, Ma: Basil Blackwell Ltd.

Schelling, T. C. 1963. *The Strategy of Conflict.* New York: Oxford University Press.

4.3 Social Agency

Social conceptions of knowledge and action: DAI foundations and open systems semantics

Les Gasser

Distributed Artificial Intelligence Group, Computer Science Department, University of Southern California, Los Angeles, CA 90089-0782, USA

Received January 1990
Revised July 1990

Abstract

Gasser, L., Social concepts of knowledge and action: DAI foundations and open systems semantics, Artificial Intelligence 47 (1991) 107–138.

This article discusses foundations for Distributed Artificial Intelligence (DAI), with a particular critical analysis of Hewitt's *Open Information Systems Semantics* (OISS). The article sets out to do five things:

- It presents a brief overview of current DAI research including motivations and concepts, and discusses some of the basic problems in DAI.
- It introduces several principles that underly a fundamentally multi-agent (i.e., *social*) conception of action and knowledge for DAI research. These principles are introduced to provide definitions, to delimit the discussion of OISS and as background against which to assess its contributions.
- It analyzes the main points of OISS in relation to these principles.
- It shows how attention to these principles can strengthen OISS approach to foundations for DAI.
- It traces some of the implications of this synthesis for theorizing and system-building in AI.

The OISS approach productively challenges some conceptions of knowledge, reasoning, and action in classical AI research. However, it sometimes ignores the sophistication and richness of contemporary DAI research. Several of the key concepts of OISS are not clearly enough defined or operationalized, and the article points out several ways to strengthen the OISS approach.

1. Introduction

All real systems are distributed
F. Hayes-Roth [20]

Artificial intelligence research is fundamentally concerned with the intelligent behavior of machines. In attempting to create machines with some degree of intelligent behavior, AI researchers model, theorize about, predict, and emulate the activities of people. Because people are quite apparently social actors, and also because knowledgeable machines will increasingly be embedded in organizations comprising people and other machines, AI research should be concerned with the social dimensions of action and knowledge as a fundamental category of analysis. But current AI research is largely *a-social*, and because of this, it has been inadequate in dealing with much human behavior and many aspects of intelligence.

In most contemporary AI research and practice, the unit of analysis and of development is a computational process with a single locus of control, focus of attention, and base of knowledge—a process organization inherited from von Neumann computer architectures and from psychology. While it is becoming easier to implement such a process as a concurrent system using an underlying distributed processing layer or a parallel language (such as concurrent PROLOG or LISP) the basic mechanisms of reasoning and problem solving generally remain bound to a single, monolithic conception of knowledge and action. Recently, however, there has been a revival of interest in approaches to analyzing and developing intelligent "communities" which comprise *collections of interacting, coordinated knowledge-based processes*. The body of research that deals with this problem-level concurrency in AI systems has come to be known as *distributed artificial intelligence* (DAI). Researchers in DAI are concerned with understanding and modeling action and knowledge in collaborative enterprises.

DAI research provides a very rich ground for re-examining some of the premises and formalisms upon which notions such as representation and reasoning, or knowledge and action, are classically located. This article analyzes open information systems semantics (OISS) from the standpoint of contemporary research in DAI, and inherently *social* conceptions of knowledge and action (actually, *interaction*). For a statement of OISS we draw mostly upon [48], which is the most recent statement in a larger coherent body of research. Since a short discussion of elements of this larger body is presented in the appendix of that paper, we also occasionally draw on [45–47, 49, 57].

We will present this investigation in several parts. First, since OISS has been proposed as a new foundation for DAI, but its differences from existing DAI foundations and research are not apparent, we briefly examine contemporary research in "classical" DAI. Following that, we introduce some principles which are desiderata for an inherently social conception of knowledge and action, consistent with the premises of open DAI systems. Next, to examine the impact of OISS, we examine it in the light of these principles and current DAI research. Finally, we discuss several ways to strengthen and extend OISS.

0004-3702/91/$03.50

2. The current state of DAI research

There are many reasons for wanting to distribute intelligence or cope with multi-agent systems. In some domains (e.g., distributed sensing, medical diagnosis, air-traffic control), knowledge or activity is inherently spatially distributed. The distribution can arise because of geographic distribution coupled with processing or data bandwidth limitations, because of the natural functional distribution in a problem, because of a desire to distribute control (e.g., for fail-soft degradation), or for modular knowledge acquisition. Other reasons for distribution include adaptability, reduced cost, ease of development and management, increased efficiency or speed, history, needs for isolation or autonomy, naturalness, increased reliability, resource limitations, and specialization. Opportunity is a second reason for studying DAI systems. Hardware and software mechanisms for distributing and controlling the interaction of multiple processes have begun to reach maturity, in both shared-memory and distributed-memory multicomputer ensembles. Third, there is interest in integrating existing AI systems to gain power and to leverage capability, which necessarily means coping with problems of discrepancies in representation and design. Fourth, problems are sometimes simply too large or complex to solve by single processes, for reasons of semantic representation as well as computational power; distributed approaches may provide solutions. Finally, it is an empirical observation that most[1] human activity involves more than one person. As researchers have tried to understand and model human problem solving and intelligent behavior, they have begun to take this observation more seriously as a foundation for theories (see, e.g., [11, 94]).

Research in DAI promises to have wide-ranging impacts in basic AI research (problem representations, epistemology, joint concept formation, collaborative reasoning and problem solving), cognitive science (mental models, social cognition), distributed systems (reasoning about knowledge and actions in distributed systems, architectural and language support for DAI), the engineering of AI systems ("cooperating expert systems", distributed sensing and data fusion, cooperating robots, collaborative design problem solving, etc.), and human–computer interaction (task allocation, intelligent interfaces, dialogue coherence, speech acts). As Nilsson has pointed out [20], DAI research is attractive for fundamental reasons: to coordinate their actions, intelligent agents need to represent and reason about the knowledge, actions, and plans of other agents. DAI research can help to improve techniques for representing and using knowledge about beliefs, action, plans, goals, etc., as well as helping us to discover the extent to which, when analyzed *from the outside in*—from the social to the individual—these concepts are useful or necessary.

[1] Or rather, all—cf. "taking the role of the other" in [77].

2.1. *Basic research problems in DAI literature*

Since OISS proposes to create new foundations for DAI, what are the existing foundations, and how adequate are they? In characterizing the recent state of DAI research, Bond and Gasser developed six basic problems that current DAI systems had begun to address [8]. These six problems are inherent to the design and implementation of any system of coordinated problem solvers, whether in open or closed worlds.

Here we give a brief exposition of these problems, each of which appears in some form in all DAI application domains. Greater detail and more citations can be found in [9, 37]. The problems include:

- *How to formulate, describe, decompose, and allocate problems and synthesize results among a group of intelligent agents.* Most approaches to these issues rely on designers. Work on the Contract Net and DVMT systems has provided mechanisms for flexible decomposition and allocation [21, 25]. Many bases for decomposition have been suggested, including abstraction levels, functional, data, or control dependencies, and interaction density. Little work has been done on automated problem formulation and description, but see [50].
- *How to enable agents to communicate and interact: what communication languages or protocols to use, and what and when to communicate.* The major approaches here include formalized interaction and negotiation protocols such as the Contact Net protocol and partial global plans (PGPs) [25, 85], Lenat's scheme based on common agent structures, and planned communications based on reasoning about the knowledge states of agents [16, 81].
- *How to ensure that agents act coherently in making decisions or taking action, accommodating the nonlocal effects of local decisions and avoiding harmful interactions.* This has been treated as the major problem of DAI research. Primary approaches include establishing organization, improving local awareness and skill [27], multi-agent planning [40], abstraction, and resource-directed coherence [57].
- *How to enable individual agents to represent and reason about the actions, plans, and knowledge of other agents in order to coordinate with them; how to reason about the state of their coordinated process (e.g., initiation and termination).* Principal approaches include the use of utility theory and game theory to represent rational choice [82], symbolic models of agents' capabilities and roles [36], belief models [14], and graph models of organizational relationships [25, 94]. Approaches to system behavioral modeling and analysis have been presented in [52].
- *How to recognize and reconcile disparate viewpoints and conflicting intentions among a collection of agents trying to coordinate their actions.* Main approaches include assumption surfacing using ATMS techniques [74],

parallel falsification and microtheories [47, 57], partial global planning [25], knowledgeable mediation, standardization, and various approaches to negotiation [26, 83, 92]. Star [89] provides another promising characterization based on malleable "boundary objects" with dual semantics.
- *How to engineer and construct practical DAI systems*; *how to design technology platforms and development methodologies for DAI.* Numerous technology platforms have been built, including testbeds such as the DVMT [27] and MACE [36]; integrative systems such as ABE [28], reflective, concurrent object-based languages such as Mering-IV [29], and blackboard or distributed blackboard systems such as GBB [19], BB1 [44], CAGE/POLIGON [79], etc.

Solutions to these problems are intertwined. For example, different procedures for communication and interaction have implications for coordination and coherent behavior. Different problem and task decompositions may yield different interaction or agent-modeling requirements. Coherent, coordinated behavior depends on how knowledge disparities are resolved, which agents resolve them, and so on.

Solving these problems in a fundamental way is quite complicated. Some of the basic DAI problems (e.g., some problems of disparate representations) can be designed away in a carefully engineered DAI system, by analyzing key questions such as what kinds of communication protocols to use, which conflicts are to be settled by people outside the system and which are to be handled autonomously by the system itself, how different conflicts interact, and how their settlement will be coordinated. In any case, we reveal the current foundations of DAI by examining how researchers have stated and solved these problems.

While these six problems appear widely in the literature, most extant theoretical and experimental solutions to them go only part way toward a basic scientific account of multi-agent collaboration, because they have not grappled with several other more basic issues. Virtually all current approaches to these problems are based on common interagent semantics with at most one or two meta- or contextual levels, correspondence theories of representation and belief, global measures of coherence, and the individual agent as the unit of analysis and interaction. Most DAI experiments and theories depend upon closed-system assumptions such as common communication protocols, a shared global means of assessing coherent behavior, some ultimate commensurability of knowledge, or some boundary to a system. While the six problems presented above still provide much fruitful ground for study, solving them still would not provide an adequate foundation for DAI. To make substantial theoretical progress, we must begin to lay firm social foundations for DAI research. As a framework in which to analyze the OISS proposal and its decentralized foundations, let us discuss some desiderata of a social framework for DAI.

3. Social conceptions of knowledge and action for AI and DAI

DAI systems, as they involve multiple agents, are *social* in character; there are properties of DAI systems which will not be derivable or representable solely on the basis of properties of their component agents. We need to begin to think through and articulate the bases of knowledge and action for DAI in the light of their social character. Here, we suggest and briefly discuss several principles that ought to underly the scientific and conceptual foundations for DAI systems from a social perspective. Since theories that support the construction of DAI systems ought to follow these principles, we will use the principles as a framework for analyzing OISS claims.

Principle 1. AI research must set its foundations in ways that treat the existence and interaction of multiple actors as a fundamental category.

Since we observe and actually are building multi-agent systems, we should investigate how to conceive aspects of representation and reasoning as fundamentally grounded in multi-agent systems. This leads directly to a serious research question for AI, namely:

> How can we usefully conceptualize representation, reasoning, problem solving and action, when we begin with multiple participants?

A social perspective on the nature of intelligent behavior is not a new idea. For example, Mead stated [77]

> We are not, in social psychology, building up the behavior of the social group in terms of the behavior of the separate individuals composing it; rather we are starting with a given social whole of complex group activity, into which we analyze (as elements) the behavior of each of the separate individuals composing it. We attempt, that is, to explain the conduct of the individual in terms of the organized conduct of the social group, rather than to account for the organized conduct of the social group in terms of the conduct of the separate individuals belonging to it. For social psychology, the whole (society) is prior to the part (the individual), not the part to the whole; and the part is explained in terms of the whole, not the whole in terms of the parts.

The traditional set of analytical categories and implementation techniques used in AI does not include fundamentally social elements; the focus is on the individual actor as the locus of reasoning and knowledge and the individual proposition as the object of truth and knowing. For example, a number of researchers are studying *commitment*, a basic concept in OISS, as a foundation of many concepts in AI and DAI, including intentions and goals, negotiation, and knowledge [7, 14, 15, 30, 96]. The research literature most often portrays commitment as a kind of rational choice made by an individual actor. Along these lines, Cohen and Levesque [14, 15] have developed a notion of commitment based on what they call a *relativized persistent goal*. Some agent A relativizes its goal g to a predicate q, so that A gives up g only when A believes that either something has satisfied g, or nothing can satisfy g, or $\neg q$. To use one of Cohen and Levesque's examples, when rain is falling, A may reason that it will be committed to the goal of getting an umbrella unless it believes that (1) it has obtained an umbrella, or (2) it cannot get an umbrella, or (3) the rain has stopped and it no longer needs an umbrella. They state that "Persistence involves an agent's *internal* commitment over time to her choices. . . . This is not a *social* commitment; it remains to be seen *if the latter can be built out of the former*" [14, p. 410] (final italics mine).

Symbolic interactionist sociologists, and authors of recent investigations in the sociology of science, have begun to provide some conceptually fruitful, though not presently computational, approaches for understanding knowledge and action in social terms. (See [13] for an illuminating review, and [18, 87] for discussions directly related to AI.) In contrast to Cohen and Levesque, for example, Becker [4] and especially Gerson [41] develop commitment as the overall organization of an agent's participation in many settings simultaneously. For example, imagine that a Los Angeles industrialist takes off in an airplane from Narita airport, bound for California, after formulating preliminary business deals in Tokyo and telephoning her associates in Los Angeles. While flying, she is participating in many settings simultaneously: the activity in the plane, the ongoing business negotiations in Tokyo and in Los Angeles (where people are planning for her arrival and making business judgements while considering her views, even in her absence).[2] Her simultaneous involvement in interlocking courses of action in all of these situations provides the commitment to her arrival in Calfornia. Both she and others balance and trade off her involvement in joint courses of action in many different situations. Moreover, whether she makes a choice or not, she is committed to landing in LA because the plane is not in her control. Her commitments in any of these settings *amount to* the interaction of many activities of many agents in many other settings. Since this multi-setting participation occurs *simultaneously* in many places, it can't be located simply to where she physically "is". In other words, the notion of commitment is distributed because the agent of commitment—"she"—is a distributed entity.

This approach rests on a somewhat untraditional idea of what an agent is: in Gerson's formulation, an agent A is a reflexive collection of processes involved in many situations. To varying degrees, the agent—that is, some component process of the agent—can take on the viewpoint of any participant in those situations. Commitment of A (i.e., continued participation of A) in a course of action in any particular setting is a product of the interactions among its simultaneous participations in many other settings—*whether* A *explicitly "knows" fully about the other settings beforehand or not*. Thus, if A has goals, they can't be effectively "relativized" because the relativizing conditions that would make A's goals contingent can't necessarily be known beforehand (a version of the qualification problem [76]). Moreover, since continued participation is distributed and simultaneous, it isn't based on localized, individual choices and goals.

In the umbrella case, from the social perspective, an infinite variety of circumstances may arise under which A's participation in other settings could change A's participation in the umbrella-getting course of action; at any time, some other agent could act in a way such that A is no longer a participant in that course (in simple cases, A could get hit by a car or unplugged); this presents problems for Cohen and Levesque's notion of commitment. Commitment from the social perspective is grounded in the actions of many agents' activities *taken together*—it is not a matter of individual choice. It is A's actions in relation to those of others (and vice versa) that maintain A's participation in a course of action (e.g., by providing resources, etc.—see below). Commitment in this sense is the outcome of a web of activity, or in OISS terms, it is "systems commitment".

Moreover, this social notion of commitment doesn't rely upon a more-primitive mental concept such as "belief" or "goal" (this is how it unifies the individual and the social). In fact, this notion of commitment cannot be grounded on individual belief or choice, because it is not located "within" the individual. Because of this, it extends in varying degrees to objects as well as people as active participants in settings, and to multiple levels of analysis. For example, for the industrialist to call Los Angeles from a coin-operated telephone, both she and a telephone system must together enter into a course of action that involves consuming coins, providing dial tones, and so on. *They are mutually committed to doing those things in that way to make a phone call*, regardless of whether she or the telephone has any mental state such as a state of belief, or any shared view of the situation. (A self-dialing modem can make phone calls. Does a telephone have a viewpoint to share?). The industrialist's other commitments (e.g., in the business deals) are simultaneously mediated by the actions of the telephone—and of course of the whole telephone network and organizations behind it: waiting time, missed connections, etc. (cf. [75]).

Many other concepts which are basic to AI researchers and AI programs, and typically (in AI) associated with individual actors or problem solvers, are, in sociological terms, reifications, constructed through joint courses of action and *made* stable by webs of commitment [4, 41], or "alliances" [60, 61] among

[2] Of course we leave out many, many others—her family, etc.—including some she may not be aware of.

the actors using them. Some examples include concepts such as *problems* [32], *knowledge* [5, 13, 63], *facts* about the world [62], and even technical objects [53]. From this perspective, stable alliances or systems of commitment even produce the demarcation and ongoing existence of individual agents as units of knowledge and interaction. In the case of people, for example, alliances among cells, chemical processes, and the environment at the lowest levels and among social actors at the more macro levels (e.g., organizations such as hospitals) yield stable and ongoing individuals.[3] In a computational intelligent agent, such a web includes (at least) the structure of the computing system and all that keeps it running "properly", including the program, the evolving content of its data stuctures (e.g., a set of represented propositional beliefs), the language processor, the hardware and the resources and activity (electricity, maintenance, and so on) that keep it active over time (cf. [56]). This is as true of a connectionist system as of a symbolic one. Perhaps the nature of this idea of alliances, and the conception of both agents and knowledge as stable systems of alliance, are easier to see if we examine what it takes to remove an agent's influence in a situation (e.g., by disabling it or discrediting its knowledge). What alliances must be broken? Actually it can be fairly simple—unplug the machine; or change the operational semantics of its program e.g., by changing the operating system, language processor, or hardware [84]; or change the behavior of another agent upon which it critically relies; or change the definition of a set of possible worlds which establishes the semantics of a proposition in its belief set.

Treating problems, knowledge, and facts as webs of commitment is a fundamentally non-local, distributed conception. Like conventional AI conceptions, such distributed conceptions account for change in knowledge and world states. They have the additional advantage of accounting for the stability and robustness of facts or agents or procedures in the face of challenges posed by alternative viewpoints or discrediting activities (sometimes known as "brittleness"), and for what OISS calls the indeterminate nature of systems.

Certain existing approaches to overcoming brittleness are theoretically problematic. For example, TMS/ATMS systems and belief networks, which do locate belief in a network of supporting evidence, rely on unwinding of assumptions and the posing of incommensurate alternative worlds or contexts—but they cannot account for how to resolve inconsistency at the assumption levels; these are battles that agents resolve outside the system. They rely on the option of keeping alternatives separate, until some unifying viewpoint or discriminating facts appear from some external source. They also don't allow for nth-order flexibility or robustness—e.g. in the choice of world representations, proof theories, etc., and they are subject to deductive indeterminacy, as the OISS proposal points out.

Principle 2. DAI theory and practice must address the basic tension between the local, situated, and pragmatic character of knowledge and action, and the ways in which knowledge and action necessarily implicate multiple contexts.

The notion that the meaning of a message is the response it generates in the system that receives it was introduced by Mead (see, e.g., [77, Chapter 11]) and was later used independently in the context of computing by Hewitt [45]. Using this conceptualization, a message that provokes no response has no meaning, and each message with impact has a *specific* meaning, played out as a set of specific response behaviors. In an asynchronous and open distributed system, no message can be guaranteed to lead to the same set of behaviors twice. Thus knowledge in an open system always means something local and situated. (See also [3, 63, 91].) As to the implications for action, actors take actions (including reasoning and planning actions) at specific times and places with specific (but of course possibly selective, incomplete, faulty, etc.) knowledge brought to bear. In a sense *action is a particular commitment to doing things a particular way*—a way conditional upon the actor's particular knowledge in and of the situation of the action (cf. [78]).

It seems, however, that some sort of generalization across situations is what makes knowledge useful and what ultimately makes knowledge knowledge. General knowledge makes possible *action-at-a-distance*:[4] reasoning about and taking control over activity located at some other place in space or time such as the future, another network site, or over actions taken by another agent—in other words, acting in a distributed fashion. There is, then, a basic tension between a local, "situated" conception of knowledge and action, and the non-local conception of action-at-a-distance. It appears that the ability to generalize across situations and the utility of doing so makes knowledge inherently *non*-local. The knowledge is derived from and can apply in many situations.

Still, any general knowledge, to be useful, has to *be applied* in a local setting, hence *made local* again. Generalization leads to transportability across contexts, and thus helps in achieving action-at-a-distance, but does not obviate the need for reintegration into a local context of use. A production rule with variables exemplifies transportability. Variables make the rule applicable in any setting where they can be bound. Such a rule is useless with variables unbound;[5] binding variables specializes the rule into a specific *rule instantia-*

[3] The issue is the nature of the individual as the locus of interaction and knowledge. Bentley [6] and Dewey [24] lay out the problems well; Buss [10] and Wimsatt [95] discuss evolutionary changes in biological units of selection from cells to higher-order aggregates and MacFarlane [71] discusses transformations of units of knowledge, action, and ownership from the social to the individual in English history.

[4] In general, "distance" here refers to some axis of distribution. Bond [8] discusses numerous axes of distribution in this sense, including space, time, and semantics.

[5] Except of course when used itself as an object of discourse; it then becomes a localized and concrete representation employed in a higher-order (meta) process.

tion, i.e. makes it local and specific again. Moreover, the localization process itself (e.g., the binding of variables) is another purely local and situated process.

Principle 3. Representation and reasoning approaches used in DAI must (1) assume that multiple representations are recursively possible at any level of analysis or action, (2) assume that actors will employ multiple representations individually and collectively, and (3) provide mechanisms for reasoning among multiple representations.

In order to understand fully the implications of the OISS analysis on the limits of deduction, we need to understand the character of what we usually view as "shared" knowledge. This is important, for example, in understanding the nature of contradiction, a concept crucial to several OISS arguments. Shared knowledge, as I think we normally conceive it,[6] is impossible; nonetheless, we have ways of pragmatically aligning our activities and acting *as though* we share knowledge (see, e.g., [91]). The difference becomes an issue precisely when conflict arises, and appeals to shared knowledge are inadequate both to explain the nature of and to resolve conflicts. Approaches to conflict that rely on logical formulations necessarily require a common semantics even to decide that conflict exists. Conflict means inconsistency and inconsistency is impossible without a common model. In an open DAI system without a priori assumptions of globality, we need another definition of conflict. The choices we have come down to conflict in action and more specifically conflict in the consumption of resources, not just conflict in representations.

Different actors necessarily have different sets of commitments, by virtue of their different histories, the different resources they use, different settings they participate in, and so on. Multiple perspectives are a fundamental feature of any multi-agent system, simply by virtue of differing commitment histories and local circumstances. The interesting phenomenon, then, would be any apparent *commonality of perspectives* or mutually aligned, mutually supportive commitments—how would they get and stay that way [35]?

If multiple perspectives are basic, disparities in perspectives are an issue. Elsewhere, we have posed this issue as a basic problem for DAI, because of its theoretical consequence and its ubiquity in DAI research [8, 37]. Moreover, multiplicity of perspectives raises the issue of the impossibility of global conceptions. As Star points out in her study of the development of a localization theory of the brain by a community of scientists [88, p. 193]:[7]

> The momentum of the theory, professional developments, turf battles between specialists and general practitioners, and the rise of specialty hospitals with their separate domains of expertise made the theory impossible to comprehend from any single point.

In effect, what the scientists involved talked about as "a theory" was in fact multiple theories by virtue of the multiple perspectives brought to the activity of expressing and understanding it.

Principle 4. DAI theory and practice must account for resource-limited activity.

All resources are limited, and real agents act in finite circumstances. Resources used by a collection of agents can be arranged and allocated in numerous ways, but the resources used to allocate resources are also limited, and in the end agents do take particular actions. "Optimal" resource allocations are in general not possible, for at least four reasons: (1) computing an optimal allocation might require infinite resources, (2) allocation actions must be taken opportunistically in a dynamic world, (3) there is no limit to how completely an allocation decision situation can be specified, and (4) agents might not agree on criteria for optimality. Moreover, no agent supplies all of its own resources. Resource allocations are the *product* of interactions of many agents, and at the same time resources serve as a key *channel* of interaction among agents—as one agent uses up a resource, others' options are restricted. Thus a complete DAI theory must integrate a treatment of limited resources with a treatment of joint actions of multiple agents.

Principle 5. DAI theory and practice must provide accounts of and mechanisms for handling the three key problems of joint qualification, representation incommensurability and failure indeterminacy.

The impossibility of fully specifying the assumptions behind a characterization of any situation, has been termed the *qualification problem* by McCarthy [76]. Given this, DAI theories must account for how agents can come to have and to act upon *mutually compatible* sets of assumptions (e.g., common defaults) in the face of partial descriptions and no global semantics. That is, how can agents leave compatible aspects of a situation unquestioned or unsupported—what accounts for how they can "stay out of each others' way" when they do? No agent can fully describe its assumptions to another, yet they must mutually take some things for granted to act jointly without conflict (see, e.g., [91]). This can be called the *joint qualification problem*, and a full DAI theory must account for it.

In the face of the assumption incompleteness, no agent can fully specify the semantics of its representations. If this is so, how are two agents to determine

[6] I.e., as several agents knowing the *same fact* interpreted the *same way*—what would this mean, and how would the agents ever be able to verify it? Cf. Principle 5.

[7] For an analysis of multiple perspectives over time, as well as over agents, see also Lakatos' study of the reconstruction of mathematical theorems in [59].

if they have the basis for joint action, or if they are in conflict? This can be called the problem of *representational incommensurability*. Bond and Gasser [8] discussed three types of disparity among agents' knowledge: incompleteness, inconsistency, and incompatibility. The first two are conventionally defined, and incompatibility referred to agents' representing the same situation with different kinds of descriptions. With incompatibility disparity, consistency could not be assessed. Incommensurability is a still deeper problem. Two agents in principle cannot have *identical* representations—any pair of similar representations can always be differentiated by more complete description. So on what basis can agents be sure that they either (1) have common (e.g., Tarskian or possible worlds) semantics (since the definition of a model or possible worlds would have to be global), or (2) common semantics based on our earlier theory of meaning as response of the system (because response can only be assessed from some particular perspective)?

Finally, when there has been some disparity at some level between two agents with different representations of the same situation, and this conflict leads to a failure of action, how are they to determine where the cause of the failure lies? For example, both Agre and Gasser have discussed the nature of agents' behavioral *routines* (Agre in the single-agent case [2], and Gasser for organized activity [35]). Suppose an agent A has a theory $\mathcal{T}$ of the routine behavior of another agent B. For example, $\mathcal{T}$ might be:

(1) If I send B a task announcement then B will reply with a bid request

Since this is a theory of a routine, it is necessarily an idealization—no routine behavior is actually carried out in precisely the same way twice [35]. Now suppose that to reason about B's behavior in a particular situation s, A qualifies or specializes $\mathcal{T}$ with some additional observations $\mathcal{I}$. (Since $\mathcal{T}$ is in idealization, $\mathcal{I}$ is necessary to make it fit s.) For example, since today is Monday and communication is via email, $\mathcal{I}$ might be:

(2) If today is Monday and bids are to be sent via email then (1)

$\mathcal{T}$ with $\mathcal{I}$ will lead to some prediction q about B's behavior:

Today is Monday
Bids are to be sent via email
I sent a task announcement to B
Thus:
q: B will reply with a bid

But suppose that A's observation q′ of B's behavior is inconsistent with q?:

q′: B does not reply with a bid

Does the problem lie with $\mathcal{T}$ or with $\mathcal{I}$?[8] (Perhaps B doesn't send bids to every task announcement, or perhaps it doesn't read email on Monday). The problem may even lie with the way $\mathcal{T}$ or $\mathcal{I}$ are interpreted in the situation (e.g., A got a message but was it a bid?). (Since interagent interaction is involved, the joint qualification and representation incommensurability problems also enter into the interpretive question.) The unfortunate problem seems to be that unless we already know that both the interpretive scheme and A's theory of B's routine are correct, A can't tell how to make them so because it can't deduce what failed—at least not using its own knowledge. This problem can be called the "failure indeterminacy" problem. It is the problem faced in any scientific experiment or court of law: Since the acceptability of a scientific theory depends on the experiment, and the experiment depends upon the apparatus, and the nature of the apparatus depends upon the theory, where is the source of experimental conviction? In court, is the defendant guilty or is the prosecution's theory wrong? Of course in either domain, like good distributed reasoners, we rely on many experiments and agreement among many participants, not just one—but this raises the joint qualification and representation incommensurability problems again [17, 62].

Principle 6. Overall, DAI theory and practice must account for how aggregates of agents can achieve joint courses of action that are robust and continuable (ongoing) despite indeterminate foulups, inconsistency, etc. which may occur recursively at any level of the system.

OISS raises the issue of self-reliance for DAI systems: how can agents preserve local autonomy (i.e. become robust to failure and challenge) while still drawing from and providing resources to the larger community? The first five principles above point to numerous possible sources of failure, discrepancy, and potentially indeterminate states of knowledge in which any agent in a multi-agent system can find itself. Principle 6 takes note of the fact that robust DAI systems that handle all of these contingencies do *exist*: many human social organizations as well as deeply embedded information systems (e.g., [35, 56, 75]). Any complete DAI theory must account for how this is possible and what the limits are; a complete set of mechanisms for DAI ought to provide us the capability to construct such systems within the limits.

4. DAI foundations and open systems semantics

With these principles in mind, then, let us move ahead to consider OISS as a proposed foundation for DAI. The OISS viewpoint has two primary compo-

[8] This exposition makes use of Laymon's argument on the difficulties of using experiments for drawing conclusions about the truth of scientific theories [64].

nents. One is an investigation of the *deductive indecision problem*, and the other is a characterization of open systems, and the nature of problem solving in them. A style of reasoning that elsewhere has been called *due process* [47], built from concepts such as trials of strength, commitments, and negotiations, glues these two together. We shall first discuss the nature of the overall OISS argument. Then we shall investigate how effectively the OISS proposal addresses the six principles presented in Section 3, contrasting the utility of the OISS approach with that of existing DAI research. The thread of the OISS argument is as follows:

(1) DAI research is concerned with work in large-scale open systems, but DAI does not yet have a clearly articulated vocabulary or common conceptual machinery. Open information systems semantics (OISS) can provide a useful and coherent set of concepts, some tractable research issues, a methodology, and a comparative vocabulary for DAI.
(2) DAI systems trade off the costs and benefits of *self-reliance*—the ability to take effective local action and to become robust against indeterminacy and conflict, with *interdependence*—contributing to the performance of the overall aggregate and drawing from it.
(3) "Deductive microtheories" are the primary competing foundation for DAI. Logical semantics are sufficient for reasoning in closed systems, and hence can be used as a foundation for reasoning within deductive microtheories. Problem solving in open systems involves interacting proposals founded in different microtheories. Different microtheories are generated and modified asynchronously, and involve differing commitments among their participants. Thus, logical and representational conflict is endemic to open systems. Logic is insufficient for reasoning in the presence of conflict and meta-conflict (i.e., conflict over the boundaries of decision making—e.g., circumscription axioms in [48]) and therefore for conflict resolution. Thus,
Conclusion 1. Because conflict is endemic, and logic is insufficient for processing under conflict, deductive microtheories are insufficient as a foundation for large-scale DAI in open systems (though they may be useful components).
(4) Alternative and more powerful foundations can be built upon the notions of *trials of strength* and *systems commitments*. Commitments are commitments because they are relatively stable or *robust* in the face of challenge or conflict.
(5) Constructing and exchanging "representations" is a basic activity; representation is not possible without communication. The "meaning" of a representation is defined to be the ways in which it modifies systems commitments.
(6) *Negotiations* (and other trials of strength) are the tools by which conflict is processed. Negotiations can occur recursively at many levels of analysis, have many potential outcomes, are inherently creative, and generate further commitments.
(7) *Conclusion* 2. Founding DAI in OISS is a different proposition from founding DAI in classical AI terms. OISS is inherently more "social", "grounded in large-scale information systems" rather than individual agents, and provides a different account of representation processes.

Up to Conclusion 1 the OISS argument is relatively strong, but within some narrow limits (which incidentally are left underspecified). It is not entirely true that DAI has failed to crystallize a common conceptual vocabulary, including a set of problems, methods, and terms. Section 2 presented a collection of these, gathered from a thorough examination of the DAI literature. Another very detailed proposal for a core set of DAI problems that coheres closely with those above can be found in [23]. With some exceptions the more basic principles presented in Section 3 above have not in general been fully artificulated or addressed in extant DAI research.

Some deeper questions are the extent to which DAI has been addressing the right set of problems at the right level of analysis, and how OISS may focus us on a different set of problems that is either more fundamental or that allows us to make better headway by changing our perspective. The implication of the OISS perspective seems to be that DAI has not chosen the appropriate set of problems. Deductive indeterminacy is clearly an issue that DAI research has certainly not openly considered until now, though other disciplines have addressed variants (see below). It is not properly subsumed in the six DAI problems of Section 2. The self-reliance/interdependence problem is a clearer and more encompassing notion than "global coherence with local control". But the only other problems posed (e.g., understanding negotiation, commitment, representation, etc.) are also precisely the set of concepts proposed as solutions, and the way they are to be woven together in a mutual foundation is unclear. There are several other key problems that must be addressed for a complete account of open DAI systems, including some of those discussed in several of the principles above. OISS actually does provide ways of thinking about them, but they are not clearly articulated as problems.

The observation that DAI is inherently concerned with work in large-scale open systems is only partially true; DAI certainly *should* be concerned with the question, but most contemporary researchers have had their hands full grappling with the (apparently) far simpler problems of coordination and performance of collections of agents under certain closure assumptions (see Section 2). An interesting open question, then, is what is the extent to which providing new foundations such as those of OISS will simplify the problems of knowledge and action in closed systems as well, and possibly go some distance toward eliminating the categories "open" and "closed".[9]

[9] Recent ferment in sociology, history, and philosophy of science is moving in precisely this direction. See, e.g., [17, 34, 42, 88, 93].

It is true that there has not been enough methodological clarity, debate or variety in DAI,[10] as has been pointed out in both [8] and [38]. But for many of the standard DAI problems, existing representation and experimentation methods have provided fruitful progress.[11] It is not entirely clear what the *methodology* of OISS is, or whether the OISS methodological focus is analytical or constructive. To what extent will it help us explain the behavior of existing DAI systems? How can a constructive methodology be built upon the explanatory theory? As an analytical theory, we are provided with a set of concepts but little guidance for how to go about finding instances, studying, comparing, or operationalizing them. Useful research methods for studying OISS questions analytically have been clearly articulated in sociology, upon which OISS has drawn for its concepts (e.g., [90]), but these or other such are not integrated into the current OISS approach as methods.

To the extent that OISS provides a mathematical or computational analysis, the Actor model for concurrent systems [1] is the chosen descriptive calculus, but at the moment, the connection is incomplete. There are three partially clear links from features of OISS to the descriptive machinery of the Actor model. *Actor configurations* are ways of providing local abstractions or closures, but are not clearly connected with OISS foundation concepts such as commitments or trials of strength. *Serializers* are one way of settling a trial of strength by arbitrating the handling of simultaneously arriving messages, and they do capture fundamental indeterminacy of open systems. *Replacement behaviors* give Actors both local autonomy and participation in joint enterprises, and thus help to address self-reliance issues. The relationship between the Actor model and other concepts such as negotiations, cooperation, commitments, etc. is not clear, and thus the formal descriptive power of OISS is currently limited.

In previous work, such features of open systems as arms-length relationships and asynchrony have been treated as the sources of difficult problems to be overcome. Now, from an OISS perspective, these also provide benefits for components of DAI systems. The notion of "self-reliance/interdependence" is used to capture the advantages and disadvantages of becoming more autonomous while somehow staying integrated with a larger community of agents. But the unit of analysis over which this self-reliance occurs is not clear—what is the self that is self-reliant? Is it a particular node in a system? If so, how are the boundaries of this node defined, by reference to a fundamentally distributed conception of knowledge and action? We can contrast the OISS notion of self-reliance to Gerson's concept of *sovereignty* which is [41, p. 798]:

> ... the overall organization of commitments associated with any delimitable social object ... the net balances of resources and constraints available to a person, organization, or other demarcatable group across the full range of settings in which he (or she, or it) participates.

Sovereignty can be seen as the kinds and degrees of constraint an object faces, over all the situations in which it participates simultaneously, and resulting from its interactions in those settings. As Gerson points out, the locus of sovereignty is any particular social object it is convenient to use for analysis, and it also "removes the distinction between 'individual' and 'society' considered as abstract entities apart from their activities and each other" [41, p. 798]. An object has its particular type of sovereignty by relationship to those other entities and situations in which it participates; it never stands alone (cf. the discussion of commitment in Section 3 above). The self-reliance/interdependence framework maintains the distinction between the individual and the larger system in which it participates.

The question of the limitations of deductive microtheories for open systems reasoning is not a new one, though I have not seen it formulated in circumscriptive terms before. Gödel's second incompleteness theorem is based on a variant of it [80], as in Garfinkel's famous description experiment[12] [33]. The importance of the OISS account is that it draws our attention to a basic limitation of a tool drawn upon by DAI theorists, and because it stresses the need for other computational approaches.

OISS also presents a proposal for alternative foundations for DAI, based on the new lexicon of trials of strength, systems commitments, representations, negotiation, cooperation, etc. Our problem is to investigate how clearly and how completely the OISS proposal addresses each of the principles for DAI foundations. One difficulty of doing this is the vagueness of some definitions. The nature and scope of concepts such as "trial of strength", "commitment", "systems commitment", or "negotiation", are matters of inference from examples, not definition. Without greater background it is sometimes difficult to see which features of an example are relevant to the concept under elucidation. For example, does "in place" mean something like "continuable" or "ongoing" (i.e., not deadlocked or otherwise become impossible)? Or does it mean something like "robust" (able to face many different challenges and withstand them)? Part of the problem may be that some concepts have not yet reached conventionalized status (e.g., "negotiation", is a term that has been used in literally dozens of different ways in the DAI literature).

[10] Or in AI in general; see, e.g., [43].

[11] One notable exception is the issue of reflexive modeling and reasoning about DAI system behavior for development purposes and as a foundation for organization self-design. See [37, 52].

[12] Garfinkel asked students to explain the meaning of a conversation by annotating it, and ultimately to give a set of instructions for unambiguously describing the meaning. Students took this as a request for more complete description, but finally realized that the task was impossible. Further description only muddled the issue because the descriptions themselves were potential sources of ambiguity. There had to be some other way of achieving conversational coherence besides shared *a priori* assumptions. This idea underlies Suchman's discussion of human–machine communication in [91]. See also our discussion of Principle 2 above.

With the specter of misconceptions of definition looming over us, let us examine how OISS addresses the six principles of Section 3, how it extends current wisdom in the DAI literature, and how it is deficient.

4.1. Principle 1: Multiple actors

Some statements of fundamental AI problems have recognized that multiple actors with different viewpoints are an important part of AI (e.g., [31, 76]). Of course, DAI research by definition deals with multiple agents, but to date, DAI research has had only limited theories. What theories do exist take certain aspects of system closure for granted, as pointed out in Sections 2 and 3. Many OISS concepts have already been in widespread use in DAI systems. For example, Mason and Johnson have designed a Distributed ATMS system for nuclear seismic analysis [74]. In this application it is essential that each node avoid compromising its local set of beliefs and assumptions by integrating faulty or malicious messages from other sensing nodes—that is, each node must maintain local autonomy and arms-length relationships while incorporating useful information generated by others. Mason and Johnson's approach is to let each node use non-local information for local focus-of-attention decisions, but never to propagate it. Similarly, the DVMT of Lesser and Corkill [67] includes mechanisms to experimentally vary a node's degree of local autonomy and how greatly it can be "distracted" by information from others; they term this "internal versus external control," and note that positive and negative distractions are sometimes hard to distinguish with a local perspective. Their definition of organization as a set of well-defined problem-solving roles and communication patterns implemented by restrictions on agent capability can be interpreted as a collection of "systems commitments"—but they are commitments by virtue of nodes' lack of sovereignty over their own roles, which is to say by virtue of the actions of designers and reflexive limits of representational theories.

OISS provides a strong foundation for DAI to the extent that it provides an account of knowledge and action from the social level to the individual (which it begins to do), recognizes the possibilities for fundamental disparities in agents' views (which it clearly does), and presents a theory of how agents act despite these disparities and without global knowledge (which it does partially).

In another light, OISS attacks in some sense the wrong problems of multi-agent systems. The important issue is not necessarily the inadequacy of closed-system microtheory techniques for OS problems, (about which there is likely to be little debate) but instead the nature of the processes of "closure"—when and how it is appropriate to make and rely upon closures, and what to do when they break down. This is my reading of one intent of circumscription and other foundations for nonmonotonic reasoning—to provide a promising but necessarily incomplete theory of how to make useful closures in a local reasoning process.

4.2. Principle 2: Tension between situated, pragmatic knowledge and action-at-a-distance

In contemporary DAI research this principle is addressed by reference to the problem of "how to achieve global coherence with local control" [22, 68], which involves the first five of the six basic DAI problems discussed in Section 2 above. Typical analyses assume that global views are possible (e.g., by an observer or oracle, to measure global coherence), that disparities that impede global coherence occur only at one level of interaction, and that general knowledge can be applied in remote settings by communicating it. For example, representations and interaction protocols are generally assumed to be fixed within the system or theory, making performance *theory-relative* to the descriptive limits imposed by them (cf. [72, 86]). The local utility approaches of Rosenschein and colleagues probably come closest to accounting for locality of knowledge because they do not depend on shared notions of utility, but they are, again, single-level analytical schemes. Agre and Chapman's "indexical" approach has promise, but it is not clear how to scale it up to aggregate interaction, and they still take the individual agent and its relationship with the world as the locus of knowledge and activity—see, e.g., [12].

OISS concepts useful for addressing Principle 2 include the self-reliance/interdependence tradeoff, the reliance on local processing of representations and the notions of systems commitments. OISS proposes negotiation as a basic mechanism. In OISS, global coherence would be conceptualized as the situated outcome of a negotiation—as long as agents collectively reach agreement (and agree that they have), their actions are coherent. But because of indeterminacy and late arriving information, a preordained concept of global coherence doesn't make sense for OISS—it is necessarily a *post-hoc* notion.

Latour provides a partial and not computational answer to the problem posed by Principle 2, that has not been fully assimilated by OISS, but that is coherent with much DAI work. The way to achieve action-at-a-distance is ". . . by *somehow* bringing home these (distant) events, places, and people. . ." [60, p. 223]. How to do this? By turning the remote entities into "immutable mobiles" which are *mobile* (transportable across contexts), *stable* (so that they keep their useful qualities in new contexts) and *combinable* (so that they can be usefully entered into associations with other such things). That is, by either bringing back preserved, representative samples (e.g., collections of animals or plants) or by bringing back *representations* of distant terrain (e.g., maps, notes, descriptions) built in a systematic (combinable) language. As indicated above, much DAI research has investigated the problems of *building models of other agents*, and of using and exchanging these models as foundations for coordination [25, 39, 65, 81, 82, 92]; from an action-at-a-distance perspective, models of other agents are the crucial immutable mobiles.

However, the stability (immutability) of any of these "mobiles," reflected in their continued representativeness, is always problematic. Transporting plants, animals, and other exemplars necessarily strips them of their context, and may render them uncombinable (e.g., if they die in a new habitat). Transporting representations raises problems of completeness (is the map detailed enough?), and of interpretation in a new context. Others in AI have begun to deal with the problem of re-interpretation in new contexts, and have suggested that it be considered in the context of the hermeneutic problem [96]. Latour's account doesn't deal fully with the mechanisms for keeping mobiles stable. OISS addresses the concern with stability of representations, in part, by delimiting its scope to open *information* systems, which are defined to be systems which manipulate digital information. The advantage of digital information is precisely its stability over time and space, and (ideally) its combinability with other digital information. It is not clear to me, however, that digital information is inherently more or less combinable than any other information, except insofar as its combinability can be automated; some studies have shown the inherent difficulty of combining digital information [35]. Moreover, the stability of interpretation over context is still problematic for OISS. Conceptually the problem can be handled by better integrating the ideas of webs of commitment developed by Becker and Gerson, but it still needs to be made computational.

It doesn't seem sensible or complete, then, to take the OISS view and say simply that representations are "information conveyed using digital communications". Instead, it seems more accurate to characterize representations as artifacts ("inscriptions" [62]) that can be passed around and reinterpreted. Latour's point is that inscriptions are useful precisely because they are transportable across spatial or semantic contexts and they are combinable (cf. Star's discussion of boundary objects in [89]). To link representation and communication, therefore, we can say that any knowledge intended to be used non-locally must be converted into a stable mobile (represented) and (re)interpreted in the local context where it is delivered. In the light of the need to keep the mobile stable, communication can be seen as the maintenance of a collection of commitments across contexts. Communication takes place via the webs of commitment. Though in OISS communication takes place digitally, that is only possible within webs of commitment [35, 56, 75].

4.3. Principle 3: Multiple perspectives

The advantages and disadvantages of multiple perspectives are well known in contemporary DAI research. Multiple views can be used to improve robustness, and several techniques for reaching reliable joint conclusions using many bits of unreliable data from multiple perspectives have been proposed. These include the functionally accurate, cooperative (FA/C) problem-solving approach of Lesser and Corkill [66], the Distributed ATMS approach of Mason and Johnson [74], and the Ether problem-solving system of Kornfeld and Hewitt [57]. The disadvantages of multiple perspectives (e.g., for global coherence) are well recognized in DAI research, and many distributed coordination mechanisms are based on reducing disparities globally by exchanging self-descriptions among agents in a process often called negotiation (e.g., [21, 26, 58, 92]). But all current approaches rely on a global perspective on some level, whether it be semantics or communication protocols, and assume that the context of negotiation cannot itself be negotiated; thus DAI as yet has no complete theory. PGPs have been suggested as a foundation for multi-level negotiations, but not for reflexively negotiating communications protocols [26].

OISS provides a deeper understanding of the basic problems of multiple viewpoints than is currently extant in most DAI. In particular, OISS accounts for the fact that negotiations can be carried out at any level of the system, including negotiations about the appropriate context of negotiations. (Others share this view to various extents. See, e.g., [26, 29, 39]). But a primary difficulty is that, despite defining negotiations as "Trials of Strength carried out using Representations", OISS provides no mechanism for integrating negotiations and more primitive (i.e., implementable) trials of strength. We do have illustrations of trials of strength at several levels of complexity, but no guidance in constructing these into multi-level negotiation mechanisms.

A *perspective* can be seen as a local organization of commitments that takes some aspects of the situation as variable or negotiable and others as fixed (cf. [39]). Strong commitment webs are ways of making things seem invisible or taken for granted—unquestioned—in dealing with the world. For example, in a logic-based agent, a perspective is manifested as the choice of a set of predicates an agent uses to describe its world, and their truth values, which the agent then uses, in a taken-for-granted way, as a world representation. It is also manifested in the decision processes the agent uses to weigh control choices it makes; these are typically commitments that cannot be changed by the agent. We can view these as *commitments* because the agent—or its designer—*could* change its representation, but that would take shifting other commitments in other contexts, e.g., commitments to using some particular communication protocol, understood by others, that relies on those predicates, or to avoiding the effort of reprogramming. Thus, the advantage of meta-level control is that it allows an agent to take on different control perspectives reflexively, but at added cost [27, 44, 72].

Multiple perspectives can be seen as differences in commitments. Moving from one perspective to another, or aligning perspectives among agents involves changing some set of commitments—i.e., the commitments that define what the local perspectives are, e.g. commitments to what predicates to use, or what assumptions to allow, or what features of a situation are important, etc.

In this way, the OISS concepts of systems commitment, representation and negotiation can be brought together, and used as a foundation for conceiving problems of disparate perspectives.

4.4. Principle 4: Resource limitations

Lesser and Erman described the DAI problem as that of enabling a collection of problem solvers to exercise sufficient control to make use of available resources and knowledge to solve a problem, assuming that the knowledge and resources were adequate for some solution [69]. Some recent DAI work has turned to resource-bounded problem solving. The issue has been inherent if not explicit in DAI due to the ways global coherence has been measured. If work is divided among nodes with potential redundancy, then one node's activities must be temporally correlated with the responses of its associates. Otherwise, these nodes may perform necessary tasks themselves, believing that they haven't been done—leading to redundancy and lowered global performance. Thus time constraints can arise purely by the need for coordination. The primary distributed AI approach to explicit resource-bounded reasoning has been *approximate processing*, introduced by Lesser et al. [70].

Problem solving under resource constraints is not clearly accounted for in the OISS framework. Earlier notions of resource *sponsors* introduced by Kornfeld and Hewitt [57] have not been incorporated into OISS at this point. This naturally raises the question of how would OISS approaches fit in real-time settings? Resource limitations are not explicit in the OISS notion of systems commitments, though they could be made so.

The oversight of OISS with respect to Principle 4 is that commitments are ways of allocating resources, and any resource-bounded activity can be represented as negotiation among participants with conflicting commitments. As the availability of resources is always linked to the activities of other agents, it is clear that the commitments of the collection of agents are an influence on resource use. In fact, remaining consistent with the social notion of commitment introduced in Section 3, we can see a commitment as simply *the use of resources*. Commitment in this sense necessarily has future implications: actor A's use of resources for one purpose in the present constrains A's (and others') choices in the future. (The economic notion is "opportunity cost".) Commitments thus "flow" through resources. (OISS would say that resources participate in systems commitments.) Moreover, the possibilities for resource allocation now (e.g., the amount of resources available) is a result of other *prior* commitments of many agents, including those of A. Becker's notion of being committed to a course of action through a collection of "side bets"—other courses of action related through resource dependencies—also falls out of this conception [4]. So do the observations that resource constraint reduces the range of practical choice of a course of action, locking the agent in ("Beggars can't be choosers.") and slack resources reduce commitment by opening a greater number of practical courses of action ("The rich can do what they want.").

4.5. Principle 5: Joint qualification, representation incommensurability, failure indeterminacy

These three problems are simply designed out of contemporary DAI systems—or rather brittleness in the face of them is designed in. There has been little or no attempt to grapple with them, in large part, because there has been so little attention to the automated formulation of problems [8] or with collaborative learning. Computational approaches to the construction of scientific knowledge and scientific explanation have in general been quite naive about scientific practice and the nature of explanation [87], a multi-agent arena in which failure indeterminacy appears routinely. In general, joint qualification and representation incommensurability are handled by assuming a global semantics for a system, and working within the constraints of the theory-relativity of the semantics. Failure indeterminacy has been dealt with via generalization [54] and model-based reasoning [52], but these are not essentially distributed approaches, nor have they been implemented under assumptions of joint qualification problems and representational incommensurability.

OISS allows us to consider several of the concepts embodied in Principle 6. First, OISS takes for granted that participants have fundamentally local and separate representations, and thus are subject to each of these problems. OISS presents a single framework—conflicting systems commitments—that integrates representational incommensurability with other levels of discrepancy mentioned in the fifth DAI problem of Section 2. The OISS approach to the joint qualification problem is to negotiate qualification discrepancies when they become manifest. OISS embeds the qualification problem in a situated process, and makes its solution responsive to local contingencies. Since negotiations can set precedents, the foundation for stable joint qualifications is laid in OISS. The OISS definition of *cooperation*, "mutually dependent roles in a Systems Commitment", is also a statement of the joint qualification problem. It does make the link to mutually supportive commitments (i.e. those that allow resources to flow in both directions) which are the foundation of an approach to joint qualification (cf. the discussions of Principle 4 above). OISS deals with representation incommensurability through the mechanism of recursive negotiation, if at all. It is not clear that OISS recognizes representation incommensurability as a key problem, and any treatment it would have would be necessarily incomplete, because the treatments of commitment and action-at-a-distance are not well-integrated. Likewise, failure indeterminacy is not accounted for, again because the development and integration of commitment is weak.

4.6. *Principle 6: Robust joint courses of action and knowledge*

Current DAI systems and theories achieve robustness through several mechanisms, which primarily are founded on either triangulation of multiple perspectives, redundancy and slack resources, or pre-specification of the causes and possibilities of failure. Several methods for robust problem solving under uncertainty that exploit multiple perspectives have been discussed in Section 4.3 above. A number of DAI systems rely upon redundancy available through parallelism to guard against failure or overload, and these have proven robust in practice. There have been few tests of the performance and overload limits of various DAI approaches, or the limits of organizational and coordination forms. Malone has given a characterization of the susceptibility of various organizational structures to node failure [73] under particularly rigid interaction assumptions. Several approaches to multi-agent planning attempt to iron out the contingencies of interaction before plan execution by interleaving partial orders of concurrent actions [40]; these are not properly in the domain of open systems approaches.

One reason that multiple agents and openness matter to DAI is because of a basic difficulty in building reliable distributed decision-making systems, that is accounted for in the conceptual machinery of OISS, but not in conventional DAI. As the nationwide nine-hour telephone network service interruption of January 1990 illustrates [75], systems which depend upon shared knowledge, common semantics, and global conceptions of coherence (e.g., identical programs at each node of a network with identical decision rules) can be subject to cascading catastropic failures (see also [38, 51]). On the other hand, without common semantics and global conceptions, interoperability and reliability become difficult for other reasons. In OISS terms, greater self-reliance produces inherent conflicts of commitment, e.g, to decision rules or communication protocols. The OISS concepts of arms-length relationships, local and multiple authority, asynchrony, self-reliance and openness are useful conceptual tools here. The fact that the network service disruptions were never complete, and operations could be restored in nine hours (i.e. the network *was* a robust and continuable process) can only be explained by reference to the existence of multiple authorities and arms-length relationships, including at least the authority of telephone engineers at multiple sites over the behavior of network nodes, and their alternative decision-making activities. The network standing alone could not restore itself, and the OISS concepts help us to focus on the actual actors doing the job, not just the network itself as a unit of analysis.

The OISS perspective makes use of the concept "in place" but this is not well-enough defined to be sensible. The notion of robustness, defined as keeping commitments in the face of conflict, is coherent with a concept of a continuable joint action. Further elaboration and mechanisms, however, are lacking. Earlier we spoke of commitment as the outcome of joint courses of action woven together. The notion of systems commitments being in place could be defined by using meta-commitment (commitment to commitment) but this has not been done in OISS.

What OISS needs is a way of linking particular negotiation contexts and particular kinds of commitment to particular ways of achieving robust joint courses of action. Latour [61] uses the image of an army made invincible by association with numerous allies, as a way of explaining robust joint courses of action. OISS must integrate similar images with computational mechanisms.

5. A synthesis

A key missing link is OISS and the other new approaches discussed in this paper, at the moment, is how to make them computational. Because commitment has been posed as a foundational concept, let us briefly examine some of the computational questions surrounding it, to see the directions we might take to construct a more computational theory based on extensions to OISS. Cohen and Levesque's construction of commitment, which is to date the most sophisticated mathematical model, is based on representing commitment using notions of "belief" and "goal", and then computing whether an agent is committed based on the logical entailments of its beliefs. Their commitment is laced into a series of decisions, and at any one of them an agent has to deduce whether it is still committed to a goal. As we discussed in Section 3, this idea of being committed is something local to the agent, and local to its viewpoint. In contrast, the OISS notion of commitment as *Systems Commitment*, though ill-defined, has roots in a basically distributed framework of multiple agents being commited together. But how can such a notion be made both computational and non-local?

One way is to begin to develop theories that dissolve the distinction between open and closed systems, that consider all systems as fundamentally open ones, and that focus on mechanisms for weaving webs of commitment as ways of achieving robustness, joint action, and plausible knowledge. When an actor is committed in the social sense of Becker and Gerson it is constrained to a course of action because of its particular local sovereignty. Establishing commitments in a manner that is both social and computational means setting up numerous side bets that constrain an agent's field of choice. Computing commitment means setting up relationships of mutual influence with additional agents.[13] There are two ways to do this that are already familiar to the world of DAI: passing self-descriptions, and developing checks and balances. Currently, these are only minimal parts of the OISS analysis.

[13] It means also being honest about what those alliances are—whether they're property of the programmer of the physical world, or of the "knowledge" in the system.

A promising approach to distributed computational commitment is based on agents modeling one another and exchanging *self-descriptions*. This approach is a foundation of the MACE system, has been exploited in DATMS [74], PGPs [26], and various network protocols, and has foundations in what Mead [77] saw as a concept that could unify concepts of the self and of society: the process of "taking the role of the other". Self-descriptions can be as simple as an address at which to receive messages, or as complex as a rich knowledge model of an agent. Variance in the ability to self-describe and to incorporate self-descriptions into action differentiate the interactive power of participants.

The flexible composition mechanism of *actor configurations* introduced by Agha and Hewitt [1], is based on actors' ability to pass self-descriptions—their mail addresses. The boundaries of a configuration are defined purely in terms of various actors' access to the addresses of other actors within and outside the configuration; this makes a configuration both flexible and distributed, and in a sense defines limits of interaction and thus provides commitment.

Self-descriptions are also ways of embedding participants in many situations simultaneously. Commitment is generated to the extent that those self-descriptions actually become a part of the calculus of action in those situations. If one agent takes another's self-description into account, it becomes committed to action in a more constrained way. For example, in the network service interruption case, most nodes' decision algorithms did react to the overload indications in passed self-descriptions, which involved them all in joint courses of action that, on the whole, interrupted service. Passing self-descriptions and meta-self-descriptions can also increase sovereignty in distributed ways, by increasing local awareness of how to adapt (e.g., [27, 67]); this was the aim of the phone network self-descriptions but there was a missing link: checks and balances.

Including a collection of checks and balances (plurality) in a DAI system, so that different participants have control over different resources in critical interactions and no participant can be ignored, is another computational approach to OISS. To some extent this notion has already been built into the convergent multi-perspective approaches such as FA/C problem solving, PGPs, and the DATMS. Building in plurality also means that self-descriptions are necessarily involved in joint courses of action. This gives us preliminary tools for implementing a balance between skepticism and involvement or self-reliance and interdependence.

Finally, by creating system-building mechanisms that treat the nature of systems as fundamentally open, we construct for ourselves another paradox—namely, do we really need new mechanisms? Suppose we change focus from problems of reasoning *across* participants with their own microtheories (which is the focus of OISS) to instead understanding the *processes of establishing and changing the boundaries of microtheories* (e.g., by understanding how to change the mix of actors participating in pragmatically common viewpoints, or by understanding how to effect closure by building denser webs of commitment). Then we have also removed the distinction between two approaches to system building (i.e. using microtheories or using OISS methods), and replaced it with a distinction in points of view toward *any* systems we build. Said another way, a viewpoint based on OISS and social foundations for DAI will provide new ways of explaining how and why *existing* reasoning paradigms work, and how they rethink their boundaries and the participants and work they leave out. In effect, we will be saying that we don't necessarily need new programming foundations, but we do need new theoretical foundations for explaining how and why existing programming foundations have the effects they do.

6. Conclusions

It is clear and not completely surprising that there are several problems with using deductive logic as a foundation for problem solving in open systems; these include Hewitt's deductive indeterminacy problem, as well as others such as the failure indeterminacy, representational incommensurability, and joint qualification problems. Since any deductive theory depends upon precursors such as a universe of discourse, a model, etc. it doesn't seem unreasonable to say that when multiple viewpoints are at stake, logic may fail.

Defining and exemplifying the problems of deduction, open systems, or DAI is an exercise—finding solutions appears to require some new foundations for knowledge and interaction, if deductive logic can't be used. OISS tells us to build our analytical foundations on trials of strength, and systems commitments. But it doesn't tell us how to win particular trials or how to organize particular sets of systems commitments, and this is typically what engineers want. OISS and others do tell us that we cannot hope to be sure of organizing and winning some of them.

Neither this paper nor OISS is trying to criticize useful reasoning mechanisms that work within bounded microtheories. It does appear to me that OISS, coupled with some of the conceptions outlined in this paper, can begin account for both the processes of delimiting microtheories in practice and the processes of reasoning employed within them, while the converse is not the case. Our major focus is upon open large-scale multi-agent systems. Both OISS and I propose approaches based upon commitments, resource allocations and interaction, and a notion of meaning independent of Tarskian semantics or possible worlds. Though thoughtful, the proposal is just that. Nonetheless, we must make a start somewhere, and the place to begin again seems to be an examination of the processes of human interaction, social organization, and concurrent systems—and thus the distributed foundations of knowledge and interaction.

Acknowledgement

Continuing discussions over many years with Elihu Gerson of the Tremont Research Institute have been invaluable in formulating the ideas in this paper. Carl Hewitt was generous enough to provide a number of clarifications of his work and critical comments on mine. I am also grateful for the comments of Phil Agre, Alan Bond, Geoff Bowker, Phil Cohen, Kari T. Eloranta, Rick Hull, Dean Jacobs, Izhar Matzkevitch, and Nick Rouquette for helping to improve the presentation of several concepts, and to David Kirsh for gently shepherding the process. I thank Susan Williams for her comments and for vigorous, unflinching editing, and M. Sue Gerson for her great herb tea at key moments. This research is partially supported by a grant from the AT&T Affiliates Program.

References

[1] G. Agha, *Actors: A Model of Concurrent Computation in Distributed Systems* (MIT Press, Cambridge, MA, 1986).
[2] P.E. Agre, Routines, AI Lab Memo 828, MIT, Cambridge, MA (1985).
[3] P.E. Agre, The dynamic structure of everyday life, Ph.D. Thesis, Department of Electrical Engineering and Computer Science, MIT, Cambridge, MA (1988).
[4] H.S. Becker, Notes on the concept of commitment, *Am. J. Sociol.* **66** (1960) 32–40.
[5] H.S. Becker, *Doing Things Together* (University of Chicago Press, Chicago, IL, 1986).
[6] A.F. Bentley, The human skin: Philosophy's last line of defense, in: S. Ratner, ed., *Inquiry into Inquiries* (Beacon Press, Boston, MA, 1954) Chapter 10, 195–211.
[7] A.H. Bond, Commitment: A computational model for organizations of cooperating intelligent agents, in: *Proceedings 1990 Conference on Office Information Systems*, Cambridge, MA (1990).
[8] A.H. Bond and L. Gasser, An analysis of problems and research in Distributed Artificial Intelligence, in: A.H. Bond and L. Gasser, eds., *Readings in Distributed Artificial Intelligence* (Morgan Kaufmann, San Mateo, CA, 1988).
[9] A.H. Bond and L. Gasser, eds., *Readings in Distributed Artificial Intelligence* (Morgan Kaufmann, San Mateo, CA, 1988).
[10] L.W. Buss, *The Evolution of Individuality* (Princeton University Press, Princeton, NJ, 1987).
[11] B. Chandrasekaran, Natural and social system metaphors for distributed problem solving: Introduction to the issue, *IEEE Trans. Syst. Man Cybern.* **11** (1) (1981) 1–5.
[12] D. Chapman and P.E. Agre, Abstract reasoning as emergent from concrete activity, in: M.P. Georgeff and A.L. Lansky, eds., *Reasoning about Actions and Plans: Proceedings of the 1986 Timberline Workshop* (Morgan Kaufmann, San Mateo, CA, 1987) 411–424.
[13] A.E. Clarke and E.M. Gerson, Symbolic interactionism in social studies of science, in: H.S. Becker and M. McCall, eds., *Symbolic Interactionism and Cultural Studies* (University of Chicago Press, Chicago, IL, 1990).
[14] P.R. Cohen and H.J. Levesque, Intention = Choice + Commitment, in: *Proceedings AAAI-87*, Seattle, WA (1987) 410–415.
[15] P.R. Cohen and H.J. Levesque, Intention is choice with commitment, *Artif. Intell.* **42** (1990) 213–261.
[16] P.R. Cohen and C.R. Perrault, Elements of a plan-based theory of speech acts, *Cogn. Sci.* **3** (3) (1979) 177–212.
[17] H.M. Collins, *Changing Order: Replication and Induction in Scientific Practice* (Sage, Beverly Hills, CA, 1985).
[18] H.M. Collins, *Artificial Experts: Social Knowledge and Intelligent Machines* (MIT Press, Cambridge, MA, 1990).
[19] D.D. Corkill, K.Q. Gallagher and K.E. Murray, GBB: A generic blackboard development system, in: *Proceedings AAAI-86*, Philadelphia, PA (1986) 1008–1014.
[20] R. Davis, Report on the workshop on distributed AI, *SIGART Newslett.* **73** (1980) 42–52.
[21] R. Davis and R.G. Smith, Negotiation as a metaphor for distributed problem solving, *Artif. Intell.* **20** (1) (1983) 63–109.
[22] K.S. Decker, Distributed problem-solving techniques: A survey, *IEEE Trans. Syst. Man Cybern.* **17** (5) (1987) 729–740.
[23] K.S. Decker, E.H. Durfee and V.R. Lesser, Evaluating research in cooperative distributed problem solving, in: L. Gasser and M.N. Huhns, eds., *Distributed Artificial Intelligence* **2** (Pitman/Morgan Kaufmann, London, 1989) 487–519.
[24] J. Dewey, The reflex arc concept in psychology, *Psychol. Rev.* **3** (1986) 357–370.
[25] E.H. Durfee and V.R. Lesser, Using partial global plans to coordinate distributed problem solvers, in: *Proceedings IJCAI-87*, Milan, Italy (1987) 875–883.
[26] E.H. Durfee and V.R. Lesser, Negotiating task decomposition and allocation using partial global planning, in: L. Gasser and M.N. Huhns, eds., *Distributed Artificial Intelligence* **2** (Pitman/Morgan Kaufmann, London, 1989) 229–244.
[27] E.H. Durfee, V.R. Lesser and D.D. Corkill, Coherent cooperation among communicating problem solvers, *IEEE Trans. Comput.* **36** (1987) 1275–1291.
[28] L.D. Erman, J.S. Lark and F. Hayes-Roth, ABE: an environment for engineering intelligent systems, *IEEE Trans. Softw. Eng.* **14** (2) (1988) 1758–1770.
[29] J. Ferber and J.-P. Briot, Design of a concurrent language for distributed artificial intelligence, Tech. Rept. LITP-88-57-RXF, Laboratoire Informatique, Theorique, et Programmation (LITP), Université Pierre et Marie Curie, Paris (1988).
[30] R.E. Fikes, A commitment-based framework for describing informal cooperative work, *Cogn. Sci.* **6** (4) (1982) 331–347.
[31] R.E. Fikes, P.E. Hart and N.J. Nilsson, Some new directions in robot problem solving, in: B. Meltzer and D. Michie, eds., *Machine Intelligence* **7** (Wiley, New York, 1972) 405–430.
[32] J.H. Fujimura, Constructing doable problems in cancer research: Articulating alignment, *Social Stud. Sci.* **17** (1987) 257–293.
[33] H. Garfinkel, *Studies in Ethnomethodology* (Prentice-Hall, Englewood Cliffs, NJ, 1967).
[34] H. Garfinkel, M. Lynch and E. Livingston, The work of a discovering science construed with materials from the optically discovered pulsar, *Philos. Social Sci.* **11** (1981) 131–158.
[35] L. Gasser, The integration of computing and routine work, *ACM Trans. Off. Inf. Syst.* **4** (3) (1986) 205–225.
[36] L. Gasser, C. Braganza and N. Herman, MACE: a flexible testbed for distributed AI research, in: M.N. Huhns, ed., *Distributed Artificial Intelligence* (Pitman/Morgan Kaufmann, San Mateo, CA, 1987) 119–152.
[37] L. Gasser and R.W. Hill, Engineering coordinated problem solvers, in: *Annual Reviews of Computer Science* **4** (Annual Reviews, Palo Alto, CA, 1990).
[38] L. Gasser and M.N. Huhns, eds., *Distributed Artificial Intelligence* **2** (Pitman/Morgan Kaufmann, London, 1989).
[39] L. Gasser, N.F. Rouquette, R.W. Hill and J. Lieb, Representing and using organizational knowledge in DAI systems, in: L. Gasser and M.N. Huhns, eds., *Distributed Artificial Intelligence* **2** (Pitman/Morgan Kaufmann, London, 1989) 55–78.
[40] M.P. Georgeff, Planning, in: *Annual Reviews of Computer Science* **2** (Annual Reviews, Palo Alto, CA, 1987) 359–400.
[41] E.M. Gerson, On quality of life, *Am. J. Sociol.* **41** (1976) 793–806.
[42] E.M. Gerson, Scientific work and social worlds, *Knowledge* **4** (1977) 357–377.
[43] R.P. Hall and D. Kibler, Differing methodological perspectives in artificial intelligence research, *AI Mag.* **6** (3) (1985) 166–178.
[44] B. Hayes-Roth, A blackboard architecture for control, *Artif. Intell.* **26** (1985) 251–321.
[45] C.E. Hewitt, Viewing control structures as patterns of passing messages, *Artif. Intell.* **8** (1977) 323–364.

[46] C.E. Hewitt, The challenge of open systems, *Byte* **10** (4) (1985) 223–242.
[47] C.E. Hewitt, Offices are open systems, *ACM Trans. Off. Inf. Syst.* **4** (3) (1986) 271–287; also in: B.A. Huberman, *The Ecology of Computation* (Elsevier Science Publishers, Amsterdam, 1988).
[48] C.E. Hewitt, Open Information Systems Semantics for Distributed Artificial Intelligence, *Artif. Intell.* **47** (1991) 79–106, this volume.
[49] C.E. Hewitt and P. de Jong, Open systems, in: M. Brodie et al., *On Conceptual Modeling* (Springer, New York, 1984) 147–164.
[50] T. Hinke, Query by committee: distributed, data-driven problem elaboration, Ph.D. Thesis, Department of Computer Science, University of Southern California, Los Angeles, CA (in preparation).
[51] B. Huberman, ed., *The Ecology of Computation* (Elsevier Science Publishers, Amsterdam, 1988).
[52] E. Hudlicka and V.R. Lesser, Modeling and diagnosing problem solving system behavior, *IEEE Trans. Syst. Man Cybern.* **17** (3) (1987) 407–419.
[53] T. Hughes P., *Networks of Power: Electric Supply Systems in the US, England and Germany* (Johns Hopkins University Press, Baltimore, MD, 1983).
[54] M.N. Huhns, U. Mukhopadhyay, L.M. Stephens and R.D. Bonnell, DAI for document retrieval: the MINDS project, in: M.N. Huhns, ed., *Distributed Artificial Intelligence* (Pitman/Morgan Kaufmann, San Mateo, CA 1987) 249–284.
[55] J.L. King and S.L. Star, Conceptual foundations for the development of organizational decision support systems, in: J.F. Nunamaker Jr, ed., *Proceedings Twenty-Third Annual Hawaii International Conference on System Sciences* **3**, Los Alamitos, CA (1990) 143–151.
[56] R. Kling and W.S. Scacchi, The web of computing: computer technology as social interaction, in: M.C. Yovits, ed., *Advances in Computers* (Academic Press, New York, 1982) 1–89.
[57] W.A. Kornfeld and C.E. Hewitt, The scientific community metaphor, *IEEE Trans. Syst. Man Cybern.* **11** (1) (1981) 24–33.
[58] K. Kuwabara and V.R. Lesser, Extended protocol for multistage negotiations, in: M. Benda, ed., *Proceedings 9th Workshop on Distributed Artificial Intelligence*, Bellevue, WA (1989) 129–162.
[59] I. Lakatos, *Proofs and Refutations: The Logic of Mathematical Discovery* (Cambridge University Press, New York, 1976).
[60] B. Latour, *Science in Action* (Harvard University Press, Cambridge, MA, 1987).
[61] B. Latour, *The Pasteurization of France, with Irreductions* (Harvard University Press, Cambridge, MA, 1988).
[62] B. Latour and S. Woolgar, *Laboratory Life: The Social Construction of Scientific Facts* (Sage, Beverly Hills, CA, 1979).
[63] J. Lave, *Cognition in Practice* (Cambridge University Press, New York, 1988).
[64] R. Laymon, Idealization and the testing of theories by experimentation, in: P. Achinstein and O. Hannaway, eds., *Observation, Experiment, and Hypothesis in Modern Physical Science* (Bradford Books/MIT Press, Cambridge, MA, 1985) Chapter 6, 147–173.
[65] D.B. Lenat, Beings: knowledge as interacting experts, in: *Proceedings IJCAI-75*, Tblisi, USSR (1975) 126–133.
[66] V.R. Lesser and D.D. Corkill, Functionally accurate, cooperative distributed systems, *IEEE Trans. Syst. Man Cybern.* **11** (1) (1981) 81–96.
[67] V.R. Lesser and D.D. Corkill, The distributed vehicle monitoring testbed: a tool for investigating distributed problem solving networks, *AI Mag.* **4** (1983) 15–33.
[68] V.R. Lesser and D.D. Corkill, Distributed problem solving, in: S.C. Shapiro, ed., *Encyclopedia of Artificial Intelligence* (Wiley, New York, 1987) 245–251.
[69] V.R. Lesser and L.D. Erman, Distributed interpretation: A model and experiment, *IEEE Trans. Comput.* **29** (12) (1980) 1144–1163.
[70] V.R. Lesser, J. Pavlin and E.H. Durfee, Approximate processing in real time problem solving, *AI Mag.* **9** (1) (1988) 49–61.
[71] A. MacFarlane, *The Origins of English Individualism* (Cambridge University Press, New York, 1978).
[72] P. Maes, Computational reflection, *Knowl. Eng. Rev.* **3** (1) (1988) 1–19.
[73] T.W. Malone, Modeling coordination in organizations and markets, *Manage. Sci.* **33** (10) (1987) 1317–1332.
[74] C.L. Mason and R.R. Johnson, DATMS: a framework for distributed assumption-based reasoning, in: L. Gasser and M.N. Huhns, eds., *Distributed Artificial Intelligence* **2** (Pitman/Morgan Kaufmann, London, 1989) 293–318.
[75] T. McCarroll and P.A. Witteman, Ghost in the machine, *Time Mag.* **135** (5) (1990) 58–59.
[76] J. McCarthy, Epistemological problems of artificial intelligence, in: *Proceedings IJCAI-77*, Cambridge, MA (1977) 1038–1044; reprinted in: R. Brachman and H.J. Levesque, eds., *Readings in Knowledge Representation* (Morgan Kaufmann, Los Altos, CA, 1985).
[77] G.H. Mead, *Mind, Self, and Society* (University of Chicago Press, Chicago, IL, 1934).
[78] R.C. Moore, Reasoning about knowledge and action, in: *Proceedings IJCAI-77*, Cambridge, MA (1977) 223–227.
[79] H.P. Nii, N. Aiello and J. Rice, Experiments on CAGE and POLIGON: measuring the performance of parallel blackboard systems, in: L. Gasser and M.N. Huhns, eds., *Distributed Artificial Intelligence* **2** (Pitman/Morgan Kaufmann, London, 1989) 319–384.
[80] W.V. Quine, *Theories and Things* (Harvard University Press, Cambridge, MA, 1981).
[81] J.S. Rosenschein, Synchronization of multi-agent plans, in: *Proceedings AAAI-82*, Pittsburgh, PA (1982) 115–119.
[82] J.S. Rosenschein and M.R. Genesereth, Deals among rational agents, in: *Proceedings IJCAI-85*, Los Angeles, CA (1985) 91–99.
[83] A. Sathi and M.S. Fox, Constraint-directed negotiation of resource reallocations, in: L. Gasser and M.N. Huhns, eds., *Distributed Artificial Intelligence* **2** (Pitman/Morgan Kaufmann, London, 1989) 163–194.
[84] R. Sethi, *Programming Languages: Concepts and Constructs* (Addison Wesley, Reading, MA, 1989).
[85] R.G. Smith, The Contract Net protocol: high-level communication and control in a distributed problem solver, *IEEE Trans. Comput.* **29** (12) (1980) 1104–1113.
[86] B.C. Smith, Varieties of self-reference, in: J.Y. Halpern, ed., *Proceedings 1986 Conference on Theoretical Aspects of Reasoning about Knowledge* (1986) 19–43.
[87] Special issue: Symposium on "Computer Discovery and the Sociology of Scientific Knowledge", *Social Stud. Sci.* **19** (4) (1989) 563–695.
[88] S.L. Star, *Regions of the Mind: Brain Research and the Quest for Scientific Certainty* (Stanford University Press, Stanford, CA, 1989).
[89] S.L. Star, The structure of ill-structured solutions: boundary objects and heterogeneous distributed problem solving, in: L. Gasser and M.N. Huhns, eds., *Distributed Artificial Intelligence* **2** (Pittman/Morgan Kaufmann, London, 1989) 37–54.
[90] A.L. Strauss, *Qualitative Analysis for Social Scientists* (Cambridge University Press, New York, 1987).
[91] L. Suchman, *Plans and Situated Actions: The Problem of Human-Machine Communication* (Cambridge University Press, New York, 1987).
[92] K.P. Sycara, Multiagent compromise via negotiation, in: L. Gasser and M.N. Huhns, eds., *Distributed Artificial Intelligence* **2** (Pitman/Morgan Kaufmann, London, 1989) 119–138.
[93] G. Teil, M. Akrich, B. Michelet and B. Latour, The Hume machine: can association networks do more than formal rules?, Centre de Sociologie de l'Innovation, École Nationale Supérieure des Mines de Paris (submitted).
[94] R.B. Wesson, F.A. Hayes-Roth, J.W. Burge, C. Stasz and C.A. Sunshine, Network structures for distributed situation assessment, *IEEE Trans. Syst. Man Cybern.* **11** (1) (1981) 5–23.
[95] W. Wimsatt, Reductionist research strategies and their biases in the units of selection controversy, in: T. Nickles, ed., *Scientific Discoveries: Case Studies* (Reidel, Boston, MA, 1980) 213–259.
[96] T. Winograd and F. Flores, *Understanding Computers and Cognition* (Ablex, Norwood, NJ, 1986).

DAI Betwixt and Between: From "Intelligent Agents" to Open Systems Science

Carl Hewitt and Jeff Inman

Abstract—**Artificial intelligence has been largely characterized by attempts to understand and develop "Intelligent Agents," which are telecomputer systems exhibiting some aspects of human intelligence. An intellectual saga of the last two decades is related, concerning distributed artificial intelligence (DAI), which began with attempts to apply and extend the study of "Intelligent Agents" to cover activities that are distributed in space and time. At the beginning in the early 1970's the enterprise did not seem especially problematical. Then things began to get sticky.The development of the *Actor* model has supported research into the fundamental principles of open distributed ultraconcurrent systems that are well suited to the coming generations of concurrent hardware. In these systems, the information of different parties can be inconsistent, incomplete, and/or incorrect. They are subject to indeterminate outcomes in their operations because of their internal concurrency and the possibility of new information arriving at any time. Such systems pose the following challenges to DAI: 1) The issue of Intelligence is supplemented with issues of Robustness, Manageability, and Scalability. 2) The maxim, "In the Knowledge lies the power," is supplemented with the maxim, "In the *Organization* lies the power," i.e., the power grows from multitudes of organized actors rather than from a few individual "Intelligent Agents." 3) Psychology and Neurophysiology are supplemented with Sociology and Anthropology. These challenges constitute deep-rooted and far-reaching change from the intellectual traditions that prevailed two decades ago.**

I. Introduction

DISTRIBUTED ARTIFICIAL INTELLIGENCE[1](DAI) systems often cover a large geography over an extended period of time with many mutual dependencies among overlapping subprojects and ongoing concurrent activities elsewhere. An example is an enterprise-wide information system of the future for flexibly managing manufacturing, including the interconnected information systems of manufacturing/production, sales, facilities maintenance, marketing, product development teams, and research. For excellent background reading for this paper see [7], [42].

In this paper, we discuss the development of open systems science (OSS) beginning with its roots in the fundamentals of concurrency (Section II). The aim of OSS (Section III) is to provide a foundation for effective technological solutions to the complex problems of large-scale open systems by providing a powerful new scientific discipline that focuses on issues of robustness, manageability, and scalability. In the large-scale Open Systems of the future (Section IV), the focus shifts from centralized systems toward decentralized ones, with an emphasis on Conflict Processing (Section V). The evolution of this paradigm presents some challenges and some fruitful new ideas for DAI (Section VI).

Manuscript received May 10, 1991; revised May 21, 1991. This work was sponsored by DARPA and monitored by ONR.

C. Hewitt is with the EECS Department, Massachusetts Institute of Technology, 545 Technology Square, Cambridge, MA 02139.

J. Inman is with the Massachusetts Institute of Technology Artificial Intelligence Laboratory, 545 Technology Square, Cambridge, MA 02139.

IEEE Log Number 9102937.

[1] This paper uses capitalization to distinguish technical usage from ordinary usage. Also, the technical words are italicized where they are introduced.

II. Actors

In this section, we discuss the nature of *Actors*, which are primitives of concurrency. We'll cover some of the factors that directed attention toward concurrency and message-passing, concentrating on what *Actors* are and how they work.

A. Precursors

One of the factors that lead to the development of *Actors* was the search for a language in which pattern-directed invocation could be used. In addition, the emergence of "objects" in programming languages in the early 1970's motivated research into what the most basic types of object could do. Some mathematical properties of *Actors* could be explored rigorously, due to the simple and concise definition of *Actors* and their semantics.

Pattern-Directed Languages for "Intelligent Agents": In pattern-directed invocation, a pattern represents what you are seeking, either to establish or to use, and acts as an advertisement for work to be done. In contrast, a programmer using procedure-directed invocation must specify a specific procedure for achieving a goal. By analogy, if one's goal is to get 300 in cash, several procedures are possible: using an automatic teller machine (e.g., of a bank) (ATM) card, asking a friend to cash a check, applying for a bank loan, etc. Procedure-directed invocation specifies directly which procedure to use. Pattern-directed invocation is more indirect, and allows the computation to choose among the alternatives, and even try them out. The pattern would be "get $300," and the alternative procedures would be "use-ATM-card," "ask-friend-to-cash-check," and "apply-for-loan." In essence, computations implemented in *Planner-69* were being performed by a community of different pattern-invoked procedures. *Planner-69* (*MicroPlanner*)[2] was the first pattern-directed planning language for "Intelligent Agent."

Planner-69 had both forward-chaining and backward-chaining rules. An example of a forward-chaining rule is "if

[2] The design of *Planner-69* was published in Hewitt [26]. The report of its first implementation is Sussman and Winograd [70]

P is asserted, then assert Q." Similarly, a backward-chaining rule is "if Q is a goal, then make P a subgoal." These two rules are procedural interpretations of the logical sentence "P implies Q." Having both forward-chaining and backward-chaining rules proved to be useful in a number of projects, including Terry Winograd's famous *SHRDLU* blocks-world program [75].

The controversial decision to use backtracking (during backward chaining) served expediency, but moved the semantics of *Planner-69* fundamentally away from the pattern-directed invocation metaphor on which it was grounded. What was needed was to take the metaphor that stood behind *Planner* more seriously.

Object-Oriented Programming Languages: Important ideas for a new conceptual basis came from *Simula* [5], [12], an object-oriented programming language that was developed in 1967 for sequential simulation of concurrent systems. In *Simula*, each simulated object kept track of its own local state instead of requiring the simulation to keep track of the global system state in a number of tables. For example, in a car-wash simulation, each simulated automobile would keep track of its position inside the car wash and the condition of its exterior at each point in simulated time. The simulator would invoke each simulated object once during each increment in simulated time. Thus, each "station" in the car wash would perform the same action on whichever simulated automobile was present in its work area.

Building on the ideas in *Simula*, Alan Kay and his colleagues at Xerox PARC developed *Smalltalk* [23]. *Smalltalk* was a more interactive version of *Simula* in that it made innovative use of object-oriented programming for bit-mapped displays. These two languages shared the common goal that they were designed to implement *sequential* simulations of concurrent systems.

B. Properties of Actors

In order to build some theoretical foundations for concurrent systems, the Message-Passing Semantics Group at MIT identified primitives of concurrent systems (called *Actors*), and began to characterize their properties. We specified laws that must hold for all *Actor* computations [28], [36], [37]. These laws state what sorts of events happen and how they are related. Causality is local in *Actor* computations. There is no global entity or process. Computation is accomplished by *Actors* sending communications to one another.

To send a communication to an *Actor A*, the sender must have a *handle* for *A*. *Handles* for an *Actor* are somewhat like phone numbers in that some people might have 3–5977 as their phone number for a person p, while others have 253–5977 as their number for p, and still others have 617–253–5977. Handles differ from phone numbers in that communication is asynchronous, as in electronic mail, and the only operation that is defined on handles is sending a communication. Also, the size of a handle is not defined, and unlike telephone numbers, if an *Actor* has a handle for *Actor A*, then the handle is valid forever, even if *A* changes location.[3] Some handles

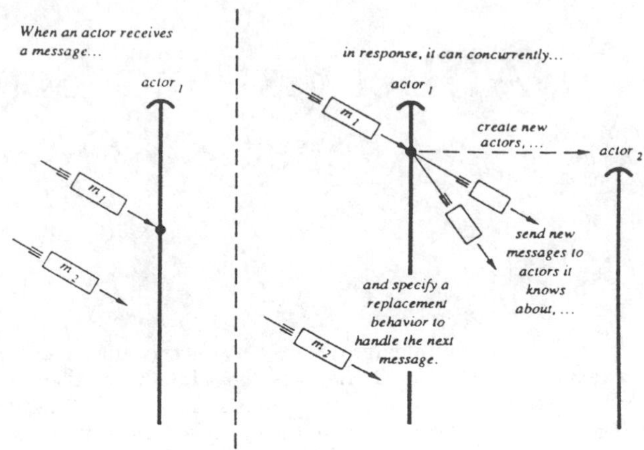

Fig. 1. The possible responses to a message.

are connected to *distributors*. Handles to distributors are like phone numbers such as 911, which connects to the *local* police department.

When a communication arrives at an *Actor*, the actions of the *Actor* are determined by its current *Behavior*. The *Actor* can process the message using any information available, but the available information is all *local*: the *Actor*'s script, the *Actor*'s acquaintances, and any information in the message itself (i.e., handles to other *Actors*). Fig. 1 illustrates this idea, in the form of an *Actor Lifeline Diagram*, in which time advances (downwards) on the vertical axis, and spatial position is shown on the horizontal axis. As suggested in the diagram, an *Actor* may concurrently do any or all of the following:

- make local decisions,
- create more *Actors*,
- send more communications, and
- replace its Behavior (i.e., specify what Behavior it will use to process the next communication it receives).

All information exists in the form of *Actors*, which are accessed only by sending messages along handles.[4] Thus, the local information available to an *Actor* consists of handles to other *Actors*, rather than the other *Actors*, themselves. Computations that need information contained in other *Actors* are achieved by passing messages to those *Actors*. Thus, *Actor* computations are conceived as orchestrations of concurrent message-passes [36], [37].

One of the fundamental partial orderings on *Actor* events is called *activation ordering*. When a communication is sent by one *Actor* (event_1) and received by another *Actor* (event_2), those two events are ordered by the activation ordering. Event_1 occurs *before* event_2. For example, consider a situation where a query is sent to a checking account. Suppose that an *Actor*, `Owner`, sends a communication to another *Actor*, `Account`, asking for the current balance. Event_1 is `Owner`-sends-communication; it always occurs before event_2, which is `Account`-receives-communication.

So activation ordering is one important notion that grew out of this early conceptual apparatus. The other is arrival

[3] Agha [2] used the term *mail address* where we use *handle*; the term "address" has connotations of physical location, which we want to avoid.

[4] There are some low-level types of *Built-in Actors*, such as integers, for which message-passing is short-circuited, for efficiency.

ordering: the order in which communications arrive at an *Actor*. In the checking account example, arrival ordering determines the balance. If a deposit does not arrive in time to cover arriving withdrawals, one or more of the checks will bounce.

In this early work, the Message-Passing Semantics Group developed a language-independent characterization of concurrent systems. This was different from the approach taken earlier by *Simula* and *Smalltalk*, in which the programming languages themselves were used to characterize "objects." So there were "objects à la *Simula*," or "objects à la *Smalltalk*," but no one could state explicitly or formally what objects were. After *Simula* was developed, it would have seemed a bit presumptuous for us to say what objects were. So *Actors* were characterized axiomatically and independently of any programming language. Another difference between objects and *Actors* is that both *Simula* and *Smalltalk* were designed for the sequential *simulation* of concurrent systems, whereas *Actors* were developed as primitives for *implementing* concurrent systems.

Having a theoretical model proved to be very helpful. For example, the *Actor* model has led directly to the notion of *ultraconcurrency*.

C. Proofs

A serializer is an *Actor* that processes the communications it receives in arrival order and that, as a result of processing a communication according to its current Behavior, can specify a different replacement Behavior to process the next communication it receives. For example, a guardian might be used to control the communications sent to two printers: it would change its Behavior for processing print requests according to which of the printers are busy. We also worked on developing ways of proving properties of *Actor* systems using serializer induction : a kind of induction for *Actor* systems. Suppose that an *Actor* A satisfies the following conditions:

- *Base condition:* A is created having the property P
- *Induction condition:* If A has property P when it receives a communication, then it will have the property P when it processes the next communication.

Then, by *Actor* induction, A will always have the property P.

D. Models

At this point, Carl Hewitt proved that Scott's model of the lambda calculus could be strictly embedded as a special subtheory within the *Actor* model [36]. Scott developed a continuity condition for his model: all the functions had to satisfy his postulated criterion of continuity. Hewitt proved that Scott's criterion of continuity is satisfied by every function that can be defined by an *Actor* system.

Will Clinger then proved the consistency of the laws for *Actor* systems by producing a mathematical model that satisfies these laws [11]. He accomplished this by showing that it was always possible to construct a (nonunique) global time for any computation that satisfied the *Actor* laws. (The consistency of non-Euclidean geometry was established in a similar way: by making a mathematical model in which straight lines are modeled as geodesics on the surface of the Earth. In this model, Euclid's parallel postulate is not viable; two longitudinal lines are parallel at the equator, yet they intersect at the poles).

Clinger's model shows that multiple frames of reference are possible in *Actor* systems, just as in relativity. The activation and arrival ordering of events remain consistent, regardless of the observer's frame of reference. Thus, if event e_1 activates event e_2, this activation order will hold true for all observers in all frames of reference. Likewise, if communication m_1 arrives at a serialized *Actor* before communication m_2, this arrival ordering of communications m_1 and m_2 will also be consistent for all observers in all frames of reference. However, if two events are not related by activation or arrival ordering, then different observations might be made in different frames of reference about which event happens first.

III. Open Information Systems

The development of the *Actor* model then became an investigation of issues in Open Information Information Systems. The first MPSG paper on Open Systems [38] pointed out limitations of the closed world assumption that had been available for use in *Planner-69* and made mandatory in *Prolog*. Open Information Systems deal with large quantities of diverse information and exploit massive concurrency. They are characterized by indeterminacy, asynchrony, decentralized control, inconsistent information, arm's-length relationships, arm's length relationships and continuous operation. Attempts to characterize Open Systems more precisely required a deeper understanding of *Actor* semantics.

Gul Agha developed an improved semantics of primitive *Actor* Behaviors [2]. He also defined *Act*, a micro-language for expressing just the primitives of *Actor* systems. Agha extended the semantics of *Actor* systems in order to analyze transitions on configurations and the concurrent composition of configurations. A configuration is basically a snapshot of an *Actor* system at one particular time. It describes the local state of each *Actor*, and what communications are currently in transit.

Agha also worked on issues of observation equivalence in *Actor* systems, especially as they relate to Robin Milner's Calculus of Concurrent Systems [55]. His analysis of the Brock-Ackerman anomaly shows the inadequacies of modeling concurrent systems purely in terms of input-output streams of messages. By ignoring local state, such "black-box" models cannot either explain or predict the behavior of such *Actors* as a line-printer manager or guardian. Agha's definition of observation equivalence does take into account the internal states of the *Actors*, and describes what's actually happening inside the configuration. (Observation equivalence is determined by doing *Gedanken* experiments with automata to see if they perform equivalently.)

Thus, Agha presented an intuitive model for *Actor* systems that provides a foundation for practical work. His model is directly applicable to the construction, engineering, and operation of *Actor* systems.

The development of the *Actor* model provided the foundations needed to rigorously address perplexing problems that had arisen in DAI.

A. *The Role of Logic in Open Information Systems*

The work of the Message-Passing Semantics Group evolved within a context of rivalry and debate between schools of thought in Artificial Intelligence (the study of Intelligent Agents). One school believes that Artificial Intelligence should be based on logic—that logic has extensive use as a foundation for mathematics which in turn is a foundation for scientific models.

Early attempts to use deductive reasoning as a basis for computation focused on the development of uniform proof procedures. The proof procedure would be given the axioms and hypothesis to be proved, and it would use logical deduction to prove the result. It was expected that more powerful and effective proof procedures would gradually be developed.

The prevailing view at MIT was that logic alone would not be enough; it would also be necessary to embed procedural know-how in these uniform proof procedures. Hewitt designed *Planner-69* for that purpose. Its pattern-directed procedures worked together to solve a problem, and it was possible to embed many kinds of procedural knowledge in the bodies of the procedures [27].

Since Deductive Inference is a powerful and well understood method for analyzing questions of meaning, its use needs to be studied in OIS Semantics. A Microtheory is defined to be a derivational calculus, together with a prespecified automaton that can check the correctness of any individual derivation step, given only the step and no additional information. Deductive Inference does not provide means adequate to decide important questions that arise in the course of operation of OIS because of the omnipresence of indeterminacy in the use of shared resources, which results in Deductive Indecision. Deductive Indecision has important operational consequences for the use of Deductive Inference for OIS. It refutes Kowalski's Thesis that Deductive Logic can be used as a universal systems implementation language [48]. Previously it has been almost universally assumed that Deductive Logic is a universal systems implementation language because it is universal for sequential Algorithmic Systems. Deductive Indecision about important operational questions (such as whether or not a withdrawal from a shared account is to be honored) is a fatal flaw in Kowalski's Thesis. OIS Semantics provides the characterization that the scope of use of Deductive Inference exactly coincides with the use of Microtheories by participants. By focusing only on the relationships internal to a Microtheory, Deductive Inference fails to address the larger issues of the use of Microtheories by OIS participants. Deductive Inference alone is inadequate to process Conflicts because the processes which actually produce the outcomes are necessarily left out.

All Conflicts are local in the sense that they occur at a particular time and place among local Participants. *Joint Activity* refers, in general, to any potentially-concurrent, Interdependent activities [32]. Often, a Joint Activity occurs without manifest strife or confrontation. In effect, one Participant says, "Let's do it this way," and everybody agrees, so no Conflict is manifested. Still, there is always the potential for Conflict in Joint Activities. No one can be certain in advance about the outcome, so Joint Activity introduces Indeterminacy.

The above result is significant because it means that there can be no logical foundations for decision making in DAI and thus fundamentally limits the kinds of logical foundations that can be provided [68], [49].

B. *Self-Reliant and Interdependent Activities*

An Activity is *Self-Reliant* to the extent that it can be carried out using only the resources that are local. Activities are *Interdependent* to the extent that they are dependent on each other. A system may be Self-Reliant in relation to some of its activities, while being Interdependent in others. For example, an automated teller machine (ATM) is Self-Reliant with respect to the cash it dispenses. However, the ATM depends on the the bank for permission to dispense the cash, and the bank depends on the ATM to dispense the allowed amount correctly. Thus, the bank and the ATM are also Interdependent.

Activities will be said to *Conflict* if they interact in a way that prevents some of them from being completed. Having both Self-Reliant and Interdependent activities often leads to Conflict.

Self-Reliant and Interdependent Activities vary along the following characteristics.

- *Late-arriving information* may be received from ongoing activities elsewhere. Ignoring such information could result in flawed decisions, but it may not be possible or practical to forestall the decision making process indefinitely, so as to make fully informed decisions. Participants may be capable, and are sometimes obliged to take new information into account as it arrives. However, when information arrives at an advanced stage of processing, acting on it may Conflict with previously initiated activities.
- *Multiple local authorities* enable participants to react immediately to changing circumstances. Otherwise, they would have to consult a nonlocal decision maker for each decision. When Conflicts arise, local authorities can immediately take action to manage the changing circumstances. However, the Joint Activities of local authorities almost inevitably Conflict over the use of shared resources, because each acts locally on the basis of its own information.
- *Division of labor* involves the creation of subactivities to physically distribute work and locally focus efforts on a narrower range of Joint Activities. These subactivities often come into conflict over the use of shared resources.
- *Arm's length relationships* enable participants to conceal their internal activities from other participants, to increase their own robustness, manageability and/or scalability. For example, a vendor might use Arm's Length Relationships with its competitors to increase its return on new product development investments. A government policing agency might use arm's length relationships,

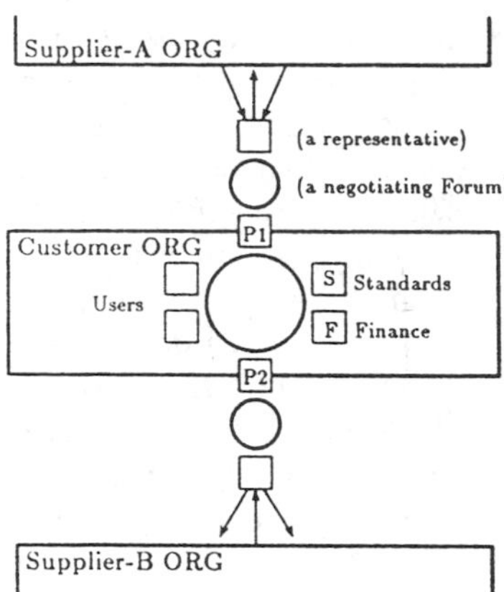

Fig. 2. Coordinating negotiations.

with parties that it regulates, to facilitate the detection of violations before they can be covered up. While increasing Self-Reliance, Arm's length relationships can also increase the severity of Conflict, because participants may develop entrenched, incompatible activities before Conflict is discovered.

Balancing the trade-offs between Self-Reliant and Interdependent Activities is one of the most fundamental issues in OSS. Powerful, well-understood methods are needed to help manage this trade-off.

IV. Organizing Large Information Agencies

Information Agencies are systems with human and telecomputer components in which the production of *all* artifacts (internal and external) is accomplished from *digital* specifications. Due to their distributed, concurrent nature, identified by Interdependent and Self-Reliant subsystems, Information Agencies are Open Systems.

Open Systems Science integrates results from the theory of concurrent systems, organization theory, and sociology to provide a foundation for the design, construction, and operation of large-scale Information Agencies that are more Robust, Manageable, and Scalable [40].

A. Background and Objectives

Large-scale work requires organization. The 'largeness' of large-scale work means that it must be divided among many resources, which are distributed across space and time, and these divisions must be organized to accomplish the work. For example, to develop and market a new commercial computer, it is not sufficient to find a few good people and immediately set to work. Instead, the product designers must cooperate with the marketing department (which is responsible for developing potential customers) and the manufacturing department (which is responsible for efficiently building the new machines). Each of these is a distinct organization within the larger organization. Each contains both humans and telecomputer systems, and is often organized into smaller suborganizations as well. An accounting department, for example, may contain separate offices for Payroll, Accounts Payable, Accounts Receivable, and so on.

All of these organizations operate concurrently, and their activities often affect one another. For example, Manufacturing needs to know what parts will be needed so that it can arrange to make or acquire them. Similarly R&D needs information about the market place so that it can design a competitive product. In fact, many decisions like these need to be made jointly because of the interdependence of the departments.

For example, consider the situation illustrated in Fig. 2. In order to make a large purchase (e.g., to assure a supply of memory chips or power supplies for the new computer), an organization might designate a Representative P1 from its Purchasing Department, to negotiate with Supplier-A, and another Representative P2 to negotiate with Supplier-B. In order to decide what to buy and from whom, Representatives P1 and P2 from Purchasing meet with a representative F from the Finance Department, a representative S from Internal Standards, and possibly other representatives of potential users of the product. These representatives then decide which supplier to use. In this way negotiation becomes an *essential* activity in large-scale work.

The decision might be reached easily and quickly, in which case the negotiation is a trivial one, or numerous Conflicts among the parties' *Joint Activities* [40] might arise. In that case, each party could present material on its view of the issue (e.g., choice of supplier), the commitments that intersect the issue, and options for dealing with the issue. We claim that these presentations are seldom ready-made. Instead, each party to the negotiation generates new material to fit the circumstances at hand. Furthermore, contradictory statements are often generated as a natural way of bringing Conflicts to the attention of other parties.

B. Relation of Actors to ORGs

ORGs[TM] address an important issue of *Actors* in that *Actors per se* are not scalable units. *ORGs* introduce technical means for *composing* larger *ORGs* out of several smaller ones. In addition, *ORGs* can be created by *Budding* in which an *Actor* can transform itself into an *ORG*. Budding is possible because the basic functions of *Actors* are sufficient to support at least rudimentary *ORG* facilities. Hence, every *Actor* can function as a rudimentary *ORG*.

C. ORG Facilities

Organizing large-scale work requires an *organizational architecture* (structure and functionality). In this section, we present such an organizational architecture called *ORGs*.

Actors are universal primitives of concurrent computation. However, the design, construction, operation, and maintenance of large-scale Information Agencies requires support for organization. Organizations of restricted generality (*ORGs*) represent an extension of the *Actor* architecture, which provide this support through the following *facilities*:

[TM] *ORG* is a trademark of the Message Passing Semantics Group.

- The *Operations* facility provides resources (e.g., processors, storage, communications) for authorized tasks.
- The *Reporting* facility provides information for other facilities concerning what happened, when it happened, and which participants were involved.
- The *Membership* facility keeps track of the *ORG* population, creates new memberships, and terminates existing memberships as the *ORG* evolves.
- The *Liaison* facility controls communications crossing the *ORG* boundary. *Reception* is a subfacility of Liaison, which fields communications sent to the *ORG* as a whole.
- The *Management* facility controls the behavior of the *ORG*. It sets policies and procedures for *ORG* behavior.

Teams of engaged activity and management (*TEAMs*) are suborganizations of an *ORG* that do not have a Liaison facility and therefore have more flexibility, but correspondingly less control. concerning communications between the *TEAM* and the rest of the containing organization. Much of the discussion in this paper applies to both *ORGs* and *TEAMs*, but we will speak in terms of *ORGs* to avoid cumbersome terminology such as "*ORGs/TEAMs*". It should be understood that points made about *ORGs* apply equally well to *TEAMs*, except where otherwise noted.

In the next few sections, we describe the *facilities* that allow *ORGs* to support the capabilities described above. Facilities are envisioned as distributed throughout an *ORG*. They are concurrent, possibly hardware-assisted capabilities that are ubiquitous in an *ORG*, just as electricity may be simultaneously available from any outlet in a building.

Operations: The purpose of the *ORG operations* facility is to provide the actual processing, storage, and communication resources that are used in an *ORG*. We single out these resources because every *task* processed by the system will require the use of each of these resources.

We should note that, in keeping with the *ORG* design philosophy, this support is the minimum of what is needed by the system. We do not specifically implement any of the "smart" allocation strategies, such as those described in [14], [16], [71]. We simply establish a very basic support structure, on top of which such schemes can be implemented.

Reporting: Each *ORG* includes a *Reporting* facility to provide information about the resources that it consumes. This will be useful for supporting the work of the Management facility and for monitoring and debugging *ORGs* and the large-scale systems built with *ORGs*.

Membership: ORGs have a *Membership* facility to provide system-level access to the population of the *ORGs*. This facility maintains information about the current memberships of an *ORG*, just as a business might maintain information concerning its current employment. Each *ORG* is in control of its own memberships. An *Actor* may have membership in several *ORGs*.

Liaison and Reception: Liaison is the *ORG* facility that is responsible for maintaining a boundary between *ORGs*. This boundary separates the resources used by different *ORGs*, helping them account for their own work without interference from others. By definition, *TEAMs* do not provide this facility.

One of the reasons for having *ORGs* is to modularize related concurrent activity, allowing management and re-organization to be applied with appropriate leverage to functionally related (i.e., Interdependent) suborganizations. Liaison implements and preserves the boundary that such modularization requires.

Communications directed to an *ORG* as a whole are handled by *Reception*, which is a subfacility of Liaison responsible for directing such communications to appropriate internal recipients. Directing all such communication through Reception may at first seem an unacceptable bottleneck. However, Reception need not be a single *Actor*, but can be a distributed facility consisting of many *Actors* working together, so traffic passing through Reception can be processed concurrently.

The Liaison boundary represents an abstraction barrier for handles to *Actors* that are members of different *ORGs*. The *ORGs* can *replace* the actual recipient of communications that are directed through the abstraction barrier. This allows them to update the behavior of their members without having to synchronize with all the external *Actors* that might possess handles to that internal *Actor*. *ORGs* thus retain local authority for their members.

We now sketch one possible mechanism for maintaining *ORG* boundaries.

Actors that manage communications leading from within an *ORG* to destinations outside the *ORG* will be called *Outsiders*. *Insider Actors* manage communications coming into an *ORG* from the outside. The Liaison facility manages the Insiders and Outsiders, as will be discussed later.

In the diagrams in this paper, we draw the Liaison facility as a shaded border around an *ORG*, to represent its function of maintaining the *ORG* boundary. An example diagram is depicted in Fig. 3. The arrows represent *handles*, which represent potential destinations for *Actor* communications. We use circles (or ovals) to represent the boundary-implementing Liaison *Actors*, whose activity would normally be transparent. Boxes represent *Actors*, and rectangles with "exhaust" behind them are used to represent messages in transit. *Actors* send messages to each other, and the messages themselves usually contain handles to other *Actors*. Note that the handle labeled r refers to the *ORG* as a whole. Any communications directed through this handle will be routed, by Reception, to some appropriate *Actor* inside the *ORG*, which is designated to handle that particular message. *Actors* labeled i and o are Insiders and Outsiders, respectively, which maintain the *ORG* boundary for communications directed to specific handles inside (or outside) the *ORG*.

In order to maintain a well-defined *ORG* boundary, we require that any communication that passes through an *ORG* boundary will pass through Liaison, allowing that facility to process the communication. Maintaining this boundary requires dynamically creating Insiders and Outsiders.

An Insider *Actor* functions as a "portal" for messages coming from outside the *ORG* to some particular member.[6] As these messages pass through the portal (i.e., the Insider *Actor*), any *Actor* handles they may contain are "translated," so that

[6] In special cases, such as the handle to the *ORG* itself (which directs messages to the Reception facility), the eventual destination may actually be one of several *Actors*.

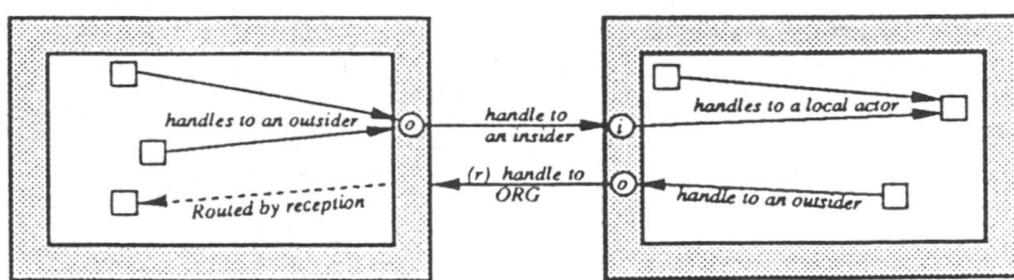

Fig. 3. Liaison between *ORGs*.

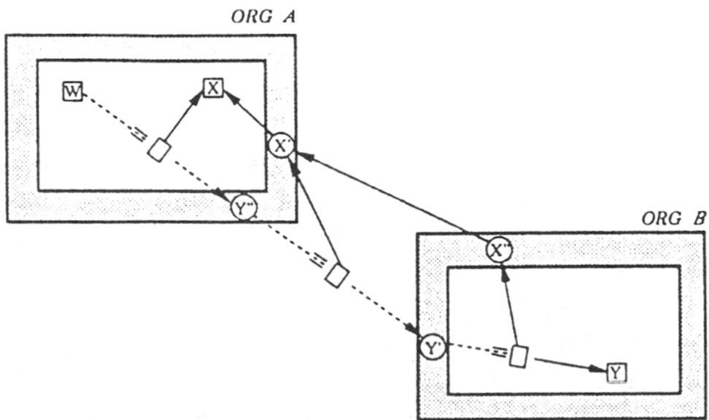

Fig. 4. Passing a communication through *ORG* boundaries.

they can be used in the internal context of the *ORG*. This translation includes the following:

- external handles to internal *Actors* (which will always be handles to other Insiders in the Liaison facility of the *ORG*) are replaced with direct handles to the internal *Actors* themselves. This promotes efficient communication within the *ORG*.
- external handles to external *Actors* (which will often be handles to Insiders in the Liaison facilities of other *ORGs*) are replaced with handles to Outsider *Actors* in the Liaison facility of the recipient *ORG*. This assures that messages sent to external *Actors* will always be processed by Outsider *Actors*.

Similarly, an Outsider will perform the reverse translation for messages sent from within the *ORG* to an external destination. This technique allows *ORG* boundaries to be implemented and maintained, using normal *Actors*. When the boundary *Actor* (i.e., an Insider or Outsider) receives a message, its Behavior is to perform the appropriate translation, and then forward the translated message to the appropriate target. The translation itself is supported through the Liaison facility.

Fig. 4 illustrates this process. Our convention for naming Insiders and Outsiders is to give the Insider the name of the destination *Actor*, appended with one prime, while giving the Outsider two primes. This reflects the necessary order of their creation, as will become clear. In this example, *Actor* W, in *ORG* A, sends a communication (which contains a handle on X) to *Actor* Y, in *ORG* B. Outsider Y'' represents the external *Actor* Y (external to *ORG* A), and Insider Y' represents the internal *Actor* Y (internal to *ORG* B). As this communication passes through Outsider Y'', the handle to X is replaced by a handle to Insider X'. Similarly, as the communication passes Insider Y', the handle to X' is replaced by a handle to the Outsider X''. Thus, the new Liaison *Actors*, Insider X' and Outsider X'', are created in just that order.

For each *Actor* mentioned in a communication, we must be able to determine if that *Actor* is resident in the *ORG* where the communication is departing or arriving. Then we must find or create any needed Liaison *Actors*. If the communication is *departing* the *ORG*, then Insiders must be found or created for arguments that are members of the *ORG*. At the same time, handles to Outsiders of this *ORG*, are replaced with the actual external handles. If the external *Actor* is a member of another *ORG*, then the external handle will actually be a handle to the Insider in that other *ORG*. In the complementary case, where the communication is *entering* an *ORG*, handles to nonmember *Actors* must be mapped to handles to Outsiders (which are either found or created), and handles to Insiders of this *ORG* must be mapped to the internal handles for the *Actors* they represent.

Management: The *Management* facility of an *ORG* is responsible for controlling the behavior of the *ORG*. It is responsible for paying the three types of resource charges that are levied (i.e., processing, communications, and storage) and can attempt to manage the activities of the *ORG* so as to utilize those resources effectively. Management will periodically receive charges for resources used by the *ORG*. It may decide to fill these requests using internal resources, or by requesting resources from other *ORGs*. It may also decline to grant the requested resources (this is known as "stifling" a subcomputation), or seek to restructure its activities so as to make some resources more accessible. Activity in large-scale systems can be controlled through the manipulation of these various resources, through the granting of requests, and through the restructuring of organizations.

D. Specialized ORGs

Transaction: ORGs Transaction *ORGs* handle activity for which an *ORG* wants to delegate some of its management and resources. A transaction *ORG* will commonly be dependent on its owning *ORG* for resources, just as the owning *ORG* will depend on still other *ORGs*.[7] The advantage in delegating resources and management to a suborganization is that concurrency is maximized and modularity is maintained. The result is that management of resources remains well distributed over the range of activities being performed by an organizational system. Small-scale, short-term, specialized

[7] This is ultimately grounded in *Workplace ORGs* [32], [39], which administer real resources on a physical module of computing machinery, such as a multiprocessor node.

projects and large-scale, long-term, general projects can have different management objectives while still being interdependent. Modularity promotes better utilization of the underlying hardware, since *ORGs* can be migrated, and is conducive to monitoring and debugging.

Project ORGs: Another way of organizing for cooperative work is for several *ORGs* to pool resources in a suborganization. They can then rely on this suborganization to help them organize their common work, without having to compromise their modularity. We refer to such shared suborganizations as *Project ORGs*, in accordance with the idea that the resources and management of the suborganization are being utilized for a shared "project" in which the *ORGs* are involved. Project *ORGs*, like transaction *ORGs*, allow modularized management to be provided for specialized activities. As before, this is conducive to design, maintenance and debugging of large-scale systems while permitting more effective utilization of the underlying hardware.[8]

E. Reorganization

De Jong [15] proposes some specific functional attributes of organizational systems, which might be automatically detected and corrected for the purpose of maintaining efficiency. Hewitt and Inman [39] suggest that *ORGs* will tend to involve Activities that are naturally modular with respect to processing, storage and communication resources.

V. Conflict Processing In Information Agencies

Activities will be said to *Conflict* if they interact in a way that prevents some of them from being completed. As suggested in Section III-B, the presence of both Self-Reliance and Interdependence in Open Information Systems is a potential source of Conflict. One mechanism by which Open Information Systems can process Conflicts, is the convening of *Forums*.

A. Forums

Forums provide a means by which information can be *Shared* with *Subscribers*. Each *Subscriber* to a *Forum* can receive all the Sharings at the *Forum*. In practice, Subscribers have *Filters* so that a Subscriber is only sent the Sharings that match its Filter. Each Sharing consists of a message and a *Respondent* which is responsible for responding to requests concerning the Sharing (e.g., questions about support, etc.). Fig. 5 diagrams the situation.

A *Forum* is naturally used as an arena for Negotiation, by which different parties can attempt to understand and resolve their differences. As noted in Section VI-B, we presume that the most common type of Conflict results from the discovery of unintended interactions in ongoing Joint Activities. *Forums*, then, will commonly be used to explore the nature of interactions in Joint Activities. Through the effects of human debugging, information about types of Conflict and various resolution techniques can be accumulated in an Information

[8]This kind of cooperative activity between *ORGs* is specially organized. The term 'Joint Activity' refers in general to any potentially-concurrent, Interdependent activities.

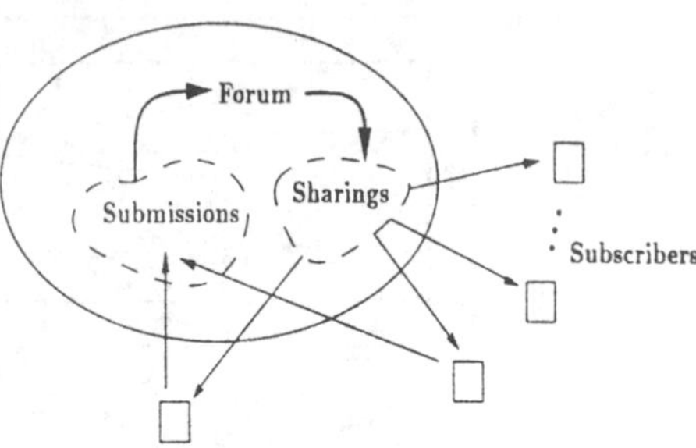

Fig. 5. Forums concurrently receive submissions from, and distribute sharings to their subscribers.

Agency. However, we don't presume that all Conflicts can or should be resolved automatically by telecomputer equipment.

We will investigate the specifics of how Negotiations might be implemented in *Forums* more thoroughly, in an upcoming paper.

Open Systems Science inherits methods from sociology (e.g., [19], [20], [51], [65]) in order to provide a suitable semantic foundation for Open Systems consisting of humans and telecomputer equipment. Ultimately, the new semantic foundations for Open Systems Science need to be represented in mathematical language, because this is the most precise language that we have. We are working to extend the mathematical semantics of [2], [11] to this end.

B. Related Work

In the following sections, we distinguish some similarities and differences between our work and other work in the areas of Blackboard architectures, Conflict Processing, and Negotiation.

C. Blackboard Architecture

Blackboard architectures are summarized in [24], as follows:

> "The blackboard architecture has three defining features: a global database called the blackboard, independent knowledge sources that generate solution elements on the blackboard, and a scheduler to control knowledge source activity."

In our own work, we make *none* of the above assumptions. We do *not* assume a global data base, because we operate in circumstances of a multiplicity of known and unknown *Forums* that are created dynamically. We also do *not* assume that information resources are independent. Subscribers to a *Forum* may communicate directly with each other as well as indirectly through various *Forums*. Subscribers to a *Forum* may often have knowledge of each other's existence, even of their behavior and expertise. Furthermore, we do *not* assume that the scheduler of a *Forum* can control its Subscribers, because Subscribers typically operate asynchronously and independently of the *Forums* to which they subscribe. Subscribers can do arbitrary processing on the Sharings that they receive (possibly from *multiple Forums*) using, in addition, any other information that they might already have, or might subsequently receive from other sources.

Some *Forums* implement *commutativity* with respect to the arrival-order of Sharings and Subscribers, so that late-arriving Subscribers will have access to all previous Sharings, but this is not mandated for all *Forums*. Anyhow, the information shared in a *Forum* is often inconsistent. It would be possible, though perhaps a bit odd, to set up a *Forum* in which it was not guaranteed that all Subscribers would receive all the Sharings that matched their filters.

Activity in *Actor* systems is event driven, but in a rather different way than in the *Blackboard* architecture. Recall that each reception of a communication by an *Actor* constitutes an event that can directly trigger the following Activities: make local decisions, create more *Actors*, send more communications, and replace its Behavior (i.e., specify what Behavior it will use to process the next communication it receives).

A *Forum* can be *concurrently* receiving and processing a large number of Sharings. In practice, many negotiations at *Forums* may fail to solve the problems that motivated the convening of those *Forums*; there are no *a priori* guarantees of success.

D. Conflict Processing

In this section, we relate our work on *Forums* to work on conflict situations in [45].

Our work differs in that we do *not* assume that in competitive situations each party has *solely* their own benefit in mind. It is true that the parties with which we deal typically have no interest in a *globally optimal* solution, because they typically have no conception of what such a solution might be. Global solutions seem impossibly hard because usually none of the parties are knowledgeable enough about the ramifications of solutions to know whether or not they are globally optimal. This is especially true when the "global" situation is dynamic, including many concurrent changes in local states, the effects and interactions of which are not instantaneous. As a result, parties commonly believe that the information systems work that would be needed to compute an optimal solution would take too long and be too expensive, and might be made obsolete by ongoing changes, anyhow.

In Open Systems Conflict frequently occurs among the parties to a *Forum*, but the reason is typically *not* because they have differing, possibly partial or incorrect, theories of how to achieve an *optimal* solution. Also, their differences do not usually depend on having different *conflict resolution strategies*. It is more likely that the parties simply discover unforeseen interactions in their Activities. Typically, the parties deliberately do not disclose certain information to others. This may be done (legitimately, in our view) so as to preserve control over Activities and information vital to the function of the party. On occasion, a party might deliver a threat (ultimatum) to another, and sometimes this activity is also legitimate, in our view.

E. Negotiation

In this section, we relate our work on *Forums* to work on negotiations in [73].

Designer-Fabricator-Interpreter research concerns development of a system for aiding negotiations between designers and fabricators of structural steel systems focusing on critiquing designs of steel beam-to-column connections in buildings based on standard steel fabrication and field erection procedures. The negotiation process is to be overseen by an arbitrator agent who assists the other agents in arriving at an agreement. This additional arbitrator "super agent" exists to assist the agents in reaching an acceptable solution. The "super agent" listens in on the communication between the design and fabrication agents. If the "super agent" notices a deadlock situation (continued failure to reach an agreement), it intervenes by analyzing the situation and *informing* one agent that the other agent would agree if only the first agent would lessen the importance or drop a connection evaluation issue. In such a case, the "super agent" is to have final say as given input from both deadlocked agents as to the importance of each issue.

We do *not* assume that negotiations in *Forums* are overseen by a "Super Agent" who assists the other agents in arriving at an agreement. However, as described in Section VI, *Forums* convened for the purpose of resolving Conflicts may *produce* (or discover) new Conflicts. It would certainly be useful to have a *capability* for expert moderation, but it needs to be available in a style that is appropriately matched to the function of specific *Forums*.

VI. Conclusion

There is a great temptation to anthropomorphize "Intelligent Agents" and to think of them as *electronic humans*. This is a great mistake because of the enormous disparity between the information systems capabilities of humans and that of existing "Intelligent Agents." Now and for the foreseeable future, "Intelligent Agents" and humans cannot participate as equal partners in Information Agencies. Instead, Information Agencies should be developed with special consideration given to the *interaction* of the humans and telecomputer equipment involved.

Artificial Intelligence has been largely characterized by attempts to understand and develop "Intelligent Agents," which are telecomputer systems exhibiting some aspects of human intelligence. Distributed artificial intelligence (DAI) began with attempts to apply and extend the study of "Intelligent Agents" to cover activities that are distributed in space and time. In addition, DAI has tended to inherit the conceptual framework of AI, which is grounded in psychology and neurophysiology.

The development of the *Actor* model has supported research into the fundamental principles of open distributed ultraconcurrent systems that are well suited to the coming generations of concurrent hardware. These systems allow information of different parties to be inconsistent, incomplete, and incorrect. They are subject to indeterminate outcomes in their operations because of their internal concurrency and the possibility of new information arriving at any time.

Such systems pose the following challenges to DAI.

- The issue of Intelligence is supplemented with issues of Robustness, Manageability, and Scalability.
- The maxim, "In the Knowledge lies the power," is supplemented with the maxim, "In the *Organization* lies the power," i.e., the power grows from multitudes of organized actors rather than from a few individual "Intelligent Agents".
- Psychology and Neurophysiology are supplemented with Sociology and Anthropology

The above challenges constitute deep-rooted and far-reaching change from the intellectual traditions that prevailed two decades ago.

ACKNOWLEDGMENT

We would like to express our appreciation to Ed Durfee for his work as an editor of this special issue. His suggestions have been invaluable in improving the presentation in this paper. Carl Manning also made numerous valuable suggestions.

We would like to thank Jeff Palmucci, whose thesis [59] developed many of the fundamental concepts and issues for *ORGs*.

The long range vision of Mario Tokoro, Yuichiro Anzai, and Shiro Iwasawa and financial support of IBM® Japan in establishing the IBM Japan Chair at Keio University is gratefully acknowledged. Thanks also to Nihon Symbolics™ for providing the use of a Lisp Machine at Keio.

REFERENCES

[1] A. B. Adler, R. Davis, R. Weihmeyer, and F. W. Worrest, "Conflict resolution strategies for non-hierarchical distributed agents," in *Distributed Artificial Intelligence, Vol. II*, L. Gasser and M. N. Huhns, Eds. London: Pitman/Morgan Kaufmann, pp. 139–162, 1989.

[2] G. Agha, *Actors: A Model of Concurrent Computation in Distributed Systems*,Cambridge, MA: MIT Press, 1986.

[3] H. J. Baker Jr. and C. Hewitt, "Incremental garbage collection of processes," MIT A. I. Memo, Dec. 1977.

[4] H. S. Becker, "Notes on the concept of commitment," *Am. J. Sociology*, vol. 66, pp. 32–40, July 1960.

[5] G. M. Birtwistle, O. J. Dahl, B. Myhrhaug, and K. Nygaard, *Simula Begin*. New York: Van Nostrand Reinhold, 1973.

[6] A. Bond, "Commitment: A computational model for organizations of cooperating intelligent agents," in *Proc. 1990 Conf. on Office Information Systems*, Cambridge, MA, Apr. 1990.

[7] A. H. Bond and L. Gasser, Eds., *Readings in Distributed Artificial Intelligence*. San Mateo, CA: Morgan Kaufmann, 1988.

[8] ——, "Organizational analysis of distributed artificial intelligence systems," Computer Res. Inst., Univ. Southern Calif., Tech. Rep. CRI-88-33, July 1988.

[9] A. Chien and W. Dally,"Concurrent aggregates," in *Proc. Second Symp. on Principles and Practice of Parallel Programming*, ACM, Mar. 1990.

[10] W. Chikayama, H. Sato, and T. Miyazaki, "Overview of the parallel inference machine operating system," in *Proc. Int. Conf. on Fifth Generation Computer Systems*, Tokyo, Japan, Nov. 28–Dec. 2, 1988.

[11] W. Clinger, "Foundation of *Actor* semantics," MIT AI Lab. Tech. Rep. AI-TR-633. May 1981. (Ph.D. dissertation,) (Portions also reprinted in *Toward Open Information Systems Science*, C. Hewitt, C. Manning, J. Inman, and G. Agha, Eds. Cambridge, MA: MIT Press, Summer 1991.)

[12] O. J. Dahl, B. Myhrhaug, and K. Nygaard, *Simula Common Base Language*, no. S-22, Norwegian Computing Center, Oct. 1970.

[13] R. Davis, "Expert systems—Where are we? And where do we go from here?" *AAAI Mag.*, Spring 1982.

[14] R. Davis and R. Smith, "Negotiation as a metaphor for distributed problem solving," MIT AI Lab Memo 624, MIT, Cambridge, MA, 1981.

® IBM is a registered trademark of International Business Machines.

™ Symbolics is a trademark of Symbolics Incorporated.

[15] Peter de Jong, "A framework for the development of organizations," *J. Computational Computing*, Feb. 1991.

[16] K. E. Drexler and M. S. Miller, "Incentive engineering for computational resource management," in *The Ecology of Computation*, B. A. Huberman, Ed., New York: Elsevier Science (North Holland), pp. 231–266, 1988.

[17] H. Durfee Edmund and Victor R. Lesser, "Negotiating task decomposition and allocation using partial global planning," in L. Gasser and M. N. Huhns, Eds., *Distributed Artificial Intelligence, Vol. II*. London: Pitman/Morgan Kaufmann, 1989, pp. **229–244.**

[18] L. Gasser and M. N. Huhns, Eds., *Distributed Artificial Intelligence, Vol. II*. London: Pitman/Morgan Kaufmann, 1989, pp. 229–244.

[19] Elihu M. Gerson, "On the quality of life," *Am.. Sociological Rev.*, vol. 41, pp. 793–806, Oct. 1976.

[20] E. M. Gerson and S. L. Star, "Analyzing due process in the workplace," *ACM Trans. Office Inform. Syst.*, vol. 4, no. 3, pp. 257–270, July 1986.

[21] S. Gibbs, A D. Tsichritzis, A E. Casais, A O. Nierstrasz, and A X. Pintado, "Class management in software information systems," *Commun. ACM*, to be published.

[22] I. Greif, "Semantics of communicating Parallel processes," MIT, Project MAC Tech. Rep. #154, 1975.

[23] A. Goldberg and D. Robson, *Smalltalk-80: The Language and Its Implementation*. Reading, MA: Addison-Wesley, 1983.

[24] B. Hayes-Roth, "Blackboard systems," in *Encycl. Artificial Intell., Vol. 1*, S. C. Shapiro, Ed. New York: Wiley, pp. 73–79, 1987.

[25] Barbara Hayes-Roth, Michael Hewett, Richard Washington, Rattikorn Hewett, and Adam Seiver, *Distributed Artificial Intelligence, Volume II* L. Gasser and M. N. Huhns, Eds. London: Pitman/Morgan Kaufmann, pp. 385–412, 1989.

[26] Carl E. Hewitt, "PLANNER: A language for proving theorems in robots,' in *Proc. IJCAI-69*, Washington, DC, May 1969.

[27] ——, "Procedural embedding of knowledge in PLANNER," in *Proc. 1971 Int. Joint Conf. on Artificial Intelligence*, pp. 167–182, Sept. 1971.

[28] ——, "Viewing control structures as patterns of passing messages," *J. Artificial Intell.*, vol. 8, no. 3, pp. 323–364, June 1977.

[29] ——, "The apiary network architecture for knowledgeable systems," in *Proc. First Lisp Conf.*, Stanford Univ., CA, Aug. 1980.

[30] ——, "The challenge of open systems," *Byte*, vol. 10, no. 4, pp. 223–242, Apr. 1985.

[31] ——, "Organizations of restricted generality," in *1989 IFIP Congress Proc.*, IFIP, San Francisco, CA, Aug. 1989.

[32] ——, "*Actor* Machine architecture," in *Toward Open Information Systems Science*, C. Hewitt, C. Manning, J. Inman, and G. Agha, Eds. Cambridge, MA: MIT Press, Summer 1991.

[33] ——, "Scientific communities and Open information systems," in *Toward Open Information Systems Science*, C. Hewitt, C. Manning, J. Inman, and G. Agha, Eds. Cambridge, MA: MIT Press, Summer 1991.

[34] ——, "Open information systems semantics," in *Toward Open Information Systems Science*, C. Hewitt, C. Manning, J. Inman, and G. Agha, Eds., Cambridge, MA: MIT Press, Summer 1991.

[35] C. Hewitt and R. Atkinson, "Specification and proof techniques for serializers," *IEEE Trans. Software Eng.*, vol. SE-5, pp. 10–23, Jan. 1979.

[36] C. E. Hewitt and H. Baker, "Actors and continuous functionals," in *Proc. IFIP Working Conf. Formal Description of Programming Concepts*, pp. 367–387, Aug. 1977.

[37] C. Hewitt and H. Baker, "Laws for communicating parallel processes," in *Proc. IFIP Congress 1977*, Toronto, Canada, pp. 987–992, Aug. 1977.

[38] C. Hewitt and P. de Jong, "Open systems," in *Perspectives on Conceptual Modeling*, M L. Brodie, J. L. Mylopoulos, and J. W. Schmidt, Eds. New York: Springer-Verlag, 1983; also, MIT AI Lab. Memo #692, 1982.

[39] C. Hewitt and J. Inman, "Organization of large-scale open information systems," in *Toward Open Information Systems Science*, C. Hewitt, C. Manning, J. Inman, and G. Agha, Eds. Cambridge, MA: MIT Press, Summer 1991.

[40] C. Hewitt, C. Manning, J. Inman, and G. Agha, Eds., *Toward Open Information Systems Science*. Cambridge, MA: MIT Press, Summer 1991.

[41] Y. Honda and A. Yonezawa , "Debugging concurrent systems based on object groups," in *Toward Open Information Systems Science*, C. Hewitt, C. Manning, J. Inman, and G. Agha, Eds. Cambridge, MA: MIT Press, Summer 1991; also in *ABCL: An Object Oriented Concurrent System*, Yonezawa Ed. Cambridge, MA: MIT Press, 1990.

[42] B. A. Huberman, Ed., *The Ecology of Computation*. New York: Elsevier Science (North Holland), 1988.

[43] K. M. Kahn and M. S. Miller, "Language design and open systems," in *The Ecology of Computation*, B. A. Huberman, Ed. New York: Elsevier Science (North Holland), 1988.

[44] M. J. Katz and J. S. Rosenschein, "Plans for multiple agents," in *Distributed Artificial Intelligence, Vol. II*, L. Gasser and M. N. Huhns,

Eds. London: Pitman/Morgan Kaufmann, 1989, pp. 197–228.
[45] Klein, Lu, and Baskin, "Toward a theory of conflict resolution in cooperative design," unpublished manuscript.
[46] W. A. Kornfeld. "Concepts in parallel problem solving," Ph. D. dissertation, Dep. of EECS, MIT, Cambridge, Feb. 1982.
[47] W. A. Kornfeld and C. Hewitt, "The scientific community metaphor," *IEEE Trans. Syst., Man, Cybern.*, vol. SMC-11, Jan./Feb. 1981.
[48] R. A. Kowalski. "Logic programming", in *1983 IFIP Congress Proc.*, IFIP, Aug. 1983.
[49] K. Kuwabara and V. R. Lesser, "Extended protocol for multistage negotiations," in *Distributed Artificial Intelligence, Vol. II*, L. Gasser and M. N. Huhns Eds. London: Pitman/Morgan Kaufmann, pp. 129–162, 1989.
[50] S. Lander and V. R. Lesser, "Conflict resolution strategies for cooperating expert agents," in *Draft Proc. Int. Working Conf. on Cooperating Knowledge-Based Systems*, Univ. Keele, U.K., pp. 129–162, Oct. 3–5, 1990.
[51] B. Latour, *Science In Action*. Cambridge, MA: Harvard Univ. Press, 1987.
[52] J. Lee, "SIBYL: A qualitative decision management system," in *Artificial Intelligence at MIT: Expanding Frontiers*, P. Winston and S. Shellard Eds. Cambridge, MA: MIT Press, June 1990.
[53] D. B. Lenat and R. V. Guha, *Building Large Knowledge-Based Systems*. New York: Addison-Wesley, 1990.
[54] C. Manning, "Introduction to programming *Actors* in Acore," in *Toward Open Information Systems Science*, C. Hewitt, C. Manning, J. Inman, and G. Agha, Eds. Cambridge, MA: MIT Press, Summer 1991.
[55] R. Milner, "A calculus of communicating systems," in *Springer-Verlag Lecture Notes in Computer Science*, vol. 92, 1980.
[56] M. Minsky, *The Society of Mind*. New York: Simon and Schuster, 1985.
[57] A. Newell, *Unified Theories of Cognition*.Cambridge, MA: Harvard Univ. Press, 1990.
[58] N. Nilsson, "Logic and artificial intelligence," *Artificial Intell. J.*, vol. 47, 1991.
[59] J. Palmucci, "*ORGs*: An architecture for constructing Large-scale *Actor* systems," Bachelor's thesis, MIT, Cambridge, MA, 1989
[60] G. L. Rein and C. A. Ellis, "rIBIS: A real-time group hypertext system," MCC Software Technology Program, Rep. STP-095–90, Mar. 1990.
[61] M. T. Rose, *The Open Book: A Practical Perspective on OSI*. Englewood Cliffs, NJ: Prentice Hall, 1990.
[62] Sathi and Fox, "Constraint-directed negotiation of resource reallocations," in *Distributed Artificial Intelligence, Vol. II*, L. Gasser and M. N. Huhns Eds. London: Pitman/Morgan Kaufmann, pp. 163–194, 1989.
[63] R. Smith and R. Davis, "Frameworks for cooperation in distributed problem solving," *IEEE Trans. Syst., Man, Cybern.*, vol. SMC-11, pp. 61–70, 1981.
[64] S. L. Star, "Simplification in scientific work: An example from neuroscience research," *Social Studies Sci.*, vol. 13, no. 2, pp. 205–228, 1983.
[65] ——, "The structure of ill-structured solutions: Boundary objects and heterogeneous distributed problem solving," *Distributed Artificial Intelligence, Vol. II*, L. Gasser and M. N. Huhns, Eds. London: Pitman/Morgan Kaufmann, 1989. pp. 37–54.
[66] G. Steele, *Common Lisp, the Language*. New York: Digital, 1984.
[67] A. Strauss, *Negotiations*. New York: Jossey-Bass, 1978.
[68] K. P. Sycara, "Multiagent Compromise via negotiation," in *Distributed Artificial Intelligence, Vol. II*, L. Gasser and M. N. Huhns Eds. London: Pitman/Morgan Kaufmann, pp. 119–138, 1989.
[69] M. Stefik, "The next knowledge medium," *AI Mag.*, vol. 7, no. 1, pp. 34–46, Spring 1986.
[70] G. Sussman and T. Winograd, "Micro-planner reference manual," MIT AI Lab Memo 203, July 1970.
[71] C. A. Waldspurger, "A distributed computational economy for using idle resources," Masters yhesis, MIT, Cambridge, MA, 1989.
[72] D. Weinreb and D. Soon, *LISP Machine Manual*. Cambridge, MA: MIT, July 1981.
[73] K. J. Werkman and D. J. Hillman, "Designer fabricator interpreter system," private communication.
[74] E. Werner, "Cooperating agents: A unified theory of communication and social structure," in *Distributed Artificial Intelligence, Volume II*, L. Gasser and M. N. Huhns Eds. London: Pitman/Morgan Kaufmann, pp. 3–36, 1989.
[75] T. Winograd, *Understanding Natural Language*. New York: Academic, 1972.
[76] T. Winograd and F. Flores, *Understanding Computers and Cognition*. Reading, MA: Addison-Wesley, 1987.
[77] A. Yonezawa, "Specification and verification. techniques for parallel programs based on message-passing semantics," Ph.D. dissertation, MIT, Cambridge, MA, LCS Tech. Rep. 191, Dec. 1977.

Carl Hewitt received the Ph.D. in mathematics in 1971 from the Massachusetts Institute of Technology, Cambridge.

He has been on the faculty of the MIT EECS Department since 1971. From September 1989 to August 1990, he held the IBM Japan Chair at Keio University, Tokyo, Japan. His research interests include open systems science, ultraconcurrent systems, information agency, panel-based computing environments, concurrent software engineering, multiprocessor workstation networks, and artificial intelligence.

Jeff Inman received the B.S. degree in computer science in 1986 from Boston University, Boston, MA.

He is a Research Scientist at the MIT Artificial Intelligence Laboratory. Previously, he worked at Symbolics QA, Inc. His research interests include social mechanisms, resource economies, and emergent behavior in natural and artificial ecosystems.

A Social Reasoning Mechanism Based On Dependence Networks

Jaime Simão Sichman [1]
Yves Demazeau [1]

Rosaria Conte [2]
Cristiano Castelfranchi [2]

Abstract. This paper describes the fundamental concepts of a *social reasoning mechanism*, designed to be part of an agent's internal model, in a multi-agent systems (MAS) context. It enables an agent to reason about the others using information about their goals, actions, resources and plans. Every agent stores this information in a data structure called external description. We have formally defined and implemented the concepts of *external description, dependence relation*, and *dependence network*. One of the main contributions of this work is that an agent can infer his dependence on others using either his own plans or those of the others. As a result, we have defined a preliminary taxonomy of *dependence situations* regarding the goal being analysed (unilateral, mutual or reciprocal) and the sets of plans used in this reasoning mechanism (mutually or locally believed). We have used this model to build a dependence network simulator, called DEPNET, which is also briefly described in this paper.

Keywords: multi-agent systems, cognitive modelling, communication and cooperation, integrating several AI components.

1 Introduction

The main goal of this work, developed in a scientific cooperation program between the LIFIA/IMAG and the IP/CNR, was to combine the complementary expertise of these groups in the multi-agent systems (MAS) domain. In particular, we have designed and implemented a computational model of the Social Power Theory [4], using the concept of dependence relation [3]. This model, as well as some of its extensions, will be used in some modules of the LIFIA's MAS platform [2] and agent models [10], mainly involving conflict management in MAS. On the other hand, we have used this model to build a dependence network simulator, called DEPNET. This simulator will enable the IP/CNR's research staff to experiment and validate some future theoretical results.

The ability of reasoning about the others is an essential issue in a so called "intelligent" agent. Moreover, if we consider a MAS as an open system [7], this feature enables an agent to adapt himself to an evolving environment, to take into account information about new members of the agency (as an example, one can think of a robot's agency, when new robots may arrive and robots may leave due to failures). Therefore, in our point of view, an agent must have a *social reasoning mechanism* in order to react properly when faced to such situations. On the other hand, structural analysis approaches have been extensively used in the last years, specially in social and political sciences [8]. More recently, these approaches are beginning to be used in Computer Science. An interesting work, closely related to this paper, is described in [12], where a model of dependence was designed to treat business reengineering problems. The difference between this work and the one presented in this paper is that in the former some of the types of dependences introduced are closely related to the target domain, while our approach claims to be domain-independent.

In section 2, we present the concept of *external description*, a data structure where an agent stores the information he has about the others. This information may be used to infer his *dependence relations* and to construct his *dependence networks*, as it is shown in section 3. Once constructed such networks, an agent may identify which is his *dependence situation* regarding the other agents for a specific goal. A preliminary taxonomy of these dependence situations is described in detail in section 4. Section 5 briefly presents the DEPNET simulator, a software tool we have built in order to test our ideas. Finally, we present in section 6 our conclusions and further work.

2 External Description

As presented in [2] [10], we consider that an essential functionality an agent has to have in order to be really autonomous (in a broader sense) is a *social reasoning mechanism.* We call social any reasoning mechanism that uses *information about the others* in order to infer some conclusions. Therefore, any agent (despite the possible different internal models an agent may have) must have a data structure where this information about the others is stored. At the LIFIA/IMAG, we call such data structure an *external description* [6]. In this paper, we define it as composed of the following elements:

- *goals:* the goals an agent wants to achieve. An agent may have more than one goal, and in this point we do not make any reference if a goal is currently active or not, this discussion is out of scope of this paper;
- *actions:* the actions an agent is able to perform;
- *resources:* the resources an agent has control on;
- *plans:* the plans an agent has, using any actions and resources, in order to achieve a certain goal. These actions

[1] LIFIA/IMAG, 46 av. Félix Viallet, 38031 Grenoble Cedex France
[2] PSCS/IP/CNR, Viale Marx 15, 00137 Rome Italy

ECAI 94. *11th European Conference on Artificial Intelligence* Edited by A. Cohn
Published in 1994 by John Wiley & Sons, Ltd.

and resources do not necessarily belong to his own set of actions and resources, and therefore an agent may *depend on others* in order to carry on a certain plan.

Let us introduce a formal notation in order to describe this concept. In the rest of this paper, we will denote ag_i as a generic agent whose social reasoning mechanism we are analysing. Therefore, for an agent ag_i, his external description Ext_{ag_i} is defined as follows:

$$Ext_{ag_i} \stackrel{def}{\equiv} \bigcup_{j=1}^{n} Ext_{ag_i}(ag_j)$$

where $Ext_{ag_i}(ag_j)$ is the corresponding entry in ag_i's external description when the information about ag_j is stored. In the previous formula, we are supposing that the agency is composed of n agents, so each agent has n entries in his external description, corresponding to each agent that belongs to the agency, including himself.

An external description entry $Ext_{ag_i}(ag_j)$ is by its way defined as follows:

$$Ext_{ag_i}(ag_j) \stackrel{def}{\equiv} \{G_{ag_i}(ag_j), A_{ag_i}(ag_j), R_{ag_i}(ag_j), P_{ag_i}(ag_j)\}$$

where $G_{ag_i}(ag_j)$ is the set of goals g_i , $A_{ag_i}(ag_j)$ is the set of actions a_i , $R_{ag_i}(ag_j)$ is the set of resources r_i and $P_{ag_i}(ag_j)$ is the set of plans p_i ag_i believes ag_j has. At this point, we must clarify that we are not interested in the moment in how an agent can gather this information about the others. This may be done by explicit communication whenever an agent enters the agency (for instance, using an introduction protocol as described in [1]) or by the agent's perception mechanisms. The important point is that this information corresponds to the beliefs an agents has regarding the others, and that these beliefs may be *neither necessarily true nor complete*. Without lacking of generality, and in order to illustrate the power of the proposed framework, we will adopt the hypothesis of external description compatibility ($Ext_{ag_i}(ag_i) = Ext_{ag_j}(ag_i) \wedge Ext_{ag_i}(ag_j) = Ext_{ag_j}(ag_j)$) in the rest of this paper, when analysing the social reasoning mechanism of two related agents.

Regarding the description of the plans, $P_{ag_i}(ag_j, g_k)$ refers to the set of plans $p_{ag_{i_l}}(ag_j, g_k)$ ag_i believes that ag_j has in order to achieve the goal g_k. Each plan $p_{ag_{i_l}}(ag_j, g_k)$ can be formally described as:

$$p_{ag_{i_l}}(ag_j, g_k) \stackrel{def}{\equiv} \{g_k, R(p_{ag_{i_l}}(ag_j, g_k)), I(p_{ag_{i_l}}(ag_j, g_k))\}$$

where g_k is the goal to be achieved by this plan, the second term $R(p_{ag_{i_l}}(ag_j, g_k))$ is a (possibly empty) set of resources used in this plan and $I(p_{ag_{i_l}}(ag_j, g_k))$ is a (possibly empty) sequence of instantiated actions used in this plan. By its way, each instantiated action $i_m(p_{ag_{i_l}}(ag_j, g_k))$ is defined as follows:

$$i_m(p_{ag_{i_l}}(ag_j, g_k)) \stackrel{def}{\equiv} \{a_m, R_{a_m}(p_{ag_{i_l}}(ag_j, g_k))\}$$

where a_m is an action and $R_{a_m}(p_{ag_{i_l}}(ag_j, g_k))$ is a (possibly empty) set of resources used in this action, with the following constraint $R_{a_m}(p_{ag_{i_l}}(ag_j, g_k)) \subseteq R(p_{ag_{i_l}}(ag_j, g_k))$.

For simplicity of notation, in the next sections we will drop the subscript referring to the generic agent ag_i we are analysing (for instance, we will use $G(ag_j)$ instead of $G_{ag_i}(ag_j)$). We will also use P_{jk} and p_{lk} respectively instead of $P_{ag_i}(ag_j, g_k)$ and $p_{ag_{i_l}}(ag_j, g_k)$. Whenever these notation assumptions are to be dropped, this fact will be explicitly stated.

3 Dependence Relations and Dependence Networks

Using the definitions cited above, an agent ag_i will be **a-autonomous** for a given goal g_k, *according to a set of plans* P_{qk} if there is a plan that achieves this goal in this set and every action appearing in this plan belongs to $A(ag_i)$:

$$a_{aut}(ag_i, g_k, P_{qk}) \stackrel{def}{\equiv} \exists g_k \in G(ag_i)\ \exists p_{lk} \in P_{qk}\ \forall i_m(p_{lk}) \in I(p_{lk})\ a_m \in A(ag_i)$$

Analogously, an agent ag_i will be **r-autonomous** for a given goal g_k, *according to a set of plans* P_{qk} if:

$$r_{aut}(ag_i, g_k, P_{qk}) \stackrel{def}{\equiv} \exists g_k \in G(ag_i)\ \exists p_{lk} \in P_{qk}\ \forall r_m \in R(p_{lk})\ r_m \in R(ag_i)$$

Finally, an agent an agent ag_i will be **s-autonomous** for a given goal g_k, *according to a set of plans* P_{qk} if he is both a-autonomous and r-autonomous for this goal:

$$s_{aut}(ag_i, g_k, P_{qk}) \stackrel{def}{\equiv} a_{aut}(ag_i, g_k, P_{qk}) \wedge r_{aut}(ag_i, g_k, P_{qk})$$

The major contribution of this work is the fact that this notion of autonomy is closely related to the set of plans used in the reasoning mechanism. In other words, an agent can use either *his own* set of plans (when $q = i$ in the definitions above) or *those of the others* in other to infer his own autonomy. Doing so, an agent can **simulate the reasoning of the others**, by using *their knowledge* (in our case, their plans).

If an agent is not autonomous for a given goal, he will depend on others to achieve it. An agent ag_i **a-depends** on another agent ag_j for a given goal g_k, according to a set of plans P_{qk} if he has g_k in his set of goals, he is not a-autonomous for g_k and there is a plan in P_{qk} that achieves g_k and at least one action used in this plan is in ag_j's set of actions. Formally:

$$a_{dep}(ag_i, ag_j, g_k, P_{qk}) \stackrel{def}{\equiv} \exists g_k \in G(ag_i) \neg a_{aut}(ag_i, g_k, P_{qk}) \wedge \exists p_{lk} \in P_{qk} \exists i_m(p_{lk}) \in I(p_{lk}) a_m \in A(ag_j)$$

In a similar way, we define that an agent ag_i **r-depends** on another agent ag_j for a given goal g_k, according to a set of plans P_{qk} if:

$$r_{dep}(ag_i, ag_j, g_k, P_{qk}) \stackrel{def}{\equiv} \exists g_k \in G(ag_i) \neg r_{aut}(ag_i, g_k, P_{qk}) \wedge \exists p_{lk} \in P_{qk} \exists r_m \in R(p_{lk}) r_m \in R(ag_j)$$

Finally, an agent ag_i **s-depends** on another agent ag_j for a given goal g_k, according to a set of plans P_{qk} if he either a-depends or r-depends on this latter:

$$s_{dep}(ag_i, ag_j, g_k, P_{qk}) \stackrel{def}{\equiv} a_{dep}(ag_i, ag_j, g_k, P_{qk}) \vee r_{dep}(ag_i, ag_j, g_k, P_{qk})$$

Once defined these dependence relations, an agent can construct a *dependence network* to represent in a same structure all of his action/resource dependences regarding the others. These networks can be used later in the agent's social reasoning mechanism, in particular to detect the dependence situations regarding two agents for a given goal, as described in the next section.

4 The Dependence Situations

Since an agent has constructed his dependence networks, he can use this information when reasoning about the others. In other words, for a given goal g_k, an agent ag_i can calculate for each other agent ag_j which is the *dependence situation* relating them for this goal. A preliminary taxonomy of dependence situations are presented in figure 1. In the rest of this section, we will analyse these situations considering only a-dependences. We will call **mutual dependence** a situation where an agent ag_i infers that he and other agent ag_j a-depend on each other for the *same goal* g_k, according to a set of plans P_{qk}:

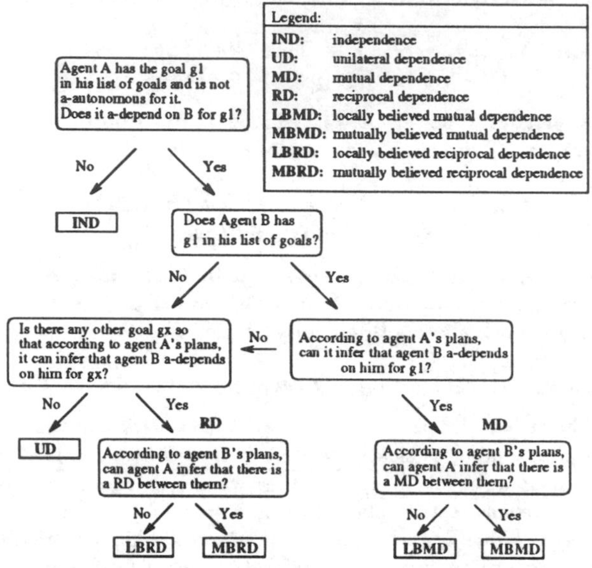

Figure 1. A Preliminary Taxonomy of Dependence Situations

$$MD(ag_i, ag_j, g_k, P_{qk}) \stackrel{def}{\equiv} a_{dep}(ag_i, ag_j, g_k, P_{qk}) \wedge a_{dep}(ag_j, ag_i, g_k, P_{qk})$$

On the other hand, we will call **reciprocal dependence** a situation where an agent ag_i infers that he and other agent ag_j a-depend on each other, but for *different goals* g_k and g_l, according to the sets of plans P_{qk} and P_{ql} (both sets belonging to the same external description entry):

$$RD(ag_i, ag_j, g_k, g_l, P_{qk}, P_{ql}) \stackrel{def}{\equiv} a_{dep}(ag_i, ag_j, g_k, P_{qk}) \wedge a_{dep}(ag_j, ag_i, g_l, P_{ql}) \wedge g_l \neq g_k$$

In the case of mutual dependence, a possible *cooperation* regarding this goal can happen. On the other hand, in the case of reciprocal dependence, one of them will have to adopt the other's goal first in order to achieve his own one in the future. This mechanism is called *social exchange*. These concepts are better explained in [3] [4].

An agent **locally believes** a given dependence (either mutual or reciprocal) if he uses exclusively his *own plans* when reasoning about the others. If he uses both *his own plans* and *those of the others* to reach such a conclusion, it will be said that there is a **mutual believed** dependence between them.

The difference between the locally and the mutually believed situations (either in mutual or reciprocal dependence) is very subtle: in the first case, one of the agents may not be aware of this dependence (for instance, when one of them has a different set of plans to achieve the considered goal and in neither of these plans he a-depends on the other). In this case, a plan negotiation will have to be made in order to achieve the desired goal.

Let us consider two agents ag_i and ag_j. If $g_k \in G(ag_i)$ and $\neg a_{aut}(ag_i, g_k, P_{ik})$, there are six different dependence situations which may occur, considering ag_i's reasoning mechanism. These situations are described next, and we will use as an example to illustrate them the external description presented in table 1, corresponding to an agency composed of 7 agents (*jaime, rosaria, cristiano, vittorio, maria, amedeo* and *paola*):

Table 1. Example of an external description

ag_j	$G(ag_j)$	$A(ag_j)$	$R(ag_j)$	$P(ag_j)$
jaime	g1 g2 g3 g4	a1	r1	g1:=a3(r1). g2:=a6(r1),a7(r2). g3:=a1(r1),a2(r3). g4:=a1(r1),a4(r5), a5(r4).
rosaria	g1	a2	r2	g1:=a2(r2).
cristiano	g5	a3	r3	g5:=a3(r3).
vittorio	g4	a4	r4	g4:=a4(r5),a5(r4).
maria	g4	a5	r5	g4:=a1(r1),a5(r7).
amedeo	g3	a6	r6	g3:=a6(r6).
paola	g2 g3	a7	r7	g2:=a5(r1),a7(r2). g3:=a1(r2),a6(r3).

1 **Independence:** using his own plans, ag_i infers that he does not a-depend on ag_j for g_k:

$$IND(ag_i, ag_j, g_k) \stackrel{def}{\equiv} \neg a_{dep}(ag_i, ag_j, g_k, P_{ik})$$

In our example, agent *jaime* is independent on agent *rosaria* regarding g_1:

```
Regarding agent:(rosaria)

Agents (jaime) and (rosaria) are independent
regarding goal g1
Agent (rosaria) is s-autonomous for goal g1
```

2 **Locally Believed Mutual Dependence:** using his own plans, ag_i infers that there is a mutual dependence between himself and ag_j for g_k, but he can not infer the same using ag_j's plans:

$$LBMD(ag_i, ag_j, g_k) \stackrel{def}{\equiv} MD(ag_i, ag_j, g_k, P_{ik}) \wedge \neg MD(ag_i, ag_j, g_k, P_{jk})$$

In our example, agent *jaime* locally believes that there is a mutual dependence between himself and agent *vittorio* for g_4 (because of a_1 and a_4):

```
Regarding agent:(vittorio)
```

```
 jaime
----------  g4
         |----------  g4:=a1(r1),a4(r5),a5(r4).
 vittorio          |----------  a4
----------  g4               |----------  vittorio
         |----------  g4:=a4(r5),a5(r4).|----------
                   |----------  a5
                             |----------  maria
                                       |----------
```

3 **Mutually Believed Mutual Dependence:** using his own plans, ag_i infers that there is a mutual dependence between himself and ag_j for g_k. Moreover, using a_j's plans, he infers the same mutual dependence:

$$MBMD(ag_i, ag_j, g_k) \stackrel{def}{\equiv} MD(ag_i, ag_j, g_k, P_{ik}) \wedge MD(ag_i, ag_j, g_k, P_{jk})$$

If we adopt the hypothesis of external description compatibility described in section 2, the two agents ag_i and ag_j will infer the same result, since it is quite easy to prove the following identity: $MBMD(ag_i, ag_j, g_k) \Longleftrightarrow MBMD(ag_j, ag_i, g_k)$.

In our example, there is a mutually believed mutual dependence between agents *jaime* and *maria* for g_4 (because of a_1 and a_5):

```
Regarding agent:(maria)

 jaime
----------  g4
         |----------  g4:=a1(r1),a4(r5),a5(r4).
 maria             |----------  a5
----------  g4               |----------  maria
         |----------  g4:=a1(r1),a5(r7).|----------
                   |----------  a1
                             |----------  jaime
                                       |----------
```

One must note that despite this mutually believed dependence, we are not supposing that *the plans involved must be the same*, as in this example. An agent may start, for instance, an interaction protocol in order to persuade to other to adopt his own plan. This feature has the advantage of not restricting unnecessarily the proposed framework.

4 **Locally Believed Reciprocal Dependence:** using his own plans, ag_i infers that there is a reciprocal dependence between himself and ag_j for g_k and g_l, but he can not infer the same using ag_j's plans:

$$LBRD(ag_i, ag_j, g_k, g_l) \stackrel{def}{\equiv} RD(ag_i, ag_j, g_k, g_l, P_{ik}, P_{il}) \wedge \neg RD(ag_i, ag_j, g_k, g_l, P_{jk}, P_{jl})$$

In our example, agent *jaime* locally believes that there is a reciprocal dependence between himself and agent *amedeo* regarding g_2 (because of a_6) and g_3 (because of a_1):

```
Regarding agent:(amedeo)

Agent (amedeo) depends on agent (jaime) for goal: g3
 jaime
----------  g2
         |----------  g2:=a6(r1),a7(r2).
                   |----------  a6
                             |----------  amedeo
                                       |----------
Agent (amedeo) is s-autonomous for goal g3
```

5 **Mutually Believed Reciprocal Dependence:** using his own plans, ag_i infers that there is a reciprocal dependence between himself and ag_j for g_k and g_l. Moreover, using a_j's plans, he infers the same reciprocal dependence:

$$MBRD(ag_i, ag_j, g_k, g_l) \stackrel{def}{\equiv} RD(ag_i, ag_j, g_k, g_l, P_{ik}, P_{il}) \wedge RD(ag_i, ag_j, g_k, g_l, P_{jk}, P_{jl})$$

Once more, the two agents ag_i and ag_j will infer the same result if we adopt the hypothesis of external description compatibility, since it is also quite easy to prove the following identity: $MBRD(ag_i, ag_j, g_k, g_l) \Longleftrightarrow MBRD(ag_j, ag_i, g_l, g_k)$.

In our example, there is a mutually believed reciprocal dependence between agents *jaime* and *paola* regarding g_2 (because of a_7) and g_3 (because of a_1):

```
Regarding agent:(paola)

Agent (paola) depends on agent (jaime) for goal: g3
 jaime
----------  g2
         |----------  g2:=a6(r1),a7(r2).
 paola             |----------  a7
----------  g3               |----------  paola
         |----------  g3:=a1(r2),a6(r3).|----------
                   |----------  a1
                             |----------  jaime
                                       |----------
```

Once again, as in the MBMD situation, we are not supposing that *the plans involved must be the same*, as in the proposed example.

6 **Unilateral Dependence:** using his own plans, ag_i infers that he a-depends on ag_j for g_k, but this latter does not a-depend on him for any of his goals:

$$UD(ag_i, ag_j, g_k) \stackrel{def}{\equiv} a_{dep}(ag_i, ag_j, g_k, P_{ik}) \wedge \neg\exists g_l \in G(ag_j)\ a_{dep}(ag_j, ag_i, g_l, P_{il})$$

In our example, agent *jaime* is unilaterally dependent on agent *cristiano* regarding g_1 (because of a_3):

```
Regarding agent:(cristiano)

 jaime
----------  g1
         |----------  g1:=a3(r1).
                   |----------  a3
                             |----------  cristiano
                                       |-----------
Agent (cristiano) have not goal g1 in his current
list of goals
```

5 The DEPNET Simulator

We have implemented a simulator, called DEPNET, which calculates both the dependence relations and situations between agents, and constructs the dependence networks of a given agent. According to the hypothesis of external description compatibility presented in section 2, there is only one external description which is shared by all agents. This simulator is composed of the following facilities:

- *agent edition module:* the user can dynamically create new agents and edit their goals, actions, resources, and plans, or modify the entry of an existing agent in the external description;
- *dependence network constructor:* this module constructs the various dependence networks of a given agent, either related to a specific goal or to all of his goals. It can construct both the a-dependence and the r-dependence networks for both cases;
- *dependence situation constructor:* this module calculates the dependence situations regarding a given agent and one of his goals. The user must specify the type of dependence situation he is interested in analysing.

The DEPNET simulator runs in UNIX workstations, and it was developed using the C++ programming language. The total number of lines of code is approximately 5800.

6 Conclusions and Further Work

In this paper, we have stressed the importance of a **social reasoning mechanism** in an agent's internal model, considering a MAS context. This feature is essential if an agent has to adapt himself to an evolving environment, to take into account information about new members of the agency, in an open system context [7].

The most obvious consequence of using such a mechanism is *decreasing the overall agency communication flow.* Even if every agent sends a broadcasting message to introduce himself, this is done only once, when he enters the agency. Since the others can take into account this information, there is no more need to send a broadcasting message every time an agent needs a given action or resource, as in [11], as he can know a priori the agents he should address.

On the other hand, the proposed framework allows an agent who wants to achieve a given goal to reason about the others in *two* different levels: *whom do I depend on* (in this case he may use only the dependence relations) and *who depends on me* (in this case he can use the dependence situations). Depending on the nature of the agents, these both levels may be used or not. Normally, the second level is hardly used in a benevolent world, where every agent wants to cooperate with the others. On the other hand, self-interested agents that want to achieve their own goals could benefit from the dependence situations in order to get their needed actions/resources more quickly, as described in [9]. Anyway, just the fact of using the first level has already a great impact in reducing the overall agency communication flow.

We intend to improve the *DEPNET simulator* (graphical interfaces, log files for storing sessions, unification mechanism for the plans) and extend the *dependence situations* (taking into account r-dependences as well). The computational models will be *integrated in LIFIA's MAS platform and agent models* (in particular by implementing both an introduction protocol [1] and an internal model of agent that uses the dependence networks in his social reasoning mechanism) and the DEPNET simulator will be used in more sophisticated *micro-social simulations* (to validate some theoretical results, specially concerning three or more party dependences [5]). Finally, we want to propose a model for the *quantification of dependence* (using goals' importance, number of actions and resources involved in a plan and so on). The main idea is to use this quantification to guide a decision mechanism in solving conflicts.

ACKNOWLEDGEMENTS

Most of the work described in this paper was developed between July/October 1993, when Jaime Sichman was working as a visiting researcher at IP/CNR. The authors would like to thank Olivier Boissier (LIFIA/IMAG) and Prof. Helder Coelho (INESC/Lisbon) for their useful comments during the revision of this paper. Yves Demazeau is a research fellow at CNRS, France. Jaime Simão Sichman is on leave from PCS-EPUSP, Brazil, and supported by FAPESP, grant number 91/1943-5.

REFERENCES

[1] S. Berthet, Y. Demazeau, and O. Boissier, 'Knowing each other better', *Proc. 11th. Int. Workshop on Distributed AI*, Glenn Arbor, USA, 1992, p. 23-41.

[2] E. Cardozo, J. S. Sichman and Y. Demazeau, 'Using the active object model to implement multi-agent systems', *Proc. 5th. IEEE Int. Conf. on Tools with AI (TAI'93)*, Boston, USA, 1993, p. 70-77.

[3] C. Castelfranchi, M. Miceli and A. Cesta, 'Dependence relations among autonomous agents', in E. Werner and Y. Demazeau (eds.) *Decentralized A. I. 3*, Elsevier Science Publishers B. V. 1992, p. 215-227.

[4] C. Castelfranchi, 'Social Power: A missing point in Multi-Agent, DAI and HCI', in Y. Demazeau and J. P. Muller (eds.) *Decentralized A. I.*, Elsevier Science Publishers B. V., 1990. p. 49-62.

[5] R. Conte, 'Three-party dependence and rational communication', *Atti del 2do. Incontro AI*IA su IA Distribuita*, Rome, Italy, 1992, p. 105-114.

[6] Y. Demazeau and J. P. Muller, 'From reactive to intentional agents', in Y. Demazeau and J. P. Muller (eds.) *Decentralized A. I. 2*, Elsevier Science Publishers B. V., 1991, p. 3-10.

[7] C. Hewitt, 'Offices are open systems', in A. Bond and L. Gasser (eds.) *Readings in Distributed Artificial Intelligence*, Morgan Kaufmann Publishers Inc., 1988, p. 321-329.

[8] D. Knoke *Political Networks: The Structural Perspective*, Cambridge University Press, 1990.

[9] M. Miceli, A. Cesta and R. Conte, ' Others as resources: cognitive ingredients for agent architecture', in K. Ryan and R. F. Sutcliffe (eds.) *AI and Cognitive Science'92*, Springer-Verlag, 1992. p.84-98.

[10] J. S. Sichman, Y. Demazeau and O. Boissier, 'When can knowledge-based systems be called agents?', *Anais do 9o. Simpósio Brasileiro de IA (SBIA'92)*, Rio de Janeiro, Brazil, 1992, p. 172-185.

[11] R. G. Smith, 'The contract net protocol: high-level communication and control in a distributed problem solver', *IEEE Transactions on Computers*, v. 29, n. 12, p. 1104-1113, Dec. 1980.

[12] E. S. K. Yu and J. Mylopoulos, 'An actor dependency model of organizational work with application to business process reengineering', *Proc. of the Conference on Organizational Computing Systems (COOCS'93)*, Milpitas, USA, 1993.

The Society of Objects

Mario Tokoro
Keio University &
Sony Computer Science Laboratory Inc.

Abstract

In this paper, I will first review the notions of objects and concurrent objects and discuss their main roles. Then, I will introduce two observations on our current computer systems and explain why we need an evolved notion of objects, which we call *autonomous agents,* to describe *open* and *distributed* systems. An autonomous agent is a software *individual* that reacts to inputs according to its situation and its goal of survival. A collection of such autonomous agents shows emergent behaviors which cannot be ascribed to individuals, eventually forming a *society.* Research into achieving a society of autonomous agents being carried out at Sony Computer Science Laboratory and Keio University will then be presented. In the last section, I will speculate about yet-to-be-realized computational modules called *volitional agents,* that could be used to create safe, evolutionarily stable, cohabitating society.

1 Introduction

Human society is characterized by a dichotomy between individuals with their goals and aspirations, and the emergence of collective behavior that cannot be ascribed to individuals. Intriguingly, computational systems and environments are beginning to exhibit some of the collective behavior that is characteristic of society.

As high speed communication networks proliferate, every computer and, thus, every software module is connected with every other. An enormous variety of software, with many variants for each type, has already been produced, and will continue to be produced by a great many software manufacturers. Hence, future software systems will consist of multi-vendor software, often dynamically integrated, residing at multiple sites as servers. Software modules, or servers, are dynamically shared by multiple users, and may be changed from time to time. Future software systems will also exhibit dynamic resource discovery. It will be useful to view such systems as forming a society that is analogous to human society and interleaved with it.

Hence, we need an evolved notion of objects, derived from a dynamic and interactive viewpoint. In this context, I will speculate on what the evolved notion of objects is, and how future software should be composed. I will first review the notions of objects and concurrent objects. Then, I will present two observations on our current computing systems operating in open, distributed environments, and illustrate the necessity for higher-level software modules called *autonomous agents.* Then, I will present some of our research work, being carried out at Sony Computer Science Laboratory and Keio University. This research is aimed at achieving a society of autonomous agents that cohabit with human society. The presentation features a personal, personified computer with a face and capable of vocal communication, called the *Intimate Computer;* an infrastructure model that abstracts future open, distributed computing environments, called the *Computational Field Model (CFM);* the *Apertos* distributed, real-time operating system; and the *Virtual Internet Protocol (VIP)* mobile host protocol. In the last section, I will be a little provocative in advocating an even more advanced notion of autonomous agents, called *volitional agents,* that could be used to create safe, evolutionarily stable, cohabitating society. I will conclude this paper with a description of recent developments toward the understanding of collective behavior in terms of dynamic, non-deterministic, stochastic, and irreversible processes taking root in various scientific fields.

2 From Objects to Concurrent Objects

The world in which we live is *concurrent* in the sense that there are multiple active entities; *distributed* such that there is a distance between entities that yields a propagation delay in communication between them; and *open,* meaning that the entities and their environment are always changing. Computation can be considered as a simulation of part of the real or an imaginary world. In doing a simulation, you can model your problem in terms of sequential computing, concurrent computing, distributed computing or open computing. To solve a simple, small problem, sequential computing is usually sufficient. However, when the problem becomes larger and more realistic, it is much easier to model it as concurrent, distributed, or open computing. For example, if you have multiple users at a time, such as in banking or airline reservation systems, you would naturally model the problem in the form of concurrent or distributed computing.

2.1 Objects

The notion of *objects* provides a very convenient way of describing problems in any of sequential to concurrent, distributed, or open computing. An object is usually considered as being a physical or logical entity with a unified communication protocol, which is usually message passing [44]. It is composed of a local storage and a set of procedures, as shown in Figure 1.

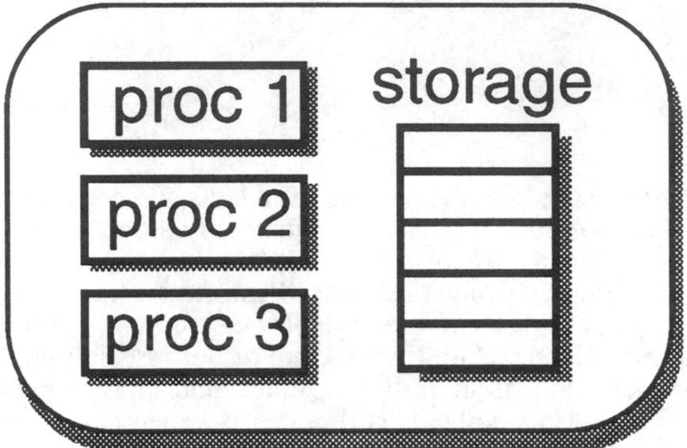

Figure 1: An Object

However, if we examine more closely what an object is, it can be seen to be an abstraction of computation as things. Chairs, pens, books, ... these are *things*. The sky, air, and water are not usually considered as being things. Things can be distinguished from others. An apple is distinguished from other apples. Water in a glass can now be distinguished from other glasses of water. This is the external view of things. The other characterization is that a thing has both an inside and an outside. This is the internal view of things. Programming and computing a problem in terms of the interaction between things is the true benefit of object orientation. It is for this reason that the notion of objects is applicable equally to concurrent, distributed, and open computing.

Object-oriented computing can be understood as being a movement from a microscopic view of computing to macroscopic view, where microscopic corresponds to computation done by executing an algorithm, and macroscopic is computation done using the mutual effects of objects.

However, objects in most existing languages and systems are sequential, and therefore, static, or passive. This is a remnant of programming styles from when the computer was centralized and based on a uniprocessor. Using this kind of object abstraction, programmers have to write execution control, or processor allocation, for objects, if they need to write a concurrent program. That is, we need the notion of *processes* on top of the notion of objects. This is very inconvenient and is a common source of errors. The fundamental reason for this is that real *things* are not like this. Every thing exists and behaves simultaneously on its own right. Analogically, every object should exist and behave simultaneously. Therefore, it should have its own processor.

2.2 Concurrent Objects

The notion of *concurrent objects* is an extremely significant development. A concurrent object contains a (virtual) processor, as shown in Figure 2. Here, we can eliminate the notion of processes which is necessary in concurrent programming using sequential objects. Programmers don't have to describe execution control. Concurrent objects are executed in the same way as in time-sharing systems.

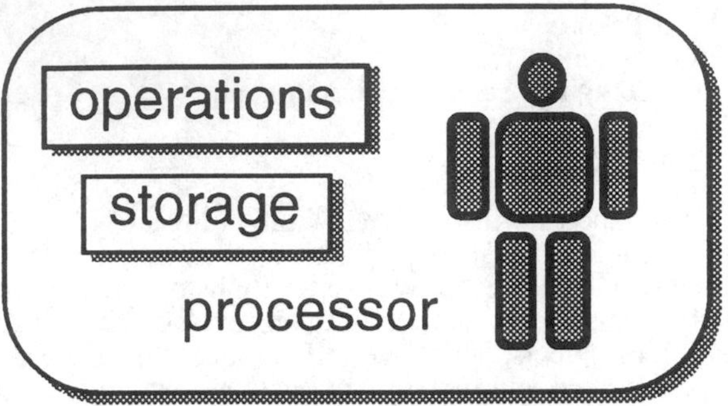

Figure 2: A Concurrent Object

We can trace the history of concurrent objects back to the early 70's when Carl Hewitt proposed Actors [16, 1]. Since then, many concurrent object-oriented languages and systems have been proposed and used. Concurrent Smalltalk [56] and Orient84/K [24] are languages which I designed with my co-researchers. ABCL [59], POOL [3], Concurrent Eiffel [7], Concurrent C++ [15], Active Objects [34], and many other languages have also been designed. It was almost ten years later when I edited the book titled, "Object-Oriented Concurrent Programming" with Aki Yonezawa [60]. The notion of concurrent objects can be found in the field of operating systems, too. Examples include Eden [5] and Apertos [57, 58]. Theoretical investigations on concurrent objects have also been pursued, such as π-calculus [30] and ν-calculus [19, 20]. Some recent accomplishments are detailed in [2].

Although the notion of concurrent objects is a more natural means of modeling things in programming, it has not yet found practical or commercial use. This is probably just a matter of the notion not yet being well known. It takes some time, say 10 years or so, until people actually feel comfortable with a new notion. Virtual memory is one such example, and (sequential) object-oriented programming is another. The notion of concurrent objects will become much more important when we need to migrate objects in a widely distributed environment. I fully expect the notion of concurrent objects to be accepted and widely utilized in the near future.

In summary, the most important role of objects (for both sequential and concurrent objects) is modularity: that is, to enable the writing of a program as a thing with interface. This affords us various benefits, such as macroscopic programming, analysis and design, classes and instances, class hierarchies, concurrency, and so on.

3 Computation in Open, Distributed Environments

I have been doing research on concurrent objects for more than ten years. The notion is neat, and provides us with a very appropriate level of abstraction. As such, it seemed as though it would be enough for describing distributed and even open systems. I tried to convince myself that concurrent objects would be enough. And, I was almost fully convinced. But something had annoyed me for a long time and prevented me from being fully convinced. In the following subsections, after presenting the essential characteristics of open, distributed systems, I will explain what it was that annoyed me by observing two example systems.

3.1 Essential Characteristics

The technical characteristics of open and distributed systems can be summarized as follows. Distributed systems are characterized by there being distance between objects, which results in communication delays. Distance, and therefore delay, has an inherent consequence that there is no unique global view of the system. The state-space of the system that one observer sees is different from the state space a distant observer sees. Since there is delay in communication, we use asynchronous communication for the sake of efficiency. Asynchronous communication means that the timing when the sender sends a message and that when the receiver receives it are different. By using asynchronous communication, we can exploit the concurrency between computation and communication.

Open systems are characterized by their entities and environments constantly changing. Widely distributed systems are usually open systems, since the topology of the networks, the component computers, and the functions, quality, and locations of the services are dynamically changing. Thus, our future computing environment will be modeled well as an open, distributed environment.

3.2 Two Observations

Here, I would like to describe two observations on our computing systems, which offer a good prediction of future computing environments.

The first observation is as follows: Assume you need a system. You write a specification, you program it or have somebody else program it, and you use it. Then, after a while, or perhaps even before the completion of the system, you need to change it. And at a later time, you need to change it again. This is the problem of version management. As everybody knows, it is not easy to follow how the current system is composed, and how it works.

Version management is much more complex in open, distributed environments. Assume your friends or colleagues happen to know that you have a good system. So, they ask you for permission to use it. They are usually at remote sites, so they want to use your system through remote procedure calls (or remote object calls). However, they also request revision of the system to tailor the system to their particular needs. This tends to be repeated over and over, in a distributed manner. Thus, after a while, nobody understands the inner workings of the system, even though the users are using the system at a reasonably satisfactory rate. However, a problem arises when somebody finds a bug. How can the system be debugged and maintained without interfering with the other users? What should be done if the system stops? Can you, in fact, depend on the system at all?

The second observation is of almost the same problem, but from a different viewpoint. Nowadays, programs with the same functions are provided by many different vendors, so that users can choose those that best fit their needs and budget. For example, user #1 buys an OS from vendor #1, and a windowing system from vendor #2, etc. This is very good situation for the users.

Vendors request software houses to develop program modules, and buy complete modules from other vendors, and combine those modules into software products for release under the vendor's own brand. I call this *nested multi-vendor software* in the sense that software vendors use other software vendors' software as their components. Up to this point, users have a *physical* copy of the software on their machines.

However, the next step is a distributed version. Here, the users don't have a copy on their machines. Instead, they only have a calling program and the right to access programs on the vendors' machines. In turn, the software on the vendors' machines will call program modules residing on machines located at software houses, and so on. I would like to call this *distributed, nested multi-vendor software.* Here, no physical copy of the programs are made. Instead, they perform *remote procedure calls,* or *remote object calls* to each other. In fact, this is already happening. You are using a program on your network through a license server. The program may use other programs remotely (Figure 3).

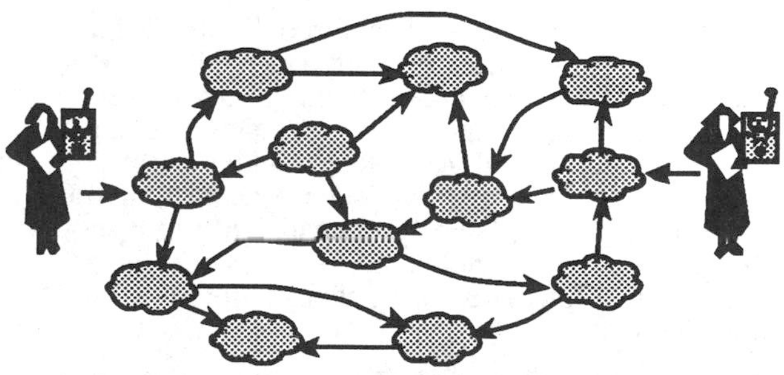

Figure 3: Distributed, Nested Servers

Once again, assume that somebody finds a bug. How can the system be debugged and maintained without interfering with the other users? What should be done if the system stops? Can you depend on the system at all?

I would like to summarize that, in open and distributed systems, we use a software module without having complete knowledge of it. Thus, it would appear to be like it is changing by itself. And, you need to discover the services you need. Then, you have to write your program in such a way that it protects the users or customers, by protecting the services and defending the computational resources you provide.

I don't think that concurrent objects provide a suitable framework for such defensive programming. First, I would like to claim that we need the notion of time for programming open, distributed systems. This necessity is derived from the fact that the essential difference between a distributed system and a concurrent system is the existence of *distance* in the system, which is equivalent to *time*. Second, we need a higher level module than a concurrent object for constructing a larger system. Hence, the above situations can be naturally modeled as a society of such modules. Let's call such a higher level module an *autonomous agent*.

4 Autonomous Agents

Now, I would like to give a rough definition of *autonomous agents*. First, I would like to clarify that the notion of autonomous agents does not conflict with the notion of objects or concurrent objects. In fact, an agent will be composed of concurrent objects, in much the same way as a person is composed of cells living concurrently. An autonomous agent is the unit of *individual* software, that interfaces with humans, other agents, and the real world in real-time. Each autonomous agent has its own goal, and reacts to stimuli, based on its situation. It behaves to survive. The collection of autonomous agents forms a society.

The definition of an individual is most important in thinking about autonomous agents. This is one kind of granularity argument, but taken from a completely different viewpoint, i.e., not for parallelism or efficiency, but for robustness or defensive programming. According to recent findings in biology and the theory of evolution, definition is very difficult, almost impossible, in fact. But we will not take such a serious approach. We instead use a naive, intuitive definition:

An individual autonomous agent is a collection of component objects (or cells) that are not physically shared with other individuals.

We assume an individual is a unit of feedback for utility or reward. An individual can be considered as being the unit of security, which corresponds to our bodies' immune system. It can also be regarded as being the unit of reliability and maintenance which corresponds to homeostasis. That is to say, security and reliability have to be provided and maintenance has to be done on an individual basis, not as a whole system. Each individual autonomous agent should provide such abilities per se.

For its functionality, each autonomous agent has an individual goal. It is reactive, in the sense that it responds to a stimulus, taking the situation or environment into consideration, in real-time. This implies that an autonomous agent is not just an object that responds to an input, but also needs to be able to learn the situation, and to have the ability to make timely decisions in real-time.

Survival is yet another important property of each individual autonomous agent. This property is, in fact, the result of only autonomous agents with a higher survivability surviving. To survive, an autonomous agent has to make its *best effort* to satisfy the users, in terms of response time and functionality; or the quality of services in general, so that it can maximize its utility. Restaurants with bad food or those that makes you wait one hour for "today's special" would never survive. To survive, an autonomous agent has to keep its losses to a minimum. This is called the *least suffering* strategy. A simple example is that, if your order doesn't come within one hour, you should decide whether to wait longer or move to a different restaurant. You have to monitor the situation and make a decision on *time-out*. That is to say, time-out is the last resort for survival in open, distributed systems. A simple programming language [47] and a formal system [42], which provide for the agents' survivability by incorporating a time-out notion, were presented at OOPSLA'92 by myself and my co-authors.

Agents should provide the facility of reflection to allow their adaptation to environments [28, 25]. Agents with negotiation ability are advantageous. Agents that can maintain a cooperative relationship for a longer duration are more profitable. They can form a group, and thus, society. Research on negotiation, cooperation, and group formation can be seen in one area of Artificial Intelligence, called "Distributed AI" [23, 13] or "Multiagent Systems" [10].

5 Current Research Activities

Here, I would like to present some of our research activities into open and distributed systems, currently being carried out at Sony Computer Science Laboratory and Keio University. The work is mainly based on concurrent objects and, as a whole, on autonomous agents.

I believe that a future computer system must be:

- *ubiquitous*, so that you can use it any time and anywhere;
- *portable and mobile*, so that you can carry it and use it on the move;
- *reliable and secure*, so that you can depend on it; and
- *friendly*, so that it is comfortable and easy to use.

With the ultimate goal of realizing such a computer system, I have been proposing two notions: *intimate computers* and *computational field* [52, 53].

5.1 Intimate Computers

Intimacy implies security, peace of mind, trustworthiness, reliability, and respect. The intimate computer is intended to inspire users with such a feeling. It has a face, and it understands natural languages, so that it presents you with a completely different user-computer interface from those we are used to today (Figure 4). An intimate computer can be seen as an autonomous agent overall, whereas it is composed of a collection of autonomous agents.

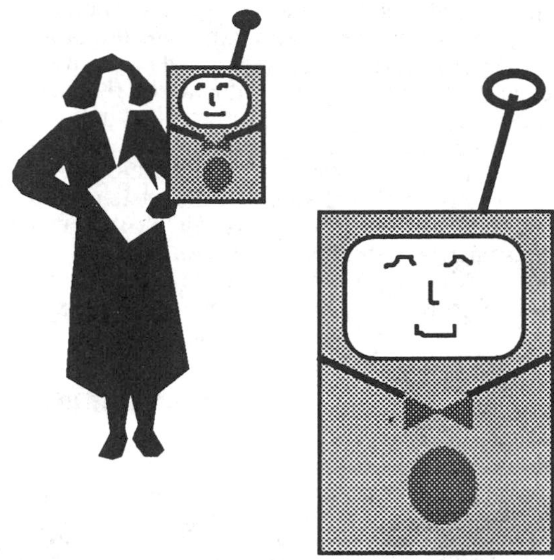

Figure 4: An Intimate Computer

An intimate computer can be thought of as an evolved version of a Personal Digital Assistant. It can be used as an access terminal to distributed computing facilities. It can be used as a communication terminal to access other intimate computers and their users. But, the ultimate purpose is the dialog itself; understanding each other and recognizing each other, rather than an interchange of ordering and inquiring.

Unfortunately, intimate computers are not yet available, but the following is an example of a possible conversation with an intimate computer in the future:

> *"Hey buddy, could you arrange a dinner meeting with Ralph?"*

My intimate computer understands who I mean by Ralph, asks Ralph's intimate computer when he is available, what kind of food he likes, makes a reservation for a restaurant, then comes back to me saying,

> *"It's done."*

On another occasion, my intimate computer suddenly talks to me

> *"Hey, Mario, how're you doing?"*

And I respond

> *"Don't bother me now!"*

Then, my intimate computer exultantly says to me

> *"Sorry, but I guess you forget something. It's your daughter's birthday. You should go back home right now!"*

5.2 Computational Field Model

To make intimate computers usable in a distributed environment, we need an infrastructure. I am proposing a higher-level abstraction of distributed computing than that of computers connected by networks. Forget about computers and networks; let's consider the field of computers. It is like a sea of computers. Concurrent objects are floating on the sea (Figure 5). The sea, the Computational Field, yields various forces between objects for the suboptimal placement of objects for moving users, grouping objects, balancing loads, and avoiding faults, such as:

- *Gravitational force* is defined for grouping objects. Frequent communication between objects yields a stronger force.
- *Repulsive force* is defined for load balancing. If two objects come very close, the repulsive force increases between them.
- *Friction* is defined for stability. It is proportional to the size, or weight of each object, so that a large object tends not to move.

Significance of the Computational Field Model is that it integrates load balancing and object grouping.

Figure 5: Computational Field Model

I will explain how the Computational Field works (Figure 6). If you place a task in the Computational Field, a mountain is formed which is a collection of concurrent objects for the given task. Then, a repulsive force between the objects arises, so that the mountain becomes lower and lower. At the same time, the gravitational force between concurrent objects increases, as they send messages to each other. Thus, they form a hill, as the two forces balance. If the user moves, the mountain follows.

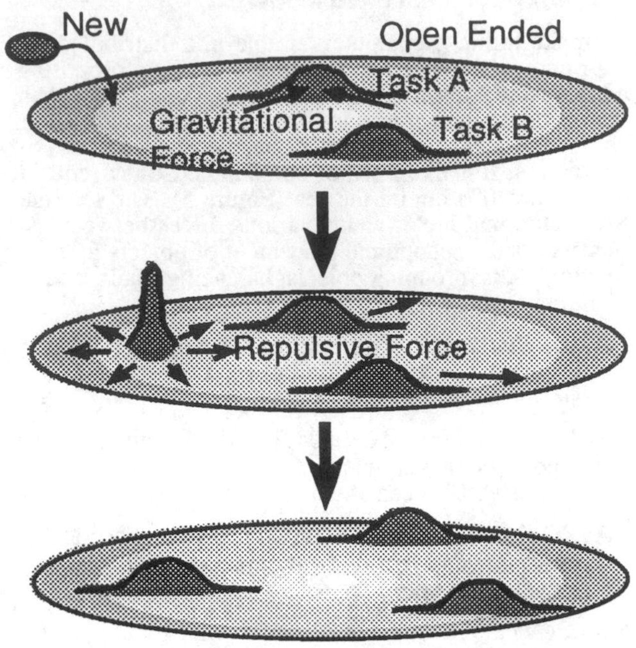

Figure 6: Dynamic Object Placement

All those properties are actually realized by an underlying distributed operating system. Also, the notion of concurrent objects is indispensable for object migration, as pointed out above.

5.3 Essential Technologies

To realize intimate computers and the computational field, many points demand our attention. We are currently concentrating our efforts on the following five topics:

- Multi-Modal Interaction
- Operating Systems
- Computer Networks
- Programming Languages, and
- Multi-Agent Systems

Demonstration videos are available for the first three topics.

Speech Dialog with Facial Displays

The first demonstration is of the speech dialog system with facial displays [48, 33]. The system was developed to verify the idea of bringing facial displays into human computer interaction as a new modality to make computers more communicative and sociable. It consists of two subsystems. One is a speech dialog subsystem. The other is a facial animation subsystem.

The speech dialog subsystem consists of a speech recognition module, a syntactic and semantic analyzer, a plan recognition module, a response generation module, and a voice synthesis module. It realizes speaker-independent speech recognition and handles the speaker's intentions. A facial animation subsystem generates a facial display by the local deformation of the polygons representing the 3D face. We adopted Keith Waters method [55] for our deformation scheme. Lip and speech synchronization was also implemented.

The speech dialog subsystem recognizes a number of typical conversational situations that are important in dialog. These situations are associated with specific conversational facial displays categorized by Nicole Chovil [8]. Upon detecting a prescribed situation, each module in the speech dialog subsystem sends a request for a specific facial display to the facial animation subsystem. An empirical study of the system with 32 subjects indicated that the speech dialog system with facial displays is helpful, especially in the first interaction with the system. An example of a session is shown in Figure 7.

Figure 7: Speech Dialog System with Facial Displays

The system uses two workstations, one for speech dialog and the other for facial display, running in real-time mode. The speech dialog subsystem is designed as a multi-agent system, whereas the facial display subsystem is currently a collection of C programs. We plan to introduce more modalities, such as reading the user's face. We are also interested in investigating the relationship between the framework of our work with social knowledge and social actions, as presented by Les Gasser [14].

Apertos Distributed Real-Time OS

The second demonstration is on the Apertos operating system [57, 58]. The Apertos OS is a pure object-oriented, real-time OS, based on concurrent objects. It clearly separates objects and meta-objects, and it can evolve by itself by using the mechanism of reflection, without stopping. Object migration and distributed naming mechanisms are provided at the system level. That is, this supports the Computational Field. The Apertos OS has been stably operating on Sony's 68030-based workstations since April 1991, and was recently ported to Sony's R3000-based workstations and 486-based IBM PC-compatible computers.

Virtual Internet Protocol

The last demonstration is of the computer network protocol that supports mobile hosts. It is called the *Virtual Internet Protocol,* or VIP for short [50, 49]. By using this protocol, you can hook-off your portable workstation from the current network, move with it, and hook it into any interconnected network. You can obtain the same computing environment there, and all messages are redirected to the new location, taking their optimal routes. You can even move with your portable workstation while preserving communication channels. The mechanism we designed is analogue to that of virtual memory. Virtual to physical address translation is done in a distributed manner by using cached mapping information. Since this protocol is implemented as a sublayer of IP, it is transparent to application programs. It has been running since spring of 1992, and has been proposed to the Internet Engineering Task Force (IETF) for standardization.

VIP protocol is running on UNIX and MS-DOS machines, but is not described in an object-oriented style at this moment. Porting to Apertos OS in an object-oriented fashion will be done very soon. We are also interested in combining this technology with real-time communication facilities [43].

Programming Languages and Multi-Agent Systems

We are intensively doing research on Programming Languages and Multi-Agent Systems. Regarding the former field, we are especially interested in persistent object programming languages [54, 31], distributed transactions [18] and the applicability of the notion of reflection to distributed and real-time programming [37, 21]. For the latter, we are interested in collaboration [38, 29].

6 Volitional Agents

I have proposed concurrent objects and autonomous agents, and have presented some of our research at Sony Computer Science Laboratory and Keio University. Here, I would like to raise the final question, that is:

> *Are autonomous agents sufficient for future computing? Are they safe? Are they stable? Are they cooperative to humans?*

In fact, I don't have any answer to these questions. But, I would like to be a little provocative and controversial in saying that the definition of autonomous agents given in section 4 may not be sufficient, safe, or cooperative to humans, and that a society composed of such autonomous agents would not be stable. Hence, I would like to propose *volitional agents.* Volition means "actions with will" or "actions of will." So, a volitional agent is an autonomous agent with will, or a spontaneous autonomous agent. A volitional agent is more active than an autonomous agent which is "reactive." It has desire, or it is aggressive [27].

I am saying that volitional agents are safer, more stable, and more cooperative with humans, compared to autonomous agents that are reactive. Reactive implies passive in a sense, since the agent doesn't perform any action unless it receives input. A society of autonomous, reactive agents may seem safe and stable, because they are passive. But that can be the very source of danger. You cannot know anything unless you give an input to the society, which may eventually result in a fatal damage.

Volitional agents are active and dynamic, and are doing something all the time. Internally, they will have antagonistic desires. Externally, they will have contentions with other agents. They will cooperate to achieve higher utility, and they will compete with each other to survive through natural selection (since computer environments are rather artificial than natural, we may need minimal legislation to ensure fair competition). They might behave selfishly [9].

Since volitional agents are active, and society is living, we can observe the behavior of the society. And, we can obtain even a higher stability of the society. Of course, it is impossible to predict the precise behavior in any ways, since the system is very large and complex. However, we can take advantage of recent developments in the study of complex dynamical systems. For example, according to the theory of *chaos* [11], it is given that under a certain condition, a system of active or dynamic components give a higher stability than that of passive or static components.

A society of agents, as well as our own society, should be evolutionarily stable. This means that society is stable for a while, but the environment changes, so that it rather quickly moves to the next stable state. This phenomenon can also be explained for a system of active or dynamic components as a phase transition by taking the same approach. Hence, we can conclude that volitional agents can provide a higher stability without sacrificing flexibility of the society than autonomous agents. This will lead to a society that is safer and more cooperative with humans.

The importance, and the necessity for aggressiveness in forming a stable society has been studied in the field of biology and ethology, such as in the work of Nikolass Tinbergen [51] and Konrad Lorenz [27]. The stability of society has also been intensively studied by political scientist Axelrod [4], biologist Maynard-Smith [45], and other researchers, taking game-theoretic approaches. Study for the behavior of society taking dynamical systems approaches are found in the new area called "Ecology of Computation" [22] or "Emergent Computation" [12]. We have also started research in this direction, particularly on chaos and collective behavior [35, 46, 36]. Distributed and massively parallel computing are expected to be powerful computing platforms [26].

7 Conclusions

I have discussed a couple of things in this paper. Objects are things which can be distinguished from others. This notion brought us "macroscopic programming." Concurrent objects are the "real" self-contained objects including virtual processors. This provided us with easy concurrent programming. Objects and concurrent objects are the cells for autonomous agents. Autonomous agents are based on the notion of the individual, are reactive, and try to survive. They form a society.

Then, I described and showed our recent research accomplishments toward the society of agents: the Intimate Computer, the Computational Field Model, the Apertos object-oriented OS and the VIP mobile host protocol. Finally, I raised a controversial proposal for volitional agents, that would provide safer and more cooperative interaction with humans and other agents, and that would provide an evolutionarily stable society, with which we can cohabit.

The notion of volitional agents is a conjecture, without any proof. We don't know how to make a volitional agent. We don't even know what "desire," or "aggressiveness" mean. But a new way of understanding collective behavior in terms of dynamic, nondeterministic, stochastic, and irreversible processes is taking root in various scientific fields. I have already mentioned this trend in biology, ethology, and the theory of evolution. We can also see similar movements in AI, such as the Society of Mind by Marvin Minsky [32] and the Subsumption Architecture by Rodney Brooks [6]. It is also happening in Chemistry and Physics. For example, a new view is given based on Thermodynamics by Ilya Prigogine [41]. It is giving us the sign of departing from the "reductionist attitude" or the "Cartesian attitude" in science.

The notion of Open Systems was advocated by philosopher Karl Popper [39, 40] and brought in to computer science by Carl Hewitt [17]. We must inevitably see Distributed and Open Systems as societies. This is already coming. In this paper, I proposed the notion of autonomous agents and volitional agents as individuals of societies. Volition might be the true meaning of autonomy, and may realize a safe, stable, cooperational society with computers.

Acknowledgment

I would like to thank Akikazu Takeuchi, Yasuhiko Yokote, Fumio Teraoka, Katashi Nagao, Hiroaki Kitano, Jun Tani, Toru Ohira, Chisato Numaoka, Shigeru Watari, Tatsumi Nagayama, and other researchers at Sony Computer Science Laboratory; Kohei Honda, Ichiro Satoh, Vasco Vasconcelos, and many other students and ex-students at Keio University; Aki Yonezawa, Satoshi Matsuoka, Gregor Kiczales, Eric Manning, Koiti Hasida, Jörg Kaiser, and many other friends of mine in computer science, for their inspiring discussions and help in preparing for the speech and this manuscript. Finally, I would like to thank the many members of the audience at the OOPSLA'93 conference who gave me useful comments and encouraged me to prepare this manuscript.

References

[1] Agha, G., *ACTORS: A Model of Concurrent Computation in Distributed Systems,* MIT Press, 1986.

[2] Agha, G., Wegner, P., and Yonezawa, A., eds, *Research Directions in Concurrent Object-Oriented Programming,* MIT Press, 1993.

[3] America, P., *POOL-T: A Parallel Object-Oriented Language, in Object-Oriented Concurrent Programming,* eds. Yonezawa, A., and Tokoro, M., MIT Press, 1987.

[4] Axelrod, R., *The Evolution of Co-operation,* Basic Books, Inc., 1984.

[5] Black, A. P., "Supporting Distributed Applications: Experience with Eden," *Proceedings of ACM Symposium on Operating System Principles,* p. 39–51, December, 1985.

[6] Brooks, R., "Intelligence Without Representation," *Artificial Intelligence,* Vol. 47, p. 139–160, 1991.

[7] Caromel, D., "Concurrency: An Object-Oriented Approach," *Proceedings of TOOL2,* p. 183–198, June, 1990.

[8] Chovil, N., "Discourse-Oriented Facial Displays in Conversation," *Research on Language and Social Interaction,* Vol. 25, p. 163–194, 1991

[9] Dawkins, R., *The Selfish Gene (2nd Edition),* Oxford University Press, 1989.

[10] Demazeau, Y., Muller, J.-P., and/or Werner, E, *Decentralized A.I. 1, 2, and 3,* North-Holland, 1990, 1991, and 1992.

[11] Devaney, R. L., An Introduction to *Chaotic Dynamical Systems (2nd Edition),* Addison-Wesley, 1989.

[12] Forrest, S. (ed.), *Emergent computation,* MIT Press, 1991.

[13] Gasser, L. and Huhns, M. (eds.), *Distributed Artificial Intelligence Vol.2,* Pittman, London, 1989.

[14] Gasser, L., "Social Knowledge and Social Action: Heterogeneity in Practice," *Proceedings of International Joint Conference on Artificial Intelligence (IJCAI'93),* p. 751–758, 1993.

[15] Gehani, N. H., "Concurrent C++: Concurrent Programming with Class(es)," *Software Practice and Experience,* Vol.16, No.12, Dec, 1988.

[16] Hewitt, C. E., "A Universal, Modular Actor Formalism for Artificial Intelligence," *Proceedings of International Joint Conference on Artificial Intelligence,* 1973.

[17] Hewitt, C. E., "The Challenge of Open Systems," *Byte,* April 1985, p. 223–242, 1985.

[18] Hirotsu, T., "A Flexible Transaction Facility for Distributed Object-Oriented Systems," *Proceedings of IEEE Workshop on Object-Orientation in Operating Systems,* September, 1992.

[19] Honda, K. and Tokoro, M., "An Object Calculus for Asynchronous Communication," *Proceedings of ECOOP'91,* LNCS 512, p. 133–147, June, 1991.

[20] Honda, K. and Tokoro, M., "Combinator Representation of Mobile Processes," *Proceedings of Symposium on Principle of Programming Languages,* January, 1993.

[21] Honda, Y. and Tokoro, M., "Soft Real-Time Programming through Reflection," *Proceedings of IMSA'92 International Workshop on Reflection and Meta-level Architectures,* 1992

[22] Huberman, B. A. (ed), *The Ecology of Computation,* North-Holland, 1988.

[23] Huhns, M. N. (ed), *Distributed Artificial Intelligence, Vol. 1,* Pitman, London, 1987.

[24] Ishikawa, Y. and Tokoro, M., "A Concurrent Object-Oriented Knowledge Representation Language Orient84/K: Its Features and Implementation," *Proceedings of OOPSLA'86,* p. .232–241, September, 1986.

[25] Kiczales, G., "Towards a New Model of Abstraction in Software Engineering," *Proceedings of the IMSA'92 International Workshop on Reflection and Meta-level Architectures,* 1992.

[26] Kitano, H. and Hendler, J., eds., *Massively Parallel Artificial Intelligence,* The MIT Press, 1994.

[27] Lorenz, K., *Das Sogenannte Böse,* Dr. G. Borotha-Schoeler Verlag, 1963.

[28] Maes, P., "Concepts and Experiments in Computational Reflection," *Proceedings of OOPSLA'87,* p. 147–155, 1987.

[29] Matsubayashi, K., "A Collaboration Mechanism on Positive Interactions in Multi-Agent Environments," *Proceedings of International Joint Conference on Artificial Intelligence (IJCAI'93),* p. 346–351, August, 1993.

[30]Milner, R., Parrow, J., and Walker, D., "A Calculus of Mobile Processes, Part 1 & 2," Technical report ECS-LFCS-89–85 & 86, University of Edinburgh, 1989.

[31] Minohara, T. and Tokoro, M., "Providing Dynamic Abstractions and Type Specifications for Persistent Information," *Proceedings of Int. Conf. on Deductive and Object-Oriented Databases,* December, 1991.

[32] Minsky, M., *The Society of Mind,* Simon and Schuster, New York, 1987.

[33] Nagao, K. and Takeuchi, A., "A New Modality for Natural Human-Computer Interaction: Integration of Speech Dialogue and Facial Animation," *Proceedings of the International Symposium on Spoken Dialogue (ISSD'93),* p. 129–132, 1993.

[34] Nierstrasz, O. M., "Active Objects in Hybrid," *Proceedings of OOPSLA'87,* p. 243–253, September, 1987.

[35] Numaoka, C. and Takeuchi, A., "Collective Choice of Strategic Type," *Proceedings of International Conference on Simulation of Adaptive Behavior (SAB92),* December. 1992.

[36] Ohira, T. and Cowan, J. D., "Feynman Diagrams for Stochastic Neurodynamics," *Proceedings of Australian Conference of Neural Networks,* January 1994.

[37] Okamura, H., Ishikawa, Y., and Tokoro, M., "Metalevel Decomposition in AL-1/D," *Proceedings of Object Technologies for Advanced Software,* LNCS No. 742, p. 110–127, November, 1993.

[38] Osawa, E., "A Scheme for Agent Collaboration in Open Multiagent Environment," *Proceedings of International Joint Conference on Artificial Intelligence (IJCAI'93),* p. 352–358, August, 1993.

[39] Popper, K. R., *The Open Society and its Enemies,* Princeton University Press, 1945.

[40] Popper, K. R. and Lorenz, K., *Die Zukunft ist Offen (The Future is Open),* R. Piper GmbH & Co., 1985.

[41] Prigogine, I. and Stengers, I., *Order out of Chaos,* Bantam Books, 1984.

[42] Satoh, I. and Tokoro, M., "A Formalism for Real-Time Concurrent Object-Oriented Computing," *Proceedings of OOPSLA'92,* p. 315–326, 1992.

[43] Shionozaki, A. and Tokoro, M., "Control Handling in Real-Time Communication Protocols," *Proceedings of SIGCOMM'93,* 1993.

[44] Shriver, B. and Wegner, P, eds., *Research Directions in Object-Oriented Programming,* MIT Press, 1987.

[45] Maynard Smith, J., *Evolution and the Theory of Games,* Cambridge University Press, 1982.

[46] Tani, J. and Fukumura, N., "Learning Goal-directed Sensory-based Navigation of a Mobile Robot," *Neural Networks,* in press.

[47] Takashio, K. and Tokoro, M., "DROL: An Object-Oriented Programming Language for Distributed Real-time Systems," *Proceedings of ACM OOPSLA'92,* p. 276–294, October, 1992.

[48] Takeuchi, A. and Nagao, K., "Communicative Facial Displays as a New Conversational Modality," *Proceedings of ACM/IFIP INTERCHI, 1993.*

[49] Teraoka, F., Yokote, Y., and Tokoro, M., "A Network Architecture Providing Host Migration Transparency," *Proceedings of ACM SIGCOMM'91,* p. 209–220, 1991.

[50] Teraoka, F., Claffy, K, and Tokoro, M., "Design, Implementation, and Evaluation of Virtual Internet Protocol," *Proceedings of 12th International Conference on Distributed Computing Systems,* p. 170–177, 1992.

[51] Tinbergen, N., *Social Behaviour in Animals,* Methuen & Co. Ltd., 1953.

[52] Tokoro, M., "Computational Field Model: Toward a New Computing Model/Methodology for Open Distributed Environment," *Proceedings 2nd IEEE Workshop on Future Trends in Distributed Computing Systems,* September, 1990.

[53] Uehara, M. and Tokoro, M., "An Adaptive Load Balancing Method in the Computational Field Model," *OOPS Messenger, Vol. 2, No. 2,* April, 1991.

[54] Watari, S., Honda, Y., and Tokoro, M., "Morphe: A Constraint-Based Object-Oriented Language Supporting Situated Knowledge," *Proceedings of International Conference on Fifth Generation Computer Systems,* 1992.

[55] Waters, K., "A Muscle Model for Animating Three-Dimensional Facial Expression," *Computer Graphics,* Vol. 21, No. 4, p. 17–24, 1987.

[56] Yokote, Y. and Tokoro, M., "The Design and Implementation of Concurrent SmallTalk," *Proceedings of OOPSLA'86,* p. 331–340, September, 1986.

[57] Yokote, Y., Teraoka, F., and Tokoro, M., "A Reflective Architecture for an Object-Oriented Distributed Operating System," *Proceedings of ECOOP'89,* p. 89–108, July, 1989.

[58] Yokote, Y., "The Apertos Reflective Operating System: The Concept and its Implementation," *Proceedings of OOPSLA'92,* p. 397–413, October, 1992.

[59] Yonezawa, A., eds., *ABCL An Object-Oriented Concurrent Systems,* MIT Press, 1990.

[60] Yonezawa, A. and Tokoro, M., eds., *Object-Oriented Concurrent Programming,* MIT Press, 1987.

Formalizing the Cooperative Problem Solving Process

Michael Wooldridge
Agent Systems Group
Zuno Ltd
Ealing Broadway Centre
London W5 5DB, United Kingdom
mjw@dlib.com

Nicholas R. Jennings
Department of Electronic Engineering
Queen Mary & Westfield College
Mile End Road
London E1 4NS, United Kingdom
N.R.Jennings@qmw.ac.uk

Abstract

One objective of distributed artificial intelligence research is to build systems that are capable of cooperative problem solving. To this end, a number of implementation-oriented models of cooperative problem solving have been developed. However, *mathematical* models of social activity have focussed only on limited aspects of the cooperative problem solving process: no mathematical model of the entire process has yet been described. In this paper, we rectify this omission. We present a preliminary model that describes the cooperative problem solving process from recognition of the potential for cooperation through to team action. The model is formalised by representing it as a theory in a quantified multi-modal logic. A key feature of the model is its reliance on the twin notions of *commitments* and *conventions*; conventions (protocols for monitoring commitments) are formalised for the first time in this paper. We comment on the generality of the model, outline its deficiencies, and suggest some possible refinements and other future areas of research.

1 Introduction

Distributed Artificial Intelligence (DAI) is concerned with all forms of social activity in systems composed of multiple computational agents [1]. An important form of interaction in such systems is *cooperative problem solving* (CPS), which occurs when a group of logically decentralized agents choose to work together to achieve a common goal. Relevant examples include a group of agents moving a heavy object, playing a symphony, building a house, and writing a joint paper. As these examples indicate, CPS is a common and important process in human societies, and there is increasing evidence to support the claim that it will be similarly important in future computer systems. A number of models of the CPS process have been devised by DAI researchers. Some of these models represent frameworks for implementing CPS systems, and for managing cooperative activities in such systems at run-time (e.g., [15; 5]). Other, more formal models have been developed in an attempt to characterise various aspects of CPS (e.g., [10; 8; 17]).

As is the case in mainstream AI, the differing motivations and approaches of formalists and system builders has meant that there has been relatively little cross-fertilisation between the two areas. The former camp has concentrated on isolated aspects of the CPS process, whereas work in the latter camp has concentrated on devising protocols for the entire CPS process. However, the key assumptions and design decisions of implementation-oriented CPS models tend to be buried deep inside the associated software; this can make it difficult to extract general principles or results from implementations.

This paper goes some way to bridging the gap between theory and practice in DAI. In §4, we develop a four-stage model of CPS, which we make precise by expressing it as a theory in a quantified multi-modal logic. The development of this model was driven by an analysis of CPS in both natural and artificial systems; the result is a theory that is accessible to both formalists and system builders. For formalists, the model represents a preliminary attempt to capture the properties of CPS in a mathematical framework. For system builders, the model can serve as a top-level specification of a CPS system, which, we believe, can inform the development of future DAI applications. The model deals with a number of issues that have hitherto been neglected by DAI theorists; for example, it considers the process by which an agent recognises the potential for cooperation, and begins to solicit assistance. Note that although we have attempted to develop a model that deals with CPS from beginning to end, we do not claim that our model is the final word on the subject; it would not be possible to present, in such a short paper, a theory that dealt with all aspects of a process as complex as CPS (see §5).

The remainder of this paper is structured as follows. The following section presents an overview of the formal framework used to represent the model. In §3, the notions of commitments and conventions, which play a key role in our model, are discussed and subsequently formalised; the model of CPS is then developed in §4. Some conclusions are presented in §5.

2 A Formal Framework

This section develops the formal framework in which the model of CPS will be expressed. This framework is a new quantified multi-modal logic, which both draws upon and extends the work described in [3; 13; 18]. Unfortunately, space restrictions prevent us relating the logic to those developed by other researchers; details may be found in the associated technical report [19].

Informally, the operators of the language have the following meanings. The operator true is a logical constant for truth. (Bel i φ) and (Goal i φ) mean that agent i has a belief, or goal of φ respectively. The $=$ operator is usual first-order equality. The $\in$ operator allows us to relate agents to groups of agents; it has the expected set-theoretic interpretation, so $(i \in g)$ means that the agent denoted by i is a member of the group denoted by g. The (Agts α g) operator means that the group denoted by g are precisely the agents required to perform the actions in the action sequence denoted by α. The A operator is a *path quantifier*: Aφ means that φ is a *path formula* that is satisfied in all the futures that could arise from the current state[1]. The operators $\neg$ (not) and $\vee$ (or) have classical semantics, as does the universal quantifier $\forall$; the remaining classical connectives and existential quantifier are assumed to be introduced as abbreviations, in the obvious way. (Happens α) is a path formula that means that the action α happens next; $\alpha;\alpha'$ means the action α is immediately followed by α'; $\alpha|\alpha'$ means either α or α' happen next; $\varphi?$ is a test action, which occurs if φ is 'true' in the current state; $\alpha*$ means the action α iterated.

Syntax

Definition 1 *The language contains the following symbols: the propositional connectives $\neg$ (not) and $\vee$ (or), and universal quantifier $\forall$; the operator symbols* Bel, Goal, Happens, Agts, $\in$, $=$, $\sqsubseteq$, *and* A*; a countable set Pred of predicate symbols — each symbol $P \in$ Pred is associated with a natural number called its arity, given by arity(P); a countable set Const of constant symbols, the union of the mutually disjoint sets $Const_{Ag}$ (agent constants), $Const_{Ac}$ (action sequence constants), $Const_{Gr}$ (group constants), and $Const_U$ (other constants); a countable set Var of variable symbols, the union of the mutually disjoint sets Var_{Ag}, Var_{Ac}, Var_{Gr} and Var_U; the punctuation symbols), (, '.' and ','; and finally, the action constructor symbols ';', '|', '?' and '*'.*

[1]There is a distinction made in the language between *path* and *state* formulae: state formulae are evaluated with respect to the 'current state' of the world, whereas path formulae are evaluated with respect to a course of events. The well-formed formulae of the language are identified with the set of state formulae [6].

Definition 2 *A term is either a constant or a variable; the set of terms is Term. The sort of a term is either Ag, Ac, Gr or U; if s is a sort then $Term_s = Const_s \cup Var_s$; thus $\tau_s \in Term_s$.*

The syntax of (well-formed) formulae ($\langle fmla \rangle$) of the language is defined in Figure 1. Note that we demand that a predicate P is applied to *arity*(P) terms.

Semantics

It is assumed that the world may be in any of a set S of *states*. A state *transition* is caused by the occurrence of a *primitive action* (or *event*): the set of all primitive actions is D_{Ac}. From any state, there is at least one — and perhaps many — possible actions, and hence resultant states. The binary relation R on S is used to represent all possible courses of world history: $(s, s') \in R$ iff the state s could be transformed into state s' by the occurrence of a primitive action that is possible in s. Clearly, R will *branch* infinitely into the future from every state. A labelling function *Act* maps each arc in R to the action associated with the transition. The world is populated by a non-empty set D_{Ag} of *agents*. A *group* over D_{Ag} is simply a non-empty subset of D_{Ag}; the set of all such groups is D_{Gr}. Agents and groups may be related to one-another via a simple (typed) set theory. Agents have beliefs and goals, and are (idealized) reasoners. The beliefs of an agent are given by a *belief accessibility relation* on S in the usual way; similarly for goals. Every primitive action α is associated with an agent, given by $Agt(\alpha)$. Finally, the world contains other individuals given by the set D_U. A complete definition of the language semantics will now be given. First, *paths* (a.k.a. fullpaths) will be defined: a path represents a possible course of events through a branching time structure.

Definition 3 *If S is a non-empty set and R is a total binary relation on S then a path over S, R is an infinite sequence $(s_u : u \in I\!N)$ such that $\forall u \in I\!N$, $s_u \in S$ and $(s_u, s_{u+1}) \in R$. The set of all paths over S, R is given by paths(S, R). The head of a path $p = (s_0, \ldots)$ is its first element s_0, and is given by hd(p).*

Next, we present the technical apparatus for dealing with the denotation of terms.

Definition 4 *The domain of quantification, D, is $D_{Ag} \cup (D^*_{Ac}) \cup D_{Gr} \cup D_U$, (where S^* denotes the set of non-empty sequences over S). If $n \in I\!N$, then the set of n-*

$$
\begin{array}{rcl@{\qquad}rcl}
\langle \textit{ag-term} \rangle & ::= & \text{any element of } \textit{Term}_{Ag} & \langle \textit{term} \rangle & ::= & \text{any element of } \textit{Term} \\
\langle \textit{ac-term} \rangle & ::= & \text{any element of } \textit{Term}_{Ac} & \langle \textit{pred-sym} \rangle & ::= & \text{any element of } \textit{Pred} \\
\langle \textit{gr-term} \rangle & ::= & \text{any element of } \textit{Term}_{Gr} & \langle \textit{var} \rangle & ::= & \text{any element of } \textit{Var}
\end{array}
$$

$$
\begin{array}{rcl}
\langle \textit{ac-exp} \rangle & ::= & \langle \textit{ac-term} \rangle \\
 & \mid & \langle \textit{ac-exp} \rangle \; ; \; \langle \textit{ac-exp} \rangle \\
 & \mid & \langle \textit{ac-exp} \rangle \text{ `}|\text{' } \langle \textit{ac-exp} \rangle \\
 & \mid & \langle \textit{state-fmla} \rangle ? \\
 & \mid & \langle \textit{ac-exp} \rangle * \\
\langle \textit{state-fmla} \rangle & ::= & (\langle \textit{pred-sym} \rangle \; \langle \textit{term} \rangle, \cdots, \langle \textit{term} \rangle) \\
 & \mid & (\mathsf{Bel} \; \langle \textit{ag-term} \rangle \; \langle \textit{state-fmla} \rangle) \\
 & \mid & (\mathsf{Goal} \; \langle \textit{ag-term} \rangle \; \langle \textit{state-fmla} \rangle) \\
 & \mid & (\mathsf{Agts} \; \langle \textit{ac-term} \rangle \; \langle \textit{gr-term} \rangle) \\
 & \mid & (\langle \textit{term} \rangle = \langle \textit{term} \rangle) \\
 & \mid & (\langle \textit{ac-term} \rangle \sqsubseteq \langle \textit{ac-term} \rangle) \\
 & \mid & (\langle \textit{ag-term} \rangle \in \langle \textit{gr-term} \rangle) \\
 & \mid & \mathsf{A} \langle \textit{path-fmla} \rangle \\
 & \mid & \neg \langle \textit{state-fmla} \rangle \\
 & \mid & \langle \textit{state-fmla} \rangle \vee \langle \textit{state-fmla} \rangle \\
 & \mid & \forall \langle \textit{var} \rangle \cdot \langle \textit{state-fmla} \rangle \\
\langle \textit{path-fmla} \rangle & ::= & (\mathsf{Happens} \; \langle \textit{ac-exp} \rangle) \\
 & \mid & \langle \textit{state-fmla} \rangle \\
 & \mid & \neg \langle \textit{path-fmla} \rangle \\
 & \mid & \langle \textit{path-fmla} \rangle \vee \langle \textit{path-fmla} \rangle \\
 & \mid & \forall \langle \textit{var} \rangle \cdot \langle \textit{path-fmla} \rangle \\
\langle \textit{fmla} \rangle & ::= & \langle \textit{state-fmla} \rangle
\end{array}
$$

Figure 1: Syntax

tuples over D is D^n. An interpretation for constants, I, is a sort-preserving bijection $I : Const \to D$. A variable assignment, V, is a sort-preserving bijection $V : Var \to D$.

The function $[\![\ldots]\!]_{I,V}$ gives the denotation of a term relative to I, V.

Definition 5 *If $\tau \in Term$, then $[\![\tau]\!]_{I,V}$ is $I(\tau)$ if $\tau \in Const$, and $V(\tau)$ otherwise. Reference to I, V will usually be suppressed.*

Definition 6 *A model, M, is a structure:*

$$\langle S, R, D_{Ag}, D_{Ac}, D_{Gr}, D_U, Act, Agt, B, G, I, \Phi \rangle$$

where: S is a non-empty set of states; $R \subseteq S \times S$ is a total binary relation on S; D_{Ag} is a non-empty set of agents; D_{Ac} is a non-empty set of actions; D_{Gr} is the set of groups over D_{Ag}; D_U is a non-empty set of other individuals; $Act : R \to D_{Ac}$ associates a primitive action with each arc in R; $Agt : D_{Ac} \to D_{Ag}$ gives the agent of each primitive action; $B : D_{Ag} \to \mathrm{powerset}(S \times S)$ associates a transitive, euclidean, serial belief accessibility relation with every agent in D_{Ag}; $G : D_{Ag} \to \mathrm{powerset}(S \times S)$ associates a serial goal accessibility relation with every agent in D_{Ag}, such that $\forall i \in D_{Ag}$, $G(i) \subseteq B(i)$; $I : Const \to D$ is an interpretation for constants; and finally $\Phi : Pred \times S \to \bigcup_{n \in I\!N} D^n$ gives the extension of each predicate symbol in each state, such that $\forall P \in Pred$, $\forall n \in I\!N$, $\forall s \in S$, if $arity(P) = n$ then $\Phi(P, s) \subseteq D^n$ (i.e., Φ preserves arity).

The semantics of the language are defined via the satisfaction relation, '$\models$', which holds between *interpretation structures* and formulae. For state formulae, an interpretation structure is a triple $\langle M, V, s \rangle$, where M is a model, V is a variable assignment and s is a state. For path formulae, an interpretation structure is a triple $\langle M, V, p \rangle$, where p is a path. The rules defining the satisfaction relation are given in Figure 3 (state formulae) and Figure 4 (path formulae). The rules make use of some syntactic abbreviations. First, we write $occurs(\alpha, u, v, p)$ if action α occurs between 'times' $u, v \in I\!N$ on the (possibly finite) path p — this metalanguage predicate is defined in Figure 2.

Two functions are required, that return all the primitive actions referred to in an action sequence, and the

$$
\begin{array}{rll}
occurs(\alpha, u, v, (s_0, \ldots)) & \text{iff} & [\![\alpha]\!] = (\alpha_1, \ldots, \alpha_n), n \leq v - u, \text{ and } \forall w \in \{1, \ldots, n\}, \\
& & Act(s_{u+w-1}, s_{u+w}) = \alpha_w \text{ (where } \alpha \in Term_{Ac}) \\
occurs(\alpha; \alpha', u, v, p) & \text{iff} & \exists w \in \{u, \ldots, v\} \text{ s.t. } occurs(\alpha, u, w, p) \text{ and} \\
& & occurs(\alpha', w, v, p) \\
occurs(\alpha | \alpha', u, v, p) & \text{iff} & occurs(\alpha, u, v, p) \text{ or } occurs(\alpha', u, v, p) \\
occurs(\varphi?, u, v, p) & \text{iff} & \langle M, V, hd(p)\rangle \models \varphi \\
occurs(\alpha*, u, v, p) & \text{iff} & \exists w_1, \ldots, w_x \in I\!N \text{ s.t. } (w_1 = 0) \text{ and } (w_1 < \cdots < w_x) \\
& & \text{and } \forall y \in \{1, \ldots, x\}, occurs(\alpha, w_y, w_{y+1}, p)
\end{array}
$$

Figure 2: The Meta-Language *occurs* Predicate

$$
\begin{array}{lcll}
\langle M, V, s\rangle & \models & \mathsf{true} & \\
\langle M, V, s\rangle & \models & (P\ \tau_1, \ldots, \tau_n) & \text{iff } \langle [\![\tau_1]\!], \ldots, [\![\tau_n]\!]\rangle \in \Phi(P, s) \\
\langle M, V, s\rangle & \models & (\mathsf{Bel}\ i\ \varphi) & \text{iff } \forall s' \in S, \text{ if } (s, s') \in B([\![i]\!]) \text{ then } \langle M, V, s'\rangle \models \varphi \\
\langle M, V, s\rangle & \models & (\mathsf{Goal}\ i\ \varphi) & \text{iff } \forall s' \in S, \text{ if } (s, s') \in G([\![i]\!]) \text{ then } \langle M, V, s'\rangle \models \varphi \\
\langle M, V, s\rangle & \models & (\mathsf{Agts}\ \alpha\ g) & \text{iff } agents(\alpha) = [\![g]\!] \\
\langle M, V, s\rangle & \models & (\tau_1 = \tau_2) & \text{iff } [\![\tau_1]\!] = [\![\tau_2]\!] \\
\langle M, V, s\rangle & \models & (i \in g) & \text{iff } [\![i]\!] \in [\![g]\!] \\
\langle M, V, s\rangle & \models & (\alpha \sqsubseteq \alpha') & \text{iff } actions([\![\alpha]\!]) \subseteq actions([\![\alpha']\!]) \\
\langle M, V, s\rangle & \models & \mathsf{A}\varphi & \text{iff } \forall p \in paths(S, R), \text{ if } hd(p) = s \text{ then } \langle M, V, p\rangle \models \varphi \\
\langle M, V, s\rangle & \models & \neg\varphi & \text{iff } \langle M, V, s\rangle \not\models \varphi \\
\langle M, V, s\rangle & \models & \varphi \vee \psi & \text{iff } \langle M, V, s\rangle \models \varphi \text{ or } \langle M, V, s\rangle \models \psi \\
\langle M, V, s\rangle & \models & \forall x \cdot \varphi & \text{iff } \langle M, V \dagger \{x \mapsto d\}, s\rangle \models \varphi \\
& & & \quad \text{for all } d \in D \text{ s.t. } x \text{ and } d \text{ are of the same sort}
\end{array}
$$

Figure 3: State Formulae Semantics

agents required for an action term, respectively.

$$
\begin{array}{rcl}
actions((\alpha_1, \ldots, \alpha_n)) & \stackrel{\text{def}}{=} & \{\alpha_1, \ldots, \alpha_n\} \\
agents(\alpha) & \stackrel{\text{def}}{=} & \{i \mid \exists \alpha' \in actions([\![\alpha]\!]) \text{ s.t.} \\
& & \quad Agt(\alpha') = i\} \\
& & \quad \text{(where } \alpha \in Term_{Ac})
\end{array}
$$

Some derived operators

A number of derived operators will now be introduced. First, the usual connectives of linear temporal logic: $\varphi \mathcal{U} \psi$ means φ is satisfied *until* ψ becomes satisfied; $\Diamond\varphi$ means φ is *eventually* satisfied; $\Box\varphi$ means φ is *always* satisfied. These connectives are used to build path formulae. The path quantifier E is the dual of A; thus $\mathsf{E}\varphi$ means φ is a path formulae satisfied on *at least one* possible future.

$$
\begin{array}{rcl}
\varphi \mathcal{U} \psi & \stackrel{\text{def}}{=} & (\mathsf{Happens}\ (\neg\psi?; \varphi?)*; \psi?) \\
\Diamond\varphi & \stackrel{\text{def}}{=} & \mathsf{true}\,\mathcal{U}\,\varphi \\
\Box\varphi & \stackrel{\text{def}}{=} & \neg\Diamond\neg\varphi \\
\mathsf{E}\varphi & \stackrel{\text{def}}{=} & \neg\mathsf{A}\neg\varphi
\end{array}
$$

$(\mathsf{Singleton}\ g\ i)$ means g is a singleton group with i as the only member. $(\mathsf{Agt}\ \alpha\ i)$ means i is the only agent of action α.

$$
\begin{array}{rcl}
(\mathsf{Singleton}\ g\ i) & \stackrel{\text{def}}{=} & \forall j \cdot (j \in g) \Rightarrow (j = i) \\
(\mathsf{Agt}\ \alpha\ i) & \stackrel{\text{def}}{=} & \forall g \cdot (\mathsf{Agts}\ \alpha\ g) \Rightarrow (\mathsf{Singleton}\ g\ i)
\end{array}
$$

To represent an action α *achieving* a goal φ, we introduce a derived operator Achieves.

$$
(\mathsf{Achieves}\ \alpha\ \varphi) \stackrel{\text{def}}{=} \mathsf{A}((\mathsf{Happens}\ \alpha) \Rightarrow (\mathsf{Happens}\ \alpha; \varphi?))
$$

We will have a number of occasions to write $\mathsf{A}(\mathsf{Happens}\ \alpha)$, (action α occurs next in all alternative futures), and $\mathsf{A}\neg(\mathsf{Happens}\ \alpha)$ (action α does not occur next in any alternative future), and so we introduce abbreviations for these.

$$
\begin{array}{rcl}
(\mathsf{Does}\ \alpha) & \stackrel{\text{def}}{=} & \mathsf{A}(\mathsf{Happens}\ \alpha) \\
(\mathsf{Doesn't}\ \alpha) & \stackrel{\text{def}}{=} & \mathsf{A}\neg(\mathsf{Happens}\ \alpha)
\end{array}
$$

Knowledge is defined as true belief, rather than by introducing it as yet another primitive modality.

$$
(\mathsf{Know}\ i\ \varphi) \stackrel{\text{def}}{=} \varphi \wedge (\mathsf{Bel}\ i\ \varphi)
$$

We also find it convenient to use the notions of *mutual* mental states. Although we recognise that such

$$
\begin{array}{llll}
\langle M, V, p\rangle & \models & (\mathsf{Happens}\ \alpha) & \text{iff } \exists u \in I\!N \text{ s.t. } occurs(\alpha, 0, u, p) \\
\langle M, V, p\rangle & \models & \varphi & \text{iff } \langle M, V, hd(p)\rangle \models \varphi \text{ (where } \varphi \text{ is a state formula)} \\
\langle M, V, p\rangle & \models & \neg\varphi & \text{iff } \langle M, V, p\rangle \not\models \varphi \\
\langle M, V, p\rangle & \models & \varphi \vee \psi & \text{iff } \langle M, V, p\rangle \models \varphi \text{ or } \langle M, V, p\rangle \models \psi \\
\langle M, V, p\rangle & \models & \forall x \cdot \varphi & \text{iff } \langle M, V \dagger \{x \mapsto d\}, p\rangle \models \varphi \\
 & & & \quad \text{for all } d \in D \text{ s.t. } x \text{ and } d \text{ are of the same sort}
\end{array}
$$

Figure 4: Path Formulae Semantics

states are idealised, in that they are not realisable in systems which admit the possibility of failed communication, they are nevertheless valuable abstraction tools for understanding multi-agent systems. The mutual belief of φ in a group of agents g is written (M-Bel g φ); the mutual goal of φ in g is written (M-Goal g φ), and the mutual knowledge of φ is written (M-Know g φ). We define mutual mental states as *fixed points*.

$$
\begin{array}{rcl}
(\mathsf{M\text{-}Bel}\ g\ \varphi) & \stackrel{\text{def}}{=} & \forall i \cdot (i \in g) \Rightarrow (\mathsf{Bel}\ i\ \varphi \wedge (\mathsf{M\text{-}Bel}\ g\ \varphi)) \\
(\mathsf{M\text{-}Goal}\ g\ \varphi) & \stackrel{\text{def}}{=} & \forall i \cdot (i \in g) \Rightarrow (\mathsf{M\text{-}Bel}\ g\ (\mathsf{Goal}\ i\ \varphi)) \\
(\mathsf{M\text{-}Know}\ g\ \varphi) & \stackrel{\text{def}}{=} & \varphi \wedge (\mathsf{M\text{-}Bel}\ g\ (\mathsf{M\text{-}Know}\ g\ \varphi))
\end{array}
$$

3 Commitments, Conventions, and Intentions

The key mental states that control agent behaviour are intentions and joint intentions — the former define local asocial behaviour, the latter control social behaviour [2]. Intentions are important as they provide both the stability and predictability (through the notion of commitment) that is needed for social interactions, and the flexibility and reactivity (through the mechanisms by which commitments are monitored) that are required to deal with a changing environment. Previous attempts to formalize (joint) intentions have made no distinction between a commitment and its underlying convention; we clearly distinguish the two concepts: a *commitment* is a pledge or a promise; a *convention* is a means of monitoring a commitment — it specifies both the conditions under which a commitment might be abandoned, and how an agent should behave, should such a circumstance arise [8].

Commitments have a number of important properties (see [8] and [3, pp217–219] for a discussion), but the most important is that *commitments persist*: having adopted a commitment, we do not expect an agent to drop it until, for some reason, it becomes redundant. The conditions under which a commitment can become redundant are specified in the associated convention — examples include the motivation for the goal no longer being present, the goal being achieved, and the realization that the goal will never be achieved [3].

When a group of agents are engaged in a cooperative activity, they have a joint commitment to the overall aim, as well as individual commitments to the specific tasks that they have been assigned. This joint commitment is parameterised by a social convention, which identifies the conditions under which the joint commitment can be dropped, and also describes how the agent should behave towards fellow team members. For example, if an agent drops its joint commitment because it believes that the goal will never be attained, then it is part of the notion of 'cooperativeness' inherent in joint action that it informs fellow team members of its change of state. In this context, social conventions provide general guidelines, and a common frame of reference in which agents can work. By adopting a convention, every agent knows what is expected both of it, and of every other agent, as part of the collective working towards the goal, and knows that every other agent has a similar set of expectations.

Formally, we define a convention as a set of rules, each rule consisting of a re-evaluation condition ρ and a goal γ: if ever an agent believes ρ to be true, then it must adopt γ as a goal, and keep this goal until the commitment becomes redundant.

Definition 7 *A* convention, *c, is an indexed set of pairs:* $c = \{(\rho_k, \gamma_k) \mid k \in \{1, \ldots, l\}\}$*, where* ρ_k *is a* re-evaluation condition*, and* γ_k *is a* goal*,* $\forall k \in \{1, \ldots, l\}$.

Joint commitments have a number of parameters. First, a joint commitment is held by a group g of agents. Second, joint commitments are held with respect to some goal φ; this is the state of affairs that the group is committed to bringing about. Third, joint commitments are held relative to a *motivation*, which characterises the justification for the commitment. They also have a *pre-condition*, which describes what must initially be true of the world in order for the commitment to be held. For example, in most types of joint commitment, we do not expect participating agents to initially believe that the object of the commitment, φ, is true. Finally, a joint commitment is parameterised by a convention c. Joint commitment is then informally defined as follows.

> **Definition: (Joint commitments)** A group g is jointly committed to goal φ with respect to motivation ψ, pre-condition *pre*, and convention c iff: (i) pre-condition *pre* is initially satis-

fied; and (ii) until the termination condition is satisfied, every agent in g either (a) has a goal of φ; or (b) believes that the re-evaluation condition of some rule in c is satisfied, and has the goal corresponding to that re-evaluation condition; where the termination condition is that the goal part of some convention rule is satisfied.

More formally:

Definition 8 *If* $c = \{(\rho_k, \gamma_k) \mid k \in \{1, \ldots, l\}\}$ *is a convention, then:*

$$(\mathsf{J\text{-}Commit}\ g\ \varphi\ \psi\ pre\ c) \stackrel{\text{def}}{=} \forall i \cdot (i \in g) \Rightarrow pre \wedge \mathsf{A}((p \vee q)\, \mathcal{U}\, r)$$

where

$$\begin{array}{lcl} p & \stackrel{\text{def}}{=} & (\mathsf{Goal}\ i\ \varphi) \\ q & \stackrel{\text{def}}{=} & \bigvee_{l=1}^{k} (\mathsf{Bel}\ i\ \rho_l) \wedge \mathsf{A}[(\mathsf{Goal}\ i\ \gamma_l)\, \mathcal{U}\, r] \\ r & \stackrel{\text{def}}{=} & \bigvee_{m=1}^{k} \gamma_m. \end{array}$$

This general model can be used to capture the properties of many different types of joint commitment. For example, we will now specify a social convention that is similar to the Levesque-Cohen model of joint persistent goals (JPGs) [10]. Let

$$\begin{array}{lcl} pre_{JPG} & \stackrel{\text{def}}{=} & \neg(\mathsf{Bel}\ i\ \varphi) \wedge (\mathsf{Bel}\ i\ \mathsf{E}\Diamond\varphi) \\ c_{JPG} & \stackrel{\text{def}}{=} & \left\{ \begin{array}{l} ((\mathsf{Bel}\ i\ \varphi), (\mathsf{M\text{-}Bel}\ g\ \varphi)), \\ ((\mathsf{Bel}\ i\ \mathsf{A}\Box\neg\varphi), (\mathsf{M\text{-}Bel}\ g\ \mathsf{A}\Box\neg\varphi)), \\ ((\mathsf{Bel}\ i\ \neg\psi), (\mathsf{M\text{-}Bel}\ g\ \neg\psi)) \end{array} \right\}. \end{array}$$

A group with a joint commitment parameterised by a pre-condition pre_{JPG}, and convention c_{JPG} will have a shared mental state identical in all important respects to that implied by the JPGs of Levesque-Cohen. We use joint commitments to define joint intentions, which are held by a group g with respect to an action α and motivation ψ. In general, it is possible to make conventions a parameter of joint intentions. However, this would complicate our subsequent formalism, and we therefore leave this refinement to future work. For the purposes of this paper, we simply assume that joint intentions are defined over the JPG-like convention c_{JPG}; this gives us a model of joint intentions similar to that in [10, p98].

$$\begin{array}{l} (\mathsf{J\text{-}Intend}\ g\ \alpha\ \psi) \stackrel{\text{def}}{=} \\ \quad (\mathsf{M\text{-}Bel}\ g\ (\mathsf{Agts}\ \alpha\ g)) \wedge \\ \quad (\mathsf{J\text{-}Commit}\ g\ \mathsf{A}\Diamond(\mathsf{Happens}\ (\mathsf{M\text{-}Bel}\ g\ (\mathsf{Does}\ \alpha))?; \alpha) \\ \qquad \psi\ pre_{JPG}\ c_{JPG}) \end{array}$$

Thus a joint intention in g to do α means having a joint commitment that eventually g will believe α will happen next, and then α happens next. An individual intention by agent i to do α with motivation ψ is a special case of joint intention.

$$(\mathsf{Intend}\ i\ \alpha\ \psi) \stackrel{\text{def}}{=} \forall g \cdot (\mathsf{Singleton}\ g\ i) \Rightarrow (\mathsf{J\text{-}Intend}\ g\ \alpha\ \psi)$$

4 The Cooperative Problem Solving Process

In this section, we present a four-stage model of CPS, which we formalize by expressing it in the logic described in §2. The four stages of the model are:

1. Recognition: The CPS process begins when some agent recognises the potential for cooperative action; this recognition may come about because an agent has a goal that it is unable to achieve in isolation, or, more generally, because the agent prefers assistance.
2. Team formation: During this stage, the agent that recognised the potential for cooperative action at stage (1) solicits assistance. If this stage is successful, then it will end with a group having a joint commitment to collective action.
3. Plan formation: During this stage, the agents attempt to negotiate a joint plan that they believe will achieve the desired goal.
4. Team action: During this stage, the newly agreed plan of joint action is executed by the agents, which maintain a close-knit relationship throughout; this relationship is defined by an agreed social convention, which every agent follows.

Although we believe that most instances of CPS exhibit these stages in some form, we stress that the model is *idealized*. We recognise that there are cases which the model cannot account for, and we highlight these wherever appropriate. Our aim has been to construct a framework that is complete, (in that it describes CPS from beginning to end), but abstract, (in that details which might obscure more significant points have been omitted). One important simplification that we have made is the assumption that CPS is strictly *sequential*, in that each stage directly follows that which preceded it, without iteration or backtracking. When CPS occurs in human societies, it is rarely sequential in this way. We intend to deal with this issue in future refinements.

4.1 Recognition

CPS begins when some agent in a multi-agent community has a goal, and recognises the potential for cooperative action with respect to that goal. Recognition may occur for several reasons:

- The paradigm case is that in which the agent is unable to achieve its goal in isolation, due to a lack of resources, but believes that cooperative action can achieve it. For example, an agent may have a goal that, to achieve, requires information only accessible to another agent; without the cooperation of this other agent, the goal cannot be achieved.

- Alternatively, an agent may have the resources to achieve the goal, but does not want to use them. There may be several reasons for this: it may believe that in working alone on this particular problem, it will clobber one of its other goals, or it may believe that a cooperative solution will in some way be better (e.g., derived faster, more accurate).

In order to more precisely define the conditions that characterise the potential for cooperative action, it is necessary to introduce a number of subsidiary definitions. First, we require definitions of single- and multi-agent *ability*: what it means to be able to bring about some state of the world. Several attempts to define multi-agent ability have appeared in the literature (e.g., [14]). However, there is currently no consensus on the appropriateness of these definitions. For this reason, we adapt the well-known model of ability proposed by Moore [11].

Definition: (Single-agent ability) Agent i can achieve φ iff there is some possibly complex action α of which i is the sole agent, such that either: (i) i knows that after it performed α, φ would be satisfied; or (ii) i knows that after it performed α, it could achieve φ.

Clause (i) is the base case, where an agent knows the identity of an action that will achieve the goal φ directly. Clause (ii) allows for the possibility of an agent performing an action in order to find out how to achieve φ. This recursive definition is easily generalized to the multi-agent case.

Definition: (Multi-agent ability) Group g can achieve φ iff there is some possibly complex action α and some group g', such that it is mutually known in g that $g' \subseteq g$, and g' are the agents of α, and it is mutually known in g that either (i) after α was performed, φ would be satisfied; or (ii) after α was performed, g would have the multi-agent ability to achieve φ.

Once again, clause (i) represents the base case, where the group is mutually aware of the identity of some action that could be performed by some subset of the group (whose identity must also be known), such that performing the action would achieve the goal directly. Clause (ii) is the recursive case, where the group is required to know the identity of some action and subset of agents such that performing the action would bring them closer to the goal.

A more precise definition of potential for cooperation can now be given.

Definition: (Potential for cooperation) With respect to agent i's goal φ, there is potential for cooperation iff: (i) there is some group g such that i believes that g can jointly achieve φ; and either (ii) i can't achieve φ in isolation; or (iii) i believes that for every action α that it could perform which achieves φ, it has a goal of not performing α.

Note that in clause (i), an agent needs to know the identity of a group that it believes can cooperate to achieve its goal. This is an overstrong assumption. It precludes an agent attempting to find out the identity of a group that can achieve the goal, and it does not allow an agent to simply broadcast its goal in the hope of attracting help (as in the CNET [15]). However, catering for these cases would complicate the formalization a good deal, and obscure some more important points. We therefore leave such refinements to future work.

The ideas introduced above are readily expressed using the language we described in §2. First, we write $(\mathsf{Can}\ i\ \varphi)$ iff i can achieve φ in isolation.

$$
\begin{array}{l}
(\mathsf{Can}\ i\ \varphi) \stackrel{\text{def}}{=} \\
\exists \alpha \cdot (\mathsf{Know}\ i\ (\mathsf{Agt}\ \alpha\ i) \wedge (\mathsf{Achieves}\ \alpha\ \varphi)) \quad \vee \\
\exists \alpha \cdot (\mathsf{Know}\ i\ (\mathsf{Agt}\ \alpha\ i) \wedge (\mathsf{Achieves}\ \alpha\ (\mathsf{Can}\ i\ \varphi)))
\end{array}
$$

Multi-agent ability is a generalization of single-agent ability.

$$
\begin{array}{l}
(\mathsf{J\text{-}Can}\ g\ \varphi) \stackrel{\text{def}}{=} \\
\exists \alpha \cdot \exists g' \cdot \left(\mathsf{M\text{-}Know}\ g \begin{array}{l} (g' \subseteq g) \wedge \\ (\mathsf{Agts}\ \alpha\ g') \wedge \\ (\mathsf{Achieves}\ \alpha\ \varphi) \end{array} \right) \\
\vee \\
\exists \alpha \cdot \exists g' \cdot \left(\mathsf{M\text{-}Know}\ g \begin{array}{l} (g' \subseteq g) \wedge \\ (\mathsf{Agts}\ \alpha\ g') \wedge \\ (\mathsf{Achieves}\ \alpha\ (\mathsf{J\text{-}Can}\ g\ \varphi)) \end{array} \right)
\end{array}
$$

We can now formally state the conditions that characterise the potential for cooperation.

$$
\begin{array}{l}
(\mathsf{PfC}\ i\ \varphi) \stackrel{\text{def}}{=} \\
\quad (\mathsf{Goal}\ i\ \varphi) \wedge \exists g \cdot (\mathsf{Bel}\ i\ (\mathsf{J\text{-}Can}\ g\ \varphi)) \wedge \\
\quad \left[\begin{array}{l} \neg(\mathsf{Can}\ i\ \varphi) \vee \\ \left(\mathsf{Bel}\ i\ \forall \alpha \cdot \begin{array}{l} (\mathsf{Agt}\ \alpha\ i) \wedge (\mathsf{Achieves}\ \alpha\ \varphi) \Rightarrow \\ \quad (\mathsf{Goal}\ i\ (\mathsf{Doesn't}\ \alpha)) \end{array} \right) \end{array} \right]
\end{array}
$$

4.2 Team Formation

Having identified the potential for cooperative action with respect to one of its goals, a rational agent will solicit assistance from some group of agents that it believes can achieve the goal. If the agent is successful, then at the conclusion of this *team formation* stage, the agent will have brought about a mental state wherein the group has a joint commitment to collective action. (There will not yet be a joint intention to act; this comes later.) An agent cannot guarantee that it will be successful in forming a team; it can only *attempt* it. We adapt the model of attempts developed by Cohen-Levesque [4, p240].

> **Definition: (Attempts)** An attempt by agent i to bring about a state φ is an action α performed by i with the goal that after α is performed, φ is satisfied, or at least ψ is satisfied.

The ultimate goal of the attempt — the thing that i hopes to bring about — is represented by φ, whereas ψ represents 'what it takes to make an honest effort' [4, p240]. If i is successful, then bringing about ψ will be sufficient to cause φ.

The team formation stage can then be characterised as an assumption made about rational agents: namely, that an agent which recognises the potential for cooperative action will solicit assistance.

> **Assumption: (Team formation)** An agent i, who believes that there is potential for cooperative action with respect to its goal φ, will eventually attempt to bring about in some group g, (that it believes can jointly achieve φ), a state wherein: (i) it is mutually believed in g that g can jointly achieve φ, and g are jointly committed to team action with respect to i's goal φ; or, failing that, to at least cause in g (ii) the mutual belief that i has a goal of φ and the mutual belief that i believes g can jointly achieve φ.

Part (i) represents the commitment that the group has towards i's goal φ if i is successful in its attempt to solicit assistance; we discuss what team action means in §4.4. Note that an agent might have its own reasons for agreeing to participate in a cooperative action, that are unconnected with the request by the agent that recognises the potential for cooperation. However, we have not attempted to deal with such cases here.

The team formation assumption implicitly states that agents are veracious with respect to their goals, i.e., that they will try to influence the group by revealing their true goal. We do not consider cases where agents are mendacious (i.e., they lie about their goals), or when agents do not reveal their goals. (We refer the interested reader to [7, pp159–165] for a discussion and formalization of these considerations.)

We write $\{\mathsf{Attempt}\ i\ \alpha\ \varphi\ \psi\}$ for an attempt by i to achieve φ by performing α, at least achieving ψ. Following Cohen-Levesque, we use curly brackets to indicate that attempts are complex actions, not predicates [4, p240].

$$\{\mathsf{Attempt}\ i\ \alpha\ \varphi\ \psi\} \stackrel{\text{def}}{=} \left[\begin{array}{l} (\mathsf{Bel}\ i\ \neg\varphi) \wedge (\mathsf{Agt}\ \alpha\ i) \wedge \\ (\mathsf{Goal}\ i\ (\mathsf{Achieves}\ \alpha\ \varphi)) \wedge \\ (\mathsf{Intend}\ i\ (\mathsf{Does}\ \alpha; \psi?)) \end{array}\right] ?; \alpha$$

We introduce an abbreviation to simplify subsequent formalization: $(\mathsf{Pre\text{-}Team}\ g\ \varphi\ i)$ means that (i) g mutually believe that they can jointly achieve φ; and (ii) g are jointly committed to becoming a team with respect to i's goal φ.

$$\begin{array}{l} (\mathsf{Pre\text{-}Team}\ g\ \varphi\ i) \stackrel{\text{def}}{=} \\ \quad (\mathsf{M\text{-}Bel}\ g\ (\mathsf{J\text{-}Can}\ g\ \varphi)) \wedge \\ \quad (\mathsf{J\text{-}Commit}\ g\ (\mathsf{Team}\ g\ \varphi\ i)\ (\mathsf{Goal}\ i\ \varphi) \\ \qquad pre_{JPG}\ c_{JPG}) \end{array}$$

(Team is defined in §4.4.) The main assumption concerning team formation can now be stated.

Assumption 1

$$\begin{array}{l} \models \forall i \cdot (\mathsf{Bel}\ i\ (\mathsf{PfC}\ i\ \varphi)) \Rightarrow \\ \quad \mathsf{A}\Diamond\exists g \cdot \exists\alpha \cdot (\mathsf{Happens}\ \{\mathsf{Attempt}\ i\ \alpha\ p\ q\}) \end{array}$$

where

$$\begin{array}{lcl} p & \stackrel{\text{def}}{=} & (\mathsf{Pre\text{-}Team}\ g\ \varphi\ i) \\ q & \stackrel{\text{def}}{=} & (\mathsf{M\text{-}Bel}\ g\ (\mathsf{Goal}\ i\ \varphi) \wedge (\mathsf{Bel}\ i\ (\mathsf{J\text{-}Can}\ g\ \varphi))). \end{array}$$

If team formation is successful then for the first time there will be a social mental state relating to i's goal, which contrasts with i's individual perspective that has guided the process until this stage.

4.3 Plan Formation

If an agent is successful in its attempt to solicit assistance, then there will be a group of agents with a joint commitment to collective action. But collective action cannot begin until the group agree on what they will actually do. Hence the next stage in the CPS process: plan formation.

We saw above that a group will not form a collective unless they believe they can actually achieve the desired goal. This, in turn, implies that there is at least one action that is known to the group that will take them 'closer' to the goal (see the definition of J-Can, above). However, it is possible that there are many agents that know of actions the group can perform in order to take the collective closer to, or even achieve the goal. Moreover, some members of the collective may have objections to one or more of these actions. For example, an agent may believe that a particular action has hitherto unforeseen and damaging consequences. It is therefore necessary for the collective to come to some agreement about exactly which course of action they will follow. *Negotiation* is the mechanism via which such agreement is reached.

Negotiation usually involves agents making reasoned arguments for and against courses of action; making proposals and counter proposals; suggesting modifications or amendments to plans; and continuing in this way until all the negotiators have reached agreement[2]. Nego-

[2]It may also involve agents lying, or being cunning and devious, though we shall not consider such cases here.

tiation has long been recognised as a process of some importance for DAI (see, e.g., [16]). Unfortunately, analyses of negotiation demonstrate that it is also extremely complex — a rigorous attempt at formalization is quite beyond the scope of this paper[3]. Instead, we simply offer some observations about the weakest conditions under which negotiation can be said to have occurred.

What can we say about negotiating a plan? First, we note that negotiation may *fail*: the collective may simply be unable to reach agreement, due to some irreconcilable differences. In this case, the minimum condition required for us to be able to say that negotiation occurred at all is that *at least one* agent proposed a course of action that it believed would take the collective closer to the goal. However, negotiation may also succeed. In this case, we expect a team action stage to follow — we shall say no more about team action here, as this is the subject of the next section.

We can make a number of other tentative assumptions about the behaviour of agents during negotiation. Most importantly, we might assume that they will *attempt to bring about their preferences.* For example, if an agent has an objection to some plan, then it will attempt to prevent this plan being carried out. Similarly, if it has a preference for some plan, then it will attempt to bring this plan about.

We shall now make the above discussion more precise. First, we define *joint attempts*: what it means for a group of agents to collectively attempt something. As might be expected, joint attempts are a generalization of single-agent attempts.

> **Definition: (Joint attempts)** An attempt by a group of agents g to bring about a state φ is an action α, of which g are the agents, performed with the mutual goal that after α is performed, φ is satisfied, or at least ψ is satisfied (where ψ represents what it takes to make a reasonable effort).

Next, we state the minimum conditions required for negotiation to have occurred.

> **Assumption: (Negotiation)** If group g are a pre-team with respect to agent i's goal φ, then g will eventually jointly attempt to bring about a state where it is mutually known in g that g are a team with respect to i's goal φ, or, failing that, to at least bring about a state where some agent $j \in g$ has made g mutually aware of its belief that some action α can be performed by g in order to achieve φ.

In other words, the group will try to bring about a state where they have agreed on a common plan, and intend to act on it. Failing that, they will bring about a state where at least one of them has proposed a plan that it believed would achieve the desired goal. The other, more tentative assumptions about agent behaviour during negotiation are as follows.

> **Assumption: (Making preferences known)** If group g are a pre-team with respect to agent i's goal φ, and there is some action α such that it is mutually believed in g that α achieves φ, and that g are the agents of α, then every agent $j \in g$ that has a preference that α does/does not occur will attempt to ensure that α does/does not occur, by at least making g mutually aware of its preference for/against α.

We are once again assuming that agents are veracious, in that they attempt to influence the team by revealing their true preferences, rather than by lying, or concealing their true preferences.

We begin by formalizing joint attempts.

$$\{\mathsf{J\text{-}Attempt}\ g\ \alpha\ \varphi\ \psi\} \stackrel{\text{def}}{=} \left[\begin{array}{l}(\mathsf{M\text{-}Bel}\ g\ \neg\varphi) \wedge (\mathsf{Agts}\ \alpha\ g) \wedge \\ (\mathsf{M\text{-}Goal}\ g\ (\mathsf{Achieves}\ \alpha\ \varphi)) \wedge \\ (\mathsf{J\text{-}Intend}\ g\ (\mathsf{Does}\ \alpha; \psi?))\end{array}\right] ?; \alpha$$

The main assumption characterising negotiation can now be given. (Team is defined below.)

Assumption 2

$$\models (\mathsf{Pre\text{-}Team}\ g\ \varphi\ i) \Rightarrow \mathsf{A}\Diamond\exists\alpha\cdot(\mathsf{Happens}\ \{\mathsf{J\text{-}Attempt}\ g\ \alpha\ p\ q\})$$

where

$$\begin{aligned} p &\stackrel{\text{def}}{=} (\mathsf{M\text{-}Know}\ g\ (\mathsf{Team}\ g\ \varphi\ i)) \\ q &\stackrel{\text{def}}{=} \exists j\cdot\exists\alpha\cdot \\ &\qquad (j \in g) \wedge \\ &\qquad (\mathsf{M\text{-}Bel}\ g\ (\mathsf{Bel}\ j\ (\mathsf{Agts}\ \alpha\ g) \wedge (\mathsf{Achieves}\ \alpha\ \varphi))). \end{aligned}$$

To formalize the assumption that members make their preferences known, we need to capture the notion of an agent trying to cause and trying to prevent a group performing an action.

$$(\mathsf{Try\text{-}to\text{-}cause}\ i\ g\ \alpha) \stackrel{\text{def}}{=} \exists\alpha'\cdot\mathsf{A}(\mathsf{Happens}\ a)$$

where

$$a \stackrel{\text{def}}{=} \left\{\mathsf{Attempt}\ i\ \alpha'\ \begin{array}{l}(\mathsf{Does}\ \alpha) \\ (\mathsf{M\text{-}Bel}\ g\ (\mathsf{Goal}\ i\ (\mathsf{Does}\ \alpha)))\end{array}\right\}$$

The definition of (Try-to-prevent $i\ g\ \alpha$) is similar to Try-to-cause, and is therefore omitted.

Assumption 3 *Agents that have a preference for some action make the team mutually aware of their preference:*

[3]See [9] for preliminary work on logical models of argumentation.

$$\models \forall g \cdot \forall i \cdot \forall \alpha \cdot$$
$$((\textsf{Pre-Team}\ g\ \varphi\ i) \wedge$$
$$(\textsf{M-Bel}\ g\ (\textsf{Agts}\ \alpha\ g) \wedge$$
$$(\textsf{Achieves}\ \alpha\ \varphi)) \Rightarrow$$
$$[\forall j \cdot (j \in g) \wedge (\textsf{Goal}\ j\ (\textsf{Does}\ \alpha)) \Rightarrow$$
$$(\textsf{Try-to-cause}\ j\ g\ \alpha)].$$

Agents that prefer some action not to be performed make the team mutually aware of their preference:

$$\models \forall g \cdot \forall i \cdot \forall \alpha \cdot$$
$$((\textsf{Pre-Team}\ g\ \varphi\ i) \wedge$$
$$(\textsf{M-Bel}\ g\ (\textsf{Agts}\ \alpha\ g) \wedge$$
$$(\textsf{Achieves}\ \alpha\ \varphi)) \Rightarrow$$
$$[\forall j \cdot (j \in g) \wedge (\textsf{Goal}\ j\ (\textsf{Doesn't}\ \alpha)) \Rightarrow$$
$$(\textsf{Try-to-prevent}\ j\ g\ \alpha)].$$

If plan formation is successful then the team will have a joint commitment to the goal, and will have agreed to the means by which they will pursue this goal. Ideally, we would like to specify that the group also negotiate a convention for monitoring team action. Unfortunately, we have no direct way of representing such behaviour: it would require quantification over formulae of the language, and such a meta-level notion cannot be represented at the object level in a normal modal language such as that used here (see §5).

4.4 Team Action

If a collective is successful in its attempt to negotiate a plan, then we expect that collective to follow up negotiation with action. This gives us the fourth, and final stage in our model: team action. For this stage, we simply require that the team jointly intend some appropriate action.

> **Definition: (Team action)** A group g are considered a team with respect to i's goal φ iff there is some action α, such that: (i) α achieves φ; and (ii) g have a joint intention of α, relative to i having a goal of φ.

The formalization of Team is simple.

$$(\textsf{Team}\ g\ \varphi\ i) \stackrel{\text{def}}{=}$$
$$\exists \alpha \cdot (\textsf{Achieves}\ \alpha\ \varphi) \wedge (\textsf{J-Intend}\ g\ \alpha\ (\textsf{Goal}\ i\ \varphi))$$

From the definition of J-Intend, we know that the group will remain committed to mutually believing they are about to perform the action, and then performing it. Moreover, if ever one of them comes to believe, for example, that i no longer has a goal of φ, then the social convention dictates that the agent will make the team aware of this, and team action will end.

5 Concluding Remarks

In this paper, we have presented an abstract formal model of cooperative problem solving, which describes all aspects of the process, from recognition of the potential for cooperation through to team action. This model considers a number of issues that have hitherto been neglected by DAI theorists. For example, it defines the conditions under which there is potential for cooperative action, and shows how an agent's individual mental state can lead it to attempt to build a social mental state in a group. The model has a number of other properties, which we shall briefly discuss in this section.

Although we have not explicitly considered communication, our model is nevertheless consistent with one of the best current theories of *speech acts*: in [4], Cohen-Levesque proposed a theory in which illocutionary acts are treated as *attempts* to bring about some mental state in a conversation participant. At a number of points, our model predicts precisely such attempts; for example, the model predicts that an agent which recognises the potential for cooperation will attempt to bring about a joint commitment to collective action in some group that it believes can achieve its goal.

Another interesting property is that the model consists of a set of *liveness* properties [12]. This is consistent with the view of agents as *intelligent reactive systems*, responding in a *reasoned* way to their goals, and events that occur in their environment.

The model also predicts that agents will attempt to initiate social interaction if they have goals that are dependent on other community members. In order to do this, the agents must have some knowledge about the abilities, skills, and interests of their acquaintances.

Finally, the model predicts that once a group of agents are formed into a collective, they will attempt to negotiate a plan that they believe will achieve the desired objective. Moreover, they will make their preferences known with respect to such plans, and are not required simply to accept another agent's proposals; they are thus autonomous, rather than benevolent.

There are a number of issues that we intend to address in future work, the most obvious of which is the need for refinement of the model, as highlighted in the main text. Additionally, there are a number of ways in which the language we have used for representing the model needs to be extended. The two most significant points are the need to quantify over complex action expressions, and the need to be able to represent meta-level notions at the object level.

References

[1] A. H. Bond and L. Gasser, editors. *Readings in Distributed Artificial Intelligence.* Morgan Kaufmann Publishers: San Mateo, CA, 1988.

[2] M. E. Bratman. *Intentions, Plans, and Practical Reason.* Harvard University Press: Cambridge, MA, 1987.

[3] P. R. Cohen and H. J. Levesque. Intention is choice with commitment. *Artificial Intelligence*, 42:213–261, 1990.

[4] P. R. Cohen and H. J. Levesque. Rational interaction as the basis for communication. In P. R. Cohen, J. Morgan,

and M. E. Pollack, editors, *Intentions in Communication*, pages 221–256. The MIT Press: Cambridge, MA, 1990.

[5] E. H. Durfee. *Coordination of Distributed Problem Solvers.* Kluwer Academic Publishers: Boston, MA, 1988.

[6] E. A. Emerson and J. Y. Halpern. 'Sometimes' and 'not never' revisited: on branching time versus linear time temporal logic. *Journal of the ACM*, 33(1):151–178, 1986.

[7] J. R. Galliers. *A Theoretical Framework for Computer Models of Cooperative Dialogue, Acknowledging Multi-Agent Conflict.* PhD thesis, Open University, UK, 1988.

[8] N. R. Jennings. Commitments and conventions: The foundation of coordination in multi-agent systems. *Knowledge Engineering Review*, 8(3):223–250, 1993.

[9] S. Kraus, M. Nirke, and K. Sycara. Reaching agreements through argumentation: A logical model. In *Proceedings of the Twelfth International Workshop on Distributed Artificial Intelligence (IWDAI-93)*, pages 233–247, Hidden Valley, PA, May 1993.

[10] H. J. Levesque, P. R. Cohen, and J. H. T. Nunes. On acting together. In *Proceedings of the Eighth National Conference on Artificial Intelligence (AAAI-90)*, pages 94–99, Boston, MA, 1990.

[11] R. C. Moore. A formal theory of knowledge and action. In J. F. Allen, J. Hendler, and A. Tate, editors, *Readings in Planning*, pages 480–519. Morgan Kaufmann Publishers: San Mateo, CA, 1990.

[12] A. Pnueli. Specification and development of reactive systems. In *Information Processing 86.* Elsevier Science Publishers B.V.: Amsterdam, The Netherlands, 1986.

[13] A. S. Rao and M. P. Georgeff. Social plans: Preliminary report. In E. Werner and Y. Demazeau, editors, *Decentralized AI 3 — Proceedings of the Third European Workshop on Modelling Autonomous Agents and Multi-Agent Worlds (MAAMAW-91)*, pages 57–76. Elsevier Science Publishers B.V.: Amsterdam, The Netherlands, 1992.

[14] M. P. Singh. Group ability and structure. In Y. Demazeau and J.-P. Müller, editors, *Decentralized AI 2 — Proceedings of the Second European Workshop on Modelling Autonomous Agents and Multi-Agent Worlds (MAAMAW-90)*, pages 127–146. Elsevier Science Publishers B.V.: Amsterdam, The Netherlands, 1991.

[15] R. G. Smith. *A Framework for Distributed Problem Solving.* UMI Research Press, 1980.

[16] K. P. Sycara. Multiagent compromise via negotiation. In L. Gasser and M. Huhns, editors, *Distributed Artificial Intelligence Volume II*, pages 119–138. Pitman Publishing: London and Morgan Kaufmann: San Mateo, CA, 1989.

[17] M. Wooldridge. Coherent social action. In *Proceedings of the Eleventh European Conference on Artificial Intelligence (ECAI-94)*, pages 279–283, Amsterdam, The Netherlands, 1994.

[18] M. Wooldridge and M. Fisher. A first-order branching time logic of multi-agent systems. In *Proceedings of the Tenth European Conference on Artificial Intelligence (ECAI-92)*, pages 234–238, Vienna, Austria, 1992.

[19] M. Wooldridge and N. Jennings. The cooperative problem solving process: A formal model. Technical report, Department of Computing, Manchester Metropolitan University, Chester St., Manchester M1 5GD, UK, 1994.

4.4 Interactive Agency

Towards a Pragmatic Theory of Interactions

Afsaneh Haddadi
Daimler-Benz AG, Research Systems Technology
Alt-Moabit 91b, 10559 Berlin, Germany
email: afsaneh@DBreserach-berlin.de

Abstract

This article provides a specification of the reasoning processes that guide communicative actions of agents towards a potential cooperation. For this purpose we develop a formal theory with an internal perspective, which enables us to identify the key data structures and specify the relationships between them. The reasoning processes are described in terms of beliefs, desires and intentions of individual agents. The logical model of these attitudes are used to formally define a number of important states including agent to agent *commitments*. The reasoning processes are in essence the transitions through these states, specified by a set of rules as part of our specification language. As a result of these processes, an agent may adopt goals to communicate. These goals are fed back into the reasoning process to find appropriate communication plans that fulfill them. Our approach is pragmatic since it enables a direct coupling of the theoretical concepts to an implementable model.

Introduction

Cooperative problem solving is considered as an important aspect in multi-agent systems. Many studies in this topic have identified *joint intentions* as the mental component that causes the cooperative activity of a group of agents. The existing theories have largely characterised such joint attitudes from an observer's perspective (*external* perspective) (e.g., (Levesque, Cohen, & Nunes 1990), (Singh 1991)). These approaches have aimed at developing theories *about* agents, rather than models that can be used *by* agents (Wooldridge & Jennings 1994). Therefore, they do not provide much insight into the design and implementation of reasoning processes of individual agents. For this purpose, we take an *internal* perspective, describing the formalisms from the perspective of individual agents on their own mental states, their environment and the other agents. This approach is more pragmatic, since internal theories typically identify the key data structures and describe the relationship between them. Therefore, coupling of the theory to the resulting design concepts is more straightforward.

The formal specification language is largely identical to the BDI model for single *situated agents* in (Rao & Georgeff 1991), but extends it to agents in multi-agent systems. Following their concept of situated agents, we adopt the view that agent-oriented reasoning can be expressed by the triple "*chance + choice + commitment*" (Rao & Georgeff 1993). While chances refer to possible future states of the environment, choices correspond to the decisions an agent makes based on what it believes to be possible and desires to bring about. Commitment then expresses *when* an agent pursues a *chosen* course of action and *under what conditions* it should give up its persistent to those choices. This view forms the fundamental concept behind reasoning about choosing appropriate communication acts which we view as part of the *means-ends reasoning* process. This process involves reasoning about appropriate means (plans) of achieving some desired ends (goals). A complete treatment of our formal framework will not be provided in this article. The formal syntax and semantics of the language and its properties can be found in a forthcoming thesis (Haddadi 1995).

Next section gives an informal description of our agent specification language. This language is used to describe a number of key constructs that take part in the means-end reasoning process of an agent. This process is then specified in a set of rules which characterise under which conditions individual and agent to agent commitments may be formed and revised. As part of this process, a subset of these rules specify an agent's reasoning about communication. Finally, a discussion and the future directions of this work is provided.

The Logical Framework

The language of formulations is a first-order, multi-modal, branching-time logic (a first-order variant of CTL* (Emerson 1990)). The world is modelled as a time tree with a single past and a branching future. Two types of formulae can be expressed in a world: *state formula* which is evaluated at a specific time point, and *path formula* which is evaluated over a specific path (sequence of time points). The formulae of the language are constructed using the usual operators of first-order logic: $\neg, \wedge, \vee, \Rightarrow, =, \exists, \forall$; the temporal operators: $\bigcirc$ (next), $\diamond$ (eventually), and $\square$ (always), which operate over state and path formulae; and the path operators E (optional) and A (inevitable) of branching time logic.

Each agent is capable of performing a number of actions. These actions are structured into *plans*, each aimed at achieving a certain state of affairs. Every agent is assumed to have a *library* of pre-compiled plans. The constructs operating on actions and plans are informally defined as follows: (Does z p) states agent z's attempt in executing plan p next. (Achieved z φ) and (Achieves z φ) denote past successful and future attempt of agent z in achieving φ. (Has_Plan z p φ) states, z has a plan p in its plan library that if executed successfully, would achieve φ.

Beliefs, desires and intentions of an agent are respectively modelled by associating a set of *belief-*, *desire-* and *intention-accessible* worlds to each situation. These worlds refer to the worlds that an agent *believes* to be possible, *desires* to bring about, or *commits* to achieve. We distinguish *goals* from *desires* in two ways: (i) goals are *chosen* desires of an agent that are consistent; and (ii) the agent should believe that the goal is achievable. A full account of modelling of these attitudes, together with their properties may be found in (Rao & Georgeff 1991). The two most important axioms related to our work are: (i) *belief-goal compatibility* axiom which states that if an agent adopts an option as a goal, it must believe that it is possible to achieve that option[1]:

Axiom 1 (GOAL z φ) $\Rightarrow$ (BEL z φ).

And (ii) *goal-intention compatibility* axiom which states that if an agent commits to an option, this option must be one of its goals.

Axiom 2 (INTEND z φ) $\Rightarrow$ (GOAL z φ).

The following abbreviation is introduced to express that an agent either believes that a formula φ holds, or that it believes that it does not hold[2], in other words, it has a belief about the value of φ:

Definition 1 (Aware z φ) $\stackrel{def}{=}$ (BEL z φ) $\vee$ (BEL z $\neg\varphi$).

Finally, the operator $\mathcal{B}$ is a variant of the *before* operator in temporal logic, meaning that if sometime in the future φ holds, ψ will hold before φ holds:

Definition 2 $\psi \, \mathcal{B} \, \varphi \stackrel{def}{=} \diamond\varphi \Rightarrow \diamond(\psi \wedge \diamond\varphi)$.

[1] R&G (Rao & Georgeff 1991) define the well-formed formulae that contain no positive occurrences of 'inevitable' (A) outside the scope of the modal operators BEL, GOAL, or INTEND *O-formulae*. In all the formulae in this article, if applicable, formula φ is an O-formula.

[2] Note that this is not be confused with the the general logics of '*awareness*' in the literature, which involve logics of implicit and explicit beliefs (see (Fagin & Halpern 1985)).

Means-Ends Reasoning

Expressing the means-end reasoning process in terms of the interplay of *chance, choice* and *commitment*, means to an end may be decided to be carried out individually – as with *individual task achievement* in single-agent systems– or cooperatively. In the context of individual task achievement we are only concerned with commitment to the choice of plan of actions, i.e., individual intention to carry out a plan. In terms of cooperative activity, in this article we restrict our attention to *task delegation* and *task adoption*. In simplest form, task delegation refers to delegation of achievement of a task to another agent, and task adoption refers to adoption of achievement of another agent's task. Agents may engage in communication and possibly negotiation in order to come to some sort of agreement about each other's attitude towards a possible cooperation. But cooperation would only commence if the two agents have agreed on the terms of cooperation, believe that they both wish to cooperate and make a commitment. Hence here we are in addition concerned with agent to agent commitments.

From a pragmatic point of view, specification of commitments would have to explicitly address the following issues:

- The semantics of intentions including the conditions an agent is committed to maintain, (*maintenance conditions*),
- The conditions which lead to the formation of commitments, (*formation conditions*), and
- The conditions under which a commitment must be re-evaluated, (*revision conditions*).

An extra requirement that may or may not be directly associates with a commitment is the specification of what an agent should do once it gives up a commitment (Wooldridge & Jennings 1994), which will not be dealt with in this article. The approach in (Cohen & Levesque 1990) and formalisms based on this approach (e.g., (Levesque, Cohen, & Nunes 1990) and (Wooldridge & Jennings 1994)) integrate these conditions in the semantics of intentions. From the practical point of view this is problematic, since one cannot say when an agent has an intention *per se*. One have to state in advance under what conditions they should be revised and in case of (Wooldridge & Jennings 1994), for each specific commitment what the agent should do once it gives up that commitment. This would be satisfactory if these conditions could be generalised. With respect to individual intentions to act, the specification of these conditions is related to certain strategies that an agent must follow, and successful strategies can only be outlined with respect to the requirement of the application in question. With respect to commitments of agents to engage in a cooperative activity, specification of these conditions is also dependent on the macro aspects of the system, such as norms, conventions and laws of the "society" or the organisation in which the

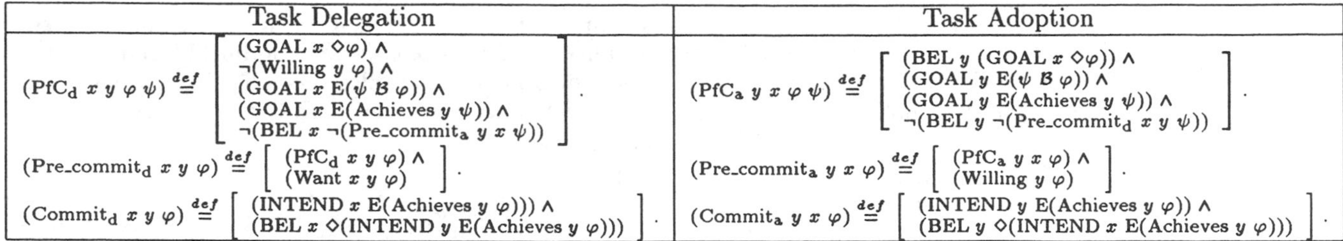

Task Delegation	Task Adoption
$(\mathsf{PfC_d}\ x\ y\ \varphi\ \psi) \stackrel{def}{=} \left[\begin{array}{l}(\mathrm{GOAL}\ x\ \Diamond\varphi) \wedge \\ \neg(\mathsf{Willing}\ y\ \varphi) \wedge \\ (\mathrm{GOAL}\ x\ \mathrm{E}(\psi\ \mathcal{B}\ \varphi)) \wedge \\ (\mathrm{GOAL}\ x\ \mathrm{E}(\mathrm{Achieves}\ y\ \psi)) \wedge \\ \neg(\mathrm{BEL}\ x\ \neg(\mathrm{Pre\_commit_a}\ y\ x\ \psi))\end{array}\right].$	$(\mathsf{PfC_a}\ y\ x\ \varphi\ \psi) \stackrel{def}{=} \left[\begin{array}{l}(\mathrm{BEL}\ y\ (\mathrm{GOAL}\ x\ \Diamond\varphi)) \wedge \\ (\mathrm{GOAL}\ y\ \mathrm{E}(\psi\ \mathcal{B}\ \varphi)) \wedge \\ (\mathrm{GOAL}\ y\ \mathrm{E}(\mathrm{Achieves}\ y\ \psi)) \wedge \\ \neg(\mathrm{BEL}\ y\ \neg(\mathrm{Pre\_commit_d}\ x\ y\ \psi))\end{array}\right].$
$(\mathrm{Pre\_commit_d}\ x\ y\ \varphi) \stackrel{def}{=} \left[\begin{array}{l}(\mathsf{PfC_d}\ x\ y\ \varphi) \wedge \\ (\mathsf{Want}\ x\ y\ \varphi)\end{array}\right].$	$(\mathrm{Pre\_commit_a}\ y\ x\ \varphi) \stackrel{def}{=} \left[\begin{array}{l}(\mathsf{PfC_a}\ y\ x\ \varphi) \wedge \\ (\mathsf{Willing}\ y\ \varphi)\end{array}\right].$
$(\mathrm{Commit_d}\ x\ y\ \varphi) \stackrel{def}{=} \left[\begin{array}{l}(\mathrm{INTEND}\ x\ \mathrm{E}(\mathrm{Achieves}\ y\ \varphi))) \wedge \\ (\mathrm{BEL}\ x\ \Diamond(\mathrm{INTEND}\ y\ \mathrm{E}(\mathrm{Achieves}\ y\ \varphi)))\end{array}\right].$	$(\mathrm{Commit_a}\ y\ x\ \varphi) \stackrel{def}{=} \left[\begin{array}{l}(\mathrm{INTEND}\ y\ \mathrm{E}(\mathrm{Achieves}\ y\ \varphi)) \wedge \\ (\mathrm{BEL}\ y\ \Diamond(\mathrm{INTEND}\ x\ \mathrm{E}(\mathrm{Achieves}\ y\ \varphi)))\end{array}\right].$

Figure 1: Formal definition of the main reasoning constructs

agents are operating. Therefore, for practical purposes we would require to disentangle these issues and identify what could be defined and specified in general and what is needed to be specified as part of the application in question.

Another problem is a technical one. Many approaches to defining joint intentions rely on the recursive notion of mutual beliefs. Under certain circumstances such a mutual state of affairs may not be attainable in practice (e.g., the coordinated attack problem (Halpern & Moses 1985)). To attain a state of mutual belief such that eventually the agents involved would indeed act on their committed terms, certain conventions must be established (Singh 1991).

In this article we aim at a more pragmatic approach and start with introducing a convention and developing our theory within the framework of this convention.

Convention: Once a *potential for cooperation* is detected, the negotiation process commences. After a series of negotiation steps, eventually one of the negotiating parties (say agent x) finalises its terms of cooperation by making a *pre-commitment*, and communicates this to the other agent (say agent y). This finalisation marks the last steps of negotiation, that is, agent y now must either make a *commitment* or else opt out. We require that if y agrees on the final terms then it commits to x on the agreed terms and communicates this to x, after which pre-commitment of x becomes a full commitment.

Our theory models this process in terms of three reasoning constructs: *potential for cooperation, pre-commitment* and *commitment* of agents to one another. These constructs will be formally defined and their properties including their formation and revision conditions will be specified.

Definitions

The reasoning constructs are defined in terms of beliefs, goals and intentions of individual agents. While goals represent choices that an agent believes to be possible in the current situation, intentions represent commitment to some of these choices. Therefore, before forming an intention, an agent has to deliberate on the choices available to it. For individual intentions to act, these choices typically correspond to the choice of actions or plans to achieve certain goals. For agent to agent commitment, these choices also include a potential cooperating partner. The final decision on these choices are respectively represented by the following decision constructs.

- $(\mathsf{Willing}\ y\ \varphi)$ denotes that agent y has chosen a plan that if executed successfully would achieve φ.
- $(\mathsf{Want}\ x\ y\ \varphi)$ denotes that agent x has chosen agent y to be the actor of achieving φ.

These constructs will not be defined in our general theory, since their value should be evaluated by some deliberation procedures that need to be defined as part of the theory of the application in question. However, there are some restrictions imposed on them as will be outlines later (see Axioms 4 and 5).

In the remainder of this article, we take the simple scenario of an agent x's attempt in delegating the achievement of one of its goals to another agent y, and an agent y's attempt in adopting the achievement of another agent's (here x's) goal. It is also important to note that hereafter in all the formulae involving agents x and y, $y \neq x$.

Since we take an internal perspective, the three reasoning constructs *potential for cooperation* (PfC), *pre-commitment* and *commitment* of two agents are defined once in the context of task delegation (agent x's perspective) and once in the context of task adoption (agent y's perspective). To distinguish the two, the corresponding operators have either the subscript 'd' (for delegation), or 'a' (for adoption). The formal definition of these states is given in Figure 1. In the context of task delegation, these constructs are defined informally as follows:

- Agent x sees a *potential for cooperation* with agent y with respect to its goal state φ, such that y achieves at least ψ, if (i) x has φ as a goal, (ii) x is not willing to achieve φ individually, (iii) x believes that one way of achieving φ is first to achieve ψ, and has ψ as a subgoal, (iv) x has it as a goal that y achieves at least ψ. and (v) up to now, x does not have any belief that y would disagree with these terms.
- Agent x is *pre-committed* to agent y such that y achieves φ, if (i) x sees a potential for cooperation with y such that y achieves φ;[3], and (ii) x wants that

[3]The representation $(\mathsf{PfC_d}\ x\ y\ \varphi)$ is used as a short form for $(\mathsf{PfC_d}\ x\ y\ \varphi\ \varphi)$. Similarly for $\mathsf{PfC_a}$.

y achieves φ.

- Agent $\underline{x}$ is *committed* to agent $\underline{y}$ achieving φ if, (i) x has committed to the choice of y achieving φ, and (ii) x believes that y will eventually commit to achieving φ.

In the context of task adoption, these constructs are defined analogously, as formally defined in Figure 1. The definition of agent to agent commitment provided a separate "semantics" including the *maintenance conditions* discussed earlier.

Axioms and Theorems

Due to the limited space, only some of the more important axioms and theorems of our theory will be outlined. A complete analysis may be found in (Haddadi 1995).

The first theorem below (derivable from our formal framework) captures the fact that if an agent has a goal to achieve φ individually, then it must have a plan in its plan library which if executed successfully would achieve that goal, and has it as a goal to carry out that plan (similarly for intentions):

Theorem 1

$$(\mathsf{GOAL}\ x\ \mathsf{E}(\mathsf{Achieves}\ x\ \varphi)) \Rightarrow \exists p \,.\, \begin{bmatrix} (\mathsf{BEL}\ x\ (\mathsf{Has\_Plan}\ x\ p\ \varphi)) \wedge \\ (\mathsf{GOAL}\ x\ \mathsf{E}(\mathsf{Does}\ x\ p)) \end{bmatrix}.$$

An important property of intentions is that they should move an agent to act. Under the assumption that an agent can only perform one action at a time, the following axiom ensures that an agent executes an action next, if it intends *inevitably* to execute that action. Note that if this action is intended *optionally*, then at the time of execution the agent must deliberate and choose one action in order to act intentionally.

Axiom 3 $(\mathsf{INTEND}\ x\ \mathsf{A}\Diamond(\mathsf{Does}\ x\ \alpha)) \Rightarrow \mathsf{A}\Diamond(\mathsf{Does}\ x\ \alpha)$

Since the decision constructs Willing and Want express certain decisions that an agent makes on the choices available and possible to it, the following two axioms are introduced to ensure that these decisions are indeed made on the choices that an agent has as a goal.

Axiom 4 $(\mathsf{Willing}\ y\ \varphi) \Rightarrow (\mathsf{GOAL}\ y\ \mathsf{E}(\mathsf{Achieves}\ y\ \varphi))$.

Axiom 5 $(\mathsf{Want}\ x\ y\ \varphi) \Rightarrow (\mathsf{GOAL}\ x\ \mathsf{E}(\mathsf{Achieves}\ y\ \varphi))$.

Furthermore we require that if an agent chooses to achieve a goal individually, it has a plan and chooses to carry out that plan in order to achieve that goal:

Axiom 6 $(\mathsf{Want}\ y\ y\ \varphi) \Leftrightarrow (\mathsf{Willing}\ y\ \varphi)$.

As was stated earlier, the common definition of joint intentions relies on the recursive definition of mutual beliefs, according to which agent x would only make a commitment to agent y, if it believes that y is also committed and believes that y believes that x is already committed and so on. Similarly for y. Therefore, it is questionable if the two agents ever end up making a commitment. Our convention makes use of a weaker condition: if an agent is pre-committed and believes that the other agent is also pre-committed, then it will make a commitment. This is expressed in Axiom 7[4].

Axiom 7

$$\begin{bmatrix} (\mathsf{Pre\_commit_d}\ x\ y\ \varphi) \wedge \\ (\mathsf{BEL}\ x\ \mathsf{Pre\_commit_a}\ y\ x\ \varphi)) \end{bmatrix} \Leftrightarrow \bigcirc(\mathsf{Commit_d}\ x\ y\ \varphi).$$

This axiom specifies under what conditions an agent makes a commitment (next) (*formation condition*). Because this is an equivalence relation, it also states that whenever any of the conditions that originally led to the formation of the commitment no longer hold, the agent should drop its commitment. Therefore, this axiom also specifies some general *revision conditions*. But we still require to impose the restriction that if an agent is committed now, it must also be pre-committed. This is to ensure that if the conditions that led to its commitment are no longer true, the agent does not maintain the conditions to which it was committed. This is captured in the next axiom[5].

Axiom 8 $(\mathsf{Commit_d}\ x\ y\ \varphi) \Rightarrow (\mathsf{Pre\_commit_d}\ x\ y\ \varphi)$.

One important theorem derivable from our model is Theorem 2, which states: as long as an agent is committed to the other agent and believes that the other agent is at least pre-committed, then it will believe that the other agent is either already committed, or will eventually make a commitment[6].

Theorem 2

$$\begin{bmatrix} (\mathsf{Commit_d}\ x\ y\ \varphi) \wedge \\ (\mathsf{BEL}\ x\ (\mathsf{Pre\_commit_a}\ y\ x\ \varphi)) \end{bmatrix} \Rightarrow (\mathsf{BEL}\ x\ \Diamond(\mathsf{Commit_a}\ y\ x\ \varphi)).$$

Finally, Theorem 3 captures the fact that if an agent has made a pre-commitment but comes to believe that the other agent will never make a commitment, then it will also not make a commitment, (i.e., drop its commitment in case it is already committed).

Theorem 3

$$\begin{bmatrix} (\mathsf{BEL}\ x\ (\mathsf{BEL}\ y\ (\mathsf{Pre\_commit_d}\ x\ y\ \varphi))) \wedge \\ (\mathsf{BEL}\ x\ \neg\Diamond(\mathsf{Commit_a}\ y\ x\ \varphi) \end{bmatrix} \Rightarrow \bigcirc\neg(\mathsf{Commit_d}\ x\ y\ \varphi).$$

Therefore the definitions, the axioms and the resulting theorems specified the three issues associated with commitment, namely, *maintenance, formation* and *revision* conditions.

[4] Because of the space restrictions we will only outline the axioms in the context of task delegation.

[5] Axiom 8 is consistent with the goal-intention compatibility axiom, i.e., $(\mathsf{INTEND}\ x\ \mathsf{E}(\mathsf{Achieves}\ y\ \varphi)) \Rightarrow (\mathsf{GOAL}\ x\ \mathsf{E}(\mathsf{Achieves}\ y\ \varphi))$.

[6] This theorem is not immediately obvious, but because of space restrictions it cannot be appropriately dealt with in this article

Specification of Means-end Reasoning

The means-end reasoning process is modelled in terms of temporal state transitions. These transitions are specified in a set of rules. According to the conditions that hold in a given state, a rule specifies the next valid state to which the transition must proceed:

Definition 3 $\varphi \longleftrightarrow \psi \stackrel{def}{=} \mathsf{A}\square(\varphi \Leftrightarrow \bigcirc\psi)$.

That is, whenever the process is in a state in which φ holds, it should proceed to a next state in which ψ holds. This is similar to the specification of *liveness properties* of concurrent programs (Manna & Pnueli 1984), which is of the form $(\varphi \Rightarrow \Diamond\psi)$ where φ and ψ are past formulas. The difference is that since by these rules we aim to specify both the formation conditions and some of the general revision conditions, we use the equivalence relation instead of the 'implies' operator.

Formation of Commitments

The formation and some of the general revision conditions associated with agent to agent commitments were already specified in Axiom 7 (which is in any case in the form of our specification rules). But we still need to specify the formation and revision conditions for individual intentions to act:

$$\forall x \,.\, (x \neq y) \land \left[\begin{array}{l} \neg(\mathsf{Pre\_commit_a}\ y\ x\ \varphi) \land \\ (\mathsf{GOAL}\ y\ \mathsf{E}(\mathsf{Achieves}\ y\ \varphi)) \land \\ (\mathsf{Willing}\ y\ \varphi) \end{array}\right] \longleftrightarrow (\mathsf{INTEND}\ y\ \mathsf{E}(\mathsf{Achieves}\ y\ \varphi)).$$

According to this rule, an agent forms and maintains its commitment to achieve φ individually iff: (i) it has not pre-committed itself to another agent to adopt and achieve φ, (ii) has it as a goal to achieve φ individually, and (iii) is willing to achieve φ individually. The first condition is to distinguish the formation of intention to act in the context of individual task achievement, from that formed as a result of task adoption, that is, it ensures that if y has made a pre-commitment, it does not intend to act for it before both agents have made a commitment.

Formation of Goals To Communicate

By communication the agents can update their belief about whether, when and how they wish to cooperate. Having in mind that we take an internal perspective, an agent's goal to communicate is directed towards two objectives: (i) update of the other agent's belief, about its own attitude towards a possible cooperation; and (ii) update of its own belief about the other agent's attitude. These goals are of the form $(\mathsf{GOAL}\ z\ \delta)$, where $\delta = \rho\ \land\ (\mathsf{Does}\ z\ \gamma?)$, ρ denoting the first objective, $(\mathsf{Does}\ z\ \gamma?)$ the second objective[7] and z is either of agents x or y, depending on which agent's goal is being expressed.

$$\left[\begin{array}{l} (\mathrm{PfC_d}\ x\ y\ \varphi\ \psi) \land \\ \neg(\mathrm{Pre\_commit_d}\ x\ y\ (\varphi \lor \psi)) \land \\ \neg(\mathrm{Aware}\ x\ (\mathrm{PfC_a}\ y\ x\ \varphi\ \psi)) \land \\ (\mathrm{BEL}\ x\ \neg(\mathrm{Aware}\ y\ (\mathrm{PfC_d}\ x\ y\ \varphi\ \psi))) \end{array}\right]$$
$$\rho_1 = (\mathrm{BEL}\ y\ (\mathrm{PfC_d}\ x\ y\ \varphi\ \psi)) \quad \gamma_1 = (\mathrm{PfC_a}\ y\ x\ \varphi\ \psi)$$

$$\left[\begin{array}{l} (\mathrm{Pre\_commit_d}\ x\ y\ \varphi) \land \\ \neg(\mathrm{Aware}\ x\ (\mathrm{Pre\_commit_a}\ y\ x\ \varphi\ \psi)) \land \\ (\mathrm{BEL}\ x\ \neg(\mathrm{Aware}\ y\ (\mathrm{Pre\_commit_d}\ x\ y\ \varphi))) \end{array}\right]$$
$$\rho_2 = (\mathrm{BEL}\ y\ (\mathrm{Pre\_commit_d}\ x\ y\ \varphi))$$
$$\gamma_2 = (\mathrm{Pre\_commit_a}\ y\ x\ \varphi\ \psi)$$

$$\left[\begin{array}{l} (\mathrm{Commit_d}\ x\ y\ \varphi) \land \\ (\mathrm{BEL}\ x\ \neg(\mathrm{Aware}\ y\ (\mathrm{Commit_d}\ x\ y\ \varphi))) \end{array}\right]$$
$$\rho_3 = (\mathrm{BEL}\ y\ (\mathrm{Commit_d}\ x\ y\ \varphi)) \quad \gamma_3 = \mathsf{true}$$

$$\left[\begin{array}{l} (\mathrm{BEL}\ x\ (\mathrm{PfC_a}\ y\ x\ \varphi)) \land \\ \forall p\,.\,(\mathrm{Contributes}\ p\ \varphi\ \psi) \Rightarrow \\ \left(\begin{array}{l} \neg(\mathrm{Pre\_commit_d}\ x\ y\ \psi) \land \\ (\mathrm{BEL}\ x\ \neg(\mathrm{Aware}\ y\ \neg(\mathrm{Pre\_commit_d}\ x\ y\ \psi))) \end{array}\right) \end{array}\right]$$
$$\rho_4 = (\mathrm{BEL}\ y \left[\begin{array}{l} \forall p\,.\,(\mathrm{Contributes}\ p\ \varphi\ \psi) \land \\ \neg(\mathrm{Pre\_commit_d}\ x\ y\ \psi) \end{array}\right])$$
$$\gamma_4 = \mathsf{true}$$

Figure 2: Communciation Rules: Task Delegation

In the context of task delegation the formation of some of these goals is specified in figure 2. For instance, based on our convention, in attempt to delegate the achievement of a goal φ (or part of it ψ) to another agent, four possible goals are identified: δ_1 is formed when x detects a potential for cooperation with y, which initiates negotiation; δ_2 is formed when x has pre-committed to y achieving φ, which finalises the negotiation process, prompting y for a commitment or opting out; δ_3 is formed when x has made a commitment (as the response to y's pre-commitment), and according to our convention should communicate this to y; finally δ_4 is formed when x does not wish to cooperate with y. There are also analogous rules in the context of task adoption which have not been included here.

Active Communication

Upon adopting a goal to communicate, an agent has to enter another round of means-end reasoning in order to find an appropriate plan that if executed successfully would achieve that goal. Among the plans in the plan library of an agent, there are a number of so called *primitive communication* plans that either consist of a send action (i.e., $\{send(msg)\}$), or the sequence of actions 'send and wait until receive' (i.e., $\{send(msg1); true{*}; receive(msg2)\}$). Primitive plans are distinguished by the message type of the message to be sent.

[7] Having the goal of $(\mathsf{Does}\ z\ \gamma_i?)$, expresses the fact that agent z has it as a goal to execute a plan in order to find out if γ_i (a fact about the other agent) holds.

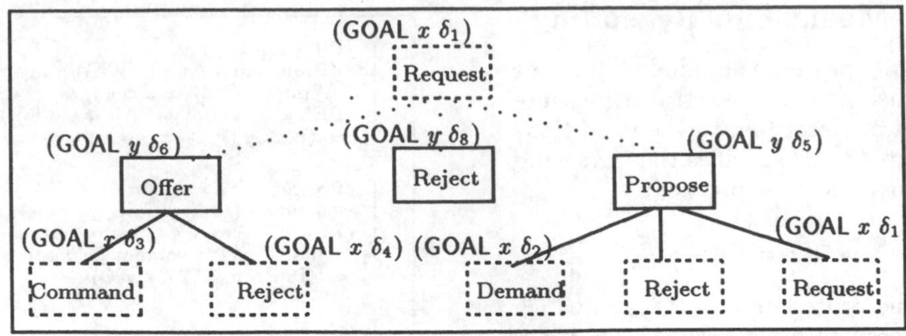

Figure 3: Demonstration

Sending and receiving messages are taken to be primitive actions[8]. Roughly, a message consists of a *sender*, a *receiver*, a *message type* and a *content*. The content of a message is a well-formed formula of (another) communication language which contains the actual proposition to be communicated.

One goal of *sending* a message is to update the receiver's belief. In the context of this article, this refers to the update of the receiver's belief about the sender's attitude towards a possible cooperation. This corresponds to (GOAL z ρ).

Message types are used to express what the sender attempts to convey to the receiver and possibly prompt the receiver for a response. This corresponds to the (GOAL z (Does z γ?)).

The language admits the following set of message types: {*'Request', 'Demand', 'Command', 'Propose', 'Offer', 'Report', 'Reject' and 'Accept'*}, and consequently primitive communication plans. To simplify, with each type of goal (i.e., δ_1 to δ_9) we associate a unique message type, and consequently a unique communication plan as shown in the table below.

Request	Demand	Command	Reject	
δ_1	δ_2	δ_3	δ_4	
Propose	Offer	Accept	Reject	Report
δ_5	δ_6	δ_7	δ_8	δ_9

However, it is possible to associate more than one communication plan to a goal, but in that case an agent has to deliberate and choose and intend one of them.

There are a number of assumptions that we make about communication: (1) If $\gamma = \textsf{true}$, the corresponding plan expression is only a *send* action meaning that the agent does not expect a response. (2) After receiving a message, the receiving agent believes the 'content' of the message. (3) After sending a message, the sending agent believes that the receiving agent has received the message and that the sending agent believes that the receiving agent believes the 'content' of the message.

An example scenario for the goals formed and the execution of the corresponding plans is demonstrated in Figure 3. In this example, to achieve its goal δ_1, agent x initiates the communication (and possibly negotiation process) by executing a *request* plan, i.e., sending a request to agent y, expressing its belief on a potential for cooperation, and waiting for a response from y. Upon receipt of this request, if y wishes to negotiate on the requested terms, it will form the goal δ_5, and *propose* its desired terms. If however, y agrees with the requested terms (or fixes some terms of its own), it will pre-commit to x, and communicate this by sending an *offer* and wait for x's response to commit or withdraw its request. Else, if y does not favour any type of cooperation in the context of the request made, it will simply *reject* the request.

[8]The formal syntax of messages can be found in (Haddadi 1995).

Summary and Future Directions

With the focus on agent to agent interactions to participate in a cooperative activity, we gave a brief overview of our internal theory. This theory allows a pragmatic approach to the specification of the reasoning processes behind communication. For this specification we identified three important reasoning states of *potential for cooperation, pre-commitment*, and *commitment* based on the beliefs, goals and intentions of individual agents. The process of reasoning was characterised as the interplay of *chance, choice* and *commitment*, and specified with a set of rules analogous to the *temporal implication* of concurrent programs. Finally, we demonstrated how our theory leads to the execution of appropriate communication plans.

Although our work extends Rao and Georgeff's single-agent BDI model to multi-agent systems, it is different from their follow up works (Rao, Georgeff, & Sonnenberg 1992) (Kinny *et al.* 1994) which embody teams of agents and their joint attitudes. Since the objective of their work has been somewhat different, many important issues concerning reasoning about communication and cooperation are simplified by encoding and compiling most of the relevant information, at design time, into the structure of social plans. Our approach however, does not rely on existence of such social plans, and allows individual agents to reason about with whom and how they wish to cooperate, and actively choose appropriate communication plans as they proceed. It is perceived that since the meta-level plans in PRS (Georgeff & Ingrand 1988) do the meta-level reasoning and decision making on the object-level plans, the model of reasoning specified in this article may be encoded in a set of *meta-level plans.*

This work was motivated by our earlier studies in (Haddadi & Sundermeyer 1993) and forms the theoretical background and specification of the cooperation protocols described in (Burmeister, Haddadi, & Sundermeyer 1993). These ideas were incorporated into the design of the general reasoning mechanism in our COSY agent architecture. The concepts behind this design directly maps into the general concepts developed in the theory briefly reviewed in this article, (see (Haddadi 1995) for details).

The future work will be concerned with studying whether and to what extend the theory and the specification of individual agent's reasoning about communication could be extended and carried over to the cooperative activities of teams of agents.

Acknowledgement

I would like to thank Michael Georgeff and Michael Wooldridge for their valuable comments on the technical details, and Kurt Sundermeyer for supporting and reviewing this paper.

References

Burmeister, B.; Haddadi, A.; and Sundermeyer, K. 1993. Configurable Cooperation Protocols for Multi-Agent Systems. In *Proc. MAAMAW-93.*

Cohen, P. R., and Levesque, H. J. 1990. Intention Is Choice with Commitment. *Artificial Intelligence* 42:213–261.

Emerson, E. A. 1990. Temporal and Modal Logic. In van Leeuwen, J., ed., *Handbook of Theoretical Computer Science*, volume B. Elsvier Science Publishers B. V.

Fagin, R., and Halpern, J. Y. 1985. Belief, Awareness, and Limited Reasoning. In *Proc. of IJCAI-85.* Morgen Kaufmann.

Georgeff, M. P., and Ingrand, F. F. 1988. Research on procedural reasoning systems. Technical report, AI Center, SRI International, Menlo park, California. Final Report, phase 1.

Haddadi, A., and Sundermeyer, K. 1993. Knowledge about Other Agents in Heterogeneous Dynamic Domains. In *ICICIS-93.*

Haddadi, A. 1995. *Reasoning about Interactions in Agent Systems: A Pragmatic Theory.* Ph.D. Dissertation, University of Manchester Institute of Science and Technology (UMIST), U.K.

Halpern, J. Y., and Moses, Y. 1985. Knowledge and Common Knowledge in a Distributed Environment. In *Proc. of the Third ACM Symposium on the Principles of Distributed Computing*, 50–61.

Kinny, D.; Ljungberg, M.; Rao, A.; Sonenberg, E.; Tidhar, G.; and Werner, E. 1994. Planned Team Activity. In Castelfranchi, C., and Werner, E., eds., *Artificial Social Systems, Lecture Notes in Artificial Intelligence, 830.* Springer-Verlag.

Levesque, H. J.; Cohen, P. R.; and Nunes, J. H. T. 1990. On Acting Together. In *Proc. AAAI-90*, 94–99.

Manna, Z., and Pnueli, A. 1984. Synthesis of communicating processes from temporal logic specifications. *ACM Transactions on Programming Languages and Systems* 6(1):68–93.

Rao, A. S., and Georgeff, M. P. 1991. Modeling Rational Agents within a BDI Architecture. In *Knowledge Representation and Reasoning, (KR-91)*, 473–484.

Rao, A. S., and Georgeff, M. P. 1993. A Model-Theoretic Approach to the Verification of Situated Reasoning Systems. In *Proc. IJCAI-93*, 318–324.

Rao, A. S.; Georgeff, M. P.; and Sonnenberg, E. A. 1992. Social Plans: A Preliminary Report. In Werner, E., and Demazeau, Y., eds., *Decentralized A. I. 3.* Elsvier Science Publishers.

Singh, M. P. 1991. Group Intentions. In *Proceedings of the 10th International Workshop on Distributed Artificial Intelligence.* MCC Technical Report Number ACT-AI-355-90.

Wooldridge, M. J., and Jennings, N. R. 1994. Towards a Theory of Cooperative Problem Solving. In *Preproceedings of MAAMAW-94.*

Designing a Family of Coordination Algorithms *

Keith S. Decker and Victor R. Lesser
Department of Computer Science
University of Massachusetts
DECKER@CS.UMASS.EDU

Abstract

Many researchers have shown that there is no single best organization or coordination mechanism for all environments. This paper discusses the design and implementation of an extendable family of coordination mechanisms, called Generalized Partial Global Planning (GPGP). The set of coordination mechanisms described here assists in scheduling activities for teams of cooperative computational agents. The GPGP approach has several unique features. First, it is not tied to a single domain. Each mechanism is defined as a response to certain features in the current task environment. We show that different combinations of mechanisms are appropriate for different task environments. Secondly, the approach works in conjunction with an agent's existing local planner/scheduler. Finally, the initial set of five mechanisms presented here generalizes and extends the Partial Global Planning (PGP) algorithm. In comparison to PGP, GPGP considers tasks with deadlines, it allows agent heterogeneity, it exchanges less global information, and it communicates at multiple levels of abstraction.

Introduction

This paper presents a formal description of the implementation of a domain independent coordination scheduling approach which we call Generalized Partial Global Planning (GPGP). The GPGP approach consists of an extendable set of modular coordination mechanisms, any subset or all of which can be used in response to a particular task environment. Each mechanism is defined using our formal framework for expressing coordination problems (TÆMS (Decker & Lesser 1993b)). GPGP both generalizes and extends the Partial Global Planning (PGP) algorithm (Durfee & Lesser 1991). Our approach has several unique features: GPGP works in conjunction with an existing agent architecture and local scheduler[1]; each coordination mechanism is defined as a response to certain features in the current task environment; the individual coordination mechanisms rest on a shared substrate that arbitrates between the mechanisms and the agent's local scheduler in a decision-theoretic manner.

The GPGP approach views coordination as *modulating* local control, not replacing it. This process occurs via a set of domain-independent coordination mechanisms that post constraints to the local scheduler about the importance of certain tasks and appropriate times for their initiation and completion. By concentrating on the creation of local scheduling constraints, we avoid the sequentiality of scheduling in the original PGP algorithm that occurs when there are multiple plans. By having separate modules for coordination and local scheduling, we can also take advantage of advances in real-time scheduling to produce cooperative distributed problem solving systems that respond to real-time deadlines. We can also take advantage of local schedulers that have a great deal of domain scheduling knowledge already encoded within them. Finally, our approach allows consideration of termination issues that were glossed over in the PGP work (where termination was handled by an external oracle).

Besides the obvious connections to the earlier PGP work, GPGP builds on work by von Martial (v. Martial 1992) in detecting and reacting to relationships (such as von Martial's "favor" relationship). GPGP also uses a notion of social commitments similar to those discussed by (Cohen & Levesque 1990; Shoham 1991; Castelfranchi 1993; Jennings 1993). Durfee's newer work (Durfee & Montgomery 1991) is based on a hierarchical behavior space representation that like GPGP allows agents to communicate at multiple levels of detail. The mechanisms presented in this paper deal with coordination while agents are scheduling (locating in time) their activities rather than while they are planning to meet goals. This allows them to be used in distributed scheduling systems, agenda-based systems (like blackboard systems), or systems where agents instantiate previous plans (like case-based planning systems). The focus on mechanisms for coordinating schedules is thus different from work that focuses on multi-agent planning (Grosz & Kraus 1993; Ephrati & Rosenschein 1994). Shoham and Tennenholtz's 'social laws' approach (Shoham & Tennenholtz 1992) can be viewed as one which tries to change the (perceived) structure of the tasks by, for example, restricting the agents' possible activities. Intelligent agents might use all of these approaches at one time or another.

*This work was supported by DARPA contract N00014-92-J-1698, Office of Naval Research contract N00014-92-J-1450, and NSF contract IRI-9321324. The content of the information does not necessarily reflect the position or the policy of the Government and no official endorsement should be inferred.

[1]Here, a "design-to-time" real-time scheduler (Garvey & Lesser 1993).

The next section will briefly re-introduce our framework for representing coordination problems, and summarize the assumptions we make about an agent's internal architecture. We then describe the GPGP substrate and five coordination mechanisms.[2] Previous work has shown how the GPGP approach can duplicate and extend the behaviors of the PGP algorithm (Decker & Lesser 1992); this paper will briefly summarize several experimental results that are reported in (Decker 1995) and concludes with a look at our future directions.

Representing The Task Environment

Coordination is the process of managing interdependencies between activities (Malone & Crowston 1991). If we view an agent as an entity that has some beliefs about the world and can perform actions, then the coordination problem arises when any or all of the following situations occur: the agent has a *choice* of actions it can take, and that choice affects the agent's performance; the *order* in which actions are carried out affects performance; the *time* at which actions are carried out affects performance. The coordination problem of choosing and temporally ordering actions is made more complex because the agent may only have an incomplete view of the entire task structure of which its actions are a part, the task structure may be changing dynamically, and the agent may be uncertain about the outcomes of its actions. If there are multiple agents in an environment, then when the potential actions of one agent are related to those of another agent, we call the relationship a *coordination relationship*. Each GPGP coordination mechanism is a response to some coordination relationship.

The TÆMS framework (Task Analysis, Environment Modeling, and Simulation) (Decker & Lesser 1993b) represents coordination problems in a formal, domain-independent way. We have used it to represent coordination problems in distributed sensor networks, hospital patient scheduling, airport resource management, distributed information retrieval, pilot's associate, local area network diagnosis, etc. (Decker 1995). In this paper we will describe an agent's current subjective beliefs about the structure of the problem it is trying to solve by using the TÆMS framework (Decker & Lesser 1993b; Decker 1995). For this purpose, there are two unique features of TÆMS. The first is the explicit, quantitative representation of task interrelationships as functions that describe the effect of activity choices and temporal orderings on performance. The second is the representation of task structures at multiple levels of abstraction. The highest level of abstraction is called a *task group*, and contains all tasks that have explicit computational interrelationships. A *task* is simply a set of lower-level subtasks and/or executable methods. The components of a task have an explicitly defined effect on the quality of the encompassing task. The lowest level of abstraction is called an executable *method.* An executable *method* represents a schedulable entity, such as a blackboard knowledge source instance, a chunk of code and its input data, or a totally-ordered plan that has been recalled and instantiated for a task. A method could also be an instance of a human activity at some useful level of detail, for example, "take an X-ray of patient 1's left foot".

A coordination problem instance (called an *episode* **E**) is defined as a set of task groups, each with a deadline $D(\mathcal{T})$, such as $\mathbf{E} = \langle \mathcal{T}_1, \mathcal{T}_2, \ldots, \mathcal{T}_n \rangle$. A common performance goal of the agent or agents is to maximize the sum of the quality achieved for each task group before its deadline.

Figure 1 shows an objective[3] task group and agent A's subjective view of that same task group. The arrows between tasks and/or methods indicate task interrelationships where the execution of some method will have a positive or negative effect on the quality or duration of another method. The presence of these interrelationships make this an NP-hard scheduling problem; further complicating factors for the local scheduler include the fact that multiple agents are executing related methods, that some methods are redundant (executable at more than one agent), and that the subjective task structure may differ from the real objective structure.

The Agent Architecture

We make few assumptions about the architecture of the agents. The agents have a database that holds their current beliefs about the structure of the tasks in the current episode; we represent this information using TÆMS. The agents can do three types of actions: they can execute methods from the task structure, send direct messages to one another, and do "information gathering". Information gathering actions model how new task structures or communications get into the agent's belief database. This could be a combination of external actions (checking the agent's incoming message box) and internal planning. Method execution actions cause quality to accrue in a task group (as indicated by the task structure). Communication actions are used to send the results of method executions (which in turn may trigger the effects of various task interrelationships) or meta-level information.

Formally, we write $B^t_A(x)$ to mean agent A subjectively believes x at time t (Shoham 1991). We will shorten this to $B(x)$ when the particular agent or time is obvious. An agent's subjective beliefs about the current episode include the agent's beliefs about task groups, subtasks, executable methods, and interrelationships (e.g., $B(\mathcal{T}_i \in \mathbf{E}), B(\mathcal{T}_a, M_b \in \mathcal{T}_i), B(\mathsf{enables}(\mathcal{T}_a, M_b)))$.

The GPGP family of coordination mechanisms also makes a stronger assumption about the agent architecture. It assumes the presence of a local scheduling mechanism (to be described in the next section) that can decide what method execution actions should take place and when. The local scheduler attempts to maximize a (possibly changing) utility function. The current set of GPGP coordination mechanisms are for cooperative teams of agents—they assume that agents do not intentionally lie and that agents believe what they are told. However, because agents can believe and communicate only subjective information, they may unwittingly transmit information that is inconsistent with an objective view (this can cause, among other things, the phenomena of *distraction*). Finally, the GPGP family approach requires domain-dependent

[2] These five mechanisms are oriented towards producing PGP-like 'cooperative team' behavior. Mechanisms for self-interested agents are also possible.

[3] The word 'objective' refers to the fact that this is the true, real structure.

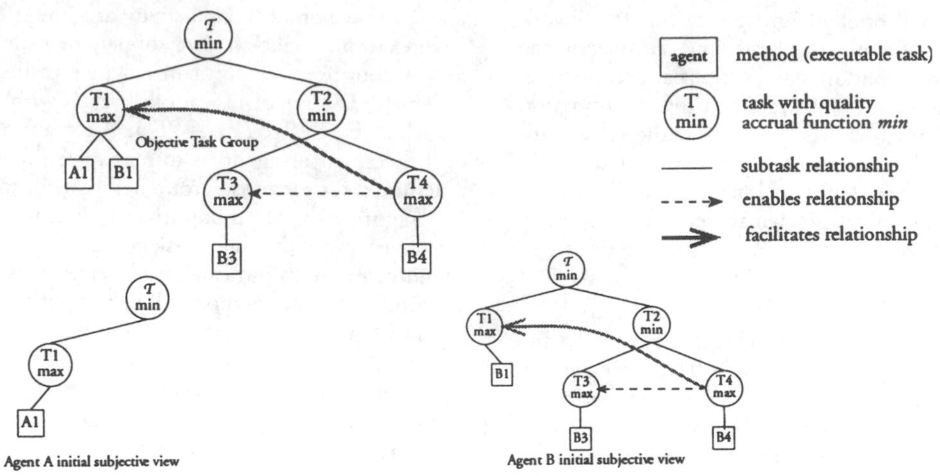

Figure 1: Agent A and B's subjective views (bottom) of a typical objective task group (top)

code to detect or predict the presence of coordination relationships in the local task structure. In this paper we will refer to that domain-dependent code as the information gathering action called *detect-coordination-relationships*; we will describe this action more in the section on Mechanism 1: Non-Local Views.

The Local Scheduler

Each GPGP agent contains a local scheduler that takes three types of input information and produces a set of schedules and alternatives. The first input is the current, subjectively believed task structure. Using information about the potential duration, potential quality, and interrelationships, the local scheduler chooses and orders executable methods in an attempt to maximize a pre-defined utility function. In this paper the utility function is the sum of the task group qualities $\sum_{\mathcal{T}\in \mathbf{E}} Q(\mathcal{T}, \mathrm{D}(\mathcal{T}))$, where $Q(T,t)$ denotes the quality of T at time t as defined in (Decker & Lesser 1993b). Quality does not accrue after a task group's deadline.

The second input is a set of *commitments* **C**. These commitments are produced by the GPGP coordination mechanisms, and act as extra constraints on the schedules that are produced by the local scheduler. For example, if method 1 is executable by agent A and method 2 is executable by agent B, and the methods are redundant, then one of agent A's coordination mechanisms may *commit* agent A to do method 1. Commitments are *social*—directed to particular agents in the sense of the work of Castelfranchi and Shoham (Castelfranchi 1993; Shoham 1991)). A local commitment C by agent A becomes a non-local commitment when received by another agent B. This paper will use two types of commitments: $C(\mathsf{Do}(T,q))$ is a commitment to 'do' (achieve quality for) T and is satisfied at the time t when $Q(T,t) \geq q$; the second type $C(\mathsf{DL}(T,q,t_{dl}))$ is a 'deadline' commitment to do T by time t_{dl} and is satisfied at the time t when $[Q(T,t) \geq q] \wedge [t \leq t_{dl}]$. When a commitment is sent to another agent, it also implies that the task result will be communicated to the other agent (by the deadline, if it is a deadline commitment).

The third input to the local scheduler is the set of non-local commitments **NLC** made by other agents. This information can be used by the local scheduler to coordinate actions between agents. For example the local scheduler could have the property that, if method M_1 is executable by agent A and is the only method that enables method M_2 at agent B (and agent B knows this), and $B_A(C(\mathsf{DL}(M_1,q,t_1))) \in B_B(\mathbf{NLC})$, then for every schedule S produced by agent B, $\langle M_2, t\rangle \in S \Rightarrow t \geq t_1$ (in other words, agent B only schedules the enabled method after the deadline that agent A has committed to.

A schedule S produced by a local scheduler will consist of a set of methods and start times: $S = \{\langle M_1,t_1\rangle, \langle M_2,t_2\rangle, \ldots, \langle M_n,t_n\rangle\}$. The schedule may include idle time, and the local scheduler may produce more than one schedule upon each invocation in the situation where not all commitments can be met. The different schedules represent different ways of partially satisfying the set of commitments. The function $\mathsf{Violated}(S)$ returns the set of commitments that are believed to be violated by the schedule. For violated deadline commitments $C(\mathsf{DL}(T,q,t_{dl})) \in \mathsf{Violated}(S)$ the function $\mathsf{Alt}(C,S)$ returns an alternative commitment $C(\mathsf{DL}(T,q,t^*_{dl}))$ where $t^*_{dl} = \min t$ such that $Q(T,t) \geq q$ if such a t exists, or NIL otherwise. For a violated Do commitment an alternative may contain a lower minimum quality, or no alternative may be possible. The function $U_{\mathrm{est}}(\mathbf{E}, S, \mathbf{NLC})$ returns the estimated utility at the end of the episode if the agent follows schedule S and all non-local commitments in **NLC** are kept.

Thus we may define the local scheduler as a function $\mathrm{LS}(\mathbf{E},\mathbf{C},\mathbf{NLC})$ returning a set of schedules $\mathbf{S} = \{S_1, S_2, \ldots, S_m\}$. More detailed information about this kind of interface between the local scheduler and the coordination component may be found in (Garvey, Decker, & Lesser 1994). This is an extremely general definition of the local scheduler, and is the minimal one necessary for the GPGP coordination module. Stronger definitions than this will be needed for more predictable performance, as we will discuss later. Ideally, the optimal local scheduler would find both the schedule with maximum utility $\hat{S}_U$ and the schedule with maximum utility that violates no commitments $\hat{S}_{\bar{V}}$. In practice, however, a heuristic local scheduler will produce a set of schedules where the schedule of highest utility S_U is not necessarily optimal: $\mathrm{U}(\mathbf{E}, S_U, \mathbf{NLC}) \leq \mathrm{U}(\mathbf{E}, \hat{S_U}, \mathbf{NLC})$.

Five GPGP Coordination Mechanisms

The role of the coordination mechanisms is to provide information to the local scheduler that allows the local scheduler to construct better schedules. This information can be in the form of modifications to portions of the subjective task structure of the episode or in the form of local and non-local commitments to tasks in the task structure. The five mechanisms we will describe in this paper form a basic set that provides similar functionality to the original Partial Global Planning algorithm as shown in (Decker & Lesser 1992). Mechanism 1 exchanges useful private views of task structures; Mechanism 2 communicates results; Mechanism 3 handles redundant methods; Mechanisms 4 and 5 handle hard and soft coordination relationships. More mechanisms can be added, such as one to update utilities across agents as discussed in the next section, or to balance the load better between agents. The mechanisms are independent in the sense that they can be used in any combination. If inconsistent constraints are introduced, the local scheduler will return at least one violated constraint in all its schedules. Since the local scheduler typically satisfices instead of optimizes, it may do this even if constraints are not inconsistent (i.e. it does not search exhaustively). The next section describes how a schedule is chosen by the coordination module substrate.

The GPGP Coordination Module Substrate

All the specific coordination mechanisms rest on a common substrate that handles information gathering actions, invoking the local scheduler, choosing a schedule to execute (including dealing with violated or inconsistent commitments), and deciding when to terminate processing on a task group. Information gathering actions include noticing new task group arrivals and receiving communications from other agents. Information gathering is done at the start of problem solving, when communications are expected from other agents, and when the agent is otherwise idle. Communications are expected in response to certain events (such as after the arrival of a new task group) or as indicated in the set of non-local commitments $\mathbf{NLC}$. This is the minimal general information gathering policy. Termination of processing on a task group occurs for an agent when the agent is idle, has no expected communications, and no outstanding commitments for the task group.

Choosing a schedule is more complicated. The agent's local scheduler may return multiple schedules because it cannot find a single schedule that both maximizes utility and meets all commitments. From the set of schedules $\mathbf{S}$ returned by the local scheduler, two particular schedules are identified: the schedule with the highest utility S_U and the best committed schedule S_C. If they are the same, then that schedule is chosen. Otherwise, we examine the sum of the changes in utility for each commitment. Each commitment, when created, is assigned the estimated utility U_{est} for the task group of which it is a part. This utility may be updated over time (when other agents depend on the commitment, for example). We then choose the schedule with the largest positive change in utility. This allows us to abandon commitments if doing so will result in higher overall utility. The coordination substrate does not use the local scheduler's utility estimate U_{est} directly on the entire schedule because it is based only on a local view. The coordination substrate may receive non-local information that places a higher utility on a commitment than it has locally.

If both schedules have the same utility, the one that is more negotiable is chosen. Every commitment has a negotiability index (high, medium, or low) that indicates (heuristically) the difficulty in rescheduling if the commitment is broken. This index is set by the individual coordination mechanisms. For example, hard coordination relationships like enables that cannot be ignored will trigger commitments with low negotiability. If the schedules are still equivalent, the shorter one is chosen, and if they are the same length, one is chosen at random.

After a schedule S is chosen, if $\mathrm{Violated}(S)$ is not empty, then each commitment $C \in \mathrm{Violated}(S)$ is replaced with its alternative $\mathbf{C} \leftarrow \mathbf{C} \setminus C \cup \mathrm{Alt}(C, S)$. If the commitment was made to other agents, the other agents are also informed of the change in the commitment. While this could potentially cause cascading changes in the schedules of multiple agents, it generally does not for three reasons: first, as we mentioned in the previous paragraph less important commitments are broken first; secondly, the resiliancy of the local schedulers to solve problems in multiple ways tends to damp out these fluctuations; and third, agents are time cognizant resource-bounded reasoners that interleave execution and scheduling (i.e., the agents cannot spend all day arguing over scheduling details and still meet their deadlines). We have observed this useful phenomenon before (Decker 1995) and plan to analyze it in future work.

Mechanism 1: Updating Non-Local Viewpoints

Remember that each agent has only a partial, subjective view of the current episode. The GPGP mechanism described here can communicate no private information ('none' policy, no non-local view), or all of it ('all' policy, global view), or take an intermediate approach ('some' policy, partial view). The process of detecting coordination relationships between private and shared parts of a task structure is in general very domain specific, so we model this process by a new information gathering action, *detect-coordination-relationships*, that takes some fixed amount of the agent's time. This action is scheduled whenever a new task group arrives.

The set $\mathbf{P}$ of privately believed tasks or methods at an agent A (tasks believed at arrival time by A only) is then $\{x \mid \mathit{task}(x) \wedge \forall a \in \mathbf{A} \setminus A,\ \neg B_A(B_a^{\mathrm{Ar}(x)}(x))\}$, where $\mathbf{A}$ is the set of all agents and $\mathrm{Ar}(x)$ is the arrival time of x. Given this definition, the action *detect-coordination-relationships* returns the set of private coordination relationships $\mathbf{PCR} = \{r \mid T_1 \in \mathbf{P} \wedge T_2 \notin \mathbf{P} \wedge [r(T_1, T_2) \vee r(T_2, T_1)]\}$ between private and mutually believed tasks. The action does not return what the task T_2 is, just that a relationship exists between T_1 and some otherwise unknown task T_2. For example, in the DVMT, we have used the physical organization of agents to detect that Agent A's task T_1 in an overlapping sensor area is in fact related to some unknown task T_2 at agent B (i.e. $B_A(B_B(T_2))$) (Decker & Lesser 1992). The non-local view coordination mechanism then communicates these coordination relationships, the private tasks, and their context: if $r(T_1, T_2) \in \mathbf{PCR}$ and $T_1 \in \mathbf{P}$ then r and T_1 will be communicated by agent A to the set of agents $\{a \mid B_A(B_a(T_2))\}$.

For example, Figure 2 shows the local subjective beliefs of agents A and B after the communication from one another due to this mechanism. We'll denote the complete set of coordination relationships as $\mathbf{CR}$; this includes all the elements of $\mathbf{PCR}$ and all the relationships between non-private tasks.

Mechanism 2: Communicating Results

The result communication coordination mechanism has three possible policies: communicate only the results necessary to satisfy commitments to other agents (the minimal policy); communicate this information plus the final results associated with a task group ('TG' policy), and communicate all results ('all' policy[4]). Extra result communications are broadcast to all agents, the minimal commitment-satisfying communications are sent only to those agents to whom the commitment was made (i.e., communicate the result of T to the set of agents $\{A \in \mathbf{A} \mid B(B_A(C(T))\}$.

Mechanism 3: Handling Simple Redundancy

Potential redundancy in the efforts of multiple agents can occur in several places in a task structure. Any task that uses a 'max' quality accumulation function (one possible semantics for an 'OR' node) indicates that, in the absence of other relationships, only one subtask needs to be done. When such subtasks are complex and involve many agents, the coordination of these agents to avoid redundant processing can also be complex; we will not address the general redundancy avoidance problem in this paper (see instead (Lesser 1991)). In the original PGP algorithm and domain (distributed sensor interpretation), the primary form of potential redundancy was simple method redundancy—the same result could be derived from the data from any of a number of sensors. The coordination mechanism described here is meant to address this simpler form of potential redundancy.

The idea behind the simple redundancy coordination mechanism is that when more than one agent wants to execute a redundant method, one agent is randomly chosen to execute it and send the results to the other interested agents. This is a generalization of the 'static' organization algorithm discussed by Decker and Lesser (Decker & Lesser 1993a)—it does not try to load balance, and uses one communication action (because in the general case the agents do not know beforehand, without communication, that certain methods are redundant[5]). The mechanism considers the set of potential redundancies $\mathbf{RCR} = \{r \in \mathbf{CR} \mid [r = \mathsf{subtask}(T, \mathbf{M}, \min)] \wedge [\forall M \in \mathbf{M}, \mathit{method}(M)]\}$. Then for all methods in the current schedule S at time t, if the method is potentially redundant then commit to it and send the commitment to $\mathsf{Others}(\mathbf{M})$ (non-local agents who also have a method in $\mathbf{M}$):

$$\begin{aligned}&[\langle M, t_M\rangle \in S] \wedge \\ &[\mathsf{subtask}(T, \mathbf{M}, \min) \in \mathbf{RCR}] \wedge [M \in \mathbf{M}] \Rightarrow \\ &\quad [C(\mathsf{Do}(M, \mathrm{Q}_{\mathrm{est}}(M, \mathrm{D}(M), S))) \in \mathbf{C}] \wedge \\ &\quad [\mathsf{comm}(M, \mathsf{Others}(\mathbf{M}), t) \in \mathcal{I}]\end{aligned}$$

See for example the top of figure 3—both agents commit to Do their methods for T_1.

After the commitment is made, the agent must refrain from executing the method in question if possible until any non-local commitments that were made simultaneously can arrive (the communication delay time δ). This mechanism then watches for multiple commitments in the redundant set and if they appear, a unique agent is chosen randomly (but identically by all agents) from those with the best commitments to keep its commitment. All the other agents can retract their commitments. For example the bottom of figure 3 shows the situation after Agent B has retracted its commitment to Do B_1. If all agents follow the same algorithm, and communication channels are assumed to be reliable, then no second message (retraction) actually needs to be sent (because they all choose the same agent to do the redundant method). In the implementation described later, identical random choices are made by giving each method a unique random identifier, and then all agents choose the method with the 'smallest' identifier for execution.

Initially, all Do commitments initiated by the redundant coordination mechanism are marked highly negotiable. When a redundant commitment is discovered, the negotiability of the remaining commitment is lowered to medium to indicate the commitment is somewhat more important.

Mechanism 4: Handling Hard Coordination Relationships

Hard coordination relationships include relationships like $\mathsf{enables}(M_1, M_2)$ that indicate that M_1 must be executed before M_2 in order to obtain quality for M_2. Like redundant methods, hard coordination relationships can be culled from the set $\mathbf{CR}$. The hard coordination mechanism further distinguishes the direction of the relationship—the current implementation only creates commitments on the predecessors of the enables relationship. We'll let $\mathbf{HPCR} \subset \mathbf{CR}$ indicate the set of potential hard predecessor coordination relationships. The hard coordination mechanism then looks for situations where the current schedule S at time t will produce quality for a predecessor in $\mathbf{HPCR}$, and commits to its execution by a certain deadline both locally and socially:

$$\begin{aligned}&[\mathrm{Q}_{\mathrm{est}}(T, \mathrm{D}(T), S) > 0] \wedge \\ &[\mathsf{enables}(T, \mathbf{M}) \in \mathbf{HPCR}] \Rightarrow \\ &\quad [C(\mathsf{DL}(T, \mathrm{Q}_{\mathrm{est}}(T, \mathrm{D}(T), S), t_{\mathrm{early}})) \in \mathbf{C}] \wedge \\ &\quad [\mathsf{comm}(C, \mathsf{Others}(\mathbf{M}), t) \in \mathcal{I}]\end{aligned}$$

---

[4]Such a policy is all that is needed in many simple environments.

[5]The detection of redundant methods is domain-dependent, as discussed earlier. Since we are talking here about simple, direct redundancy (i.e. doing the exact same method at more than one agent) this detection is very straight-forward.

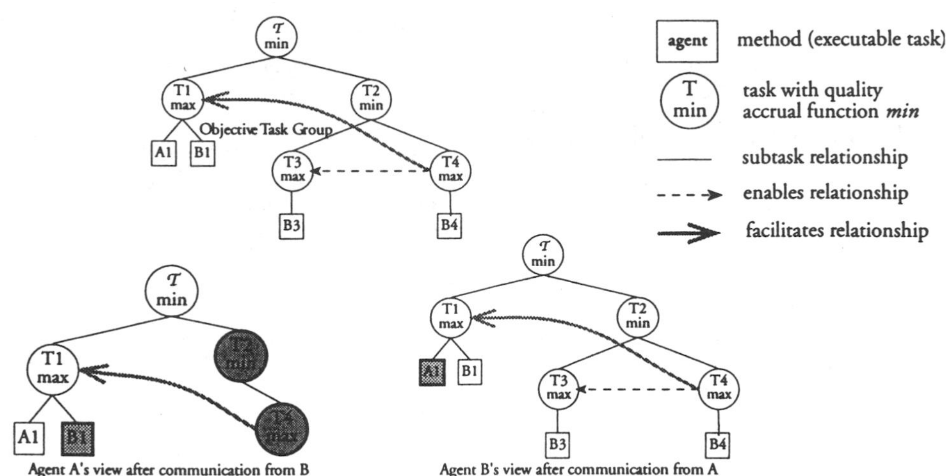

Figure 2: Agents A and B's local views after receiving non-local viewpoint communications via mechanism 1 (shaded objects). Figure 1 shows the agents' initial states.

The next question is, by what time (t_{early} above) do we commit to providing the answer? One solution, usable with any local scheduler that fits our general description of a Local Scheduler, is to use the min t such that $\text{Q}_{\text{est}}(T, \text{D}(T), S) > 0$. In our implementation, the local scheduler provides a query facility that allows us to propose a commitment to satisfy as 'early' as possible (thus allowing the agent on the other end of the relationship more slack). We take advantage of this ability in the hard coordination mechanism by adding the new commitment $C(\text{DL}(T, \text{Q}_{\text{est}}(T, \text{D}(T), S), \text{"early"}))$ to the local commitment set $\mathbf{C}$, and invoking the local scheduler $LS(\mathbf{E}, \mathbf{C}, \mathbf{NLC})$ to produce a new set of schedules $\mathbf{S}$. If the preferred, highest utility schedule $S_U \in \mathbf{S}$ has no violations (highly likely since the local scheduler can simply return the same schedule if no better one can be found), we replace the current schedule with it and use the new schedule, with a potentially earlier finish time for T, to provide a value for t_{early}. The new completed commitment is entered locally (with low negotiability) and sent to the subset of interested other agents.

If redundant commitments are made to the same task, the earliest commitment made by any agent is kept, then the agent committing to the highest quality, and any remaining ties are broken by the same method as before.

Currently, the hard coordination mechanism is a pro-active mechanism, providing information that might be used by other agents to them, while not putting the individual agent to any extra effort. Other future coordination mechanisms might be added to the family that are reactive and request from other agents that certain tasks be done by certain times; this is quite different behavior that would need to be analyzed separately.

Mechanism 5: Handling Soft Coordination Relationships

Soft coordination relationships are handled analogously to hard coordination relationships except that they start out with high negotiability. In the current implementation the predecessor of a facilitates relationship is the only one that triggers commitments across agents, although hinders relationships are also present. The positive relationship facilitates$(M_1, M_2, \phi_d, \phi_q)$ indicates that executing M_1 before M_2 decreases the duration of M_2 by a 'power' factor related to ϕ_d and increases the maximum quality possible by a power factor related to ϕ_q (Decker & Lesser 1993b). A more situation-specific version of this coordination mechanism might ignore relationships with very low power. Figure 3 shows Agent B making a D commitment to do method B_4, which in turn allows Agent A to take advantage of the facilitates$(T_4, T1, 0.5, 0.5)$ relationship, causing method A_1 to take only half the time and produce 1.5 times the quality.

Overhead

The primary sources of overhead associated with the coordination mechanisms include action executions (communication and information gathering), calls to the local scheduler, and any algorithmic overhead associated with the mechanism itself. Table 1 summarizes the total amount of overhead from each source for each coordination mechanism setting and the coordination substrate. L represents the length of processing (time before termination), and d is a general density measure of coordination relationships. Interactions between the presence of coordination mechanisms and these quantities include: the number of methods or tasks in $\mathbf{E}$, which depends on the non-local view mechanism; the number of coordination relationships $|\mathbf{CR}|$ or the subsets $\mathbf{RCR}$ (redundant coordination relationships), $\mathbf{HPCR}$ (hard predecessor coordination relationships), $\mathbf{SPCR}$ (soft predecessor coordination relationships), which depends on the number of tasks and methods as well; and the number of commitments $|\mathbf{C}|$, which depends on each of the three mechanisms that makes commitments.

Conclusions, Status, and Future Work

This paper discusses the design of an extendable family of coordination mechanisms, called Generalized Partial Global

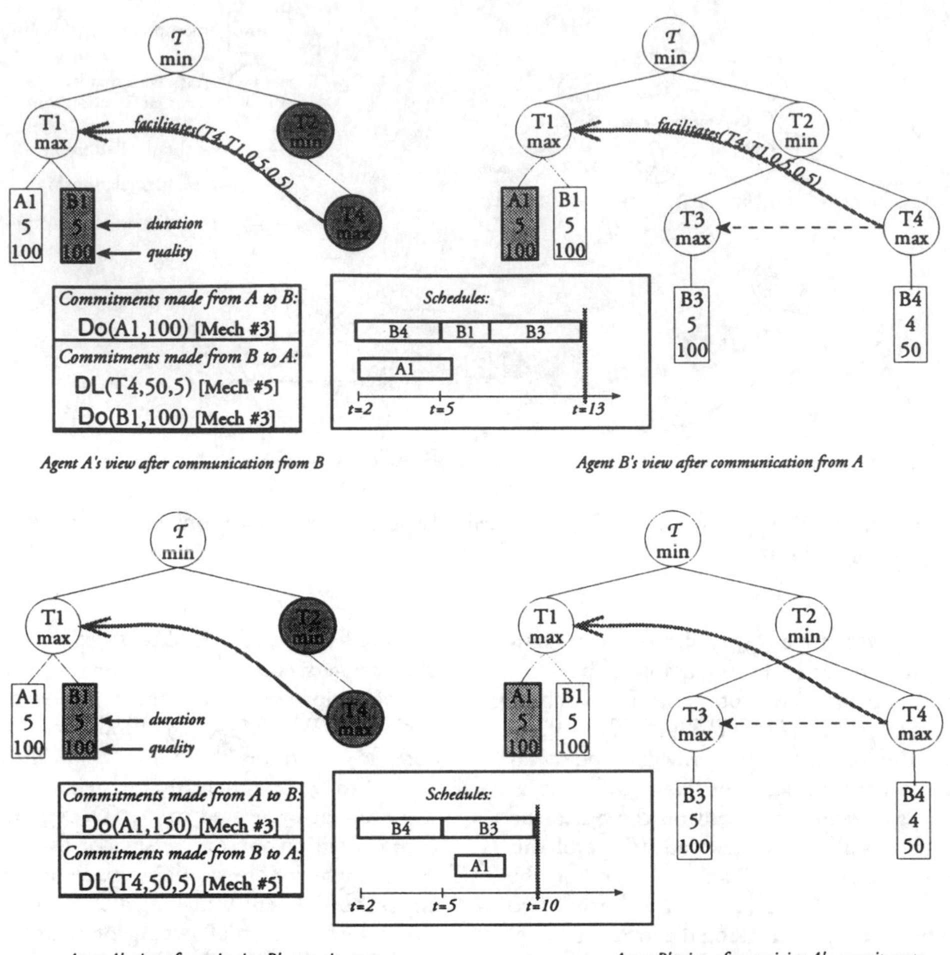

Figure 3: A continuation of Figures 1 and 2. At top: agents A and B propose certain commitments to one another via mechanisms 3 and 5. At bottom: after receiving the initial commitments, mechanism 3 removes agent B's redundant commitment.

Planning (GPGP), that form a basic set of schedule coordination mechanisms for teams of cooperative computational agents. An important feature of this approach includes an extendable set of modular coordination mechanisms, any subset or all of which can be used in response to a particular task environment. This subset may be parameterized, and the parameterization does not have to be chosen statically, but can instead be chosen on a task-group-by-task-group basis or even in response to a particular problem-solving situation. For example, Mechanism 5 (Handle Soft Predecessor CRs) might be "on" for certain classes of tasks and 'off' for other classes (that usually have few or very weak soft CRs). The general specification of the GPGP mechanisms involves the detection and response to certain abstract *coordination relationships* in the incoming task structure that were not tied to a particular domain—we have used TÆMS to describe tasks as diverse as distributed sensor networks, hospital scheduling, and Internet information gathering. A careful separation of the coordination mechanisms from an agent's local scheduler allows each to better do the job for which it was designed. We believe this separation is not only useful for applying our coordination mechanisms to problems with existing, customized local schedulers, but also to problems involving humans (where the coordination mechanism can act as an interface to the person, suggesting possible commitments for the person's consideration and reporting non-local commitments made by others) (Decker & Lesser 1995).

The GPGP coordination approach as described in this paper has been fully implemented in the TÆMS simulation testbed. Significant experimental validation of the GPGP approach is documented in (Decker 1995). These experiments have demonstrated the effective performance of the current mechanisms and the range of behaviors possible. We demonstrate that in complex task environments agents that use the appropriate mechanisms perform better than agents that do not for several performance measures. We show how to test that a particular mechanism is useful. We show that different combinations of mechanisms are, in fact, needed in different environments. We describe a way to structure the search for a particular combination of mechanisms in a particular envi-

Mechanism *setting*	Communications	Information Gathering	Scheduler	*Other Overhead*
substrate	0	$\mathbf{E}+idle$	L	$O(L\mathbf{C})$
nlv *none*	0	0	0	0
some	$O(d\mathbf{P})$	$\mathbf{E}$*detect-CRs*	0	$O(T \in \mathbf{E})$
all	$O(\mathbf{P})$	$\mathbf{E}$*detect-CRs*	0	$O(T \in \mathbf{E})$
comm *min*	$O(\mathbf{C})$	0	0	$O(\mathbf{C})$
TG	$O(\mathbf{C}+\mathbf{E})$	0	0	$O(\mathbf{C}+\mathbf{E})$
all	$O(M \in \mathbf{E})$	0	0	$O(M \in \mathbf{E})$
redundant *on*	$O(\mathbf{RCR})$	0	0	$O(\mathbf{RCR} * S + \mathbf{CR})$
hard *on*	$O(\mathbf{HPCR})$	0	$O(\mathbf{HPCR})$	$O(\mathbf{HPCR} * S + \mathbf{CR})$
soft *on*	$O(\mathbf{SPCR})$	0	$O(\mathbf{SPCR})$	$O(\mathbf{SPCR} * S + \mathbf{CR})$

Table 1: Overhead associated with individual mechanisms at each parameter setting

ronment, starting from certain architypical clusters of mechanisms. Our experiments have also shown the value of structuring coordination in terms of a family of algorithms and the ease of adding new mechanisms such as a cooperative load balancing mechanism. The cooperative load-balancing coordination mechanism works by providing better information to the agents with which to resolve redundant commitments.

Eventually we intend to develop a library of reusable coordination mechanisms. For example, mechanisms that work from the successors of hard and soft relationships instead of the predecessors, negotiation mechanisms, mechanisms for behavior such as contracting, or mechanisms that can be used by self-motivated agents in non-cooperative environments. Many of these mechanisms can be built on the existing work of other DAI researchers. Future work will also examine expanding the parameterization of the mechanisms and using machine learning techniques to choose the appropriate parameter values (i.e., learning the best mechanism set for an environment). Finally, we are also beginning work on using the GPGP approach in applications ranging from providing human coordination assistance to distributed information gathering.

References

Castelfranchi, C. 1993. Commitments:from individual intentions to groups and organizations. In Prietula, M., ed., *AI and theories of groups & organizations: Conceptual and Empirical Research.* AAAI Workshop. Working Notes.

Cohen, P. R., and Levesque, H. J. 1990. Intention is choice with commitment. *Artificial Intelligence* 42(3):213–261.

Decker, K. S., and Lesser, V. R. 1992. Generalizing the partial global planning algorithm. *Intnl. Jrnl. of Intelligent and Cooperative Information Systems* 1(2):319–346.

Decker, K. S., and Lesser, V. R. 1993a. An approach to analyzing the need for meta-level communication. In *Proceedings of the Thirteenth International Joint Conference on Artificial Intelligence*, 360–366.

Decker, K. S., and Lesser, V. R. 1993b. Quantitative modeling of complex computational task environments. In *Proc. of the Eleventh National Conference on AI*, 217–224.

Decker, K. S., and Lesser, V. R. 1995. Coordination assistance for mixed human and computational agent systems. UMass Technical Report 95–31.

Decker, K. S. 1995. *Environment Centered Analysis and Design of Coordination Mechanisms.* Ph.D. Dissertation, University of Massachusetts.

Durfee, E., and Lesser, V. 1991. Partial global planning: A coordination framework for distributed hypothesis formation. *IEEE Trans. on Systems, Man, and Cybernetics* 21(5):1167–1183.

Durfee, E. H., and Montgomery, T. A. 1991. Coordination as distributed search in a hierarchical behavior space. *IEEE Trans. on Systems, Man, and Cybernetics* 21(6):1363–1378.

Ephrati, E., and Rosenschein, J. 1994. Divide and conquer in multi-agent planning. In *Proceedings of the Twelfth National Conference on Artificial Intelligence*, 375–380.

Garvey, A., and Lesser, V. 1993. Design-to-time real-time scheduling. *IEEE Transactions on Systems, Man, and Cybernetics* 23(6):1491–1502. See also updated UMass TR 95–03.

Garvey, A.; Decker, K.; and Lesser, V. 1994. A negotiation-based interface between a real-time scheduler and a decision-maker. UMass Technical Report 94–08.

Grosz, B., and Kraus, S. 1993. Collaborative plans for group activities. In *Proceedings of the Thirteenth International Joint Conference on Artificial Intelligence.*

Jennings, N. R. 1993. Commitments and conventions: The foundation of coordination in multi-agent systems. *The Knowledge Engineering Review* 8(3):223–250.

Lesser, V. R. 1991. A retrospective view of FA/C distributed problem solving. *IEEE Transactions on Systems, Man, and Cybernetics* 21(6):1347–1363.

Malone, T. W., and Crowston, K. 1991. Toward an interdisciplinary theory of coordination. Center for Coordination Science Technical Report 120, MIT Sloan School.

Shoham, Y., and Tennenholtz, M. 1992. On the synthesis of useful social laws for artificial agent societies (preliminary report). In *Proceedings of the Tenth National Conference on Artificial Intelligence*, 276–281.

Shoham, Y. 1991. AGENT0: A simple agent language and its interpreter. In *Proceedings of the Ninth National Conference on Artificial Intelligence*, 704–709.

v. Martial, F. 1992. *Coordinating Plans of Autonomous Agents.* Berlin: Springer-Verlag. Lecture Notes in AI #610.

A semantics for speech acts*

Munindar P. Singh[1,2]
El-Carnot Project, MCC, Austin, TX 78759, USA
and
Department of Computer Sciences, University of Texas, Austin, TX 78712, USA

Abstract

Speech act theory is important not only in Linguistics, but also in Computer Science. It has applications in Distributed Computing, Distributed Artificial Intelligence, Natural Language Processing, and Electronic Data Interchange protocols. While much research into speech acts has been done, one aspect of them that has largely been ignored is their semantics, i.e. their conditions of satisfaction. A formal semantics for speech acts is motivated and presented here that relates their satisfaction to the intentions, know-how, and actions of the participating agents. This makes it possible to state several potentially useful constraints on communication and provides a basis for checking their consistency.

1. Introduction

One of the most significant developments in the study of language was the formulation of speech act theory by Austin, Grice, Searle, and others. Austin's main contribution was in pointing out that the major role of language, communication, is a kind of action *par excellence* [3]. This idea has inspired much work in the Philosophy of Language, Linguistics, and Artificial Intelligence. Unfortunately, research in each of these three areas has been concentrated on what are, from the point of view of semantics, somewhat peripheral matters. Typically, the issues addressed in the study of speech acts concern such things as the heuristics that may be used to determine when what sort of a speech act may be said to have occurred, or the syntactic forms that different kinds of utterances might take. Occasionally, one may see a paper on the definitions of speech acts in terms of how the cognitive states of the participants are updated as a consequence of a speech act. However, the crucial matter of the *semantics* of speech acts *per se* is never addressed. In other words, extant theories tell us when a specific kind of speech act occurred and what should happen as a result of it in ordinary or ideal circumstances, but they do not tell us when it is, in fact, satisfied.

A semantics for speech acts is direly needed to provide a rigorous foundation for our understanding of languages, both artificial and natural, and to further advance the many applications of speech act theory. These applications are in a number of areas of Computer Science, including the following:

(1) *Distributed Computing*. The initial specifications of distributed systems and protocols that human designers and ultimate users come up with often are in terms of the speech acts performed by the processes in a system [24]. A semantics would make precise notions such as permission and promise that are commonly used – though used only informally. Having precise definitions would help in designing reliable systems and would facilitate the debugging of their specifications relative to the desires of their ultimate users.

(2) *Distributed Artificial Intelligence*. The messages exchanged by intelligent agents may usefully be considered to be speech acts [6,14]. A semantics of speech acts would be useful in setting down the objective criteria for the evaluation of the communications and other actions of agents. Such criteria could be used by the designers of multiagent systems and by the agents who compose such systems.

(3) *Natural Language Understanding and Generation*. This application is perhaps the easiest to identify, since ultimately all of natural language involves speech acts. In particular, it helps to consider speech acts as first-rate actions that discourse participants plan, and then perform [2]. A formal semantics would provide clear criteria for success and failure that can be used to better integrate the natural components of an intelligent system with other parts of it. It may also be used in planning and replanning speech acts and in clearing up misunderstandings between participants.

(4) *Electronic Data Interchange Protocols*. The documents exchanged among organizations may fruitfully be seen as speech acts performed by them [8,16]. A semantics for speech acts would provide a uniform basis for standardization and formal specification of such protocols that is critically needed.

Thus, a semantics for speech acts is needed to fully develop each of the above applications. Further, a semantics for speech acts is also needed in classical linguistics. This is because most languages have verbs such as "obey" (as in "obey a command"), "follow" (as in "follow an instruction"), "keep" (as in "keep a promise"), and so on. The semantics of each of these verbs and their derived forms depends crucially

* An earlier version of this paper was presented at the Second Meeting on the Mathematics of Language, Tarrytown, NY, May 1991. Some parts of this paper overlap with [23].
[1] This research was supported by the National Science Foundation (through Grant No. IRI-8945845 to the Center for Cognitive Science, University of Texas, Austin) and by the Microelectronics and Computer Technology Corporation, Austin.
[2] The author is indebted to the anonymous referees for comments.

on what it means to, respectively, obey a command, follow an instruction, or keep a promise. However, this is a component of the semantics of speech acts as motivated and defined here.

We present a formal theory that gives the semantics of several different kinds of speech acts. This theory uses the concepts of know-how and intentions as primitives. The technical framework of this paper follows the ones developed previously to formalize know-how and intentions [25,26]. This connection to other theories is reason to be reassured that the primitives can in fact be formalized and that this theory will fit into a bigger picture. It also helps us to capture many of the intuitive properties of speech acts. The original contributions of this paper include the following:

(1) This paper argues that there is a level of formal semantics of speech acts that is distinct from both (a) what is traditionally considered their semantics, namely, the conditions under which they may be said to have occurred, and (b) their pragmatics, namely, the effects they may or ought to have on the speaker's and hearer's cognitive states. That is, it proposes a novel semantics that differs from both the illocutionary and the perlocutionary aspects of speech acts.

(2) This paper argues that the semantics of speech acts roughly corresponds to the conditions under which we would affirm that the given speech act had been satisfied, e.g. a command is satisfied if it is obeyed and a promise is satisfied when it is kept. That is, this paper extracts a component of our pretheoretic intuitions concerning the satisfaction of speech acts that has been largely ignored in past work.

(3) This paper proposes that this suggested notion of semantics be captured in the usual model-theoretic framework by introducing a modal operator that distinguishes the satisfaction of a speech act from its mere occurrence.

(4) This paper argues that the actual definitions of the semantics be given in terms of the intentions and know-how of the agents participating in the given speech act, as well as the state of the world (at some salient time or times).

The ideas developed in this paper can be used to motivate a taxonomy of speech acts on semantic grounds, rather than on syntactic or pragmatic ones alone. This is the first such attempt known to the author – existing taxonomies fall into the latter two categories. The formalization is presented in the simple and fairly well-known framework of modal and temporal logics. This formalization can be used to provide a model-theoretic basis for normative constraints on communication among agents, and for felicity conditions for different kinds of speech acts.

In section 2, we give a brief overview of speech act theory. In section 3, we motivate the semantics presented in this paper. In section 4, we give the technical framework of this paper and describe the formal language and the formal model used. In section 5, which is the core of this paper, we give the actual satisfaction conditions. In section 6, we outline a novel application of this theory to the semantics of the verbs of fulfillment and present some example constraints that make communication felicitous in various respects in section 7. In section 8, we compare the approach of this paper with some recent work on speech acts.

2. Speech acts and their semantics

When speech act theory first arose as a research area, the doctrine of *verificationism* was still quite powerful in Philosophy and Logic. This doctrine held that only those sentences of a language (natural or artificial) were meaningful that could be verified, at least in principle. That is, all sentences that even in principle were neither true nor false were deemed to be nonsense. The standard logical notion of semantics, e.g. as captured by the Tarskian $\models$, reflects this doctrine. Unfortunately, the above doctrine is unduly restrictive: most utterances are neither true nor false. Sentences such as "I declare you man and wife" and "I plead not guilty" are perfectly meaningful, but their meaning is not captured by the fact of their truth or falsity. Furthermore, sentences such as "Please shut the door", which are also perfectly meaningful, cannot be assigned a truth value at all. Thus, from its very roots, speech act theory has been against the standard logical notion of semantics.

It is useful to see speech act theory as arising in reaction to this doctrine. Speech act theory concerns itself primarily with the role of language as action, and this view forces the rejection of verificationism. This is presented as a sort of historical explanation of the tendency of speech act theory to shun standard semantics. However, as we hope to show, there is no real technical reason why this should be so – one can retain the key ideas of speech act theory and still give a formal semantics.

In his early work, Austin made a distinction between what he termed *constative* and *performative* sentences. The former included most ordinary sentences in language; the latter were those like "I declare you man and wife", whose utterance constitutes an action being done. Later, this distinction was collapsed when it was realized that all sentences could be put in the form of performatives, by using appropriate performative verbs. For example, the sentence "Shut the door" could be seen as a variant of "I ask you to shut the door", which is an explicit performative. This observation is usually taken as the starting point for speech act theory.

There has been much work done in speech act theory from various angles, in particular, those of Syntax, Pragmatics, and Artificial Intelligence. We briefly discuss each of these below.

2.1. SYNTAX

Syntactic work on speech act theory has drawn inspiration from the fact that there is a close relationship between the surface form of a sentence and the kind of performative is represents. For example, it is easy to see that the proposition "the door is shut" underlies both the indicative "The door is shut" and the imperative "Shut the door". Different performative verbs can be combined with a given proposition, appropriately linguistically represented, to yield different kinds of speech acts. For example, the above indicative and imperative may be recast as "I tell you that the door is shut" and "I order you to shut the door", respectively. This sort of syntactic regularity has driven much work in generative grammar, e.g. that of Ross [18]. The performative form of a sentence is taken to be the deep structure from which the appropriate surface structure is derived. This approach nicely explains some other data involving performatives, e.g. about the so-called dangling clauses of the form "Since you ask me, buy new tires", where the subordinate clause really makes sense with the missing performative verb inserted, e.g. as " . . . , I *tell* you to buy new tires". In other syntactic work, Vendler classified the so-called performative verbs, such as "order" and "entreat", on various dimensions, e.g. of the kinds of objects they take [29]. This data explains certain facts about performatives and their differences from, and similarities with, attitudinal verbs.

2.2. PRAGMATICS

Much of the work on speech acts in pragmatics has been about identifying the illocutionary force of a speech act. Speech acts with the same locutions can have different illocutionary forces depending on the speaker's intentions and beliefs. For example, "It is cold in here" might serve as both an assertion, namely, that it is cold, and as a request, namely, to turn up the heater. Research in pragmatics has mostly concerned itself with giving the felicity conditions for speech acts. A possible condition stated, and debated, here would be that a speech act succeeds when it is the true cause of the appropriate effect on the cognitive states of the speaker and the hearer. The appropriate effect would include the instantiation of various mutual beliefs, perhaps with further restrictions enforced on them [10,20].

2.3. ARTIFICIAL INTELLIGENCE

Work in Computational Linguistics on speech acts has borrowed heavily from the tradition in Pragmatics. It too is primarily concerned with the linguistic or discourse-related aspects of this problem, e.g. for identifying the illocutionary forces of indirect speech acts [1], or for defining their effects on the mutual beliefs of agents [7]. Speech acts are defined in terms of the effects of the cognitive state of the hearer that are intended by the speaker. They are seen as parts of plans that the participants find and execute [2]. This idea helps to explain the true illocutionary force of a speech act and also sheds some light on the phenomena of presuppositions and implicature. Thus, it is useful for many aspects of natural language understanding.

Most other Artificial Intelligence (AI) work on speech acts is in the area of Distributed AI. Here, the classification of speech acts is used to motivate different sets of message types for communications among different intelligent agents [6,14]. Different heuristics are studied that shed light on how agents ought to generate and process different kinds of speech acts. No formal semantics for these message types has been available.

2.4. LOGIC

Classical logic is concerned only with statements that are true or false or which, at least in principle, can be found to be either. Thus, it applies only to assertives. Even other work in logic is different in spirit from the research reported in this paper. For example, deontic logics are about the nature of what an agent is permitted or obliged to do. They would validate inferences of the form: if an agent is permitted A, then he is also permitted B, for appropriate actions or propositions, A and B. This issue is orthogonal to the matter of when a speech act that issues a permission is satisfied. Logics of commands are similar to deontic logics in this respect. In any case, the approach proposed here is model-theoretic rather than proof-theoretic. However, some of the ideas of these logics are useful when adapted to the framework of this paper. In particular, work on the semantics of questions can be used to motivate the definition of satisfaction for interrogatives, which are treated as special kinds of directives here.

3. Intuitive motivation for semantics

While much useful work has been done on various aspects of speech acts, one obvious facet of them has never been studied properly. This is the facet of their semantics, in the mundane sense of success. The satisfaction of a speech act is very different from its being understood – most work related to semantics has addressed the latter, and not the former, problem. The problem of formally describing the conditions of satisfaction for the different kinds of speech acts is of interest here. The reduction of all speech acts to performatives makes a performative verb, e.g. "tell" or "request", the main verb of a sentence. Thereby, a lot is gained in the understanding of speech acts. Unfortunately, it has also tended to restrict the attention of semanticists to the performative verb itself. The verb of the nested clause, which is likely to be the verb of the sentence in its usual surface form, is not paid sufficient attention. The sentence "I request you to open the door" is thus true, if I succeed in so requesting you, i.e. if I can in an appropriate manner convince you of my intention to communicate that request (e.g. see [19, p. 43]). What I requested, and whether that request was satisfied, are two factors that are simply left out of the picture. These factors are central to the picture of this paper.

A problem not addressed here concerns the effects a speech act has on the hearer. These depend on issues such as the social relationship of the agents or on matters of performance – these are not easy to describe, and are connected to processes of deliberation and belief revision [17], rather than to the semantics of speech acts *per se*. Similarly, how an agent ought to respond to a speech act is a matter of pragmatics. In any case, a semantics such as the one presented here would help to clarify our intuitions even about the pragmatic aspects of speech acts. Indeed, in section 8 we discuss some possible normative constraints on communications: when such constraints apply, they restrict the communications and other actions of agents in response to different speech acts. As a clarification of our goals, note that the role of the proposed semantics is akin to that of classical semantics for assertives. Classical semantics only tells us when an assertive is objectively satisfied – it makes no claims about when a given assertive should actually be uttered or believed.

3.1. ILLOCUTIONARY FORCE AND PROPOSITIONAL CONTENT

Traditionally, speech act theory classifies speech acts into several kinds of *illocutionary acts* [19,21]. In this paper, we consider the classes of *assertives, directives, commissives, permissives, prohibitives*, and *declaratives*. Briefly, assertives are statements of fact; directives are commands, requests or suggestions; commissives, e.g. promises, commit the speaker to a course of action; permissives issue permissions; and prohibitives take them away. Declaratives entail the occurrence of an action in themselves. For example, the declarative "I plead not guilty" differs from the mere assertive "I pleaded not guilty yesterday". The former speech act, which succeeds only in certain situations, not only reports the fact of the speaker pleading not guilty, but also constitutes the occurrence of the reported action.

The classification of speech acts given above is necessarily coarse. Speech acts of varying strengths and of differing pragmatic effects are lumped together here. For example, assertives include statements, tellings, claims, and so on; directives include commands, entreaties, requests, suggestions, and so on. This should not be taken to mean that the proposed theory cannot accommodate different kinds of speech acts, or that it cannot capture the distinction between, e.g. requests and commands. It just means that the distinctions between them are not seen to be *semantic*. The conditions of the satisfaction of different speech acts in the same class are identical; their differences lie in pragmatic factors, e.g. cultural conventions and the social stature of the participants. For example, a command can be successfully issued only to subordinates; however, one can request almost anyone. Further constraints on when requests and commands are satisfied may be stated that capture their non-semantic aspects properly.

In speech act theory, an *illocution* or speech act is usually seen to have two parts: an *illocutionary force* and a *proposition* [19]. The illocutionary force distinguishes, for example, a command from a promise; the proposition describes the state of the world that is, respectively, commanded or promised. This suggests a simple syntax for our formal language – an illocution or *message*, m, is a pair $\langle i, p \rangle$, where i identifies the illocutionary force, and p the proposition. Here, i is an atomic symbol from the set {assertive, directive, commissive, permissive, prohibitive, declarative}, and p a logical formula. The propositional part of an illocution specifies the state

Table 1

Classification of speech acts.

Force	Example
Assertive	The door is shut
Directive	Shut the door
Commissive	I will shut the door
Permissive	You may shut the door
Prohibitive	You may not shut the door
Declarative	I name this door the Golden Gate

of the world that it is, in some sense, about. For example, an assertive asserts of that state that it holds currently (although the proposition could be temporally indexed); a directive asks the hearer to bring that state about; a commissive commits the speaker to bringing it about, and so on. Paradigmatic examples of speech acts of different illocutionary forces are given in table 1. Thus, the satisfaction of a speech act depends both on its illocutionary force and on its proposition.

3.2. WHOLE-HEARTED SATISFACTION

We now present the definition of satisfaction intuitively, so as to motivate the formal framework of section 4. In the context of imperatives, Hamblin distinguishes between what he called *extensional* and *whole-hearted* satisfaction [12, pp. 153–157]. Briefly, the former notion admits accidental or contingent success, while the latter does not. Here we consider only the latter, although we extend it to other important kinds of speech acts. Also, our aim is to obtain a semantics of speech acts. Hamblin's aim was simply to be able to state prescriptive conditions on when what kind of imperatives ought to be issued, and the philosophical problems that arise when one is in a quandary. That is, his focus was largely pragmatic.

As motivation, we informally discuss the case of directives in this section. The *whole-hearted* satisfaction of a directive requires not only that the specified proposition be made true, but be made true in a surefire manner. The concerned agent should not only bring about the right state of the world, but know how to bring it about and intend to bring it about. We know that the proposed condition is correct because, and only because, it matches our pretheoretic sense of when a directive is satisfied. We know, as language users ourselves, that our requests are whole-heartedly satisfied when the person requested goes about making the appropriate conditions occur. This is the only kind of justification we could have for a semantics.

Indeed, this methodology is common in all of logic, e.g. that of belief. Furthermore, whole-hearted satisfaction allows us to capture other intuitions as well. For example, we can normatively require that an agent not issue two commands that cannot both be whole-heartedly satisfied, even if they can both be extensionally satisfied. This is a useful constraint for communication to be felicitous.

The definition of the satisfaction of speech acts as proposed here depends on the definitions of know-how and intentions. These concepts have been formalized in models of branching time (that allow the possible actions of agents to be considered) [26,22,25]. We use essentially the same framework here as in the cited work, extending it only to accommodate speech acts.

Briefly, an agent knows how to achieve *A*, if he can achieve *A* if he so intends. Intuitively, an agent knows how to achieve *A*, iff he possesses the skills required to act in such a way as to achieve *A*. For example, I know how to open a door in a certain variety of circumstances in which I can perform actions, such as opening a bolt and pulling at the handle, that would result in the door being open. I would not know how to open a door if a stronger person than I were to hold the door from the other side, or if the door were locked. The key idea is that the given agent forces the appropriate conditions to come to hold. An agent's intentions can be taken as primitives of his cognitive state, or derived from an abstract characterization of the extended actions he is currently engaged in. Their important properties are that they are "pro-attitudes" of agents, agents usually act for them and tend to persist with them. Intentions are also usually associated with agents' rationality in that they are supposed to be mutually consistent and consistent with the beliefs of the agent holding them.

An important intuitive property to keep in mind is that neither an intention nor some know-how is by itself sufficient for the agent to achieve something: one can intend things beyond one's capacities, or not intend things within one's capacities. However, if an agent intends something, persists with it, acts on his intentions and knows how to achieve it, then he will eventually succeed. The above properties are not used in the technical development of this paper, although they are an important part of our understanding of these concepts.

The ideas of this paper are modular with respect to the exact underlying theory of intentions and know-how that one might choose. This is a good thing for the following reasons. Several applications of this theory were discussed in section 1. The particular formalization that one chooses depends on the application at hand. For example, the closure of intentions, as of knowledge, under logical consequence is problematic for humans [26], but is acceptable for processes in distributed computing [5]. Secondly, we do not wish to debate the relative merits of different theories here: our claim is that no matter how one understands the primitives involved, the satisfaction of a speech act requires that certain conditions hold among them. These primitives are an important layer of abstraction because our pretheoretic intuitions are most natural in their terms. Using these primitives thus boosts our confidence that we are capturing our intuitions properly.

4. The formal framework

The formal model of this paper is a set of possible *times*, each of which is intuitively associated with a state of the world. We describe it informally before coming to the formal definitions. As diagrammed in fig. 1, from each possible time the world may develop in any of several ways depending on the agents' actions and other events. That is, there is a partial order on the times that may branch into the future but, for simplicity, is taken to be linear in the past.

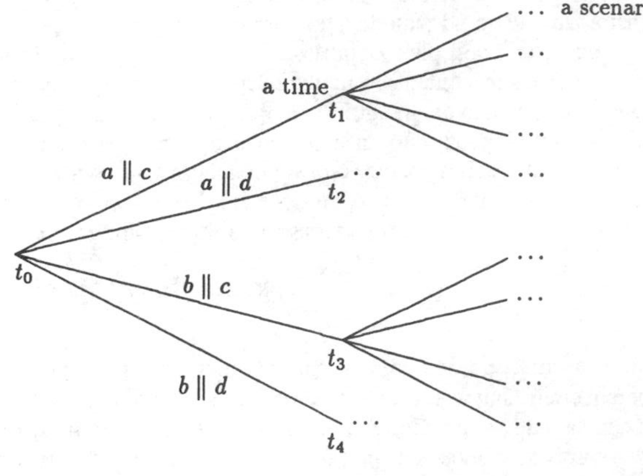

Fig. 1. The formal model.

Two agents are considered in fig. 1, whose actions label the branches out of t_0. At time t_0, if the first agent does action *a*, the state of the world may change to t_1, or to t_2, depending on what the other agent does then. Each of the agents influences the future by acting, but the outcome also depends on other events. For example, in fig. 1 the first agent can constrain the future to some extent by choosing to do action *a* or action *b* – if he does action *a*, then the world progresses along one of the top two branches out of t_0; if he does action *b*, then it progresses along one of the bottom two branches. However, the agent cannot control what exactly transpires, since that also depends on the other agent's actions.

Each of the different branches of time that begins at a point in the model is called a *scenario* (at that time) and is equivalent to a possible course of events. That is, a *scenario* at a time is any branch of the future beginning there – this corresponds to a particular run or trace of the given system. A *subscenario* is a triple $\langle S, t, t' \rangle$ which denotes a section of scenario *S* from time *t* to *t'*.

4.1. THE FORMAL LANGUAGE

The formal language of this paper $\mathcal{L}$ is based on CTL* (a propositional branching time logic [9]) augmented with a predicate for intention, "intends", and two predicates for know-how, "K_{how}" and "K_{prev}". Each of these applies to an agent and a formula. The predicate for communication, "comm", is as defined above, as is the operator WSAT.

Now we formally define the syntax of $\mathcal{L}$. $\mathcal{L}$ is the minimal set closed under the following rules. Here, Φ is a set of atomic proposition symbols, $\mathcal{B}$ a set of actions, and $\mathcal{B}'$ a set of basic action symbols. $\mathcal{F}$ = {assertive, directive, commissive, permissive, prohibitive, declarative} is the set of illocutionary forces. $\mathcal{A}$ is the set of agent symbols. $\mathcal{M}$ is the set of *messages* as defined below. $\mathcal{L}_s$ is the set of *scenario-formulae* that is used as an auxiliary definition. It contains formulae that are evaluated relative to scenarios in the model, rather than relative to times.

(1) $\psi \in \mathcal{L}$, where $\psi \in \Phi$;

(2) $p, q \in \mathcal{L}$ implies $p \wedge q \in \mathcal{L}$;

(3) $p \in \mathcal{L}$ implies $\neg p \in \mathcal{L}$;

(4) $p \in \mathcal{L}_s$ implies $\mathsf{WSAT}p \in \mathcal{L}_s$;

(5) $p \in \mathcal{L}_s$ implies $\mathsf{A}p \in \mathcal{L}$, where A is the universal scenario-quantifier;

(6) $p \in \mathcal{L}$ and $x \in \mathcal{A}$ implies $K_{how}(x, p)$, $K_{prev}(x, p)$, $\text{intends}(x, p) \in \mathcal{L}$;

(7) $\mathcal{L} \subseteq \mathcal{L}_s$;

(8) $p, q \in \mathcal{L}_s$ implies $p \wedge q \in \mathcal{L}_s$;

(9) $p \in \mathcal{L}_s$ implies $\neg p \in \mathcal{L}_s$;

(10) $p, q \in \mathcal{L}_s$ implies $p \cup q \in \mathcal{L}_s$;

(11) $p \in \mathcal{L}$ implies $\mathsf{P}p \in \mathcal{L}$, where P is the past operator;

(12) $p \in \mathcal{L}$ and $i \in \mathcal{F}$ implies $\langle i, p\rangle \in \mathcal{M}$;

(13) $x, y \in \mathcal{A}$ and $m \in \mathcal{M}$ implies "comm(x, y, m)" $\in \mathcal{L}_s$;

(14) $\mathcal{B}' \subseteq \mathcal{B}$;

(15) $x, y \in \mathcal{A}$ and $m \in \mathcal{M}$ implies "says-to(x, y, m)" $\in \mathcal{B}$;

(16) $p \in \mathcal{L}$ and $a \in \mathcal{B}$ implies $[a]p \in \mathcal{L}_s$.

Throughout this paper, the agent is elided over when obvious from the context. A denotes "in *all* scenarios at the present time". A useful abbreviation is E, which denotes "in *some* scenario at the present time" – i.e. $\mathsf{E}p \equiv \neg\mathsf{A}\neg p$. $p \cup q$ means that q holds sometimes in the future in the given scenario and p holds from now to then. $\mathsf{F}p$ denotes "p holds sometimes in the future in this scenario" and abbreviates "true $\cup p$". $\mathsf{G}p$ denotes "p always holds in the future in this scenario" and abbreviates "$\neg\mathsf{F}\neg p$". $\mathsf{P}p$ denotes "p held at some point in the past". Implications $(p \rightarrow q)$ and disjunctions $(p \vee q)$ of formulae are defined as the usual abbreviations. For an action a, an agent x, and a formula p, $x[a]p$ denotes that in the given scenario, if a is ever done by x starting now, then p holds at some time during the period when a is being done. Let $x\langle a\rangle p$ abbreviate $\neg x[a]\neg p$. Thus, $\mathsf{A}[a]p$ denotes that in all scenarios at the present moment, if a is ever done then p holds at a time during the period over which a is done.

4.2. THE FORMAL MODEL

Let $M = \langle F, [\,]\rangle$ be an intensional model for the language $\mathcal{L}$, where $F = \langle \mathbf{T}, <, \mathbf{A}\rangle$ is a frame and $[\,]$ is an interpretation. Here, $\mathbf{T}$ is a set of possible times ordered by $<$; $\mathbf{A}$ assigns agents to different times; i.e. $\mathbf{A} : \mathbf{T} \mapsto \mathcal{A}$. As described below, $[\,]$ assigns intensions to atomic propositions and to pairs of agent symbols and actions.

A scenario at a time is any single branch of the relation $<$ that begins at the given time, and contains *all* times in some linear subrelation of $<$. Different scenarios correspond to different ways in which the world may develop in the future as a result of the actions of agents and events in the environment. Formally, a scenario at time t is a set $S \subseteq \mathbf{T}$ of which the following conditions hold.

- *Root*: $t \in S$.
- *Linearity*: $(\forall t', t'' \in S : (t' = t'') \vee (t' < t'') \vee (t'' < t'))$.
- *Density*: $(\forall t', t'' \in S, t''' \in \mathbf{T} : (t' < t''' < t'') \rightarrow t''' \in S)$.
- *Maximality*: $(\forall t' \in S, t'' \in \mathbf{T} : (t' < t'') \rightarrow (\exists t''' \in S : (t' < t''') \wedge (t''' \not< t'')))$.
  Intuitively, this property means that if it is possible to extend the scenario S (here to t''), then it is extended, either to t'' (when $t''' = t''$), or along some other branch.

$\mathbf{S}_t$ is the class of all scenarios at time t. The classes of scenarios at different times are disjoint, i.e. $t \neq t' \Rightarrow \mathbf{S}_t \cap \mathbf{S}_{t'} = \varnothing$. The tuple $\langle S, t, t'\rangle$ denotes a subscenario of S from t to t', inclusive. Whenever $\langle S, t, t'\rangle$ is written, it may be assumed that $t, t' \in S$ and $t \leq t'$. This captures the essential intuition behind subscenarios, namely that they are periods of time, and helps to simplify the formalism somewhat.

The intension $[\,]$ of an atomic proposition is the set of times where it is true. The intension of an action is, for each agent x, the set of subscenarios in the model in which an instance of it is done by x. Thus, $[\,]$ is the union of two functions of types $\Phi \mapsto \mathcal{P}(\mathbf{T})$ and $\mathcal{A} \times \mathcal{B} \mapsto \mathcal{P}(\mathcal{P}(\mathbf{T}) \times \mathbf{T} \times \mathbf{T})$, respectively. $t \in [p]$ means that p is true at time t and $\langle S, t, t'\rangle \in [a]^x$ means that agent x does action a in the subscenario of S from time t to t'. We require that all actions in $\mathcal{B}$ take time; i.e. $t < t'$ holds in the above. The superscript is deleted when it can be understood from the context.

The following coherence conditions on models are imposed to make them intuitively reasonable and to preserve certain technical properties [25]: (1) if begun at a particular time in a scenario, an action can end at most once in that scenario; (2) subscenarios are uniquely identified by the times over which they stretch, i.e. the scenario used to refer to them is not important; (3) there is always a future time available in the model; (4) something must be *done* by each agent along each scenario in the model, even if it is a dummy action; (5) for any time in the future of a given time, there is a finite sequence of actions that would reach it; and (6) if an action is performed from t to t', it may be taken to be performed from any time in the middle to t'.

4.3. FORMALIZING SPEECH ACTS

Speech acts are, first of all, actions. We take them to be the actions of just their speakers, and as occurring over subscenarios. Let "says-to" be a parametrized speech act, to be used as in "says-to(y, m)". This action will be seen as an action done by agent x. $\langle S, t_b, t_e\rangle \in [\text{says-to}(y, m)]^x$ means that, on scenario S, agent x performed the speech act of saying m to agent y in the time from t_b (the time of beginning) to t_e (the time of ending). This just means that the illocution was successfully made. There is no commitment at this stage as to whether it was satisfied or not. We require that $t_b < t_e$; i.e. the above action, like all actions, takes time.

The semantics of speech acts is captured in the theory of this paper by means of a new modal operator. The operator WSAT captures the *whole-hearted satisfaction* of speech acts, which is described in section 5. It is convenient to have a special predicate in the language that allows us to speak of the performance of a speech act. This allows us to apply our modal operator to formulae that denote propositions, rather than to those that denote actions. In addition to allowing us to follow the usual way of defining a modal operator, the definition of "comm" also allows speech acts to be nested as in "I tell you that he pleaded guilty".

Let the new predicate be "comm" that applies to two agents, and an illocution. Since actions take place over scenarios, it is most convenient to evaluate "comm(x, y, m)" at scenarios and times. "Comm(x, y, m)" is true at S, t just if y said (or started to say) m to x then. A performed illocution may not, of course, be satisfiable – e.g. some commands may be issued that are impossible to obey. WSAT, then, applies on formulae of the form "comm(x, y, m)" and denotes the satisfaction of the associated speech act.

4.4. SEMANTICS OF THE FORMAL LANGUAGE

The semantics of sentences, i.e. formulae, in the formal language is given relative to a model and a time in it. $M \models_t p$ expresses "M satisfies p at t". This is the main notion of satisfaction in this paper. For formulae in $\mathcal{L}_s$, it is useful to define an auxiliary notion of satisfaction, $M \models_{S,t} p$, which expresses "M satisfies p at time t on scenario S". This presupposes that $t \in S$; however, t may not be the root of S. The satisfaction conditions for the temporal operators are adapted from those in [9]. Formally, we have the following definitions:

(1) $M \models_t \psi$ iff $\langle t\rangle \in [\psi]$;

(2) $M \models_t p \wedge q$ iff $M \models_t p$ and $M \models_t q$;

(3) $M \models_t \neg p$ iff $M \not\models_t p$;

(4) $M \models_t \mathsf{A}p$ iff $(\forall S : S \in \mathbf{S}_t \rightarrow M \models_{S,t} p)$;

(5) $M \models_t \mathsf{P}p$ iff $(\exists t' : t' < t \wedge M \models_{t'} p)$;

(6) $M \models_{S,t} p \cup q$ iff $(\exists t' : t \leq t' \wedge M \models_{S,t'} q \wedge (\forall t'' : t \leq t'' \leq t' \rightarrow M \models_{S,t''} p))$;

(7) $M \models_{S,t} [a]p$ iff $(\exists t' : \langle S, t, t'\rangle \in [a]) \rightarrow (\exists t' : \langle S, t, t'\rangle \in [a]$
$\wedge (\exists t'' : t \leq t'' \leq t' \wedge M \models_{S,t''} p))$;

(8) $M \models_{S,t} p \wedge q$ iff $M \models_{S,t} p$ and $M \models_{S,t} q$;

(9) $M \models_{S,t} \neg p$ iff $M \not\models_{S,t} p$;

(10) $M \models_{S,t}$ comm(x, y, m) iff $(\exists t' : t' \in S \wedge \langle S, t, t'\rangle \in [\text{says-to}(y, m)]^x)$;

(11) $M \models_{S,t} p$ iff $M \models_t p$, if $p \in \mathcal{L}$, and t is the unique time such that $S \in \mathbf{S}_t$.

The semantic conditions for the rest of the language are motivated and presented below.

5. Whole-hearted satisfaction formalized

Whole-hearted satisfaction is defined relative to a scenario and a time. A performative is taken to be in force as soon as it is completed, but not sooner. This is done to allow the possibility of a communication being aborted midway. That is, a speaker's failed attempts to say something, i.e. to get his point across, do not count as communications.

As we have already argued, the primary considerations in this paper are semantic, rather than syntactic or pragmatic. As we shall see, this justifies the particular taxonomy of speech acts considered here. The advantages of not partitioning the space of speech acts in terms of their syntax are that (1) intuitively disparate speech acts like permissions and request are kept apart in the theory; and (2) the phenomenon of indirect speech acts can be accounted for with ease (of course, the problem of determining, given an utterance, which speech act really has occurred is not addressed here). The advantage of not considering the pragmatics directly is that the semantics can be more systematically and rigorously defined, whereas the pragmatics, which rely on performance issues, would be difficult to pin down exactly. In the following, the satisfaction of a speech act requires that it has actually been performed in the given scenario. While we could possibly have stated conditions about scenarios that would tell us whether a given speech act, if performed in them, would be satisfied, this would not be intuitive. It would also leave open the possibility of a speech act being satisfied in scenarios in which it could not have occurred given the physics of the world, or the communicative conventions in force.

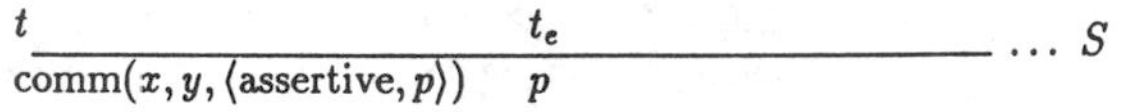

t —— t_e —— $\ldots S$
comm$(x, y, \langle \text{assertive}, p \rangle)$ p

Fig. 2. The satisfaction condition for assertives.

(1) $M \models_{S,t}$ WSAT(comm$(x, y, \langle \text{assertive}, p \rangle)$) iff
$$(\exists t_e : \langle S, t, t_e \rangle \in [\text{says-to}(x, y, \langle \text{assertive}, p \rangle)]^x \wedge M \models_{S,t_e} p).$$

An assertive is satisfied simply if its proposition is true at the time the utterance is made. Thus, the assertive "The door is shut" is satisfied in all scenarios where the door is, in fact, shut. The satisfaction conditions for the other kinds of speech acts are more interesting than this.

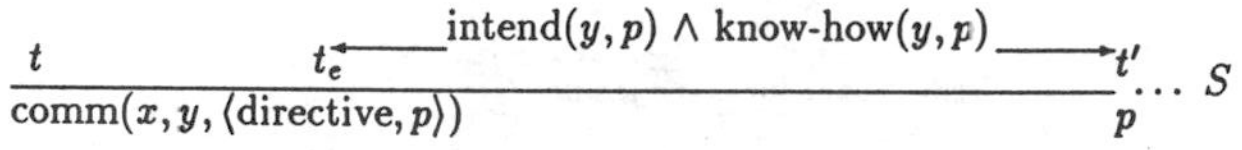

t —— $t_e \leftarrow$ intend$(y, p) \wedge$ know-how$(y, p) \rightarrow t'$ $\ldots S$
comm$(x, y, \langle \text{directive}, p \rangle)$ p

Fig. 3. The satisfaction condition for directives.

(2) $M \models_{S,t}$ WSAT(comm$(x, y, \langle \text{directive}, p \rangle)$) iff
$$(\exists t_e : \langle S, t, t_e \rangle \in [\text{says-to}(x, y, \langle \text{directive}, p \rangle)]^x \wedge (\exists t' \in S : t' \geq t_e$$
$$\wedge M \models_{S,t'} p \wedge (\forall t'' : t_e \leq t'' < t' \rightarrow M \models_{S,t''} K_{how}(y, p) \wedge \text{intends}(y, p)))).$$

A directive is satisfied only if (1) its proposition p becomes true at a point in the future of it being said, and (2) all along the scenario from now to then, the hearer has the know-how, as well as the intention to achieve it. For example, a directive to open the door is satisfied if the door ends up open (within some salient period of time, perhaps) and, furthermore, the hearer continuously planned to open the door and was in a position to be able to execute the plan to open it. Note that this definition does not finally require that the door open because of the hearer's actions. In our view, this would not be an important requirement to impose, and would only cause action–theoretic complications about the matter of when an agent can be said to have performed a certain action, especially when that action is not a single-step basic action.

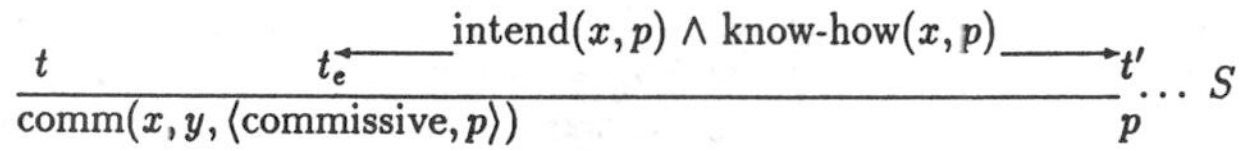

t —— $t_e \leftarrow$ intend$(x, p) \wedge$ know-how$(x, p) \rightarrow t'$ $\ldots S$
comm$(x, y, \langle \text{commissive}, p \rangle)$ p

Fig. 4. The satisfaction condition for commissives.

(3) $M \models_{S,t}$ WSAT(comm$(x, y, \langle \text{commissive}, p \rangle)$) iff
$$(\exists t_e : \langle S, t, t_e \rangle \in [\text{says-to}(x, y, \langle \text{commissive}, p \rangle)]^x \wedge (\exists t' \in S : t' \geq t_e$$
$$\wedge M \models_{S,t'} p \wedge (\forall t'' : t_e \leq t'' < t' \rightarrow M \models_{S,t''} K_{how}(x, p) \wedge \text{intends}(x, p)))).$$

Similarly, a commissive is satisfied only if (1) its proposition becomes true at a point in the future of it being said, and (2) all along the scenario from now to then, the *speaker* has the know-how as well as the intention to achieve it. Technically, a commissive is just like a directive except that the role of the hearer is taken over by the speaker. For example, the commissive "I promise to shut the door" is satisfied in all scenarios in which the door eventually gets shut and until it does, the speaker intends and knows how to shut it.

A difference between commissives and directives that is of significance in some applications is that the satisfaction condition of a commissive depends on the actions, intentions, and know-how of just one agent. This can make the satisfaction of commissives easier to enforce in artificial systems. A related observation which is also interesting is that there seem to be fewer forms of commissives in natural languages than directives. This seems to be related to that fact that the satisfaction of directives involves actions by agents other than the speaker, and so different kinds of social considerations come into play – one may request or command or beseech or advise someone to do something, but one can simply do it on one's own (one can, of course, issue commissives on the basis of others' actions, and even issue a commissive to do something if another agent acts in a certain way).

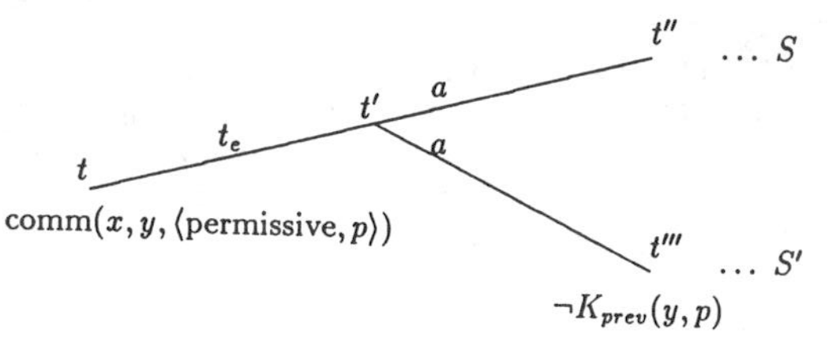

Fig. 5. The satisfaction condition for permissives.

(4) $M \models_{S,t}$ WSAT(comm$(x, y, \langle \text{permissive}, p \rangle)$) iff
$$(\exists t_e : \langle S, t, t_e \rangle \in [\text{says-to}(x, y, \langle \text{permissive}, p \rangle)]^x \wedge (\exists t' \in S : t' \geq t_e$$
$$\wedge (\forall a : (\exists t'' : \langle S, t', t'' \rangle \in [a]^y) \rightarrow (\exists S', t''' : \langle S', t', t''' \rangle \in [a]^y$$
$$\wedge M \not\models_{S',t'''} K_{prev}(y, p))))).$$

A permissive is satisfied in a scenario and a time only if it is taken advantage of by the hearer at a future point in that scenario. However, when a permissive is taken advantage of, it allows the hearer to do actions at certain times that he could not have done before, because those actions might possibly have led to the condition becoming true. Thus, a permissive is satisfied in a scenario in which the hearer does at least one action whose performance can lead to a situation where he is unable to prevent that condition from occurring. That is, the hearer can now risk letting that condition hold. For example, a permissive allowing a hearer to let the door be open is satisfied in a scenario if (as a result of the given permissive, as it were) the hearer can, e.g. risk opening the window, even though the breeze may open the door. Without this permissive, the hearer would have to take some precaution, e.g. latch the door, before opening the window. The satisfaction of a permissive tends to increase the know-how of the hearer by giving him more options. Unfortunately, no closed-form characterization of this increase in know-how is available at present.

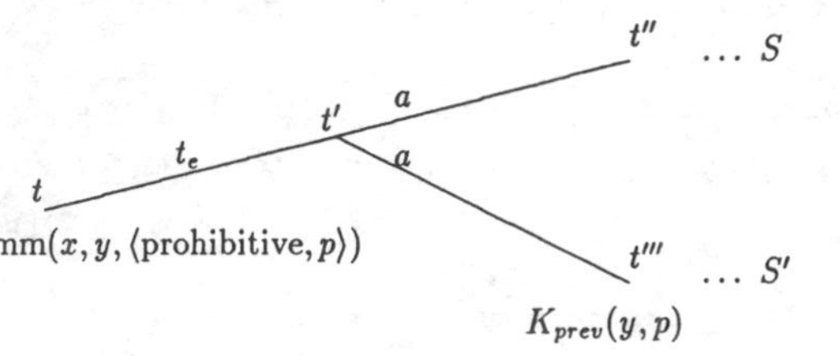

Fig. 6. The satisfaction condition for prohibitives.

(5) $M \models_{S,t}$ WSAT(comm(x, y, ⟨prohibitive, p⟩)) iff

$$(\exists t_e : \langle S, t, t_e\rangle \in [\text{says-to}(x, y, \langle \text{prohibitive}, p\rangle)]^x \wedge (\forall t' \in S : t' > t_e$$
$$\rightarrow (\forall a : (\exists t'' : \langle S, t', t''\rangle \in [a]^y) \rightarrow (\forall S', t''' : \langle S', t', t'''\rangle \in [a]^y)$$
$$\rightarrow M \models_{S',t'''} K_{prev}(y, p))))).$$

A prohibitive is satisfied in a scenario and a time if none of the actions done by the hearer in that scenario (in the future) can lead to a situation where the hearer would be unable to prevent the condition from occurring. That is, the hearer cannot risk violating the prohibition. For example, a prohibitive to not let the door be open can be satisfied only if the hearer does not let the window be open, where the opening of the window may lead to the door being opened.

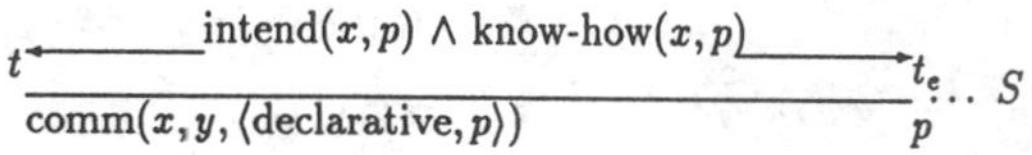

Fig. 7. The satisfaction condition for declaratives.

(6) $M \models_{S,t}$ WSAT(comm(x, y, ⟨declarative, p⟩)) iff

$$(\exists t_e : \langle S, t, t_e\rangle \in [\text{says-to}(x, y, \langle \text{declarative}, p\rangle)]^x \wedge M \models_{S,t_e} p$$
$$\wedge (\forall t' : t \leq t' < t_e \rightarrow M \models_{S,t'} (\neg p \wedge K_{how}(x, p) \wedge \text{intends}(x, p)))).$$

A declarative is satisfied only if (1) its proposition p becomes true at the time that it is said, and (2) all along while the speaker is saying it, he intends that condition to occur and knows how to make it occur. For example, a declarative to name a certain door the Golden Gate is satisfied if the door ends up named thus, and the speaker intended it to be so named and knew how to name it. The door has its new name as soon as the declarative is completed. The condition about the know-how is included to ensure that the speaker at each point is able to force the completion of the declarative and thereby force the occurrence of the appropriate condition. This helps to eliminate cases where the speaker has the intention, but is not in the right social or conventional position to make the declarative succeed – the naming should succeed, but not because of some contingent features of the given scenario. According to some traditional theories, e.g. that of Vanderveken [27], the occurrence of declaratives merely coincides with their success. This seems too weak, since it allows a declarative to succeed even if the speaker did not have full control over its occurrence, i.e. even if the speaker could not have forced the given condition to occur.

Since declaratives epitomize doing things by saying, they occur exactly when they are satisfied. In other words, we have the following condition:

- comm(x, y), ⟨declarative, p⟩) ≡ WSAT(comm(x, y, ⟨declarative, p⟩)).

That is, a declarative can be successfully uttered only when it is satisifed. As a consequence, the appropriate intentions and know-how are presupposed for a declarative to even be uttered.

An interesting observation can be made about the relationship between declaratives and other speech acts. All speech acts can be expressed as declaratives. In fact, this is the core claim of the account of performatives as given by Austin. It would seem, then, that if we reduce, say, a promise to a declarative, we would have to say that it was satisfied precisely when it was uttered. Thus, the intuitions captured by WSAT would be lost. However, this is not really the case in the theory of this paper. We used the performative account to motivate the syntax of the formal language used here. If a speech act that is not naturally a declarative is interpreted as a declarative, we have to wrap an extra illocution around it, i.e. we obtain something like comm$(x, y, \langle \text{declarative}, \text{comm}(x, y, \langle \text{commissive}, p\rangle)\rangle)$. The satisfaction of this does indeed coincide with the successful issuing of the appropriate promise; however, it is not the same as the promise nested within it. Of course, this leaves the question open of how to distinguish different speech acts in natural language but, as explained in section 1, we are not addressing the problem of determining the appropriate illocutionary force of natural language utterances. One should note, though, that the proposed formal framework is rich enough to capture the relevant distinctions. Also, when the above complex speech act is considered, we can see that the act of issuing a promise involves at least intending to issue it, and knowing how to do so.

Interrogatives are semantically quite like directives; for example, see Searle and Vanderveken [21, p. 199] and Harrah [13, pp. 740, 747]. However, they need special treatment to allow for answers to be defined and received. An interrogative is treated as a directive to perform an assertive speech act (back to the speaker of the question) that provides the answer to the question posed in the original interrogative. Thus, it is satisfied when a true answer to it is given, i.e. the assertive containing the answer is itself satisfied. This derives from an intuition about treating interrogatives as imperatives of the form "Tell me Truly" [13, pp. 747–748].

We need to introduce "interrogative" as a new force in $\mathcal{F}$. This is a subcategory of directives. Questions can be thought of as lambda expressions of the form $(\lambda\vec{a}p)$. An interrogative is then a directive to assert the correct answer to the given question, i.e. the set of substitutions for which the above expression evaluates to true. This corresponds to the semantics of questions, e.g. as proposed by Groenendijk and Stokhof [11]. Let $\mathfrak{R}$ be a set of tuples. Let "answer-to$((\lambda\vec{a}p), \mathfrak{R})$" hold iff $(\forall\vec{b} : \vec{b} \in \mathfrak{R} \leftrightarrow (\lambda\vec{a}p)[\vec{b}])$; i.e. $\mathfrak{R}$ is the answer to $(\lambda\vec{a}p)$. $\mathfrak{R}$ must be finite if it is to be explicitly communicated, but could be infinite if it is communicated by reference, e.g. as "the set of all even numbers". For simplicity, let $\mathfrak{R}$ denote a representation of itself in the formal language. It is useful to have the following abbreviations: m_q stands for $\langle$interrogative, $(\lambda\vec{a}p)\rangle$, m_r stands for $\langle$assertive, answer-to$((\lambda\vec{a}p), \mathfrak{R})\rangle$, and c_r stands for comm(y, x, m_r).

(7) $M \models_{S,t} \text{WSAT}(\text{comm}(x, y, m_q))$ iff

$$(\exists t_e : \langle S, t, t_e\rangle \in [\text{says-to}(x, y, m_q)]^x \wedge (\exists \mathfrak{R}, t' : t_e \leq t' \wedge M \models_{S,t'} \text{WSAT}(c_r))$$

$$\wedge (\forall t'' : t_e \leq t'' < t' : M \models_{S,t'} \text{intends}(x, \text{WSAT}(c_r)) \wedge K_{how}(x, \text{WSAT}(c_r))))$$

$$\wedge (\forall \mathfrak{R}, t''' : t_e \leq t''' \rightarrow [M \models_{S,t'''} c_r \rightarrow M \models_{S,t'''} \text{WSAT}(c_r)])).$$

The last conjunct is included to capture the restriction that all answers asserted by the hearer of the interrogative must be WSAT. That is, only correct answers may be produced. This takes care of interrogatives that contain the so-called Wh-questions; those that contain yes–no questions are analogous. A yes–no question for q is of the form $(\lambda\upsilon(q \equiv \upsilon))$, where υ is of the sort *truth-value*; thus, the lambda expression evaluates to true iff υ is the Boolean value of q.

6. Verbs of fulfillment

Table 2

Some verbs of fulfillment.

Force	Example
Directive	He acceded to my request to shut the door
Commissive	I kept my promise to shut the door
Permissive	He enjoyed the permission to let the door be shut
Prohibitive	He upheld the prohibition against shutting the door
Declarative	He named this door the Golden Gate

One of the applications of the theory developed in this paper is to systematically give a rigorous semantics to what we call the *verbs of fulfillment*. These are verbs such as "obey", "follow", "keep", "enjoy", and "uphold". The connotations of them that are of interest here are the ones used in, for example, "obey an order", "follow a suggestion", "keep a promise", "enjoy some privileges", and "uphold the law (which corresponded to a prohibition)". There are no special such verbs for declaratives; however, the verbs used for declaratives can themselves be used in the appropriate sense to indicate fulfillment, e.g. as in "He named the door the Golden Gate". These verbs correspond to the different kinds of speech acts, and denote their fulfillment. It is perhaps no accident that there are no verbs of fulfillment for assertives. The truth of assertives can be referred to in various ways, but there are no special conditions of fulfillment for them. This is because their conditions of satisfaction are themselves trivial, and they call for no further action or inaction. Assertives describe their own conditions of satisfaction; these conditions can also be referred to with predicates such as "is true". However, there is no explicit fulfillment of assertives as we have defined the term here.

Work on the semantics of speech acts is usually taken to be about the performative verbs. By contrast, it is suggested here how the corresponding fulfillment verbs may be given a semantics. The idea is really quite simple. The semantic content of a fulfillment verb is the set of scenarios where the corresponding speech act is WSAT. Different fulfillment verbs correspond to different kinds of speech acts. For each, the appropriate definition may be invoked, and plugged into whatever kind of natural language semantics one cares to employ.

In a way, the exercise of giving a semantics to different verbs of fulfillment is no different to the exercise of giving special semantics to verbs such as "believes", "knows", and "intends". Such verbs have been carefully considered for decades. We believe that verbs of fulfillment are on par with attitudinal verbs, at least insofar as they cannot be given a reasonable extensional semantics.

7. Normative constraints for felicitous communication

The conditions of the satisfaction of speech acts can be used to motivate some normative constraints on communication among agents. The particular constraints stated below are given primarily as examples; some entail the others, and not all would make sense simultaneously. However, if some of these constraints or others like them are satisfied, the scenarios that are actualized are "good" – i.e. those where maxims akin to the Gricean maxims may be said to hold, and where communication is not only successful, but also cooperative and felicitous. In other words, these constraints restrict the possible models to those that have some properties of felititous communication.

(1) *Intending one's directives*:

The proposition of a directive should be intended by its issuer. If the speaker does not intend that something occur, he should not go about directing others to achieve it.

$\text{comm}(x, y, \langle \text{directive}, p\rangle) \rightarrow \text{intends}(x, p)$.

(2) *Weak consistency for directives*:

A directive issued by an agent should not clash with the agent's own intentions; i.e. at least in some scenarios, the speaker's intentions and his directives should be compatible. This differs significantly from constraint (1), which says that the issuer intends the given directive; this constraint says that all of the issuer's intentions are consistent with the directive.

$$\text{intends}(x, q) \wedge \text{comm}(x, y, \langle \text{directive}, p\rangle) \rightarrow \mathsf{E}[\mathsf{WSAT}\ \text{comm}(x, y, \langle \text{directive}, p\rangle) \wedge \mathsf{F}q].$$

(3) *Consistency with intentions*:

All speech acts must be WSAT over all scenarios compatible with the speaker's current intentions.

$$\text{intends}(x, q) \wedge \text{comm}(x, y, m) \rightarrow \mathsf{A}[\mathsf{F}q \rightarrow \mathsf{WSAT}\ \text{comm}(x, y, m)].$$

(4) *No loss of know-how for issuers of directive*:

A speech act made by an agent should not clash with his own intentions. Its satisfaction should not reduce his ability to achieve his intentions. That is, in all scenarios in which the given speech act is satisfied, the speaker should, in the future of making the speech act, know how to achieve the intentions he had at the time he issued it. In other words, speech acts should not backfire on their issuers.

$$\text{intends}(x, q) \wedge \text{comm}(x, y, m) \rightarrow \mathsf{A}[\mathsf{WSAT}\ \text{comm}(x, y, m) \rightarrow [\text{says-to}(x, y, m)]\mathsf{F}K_{how}(x, q)].$$

(5) *Weak consistency for prohibitives*:

A prohibitive is issued by an agent only if the agent himself does not intend that it be violated. That is, the agent who prohibits another from letting a certain condition occur should not himself try to make it happen. This is a minimal level of cooperation or rationality one would expect from the issuers of prohibitions.

$\text{comm}(x, y, \langle \text{prohibitive}, p\rangle) \rightarrow \neg\text{intends}(x, p)$.

(6) *Intending to uphold the law*:

An agent must never intend to violate a prohibitive issued to him. That is, not only must the agent never violate a prohibitive in practice, he should not even intend its violation in any scenario.

$$\text{comm}(x, y, \langle \text{prohibitive}, p\rangle) \rightarrow \neg\mathsf{EF}[\text{intends}(y, \neg\,\mathsf{WSAT}\ \text{comm}(x, y, \langle \text{prohibitive}, p\rangle))].$$

(7) *Mutual consistency of speech acts*:

All the speech acts performed by one speaker in any single situation must be mutally consistent in the sense of being jointly satisfiable in at least some scenario in the future of the world and time at which they have both been uttered. This prevents many unacceptable situations. It also requires in practice that the agents be able to check the consistency of their speech acts, which can be a difficult task if their speech acts involve complex propositions.

$$\mathsf{P}\ \text{comm}(x, y, m_1) \wedge \text{comm}(x, y, m_2) \rightarrow \mathsf{E}[\mathsf{WSAT}\ \text{comm}(x, y, m_1) \wedge \mathsf{WSAT}\ \text{comm}(x, y, m_2)].$$

8. Comparisons

The taxonomy of speech acts of this paper is motivated by the semantic definitions given above, which are different for permissives, prohibitives, and directives. This distinguishes the taxonomy of this paper from other classifications of speech acts. Since syntactically, permissives, prohibitives, and directives are all imperatives, they are usually classified together, e.g. by Bach and Harnish [4, pp. 39–54] and

Searle and Vanderveken [21, ch. 9]. This is surprising in the case of Searle and Vanderveken, since their focus is pragmatic, rather than syntactic.

We have argued in many places in this paper that traditional approaches to formalizing speech acts ignore the aspects of them focused on here. In this section, we compare this paper to some semantics of speech acts that others have proposed. One important work is that of Searle and Vanderveken [21]. However, they do not relate the satisfaction conditions of different sorts of speech acts with the intentions and know-how of the speaker or the hearer. Their greater aim seems to be to derive the possible illocutionary forces from a set of core features, e.g. what they call the illocutionary point and the direction of fit.

Searle and Vanderveken's approach has been challenged by Cohen and Levesque, who argue that the illocutionary point is theoretically redundant and can be derived from the inferences that a speech act sanctions [7]. These inferences involve the updating of the beliefs, intentions, and mutual beliefs of the speaker and the hearer – for this reason, Cohen and Levesque's approach is largely of pragmatic interest. Perrault has argued that, despite Cohen and Levesque's attempts, how the participant's cognitive states ought to be updated cannot be monotonically specified [17]. He proposes that a default mechanism, in his paper Reiter's default logic, be used to characterize the effects of speech acts and, hence, their pragmatic content.

In more recent work, Vanderveken has independently addressed the problems of the "success and satisfaction" of speech acts [27,28]. Vanderveken's goal is a general illocutionary logic, and a large part of his theory is focused on the conditions of when a performative succeeds, i.e. when a speech act of a particular illocutionary force is made. His goal is to give the semantics of performative verbs in an extension of Montague grammar. He also considers the degree of strength of different speech acts explicitly, and classifies a variety of speech act verbs, as special as the declaratives "homologate" and "ratify", which differ primarily in their pragmatic aspects. The particular definitions given by Vanderveken are extensional in that no reference is made to the intentions or the know-how of the agents. For example, to Vanderveken a directive is satisfied if the appropriate condition comes to hold, and a prohibitive, merely a special kind of directive to him, is satisfied if the appropriate condition does not occur. Vanderveken lumps permissives and prohibitives with directives [27, pp. 189–198], which we have argued should not be done. He also does not consider the temporal aspect of speech acts explicitly. In sum, while the results of the theory of this paper are more refined than the corresponding results of Vanderveken's theory, they could fruitfully be combined with the pragmatic and other aspects of speech acts that he has studied in much greater detail.

9. Conclusions

We have presented a formal semantics of speech acts that is not only quite intuitive, but also has many applications. A question may be raised about its relationship with the traditional work on speech acts, especially in AI. The relationship is essentially one of complementarity. As already mentioned, traditional theories have addressed the problem of determining when what kind of a speech act occurs. Those theories can thus be used to feed into the theory of this paper: One simply has to use those theories under appropriate assumptions to determine the truth of different instances of "comm(x, y, m)" and then apply the present theory to determine the satisfaction conditions of those instances.

This way of looking at things places the semantics presented here at the natural boundary of deciding what to say, on the one hand, and deciding how to say it, on the other. That is, on the one hand, we have the concerns of deciding what speech act to make, and on the other, the concerns of how to get a point across. This is a useful way to organize an AI system that is designed to also communicate with humans – the first aspect mentioned above is a part of Distributed AI, the second aspect a part of Computational Linguistics.

An important contribution of this paper is that it brings the satisfaction conditions for speech acts into the fold of logic. Using definitions of the intentions and know-how of an agent, we were able to systematically give rigorous and accurate definitions of the conditions of satisfaction for speech acts of different illocutionary forces. The theory presented here can yield some well-motivated normative constraints on communication among agents. An advantage of the model-theoretic approach is that it allows our intuitions to be expressed directly and formally, and thus can be used in clarifying and debugging them.

References

[1] J.F. Allen and C.R. Perrault, Analyzing intentions in utterances, Art. Int. 15(1980)143–178.
[2] D. Appelt, *Planning English Sentences* (Cambridge University Press, Cambridge, UK, 1986).
[3] J.L. Austin, *How to do Things with Words* (Clarendon, Oxford, UK, 1962).
[4] K. Bach and R.M. Harnish, *Linguistic Communication and Speech Acts* (MIT Press, Cambridge, MA, 1979).
[5] K.M. Chandy and J. Misra, How processes learn, Distr. Comp. 1(1986)40–52.
[6] M.K. Chang, SANP: A communication level protocol for supporting machine-to-machine negotiation in organization, Master's Thesis, University of British Columbia, Vancouver, B.C., Canada (1991).
[7] P.R. Cohen and H.J. Levesque, Rational interaction as the basis for communication, Technical Report No. 433, SRI International, Menlo Park, VA (1988).
[8] S.K. Dewitz and R.M. Lee, Legal procedures as formal conversations: Contracting on a performative network, in: *Int. Conf. on Information Systems* (1989).
[9] E.A. Emerson, Temporal and modal logic, in: *Handbook of Theoretical Computer Science*, ed. J. van Leeuwen (North-Holland, Amsterdam, 1989).
[10] P. Grice, Utterer's meaning and intentions, Philos. Rev. (1969); reprinted in ref. [15].
[11] J. Groenendijk and M. Stokhof, On the semantics of questions and the pragmatics of answers, in: *Varieties of Formal Semantics*, ed. F. Landman and F. Veltman (Foris, Dordrecht, 1984) pp. 143–170.
[12] C.L. Hamblin, *Imperatives* (Basil Blackwell, Oxford, UK, 1987).
[13] D. Harrah, The logic of questions, in: *Handbook of Philosophical Logic*, ed. D. Gabbay and F. Guenthner (Reidel, Dordrecht, 1984).

[14] M.N. Huhns, D. Bridgeland and N. Arni, A DAI communication aide, Technical Report No. ACT-RA-317-90, Artificial Intelligence Laboratory, Microelectronics and Computer Technology Corporation, Austin, TX (1990).

[15] A.P. Martinich (ed.), *The Philosophy of Language* (Oxford University Press, New York, NY, 1985).

[16] J. McCarthy, Common business communication language, in: *Textverarbeitung und Bürosysteme*, ed. A. Endres and J. Reets (Oldenbourg, Vienna, 1982).

[17] R. Perrault, An application of default logic to speech act theory, Technical Report No. 90, Center for the Study of Language and Information, Stanford, CA (1987).

[18] J.R. Ross, On declarative sentences, in: *Readings in English Transformational Grammar*, ed. R.A. Jacobs (Ginn & Co., Waltham, MA, 1970).

[19] J.R. Searle, *Speech Acts* (Cambridge University Press, Cambridge, UK, 1969).

[20] J.R. Searle, Indirect speech acts, in: *Syntax and Semantics*, Vol. 3, ed. P. Cole and J.L. Morgan (Academic Press, New York, 1975); reprinted in ref. [15].

[21] J.R. Searle and D. Vanderveken, *Foundations of Illocutionary Logic* (Cambridge University Press, Cambridge, UK, 1985).

[22] M.P. Singh, A logic of situated know-how, in: *National Conf. on Artificial Intelligence (AAAI)* (1991).

[23] M.P. Singh, Towards a formal theory of communication for multiagent systems, in: *Int. Joint Conf. on Artificial Intelligence (IJCAI)* (1991).

[24] M.P. Singh, On the semantics of protocols among distributed intelligent agents, in: *IEEE Int. Phoenix Conf. on Computers and Communications* (1992).

[25] M.P. Singh, A theory of actions, intentions, and communications for multiagent systems, Ph.D. Thesis, University of Texas, Austin, TX (1992).

[26] M.P. Singh and N.M. Asher, A logic of intentions and beliefs, J. Philos. Logic (1992), in press.

[27] D. Vanderveken, *Meaning and Speech Acts*, Vol. 1: *Principles of Language Use* (Cambridge University Press, Cambridge, UK, 1990).

[28] D. Vanderveken, *Meaning and Speech Acts*, Vol. 2: *Formal Semantics of Success and Satisfaction* (Cambridge University Press, Cambridge, UK, 1991).

[29] Z. Vendler, On saying something, in: *Res Cogitans: A Study in Rational Psychology* (Cornell University Press, Ithaca, NY, 1972); reprinted in ref. [15].

Understanding Cooperation: an Agent's Perspective

Andreas Lux
DFKI *
PO-Box 2080
67608 Kaiserslautern
Germany
lux@dfki.uni-kl.de

Donald Steiner
Siemens AG, c/o DFKI
PO-Box 2080
67608 Kaiserslautern
Germany
steiner@dfki.uni-kl.de

Abstract

The Multi-agent Environment for Constructing Cooperative Applications (MECCA) is based upon a framework unifying the internal behavior of agents and cooperation among agents. This paper presents a formalized view of agent behavior relying on the basic loop of goal activation, plan execution and scheduling followed by task execution. This allows for a presentation of the semantics of cooperation primitives: interagent messages supporting cooperation, comprised of speech acts operating upon objects occuring in the basic loop. The formal semantics of cooperation primitives gives a meaning to individual messages, independent from the cooperation protocol. Thus, agents can reason about exchanged messages and are able to dynamically create their own methods for cooperation.

1 Introduction

The Multi-agent Environment for Constructing Cooperative Applications (MECCA)[1] establishes a basic loop guiding the behavior of agents incorporating reactivity and deliberation (Steiner et al. 1993). As all agents act according to this loop, cooperation can also be based upon it. Messages are fundamental for supporting cooperation in MECCA; their content is clearly important for successful cooperation. This content is determined not only by the agents' local behavior, but also by the previous messages and the expected direction the conversation will take. Human conversations have been extensively analyzed; speech act theory arose as a result (Austin 1962; Searle 1969), classifying messages into a variety of types. Attention has been directed towards embedding (illocutionary) speech acts in planning theory (Grosz & Sidner 1990), but has, up to now, been limited to the speech acts and not the entire content of the message.

We argue that a sender of a message should have a sufficient model of the recipient to know the recipient's behavior upon receipt of the message. Exactly this model is what determines which message the sender sends and, correspondingly, the entire cooperative process. Thus, sender and receiver must agree upon the meaning (semantics) of the exchanged messages. Furthermore, the semantics of the speech acts vary according to the objects under discussion - the proposal of a goal has a different meaning than the proposal of a plan to achieve the goal. Only until these semantics have been determined, can agents reason about the messages they send and receive to influence the cooperation.

In this paper, we present the formal representations of the basic loop determining both agent behavior as well as cooperation among agents.

*German Research Center for Artificial Intelligence

[1] This work has been supported by Siemens as part of the KIK-Teamware and CoMMA-Plat projects

2 The Agent Model

An agent is the central computational entity, which serves as an explicit model of all entities participating in a cooperation.[2] It can be decomposed into the following three components: the functional, task-solving component (*agent body*), the cooperative superstrate (*agent head*), and the communication functionality (*agent communicator*) (Steiner, Mahling & Haugeneder 1990).

We assume that functional interfaces to an agent's body and communicator are given and concentrate here on a formal description of the agent's head. The resulting cooperative interaction among agents will be examined in Section 3.1. The agent behaves according to a basic *agent loop* (Steiner et al. 1993) which consists of the four phases of *goal activation*, *planning*, *scheduling* (temporal synchronization) and *execution/evaluation*.

2.1 Formalization of the Agent Model

An agent is formally defined by sets and by functions which operate on these sets. According to the above mentioned phases, the following sets are fundamental to an agent A.

$\mathcal{W}_A$ a set of possible world states of A; the current world state of A is denoted $\mathcal{W}_{A,c}$.

[2] both human and machine agents

$\mathcal{A}_A$ a set of actions A can perform; actions have preconditions, which must hold in $\mathcal{W}_c$ before execution, procedures, which are function calls to either body, head or communicator, and effects, which alter the world state $\mathcal{W}_c$; actions are primitive, non-decomposable plans.

$\mathcal{G}_A$ a set of A's active goals; an active goal $g \in \mathcal{G}_A$ is represented by a particular world state, i.e. $\mathcal{G}_A \subseteq \mathcal{W}_A$.

$\mathcal{P}_A$ a set of hypothetical plan sets for A's goals; plans are similar to actions in that they have preconditions and effects on the world state $\mathcal{W}_c$; their procedures, however, are compositions of actions and other plans; formally, $\mathcal{P}_A = \bigcup_{g \in \mathcal{G}_A} \{\mathcal{P}_g\}$, where $\mathcal{P}_g$ is a set of hypothetical plans for g.

$\mathcal{S}_A$ a set of plans to whose execution A is committed; thus, $\mathcal{S}_A \subseteq \bigcup \mathcal{P}_A$.

$\mathcal{F}_A$ a set of functions which are used by A to activate goals (*new_goal*), to find plans (*find_all_plans*), to perform actions (*perform*) etc.; these functions are used to control A's basic loop; the functions might be different among agents.

Thus, an agent A is formally defined by the 6-tuple

$A = (\mathcal{W}_{A,c}, \mathcal{G}_A, \mathcal{P}_A, \mathcal{S}_A, \mathcal{A}_A, \mathcal{F}_A)$, where $\mathcal{W}_{A,c} \in \mathcal{W}_A$.[3]

In the following, we formally describe an agent's basic loop based upon the aforementioned sets. The functions in $\mathcal{F}$ are described briefly, with more detail to follow in Section 3.1 where the cooperative aspects are considered.

Goal Activation Assume a set of current goals $\mathcal{G}$ is given. The set is extended with the goal g by the function *new_goal:* $\mathcal{W} \times \{\mathcal{G}\} \rightarrow \mathcal{G}$. According to the current world state $\mathcal{W}_c$, the function *new_goal* selects a world state g which is inserted into the set of active goals $\mathcal{G}$. *new_goal* can be triggered by the agent itself as well as by an external event, e.g. receipt of a message from another agent or effect of the execution of another agent's action. Algorithmically, this phase of the basic loop can be described by:[4]

```
while (g := new_goal(Wc,G)) do
    G := {g} ∪ G
od.
```

Planning The planning approach pursued (Burt 1995) can be characterized as follows: Cooperative plans are built by hypothetical reasoning on the basis of a temporal knowledge representation. Hypothetical reasoning is done by means of abduction (Shanahan 1989); event calculus (Kowalski & Sergot 1986; Eshghi 1988) is used for knowledge representation. Thus, a plan p is a set of events. An event e of a plan p is defined by an instantiated action, a partial ordering, the executing agent and a set of constraints on necessary resources.[5]

$$e = (a_e, ag_e, V_e, N_e, s_e, ((r_1, C_1), \ldots, (r_n, C_n)))$$

with
a_e = action to be executed
ag_e = executing agent
V_e = set of direct predecessor events
N_e = set of direct successor events
s_e = status of the event,
$s_e \in \{hyp, committed, done\}$
r_i = i-th resource
C_i = set of constraints on the i-th resource, possibly empty

The agent function *plan_goal* : $\{\mathcal{G}\} \times \mathcal{W} \rightarrow \mathcal{G}$ selects a goal $g \in \mathcal{G}$ from the set of active goals. The function *find_all_plans* : $\mathcal{G} \times \{\mathcal{A}\} \times \{\mathcal{S}\} \times \mathcal{W} \rightarrow \mathcal{P}$ returns a set of hypothetical plans $\mathcal{P}_g$ which will achieve the goal $g \in \mathcal{G}$, from the world state $\mathcal{W}_c$, ensuring that the plans are compatible with the already scheduled events from $\mathcal{S}$. Knowledge about the post- and preconditions of actions is contained in $\mathcal{A}$. The planning phase can be described by:

```
while (g:= plan_goal(G,Wc)) do
if Pg := find_all_plans(g,A,S,Wc))
then P := Pg ∪ P;
fi;
od.
```

Scheduling The function *schedule_plan* : $\{\mathcal{P}\} \times \mathcal{W} \rightarrow \mathcal{P}$ selects a set of alternative plans $\mathcal{P}_g$ for the goal g from the set of hypothetical plans. Using a cost function *cost* : $\{\mathcal{A}\} \times \mathcal{W} \times \{\mathcal{S}\} \times \mathcal{P} \rightarrow \Re$[6] the function *find_optimal_plan* : $\mathcal{P} \times \{\mathcal{A}\} \times \{\mathcal{S}\} \times \mathcal{W} \rightarrow \mathcal{P}$ calculates the "cheapest" plan $p_g^\star$ out of this set. In deciding the overall utility of the plan, not only costs for necessary ressources should be taken into account but also cooperative aspects like e.g. the confidence in partner agents.

After that, the plan $p_g^\star$ is scheduled into the global schedule $\mathcal{S}$ of the agent, thereby updating information about predecessor and successor events. A successful scheduling corresponds to a commitment of the agent to the plan; the status of the events of the plan is modified to *committed*. $p_g^\star$ must be removed from $\mathcal{P}$, and the other sets in $\mathcal{P}$ must be updated so that they only contain plans which are still correct with the new schedule $\mathcal{S}$. We thus ensure that $\mathcal{P}$ always contains

[3] Where it is unambiguous, an agent's index is omitted, i.e. $\mathcal{W} = \mathcal{W}_A$, $\mathcal{G} = \mathcal{G}_A$, etc.

[4] The formal description of the agent loop is based on a mixture of logic and programming language-like notation. As e.g. in Lisp it is assumed that failure of a function (= boolean value *false*) returns *nil* and that each value not *nil* corresponds to boolean value *true*.

[5] The executing agent can be seen as a "special" kind of resource.

[6] $\Re$ is the set of real numbers

correct plans. Algorithmically, this can be described as follows:

```
while (𝒫_g:= schedule_plan(𝒫, 𝒲_c)) do
    p*_g := find_optimal_plan(𝒫_g, min_<𝒫_g);⁷
    𝒮 := merge_events(p*_g, 𝒮) ∪ p*_g;
    𝒫 := 𝒫\{𝒫_g}
od.
```

Execution The selection of the next event to be executed is made by the function *select_event* : $\{\mathcal{S}\} \rightarrow \mathcal{S}$. From the global schedule $\mathcal{S}$, this function searches the event e for which holds: $\forall e' \in V_e : s_{e'} = done$. Let a_e be the action associated with the event e. To be executable the preconditions of the associated action have to be consistent with the actual world state $\mathcal{W}_c$. This fact is proven by the predicate *applicable* : $\mathcal{A}\times\mathcal{W}\rightarrow \{true, false\}$.

Within the execution phase those events of the agent's global schedule $\mathcal{S}$ can be executed by the function $perform : \mathcal{A}\rightarrow \{true, false\}$ for which no temporal restrictions exist because the predecessor events have already been performed. If several such events exist, they are executed in parallel (if possible) or one is selected on a non-deterministic basis. On correct execution of the action - the predicate $perform(a_e)$ yields the result value *true* - the agent's world state $\mathcal{W}_c$ changes. The world state is actualized by the function *update_state* : $\mathcal{A}\times\mathcal{W}\rightarrow \mathcal{W}$ according to the effects of the instantiated action a_e. The status s_e of the executed event e is changed by the function *mark_as_done* : $\mathcal{S}\rightarrow \mathcal{S}$ from *committed* to *done*. This part of the basic agent loop can be described by:

```
while (e:= select_event(𝒮)) do
    if (applicable(a_e, 𝒲_c) ∧ perform(a_e))
    then 𝒲_c := update_state(a_e, 𝒲_c);
    𝒮 := mark_as_done(e)
    else replan(g)⁸
od.
```

Evaluation In the evaluation phase it is examined whether all events of plan $p_g^\star$ have been executed correctly to achieve goal g, i.e. $\forall e \in p_g^\star$ must hold: $s_e = done$. To check this status, the predicate *all_events_marked_done* : $\mathcal{P}\rightarrow \{true, false\}$ is used. In other words, the agent has to monitor the execution of its scheduled events. Failed actions or actions not being executable due to un-kept commitments from partner agents are reasons why a plan can fail to achieve the goal. For that reason, the agent should consider each new observation, how it effects the actual world state $\mathcal{W}_c$ and whether the scheduled plan $p_g^\star$ is still on track to achieve the goal g.

Thus, observations - when made several times - can even result e.g. in a revision of an agent's knowledge about actions if the actions did not lead to the desired effects. The function *assimilate* : $\mathcal{O}\times\{\mathcal{A}\} \times \mathcal{W}\times\{\mathcal{S}\} \rightarrow \mathcal{W}$[9] handles both of these issues - modification of the world state and revision of the agent's knowledge. The predicate *consistent* : $\mathcal{W}\times\{\mathcal{S}\} \times \mathcal{P}\times\mathcal{G}\rightarrow \{true, false\}$ checks whether the scheduled plan $p_g^\star$ leads to the desired goal g when the agent's world state has changed.

If an agent observes the successful execution of a plan's last event, the desired goal is achieved and is deleted from the active goal list; the predicate *all_events_marked_done* yields the result *true*, and the following holds: $g \subseteq \mathcal{W}_c$. In the other case, a rescheduling process has to be initiated by the function *reschedule* : $\mathcal{W}\times\{\mathcal{S}\} \times \mathcal{P}\times\mathcal{G}\rightarrow \mathcal{S}$ which, in turn, triggers a re-planning process for goal g if it does not succeed. The evaluation sub-process can be described by:

```
while (o:= observation()) do
    𝒲_c := assimilate(o, 𝒜, 𝒲_c, 𝒮);
    if ¬ consistent(𝒲_c, 𝒮, p*_g, g) then
    reschedule(𝒲_c, 𝒮, p*_g, g)
    fi;
    if all_events_marked_done(p*_g) then
    𝒢 := 𝒢\{g}
    fi;
od.
```

3 The Cooperation Model

The formal agent model serves as the basis for the description of the cooperation model. However, agents do not always plan and act alone in a world, but must often cooperate with each other to commonly achieve their goals. Cooperation arises as several agents plan and execute their actions in a coordinated way. In MECCA, not only single-agent behavior but also cooperation is seen from a goal-based viewpoint. The basic elements of cooperation are the so-called *cooperation primitives* (Lux, Bomarius & Steiner 1992). They are a combination of *cooperation types*[10] and *cooperation objects*, which are either a goal, a plan, a task or unspecific information such as results, parameters, or other knowledge. Cooperation primitives are basic agent head functions, describing communication among agents with a specific intention. They are represented as plans, whose preconditions and effects fix the semantics/intention of the primitives and whose plan procedures consist of a call to the head function handling the communication (head-communicator-interface).

[7] Let p_1, p_2 be plans with $p_1, p_2 \in \mathcal{P}_g$. It holds: $p_1 < p_2$, iff $cost(\mathcal{A}, \mathcal{W}_c, \mathcal{S}, p_1) < cost(\mathcal{A}, \mathcal{W}_c, \mathcal{S}, p_2)$.

[8] where $e \in p_g^\star$

[9] $\mathcal{O}$ is the set of observations made by an agent due to its sensoring or communication facilities.

[10] drawn from speech-act theory (Searle 1969)

Speaker	Hearer
Pre: *Preconditions* Proc: send (coop_prim) Eff: *Effects*	Pre: *Preconditions* Proc: recv (coop_prim) Eff: *Effects*

Table 1: Generic semantic representation of cooperation primitives

3.1 Formalization of the Cooperation Model

In the extended process view of cooperating agents, local goals of an agent become *shared goals* if they are solved in cooperation with other agents. The common planning phase leads to the development of so-called *multi-agent plans*, plans which are executed by more than one agent. During the planning and scheduling process, a multi-agent plan is subdivided - as far as possible - into several single-agent plans which can be executed by the agents. The execution of single-agent tasks does not only comprise head or body actions but also communicator actions (i.e. sending cooperation primitives) to coordinate the behavior of other agents.

The semantics and pragmatics of cooperation primitives are dependent on the current phase and on the involved cooperation objects. The functions $f \in \mathcal{F}$ have to be extended to react appropriately to the receipt of a cooperation request. The decision whether a cooperation between agents is at all possible, is also made via these functions. The decision process either ends in sending an answer, in executing a body or head action or in ignoring the received message. Cooperation requests for goals are decided by the function *new_goal*, for plans by the function *find_all_plans*, for schedules by the function *schedule_plan* and for queries by the function *answer_query*.

Cooperation primitives are represented as multi-agent actions with specific preconditions and effects. The procedure (Proc:) of cooperation primitives calls the send and receive communication functions on the sender (Speaker) and receiver (Hearer) sides, respectively (cf. Table 1).

According to Table 1, the following formal semantic and pragmatic representation describes the preconditions and effects (P: and E:, resp.) with respect to the sender and receiver of the cooperation primitive. The description is split according to the agent's basic loop phases and the tackled cooperation objects. The preconditions of the cooperation primitives can be seen as applicability conditions. Together with the speech act class and the message type, they yield the semantics of the cooperation primitives. The effects of the cooperation primitives enhance the knowledge of the cooperating agents and trigger functions in the agents' basic loops. Therefore, they can be seen as the pragmatics of the cooperation primitives. In addition to the notation in Section 2.1 we assume the following:

S, H cooperating agents (S = Speaker, H = Hearer); note that agents alternate roles when issuing successive cooperation primitives, e.g. the initiator S of a PROPOSE can be the recipient of a following ACCEPT message. Furthermore, in this discussion we restrict the hearer H to be one agent, although in principle H can be a set of agents.

RC_e set of resource constraint pairs

$$((r_1, C_1), \ldots, (r_n, C_n))$$

which have to hold for event e; the consistency of an event is defined by the predicate *consistent* : $\mathcal{P}\times\mathcal{S}\times\mathcal{W}_c \times \mathcal{A} \rightarrow \{true, false\}$; the predicate yields *false*, if $RC_e \cup \mathcal{W}_c \cup \mathcal{S} \cup \mathcal{A} \Rightarrow \neg < x > \wedge < x >$; a plan p is consistent with an agent's global schedule $\mathcal{S}$ iff all events e of the plan are consistent with $\mathcal{S}$, i.e. : $\forall e \in p : consistent(\{e\}, \mathcal{S}, \mathcal{W}_c, \mathcal{A})$.

RC'_e modified constraints of an event e, where the following cases can occur: $RC'_e \Rightarrow RC_e$, i.e. RC'_e is a refinement of RC_e; $RC'_e \not\Rightarrow RC_e$, i.e. RC'_e is a modification of RC_e

$p' \Rightarrow p$ the plan p' is a refinement of the plan p, i.e. : $\forall e' \in p' : RC'_e \Rightarrow RC_e$

$p' \not\Rightarrow p$ the plan p' is a modification of the plan p, i.e. : $\exists e' \in p' : RC'_e \not\Rightarrow RC_e \vee (\exists e' \in p' \wedge e' \notin p) \vee (\exists e \in p \wedge e \notin p')$

C_g constraint set associated with the active goal g; for C_g the same cases can occur as for RC_e; a variation of the above mentioned predicate *consistent* applied to the pair (g, C_g) is used to check for consistency of goal constraints

$g' \Rightarrow g$ goal g' is a refinement of goal g, i.e. : $C'_g \Rightarrow C_g$

$g' \not\Rightarrow g$ goal g' is a modification of goal g, i.e. : $C'_g \not\Rightarrow C_g$

$\oplus (x)$ abbreviation for $\mathcal{W}_c = \mathcal{W}_c \cup \{(x)\}$

$\ominus (x)$ abbreviation for $\mathcal{W}_c = \mathcal{W}_c \backslash \{(x)\}$

$y + \mathtt{TYPE}(y)$ abbreviation for: if y is the direct result of a function, it should also be sent in a message of cooperation type TYPE to the cooperating agent

When working in cooperation with other agents, the basic loop presented in Section 2.1 becomes distributed (Steiner et al. 1993). Thus the following holds:

Goal Activation In the goal activation phase, a cooperation is instantiated if an agent can not find a local plan for the goal or finds a plan which would involve actions to be carried out by other agents. The agent can also propose a goal to a cooperating agent if it thinks that a cooperative plan is cheaper or more effective than a local plan. The proposal of a goal g is answered by the partner after examining the function new_goal. The situation is as in Figure 1.

Derived from this agent behavior, **benevolence** of an agent can be defined as follows: an agent always accept a partner's proposal (also in the phases of planning, scheduling, execution), if the proposal does not contradict its current world state.

Thus, in the cooperative context, the function new_goal with parameters $(\mathcal{W}_c, \mathcal{G})$,[11] returns the following values:[12]

$$\begin{cases} g + \texttt{ACCEPT}(g), if\ consistent((g, C_g), \mathcal{S}, \mathcal{W}_c, \mathcal{G}) \\ \{\} + \texttt{REJECT}(g), if\ \neg consistent((g, C_g), \mathcal{S}, \mathcal{W}_c, \mathcal{G}) \\ g' + \texttt{REFINE}(g, g'), where\ g' \Rightarrow g \\ g' + \texttt{MODIFY}(g, g'), where\ g' \not\Rightarrow g \end{cases}$$

Planning During the planning phase an agent creates all hypothetical plans $\mathcal{P}_g$ for a selected goal g thereby keeping them consistent with already existing hypothetical plans $\mathcal{P}$. The agent can find plans which are incomplete. These partial plans have gaps which are conceptually represented in the event-based representation by "abstract events". Finding appropriate sub-plans, i.e. refinement of an "abstract event" into a set of events, can be done in cooperation with other agents. A second kind of plans which are treated in a cooperation with other agents are those which contain "foreign events". "Foreign events" are events the agent can not execute on its own, but which it knows other agents can possibly execute. See Figure 2.

When cooperating about hypothetical plans, the partner agent can also find alternative plans which are not yet in $\mathcal{P}_g$ and propose them as hypothetical plans. To realize this cooperative aspect, *find_all_plans* $(g, \mathcal{A}, \mathcal{S}, has\_hyp\_plan(< Agent >, \mathcal{P}_g) \cup \mathcal{W}^*)$ yields the following values:[13]

$$\begin{cases} \mathcal{P}_g + \texttt{ACCEPT}(P_g), if\ \forall p \in \mathcal{P}_g : consistent(p, \mathcal{S}, \mathcal{W}_c, \mathcal{A}) \\ \{\} + \texttt{REJECT}(P_g), if\ \forall p \in \mathcal{P}_g : \neg consistent(p, \mathcal{S}, \mathcal{W}_c, \mathcal{A}) \\ \mathcal{P}'_g + \texttt{REFINE}(P_g, P'_g), where\ \forall p' \in \mathcal{P}'_g : p' \Rightarrow p \in \mathcal{P}_g \\ \mathcal{P}'_g + \texttt{MODIFY}(P_g, P'_g), where\ \exists p' \in \mathcal{P}'_g : p' \not\Rightarrow p \in \mathcal{P}_g \end{cases}$$

Scheduling In the scheduling phase, the optimal plan p^* for the goal g has to be inserted in the agents' global schedules. To select the optimal plan p^* out of the set of hypothetical plans an agent must know the costs for the plan's actions, especially for the actions which have to be executed by the cooperating agents. If the agent does not know these costs, it has to ask the cooperating agents. Within the function $find\_optimal\_plan$ it has to send an ASK message to the cooperation partners which themselves provide the agent with the requested information by a TELL message.[14] After that, the agent has sufficient knowledge to evaluate the list of hypothetical plans. It can decide on the optimal plan $p^* \in \mathcal{P}_g$ which in turn should be accepted by the cooperating partners. Only for weighty reasons - unforeseen change of a world state - should the cooperating agent be able to reject the optimal plan.

The agent proposing the optimal plan p^* "tentatively' 'commits to it. The acceptance of the optimal plan by the cooperating agent is a commitment to execute the corresponding actions, and triggers a definitive commitment by the receiving agent.

The receiving agent looks at the optimal[15] plan calling the function $find\_optimal\_plan : \{\mathcal{P}\} \times \mathcal{A} \times \{\mathcal{S}\} \times \mathcal{W} \rightarrow \mathcal{P}$, which results in

$$\begin{cases} p^* + \texttt{ACCEPT}(p^*), if\ consistent(p^*, \mathcal{S}, \mathcal{W}_c, \mathcal{A}) \\ \{\} + \texttt{REJECT}(p^*), if\ \neg consistent(p^*, \mathcal{S}, \mathcal{W}_c, \mathcal{A}). \end{cases}$$

For reasons of space, we skip the formal descriptions of PROPOSE(p^*), ACCEPT(p^*) and REJECT(p^*), which are very similar to the ones in the planning phase.

Execution Actions of a plan are executed by the agents by calling the function $perform$. Depending on whether the result res of the execution should be transferred to another agent A, the function $perform$ creates as effect a new goal $goal(knows(A, res))$ which, in turn, triggers sending a TELL message. Also, failure of an action has to be transmitted to the partner. Cooperation in the execution phase thus comprises message exchange between the cooperation partners. See Figure 3.

For reasons of space, we conclude with a short informal look at the remaining cooperation primitives REQUEST, ORDER, and ASK.

REQUEST und ORDER can be treated as special cases of PROPOSE. The difference from the cooperation primitive PROPOSE is that the recipient of a REQUEST message can only answer with an ACCEPT message or a REJECT message; the recipient of an ORDER message can only answer with an ACCEPT message. The functions *new_goal, find_all_plans, find_optimal_plan* are thus restricted in their decision about the cooperation object, e.g. *find_all_plans* $(g, \mathcal{A}, \mathcal{S}, has\_hyp\_plan(< Agent >, p) \cup request(< Agent >, p) \cup \mathcal{W}^*)$ yields

$$\begin{cases} p \in \mathcal{P}_g + \texttt{ACCEPT}, if\ consistent(p, \mathcal{S}, \mathcal{W}_c, \mathcal{A}) \\ \{\} + \texttt{REJECT}, if\ \neg consistent(p, \mathcal{S}, \mathcal{W}_c, \mathcal{A}). \end{cases}$$

---

[11] where $(has\_goal(< Agent >, g) \in \mathcal{W}_c)$

[12] Clearly, if $g' \Rightarrow g$ and $g' \in \mathcal{G}$, then g is consistent with $\mathcal{G}$. We do not go into the details in this paper, but the result of *new_goal* also depends upon the expected reply, e.g. {ACCEPT/REJECT} vs. {MODIFY/REFINE}.

[13] As with *new_goal*, exactly which value is returned depends among others upon the expected reply.It has to be noted that a given ACCEPT is not yet a commitment for execution rather that the plan proposed is consistent with its current plans. The agent commits to a plan in the scheduling phase.

[14] See next paragraph for the formal semantics of ASK and TELL.

[15] from the partner's perspective

[16] in general: $knows(self, x) \Leftrightarrow x \in W_c$.

		Speaker	Hearer
PROPOSE(g)	Pre:	$g \in \mathcal{G}$	-
	Eff:	$\oplus$ *proposed*(g, H)	$\oplus$ *has_goal*(S, g)
ACCEPT(g)	Pre:	*has_goal*(H, g) $\wedge$ $g \in \mathcal{G}$	*proposed*(g, S) $\wedge$ $g \in \mathcal{G}$
	Eff:	-	$\oplus$ *has_goal*(S, g)
REJECT(g)	Pre:	*has_goal*(H, g) $\wedge$ $g \notin \mathcal{G}$	*proposed*(g, S) $\wedge$ $g \in \mathcal{G}$
	Eff:	$\ominus$ *has_goal*(H, g)	-
MODIFY/REFINE(g, g')	Pre:	*has_goal*(H, g) $\wedge g \notin \mathcal{G}$ $\wedge g' \in \mathcal{G}$	*proposed*(g, S) $\wedge$ $g \in \mathcal{G}$
	Eff:	*proposed*(g', H)	$\oplus$ *has_goal*(S, g')

Figure 1: Cooperation Primitives for Goal Activation

		Speaker	Hearer
PROPOSE($\mathcal{P}_g$)	Pre:	$\mathcal{P}_g \in \mathcal{P}$	-
	Eff:	$\oplus$ *prop_hyp_plan*$(\mathcal{P}_g, H)$	$\oplus$ *has_hyp_plan*$(S, \mathcal{P}_g)$
ACCEPT($\mathcal{P}_g$)	Pre:	*has_hyp_plan*$(H, \mathcal{P}_g)$ $\wedge$ $\mathcal{P}_g \in \mathcal{P}$	*prop_hyp_plan*$(\mathcal{P}_g, S)$ $\wedge$ $\mathcal{P}_g \in \mathcal{P}$
	Eff:	-	$\oplus$ *has_hyp_plan*$(S, \mathcal{P}_g)$
REJECT($\mathcal{P}_g$)	Pre:	*has_hyp_plan*$(H, \mathcal{P}_g)$ $\wedge$ $\mathcal{P}_g \notin \mathcal{P}$	*prop_hyp_plan*$(\mathcal{P}_g, S)$ $\wedge$ $\mathcal{P}_g \in \mathcal{P}$
	Eff:	$\ominus$ *has_hyp_plan*$(H, \mathcal{P}_g)$	-
MODIFY/REFINE($\mathcal{P}_g, \mathcal{P}'_g$)	Pre:	*has_hyp_plan*$(H, \mathcal{P}_g)$ $\wedge$ $\mathcal{P}_g \notin \mathcal{P} \wedge \mathcal{P}'_g \in \mathcal{P}_g$	*prop_hyp_plan*$(\mathcal{P}_g, S)$ $\wedge$ $\mathcal{P}_g \in \mathcal{P}$
	Eff:	*prop_hyp_plan*$(\mathcal{P}'_g, H)$	$\oplus$ *has_hyp_plan*$(S, \mathcal{P}'_g)$

Figure 2: Cooperation Primitives for Planning

The cooperation primitive **ASK** is needed to ask another agent for some information. Information can be either hypothetical knowledge under cooperation as e.g. the current goal, the current plan etc. or world knowledge like e.g. the costs of an action.

This section has introduced the operational semantics and pragmatics of the cooperation primitives. The cooperation primitives are the basis of our cooperation model. By composing cooperation primitives, so-called cooperation methods can be build as multi-agent plans (Lux, Bomarius & Steiner 1992).

4 Related Work and Outlook

The work presented in this paper is based on embedding the philosophical notion of speech acts (Austin 1962; Searle 1969) in a planning framework (cf. (Cohen & Perrault 1979) as a seminal work in this area).

Recently, general theories of communication and coordination in human work environments have been proposed (Winograd & Flores 1986; Malone & Crowston 1991), but the main idea looking at cooperation in multi-agent environments in terms of communication structures goes back to Hewitt's pioneering work on actors and open systems (Hewitt 1977; Hewitt 1986). However, he gives no formal syntax or semantics for such communication structures. Halpern and others (Halpern & Moses 1985; Fischer & Immerman 1986) analyzed the process of communication to prove certain properties such as correctness of distributed protocols. Their work is based on a logic of common knowledge and belief, however, they missed formalizing concepts like intention, commitment, capability etc. which are important for cooperation and coordinated action. Cohen and Levesque were the first to set up a formal theory of belief, goal (choice), intention and commitment (Cohen & Levesque 1987; Cohen & Levesque 1990). This was recently criticized by Singh (Singh 1992a) as being conceptually problematic and in parts unduly complicated. Furthermore, Singh shows that their theory is false or counterintuitive in most natural scenarios. Singh himself proposed a clear formalization of intentions and know-how in a general model of logic and time (Singh 1992b). He uses this formalization to provide a new semantics for communication in multi-agent systems. This formal semantics yields a rigorous framework for establishing various design rules regarding communication among agents. Whereas Cohen/Levesque and Singh were interested in speech acts and mental states as building blocks for coordination and analysis of behavior, Shoham was the first who attempted to base a programming language in part on speech acts (Shoham 1993). This most closely resembles our work as the main emphasis is not only on a formal underpinning but also on an algorithmic design and on the implementation of cooperating agents. However, the first version of **AGENTO** lacks notions such as desires, intentions and plans and is thus less suitable for constructing high-

		Speaker	Hearer
TELL(res)	Pre:	$res \in \mathcal{W}_c \wedge goal(knows(H, res))$	-
	Eff:	$\oplus\ knows(H, res)$	$\oplus\ knows(S, res) \wedge res \in \mathcal{W}_c$[16]

Figure 3: Cooperation Primitives for Execution

level cooperative commands and agent behavior.

Our work on cooperation primitives emphasizes the semantics of the exchanged messages, thus following Singh's work, but extends it by also taking into account the cooperation context. This is achieved by a planning formalism where fundamental work on reasoning about actions has been done e.g. in (Allen 1984) and (Georgeff & Lansky 1987). Because our model deals with human-computer cooperation, it was greatly influenced by work on discourse modeling, which addresses the relationship between mental state and acting by speaking (cf. e.g. the work of Allen, Grosz, Kautz, Litman, Pollack, Sidner and others in (Cohen, Morgan & Pollack 1990)).

In summary, based upon the conceptual view of the MECCA agent and cooperation models, this paper has demonstrated a first viable approach towards a formalism tightly integrating cooperation with an agent's basic loop.

As described in (Steiner et al. 1993) cooperation primitives can be combined to form special plans called cooperation methods (such as contract net). Future work will investigate how the described semantics of cooperation primitives can be used to dynamically alter a cooperation method during the cooperative process. For example, after receiving a request for bids with a deadline in the contract net method, a potential bidder could request an extension of this deadline. The manager would then need to determine how long of an extension, if any, would be compatible with its current plan.

Further, as common within human cooperation, "merging" cooperation primitives may reduce communication overhead. For example, the classic "Shall we have lunch tomorrow" expresses not only the goal of having lunch but also a partial plan for executing this goal tomorrow.

Acknowledgment

We thank our colleagues Alastair Burt, Michael Kolb (both DFKI) and Hans Haugeneder (Siemens) for stimulating discussions and fruitful comments on the reported work. Michael Kolb did a great job by implementing most parts of the MECCA system.

References

J. F. Allen. Towards a general theory of action and time. *Artificial Intelligence*, 23:123–154, 1984.

J. L. Austin: How to Do Things with Words. Oxford University Press, 1962.

A. Burt. Abduction Based Cooperative Planning in Multi-Agent Systems. PhD Thesis. Imperial College, London, forthcoming.

P. Cohen, J. Morgan, M. Pollack (eds.). Intentions in Communication. Bradford Books at MIT Press, 1990.

P. R. Cohen, H. J. Levesque. Persistence, Intention, and Commitment, *in: M. P. Georgeff, A. L. Lansky (eds.): Reasoning about Actions and Plans*, Morgan Kaufman, 1987.

P. R. Cohen, H. J. Levesque. Intention is choice with commitment, *in: Artificial Intelligence, 42(3)*, 1990.

P. R. Cohen, C. R. Perrault. Elements of a Plan-Based Theory of Speech Acts. *in: Cognitive Science 3: 177-122*, 1979.

K. Eshghi. Abductive planning with event calculus. *in: R. A. Kowalski, K. A. Bowen (eds.): Proceedings of the 5th International Conference on Logic Programming.* 1988.

M. J. Fischer, N. Immerman. Foundations of Knowledge for Distributed Systems, *in: Proc. of the 1986 Conference on Theoretical Aspects of Reasoning about Knowledge, 171-185*, Monterey, CA., 1986.

M. P. Georgeff and A. L. Lansky (eds.). *Reasoning about Actions and Plans.* Morgan Kaufman, 1987.

B.J. Grosz, C. Sidner. Plans for discourse. *in: P. Cohen, J. Morgan, M. Pollack (eds.) Intentions in Communication.* Bradford Books at MIT Press. 1990.

C. Hewitt. Offices are Open Systems. *in: ACM Transactions on Office Information Systems, 4(3):271-287*, 1986.

C. Hewitt. Viewing Control Structures as Patterns of Passing Messages. *in: Artificial Intelligence 8, 323-364*, 1977.

J. Y. Halpern, Y. Moses. A guide to the modal logics of knowledge and belief: preliminary draft, *in: Proceedings IJCAI-85, 480-490*, Los Angeles, CA., 1985.

R. A. Kowalski, M. Sergot. A logic based calculus of events. New Generation Computing 4, 67-95, 1986.

A. Lux, F. Bomarius, D. Steiner. A Model for Supporting Human Computer Cooperation. *in: Proceedings of the AAAI Workshop on Cooperation among Heterogeneous Intelligent Systems.* San Jose, CA., July 1992.

T. W. Malone, K. Crowston. Toward an Interdisciplinary Theory of Coordination. Technical Report

CCS TR #120. Center for Coordination Science, MIT, Sloan School of Management, Cambridge, MA., 1991.

J. R. Searle. *Speech Acts*. Cambridge University Press, Cambridge, 1969.

M. Shanahan. Prediction is deduction but explanation is abduction. *in: Proceedings IJCAI-89, 1055-1060*, 1989.

Y. Shoham. Agent-oriented programming. *in: Artificial Intelligence, 60: 51-92*, 1993.

M. P. Singh. A Theory of Actions, Intentions, and Communications for Multiagent Systems. PhD thesis, University of Texas, Austin, 1992.

M. P. Singh. A Critical Examination of the Cohen-Levesque Theory of Intentions. *in: Proceedings of the 10th ECAI*, Vienna, Austria, 1992.

D. Steiner, D. Mahling, and H. Haugeneder. Human Computer Cooperative Work. *in: M. Huhns (ed.): Proc. of the 10th International Workshop on Distributed Artificial Intelligence*. MCC Technical Report Nr. ACT-AI-355-90, 1990.

D. Steiner, A. Burt, M. Kolb, C. Lerin. The Conceptual Framework of MAI^{2}L. *in: Proceedings of MAAMAW-93*, Neuchâtel, Switzerland, August 1993.

T. Winograd, F. Flores. Understanding Computers and Cognition: A New Foundation for Design. Addison Wesley, Reading, MA., 1986.

4.5 Adaptive Agency

Learning to Coordinate Actions in Multi–Agent Systems

Gerhard Weiß
Institut für Informatik, Technische Universität München
Arcisstr. 21, 8000 München 2, Germany
weissg@informatik.tu-muenchen.de

Abstract

This paper deals with learning in reactive multi–agent systems. The central problem addressed is how several agents can collectively learn to coordinate their actions such that they solve a given environmental task together. In approaching this problem, two important constraints have to be taken into consideration: the incompatibility constraint, that is, the fact that different actions may be mutually exclusive; and the local information constraint, that is, the fact that each agent typically knows only a fraction of its environment.

The contents of the paper is as follows. First, the topic of learning in multi–agent systems is motivated (section 1). Then, two algorithms called ACE and AGE (standing for "ACtion Estimation" and "Action Group Estimation", respectively) for the reinforcement learning of appropriate sequences of action sets in multi–agent systems are described (section 2). Next, experimental results illustrating the learning abilities of these algorithms are presented (section 3). Finally, the algorithms are discussed and an outlook on future research is provided (section 4).

1 Introduction

Multi–Agent Systems. In computer science and artificial intelligence the concept of multi–agent systems has influenced the initial developments in areas like cognitive modelling [Selfridge, 1959; Minsky, 1979], blackboard systems [Erman and Lesser, 1975], object–oriented programming languages [Hewitt, 1977], and formal models of concurrency [Petri, 1962; Brauer *et al.*, 1987]. Nowadays multi–agent systems establish a major research subject in distributed artificial intelligence; see [Bond and Gasser, 1988; Brauer and Hernández, 1991; Gasser and Huhns, 1989; Huhns, 1987]. The interest in multi–agent systems is largely founded on the insight that many real–world problems are best modelled using a set of agents instead of a single agent. In particular, multi–agent modelling makes it possible *(i)* to cope with natural constraints like the limitation of the processing power of a single agent or the physical distribution of the data to be processed and *(ii)* to profit from inherent properties of distributed systems like robustness, fault tolerance, parallelism and scalability.

Generally, a multi–agent system is composed of a number of agents that are able to interact with each other and the environment and that differ from each other in their skills and their knowledge about the environment. (Usually an individual agent is assumed to consist of sensor component, a motor component, a knowledge base, and a learning component.) There is a great variety in the multi–agent systems studied in distributed artificial intelligence [Huhns, 1987, foreword]. This paper deals with *reactive* multi–agent systems, where "reactive" means that the behavior and the environment of the system are strongly coupled (there is a continuous interaction between the system and its environment).

Learning. There is a common agreement that there are two important reasons for studying learning in multi–agent systems: to be able to endow artificial multi–agent systems (e.g., systems of interacting autonomous robots) with the ability to automatically improve their behavior; and to get a better understanding of the learning processes in natural multi–agent systems (e.g., human groups or societies). In a multi–agent system two forms of learning can be distinguished [Shaw and Whinston, 1989]. First, *centralized* or *isolated learning*, i.e. learning that is done by a single agent on its own (e.g. by creating new knowledge structures or by practicing motor activities). And second, *distributed* or *collective learning*, i.e. learning that is done by the agents as a group (e.g. by exchanging knowledge or by observing other agents). This paper focusses on collective learning, and the central question addressed is: "How can each agent learn which action it shall perform under which circumstances?" In answering this question, two important constraints have to be taken into consideration [Weiß, 1993a, 1993b]. First, the *incompatibility constraint*, i.e. the fact that different actions may be incompatible in the sense that the execution of one action leads to environmental changes that impair or even prevent the execution of the others. And second, the *local information constraint*, i.e. the fact that an agent typically has only local information about the actual environmental state, and this information may differ from the one another agent has; this situation is illustrated by figure 1.

Two algorithms called the *ACE algorithm* and the *AGE algorithm* for reinforcement learning in reactive multi–agent systems are described (ACE and AGE are acronyms for "ACtion Estimation" and "Action Group Estimation", respectively). These algorithms base on the action–oriented version [Weiß, 1992] of the bucket brigade learning model for classifier systems [Holland, 1986]. According to both algorithms the agents collectively learn to estimate the goal relevance of their actions and, based on their estimates, to coordinate their actions

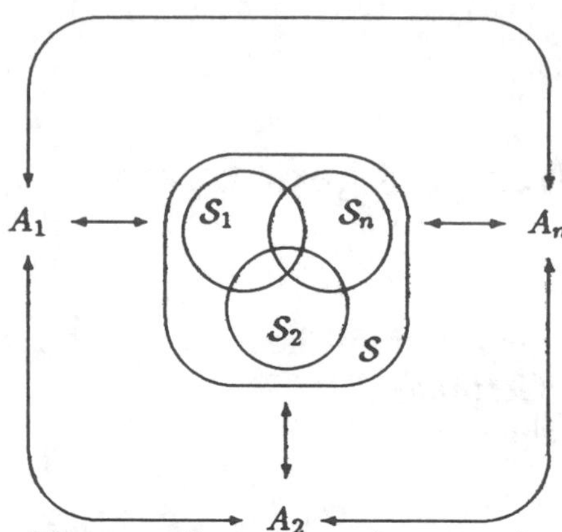

Figure 1: System—environment interaction. Each agent A_i only knows a fraction S_i of the actual environmental state S. The agents may know different aspects of the actual state, and there may be environmental aspects that none of the agents knows. The agents interact with each other as well as with the environment.

and to generate appropriate action sequences.

Notational Preliminaries. For a description of the ACE and the AGE algorithm the following elementary notation is used throughout the rest of this paper. $\mathcal{A}g = \{A_1, \ldots, A_n\}$ $(n \in \mathbb{N})$ denotes the set of all agents. $\mathcal{S}$ $(\mathcal{T}, \mathcal{U}, \ldots)$ refers to an environmental state, and $\mathcal{S}_i$ refers to the part of $\mathcal{S}$ that is known to the agent $A_i \in \mathcal{A}g$ $(\mathcal{S}_i \subseteq \mathcal{S})$; $\mathcal{S}_i$ is called *A_i's knowledge about* $\mathcal{S}$. $\mathcal{A}c_i^{poss} = \{a_i^1, \ldots, a_i^{m_i}\}$ $(m_i \in \mathbb{N})$ denotes the set of all possible actions of the agent A_i, and it is called the *action potential* of A_i. $\mathcal{A}c_i^{poss}[\mathcal{S}]$ denotes the set of all actions that A_i could carry out (identifies as "executable") in the environmental state $\mathcal{S}$ $(\mathcal{A}c_i^{poss}[\mathcal{S}] \subseteq \mathcal{A}c_i^{poss})$.

It is worth emphasizing that $\mathcal{S}_i \cap \mathcal{S}_j$ may but need not be empty, and that $\bigcup_{i=1}^{n} \mathcal{S}_i$ is not necessarily equal to $\mathcal{S}$ (i.e. the agents may have incomplete information about an environmental state, see figure 1). Similarly, if $\mathcal{S}$ and $\mathcal{T}$ are two different environmental states, then $\mathcal{S}_i \cap \mathcal{T}_i$ may but need not be empty; in particular, it may be the case that $\mathcal{S}_i = \mathcal{T}_i$ (i.e. an agent may be unable to distinguish between different environmental states).

2 Collective Learning

The ACE Algorithm. According to the ACE algorithm the learning activity of the multi-agent system results from the repeated execution of a basic *working cycle* which consists of the three activitities *action determination*, *competition*, and *credit assignment* as follows.

First, each agent $A_i \in \mathcal{A}g$ determines, in dependence on its knowledge $\mathcal{S}_i$ about the actual environmental state $\mathcal{S}$, the set $\mathcal{A}c_i^{poss}[\mathcal{S}]$ of actions that it could carry out.

Then the agents compete for the right to become active. This competition encompasses the calculation and announcement of bids and the selection of the actions that are actually carried out:

(i) Each agent A_i makes a bid $B_i^j[\mathcal{S}]$ for each of its possible actions $a_i^j \in \mathcal{A}c_i^{poss}[\mathcal{S}]$ and announces it to the other agents. The bid is calculated by

$$B_i^j[\mathcal{S}] = \begin{cases} (\alpha + \beta) \cdot E_i^j[\mathcal{S}] & : E_i^j[\mathcal{S}] > \Theta \\ 0 & : \textit{otherwise} \end{cases}, \qquad (1)$$

where α is a small constant called ***risk factor***, β is a small random number called ***noise term***, Θ is a constant called ***estimate minimum***, and $E_i^j[\mathcal{S}]$ is A_i's estimate of the goal relevance of a_i^j in dependence on its knowledge $\mathcal{S}_i$ about $\mathcal{S}$. The α indicates the fraction of $E_i^j[\mathcal{S}]$ the agent A_i is willing to risk for being allowed to perform the action a_i^j; the β introduces noise into the competition in order to avoid getting stuck into local learning minima; and the Θ helps to prevent executing useless (low–estimated) actions. (Whenever an agent A_i can execute an action under some knowledge $\mathcal{S}_i$ for the first time, it initializes the estimated goal relevance of this action with a predefined value E^{init}; afterwards the estimated goal relevance is adjusted during credit assignment as it is described below.)

(ii) After the agents have announced their bids, they select the actions to be carried out. The agent having made the highest bid is allowed to execute its corresponding action, and all agents withdraw the bids for those actions that are incompatible to this selected action; this is repeated until no further action being associated with a non–zero bid can be selected. This action selection may be formally described as follows:

- $\mathcal{A}c^{poss}[\mathcal{S}] = \bigcup_{i=1}^{n} \mathcal{A}c_i^{poss}[\mathcal{S}]$ and $\mathcal{A} = \emptyset$
- until $\mathcal{A}c^{poss}[\mathcal{S}] = \emptyset$ do
  - select $a_i^j \in \mathcal{A}c^{poss}[\mathcal{S}]$ with $B_i^j[\mathcal{S}] \geq B_k^l[\mathcal{S}]$ for all $a_k^l \in \mathcal{A}c^{poss}[\mathcal{S}]$
  - $\mathcal{A} = \mathcal{A} \cup \{a_i^j\}$
  - $\mathcal{A}c^{poss}[\mathcal{S}] = \mathcal{A}c^{poss}[\mathcal{S}] \setminus (a_i^j \cup \{a_k^l \in \mathcal{A}c^{poss}[\mathcal{S}]:$ a_k^l and a_i^j are incompatible$\}$)

The set $\mathcal{A}$ is called the actual ***activity context***, and the actions contained in in this set are called the ***actual actions*** (in state $\mathcal{S}$). (The selection requires a rational or non–egoistic behavior of the agents in the sense that none of the agents insists the execution of a low–bid or an incompatible action.)

Finally, the agents assign credit to each other by adjusting the estimates of the goal relevance of their actions. This adjustment is done according to the action–oriented bucket brigade mechanism [Weiß, 1992]. Informally, the agents reduce the estimates of their actual actions (the actual winners pay for their previlege to carry out their actions), and hand the amount of all reductions back to the agents that won the previous competition (the previous winners are rewarded for appropriately setting up the environment). The previous winners, in turn, add the received amount to the estimates of the actions they performed last. Additionally, if there is an external reward from the environment, then the agents distribute this reward among the actual actions. Formally, this can be described as follows:

(i) For each actual action $a_i^j \in \mathcal{A}$ the agent A_i modifies its estimate $E_i^j[\mathcal{S}]$ according to

$$E_i^j[\mathcal{S}] = E_i^j[\mathcal{S}] - B_i^j[\mathcal{S}] + R^{ext}/|\mathcal{A}| \ , \quad (2)$$

where $B_i^j[\mathcal{S}]$ is the corresponding action–specific bid and R^{ext} is the external reward (if there is any).

(ii) The agents sum up the bids they made for the actual actions. The resulting sum $B_{\mathcal{A}}[\mathcal{S}]$,

$$B_{\mathcal{A}}[\mathcal{S}] = \sum_{a_i^j \in \mathcal{A}} B_i^j[\mathcal{S}] \ , \quad (3)$$

is distributed in equal shares among those actions that were carried out during the previous competition. Suppose that $\mathcal{T}$ is the previous environmental state, $\mathcal{B}$ is the previous activity context, and $a_k^l \in \mathcal{B}$. Then $E_k^l[\mathcal{T}]$ is increased by

$$E_k^l[\mathcal{T}] = E_k^l[\mathcal{T}] + B_{\mathcal{A}}[\mathcal{S}] \ / \ |\mathcal{B}| \ . \quad (4)$$

This credit assigment mechanism has two major effects [Holland, 1985]: the estimates of actions that are involved in a successful sequence of action sets (i.e. a sequence that leads to external reward) increase over time and, by the way, stabilize this sequence; and conversely, the estimates of actions that are involved in an unsuccessful sequence decrease over time and destabilize this sequence.

The AGE Algorithm. The AGE algorithm retains the basic working cycle of the ACE algorithm — repeated execution of action determination, competition and credit assignment — but realizes competition in a different way. Now an agent estimates the goal relevance of an action not only in dependence on its knowledge about the actual environmental state but also in dependence on the *possible activity contexts*, and the agents do not compete for carrying out individual actions but for carrying out *groups of actions*. Generally, an activity context is a group of mutually compatible actions. Formally, the set of all possible activity contexts in an environmental state $\mathcal{S}$ is given by

$$\mathcal{A}[\mathcal{S}] = \{\mathcal{A} \subseteq \bigcup_{i=1}^{n} \mathcal{A}c_i^{poss}[\mathcal{S}] :$$
$$(\forall a_k^l, a_p^q \in \mathcal{A} : a_k^l \text{ and } a_p^q \text{ are compatible})\} \ . \quad (5)$$

The competition is organized as follows (let $\mathcal{S}$ be the actual environmental state).

(i) For each $\mathcal{A} \in \mathcal{A}[\mathcal{S}]$ the agents calculate a bid $B_{\mathcal{A}}[\mathcal{S}]$ for being allowed to carry out *all* the actions contained in $\mathcal{A}$ by

$$B_{\mathcal{A}}[\mathcal{S}] = \sum_{a_i^j \in \mathcal{A}} B_i^j[\mathcal{S}, \mathcal{A}] \quad (6)$$

with

$$B_i^j[\mathcal{S}, \mathcal{A}] = (\alpha + \beta) \cdot E_i^j[\mathcal{S}, \mathcal{A}] \ , \quad (7)$$

where α is a risk factor, β is a noise term, and $E_i^j[\mathcal{S}, \mathcal{A}]$ is A_i's estimate of the goal relevance of a_i^j in dependence on $\mathcal{S}_i$ and $\mathcal{A}$.

(ii) The activity context $\mathcal{A} \in \mathcal{A}[\mathcal{S}]$ being associated with the greatest bid $B_{\mathcal{A}}[\mathcal{S}]$ is selected, and all actions contained in this context are carried out.

Credit assignment is done analogously to the ACE algorithm (suppose that the activity context $\mathcal{A}$ has been selected):

(i) For each $a_i^j \in \mathcal{A}$ the agent A_i modifies its estimate $E_i^j[\mathcal{S}, \mathcal{A}]$ according to

$$E_i^j[\mathcal{S}, \mathcal{A}] = E_i^j[\mathcal{S}, \mathcal{A}] - B_i^j[\mathcal{S}, \mathcal{A}] + R^{ext}/|\mathcal{A}| \ . \quad (8)$$

(ii) The total bid $B_{\mathcal{A}}[\mathcal{S}]$ is distributed among the actions that were carried out in the previous competition. Suppose that $\mathcal{T}$ is the previous environmental state and that $\mathcal{B}$ is the previously selected activity context. For each $a_k^l \in \mathcal{B}$ the agent A_k increases $E_k^l[\mathcal{T}, \mathcal{B}]$ by

$$E_k^l[\mathcal{T}, \mathcal{B}] = E_k^l[\mathcal{T}, \mathcal{B}] + B_{\mathcal{A}}[\mathcal{S}] \ / \ |\mathcal{B}| \ . \quad (9)$$

Like the ACE–type adjustment does, this AGE–type adjustment of the estimates induces the stabilization of successful sequences of action sets and to the destabilization of unsuccessful ones.

3 Experimental Results

Task Domain. As a task domain the blocks world is chosen. This domain is clearly enough for experimental studies in an unknown field like collective learning, and it is well suited for illustrating the essential features of the ACE algorithm and the AGE algorithm.

The task to be solved by the agents is to transform a start configuration of blocks into a goal configuration within a limited time interval. Figure 2 shows such a task together with the actions that can be carried out by the agents. In this example each agent is assumed to have limited motor capabilities and to be specialized in moving one specific block; for instance, agent A_1 is responsible for block A, and is able to put this block on block B ($put(A, B)$) or on the ground ($put(A, \perp)$). The precondition for the application of an action $put(x, y)$ is that the blocks x and y are empty, i.e. that no other blocks are placed on them. (Note that an agent's action is quite complex and involves a number of activities; for instance, in order to put A on B the agent has to walk to A, to pick up A, to walk to B, and to place A on B.)

Each agent is assumed to have limited sensor capabilities (it only "sees" what is directly relevant to its actions) and, as a consequence, to have only local information about each environmental state. The part $\mathcal{S}_i$ of an environmental state $\mathcal{S}$ that is known to an agent A_i is specified as follows. For each of its actions $a_i^j \equiv put(x, y)$ an agent only knows *(i)* the block on which $z \in \{x, y\}$ is positioned and *(ii)* whether $z \in \{x, y\}$ is empty. The knowledge specified by *(i)* and *(ii)* is called the *environmental context* of the action $put(x, y)$.

Furthermore, two actions are considered to be incompatible if the execution of one of them changes the environmental context of the other. Formally, this can be expressed as follows: two actions, $put(x, y)$ and $put(u, v)$, are incompatible if $x \in \{u, v\}$ or $u \in \{x, y\}$ or $y = v \neq \perp$. Examples of sets of incompatible actions are $\{put(B, C), put(B, D)\}$ ("a block cannot be put on different blocks at the same time"), $\{put(D, C), put(E, C)\}$ ("two different blocks cannot be put on the same block at the same time"), and $\{put(E, B), put(B, C)\}$ ("a block cannot be put on a block which at the same time is put on another block"). It is assumed that the agents know these incompatibility constraints.

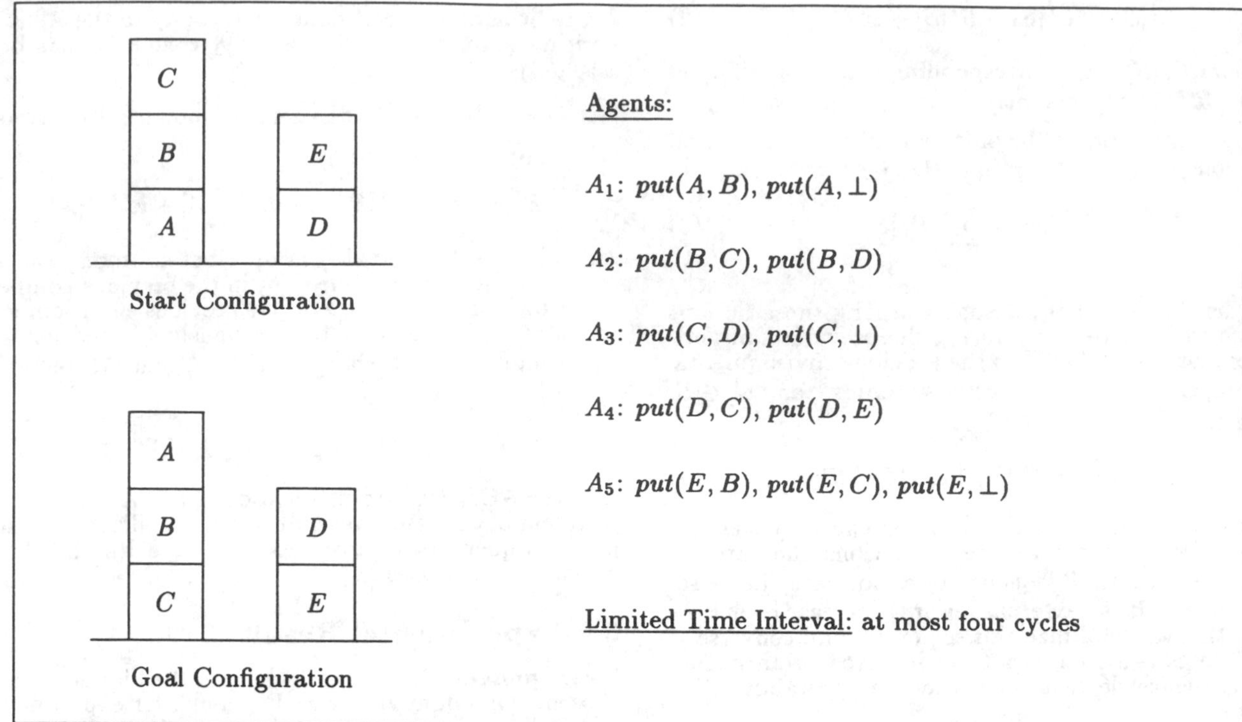

Figure 2: A blocks world task.

As it is described in section 2, learning proceeds by the repeated execution of the basic working cycle. A *trial* is defined as any sequence of at most four cycles that transforms the start into the goal configuration (successful trial), as well as any sequence of exactly four cycles that transforms the start into a non–goal configuration. At the end of each trial the start configuration is restored, and it is again presented to the agents. Additionally, at the end of each successful trial a non–zero external reward R^{ext} is provided.

Task Analysis. As a consequence of the local information constraint, an agent may be unable to distinguish between environmental states in which its actions are useful and relevant to goal attainment and environmental states in which its actions are useless. (This situation is sometimes called the *Sussman anomaly*.) Consider the environmental states $\mathcal{T}$, $\mathcal{U}$ and $\mathcal{V}$ shown in figure 3. Based on the usual blocks world notation, these three states are completely described by

$$\begin{aligned} \mathcal{T} &= \{on(A,\bot), on(B,C), on(C,\bot), on(D,E), \\ &\quad on(E,\bot), empty(A), empty(B), empty(D)\}\ , \\ \mathcal{U} &= \{on(A,\bot), on(B,D), on(D,\bot), on(C,\bot), \\ &\quad on(E,\bot), empty(A), empty(B), empty(C), \\ &\quad empty(E)\}\ and \\ \mathcal{V} &= \{on(A,\bot), on(B,C), on(C,D), on(D,\bot), \\ &\quad on(E,\bot), empty(A), empty(B), empty(E)\}\ . \end{aligned}$$

As it is easy to see, the action $put(A, B)$ of the agent A_1 is useful in state $\mathcal{T}$ but not useful in state $\mathcal{V}$. However, because A_1's local information $\mathcal{T}_1$ and $\mathcal{V}_1$ about the states $\mathcal{T}$ and $\mathcal{V}$, respectively, are identical, the agent A_1 is unable to distinguish between these two states. (Of course, an agent does not always fail to distinguish between "useful and useless states"; see e.g. the states $\mathcal{T}$ and $\mathcal{U}$. A_1's local information is given by $\mathcal{T}_1 = \mathcal{V}_1 = \{on(A,\bot), on(B,C), empty(A), empty(B)\}$ and $\mathcal{U}_1 = \{on(A,\bot), on(B,D), empty(A), empty(B)\}$.)

An analysis of the search space of the task depicted in figure 2 shows that there are only 3 successful trials of length 3, and 13 successful trials of length 4. The probability that a randomly generated sequence of applicable sets of compatible actions transforms the start into the goal configuration is 2.6 percent, if the sequence has the length 3, and 3.3 percent, if the sequence has the length 4. With that, the probability that a random trial solves the task to be learnt is less than 6 percent. (An example of a successful trial of length 3 is given by $\langle \{put(C,\bot), put(E,\bot)\}, \{put(B,C), put(D,E)\}, \{put(A,B)\} \rangle$. Note that a sequential "one–action–per–cycle" approach would require five cycles in order to implement this sequence.)

Experimental Results. A series of experiments was performed to test the ACE and the AGE algorithm. Figure 4 shows the performance profiles of the ACE algorithm, the AGE algorithm, and a random walk algorithm (i.e. an algorithm which randomly chooses an applicable set of compatible actions in each cycle). The parameter setting underlying these performance profiles was as follows: $E^{init} = R^{ext} = 1000$, $\alpha = 0.1$, $\beta \in [-\alpha/5 \ldots +\alpha/5]$ (randomly chosen), and $\Theta = 0.7 \cdot E^{init}$. (It has to be mentioned that the learning effects reported below can be observed for a broad range of parameters and are not limited to this setting.) Each data point in figure 4 reflects the average external reward per episode obtained during the previous 50 episodes. There are several important observations. First, the ACE and the AGE algorithm performed significantly better than the random walk algorithm, and they reached their maximum performance level after about 250 trials. After that, the performance levels remained almost constant; this shows that the ACE/AGE algorithms were able to learn stable sequences of action sets. Second, the perfor-

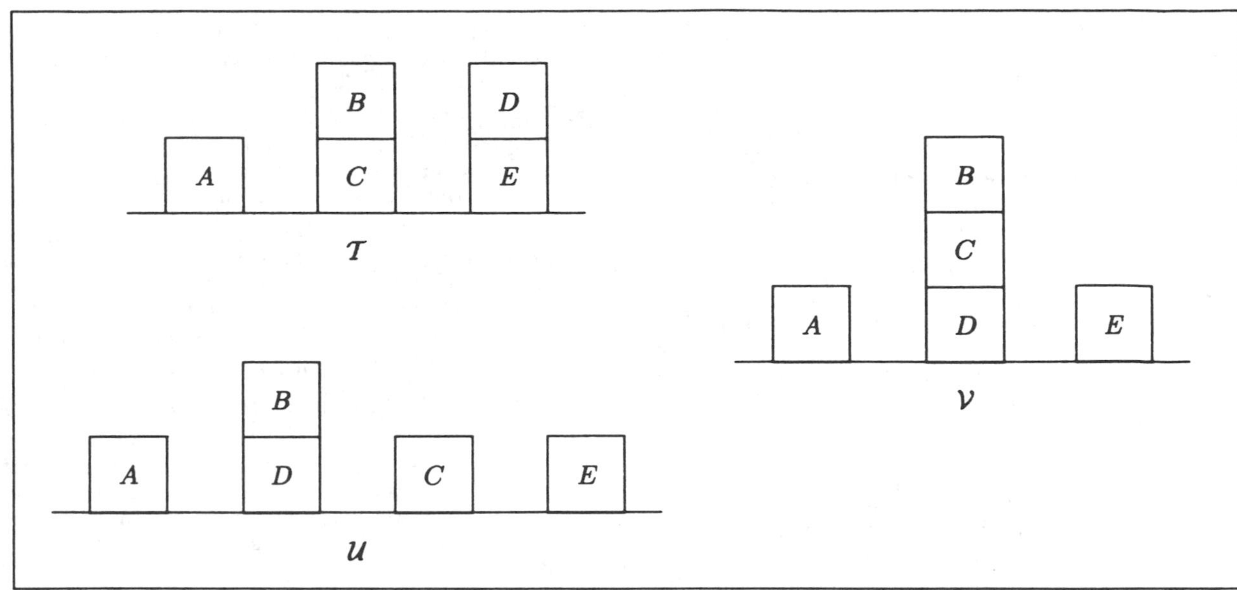

Figure 3: Blocks world states.

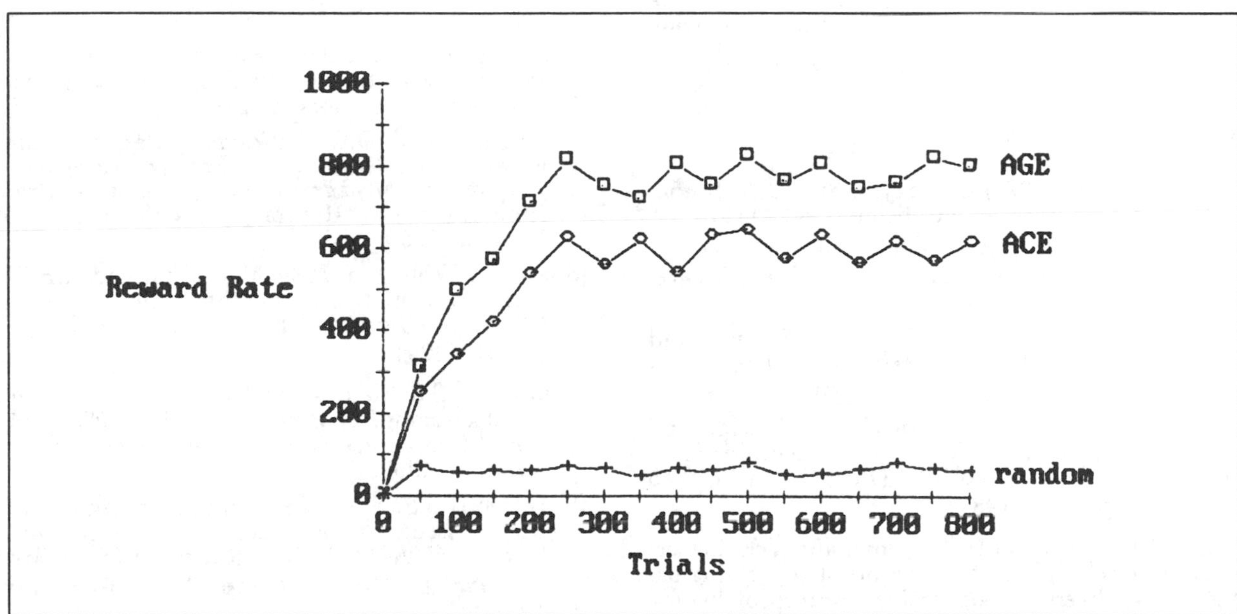

Figure 4: Performance profiles.

mance level of the AGE algorithm is clearly above the performance of the ACE algorithm. This illustrates the importance of estimating the goal relevance of an action, as it is done by the AGE algorithm, in dependence on other (concurrent) actions. The reason for that is that an action may be useful in one activity context but useless in another. However, the improved performance is achieved at the cost of higher space and computation time: whereas the costs of the ACE algorithm are proportional to the number of possible actions that can be carried out by the agents, the costs of the AGE algorithm are proportional to the number of possible action sets. And third, despite their learning abilities both algorithms remain below the possible maximal reward level (which is 1000). The reason for that is the local information constraint and, with that, the inability of the agents to distinguish between all different environmental states; as a consequence, the same estimates are used for different environmental states and necessarily remain inaccurate on some scale.

4 Concluding Remarks

This paper took the first steps towards learning to coordinate actions in multi-agent systems. Two algorithms called the ACE algorithm and the ACE algorithm for the delayed reinforcement learning of sequences of action sets were introduced and experimental results illustrating the learning abilities of these two algorithms were presented. Both algorithms are "elementary" in a twofold sense. On the one side, they make only weak demands on the cognitive abilities of the individual agents. For instance, they do not require that the agents are able to reason about the other agents' knowledge or intentions and they do not require that the agents possess complex decision making strategies. As a consequence, the algorithms are even applicable to systems that are composed of rather simple agents. On the other side, both algorithms are very flexible learning schemes that can be extended in a number of ways. For instance, they allow to incorporate high–level problem solving and planning mechanisms known from the field of single–agent systems, as well as a number of refinements that have been proposed for the bucket brigade learning model (e.g., tax payment, support and look–ahead mechanisms).

Our future research will concentrate on these possible extensions of the ACE/AGE algorithms. A major topic is the development of algorithms that implement multi–agent learning of sequences of compatible actions like the ACE/AGE algorithms do, but that better cope with the local information constraint.

Another goal of future research is the development of learning algorithms for more complex structured (e.g. hierarchically organized) multi–agent systems [Fox, 1981]. Up to now this topic has been not addressed in the field of distributed artificial intelligence. However, there are various related works from other disciplines like psychology (e.g., [Guzzo, 1982; Laughlin, 1988]) and economics (e.g., [Argyris and Schön, 1978; Galbraith, 1973; Hedberg, 1981; Sikora and Shaw, 1989]) that are likely to be very stimulating and useful for achieving this challanging goal.

References

[Argyris and Schön, 1978] C. Argyris and D.A. Schön. *Organizational learning.* Addison Wesley. 1978.

[Bond and Gasser, 1988] A.H. Bond and L. Gasser, editors. *Readings in distributed artificial intelligence.* Morgan Kaufmann. 1988.

[Brauer and Hernández, 1991] W. Brauer and D. Hernández, editors. *Verteilte Künstliche Intelligenz und kooperatives Arbeiten.* Springer. 1991.

[Brauer *et al.*, 1987] W. Brauer, W. Reisig, and R. Rozenberg, editors. *Petri nets.* Lecture Notes in Computer Science, Vol. 254 (Part I) and Vol. 255 (Part II). Springer. 1987.

[Erman and Lesser, 1975] L.D. Erman and V.E. Lesser. A multi–level organization for problem–solving using many, diverse, cooperating sources of knowledge. In *Proceedings of the 1975 International Joint Conference on Artificial Intelligence* (pp. 483–490). 1975.

[Fox, 1981] M.S. Fox. An organizational view of distributed systems. In *IEEE Transactions on Systems, Man, and Cybernetics* (Vol. SCM–11, No. 1, pp. 70–80). 1981.

[Galbraith, 1973] J.R. Galbraith. *Designing complex organizations.* Addison Wesley. 1973.

[Gasser and Huhns, 1989] L. Gasser and M.N. Huhns, editors. *Distributed artificial intelligence* (Vol. 2). Pitman. 1989.

[Guzzo, 1992] R.A. Guzzo, editor. *Improving group decision making in organizations - Approaches from theory and research.* Academic Press. 1992.

[Hedberg, 1981] B. Hedberg. How organizations learn and unlearn. In P. C. Nystrom & W. H. Starbuck (Eds.), *Handbook of organizational design* (Vol. 1, pp. 1–27). Oxford University Press. 1981.

[Hewitt, 1977] C.E. Hewitt. Viewing control structures as patterns of passing messages. *Artificial Intelligence, 8(3),* 323–364. 1977.

[Holland, 1985] J.H. Holland. Properties of the bucket brigade. In J. J. Grefenstette, editor, *Proceedings of the First International Conference on Genetic Algorithms and Their Applications* (pp. 1–7). 1985.

[Holland, 1986] J.H. Holland. Escaping brittleness: the possibilities of general–purpose learning algorithms to parallel rule–based systems. In R. S. Michalski, J. G. Carbonell, & T. M. Mitchell (Eds.), *Machine learning: an artificial intelligence approach* (Vol. 2, pp. 593–632). Morgan Kaufmann. 1986.

[Huhns, 1987] M.N. Huhns, editor. *Distributed artificial intelligence.* Pitman. 1987.

[Laughlin, 1988] P.R. Laughlin. Collective induction: group performance, social combination processes, and mutual majority and minority influence. *Journal of Personality and Social Psychology, 54(2),* 254–267. 1988.

[Minsky, 1979] M. Minsky. The society theory of thinking. In *Artificial intelligence: an MIT perspective* (pp. 423–450). MIT Press. 1979.

[Petri, 1962] C.A. Petri. *Kommunikation mit Automaten.* Schriften des Instituts für Instrumentelle Mathematik, Universität Bonn, Germany. 1962.

[Selfridge, 1959] O.G. Selfridge. Pandemonium: a paradigm for learning. In *Proceedings of the Symposium on Mechanisation of Thought Processes* (pp. 511–529). Her Majesty's Stationery Office, London. 1959.

[Shaw and Whinston, 1989] M.J. Shaw and A.B. Whinston. Learning and adaptation in distributed artificial intelligence. In (Gasser & Huhns, 1989, pp. 413–429).

[Sian, 1990] S.S. Sian. The role of cooperation in multi–agent learning. In *Proceedings of the First International Conference on Cooperating Knowledge Based Systems.* 1990.

[Sian, 1991] S.S. Sian. Extending learning to multiple agents: issues and a model for multi–agent machine learning (MA–ML). In Y. Kodratoff (Ed.), *Machine learning — EWSL-91* (pp. 440–456). Springer. 1991.

[Sikora and Shaw, 1990] R. Sikora and M. Shaw. *A double–layered learning approach to acquiring rules for financial classification.* Faculty Working Paper No. 90–1693, College of Commerce and Business Administration, University of Illinois at Urbana–Champaign. 1990.

[Weiß, 1992] G. Weiß. Learning the goal relevance of actions in classifier systems. In B. Neumann (Ed.), *Proceedings of the 10th European Conference on Artificial Intelligence* (pp. 430–434). Wiley. 1992.

[Weiß, 1993a] G. Weiß. Action selection and learning in multi–agent environments. Appears in *Proceedings of the Second International Conference on Simulation of Adaptive Behavior.* 1993.

[Weiß, 1993b] G. Weiß. Collective learning of action sequences. Appears in *Proceedings of the 13th International Conference on Distributed Computing Systems.* 1993.

Multi-Agent Reinforcement Learning: Independent vs. Cooperative Agents

Ming Tan

GTE Laboratories Incorporated
40 Sylvan Road
Waltham, MA 02254
tan@gte.com

Abstract

Intelligent human agents exist in a cooperative social environment that facilitates learning. They learn not only by trial-and-error, but also through *cooperation* by sharing instantaneous information, episodic experience, and learned knowledge. The key investigations of this paper are, "Given the same number of reinforcement learning agents, will cooperative agents outperform independent agents who do not communicate during learning?" and "What is the price for such cooperation?" Using independent agents as a benchmark, cooperative agents are studied in following ways: (1) sharing sensation, (2) sharing episodes, and (3) sharing learned policies. This paper shows that (a) additional sensation from another agent is beneficial if it can be used efficiently, (b) sharing learned policies or episodes among agents speeds up learning at the cost of communication, and (c) for joint tasks, agents engaging in partnership can significantly outperform independent agents although they may learn slowly in the beginning. These tradeoffs are not just limited to multi-agent reinforcement learning.

1 INTRODUCTION

In human society, learning is an essential component of intelligent behavior. However, each individual agent need not learn everything from scratch by its own discovery. Instead, they exchange information and knowledge with each other and learn from their peers or teachers. When a task is too big for a single agent to handle, they may cooperate in order to accomplish the task. Examples are common in non-human societies as well. For example, ants are known to communicate about the locations of food, and to move objects collectively.

In this paper, I use reinforcement learning to study intelligent agents (Mahadevan & Connel 1991, Lin 1991, Tan 1991). Each reinforcement-learning agent can incrementally learn an efficient decision policy over a state space by trial-and-error, where the only input from an environment is a delayed scalar reward. The task of each agent is to maximize the long-term discounted reward per action.

Although most work on reinforcement learning has focused exclusively on single agents, we can extend reinforcement learning straightforwardly to multiple agents if they are all independent. They together will outperform any single agent due to the fact that they have more resources and a better chance of receiving rewards. Recently, Whitehead (1991) has also demonstrated the potential benefit of multiple "complete-observing" cooperative agents over a single agent. However, the more practical study is to compare the performance of n independent agents with the one of n cooperative agents and to identify their tradeoffs. Yet, no such study has been done previously. It is the subject of this paper.

How can reinforcement-learning agents be cooperative? I identify three ways of cooperation. First, agents can communicate instantaneous information such as sensation, actions, or rewards. Second, agents can communicate episodes that are sequences of (sensation, action, reward) triples experienced by agents. Third, agents can communicate learned decision policies. This paper presents three case studies of multi-agent reinforcement learning involving such cooperation and draws some related conclusions that are not limited to multi-agent reinforcement learning. The main thesis of this paper is that *if cooperation is done intelligently, each agent can benefit from other agents' instantaneous information, episodic experience, and learned knowledge.*

Specifically, in case study 1, I investigate the ability of an agent to utilize sensation input provided by another agent. I demonstrate that sensory information from another agent is beneficial only if it is relevant and sufficient for learning. I show one instance where cooperative agents were not able to efficiently learn decision policies (compared with independent agents) due to insufficient sensation from other agents.

Case study 2 focuses on sharing learned policies and episodes. I show that in these cases cooperation speeds up learning, but does not affect asymptotic performance. I also provide upper bounds on their communication costs incurred during cooperation. While sharing policies is limited to homogeneous agents, sharing episodes can be used by heterogeneous agents as long as they can interpret episodes.

Case study 3 concerns joint tasks which require more than one agent in order to be accomplished. I demonstrate that cooperative agents who sense their partners or communicate their sensations with each other can learn to perform the tasks at a level that independent agents cannot reach even though they start out slowly. If a cooperative agent must sense other agents, the size of its state space can increase exponentially in terms of the number of involved agents.

Ideally, intelligent agents would learn when to cooperate and which cooperative method to use to achieve maximum gain. This paper is a starting point for the examination of these fundamental open questions.

2 RELATED WORK

Several multi-agent learning systems have been developed for speed and/or accuracy. GTE's ILS system (Silver et. al 1990) integrates heterogeneous (inductive, search-based, and knowledge-based) learning agents by a central controller through which the agents critique each other's proposals. The MALE system (Sian 1991) uses an interaction board (similar to a blackboard) to coordinate different learning agents. DLS (Shaw & Sikora 1990) adopts a distributed problem-solving approach to rule induction by dividing data among inductive learning agents. Recently, Chan and Salvatore (1993) advocate meta-learning for distributed learning. Most of these systems deal with inductive learning from examples, rather than autonomous learning agents that involve perception and action. One exception to this is the complexity analysis of cooperative mechanisms in reinforcement learning by Whitehead (1991). His main theorem is that n reinforcement-learning agents who can observe everything about each other can decrease the required learning time at a rate that is $\Omega(1/n)$.

Recent work in the field of *Distributed Artificial Intelligence* (DAI) (Gasser & Huhns 1989) has addressed the issues of organization, coordination, and cooperation among agents, but not for multi-agent learning. In the terms of DAI, my case studies 1 and 2 explore reinforcement learning in *collaborative reasoning systems* (Pope et. al 1992) which are concerned with coordinating intelligent behavior across multiple self-sufficient agents, and my case study 3 studies reinforcement learning in *distributed problem-solving systems* (Durfee 1988, Tan & Weihmayer 1992) in which a particular problem is divided among agents that cooperate and interact to develop a solution. Unlike DAI, this work does not deal with issues such as communication language, agent beliefs, resource constraint, and negotiation. It also mainly focus on homogeneous agents.

3 REINFORCEMENT LEARNING

Reinforcement learning is an on-line technique that approximates the conventional optimal control technique known as *dynamic programming* (Bellman 1957). The external world is modeled as a discrete-time, finite state, Markov decision process. Each action is associated with a reward. The task of reinforcement learning is to maximize the long-term discounted reward per action.

In this study, each reinforcement-learning agent uses the one-step *Q-learning* algorithm (Watkins 1989). Its learned decision policy is determined by the state/action value function, Q, which estimates long-term discounted rewards for each state/action pair. Given a current state x and available actions a_i, a Q-learning agent selects each action a with a probability given by the Boltzmann distribution:

$$p(a_i|x) = \frac{e^{Q(x,a_i)/T}}{\sum_{k \in actions} e^{Q(x,a_k)/T}} \quad (1)$$

where T is the temperature parameter that adjusts the randomness of decisions. The agent then executes the action, receives an immediate reward r, moves to the next state y.

In each time step, the agent updates $Q(x,a)$ by recursively discounting future utilities and weighting them by a positive learning rate β:

$$Q(x,a) \leftarrow Q(x,a) + \beta(r + \gamma V(y) - Q(x,a)) \quad (2)$$

Here γ $(0 \leq \gamma < 1)$ is a discount parameter, and $V(x)$ is given by:

$$V(x) = \max_{b \in actions} Q(x,b) \quad (3)$$

Note that $Q(x,a)$ is updated only when taking action a from state x. Selecting actions stochastically by (1) ensures that each action will be evaluated repeatedly.

As the agent explores the state space, its estimate Q improves gradually, and, eventually, each $V(x)$ approaches: $E\{\sum_{n=1}^{\infty} \gamma^{n-1} r_{t+n}\}$. Here r_t is the reward received at time t due to the action chosen at time $t-1$. Watkins and Dayan (1992) have shown that this Q-learning algorithm converges to an optimal decision policy for a finite Markov decision process.

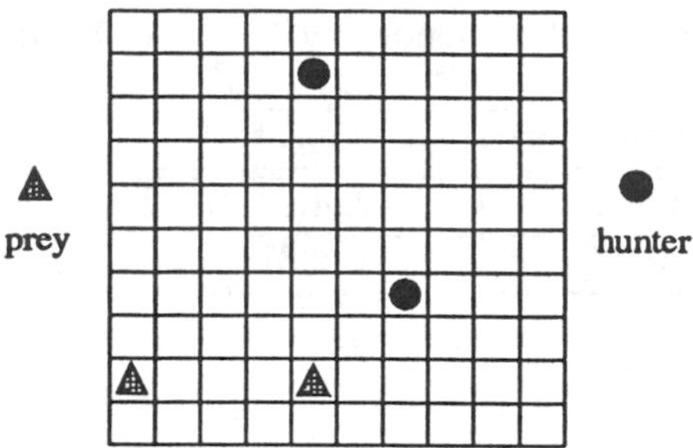

Figure 1: A 10 by 10 grid world.

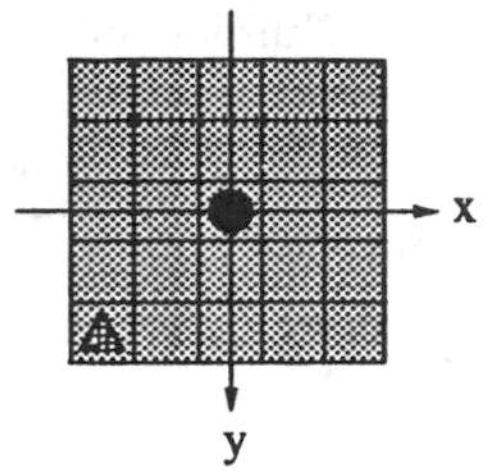

A perceptual state represented by (-2, 2)

Figure 2: A visual field of depth 2.

4 TASK DESCRIPTION

All the tasks considered in this study involve hunter agents seeking to capture randomly-moving prey agents in a 10 by 10 grid world, as shown by Figure 1. On each time step, each agent (hunter or prey) has four possible actions to choose from: moving up, down, left, or right within the boundary. Initially, hunters also make random moves as they have equal Q values. More than one agent can occupy the same cell. A prey is captured when it occupies the same cell as a hunter (in case study 1 and 2) or when two hunters either occupy the same cell as the prey or are next to the prey (in case study 3). Upon capturing a prey, the hunter or hunters involved receive +1 reward. Hunters receive −0.1 reward for each move when they do not capture a prey. Each hunter has a limited visual field inside which it can locate prey accurately. Figure 2 shows a visual field of depth 2. Each hunter's sensation is represented by (x, y) where x (y) is the relative distance of the closest prey to the hunter according to its x (y) axis. For example, (-2, 2) is a perceptual state when the closest prey is in the lower left corner of the hunter's visual field (see Figure 2). If two prey are equally close to a hunter, only one of them (chosen randomly) will be sensed. If there is no prey in sight, a unique default sensation is used.

Each run of each experiment consisted of a sequence of trials. In the first trial of each run, all agents were given a random location. Afterwards, each trial began with only rewarded hunters in random locations. Each trial ended when the first prey was captured. Each run was given a sufficient number of trials until the decision policies of hunters converged (i.e., the performance of hunters stabilized). I measured the average number of time steps per trial in *training* where actions were selected by the Boltzmann distribution, at intervals of every 50 trials. After convergence, I also measured the average number of time steps per trial in *test* where actions were selected by the highest Q value, over at least 1000 trials. Results were averaged over at least 5 runs.

The Q-learning parameters were set at $\beta = 0.8$, $\gamma = 0.9$, and $T = 0.4$. These values are reasonable for these tasks. Task parameters include the number of prey, the number of hunters, and the hunters' visual-field depth.

Without learning, hunters move randomly with baseline performances for four different prey/hunter tasks given in Table 1. The table shows the average number of steps for random hunters to capture a prey over 200 trials. I also tested the performances of independently learning hunters for the corresponding tasks. Table 1 gives their average number of steps to capture a prey in training calculated after a sufficient number of trials, where the hunters' visual-field depth was 4. Clearly, learning hunters significantly outperform random hunters. The real question is whether or not cooperation among learning hunters can further improve their performance.

5 CASE 1: SHARING SENSATION

First, I study the effect of sensation from another agent. To isolate sensing from learning, I choose the one-prey/one-hunter task and add a scouting agent that cannot capture prey. Later I extend this concept to hunters that perform both scouting and hunting. I demonstrate that sensory information from another (scouting) agent is beneficial if the information is relevant and sufficient for learning.

The scout makes random moves. At each step, the scout send its action and sensation back to the hunter. Assume that the initial relative location between the scout and the hunter is known. Therefore, the hunter can incrementally update the scout's relative location and also compute the location of the prey sensed by the scout. For example, if the relative locations of a prey to the scout (known) and the scout to the hunter (sensed) are (-2, 2) and (2, 5) respectively, then the relative location of the prey to the hunter is (0, 7). To keep the same dimension of a state representation (i.e., still use (x, y)), I combine sensation inputs from the hunter and the scout as follows: use the hunter's sensation first, if the hunter cannot sense any prey, then use the scout's sensation.

Table 2 shows the average numbers of steps to capture

Table 1: Average Number of Steps to Capture a Prey: Random vs. Independently Learning Hunters.

N-of-prey/N-of-hunters	1/1	1/2	1/2 (joint task)	2/2 (joint task)
Random hunters	123.08	56.47	354.45	224.92
Learning hunters	25.32	12.21	119.17	100.61

Table 2: Scouting vs. No Scouting.

Hunter Visual Depth	Scout Visual Depth	Average Steps to Capture a Prey	
		Training	Test
2	no scouting	47.14 (±1.28)	49.49 (±1.60)
2	2	46.33 (±1.39)	42.91 (±1.48)
2	3	39.78 (±1.06)	32.08 (±1.22)
2	4	32.67 (±1.03)	25.07 (±0.89)

a prey in training after 2000 trials and the ones in test after convergence with or without a scout. Their 90% confidence intervals calculated by a *t-test* are listed in the parentheses. The hunter with a scout took fewer steps in both training and test to capture a prey than the one without.[1] As the scout's visual-field depth increases, the difference in their performances becomes larger. This observation held when the hunter's visual-field depth was given other values (other than 2). Based on this state representation, the maximum number of perceptual states in the 10 by 10 grid world is 442 ($= (2\times10+1)^2+1$). After introducing a scout, the size of the state space for the hunter was effectively increased from 26 ($= 5^2 + 1$) to 442. This increase was traded for extra sensory information and paid off in the end. In fact, when the scout's visual-field depth was 4, no obvious slowdown was observed after only 50 trials.

Once establishing the benefit of additional sensory information from a scout, I then extended this concept to the one-prey/two-hunter task with each hunter acting as a scout for the other hunter. Table 3 gives the similar measures for both independent and mutual-scouting agents. Their 90% confidence intervals calculated by a *t-test* and the resulting *t-test* comparisons within each pair are given in the parentheses. As their visual-field depth increases, (a) both independent and mutual-scouting agents take fewer and fewer steps to capture a prey; (b) mutual-scouting agents gradually outperform independent agents; and (c) the advantage of mutual-scouting agents over independent agents shows up sooner in test than in training. As an example, when the visual-field depth was 4, mutual-scouting hunters took, on the average, 8.83 steps in test to capture a prey comparing with 11.53 steps for independent hunters. However, when the visual-field depth was limited to 2, sharing sensory information hindered *training*, because a short-sighted scouting hunter could not stay with a prey long enough for the other hunter to learn to catch up with the prey. This suggests that sensory information from another agent should be used prudently, and extra, insufficient information can interfere with learning. Scouting also incurs communication cost. The information communicated from a mutual-scouting agent to another agent per step is bounded by the size (in bits) of its sensation and action representation. In this experiment, it is $2\log_2(2V_{depth}+1)+2$ where V_{depth} is the visual-field depth.

[1] Although the average steps of the hunter in training with a scout whose visual-field depth was 2 (= 46.33) is less than the one of the hunter without a scout (= 47.14), the difference is not significant according to the *t-test*.

6 CASE 2: SHARING POLICIES OR EPISODES

Assume that agents do not share sensation. If each agent is adequate to accomplish a task (e.g., each hunter can capture a prey by itself), is cooperation among agents still useful? I studied several ways of sharing learned policies and episodes in the one-prey/two-hunter task. Hunters can either (1) use the same decision policy or (2) exchange their individual policies at various frequencies. Episodes can be exchanged (a) among peer hunters or (b) between peer and expert hunters. I will show that such cooperative agents can speed up learning, measured by the average number of steps in training, even though they will eventually reach the same asymptotic performance as independent agents. This study presents the experimental results when the hunters' visual-field depth is

Table 3: Two Independent Agents vs. Two Mutual-Scouting Agents.

	Visual Depth	Average Steps to Capture a Prey	
		Training	Test
Independent agents	2	20.38 (±0.57)	24.04 (±1.00)
Mutual-scouting agents	2	25.20 (±0.79) (worse)	24.52 (±1.24) (same)
Independent agents	3	14.65 (±0.53)	16.04 (±0.56)
Mutual-scouting agents	3	14.02 (±0.75) (same)	12.98 (±0.65) (better)
Independent agents	4	12.21 (±0.65)	11.53 (±0.61)
Mutual-scouting agents	4	11.05 (±0.56) (better)	8.83 (±0.78) (better)

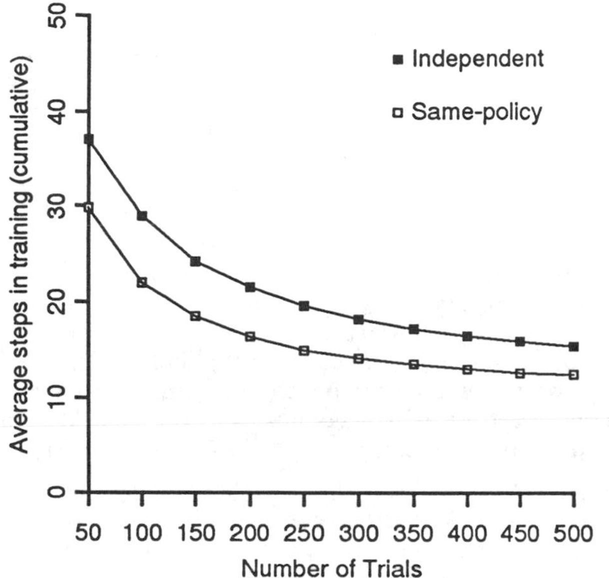

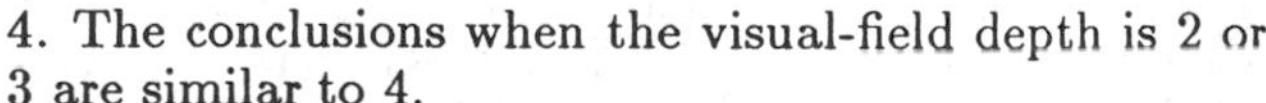

Figure 3: Independent agents vs. same-policy agents.

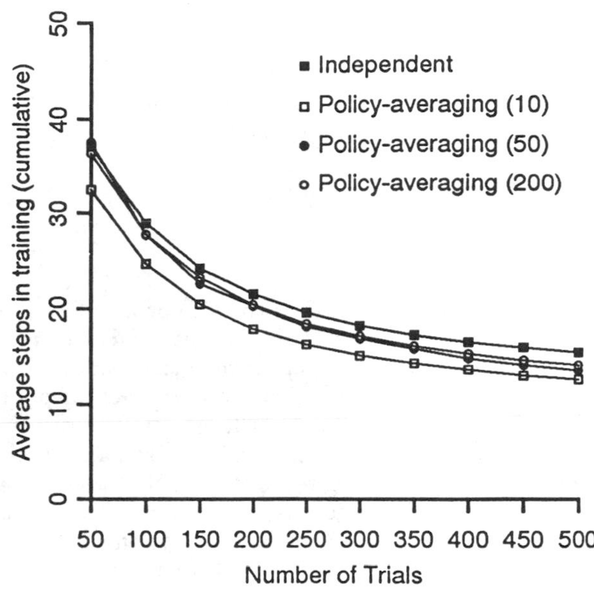

Figure 4: Independent agents vs. policy-averaging agents.

4. The conclusions when the visual-field depth is 2 or 3 are similar to 4.

One simple way of cooperating is that hunters use the same decision policy. Although each hunter updates the same policy independently, the rate of updating the policy is multiplied by the number of hunters per step. Figure 3 shows that when two hunters used the same policy, they converged much quicker than two independent hunters did. The average information communicated by each same-policy hunter per step is bounded by the number of the bits needed to describe a sensation, an action and a reward.[2] In this experiment, it is $2\log_2(2V_{depth} + 1) + 3$.

If agents perform the same task, their decision policies during learning can differ because they may have explored the different parts of a state space. Two hunters can complement each other by exchanging their policies and use what the other agent had already learned for its own benefit. Assume that each agent can simultaneously send its current policy to other agents, I adopted the following policy assimilation: agents average their policies at certain frequency. Figure 4 shows the performance results when two hunters averaged their policies at every 10 steps, 50 steps, or 200 steps. All of them converged quicker than two independent hunters. One interesting observation is that when the visual-field depth was 4, the best frequency was every 10 steps (see Figure 4) while when the visual-field depth was 2, the best frequency was every 50 steps (not shown here). In general, the information communicated by each policy-exchanging hunter per step is bounded by $(N-1) \cdot P \cdot F$ where N is the number

[2] I assume that only one agent keeps a decision policy. At each step, the rest of the involved agents send their current sensation to the policy-keeping agent, receive corresponding actions in return, and then send the rewards of their actions back to the policy-keeping agent.

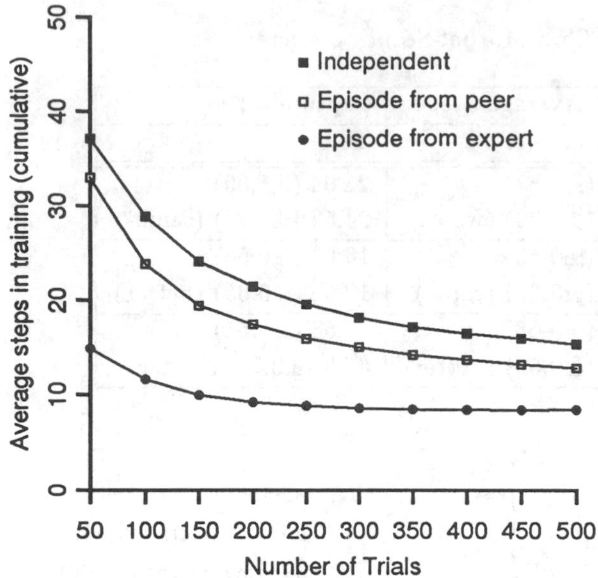

Figure 5: Independent agents vs. episode-exchanging agents.

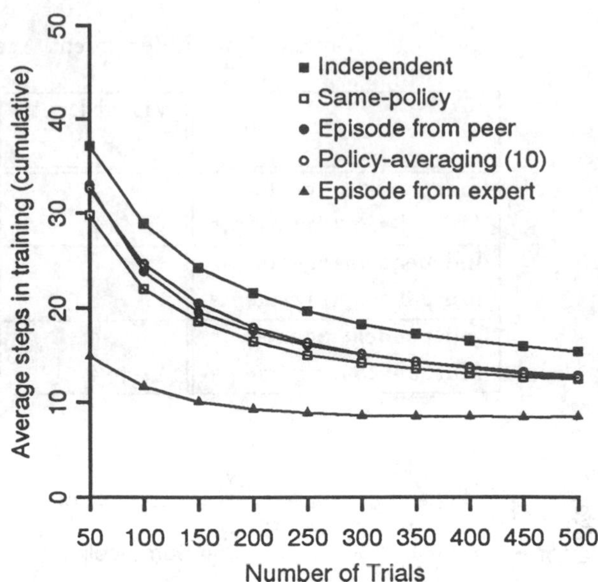

Figure 6: Summary.

of participating hunters, P is the size of a policy (i.e., number of perceptual states $\times$ number of actions $\times$ number of bits needed to represent a sensation, an action and a Q value), and F is the frequency of policy exchanging. When P or F is large, communication can be costly. On the other hand, unlike same-policy agents, a policy-exchanging agent can be selective in assimilating another agent's policy. For example, an agent could adopt another agent's decision only when it did not have confidence in certain actions.

Instead of sharing learned knowledge such as a policy, agents can share their episodes. An episode is a sequence of (sensation, action, reward) triples experienced by an agent. I used the following episode exchanging: when a hunter captured a prey, the hunter transferred its entire solution episode to the other hunter. The other hunter then "mentally replayed" the episode forward to update its own policy. As a result, two hunters doubled their learning experience. The middle curve in Figure 5 shows the speedup in training of two hunters after exchanging their episodes. The average information communicated by each episode-exchanging hunter per step is bounded by $(N-1) \cdot E$ where E is the number of bits needed to represent a sensation, an action, and a reward ($E = 2\log_2(2V_{depth}+1)+3$ in this experiment). In addition to the flexibility of assimilating episodes, exchanging episodes can be used by heterogeneous reinforcement-learning agents as long as they can interpret episodes (e.g., hunters can have different visual-field depths). To demonstrate this point, I let two hunters learn from an expert hunter that always moves towards the prey using the shortest path. Figure 5 shows significant improvement for the two novice hunters when the episodes they received were from an expert hunter (see the bottom curve). Note that an expert hunter could be just another hunter who has already learned hunting skills. This result demonstrates another benefit of learning in a cooperative society where novices can learn quickly from experts by examples (Lin 1991, Whitehead 1991).

Figure 6 summarizes the experimental results of this case study. Generally speaking, during the early phase of training, cooperative learning outperforms independent learning, and learning from an expert outperforms both. Their differences in performance are statistically significant according to *t-tests*. However, among different ways of cooperation (excluding learning from an expert), there is no conclusive evidence that one performs better than the others. In terms of the average information communicated, if the number of participating agents is limited to 2, exchanging episodes is comparable to using the same policy. Exchanging policy is plausible if the size of a policy is small and the proper frequency of policy exchanging can be determined.

7 CASE 3: ON JOINT TASKS

In the previous two case studies, each hunter can capture prey by itself. Here, I study joint tasks where a prey can only be captured by two hunters who either occupy the same cell as the prey as or are next to the prey. Hunters cooperate by either passively observing each other or actively sharing their sensations and locations. I demonstrate that cooperative agents can learn to perform the joint task significantly better than independent agents although they start slowly.

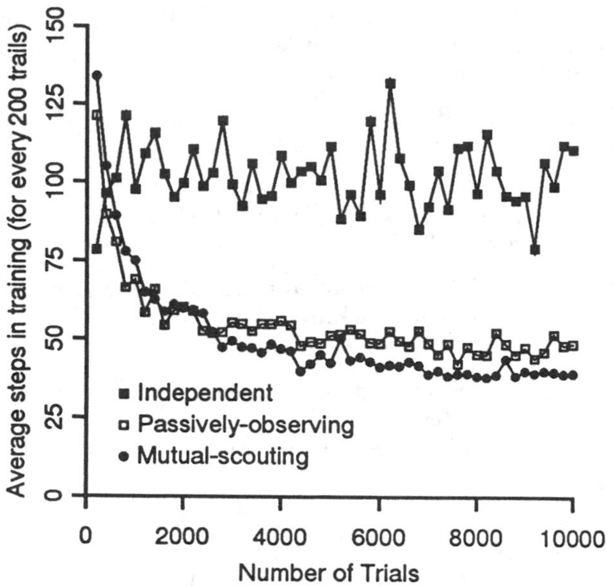

Figure 7: Typical runs for the 2-prey/2-hunter joint task.

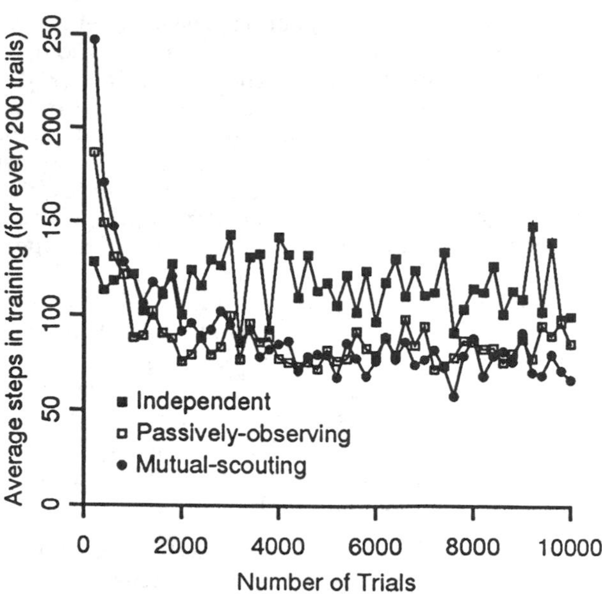

Figure 8: Typical runs for the 1-prey/2-hunter joint task.

Assume that the hunters' visual-field depth is 4 (again, the conclusions are similar when the visual-field depth is 2 or 3). Let us first consider the two-prey/two-hunter joint task. When two independent hunters were given this task, each hunter tended to learn to approach a prey directly. When both hunters approached the same prey, they succeeded and received rewards. When they chased two different prey, they failed and were penalized. As training continued, their performance fluctuated noticeably around the level of taking, on the average, 101 steps to capture a prey (see the top curve in Figure 7).

The problem with independent hunters is that they ignore each other. They cannot distinguish the situation where another hunter is nearby from the one far away. If each hunter can also sense the other hunter, cooperative behavior can emerge from greedy learning hunters. To address this problem, I extended the sensation of a hunter to two pairs $\{(x_{prey}, y_{prey})(x_{ptn}, y_{ptn})\}$ where (x_{prey}, y_{prey}) is the relative location ($\leq$ visual-field depth) between a prey and the hunter, and (x_{ptn}, y_{ptn}) between a partner and the hunter. Note that the state space is increased exponentially in terms of the number of agents. A large state space means more state exploration for a hunter, and slower learning. Nevertheless, although starting slowly, such passively-observing hunters began to overtake independent hunters soon after 400 trials, and eventually reduced the average number of steps to only 49 (see the middle curve in Figure 7).

Two hunters can cooperate passively by observing each other in addition to prey. Given the encouraging results from case study 1, I proceeded to let hunters also actively share their sensory information. This means that the state space is further enlarged although there is no increase in the dimension of a state representation. This enlargement made initial learning even slower than passively-observing hunters. Yet, mutual-scouting hunters soon outperformed passively-observing agents after about 1400 trials, and settled down at average 39 steps in training (see the bottom curve in Figure 7). The average number of steps per trial in test for independent, passively-observing and mutual-scouting hunters are 49, 42 and 34, respectively.

People may wonder what would happen if there was only one prey in the joint task. Independent hunters might do well because both hunters can just learn to approach the prey directly. This, however, is not the case. By knowing where its partner is, a hunter can learn better approach (herding) patterns. Figure 8 shows the typical runs of the three types of hunters when there was only one prey. As you can see, independent agents, passively-observing agents, and mutual-scouting agents settled down at average 116, 84, and 76 steps in training, respectively. Although it is difficult to analyze the hunters' specific approach patterns, the fact that cooperative hunters outperformed independent hunters by at least 32 steps per trial suggests the existence of such patterns.

8 CONCLUSIONS AND FUTURE WORK

This paper demonstrates that reinforcement-learning agents can learn cooperative behavior in a simulated social environment. Although this paper's results are based on simulated prey/hunter tasks, I believe the conclusions can be applied to cooperation among autonomous learning agents in general. This paper identifies three ways of agent cooperation, i.e., by communicating instantaneous information, episodic experience, and learned knowledge. Specifically, cooperative reinforcement-learning agents can learn faster and converge sooner than independent agents via sharing learned policies or solution episodes. Cooperative agents can also broaden their sensation via mutual scouting, and can handle joint tasks via sensing other partners. On the other hand, this paper also shows that extra sensory information can interfere with learning, sharing knowledge or episodes comes with a communication cost, and it takes a larger state space to learn cooperative behavior for joint tasks. These tradeoffs must be taken into consideration for autonomous and cooperative learning agents.

This research raises several important issues of multiagent reinforcement learning. First, sensation must be selective because the size of a state space can increase exponentially in terms of the number of involved agents. One heuristic used here is that each hunter only pays attention to the nearest prey (or hunter). Can such selective sensation strategies be learned? Second, on a related issue, one needs to use generalization techniques to reduce a state space and improve performance for complex, noisy tasks. Third, learning opportunities are hard to come by for nontrivial cooperative behavior. If a prey were smart enough to know how to escape, it could take a long time for hunters to get enough learning experience. How can learning be more focused (e.g., by learning from a teacher)? Fourth, information exchanging among agents incurs communication costs. Can agents learn to communicate? This learning task gets complicated when the content of communication can be instantaneous information, episodic experience, and learned knowledge. Fifth, other cooperative methods need to be explored. For example, what if hunters share their action intentions to avoid collision, or share their rewards to sustain hunger? Finally, can homogeneous agents learn to have job division and to specialize differently? Can heterogeneous agents (such as scouting agents vs. blind hunting agents) learn to cooperate? These are directions for future work.

Acknowledgments

I am grateful to Rich Sutton, Steve Whitehead, and Chris Matheus for useful discussions and careful comments. I would like to thank Shri Goyal for his support of this research.

References

Bellman, R. E. (1957). *Dynamic Programming.* Princeton University Press, Princeton, NJ.

Chan, P. K. & Salvatore, J. S. (1993). Experiments on parallel and distributed learning by meta-learning. Submitted for publication.

Durfee, E. H. (1988). *Coordination of Distributed Problem Solvers*, Kluwer Academic Publishers, Boston.

Gasser, L. & Huhns, M. (1989). *Distributed Artificial Intelligence, 2*, (eds.) Pitman, London.

Lin, L. J. (1991). Programming robots using reinforcement learning and teaching. In Proceedings of AAAI-91. (pp. 781-786).

Mahadevan, S. & Connel, J. (1991). Automatic programming of behavior-based robots using reinforcement learning. In Proceedings of AAAI-91. (pp. 768-773).

Pope, R., Conry, S., & Meyer, R. (1992). Distributing the planning process in a dynamic environment. Proceedings of the 11th International Workshop on Distributed AI, Glen Arbor, MI.

Shaw, M. J. & Sikora, R. (1990). A distributed problem-solving approach to rule induction: learning in distributed artificial intelligence systems. Technical Report, CMU-RI-TR-90-28, The Robotics Institute, Carnegie Mellon University.

Sian, S. S. (1991). Extending learning to multiple agents: issues and a model for multi-agent machine learning. In Y. Kodratoff (Ed.), *Machine Learning – EWSL 91.* Springer-Verlag, pp. 440-456.

Silver, B., Frawely, W., Iba, G., Vittal, J., & Bradford, K. (1990). A framework for multi-paradigmatic learning. In Proceedings of the Seventh International Conference on Machine Learning, 348-358. Austin, Texas.

Tan, M. (1991). Cost-sensitive reinforcement learning for adaptive classification and control. In Proceedings of AAAI-91. (pp. 774-780).

Tan, M. & Weihmayer, R. (1992). Integrating agent-oriented programming and planning for cooperative problem solving. Proceedings of the AAAI-92's Workshop on Cooperation among Heterogeneous Intelligent Agents, San Jose, CA,

Watkins, C. J. C. H. (1989). Learning With Delayed Rewards. Ph.D. thesis, Cambridge University Psychology Department.

Watkins, C. J. C. H. & Dayan, P. (1992) Technical Note: Q-Learning. *Machine Learning*, 8(3/4), Kluwer Academic Publishers.

Whitehead, S. D. (1991). A complexity analysis of cooperative mechanisms in reinforcement learning. In Proceedings of AAAI-91. (pp. 607-613)

Learning policies for partially observable environments: Scaling up

Michael L. Littman
mlittman@cs.brown.edu

Anthony R. Cassandra
arc@cs.brown.edu

Leslie Pack Kaelbling
lpk@cs.brown.edu

Department of Computer Science
Brown University
Providence, RI 02912-1910

Abstract

Partially observable Markov decision processes (POMDP's) model decision problems in which an agent tries to maximize its reward in the face of limited and/or noisy sensor feedback. While the study of POMDP's is motivated by a need to address realistic problems, existing techniques for finding optimal behavior do not appear to scale well and have been unable to find satisfactory policies for problems with more than a dozen states. After a brief review of POMDP's, this paper discusses several simple solution methods and shows that all are capable of finding near-optimal policies for a selection of extremely small POMDP's taken from the learning literature. In contrast, we show that none are able to solve a slightly larger and noisier problem based on robot navigation. We find that a combination of two novel approaches performs well on these problems and suggest methods for scaling to even larger and more complicated domains.

1 INTRODUCTION

Mobile robots must act on the basis of their current and previous sensor readings. In spite of improvements in technology, a robot's information about its surroundings is necessarily incomplete: sensors are imperfect, objects occlude one another from view, the robot might not know its initial status or precisely where it is. The theory of *partially observable Markov decision processes* (POMDP's) (Astrom, 1965; Smallwood and Sondik, 1973; Cassandra et al., 1994) models this situation and provides a basis for computing optimal behavior.

A variety of algorithms have been developed for solving POMDP's (Lovejoy, 1991), but because the problem is so computationally challenging (Papadimitriou and Tsitsiklis, 1987), most techniques are too inefficient to be used on all but the smallest problems (2 to 5 states (Cheng, 1988)). Recently, the Witness algorithm (Cassandra, 1994; Littman, 1994) has been used to solve POMDP's with up to 16 states. While this problem size is considerably larger than prior state of the art, the algorithm is not efficient enough to be used for larger POMDP's.

Thus, the generality and expressiveness of the POMDP framework comes with a cost: only extremely small problems can be solved using available techniques. This paper is an incremental attempt at narrowing the gap between promise and practice. Using reinforcement-learning techniques and insights from the POMDP literature, we show how a satisfactory policy can be found for a POMDP with close to 100 states and dozens of observations.

We assume that a complete and accurate model of the state transition dynamics is given and use various techniques to construct a policy that achieves high reward. Even with these restrictions, the problem of finding optimal behavior is still too difficult and we have chosen to simplify it in several respects. First, we will be satisfied if we can find reasonably good suboptimal policies. Secondly, our training and testing is done using simulated runs from a fixed initial distribution, limiting the set of situations for which the algorithms need to find good behavior.

The structure of the paper is as follows. The introduction summarizes formal results concerning the POMDP model. The next section describes several methods for finding approximately optimal policies and provides evidence that all perform comparably on a collection of extremely small problems. Of these, a simple approach based on solving the underlying MDP is clearly the most time efficient. None of these approaches can solve two slightly larger navigation problems and so the next section presents a more successful hybrid approach that seeds learning using the Q values of the underlying MDP. The concluding section considers a class of problems that require a richer representation for policies and presents preliminary results on a technique for learning such policies.

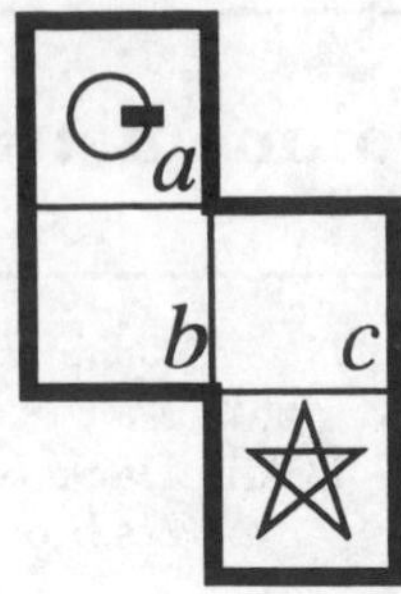

Figure 1: A tiny navigation environment.

2 PARTIALLY OBSERVABLE MARKOV DECISION PROCESSES

This section reviews the operations research literature on POMDP's.

2.1 DEFINITIONS AND EXAMPLE

A POMDP is a tuple $< S, A, T, R, O, \Omega >$ where S is a set of states, A a set of actions, and Ω a set of observations. We will only consider the case in which these sets are finite.

The functions T and R define a Markov decision process (MDP) (Bertsekas, 1987) with which the agent interacts without direct information as to the current state. The transition function, $T : S \times A \rightarrow \Pi(S)$, specifies how the various actions affect the state of the environment. ($\Pi(\cdot)$ represents the set of discrete probability distributions over a finite set.) The agent's immediate rewards are given by $R : S \times A \rightarrow \Re$. The agent's decisions are made based on information from its sensors (observations) formalized by $O : S \times A \rightarrow \Pi(\Omega)$.

Our goal in this work is to take a POMDP and find a *policy*, which is a strategy for selecting actions based on the information available to the agent, that maximizes an infinite-horizon, discounted optimality criterion.

Figure 1 depicts a tiny navigation POMDP that we use for explanatory purposes. It consists of 13 states (4 possible orientations in each of 3 rooms and a goal state which is denoted by a star), 9 observations (relative location of the surrounding walls, plus "star"), and 3 actions (forward, rotate left, rotate right). The problem is intended to model a robot in a simple office environment. In the figure, the robot symbol occupies the "East in Room a" state. The agent's task is to enter the room marked with the star, at which point it receives a reward of +1. After receiving the reward, the agent's next action transports it at random into one of the 12 non-goal states. Otherwise, transitions and observations are deterministic in this example.

2.2 THE BELIEF MDP

In the tiny navigation environment, the immediate observations do not supply enough information for the agent to disambiguate its location nor are they sufficient for indicating the agent's best choice of action. For example, if the agent sees a wall behind it and to its left, it might be in "North in Room b" (optimal action is to turn right) or "South in Room c" (optimal action is to go forward to the goal).

Some form of memory is necessary in order for our agent to choose its actions well. Although many architectures are possible, one elegant choice is to maintain a probability distribution over the states of the underlying environment. We call these distributions *belief states* and use the notation $b(s)$ to indicate the agent's belief that it is in state s when the current belief state is $b \in \Pi(S)$. Using the model, belief states can be updated based on the agent's actions and observations in a way that makes the beliefs correspond exactly to state occupation probabilities.

From a known starting belief state, it is easy to use the transition and observation probabilities to incorporate new information into the belief state (Cassandra et al., 1994). As an example, consider an agent that is started in any of the 12 non-goal states of the tiny navigation environment with equal probability: $b(s) = 1/12$ for all non-goal states. If the agent chooses to turn right and then sees walls in front of it and to its right, only two states are possible:

$$b(\text{ South in Room } b\ ) = b(\text{ North in Room } c\ ) = 1/2\ .$$

After next moving forward and seeing walls in all directions except behind, the agent is sure of where it is:

$$b(\text{ North in Room } a\ ) = 1.$$

Since the agent's belief state is an accurate summary of all the relevant past information, it is a *sufficient statistic* for choosing optimal actions (Bertsekas, 1987). That is, an agent that can choose the optimal action for any given belief state is acting optimally in the environment.

An important consequence is that the belief states, in combination with the updating rule, form a completely observable Markov decision process (MDP) with a continuous state space, similar to problems addressed in the reinforcement-learning literature (Moore, 1994). Our goal will be to find an approximation of the Q function over the continuous space of belief states and to use this as a basis for action in the environment. We restrict our attention to stationary, deterministic policies on the belief state, since this class is relatively simple and we are assured that it includes an optimal policy (Ross, 1983).

2.3 PIECEWISE-LINEAR CONVEX FUNCTIONS

A particularly powerful result of Sondik's is that the optimal value function for any POMDP can be approximated arbitrarily well by a piecewise-linear and convex (PWLC) function (Smallwood and Sondik, 1973; Littman, 1994). Further, there is a class of POMDP's that have value functions that are exactly PWLC (Sondik, 1978). These results apply to the optimal Q functions as well: the Q function for action a, $Q_a(b)$ is the expected reward for a policy that starts in belief state b, takes action a, and then behaves optimally. By choosing the action that has the largest Q value for a given belief state, an agent can behave optimally.

PWLC functions are particularly convenient because of their representational simplicity. If $Q_a(b)$ is a PWLC function, then $Q_a(b)$ can be written:

$$Q_a(b) := \max_{q \in L_a} q \cdot b$$

for some finite set of $|S|$-dimensional vectors, L_a. That is, Q_a is just the maximum of a finite set of linear functions of b.

So, although we are trying to find a solution to a continuous-space MDP, we have constraints on the form of the optimal Q functions that make this search a great deal simpler.

3 SOME SOLUTION METHODS FOR POMDP's

This section sketches several methods for finding linear or PWLC approximations to the optimal Q functions for POMDP's. The goal in each of them is to find Q functions that can be used to generate good behavior; that is, we will judge the methods by the policies they produce and not by the accuracy with which they estimate the optimal Q values. None of these methods are entirely original, but none have been used to find fast approximations to optimal policies for POMDP's given the POMDP models.

3.1 TRUNCATED EXACT VALUE ITERATION

The Witness algorithm (Cassandra et al., 1994; Littman, 1994) finds exact solutions to discounted finite-horizon POMDP's using value iteration. After its k-th iteration, the algorithm returns the exact k-step Q functions as collections of vectors, L_a, for each action, a. The algorithm can be used to find arbitrarily accurate approximations to the optimal infinite-horizon Q functions and therefore policies that are arbitrarily close to optimal (Williams and Baird, 1993). Unfortunately, the algorithm can take many, many iterations to find an approximately optimal value function, and for problems with a large number of observations, the size of the L_a sets can grow explosively from iteration to iteration. Nonetheless, it is often the case that a near-optimal policy is reached long before the Q values have converged to their optimal values, so truncating the value iteration process prematurely can still yield excellent policies. We call this approach "truncated exact value iteration" and denote it as Trunc-VI.

3.2 THE Q_{MDP} VALUE METHOD

Another natural approach to finding Q functions for POMDP's is to make use of the Q values of the underlying MDP. That is, we can temporarily ignore the observation model and find the $Q_{\text{MDP}}(s,a)$ values for the MDP consisting of the transitions and rewards only. These values can be computed extremely efficiently for problems with dozens to thousands of states and a variety of approaches are available (Puterman, 1994).

With the Q_{MDP} values in hand, we can treat all the Q_{MDP} values for each action as a single linear function and estimate the Q value for a belief state b as $Q_a(b) = \sum_s b(s)\; Q_{\text{MDP}}(s,a)$. This estimate amounts to assuming that any uncertainty in the agent's current belief state will be gone after the next action. Thus, the action whose long-term reward from all states (weighted by the probability of occupying the state) is largest will be the one chosen at each step.

Policies based on this approach can be remarkably effective. One drawback, though, is that these policies will not take actions to gain information. For instance, a "look around without moving" action and a "stay in place and ignore everything" action would be indistinguishable with regard to the performance of policies under an assumption of one-step uncertainty. This can lead to situations in which the agent loops forever without changing belief state.

3.3 REPLICATED Q-LEARNING

Chrisman (1992) and McCallum (1992) explored the problem of learning a POMDP model in a reinforcement-learning setting. At the same time that their algorithms attempt to learn the transition and observation probabilities, they used an extension of Q-learning (Watkins, 1989) to learn approximate Q functions for the learned POMDP model. Although it was not the emphasis of their work, their "replicated Q-learning" rule is of independent interest.

Replicated Q-learning generalizes Q-learning to apply to vector-valued states and uses a single vector, q_a, to approximate the Q function for each action a: $Q_a(b) = q_a \cdot b$. For many POMDP's, a single vector per action is not sufficient for representing the optimal policy. Nonetheless, this approximation is simple and can be remarkably effective.

The components of the vectors are updated using

$$\Delta q_a(s) = \alpha\, b(s)(r + \gamma \max_{a'} Q_{a'}(b') - q_a(s)) .$$

The update rule is evaluated for every $s \in S$ each time the agent makes a state transition; α is a learning rate, b a belief state, a the action taken, r the reward received, and b' the resulting belief state. This rule applies the Q-learning update rule to each component of q_a in proportion to the probability that the agent is currently occupying the state associated with that component.

By simulating a series of transitions from belief state to belief state and applying the update rule at each step, this learning rule can be used to solve a POMDP. If the observations of the POMDP are sufficient to ensure that the agent is always certain of its state (i.e., $b(s) = 1$ for some s at all times), this rule reduces exactly to standard Q-learning and can be shown to converge to the optimal Q function under the proper conditions (Jaakkola et al., 1994; Tsitsikilis, 1994).

The rule itself is an extremely natural extension of Q-learning to vector-valued state spaces, since it basically consists of applying the Q-learning rule at every state where the magnitude of the change of a state's value is proportional to the probability the agent is in that state. In fact, in addition to its use by Chrisman and McCallum, an elaboration of this rule is used by Connell and Mahadevan (1993) for solving a distributed-representation reinforcement-learning problem.

Although replicated Q-learning is a generalization of Q-learning, it does not extend correctly to cases in which the agent is faced with significant uncertainty. Consider a POMDP in which the optimal Q function can be represented with a single linear function. Since replicated Q-learning independently adjusts each component to predict the moment-to-moment Q values, the learning rule will tend to move all the components of q_a toward the same value.

3.4 LINEAR Q-LEARNING

Linear Q-learning is extremely similar to replicated Q-learning but instead of training each component of q_a toward the same value, the components of q_a are adjusted to match the coefficients of the linear function that predicts the Q values. This is accomplished by applying the delta rule for neural networks (Rumelhart et al., 1986), which, adapted to the belief MDP framework, becomes:

$$\Delta q_a(s) = \alpha\, b(s)(r + \gamma \max_{a'} Q_{a'}(b') - q_a \cdot b) .$$

Like the replicated Q-learning rule, this rule reduces to ordinary Q-learning when the belief state is deterministic.

In neural network terminology, linear Q-learning views $\{b,\ r + \gamma \max_{a'} Q_{a'}(b')\}$ as a training instance for the function $Q_a(\cdot)$. Replicated Q-learning, in contrast, uses this example as a training instance for the component $q_a(s)$ for every s. We should expect the rules to behave differently when the components of q_a need to have widely different values to solve the problem at hand.

Like replicated Q-learning, linear Q-learning has the limitation that only linear approximations to the optimal Q functions are considered. In general, this can lead to policies that are arbitrarily poor, although this does not appear to be true for the extremely small POMDP's we studied.

Note that, since the transition probabilities and rewards are known, it is possible to perform full backups instead of the sampled backups used in traditional Q-learning. Our preliminary experiments indicate that full backups do not appear to speed convergence (at least not consistently across POMDP's) and require significant computational overhead (Littman et al., 1995). More study will be necessary to fully address this issue. All of the results reported here use sample backups.

3.5 EMPIRICAL COMPARISON ON EXTREMELY SMALL PROBLEMS

We ran each of the above methods on a battery of POMDP's selected from the literature, summarized in Table 1. The details of the problems are not crucial and there is not space here to describe them—the reader is referred to the appropriate references for descriptions.

Interestingly, all 6 POMDP's have the property that optimal policies periodically reset to a problem-specific belief state. We used a discount factor of 0.95 for all problems. The column of Table 1 labeled "Noise" indicates whether there is noise in the transitions, observations, or both. The part-painting problem has been adapted from its original form (Littman et al., 1995). The 4x3 grid problem was introduced by Russell and Norvig (1994) and the version here includes a discounted criterion and returns to the initial belief state after a goal instead of entering an absorbing state.

For the experiments on truncated exact value iteration, we ran the exact algorithm for approximately 100 seconds and used the output of the last complete iteration as a solution.

The learning approaches have a large number of free parameters which we did not optimize carefully for either speed or performance. For each of 21 runs, we performed 75,000 steps of learning starting from the problem-specific belief state. During learning, actions were selected to maximize the current Q functions with

Name	$\|S\|$	$\|A\|$	$\|\Omega\|$	Noise
Shuttle (Chrisman, 1992)	8	3	5	T/O
Cheese Maze (McCallum, 1992)	11	4	7	–
Part Painting (Kushmerick et al., 1993)	4	4	2	T/O
4x4 Grid (Cassandra et al., 1994)	16	4	2	–
Tiger (Cassandra et al., 1994)	2	3	2	O
4x3 Grid (Parr and Russell, 1995)	11	4	6	T

Table 1: A suite of extremely small POMDP's.

	Shuttle	Cheese Maze	Part Painting	4x4 Grid	Tiger	4x3 Grid
Trunc VI	1.805 ± 0.014	0.188 ± 0.002	0.179 ± 0.012	0.193 ± 0.003	0.930 ± 0.205	0.109 ± 0.005
Q_{MDP}	1.809 ± 0.012	0.185 ± 0.002	0.112 ± 0.016	0.192 ± 0.003	1.106 ± 0.196	0.112 ± 0.005
Repl Q	1.355 ± 0.265	0.175 ± 0.017	0.003 ± 0.005	0.179 ± 0.013	1.068 ± 0.047	0.080 ± 0.014
Linear Q	1.672 ± 0.121	0.186 ± 0.000	0.132 ± 0.030	0.141 ± 0.026	1.074 ± 0.046	0.095 ± 0.007
optimal	—	0.186 ± 0.002	0.170 ± 0.012	0.192 ± 0.002	1.041 ± 0.180	—

Table 2: Results of POMDP solution methods on the suite of extremely small problems.

a 0.10 probability of being overridden by a uniform random action. The learning rate was decreased according to the following schedule: 0.1 for steps 0 to 20,000, 0.01 from 20,000 to 40,000, 0.001 from 40,000 to 60,000, and then 0.0001 thereafter. The $q_a(s)$ component values were initialized to random numbers uniformly chosen between -20.0 and 20.0. The parameter values were chosen by informally monitoring the performance of linear Q-learning on several of the problems.

Each method returned a set of vectors that constitute linear or PWLC approximations of the Q functions. An agent that chooses actions to maximize the Q functions was then simulated to evaluate the quality of the induced policy. Each simulation started with the agent in the problem-specific belief state and ran for 101 steps. This procedure was repeated 101 times and the performance is reported as the mean reward received with a 95% confidence interval.

Table 2 reports the results. The data for the two learning algorithms are pooled over 21 independent experiments. For four of the problems, we were able to compute the optimal Q functions using the Witness algorithm in 25 to 120 minutes. We then simulated the optimal vectors to obtain the row marked "optimal" in the table. The two other problems possibly do not have PWLC optimal Q functions.

The most overwhelming result is that almost every method on almost every problem achieves practically optimal performance. Truncated exact value iteration is always statistically indistinguishable from optimal and tends to do no worse than the Q_{MDP} value method. The Q_{MDP} value method tends to do no worse than linear Q-learning which tends to do no worse than replicated Q-learning. The Q_{MDP} value method, which consistently performed quite well, was the most time-efficient algorithm, requiring no more than half a second on any problem. The learning algorithms, by contrast, took between 16 seconds and 80 seconds, depending mostly on the size of the problem. The truncated exact value iteration algorithm always took 100 seconds, by design.

There are two significant exceptions to the overall trend mentioned above: the Q_{MDP} value method was worse than linear Q-learning on the part-painting problem and linear Q-learning was worse than replicated Q-learning on the 4x4 problem. The former is a result of the Q_{MDP} value method not choosing actions to gain information, which are necessary for optimal behavior in this problem. The latter occurs because of the determinism in the state transitions and the relatively small probability of taking random actions; this problem can be easily fixed by adjusting the random-action probability (Littman et al., 1995). This combination can cause the goal to be infrequently visited during learning in cases where the random initial policy leads to cyclic behavior.

4 HANDLING LARGER POMDP's: A HYBRID APPROACH

It is worth asking whether the results of the previous section apply to larger or more complicated domains. We constructed two POMDP's designed to model a robot navigation domain, shown in Figures 2 and 3.

One environment has 57 states (14 rooms with 4 orientations each, plus a goal) and 21 observations (each possible combination of the presence of a wall in each of the 4 relative directions, plus "star" and three landmarks visible when the agent faces south in three particular locations). The other has 89 states (4 orientations in 22 rooms, plus a goal) and 17 observations (all combinations of walls, plus "star"). Both include 5 actions (stay in place, move forward, turn right, turn

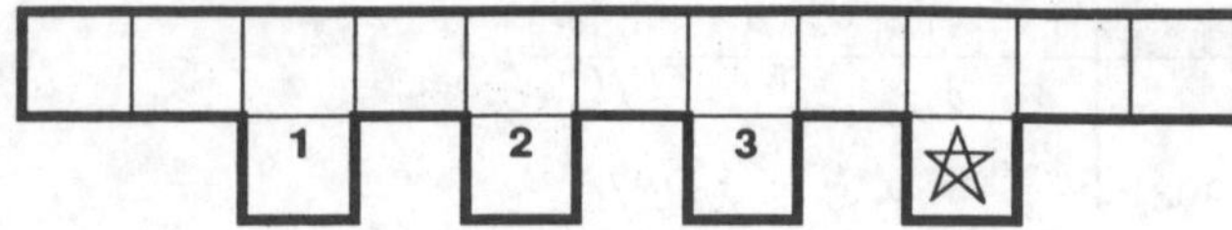

Figure 2: Navigation environment with 57 states.

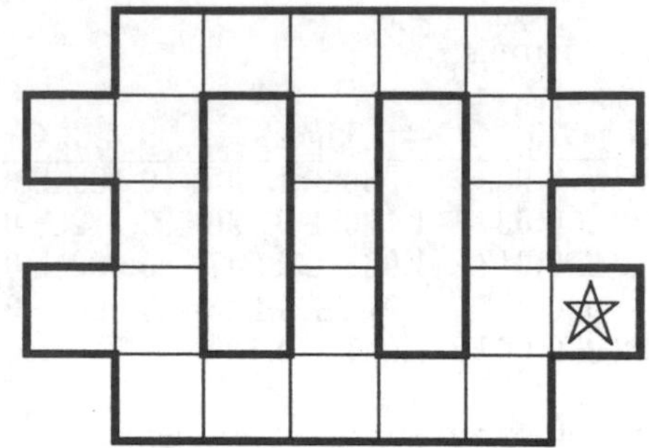

Figure 3: Navigation environment with 89 states.

left, turn around) and have extremely noisy transitions and observations (Littman et al., 1995).

We ran the same collection of algorithms on these two environments with a slight change: truncated exact value iteration was given roughly 1000 seconds. Performance was measured slightly differently. The policies were evaluated for 251 trials, each consisting of a run from a problem-specific initial belief state to the goal. For these two environments the initial belief state was a uniform distribution over all states except the goal state. If the agent was unable to reach the goal in 251 steps, the trial was terminated.

Table 3 reports the percentage of the 251 runs in which the agent reached the goal and the median number of steps to goal over all 251 runs. For the learning algorithms, performance was measured as a median of 21 independent runs.

This time, none of the approaches gave even passable results, with many test runs never reaching the goal after hundreds of steps. Truncated exact value iteration was able to complete two iterations in about 4 seconds and made no additional progress for up to 1500 seconds. The Q_{MDP} value method is deterministic, so the reported results are based on the best policy it can achieve. The learning approaches have the capability of adapting and improving but are unable to reach the goal state often enough to learn anything at all. Thus, all 4 methods fail, but for different reasons.

	57 states		89 states	
	goal%	median	goal%	median
Trunc VI	62.9	150	44.6	> 251
Q_{MDP}	47.4	> 251	25.9	> 251
Repl Q	5.2	> 251	2.8	> 251
Linear Q	8.4	> 251	5.2	> 251

Table 3: Results of POMDP solution methods on the two navigation environments.

	57 states		89 states	
	goal%	median	goal%	median
Repl Q	72.9	21	10.8	> 251
Linear Q	96.0	15	58.6	51
Human	100.0	15	100.0	29
Q_{MDP}-no stay	100.0	16	57.8	40
Random Walk	46.2	> 251	25.9	> 251

Table 4: Results of POMDP solution methods when seeded with the Q_{MDP} values on two navigation environments.

This suggests the possibility of a hybrid solution. By computing the Q_{MDP} values and using them to seed the q_a vectors for learning, we can take advantage of the strengths of both approaches. In particular, the hope is that the Q_{MDP} values can be computed quickly and then improved by the learning algorithms.

Table 4 summarizes the results of initializing the two learning algorithms using the Q_{MDP} values in place of random vectors. Training and testing procedures followed those of the other navigation experiments.

In both environments, the linear Q-learning algorithm was able to use the initial seed values to find a better policy (almost doubling the completion percentage and halving the steps to the goal). The replicated Q-learning algorithm, on the other hand, actually made the performance of the Q_{MDP} value method worse.

The performance of the hybrid algorithm appears quite good. However, the complexity of the navigation environments makes direct comparison with an optimal policy out of the question. To get a qualitative sense of the difficulty, we created an interactive simulator for the two navigation environments which included a graphical belief state display. A single human subject (one of the authors) practiced using the simulator and then carried out testing trials with the results reported in Table 4. In the smaller environment, the testing period lasted for 45 trials and the longest run was 57 steps. The median performance of 15 steps per trial is exactly the same as that of the hybrid algorithm. In the larger environment, the testing period lasted for 31 trials and the longest run was 73 steps indicating substantial room for improvement in the existing algorithms.

After further study, we discovered that the primary reason for the poor performance of the straight Q_{MDP} value method is that the agent chooses the "stay in place" action in some belief states and sometimes becomes trapped in a cycle. As a test of this hypothesis, we removed this action from the set of actions that can be chosen by the Q_{MDP} value method and reran the evaluation with results given in Table 4. Surpris-

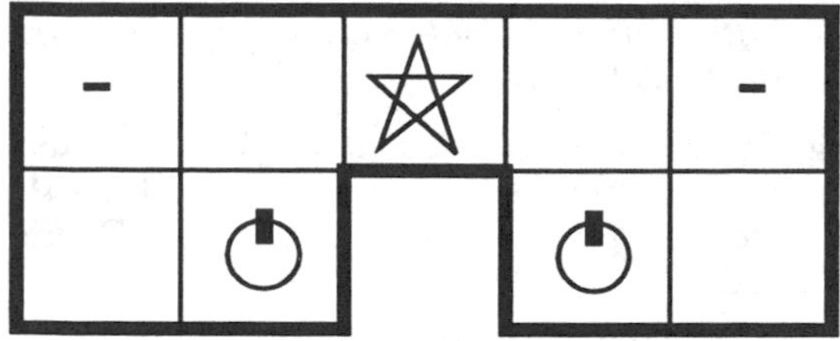

Figure 4: A 33-state navigation environment that cannot be solved with a single linear function per action.

ingly, decreasing the set of options *helped* the Q_{MDP} value method reach a level of performance comparable to that of linear Q-learning. Thus, the learning algorithm applied to the navigation environments may be retaining the important parts of the Q_{MDP} policy while simply learning to suppress the "stay in place" action—a reasonable approach to attaining good performance on these POMDP's. For comparison purposes, we have included the performance of a random walk policy where actions (except "stay in place") are chosen randomly.

Seeding linear Q-learning using the Q_{MDP} values leads to a promising method of solving larger POMDP's than have been addressed to date. More study is needed to understand the strengths and limitations of this approach.

5 MORE ADVANCED REPRESENTATIONS

None of the algorithms reach the goal in the 89-state problem all the time: clearly optimal performance has not yet been reached. As discussed in Section 2.3, piecewise-linear convex functions can approximate the optimal Q functions as closely as necessary. In contrast, the linear functions used by the learning algorithms can result in arbitrarily bad approximations.

5.1 THE NEED FOR A MORE ADVANCED REPRESENTATION

To drive this point home, we designed a navigation problem (see Figure 4) for which any linear approximation to the Q functions is guaranteed to be suboptimal. The parameters of the environment follow those of the navigation environments discussed previously. There are two significant differences: the two rooms marked with minus signs in the figure are associated with negative reward, and the agent starts with equal probability facing North in one or the other of the two rooms marked with robot symbols in the figure.

An agent starting in the left start state should move forward, turn right, and move forward again. From the right start state, the agent should move forward, turn *left* and move forward again. The difficulty is that the two scenarios are distinguished *only* by the configuration of walls in the initial state, which can only be perceived if the agents chooses to stay in place for a step so that it may receive an observation for the initial state. Because actions precede observations, staying in place is an action to gain information in this problem.

The fact that the agent needs to take an action to gain information and then execute the same action (forward) regardless of the outcome, is sufficient to destroy any single-vector-per-action approximation of the optimal policy (Littman et al., 1995). Although we understand the nature of this particular problem, a very interesting (and open) problem is how to determine the number of vectors needed to represent the optimal policy for any given POMDP.

5.2 A PWLC Q-LEARNING ALGORITHM

A simple approach to learning a PWLC Q function is to maintain a set of vectors for each action and use a competitive updating rule: when a new training instance (i.e., belief state/value pair) arrives, the vector with the largest dot product is selected for updating. The actual update follows the linear Q-learning rule. It is possible that the different vectors will come to cover different parts of the state space and thereby represent a more complex function than is possible with a single vector.

To show the potential gain of utilizing multiple vectors per action, we ran experiments on the 33-state navigation environment. We ran 21 independent trials of 75,000 learning steps of linear Q-learning as well as truncated exact value iteration and the Q_{MDP} value method. We compared these to the 3-PWLC Q-learning algorithm, which uses the competitive approach described above with 3 vectors per action. In analogy to the hybrid algorithm of the previous section, we initialize all 3 vectors for each action with the appropriate Q_{MDP} values.

The evaluation criterion was the same as for the 57 and 89-state navigation environment experiments. Table 5 shows the results and, as anticipated, the single vector methods perform poorly.

Although the 3-PWLC algorithm performs astonishingly well on this problem, its performance on other problems has been inconsistent. The primary difficulty is that noisy updates can cause a vector to "sink" below the other vectors. Since this approach only updates vectors when they are the largest for some belief state, these sunken vectors can never be recovered. A related problem plagues almost all competitive learning methods and in our informal experiments, we found this to occur quite often. We have considered some extensions to address this problem, but we have not yet found a reliable solution.

	33 states	
	goal%	median
trunc VI	39.8	> 251
Q_{MDP}	17.9	> 251
Linear Q	46.6	> 251
3-PWLC Q	98.4	5
Q_{MDP}-no stay	14.3	> 251

Table 5: Results of POMDP solution methods on the specially-constructed 33-state navigation environment.

A classic approach to the sunken-vector problem is to avoid hard "winner-take-all" updates. Parr and Russell (1995) use a differentiable approximation of the max operator and find they can produce good policies for the 4x4 and 4x3 grid problems. The approach is promising enough to warrant further study including comparisons on the difficult navigation environments described in this paper.

6 CONCLUSIONS

We can now obtain high quality policies for a class of POMDP's with nearly 100 states. We predict that these techniques can be honed to produce good policies for a wide variety of problems consisting of hundreds of states. But to handle the thousands of states needed to address realistic problems, other techniques will be needed.

Other approaches to scaling up, including various kinds of factoring and decomposition of the transitions and belief states (e.g., the sort of approach Boutilier et al. (1995) and Nicholson and Kaelbling (1994) used in fully observable domains), may be able to be used in concert with techniques described in this paper to yield practical results in moderately large POMDP problems.

References

Astrom, K. J. (1965). Optimal control of Markov decision processes with incomplete state estimation. *J. Math. Anal. Appl.*, 10:174–205.

Bertsekas, D. P. (1987). *Dynamic Programming: Deterministic and Stochastic Models.* Prentice-Hall.

Boutilier, C., Dearden, R., and Goldszmidt, M. (1995). Exploiting structure in policy construction. In *Proceedings of the International Joint Conference on Artificial Intelligence.*

Cassandra, A. (1994). Optimal policies for partially observable Markov decision processes. Technical Report CS-94-14, Brown University, Department of Computer Science, Providence RI.

Cassandra, A. R., Kaelbling, L. P., and Littman, M. L. (1994). Acting optimally in partially observable stochastic domains. In *Proceedings of the Twelfth National Conference on Artificial Intelligence*, Seattle, WA.

Cheng, H.-T. (1988). *Algorithms for Partially Observable Markov Decision Processes.* PhD thesis, University of British Columbia, British Columbia, Canada.

Chrisman, L. (1992). Reinforcement learning with perceptual aliasing: The perceptual distinctions approach. In *Proc. Tenth National Conference on AI (AAAI).*

Connell, J. and Mahadevan, S. (1993). Rapid task learning for real robots. In *Robot Learning.* Kluwer Academic Publishers.

Jaakkola, T., Jordan, M. I., and Singh, S. P. (1994). On the convergence of stochastic iterative dynamic programming algorithms. *Neural Computation*, 6(6).

Kushmerick, N., Hanks, S., and Weld, D. (1993). An Algorithm for Probabilistic Planning. Technical Report 93-06-03, University of Washington Department of Computer Science and Engineering. To appear in *Artificial Intelligence.*

Littman, M., Cassandra, A., and Kaelbling, L. (1995). Learning policies for partially observable environments: Scaling up. Technical Report CS-95-11, Brown University, Department of Computer Science, Providence RI.

Littman, M. L. (1994). The Witness algorithm: Solving partially observable Markov decision processes. Technical Report CS-94-40, Brown University, Department of Computer Science, Providence, RI.

Lovejoy, W. S. (1991). A survey of algorithmic methods for partially observable Markov decision processes. *Annals of Operations Research*, 28:47–66.

McCallum, R. A. (1992). First results with utile distinction memory for reinforcement learning. Technical Report 446, Dept. Comp. Sci., Univ. Rochester. See also Proceedings of Machine Learning Conference 1993.

Moore, A. W. (1994). The parti-game algorithm for variable resolution reinforcement learning in multidimensional state spaces. In *Advances in Neural Information Processing Systems 6*, San Mateo, CA. Morgan Kaufmann.

Nicholson, A. and Kaelbling, L. P. (1994). Toward approximate planning in very large stochastic domains. In *Proceedings of the AAAI Spring Symposium on Decision Theoretic Planning*, Stanford, California.

Papadimitriou, C. H. and Tsitsiklis, J. N. (1987). The complexity of Markov decision processes. *Mathematics of Operations Research*, 12(3):441–450.

Parr, R. and Russell, S. (1995). Approximating optimal policies for partially observable stochastic domains. In *Proceedings of the International Joint Conference on Artificial Intelligence.*

Puterman, M. L. (1994). *Markov Decision Processes—Discrete Stochastic Dynamic Programming.* John Wiley & Sons, Inc., New York, NY.

Ross, S. M. (1983). *Introduction to Stochastic Dynamic Programming.* Academic Press, New York.

Rumelhart, D. E., Hinton, G. E., and Williams, R. J. (1986). Learning internal representations by error backpropagation. In Rumelhart, D. E. and McClelland, J. L., editors, *Parallel Distributed Processing: Explorations in the microstructures of cognition. Volume 1: Foundations*, chapter 8. The MIT Press, Cambridge, MA.

Russell, S. J. and Norvig, P. (1994). *Artificial Intelligence: A Modern Approach.* Prentice-Hall, Englewood Cliffs, NJ.

Smallwood, R. D. and Sondik, E. J. (1973). The optimal control of partially observable Markov processes over a finite horizon. *Operations Research*, 21:1071–1088.

Sondik, E. J. (1978). The optimal control of partially observable Markov processes over the infinite horizon: Discounted costs. *Operations Research*, 26(2).

Tsitsikilis, J. N. (1994). Asynchronous stohcastic aproximation and Q-learning. *Machine Learning*, 16(3).

Watkins, C. J. (1989). *Learning with Delayed Rewards.* PhD thesis, Cambridge University.

Williams, R. J. and Baird, L. C. I. (1993). Tight performance bounds on greedy policies based on imperfect value functions. Technical Report NU-CCS-93-13, Northeastern University, College of Computer Science, Boston, MA.

Adaptive Agent Tracking in Real-world Multi-Agent Domains: A Preliminary Report

Milind Tambe, Lewis Johnson and Wei-Min Shen
Information Sciences Institute and Computer Science Department
University of Southern California
4676 Admiralty Way, Marina del Rey, CA 90292
{tambe,johnson,shen}@isi.edu

Abstract

In multi-agent environments, the task of *agent tracking* becomes increasingly difficult when a tracker only has an imperfect model of the trackee. This difficulty is unavoidable in any real-world situation where the amount of perception information is overwhelming in comparison to a tracker's limited resource and response time, and trackees may dynamically change their action models for a number of reasons. In this paper, we analyze this *adaptive agent tracking* problem in detail and describe an initial solution using discrimination-based learning. The main idea is to identify the deficiency of a model based on prediction failures, and revise the model by using features that are critical in discriminating successful and failed episodes. Our experiments in simulated air-to-air combat environments have shown some interesting results but many problems remain open for future research.

Introduction

In multi-agent environments, intelligent agents interact with each other, either collaboratively or non-collaboratively, to achieve their goals. Many of these multi-agent domains are real-time and dynamic, requiring the interaction to be highly flexible and reactive. For instance, in the education arena, intelligent tutoring systems need to interact with students while they are solving problems (Ward 1991). In the arena of entertainment, recent work has focused on real-time, dynamic interactivity among multiple agents within virtual reality environments (Bates, Loyall, & Reilly 1992; Hayes-Roth, Brownston, & V. 1995). Similarly, in the arena of training, there is a recent thrust on dynamic, real-time interactive simulations — e.g., realistic traffic environments (Cremer *et al.*), or realistic combat environments (steering committee 1994; Tambe *et al.* 1995) — where humans may interact with tens or hundreds of collaborative and non-collaborative intelligent agents. Such real-time interaction is also seen in robotic environments (Kuniyoshi *et al.* 1994).

In all these environments, *agent tracking* is a key capability required for intelligent interaction (Tambe & Rosenbloom 1995; Ward 1991; Rao 1994). It involves monitoring other agents' observable actions and inferring their unobserved actions or high-level goals, plans and behaviors. This capability is closely related to plan recognition (Kautz & Allen 1986; Azarewicz *et al.* 1986), which involves recognizing agents' plans based on observations of their actions. One key difference is that plan-recognition efforts generally assume that agents are executing plans that rigidly prescribe the actions to be performed. Agent tracking, in contrast, involves recognizing a broader mix of goal-driven and reactive behaviors. It is appropriate in domains where agents exhibit dynamic behaviors in response to the changing environment and the actions of other agents.

This paper focuses on *adaptive agent tracking*, an important requirement to scale up tracking to real-world domains. In particular, agent tracking is typically based on *model tracing* (Anderson *et al.* 1990), where a tracker (tracking agent) executes a runnable model of the trackee (tracked agent), matching the model's predictions with actual observations. However, in real-world domains, a tracker's model of the trackee's behaviors is often imperfect, i.e., incomplete or incorrect. The trackee further contributes to this imperfections, since its behaviors are not static, but alter over time. Of course, eradicating all such model imperfections is difficult (if not impossible) — and thus tracking must proceed despite such imperfections. Nonetheless, the tracker must engage in some adaptive tracking, i.e., it must adapt its model of the trackee to remdey at least some of these imperfections.

The remainder of the paper is organized as follows: Section 2 discusses a real-world domain that forms the basis of our work on agent tracking, and the challenges it poses. Section 3 outlines specific issues in adaptive agent tracking, and describes a detailed real-world example. Section 4 presents our approach to adaptive agent tracking. Section 5 presents experimental results; while Section 6 concludes the paper and outlines the future research.

Agent Tracking in Real-world Domains

The domain of our work on agent tracking is one of virtual battlefields based on Distributed Interactive Simulation Environments (DIS) (steering committee 1994). These are synthetic, yet real-world environments, and they have already been used in large-scale operational military exercises. These environments promise to provide cost-effective and realistic environments for training and rehearsal, as well as for testing new doctrine, tactics and weapon system concepts. The realization of this promise is critically dependent on intelligent automated agents that can act as effective human surrogates — interacting intelligently with humans as well as other agents. Agent tracking is of course one key aspect of such an intelligent interaction (Tambe & Rosenbloom 1995). Certainly, an adversary will not communicate information regarding its goals and plans to an agent voluntarily — such information must be inferred via tracking. Furthermore, even in collaborative situations, tracking often assumes importance due to communication difficulties.

Given that agent tracking occurs here on a synthetic battlefield, there are some key challenges that it poses:

- *Imperfect models:* A tracker's model of the trackee is often imperfect. Such imperfection could be divided into two categories:
  1. Dynamic model imperfections: The tracker possesses a perfect static model of the trackee — so that the trackee's set of possible goals, plans, and beliefs is known. Here, the tracker has to infer the trackee's currently active goals, plans and beliefs. This task is, of course, at the heart of agent tracking.
  2. Static model imperfections: The tracker's model of the trackee is itself incomplete, i.e., the trackee's overall set of possible goals, plans and beliefs is itself not known. This situation may arise due to *adaptiveness*: an intelligent adversary will very likely adapt its tactics to exploit possible weaknesses in a tracker's behaviors.
- *Real-time and dynamism:* The tracker and trackee interact in real-time; for example, in simulated air-to-air combat, *speed is life* (Shaw 1988) in the real-world, and in the simulated combat environment.
- *Complexity of environment:* This is a realistic environment, in which entities and objects have a rich set of properties.
- *Cost of trial:* Trials are not straightforward to run. Indeed, trials with same initial conditions may have very different outcomes due the "chaotic" nature of the environment.

While our analysis focuses on the combat-simulation environment, given its real-world character, we expect that the lessons will generalize to some of the other multi-agent environments mentioned above.

Issues in Adaptive Agent Tracking

As mentioned earlier, to track a trackee, tracker executes a runnable model of the trackee, matching the model's predictions with actual observations. One key reason that tracking in this fashion remains a challenging problem is dynamic model imperfections. Dynamic imperfections introduce ambiguity in tracking. For instance, in air-combat simulations, a tracker cannot directly observe a missile fired by its opponent (the trackee). It needs to infer a missile firing from the trackee's observable maneuvers, even though those are often ambiguous. Nonetheless, given a reasonably accurate model of the trackee, the tracker agent can hope to address such ambiguity in real-time (Tambe & Rosenbloom 1995).

Given adaptiveness on part of the trackee (static model imperfections), however, the situation becomes much more complex. The tracker cannot necessarily assume its model of the trackee is accurate, or that it will stay accurate over time. Such a situation does arise in the synthetic battlefield environment, given the adaptive character of intelligent adversaries. In particular, human adversaries will very likely adapt and evolve their tactics to exploit weaknesses in an intelligent agent's behaviors. For instance, in the simulated theatre of war (STOW-E) exercise held in November of 1994, human pilots deliberately changed their missile firing tactic — instead of pointing their aircraft nose straight at the target before firing a missile (0-5 degrees "nose-off" as shown in Figure 1), they began firing missiles while maintaining a 25-degree nose-off from the target (as shown in Figure 2). This was intended to confuse the participating intelligent pilot agents, and indeed it did (Tambe *et al.* 1995). Unable to track this changed missile firing tactic, intelligent pilot agents got shot down. Of course, human pilots are bound to come up with novel variations on known maneuvers, and intelligent agents cannot be expected to anticipate them. Yet, at the same time, intelligent agents cannot remain in a state of permanent vulnerability — for instance, getting shot down each time the 25-degree nose-off variation gets used — otherwise they would be unable to continue to provide a challenging and appropriate training environment for human pilots.

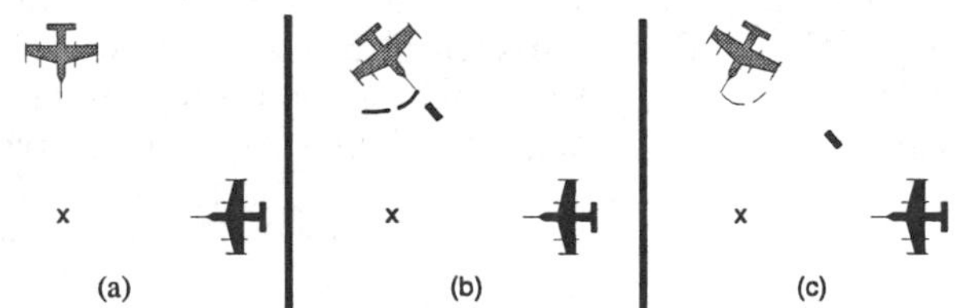

Figure 1: A simulated air-combat scenario illustrating the "normal" missile firing maneuvers: (a) aircraft approach each other; (b) the trackee points straight at the tracker to fire a missile; (c) the trackee executes an Fpole turn to continue supporting the missile without flying right behind the missile. An arc on an aircraft's nose shows its turn direction.

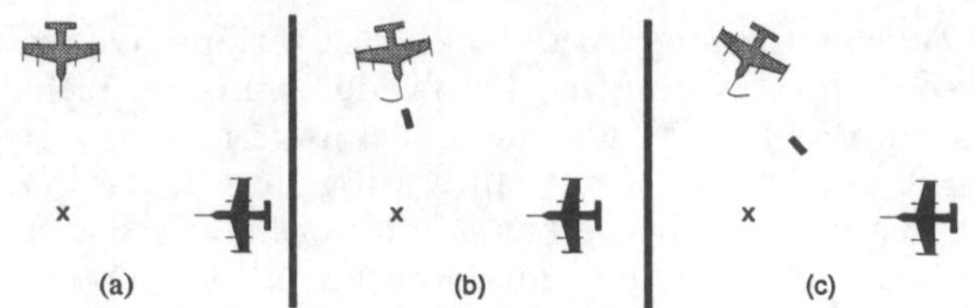

Figure 2: A simulated air-combat scenario illustrating a change in the missile firing maneuver.

To deal with such imperfections in the trackee's model, the tracker must:

- Recognize the deficiency of its model;
- Adapt the model by either revising its assumptions regarding known agent actions or postulating the existence of heretofore unknown actions.

Unfortunately, characteristics of the combat simulation environment outlined in the introduction section conspire to make this difficult. Thus, given imperfect information, it is difficult for the tracker to pinpoint the deficiencies in its model of the trackee. For instance, in the above STOW-E example, the tracker failed to recognize that 25-degree "nose off" is also a legitimate condition for missile firing (for its model is that missile firing is possible only if the nose-off angle is within 0-5 degrees). Yet, since it cannot observe the missile, and thus cannot know when it was fired, the tracker cannot easily pinpoint this precise deficiency. All it does detect is that it was unexpectedly shot down. (One simplifying assumption here is that the tracker assumes that it is the trackee's missile that shot it down).

The complexity of the environment and its real-time nature further complicate matters. Basically, it is difficult for the tracker to obtain a perfectly accurate model of the trackee, and access all of the relevant information for accurate tracking. For instance, in some situations, to predict whether an opponent pilot (trackee) will engage in an offensive or defensive maneuver, it is useful to know whether or not the trackee is willing to enter into risky situations in pursuit of its goals. However, it is difficult obtain such information in advance or during a real-time air-combat simulation — in fact, the tracker may end up jeopardizing its own survival in such a test.

Therefore, we believe that attempting to learn an exact model of the trackee will not be a very fruitful enterprise for the tracker. Instead, it should focus its learning effort on situations involving catastrophic failures, such as the unexpected missile firing in the STOW-E example. With respect to other less harmful imperfections, using a flexible tracking strategy — one that can work with an imperfect model of the trackee — would appear to be a more fruitful approach. Such a strategy would need the capability to switch inferences dynamically in real-time (Tambe & Rosenbloom 1995). For instance, if the tracker is not sure if the trackee is performing an offensive maneuver or a defensive maneuver, it may first assume that the maneuver is offensive (worst-case scenario), and then flexibly modify this assumption as soon as warranted by further observations. Thus, the tracker need not depend on acquiring information regarding risk.

Our Current Approach to Adaptive Agent Tracking

We are currently investigating an approach to agent tracking that involves learning prediction rules based on discrimination (Shen 1993; 1994). The discrimination-based approach is used to locate deficiencies in tracker's model of the trackee. This approach is augmented using discovery learning techniques for explaining successful and unsuccessful agent tracking experiences (Johnson 1994), to further specialize the analysis of such deficiencies.

The main idea of discrimination-based learning is the framework of predict-surprise-revise. The agent always makes predictions that can be verified or falsified by the actual observations, and if a prediction fails in the current situation, then the current episode will be compared with an earlier episode where the prediction was successful. The agent compares the features of the two situations looking for differences in the features, and incorporates those features into a revised prediction rule. In the event that no known features are effective in discriminating the situations, it may be necessary to hypothesize that new unknown features exist.

In order to apply discrimination-based learning to the agent tracking problem, two issues must be resolved.

- The agent must decide which points of time to compare between episodes. Each episode consists not of a single situation, but of a sequence of situations, each of which may be different from the previous one. It is impractical to discriminate all of the situations that arise in each episode; rather, we must select specific situations in each episode which are likely to yield meaningful differences when compared. Then, once a situation is selected within one episode, it is necessary to determine which situation corresponds to it in the other episode, so that an effective discrimination can be performed.
- The agent must determine which features to discriminate, and decide whether the existing features are effective in discriminating the situations.

Our tracker agents record important events during each episode, such as an air-combat engagement, in its memory. In the case of a catastrophe, such as being unexpectedly shot down, it does a backward scan of this event memory (from the point of the catastrophe), and locates the last point of prediction failure. Note that since a tracker is continuously making predictions about the trackee, it is difficult to determine which of the tracker's series of predictions needs to be revised. We assume here that the last occurrence of a prediction failure is the point where revision is required. Thus, in the 25 degree nose-off example, the tracker last predicts the opponent to move to a nose-off of 0-5 degrees, to fire a missile. This never occurs, and remains the last point of prediction/tracking failure. This case is compared with a successful case of tracking a missile firing. (Thus, we also assume that there is some good way of retrieving from memory a "successful" previous episode to compare against).

Unfortunately, in complex domains such as battlefield simulations, discrimination-based learning can be difficult to apply without knowledge and/or heuristics for deciding which features to attend to. A feature description of the environment can be quite complex: our agent models typically have hundreds of features, many of which change constantly. Thus, comparing the feature set where the missile firing was successfully tracked with one where the tracking failed may yield differences in a large number of irrelevant features, e.g., the altitude or speed of the trackee.

Under these circumstances, techniques akin to *incremental enlargement* (Shen 1993) or learning via experimentation (Gil 1993) can be employed to determine which features to discriminate.

Incremental enlargement is a heuristic applicable to finding relevant features that are crucial in discriminating two environmental states that contain a large number of differences. The idea is to first focus on the features that are mentioned in the action or operator involved in the prediction failure. If difference can be found in this core set of features, then the search for difference stops. Otherwise, this core set will be enlarged to include other features that are related to some core features and the search for difference continues. This process of enlargement stops as soon as differences are found among the two states. To illustrate the idea, consider the STOW-E example again. The feature "nose-off" is mentioned in the operator "steering-circle-achieved" which is involved in the current prediction failure. Since this feature has different values in the two states, it is identified as the cricial feature that can discriminating the two states, although in these two particular enironmental states there are many other features that have different values as well.

In learning via experimentation, the agent recalls a similar situation in which prediction was successful, and analyzes that situation to determine which features of the situation are critical for the decision. That is, the agent experiments with selectively removing features from the feature set, and trying to replay the decision making process that led to the prediction, to see whether or not a similar prediction results. This process typically identifies a small number of features that are determined to be relevant, even if a decision involves multiple reasoning steps (Johnson 1994). This reduced feature set becomes the focus of discrimination-based learning, instead of the full feature set. In the case under discussion, experimentation reveals that nose-off is one of the features that is critical to the decision-making process, and this is one of the features that discriminates the situations being compared. The prediction rules are therefore revised in order to make a different prediction — that missile firing is possible when the nose-off is 0-25 degrees. Experience with further episodes will then be required to determine whether the revised rule makes the right prediction; if not, the set of discrimination features will have to be broadened.

Experimental Results

We are taking a two-pronged approach in implementing the above approach. First, we have begun implementing the approach in intelligent pilot agents for the air-combat simulation environment (Tambe *et al.* 1995). To this end, two versions of the pilot agents — one developed for tracking (Tambe & Rosenbloom 1995; Tambe 1995) and one that learns models of decisions for explanation (Johnson 1994) — have been integrated. We are experimenting with this integrated agent to address the 25-degree nose-off example discussed above. (These agents are based on the Soar integrated architecture (Newell 1990), and use chunking, a form of EBL, as the basis of all of their learning (Laird, Rosenbloom, & Newell 1986)).

We are also in the process of implementing the above approach in a simple test-bed, where agents mimic the behavior of fighter aircraft, and are provided limited information about other agents. The goal here is to engage in controlled experiments, and gain some understanding of the tradeoffs involved. We have begun with two sets of experiments: one is to give the tracker a good model of the opponent and see how it can deal with imperfect information and make flexible and safe predictions, and the other to have the tracker learn the model from scratch. In the workshop, we expect to have demos or performance analysis from both the real-world simulator and the testbed.

Conclusions and Future Research

In this paper, we have identified the problem of adaptive agent tracking as a special case of agent tracking, where the tacker only has an imperfect model of the trackee. This problem is especially important in real-world situations where the amount of perception information is overwhelming in comparison to a tracker's limited resource and response time, and trackees may dynamically change their action models for a number of reasons. We have investigated possible solutions to the problem by using discrimination-based learning techniques and obtained some interesting initial experimental results. Furthermore, this research has revealed several important future research directions for adaptive agent tracking. In particular, we would like to investigate more cases of adaption such as creating new actions in the model, modifying existing actions by generalizing or specializing existing actions, and inventing new features that are critical for making corect predictions in life-threaten situtions.

Acknowledgments

This research was supported under subcontract to the University of Southern California Information Sciences Institute from the University of Michigan, as part of contract N00014-92-K-2015 from the Advanced Systems Technology Office (ASTO) of the Advanced Research Projects Agency (ARPA) and the Naval Research Laboratory (NRL); and under contract N66001-95-C-6013 from the Advanced Systems Technology Office (ASTO) of the Advanced Research Projects Agency (ARPA) and the Naval Command and Ocean Surveillance Center, RDT&E division (NRAD). Critical expertise and support has been provided by BMH Inc.

References

Anderson, J. R.; Boyle, C. F.; Corbett, A. T.; and Lewis, M. W. 1990. Cognitive modeling and intelligent tutoring. *Artificial Intelligence* 42:7–49.

Azarewicz, J.; Fala, G.; Fink, R.; and Heithecker, C. 1986. Plan recognition for airborne tactical decision making. In *Proceedings of the National Conference on Artificial Intelligence*, 805–811. Menlo Park, Calif.: AAAI press.

Bates, J.; Loyall, A. B.; and Reilly, W. S. 1992. Integrating reactivity, goals and emotions in a broad agent. Technical Report CMU-CS-92-142, School of Computer Science, Carnegie Mellon University.

Cremer, J.; Kearney, J.; Papelis, Y.; and Romano, R. The software architecture for scenario control in the Iowa driving simulator. In *Proceedings of the Conference on Computer Generated Forces and Behavioral Representation.*

Gil, Y. 1993. Efficient domain-independent experimentation. Technical Report ISI/RR-93-337, USC / Information Sciences Institute. Appears in the Proceedings of the Tenth International Conference on Machine Learning.

Hayes-Roth, B.; Brownston, L.; and V., G. R. 1995. Multiagent collaobration in directed improvisation. In *Proceedings of the International Conference on Multi-Agent Systems (ICMAS-95).*

Johnson, W. 1994. Agents that learn to explain themselves. In *Proceedings of the National Conference on Artificial Intelligence*, 1257–1263. Seattle, WA: AAAI.

Kautz, A., and Allen, J. F. 1986. Generalized plan recognition. In *Proceedings of the National Conference on Artificial Intelligence*, 32–37. Menlo Park, Calif.: AAAI press.

Kuniyoshi, Y.; Rougeaux, S.; Ishii, M.; Kita, N.; Sakane, S.; and Kakikura, M. 1994. Cooperation by observation: the framework and the basic task pattern. In *Proceedings of the IEEE International Conference on Robotics and Automation.*

Laird, J. E.; Rosenbloom, P. S.; and Newell, A. 1986. Chunking in soar: The anatomy of a general learning mechanism. *Machine Learning* 1(1):11–46.

Newell, A. 1990. *Unified Theories of Cognition.* Cambridge, Mass.: Harvard Univ. Press.

Rao, A. S. 1994. Means-end plan recognition: Towards a theory of reactive recognition. In *Proceedings of the International Conference on Knowledge Representation and Reasoning (KR-94).*

Shaw, R. L. 1988. *Fighter combat: tactics and maneuvers.* Annapolis, Maryland: Naval Institute Press.

Shen, W. 1993. Discovery as autonomous learning from the environment. *Machine Learning* 12:143–165.

Shen, W. 1994. *Autonomous Learning from the Environment.* W. H. Freeman, Computer Science Press.

steering committee, T. D. 1994. The dis vision: A map to the future of distributed simulation. Technical Report IST-SP-94-01, Institute for simulation and training, University of Central Florida, Orlando.

Tambe, M., and Rosenbloom, P. S. 1995. RESC: An approach for real-time, dynamic agent tracking. In *Proceedings of the International Joint Conference on Artificial Intelligence (IJCAI).*

Tambe, M.; Johnson, W. L.; Jones, R.; Koss, F.; Laird, J. E.; Rosenbloom, P. S.; and Schwamb, K. 1995. Intelligent agents for interactive simulation environments. *AI Magazine* 16(1).

Tambe, M. 1995. Recursive agent and agent-group tracking in a real-time dynamic environment. In *Proceedings of the International Conference on Multi-agent systems (ICMAS).*

Ward, B. 1991. *ET-Soar: Toward an ITS for Theory-Based Representations.* Ph.D. Dissertation, School of Computer Science, Carnegie Mellon Univ.

Learning to coordinate without sharing information

Sandip Sen, Mahendra Sekaran, and John Hale
Department of Mathematical & Computer Sciences
University of Tulsa
600 South College Avenue
Tulsa, OK 74104-3189
sandip@kolkata.mcs.utulsa.edu

Abstract

Researchers in the field of Distributed Artificial Intelligence (DAI) have been developing efficient mechanisms to coordinate the activities of multiple autonomous agents. The need for coordination arises because agents have to share resources and expertise required to achieve their goals. Previous work in the area includes using sophisticated information exchange protocols, investigating heuristics for negotiation, and developing formal models of possibilities of conflict and cooperation among agent interests. In order to handle the changing requirements of continuous and dynamic environments, we propose learning as a means to provide additional possibilities for effective coordination. We use reinforcement learning techniques on a block pushing problem to show that agents can learn complimentary policies to follow a desired path without any knowledge about each other. We theoretically analyze and experimentally verify the effects of learning rate on system convergence, and demonstrate benefits of using learned coordination knowledge on similar problems. Reinforcement learning based coordination can be achieved in both cooperative and non-cooperative domains, and in domains with noisy communication channels and other stochastic characteristics that present a formidable challenge to using other coordination schemes.

Introduction

In this paper, we will be applying recent research developments from the reinforcement learning literature to the coordination problem in multiagent systems. In a reinforcement learning scenario, an agent chooses actions based on its perceptions, receives scalar feedbacks based on past actions, and is expected to develop a mapping from perceptions to actions that will maximize feedbacks. Multiagent systems are a particular type of distributed AI system (Bond & Gasser 1988), in which autonomous intelligent agents inhabit a world with no global control or globally consistent knowledge. These agents may still need to coordinate their activities with others to achieve their own local goals. They could benefit from receiving information about what others are doing or plan to do, and from sending them information to influence what they do.

Coordination of problem solvers, both selfish and cooperative, is a key issue to the design of an effective distributed AI system. The search for domain-independent coordination mechanisms has yielded some very different, yet effective, classes of coordination schemes. Almost all of the coordination schemes developed to date assume explicit or implicit sharing of information. In the explicit form of information sharing, agents communicate partial results (Durfee & Lesser 1991), speech acts (Cohen & Perrault 1979), resource availabilities (Smith 1980), etc. to other agents to facilitate the process of coordination. In the implicit form of information sharing, agents use knowledge about the capabilities of other agents (Fox 1981; Genesereth, Ginsberg, & Rosenschein 1986) to aid local decision-making. Though each of these approaches has its own benefits and weaknesses, we believe that the less an agent depends on shared information, and the more flexible it is to the on-line arrival of problem-solving and coordination knowledge, the better it can adapt to changing environments.

In this paper, we discuss how reinforcement learning techniques of developing policies to optimize environmental feedback, through a mapping between perceptions and actions, can be used by multiple agents to learn coordination strategies without having to rely on shared information. These agents, though working in a common environment, are unaware of the capabilities of other agents and may or may not be cognizant of goals to achieve. We show that through repeated problem-solving experience, these agents can develop policies to maximize environmental feedback that can be interpreted as goal achievement from the viewpoint of an external observer. This research opens up a new dimension of coordination strategies for multiagent systems.

Acquiring coordination knowledge

Researchers in the field of machine learning have investigated a number of schemes for using past experience to improve problem solving behavior (Shavlik & Dietterich 1990). A number of these schemes can be effectively used to aid the problem of coordinating multiple agents inhabiting a common environment. In cooperative domains, where agents have approximate models of the behavior of other agents and are willing to reveal information to enable the group perform better as a whole, pre-existing domain knowledge can be used inductively to improve performance over time. On the other hand, learning techniques that can be used incrementally to develop problem-solving skills relying on little or no pre-existing domain knowledge can be used by both cooperative and non-cooperative agents. Though the latter form of learning may be more time-consuming, it is generally more robust in the presence of noisy, uncertain, and incomplete information.

Previous proposals for using learning techniques to coordinate multiple agents have mostly relied on using prior knowledge (Brazdil et al. 1991), or on cooperative domains with unrestricted information sharing (Sian 1991). Even previous work on using reinforcement learning for coordinating multiple agents (Tan 1993; Weiß1993) have relied on explicit information sharing. We, however, concentrate on systems where agents share no problem-solving knowledge. We show that although each agent is independently optimizing its own environmental reward, global coordination between multiple agents can emerge without explicit or implicit information sharing. These agents can therefore act independently and autonomously, without being affected by communication delays (due to other agents being busy) or failure of a key agent (who controls information exchange or who has more information), and do not have to be worry about the reliability of the information received (Do I believe the information received? Is the communicating agent an accomplice or an adversary?). The resultant systems are, therefore, robust and general-purpose.

Reinforcement learning

In reinforcement learning problems (Barto, Sutton, & Watkins 1989; Holland 1986; Sutton 1990), reactive and adaptive agents are given a description of the current state and have to choose the next action from a set of possible actions so as to maximize a scalar *reinforcement* or *feedback* received after each action. The learner's environment can be modeled by a discrete time, finite state, Markov decision process that can be represented by a 4-tuple $\langle S, A, P, r\rangle$ where $P : S \times S \times A \mapsto [0,1]$ gives the probability of moving from state s_1 to s_2 on performing action a, and $r : S \times A \mapsto \Re$ is a scalar reward function. Each agent maintains a policy, π, that maps the current state into the desirable action(s) to be performed in that state. The expected value of a discounted sum of future rewards of a policy π at a state x is given by $V_\gamma^\pi \stackrel{\text{def}}{=} E\{\sum_{t=0}^{\infty} \gamma^t r_{s,t}^\pi\}$, where $r_{s,t}^\pi$ is the random variable corresponding to the reward received by the learning agent t time steps after if starts using the policy π in state s, and γ is a discount rate $(0 \le \gamma < 1)$.

Various reinforcement learning strategies have been proposed using which agents can can develop a policy to maximize rewards accumulated over time. For our experiments, we use the Q-learning (Watkins 1989) algorithm, which is designed to find a policy π^* that maximizes $V_\gamma^\pi(s)$ for all states $s \in S$. The decision policy is represented by a function, $Q : S \times A \mapsto \Re$, which estimates long-term discounted rewards for each state–action pair. The Q values are defined as $Q_\gamma^\pi(s,a) = V_\gamma^{a;\pi}(s)$, where $a;\pi$ denotes the event sequence of choosing action a at the current state, followed by choosing actions based on policy π. The action, a, to perform in a state s is chosen such that it is expected to maximize the reward,

$$V_\gamma^{\pi^*}(s) = \max_{a \in A} Q_\gamma^{\pi^*}(s,a) \text{ for all } s \in S.$$

If an action a in state s produces a *reinforcement* of R and a transition to state s', then the corresponding Q value is modified as follows:

$$Q(s,a) \leftarrow (1-\beta)\, Q(s,a) + \beta\, (R + \gamma \max_{a' \in A} Q(s',a')). \quad (1)$$

Block pushing problem

To explore the application of reinforcement learning in multi-agent environments, we designed a problem in which two agents, a_1 and a_2, are independently assigned to move a block, b, from a starting position, S, to some goal position, G, following a path, P, in Euclidean space. The agents are not aware of the capabilities of each other and yet must choose their actions individually such that the joint task is completed. The agents have no knowledge of the system physics, but can perceive their current distance from the desired path to take to the goal state. Their actions are restricted as follows; agent i exerts a force $\vec{F_i}$, where $0 \le |\vec{F_i}| \le F_{max}$, on the object at an angle θ_i, where $0 \le \theta \le \pi$. An agent pushing with force $\vec{F}$ at angle θ will offset the block in the x direction by $|\vec{F}|\cos(\theta)$ units and in the y direction by $|\vec{F}|\sin(\theta)$ units. The net resultant force on the block is found by vector addition of individual forces: $\vec{F} = \vec{F_1} + \vec{F_2}$. We calculate the new position of the block by assuming unit displacement per unit force along the direction of the resultant force. The new block location is used to provide *feedback* to the agent. If (x,y) is the new block location, $P_x(y)$ is the x-coordinate of the path P for the same y coordinate, $\Delta x = |x - P_x(y)|$ is the distance along the x dimension between the block and the desired path, then $K * a^{-\Delta x}$ is the feedback given to each agent for their last action (we have used $K = 50$ and $a = 1.15$).

The field of play is restricted to a rectangle with endpoints $[0,0]$ and $[100,100]$. A trial consists of the agents starting from the initial position S and applying forces until either the goal position G is reached or the block leaves the field of play (see Figure 1). We abort a trial if a pre-set number of agent actions fail to

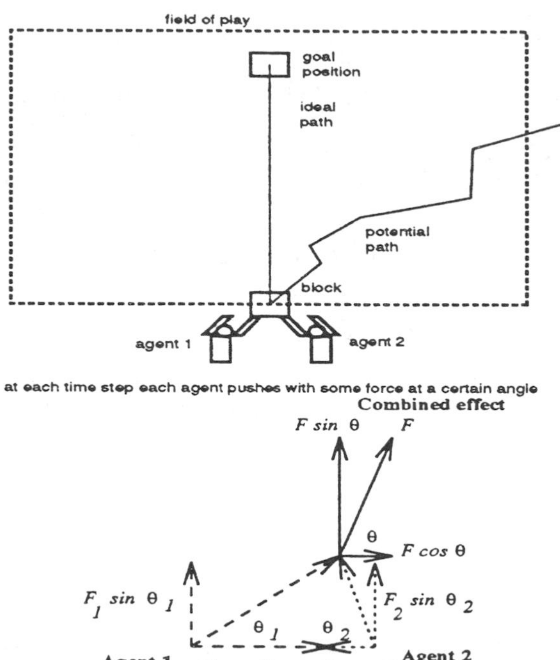

Figure 1: The block pushing problem.

take the block to the goal. This prevents agents from learning policies where they apply no force when the block is resting on the optimal path to the goal but not on the goal itself. The agents are required to learn, through repeated trials, to push the block along the path P to the goal. Although we have used only two agents in our experiments, the solution methodology can be applied without modification to problems with arbitrary number of agents.

Experimental setup

To implement the policy π we chose to use an internal discrete representation for the external continuous space. The force, angle, and the space dimensions were all uniformly discretized. When a particular discrete force or action is selected by the agent, the middle value of the associated continuous range is used as the actual force or angle that is applied on the block.

An experimental run consists of a number of trials during which the system parameters (β, γ, and K) as well as the learning problem (granularity, agent choices) is held constant. The stopping criteria for a run is either that the agents succeed in pushing the block to the goal in N consecutive trials (we have used $N = 10$) or that a maximum number of trials (we have used 1500) have been executed. The latter cases are reported as non-converged runs.

The standard procedure in Q-learning literature of initializing Q values to zero is suitable for most tasks where non-zero feedback is infrequent and hence there is enough opportunity to explore all the actions. Because a non-zero feedback is received after every action in our problem, we found that agents would follow, for an entire run, the path they take in the first trial. This is because they start each trial at the same state, and the only non-zero Q-value for that state is for the action that was chosen at the start trial. Similar reasoning holds for all the other actions chosen in the trial. A possible fix is to choose a fraction of the actions by random choice, or to use a probability distribution over the Q-values to choose actions stochastically. These options, however, lead to very slow convergence. Instead, we chose to initialize the Q-values to a large positive number. This enforced an exploration of the available action options while allowing for convergence after a reasonable number of trials.

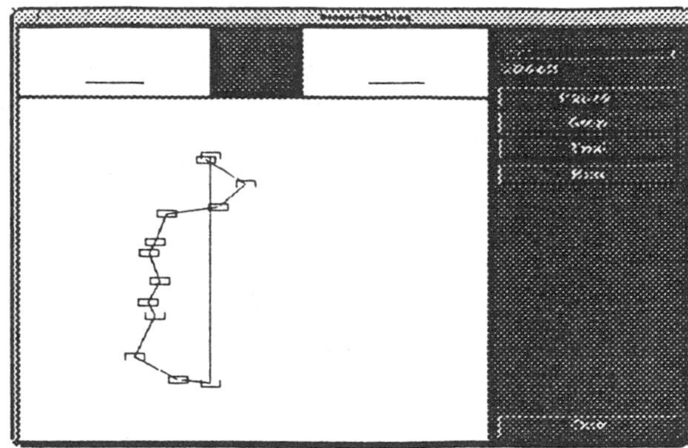

Figure 2: The X/Motif interface for experimentation.

The primary metric for performance evaluation is the average number of trials taken by the system to converge. Information about acquisition of coordination knowledge is obtained by plotting, for different trials, the average distance of the actual path followed from the desired path. Data for all plots and tables in this paper have been averaged over 100 runs.

We have developed a X/Motif interface (see Figure 2) to visualize and control the experiments. It displays the desired path, as well as the current path along which the block is being pushed. The interface allows us to step through trials, run one trial at a time, pause anywhere in the middle of a run, "play" the run at various speeds, and monitor the development of the policy matrices of the agents. By clicking anywhere on the field of play we can see the current best action choice for each agent corresponding to that position.

Choice of system parameters

If the agents learn to push the block along the desired path, the reward that they will receive for the best action choices at each step is equal to the maximum possible value of K. The steady-state values for the Q-values (Q_{ss}) corresponding to optimal action choices can be calculated from the equation:

$$Q_{ss} = (1 - \beta)\, Q_{ss} + \beta\, (K + \gamma\, Q_{ss}).$$

Solving for Q_{ss} in this equation yields a value of $\frac{K}{1-\gamma}$. In order for the agents to explore all actions after the Q-values are initialized at S_I, we require that any new Q value be less than S_I. From similar considerations as above we can show that this will be the case if $S_I \geq \frac{K}{1-\gamma}$. In our experiments we fix the maximum reward K at 50, S_I at 100, and γ at 0.9. Unless otherwise mentioned, we have used $\beta = 0.2$, and allowed each agent to vary both the magnitude and angle of the force they apply on the block.

The first problem we used had starting and goal positions at (40, 0) and (40, 100) respectively. During our initial experiments we found that with an even number of discrete intervals chosen for the angle dimension, an agent cannot push along any line parallel to the y-axis. Hence we used an odd number, 11, of discrete intervals for the angle dimension. The number of discrete intervals for the force dimension is chosen to be 10.

On varying the number of discretization intervals for the state space between 10, 15, and 20, we found the corresponding average number of trials to convergence is 784, 793, and 115 respectively with 82%, 83%, and 100% of the respective runs converging within the specified limit of 1200 trials. This suggests that when the state representation gets too coarse, the agents find it very difficult to learn the optimal policy. This is because the less the number of intervals (the coarser the granularity), the more the variations in reward an agent gets after taking the same action at the same state (each discrete state maps into a larger range of continuous space and hence the agents start from and ends up in physically different locations, the latter resulting in different rewards).

Varying learning rate

We experimented by varying the learning rate, β. The resultant average distance of the actual path from the desired path over the course of a run is plotted in Figure 3 for β values 0.4, 0.6, and 0.8. The average number of trials to convergence is 784, 793, and 115 respectively with 82%, 83%, and 100% of the respective runs converging within the specified limit of 1200 trials.

In case of the straight path between (40,0) and (40,100), the optimal sequence of actions always puts the block on the same x-position. Since the x-dimension is the only dimension used to represent state, the agents update the same Q-value in their policy matrix in successive steps. We now calculate the number of updates required for the Q-value corresponding to this optimal action before it reaches the steady state value. Note that for the system to converge, it is necessary that only the Q-value for the optimal action at $x = 40$ needs to arrive at its steady state value. This is because the block is initially placed at $x = 40$, and so long as the agents choose their optimal action, it never reaches any other x position. So, the number of updates to reach steady state for the Q-value associated with the optimal action at $x = 40$ should be proportional to the number of trials to convergence for a given run.

In the following, let S_t be the Q-value after t updates and S_I be the initial Q-value. Using Equation 1 and the fact that for the optimal action at the starting position, the *reinforcement* received is K and the next state is the same as the current state, we can write,

$$\begin{aligned} S_{t+1} &= (1-\beta)\, S_t + \beta\,(K + \gamma\, S_t) \\ &= (1-\beta\,(1-\gamma))\, S_t + \beta\, K \\ &= A\, S_t + C \end{aligned} \quad (2)$$

where A and B are constants defined to be equal to $1 - \beta * (1-\gamma)$ and $\beta * K$ respectively. Equation 2 is a difference equation which can be solved using $S_0 = S_I$ to obtain

$$S_t = A^{t+1}\, S_I + \frac{C\,(1 - A^{t+1})}{1-A}.$$

If we define convergence by the criteria that $|S_{t+1} - S_t| < \epsilon$, where ϵ is an arbitrarily small positive number, then the number of updates t required for convergence can be calculated to be the following:

$$\begin{aligned} t &\geq \frac{\log(\epsilon) - \log(S_I\,(1-A) - C)}{log(A)} \\ &= \frac{\log(\epsilon) - \log(\beta) - \log(S_I\,(1-\gamma) - K)}{log(1-\beta\,(1-\gamma))} \end{aligned} \quad (3)$$

If we keep γ and S_I constant the above expression can be shown to be a decreasing function of β. This is corroborated by our experiments with varying β while holding $\gamma = 0.1$ (see Figure 3). As β increases, the agents take less number of trials to convergence to the optimal set of actions required to follow the desired path. The other plot in Figure 3 presents a comparison of the theoretical and experimental convergence trends. The first curve in the plot represents the function corresponding to the number of updates required to reach steady state value (with $\epsilon = 0$). The second curve represents the average number of trials required for a run to converge, scaled down by a constant factor of 0.06. The actual ratios between the number of trials to convergence and the values of the expression on the right hand side of the inequality 3 for β equal to 0.4, 0.6, and 0.8 are 24.1, 25.6, and 27.5 respectively (the average number of trials are 95.6, 71.7, and 53; values of the above-mentioned expression are 3.97, 2.8, and 1.93). Given the fact that results are averaged over 100 runs, we can claim that our theoretical analysis provides a good estimate of the relative time required for convergence as the learning rate is changed.

Varying agent capabilities

The next set of experiments was designed to demonstrate the effects of agent capabilities on the time required to converge on the optimal set of actions. In the first of the current set of experiments, one of the agents was chosen to be a "dummy"; it did not exert

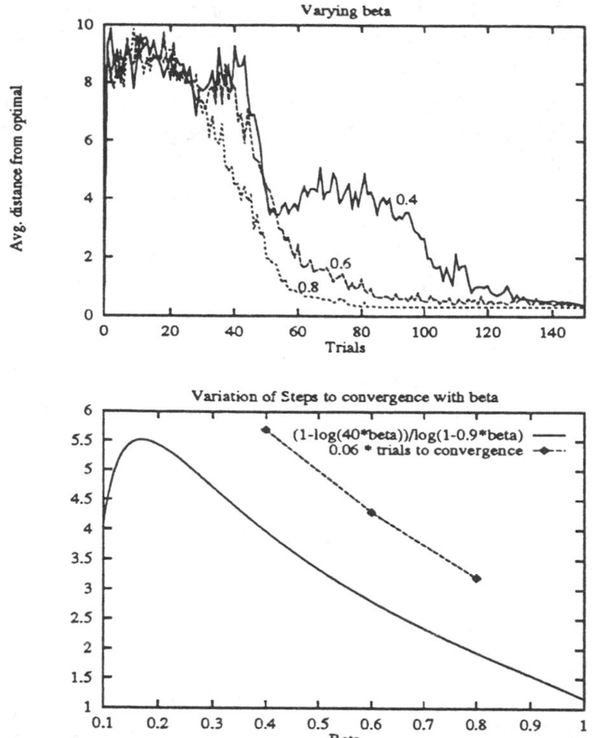

Figure 3: Variation of average distance of actual path from desired path over the course of a run, and the number of updates for convergence of optimal Q-value with changing β ($\gamma = 0.1$, $S_I = 100$).

any force at all. The other agent could only change the angle at which it could apply a constant force on the block. In the second experiment, the latter agent was allowed to vary both force and angle. In the third experiment, both agents were allowed to vary their force and angle. The average number of trials to convergence for the first, second, and third experiment are 431, 55, and 115 respectively. The most interesting result from these experiments is that two agents can learn to coordinate their actions and achieve the desired problem-solving behavior much faster than when a single agent is acting alone. If, however, we simplify the problem of the only active agent by restricting its choice to that of selecting the angle of force, it can learn to solve the problem quickly. If we fix the angle for the only active agent, and allow it to vary only the magnitude of the force, the problem becomes either trivial (if the chosen angle is identical to the angle of the desired path from the starting point) or unsolvable.

Transfer of learning

We designed a set of experiments to demonstrate how learning in one situation can help learning to perform well in a similar situation. The problem with starting and goal locations at (40,0) and (40,100) respectively is used as a reference problem. In addition, we used five other problems with the same starting location and with goal locations at (50,100), (60,100), (70,100), (80,100), and (90,100) respectively. The corresponding desired paths were obtained by joining the starting and goal locations by straight lines. To demonstrate transfer of learning, we first stored each of the policy matrices that the two agents converged on for the original problem. Next, we ran a set of experiments using each of the new problems, with the agents starting off with their previously stored policy matrices.

We found that there is a linear increase in the number of trials to convergence as the goal in the new problem is placed farther apart from the goal in the initial problem. To determine if this increase was due purely to the distance between the two desired paths, or due to the difficulty in learning to follow certain paths, we ran experiments on the latter problems with agents starting with uniform policies. These experiments reveal that the more the angle between the desired path and the y-axis, the longer the agents take to converge. Learning in the original problem, however, does help in solving these new problems, as evidenced by a $\approx 10\%$ savings in the number of trials to convergence when agents started with the previously learned policy. Using a one-tailed t-test we found that all the differences were significant at the 99% confidence level. This result demonstrates the transfer of learned knowledge between similar problem-solving situations.

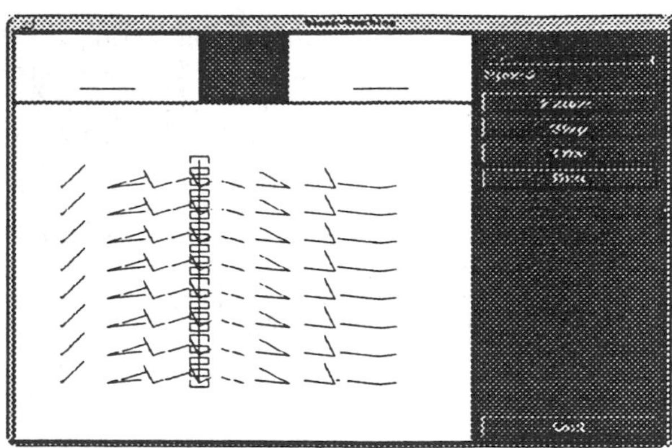

Figure 4: Visualization of agent policy matrices at the end of a successful run.

Complimentary learning

If the agents were cognizant of the actual constraints and goals of the problem, and knew elementary physics, they could independently calculate the desired action for each of the states that they may enter. The resulting policies would be identical. Our agents, however, have no planning capacity and their knowledge is encoded in the policy matrix. Figure 4 provides a snapshot, at the end of a successfully converged run, of what each agent believes to be its best action choice for each of the possible states in the world. The action choice for each agent at a state is represented by a straight line at the appropriate angle and scaled to represent the magnitude of force. We immediately notice that the individual policies are complimentary rather than being identical. Given a state, the combination of the best actions will bring the block closer to the desired path. In some cases, one of the agents even pushes in the wrong direction while the other agent has to compensate with a larger force to bring the block closer to the desired path. These cases occur in states which are at the edge of the field of play, and have been visited only infrequently. Complementarity of the individual policies, however, are visible for all the states.

Conclusions

In this paper, we have demonstrated that two agents can coordinate to solve a problem better, even without a model for each other, than what they can do alone. We have developed and experimentally verified theoretical predictions of the effects of a particular system parameter, the learning rate, on system convergence. Other experiments show the utility of using knowledge, acquired from learning in one situation, in other similar situations. Additionally, we have demonstrated that agents coordinate by learning complimentary, rather than identical, problem-solving knowledge.

The most surprising result of this paper is that agents can learn coordinated actions without even being aware of each other! This is a clear demonstration of the fact that more complex system behavior can emerge out of relatively simple properties of components of the system. Since agents can learn to coordinate behavior without sharing information, this methodology can be equally applied to both cooperative and non-cooperative domains.

To converge on the optimal policy, agents must repeatedly perform the same task. This aspect of the current approach to agent coordination limits its applicability. Without an appropriate choice of system parameters, the system may take considerable time to converge, or may not converge at all.

In general, agents converged on sub-optimal policies due to incomplete exploration of the state space. We plan to use Boltzmann selection of action in place of deterministic action choice to remedy this problem, though this will lead to slower convergence. We also plan to develop mechanisms to incorporate world models to speed up reinforcement learning as proposed by Sutton (Sutton 1990). We are currently investigating the application of reinforcement learning for resource-sharing problems involving non-benevolent agents.

References

A. B. Barto, R. S. Sutton, and C. Watkins. Sequential decision problems and neural networks. In *Proceedings of 1989 Conference on Neural Information Processing*, 1989.

A. H. Bond and L. Gasser. *Readings in Distributed Artificial Intelligence*. Morgan Kaufmann Publishers, San Mateo, CA, 1988.

P. Brazdil, M. Gams, S. Sian, L. Torgo, and W. van de Velde. Learning in distributed systems and multi-agent environments. In *European Working Session on Learning*, Lecture Notes in AI, 482, Berlin, March 1991. Springer Verlag.

P. R. Cohen and C. R. Perrault. Elements of a plan-based theory of speech acts. *Cognitive Science*, 3(3):177–212, 1979.

E. H. Durfee and V. R. Lesser. Partial global planning: A coordination framework for distributed hypothesis formation. *IEEE Transactions on Systems, Man, and Cybernetics*, 21(5), September 1991.

M. S. Fox. An organizational view of distributed systems. *IEEE Transactions on Systems, Man, and Cybernetics*, 11(1):70–80, Jan. 1981.

M. Genesereth, M. Ginsberg, and J. Rosenschein. Cooperation without communications. In *Proceedings of the National Conference on Artificial Intelligence*, pages 51–57, Philadelphia, Pennsylvania, 1986.

J. H. Holland. Escaping brittleness: the possibilities of general-purpose learning algorithms applied to parallel rule-based systems. In R. Michalski, J. Carbonell, and T. M. Mitchell, editors, *Machine Learning, an artificial intelligence approach: Volume II*. Morgan Kaufman, Los Alamos, CA, 1986.

J. W. Shavlik and T. G. Dietterich. *Readings in Machine Learning*. Morgan Kaufmann, San Mateo, California, 1990.

S. Sian. Adaptation based on cooperative learning in multi-agent systems. In Y. Demazeau and J.-P. Müller, editors, *Decentralize AI*, volume 2, pages 257–272. Elsevier Science Publications, 1991.

R. G. Smith. The contract net protocol: High-level communication and control in a distributed problem solver. *IEEE Transactions on Computers*, C-29(12):1104–1113, Dec. 1980.

R. S. Sutton. Integrated architecture for learning, planning, and reacting based on approximate dynamic programming. In *Proceedings of the Seventh International Conference on Machine Learning*, pages 216–225, 1990.

M. Tan. Multi-agent reinforcement learning: Independent vs. cooperative agents. In *Proceedings of the Tenth International Conference on Machine Learning*, pages 330–337, June 1993.

C. Watkins. *Learning from Delayed Rewards*. PhD thesis, King's College, Cambridge University, 1989.

G. Weiß. Learning to coordinate actions in multi-agent systems. In *Proceedings of the International Joint Conference on Artificial Intelligence*, pages 311–316, August 1993.

Index

A

D

E

F

G

H

I

J

K

L

M

N

O

P

T

U

V

W

Z